D1241441

Essays in

Economic

Thought

ARISTOTLE TO MARSHALL

ESSAYS IN Economic Thought:

ARISTOTLE TO MARSHALL

EDITED BY
JOSEPH J. SPENGLER
Duke University

AND

WILLIAM R. ALLEN
University of California, Los Angeles

Rand McNally & Company

CHICAGO

RAND McNALLY

ECONOMICS SERIES

WALTER W. HELLER

Consulting Editor

BARGER

Money, Banking and Public Policy

COONS

The Income of Nations and Persons

DEWEY

Monopoly in Economics and Law

HOLZMAN

Readings on the Soviet Economy

KURIHARA

National Income and Economic Growth

WHITTAKER

Schools and Streams of Economic Thought

SPENGLER and ALLEN

Essays in Economic Thought: Aristotle to Marshall

to

DOT

FRAN

and

JAN

Preface

Economists responsible for courses dealing with the history of their science usually are handicapped when they seek to make periodical literature and reference material readily available to students. Journals seem always to be missing, or in use elsewhere, or not to be had for ordinary class-assignment purposes; library encyclopedias are not allowed to circulate and are available in only one or a few copies. A partial solution to the problem of nonaccessibility of materials is to be found in a collection of relevant and excellent essays and excerpts drawn from leading sources. The present collection is intended to afford such a partial solution. It is the hope of the editors that these selections will significantly supplement handbooks and collections of original writings currently in use in courses dealing with the evolution of economic analysis and practice.

By means of a short introduction to each section, the editors have endeavored both to assist in placing the subjects treated by these essays in the developmental history of economics and also to present pertinent material which is treated either differently or not at all in the essays. No attempt has been made to supply a selected bibliography, for there will soon be issued, under the auspices of the American Economic Association, a classified bibliography of post-1880 economic periodical literature.

Undoubtedly, readers will sometimes quarrel with the selective princi-ples that prompted the editors to include the particular papers chosen and to exclude others. However, the hurdle of space is not to be surmounted, and, given this constraint, a selector's power to include is severely limited. At best he functions in the neighborhood of a Pareto optimum of his own definition which he may roughly approximate in a variety of ways. It is the belief of the editors that they have approximated such an optimum, though not in the only manner possible. They have sought to represent the develop-ment of economics from the period of the ancient Greeks through the neo-classical formulation of Marshall. To cover at all adequately the last three decades or so of "contemporary" analysis — a body of material which is the proper concern of other courses in the economics curriculum — would neces-sitate either a vast expansion of the book or the imposing of an unacceptably high alternative cost in the form of deleting many of the pieces here in-cluded. The papers selected and the editorial introductions deal with impor-tant authors or with significant and integrating ideas reflective of the thought-ways of Western economics as it evolved through time. Periods and schools are thus exhibited as well as ideas and writers.

Professor George H. Hildebrand has given assistance at several points in the preparation of the volume. The editors appreciate the permissions of the authors of the essays and of their publishers to reprint the selections. The following publishers and associations have kindly allowed use of their material in the introductions: The American Economic Association; *The Canadian Journal of Economics and Political Science;* The Free Press of Glencoe; Longmans, Green and Company; Macmillan and Company; The Macmillan Company; Oxford University Press; Random House; and The Royal Economic Society.

J. J.

W. R. A.

Contents

PART ONE

INTRODUCTION

MEN UNDOUBTEDLY BEHAVED economically for many centuries before they undertook to analyze economic behavior and arrive at explanatory principles. At first, this analysis was more implicit than explicit, more inarticulate than articulate, and more philosophical and political in mode than economic. But in face of ubiquitous and inevitable scarcity, the study, in various forms and for various proximate purposes, went on. In the essays and introductions that follow, the long and difficult evolvement of what has now become a highly formalized and scientific body of thought is surveyed. In this introduction, however, attention will be given only to certain very general aspects of the development of economic thought and analysis.

(1) As a society evolves it undergoes a twofold evolution of concern to economists. Both its objective and its subjective economic components change. Its concrete economic-institutional arrangements undergo modification, and so does that which men think about these arrangements, their efficiency, their impacts, their capacity to influence economic welfare, and so on. Changes in economic-institutional arrangements tend to be accompanied by changes in what is thought of them, and changes in how and what men think of these arrangements tend to be accompanied by changes in the arrangements themselves. There is no hard and fast set of interrelations between these two sorts of change, though some students of social change find its primary source in the objective sector whereas others find it in the subjective sector. Economists have usually concerned themselves with the history of ideas as such. Sociologists of knowledge, on the contrary, even when relatively well informed concerning the content of ideas, have tended to play up the role of circumstances external to the body of economic thought as such and to neglect the strong tendency of such a body of thought to immanent change (*i.e.*, to change originating within itself). To the student of the development of economic analysis both sources of change are likely to be of concern.

Here it is possible only to suggest in broad terms several ways in which the development of economic thought is affected by what takes place outside this body of thought. The questions to which economical writers directed their attention, particularly in and after the early modern period when economic science began to develop more systematically, were inspired largely by specific problems troubling the communities in which these writers lived. For example, problems associated with money, trade, taxation, and the fomenting of economic development have long commanded attention, though the specific guises in which they have presented themselves have often changed. How these problems have been dealt with analytically at any point in time has been largely governed, of course, by the state of development of economics and its concepts and tools at that time. This

2

state of development has been affected, however, by conceptual and other changes taking place outside economics. For example, the analytical tools of which economists avail themselves depend in part upon noneconomic technological changes (*e.g.*, the development of electronic computers), the introduction of which may also encourage new lines of inquiry (*e.g.*, in seasonal aspects of economic processes). Similarly, the problems and the conceptual approaches selected by economists have been affected in varying measure, as has the development of economic analysis as such, by philosophical predispositions subscribed to by economists as well as by the *Zeitgeist* or *Weltanschauung* ruling in the communities in which they lived. Witness the recourse economic writers have had to historical, evolutionary, or dialectical-materialistic approaches, or to the use of concepts drawn from mechanics, biology, etc.

The development of economics has been affected also by the manner in which the economic life of a society has been organized. It may be organized in terms of free, competitive markets and animated by profit- and income-prospects. It may be organized along the lines of the Soviet economy. It may be organized largely in terms of comparatively self-sufficient demesnes, temple-estates, etc. There are still other possible arrangements. In each type of organization the constraint of economic scarcity operates, but it remains highly probable that, at least until recently, how economics was envisaged and how economic questions were posed depended largely upon the sort of economic organization with which an economical writer was familiar. His views were affected also by the extent to which he looked upon the economic sector of a society as distinct from other sectors and hence as essentially self-contained and autonomous. For these reasons, economical writers long tended to envisage the economy of other societies or periods in terms of that economic organization with which they were familiar. In recent decades, however, economical writers have become relatively free of this tendency to interpret all economic behavior in terms of their own economies. For the past three or four centuries the economic sector has come to be increasingly differentiated from other sectors of society, and it has thus come to be looked upon as enjoying a high degree of behavioral autonomy. Of greater importance, economics itself has become highly conceptualized, and many specific economic functions have been identified and made analytically and operationally utilizable, with the result that even the behavior of relatively nonautonomous economies, such as are found in the primitive world or were found in the ancient world, can be efficiently analyzed.

(2) The development of the social sciences has been more subject than has that of the natural sciences to influences flowing from accidental or extraneous happenings. Economics has not been a clear exception, but it seems to have been somewhat more immune than other social sciences to these influences. It has also become freer of these external influences as it has become more technical and hence more subject to changes of the sort immanent in the subject as such or originating with its professional custodians. This tendency to greater freedom from external influences has been

3

offset at least in part, however, by the fact that as economics, together with other social sciences, has become more conceptualized, it has become more sensitive to conceptual developments in other social sciences, when these developments have become mobile and transferable to economics and assimilable to it.

(3) Central economic problems persist. Only the empirical forms in which they present themselves undergo great change. Economic scarcity is as much a problem today in Western society as it was in ancient Mesopotamia in the time of Sargon I, even though its concrete manifestations are quite different. Hence, allocative mechanisms are as essential today as they were thousands of years ago, and their construction and assessment engage the attention of economists as they probably engaged that of Sargon's administrators. What earlier we called specific problems were really new forms of problems that had persisted from age to age, though subject, at the practical level, to variation in the comparative degree of importance attached to them. Thus, making provision for the performance of monetary functions has long been a societal problem, even though interest manifested in the effectiveness of its performance varies greatly in time and space. The essay included in Part One shows that the central problem of economic order has long persisted and has had attention from economical writers since the time of Socrates if not longer. It shows also that how men envisage or conceptualize a central problem tends to change in time for a variety of reasons, with the result that economic thought itself changes. Later (see Selection 10) it is suggested that when a satisfactory way of conceptualizing a problem is developed, its essential features are likely to persist.

(4) It may be useful to touch upon the problem of organizing the history of the development of economic thought. As a rule, its preninteenth-century history is organized on a chronological basis, with accounts of Graeco-Roman, medieval, mercantilistic, pre-Smithian, physiocratic, and Smithian economics succeeding one another. This arrangement has been followed in the present work. For, while no article dealing exclusively with Graeco-Roman economics has been included, Selection 1 and the Introduction to Part Two have to do, in part, with Greek and Roman views. Furthermore, in Selection 2, Roman and early Christian contributions to the formulation of the doctrine of "just price" are indicated, while in Selection 10 it is shown that the concept of utility, already touched upon by Aristotle, continued to have exponents until in the nineteenth century it was made the basis of economic administration by Carl Menger and his followers. The contributions of the classical economists and Marx are dealt with in Part Four; the views of the historical and institutional economists are treated in Part Five; the theories of the nineteenth-century marginalists and the neoclassicists are discussed in Part Six.

Economic literature may be grouped also in terms of the objectives that economic organization was intended to serve and of the role of the state in economic organization. At least five such groups may be identified. (1) In the time of Plato and Aristotle, major emphasis was placed upon the mental and ethical development of citizens, largely through the instrumentality of the city-state; not much emphasis was put upon improving men's material conditions, partly because they were not deemed susceptible of much improvement. (2) Between the fall of the Roman Empire and the late Middle Ages, major emphasis was placed upon other-worldly objectives; material ends, while sometimes less neglected than in Greek times, were not stressed; governmental agencies, now less developed than in Roman times, were conceived of as supplementing ecclesiastical organizations and objectives. (3) With the advent of nationalism and the partial replacement of other-worldly ends and motives by this-worldly incentives and aspirations, the existence of an economic system began to be recognized, and it began to be taken for granted that the state, through recourse to appropriate measures, could channel men's economic behavior and make the economic system serve political as well as economic ends. (4) In the eighteenth century if not earlier, there came into being, for a variety of reasons, the belief that the economic system was relatively automatic and machine-like in character, and that men, when left essentially free, responded to each other and to changing circumstances in a manner well suited to further the advantage of themselves and the collectivity. This view, while always subject to qualification, held sway until the latter part of the nineteenth century. It permeated even Marxian anticipations in that Marx seems confidently to have expected the capitalistic system to collapse without much active intervention on the part of the proletariat until its dictatorship was established. (5) In the late nineteenth century there began to come into being the Age of Governmental Intervention, its development assisted by the demands of war, the rise of an organized working class, and the decline of faith in the capacity of unassisted economic homeostasis to maximize the welfare of the common man. This shift in point of view is evident in Lenin's espousal of an activist revolutionary policy in place of Marx's more placid approach. It is equally evident in the espousal by some of a program of governmentally sustained employment within frameworks of either mixed or essentially collectivistic economies.

1.

JOSEPH J. SPENGLER
Duke University

The Problem of

Order in

Economic Affairs

> The art of progress is to preserve order amid change, and to preserve change amid order . . . . Order is not sufficient . . . . What is required, is . . . . order entering upon novelty; so that the massiveness of order does not degenerate into mere repetition; and so that the novelty is always reflected upon a background of system.
>
> A. N. Whitehead, *Process and Reality*

The problem of economic order is taking on the importance it had in classic Rome about the time Augustus substituted the principate for the republic, and in Western Europe during the period of religious strife when Bodin and others were searching for a means of unifying the community. In this paper I deal with the problem of economic order and with economists' and others' treatment of it at various epochs in man's ideological history. In the first section I discuss analytically a principal source of error in economic theory, of which the treatment of the problem of economic order is later shown to be a prime example. In Section II, I define the problem of economic order. In Sections III, IV, and V, I summarize the treatment of this problem by representative ancient, medieval, and modern writers. In Section VI, I examine some of the consequences of Smith's views'

Reprinted from *The Southern Economic Journal*, XV (July 1948), 1–29, by permission of the publisher.

having been followed to the exclusion of relevant views of the Physiocrats. In Section VII, I consider the implications of the preceding analysis for the contemporary American economy.

I

Man, as represented by the social theorist, inhabits two realms of being, a realm that is *real* and a realm that is *analytical* or *hypothetical*. The realm that is real comprehends the earthy, dissonant, bumbled, and seemingly confused (albeit not wholly disorderly) world of affairs of which an all-perceiving, all-understanding, and hypothesis-free observer from another planet would be sensible. The realm that is hypothetical consists of the mental constructs more or less wittingly built by the social theorist (and, for that matter, though less wittingly, by every human observer) out of his percepts and concepts of the real realm, with the object in view of mirroring the significant components of the real realm and attaining understanding of and (possibly) control over this realm. The hypothetical realm, moreover, although sharply distinguishable from the real realm, is an integral part of the latter, inasmuch as man's behavior through time is conditioned by his percepts, concepts, and hypotheses of the elements composing the aggregate environment impinging upon him.

The hypothetical, abstract realm of being generated by social theorists constitutes a part of their society's ideology, itself an important component of this society's spiritual equipment, which, together with its substantial equipment, determines the well-being of the individuals composing the society. The hypothetical realm of being may be distinguished into its irrational and its rational components, and the latter may be divided, in turn, into that which appears to consist with the real realm of being and that which does not. Progress in social theory and (in considerable degree) in man's ability to shape his spiritual and physical environment consists in the supersession of irrational by rational mental constructs, and in the replacement of mental constructs which do not consist with the real realm of being by those which do.

At different times in man's ideological history his hypothetical realm of being has been variously divided into subrealms by social scientists. Moreover, with the differentiation of social science and social scientists, particular hypothetical subrealms of being have fallen under the dominion of particular groups of social scientists who have been implicitly charged, somewhat after the manner of priesthoods in ancient Egypt, to make their respective hypothetical subrealms of being adequately represent the corresponding and referent real subrealms of being.

The subdivision of the hypothetical realm of being, coupled with the manner of parcelling out of the custody of these hypothetical subrealms, has not been unmixed blessing. This arrangement has been in accord with the time-tested principle of specialization; but it has not always been accompanied by adequate coördination. In consequence, certain hypothetical subrealms have been neglected while others have been given undue attention

7

and have been allowed to masquerade as both themselves and cognate hypothetical subrealms. Such disproportionality in attention would be of no material concern to man were it not for the fact that the hypothetical realm is, as has been noted, an integral part of the real realm of being; that the hypothetical subrealms of being are interdependent; and that consequently the substantial welfare of man is sensitive to overemphasis of some hypothetical subrealms of being at the expense of undervaluation of others.

The subject matter of economics constitutes one of these hypothetical subrealms of being, respecting whose boundaries, however, economists have differed. Exponents of operational definition have been content to say that economics is what economics does. Others have accepted Robbins's definition of economics as "the science which studies human behaviour as a relationship between ends and scarce means which have alternative uses."[1] Still others have agreed with Fraser that connecting economics with the idea of wealth need not be inconsistent with centering it about the concept of scarcity.[2] For our purposes Parsons' description is more satisfactory: that economics is a science of action, concerned with the ramifications of economic rationality "in its various relations to the concrete facts of action," and to be distinguished both from politics (which has to do with coercive rationality, power relations, and social order) and from sociology (which treats of the "integration of individuals with reference to a common value system, manifested in the legitimacy of institutional norms, in the common ultimate ends of action, in ritual and in various modes of expression").[3]

It is the adequacy of the aggregate content of the definitions of the various hypothetical subrealms of being that is important rather than the specific content of the definition of any particular subrealm. For example, it does not make too much difference how we circumscribe the hypothetical subrealm assigned to economics provided that: (a) this subrealm accurately represents its corresponding real subrealm of being; (b) other hypothetical subrealms are so defined that in the aggregate they adequately represent those portions of the real realm of being not represented by economics; and (c) economists are fully aware that, just as in the real realm of being, economic, political, sociological, and other elements are more or less interdependent, so in the hypothetical realm of being the analytical elements corresponding to these real elements are more or less interdependent. If condition (c) is not met, and at the hypothetical level reliance is placed in the capacity of the economic subrealm per se to reflect comprehensively all significant objects and events relevant to the real economic subrealm of being, an adequate representation and explanation of the latter will not be forthcoming. Moreover, even though condition (a) is observed, condition (c) cannot be met unless condition (b) is satisfied.

Our present incapacity to deal with the problem of economic order arises in large measure from the compounded failure of economists (1) to devise a hypothetical subrealm that adequately represents economic objects and events in the real subrealm of being, and (2) to take fully into account at the hypothetical level the interdependence of the economic subrealm with other relevant subrealms. In particular, economists have failed sufficiently to recognize that what takes place in the real subrealm of being they are studying is conditioned by the prevailing state of power relations and by the extent to which conduct influencing common values and value attitudes have been integrated.[4] In the historical sections that follow it will be shown how this neglect of the rôles of common values and the distribution of power originated.

II

Three somewhat incompatible conditions have combined, at all times and in all economies, to create the problem of economic order: the *autonomy* of many consuming and factor-organizing and supplying agents; the necessity that these autonomous agents behave in an appropriately coöperative and *coördinate* fashion; and the generally felt need that economic activity be *continuous* and uninterrupted. The problem has been aggravated, moreover, by the force of secular and random change which is continually playing upon these three conditions as well as upon other aspects of man's real realm of being, and which has been the principal source of the recorded improvement in man's material lot.

Economic activity issues ultimately out of the pressure men are under to transform more or less undifferentiated factors of production into goods and services. Economic activity therefore entails autonomy at two levels, at that of the consumer-agent and at that of the agent who combines and organizes factors of production, or conditions their supply. Decisions regarding what and how much is utilized for ultimate consumption are made chiefly by individual consumers, by familial units, by eleemosynary institutions, and by governmental units. Accordingly, since each decision maker enjoys a greater or lesser degree of autonomy, it is not possible for any one to gauge at any moment the full significance of the aggregate of consumer decisions being made. Decisions regarding what and how much is to be produced, and by what methods, are made by private and public entrepreneurs (i.e., proprietorships, partnerships, corporations, and other *plural* enterprises) in the light both of their surmises and appraisals respecting actual and prospective decisions at the consumer level and of other supposedly relevant circumstances. Again, since each of these decision makers enjoys a greater or lesser measure of autonomy, it is impossible for any one to predict at any moment just what the aggregate of producer decisions then being made signifies. Decisions regarding the provision of factors and materials of production are also made by autonomous agencies, the supply of labor being under the dominion of the individual worker and/or a trade union[5] (bent upon both perpetuating itself and maximizing the remuneration of its members),[6] and the supply of other productive agents being under the governance of owners who usually are entrepreneurs.

In the absence of coöperation-producing coördinating arrangements, autonomy, at the consumer, supplier, and producer levels must generate unpredictability, conduce to economic disorder, and, in conjunction with the continual stimulus of change, make for frequent interruption of the

9

circular economic flow. In theory these coördinating arrangements may assume a number of forms. But these forms are not equally satisfactory; whereas some secure the coöperation of the discretionary agents without interfering unduly with their autonomy, others operate, actually or in effect, to destroy the autonomy of the agents whose economic behavior they are supposed to coördinate. Thus coördination may be accomplished by centering in the state the determination of what is to be produced, how it is to be produced, and to whom it is to be distributed; yet this arrangement, except when it is executed under the guidance of a flexible price system, strips the theretofore autonomous agents of their independence. Again coöperation may be secured by imbedding in the underlying value system an appropriate set of tastes and a preference for appropriate productive methods; but this arrangement, while it does not actually destroy the autonomy of the agents whose activities are being coördinated, in effect solves the problem of order by terminating its existence. Yet again, coöperation may be secured by allowing the several agents their respective autonomy while requiring them to conform their behavior to certain rules calculated to coördinate their activities; this method circumscribes autonomy and coöperation without destroying either, thereby making possible their reconciliation. If it be granted that a large measure of autonomy is desirable, it follows that coöperation may best be secured through (i) a considerable and appropriate integration of underlying values; (ii) the establishment and enforcement by the state of norms and rules suited to produce coördination without destroying autonomy; and (iii) action by the state to prevent any appreciable interruption of the continuity of the aggregate flow of goods and services.

I shall not attempt to define economic order and its requisites with precision; for its meaning and content have undergone modification pari passu with changes in man's environment, in his conduct-determining ends and norms, and in the means he has at hand to make his environment subserve his ends. In general, it may be said that the problem of economic order is solved in proportion as the three objectives, autonomy, coöperation, and continuity, are achieved and reconciled both with one another and with the force of secular and random change.

Present-day economists will probably agree that, given a distribution of income both realizable and generally acquiesced in, economic order exists in proportion as: (a) disguised unemployment is absent; (b) technological and related progress is at a rate consistent with the maximization of the annual increment of output per capita; (c) productive processes are not subject to interruption by political strife, by conflict over the division of output, or by cyclical depressants removable, or mitigatable, consistently with (b) and (d); and (d) conditions (a), (b), and (c) are compatible with relevant elements in the prevailing common value system. Condition (d) is introduced to allow for value elements whose full or adequate realization is, or was, inconsistent with the full realization of conditions (a), (b), and (c). For example, it is necessary to allow for the fact that economic activity has, or may have, value for the actor both as means and as end — both the game itself and its favorable outcome may yield satisfaction to the player; and it is essential to remember that when slave or feudal relationships were dominant, full realization of conditions (a) and (b) was not practicable.

III

Before I consider the treatment of the problem of economic order by Europeans who wrote prior to Quesnay and Smith,[7] I should like to pose the problem in purely abstract terms. So let us imagine an economy composed of individuals who are without conduct-regulating institutions and free of the coercive influence of an external coördinating agent. If these individuals are animated by appropriate automatic behavior mechanisms, or are under the governance of appropriate conduct-determining norms, they will carry on the interdependent activities of the economy harmoniously and coöperatively. If, although neither of these conditions holds, a powerful external agent is present to coördinate these activities, like coöperation and harmony will result. In each of these three situations, our supposed human world is completely atomized; yet the activities of these autonomous atoms are coördinated and harmonized, respectively, by internal automatisms, by norms, and by a coercive agent. In the absence of each of the stipulated coöperation-producing conditions, there would be disharmony and disorder.

The real realm of being, of course, does not correspond to any one of these hypothetical realms; for in the real world the behavior of individuals, while more or less autonomous in character, is subject to the unobtrusive and/or overt regulatory influence of the institutions, associations, laws, folkways, mores, and other habit-patterning arrangements operative in the community. These regulatory influences are designed and help to produce harmony within circumscribed segments of the real realm of being. These influences also can and do contribute to the solution of the larger problem, the harmonizing of the diverse economic ends and activities of the more or less autonomous individuals and groups composing the economy. At different times in history men have employed various methods to establish compatibility among the economic ends and activities of individuals and the commonwealth; and economists have fashioned theories respecting the achievement of economic harmony. While these theories have always reflected the premises underlying the regnant complex of philosophical ideas, they usually consisted, in the works of the pre-Smithian writers, of differently weighed combinations of coercive principles, ethical norms, and religious sanctions.

The problem of economic order and its solution was dealt with at length by the Socratic philosophers. I shall confine myself to Aristotle, however, since his treatment of the problem, while somewhat unique, is representative of the approach of the Socratic school. Man, as conceived by Aristotle, is a form of matter whose potentiality and excellence can be fully actualized only in the city-state, or *polis*, which, being the "highest" form of "community," aims "at the highest good." Within it, presumably, was to be found that harmony with which so many of the classical writers were concerned. From Aristotle's discussion of the constitution of Athens and other politico-economic subjects, it is evident that, for him, disorder had its origin in the unrestricted striving of man after the necessarily limited means of wealth and power, while order could be achieved through the appropriate adjustment of man's strivings to the means available for their satisfaction. This adjustment was most likely to be found when there was private property, but accompanied by generosity; when men sought to gratify modest bodily pleasures through "household management" rather than to satisfy a desire for limitless gain by acquiring money through unnecessary kinds of exchange; and when the state was one in which citizenship was duly restricted, the rich balanced the poor, the middle class was supreme, and the government was one of laws rather than one of men.[8] Aristotle's contribution to the analysis of the problem of order thus consisted in his supposition that individual and household autonomy can best conduce to the development of man's faculties in a middle-class-dominated state where the other classes are in balance and where properly enacted laws are sovereign. Because he did not grasp the possible rôle of competition or conceive of a self-adjusting economy Aristotle did not effectively apply ethical norms and coercive power to the sustentation of such a self-adjusting process.[9]

Aristotle's *polis* could not withstand the impact of the military prowess of his most famous student, or the bellicosity of the Greeks and the defectiveness of their economic institutions.[10] Nor could the essentially Hobbesian theory of the Epicureans.[11] In the hands of the Roman writers, particularly Cicero, the community-like *polis* becomes the much more association-like *res publica*, founded upon a sharp distinction between *res privata* and *res publica* and "on a basis of agreed rights and common interests," yet designed through the use of adequate social controls to develop man's potentialities and secure justice. Law is the cement which holds economy and *res publica* together, whilst preserving freedom and a proper measure of autonomy. The state is "an association of citizens united by law."[12] In a much greater degree than Aristotle, therefore, Cicero grasped the function of impersonal laws and rules; but he did not recognize their peculiar fitness as instruments, if properly contrived, to produce economic order.

Ideological and material change gradually dissolved the Roman mode of life and the classical culture on which it rested until, in the fifth century, they were finally replaced by barbarism and the Christian culture. Two Stoic philosophers, Cicero (106–43 B.C.) when he declared all men to be equal in light of the providential law of nature, and Seneca (d. 65 A.D.) when he described (as did St. Paul and as did Malthus centuries later) government and property as institutions necessary to curb the wickedness of man, undermined the classical belief in the individual-perfecting rôle of the state and in the supreme value of citizenship in such state.[13] Subsequently, Ambrose (c. 340–397) envisaged man's institutions as means to moderate fallen man's passionate desires.[14] St. Augustine (354–430), reasoning somewhat as did Hobbes later, observed that conflict and oppression rose "so long . . . as the object of appetition is insufficient for any or for all," and that the competition of men for wealth and power produced disorder. Happiness is to be found in the appropriate ordering of the hierarchy of beings and of values, and in the subordination of inferior ends to the ultimate value of eternal salvation. Order could not be permanently established in a secular state, however, even through use of force. Felicity and concord must be sought in Christian brotherhood and discipline under the leadership of the episcopate.[15] Augustine, therefore, conceived neither of a self-adjusting economic system nor of a state either totalitarian or perfection producing. But he condemned buying "cheap to sell dear," indicating, as had Roman lawyers, that there is a just (albeit not invariant) price to which buyer and seller, under the impelling influence of moral principle, should conform.[16]

The problem of economic order and its solution received greater attention from the medieval scholastics than from Augustine, for they wrote under the influence of Aristotle instead of under that of the neo-Platonists, and while their emphasis was other-worldly rather than this-worldly, they attached greater importance to this-worldly instruments than did Augustine. Thus, St. Thomas Aquinas, their most outstanding spokesman, unlike Augustine, looked upon the state as an association divinely instituted to impel "towards the common good of the many, over and above that which impels toward the private good of each individual"; to make possible "virtuous living" through establishment of peace, guidance to good deeds, and provision of a sufficiency of "the things required for proper living"; and to enable men "through virtuous living to attain to the possession of God."[17] But Thomas, like Augustine, restricted the rôle of the state, subordinating it to man's needs, and emphasized the ultimate regulative influence of the moral principles to which the Church sought to induce man to conform. While Thomas conceived of economic society as a kind of organism whose specialized parts are interdependent, and while he looked upon economic order and liberty as complementary, he did not find in competition a means of securing economic order while preserving economic liberty. Coöperation was to be sought rather through the coördinating and regulatory operations of essentially autonomous lesser associations, or gilds, whose activities were to be coördinated in turn (presumably) by the principles of commutative and distributive justice which individuals and groups were morally bound to observe. Only when necessary was coöperation to be achieved through the intervention of the hierarchically supreme "commonwealth which is ordained to procure by itself a sufficiency of goods for human life." In just price, therefore, to the formal and the practical definition of which they contributed greatly, Thomas and his school found the principal guide to economic order;[18] and, under the pressure of ethical and religious and related sanctions, it did exercise considerable influence.[19]

With the sundering of medieval ideological unity by the Renaissance and the Reformation, man's theorizing about his behavior tendencies underwent great modification, and the problem of economic order was reformulated. To this development various changes contributed: the supersession of medieval society and pre-capitalist town economy by bourgeois society and nascent capitalism; the rise of religious particularism; the ascendancy of the national state, together with the diminution in the regulatory influence of moral principle and communal precept; and the growth of *Gesellschaft*-like at the expense of *Gemeinschaft*-like organizational elements. Political and ethical theory began to emphasize that egoism which is so prominent in Machiavelli's (1469–1527) writings. The new formulation implicit in these ideological tendencies was not forthcoming, however, until the midseventeenth century when Thomas Hobbes (1588–1679) greatly elaborated the view, suggested already by Machiavelli, that a society of essentially egoistic individuals must be held together ultimately by the fear of force.[20]

Hobbes treated the problem of economic order in a manner befitting a century notable for its creative work in mathematics, mechanics, and physics; for its rejection of anthropomorphism, moralism, and hierarchism; and for its espousal of the objective view that man is a physical automaton.[21] The problem arises in Hobbes's world of human atoms from the fact that men are animated by appetites and aversions which are without limit whereas that which exists to satisfy these appetites and aversions is restricted in actual and potential amount. For man "felicity is a continuall progresse of the desire, from one object to another"; and life is an unending struggle after power which consists in "his present means, to obtain some future apparent Good." Moreover, since men differ in constitution and taste from bees and ants, they do not automatically live sociably together as do these creatures. Quite the contrary. Out of desire for gain, safety, glory, and reputation men necessarily quarrel, and this tendency is strengthened by the fact that in the state of nature men differ little in ability and expectation. Consequently, so long as "men live without a common Power to keep them all in awe, they are in that condition which is called Warre; and such a warre, as is of every man against every man." Under these conditions industry, agriculture, commerce, security, capital formation, and collective activity are impossible; the "Laws of Nature" are not well observed; and man's life is "solitary, poor, nasty, brutish, and short." But a way of escape is open. In fact man is obligated to choose this way by the "fundamental law of nature," which commands him to seek peace and avert the destruction of his life. Escape consists in the establishment by men, under mutual covenant, of an absolute personal sovereign (embodying "the Essence of the Common-Wealth"), or "Common Power, to keep them in awe, and to direct their actions to the Common Benefit." Only in this wise can harmony be maintained.

Although Hobbes did not sequester the economic from other realms of being, his basic contribution may nonetheless be said to consist in his explicit recognition of the dependence of the functioning of an essentially free-enterprise economy upon the existence of a sovereign agent competent to establish appropriate rules and capable of enforcing their observance. While Hobbes indicated that the right of property in goods is limited, that the formation of contracts is subject to regulation, that monopolies are hurtful, etc., he did not indicate in detail what economic rules are needed, or how a sovereign should proceed to formulate them. He was content to urge the criterion of "common benefit." For his knowledge of economic affairs and of the functioning of economic systems was limited; and his grasp of the growing rôle of autonomy was inadequate. Notwithstanding, he demonstrated, as no economist was to demonstrate for more than 250 years, the very great importance of the element of coercion in the determination of the sequence of economic events.[22]

We have spanned two millenniums, moving from the elementary Greek community-state through the complex Roman state and the simpler medieval economy into the burgeoning mercantilist state. In no instance have we found an economically harmonious real realm of being, or writers with a thorough grasp of the operations of an economic system. But we have found recognition of sources of economic disharmony, and descriptions, however inadequate as to detail, of means by which economic harmony may be achieved. The means uncovered are the small community-like state, commonly accepted ethical and legal norms, religious sanctions, and an unrestricted coercive agent. Of these means and the need to employ them economists were soon, however, to lose sight.

IV

A number of circumstances contributed to the formulation of the belief that the harmony-producing agencies I have described — state, common ethical norms, religious sanctions — were not really necessary. The Mercantilists criticized the older ethico-religious appraisals of usury, luxury, etc., and, as a rule, objected to the conduct of business enterprise by the state as such. Although some of them believed the state to be essentially incapable of fixing prices at a "just" or any other level,[23] many conceived in large nature "of the economic system as a mechanism which could be manipulated,"[24] and of man as an egoist animatable and directable through his desire for gain. Whence they supposed that the state, by the use of rewards and penalties, could in some degree canalize the endeavors of undertakers.[25] It began to appear that, if this economic mechanism could be shown to work automatically and in a fashion to harmonize the interests of individuals, there would not be much need for a regulative and coercive agency. To this denouement several elements in the pre-Smithian stream of thought were contributing. From the rationalist thought of the Middle Ages philosophy had received a sense of coherence and order which affected the shaping of subsequent thought.[26] The mercantilist assertion of an identity between national and class interests, together with the supposition of some students of juristic natural law that a reasonable harmony of interests tended to be realized, must have contributed to the development of the later view that individual and general interests, if not naturally identical, were reconcilable either through a fusion of interest or through an artificial identification of interest.[27] The actual operation of the economy was illuminated, at a time when the entrepreneur was demonstrating his key rôle, by Cantillon's description of the organizing and uncertainty-assuming rôles of the entrepreneur and of his response to effective demand (principally that of the landed proprietors).[28] Still additional elements out of which a more or less self-adjusting and harmony-producing mechanical economic system could be constructed were supplied by Hume and others.[29]

Locke and Hume contributed appreciably to the rejection of Hobbes's central thesis, Locke proceeding from a different view of human nature, and Hume from a different conception of the manner in which social controls develop.[30] Locke starts, much as did Hobbes, with a state of nature in which man's rights are insecure, albeit much less so than in Hobbes's state of nature. This insecurity has its origin in the limitedness of resources and man's inability to work them effectively in a lawless world. Solution is found in the compacting of men to establish a government. But this government differs from that of Hobbes; it is distinct from the society of which it is the instrument, and its sovereignty lies in the community as a whole, to which it is subordinate. The "chief end" of this government is the "preservation of . . . property." This end is accomplished through the establishment of "settled, known" and commonly accepted law, together with a judiciary to interpret it and a coercive power to enforce it. More specifically, the purpose of government is to preserve the fruits of that labor by which men are enabled to escape want and economic insecurity; for property consists essentially in these fruits, since "of the products of the earth useful to the life of man" ninety to ninety-nine hundredths "are the effects of labor." Accordingly, Locke's argument suggests, something like economic order can prevail only where there is law and a government that is democratic in spirit, and where consequently, the worker receives the imputed product of his labor.[31] Presumably, where such order does prevail, pronounced economic inequality does not tend to develop.

Hume, in his discussion of the problem of economic order, considered the various ways in which private and general interests might be reconciled, but he failed adequately to synthesize these ways. The problem of economic order issues, he believed, out of man's nature and the limitedness of resources. There would be no problem if things were to be had for the asking; or if men were animated solely by benevolence; or if, there being extreme want of all necessities, men, from motives "of necessity and self-preservation," were to establish an egalitarian collectivism. Actually, however, enjoyments are limited, although augmentable in supply by human effort, and men act from self-love, albeit tempered somewhat by benevolence, fellow-feeling, and a disposition to be engaged by "a tendency to public good, and to the promoting of peace, harmony, and order in society." There is need, therefore, for the institution of property, to preserve an equitable balance between wants and the means of satisfying them. This institution cannot stand by itself, however, Hume's analysis discloses; for he declared that "property should be regulated by general inflexible rules" and that "*authority*," while subject to the control of law, is "essential" to the existence of its antithesis, "*liberty*," which "is the perfection of civil society." Hume thus dwelt upon both autonomy and coöperation and noted the complementary aspects of their rôles. Notwithstanding, in his able exposition of the self-regulating specie-distributing mechanism, and in his anticipations of a self-

16

regulating competitivism, he failed to note explicitly the importance of the overhanging presence of a coercive factor, perhaps because he took it for granted.[32]

The closing third of the eighteenth century witnessed the formation of two dissimilar, yet not wholly unlike, systems of economic thought, that of Quesnay and that of Adam Smith, of which the latter, being more in concord with the prevailing climate of opinion, eventually triumphed and gave to economic theory a bias it was to retain for more than a century.

In the somewhat doctrinaire writings of Quesnay and his competent disciples three theses, of import for the present discussion, are to be found: (a) that a *contingently* self-adjusting competitive system can conciliate diverse economic interests and produce justice; (b) that the continuance of economic activity at a high level presupposes sufficient and appropriately distributed expenditure; and (c) that objectives (a) and (b) are realizable so long as men observe, or are made to observe, the knowable laws and rules expressing that "essential and general" natural order which "comprehends the constitutive and fundamental laws of all societies." Where there is competition and complete freedom of exchange, declared Le Trosne, "natural price" (or "*bon prix*," the homologue of the scholastics' "just price") results, the interest of everyone is subserved, the interest of no one is hurt, and the interests of all individuals are equilibrated in such wise as to preserve the social order.[33]

It is competition which conciliates all interests: it is perfect only under the absolute reign of freedom of trade, which is the premier consequence of the right of property, and in consequence one of the most essential laws of the social order. It alone can establish products at their natural price, so that they feel only the variations of the physical order, which it also renders very much less perceptible.[34]

Competition serves also to increase the probability that economic activity will continue at a high level. For persistence of prosperity is dependent upon continuity of expenditure, and the flow of a sufficient fraction thereof into agriculture and other industries yielding a "net product"; and these circumstances are favored by competition. In their emphasis upon the necessity of continuity of expenditure, and in their denial that it results automatically, the Physiocrats both anticipated certain of the views of Lord Keynes and stimulated Say and Mill to formulate the Law of Markets, for more than a century a pillar of received economic theory.[35]

The Physiocrats differed from Smith and his successors: they did not suppose that continuity of expenditure, or the conciliation of interests through competition, resulted necessarily and automatically. These ends were achieved only when men and the community acted in consistence with the natural order and its inviolable natural laws. Then only were liberty, property, and security, together with harmony and prosperity, ensured; then only, in our terms, could autonomy be reconciled with coördination and continuity, consistently with change. The basic laws of the natural order were knowable. The Physiocrats, therefore, proposed to secure economic order in two ways. Through education knowledge of the necessary

17

laws and rules would be diffused and, in our terms, underlying values would be more completely integrated. Provision was made for the use of coercion when necessary and compatible with the basic natural order. The prince, or legal despot, would declare positive laws which expressed the laws of the natural order and which were calculated to maximize the welfare of the population. The formulation of such positive laws could not, however, be entrusted solely to the prince and his legislative aides; they might err, in which event the state would be weakened and the welfare of the people would be adversely affected. The Physiocrats, therefore, advocated the creation of a supreme magistracy, or judiciary, consisting of judges adept in the laws and principles composing the fundamental natural order. It would be the duty of these judges to void all positive laws which failed to conform to the natural order and thus deny them enforcement. While it is true that the Physiocrats gave concrete content only to a small number of positive principles, all of which have since been found more or less wanting, they clearly posed the problem of economic order and noted the basic importance of both the coercive factor and values integration.[36]

Throughout the nineteenth century and for a time thereafter three presumptions pervaded the hypothetical realm of being fashioned by orthodox economists: (a) that the economic system is an automatically self-adjusting mechanism; (b) that the economic rôle of the state should be narrowly restricted; (c) and that, given conditions (a) and (b), the interests of individuals are harmonized with each other and with the general interest about as well as may be expected. These propositions had their origin in the writings of Adam Smith.[37]

Competition, together with the disposition of men speedily to spend their money receipts, made the economic system self-adjusting, Smith inferred. For competition, through its influence upon prices, directed men where to work, what to produce, and how much to supply. Man's disposition to expend his receipts with alacrity, which later was reformulated as Say's Law,[38] served to prevent protracted unemployment. The self-adjusting economic system would therefore maximize wealth and per capita income, distribute it fairly equitably, and ensure a satisfactory level of employment.

Because Smith believed that, in the absence of restraint, the economic system tended to operate automatically, and that governments were less competent than individuals to deal with matters of private economy, he assigned to "the obvious and simple system of natural liberty [which] establishes itself of its own accord" all duties but those of defense, administration of justice, and maintenance of useful and desirable public works whose effectuation the profit motive cannot bring about. Actually, Smith's definition of what the state could do was quite elastic, and his list of specific tasks which the state should perform was rather long;[39] yet because these tasks were not all assembled in one place, and because his emphasis usually was upon the superior competence of the "system of natural liberty," Smith left the impression of circumscribing the rôle of government even more than he in fact proposed. It is this somewhat misleading impression which set the tone for subsequent writers. Even so Smith's account suggests that "with some important qualifications, . . . the interests of society, by which he understood the interests of the sum of individuals in the group, would be best served by permitting each one to pursue his own interests in his own way."[40]

Smith did not assert the existence of a natural identity of private and public interest, even though he is sometimes credited with having done so.[41] He was aware of too much evidence to the contrary. Notwithstanding, he supposed that man's propensities (in especial, self-interest, sympathy, and the tendency to truck and barter) were such as to bind men together in a politico-economic community and to make for a harmony rather than for a disharmony of egoisms.[42] In fact, so long as competition remained free, a high degree of harmony tended to result. Although Smith implied that disharmony had its origin principally in monopolistic and other exploitation of buyers and in monopsonistic and other exploitation of sellers, he did not advocate positive governmental intervention to enforce competition. He apparently supposed that if the government did not support monopolistic arrangements, they would not be very effective; and that if it espoused a program of positive action, it probably would not know what to do and therefore would accomplish more harm than good. Accordingly, his analysis suggests, the most that the government could do respecting the enforcement of competition was to refrain from establishing or supporting anticompetitive arrangements. If this policy were pursued, reasonable harmony would result; and, if the history of Europe and the prospects of America constituted an augury, this harmony would increase.[43]

Without an organized school, a body of doctrine is not likely to be widely disseminated. For Smith's views this school was initially provided in England by the Benthamite Utilitarians and on the continent by those who subscribed to the analogous "juristic and spiritualistic philosophy of the Rights of Man."[44] Bentham went beyond Smith, rejecting even the latter's defense of the fixation of maximum interest by the state and of governmental interference in international trade when necessary to national defense. For in a world such as the British, Bentham held, economic liberty consisted with the springs of human action and the interests of men were approaching natural identity. Men were potentially equal. The nation was moving towards economic equality, and this progress would be accelerated by education, savings institutions, and estate-decomposing death taxes. The eighteenth century realm of equality, which was based upon individual property, and in which the interest of each naturally concurred with that of all, was nearly at hand,[45] and with it the solution of the problem of economic order.

Until the early part of the present century British orthodox economists continued to believe the economic system to be essentially self-contained and self-regulating, and the most salutary governmental policy to be one of minimal state interference. Respecting wages, for example, it was supposed that nothing could be accomplished by trade union activity until Jenkin, Edgeworth, and others showed that in an imperfectly competitive labor market collective action might influence the outcome.[46]

Both the classical and the neoclassical economists were keenly aware of the disharmony of the interests of individuals. Yet they believed that harmony was most likely to be maximized, given security of private property, free competition, and minimal state action; and they failed to advocate state intervention either for the purpose of enforcing competition or for that of maintaining purchasing power. The propensities of men would be appropriately channelized and their interests harmonized as much as possible, Malthus implied, in an economic system founded upon private property and the family, each guarded by the state and supplemented by education in individual responsibility.[47] Wage and other contracts, Ricardo declared, "should be left to the fair and free competition of the market, and should never be controlled by the interference of the legislature."[48] Both the Manchester School, with laissez faire as its maxim, and the followers of Herbert Spencer, who declared the "wisest plan" to be "to let things take their own course,"[49] deemed competitivism adequate if allowed full play. So also believed Walter Bagehot.[50] J. S. Mill observed that the distribution of wealth "is a matter of institutions solely" while that of produce is subject in part to custom; he was critical of the society about him, and gave a favorable hearing to socialism. Yet he considered "every restriction of [competition] . . . an evil, and every extension of it . . . always an ultimate good"; he predicted that the principle of private property would long survive; he insisted on the supreme importance of liberty; and he narrowly circumscribed the functions of government, although not so much so as had Smith.[51] Jevons acted on a presumption against state interference, qualified, however, by its subordination to the Benthamite principle of the greatest happiness of the greatest number; but although he favored state control of some economic relationships and public utilities and state management of others, he placed his trust mainly in free competition.[52] Sidgwick presented a qualified defense of the "system of natural liberty," saying that "the general presumption . . . is not in favour of leaving industry altogether to private enterprise . . .; but is on the contrary in favour of supplementing and controlling such enterprise in various ways by the collective action of the community."[53] Alfred Marshall, most influential British economist in 1890–1920, while admitting the need for state control of public utilities, and while alert to the deviation of the position of "maximum satisfaction" from that of stable competitive equilibrium, greatly preferred smaller scale private enterprise. But Marshall's reason for this conclusion, while akin to Mill's reason for defending individual liberty, sets him apart from his utility-dominated forebears. An economy, Marshall believed, was not merely a mechanism to provide utilities; it was also, if it consisted primarily of smaller scale enterprise, a social arrangement that tended to bring out the best in men.[54]

The belief in minimal state interference, self-regulating competitivism, and the consequent realization of essential harmony held sway also outside England. In France J. B. Say, having praised the separation of economics from politics, gave expression to an economic liberalism that found state intervention objectionable even when necessary and that assumed laissez faire to produce a high degree of harmony between individual and public interest.[55] This liberalism received its most optimistic expression at the hands of the vulgariser Bastiat who appropriately named his work *Harmonies économiques*.[56] These doctrines, except for occasional protectionist and populationist modifications and a reduction in emphasis upon harmony, received support until the eve of World War I.[57] In the United States, too, optimistic economic liberalism, though less explicit than the French and sometimes mixed with protectionism, prevailed until the close of the century.[58] On the continent outside France, with the exception of Germany, political economy also was essentially liberal in character.[59] In the latter part of the nineteenth century and in the early twentieth the analytical advantage associated with the assumption of free competition may also have subtly operated to win some support for economic liberalism.[60]

V

Throughout the nineteenth century and thereafter orthodox political economy, with its emphasis upon laissez faire, was subjected to criticism. It was criticized by those who supposed the state, as did Adam Müller and some Romantics, to be essential to the development of the individual; by the Utopian socialists and the Godwinian anarchists, who denied the need even of a coördinating competitive system, since, given an appropriate world, men rationally and spontaneously coöperate; and by those who believed the followers of Smith were underestimating the effects of social change. It was criticized by the historical economists who denied that competition could produce interpersonal concord any more than it could produce international concord; and who concerned themselves, as did later institutionalists, with (among other matters) the contribution of ideals, institutions, and the state to the coördination of the economic activities of individuals; but who contributed relatively little to the solution of the problem of economic order, since they lacked a unifying theory to guide them in the assembly and organization of facts. It was criticized by those evolutionists who found in the economic realm the same purposeless struggle they believed they had discovered in the animal realm.

It was criticized by those who believed that, because of the uneven distribution of bargaining power issuing out of the class structure, many members of society received less than they had produced in terms of the marginal principle, or were denied the opportunity to move into employments where productivity and remuneration were relatively high. Even Boehm-Bawerk and Von Wieser admitted this discrepancy between the harmonious hypothetical equilibrium that would result under conditions of pure competition and the actual "equilibrium" that is found in the real realm of being.[61]

The socialists denied that economic harmony would result under conditions of laissez faire. Both Saint-Simon and Comte, founders of modern authoritarian socialism, rejected liberty and sought an economy essentially totalitarian in character and subject to centralized direction through the medium of the banking system.[62] Marx and his followers described the existing capitalistic economy as shot through with disharmony and the exploitation of class by class; and they predicted its eventual supersession by a planned, propertyless, and competitionless economic order.[63]

Although students of the business cycle were not usually concerned with the problem of economic order in general, they were concerned with the *continuity* of a high level of economic activity, and they therefore contributed, as did Marx, to the rejection of one of the props of the belief in automatic self-adjustment and economic harmony, namely, Say's Law. This law was taken to mean in effect that general overproduction, general involuntary unemployment, and the destruction of purchasing power are impossible. The rejection of this prop prepared the way for Keynesian and related forms of anticyclical state interventionism.[64]

Of the contributions of the critics of Smithian harmony economics, the two most relevant to the present discussion are those of Commons and Pareto. Commons added collective action to the body of subject matter with which economists must concern themselves. Building upon Hume, he developed in detail how economic scarcity gives rise to both conflicts of interest and mutual coöperation. Conflicts of interests center in the transactions of individuals and other bargaining units with one another. In the absence of appropriate restrictions these conflicts would generate continuing anarchy and disorder which increasing efficiency in the use of resources would be powerless to correct. Accordingly, since the establishment of a new and complete harmony of interests is out of the question, individual transactions must be subjected to collective control which is designed to produce order. This collective control issues out of persuasion, coercion, and duress; it consists in the working rules of collective action; and it manifests itself in the various rationing arrangements by which access to resources is peacefully and lawfully restricted to the limited amounts available.[65]

Pareto was largely responsible for the destruction of the utilitarianism with which economics was intimately associated in the nineteenth and early twentieth century, and for the recognition that the findings of economic theory, if they are to make possible solutions of concrete problems, must be synthesized with those of other relevant social sciences.[66] Pareto denied both the utilitarian premise that the ends of human action are random, and the counter-proposition that the interests of men are naturally identical. He noted that wealth and power are the principal means to ends, and that economic activities can be effectively carried on only where "a relatively stable settlement of the power relationships between individuals and groups is attained." Accordingly, it is essential to the realization and maintenance of a social equilibrium conducive to stability in economic relationships that "the value element in the form both of ultimate ends and of value attitudes is in a significant degree common to the members of the society." (When such social integration is lacking it may sometimes be established through the use of force by an elite newly risen to power.)[67] Pareto's inference was made even more explicit by Durkheim who showed that the sanctions and the sense of moral obligation, which cause men to conform to the common system of normative rules by which order and social equilibrium are sustained and the centrifugal forces in society are contained, rest finally upon "a common system of ultimate-value attitudes."[68] Economic order is not attainable, the argument implies, so long as this common system is lacking.

VI

I have said that the social theorist gets into trouble when he fashions a subrealm of *hypothetical* being to represent a corresponding subrealm of *real* being, and then supposes that analysis of this hypothetical subrealm, to the exclusion of all other relevant hypothetical subrealms, can adequately explain the objects and events constituting the corresponding real subrealm or provide solutions for concrete problems arising in this real subrealm. For since the subrealms of real being are interdependent, the use of a hypothetical subrealm to discover explanations and solutions pertinent to the real realm of being must take this interdependence into account.

I also stated that solution of the problem of economic order consists in reconciling economic autonomy, coördination, and continuity with each other and with the forces of productivity-increasing change. I said, furthermore, that economists had failed to solve this problem because they had relied upon analysis of a circumscribed hypothetical economic subrealm to explain objects and events in a more extended real subrealm. Specifically, economists have ignored the fact that the real economic, political, and moral subrealms of being are intertwined; and they have acted as if the conduct of affairs in the real economic subrealm of being is essentially independent of what takes place in the real political and the real moral subrealms.

Let us see how this situation came about. It had been recognized long before Adam Smith and Quesnay wrote that the interests of men are not naturally identical but must be harmonized either through coercion, or through commonly held ethical and/or religious beliefs and norms which govern conduct and cause men to coöperate, or through a combination of coercion and norms. The relative weights attached to these two coördinating agents by social scientists had varied: in Greco-Roman times the state was deemed of greater importance; in the early centuries of Christianity ethico-religious norms dominated; by the late Middle Ages the rôle of state had become greater than in the period of Augustine, and it continued to grow in importance until the eighteenth century. At this time, however, both Smith and Quesnay made the great discovery that, even in the absence of a preconceived design, the conscious action of many men in an economy produces results which, though undesigned, are orderly, essentially consistent with their separate interests, and (usually) superior to those which an individual or group might achieve through deliberate planning of the activities of a whole economy.[69] Smith and his followers thus established the extreme importance of economic autonomy, particularly that of the entrepreneur who must function in a dynamic world.

The case for economic autonomy was made even stronger by subsequent economists. It was strengthened by the finding of Walras and his followers that free competition tends to maximize effective utility.[70] It has been strengthened on administrative grounds so far by the inability of proponents of centralized planning, despite their refutation of the thesis of Von Mises and others that correct pricing is *theoretically* impossible in a socialist state, to demonstrate how correct prices can be established *in practice* under authoritarian socialisms.[71] It was strengthened also by the extra-economic arguments of Mill and Marshall to the effect that man can develop his inherent excellences only under a system that allows great liberty to the individual.[72]

Unfortunately Smith and his followers, because of their emphasis upon the value of autonomy, made a mistake which the Physiocrats did not make: they overlooked the fact that, in the absence of appropriate rules and of a coercive agent to enforce these rules if necessary, the actions of autonomous agents will not be so coördinated as to produce harmony; and they ignored the fact that economic activity can continue at a high level only if satisfactory conditions are present. If the followers of Smith had recognized the contingent character of the harmony and the continuity which, they supposed, tended automatically to be realized, they would have sought to discover what these necessary conditions are; and they would have formulated rules and principles out of which statesmen, armed with practical wisdom, could fashion institutional and governmental controls suited to establish these conditions and reconcile autonomy with coördination and continuity in a dynamic world. Had this been done, much bad legislation and many costly failures to take collective action would have been avoided.

The cost to the Western world of its failure to combine Quesnay's principles with those of Smith has been accentuated by three changes, the last two of which are attributable in part to the decision of economists to follow Smith to the exclusion of Quesnay. First, because of the decline in the conduct-determining influence of the Christian ethic, the underlying common value system has lost some of its homogeneity and, therefore, some of its capacity to coördinate the economic behavior of autonomous agents; whence, as Pareto observed, the need for a harmony-producing coercive agent has increased. Second, the four pillars — the balance-of-power system, the international gold standard, the liberal state, and the self-regulating market — of nineteenth century civilization and Smithian harmony finally collapsed.[73] Third, the supposedly egoistic *individual* bargaining units of the early nineteenth century have been largely replaced by *plural* bargaining units — trade unions, corporations, etc. — whose psychology, objectives, and methods of procedure differ markedly from those of the bargaining egoisms postulated by nineteenth century economic theory.[74] Whence the determinate economy of yesterday in which the forces of competition supposedly produced something like a satisfactory equilibrium is giving way to an indeterminate economy in which essentially amoral economic interest groups will struggle for power and income until, if this struggle is not otherwise composed, a Hobbesian sovereign takes over.[75] A foretaste of what may be in prospect was supplied in the post-V-J-Day period by the struggle of business, agriculture, and labor, always abetted by opportunistic politicians, each to rid itself prematurely of the wartime controls imposed on it in the interest of the common welfare.

This Hobbesian denouement is by no means a foregone conclusion; and we could not confidently predict this outcome even if it were assured in fact. We have at our disposal knowledge which may be mobilized to reconcile autonomy, coördination, continuity, and change. Keynesianism may yet enable us to ensure the continuity which belief in Say's Law was unable to produce. The allocational principles developed by the Austrian, Lausanne, and related schools may yet be fashioned into economic rules suitable for the guidance of agents, coercive and otherwise, appointed to suppress anti-competitive behavior and bring about a correct allocation of the factors of production.[76] The studies of Pareto, Commons, and others, which have made explicit the coördinating rôle of coercive agents, institutions, and common value-attitudes, may help us to implement the information they have provided.

VII

I turn now to the import of what I have said for the American economy. This economy, as presently conceived and operated, does not appear likely to persist. For it has failed to solve the problem of economic order; and an economy that fails to solve this problem does not tend to survive unchanged. It has provided a large amount of economic *autonomy*, to be sure. But it has been unable to ensure *continuity* of a high level of economic activity, and its capacity to *coördinate* and harmonize the diverse interests of individuals and groups has been declining and probably will continue to decline so long as present conditions persist. Today powerful groups — I refer particularly to those elements in the business, agricultural, and labor sectors which are seeking to establish quasi-monopolistic prices for their goods and services — are engaged in a struggle for wealth and power, which the coercive power of the state is at present unable to compose, and which is affecting adversely the well-being of a large fraction of the population. This struggle is aggravated by the fact that in the cases of agriculture and labor the two primary forms of power, the economic and the political, are united as they have never before been united in this country. There is great danger, therefore, that this struggle, if permitted to continue, will generate a totalitarian economic state and thus destroy the very autonomy that most thinking men would like to see preserved.

Struggles of this sort may in theory be composed in one of two ways, either of which can produce a coördination of activities and an artificial identity of interests. A centrally planned economy, dominated and largely operated by the state, may be brought into existence. This solution is out of the question, however. It involves rejection of the very values and ideals to the realization of which the attainment of economic order is merely a means. It entails denial of the autonomy we are seeking to preserve. It almost certainly will neither maximize the rate of growth of per capita income nor bring about the particular kind of coördination that most men want. For the entrepreneurial state lacks and probably will continue to lack the know-how, the moral integrity, the inventiveness, the capacity to give incentive, and the flexibility of economic behavior requisite in a dynamic world. Moreover, because of the uncertainty inherent in human society and characteristic of human endeavor, the state is incapable of establishing for large numbers those complex arrangements which are presently brought about in the democratic world by continual mutual adjustments of the participating autonomous agents.[77]

A solution may be found, secondly, in the establishment and enforcement by the state and by inferior associations, of a body of rules,[78] suited to produce a workable and stable harmony of diverse interests, while probably allowing to individuals and entrepreneurs even more autonomy than they now enjoy in the aggregate. These rules would be designed: (a) to produce an economically correct allocation of factors of production and thus remove short-run and long-run disguised unemployment; (b) to prevent major disturbances in the monetary system and in the orderly growth of the media of exchange. These rules, by reducing diminishable uncertainties and narrowing the range of expectations, would give greater stability and certitude to the expectations of men regarding future prices, the character of prospective institutional controls, and the probable scope of the use of coercion in the economic realm of being.

The general effect of these rules would be to prevent monopolistic and related practices and to compel buyers and sellers, whether many or few in number, to behave as if they were operating under conditions of pure competition.[79] Given these rules, collective bargaining between employers and trade union representatives could no longer serve, as it so frequently does today, particularly in the case of industry-wide agreements, to establish supra-competitive wages and prices at the expense of the rest of the community; organized agriculture could no longer, through government-sponsored arrangements, collect from American consumers both supra-competitive prices for agricultural products and tax receipts for distribution to farmers participating in these monopolistic operations;[80] particular sheltered business groups could no longer overcharge their customers; periodic raids upon the federal treasury by groups such as the "silver interests" would become a thing of the past; and banks would no longer be so free to manufacture or to destroy means of exchange irrespective of the effects of such action upon the economy. In short, effective application of appropriate rules would restore to the consumer, the Forgotten Man of the American economy, his seat at the bargaining table which was taken away from him by the monopoly-seekers and their political henchmen.

The establishment and enforcement of these rules will not only serve to produce competition, or its similitude, and an acceptable artificial and dynamic identity of interests. It will also help to make possible what so far has been achieved only in regimented police states dedicated to war or to preparation for war, namely, economic *continuity*. Something like continuous high-level activity can be achieved only if the state and other associations make use, when necessary, of the instruments of control which contemporary economic theory has fashioned or may fashion. These instruments cannot safely be applied, however, in a dynamic society under the sway of monopoly-seekers and shot through with the bottlenecks to which full employment gives rise even when free competition prevails. For in such a society the use of these instruments makes for the prevention of necessary price adjustments, the perpetuation of monopolistic arrangements, and the generation of inflation; it cannot, therefore, bring about real continuity in such a society.

The establishment of rules, even when supported by the coercive power of the state, will not suffice per se to secure and preserve economic order. First, the basic common value-attitudes of the population must be sufficiently consistent with these rules to mobilize in their support a strong sense of moral obligation to comply with these rules. Otherwise there will be need for a much stronger external coercive agent than is likely to be compatible with a high degree of autonomy.

What I have said respecting rules and autonomy is well illustrated and attested in particular branches of athletics such as football. Everyone with any interest in football — coaches, players, spectators — is concerned above all that the game both survive and improve. Everyone is willing, therefore, even at the expense of temporary disadvantage to himself, to accept and abide by whatever rules are essential to the survival and improvement of the game. So the rules are enforced both by appointed regulatory bodies armed with sanctions and by the commonly felt sense of moral responsibility for the maintenance and observance of an appropriate body of rules. While these rules circumscribe the behavior of each team, they do not deprive it of its creative autonomy. Each coach plans his offense and defense within the boundary of these rules, incorporating his offensive and defensive plans in a set of plays, maneuvers, and action-directing maxims. This set allows considerable autonomy to the individual player just as the overriding body of rules allows considerable autonomy to each coach and team. A coach does not imagine and describe and plan in detail every possible disposition, and series of dispositions, of men by which his team may be confronted, or with which his team may face the opposing team. It is impossible in practice for a coach to do this, let alone to communicate to his players every possible disposition and counterdisposition of his men and their opponents. If this were attempted the game would be frozen. The coach is content, therefore, to plan broader initial dispositions and counterdispositions of players, to indicate their manner of execution, and otherwise to rely upon action-directing maxims which allow each player a large and necessary amount of autonomy. In sum, in athletics we find autonomy and coördination nicely balanced at all relevant levels.

Second, intranational economic order can be achieved only in a world of international political order; it cannot be achieved so long as unrestricted national sovereignty and, therefore, international anarchy prevail. It is already evident, in fact, that as the cold war of the totalitarian East against the freedom-loving West becomes warmer, the economies of the Western world will tend gradually to be transformed into highly militarized and essentially totalitarian systems. The ultimate way out lies in the establishment of a regime of international law under which *all individuals and states* must live, and to which they must be made to conform, if and when necessary, by the coercive power lodged at the international level in the United Nations or its successor. If, as is likely, the totalitarian East refuses to participate in such a government of laws at the international level it must be pressed to participate and without too much delay; for the economic and moral cost to the freedom-loving West of delay in this matter is not one that can long be tolerated without serious adverse effects.

Third, it will be difficult to secure and enforce rules of economic order in an economy in which the distribution of wealth is both markedly unequal and without the general approval of the population. For marked inequality tends to worsen socio-economic selection; it operates to check incentive and effort, and this tendency is accentuated by the progressive character of the present system of taxation, which is based largely upon income instead of upon capacity to produce income; and it serves to create social dissatisfaction, since few men include in the category of an individual's productivity his having been born in a gilded cradle. A reconsideration of the findings of Rignano, Dalton, and Wedgewood is in order, therefore. Presumably, despite past unsatisfactory experience with death and gift taxes, inequality could be greatly reduced through the use of these taxes and the imposition of ceilings upon the amount of property donatable and/or bequeathable in the aggregate and to individual direct, or collateral, heirs.[81] The preservation of autonomy would require, however: (a) that, as a rule, property gathered into the hands of the state through such taxation be transferred to private ownership and management; and (b) that gifts and bequests to eleemosynary institutions not be subject to limitations, since these institutions constitute bulwarks against the encroachment of the state bureaucracy in many spheres of life in which considerable privately dominated activity is desirable.

I have indicated the direction in which the solution of the problem of economic order lies. Whether it will be solved by our society no one knows. Certainly past history does not augur too well for the future. Solution involves action at three levels. First, the problem must be clearly envisaged. Second, the solution must be stated in theoretical terms. I have limited my historical and other discussion to these first two levels. Action at the third level consists in the translation of the theoretical solution into practice; therefore it is by far the most difficult. Yet it is not impossible of realization. And economists can contribute tremendously to its realization by reorienting their economic thinking in terms of this all-inclusive and paramount problem of economic order.

NOTES

1. L. Robbins, *An Essay on the Nature & Significance of Economic Science*, 2d ed., London, 1935, p. 16.

2. L. M. Fraser, *Economic Thought and Language*, London, 1937, chap. 2.

3. Talcott Parsons, *The Structure of Social Action*, pp. 757–75, especially 765–768. This important study has been very helpful to me in the preparation of the present paper. See also on this question F. H.

Knight, "Economic Science in Recent Discussion," *American Economic Review,* XXIV, 1934, pp. 225–38, and my "Sociological Presuppositions in Economic Theory," *Southern Economic Journal,* VII, 1940, pp. 131–57.

4. The conditions of action (heredity and environment), as Parsons states, "may be conceived at one pole, ends and normative rules at the other, means and effort as the connecting link between them." *Op. cit.,* pp. 732, 717–19. Of particular importance (see notes 27, 66 below) are the ends and normative rules. For when many persons coexist in the same physical space, their ultimate values cannot be random and multiple; they "must be, to a significant degree, integrated into a system common" to the members of the community; and in fact they "are developed in the processes of social interaction." See Parsons's analysis of Durkheim's views, *ibid.,* pp. 400–401. It is interesting to note that Leibniz accounted for the harmony of minds by supposing them under one moral government. See H. W. Carr, *Leibniz,* London, 1929, pp. 131–32, 133–34.

5. It may also be under the control of others with power over individual workers (e.g., slave owners).

6. On some of the factors which influence corporate decisions, see R. A. Gordon, *Business Leadership in the Large Corporation.* On factors which influence trade-union decisions see A. M. Ross, "Trade Unions as Wage-Fixing Institutions," *American Economic Review,* XXXVII, 1947, pp. 566–88; J. Shister, "The Locus of Union Control in Collective Bargaining," *Quarterly Journal of Economics,* LX, 1946, pp. 513 ff., "The Economics of Collective Bargaining," *Journal of Political Economy,* LI, 1943, pp. 338 ff., "The Theory of Union Bargaining Power," *Southern Economic Journal,* X, 1943, pp. 151 ff.

7. Limitations of time and space prevent our discussing the manner in which the problem of economic order was solved and the good of the individual was harmonized with that of his fellows and that of the community by other cultures and their social scientists. Aspects of the problem as it has been dealt with in primitive cultures are treated in M. J. Herskovits's *The Economic Life of Primitive Peoples.* On the Chinese solutions see Chen Huan-Chang, *The Economic Principles of Confucius and His School.* F. C. S. Northrop's analysis (*The Meeting of East and West,* chap. 10, esp. pp. 352–354, 383–393) suggests that the Oriental emphasis upon the indeterminate and undifferentiated aesthetic continuum entails an approach to the problem of order different from that prevalent in the West.

Because of limitations of time and space I have limited my discussion to the views of the leading representatives of different schools and/or epochs. There were differences between members of given schools (e.g., between Plato, Aristotle, and Xenophon); but these have been ignored.

8. See Aristotle, *Politics,* I–IV, VI–VII; *Rhetoric,* I, 4; *Ethica Nichomachea,* I, 5; IV, 1–2, V, VII, 9; *Oeconomica;* and *Atheniensum Respublica.* See also G. Sabine, *A History of Political Theory,* chaps. 1–6; C. N. Cochrane, *Christianity and Classical Culture,* pp. 74–84, 98, 111, 160; R. G. Collingwood, *The Idea of Nature,* Oxford, 1945, Part I; W. Jaeger, *Paideia,* I, chap. 9, esp. pp. 164–165, also 266–267, 277. Stressing the importance of the rule of law even more than did Plato, Aristotle said (*Politics,* III, 16): "He who bids the law rule may be deemed to bid God and Reason alone rule, but he who bids man rule adds an element of the beast; for desire is a wild beast, and passion perverts the minds of rulers even when they are the best of men. The law is reason unaffected by desire." In the *Rhetoric* (I, 4) he says that "it is on a country's laws that its welfare depends."

9. "A man ought to know," says Aristotle, which of the useful parts of wealth getting "pay better than others, and which pay best in particular places." *Politics,* I, 11.

10. H. Michell, *The Economics of Ancient Greece,* Cambridge, 1940, pp. 36–37; also Sabine, *op. cit.,* chap. 7.

11. Sabine, *op. cit.,* p. 133.

12. Cochrane, *op. cit.,* pp. 47, 56–57; Cicero, *On the Commonwealth,* translated with notes and introduction by G. H. Sabine and S. B. Smith, pp. 52, 55, 136–139, 177n., 191n., 196; Sabine, *Political Theory,* chaps. 8–9.

13. Sabine, *ibid.,* pp. 164 ff., 179–182.

14. Cochrane, *op. cit.,* pp. 347–348.

15. *Ibid.,* pp. 351–357, 440–516; Augustine, *The City of God,* XVIII, 2, XIX, 5.

16. B. Dempsey, "Just Price in a Functional Economy," *American Economic Review,* XXV, 1935, pp. 473–476; R. Kaulla, *Theory of Just Price,* London, 1940, pp. 21–35; A. Gray, *The Socialist Tradition,* pp. 38–54.

17. Thomas Aquinas, *On the Governance of Rulers* (translated by B. G. Phelan), pp. 35–36, 97–104.

18. Dempsey, *op. cit.,* pp. 476–485; Kaulla, *op. cit.,* pp. 35–45; Aquinas, *Summa Theologica,* Part II, Second Part, Questions LXI, LXXVII, LXXVIII. See also B. W. Dempsey, *Interest and Usury,* chaps. 6–8; G. Biel (c. 1430–1495), *Powers and Utility of Money* (Nuremberg, 1542) Philadelphia, 1930. Aquinas, of course, approved private property, when conjoined with liberality in its use (Gray, *op cit.,* pp. 55–60).

19. See B. N. Nelson, "The Usurer and the Merchant Prince," in Supplement VII (1947) to *The Journal of Economic History.* On the change in values as the medieval economy declined, see R. H. Tawney, *The Acquisitive Society,* chap. 2.

20. In his *Six livres de la republique* (1576) J. Bodin also anticipated Hobbes in part. However, while Bodin sought to formulate the bases of peace, order, and unity within the bounds of the modern state, his concern was primarily to solve the problems originating in feudal particularism and diversity of religion, and his solution involved greater restriction than did Hobbes's upon the power of the individual sovereign.

21. See P. A. Sorokin, *Contemporary Sociological Theories,* chap. 1, esp. pp. 4 ff.

22. See T. Hobbes, *Leviathan* (1651), Everyman edition, pp. 23 ff., 43, 49, 63–67, 87–90, 93, 115, 122, chaps. 24, 29–30. See also C. B. Macpherson, "Hobbes Today," *Canadian Journal of Economics and Political Science,* XI, 1945, pp. 524–534.

23. E.g., Sir Dudley North, in his *Discourses Upon Trade* (1691), an essay that however exercised little influence, declared that "no Laws can set Prizes in Trade, the Rates of which, must and will make themselves: But when such Laws do happen to lay any hold, it is so much Impediment to Trade, and therefore prejudicial"; that "Interest . . . should be left freely to the Market"; and that "there can be no Trade unprofitable to the Publick; for if any prove so, men leave it off." See edition edited by J. H. Hollander, Baltimore, 1907, pp. 10, 13.

24. O. H. Taylor, "Economics and the Idea of 'Jus Naturale,'" *Quarterly Journal of Economics,* XLIV, 1930, p. 211; this is really the second part of an article of which the first part (*ibid.,* pp. 1–39) is entitled "Economics and the Idea of Natural Laws."

25. A good summary of the views of the mercantilists is to be found in E. Hecksher, *Mercantilism,* Part V of which relates particularly to the discussion in the text above. See also H. Heaton's criticisms of Hecksher's interpretation (*Journal of Political Economy,* XLV, 1937, pp. 370–394) and Hecksher's reply to earlier criticisms (*Economic History Review,* VII, 1936, pp. 44 ff.). The international bellicosity of mercantilism is stressed particularly by E. Silberner, *La guerre dans la pensée économique de XVIIᵉ au XVIIIᵉ siècle,* Paris, 1939, pp. 117 ff.

26. A. N. Whitehead, *Science and the Modern World,* pp. 16 ff.

27. Taylor, *op. cit.,* pp. 213 ff.; P. W. Buck, *The Politics of Mercantilism,* chap. 3. E. Halévy treats of the reconciliation of individual and general interest as follows (*The Growth of Philosophical Radicalism,* pp. 13–18): There are three conditions under which the individual, who naturally desires pleasure and averts pain, will "pursue the general utility and not [his] private interest." (i) There is a "fusion of interests" when "personal and general interest" are spontaneously identified "within each individual conscience by means of the feeling of sympathy" which interests the individual in the happiness of his neighbor. (ii) A natural identity of interests may be supposed to exist; for, since the human species lives and survives despite the predominance of egoistic motives in human nature, "it must be admitted that the various egoisms harmonise of their own accord and automatically bring about the good of the species," and it may be inferred that egoistic motives are essential to survival. (iii) There is an artificial identification of interests if, it being denied that egoism do or ever will harmonize, it is necessary to suppose it to be the business of the legislator, by means of punishments and rewards, to identify the interest of the individual with the general interest, since this is in the interest of the individual.

28. R. Cantillon, *Essai sur la nature du commerce en général* (1755), translated by Henry Higgs, London, 1931, Part I, chaps. 13–16. As A. H. Cole has observed ("An Approach to the Study of Entrepreneurship," *Journal of Economic History,* Supplement VI, 1946, pp. 2 ff.) Cantillon's emphasis upon the importance of the entrepreneur was not characteristic of the English classical school; in France Condillac and J. B. Say did continue this emphasis. "The sort of men we call Undertakers are very instrumental in the public by advancing manufactures," it was written shortly before 1700. See E. Lipson, *A Planned Economy or Free Enterprise,* London, 1944, p. 110; also pp. 86–88, 104, on the already all-permeating influence of the entrepreneur in the early modern period in Great Britain.

29. See J. Viner, *Studies in the Theory of International Trade,* pp. 91–109.

30. For other criticisms see H. Sidgwick, *Outlines of the History of Ethics,* London, 1939, pp. 174 ff., 184 ff., 200. Cumberland, a precursor of the later utilitarians, assigned considerable weight to benevolence as a determiner of conduct; Shaftsbury reasoned that normally there is much harmony between a man's social affections and his "reflective self-regard."

31. John Locke, *Of Civil Government,* 1690, Everyman edition, pp. 118–121, 126–141, 158–165, 180–181, 189–190, 205, 224.

32. David Hume, *Essays Moral, Political, and Literary,* edited by T. H. Green and T. H. Grosse, I, pp. 113–117, 156 ff., 330 ff., 443–460, II, pp. 179–217, 271–274. Both Plato and Cicero had anticipated Hobbes, Hume noted (*ibid.,* pp. 184–185n.). See Viner, *op. cit.,* pp. 74 ff., 84 ff.; E. A. J. Johnson, *Predecessors of Adam Smith,* pp. 161 ff. According to Halévy (*op. cit.,* p. 13; see also note 27 above) Hume, in his endeavors to reconcile private and public interest, made use of fusion, natural identity, and artificial identification of interests.

33. *De l'intérêt social,* Paris, 1777, pp. 557–558, 603–605. See also Le Mercier

de la Rivière, *L'ordre naturel et essentiel de sociétés politiques,* Paris, 1767, chaps. 39–40. Similar opinions were expressed by other members of the school.

34. Le Trosne, *op. cit.,* p. 603.

35. These views of the Physiocrats are recounted in my "The Physiocrats and Say's Law of Markets," *Journal of Political Economy,* LIII, 1945, pp. 193 ff., 317 ff. The contradictions which developed in their writings are noticed in *ibid.,* pp. 327 ff. See also my *French Predecessors of Malthus,* chap. 5.

36. For a brief but careful account of questions considered in this paragraph see M. Einaudi, *The Physiocratic Doctrine of Judicial Control,* Cambridge, 1938. See also Taylor, *op. cit.,* pp. 215–226. Bibliography will be found in the former study. According to M. Beer there was much of Aquinas and scholasticism in the views of the Physiocrats, most of whom presumably were Catholic in religion (*An Inquiry into Physiocracy,* London, 1939).

37. For a brief account of the introduction of Smith's views into Europe and their widespread influence see M. Palyi's essay in *Adam Smith, 1776–1926.*

38. On Smith's anticipation of Say's law, see my paper cited in note 35 above.

39. See J. Viner, "Laissez Faire," in work cited in note 37, esp. pp. 138–153. Smith's views on the role of government are found principally in Book V of *The Wealth of Nations.* He dealt with it also in his lectures as of 1763 (*Lectures on Justice, Police, Revenue and Arms,* edited by E. Cannan, London, 1896). On the formation of Smith's views see also W. R. Scott, *Adam Smith as Student and Professor,* Glasgow, 1937, chap. 5, and pp. 111–115.

40. This is H. J. Bitterman's conclusion in his careful "Adam Smith's Empiricism and the Law of Nature" (*Journal of Political Economy,* XLVIII, 1940, pp. 487–88; see also 488 ff., 703 ff.) in which Smith's empiricism is demonstrated. See notes 41, 43 below. That allowing great autonomy to the individual and the individual business man would make for the interests of all must have been suggested to Smith by Mandeville's *Fable of the Bees* (E. Cannan, introduction to *Wealth of Nations,* p. liv of Modern Library edition). That Smith was influenced in this and other respects by Boisguilbert is the conclusion of H. V. Roberts (*Boisguilbert,* chaps. 15–17). On Scottish opinion in this matter see G. Bryson, *Man and Society.*

41. See Halévy, *op. cit.,* pp. 89–92, 97, 101–107, 212–213, 237. In his *Theory of Moral Sentiments,* which was speculative in character, Smith wrote as if the order of nature is harmonious, under divine guidance, and conducive to man's welfare. In the *Wealth of Nations,* which was empirical in character, Smith had to take disharmonies into account. The differences are well summarized by Viner

("Laissez Faire," pp. 125–127). Bitterman concludes that "Smith's theory of ethics did not rest directly on the doctrine of the order of nature" (*op. cit.,* p. 717).

42. F. H. Giddings transmuted Smith's "sympathy" or "fellow-feeling" into "consciousness of kind" and made it "the principal cause of social conduct." See preface to 3rd edition of Giddings's *Principles of Sociology.* A. W. Small (*Adam Smith and Modern Sociology*) impressed by Smith's historical and institutional analysis, found the object of modern sociology implicit in Smith's moral philosophy.

43. This paragraph is based upon my reading of Smith's two chief works. According to Taylor (*op. cit.,* p. 208) late eighteenth and early nineteenth century economic liberalism "was not a doctrine that selfish interests should be given free play while the state and society remained passive. It was a particular theory of an ideal legal order, imposing equal restraints upon all in order to give equal and maximum liberty to all, so that a 'natural' interplay and adjustment of interests might ensure the welfare of all." Bitterman's (see *op. cit.*) interpretation is somewhat at variance with Taylor's. Smith's interest in the welfare of the common man is brought out in E. Ginzberg's *House of Adam Smith.*

44. Cp. Halévy, *op. cit.,* p. xvi. F. A. Hayek points out that the Liberalism of the French Revolution was not yet founded upon an understanding of the free market. See "The Counter-Revolution of Science," *Economica,* VIII, 1941, p. 11n.

45. For a careful summary of Bentham's views see W. Stark, "Jeremy Bentham as an Economist," *Economic Journal,* LI, 1941, pp. 56–79, esp. pp. 59 ff., 67 ff., 75 ff., and *ibid.,* LVI, 1946, pp. 583–608, esp. 583–591. See also W. C. Mitchell, *The Backward Art of Spending Money,* pp. 177–202.

46. S. and B. Webb, *Industrial Democracy,* London, 1902, pp. 573–574, 605, 612, 615, 647 ff. Even arbitration and conciliation, wrote J. G. Stirling in 1869, implicitly sanctioned "the substitution of an artificial mechanism for that natural organism which Providence has provided for the harmonious regulation of industrial interests." Cited in *ibid.,* pp. 224n. On the wages fund and its eventual rejection see F. W. Taussig, *Wages and Capital.*

47. See my "Malthus's Total Population Theory: A Restatement and Reappraisal," *Canadian Journal of Economics and Political Science,* XI, esp. pp. 250–255. Because he did not subscribe to Say's Law, Malthus favored the construction of public works in times of crisis; and because, unlike Ricardo, Malthus anticipated the advent of a situation such as that in which England now finds herself, he opposed her becoming dependent upon foreign food supplies.

48. *Principles of Political Economy and Taxation* (E. C. K. Gonner, ed.), Lon-

don, 1903, p. 82. See also Mitchell's "Postulates and Preconceptions of Ricardian Economics," in *op. cit.*, pp. 203 ff.

49. *Social Statics*, New York, 1883, p. 334; Halévy, *op. cit.* p. 514.

50. "Nothing can be more surely established or [by] a larger experience than that a government which interferes with any trade injures that trade . . . let it take care of itself." (See W. Bagehot, *Lombard Street*, London, 1873, chap. 4).

51. *Principles of Political Economy* (W. Ashley, ed.), pp. 200, 211, 242, 793, 984–989, Bk. V. Mill believed that economists exaggerated the effect of competition at the expense of custom; but he added that "only through the principle of competition has political economy any pretension to the character of a science" (*ibid.*, p. 242). The ease with which economic questions can be formulated when pure competition is assumed commended this assumption to later economists as well.

52. *The State in Relation to Labour*, London, 1882; *Methods of Reform*, London, 1883.

53. H. Sidgwick, *The Principles of Political Economy*, London, 1887, p. 418, also Bk. 3, and Bk. 2, chaps. 9–10.

54. *Principles of Economics*, London, 1920, Bk. 3, Bk. 5, chap. 13, Appendix A, p. 304; *Memorials* (A. C. Pigou, ed.), London, 1925, pp. 256 ff., 323 ff.; Parsons, *op. cit.*, chap. 4. Modern welfare economics, as developed by Pigou, Harrod, J. Robinson, Hutt, Hicks, Henderson, Kahn, Kaldor, Samuelson, and others, is more or less in the Marshallian tradition. See note 79; also M. W. Reder, *Studies in the Theory of Welfare Economics*.

55. *Traité d'économie politique; Cours complet d'économie politique.*

56. E.g., see Bastiat, *Harmonies of Political Economy*, Edinburgh, 1880.

57. Typical though not identical in emphasis are the works of De Molinari, Colson, Leroy-Beaulieu, and Courcelle-Seneuil. Even advocates of protectionism in France and America otherwise accepted the tenets of liberal economics.

58. E.g., the works of H. Carey, A. L. Perry, F. A. Walker, J. B. Clark, and F. M. Taylor.

59. E.g., see accounts of various national schools in Palgrave's *Dictionary of Political Economy*.

60. Walras, first formulator of the theory of general equilibrium, "was the first economist to show that under perfect competition, full employment of resources is compatible with the desire of each individual to maximize the return from his resources." See G. Stigler, *Production and Distribution Theories*, pp. 241–242. See L. Walras, *Etudes d'économie politique appliquée*, Paris, 1936, p. 476.

61. See E. von Boehm-Bawerk, "Macht oder Oekonomisches Gesetz" (1914), included in his *Gesammelte*

Schriften, Vienna, 1924; F. von Wieser, *Social Economics*. Concerning writers who have dwelt upon the power factor see T. Suranyi-Unger, *Economics in the Twentieth Century*, pp. 109–114, 119–123, 192–193, 203–206. In Japan the power theory of distribution has been developed by Yasuma Takata, in "The Bankruptcy of Wage Theories: Prolegomena to a Power Theory of Economy," *Kyoto University Economic Review*, XI, 1936, pp. 17–36; and elsewhere in this same journal, XII, 1937, pp. 1 ff., X, 1935, pp. 18 ff., 54 ff., IV, 1928, pp. 81–83.

62. See F. A. Hayek, "The Counter-Revolution of Science," *Economica*, VIII, 1941, esp. Part II, pp. 127–128, 131–132, 141–145; E. Silberner, *The Problem of War in Nineteenth Century Economic Thought*, chaps. 13–14. See also E. Halévy ("The Age of Tyrannies," *Economica*, VIII, 1946, pp. 77 ff.) who shows that socialism in its original form was neither liberal nor democratic.

63. *Ibid.*, chap. 14; discussions of Marx's work by S. F. Bloom and H. Grossman in *Journal of Political Economy*, LI, 1943, pp. 494 ff., 506 ff.; P. M. Sweezy, *The Theory of Capitalist Development*, New York, 1942; W. Leontief, "The Significance of Marxian Economics for Present-Day Economic Theory," *American Economic Review, Supplement*, XXVIII, 1938, pp. 1 ff.

64. L. Klein, *The Keynesian Revolution*. On the differences between the classical, the Marxian, and the Keynesian theories see Klein's "Theories of Effective Demand and Employment," *Journal of Political Economy*, LV, 1947, pp. 108–131.

65. J. R. Commons, *Institutional Economics; The Legal Foundations of Capitalism*. A careful study of Commons's economics would reveal how the importance attached by him to collective institutional controls grew from its small beginnings in his *Distribution of Wealth*.

66. V. Pareto, *The Mind and Society*, sec. 34. His purely economic theories are summarised in his *Manuel d'économie politique* (Paris, 1907). For a treatment of his views from one point of view see my "Pareto on Population," *Quarterly Journal of Economics*, LVIII, 1944, pp. 571 ff., LIX, 1944, pp. 107 ff.

67. See Parsons's analysis of Pareto's system, *op. cit.*, pp. 236, 707, also 206, 237–241, 263–264, 267–268, 291, 457–458.

68. *Ibid*, pp. 463–465, 709–710, 713; also R. K. Merton, "Social Structure and Anomie," *American Sociological Review*, III, 1938, pp. 672 ff. Max Weber too, and in some measure, Marshall, reached a conclusion similar to that of Pareto and Durkheim (see Parsons, *op. cit.*).

69. See F. A. Hayek, "Scientism and the Study of Society," *Economica*, IX, 1942, pp. 288–291, XI, 1944, pp. 27–30.

70. See note 60 above. The Lausanne

school for reasons of mathematical convenience postulated a finely articulated economic system. Elsewhere ("The Role of the State in Shaping Things Economic," *Journal of Economic History*, Supplement VII, 1947) I have suggested that the economic system, being shot through with play, is not so tightly articulated as is sometimes supposed. Professor C. L. Allen has recalled to my attention T. Veblen's observation that "the system has not yet reached a fatal degree of close-knit interdependence, balance, and complication; it will run along at a very tolerable efficiency in the face of a very appreciable amount of persistent derangement" (*The Engineers and the Price System*, p. 57). Here Veblen refers primarily to level of activity; my reference is to the sensitivity of one part of the system to a change in some other part independently of the level of activity. The condition of sensitivity, of course, is far more important than that of insensitivity.

71. For a discussion of the problem and reference to some of the relevant literature see my review of Hayek's *The Road to Serfdom* in *Southern Economic Journal*, XII, 1945, pp. 48–55.

72. The psychologist I. P. Pavlov said there exists a "freedom reflex." Cited by P. A. Sorokin, *Social and Cultural Dynamics*, III, p. 174; see the whole of chap. 6, pp. 161 ff.

73. The collapse of these pillars is described by K. Polanyi in *The Great Transformation*.

74. See references cited in note 6 above.

75. "The Keynesian revolution in theory . . . may turn out to be the opening stage of a greater revolution, precipitating us into the theory and practice of an indeterminate economy of organized groups, whose social roots go far deeper, and whose social effects are far wider, than questions of wages and prices." See J. M. Clark, "Some Current Cleavages Among Economists," *American Economic Review*, Supplement, XXXVII, 1947, p. 2. See also my paper cited in note 70 above. It is significant that six of the ten principal causes of inflation listed in the *Monthly Business Review* (Oct. 1947, p. 4) of the Cleveland Federal Reserve Bank are the result of action by politicians; the other four causes are attributable in part to actions of politicians.

76. Some of these principles have been expressed formally by A. P. Lerner in his *The Economics of Control*. Since Lerner's statement of some principles is unsatisfactory at the formal level, and since he does not show how the formally satisfactory principles may be translated into administratively feasible rules, his study, while useful and clarifying, is of quite limited applicability. See also M. W. Reder, *op. cit.*

77. See K. Polanyi, "The Growth of Thought in Society," *Economica*, VIII, 1941, pp. 428–457. See my papers cited in notes 70 and 71 above.

78. "The substance of society, in so far as it is free or moral, is the body of such rules made by human beings for their own association, with a view either to making their activity itself as interesting and satisfying as possible, or else to fulfilling what they conceive to be their 'task' as human beings." See F. H. Knight, "Economic Science in Recent Discussion," *American Economic Review*, XXIV, 1934, p. 237. This view was effectively stated by the late Henry Simons. See references to his work in my paper cited in note 70 above.

79. In this section I use the terms monopoly and competition, and their adjectival forms, in a not too rigorous sense. The term monopoly is intended to cover all economically adverse deviations from pure competition except those no more extreme than monopolistic competition when selling is aggressive. The use of the concept competitive equilibrium is not intended to suggest that this particular equilibrium necessarily yields the maximum of satisfaction; it is here used as a first approximation on grounds of convenience. It is not possible in this paper to take into account the ways in which a purely competitive equilibrium may differ from an equilibrium yielding maximum satisfaction. It is the latter which is the desideratum and which, in so far as is practicable, the rules should be contrived to realize. See note 54 above.

80. Evidence that schemes such as the tobacco allotment plan elevate prices above the competitive level is suggested by a study of the price of tobacco land which reveals that "a majority of farms in the tobacco areas that were sold in 1945 and which had appropriate tobacco allotments were enhanced in market value by from $300 to $600 for each allotment acre." See J. E. Mason, "Acreage Allotments and Land Prices," *The Journal of Land & Public Utility Economics*, XXII, 1946, p. 181. On the basic problem which agriculture controls are intended to solve see T. E. Schultz, *Agriculture in an Unstable Economy*.

81. Death and gift taxes have not been an important source of income in the past because of difficulties attendant upon their administration. See H. M. Groves, *Postwar Taxation and Economic Progress*, chap. 9. How much death and gift taxes would contribute if a ceiling were placed upon gifts and bequests as suggested is difficult to determine. Suppose the national wealth is equal to five times the national income and that government absorbs one-fourth of the national income. Then, if 1.5 per cent of the property holders died every year, and the government took all their

property, the amount taken would aggregate only 30 per cent of tax income ($[.015 \times 500] \div 25 = 0.3$). This percentage is very much reduced, however, by allowances for gifts and bequests subject to little or no taxation. It is not likely, therefore, that death and gift taxes will supply a sizeable fraction of governmental receipts. Death and gift taxes provided 2.3 per cent of federal, state, and local tax revenue in 1942; 1.3 in 1945; and 1.6 in 1946 (see U.S. Bureau of the Census release G-GF46-No. 3 on "Governmental Revenue in 1946").

PART TWO

SCHOLASTICISM

AND

MERCANTILISM

IT IS NOT CLEAR just when economic behavior began to be manifested through commercial rather than through household and other noncommercial channels in a measure significant enough to command the attention of analysts. For these were slow to concern themselves with the explanation of economic behavior. The interests of philosophers in the Near East and in the Mediterranean world, for example, were centered initially upon questions lying within the realm of ethics and religion, and, in some instances, upon the behavior of physical rather than of human phenomena. Only occasionally, however, were their interests focused upon the behavior of men as members of groups, and then it was political rather than economic behavior that commanded major attention. Even when Greek philosophers concerned themselves with the economic preconditions of political stability, their attention seems to have been concentrated upon the establishment of suitable rules and practices rather than upon the analysis of economic behavior as such. Similarly, those who had to concern themselves with military logistics, or with elements of public housekeeping and finance, viewed their problems essentially from the vantage point of workable administrative rules. With few if any exceptions, therefore, ancient authors confined themselves to implicit and protoeconomics. The extent to which they were aware of economic principles must, therefore, be inferred largely from laws and legal codes, from law-court speeches and records, from reported administrative rules, from accounts of business practice, from political and ethical works, and so on. These sources receive almost no attention in the present work. In Part Two, together with Selection 10, a brief review is presented of the notions current before economics began to assume the form of a social science in the seventeenth century, subsequently to acquire a comparatively stable form at the hands of the physiocrats and Adam Smith.

The essays included in this part encompass a period of some six centuries. They serve, in combination with this introduction and Selection 10, to bridge both the gap between Graeco-Roman and scholastic economics and that between scholastic economics and the beginnings of liberal, classical economics in the early eighteenth century. Selection 2 describes phases of what may be called city-state economics, whereas Selection 3 describes elements present in national-state economics. Selection 4 illustrates that to a considerable extent continuity characterizes the development of economic thought; it demonstrates that a number of elements present in medieval economical writings survived into pre-Smithian and Smithian economics, even as Aristotelian ideas dominated scholastic economics and Smithian ideas permeated nineteenth-century economics. Ideational change rarely entails complete ideational annihilation or supersession, at least outside the realm of Animal Farm.

Toward the close of the Introduction to Part One, it was implied that at times severe breaks have characterized the development of economic thought. There at least five types of economic thought, or of approaches to economic questions, were identified. It may be inferred, therefore, that the continuity present in economic thought sometimes is accompanied also by discontinuity. Comparison of the views summarized in Selection 2 with those in Selection 3 may serve to suggest this discontinuity. For, in the thought discussed in Selection 3 there is much concern, not present in that in Selection 2, about this-worldly ends and a measure of concern with modes of analysis suitable to facilitate the realization of these ends. Selection 3, therefore, indicates that a modernization of thought and a change in *Weltanschauung* were under way, despite the continued endorsement of various earlier ideas by the mercantilist authors. A part of this shift in view is attributable, of course, to the fact that the earlier writers were generally ecclesiastics, whereas the mercantilist writers were generally men of commerce and governmental officials.

As was shown in Selection 1, scholastic economics resembles rather closely the economics of Aristotle, who, along with his contemporaries, may be looked upon as the first of the writers whose discussion of economic questions had an impact upon the course of development of recorded economic thought. (Biblical economic phrases, some of economic-historical significance, had considerable currency in the later Christian world, but they were not of analytical relevance, serving rather to support ethical prescriptions and prohibitions such as that of usury.) A number of factors account for the extent to which St. Thomas Aquinas and his successors were influenced by Aristotle. They found his philosophy as a whole, so inclusive and orderly, admirably adapted to support the philosophical views of the spokesmen for the Church and to supply needed opinions when these were lacking. Aristotle's economic and political philosophy specifically was found similarly adaptable, in part because both St. Thomas and Aristotle were writing about ideal and somewhat conceptualized societies, and in part because the civil society of which St. Thomas found exemplars in his thirteenth-century world resembled that of Aristotle's Athens in a number of respects. There were differences, of course: slavery was important in Athens but not in the medieval city-states; merchants dominated the life of the latter but not that of the former; applied invention and work and workers were held in somewhat greater esteem in the medieval than in the Greek city-states; and material conditions, though poor by present-day standards, often were better in the medieval communities. At the same time, medieval city-states were comparable in size with Athens and similarly dependent in large measure upon imported subsistence. Even the relatively large state of Florence in the early fourteenth century embraced only about twice as many inhabitants as did a weakened fourth-century Athens numbering perhaps 144,000 (of whom about 20,000 were slaves) and with a density similar to that of Florence. Of greatest importance, however, is the fact that in the city-states known to Aristotle and St. Thomas the economy remained nonautonomous, imbedded in society, and under a large amount of control by the community;

economic activity and motives were mingled with other activities and motives, and the forces operative in a free market were not counted upon to govern in entirety the allocation of productive agents and their earnings. The actual city-state Aristotle and St. Thomas knew was too small, as was the ideal state each envisaged, to give full play to free-market forces; it was also conceived of as a community within which men could realize spiritual and social aspirations to which purely material considerations were subordinate.[1]

Economic growth and its determinants were not of much concern to Aristotle or to St. Thomas; indeed they were not of much concern to economical writers until after the modern national state had begun to take shape and its mercantilist spokesmen had formulated an economic philosophy suitable to its destiny. Distribution rather than production engaged the interest of both the Socratic and the scholastic philosophers. The productivity-increasing role of organizational change, capital, and invention was not greatly appreciated, nor was the stimulus flowing from the reward of incentive. Plenty was not expected to smile upon a community in continually increasing measure; therefore, what it provided, if not devoted to religious or other public purpose, should be equitably distributed. Otherwise political turmoil might result. That the devotion of much of the social surplus to extravagant private consumption or to unproductive public purposes retarded economic development was disregarded.

The role of economic activity, Plato and Aristotle believed, was to make possible realization of the excellence or well-being of the citizen of the polis (*i.e.*, city-state) and of such other of its inhabitants as acquired a status approximating closely enough that of the citizen. The polis itself was a natural social organization within which functionally differentiated and hierarchically ordered individuals or groups co-operated to accomplish its purposes; it embraced man in his economic, political, ethical, and other capacities, all of which were more or less organically interrelated. Co-operation essential to realization of the purposes of the polis entailed reciprocity and exchange, in accordance with the principles of *particular* justice which, as it was put centuries later in Justinian's *Institutes* and repeated for many centuries thereafter, "gives to every man his due"; the persistence and the stability of the polis in fact depended upon the presence of particular justice.

This genus of justice included several species, the most important and relevant of which were distributive and commutative justice. Distributive justice had to do with the distribution of wealth, income, honors, and con-

---

1. See Karl Polanyi, C. M. Arensberg, and H. W. Pearson, eds., *Trade and Market in the Early Empires* (Glencoe: The Free Press, 1957), Chap. 5. See also Chaps. 2–3 and 18, in which it is argued that not until around Aristotle's time did a free-market economy begin to come into being, trading and related activities having been largely administered up to that time by states, temple-estates, etc., in Mesopotamia and elsewhere. On Athens see Alfred Zimmern, *The Greek Commonwealth* (New York: Modern Library, n.d.); A. H. M. Jones, "The Social Structure of Athens in the Fourth Century B.C.," *Economic History Review*, VIII (December 1955), 141–55. On the medieval city-state see M. V. Clarke, *The Medieval State* (London: Methuen & Co., Ltd., 1926); M. Poston and E. E. Rich, *The Cambridge Economic History of Europe*, II (Cambridge: Cambridge University Press, 1952).

tributions; it entailed reward or assumption of responsibility in accordance with certain criteria that varied with person or with class of persons. These criteria were not well defined; they seem to have included social position, manifestations of performance or of capacity to perform, amount invested in a business venture, and ability to contribute, but not apparently relative scarcity or imputed productivity as such. Commutative justice had to do with trade, exchange, etc.; it entailed that when a transaction took place, equivalent values must be exchanged. What constituted equivalence was not in the end very concretely specified, even though it apparently was taken for granted that each participant in a "just" transaction would be rewarded in accordance with his merit or performance as indicated by the requirements of distributive justice; for, as has been noted, these requirements were not defined with enough specificity. It apparently was assumed that the requirements of the two species of justice not only could be met simultaneously but could be met without great difficulty. It was taken for granted, consequently, that when commutative justice ruled, the price or exchange ratio that resulted was just and in keeping with the comparative want-satisfying powers of the goods exchanged. No attempt was made, therefore, to determine whether the possibility of the compatibility of distributive and commutative justice existed, or whether it was easily realized.

Aristotle's emphasis (more in keeping with Plato's *Laws* than with his *Republic*), in his political writings relating to life in the polis and in his ethical writings relating to individual behavior, was upon justice, its role in human relations, and its content. In his rhetorical and in some of his logical writings he dealt with the imputation of cause, but he did not bring the concept of imputation to bear effectively upon questions relating to justice in distribution and exchange. Though his arguments often were founded upon empirical observation, his prescriptions related to an ideal polis; they frequently were not descriptive of Athenian or other practice. Moreover, it apparently was not his intent to inquire into empirical aspects of price determination, or to set down a theory designed to explain pricing under conditions of competition or in situations, perhaps still dominant in his day, in which administrative allocation played a large role. He did not, therefore, isolate the various factors that helped to fix price in the transactions he discussed, nor did he note carefully (as finally did the Austrians) the connection between cost and utility, or translate criteria of merit into explicitly economic terms. Empirical observations appear in his writings, however, such as that monopoly makes for relatively high prices and profits.[2]

Preceding upon the supposition that every instrument has its natural function, and that realization of the good life within the polis was contingent upon there being available a moderate but not excessive amount of useful and necessary goods, Aristotle arrived at ethical conclusions in keeping with the very simple mode of living prevalent in Athens. Acquisition was

2. There is much dispute about what Aristotle meant, in part because of variation in the meanings assigned Greek terms. Sir Ernest Barker's *The Political Thought of Plato and Aristotle* (New York: Dover Publications, 1959), is helpful, though some of the interpretations may be questioned.

natural only in so far as it made goods available in a measure compatible with the moral purpose of the household and the polis; commercial trading for profit was unnatural, therefore. Similarly, lending money at interest was unnatural inasmuch as the proper function of money was the facilitation of exchange within the limits of the moral purpose of the state.

Because he considered political stability essential to the realizability of the good life within the polis, Aristotle inquired empirically and otherwise into the economic preconditions of political stability. He inferred (much as had Plato) that excessive inequality, want of subsistence, and mistreatment of the underprivileged were to be avoided. He did not really make use of his partial recognition of diminishing utility when assessing the effects of inequality, but he did stress (as had Plato) that the size of the population occupying the polis must be adequately restricted in order that its inhabitants might have sufficient land and means. While he supposed private property to be conducive to political stability, he believed that ownership of land, in so far as it was not in the hands of the state, ought to be restricted to citizens so they might have the leisure to serve the community. There was need for a middle class sufficiently strong and educated to mediate between the poor and the rich. It would help also if the virtues relating to the use of money (*i.e.*, liberality and munificence) animated men, since then their behavior would cushion the impact of inequality. In sum, Aristotle's views, like those of his contemporaries, were ethical and policy-oriented much more than analytical.

The age of the classical city-state or polis came to an end with the rise of Alexander's empire and its successor states and with the final ascendancy of the Romans over these states and Phoenician and Hellenic city-states. But economic thought was not really accommodated to these changes, to the ascendancy of free-market influences and many manifestations of capitalistic production, widening markets, and competition, and to the impact of comparative advantage upon the distribution of economic activities in the Mediterranean world. Ethical and legal philosophy were adjusted to the requirements of a larger world, especially by the Stoics, and Roman law, itself much inspired by Greek thought, was gradually made to satisfy many of the requirements of an ecumenical economy. But no systematic analysis of economic practice and tendencies was undertaken, nor were notable additions made to such analysis as Aristotle undertook or to such discussions of fiscal and related policy as Xenophon prepared. As in the later mercantilist times, so in greater measure in Roman times, one must look to practice for evidence of the economic principles presumed to obtain. One must look particularly to legal and business practice and similar sources as well as to administrative and managerial procedure, Rome's outstanding contribution to world politico-economic progress. For in Roman as in Greek belletristic, philosophical, and historical writings, one encounters economic information and occasional recognition of functional relationships (*e.g.*, Aristophanes' illustration of Gresham's Law) but no ordered economic analysis.

In time, circumstances became less favorable to the development of economic analysis. Christian thought and practice attached primary importance to other-worldly objectives and much less importance than did earlier Roman thought to this-worldly, material purposes, with the result that there was less occasion to be concerned with economics. Steps taken to solve the dire problems which troubled third-century Rome eventuated in a diminution in economic freedom and mobility and in the ascendancy of status — at the expense of contractual — relationships. Of this ascendancy the carefully administered Byzantine economy was an outcome, but, despite the persistence of a strong intellectual tradition, the spokesmen for this tradition seem to have been interested very little in economic analysis other than the implicit notions set down in works on administration.

In the West, upon the passage of the empire under the control of the Germans in the fifth century and its subsequent decomposition, the Graeco-Roman intellectual tradition was greatly damaged, with the result that for a long time there was little serious discussion of economic and related ethical matters. Moreover, in most parts, the population, now predominantly rural, became functionally divided into laborers, soldiers, and the clergy; few of these other than the clergy were capable after 800 A.D. of performing tasks requiring literacy. It is not surprising, therefore, that economic discussion was neglected, beyond the uttering of condemnations of usury and inequity. With the economic and cultural revival of Europe after the tenth century, however, and the rise of towns and associated conditions favorable to intellectual progress, the role of price and interest began to be examined more carefully until, in the thirteenth century, St. Thomas gave classic form to the scholastic treatment of interest, price, and related subjects, a treatment that served as a point of departure for subsequent Catholic authors.[3]

What St. Thomas and the scholastics had to say about economic questions centered largely on the subject of justice (which guarded a man's property against seizure) and the place of economic activities in the scheme of life man ought to pursue in order to realize his destiny. It thus was ethically oriented and reflected a particular conception of the economy, as did Aristotle's view. It had to be kept adjusted, however, to the changing economic circumstances which confronted expounders of canon law and others making practical application of scholastic economic principles. The scholastic system continued to incorporate adaptations to new or newly recognized empirical circumstances, even though it was not designed to formulate abstract economic principles and to use them to promote empirical inquiry.

Much of what the scholastics said flowed out of their discussions of two usually distinct subjects, just price and usury. The first is treated in Selection 2. Regarding the second, the determination of when a return might be allowed on a loan, it may be said that the scholastics, whose views were first synthesized by St. Thomas Aquinas, sought to rationalize the Church's

3. For summaries of the historical changes taking place, see Richard M. Haywood, *The Myth of Rome's Fall* (New York: Thomas Y. Crowell Co., 1958); R. W. Southern, *The Making of the Middle Ages* (London: Hutchinson's University Library, 1953). Excellent accounts of usury and related matters are to be found in John T. Noonan, Jr., *The Scholastic Analysis of Usury* (Cambridge: Harvard University Press, 1957). Functional aspects of the economic thought of St. Thomas and others, as applied at various times, are dealt with by the author of Selection 2, Father Bernard W. Dempsey, in *The Functional Economy* (Englewood Cliffs, N.J.: Prentice-Hall, Inc., 1958).

long-standing prohibition of usury, to bring natural-law and Aristotelian principles to bear upon the matter, and to establish juristic formulae and rules intended to disclose explicitly when usury was present in a transaction and when not. Much subtlety and considerable empirical observation therefore entered into their discussions. These never eventuated in a complete consensus, but they tended to restrict the set of transactions in which usury might be held to be present. The rules relating to the determination of justice in pricing were not, as a rule, found applicable in the determination of the presence of usury. For, whereas the just price of a vendible commodity was fixed by common estimation and varied with circumstances, the value of money, which was nonvendible, was fixed by law and hence was invariable unless changed by the state or (a few held) was involved in foreign-exchange transactions. Thus usury and just-price theories overlapped only when commodities were sold on credit and either overcharging or usury might be involved. The argument that a prince might not reduce the legal value (*i.e.*, metallic content) of money unless the whole community stood to benefit, was not tied into usury analysis.[4]

At least four sorts of change gradually resulted in modification of medieval approaches to economic questions. First, as economic conditions became more complex, the criteria pointing to the presence of usury were narrowed until in the early nineteenth century whatever interest was allowed by civil law was declared permissible by the Holy Office of the Roman Catholic Church. Second, as the economic, allocative, and developmental roles of price and profit came to be recognized, the concept of just price, though always influential, lost much of its original appeal. Third, values, ethical attitudes, and the ruling *Weltanschauung* gradually changed in and after the later Middle Ages, with the rise of commercial and urban interests and later the pluralizing of religious belief and doctrine. As a result emphasis upon material ends greatly increased, and the conduct-determining influence of antiusury and just-price injunctions was greatly weakened. Fourth, with the rise of federations of cities and (particularly) national states, together with the consequent absorption of the city-state, the politico-economic milieu (in which men lived and in the light of which political and economic decisions were made) underwent great enlargement and change. It was no longer easy and practicable to organize economic life in the simple, functional terms that the scholastics had in mind. It is with these last two sorts of change that mercantilist theory and practice, discussed in Selections 3 and 4, are associated.

There were manifestations of mercantilism throughout Europe, though at first only in western parts, in and after the fifteenth century if not earlier. It embodies a variety of policies and opinions formulated by a large and heterogeneous body of writers. Many of the objectives were oriented, as also were some nonmercantilist views, to emphasizing the significance of material values and objectives, the importance of commerce and industry, and the need to employ the apparatus of state to foment national economic

4. This paragraph is based largely on Noonan, *op. cit.*

development and release economies from their currently backward state. Their economic analysis, most unsystematic by scholastic standards, was usually of a low order. Yet to them largely belongs the credit for interesting man in economics as a science, for preparing the way for its modern formulation, and for recognizing its empirical applicability. While the mercantilists had a better grasp of the role of prices than did medieval writers, they had not yet learned to conceive of a price system and its allocative and distributive roles, or even of a simpler automatic mechanism such as that which in the eighteenth century was discovered to underly the distribution of precious metals. Just as they emphasized this-worldly values far more than did medieval writers, so also did they esteem merchants, traders, and manufacturers more and agriculturalists and the clergy less, though they usually were alert to the economic importance of agriculture and raw materials. Since mercantilist policy was intended to foster economic growth and make the nation economically and politically strong, mercantilists attached considerable importance to maritime activities and to the availability of requisite naval and military personnel. They counted upon self-interest, properly channeled by the state when necessary, to animate entrepreneurs and capitalists but not the working classes, the elasticity of whose demand for income in terms of effort was generally assumed, prior to the eighteenth century, to be quite low.

Of the agents of production, upon which economic growth depended, labor was considered to be the most important by far, with some writers recognizing that the rural labor force needed to be adapted to industry. It was supposed, therefore, that growth of the labor force should be encouraged by fostering natural increase, stimulating immigration, and regulating emigration — that is, by pursuit of a policy whose premises were rejected in the eighteenth century when it became accepted that numbers adjusted themselves to the means of existence. Stress was put also upon keeping the unemployed and the partially employed fully occupied. Although invention and innovation were emphasized, they do not seem to have been counted upon to increase output per head significantly or continuously, probably because signs of such increase had not yet become conspicuous. After labor, land was considered the most important of the factors of production, and attention was given to increasing its use and the efficiency with which it was used and thereby reducing the cost of wage goods and raw materials. The importance of fixed and circulating capital, together with its increase, was remarked, but the determinants of its growth were not skilfully discussed. The dynamic quality of the enterpriser's role was noted, but no entrepreneurial theory was formulated (see Selection 9).

Treatment of the role of money was often mixed with that of external trade. Money was thought of as playing a dynamic part in economic development, a view eighteenth-century writers became concerned to controvert; for its plenty supposedly held down the interest rate or prevented adverse price movements. Maintenance of a favorable balance of trade was deemed important, in part, therefore, because it served to increase the supply of money and precious metals. Import, export, maritime, and other policies

43

were oriented to the maintenance of a favorable balance, and the relation of colonies to the mother country was thought of in similar terms. Toward the close of the seventeenth century, however, when many were becoming aware of the substitutability of paper money and possibly of bank credit for hard money, emphasis upon the maintenance of a favorable balance diminished, and this tendency was re-enforced by a growing appreciation of the quantity theory of money.

As has already been implied, the state was assigned a key economic role in mercantilistic theory and practice, with the result that in the eighteenth century this role was as much attacked by liberal and physiocratic economists as were some of the fallacious economic principles the state was supposed to translate into action. The state intervened, or was urged to intervene, directly and indirectly, to accomplish mercantilist objectives, especially in respect of external trade, colonies, and the fomenting of domestic industry. Usually a system of privileges, rewards, and penalties was relied upon to keep capital and enterprise in sectors selected for support, though at times the state itself carried on favored economic activities. The state was also urged by some mercantilist writers to support science, innovation, technical education, and enough elementary training to enable the common man to perform tasks essential in an industrializing society.

It is evident that mercantilist emphasis was primarily upon policy. Its principles were given expression principally in legislation, administrative decrees, pamphlets, polemical literature, etc. The economic principles present in these various sources usually were implicit in form. Even when expressed explicitly, they were not supported by a systematic exposition such as some eighteenth-century writers were to provide. Mercantilism could not therefore make many significant contributions to the body of economic theory as such, and, because of its lack of systematic formulation, it could not cope effectively with the more systematic antimercantilistic presentations that appeared in the eighteenth century. Even so, as was remarked earlier, it directed attention to economic issues and to the potential usefulness of a science of economics.[5]

5. The above account is based upon J. J. Spengler's essay on mercantilism in B. F. Hoselitz, ed., *The Theory of Economic Growth: Botero to Keynes* (Glencoe: The Free Press, 1960). See also Eli F. Heckscher, *Mercantilism*, trans. Mendel Shapiro (rev. ed.; 2 vols.; London: George Allen & Unwin, Ltd., 1955); and Jacob Viner's detailed critical account of mercantilist trade theory in *Studies in the Theory of International Trade* (New York: Harper & Brothers, 1937).

2.

BERNARD W. DEMPSEY
Marquette University

Just Price

in a

Functional Economy

The current recrudescence of corporate economy bestows importance on historical analogies hitherto neglected. Medieval economy combined a corporate and functional concept of economic society with political ideals close kin to American constitutional principles. But at present, very incorrect notions of just price, widely accepted, preclude an objective examination of medieval economic theory by American economists. Just price is here examined in its historical sources, the Roman law and the writings of Augustine; development is then traced by quotation from the leading medieval thinkers. Just price thus appears as an integral part of a consistent social philosophy and properly applied as a workable general principle.

I

When the record of economic history is viewed in its full length, that lack of a system which we call the system of individualism is seen to be a recent episode. Historically speaking, only the last century and a half have endeavored to live an economic life without organization or control; and even

Reprinted from *The American Economic Review*, XXV (September 1935), 471–86, by permission of the author and the American Economic Association. This article forms Chapter 21 of Bernard W. Dempsey, *The Functional Economy* (Englewood Cliffs, N.J.: Prentice-Hall, Inc., 1958). At the time of original publication, the author was with Saint Louis University.

45

within that century and a half, individualism has never held the field uncontested. Since the war, as is perfectly evident, the nineteenth century individualistic mood has been replaced by a powerful twentieth century trend toward a corporate economy. Moreover, the economists of the English-speaking world who do not like the Hegelian outlook of Stalin, Mussolini and Hitler, face this world of facts under a severe handicap with the postulates of their own system challenged on various scores.

In all the years of economic activity, and all the types of economic organization before and since the brief day of liberalism, one only attempted to combine the ideas that "all men are by nature equal";[1] that the state is for man and not man for the state;[2] and that there is a measure and a limit and a norm for government interference with individual effort.[3] When we are being pushed into a corporate economy, an historical example of a system that could maintain those three objectives is worthy of consideration. Any economy based on such theory, however faulty in practice, can in our present situation be profitably studied. From this emphasis on principle, it should be clear that we shall not describe the archaic external trappings of medieval economic life, upon which undue emphasis has been placed by enthusiasts and critics alike. The question is one of radical economic principles, not of gargoyles or stained glass windows.

Yet the American economist does not consider the medieval system of economic thought a fruitful field of study. The reason is that he approaches the subject with a fundamental misconception; at the mere mention of just price or objective value, the matter is closed. Regardless of practical considerations, a concern for objective truth would alone justify a re-examination of basic medieval economic concepts. There are few subjects in the field of social science upon which misinformation can be more readily obtained. Scholastic philosophy has recently enjoyed a renascence, both in development as neo-scholasticism, and in historically accurate studies. That the fruit of these studies has not penetrated into the economic world is evident from the fact that it was possible, as late as 1928, to reprint pages 90–96 of Dr. Lewis H. Haney's *History of Economic Thought*, with the statement among others that:

The general notion appears to have been that value is absolute, and objective, and independent of price.[4]

Nor can much be said for Dr. James Westfall Thompson's summary save that it is in harmony with the tall gratuities found elsewhere in his volume. Relying on a second-hand quotation from Thomas Aquinas, through an unidentified Miss Davidson, Dr. Thompson commits himself to the unequivocal position that:

The Church's concept of value was something absolute and apart from value in use and value in exchange, something independent of supply and demand, something intrinsic and fixed.[5]

46

Even so carefully objective an investigator as Dr. Norman S. B. Gras is able to remark of medieval economics rather complacently:

It was assumed that there was such a thing as an objective value, something inherent in the object rather than in the minds of the buyer and seller. We now have had enough experience and have made enough examination of the problem, of course, to know that no such value ever existed.[6]

Medieval schoolmen are frequently criticized for their lack of scientific method, though Hugo Grotius felt that:

Whenever they are found to agree on moral questions they can scarcely be wrong, they who are so keen in discovering the flaws in each other's arguments.[7]

But whatever may be said for the methods of the schoolmen, one can scarcely approve of the critical technique of the writers cited above or indeed of most writers in English on this subject. In such case, it behooves us to let the schoolmen speak for themselves, and thus to remove the principal misconception which has prevented modern writers from seeing in realistic perspective the medieval organic economy which is the only historical analogy which can now be of service to us. Our present purpose is to look the bogey of just price squarely in the eye, and thus to clear the air. Around the correct conception of just price, we shall then seek to sketch some of the leading principles of scholastic economic organization. The space devoted to the question of price is objectively disproportionate but the disproportion is necessary under the circumstances.

II

The scholastic moralist in questions of right and justice founds his general principles on the natural law. The principles of the natural law, however, are in many matters not sufficiently detailed to offer solutions for concrete cases. For this reason, schoolmen have always conceded to the civil law a competence in determining the scope of certain rights, if not in constituting the rights themselves. For example, the right of acquisition by prescription is founded upon natural law, but it is for the civil law to determine after what period of time a title by prescription becomes valid. Acquisition by accession, by the finding of treasure, the determination of the formalities which are required for a binding contract, are other matters which, though grounded in the natural law, may in a specific instance receive their final determination from the civil law. Not only is this true in general, but the moralist also regarded the statement of the natural law as contained in Roman law and, in particular, in the Justinian Code as very satisfactory in many respects. Thomas Aquinas devotes a whole special article to the corroboration of Ulpian's definition of justice set down in the first sentence of the *Institutes*,[8] a definition which had already been accepted, probably from legal sources by Ambrose,[9] and by Augustine.[10] Later when specialists in moral theology would separate the treatise *De Jure et Justitia* from dogmatic tracts and commentaries, the sequence and structure of the treatise would follow that of the Code very closely.

The Justinian Code discusses the Falcidian law[11] "which required that there remain entire to each heir a fourth part of his hereditary portion. But this law regarded only those estates unduly burdened with legatees."[12] The law itself sought to settle a prolonged legal dispute which lies outside our present purpose. But what is to our present purpose is the commentary of the legist Paul in the *Digests*. Question has arisen concerning the manner of the computation of this one-fourth portion.

The prices of things function not according to the whim or utility of individuals, but according to the common estimate. A man who has a son whom he would ransom for a very large sum is not richer by that amount. Nor does he who possesses another man's son possess the sum for which he could sell him to his father; nor is that amount to be expected when he sells him. In the present circumstances he is evaluated as a man and not as somebody's son. . . . Time and place, however, bring about some variation in price. Oil will not be evaluated the same in Rome as in Spain, nor, since here as well prices are not constituted by momentary influences, nor by occasional scarcity, will it be evaluated the same in times of prolonged sterility as in times of abundant harvest.[13]

"Even after the extinction of the Western Empire in the year 476, the Roman law did not cease to have force. First of all, the clergy settled among the various German peoples were not hindered from using the Roman law in their own affairs even when these affairs were secular."[14] The case with reference to which this price doctrine occurs in the code was that of the settlement of inheritances. From very early times, the administration of wills and similar questions of the "orphans' courts" were under ecclesiastical jurisdiction.[15] Later scholastic writers of the highest authority refer specifically and approvingly to this passage in substantiation of their doctrine of just price and the theory of prices underlying it.[16]

In view therefore of the place held by the Roman law in the schoolmen's discussion of right and justice, in view of the close connection of ecclesiastical and civil law on the precise point involved, in view of the general pre-eminence of Roman law in the training of the clergy, and in view of subsequent specific quotation by weighty authorities of the same tradition, the commentary of Paul on the Falcidian law can scarcely be denied a place among the influences forming medieval price and value theory. And that influence was certainly not in the direction of an objective and absolute value and price.

III

Aurelius Augustinus, bishop of Hippo Regius in Africa, saint, Father and Doctor of the Church, would by some be placed outside the scholastic tradition because of his platonist leanings. Yet so great was his influence upon all subsequent western thought, especially in the domain of psychology and epistemology, that the distinction would do violence to historical sequence in spite of the truth it seeks to emphasize. In the theory of value his influence is great as elsewhere.

There is, however, a different value set upon each thing proportionate to its use. Wherefore we set a greater value upon some insentient objects than we do upon some sentient objects. So much so in fact, that were it within our power we should like to remove these living things from the order of nature, either because we do not know what place they hold in the scheme of nature, or, even if we did know, because we value these living things less than our own convenience. Who does not prefer to have bread in the house rather than mice, or money rather than fleas? But why be surprised since in the value set upon men themselves, whose nature is certainly of paramount dignity, very frequently a horse is held more dear than a slave, or a jewel more precious than a maid servant. Since every man has the power of forming his own mind as he wishes, there is very little agreement between the choice of a man who through necessity stands in real need of an object, and of one who hankers after a thing merely for pleasure.[17]

This passage resounds through centuries of writing by scholastics and is found either in direct quotation or in paraphrase in almost every important treatment of the subject. Aquinas gives the substance of it;[18] Scotus refers to it specifically;[19] and its influence is clear in Antoninus of Florence,[20] in Bernardine of Sienna,[21] in the great Dominican moralist, Dominic Soto,[22] and Cardinal de Lugo[23] among others. This is a decidedly imposing array of scholastic authorities who accept, approve and adapt the quotation from Augustine. And that analysis of Augustine's can in no sense be interpreted as setting up an objective and absolute standard of value.

And yet Augustine could say that "to wish to buy cheap and sell dear is a vice." He narrates the story of an actor who promised on a certain day to reveal to the members of his audience:

. . . what they had in their hearts and what they all wanted, and a large crowd assembled on the appointed day, silent and expectant, to whom he is said to have announced, "You wish to buy cheap and sell dear." That actor, either from self-examination or from experience of others, came to the conclusion that to wish to buy cheap and sell dear was common to all men. . . . As a matter of fact, it is a vice. . . . I myself know a man to whom the sale of a book was offered; he saw that the seller was unaware of its real price and for that reason was asking very little for it. And yet he gave the seller, ignorant as he was, the just price which was far greater. . . . We have known people from humanitarian motives to have sold cheaply to their fellow citizens grain for which they had paid a high price.[24]

The inability to reconcile these apparently contradictory points of view — namely, that there is a powerful subjective element in our evaluations, and yet that there is a just price which is independent of my subjective judgments, seems to be the reason why modern writers of ability and authority are led to make statements concerning scholastic price and value theory which are at variance with the truth to the point of being bizarre. How scholastic writers themselves effected this reconciliation, we shall seek to show by quotation as we proceed. But it may now be observed in general that the resultant of a large number of personal judgments, the community estimate, though partly subjective in origin, and partly objective, insofar as it is based on a consideration of the actual physical qualities of the object for sale, is for me in practice wholly objective. The matter is analogous to a political election; my vote may have gone for Mr. Hoover; the community estimate went for Mr. Roosevelt. Though my subjective choice was one of the factors determining the election, the ultimate outcome, Mr. Roosevelt's presidency, is for me a wholly objective consideration. Similarly, my estimate of the worth of an object to me will be one of the factors determining the community estimate which will determine the just price. Yet that just price, resultant of many objective and subjective forces, once determined is for me a wholly objective fact.

IV

The Dark Ages, if there were any such, offer us little new on price and value save the work of the canonists properly so-called who lie beyond the scope of this present writing. The next writer of importance to whom we turn is Albertus Magnus (1193–1280), a Suabian of the noble family of Bollstadt, teacher at Paris and Cologne, bishop of Ratisbon and founder of the theological tradition of the Dominican order. Albert, though one of the few writers who quotes neither the commentary of Paulus, nor the famed passage of Augustine, is on his own grounds an advocate of just price. He is commenting on the *Ethics* of Aristotle:

There is accordingly always a just mean between gain and loss. This mean is preserved when in a voluntary contract the antecedent situation is equivalent to the consequent, that is to say, before and after the contract. A couch, for example, prior to the contract had a value of five; if one received five for it, the situation consequent to the contract is equal to that which was antecedent. No one can complain that he has been in any way injured thereby.[25]

Such exchange, however, does not take place through an equality of the things exchanged but rather according to the value of one thing in relative proportion to the value of the other with due regard for the need which is the cause of the transaction.[26]

This "need" of which Albert speaks includes not only my personal need of this particular object but also and more significantly the need which all men have of living in society and of exchanging with one another the products of their labor, if human life is to be carried out on a level in any way proportionate to human capacity and dignity. My need is included, to be sure, but the principles of justice involved derive from the general nature of human needs in society, as the writer proceeds to show in the continuation of the passage cited above.

According to this analysis, the carpenter ought to receive the product of the tanner and in turn pay the tanner that which according to a just exchange is his. . . . And when this equality is not preserved, the community is not maintained, for labor and expense are not repaid. For all would, indeed, be destroyed if he who makes a contract for so much goods of such a kind, does not receive a similar quality and quantity. For the state cannot be built up of one type of workers alone. Properly, therefore, these things are exchanged not absolutely but with a certain comparison to their value according to use and need. Otherwise, there would be no exchange.[27]

To this end, money was invented, that community life might be facilitated and preserved through just contracts which through the device of money are made both easier and more just:

Wherefore all exchangeable goods are properly priced in money and thus there will always be exchange. . . . While there is exchange, there is also a community. Now money equals all exchangeable goods just as the unit of a ruler by addition and subtraction equals all things ruled. We have just said that without an exchange of products there will be no community life. But community life cannot be unless the products are reduced to proportionate equality. . . . And this is the reason why the first and primary measure of all exchangeable goods (money, to wit) was of necessity invented.[28]

Lest his doctrine be misunderstood, Albert is careful to explain how what he says fits in with the traditional scholastic doctrine of immutable essences and final values with reference to a last end. Time has shown the wisdom and need of the warning.

. . . In a certain way, natural objects are immutable, as for example, with regard to those first principles by which man is ordained for the good and the true, for these are imprinted on humankind and do not change. However, the use of these things when applied in practice varies with many customs and institutions. Thus, although with the gods every just thing is precisely so and in absolutely no degree otherwise, for with the gods nothing suffers change, with us, however, an object is by nature in a certain sense changeable, for whatever is human is changeable, and as this is the case, so there is in human justice an element that is of nature and an element that is not.[29]

These citations manifest an intimate connection in the writer's mind between just price and social organization. Because men must live in community, because life can be sustained only by mutual exchange of products for the subvention of mutual needs, the contracts arising from these exchanges must be equitable. And if they must be fundamentally equitable, the expression of that basic equity in money must be a just price. The process, as a whole, is radically a social phenomenon arising from man's need for life in society, and his inability adequately and congruously to develop his personality alone; "the commonwealth cannot be built up of one type of workers alone." Albert is talking not only of a division of labor but more particularly of the organic interrelation arising from this specialization of function. Because exchange is socially necessary, money is socially necessary, and because both money and exchange are designed to serve the development of persons in community, the quantitative determination of price is necessarily social. Prices must be equitable because all of the functional

51

groups are necessary to each other and live in mutual interdependence. By fair exchange manifested in a fair price, is progress made and the commonwealth maintained.

Had Albertus Magnus no greater claim to distinction than his part in the intellectual formation of Thomas Aquinas (1225–1274), it should be enough. Master and pupil are both Doctors of the Church, and the works of Thomas are rightly regarded as an epitome of medieval thought. Before we turn to the question as to whether Thomas thought that value and price were exclusively objective, it is necessary to consider briefly the structure of the society in which these transactions would take place.

That human societal relations are natural and, therefore, both normal and normative is axiomatic in the work of Thomas Aquinas as indeed in all scholasticism. The principle of Aristotle, "Man is by nature a social animal,"[30] is cited almost every time a social topic is discussed. Out of the innumerable places in Thomas's vast works that touch upon social analysis, we limit ourselves to a few which indicate in what manner he regarded society, economic society included, as organic.

Economic need is one of the most powerful motive forces impelling to social organization, in the mind of Aquinas as well as in that of Albert.

"Man is naturally a social animal." This is evident from the fact that one man does not suffice for himself if he lives alone because the things are few in which nature makes adequate provision for man, since she gave him reason by means of which to provide himself with all the necessities of life such as food, clothes, and so forth, for the production of which one man is not enough. Wherefore man has a natural inclination to social life.[31]

In a totally different connection, and in a different work, after an introduction which is almost *verbatim* with the above, Aquinas continues:

Just as one man has various members by which he functions in various capacities, all ordered to supply any need, since all functions cannot be supplied by one member, so the eye sees for the whole body and the foot carries the whole body. Likewise, in what pertains to all mankind, one man is not able to do all the things which are needed in a society, and, accordingly, different people properly work at different tasks.

But since in Thomas's thought, order and liberty when properly conceived are not exclusive notions but complementary ones, he explains:

This diversity of men in different functions, happens, in the first place, by divine providence which has so distributed the types of men that nothing necessary for life will ever be found wanting. But this also comes about from natural influences by which different men have different inclinations for this function of that manner of life.[32]

The thought is also developed by an analogy from the animal world, the division of labor in the bee-hive.

For, as many things are needed for man's livelihood for which one man is not sufficient for himself, it is necessary that different things be done by different men, that some, for instance, should cultivate the land, that some build houses, and so forth.[33]

All of which may thus be summarized:

In civic relationships, all men who belong to the same community are regarded as one body, and the whole community as one man.[34]

A division of labor, therefore, is fundamental in Aquinas's idea of social organization and progress:

For the welfare of human society, many things are necessary; divers offices are done better and more expeditiously by divers persons than by men singly.[35]

But, though there be a division of labor, competition as a ruling principle is far from his mind. Scholastic economic organization is pre-eminently one of non-competing groups.

In the temporal commonwealth, peace departs because the individual citizens seek only their own good. . . . Rather through diversity of function and status is the peace of temporal commonwealths promoted inasmuch as thereby there are many who participate in public affairs.[36]

When there is combined with this organic concept of economic society, the scholastic doctrine on private property, which cannot be here elaborated, we achieve a conclusion which sounds odd to modern ears.

All particular goods which men procure are ordained for the common good as for their end.[37]

And we come also to that fundamental notion of the basic community of goods which the institution of private property is to promote and not impede.

And, therefore, the division and appropriation of goods that proceeds from human law cannot come in the way of man's need of being relieved out of such goods. . . . To use the property of another, taking it secretly in a case of extreme need, cannot, properly speaking, be characterized as theft.[38]

In the economic society of which Thomas had practical experience, these diverse functions and various tasks and offices and duties of which he speaks were carried out not by isolated individuals but by well-defined *universitates* and *corpora*, gilds, in other words, each of which was an organ of the state for fulfilling some requisite of community life. Thomas was no advocate of the modern "monolithic" state, ruled with high hand from above. Association took place naturally on many levels.

Since there are various grades and orders in these communities, the highest is that of the commonwealth which is ordained to procure by itself a sufficiency of goods for human life.[39]

Thus, though the state has a proper regulatory office, these lesser associations should be left to carry out their organic functions freely within the
limits of justice.

The optimum in any government is that things should be provided for according to their own measure for in this does the justice of an administration consist.
Accordingly it would be against the principle of human government if men were
to be prevented by the governor of the commonwealth from carrying out their
own functions, unless perchance for a brief time because of some emergency.[40]

From this brief sketch, of necessity inadequate,[41] we wish to point out
those factors in Thomas's analysis which bear on our present problem. The
state is a natural society within which flourish many lesser coördinate societies, each enjoying within its own sphere an ordinate autonomy, all, however, designed through coöperation to serve the interests of the persons who
compose the state, and all attaining these ends through an observance of
justice which regulates those acts of men which concern a second person.

With these observations in mind, what Thomas has to say on the subject
of just price becomes more intelligible. On the origins of money and exchange, he comments approvingly upon the words of Aristotle,[42] but a fuller
discussion is given elsewhere.

To the end that exchange be just, as many shoes should be exchanged for a
house, or for a man's food, as the labor and expense of the builder or farmer is
greater than that of the tanner because, if this be not observed there will be
no exchange, nor will men share their goods with one another. . . . This one
thing which measures all other things is, in truth, the need which embraces all
exchangeable goods insofar as all things are referred to human needs. *For things
are not valued according to the dignity of their natures,* otherwise a mouse which
is a sentient thing would have a higher price than a pearl which is an inanimate
thing. This is manifest because, if men had no needs, there would be no exchange.
. . . In other words, insofar as the farmer, whose function is the provision of food,
is more necessary than the tanner whose function is the provision of shoes, by that
amount in numerical proportion must the work of the tanner exceed that of the
farmer so that many shoes are exchanged for one measure of grain. . . . Moreover,
it is true that money also suffers the same as anything else. . . . That is to say that
it has not always the same value but ought, nevertheless, to be so instituted that
it have greater permanency in the same value than other things.[43]

If, however, this reciprocity is absent, there will be no equality of the things
exchanged, and thus men are no longer able to dwell together. . . . All the crafts
would be destroyed if each would not receive an amount proportionate to that
which he produced.[44]

In the light of these considerations of the natural and all-inclusive mutual interdependence of men, of the close articulation of all parts of the
community for the maintenance and progress of all, and of the necessary
observance of justice if these ends are to be obtained, the jejune remarks of
Thomas in the passage usually cited from his works in this connection,
acquire a fuller meaning.

Buying and selling were instituted for the common good of both parties since each needs the products of the other and vice versa as is evident from the Philosopher. But what was introduced for the common utility ought not to bear harder on one party than on the other, and therefore, the contract between them should rest upon an equality of thing to thing. The quantity of a thing which comes into human use is measured by the price given, for which purpose money was invented, as said. Therefore, if the price exceeds the quantity of the value of the article, or the article exceeds the price, the equality of justice will be destroyed. And, therefore, to sell a thing dearer or to buy it cheaper than it is worth, is, in itself, unjust and illicit. . . . The just price of things, however, is not determined to a precise point but consists in a certain estimate. . . . The price of an article is changed according to difference in location, time, or risk to which one is exposed in carrying it from one place to another or in causing it to be carried. Neither purchase nor sale according to this principle is unjust.[45]

Elaborate demonstration that scholastic writers are not concerned with an absolute, immobile, intrinsic value should, in the light of the quotations given, be quite superfluous; for "things are not valued according to the dignity of their natures." Value rests upon a kind of estimate, not of the buyer and seller alone, but of the whole community. This is true because man is social by nature and for him production and progress are possible only in association. That society which arises through this association is a commonwealth in the fullest sense of the word, and will flourish only when all its parts are sound. By the production of a useful commodity, man makes his contribution to the commonweal for which contribution he expects a reciprocal support. Because social relations are governed by justice, (which we do not here prove, but assume as axiomatic in scholasticism, or in any other civilized philosophy) the exchange must take place according to the community's estimate of the social utility of the two products because the producer who expects sustenance from society in return for his labor, by performing his function in the social organism, has earned his right to a just return. The factors which will normally determine the community estimate of social utility are labor, cost of materials, risk and carriage charges.

V

There remains, for the sake of completeness, to consider the writings of a few other thinkers who each in his day enjoyed great authority and who, though accepting without qualification the traditional scholastic position, extended it in one or other minor point arising from the circumstances of his own time. John Duns Scotus, for example, Aquinas's much younger contemporary (1265–1308) and the principal ornament of the Order of St. Francis in the field of speculative thought, extends or makes explicit several principles. After citing the two quotations from Augustine and setting down general principles substantially the same as those of Aquinas, Scotus continues:

Beyond the rules which have been given above as to what is just and what is not, I add two. The first is that such an exchange be useful to the community, and the second, that such a person shall receive in the exchange recompense according to his diligence, prudence, trouble, and risk. . . . This second rule follows because every man who serves the community in an honest function ought to live by his work. But such a one as transports or stores goods is of honest and useful service to the community, and should, therefore, live by his work. And, moreover, one can sell his effort and care for a just price. But great industry is required of one who transports goods from one country to another inasmuch as he must investigate the resources and needs of the country. Therefore, may he take a price corresponding to his labor beyond the necessary support for himself and those of his establishment employed according to his requirements, and thirdly, something beyond this corresponding to his risk. For if he is a transporter or custodian of goods (*e.g.,* in a warehouse), he does this at his own risk and for this risk he is in all conscience entitled to some recompense. And this is especially true if, now and then, through no fault of his own in such a service to the community he suffers a loss; for a merchant engaged in transport now and then loses a ship laden with fine wares, and the custodian occasionally loses in an accidental fire, the valuable goods which he stores for the use of the commonwealth.

It is evident from these two conditions requisite in just business how some are called business men in a vituperative sense, those to wit who neither transport, nor store, nor by their own industry better a salable article, nor guarantee the worth of some object for sale to one who lacks the necessary knowledge of it. These people who buy only to sell immediately, under none of the above conditions ought to be crushed by the community and exiled. Such persons are called by the French *regratiers* because they prevent the unhampered exchange of those who wish to buy or make an economic exchange, and as a result, they render a salable and usable article dearer to the buyer than it should be, and dearer to the seller. Thus the contract is defective on both sides.[46]

The emphasis given to cost factors on the supply side by Scotus caused certain sixteenth century scholastics to object to his theory as they understood it.[47] The version of the theory which they took they promptly riddled with objections very similar to those which the Austrian School brought against the classical cost analysis. Not even in this sense would the scholastic moralists tolerate an objective theory of economic value. However, as the commentator on Scotus justly remarks, "They object in vain, for the Doctor assigns justice and the causes thereof to the nature of the object . . . and the common estimate."

The increasing mercantile activity of the Italian cities brought new moral problems to the desk of Antoninus, saint, archbishop of Florence, and a moral theologian of great repute (1389–1459). Antoninus was not loath to recognize changed conditions and to apply the old principles to the new facts, and for this reason some have regarded his ideas as involving new principles. We shall here note merely that his approach is substantially that of Albertus Magnus two centuries before.

Many unsupportable statements have been made concerning the medieval attitude toward trade; the neat summary of Antoninus will bear repeating.

The notion of business implies nothing vicious in its nature or contrary to reason. Therefore, it should be ordered to any honest and necessary purpose and is so rendered lawful, as for example, when a business man orders his moderate gain which he seeks to the end that he and his family may be decently provided for according to their condition, and that he may also assist the poor. Nor is condemnation possible when he undertakes a business as a public service lest necessary things be wanting to the state, and seeks gain therefrom, not as an end, but in remuneration for his labor observing all other due considerations which we mention. But if he places his final purpose in gain, seeking only to increase wealth enormously and to keep it for himself, his attitude is to be condemned.[48]

So close is the resemblance of the doctrine of Antoninus to that of his predecessors, that the first sections consisting of paraphrase and quotation from Aristotle and Aquinas may be omitted. We begin where he, paraphrasing Augustine, and accepting Scotus's conclusions, proceeds to develop them.

The value of an article rests on a three-fold consideration, (1) its intrinsic qualities, (2) its scarcity, and, (3) the desire which it arouses in us.

The intrinsic qualities of a thing are known from the way in which, due to its inherent properties, it is more effective for our use. Thus, good wheaten bread has greater value for us than barley bread, and a powerful horse has greater value for traveling than an ass.

Secondly, the value of a salable object is judged according to its scarcity, that is, things which are found rarely or with difficulty are more necessary in proportion as, because of their scarcity, we feel a greater need of them and there is less opportunity of owning and using them. According to this principle, grain is worth more in time of famine and scarcity than at a time when there is plenty for all. . . .

Thirdly, a salable object is judged from its pleasant effect upon us, that is, according to the degree in which it pleases our fancy to own and use such an object. Thus no small part of the value of salable objects arises from the pleasure of the will taking greater or less satisfaction in the use of this thing or that. One horse is more pleasing to one person than to another, and an ornament pleases this person more than that.

The third thing to be considered regarding the value of an object is that we can hardly ever determine it except conjecturally and with probability, and this not at a mathematical point but within a certain range respecting times, places, and persons. . . . With regard to the second principle division, namely, that there is an appropriate range within the limits of which prices may vary, it should be observed that this may be known in three ways; from law, from custom, and from practical judgment. First of all, from the law — extra De empt. et vend., Cum Dilecti.[49] This same proper range is known also in a second way. For as Scotus says in his commentary referred to above, experience shows clearly enough that the matter is ordinarily left to those making the exchange so that, having due regard for each other's wants, they judge themselves to give and receive equivalents. . . . Thus a certain real gift or concession commonly accompanies contracts. It is therefore probable enough that when the contracting parties are mutually satisfied, they wish to concede something to each other as long as they do not too grossly depart from perfect justice.

This same appropriate range of price is known, in the third place, from practical judgment. For practical judgment dictates that when a thing, which in itself is worth ten, is as dear to the owner as though worth twelve, if I propose to own it, I must give not only the ten but as much as it is worth to him according to his desire of retaining it.[50] One reason why things are worth more or less is the shortage or abundance of money among the townspeople. When they have money, they buy and then things sell dearer, but when those who have power in the community need money, things are bought and sold for less.[51]

We observe here that with the passage of time and with the expansion of Europe's economic outlook, the just price analysis was not changed but developed. In Antoninus, accepting and building upon his early medieval predecessors, we find a doctrine of value based upon three factors: (1) intrinsic qualities, which are the foundation of value in any system save that of the hopeless idealist; (2) scarcity, which, as explained by Antoninus following Scotus, includes the element of cost; and (3) the subjective influence of these objective qualities (*complacibilitas*). Finally, some hint is given that money is becoming an independent factor in the process of translating value into price. These elements are, and must be the leading components in any value theory. Whatever may have been the source of the prevailing opinion that medieval value theory was inherent, fixed, absolute, objective, independent of supply and demand, that source was not the writings of the men who are the acknowledged spokesmen for medieval intellectual life.

VI

Scholastic writers demanded a just price because purchase and sale is a social transaction and social transactions are governed by justice. Purchase and sale is a social transaction because man is social by nature, and only through exchange is he able to provide himself with congruous sustenance. Man is a person with the right and obligation to develop and perfect his personality. But this he can do only in society. The two societies in which he invariably seeks and finds the proper medium for development are the family and the state, which are for this reason called natural societies. Among the functions of the state, one of the principal is the procuring of economic prosperity for its members, yet, for this purpose the state is not directly equipped. Men, ever social in tendency, in this as in everything else, lean naturally toward association for the more efficient fulfillment of their material needs, and the state achieves its purpose by fostering, protecting, or, if need be, restraining these associations. Functional associations of this sort are not absolutely indispensable to social life as are the family and the state but they are requisite for a healthy commonwealth for which reason they are called quasi-natural societies. They stand lower than the family and the state but above the purely conventional society like a joint stock corporation or a club.

The achievement of prosperity is patently a coöperative enterprise to which each producer brings his labor as his means of production and his title to subsistence. For the protection of that right and the improvement of those powers, it is natural that man should associate with all, owners or workers, who function in the same industry where each makes his contribution, whence each receives his sustenance. Such associations are the economic organs of the body politic; they are the vertical girders furnishing structural balance in the social edifice along with the horizontal, geographical, political framework. The exchange of the increased product made possible by the diversification of function must take place at a fair price, else the commonwealth will suffer. In an organism, the diminution of function in one organ means a diminution of function in all. When society permits transactions at other than just prices, it is cutting off its nose to spite its face, or is enacting the ancient pantomime of the hands that would not feed the lazy stomach.[52]

In such an organization of society, the tension of class conflict, which is unnatural and philosophically as well as practically inhuman, is relieved because men, on a basis of what they are, stand united according to what they do, not divided according to what they have or have not. There is achieved, not a sterile and futile socialization of goods, but a natural and fruitful socialization of men.

NOTES

1. Thomas Aquinas, *Summa Theologica*, 2a 2ae quaestio 104, ad 5um.
2. Thomas Aquinas, *De Regimine Principum* (De Regno) Lib. 3, cap. ii.
3. Thomas Aquinas, *Summa Contra Gentiles*, Lib. 3, cap. 71.
4. Haney, *op. cit.*, p. 90.
5. Thompson, *Economic and Social History of the Middle Ages*, New York, 1928, pp. 697–698.
6. Gras, "Economic Rationalism in the Late Middle Ages," *Speculum*, viii, 3, July, 1933, p. 305.
7. Grotius, *De Jure Belli et Pacis*, reproduction of the edition of 1646, Washington, 1916, pages unnumbered (17).
8. Aquinas, *Summa Theologica*, 2a 2ae, Quaestio 58, art. 1.
9. Ambrose, *De Officiis Ministrorum*, Lib. I, c. 24, Migne PL., vol. 16, p. 57.
10. Augustine, *De Civitate Dei*, Lib. XIX, c. 21, CSEL (CV), vol. 40:2, p. 409.
11. *Corpus Iuris Civilis*, Krueger-Mommsen ed., Berlin, 1928, Institutes, xxii, p. 25.
12. P. Vidal, S. J., *Institutiones Iuris Romani*, Prati, 1915, p. 594.
13. *Op. cit.*, Ad Legem Falcidiam, Digests, xxxv, 2, 63, p. 556.
14. F. X. Wernz, S. J. *Ius Decretalium*, Prati, 1913, vol. i, Pars 2a, tit. xi, no. 10, p. 346.
15. Wernz, *op. cit.*, vol. v, Pars 2a, tit. IX, no. 2, p. 221. Blackstone, *Commentary on the Laws of England*, Philadelphia, 1860, Book III, ch. 7. nos. 5–6 (pp. 95–103), vol. 2, p. 72 sq.

16. Luis Molina, S. J. (d. 1600), *De Jure et Justitia*, Antwerp, 1615, Tomus II, Disp. 348, sec. 4, p. 166. Joannis Cardinalis de Lugo, S. J. (d. 1660), *Disputationes Scholasticae et Morales*, Paris, 1869, vol. vii, Disp. 26, no. 38, p. 273.
17. Augustine, *De Civitate Dei*, Book XI, cap. 16, CSEL (CV), vol. 40, p. 535.
18. Aquinas, *Summa Theologica*, 2a 2ae quaestio 77, art. 2, add 3um.
19. Joannis Duns Scoti *Opera Omnia*, Paris, 1894, vol. 18, "Quaestiones in Quartum Librum Sententiarum," Dist. XV, quaestio 2a, n. 14.
20. Antonini *Summa Theologica*, Verona, 1740, Lib. II, tit. 1, cap. 16, no. 3.
21. Bernardine of Sienna, *Quadragesimale de Evangelio Aeterno*, Venice, 1745, Serm. 35, a. 1, c. 1.
22. Dominic Soto, *De Jure et Justitia*, Lyons, 1558, Lib. 1, cap. 6, q. 2, a. 3.
23. de Lugo, *op. cit.*, sec. 4, no. 42.
24. Augustini, *Opera Omnia*, St. Maur's ed., Paris, 1841, vol. 8, *De Trinitate*, Liber XIII, cap. 3, sec. 6, cols. 1017–1018.
25. B. Alberti Magni, *Opera Omnia*, Paris, 1891, vol. vii, *In Librum V Ethicorum*, Tract. 2, cap. 7, no. 30.
26. *Ibid.*, cap. 9, no. 31.
27. *Ibid.*, cap. 9, no. 31.
28. *Ibid.*, cap. 10, no. 36.
29. *Ibid.*, Tract 3, cap. 1, no. 49.
30. Aristotle, *Nichomachean Ethics*, Book I, c. 7.
31. Aquinas, *Summa contra Gentiles*, Book III, c. 85.

32. Aquinas, *Quaestiones Quodlibetales*, Quodlibetum 7um, quaestio 7, art. xvii, ad corpus.

33. Aquinas, *Summa contra Gentiles*, Book III, c. 134.

34. Aquinas, *Summa Theologica*, 1a 2ae, quaestio 81, art. 1, ad corpus.

35. Aquinas, *Summa Theologica*, 2a 2ae, quaestio 40, art. 2, resp.

36. Aquinas, *Summa Theologica*, 2a 2ae, quaestio 183, art. 2, ad 3um.

37. Aquinas, *De Regimine Principum*, Book I, c. 15.

38. Aquinas, *Summa Theologica*, 2a 2ae, quaestio 66, art. 7.

39. Aquinas, *In Libros Politicorum*, prologus.

40. Aquinas, *Summa contra Gentiles*, Book III, c. 71.

41. Among the many writings on the political thought of Thomas Aquinas few compendious statements will be found to excel the work of Dr. Clare Q. Riedl of Marquette University, "The Social Theory of Thomas Aquinas" in *Philosophy of Society*, Philadelphia, 1934. For a scholastic interpretation of general modern "value" theory see, *Philosophy of Value* by Leo R. Ward, of the University of Notre Dame, New York, 1930.

42. Aquinas, *In Primum Librum Politicorum*, lect. 7.

43. Aquinas, *In Decem Libros Ethicorum*, Liber V, lect. 9 (italics inserted).

44. *Ibid.*, lect. 8.

45. Aquinas, *Summa Theologica*, 2a 2ae, quaestio 77.

46. Scotus, *op. cit.*, nn. 21–22.

47. Soto, *op. cit.*, Book VI, quaestio 2, art. 3; Molina, *op. cit.*, Disp. 348; de Lugo, *op. cit.*, Disp. 26, sec. 4, no. 41.

48. Sancti Antonini, Archiepiscopi Florentini, O. P., *Summa Theologica*, Verona, 1740, vol. 4, Pars 2a, Tit. lus, c. 16, n. 2, col. 250. For an interesting comparison see Mill, Ashley ed., Bk. I, ch. 7, sec. 3, p. 106.

49. This reference is given as written by Antoninus. The passage will be found in *Decretalium Gregorii IX*, Lib. III, tit. XVII, De Emptione et Venditione, cap. III, Alexander III, Attrebatensi Episcopo, *Corpus Juris Canonici*, Editio Lipsiensis 2a, Leipzig, 1922, p. 518.

50. Antoninus, *op. cit.*, col. 255.

51. Antoninus, *ibid.*, col. 186.

52. The application of scholastic principles to modern economy will be found in the five volume work of Heinrich Pesch, S.J., *Lehrbuch der National Ökonomie*, Freiburg, 1907. Pesch was a pupil of Adolph Wagner, and Spann rates his work as "the most comprehensive economic treatise in the German language."

3.

WILLIAM D. GRAMPP

University of Illinois in Chicago

The Liberal

Elements in

English Mercantilism

I. The goal of full employment — II. The means to full employment — III. Economic freedom in mercantilist doctrine — IV. The exceptions to free exchange — V. The historical roots of mercantilism — VI. Economists on mercantilism.

The period of mercantilism in England extended from roughly 1500 to 1750, and it is customary to apply that word both to the economic writings of the period and to its economic practices. It is also customary to describe mercantilism as the antithesis of liberal, or classical, economic doctrine. Adam Smith used some of his strongest invective against it, and since his time mercantilism has been thoroughly condemned by liberal economists because its practices were the very kind of interference which they always have regarded as useless, unwise, or mischievous.

By reasoning from the actual practices of the mercantilist states, economists and historians usually have supposed that the doctrines of the period of mercantilism were a justification of its institutions. It is common in studies of mercantilism for the author to explain, say, the restriction of imports by referring both to the tariff duties of the age and to the concurrent doctrine of a favorable balance of trade, or for him to move freely among expressions

Reprinted from *The Quarterly Journal of Economics*, LXVI (November 1952), 465–501, by permission of the author and The Harvard University Press. Copyright, 1952, by the President and Fellows of Harvard College.

of public officials, laws, economic tracts and discourses, and to suppose that because particular controls were exercised, like price fixing, they must have been justified in the economic writing of the time. No one, of course, would write of recent economic policy this way. It would be unthinkable to describe the New Deal by an indiscriminate reference to the works of Keynes and Hansen and to the public papers of Franklin D. Roosevelt and the private memoranda of Harry Hopkins and always to suppose that whatever the state did or wanted to do found its rationalization in economic doctrine.

When studies of mercantilism use a method of this kind, they leave an impression with the reader that in many ways is distressingly wrong. He must be led to think that because the mercantilist states did not believe in the market as the mechanism for discharging the economic functions of society, the economists of the age held the same belief and were in favor of the intricate kind of regulation which was practiced. More indeed than this is implied. If the practitioners of mercantilism did not understand prices, money, foreign trade, and other matters, it follows that the economists also were wanting in a knowledge of these matters. Especially is it implied that the mercantilists did not understand the mechanism by which the economic problem is solved in a free society and that this knowledge was the signal discovery of classical economics. From this it must be concluded that the mercantilist writers were particularly deficient because they did not understand how the price system directs resources to particular employments and causes the product to be distributed in a certain way.

None of these impressions about mercantilist *doctrine,* as distinct from mercantilist *practice,* is correct. Yet they are unavoidable if the doctrine and the practice are thought to be parts of a unified system. It is the purpose of this essay to re-examine the ideas expressed by the mercantilist writers of England between about 1550 and 1750 in order to show that the mercantilists anticipated many important elements of classical economic doctrine, including the classical conception of self-interest, the price mechanism, the mutual advantage in exchange, and the place of the state in the economic organization. To this end, it is necessary first to explain that the objective of mercantilist doctrine was different from what is is usually thought to be.

Although I do not know that the doctrine has ever been interpreted as it will be here, a number of writers have in fact suggested that English mercantilism was not wholly mistaken, and that it was in some ways a necessary preliminary to classical economics. Marshall thought of it this way.[1] Viner is charitable to the later writings for their traces of free trade theory.[2] Keynes observed that the mercantilists' monetary theory was a valid effort to connect the money supply with the rate of interest.[3] Heckscher clearly noted the mercantilist expressions in favor of a free market, even though he thought they were not sincere.[4] Lipson contends that the mercantilists ought not to be dismissed in quite the cavalier fashion in which it has been common to treat them.[5] Edmund Whittaker finds evidences of individualism in the writings of some of them.[6] Although none of these men came to the conclusion of this essay, and cannot be cited in any way to substantiate it, I mention their work in order not to appear to claim for my views more novelty than they actually have.

In what follows, the words "mercantilism" and "mercantilist" refer always to English doctrine and to the Englishmen who expressed it, and, except when explicitly stated, never refer to economic institutions, practices, historical circumstances, or the rulers or administrators of the age.

I

It is not in an obvious way that mercantilist and liberal economic policy are related. What indeed is obvious is the great difference between the measures which each proposed to advance its policy. The liberals wanted the functions of economic organization performed by a market which was as free as possible, and the mercantilists believed the functions would be performed better if the market were controlled in certain ways. However, there is another way to analyze mercantilist doctrine, different from the common one of comparing its proposed controls with the relative absence of control in liberal doctrine. It is to examine the presuppositions of mercantilist doctrine and to ask: What did the mercantilist writers believe was the objective of economic policy? What were their measures of control meant to achieve? The answer must be taken from diverse writings of a period covering some two centuries. In generalizing from them, there is the danger of supposing them to be more consistent than they actually are, just in order to make the question manageable. But the hazard is worth taking. Mercantilism was an important stage in the development of economic ideas, and a fresh approach to it may aid in making it more comprehensible.

Had the mercantilist writers been asked for an explicit statement of their objective, they undoubtedly would have said it was to create a strong and secure England. Although their motives were mixed (as most writers' are) the principal motive was the national interest. It was not this, however, which made mercantilism different from classical economics. The classical economists also were nationalists; they valued the political and military interest of England above all things and were ready to sacrifice efficiency and even justice in return for greater national power. The title of Smith's work describes the purpose of his policy of laissez faire. The purpose of John Hales's policy is also indicated by the title of his work, written about 1549, *A Discourse of the Common Weal of This Realm of England*. Now the word "nationalism" is a piece of intensional language, and when applied to the economists, has to be shorn of its inflammatory connotation. They were not like Lord Copper, who stood for "strong mutually antagonistic governments everywhere, self-sufficiency at home, self-assertion abroad." Rather they were devoted to God, St. George, and particularly England.

What separated the mercantilists from the liberal economists was their different means of advancing the national interest. The mercantilists believed the latter required a prosperous, fully employed, and growing economy. The connection between power and wealth was expressed about 1548 in the *Pleasant Poeyse of Princelie Practise* by Sir William Forest:

> For kings of their commons sometime must aid true.
> The more therefore the public weal doth afflow;
> The more is their wealth: this reason proveth now.

Among the conditions necessary for a growing economy the mercantilists cited: a brisk trade, adequate domestic spending, a proper wage and price structure, a particular distribution of income, an excess of exports over imports, a diligent and obedient working class, security of private property, the elimination of monopoly, the full utilization of agricultural lands, an adequate money supply, a low rate of interest, and the full employment of the labor force.

The greatest attention was given to the money supply, spending, and employment. Spending, or in today's language, effective demand, and employment were regarded as mutually determined: whatever changed one would change the other in the same direction. The money supply in some writings was made a determinant of spending while in others it was not directly related to spending. To most of the mercantilists, the condition of national prosperity was an amount of spending sufficient to maintain full employment, and these writers subordinated the accumulation of bullion and other methods of increasing the money supply to the position of determinants of spending. Full employment was taken to be a measure of the quantity of goods produced by the economy, and full employment was the economic objective of mercantilist policy, as distinct from its political objective which was national power.

The objective of full employment was expressed early in the period of mercantilism by John Hales, who wrote that the state should adopt measures which would assure a "great plenty" of goods and that this required the employment in agriculture and the towns of all those able to work.[7] At the time Hales' work appeared, there also appeared an anonymous tract called *Policies to Reduce This Realme Unto a Prosperous Wealthe and Estate,* in which the author stated that foreign and domestic trade would be increased "if every laborer and artificer, and all other [of] the common people were well set at work."[8] The mercantilist objective of full employment, its connection with a flourishing trade, and the importance of trade to the nation, were summarized by Edward Misselden in 1622:

And what has more relation to matters of state, than Commerce of merchants? For when trade flourishes, the King's revenue is augmented, lands and rents improved, navigation is increased, the poor employed. But if trade decay, all these decline with it.[9]

The importance of employment was expressed by William Petty (1662) in his familiar proposition that as the nation's population increased its wealth increased in greater proportion (on the assumption, it is clear, that employment increased as much or more than the population). He believed the state should take the greatest care to utilize the labor force and to keep its skills in order. If necessary the idle workers should be employed to build a useless pyramid upon Salisbury Plain, bring the stones at Stonehenge to Towerhill, or the like, for at worst this would keep their mindes to a discipline and obedience, and their bodies to a patience of more profitable labours when need shall require it.[1]

Petty's expedient was ridiculed sixty-six years later by the author of the anonymous *Considerations on the East India Trade*, but Petty's principle was accepted. The later author wrote:

A people would be thought extravagant and only fit for bedlam which with great stir and bustle should employ itself to remove stones from place to place.

Yet as a method of increasing employment, the later author held, such a shift was no more silly than the restricting of imports. If trade were free, "every individual man in England might be employed to some profit of the kingdom."[11] It is clear that the later author believed a wise economic policy sought to maximize the national output, which of course was exactly what Petty believed. Where their views differed was on the means of achieving the objective. The later author must have assumed that labor was mobile, or possibly that free trade would make labor mobile, and he then could argue that the greatest output requires the specialization which free trade provides. Petty, on the other hand, made no such assumptions, and therefore the maximizing of output seemed to him to require the full utilization of labor by whatever means were appropriate to the circumstances of the moment.

William Temple (1671) maintained that the riches of a nation were in its people and that they would add to the country's wealth in proportion to necessity's driving them to industry and enterprise.[12] Nicholas Barbon (1690) believed that employment was more important than efficiency in consumption and in the use of resources.[13] Josiah Child (1690) believed that the obstacles to greater national wealth were those which restricted free exchange and consequently reduced employment, and the reforms he submitted gave attention to increasing employment.[14] Sir Dudley North (1691), who has been called one of the first free traders, wrote: "Commerce and trade, as hath been said, first spring from the labour of man, but as the stock increases, it dilates more and more." As trade expands, or "dilates," it "never thrives better than when riches are tossed from hand to hand."[15] Charles Davenant (1695) reasoned that security of employment increased the industry of the worker, encouraged him to be thrifty, and thereby was favorable to economic growth.[16] John Law (1720) argued that one of the main benefits of an increase in the money supply would be an increase in employment.[17] Daniel Defoe in his famous defense of tradesmen (1732) held that the main benefit of trade was in the numbers it employed.[18] John Cary (1745) believed that the wealth of the nation was in the "labour of its people."[19] Josiah Tucker (1750) wrote that the country was the more prosperous, "the more persons there are employed in every branch of business."[20] Bishop Berkeley (1751), another mercantilist who was quite near the classical economists, argued that the satisfaction of wants is the ultimate objective of economic organization and that the complete and efficient employment of resources is necessary thereto.[21] Malachy Postlethwayt (1759) reasoned that the satisfaction of individual wants required full employment and competition.[22]

The preceding summary is meant to show the importance of full employment in mercantilist policy. The writers indicated how important they felt it to be by their frequent assertion that the wealth of the nation depended on its "labor"; by the significance they attached to the size of the population; by the common statement that the advantage of trade was in the numbers it employed; by the grave concern expressed over the extent of unemployment, idleness, and poverty, in the numerous remedies by which these problems were to be eliminated and the productivity of labor was to be increased. Most of the measures of policy can be explained more simply and completely by assuming that full employment was the mercantilists' objective than by supposing that some other purpose directed their ideas.

It is, however, possible to assume that the amount of "trade" was the keystone of policy, if one uses the word, as the mercantilists usually did, to include *all* economic activity. Their designs for "a brisk trade" then become methods of assuring the maximum amount of productive effort which is what full employment is also meant to provide. But the word, "trade," has a narrower meaning in modern usage, denoting one aspect of the distributive process, and therefore its use can mislead one into thinking the mercantilists ignored manufacturing, agriculture, shipping, and other industries, which in fact they did not. Moreover, many of the mercantilists' ideas can be related more directly to the amount of employment than to the amount of trade (as their ideas about psychological motivation). Of course, the words "full employment" also can be misleading, but less so, I believe, than any others which can describe the objective of mercantilist policy.

The objective was not, as often supposed, the accumulation of bullion, a favorable balance of trade, the advancement of private interests, the subordination of the working class, low interest rates, the elevation of trade at the expense of other industries. Some of these considerations were means to the end of full employment; some were not entertained by the majority of writers at all. A few of the mercantilists may have confused money with wealth and so made bullionism an end. None of the considerations occupied as important a place in the doctrine as full employment did, and none serves so well to unify the particular measures of control which were proposed.

Once full employment is taken as the objective of mercantilist policy, that policy's difference from liberal policy narrows considerably. Although the difference is not eliminated, it is much less than if one supposes that the objective of mercantilism was, say, a favorable balance of trade, which the liberals never could have accepted as an end.

As many of the commentaries assume a favorable balance of trade to be the objective of mercantilist policy, it perhaps is necessary to explain why that view is not accepted in this essay. If this had been the mercantilists' objective, it is unlikely that they would have given much attention to the money supply, employment, spending, domestic trade, and to other matters which have only an indirect connection, if any at all, with a favorable trade balance. Moreover, they would have emphasized a restriction of imports at least as much as an increase in exports, since by either method a favorable balance could have been realized. One can try, of course, to explain away their doctrine by assuming they were ignorant and illogical. But this does them less than justice. It also leaves one puzzled over why later generations have studied what they said so closely, if they were merely unenlightened and unreasonable scribblers.

It is my opinion that their desire to maintain a favorable balance of trade was based on the assumption that England would be able to increase employment by exporting more than it imported — an assumption which is plausible in the short run. In the long run, the policy would have supported domestic employment if England had invested its net receipts abroad; and it is of interest that some mercantilists, like Thomas Mun (1630), recommended this practice. The favorable balance of trade doctrine is sometimes explained as a device to secure bullion, which, it is said, was thought to increase the national wealth. Since the mercantilists' monetary theory is explained below, it need only be said here that this was not the belief of most of them.

II

In order to achieve full employment, the mercantilists proposed a variety of measures. Most of the measures have often been called wonderful examples of what an economy should not undertake. However, they become sensible if related to the objective of policy. The measures can be grouped into those which affected: (1) the total spending of the economy, (2) prices, wages, and the distribution of income, (3) interest rates, and (4) the supply of labor. The measures in the first three groups were meant to increase employment mainly by increasing the demand for labor while those in the fourth group were meant to increase the labor supply.

(1) Most of the mercantilists believed the economy would prosper if there was the maximum amount of spending by individuals, business enterprise, and foreigners, to which Petty added the government. Although most mercantilists thought of spending on exports as the principal support of employment, some noted that spending in wholly domestic markets was also important. Petty noted that there were circumstances which justified public extravagance, because it put money into the hands of the tradesman; he did, however, think it more prudent for the state, whenever possible, to use its fiscal powers to direct spending to capital goods (or encourage investment).[23] Barbon observed that covetousness (a high propensity to save) reduced consumption, income, government revenues, and employment. He submitted that the most powerful stimulant to trade, even though he thought it wasteful in itself, was spending on goods which quickly became obsolete.[24] Defoe believed the economy prospered when consumers spent a large proportion of their income, although he urged the tradesman himself to be frugal in order that trade and employment would be secure.[25]

North was less concerned with the solvency of the tradesman than with the state of all trade, which, he said, will decline if "the consumption fails, as when men by reason of poverty, do not spend so much in their houses as formerly they did." Many of the mercantilists were alarmed by the hoarding of gold and silver, and showed their alarm by frequent aspersions on individuals who fancied "plate" and on those who were covetous. North deferred to the common view of hoarding to the extent of defending a miser by saying that even he spends occasionally and when he does "those he sets on work benefit by their being employed."[26]

However, it was foreign trade more than domestic trade which interested the mercantilists, because they believed it contributed more to employment, to the nation's wealth, and to its power. The writers *after* 1600 stressed the inflationary effect of an excess of exports over imports and the consequent increase in employment produced by inflation. They reasoned that a favorable balance of trade brought gold and silver to England, that the greater money supply caused spending to increase, and that the greater spending would increase employment. Some viewed exports more directly and naively, thinking that greater exports meant greater employment. Few of the mercantilists distinguished carefully between the short- and long-run effects of a favorable trade balance, a deficiency, however, which would be more noteworthy if it were not that many of their critics also failed to make the distinction carefully.

In order to secure a favorable balance, the mercantilists proposed their familiar commercial policy: duties on imports, with rebates on raw materials used in making exports; the prohibition of certain imported goods; the removal of export duties; subsidies and other assistance to the export industries; monopoly grants to certain joint stock companies engaged in foreign trade; a prohibition of the export of coin and bullion; and an aggressive foreign policy by which England would help its exporters capture markets from their competitors.

The mercantilists who wrote *before* 1600 believed a favorable balance would enable England to accumulate bullion for war purposes. For this reason Hales regarded the export industries as most valuable to the nation, saying: "I would have them most preferred and cherished that bring in most commodity and treasure to the country," commodity and treasure being synonyms here.[27]

Not every one of the measures of policy noted above is proposed in all of the mercantilist writings. In some they even appear to be contradicted, especially the central idea that an increase in spending causes an increase in employment. For example, Temple was opposed to indiscriminate spending on consumption. Other writers deplored the taste for luxuries and urged their use be restricted. However, this kind of opposition to spending rested on one or more of three arguments, and each reveals that the mercantilists did, in fact, relate spending to employment and wished spending regulated in order that it would increase employment. Temple, like his contemporary, Petty, believed that England required more capital, and he urged less consumption out of income in order that there be greater spending on capital goods (which in turn would increase the productivity of labor). The mercantilists who opposed spending on luxuries did so partly because luxuries were imported and partly because their use by the working class reduced its willingness to work.

(2) The mercantilists' ideas about wages and prices were related to employment in four ways. One view was that wages determined export prices and the amount of exports, and hence determined spending and employment. Another was that the relationship between money wages and prices, or real wages, determined the distribution of income which in turn affected the amount of spending and employment. A third was that selling prices determined the amount of spending and employment. A fourth was that real wages determined the quantity of labor supplied.

Those mercantilists who regarded the net export balance as the chief determinant of employment usually favored a policy of low wages, reasoning that low wages meant low costs and prices and increased unit sales. Some writers, however, favored the opposite policy. Cary believed that high labor costs did not reduce exports. Arguing from the labor theory of value, he stated that the greater the amount of labor used in the manufacture of exports the greater their price would be and the greater the return in bullion from their sale, a viewpoint which assumed demand conditions different from those assumed by the mercantilists who favored low wages.[28] It was Mun who made clear the importance of demand conditions in the export market. He said that England should take care to keep its costs down in the manufacture of those exports for which foreigners had no great need (*i.e.*, those for which the demand was elastic), and that England need be less concerned about high costs for those exports which foreigners found necessary (for which the demand was inelastic).[29]

Cary also favored high wages because he believed they supported employment in wholly domestic industries. He thought wage reductions would reduce spending on food and in turn the income of landlords.[30] Of all of the mercantilists who believed the distribution of income determined spending and employment, it was Defoe who was most explicit:

The consumption of provisions increases the rent and value of the lands, and this raises the gentlemen's estates, and that again increases the employment of people, and consequently the numbers of them. . . .

As the people get greater wages, so they, I mean the same poorer part of the people, clothe better, and furnish better, and this increases the consumption of the very manufactures they make; then that consumption increases the quantity made, and this creates what we call the inland trade, by which innumerable families are employed, and the increase of the people maintained; and by which increase of trade and people the present growing prosperity of this nation is produced.[31]

Berkeley expressed a similar idea in one of his rhetorical queries:

Whether as seed equally scattered produceth a goodly harvest, even so an equal distribution of wealth doth not cause a nation to flourish.[32]

69

Davenant and Postlethwayt also favored a more equal distribution of income or of wealth.[33]

A policy of high real wages implies a policy of low prices for any given money wage structure. Therefore one should think that these mercantilists were not averse to price reductions. Many, however, were. Defoe was opposed to price cutting because he believed it damaged the interests of the tradesman who by his central position in the economy had greatest influence on the amount of employment. Defoe, in fact, seems to have wanted high prices *and* high wages, and the difficulty of having both does not seem to have troubled him. He proposed that wages be kept high by the tradesman's avoiding all practices which would reduce the amount of labor required in enterprise. "There is a maxim," he said, "that the more hands it [trade] goes through, the greater public advantage it is to the country." In order to maintain high prices, he proposed that production be restricted if necessary:

There is another fundamental in the prosperity of a nation, which will never fail to be true, viz., that no land is fully improved until it is made to yield its utmost increase: But if our lands should be made to yield their utmost increase, and your people cannot consume the increase, or foreign trade take it off your hands, 'tis then no increase to us, and must not be produced; so that the lands must be laid down, that is to say, a certain proportion of them, and left to bear no corn, or feed no cattle, because your produce is too great for your consumption.[34]

This idea was revived about thirty years later by Postlethwayt, and from it he developed the notion of maintaining the spending power of farmers by fixing the prices they received in a particular proportion to nonagricultural prices, a notion which contained the rudiments of parity pricing.[35] About a century prior to Defoe, Gerard Malynes (1656) wrote that the national interest required high prices.[36] Still earlier, Hales wrote that spending should be directed to high-priced domestically produced goods in preference to lower-priced imports, although he believed the price *level* was too high and should be reduced by lowering the price of silver.[37]

The mercantilist attachment to high prices came of the inflationary persuasion common to most of them after 1600. (Before 1600, there were several proposals to increase the silver content of the coin, which, it was believed, would have been deflationary.) They seem to have observed that unemployment was accompanied by declining prices and severe price competition. They probably reasoned that in order to keep the economy prosperous prices had to be kept high, by means of maximum spending supported by an adequate money supply. Misselden wrote:

And it is much better for the kingdom, to have things dear with plenty of money, whereby men may live in their several callings: than to have things cheap with want of money, which now makes every man complain.[38]

It is important to note that it was by monetary means that most mercantilists believed prices should be raised and supported. Almost all of them were opposed to raising prices by a monopolistic organization of the market.

Although this device would have raised prices it also would have reduced employment, or at least would have made full employment more difficult to achieve. As the mercantilists were strongly against monopoly, they were much in favor of competition. How they conceived of competition is explained below, but it is in order here to note what they thought was the effect of competition on prices, wages, and employment.

Child believed that competition in domestic and foreign markets, including free entry into all occupations, would increase employment and the national wealth.[39] Tucker reasoned that a free price system within wholly domestic markets would produce greater employment than any other system.[40] Similar ideas were expressed by the author of the anonymous *Policies, etc.*, by Hales, Malynes, Petty, Barbon, North, Davenant, Berkeley, and Postlethwayt.[41] In view of the common belief that the mercantilist writers supported the mercantilist practice of price fixing, it is interesting to note the observations of the author of *Policies, etc.*, about the fixing of food prices in London in the first half of the sixteenth century. It was his view that price fixing reduced the supply of farm products brought to London and thereby made worse the condition it was meant to alleviate. He wondered how anyone could believe "this present dearth of victual may be redressed by setting prices upon victual," and continued: "but surely it is not the setting of low prices that will anything amend the matter. But it must be the taking away of the occasion of high prices," which was, he said, the small supply of goods. The author observed also the inconvenience experienced by buyers. When prices are set below their market value, "what throng and strife is there then like to be who shall first catch upon that which cometh." He concluded that it is much better "to suffer all kind of persons quietly to sell all kind of victual in the market at what price he can."[42]

Another argument advanced for a free market was its salutary effect on the laboring classes. Postlethwayt believed that competition among workers forced them to be efficient, responsible, and enterprising, and that it lowered wages.[43] The mercantilists holding this view associated low wages with competition and high wages with restrictions on the labor supply, such as apprenticeship and journeymen rules. They argued for a market determination of wages and not, as sometimes asserted, for the subordination of the working class. There were mercantilists who did believe the workers should be disciplined in order that the amount of labor offered for sale would be increased. Petty and one of his eighteenth century admirers, Thomas Man (1739), argued that as real wages exceeded a certain amount the quantity of labor supplied decreased and therefore if the maximum amount of effort was to be obtained real wages should not exceed this amount.[44]

(3) In addition to achieving full employment by measures related to spending and to wages and prices, some of the mercantilists wished to use the rate of interest for this purpose. There was more agreement about the rate of interest than about the correct wage and price policy but less than about the importance of adequate spending. Those who wished to use the interest rate believed a low rate would enable the merchant to increase his

inventories, that it would lower the price of exports, and that both these effects would in turn cause an increase in employment. Those who favored a low rate included Misselden, Malynes, Temple, Barbon, Child, Law, and the author of *Britannia Languens* (1680).[45]

Except for Barbon who proposed a maximum rate of three per cent to be fixed by law, these mercantilists favored indirect means of reducing the rate. Most believed that the development of financial institutions, like banking and the money market, would exert a downward influence on the rate. One of the most interesting ideas held that the rate varied inversely with the money supply and was expressed by Misselden, Malynes, and Law. According to Misselden "The remedy for usury may be plenty of money," and Malynes wrote of "the abundance of money which maketh the price of usury to fall, more than any law or proclamation can ever do."[46] Law wrote:

. . . indeed, if lowness of interest were the consequence of a greater quantity of money, the stock applied to trade would be greater, and merchants would trade cheaper, from the easiness of borrowing, and the lower interest of money, without any inconveniences attending it.[47]

(The "inconveniences" are those of usury laws.)

This view of the interest rate was not wholly shared by Petty and North. Petty conceded that an increase in the money supply would lower the rate on loans, but he was averse to this sort of manipulation, probably because he believed that as many economic matters as possible should be regulated by "the laws of nature," by which he seems to have meant a free market. He held that the interest on a sum of money at loan must be equal to the net rent which the same sum would yield if used to purchase land, except where the risk in the two transactions differed.[48] This implies that the money rate of interest must conform to the real rate and can fall only as the productivity of capital declines. This was a long-term view which does not preclude the possibility of short-term differences between the two rates. There was, therefore, no necessary contradiction between Petty's theory and the conventional one (although the mercantilists themselves might very well have insisted there was). North, too, believed the long-run determinant of the interest rate was the productivity of capital and that the rate could fall only as the "stock in trade" (capital) increased. A low rate was therefore the consequence of an increase in the quantity of capital and not the cause of the increase. North was strongly opposed to regulating the rate by altering the money supply, believing that the money supply adjusted itself to the volume of trade rather than determined it. He also was opposed to usury laws, which he believed would decrease the quantity of loans supplied.[49] One can observe that the proponents of a low rate based their argument on the assumption that a decrease in the rate would increase the quantity of loans demanded while North argued from the assumption that a decrease in the rate would decrease the quantity of loans supplied. Neither seemed to want to consider the other's premises, and so it is not surprising that the debate was inconclusive.

In addition to believing that it determined the rate of interest, there were two other reasons why the mercantilists attended so closely to the money supply. One was the belief that for any given amount of trade there was an appropriate supply of money and that as the supply increased there would be an increase in trade and employment. In this conception, a change in the money supply was thought to operate directly on spending rather than indirectly through changing the interest rate. It happens that Law used both ideas to support his scheme for increasing the money supply. About the direct effect of an increase he wrote:

Domestic trade depends on the money: A greater quantity employs more people than a lesser quantity. A limited sum can only set a number of people to work proportioned to it, and it is with little success laws are made, for employing the poor and idle in countries where money is scarce; good laws may bring the money to the full circulation it is capable of, and force it to those employments that are most profitable to the country: But no laws can make it go further, nor can more people be set to work, without more money to circulate so as to pay the wages of a greater number.[50]

The argument assumes a downward rigidity of prices such that a decrease in the money supply, by causing less spending, produces a decrease in employment and output.

The other reason for the mercantilists' attention to money was the belief that an accumulation of bullion could be desirable in itself. Those who held this belief included Hales, Temple, Cary, and Tucker, the last of whom said:

. . . the whole science of gainful commerce consists, ultimately in procuring a balance of gold and silver to ourselves from other nations.[51]

This has been taken to mean, by Smith and John Stuart Mill for example, that the mercantilists believed money was wealth and that they made no distinction between things exchanged and the medium by which they were exchanged. Some of the mercantilists may have believed this, but it is very doubtful that many did. Hales observed that accumulation was desirable because treasure was the "sinews of war."[52] Petty believed that the nation should accumulate gold and silver,

because those things are not only not perishable, but are esteemed for wealth at all times and everywhere.[53]

The statements of Hales and Petty do not imply that a nation should accumulate specie because it is wealth but because it is a store of wealth. Even Mun, who has come down to us as one of the first to expose the fallacy of bullionism, conceded there were circumstances in which a prince would be wise to lay by a store of treasure. It is debatable whether the accumulation of bullion would have given England a more certain command over the goods of other nations than would its commodity exports. However, the mercantilists assumed that it would, and in this assumption, however unrealistic or otherwise, there was no logical confusion of money with wealth.

Nor was there in the alternative conceptions which related the money supply to the rate of interest and to spending. Moreover, when it is realized that some of the mercantilists were opposed to accumulation, or to restrictions on the export of bullion and coin, there is no warrant at all for stating that the characteristic fallacy of mercantilism was the confusion of money with wealth. North and Berkeley were opposed to accumulation; Child opposed restriction of the export of coin because he thought it reduced employment, and Petty because it was "against the laws of nature, and also impracticable."[54]

(4) There was a final group of measures by which the mercantilists meant to increase employment. It consisted of means of increasing the quantity of labor supplied (the relationship of real wages to which was explained above), of increasing the labor supply, and of increasing the productivity of labor. That the mercantilists looked at employment from the supply as well as demand side of the market indicates their policy sought to increase the quantity of resources and was not a make-shift for creating jobs.

Their methods of increasing the labor force are harsh by today's standards and often are interpreted as revealing an animosity toward the lower classes. Those who interpret the mercantilists this way usually imply that the classical economists had a more enlightened view of the working class.[55] Certainly more sympathy was expressed by the classicists; there was less carping, less preaching of the early-to-bed, early-to-rise variety, and there was more tolerance of distinctively human behavior. But when all this is said, there still remains the fact that the classical economists did not make any important proposals to redistribute income or otherwise to ameliorate the condition of the lower classes except to urge that the best hope for them, as for all other classes, was the steady growth of national output, a goal which the mercantilists just as persistently sought although by somewhat different means.

Actually, most of the mercantilist labor policy came from the assumption that self-interest governs individual conduct, an assumption as fully entertained today as it was two and three hundred years ago. The principle which directed the mercantilists to believe that the unemployed should receive only a subsistence allowance is no different from that which leads modern economists to believe unemployment compensation should be set much below prevailing wages in order that the idle shall not come to prefer leisure to work. The point was made very clear by J. S. Mill who argued that the best way to treat the poor is to make them wish they were rich.

The mercantilist labor policy consisted of measures to increase the population; to increase the size of the labor force within a given population, in numbers of workers and in the amount of work supplied by each laborer; and to increase the productivity of the labor force. In order to increase the population some writers proposed that subsidies be given to large families; and occasionally they attached the ingenious scheme of financing the subsidies by a tax on bachelors (which makes one wonder what would have happened had the subsidies been successful). Other methods were to encourage the immigration of skilled workers and tradesmen which, it was believed, would be easier if there were greater religious tolerance. The percentage of the labor force to the total population was to be increased by bringing children into employment. Petty estimated that if all those between six and sixteen were employed the national income of England would be increased by five million pounds (about the year 1662).[56] Almost all mercantilists considered ways of bringing more persons into the labor force. They wished to reduce the enlistments in the army and navy and to direct men into gainful employment, to turn criminals to legitimate activity, and, above all, to rehabilitate the poor and indigent whom circumstances or choice had deprived of the will to work.

Petty held that enlistments could be reduced by raising wages in civilian employments.[57] The unemployed were to be rehabilitated by work houses into which they were to be forced on pain of receiving no public assistance whatever and in which they would learn the virtue of work. More severe treatment was thought proper for criminals who, it was believed, had to be shown that crime was not to their interest. Temple thought the forms of punishment should be made more lasting, and he proposed "to change the usual punishment by short and easy deaths, into some others of painful and uneasy lives," a change which involved branding the cheeks of criminals, slitting their noses, and condemning them to slavery in the colonies.[58] Berkeley believed that all who would not work should be impressed into labor gangs and used for public projects.[59] However, not all mercantilists were as ruthless. Child pleaded for understanding and patience. He proposed a reconstruction of the system of providing relief to the poor in order to help them and to demonstrate to others that the lower classes were an asset and not a liability to the nation.[60]

In order to increase the amount of work offered, it was proposed that the state remove the many distractions which kept the workers from being industrious. Drinking was the first to be attended to. According to Defoe:[61]

> In English ale their dear enjoyment lies,
> For which they'll starve themselves and families.
> An Englishman will fairly drink as much
> As will maintain two families of Dutch.

Tucker would have done away with cockpits, skittle-alleys, stages for cudgel playing, making book on horse races, the selling of liquor, cakes, fruit, "or any like temptations to draw people together" and away from their jobs.[62] Other mercantilists asked for sumptuary control, because they thought the wearing of ribbons and ruffles and the drinking of tea made workers prideful and lazy. It is interesting that such proposals hardly ever expressed the fear of insubordination turning into sedition. It was sloth which alarmed the mercantilists.

For the purpose of increasing labor productivity, it was proposed the workers be shown that industry, skill, and enterprise were to their advantage. Rewards were to be given for excellence of work, some in money, some in the form of distinction. Industrious and skilled immigrants were to be attracted to England in order to set an example to native workers. Children were to be trained to the habit of work from an early age, and older persons were to be shown in a variety of ways the rewards from industry. In his program for improving the poor, Tucker asked that courts be formed in each district to supervise the working class, each court to be presided over by "Guardians of the Morals of the Manufacturing Poor." By precept, inducement, and punishment, the poor would be transformed into a national asset. One of the rewards was to be "a good book" stamped in gold on one side with "The Hand of the Diligent Maketh Rich" and on the other, "To the Praise of Them that Do Well."[63]

The labor policy of the mercantilists was a logical derivation of their economic psychology. Almost all believed there were three factors which directed individuals to economic activity: the stimulus given by physical environment, the desire of men to emulate their betters (a desire partly created by social environment), and the eagerness for pecuniary rewards. It was believed that men were the more industrious, the more difficult were the conditions in which they lived: the climate, soil fertility, the national wealth in relation to the population. The less favorable was their environment, the more likely they were to become rich. Temple wrote:

I conceive the true and original grounds of trade to be, a great multitude of people crowded into small compass of land, whereby all things necessary to life become dear, and all men, who have possessions, are induced to parsimony; but those, who have none, are forced to industry and labour, or else to want. Bodies that are vigorous fall to labour; such as are not, supply that defect by some sort of inventions or ingenuity. These customs arise first from necessity, but increase by imitation, and grow in time to be habitual in a country.[64]

Postlethwayt summarized the idea by saying, "The greatest industry has ever been the effect of the greatest necessity."[65]

The second factor which made men industrious was their desire to emulate those above them in social position and income. Petty wrote that men always seek to excel, and when placed together, as in large cities, their emulative instinct becomes all the keener, evoking their industry, increasing spending, and providing opportunity for still greater industry.[66] Other writers, like Defoe, doubted the beneficence of emulation, believing it often made men imprudent, but they admitted the motive was a strong one.[67]

The third factor was the desire for monetary returns. It was thought to be the principal cause of industry, and that the greater were the money returns from a particular employment the greater usually would be the quantity of resources supplied to that employment. The idea was expressed quite early and repeated down to the end of the mercantilist period when it was carried forward by the classical economists in their doctrine of self-interest. Hales wrote that "profit or advancement nourishes every faculty; which saying is so true, that it is allowed by the common judgment of all men."[68] The idea was expressed by other mercantilists, among them Petty, North, Davenant, and Defoe, the last of whom said, somewhat prodigally:

Gain is the tradesman's life, 'tis the essence of his being, as a qualified trades-man. Convenience, and supply of necessary things for life, were the first causes indeed of trade; but the reason and end of the tradesman is to get money: 'Tis the polestar and guide, the aim and design of all his notions; 'tis the center and point to which all his actions tend; 'tis the soul of business, the spur of industry, the wheel that turns within all wheels of his whole business, and gives motion to the rest.[69]

What Defoe said of the tradesman (and Lamb described more econom-ically as "the quick pulse of gain") was believed true of all in the economy and true in a special way of the worker. An increase in real wages would be accompanied by an increase in the quantity of labor supplied until real wages reached a certain amount, and if they went beyond this amount the quantity of labor supplied would decrease. The mercantilists who thought of the labor supply function in this way believed that pecuniary self-interest had less of an effect on the worker than on others in the economy; or that before the pecuniary motive could operate effectively the worker had first to become accustomed to high real wages. It had, therefore, to be reinforced by other factors. One was emulation. This trait could be exploited by placing before the working man the rewards which others had acquired by their industry, and so developing his wants. Wants, however, had to be guided prudently, for they could turn men toward the ale houses as well as the shops and factories. Most certain of all conditions leading them to industry was environment. If the poor could not be brought to gainful activity by monetary rewards or enticed to it by the desire to excel, they could be forced to it by necessity. Moreover, as Temple explained, the habits they formed while overcoming necessity would remain with them, and they would continue to be industrious when the original cause had disappeared.

III

In these observations on individual motivation, the mercantilist writers anticipated the economic psychology in classical doctrine. In addition, they anticipated two other of its important features: the nature of the price mechanism and the political presuppositions of economic policy.

It was the classical view that self-interest operating in a competitive market directed resources to their most efficient employments and enabled individuals to spend their income in a way which would maximize their satisfaction as consumers. Whatever interfered with the operation of self-interest, as it directed the choices of individuals in their capacity as pro-ducers or consumers, usually reduced the efficiency of the economy or, what is the same thing, its real income. The classicists did make exceptions to laissez faire, some of them insistent, but laissez faire was certainly their rule of policy. So great was their emphasis on the efficiency of resource use which the market created that one must suppose they believed the market would provide for the full employment of resources as well as their direc-tion to the best particular uses. Apart from Malthus and Sismondi, none of the classicists admitted a conflict between efficient employment and full employment.

The mercantilists' conception of the price mechanism was similar to that of the classicists on these matters: the directive power of self-interest (that is, its economic as well as psychological aspect); the determination of prices by supply and demand; the desirability of competition; and the mutual advantage of exchange in domestic markets. The mercantilists, however, did not believe that universal efficiency could be established by the price system; they did believe that a limited operation of the system was desirable. They also held a qualified notion of the harmony of self-interest. On the issue of full employment, there was the greatest difference between the mercantilists and the classical economists. It was the mercantilist view that free international trade would reduce employment, that inattention to the monetary system would have the same result, and that a highly unequal distribution of income could reduce spending which in turn would reduce employment.

From the mercantilist conception of self-interest followed the belief that under certain conditions the free allocation of resources would yield the greatest possible efficiency and employment. It is noteworthy that the mechanics of the price system should have been explained by one of the earliest writers, Hales, and it is especially interesting that he should have suggested that the idea was a common one in his age. His work is a dialogue between a doctor and a knight. At one point they consider the best means of eliminating the scarcity of corn, and the doctor says its price should be free to find its market value just as the price of wool is free.

Knight: How would you have them [the husbandmen] better cherished to use the plough?

Dr.: To let them have more profit from it than they have, and liberty to sell it at all times, and to all places, as freely as men do their other things. But then no doubt the price of corn would rise, specially at the first more than at the length; yet that price would provoke every man to set plough to the ground, to husband waste grounds, yes to turn the lands which be enclosed from pasture to arable land; for every man will gladder follow that wherein they see the more profit and gains. And thereby must needs ensue both great plenty of corn, and also much treasure should be brought into this realm by occasion thereof; and besides that plenty of other victuals increased amongst us.[70]

If these remarks were taken out of context, they easily could be interpreted as an argument for the unrestricted operation of the price system. That "every man will gladder follow that wherein they see the more profit and gains" is in agreement with Smith's statement that "every individual is constantly exerting himself to find out the most advantageous employment for whatever capital he can command."[71] Hales also anticipated the classical economists in his statement that "the workman never travails but as the master provokes him with good wages"; in his belief that the common ownership of capital is less productive than individual ownership — "that which is possessed of many in common is neglected of all"; and in his conviction that many forms of economic control are ineffective before the power of self-interest — "for many heads will devise many ways to get anything by."[72] So long as only the positive aspects of Hales' ideas are compared with those of Smith, the two writers are in agreement. Both held the same view of the fact of self-interest and of its power to direct labor and capital to their most profitable uses. The agreement is implied in the above passages and it is clear when the passages are placed in their context. About the normative aspect, however, there was disagreement, and this is explained farther along.

Many of the mercantilists explained how prices are determined by supply and demand. Malynes, in a passage arguing against the fixing of prices by the state, wrote:

> Everyman knoweth, that in the buying and selling of commodities there is an estimation and price demanded and agreed upon between both parties, according to a certain equality in the value of things, promoted by a true reason grounded upon the commodious use of things. So that equality is nothing else but a mutual voluntary estimation of things made in good order and truth wherein equality is not admitted or known.[73]

This statement actually goes beyond an expression of the fact of supply and demand. It suggests that utility is the basis of value ("commodious use"), that utility is a subjective magnitude ("estimation . . . wherein equality is not admitted or known"), and that there is an advantage in exchange to both buyer and seller ("a mutual voluntary estimation of things").

The words "true reason" have a special significance, both for Malynes' statement and for the doctrine of other mercantilists. In the quotation above, true reason should be interpreted to mean accurate perception or understanding, which makes the statement an expression of the idea that price or value is determined by individual evaluation and that this evaluation is the only true kind. It is the idea that individuals are the best judges of their welfare. Malynes again remarked on true reason in his exposition of the Law of Merchants, which, he said, was the only law that was universal and absolute, the same everywhere and at all times, and that it had its origin in Cicero's conception of true law as right reason agreeable to nature.[74] Malynes' remarks anticipate the conception of natural law held by the classical economists. They identified natural law with reason and made reason an individual trait, which was in contrast to conceptions of natural law that made reason an immanent quality of social institutions or of a supernal power. The doctrine suggested by Malynes was the doctrine of natural rights or of individual prerogatives which are beyond the power of the state or of society to abridge. It was first enunciated by the Stoics, was applied to social philosophy by Cicero, and then was allowed to lapse for many hundreds of years until it was returned to social thought by the philosophers of liberalism in the seventeenth century.[75] That which Malynes incorporated in economic policy, if only by intimation, was not natural law, *sui generis* — this had been done when economic problems first were recognized — but that particular version of natural law which was the touchstone of political and economic liberalism.

79

The practical result of the natural rights doctrine was a policy of individual economic freedom. Petty, for example, argued against the many economic controls imposed by the state, and attributed England's difficulties to the fact that "too many matters have been regulated by laws, which nature, long custom, and general consent ought only to have governed." Positive laws, he stated, should consist of "whatsoever is right reason and the Law of Nature," a statement which is best interpreted by placing the word, "therefore" before "the Law of Nature," since Petty did not make a substantive distinction between reason and natural law.[76]

As they believed prices ought to be determined by supply and demand, most of the mercantilists were opposed to price fixing and to many other forms of market control. Barbon stated that "the value of all wares arises from their use," that a "plenty" of wares makes them cheap, while a "scarcity" makes them expensive. He concluded, "the market is the best judge of value."[77] North asserted the "universal maxim" of price is that a "plenty of anything makes it cheap," on the assumption that demand is constant.[78] Law stated that the price of a commodity is determined by the quantity offered for sale in relation to the demand, and that as the quantity offered increases, the price or value declines. He illustrated the point most interestingly by water and diamonds, explaining that diamonds were more valuable than water, despite the greater "usefulness" of the latter, because the quantity supplied of diamonds was less than that of water. This paradox was noted independently by Smith, about fifty years later, and illustrated by the same commodities, but he did not as explicitly resolve it as Law did.[79] Berkeley expressed the principle of price determination in one of his queries:

Whether the value or price of things, be not a compounded proportion, directly as the demand, and reciprocally as the plenty?[80]

The opposition to market control was made explicit by Child, who presented a list of nine laws which he said were impediments to trade and employment. Included were laws which prohibited the export of coin, raised the price of exports, reduced the price of beer, forbade engrossing ("there being no more useful trade in a nation"), and limited the supply of labor by restricting entry into skilled trades. He stated:

It is the care of law makers first and principally to provide for the people in gross, not particulars.[81]

Davenant expressed the same conclusion:

Trade is in its nature free, finds its own channel, and best directeth its own course: and all laws to give it rules and directions, and to limit and circumscribe it, may serve the particular ends of private men, but are seldom advantageous to the public.[82]

Petty (as noted above) believed that economic relations among individuals should be directed by "whatsoever is right reason" and not by the state. Of all the mercantilists, North endorsed free exchange most thoroughly:

Now it may appear strange to hear it said,

That the whole world as to trade, is but as one nation or people, and therein nations are as persons.

That the loss of a trade with one nation, is not that only, separately considered, but so much of the trade of the world rescinded and lost, for all is combined together.

That there can be no trade unprofitable to the public; for if any prove so, men leave it off; and wherever the traders thrive, the public, of which they are a part, thrives also.

That to force men to deal in any prescribed manner, may profit such as do happen to serve them; but the public gains not, because it is taking from one subject, to give to another.

That no laws can set prizes in trade, the rates of which must and will make themselves: but when such laws do happen to lay hold, it is so much impediment to trade, and therefore prejudicial.[83]

The mercantilist conception of free exchange had a political as well as economic aspect, and both anticipated the ideas of the classical economists. Although the mercantilists differed about the origin of government they agreed upon the extent of its powers, which, they said, should be limited by law; and the consequent economic liberty would be favorable to the growth of the economy. Temple said the economy could prosper "under good princes and legal monarchies, as well as under free states" and that it must decline under a "tyrannical power," "free states" here meaning republican governments.[84] The words also were used to mean any form of government whose power was limited, as when Barbon wrote that trade could flourish only in a "free government," of which a constitutional monarchy was one form. "Men are most industrious where they are most free and secure to enjoy the effects of their labours," he stated.[85] In its economic application, the doctrine of limited power meant that regulation of the market should be minimized and made to apply uniformly to all persons and trades. "All favor to one trade or interest against another, is an abuse, and cuts so much of profit from the public," North observed.[86]

As among the classical economists, there was among the mercantilists considerable disagreement about the foundation of government. Some mercantilists insisted, as Hume did later, that the authority of government rested upon the "greatest and strongest" among the people. This was Temple's conception. Others, Defoe among them, accepted the contract theory of government which then enjoyed its eminent hour. But these differences did not lead to disagreement over the proper structure of government. The mercantilists were united in opposing absolute rule by a single individual and unlimited rule by the people, and the opposition to both autocracy and democracy came of a profound distrust of power per se. Temple wrote:

Many men are good and esteemed when they are private, ill and hated when they are in office . . . and many men *come out,* when they *come into* great and public employments.[87]

Barbon and Davenant were forcible in advocating constitutional procedures, asserting that only by these means could the liberty of the individual be secured.[88]

Their opposition to democratic government did not make the mercantilists uncritical apologists for an aristocracy; and they disapproved of many of the grosser forms of illiberalism which they saw about them. Most of them were opposed to religious intolerance, and insisted upon the practicability of allowing each person to seek his salvation in his own way. Defoe was very critical of the ruling classes, believing their attitude toward trade was an obstacle to economic progress. *The Complete English Tradesman,* parts of *The Complete English Gentleman,* and the parabolical meaning of *Robinson Crusoe* can be read as an effort to persuade the aristocracy of the national value of trade and the tradesman. Other mercantilists wrote persuasively of the usefulness of the tradesman and of the wisdom of giving him greater political power and a higher social position.

IV

The ideas of politics and of the price mechanism have a curious relation to the economic policy which the mercantilists advanced. If one read only their expressions about economic and political liberty, one easily could conclude that their policy must be laisser faire. If, on the other hand, one looked only at the measures of control they proposed, one would have great doubts of their laissez faire. There is a paradox in the mercantilists' anticipating many of the positive and some of the normative elements of classical economics and at the same time proposing a policy quite different from the classical policy. The mercantilists were reluctant to follow the principle of freedom to all of the practical results which they thought it would bring, and, it is equally clear, they were reluctant to modify their ideas of liberty in order to achieve the practical results they wanted.

It is illuminating to compare the ideas of Hales and Smith on the normative aspects of free exchange. When Smith observed that each individual always tries to discover "the most advantageous employment for whatever capital he can command," he concluded that the "study of his advantage naturally, or necessarily, leads him to prefer that employment which is most advantageous to society." Hales did not think this would always be so. In another colloquy, it is said:

Knight: Every man is a member of the commonweal, and that that is profitable to one may be profitable to another, if he would exercise the same feat. Therefore that is profitable to one, and so to another, may be profitable to all, and so to the commonwealth. . . .

Dr.: That reason is good (adding so much and more to it). True, it is that thing which is profitable to each man by himself (*so it be not prejudicial to any other*) is profitable to the whole commonwealth, and not otherwise; or else robbing and stealing, which perchance is profitable to some men, were profitable to the whole commonweal, which no man will admit.[89]

Malynes, too, was unable to endorse free exchange completely. He believed it might conflict with the "good of the commonwealth, which is the cause that princes and governors are to set at the stern of the course of trade and commerce." He held that to allow merchants to set the course of trade would be as imprudent as to consult vintners about laws against drunkedness.[90] A similar qualification was made by Child:

. . . the profit of the merchant, and the gain of the kingdom, which are so far from being always parallel, that frequently they run counter one to the other, although most men . . . do usually confound the two.[91]

Although favorable to competition Postlethwayt hesitated to approve of it wholly. "Exchange of merchandise for merchandise is advantageous in general; but not in cases where it is contrary to the foregoing maxims," he wrote, the maxims being that trade should increase the money supply and employment.[92] Even the enlightened North was doubtful of the universal harmony of self-interest, although he viewed the disharmony oppositely from the usual way. He was less troubled that the individual could gain at the nation's expense than interested in the possibility of the nation gaining at the expense of the individual (as when unwise investment led to greater employment).[93] Some mercantilists believed the economy could prosper at the expense of individuals, if they engaged in extravagant expenditure which, however damaging to them, was a stimulant to trade. The idea was set forth by Mun in a chapter called, "Of some Excesses and Evils in the Commonwealth, which not withstanding decay not our Trade nor Treasure."[94] The idea was made notorious by Mandeville in his fable of the bees whose private vices were public benefits. It was not, however, quite as widely accepted as the notoriety of Mandeville's verse suggests. Davenant, while admitting the possibility, denied that private extravagance was the way to wealth, and submitted that a wise levying of excises would give the lie to the notion that "riot and expense, in private persons, is advantageous to the public."[95]

These passages indicate that the mercantilists were aware that some of their measures of policy would abridge economic freedom. It can be shown that they were aware of why freedom should be limited.

One reason was that a free market was not entirely favorable to an increase in the nation's wealth. The other reason was less significant and the limitation it implied was in no way inconsistent with classical policy. When, for example, Hales denied that self-interest always produced universal harmony, he cited the act of theft as a proof (actually he had more than this in mind, and the example does not illustrate his position completely). The prohibiting of crime is not, of course, a denial of freedom. Other mercantilists argued that the unlimited freedom of the tradesman would lead eventually to monopoly, which again was a trivial exception because free exchange is, by definition, competitive exchange. Indeed the mercantilists' opposition to monopoly is an affirmation of liberal doctrine, and many of them anticipated the doctrine in their endorsement of competition. Tucker excoriated the regulated companies (which had certain monopolistic powers) in language suggestive of Smith at a peak of indignation:

> This is the greatest and most intolerable of all the evils of monopolies. It is a prostitution of the trade and welfare of the public to the merciless ravages of greedy individuals.[96]

Postlethwayt anticipated the classical conception of the advantages of competition, writing:

> Domestic rivalship in trade produces plenty; and plenty cheapness of provisions, of the first materials, of labour, and of money. Rivalship is one of the most important principles of trade, and a considerable part of its liberty. Whatever cramps or hurts it in these four points is ruinous to the state, and diametrically contrary to its intent, which is the happiness of the greatest number possible of men.[97]

North warned of the devious forms which monopoly could assume:

> For whenever men consult for the public good, as for the advancement of trade, wherein all are concerned, they usually esteem the immediate interest of their own to be the common measure of good and evil.[98]

It will be remembered that Smith said dryly: "I have never known much good done by those who affected to trade for the public good."[99]

When they insisted that one individual should not be free to deprive another of his freedom the mercantilists did not take important exception to the principle of the free market. When, however, they insisted that the market could not be relied upon to guarantee full employment, the exception was important. They believed that if the economy were directed by the market, even a competitive one, spending would not always be sufficient, specie could be lost through excessive imports, the supply of money for other reasons could be inadequate, the rate of interest might be too high, and the labor force too small and insufficiently productive.

Hence, instead of the classical policy of laissez faire, the mercantilists proposed a policy which would utilize the market wherever possible, supplement and control it where not, and which would have full employment as its proximate objective. There was, then, this difference of *means* between the mercantilists and the classicists: the former proposed a relatively controlled market and the latter a relatively uncontrolled one. There also was a difference in emphasis on proximate *ends:* the mercantilists stressed the full employment of resources and the classicists stressed the efficiency of the use of particular resources.

Yet it will not do to carry these differences much farther. The difference about means was not a fundamental one. The mercantilists did not believe in an economy wholly or mainly directed by the state, and the classicists did not believe in an economy entirely controlled by a competitive market. The difference about means was a difference over the amount and kinds of control. Both classicists and mercantilists believed in what we now call a mixed economy, and they differed over the ingredients in the mixture. This kind of difference, we know today, is singularly hard to define and to resolve.

The difference on immediate ends — full employment versus efficiency of employment — also is one which must not be made fundamental. It is very probable that neither the mercantilists nor the classicists would have admitted such a distinction. The former, I suspect, would have insisted that their policy achieved a greater output, and therefore more efficiency, than a policy which ignored the problem of full employment. Their implicit assumption was that a nation was not free to choose between using *all* of its resources in one way or another, in order to satisfy the criterion of maximum output, but that the nation must choose between a policy which would produce full employment and one which would not. The classicists probably would have insisted that once the market had been made competitive and the conditions established for an efficient use of resources there would be no problem of full employment. They would have granted, perhaps insisted, that unwise interference with the market could create underemployment but they would not have admitted underemployment as a problem once the market was properly organized. It is only a later age which can make the distinction between full employment and efficient employment a certain one; and in order to do this it must define each of these objectives differently from the way they were defined by the mercantilists and the classicists. It must assume that a policy which provides full employment probably would be accompanied by some inefficiency in the use of particular resources, and that a policy which yields efficiency in the use of employed resources would be accompanied by a condition of some idle labor and capital. When the objectives are so defined, a choice can be made between the two policies, and that will be chosen which yields the largest national product. No clear choice is, however, implied by the distinction between the mercantilist and the classical policies. Not only is it unnecessary to speculate over which was correct, but, it seems to me, the speculation is a little pointless.

V

It is more promising to speculate over the reasons for the difference between the mercantilist and the liberal objectives. The most plausible reason is that the two policies were developed in different periods in which there were different economic problems. The great concern of the mercantilists over employment, particularly of labor, may have been forced on them by the unemployment of the sixteenth, seventeenth, and early eighteenth centuries, which, economic historians tell us, and we can infer from contemporary tracts, was considerable. The enclosure movement seems to have been the major cause of unemployment in the first part of the mercantilist period. By replacing tillage with grazing, the enclosures reduced the amount of labor required in agriculture and drove large numbers of persons off the land into rural slums and into the towns and cities. The transfer of large numbers from one occupation to another is difficult even under favorable circumstances; and circumstances in the sixteenth century were not favorable. The craft guilds were not eager to increase their output at any time, and one can easily suppose that they were not pleased by the hordes who were swept off the land and sought employment in the towns.

Another cause of unemployment was the frequent commercial crises which by their strangeness must have baffled the early economists (no less than the later). Although the fluctuations seem not to have been of regular occurrence, as later cyclical movements were, yet these were more than occasional and sporadic changes. In addition to these two types of unemployment, which today would be called frictional and cyclical, there seems also to have been much seasonal unemployment. Petty's statistics on annual and weekly wages in the third quarter of the seventeenth century suggest that the average worker was employed about thirty-five weeks of the year.[100]

It is fairly clear that unemployment was extensive and quite clear that poverty was common. The management of these two problems was made more than usually difficult by a circumstance arising from the Reformation. When the power of the Catholic church was destroyed there went with it an organized method of caring for the poor. An effort was made to place the responsibility on local governments, but this was not successful. The craft guilds, it is true, looked out for their members, but were unable to care for the newly created poor from agriculture even if they had wished to.

Not only was there less provision for the lower classes, but after the middle of the seventeenth century there was less interest in their welfare and less concern over the problem of unemployment. Under the Tudors there seems to have been a genuine solicitude for the lower classes, a feeling which perhaps came of the knowledge that disaffection with an absolute monarch can have disastrous results. After the revolution of 1688, the monarchy was severely abridged and therefore was less responsible for the general welfare, while Parliament could be only a diffuse object of resentment to those who thought the state was not looking after them properly. Elizabeth could say with reason, "Yet this I account the glory of my crown, that I have reigned with your loves." It is difficult to imagine words of the same sincerity coming from a sovereign after 1688.

It seems, to use today's language, that the unemployment of the sixteenth and seventeenth centuries was the result of immobility, of seasonal fluctuations, of the rigidity of certain prices and wages which was produced by the monopolistic practices of the guilds, and of frequent and severe deflations. The nonseasonal unemployment might have been eliminated (it now is easy to say) had it been possible to move labor from areas where it was abundant to where it was scarce and to force a reduction of certain wages and prices in order to make increased employment profitable to the entrepreneurs of the age. But it does not seem, from their writings, that the mercantilists thought such measures would have been adequate. Although they made proposals for increasing labor mobility and for making wages and prices more flexible, they do not seem to have put much reliance on them. Instead, it seems they had greater confidence in inflationary measures: those which, by increasing the money supply, would have increased spending and employment.

It is interesting to observe that Great Britain had a similar unemployment problem about 200 years after the close of the mercantilist period and solved it by methods quite suggestive of the mercantilists' proposals. After the first World War there was considerable frictional unemployment and money wages could not easily have been lowered. A few years after the second World War, after the inflationary measures of the Labor Government had shown their effect, it was observed by a United Nations report on economic stability, that the frictional unemployment "which had previously been attributed mainly to lack of mobility of labour, melted away, leaving an acute labour shortage."[101] This report was written mainly from the viewpoint of Keynesian economics which, it is clear, has an affinity to mercantilist doctrine.

In the period when liberal economic doctrine developed circumstances were much different from those of the mercantilist period. There was no longer the problem of managing a large amount of permanent unemployment, as this effect of the enclosure movement had disappeared. The internal market of Great Britain was much better organized, in the sense of there being less immobility of commodities and capital as well as of labor. By 1750, the government no longer enforced any important controls over the internal market. The obstacles to price and wage flexibility were much less formidable than they had been in the preceding three centuries. Improvements in transportation, especially after 1800, brought the parts of the economy into closer connection and made competition more feasible. Finally, there was an expansion of British foreign trade, resulting from the decline of the Dutch empire at the end of the seventeenth century, from the weakening of the imperial power of Spain, and from the increased efficiency of manufactures and shipping which gave Britain a cost advantage in the world market. These circumstances dictated a much wider use of the market as the appropriate economic policy, just as the different circumstances confronting the mercantilists required restrictions on the market.

VI

The interpretation of this essay makes English mercantilist doctrine a predecessor of economic liberalism. In order that the meaning be clear, it may be helpful to compare it to other interpretations of mercantilism. It is common for works on the history of economic thought to abide by the judgment of Smith and Mill, that the mercantilists believed money was wealth and therefore believed the nation became richer as its supply of monetary metal increased. It is understandable that the mercantilists should be judged this way. If their goal of full employment is neglected, there is no way to explain their preoccupation with the money supply but to suppose they thought money was wealth. The exposition above of their monetary theory should make clear that few of them made the simple error of which they have so often been accused.

Another interpretation looks upon mercantilist doctrine as a collection of mistaken ideas, not only in the area of monetary theory but in other areas as well. The mercantilists, by this view, are regarded as rudimentary economists who sensed the importance of the problems they addressed but were defeated by them. The mercantilists did express certain ideas crudely and they made mistakes (which is not at all singular). But there was nothing primitive about their central ideas. The most important aspects of the price mechanism, for example, were understood as long ago as 1549 when Hales's *Discourse* was published, and the way in which he wrote of them suggests they were known even earlier. Modern economics has expressed these principles more rigorously but it has not altered them. We still believe that unequal rates of profit will cause a re-allocation of transferable resources. Indeed, it is only in recent years that economics has tried to reintegrate monetary and price theory, in order to bring together the money and the real sides of the economy, which is a theoretical achievement sought by the mercantilists.

A third interpretation makes the mercantilists into apologists for the kind of economy in which they lived. It has become increasingly common in recent years to look upon social thought as an apology or rationalization of the social institutions which are dominant when the thought is expressed. When the mercantilists are regarded this way, two conclusions usually result. One is that their doctrine was an effort to explain the circumstances of their age. If this means the mercantilists were interested only in their period, it is wholly — and trivially — correct. Economists always are interested in the problems of the time, some of which are transitory and others nearly everlasting. The other conclusion is that the mercantilists sought to advance private interests by disguising them in a tissue of abstraction. I do not know how such an interpretation can be upheld (in addition to contrary statements in their works, there is the awkward difficulty of uncovering the private thoughts of men who have been dead 200 years and more), nor do I see just what significance the proof would have. Perhaps John Hales was trying to increase the income of corn growers and Thomas Mun wanted greater dividends for the East India Company. Nevertheless, they had something of lasting interest to say.

The most cogent of all interpretations makes mercantilism a continuation of the ideas of medieval society. This is the view of Schmoller and of Heckscher.[102] Schmoller stated that the principal tenet of mercantilism was the identity between political and economic institutions, such that the economic conduct of the individual was made to conform to the objectives of the state. Mercantilism was thus a system of national power and one of a number of forms which idealism as a political philosophy can take. Prior to the twentieth century dictatorships, the most notable expression of idealism was medieval society. In their remarks on economic conduct, the Schoolmen stated that free individual behavior was inimical to the welfare of society. They adopted the Aristotelean idea that exchange was "unnatural" because it caused men to lose sight of the proper use of commodities, which was consumption, and to make an improper use of them, which was unlimited accumulation.[103] In the Aristotelean and medieval conception, exchange is condemned if its purpose is anything more than the satisfaction of limited wants. It is wrong if it becomes a means of expressing acquisitive desires because these in themselves are improper. In its practical aspect, the conception makes exchange a useless, or barren, act, and imposes numerous controls over it. This was the medieval view after about the twelfth century, although there were exceptions to it.

In English mercantilist writings I have found only one statement which in any way suggests the medieval notion of exchange. It is Cary's assertion that the buying and selling "whereby one man lives by the profit of another, brings no advantage to the public."[104] However, it is not certain that Cary endorsed the medieval idea. His observations on the price mechanism are anything but medieval. Admittedly, the mercantilists stated that self-interest was inimical to the public good, but the statement is, I believe, of no significance. The kind of economy they proposed could not possibly have operated without the expression of self-interest, just as the economy proposed by the classicists could not have operated without it. They too condemned self-interest, but neither they nor the mercantilists believed it wholly bad or even mainly so, and they did not want it suppressed. Both wanted the power it gave to men to be used in the national interest. Hales wrote:

> To tell you plainly, it is avarice that I take for the principal cause thereof [of enclosures]; but can we devise that all covetousness may be taken from men? No, no more than we can make men to be without ire, without gladness, without fear, and without all affections. What then? We must take away from men the occasion of their covetousness in this part. What is that? The exceeding lucre that they see grow by these enclosures, more than by husbandry. And that may be done by any of these two means that I will tell you: either by minishing the lucre that men have by grazing; or else by advancing of the profit of husbandry, till it be as good and as profitable to the occupiers as grazing is.[105]

To exploit the selfishness in men, to reward them for it, to see in it a power for good as well as harm, were ideas as remote from the ruling thought of the Middle Ages as ideas could be. It is quite impossible there to discover the roots of English mercantilist doctrine. They took hold after the power of medievalism in England had passed. The direction of the doctrine laid not to the past but to the future, to the ideas of the classical economists, however much they disdained their predecessors. It is ironic that the doctrine should have been disparaged most by the men whose ideas it anticipated and that it should have been pushed back into an age with which it could have nothing in common.

NOTES

1. Alfred Marshall, *Principles of Economics* (8th ed.), p. 755.
2. Jacob Viner, *Studies in the Theory of International Trade* (New York, 1937), pp. 74 *et seq.*
3. J. M. Keynes, *The General Theory of Employment Interest and Money*, p. 341.
4. Eli F. Heckscher, *Mercantilism* (London, 1935), II, 323.
5. E. Lipson, *A Planned Economy or Free Enterprise* (London, 1944), chap. 2.
6. Edmund Whittaker, *A History of Economic Ideas* (New York, 1943), pp. 141–42, 145–47.
7. John Hales, *A Discourse of the Common Weal of This Realm of England,* ed. Elizabeth Lamond (Cambridge, 1893), pp. 59, 98.
8. *Tudor Economic Documents,* ed. R. H. Tawney and Eileen Power, III, 323.
9. Edward Misselden, *Free Trade, or the Meanes to Make Trade Florish* (London, 1622), p. 4.
10. Sir William Petty, *Economic Writings,* ed. Charles Henry Hull (Cambridge, 1899), I, 31, 35.
11. *A Select Collection of Early English Tracts on Commerce* (London, 1856), pp. 581, 582.
12. Sir William Temple, *Works* (Edinburgh, 1754), II, 59–60.
13. Nicholas Barbon, *A Discourse of Trade* ([London: 1690] *A Reprint of Economic Tracts,* ed. Jacob Hollander, Baltimore, 1905), p. 32.
14. Josiah Child, *A New Discourse of Trade* (5th ed.; Glasgow, 1751), pp. 54–56.
15. Sir Dudley North, *Discourses Upon Trade* ([London, 1691] *A Reprint of Economic Tracts,* ed. Jacob Hollander, Baltimore, 1907), pp. 25, 27.
16. Charles Davenant, *An Essay Upon Ways and Means of Supplying the War* (London, 1695), p. 143.
17. John Law, *Money and Trade Considered, with a Proposal for Supplying the Nation with Money* (London, 1720), p. 11.
18. Daniel Defoe, *The Complete English Tradesman, etc.* (London, 1732), II, 109, 111.
19. John Cary, *A Discourse on Trade* (London, 1745), p. 82.
20. Josiah Tucker, *A Brief Essay on . . . Trade* (2d. ed.; London, 1750), xii.
21. The Right Rev. George Berkeley, *The Querist* (Glasgow, 1751), Queries 46, 47, 168.
22. Malachy Postlethwayt, *Great Britain's Commercial Interest Explained and Improved* (2d ed.; London, 1759), II, 367, 370–71, 377.
23. Petty, *op. cit.,* I, 33, II, 269.
24. Barbon, *op. cit.,* p. 32.
25. Defoe, *op. cit.,* II, 118.
26. North, *op. cit.,* pp. 25, 27–28.
27. Hales, *op. cit.,* p. 127.
28. Cary, *op. cit.,* p. 12.
29. Thomas Mun, *England's Treasure by Forraign Trade* (New York, 1928), p. 8.
30. Cary, *op. cit.,* pp. 96–102.
31. Defoe, *op. cit.,* I, 318–19.
32. Berkeley, *op. cit.,* Q. 214.
33. Davenant, *op. cit.,* p. 103. Postlethwayt, *op. cit.,* II, 389.
34. Defoe, *op. cit.,* II, 109, 115–16.
35. Postlethwayt, *op. cit.,* II, 405.
36. Gerard Malynes, *Consuetudo, vel, Lex Mercatoria: Or the Ancient Law Merchant* (London, 1656), p. 65.
37. Hales, *op. cit.,* p. 67.
38. Misselden, *op. cit.,* p. 107.
39. Child, *op. cit.,* pp. 54–56, 127.
40. Tucker, *op. cit.,* p. 83.
41. Hales, *op. cit.,* p. 60. Gerard Malynes, *The Maintenance of Free Trade* (London, 1622), p. 79. Petty, *op. cit.,* I, 9, II, 243. Barbon, *op. cit.,* p. 16. North, *op. cit.,* p. 12. Davenant, *op. cit.,* pp. 56–60. Berkeley, *op. cit.,* Q. 47. Malachy Postlethwayt, *The Universal Dictionary of Trade and Commerce* (London, 1774), cap. "Forestalling," "Engrossing," "Regrating."
42. Tawney and Power, *op. cit.,* III, 340, 342.
43. Postlethwayt, *Great Britain's Commercial Interest, etc.,* II, 425.
44. Petty, *op. cit.,* I, 274–75. Thomas Man, *The Benefit of Procreation* (London, 1739), pp. 20–21.
45. Misselden, *op. cit.,* pp. 29–30. Malynes, *The Maintenance of Free Trade,* p. 39. Temple, *op. cit.,* I, 129. Barbon, *op. cit.,* p. 41. Child, *op. cit.,* p. ix. Law, *op. cit.,* p. 17. *Early English Tracts,* p. 318.
46. Misselden, *op. cit.,* p. 117. Malynes, *The Maintenance of Free Trade,* pp. 39–40.
47. Law, *op. cit.,* p. 17.
48. Petty, *op. cit.,* I, 48, II, 445.
49. North, *op. cit.,* pp. 17–19.
50. Law, *op. cit.,* p. 11.
51. Temple, *op. cit.,* I, 131–32. Cary, *op. cit.,* p. 2. Tucker, *op. cit.,* p. iii n.
52. Hales, *op. cit.,* pp. 87, 127.
53. Petty, *op. cit.,* I, 269.
54. Mun, *op. cit.,* p. 66. North, *op. cit.,* pp. 25–26. Berkeley, *op. cit.,* passim. Child, *op. cit.,* p. 55. Petty, *op. cit.,* II, 445.
55. See Edgar J. Furniss, *The Position of the Laborer in a System of Nationalism* (Boston, 1920).
56. Petty, *op. cit.,* I, 308.
57. Petty, *op. cit.,* I, 23.
58. Temple, *op. cit.,* II, 380–81.
59. Berkeley, *op. cit.,* Q. 381.
60. Child, *op. cit.,* chap. 2.
61. Daniel Defoe, *True Born English-*

man in *Essays and Studies by Members of the English Association*, collected by C. H. Herford (Oxford, 1913), IV.

62. Tucker, *op. cit.*, pp. 53 ff.

63. Tucker, *op. cit.*, p. 57.

64. Temple, *op. cit.*, I, 119.

65. Postlethwayt, *Great Britain's Commercial Interest, etc.*, II, 367.

66. Petty, *op. cit.*, I, 32.

67. Defoe, *The Complete English Tradesman*, I, 56.

68. Hales, *op. cit.*, p. 57.

69. Petty, *op. cit.*, I, 48. North, *op. cit.*, p. 13. Davenant, *op. cit.*, p. 109. Defoe, *Complete English Tradesman etc.*, II, 79–80.

70. Hales, *op. cit.*, p. 59.

71. Adam Smith, *The Wealth of Nations*, ed. Edwin Cannan (New York, 1937), p. 421.

72. Hales, *op. cit.*, pp. 46, 49, 99.

73. Malynes, *Consuetudo, etc.*, p. 67.

74. Malynes, *Consuetudo, etc.*, p. 2. Cicero, *De officiis* (trans. C. W. Keyes), i, 4.

75. See my study of the elements of Stoicism in liberal economic doctrine, "The Moral Hero and the Economic Man," *Ethics*, LXI, 2.

76. Petty, *op. cit.*, I, 9, II, 243.

77. Barbon, *op. cit.*, pp. 13, 16.

78. North, *op. cit.*, p. 34.

79. Law, *op. cit.*, p. 4. Smith, *op. cit.*, p. 28.

80. Berkeley, *op. cit.*, Q. 24.

81. Child, *op. cit.*, pp. 55–56, 80.

82. Davenant, *An Essay on the East India Trade*, quoted by Whittaker, *op. cit.*, p. 147.

83. North, *op. cit.*, p. 13.

84. Temple, *op. cit.*, I, 121.

85. Barbon, *op. cit.*, pp. 27–28.

86. North, *op. cit.*, p. 14. See, however, Philip W. Buck, *The Politics of Mercantilism* (New York, 1942).

87. Temple, *op. cit.*, II, 366.

88. Barbon, *op. cit.*, p. 20. Davenant, *An Essay on Ways and Means, etc.*, passim.

89. Hales, *op. cit.*, pp. 50–51, my italics.

90. Malynes, *The Maintenance of Free Trade*, pp. 3–5.

91. Child, *op. cit.*, pp. xxvi–xxvii.

92. Postlethwayt, *Great Britain's Commercial Interest, etc.*, II, 371.

93. North, *op. cit.*, pp. 27–28.

94. Mun, *op. cit.*, chap. xv.

95. Davenant, *op. cit.*, pp. 56–57, 139.

96. Tucker, *op. cit.*, p. 74.

97. Postlethwayt, *Great Britain's Commercial Interest, etc.*, II, 377.

98. North, *op. cit.*, p. 12.

99. Smith, *op. cit.*, p. 423.

100. Petty, *op. cit.*, I, 244, 305.

101. *National and International Measures for Full Employment* (New York, 1949), § 25.

102. Gustav Schmoller, *The Mercantile System and Its Historical Significance* (New York, 1896), p. 7. Heckscher, *op. cit.*, II, 324.

103. Aristotle, *Politics*, I, 9.

104. Cary, *op. cit.*, p. 4.

105. Hales, *op. cit.*, p. 122.

4.

RAYMOND DE ROOVER
Boston College

Scholasticism and

Mercantilism:

A Contrast

The differences between mercantilism and scholastic economics are striking and profound. Yet, I do not know that a comparison has ever been attempted, although a clear perception of the contrasts has its importance for an understanding of the development of economic thought. There are even historians who profess to find the "prehistory" of economics among the vagaries of the mercantilistic pamphleteers, thus completely ignoring the contributions of the Doctors.[1]

Unlike mercantilism, scholastic economics enjoyed the unquestioned superiority of being an integral part of a coherent philosophical system. Although economics was not yet acknowledged as an independent discipline, it formed a consistent body of doctrine according to which economic relations ought to be ruled by the laws of distributive and commutative justice. In contrast, mercantilism was never more than a conglomerate of unco-ordinated prescriptions by which the authors of the mercantilistic tracts sought to influence economic policy, usually in a sense favorable to their private interests.[2]

The Doctors, as this name indicates, were all university graduates,

Excerpt reprinted by permission of the author and The Harvard University Press from "Scholastic Economics: Survival and Lasting Influence from the Sixteenth Century to Adam Smith," *The Quarterly Journal of Economics*, LXIX (May 1955), 161–90; pp. 177–85 excerpted. Copyright, 1955, by the President and Fellows of Harvard College.

trained in theology or in canon and civil law (*doctor utriusque juris*). Most of them were clerics, though there are some notable exceptions among the jurists, especially among the civilians, for instance, Messer Lorenzo di Antonio Ridolfi, who was a layman, a diplomat and a lecturer at the Florentine athenaeum.[3] The mercantilists, on the contrary, were with few exceptions self-trained merchants, with some literary talents, but without university degrees. Essentially, they were empiricists who, for better or for worse, were not encumbered by scholastic traditions. In this way they made their major contribution by developing the balance-of-trade theory, whereas the Doctors were unable to cut themselves loose from their traditional approach to the foreign exchange problem.

As a rule, the mercantilist writings were brief tracts on specific and controversial issues, which contrast markedly with the weighty and often pedantic treatises of the Doctors. Whereas the mercantilist pamphlets rarely refer to sources or provide marginal notes, the scholastic treatises literally bristle with references in support of nearly every statement, even the most commonplace. This sometimes annoying display of erudition, first introduced by the post-glossators, received further encouragement from the humanists, who developed the habit of invoking the authority of the Ancients for everything.

By the very fact that the Doctors were moralists, their main preoccupation was with social justice and general welfare, but naturally with these ideals as they were conceived in the Middle Ages and the sixteenth and seventeenth centuries. The mercantilists, too, professed to further the cause of the commonwealth; however, their declarations in this respect should not always be taken at their face value. All too often they serve as a screen for private interests. Most of the authors of mercantilist tracts had an ax to grind. This is especially true of the early mercantilists. Gérard de Malynes (fl. 1586–1641) was a perennial office-seeker who advocated exchange control in the hope that he himself would be appointed the controller. Misselden (fl. 1608–1654) and John Wheeler (fl. 1601–1608) were spokesmen for the Merchant Adventurers; and Thomas Mun (1571–1641) wrote his tracts in defense of the East India Company. As for Gresham (1519–1579), he was a shrewd and none too scrupulous manipulator of the money market, whose recommendations, although advantageous to the Queen, were apt to have unfavorable repercussions on English trade and on the volume of employment. The later mercantilists were less prejudiced, but their views were still warped by their narrow nationalism. Most of them rallied to the defense of the colonial system and sponsored aggressive measures to combat or to exclude foreign competition, an attitude which is alien to the spirit of scholasticism. Did not St. Thomas justify international trade by pointing out the fact that no nation is self-sufficient?[4]

As we have seen, the casuists of the seventeenth century were either unwilling or unable to rejuvenate their methods. They continued in the old ruts and made no effort to incorporate new discoveries, such as the balance-of-trade theory, into their traditional doctrines. The conservatism of the late scholastic writers thus became an impediment to further progress, and it is fortunate that the mercantilists displayed more initiative and did not hesitate to blaze new trails. True, their methods were not always sound, nor always successful, but they opened up new avenues for further research. The controversy of the early mercantilists about exchange control led to a premature proposal for the creation of a stabilization fund and eventually culminated in the formulation by Thomas Mun of the balance-of-trade theory.[5] The mercantilists also made the first clumsy attempts to use statistical data, and Sir William Petty (1623–1687) even made statistics the basis of his *Political Arithmetick*. Others pondered over banking schemes; and the studies of Charles Davenant (1656–1714) and Gregory King (1648–1712) on the behavior of grain prices put them on the track of the elasticity of demand.[6] The seventeenth century was the age of projectors. Nearly always, the aim was to influence public policy, whereas the scholastic writers were content to set up ethical standards, but left their practical realization to the often inefficient government authorities.

The scholastic writers regarded trade as an occupation which, although not evil in itself, endangered the salvation of the soul, as the merchants almost unavoidably succumbed to the temptations of usury, cheating, and unlawful gain: *et de hoc rarissime evadunt mercatores,* as St. Bonaventure (1221–1275), the Seraphic Doctor, testifies.[7] In this opinion, the other Doctors concur: without exception, they much prefer agriculture to trade. The mercantilist writers, of course, take exactly the opposite point of view.[8] In their eyes trade is the noblest of all professions.[9] Both agriculture and industry depend on trade to provide a market for their products and to give employment to the "poor."[10] The merchant, far from being regarded with distrust, is extolled as the benefactor of humanity and the principal pillar of the State. This is what one might expect, since mercantilism was the economic system developed by, and for, the merchants.

In contrast to scholastic economics, mercantilism was amoral. The later mercantilists were interested in a large population and full employment only because they thought such conditions would stimulate trade and increase the economic power of the state.[11] Usury was no longer considered a voracious monster: Sir Josiah Child (1630–1699), Sir Thomas Culpeper the Elder, and others complained only that the interest rate, being higher in England than in Holland, favored the competition of the Dutch.[12] Trade has no soul and the individual did not count: why should the mercantilists be disturbed by moral issues?

One of the most striking characteristics of scholastic economics was universalism: regardless of origin and nationality, the Doctors are in fundamental agreement on method and principles. Although there may be, sometimes, sharp differences on points of detail or of practical application, all their treatises follow more or less the same pattern easily recognizable by anyone acquainted with scholastic literature. In the mercantilist camp, on the contrary, such uniformity in doctrine or method does not exist: neither between national schools nor between individual writers.

Among the mercantilists, "everyone is his own economist," according to the phrase so aptly coined by Professor E. A. J. Johnson. No one considers himself bound by precedent, and each author follows his own inspiration in selecting the appropriate method for dealing with his chosen topic.

Notwithstanding the great prestige of Eli F. Heckscher, I disagree with his statement that mercantilism strove toward unity.[13] As a matter of fact, non-scholastic economics in the seventeenth and eighteenth centuries varied greatly from country to country. In my opinion, the name "mercantilism" is appropriate only for British economics during that period. In Germany, one should speak of cameralism. One of its leading exponents, Johann Joachim Becher (1635–1682), "was still strongly influenced by the venerable Aristotelian tradition," albeit that he considerably modified the scholastic views.[14] In France, the expression "Colbertism," rather than "mercantilism," should be used to designate the economic policy of Colbert. Moreover, this policy aroused much criticism from writers such as Vauban (1633–1707) and his cousin Boisguilbert (1646–1714), whose comments on the iniquities of the French tax system anticipated the physiocrats instead of owing something to mercantilist ideas.[15]

Although the United Provinces were the leading economic power in the seventeenth century, there exists as yet no adequate study on Dutch economic thought during this period.[16] At any rate, Hugo Grotius or de Groot deserves a niche in the gallery of famous economists. One can hardly classify him as a mercantilist; he was rather an Aristotelian who used scholastic methods to defeat scholasticism.[17] Even Pieter de la Court (1618–1685), although not an Aristotelian, is far too liberal to pass for a mercantilist.[18]

In Spain, after 1600, economic writers, without breaking with scholasticism, were mainly concerned with the country's ailments: vellon inflation, vagrancy, depopulation, and economic decline. Whether this concern with pressing social and economic problems labels them as mercantilists remains a debatable point.[19] As in Spain, so also in Italy the scholastic traditions were particularly strong, and persisted well into the eighteenth century along with other currents of thought originating in the merchant manuals of the Middle Ages.[20] In 1613, a Neapolitan writer, Dr. Antonio Serra, in fighting a scheme to regulate foreign exchange, formulated independently the balance-of-trade theory developed contemporaneously by the English mercantilists.[21] His proposals were dismissed, and his book was ignored for more than a century until abbé Ferdinando Galiani praised it as an outstanding performance. The witty abbé expresses his surprise that a book like Serra's was conceived "in an age of ignorance about economic matters," but he complains that the work is "tedious" reading because of its obscure style, its poor organization, and its "divisions and subdivisions" reminiscent of scholastic literature.[22] In other words, the abbé is a typical example of the eighteenth-century point of view. Another interesting fact is that Galiani considers the work of Serra to be scholastic, whereas most modern authors have classed it as a mercantilist pamphlet.[23]

The trouble is that the word "mercantilism" does not stand for a clear concept, but lends itself to confusion. The great specialist Heckscher, himself, has to admit that "mercantilism is simply a convenient term for summarizing a phase of economic policy and economic ideas."[24] It should be added that the term covers only those heterogeneous ideas that are non-scholastic in inspiration.

There are remnants of scholastic influence in many mercantilist writings, but surprisingly those traces have not been recognized, though they are not so difficult to spot. The mercantilists, of course, were unable to escape from the impact of several centuries of culture. Whether or not they knew it, they absorbed some of the ideas bequeathed by former generations.[25]

Gerard de Malynes is the writer in whose works the traditional views are the most perceptible. Whether he should be considered as a mercantilist or as a scholastic writer, is to my mind a moot question.[26] In any case, there can be no doubt that he forms the link between the two schools of thought. His insistence on the par as the only fair rate of exchange is simply a variant of the just price theory taken over from Dr. Thomas Wilson, himself a Doctor still imbued with scholastic traditions. According to Professor Jacob Viner, Malynes was poor in market analysis,[27] but there can be no question about his being well read and well acquainted with ancient and scholastic literature.[28] In his *Saint George for England,* a tract against usury, he describes the dragon called *Foenus politicum* as having two wings, *usura palliata* and *usura explicata,* and a tail, "inconstant *Cambium.*"[29] This allegory is obviously sheer and unadulterated scholasticism. Malynes has also received credit for distinguishing between changes in the price level due to monetary factors and changes in the price of particular commodities due to the operation of the law of supply and demand. I strongly suspect that this idea did not originate with him but that he took it from a continental treatise, for he was by no means an original thinker and was addicted to plagiarism.[30]

In a recent article, the mercantilists have been praised for the "liberalism" of their concepts.[31] Contrary to the conclusions of the author, it appears, however, that those so-called "liberal elements" are rooted in the doctrines of the medieval Schoolmen.[32] For one thing, the Doctors were uncompromising in their condemnation of monopoly for the reason that the monopolist exploits the public and makes an illicit gain by raising the price of his articles above the competitive level. For example, Cardinal Cajetan, commenting on the *Summa* of Thomas Aquinas states that monopoly offends freedom by compelling the public to pay a price higher than the one that would prevail in the market, if there were no such monopoly (*si huiusmodi monopolium non esset*).[33] The traditional feeling against monopoly was so strong that no mercantilist writer dared openly defy public opinion, even when his purpose was to justify the monopolistic practices of this or that trading company.[34] In the parlance of the mercantilists, "free trade," as I have pointed out in this *Journal,* meant freedom from restraints of any sort in internal as well as in foreign trade. Consequently, it corresponded to the French expression *liberté du commerce* and not to *libre échange.*[35] In the seventeenth century, protection in the modern sense was not yet born; the struggle was still a medieval struggle for the control of the carrying trade.[36] In dealing with the history of economic thought, it is not enough to know the writings of the economists; one must also know something about the institutional framework and the social environment of the period.

Certainly, the English "mercantilists did not believe in an economy wholly or mainly directed by the State,"[37] but they wanted the state to pursue a policy favorable to the trading interests and they tended to defend the exclusive privileges of chartered companies and corporations.[38] Owing to the persistent influence of scholastic ideals, the mercantilists paid lip service to the goddess of "free trade," though the sincerity of their devotion is very much open to question, inasmuch as their pretenses conflict with their other aims. But then, mercantilism was not a logical system. It may even plausibly be argued that, unlike scholasticism, the much vaunted mercantile system was not a system at all.

NOTES

1. For instance, Edward Heimann, *History of Economic Doctrines*, pp. 22–47.

2. A. V. Judges, "The Idea of a Mercantile State," *Transactions of the Royal Historical Society*, 4th Series, XXI (1939), 50.

3. For his biography, see Vespasiano da Bisticci, *Vite di uomini illustri del secolo XV* (Florence, 1938), pp. 401–5.

4. Amintore Fanfani, *Storia delle dottrine economiche: il volontarismo* (3d ed.; Milan, 1942), p. 112. The reference is to *De regimine principum*, Book 2, chap. 4.

5. R. de Roover, *Gresham on Foreign Exchange; an Essay on Early English Mercantilism* (Cambridge, Mass.: Harvard University, Press, 1949), pp. 226–31, 250–65.

6. I take advantage of this opportunity to call the attention of the economists to an article by Luigi Einaudi, "La paternità della legge detta di King," *Rivista di storia economica*, VIII (1943), 33–38. The author attributes to both Davenant and King the discovery of the law stating that grain prices vary more than proportionately to the deviations of the harvest from the normal.

7. *Decretum Gratiani:* canon *Quoniam non cognovi*, Dist. LXXXVIII, canon 12; and canon *Qualitas lucri*, Dist. V, "de paenitentia," canon 2; *quia difficile est inter ementis vendentisque commercium non intervenire peccatum.* Cf. Edmund Schreiber, *Die volkswirtschaftlichen Anschauungen der Scholastik seit Thomas von Aquin* (Jena, 1913), p. 129.

8. Jelle C. Riemersma, "Usury Restrictions in a Mercantile Economy," *Canadian Journal of Economics and Political Science*, XVIII (1952), 22.

9. See the encomium of trade by Thomas Mun, *England's Treasure by Forraign Trade* (London, 1664), chap. 21. Cf. Eli F. Heckscher, *Mercantilism* II, 281.

10. William D. Grampp, "The Liberal Elements in English Mercantilism," this *Journal*, LXVI (1952), 469. These ideas must have been current among the merchants on the continent as well as in England, since we find them also in Lodovico Guicciardini's famous description of Antwerp, first published in 1567: *Description de tous les Pays-Bas*, trans. François de Belleforest (Antwerp, 1582), p. 182; republished in *Tudor Economic Documents*, eds. R. H. Tawney and Eileen Power, III, 161.

11. E. A. J. Johnson, *Predecessors of Adam Smith*, pp. 247–52; Heckscher, *Mercantilism*, II, 159; Philip W. Buck, *The Politics of Mercantilism*, pp. 44–48, 65–66, 89–90.

12. Heckscher, *Mercantilism*, II, 286–89.

13. Heckscher, himself, in response to criticism of his book, was forced to concede that mercantilism failed as a unifying system: "Mercantilism," *Economic History Review*, VII (1936), 48. Cf. Herbert Heaton, "Heckscher on Mercantilism," *Journal of Political Economy*, XLV (1937), 374; J. F. Rees, "Mercantilism," *History*, New Series, XXIV (1939–1940), 130.

14. R. de Roover, "Monopoly Theory prior to Adam Smith: a Revision," this *Journal* (Nov. 1951), p. 519. There is a new book on Becher by H. Hassinger, *Johann Joachim Becher* (1635–1682): *ein Beitrag zur Geschichte des Mercantilismus* (Vienna, 1951). The author apparently regards Becher as a mercantilist. Heckscher, however, states that the German cameralists "were imbued with a spirit of their own" (*Mercantilism*, II, 263).

15. *Ibid.*, II, 264. Cf. Hazel van Dyke Roberts, *Boisguilbert, Economist of the Reign of Louis XIV*, p. 255: "Boisguilbert had completely shaken off mercantilist thought."

16. The best study is still that of Etienne Laspeyres, but it is almost a century old: *Geschichte der wirtschaftlichen Anschauungen der Niederländer und ihrer Litteratur zur Zeit der Republik* (Preisschriften gekrönt und herausgegeben von der Fürstlich Jablonowski'schen Gesellschaft, Vol. XI, Leipzig, 1863).

17. de Roover, "Monopoly Theory prior to Adam Smith," *op. cit.*, pp. 521–22.

18. Heckscher (*Mercantilism*, I, 351) admits that the Dutch were "less affected by mercantilist tendencies than most other countries." His treatment of Dutch writers is based entirely on the study of Laspeyres (*op. cit.*, II, 263) and, moreover, is very superficial. See the pertinent remarks of Heaton (*op. cit.*, pp. 371 f.) about Heckscher's neglect of Dutch economic thought and policy in the seventeenth century.

19. They are mercantilists according to Earl J. Hamilton, "Spanish Mercantilism before 1700," *Facts and Factors in Economic History: Articles by former Students of Edwin Francis Gay*, pp. 214–39. This is an introductory survey which lists a few tracts and makes some general comments on the contents of the economic literature in Spain from about 1600 to 1700. The Latin treatises, including the important work of Luis de Molina, are not discussed. After stating that most of the Spanish economic writers were ecclesiastics with no intimate knowledge of business or finance (pp. 229–30), Professor Hamilton calls them "mercantilists." Sancho de Moncada, one of the so-called Spanish mercantilists, was professor of theology in the University of Toledo, as Hamilton himself points out (*American Treasure and the Price Revolution in Spain, 1501–1650*, p. 294). Other authors, including Andrés Villegas Castillo, Ramón Carande, Bernard W. Dempsey, Marjorie Grice-Hutchinson, and José Larraz, do not agree with Hamilton's classification. Only Gerónimo de Uztáriz (1670–1732), a late writer and statesman, seems to have come strongly under the influence of mercantilist thought. Cf. Ramón Carande, *Carlos V y sus Banqueros, la vida económica de España en una fase de su hegemonía, 1516–1556* (Madrid, 1943), p. 89.

20. Heckscher (*Mercantilism*, II, 263) implicitly admits that he is unacquainted with Italian economic literature. The famous tract of Bernardo Davanzati (1529–1606), *Notizia dei cambi*, written in 1581, was certainly based on merchant manuals, as appears clear from two manuscripts in the State Archives of Pisa: Fondo Alleati, Nos. 17 and 69. I owe this information to the kindness of Professor Federigo Melis of the University of Pisa.

21. *Breve trattato delle cause che possono far abbondare li regni d'oro e argento dove non sono miniere con applicazione al Regno di Napoli* in *Economisti del cinque e seicento*, ed. Augusto Graziani (Bari, 1913), 141–233. Selections from Serra's treatise, in English translation, are found in Arthur Eli Monroe, *Early Economic Thought, Selections from Economic Literature prior to Adam Smith*, pp. 143–67.

22. Ferdinando Galiani, *Della moneta* (Bari, 1915), p. 344.

23. Monroe, *op. cit.*, p. 144; Luigi Cossa, *An Introduction to the Study of Political Economy* (London, 1893), p. 178; Fanfani, *Storia, il volontarismo*, p. 171; Lewis H. Haney, *History of Economic Thought* (3d ed.), pp. 112–13; John M. Ferguson, *Landmarks of Economic Thought*, pp. 36–37.

24. "Mercantilism," *Economic History Review*, VII (1936–37), 54.

25. Heckscher (*Mercantilism*, II, 277) states: "Here one may perceive a tendency towards economic liberty that was never entirely broken off and therefore connected medieval and laissez-faire ideals."

26. de Roover, *Gresham on Foreign Exchange*, pp. 285 f.

27. *Studies in the Theory of International Trade* (New York, 1937), p. 76.

28. Helen E. Sandison, "An Elizabethan Economist's Method of Literary Composition," *Huntington Library Quarterly*, VI (1942–43), 205–11. Professor Sandison shows that Malynes certainly "borrowed" from Sir Thomas More's *Utopia*. I may add that he also was acquainted with the works of Jean Bodin, Lodovico Guicciardini, Dr. Thomas Wilson, Aristotle, and most probably, Leonardus Lessius.

29. *Saint George for England allegorically described* (London, 1601); "Foreword to the Reader." On p. 61, Malynes mentions the extrinsic titles, *damnum emergens* and *lucrum cessans*.

30. In the sixteenth century, most of the scholastic writers accepted the quantity theory of money and stated that prices "generally" go up or down with the abundance or scarcity of money. Such a statement had even become commonplace.

31. Grampp, *op. cit.*, pp. 465–501.

32. *Ibid.*, pp. 500 f. So far as I know, the Schoolmen have never stated "that free individual behavior was inimical to the welfare of society." Heckscher (*Mercantilism*, II, 277) asserts the contrary and rightly states: "that even the medieval tradition was sympathetic to a certain sort of freedom. The medieval influence was thus not without importance to the notion of economic liberty under mercantilism." As late as the seventeenth century, the Anglican and Puritan divines continued to propound scholastic doctrine on just price, monopoly, and price discrimination. See the characteristic passages of Richard Baxter (1615–1691), a popular preacher, which are quoted by H. M. Robertson, *Aspects of the Rise of Economic Indi-*

vidualism: A Criticism of Max Weber and his School (Cambridge, 1935), p. 17.

33. Text quoted by Amintore Fanfani, *Le origini dello spirito capitalistico in Italia* (Milan, 1933), p. 123. Cf. Joseph Höffner, *Wirtschaftsethik und Monopole im fünfzehnten und sechzehnten Jahrhundert* (Jena, 1941), p. 107.

34. de Roover, *Gresham on Foreign Exchange,* p. 284. Such was certainly the purpose of John Wheeler, Edward Misselden, Thomas Mun, Sir Josiah Child, and Charles Davenant.

35. When French authors of the period mean *libre échange,* they use the expression: *liberté du commerce entre les nations.*

36. de Roover, *Gresham on Foreign Exchange,* pp. 282 f.

37. Grampp, *op. cit.,* p. 495.

38. In order to enlist the support of the government, mercantilist writers and projectors never failed to stress the benefits which would accrue to the Royal Treasury, if their schemes were carried out (Heaton, "Heckscher on Mercantilism," *op. cit.,* p. 376).

PART THREE

PRE-SMITHIAN

EIGHTEENTH-CENTURY

ECONOMICS

THE WRITERS DEALT WITH in this part represent a reaction, sometimes qualified, to the mercantilist views described in Part Two, a reaction that began in the late seventeenth century and was reflected both in post-1700 neo-mercantilist literature and in the essays of economical writers more strictly in what became the liberal tradition. This shift in view, this manifestation of an increasingly liberal climate of opinion, reflected both a change in what was deemed best for business enterprise and a growing acceptance of the opinion that an economy is essentially autonomous. It probably reflected also an increase in optimism in Britain and France, which stood to gain as the Mediterranean world stood to lose, at least relatively, by the shift of the center of economic gravity toward the Atlantic.

Although the industrial revolution did not get under way effectively until a few years after the appearance of Smith's *Wealth of Nations,* there had come into being, especially in England, a self-reliant middle class which included many representatives of commerce and industry. There thus existed in the early eighteenth century, in France as well as in England, many business people who believed that they could operate to better advantage when they were on their own and free of governmental restrictions. They believed that greater economic progress could be made by themselves as individuals and by the nation if largely *laissez faire* conditions superseded restrictive conditions inherited from the past. This belief was given ideological and, within limits, scientific form by late seventeenth-century and eighteenth-century writers.

What was accomplished by these writers must have been facilitated by the developments that had taken place up to and after the late seventeenth century, at least in the English economy. The economic sector was beginning to take on the character of a self-subsisting and self-perpetuating social organism, seemingly under the governance of its own laws. So at least it evidently appeared to various writers who were familiar with recent discoveries of the simple, mechanical laws that regulated a self-subsisting physical universe. Similar laws might be found to permeate economies, since presumably they were as much under the governance of law as was the physical world. Hence a nomothetic point of view and a law-discovering search were initiated. In sum, then, economic and ideological progress were co-operating, so to speak, to animate inquiring minds to conceive of economies as comparatively autonomous, law-bound systems.

Manifestations of this liberal trend in economic thinking were more pronounced in England than elsewhere, though it early had its spokesmen in France and Holland. In Italy, despite the acuteness of some of its economic analysts (see Selection 10), mercantilist views persisted, those of Belloni (1750) receiving the commendation of the English economist Sir

James Steuart (1712–1780), in whose works, speedily blanketed out by Smith's epochal treatise, liberal and nonliberal ideas mingled (see Selection 20). In Germany, despite the hospitality later shown physiocratic views, liberal views were slow to receive expression. The contributions of English writers may best serve, therefore, to illustrate this new way of thinking which gradually dissipated mercantilist economic philosophy and prepared the British mind for Smith's interpretation of economies and their behavior. Liberal elements, as implied, are to be found even in the works of such exponents of a philosophy of state intervention as Bishop George Berkeley (1685–1753) and Sir James Steuart, for they were in the air.

In and after the late seventeenth century the newer, liberal view appears in writings of Nicholas Barbon (1640–1698), of an author tentatively identified as Henry Martins,[1] and of John Locke (1632–1704). The work of the great political arithmetician, Gregory King (1648–1712), is not included here, since he was interested primarily in income measurement. Nor is that of Sir William Petty (1623–1687), whose notion of surplus led Marx to describe him as "the founder of modern political economy"; for Petty's primary concern was measurement and the discovery of empirical generalizations descriptive of economies. The work of John Locke, often loosely formulated, belongs in the liberal category even though it included mercantilist elements; for he controverted the view that the interest rate could be fixed by law below its "natural" or market-determined level, and he held generally, though less clearly than Cantillon, that the value of metallic money was governed as was that of commodities by the ruling conditions of supply and demand. In Barbon's work one finds a refutation of mercantilist balance-of-trade theory, an account of the restrictive impact of England's import restrictions upon her exports, and the argument that "the Market," which reflects costs and wants, "is the best Judge of Value." In Martins' work, objections to the "East-India Trade" on the ground that it depressed activity and income within Britain were refuted in a manner anticipatory of Smith.

Most striking of those writing around the turn of the century was Sir Dudley North (1641–1690), or his brother, Roger, in so far as the latter is responsible for views included in Sir Dudley's *Discourses upon Trade* (1691), a work that unfortunately remained without influence. In the preface to the *Discourses* it was argued "that no Laws can set Prizes [*i.e.,* prices] in Trade, the rates of which must and will make themselves," that the determination of "Interest of Money" should "be left freely to the Market," that every attempt to fix prices "is so much Impediment to Trade, and therefore prejudicial," and that in the world as well as in any nation "there can be no Trade unprofitable to the Publick; for if any prove so, men leave it off." Of greater analytical importance is the observation that the student of trade must emulate the method of Descartes, abstract from the

---

1. See Marcus Arkin's account of Martins' *Considerations on the East India Trade* (1701), in "A Neglected Forerunner of Adam Smith," *South African Journal of Economics*, XXIII (December 1955), 299–314.

world of reality, and express himself "philosophically" or in terms of a model. "He begins at the quick, from Principles indisputably true . . . he reduceth things to their Extreams, wherein all discriminations are most gross and sensible, and then shows them; and not in the state of ordinary concerns, whereof the terms are scarce distinguishable."

There already appears in the early eighteenth century another vein of thought which had to be incorporated into a system of economics whose functioning depended so largely as did the classical upon the pursuit of private advantage and the receipt of reward for successful effort. So hedonistic a philosophy was incompatible with the medieval scheme of values, and it had only partial endorsement of the mercantilists; for these usually held that while it was primarily the reward of successful enter-prisers that counted, payment of labor much in excess of subsistence would reduce the amount of work which labor was prepared to do. This last view persisted into the eighteenth century, being adhered to even by Mandeville (1670?–1731), probably the most effective of the early spokesmen for the essentiality of psychological-hedonistic theory and practice to the function-ing of a free enterprise economy. Without such a philosophy, without a removal of ethical and religious as well as of economic barriers to the aug-mentation of personal demand and consumption, Mandeville argued in effect, economic expansion would come to a halt. Subsequent writers ex-tended the application of this view to all classes and argued that a society functioned best when each and all stood to benefit from output-increasing activities. Then the stimulus of self-interest and the prospect of rising per capita consumption, later approved by Smith, would be most likely to foster economic progress.

The eighteenth century witnessed various anticipations of Say's Law, a bulwark of economics until its subjection to powerful attack by J. M. Keynes in 1936. Some of these are noted in Selection 5; for later periods, see Selections 18 and 31. It is evident that as early as 1701, Martins, referred to earlier in this introduction, had something like Say's principle in mind, though in primitive form at best. Undoubtedly other anticipations might be noted; the names of Josiah Tucker (1712–1799) and F. Mengotti (1749–1830) are sometimes mentioned. Among the physiocrats, Le Trosne wrote about "products being paid for only with products." J. B. Say went beyond this, Lambert notes, and emphasized as early as 1803 the role, not of prod-ucts as such, but of the production of products in opening markets; this principle he stated most concisely in 1821: "it is [production alone] which opens a market for the sale of produce."[2] Lambert thus endorses the view that Say formulated his law in the 1803 edition of his treatise, before James Mill stated it. Lambert also supports McCulloch's opinion that the principle of Say's Law was succinctly but fully expressed as early as 1795, by the

2. See Paul Lambert, "The Law of Markets Prior to J. B. Say and the Say-Malthus Debate," translated from the French by A. A. Maitland and reprinted in *International Economic Papers*, No. 6 (London: Macmillan & Co., Ltd., 1956), pp. 7–22; the quota-tions appear on pp. 8–9.

anonymous author of the *Sketch of the Advance and Decline of Nations.*[3] It was, however, the formulations of Say and Ricardo that gave the principle currency and incorporated it into the classical engine of analysis.

Of the writers principally dealt with in Part Three, Quesnay and Cantillon much more than Hume are describable as the most systematic and outstanding of those who preceded Smith. While Cantillon may be rated above Quesnay in that he anticipated the latter in time and ideas, some of which continued to recur in the nineteenth century, Quesnay's contribution is very impressive and frequently underrated. Cantillon is usually reputed to have been the first to recognize the role of the entrepreneur, the strategic significance of which the classical writers, other than Say and perhaps Cournot and von Thünen, tended to pass over. The early development of entrepreneurial theory, so important in modern accounts of economic growth and decision-making, is reviewed in Selection 9, where the contributions of noneconomist writers receive due attention.

3. *Ibid.*, pp. 14–16.

5.

JOSEPH J. SPENGLER
Duke University

Richard Cantillon:

First of

the Moderns

It is the fate of anonymous works . . . to have their ideas pilfered by contemporaries and to be forgotten by later generations. — CHARLES RIST.

The appearance of Professor Alfred Sauvy's splendid new edition of Richard Cantillon's *Essai sur la nature du commerce en général*[1] raises once again the question: Who is the founder of modern political economy? According to Karl Marx,[2] it was Sir William Petty; according to others, Quesnay or Adam Smith. A review of Cantillon's system of principles and injunctions suggests, however, that if the multiple origin of political economy is ignored, Cantillon has a very good claim to having been the principal forerunner of both the classical and the neoclassical schools.

I

Considerable information has been assembled respecting the publication of the *Essai* and the fluctuations in public esteem undergone by its various parts.[3] Written between 1730 and 1734, the *Essai* was not published in entirety until 1755. The English original must have gotten into the hands

Reprinted from *The Journal of Political Economy*, LXII (August, October 1954), 281–95, 406–24, by permission of The University of Chicago Press. Copyright 1954 by The University of Chicago.

of Malachy Postlethwayt, who incorporated some six thousand words of the *Essai* in a 1749 publication and most of it in his *Universal Dictionary of Trade and Commerce* (1751–55) and a portion of the eleventh chapter of Part I of the *Essai* in his *Great Britain's True System* (1757).[4] The French translation of the *Essai*, reportedly by Cantillon himself, after supposedly remaining sixteen years in the hands of the Marquis of Mirabeau, was restored to its rightful owner at the latter's request; and from this manuscript, presumably, the *Essai* was printed in London in 1755.[5] Two reprints were issued in 1756, one in France and one as part of a collection put out in Amsterdam by Eleazar de Mauvillon, father of the German Physiocrat, Jakob Mauvillon; but neither appears to have sold well. In 1767 an Italian translation was brought out. Presumably because of the lapse, even before the close of the eighteenth century, of interest in Cantillon's work, no additional edition appeared until 1892, when Harvard University Press brought out an essentially facsimile reproduction of the French original.[6] This issue apparently was prompted by W. S. Jevons' discovery of the *Essai's* great merit to the world of economists and by Henry Higgs's continuation of the work initiated by Jevons. In 1931 appeared two translations of the *Essai*, one German, edited with an introduction by F. A. Hayek, and one English,[7] accompanied by much supplementary material, most of it by Higgs.

The influence of the *Essai* upon the development of economic thought seems to have been considerable. Many who wrote on economic subjects in the eighteenth century were familiar with Cantillon's work and made use, with or without acknowledgment, of his materials and ideas or were influenced by them. Among those appreciably influenced were Postlethwayt, Harris, Mirabeau (especially before he became a Physiocrat), Quesnay,[8] Gournay, Graumann, Accarias de Serionne, James Steuart, Adam Smith, Condillac, J. G. Büsch, Pluquet, Germaine Garnier (in his earlier writings), and Peuchet. Among those somewhat influenced were Turgot, Filangieri, Beccaria, Roederer, and, at least indirectly, Genovesi, Paley, and Malthus. Dubuat-Nançay, De Meilhan, Moheau, Forbonnais, Necker, Butel-Dumont (in part a critic), and Say may have been influenced by Cantillon's ideas. Among those who at least knew Cantillon's work are numbered Dupont de Nemours, Ferrara, Freron, Grimm, Mably, Morellet, Savary, Graslin, J. F. von Pfeiffer, and G.-A. Will. Arthur Young referred to Cantillon's work but was reportedly not influenced by it, having gotten elsewhere his idea that population growth depends upon the state of employment and the demand for labor. Hume must have known of Cantillon's manuscript, but he was little if at all influenced by it, missing the import of Cantillon's brilliant analysis (which compares favorably with Keynes's) of the response of the price structure to changes in the quantity of money. Except for occasional references to his work before 1860 (e.g., by Ganilh, Rae, and Daire) and occasional short appreciations of his work (e.g., those of G. Kautz, De Lavergne, Von Sivers, and Roscher) in 1860–80, Cantillon's work received no critical attention in the nineteenth century until after Jevons' fine paper (1881) had recalled its merits to the attention of economists.[9]

II

Much of the life of Richard Cantillon, author of the *Essai*, remains enveloped in mystery. He was born in Ireland, in March, 1697, according to Hone, and some seven to seventeen years earlier, according to others.[10] His ancestors had come to England with William the Conqueror, and at least some of their descendants had settled in Ireland, among them Richard's ancestor, Roger Cantillon of Ballyheigue, in county Kerry, who married a Stuart, Elizabeth, in 1556.[11] Richard, the economist, was the son of Philip Cantillon of Ballyheigue and the nephew of the chevalier Richard Cantillon, banker to the Stuart Pretender in Paris, whither young Richard went in 1716.[12] Most of the Cantillons were Catholic as well as Jacobite, though religion sat lightly on some, among them Richard, the economist.[13] The French Cantillons (become extinct in 1940), Hone believes, are descended from the economist's brother, James, probably through his son Thomas. Richard, the economist, was murdered in London on the night of May 13, 1734, by his former cook, and his body was burned to ashes along with many of his literary documents, the house probably having been set on fire to hide the murder.

While Cantillon was engaged principally in banking, he also appears to have traded in wine, silk, and copper. Apparently he began his banking operations in France rather than in England, perhaps because his uncle, the chevalier, was established in Paris. Richard is reported as having been engaged in banking in Paris during most of 1716–20, in the latter part of which period he profited greatly at the expense of John Law's "System." He quit Paris in 1720 and was away for most of eight years, traveling extensively on the Continent and in England. He lived in Paris in 1729–32, his stay including a few days in prison; then he moved to Utrecht and Brussels and, in 1734, to London. His fortune (much of it made possible by the failure of Law's scheme) at the time of his death was extensive, varied, and dispersed; it included houses and holdings in a number of countries and places.[14]

The *Essai*, embodying as it does Cantillon's reactions to views of contemporaries and his reflections upon his and other experiences in the world of affairs, reveals something of his mind and its operations. A man of "profound erudition" (reports Mirabeau) who usually "read for three hours or so in bed," Cantillon was well informed concerning monetary history and economic literature, though not so well as Adam Smith. Cantillon refers, in the *Essai*, to Cicero, Livy, the two Plinys, Petty, Davenant, Locke, Halley, King, Newton, Vauban, Boizard, casuist writers on usury, the Book of Genesis, and the author (probably Boisguillebert or Boulainvilliers) of an *État de la France*. He must have been familiar with the works of Dupuy, Savary, and others on foreign exchange, and he was familiar with literature reporting travelers' observations. Of the authors he specifically mentions, Locke and Petty seem to have stimulated him most, though he criticized various ideas of each. Cantillon must also have been familiar with and even influenced by the writings of authors whom he does not identify. He does not mention Law, with whom he agreed on a minor point and against whose theories much of Cantillon's treatment of monetary matters is directed. His description of land as "the Source or Matter from whence all Wealth is produced" and of man's labor as "the Form which produces it" is remindful of Aristotle (I, 1, 10).[15] Certain of his views resemble views expressed by Boisguillebert.[16] Cantillon's stress upon the homeostatic and self-adjusting character of the economy and upon the role of self-interest in bringing adjustment about may reflect the influence of Mandeville, North, and others,[17] just as his account of the origins of property may reflect the influence of Hobbes rather than that of Locke.[18]

Explicit theory and empiricism are fruitfully combined in the *Essai*. Though, as Marx implied,[19] Cantillon remained under the influence of his feudal, land-economy surroundings, his theory, the outlines of which will be presented, usually is potentially generalizable even when it was not actually generalized. His empiricism is manifested in the information with which the *Essai* is shot through[20] and in Mirabeau's report of his field-work methods:

> One of his friends told me that he found him one day at home in Paris in his dressing gown with Livy on his desk. "I am going," he said, "to make a little trip. There has always been a blunder as to the value of the coins with which the Romans ransomed their city from the Gauls. One of these coins is in the collection of the Grand Duke and I am going to verify its weight and alloy." At this moment the horses arrived and he took leave of my friend to get into the coach. In these voyages he made certain of everything, got out of his carriage to question a labourer in the field, judged the quality of the soil, tasted it, drew up his notes, and an accountant whom he always took with him put them in order when they stopped for the night. A mass of precious manuscripts perished with him. . . .[21]

That in Cantillon's mind qualities essential to both speculator and economist were combined in an unusual degree is testified to by Higgs as well as by Mirabeau, who remarked also on his cosmopolitan temper, a temper probably nourished both by the need of the speculator to be rootless, impersonal, and flexible and by the need of one required to live in divers religious spheres to avoid heavy psychological commitment to any. Higgs wrote:

> The lengthy English correspondence shows Cantillon to have been a person of extreme ability and very great energy. . . . The impression left on the mind by a perusal of Cantillon's letters is that the writer was possessed of great clearness and grasp, quick to penetrate ambiguity or weakness of argument, able at combination and calculation, and so thorough a master of the foreign exchanges that his speculations exhibit a scientific prevision amounting almost to certainty.[22]

Mirabeau testified:

He foresaw the complete course of the famous system of Mr. Law, and, compelled by circumstances to take part in it, he quitted the theatre of this astonishing revolution leaving his correspondent with orders in advance as to the different stages of the cycle which this catastrophe would run.[23]

Cantillon's gifts as a theorist, gifts reinforced (as Higgs observes) by a cosmopolitan experience which sharpened his capacity to distinguish the persisting and the general from the accidental and the particular, and gifts favorably commented upon by many students of the *Essai,* may be illustratively suggested here, with more detailed evidence reserved until later. For example, Cantillon apparently conceived of the elements composing the European economy as constituting an organized system under the empire of mechanisms which operated to achieve a kind of equilibrium. This equilibrium was accomplished principally through the activities of an entrepreneurial class whose members assumed the risk and the uncertainty inherent in the prevailing economic society and, guided by the behavior of buyers and sellers and by the movements of prices, continually brought particular supplies and particular demands into balance. Cantillon thus looked upon the European economic society as a kind of network of reciprocity, given hierarchical form by prevailing institutions and kept in adjustment by the play of self-interest, into which individuals and groups were bound by "need and necessity."[24] Again, the term "nature" in the title of the *Essai* apparently referred to the system of links binding men and groups together in an economic society, while the terms "natural" and "naturally," used some thirty times by Cantillon, implied the existence of functional or cause-effect relationships which, though sometimes hidden by extraneous circumstances, were fundamental, persistent, and comparatively immutable, economic systems being what they then were. Presumably because Cantillon considered these relationships relatively immune to interventionism and because he was interested almost entirely in describing and analyzing the economic system and the behavior of the individuals and institutions constituting it, he frequently, but not always, eschewed making ethical evaluations of economic outcomes. "Cela n'est pas de mon sujet," he remarked with respect to matters such as the sanctionability of monopolistic pricing or the preferability of a smaller higher-income to a larger lower-income population.[25] His theoretical acumen was manifested also in his use of concepts of both closed and open states (i.e., economies) and in his employment of relatively simple models occasionally involving what later came to be known as conjectural history.[26] Finally, his theoretical skill in treating monetary and related questions, together with his handling of empirical information, probably contributed appreciably to the formulation of what later became the theory of liberalistic-capitalistic economics.[27]

III

Having treated of the fortunes of the *Essai* and its author, we turn to its contents. In this section we review his opinions respecting population and related questions, since the materials falling in this category illustrate the institutional background and premises Cantillon had in mind when discussing nondemographic questions — premises, incidentally, which sometimes prevented his generalizing and universalizing as much as possible the principles he set down. In the next section we treat of his value and distributive theory; in Sections V–VI his monetary, banking, price, and related theories are discussed. In the closing section some attention is given to the influence of certain of his views.

Cantillon's views on population and related matters may be grouped under five heads: (1) the mechanisms by which numbers are adjusted in time and space; (2) the demand for labor and population; (3) foreign trade, population capacity, and population growth; (4) the genesis of living standards; and (5) the distribution of population in space.

1. The mechanisms through whose operation population becomes adjusted to the means available for its support are three. (i) When the demand for labor declines in a locality, internal migration tends to remove labor and population from that locality; and, when the demand declines in a country generally, external migration removes some of the population to lands of greater opportunity.[28] (ii) Increases in infant mortality (whose absolute levels always were high), supplemented sometimes by increases in adult mortality, eliminate excess population in low-income areas when there is unemployment and great poverty (pp. 15–16, 19–20, 38–39, 54). (iii) Nuptiality in each of the classes composing a population increases in response to improvement, and decreases in response to deterioration, in the economic condition and prospects of its members. For most men wish to support their families according to a scale they have in view, and this scale usually is the one customary for the class of which one is a member. It was maintenance of the customary standard, not acquisition of a higher standard, that Cantillon stressed. "Most men desire nothing better than to marry if they are set in a position to keep their families in the same style as they are content to live themselves" (p. 43). For, with the exception of younger sons of the nobility who tend to defer marriage until they come into a fortune and of those members of "the lower classes" who, "from pride" and the desire to live better than they could if they married, remain single (pp. 21–22, 43), most individuals prefer to set up a family provided that there is a good prospect of their supporting it as they wish and thereby preventing their children from descending into a lower class. Men who do not believe the prospect good enough will postpone marrying and may not marry at all. Those who believe the prospect sufficiently good will marry, at least after they have saved enough to establish a household (pp. 43–44). In sum, then, whatever improves this prospect will make for an increase in nuptiality and population; what worsens it will make for a decrease in nuptiality and thus check population growth. In like manner, whatever makes for an increase in the scale of living will diminish nuptiality, production remaining the same; and conversely. It should be noted that Cantillon, who has been called an anticipator of the modern French theory of "social

capillarity,"[29] had in mind, much as did the later formulators of this theory, not an economy so dynamic as the nineteenth-century British or German, but one that, being comparatively static, was characterized by redistributions of social positions rather than by improvements in the emoluments attaching to most positions.[30]

2. Cantillon based his explanation of the growth and distribution of population upon a cost-of-production theory of value, which is discussed in Section IV. First, labor, whose supply was highly correlated with population,[31] had a cost of production.[32] The labor of a peasant or worker approximated in value to double the produce of the land required to maintain him, and that of an entrepreneur to treble his own support; for the earnings of individuals needed to be high enough to insure maintenance of the population (I, 11). The upkeep of an adult male, being determined largely by the custom of a place, varied greatly, ranging in Europe from 1.5 acres of medium goodness (if he ate meat rarely and drank little beer or wine) to 4–5 acres (if he ate meat daily and drank moderately of wine or beer); in China, where three crops of rice were raised yearly, a fraction of an acre sufficed.[33] Accordingly, the maintenance of the population called for a wage per adult worker approximating in produce the yield of 3–10 acres in Europe and of less than an acre in China. But were yields per acre greater (smaller), Cantillon implied, fewer (more) acres would be required per adult male and per family.[34]

Second, since labor and population had production costs, the amounts of them forthcoming depended upon the state of demand for them. The number of workers in any category "is naturally proportioned" to the demand obtaining for them in a country or a locality (I, 9). In like manner the inhabitants of a country "are necessarily proportioned to their Means of Living" (p. 38). Since these means of living consisted predominantly of the produce of land, the demand for labor, Cantillon implied, was determined by the volume of such produce available for the purchase and support of workers and their dependents. Cantillon reached the conclusion, therefore, that, since the owners of land directly and indirectly govern the uses to which land is put, "the Increase and Decrease of the number of People in a State chiefly depend on the Taste, the Fashions, and the Modes of Living of the Proprietors of Land"; theirs was the power of the purse (I, 15).[35] The "Prince," most important of the proprietors, is described as "generally capable of determining the inspiration and tastes" of the other proprietors; and these are said to determine what occupations the people should pursue (pp. 52–53).

Cantillon's argument, the germ of which he may have gotten from Locke,[36] made the demand for labor and hence the level of wages and/or the size of the population depend upon the consumption and spending patterns of the rich landed proprietors.[37] If they so spent their incomes and otherwise acted as to cause their lands to be used in the production of subsistence to which the inhabitants had access, numbers would speedily grow to the limit of the capacity of the land to support population at the prevailing scale of living. If, on the contrary, the proprietors concentrated in towns and cities and so spent their money as to cause much of their land to be diverted to the support of superfluous horses and the serving of ornamental purposes, the production of subsistence for men would be diminished, since farmers are prompted by self-interest to produce what is in demand (I, 14).[38] The diversionary influence of the proprietors was accentuated by the fact that their modes of consumption tended to be imitated and emulated by successful entrepreneurs and "all the lower ranks."[39] Given any resulting diminution in the domestic supply of agricultural produce, the demand for labor would fall and with it (temporarily) the current wage level and (eventually) the size of the population, since the worker's customary scale of living did not readily adjust downward. In support of this thesis Cantillon suggested that, because of increased consumption per head, the population of England had declined as had that of other countries; and he indicated that, given a fixed quantity of land or a rising scale of living, population could not increase geometrically, men multiplying "like Mice in a barn" only when "they have unlimited Means of Subsistence."[40]

3. So long as an economy was closed, Cantillon reasoned, whether numbers grew or not turned on what domestic fancies the land was made to serve. If, however, an economy was open and linked with other economies by trade, it turned also on whether labor-embodying products were imported or a converse exchange obtained. Suppose, said Cantillon, that France exchanges 16,667 muids of wine for its value in Brussels lace. The wine represents the output of about 6,000 acres in all, 4,000 acres of vineland and 2,000 acres of pasture and arable land for the support of the cart horses engaged in the production of the wine. The lace represents the flax output of 0.25 acre and the labor input of about 2,000 people, the maintenance of whose families requires the output of about 6,000 acres. The exchange in question has operated, therefore, to subtract about 6,000 acres of land and 2,000 families from France and add them to Belgium. In effect, Belgium has swapped labor for land and thereby gained at the expense of France much as Rome gained at the expense of other nations when it levied tribute upon them.[41]

Cantillon argued in general that "the exportation of all Manufactured articles is advantageous to the State, because in this case the Foreigner pays and supports Workmen useful to the State"; and he pointed to "trading States" (e.g., Hamburg, Danzig, Holland, Venice, etc.) which, though much more vulnerable to adverse events than "great States" (e.g., France, Spain, England), were supporting or had supported "great numbers at the expense of Foreigners." While he believed that a country which exchanged raw produce for wrought goods had a lower population in consequence, he did not emphasize this point with respect to "great States" which had "no need to increase the number of their inhabitants." But he did contend that pursuit of a policy of exporting only wrought goods and of retaining raw products at home, especially if it were complemented by a strong and well-secured merchant marine, would make for "greater ease and abundance" of produce in great states, would bring about an influx of gold and silver, and would produce the advantages associated with abundance of money (at least until internal prices became so high that the value of imports exceeded that of exports and the trade balance became negative).[42]

Cantillon's doctrine, derivative of a long-held thesis that foreigners paid the incomes of persons engaged in production for export, received its classic expression in 1767 at the hands of James Steuart, who declared that a country gained in proportion as it exported "work" and imported "matter."[43] Quesnay and the Physiocrats, proponents of *luxe de subsistance,* rejected Cantillon's argument in support of what could be *luxe de décoration.* For, believing that France's net product and national income would thus be augmented, the Physiocrats favored both a high per capita domestic consumption of agricultural produce and, at least so long as domestic agricultural output exceeded domestic consumption under competitive conditions, a sufficient exportation of farm produce.[44] Cantillon would have agreed that a state might export temporary surpluses of farm produce, but he would have stipulated that they be exchanged not for manufactures, whose influx would depress domestic employment and population growth, but for gold and silver, whose influx contributed (within limits) to a state's strength and advantage.[45] Because Cantillon believed raw produce to be the principal population-limiting factor, because he was interested in the strengthening of the state instead of in the maximizing of per capita output and income,[46] and because he wanted to expand exports, he overlooked both the output-increasing effect of international specialization and the fact that, if labor were relatively plentiful, labor-embodying products would most likely be exported.[47]

4. In Part I Cantillon looked upon the scale of living of the lower orders as set by custom and relatively fixed. At the same time he indicated that it had risen in the course of time. But he advanced no dynamic theory to explain this rise. Presumably, on his principles, he could have accounted for it in two ways. (i) He could simply have assumed that for divers reasons the real incomes of the lower orders had risen to new and higher levels and remained there long enough to establish new customary scales.[48] (ii) He could have supposed that an increase in the consumption level of the landed proprietors had been imitated by entrepreneurs and others who were receiving incomes temporarily in excess of their customary requirements, with the result that their customary standards had risen only to be imitated in turn by individuals situated still lower in the social hierarchy. But he did not employ these principles in Part I; in fact, unlike Petty, he seems to have been thinking in terms of a relatively static economy.

In Part II, in the course of his discussion of changes in the price structure, he dealt incidentally with the dynamics of living standards, recognizing (among other things) the principle of intercommodity substitution by consumers (pp. 96–97). In this discussion he did not assign so important a role to the proprietors, perhaps because, under the conditions he assumed, the real income of the proprietors had declined as a result of rising prices, while that of many others had risen. Increases in the quantity of hard money in circulation, he said, operated to increase both subjective and objective standards of living.[49] "I conclude that an increase of money circulating in a State always causes there an increase of consumption and a higher standard of expense" (p. 100). Presumably not much time is required for an increment in income to generate new and higher customary standards of living in the various classes composing a population; "for nothing is easier or more agreeable than to increase the family expenses, nothing more difficult or disagreeable than to retrench them" (p. 94). Cantillon does not stress, as did J. S. Mill later,[50] that only relatively large increments in income are likely to generate new customary standards. Cantillon's argument implies that an increase in real income consequent upon an increase in the amount of hard money in circulation would tend to diminish the population unless enough produce were imported from abroad.[51] For, while production would rise in consequence of the rise in prices (pp. 91–92, 96–97, 104), it apparently would not rise enough to offset the increase in demand for the means of living. Furthermore, the increase in income would tend, as would price rises, to be unevenly distributed, with important segments of the population suffering decreases in real income as a result either of price rises or of unemployment (pp. 91–93, 100). Some of these adversely affected persons would tend to emigrate (pp. 91–93, 101–2), while others, on Cantillon's principles, presumably would defer marriage. At all events, in the end the customary standards of living would generally be higher. A "rarity" of money presumably, since it would occasion a fall in income but not in the subjective standard of living, would tend to occasion emigration and a decline in nuptiality.[52]

Although Cantillon did not relate luxury and population movements closely, he did imply a general relationship. Inasmuch as only half a nation's wage-earners were engaged in agriculture, and as there was not always enough nonluxury employment to engage the other half, it often was necessary for a part — presumably a small part (p. 28) — to supply "ornament and amusement" (pp. 50–52). Luxury, which tended to become installed when money was too abundant, could also be harmful. It discouraged population growth when it retarded the development of manufactures in a state or entailed the continuing export of raw produce (pp. 42–43). Luxury affected an economy adversely also when it entailed an efflux of gold and silver; it had brought about the decline of Rome by occasioning a diminution of the money in circulation (p. 108–10).[53]

5. The spatial distribution of both a state's inhabitants and their economic activities, according to Cantillon, assumed a regular and orderly pattern which tended to be preserved by the network of market and price relationships that had gradually come into being as this pattern had evolved. This distribution reflected, above all, the extent to which the ownership of agricultural land was concentrated in the hands of a few and the constraints which were imposed by the impossibility of transporting services and by the tendency of the carriage costs of transportable goods to increase with distance. In his discussion, Cantillon, having noted (though perhaps less than Petty) the importance of secondary and tertiary employments, made use implicitly of the concept of a geographical multiplier, even

to the extent of calculating it (I, 3, 5; pp. 35–36). Perhaps, had he concentrated upon locational questions instead of discussing them incidentally to his analysis of price behavior, he might have anticipated modern attempts to integrate locational and populational theory; for he emphasized the importance of transfer costs and arrangements for reducing them (e.g., I, 4, 8).

The population was distributed among villages, market towns, and cities, one of which served as the capital city. The villages were oriented to agriculture, having been brought into being by the fact that farmers and farm workers, if they are to avoid loss of time going to and from work, must live near the fields they till. The size of a village thus depended immediately upon the number of agriculturalists settled there and the number of artisans required to minister to the needs of these agriculturalists and ultimately upon the fertility of the soil and the kinds of crops raised, together with the extent to which the services of artisans were to be had at little time cost in near-by towns. The size of a village usually was augmented somewhat by the fact that they had one or several less wealthy proprietors, who brought with them domestic servants and provided additional demand for the services of artisans.

The villages were economically clustered about bourgs, each of which ministered to the distributive requirements of a number of surrounding villages. A bourg was simply a somewhat larger village where markets were held once or twice a week. The function of the bourg was to permit merchants, at minimum transport and time costs, to collect for consumers situated in cities the products of the farmers from villages surrounding the bourgs, to distribute to these farmers and their dependents the merchandise which they sought from the city, and to carry on these exchanges at prices which were both satisfactory and stable.[54] Bourgs, though subject to the same growth determinants as were villages, became somewhat larger inasmuch as relatively more artisans and domestics located there and ministered to the needs of the landlords, agriculturalists, merchants, and one another.

Cities, particularly those situated within the interior of a country, owed their origin and being most of all to wealthy landlords who realized enough from the net value of their one-third of the produce to enable them to live, not in villages or bourgs, but in large places where they could enjoy the "agreeable society" of people of their own condition. The purchasing power of these great proprietors attracted to the cities, besides their own retinues and domestics, "an infinity" of merchants and artisans who in effect ministered primarily to the wants of the landlords and their dependents and secondarily to the wants of others. So the advent of the landlords produced a geographical multiplier effect (e.g., I, 5; pp. 35–36). The size of a city was further augmented if law courts were established there, since these increased the demand for domestics and artisans. Presumably, because cities constituted large markets for the output of workshops and manufactories, these tended to take hold there. These manufactories tended to become very large when a city was situated along the seacoast or on the banks of a large river and therefore had access (because of the resulting economy and convenience of its transport connections with the interior and exterior) to large domestic and foreign markets. The establishment of workshops and manufactories brought to a city not only entrepreneurs and operatives but also merchants, artisans, and domestics who could serve the wants of persons employed in manufacture. The capital city, though brought into being as were other cities, differed from them in that it was the place where the king, the government, the courts of last resort, and the largest landowners were situated and where were spent the revenue of the government, the incomes of the great landowners, and the moneys of the many (e.g., visiting landlords, students, etc.) who, drawn by the city's attractions, passed some time in the capital.[55]

Agricultural produce moved after harvest from the countryside to the cities in response principally to the prior movement, in the form of money, of proprietary rents, taxes, and farmers' profits to the cities.[56] Prices, accordingly, were much higher in cities than in the countryside, being highest in the capital city and lowest in agricultural surplus areas far removed from cities. Cantillon writes as though the prices of transportable produce were determined in the capital city, with farmers and proprietors in any area getting these prices *less* allowances for the risk and the transport costs incidental to the carriage of the produce from the area of provenience to the capital city. Even greater differences characterized the prices for nontransportable and perishable products (garden produce, eggs, fuel, etc.) which had to be supplied from points near by the consumers. The cost of living was high, therefore, in the cities and low in the hinterland; and, because transport was so expensive, the *net* prices realized by agricultural producers were low except in the vicinity of the capital city and adjacent to rivers and the sea where cheap water transport was to be had.

The geographical price pattern being what it was, a greater dispersal of industry and population was indicated. In so far as practicable, manufacturing should be conducted in provinces far removed from the capital. Cloth, linen, and lace production should be carried on in the provinces, and the manufacture of metal tools near coal mines and forests. For such locations, by making largely unnecessary the carriage of foodstuffs and raw materials to the city, would save for better employment the labor of many horses and wagoners and thereby greatly reduce transport costs. The population of the provinces would increase, and net price in local markets for agricultural produce would rise. He suggested, however, with respect to remote provinces, that capital would have to be provided, markets for products would have to be developed, and ventures which could better be carried on close to the capital or near rivers and the sea would have to be avoided.[57] Cantillon failed to show, perhaps because he was concerned with monetary questions, how comparative plenty of produce, in consequence of its effects upon the price structure and the distribution of the labor supply, might draw manufactures to an area. The same oversight marked his discussion of international trade.

IV

Cantillon, as in effect had many writers before him, distinguished the market value or price of a commodity from its intrinsic value or cost of production; but he made the distinction more explicit than had earlier writers, among them authors whose works he probably had read.[58]

> The Price or intrinsic value of a thing is the measure of the quantity of Land and of Labour entering into its production, having regard to the fertility of the produce of the Land and to the quality of the Labour. . . . But it often happens that many things which have actually this intrinsic value are not sold in the Market according to that value: that will depend on the Humours and Fancies of men and on their consumption.

The value of money (I, 17; II, 7) and the value of labor (II, 4; p. 81) constitute special cases of the theory of value in general. In his discussion of the gravitation of market value toward cost of production, however, he did not take into account, as he was to take into account in his later discussion of effects consequent upon changes in the quantity of money, the role of the passage of time, and he neglected the susceptibility of cost to variation, presumably because, as has been noted, he usually had in mind something resembling Schumpeter's "circular flow which consists of given processes already in working order."[59] In fact, he observes that, since "there is never a variation in intrinsic values," and since "in well organised Societies the Market Prices of articles whose consumption is tolerably constant and uniform do not vary much from the intrinsic value," it is possible "to fix the Market Prices of many things, like bread and meat, without any one having cause to complain." He took it for granted, nonetheless, that the supply and/or demand of widely used goods may and does vary and that individuals differ greatly respecting the worth they attach to uncommon articles.

Cantillon's discussion (e.g., I, 12) of the manner in which market prices are arrived at through bargaining indicates that the supply of an item tended to increase (decrease) when its market price exceeded (fell short of) its intrinsic value. The market price of a good is fixed, through bargaining, on the basis of the quantity offered in a market, in proportion to the demand (amount of money "destined for its purchase") or number of buyers seeking this good.[60] In a market, which resembles an auction or an exchange, demand, of which Cantillon conceived in a schedule[61] sense, and supply, of which he usually conceived in a comparatively fixed sense, came into balance when, allowing for such sales as had already been made at higher or lower prices, there was established a price at which the sum of the quantities sought by buyers (at this or higher prices) equaled the sum of the quantities offered by sellers (at this or lower prices). On occasion this equilibrating price might be established by a few buyers and sellers whom the others were inclined to follow; but it could not descend below a level fixed by sellers' reservation prices or by opportunities to sell in other accessible markets.[62] Elsewhere (I, 14; II, 5–6) Cantillon shows how farmers and others, animated by self-interest, guided by the behavior of market prices and alert to the opportunity costs of particular courses of action, change their activities until they arrive at a combination which, under the circumstances, is satisfactory; and how consumers substitute lower-priced for higher-priced commodities.

Returning to Cantillon's analysis of intrinsic value, we find (a) that, though he apparently felt the lack of a *representative* unit of land into terms of which to convert heterogeneous units of land and similarly the lack of a comparable *representative* unit of labor, he did not attempt to overcome this lack; (b) that he expressed himself in terms of a tradition, running back to medieval times, that made land and labor the only significant factors of production;[63] (c) that, inspired by Petty's analysis, which he considered incorrect, he sought to establish a "par" between land and labor; and (d) that, despite his emphasis upon land and labor, he mentioned other factors which, by entering into cost or otherwise restricting supply, augmented price and intrinsic value. Among these cost items — items to which incidentally medieval and later writers had called attention — he specified risk and uncertainty (I, 13), net interest and other elements making up gross interest and gross profit (I, 10; II, 9), elements that enter into the cost of transport (I, 4, 6; II, 5), and length of apprenticeship, training expenses, risks, responsibilities, dangers, etc., incidental to various jobs and occupations (I, 7–8, 11).

When Cantillon sought to discover "the par or relation between the value of land and labour," he proceeded, not from the fact that labor and land were intersubstitutable in terms of their imputed productivities, but from the fact that "those who labour must subsist on the produce of the Land." Accordingly, as has been noted, he attempted to establish that, given population replacement, the value (or cost) per day of most forms of labor (slave, peasant, craftsman, overseer) approximated twice the individual worker's upkeep and that the value of entrepreneurial labor approximated three times the entrepreneur's upkeep. Accordingly, given the amount of land required (on the basis of its yield and the individual's customary scale of living) to support an individual, labor input could be expressed in terms of land input; and, given the amount of labor and of land (if any)[64] entering into the production of an article, its whole value became expressible in terms of land.[65] Hence "the intrinsic value of any thing may be measured by the quantity of Land used in its production and the quantity of Labour which enters into it, in other words by the quantity of Land of which the produce is allotted to those who have worked upon it."[66] This intrinsic value, whether of a thing or of labor, was reflected in money price, with the result that, "in the same place," one ounce of silver represented twice as much produce as did one half-ounce; subsistence thus became a kind of numeraire. A close connection existed in Cantillon's system between his reduction of value to terms of land and his proposal that, since a country's land is limited, it might overcome this limitation by exchanging fabricated goods for produce.[67]

Cantillon did not integrate his views regarding particular forms of income into a general theory of distribution; nor did he effectively bridge either the gap between his analysis of price formation and his views on distribution or the gap between these views and his expectation (I, 2, 11) that strife, laws (e.g., that relating to primogeniture), and interpersonal differences in family size, frugality, health, industry, etc., would cause the ownership of land to remain highly concentrated. In fact, except for his treatment of profit and interest, Cantillon's distributive theory did not differ markedly from that of his immediate predecessors who looked upon land and labor as the overwhelmingly significant factors of production. For them, wages (based upon some sort of a downwardly inflexible scale of living) and the labor force being given, what remained of the total product after wages had been deducted constituted a gross rent out of which may be paid the supposedly minor[68] interest claims of owners of "stock," etc.

Cantillon, as has been shown, believed the level of wages for any kind of labor to depend primarily on the scale of living customary for that kind of labor — on a scale that was upwardly elastic and downwardly inelastic. The daily wage for a member of any one of most categories of workers tended roughly to approximate an amount double his daily upkeep, with only the entrepreneur tending to receive treble his upkeep (I, 11). Cantillon, as has been said, noted the upward response of this scale to certain changes in the monetary supply; but, except for an occasional observation (e.g., p. 23) that wages might rise with output, he did not give attention to the possible influence of increases in worker-productivity or to the fact that output per worker set a limit to the upward movement of real wages. Nor did productivity differences receive much attention in his analysis of wage differences. He attributed the fact that craftsmen received more pay than common laborers and husbandmen to the need that craftsmen must be compensated for "the time lost in learning the trade and the cost and risk incurred in becoming proficient" and to their not making "all their Children learn their own mystery" and thereby overcrowding the craft (I, 7). Among the circumstances accounting for differences, by individual and craft, in the earnings of craftsmen Cantillon included cost of training, skill, ability, degree of trustworthiness required, risk, and danger; but he did not explicitly translate these factors into terms of relative scarcity.[69]

Cantillon treated rent as a surplus, but, despite his emphasis upon transport costs and their influence upon the geographical price structure and the magnitude of net realized prices (II, 5), he did not elaborate a locational theory of rent or treat at length of the determinants of rent levels.[70] Cantillon, inspired perhaps by Bellers and others, looked upon agricultural land as yielding three rents of equal magnitude,[71] two of which went to farmers, "one for their costs and the support of their Assistants [and Horses], the other for the Profit of their Undertaking," and one of which went to the owners or proprietors of land; only the last, which elsewhere (I, 2) he called "the overplus of Land," approximated a true rent. The farmers' two rents directly or indirectly subsisted all who lived in the country, together with urban "Mechanicks or Undertakers" who were involved in supplying merchandise consumed in the country. The proprietors' rent served to maintain mechanics and others employed by the proprietors, together with "the Carriers who bring the Produce of the Country to the City." On the supposition that one-half the inhabitants lived in cities (and towns), somewhat more than half the produce of the land was consumed by the city population (i.e., the proprietors' rent, together with somewhat in excess of one-fourth of the farmers' two rents).[72] Cantillon does not explain why the product of agriculture is divided into three such equal shares, only to be redistributed as indicated, perhaps because he is thinking in terms of a model. But he suggests that if the owner of a large estate were to bargain intelligently with his overseers, now become farmers or entrepreneurs, and these in turn were to maintain their laborers "in the usual manner," the product would be distributed as indicated (I, 14).

Though Cantillon looked upon interest as the price of money, and though he stressed the advantages of an abundance of money, he denied that mere "Plenty or Scarcity of Money" governed the rate of interest. The "price of everything" (i.e., the level of prices), rising and falling with increases and decreases in the amount of money (and monetary requirements being variously affected thereby), changes in this amount and in prices had no "necessary connection with the rate of interest," of which Cantillon usually thought as a structure of rates.[73] One variously found high and low rates associated with both plenty and scarcity of money, and one might find an increase in the plenty of money initially lowering and eventually raising the rate of interest. The outcome depended upon what individuals got the money; for interest is "settled by the proportionate number of Lenders and Borrowers." Accordingly, most of his discussion relates to circumstances affecting the comparative number of borrowers and lenders.[74] Borrowers comprised entrepreneurs, would-be entrepreneurs (e.g., journeymen who wished to become masters, and laborers who wished to become farmers), and individuals bent upon making consumption expenditures in advance of their receipt of income. Lenders were made up primarily of professional moneylenders and landowners who expended only a part of their rental incomes; apparently but few of those who saved to invest or spend later fell in the lender category.[75] Loans were contracted primarily to bridge the interval between when the borrower wanted to make outlays and when he would realize income from sales, rents, or other sources.[76] Since the most important of the borrowers were landowners wishing to spend their rents even before receiving them, together with entrepreneurs who ministered to the wants of prodigals, and since lenders comprised principally professional moneylenders and such landowners as were content to live on less than the whole of their incomes, Cantillon made the interest rate depend largely upon the extent to which landowners were willing to live economically, save, and make their savings available. He drew attention, however, to particular circumstances that tended to raise or lower the interest rate. Whatever increased entrepreneurial profit prospects and the number wanting to be entrepreneurs increased the rate, as also did whatever augmented the lenders' risk (e.g., war, rumors, prospect of adverse price change, fear of borrower's solvency). The advent of peace, entailing as it did a reduction in some risks and in the number of entrepreneurs, tended to be succeeded by a decline in the interest rate, particularly when accompanied by a partial repayment of state debts to holders who were potential lenders. A favorable balance of trade, when not offset by increased expenditures on the part of landowners, tended to increase monetary supplies and reduce entrepreneurial monetary demands enough to diminish the rate of interest. Because he believed that the interest rate was fixed by the "altercations" (competition) of borrowers and lenders, Cantillon did not think that regulations could reduce the rate below the level obtaining in the free market. Respecting the relationship between the interest rate and the price of land, Cantillon noted that the rate at which land rents were capitalized was lowest around the capital city, where "the proportion" of buyers to sellers was high, and highest in the remote provinces, where the proportion was low.[77]

Cantillon understood well the use, by the Bank of England, of the purchase of securities on the open market "to lower the rate of interest or for other reasons." At the request of a minister of state the bank would "issue a quantity of bank notes without backing" and use them discreetly to buy and force up "the price of public stock" and thereby reduce the yield of this stock. It was sometimes possible, by this means, to instil in the security-buying public an expectation of sufficient further rises in stock prices and further falls in their yields to permit the bank to resell the purchased stock at enough profit to "retire and cancel all the extraordinary banknotes which it had issued."[78]

Noting that the inhabitants of a state, other than the proprietors of land, are divisible into "two classes," the entrepreneurs who are "as it were on unfixed wages" and the "hired people" who are on "fixed" wages, Cantillon undertook to explain by what circumstances these "unfixed wages" were governed. Some entrepreneurs (e.g., farmers, manufacturers, mastercraftsmen, wholesalers, retailers) bought at "fixed" or "certain" prices, hoping to sell at prices which, though "uncertain," would "leave them a profit"; while other entrepreneurs (e.g., lawyers, physicians, robbers) merely hoped to sell their services profitably; but there is "much uncertainty," since no entrepreneur can foresee "the extent of the demand" for what he sells, and many must sell at a loss and even at prices resulting in bankruptcy.[79] Cantillon did not, however, develop anything like an uncertainty theory of profit. Instead he thought of profit both as a composite gross return and as a supply price that reflected the scale of living characteristic of the relevant entrepreneurial group. The "Labour or Superintendence" of entrepreneurs tended to be "valued at about thrice . . . their maintenance"; and the number of entrepreneurs in any line increased (decreased) when profits were relatively high (low) until they had become suitably proportioned "to the Customers or consumption." Even after this adjustment had been achieved, however, the distribution of entrepreneurial incomes within any line remained highly dispersed relatively to that of persons in the same line who were on "fixed wages." Presumably also the profit rate exceeded the interest rate sufficiently, since otherwise entrepreneurial services would not be forthcoming.[80]

V

In this section we shall consider Cantillon's views respecting the value of money in exchange (as distinguished from its function as a unit of account, which he took for granted), monetary velocity, the monetary requirements of economies, and the role of money in international trade.

Cantillon treats the value of money as but a special case of value in general.

> The real or intrinsic Value of Metals is like everything else proportionable to the Land and Labour that enters into their production. . . . The Market Value of Metals, as of other Merchandise or Produce, is sometimes above, sometimes below, the intrinsic Value, and varies with their plenty or scarcity according to the demand. . . . The quantity of money, as of all other commodities, determines its value in the bargaining of the Market against other things.[81]

For this reason the purchasing power of gold and silver coins always became adjusted to their metallic content, which, together with their transport cost, made up all or nearly all of their intrinsic value (pp. 62–63, 147–48, 154–55). If the mint ratio between gold and silver coins departed from the ratio of the price of gold to that of silver which had been established in the international network of markets among which each metal moved at negligible cost,[82] the undervalued coins would disappear from circulation (III, 4). The aggregate stock of gold and silver would be added to only if its market value approximated or exceeded its intrinsic value (pp. 62–63). When the denomination of silver (or gold) coins of given metallic content, or the metallic content of coins of given denomination, was changed, market prices would adjust to the metallic content; but the adjustment would take time, its rapidity depending in part upon "the spirit of the Nation," upon how the people gauged the government's prospective policy respecting coinage, and upon the manner in which the economy was linked with foreign economies.[83] While Cantillon agreed with Locke's opinion (shared by Newton) that mankind's consent had given value to gold and silver, he insisted that this was not merely an "imaginary value" but one reflecting scarcity and intrinsic value.[84]

Believing that silver (which fluctuated in value less than gold) "alone is the true sinews of circulation," Cantillon distinguished between hard money and bank notes and between bank notes which constituted receipts for specific metal deposits and checks and bank notes which were not fully supported by metal deposits.[85] While Cantillon thought (perhaps because he had clearings in mind) "public banks of very great utility in small States and those where silver is rather scarce," he considered "a general Bank" of "very little solid service in a great State," though sometimes capable of producing seemingly "astonishing" effects. Bankers' and goldsmiths' receipts

122

(or notes) served "to accelerate the circulation of money." For whereas the gold and silver deposited with a bank or goldsmith would circulate very little in that form, half or more of it would circulate from payor to payee if notes in this amount were issued to borrowers. But, even so, bank notes comprised only about one-tenth of the money in circulation in England and Venice. When notes or "Bank money" were not wholly backed by silver or gold, difficulties were to be expected; apprehensive note-holders might precipitate runs on banks, and, if there were more "sellers" than "buyers" of notes or "Bank money," it would begin "to be at a discount against silver." The effect of bank notes and checks upon the demand for commodities and services depended upon the uses to which these mediums were put. So long as they moved only in financial circuits, there facilitating the sale of stocks, they did not affect the demand for commodities. When, however, security sellers converted their profits into hard cash, the aggregate expenditure of cash upon goods and services increased. Cantillon noted also that, if, in the absence of notes and bank money, silver (or gold) had to be used to facilitate the sale of stock in financial circuits, the amount available for ordinary purposes would probably be less, and there would be less stock selling.[86]

Cantillon conjectured that "the real cash or money necessary to carry on the circulation and exchange in a State is equal in value to one third of all the annual Rents of the proprietors of the said State," or to "the ninth part of all the annual produce of the soil." He arrived at this estimate by reasoning as follows: (a) if two-thirds of the agricultural produce (i.e., the shares of the landlords and the farmers) moved from country to city and payments were made once a year, silver equal in amount to the value of this two-thirds would be required to circulate it; (b) but, since the frequency with which payments actually were made ranged from something like four per year in the case of rents and taxes to many times a year in the case of petty trade, the average frequency with which payments were made for the purpose of circulating the shares of the landlords and the farmers might approximate six times per year; (c) since at least one-third the produce was distributed without the intervention of money, the money-product ratio must be raised from a 1:6 level, based on the two-thirds distributed with the assistance of money, to a 1:9 level for the whole agricultural output; (d) the 1:9 ratio was little affected by foreign trade so long as foreign sales and purchases were in balance, since bills of exchange were used to clear such sales. His supposition that a state's monetary requirements approximated one-ninth of the value of its gross agricultural product amounted to the supposition that they approximated something like 5–6 per cent of the value of its gross national product.[87]

As his argument implies, Cantillon looked upon "an acceleration . . . in circulation of money in exchange [as] equivalent to an increase of actual money up to a point," thus giving support to the views of those economists who, when replying to opinions that certain specific amounts of money were needed to conduct trade, stressed the importance of velocity. Cantillon, of course, had in mind a kind of circular velocity, though he indicated (p. 135) that an increase in the number of transactions separating the consumer from the producer would decrease circular velocity (presumably because he supposed that transaction velocity would not undergo a compensatory increase). Among the conditions that governed the "rapidity or slowness of the circulation" of "real" money he included (besides the size and nature of transactions which determined whether they could be completed with substitutes for hard money) the following: (a) the amount of recourse to barter; (b) the extent to which the distribution of securities and goods was facilitated by the use of notes, of bank-clearing and compensation arrangements, and of "book debts" or mercantile credit that required only an annual settlement of net balances;[88] (c) the frequency with which payments were made; (d) the number of entrepreneurial hands through which products and money passed before raw materials were transformed into finished goods and these were put into consumers' hands; (e) how much the "timid" hoarded and others held "against unforeseen emergencies"; (f) how much needed to be saved before it could be invested "at interest or profit"; and (g) how much was kept in idle cash for the accounts of "Minors and . . . Suitors."[89]

Having remarked that he would confine himself to "simple views" and avoid the encumbrance of a "multiplicity of facts," Cantillon indicated that international payments were made in much the same way as large intranational payments. Bills of exchange were "set off" against one another and cleared. Only "the balance of trade" had to "be sent in specie." The "par" between national moneys was "regulated by the intrinsic value of specie." Because some countries, having bought more than they had sold, were in debt to other countries, their money was at a discount with respect to gold and to the money of creditor countries. The magnitude of the discount (or premium) was limited by "the costs and risks" of transporting money from "one place to another"; but it was made greater when a debtor country prohibited the export of bullion and specie, hoping thereby to retain them, for "the only way to keep them in a State is so to conduct foreign trade that the balance is not adverse to the State." Extension of credit to a debtor country could delay but could not finally prevent the "transport of the sums" required to pay an unsettled debt occasioned by an unfavorable balance. Accordingly, in a debtor country the market price of gold would be relatively high and, were the export of gold coin prohibited, would exceed the mint price of gold. While a country's rate of exchange depended primarily upon the state of its trade balance, it could be affected also by other transactions (e.g., political, military, investment) involving payments to or from abroad.[90]

VI

In this section we review Cantillon's opinion respecting the advantages attendant upon a state's having an abundance of money and his description of "in what way and in what proportion the increase of money raises prices." Generalizing, Cantillon indicated that not all prices would increase in the same proportion as the "quantity of money in a state" and that the average increase would be relatively greater if the advent of new money gave "a new speed to circulation." Since some goods would be wanted much more than others by those into whose hands the new money passed, the consumption of some goods would be increased much more than that of others. At the same time it was not equally easy to meet all of these new consumption requirements. If the supply of a good was not very transportable, or was not legally importable, or was not highly augmentable for other reasons, its price would rise appreciably in response to the increase in demand. If, however, a good was importable, its price would not rise to a level in excess of its foreign cost plus its cost of transport. He sought to show in general that the process and outcome depended largely upon whence the money came, how it was spent, and what were the conditions of supply of particular goods. Unfortunately, he did not indicate explicitly how great he believed the amount of unutilized productive power tended to be under various circumstances, and so he did not make plain how elastic to a rising money price level, therefore, he considered output in general to be. Of necessity, elasticity could not be so great with him as with Petty, who attached more importance to technology and to the transfer of labor from agriculture to manufacturing.

1. An increase in money originating in domestic gold (or silver) mines initially augments the incomes of mineowners, workers, smelters, and others variously dependent upon gold production for their livelihood, and these in turn augment their expenditures, thereby giving fuller employment to some artisans, while nearly all lend at interest what they do not spend. Agricultural prices rising in consequence, farmers cultivate more land and gross more income, which they in turn spend. Meanwhile the rise in prices reduces the real incomes of those (including landowners whose leases are not yet up for renewal, together with their servants) on fixed incomes, with the result that some emigrate, therewith making possible "greater expense among those who remain." As landowners' leases expire, they raise their rents and the wages of their servants. Because of the height to which prices have risen, it becomes cheaper to import many manufactured articles, to the ruination of domestic manufactures and real incomes derived from them. In the end the only beneficiaries of the increased output of gold are those engaged in its production, together with the foreign manufacturers; the lot of the rest is "poverty and misery." This "is approximately what has happened to Spain since the discovery of the Indies."

2. An increase in money originating in a favorable balance of foreign trade enriches many entrepreneurs who in consequence employ more artisans and workers (who presumably were unemployed or underemployed). Their consumption, together with "the price of Land and Labour," rises, but slowly at first, since many initially save to acquire income-yielding property, having gotten which they step up their consumption (often at the expense of their capital) "and raise the price of everything" (presumably because output cannot be sufficiently increased). As a final result of the rise in prices, more goods are imported, and some foreign sales and even

some workmen are lost to manufactories newly erected in countries where "money is rare" and land and labor are cheap. The state will end up either with a small continuing trade balance "against the foreigner" or with a sufficient exportation of "work and manufactures" (for which it has a reputation) to pay for the commodities it imports. If it is a maritime state (as England) capable of transporting manufactures cheaply, the lowness of its transport charges may somewhat offset the highness of its manufacturing wages and even enable it to sell manufactures in a third country at lower prices than can a country "where Labour is less highly paid." If other maritime states with lower prices enter this export trade, however, these states will take away some of the sales, and the state with higher prices "will begin to lose its balance of trade." In all this argument there is the suggestion of an alternation of periods of prosperity and periods of depression issuing out of changes in the balance of trade and the underlying movements of prices, consumption, and sales abroad.

3. When money is brought into a state by subsidy or by foreign ambassadors, travelers, etc., its expenditure raises "the prices of all things in the channels of exchange into which money enters." Those who supply the foreigners, upon experiencing increases in income as a result, step up their consumption and expenditure. Velocity increases, and prices rise, especially those of things formerly consumed only by "a small section of the people" and those of goods which cannot be imported.

Money flowing into a state as a result of foreign loans increases wages and prices and may stimulate the establishment of manufactories. But the loans have disadvantages. They increase interest charges much more than they increase the public revenue, and, if the interest cannot be paid, distrust develops and the "Public stocks fall." Cantillon did not discuss the sequence of events following the introduction of tribute, remaining content to indicate that all states which had resorted thereto had "not failed to decline."[91]

It was essential, Cantillon believed, that a state have enough money, but not too much, since in the latter event it would, "in the ordinary course of things," fall "into poverty" and experience "collapse"; and yet he seems to have doubted that what was for him an optimum situation could be maintained. Certain advantages attached to a state's having enough — even an abundance of — money. Then consumption and expenditure would be relatively great, and stimulus would be given to economic activity, especially to the cultivation of land (and probably to the employment of unemployed and underemployed artisans and workers).[92] Then the power of the state would be great, for governmental revenue would be relatively plentiful and easy to raise, and the state could readily acquire "munitions of war and food" and military personnel. Then the terms of trade would be more favorable than if money had been less abundant and domestic prices less high.[93] If, however, money became overabundant, and the prince did not withdraw the excess from circulation and "keep it for emergencies," the advantages associated with an abundance of money would disappear. For since the markets of various nations were interconnected, price and income effects could develop and turn the export surplus into an import surplus. The continuing increase in the amount of money in circulation would generate (a) rising domestic prices and a substitution effect, in both the domestic and the international market, against goods produced by the country in question and in favor of the goods of competitor countries and (b) rising money incomes and consumption, much of which might or would be directed into foreign markets, especially those supplying luxuries. The balance of trade becoming unfavorable, as a result, money would flow abroad, and the state would become weak and impoverished. Presumably therefore he did not think the advantages associated with an abundance (or an optimum amount) of money could be permanently retained.[94]

Whether Cantillon believed that, in time, the process just described would usually become reversed, and that the lost prosperity would be restored, is not absolutely clear. But the burden of his argument appears to be in the affirmative. The persistence of luxury importation could, as the experience of the Roman Empire indicated, produce a net outflow of money, falling prices, and politico-economic decline.[95] The "brilliant situation" of small commercial states, having been undermined, could not be restored. But "a considerable State which has both capital and industrious inhabitants" could, with "good administration" and "by trade alone," produce an inflow of money and a sufficiency of circulation (pp. 108–9). He pointed also (pp. 157 ff.) to the experience of France, where, when her prices fell, what had been an unfavorable balance was converted into a favorable balance.[96] Cantillon's discussion, however, though it incorporates much of what went into the theory of a "self-regulating mechanism of specie distribution," lacks the precision and roundedness of the exposition of Hume and Gervaise.[97] This lack may be due to the fact that Cantillon was concerned not with the balance of trade as such but with the response of the price structure to increases in the quantity of money and with the maximization of a state's international position in terms of his criteria of national welfare. It is not unlikely, therefore, that, had he directed himself solely and specifically to an analysis of the international distribution of specie, he would, despite his mercantilist leanings and his rejection of a simple quantity theory of money, have produced a complete formula.[98]

VII

It is not easy to determine with precision how great Cantillon's influence has been or what particular forms it assumed. Economic thought is collective in origin, cumulative and transiently selective in character, being subject, as a rule, only to small accretions, deletions, and modifications and but rarely to major displacements of the order produced by a Smith or a Keynes through recombinations and reorientations of relatively familiar and accepted subject matter. Any man's ideas, once introduced into the stream of thought, may influence succeeding generations long after these ideas have become anonymous. Cantillon's name had already been stripped from most if not all of his ideas by the closing years of the eighteenth century —

a century, incidentally, whose authors are not noted for their recognition of sources of inspiration — and, even if it had not, it is quite possible that his association in men's minds with supposedly discredited neomercantilistic and physiocratic ideas would have made later liberalistic writers less prone to cite his work. His ideas were important, and his contributions to the development of economic thought, not the least among them being his introduction of English ideas into the stream of French political economy, were significant. Space being limited, I shall trace in some detail the fortunes of his theory concerning the connection obtaining between the fancies of proprietors and the demand for labor and population and much more sketchily the outcome of some of his views respecting location, price, distributive, and monetary theory which may have filiated from the *Essai* into the body of economic thought.

Cantillon's thesis, put in modern terminology and generalized, may be expressed as follows. (i) The income elasticity of demand for children is greater in some social strata than in others, being especially great among those — let us call them "workers" — who derive their income principally from the sale of their services. (ii) Any change in income distribution that results in an increase in the *absolute* amount of income going to workers will almost certainly increase a society's aggregate demand for children, since the increase in the workers' demand will suffice to offset any decrease in the demand of the propertied class. (iii) When, factor supplies and technical conditions of production being given, the preferences of the community favor labor-using as compared with capital-using types of goods, the amount of income going to the workers is relatively and absolutely greater than when a converse set of preferences rules, and the amount of employment resulting may be greater.[99] (iv) Accordingly, given (i)–(iii), when the preferences of a community shift in favor of labor-using types of goods, other conditions (including the workers' tastes for children) being given, the demand for workers, together with their incomes, rises, "population pressure" (along with consciousness of it) is relaxed, and the aggregate demand for children increases.

After Malthus wrote, Cantillon's theorem, as posed by him, was lost sight of, being appreciated not even by his late-nineteenth-century admirers. Much of the theory got into Mirabeau's *L'Ami des hommes* and the works of Condillac, Pluquet, Garnier (before he became a Smithian), and Peuchet. Malthus, probably because of Paley's influence, dealt extensively with the issue. Traces of the theory got into other works. But the question ceased to be dealt with as Cantillon had dealt with it, and Cantillon's name did not become associated with the theory of the demand for labor and population. Not until 1888 was a part of the theorem revived by Effertz, a German writer, who apparently was unfamiliar with Cantillon's work and who approached the problem from the point of view of the source of social antagonisms. The theory was lost sight of principally, Landry infers, because it had been given not a generalized but a particularized form, the institutional basis of which — highly concentrated landownership — was dissolved by the French Revolution. Responsible also must have been the rise of the well-organized Physiocratic school, which was essentially hostile to Cantillon, and its subsequent and complete supersession by the system of Smith, Say, and their followers, many of whom, probably, thought of Cantillon, if at all, as a predecessor of the Physiocrats. In 1910, in a much too little appreciated paper, Landry, making use of both the marginal productivity theory and a diffusion principle, generalized Cantillon's theory of the demand for labor and showed that a relative increase in the aggregate preference of consumers for labor-embodying goods would increase the demand for labor and hence serve to augment wages, employment,[100] and worker income. In the consumer category were included, of course, not only the proprietary class but all classes who, by their spending, generated the demand for labor. Whether an increase in the demand for labor would stimulate population growth, as Cantillon had suggested, turned, Landry indicated, on how workers responded to increases in worker income.[101]

Ricardo reintroduced the Cantillon type of argument into the body of received economics by a path not wholly different from that utilized by Cantillon. Ricardo reasoned that the demand for labor (a) would be reduced if expenditure upon menials were replaced by expenditure upon luxury goods, (b) probably would be reduced if the labor of horses were substituted for that of men, and (c) might be reduced if machinery were introduced. Such reduction in demand, if it persisted, his reasoning elsewhere indicates, would tend to diminish population. Case (a) resembles Cantillon's argument closely; cases (b) and (c) only remotely, since here the substitution may be said to originate on the supply side, though the effect upon population will be the same unless there results an increase in aggregate income that offsets the substitution effect against labor.[102] The controversy over protectionism and wages likewise involved the question of income distribution; but it has not been integrated into population theory. All these arguments may be said, however, to belong to the same genus as does Cantillon's and to be capable of being related to the population question.

Cantillon's theory of city formation, Maunier reports, was accepted in large measure by Condillac, Beccaria, and Roederer and, in some measure, by Quesnay and Steuart. It may have influenced Say and Forbonnais. It apparently did not influence D'Arco, who placed major stress upon the importance of the governmental bureaucracy.[103] While the context of Smith's analysis is different, it attaches importance to some of the things Cantillon considered important, among them transportation and transfer relations generally.[104] Twentieth-century inquiries into the origins of European cities, together with some of the more recent studies of population distribution, lend support to the pertinence of Cantillon's observations.

Both value theory and distributive theory came to reflect Cantillon's influence. Adam Smith seems to have gotten from Cantillon his use of the concepts of market price and natural price to account harmoniously for the behavior of exchange value in both the shorter and the longer run. From Smith's work this approach passed, with some modification, into classical and subsequently into neoclassical economics, apparently serving also to stimulate time-period analysis. Cantillon's account of wage differences influenced both Smith and the Physiocrats, and some of the factors to which he called attention continue even to this day to be given weight.[105] The wages-fund theory, derivative of a simple and predominantly agricultural economy, seems to have been a product of the disposition of seventeenth- and early-eighteenth-century economists to think of wage goods in organic terms and of land as yielding a surplus that was somehow divided. Cantillon's treatment could have lent some support to the formulation of this approach by Smith. Though Cantillon did not give expression to a law of diminishing returns, his treatment of proprietors' rent, by facilitating Quesnay's isolation of net product, may have contributed to the gradual sequestration of what came to be known as Ricardian rent. While Cantillon's conception of profit was in accordance with the English tradition, his emphasis upon the fundamental importance of the entrepreneur and his recognition of the significance of uncertainty were not. Yet, though Condillac noticed the entrepreneur, it remained for J. B. Say, quite possibly under the influence of Cantillon, to win for the entrepreneur the role he was to occupy in economics and prepare the way for the Walrasian approach; and it remained for still later writers to develop the full importance of uncertainty as a factor in economic behavior and profit theory.[106] That Cantillon's views on interest might have done much to explain whereon the behavior of interest depended, and to undermine the opinion that plenty of money had the most to do with interest, is plain; but that his analysis rather than that of Hume was responsible for the change that took place would be hard to support. It was not until the time of Newmarch, Rist finds, that Cantillon's proposition, that an influx of money may at first depress the interest rate and only subsequently raise it, was again understood.[107]

Though Cantillon's analysis of the sequence of changes, which take place in the prices of particular kinds of labor and goods subsequent to an influx of gold or silver, should have served as a model for subsequent writers, it did not do so, even though several writers (e.g., Condillac, Büsch), under the inspiration of Cantillon, did employ his approach; for Smith and his followers missed its import.[108] So Cantillon's role as forerunner of the "income approach" was not so influential as it might have been, though Keynes had little more to say on this head than did Cantillon.[109] In consequence the effective integration of value theory in the realm of money and prices and value theory in general was retarded, as was also the development of a satisfactory empirical approach. Appreciation of the fact, noted by Cantillon and Verri, that increases in the supply of money may intensify rather than reduce velocity, might then also have been greater.[110]

While Cantillon has been accredited with producing the first substantial change in French monetary and international price theory after Montchrétien, it remains unclear whether Forbonnais's attempt, to reconcile emphasis upon the supposed importance of the accumulation of precious metals with the quantity theory, was influenced by Cantillon.[111] As has been indicated, Cantillon's rejection of a simple and unqualified quantity theory prevented his setting down an equally simple theory of the international distribution of specie, much as his emphasis upon a labor-land cost theory instead of upon a simple labor-cost theory may have prevented his bringing to the surface such comparative cost theory as lurked in his argument. Forbonnais, an interventionist, seems to have taken a stronger position against falling prices than did Cantillon, who, however, noted the importance of price stability; and he seems to have supposed output susceptible of much greater increase in the short run, given the stimulus of an increase of money issuing out of a favorable balance of trade, than did Cantillon. The views of both men, however, disappeared from the stream of French monetary theory after the French Revolution.

Cantillon was the first writer to describe at so great length the supposedly self-adjusting and essentially autonomous character of the economic system and to suggest the inadvisability (if not the impossibility) of attempting, by legislative action, to modify the behavior of that system. Even so, Cantillon was reflecting a climate of opinion to which he in turn contributed; and, although he did not make specific recommendations, he wrote at times as though some interventionism was indicated and might succeed. His most significant contribution to the theory of self-adjustment was his account of the workings of the price system — an account that to this day retains its freshness, as, in fact, does much of the *Essai*.

NOTES

1. This edition (hereafter cited as "Sauvy, *Essai*") includes studies and commentaries by Anita Page, A. Fanfani, Louis Salleron, the editor, and the author of the present essay, notes by Louis Salleron, and a list of the works in which there is reference to Cantillon's *Essai;* it was published in Paris, in 1952, under the auspices of the Institut National d'Etudes Démographiques. I have included in the present essay portions of my commentary, in French, in the Sauvy edition. For the reader's convenience I shall refer to the *Essai* by book and chapter, using for this purpose Roman and Arabic numerals; occasional page references are to the Sauvy edition; the English is that of Cantillon as rendered by Higgs (see n. 3 below).

2. *Theories of Surplus Value*, trans. G. A. Bonner and Emile Burns (New York, 1952), p. 15.

3. Sauvy's new edition is the principal repository of this information. The Henry Higgs edition (hereafter cited as "Higgs, *Essai*") includes both the French original and Higgs's English version, together with a summary of his own research and W. S. Jevons' important paper, "Richard Cantillon and the Nationality of Political Economy" (which first appeared in the *Contemporary Review*, January,

1881). On Cantillon's life and his relations with the Marquis de Mirabeau see also Higgs, "Richard Cantillon," *Economic Journal*, I (1891), 262–91. Higgs's other studies of Cantillon include *The Physiocrats* (London, 1897) and "Cantillon's Place in Economics" (*Quarterly Journal of Economics*, VI [1892], 436–56). An excellent account of Cantillon's life and the fortunes of his *Essai* is given by F. A. Hayek in his introduction to the German translation (Jena, 1931); this introduction appears in French translation in *Revue des sciences économiques* (Liége), Vol. X (1936), and in Italian translation in *La Reforma sociale* (1932). J. Hone, in his "Richard Cantillon, Economist—Biographical Note" (*Economic Journal*, LIV [1944], 96–100), supplies Cantillon's genealogy and the supposed date of his birth. In "A Forgotten Quotation about Cantillon's Life" (*Economic Journal*, XLIII [1933], 534–37) Luigi Einaudi recalls Du Hautchamp's report about Cantillon, one of the forty-six acquiring first-class fortunes through John Law's "System" in 1719–20, who made 20,000,000 livres on his "Mississippi" speculations in this interval. Cantillon's contributions to the physiocratic system are treated by Georges Weulersse in *Le Mouvement physiocratique en*

France (Paris, 1910); see also my *French Predecessors of Malthus* (Durham, N.C., 1942) and my "The Physiocrats and Say's Law of Markets," *Journal of Political Economy*, LIII (1945), 193 ff., 317 ff.

4. Postlethwayt, who usually acknowledged his sources, did not refer to Cantillon's manuscript, perhaps because he was under obligation not to reveal the source. From Postlethwayt's *Dictionary* perhaps Joseph Harris drew the Cantillon material included in his *Essay upon Money and Coins* (London, 1757). On Harris and Postlethwayt see E. A. J. Johnson, *Predecessors of Adam Smith* (New York, 1937), esp. chap. x and pp. 405 ff.

5. While the identity of this rightful owner is not known, he may, as Hayek suggests, have been Francis Bulkeley, husband of Cantillon's widow; for the latter died in 1749 or 1750, while Bulkeley lived until January 14, 1756. Mirabeau, who professedly was held back from publishing the manuscript by its stylistic imperfections and the lack of the statistical supplement, proposed to write a book based on the manuscript; whereupon presumably the rightful owner, preferring the manuscript to be printed as it stood, called it back and had it printed. Mirabeau actually had done an abridgment of the *Essai* manuscript, supplemented by additions of his own, and a closet copy under the head of *Mémoire sur la population;* but these papers were not printed. Instead, in 1756, he composed his famous *L'Ami des hommes* (Avignon, 1757), in which he incorporated some of Cantillon's ideas (see Higgs, "Richard Cantillon," *op. cit.,* pp. 263–70; Georges Weulersse, *Les Manuscrits économiques de François Quesnay et du Marquis de Mirabeau aux Archives nationales* [Paris, 1910], pp. 2–3, 19–20; Sauvy, *Essai,* pp. lxviii–lxxiii).

6. A much-mutilated abridgment, based upon the French edition, by Philip Cantillon, one-time London merchant and a first or second cousin of Richard Cantillon, is hardly definable as an edition (see Higgs, *Essai,* pp. 376–78).

7. Higgs describes his translation, much of it based upon Postlethwayt's reproductions of the English original, as "near to a reconstruction of the English original" (*ibid.,* p. 384).

8. While some of the Physiocrats' views (e.g., on the role of land, rent, circular flow, money) were influenced by Cantillon, other of their views (e.g., on luxury, consumption, production, trade) differed from his. Upon Mirabeau's becoming associated with Quesnay, his esteem for Cantillon's ideas declined greatly (see my studies cited in n. 3).

9. The above paragraph is based upon Sauvy, *Essai,* pp. 177 ff.; Higgs, "Richard Cantillon," *op. cit.,* pp. 262–63, and *Essai,* pp. 391–92; Hayek, *loc. cit.;* Johnson, *op. cit.,* chap. ix; A. Fanfani, *Del*

Mercantilismo al liberismo (Milan, 1936), chap. iv; A. W. Marget, *The Theory of Prices* (New York, 1938–42), I, 307–10, II, 24, 29, 125, 130, 308–10; René Maunier, "Theories sur la formation des villes," *Revue d'économie politique*, XXIV (1910), 639–49; A. Landry, "Une Théorie négligée: De l'influence de la direction de la demande sur la productivité du travail, les salaires et la population," *Revue d'économie politique*, XXIV (1910), 314–23, 326–74; Jacob Viner, *Studies in the Theory of International Trade* (New York, 1937), pp. 74, 78 ff.; my *French Predecessors of Malthus*, esp. chaps. iv–v; Charles Rist, *History of Monetary and Credit Theory* (New York, 1940), *passim;* J. M. Keynes, *Treatise on Money* (New York, 1930), chap. vii; James Bonar, *Theories of Population from Raleigh to Young* (London, 1931), p. 234. The *Essai* referred to in E. Daire (ed.), *Oeuvres de Turgot* (Paris, 1844), I, 344–45 n., is not Cantillon's.

10. See Hone, *op. cit.,* p. 97, and Higgs, *Essai,* p. 366. Professor Page considers Hone's finding incontestable (Sauvy, *Essai,* p. xxiv).

11. Hone gives the date of this marriage as 1556 (*op. cit.,* p. 99) and Higgs (*Essai,* p. 365) as 1536.

12. Upon his death in 1717 the chevalier was found to be insolvent. Richard, the economist, himself a principal creditor, paid the unrequited claims of the other creditors.

13. Mirabeau, in *L'Ami des hommes,* characterized the author of the *Essai* as a Protestant, presumably, suggests Higgs, because Cantillon (in *Essai,* I, 16), like Petty, had described holy days and the activities of monks as wasteful, Petty (see C. H. Hull [ed.], *Economic Writings of Sir W. Petty* [Cambridge, 1899], pp. 216, 218) estimating that the Protestants worked about one-tenth more days per year than Catholics in Ireland (see Higgs, "Richard Cantillon," *op. cit.,* p. 273; and Mirabeau's defense of holidays, cited in Sauvy, *Essai,* pp. 52–53 nn.). Cantillon (*ibid.,* p. 103) attributed the decline in French cloth manufacture to the driving-out of the Huguenots.

14. This paragraph and the preceding one are based on Hayek, Higgs, Hone, and Page. Cantillon's seeming passion for anonymity is symbolized by the word "inconnu," which Du Hautchamp inserted after Cantillon's name in a column headed "Remarques" intended to provide supplementary information respecting the "Mississippiens" (see Einaudi, *op. cit.,* pp. 535–36).

15. E.g., cf. Aristotle *Metaphysics* vii. 8. This Aristotelian formulation, still substantially present in J. B. Say's *Treatise on Political Economy* (e.g., see 4th ed. [Philadelphia, 1841], Book I, chap. i), could have been suggested by French legal or

other sources, Higgs believes (see "Richard Cantillon," *op. cit.*, pp. 262–63).

16. See Fanfani (*op. cit.*, pp. 75–89), who treats also (*ibid.*, chap. ii) of Cantillon's indebtedness to Locke and Petty. Cantillon's definition of wealth as "la nouritture, les commodités & les agrémens de la vie" resembles Boisguillebert's; but the latter stressed far more than did Cantillon the importance of mass consumption (see Hazel Van Dyke Roberts, *Boisguilbert* [New York, 1935], pp. 285 ff.; Sauvy, *Essai*, p. 104 n.).

17. E.g., cf. Cantillon's comment (I, 9) on the uselessness of charity schools with the similar comment of Mandeville in *The Fable of the Bees* (see F. B. Kaye ed. [Oxford, 1924], I, 299–300) or the place of self-interest in Cantillon's system with that in Mandeville's system. Petty observed that men are more likely to put forth effort when it is to their advantage to do so (cf. Hull ed., e.g., pp. 201–2), but he did not apparently consider this disposition sufficient to organize men into an adequately functioning economy. In the Preface (now attributed to Roger North) to Sir Dudley North's *Discourses upon Trade* (London, 1691) it is said that "no Laws can set Prizes in Trade, the Rates of which, must and will make themselves" and that such laws are "prejudicial" to trade. Mandeville (*op. cit.*) wrote that the required "Proportion as to Numbers in every Trade finds it self, and is never better kept than when no body meddles or interferes with it." Mandeville may have been influenced by North (see Kaye's, under "North," in index to Kaye's commentary).

18. Possession, Cantillon believed, commonly originated in violence, with ownership sooner or later passing into the hands of a few (I, 2, 11). Presumably Cantillon found to his liking Hobbes's description of human behavior as self-regarding (e.g., see the latter's *Leviathan* [1651], Part I, chaps. xi–xv).

19. *Capital*, Kerr ed., III, 910.

20. This information is but a fraction of that assembled in the lost statistical supplement to the *Essai* which apparently included, along with other matter, "a rudimentary study of workmen's budgets in the different countries of Europe which would have afforded interesting comparison with Le Play's great work, *Les Ouvriers Européens*" (see Higgs, *Essai*, p. 385). Though Mirabeau reported the supplement to have been destroyed (see Sauvy, *Essai*, p. lxxi), scholars still hope that a copy may be found hidden away in some archives.

21. See Sauvy, *Essai* (where Mirabeau's remarks, put down about 1750 and now in Arch. Nat. M. 780, are cited *in extenso*), p. lxx; the translation is Higgs's (cf. *Essai*, p. 382). While Cantillon considered approximations to reality useful, he did not represent them as more than approximations; and, while he considered

"Statistics . . . left to imagination" especially "subject to error," he believed there was no branch of knowledge "more demonstrable" than statistics "based upon detailed facts" (see Sauvy, *Essai*, pp. 74–75).

22. See "Richard Cantillon," *op. cit.*, pp. 285–289. Cf. Rist, *op. cit.*, chap. i, sec. 3.

23. See Sauvy, *Essai*, p. lxix; Higgs, *Essai*, p. 381.

24. I, 2, 12 (p. 28), 13; II, 2.

25. I, 13, 15; II, 5; III, 5. Cantillon, after characterizing Petty's "research" into the "par" between land and labor as "fanciful and remote from natural laws, because he has attached himself not to causes and principles but only to effects," extended this criticism to Locke, Charles Davenant, and other English authors (I, 11).

26. I, 12, 14–15, 17; III, 3; p. 85. On the use of conjectural historical models in eighteenth-century Europe see F. J. Teggart, *Theory of History* (New Haven, 1925), *passim*.

27. On his contribution to liberalistic-capitalistic economics see Fanfani, *op. cit.*, esp. pp. 121–26, and Sauvy, *Essai*, pp. xxi ff.

28. See pp. 13–14, 40–41, 101. Though unequipped with a marginal productivity theory, Cantillon reasoned that wage differences consequent upon differences in local supply-demand situations would set in motion equilibrating movements, particularly since men were animated by economic self-interest.

29. See R. Gonnard, *Histoire des doctrines de la population* (Paris, 1923), p. 143; also my *France Faces Depopulation* (Durham, N.C., 1938), esp. pp. 157 ff., 205.

30. See *Essai*, pp. 13, 43–47; also p. 38, where it is noted that in China religious principles obliged all to marry. A. Landry (*La Révolution démographique* [Paris, 1934], pp. 169–92) distinguishes Cantillon's law, according to which population is *conditioned* by subsistence and regulated by variation in nuptiality, from Townsend's law, according to which population is determined by subsistence and regulated by mortality, and from the modern principle, according to which population is conditioned by subjective and objective factors and regulated principally through birth limitation. At and before the time Cantillon wrote, apparently very little weight was attached to the role of variation in nuptiality as a voluntaristic means of regulating natural increase. C. E. Stangeland (*Premalthusian Doctrines of Population* [New York, 1904], pp. 112, 164), mentions only Sir Walter Raleigh and S. Dugard. Petty (Hull ed., p. 608) merely refers to the marriage-delaying effect of "Portions, Jointures, Settlements, & c." Halley (to whom Cantillon refers at p. 44, and whose life-table apparently is the basis of

Cantillon's misinterpretation when he assigns [I, 7] but ten to twelve years to a man's [working?] life) observed (*Philosophical Transactions of the Royal Society of London*, XCII, No. 198 [1693], 654–56): "It is from the cautious difficulty most People make to adventure on the state of *Marriage,* from the prospect of the Trouble and Charge of providing for a Family," that population growth is "stinted." Variation in nuptiality, after having been given a place of importance in the system of thought of Malthus and some of his disciples, underwent a decline in significance as a check in late-nineteenth-century population theory, only to be treated as the major regulator of numbers by G. Cauderlier around the close of the century (see my *France Faces Depopulation*, pp. 143–44).

31. He put at 50 per cent of the population the number of persons who work for others; landowners and proprietors along with the sick comprise another 17 per cent (I, 16).

32. Differences in the wages received by various categories of labor he accounted for in terms of differences in their cost of production and, consequently, in their conditions of supply (I, 7–8).

33. See I, 11, 15, and p. 34. In these estimates Cantillon allowed only for the food for horses for the plow and for the carriage of the produce a distance of ten miles (p. 40).

34. Cantillon indicated that, because of variation in the quality of the soil, in the number of crops harvested per year, and in the skill of cultivation, yields per acre varied widely (pp. 37–39, 111). While he indicated that yields per acre are limited (pp. 37–38), he developed no law of diminishing returns, resembling, in this regard, Petty, who, however, implied the operation of increasing returns in England (Hull ed., pp. 34, 68).

35. Petty (Hull ed., p. 90) remarked that demand and price are affected by the "example of Superiors," and a similar opinion was expressed by Locke ("Some Considerations of the Consequences of Lowering the Interest, and Raising the Value of Money" [1691], in *Works* [London, 1801], V, 58–60, 72). Cantillon (I, 12–13; also II, 3–4) described the landed proprietors as the only naturally independent class in the state because, raw produce being so essential and (apparently) the support of labor being so largely reducible to terms of organic materials, the economic situation of the proprietors (who could exercise great control over the supply of organic materials) was more secure than that of workers, entrepreneurs, and possessors of nonlanded wealth, all of whom had to have produce for their maintenance. Cantillon's argument, in so far as it stressed the autonomy of the role of the large landowner, underestimated the importance of the peasant in the then social structure and

the routine character of the principles according to which the lands of large owners were cultivated; it, of course, underestimated the influence of the power of the purse of other income-receivers.

36. See John Locke, *Of Civil Government* (1690), Book I, par. 41; cf. *Essai,* pp. 25–26.

37. Their incomes, supposedly in money, approximated in value one-third of the agricultural produce of the land they owned (see Sec. IV below).

38. Urban growth increased the horse requirement of the transport system, with each horse consuming the produce of 3–4 acres (pp. 97–98). According to Petty (Hull ed., pp. 173, 175, 287–88), the support of a man required about the same amount of land as that of a horse.

39. See pp. 35–36, 41–42, 52, 56–58.

40. I, 15. He added that (*ibid.*) in the colonies where land was freely to be had population grew ten times as fast as in a country like England. That numbers were less than formerly had been asserted by Continental contemporaries of Cantillon (e.g., by Vossius, Bayle, and Montesquieu [see my *French Predecessors of Malthus,* and D. V. Glass, "The Population Controversy in Eighteenth-century England, Part I: The Background," *Population Studies,* VI (1952), 83–91]), though for reasons somewhat different than those advanced by Cantillon; but this opinion seems not to have had supporters in England until after 1750, when it was questioned whether numbers had increased since the Glorious Revolution (see Glass, *op. cit.,* pp. 69–71). Petty (Hull ed., pp. 462–64) and Davenant (*Essay upon the Probable Methods of Making a People Gainers in the Balance of Trade* [London, 1699], pp. 15–20), who cites Gregory King, supposed that England's population increased at a low but steady rate. Hume, Voltaire, and others later denied that numbers had decreased, but they made no reference to Cantillon's argument as such.

41. See III, 1; I, 15; also pp. 51, 132–34, on the difficulty of expanding foreign markets; also p. 48 on land-saving effect of coal consumption.

42. III, 1; pp. 28–34, also pp. 47–48, 75–76, 107–8. The Physiocrats also distinguished between small trading states and large land-rich states, saying that their policies applied only to the latter (see my studies cited in n. 3).

43. *Works* (London, 1805), Book II, chap. xxiv; Johnson, *op. cit.,* chaps. xi and xv.

44. See A. Landry, "Les Idées de Quesnay sur la population," *Revue d'histoire des doctrines économiques et sociales,* II (1909), 41–87; also my "The Physiocrats and Say's Law of Markets," *op. cit.,* pp. 208 ff. Cantillon did not distinguish between "productive" and "unproductive" labor.

45. See III, 1; II, 8; pp. 129–30. If

too much of the silver got into circulation, prices would rise above a point where the terms of trade, together with volume, were very favorable, to a point where exports would decline and imports would increase (pp. 129–30). On military advantages arising from state's possession of gold and silver, the best form of "reserve Stock," see pp. 50–51, 104–5.

46. Here, despite his refusal (I, 15) to say whether a higher-income small population was to be preferred to a lower-income large population, he declares for a strong state which derives its power from the magnitude of its usefully employed labor force and its consequent ability to exchange wrought goods for gold and silver (I, 16; III, 1). Yet whereas, reasoning similarly, he condemned the idleness of monks, he described the "Nobleman" as useful in military service and the magistracy and as always "a great ornament to the Country" (see I, 16).

47. Cantillon was not thinking in terms of a foreign-trade multiplier, although he did conceive implicitly of a geographical multiplier (pp. 4–5, 8, 36–37), and, as Landry later demonstrated ("Une Théorie négligée," op. cit., pp. 750–57), his theory of the demand for labor contained a multiplier principle.

48. This approach would have had to be reconciled with his assertion that war losses were made up rapidly (p. 47).

49. Cantillon's analysis is remindful of both Simiand's theory of economic change (see R. Marjolin, "François Simiand's Theory of Economic Progress," Review of Economic Studies, V [1938], 159–71) and Keynes's thrilling account of the impact of price changes (op. cit., chap. xxx).

50. Principles of Political Economy (Ashley ed.), pp. 348, 371, 380–84.

51. See pp. 94 ff. The increase is the result of mining or of an export surplus. While he showed that in England the increase in meat production had diminished corn production and increased the relative value of pastures and meadows, he did not trace the impact of the shift upon population. Cantillon did not recognize what V. G. Simkhovitch has called the "grass revolution" (Toward the Understanding of Jesus [New York, 1937], pp. 150 ff.).

52. Cantillon does not say this, but his argument (pp. 103–4, 109–10) carries this implication.

53. On Rome cf. Keynes, op. cit., II, 151 ff.

54. Only if a market was organized and supply and demand had become relatively stable were market prices relatively stable (pp. 17–18).

55. I, 2–6; p. 52. On transport costs see, e.g., I, 6; pp. 41, 87; and on trading cities (e.g., Hamburg), treated as a special class by the Physiocrats, pp. 75, 108, 129. Unlike Petty (Hull ed., pp. 462–65), Can-

tillon did not attempt to fix the maximum size of the capital city. In Cantillon's day students of rural economy were aware of location problems, and a number of eighteenth-century economists (e.g., Melon, Galiani, Forbonnais) argued in favor of the diffusion of industry (see Sauvy, Essai, pp. 85–87 nn.).

56. One half the population lived in the country and one half in the cities, with somewhat more than half the agricultural produce moving into the city or away from the country (I, 12; II, 5).

57. The last two paragraphs are based upon II, 4–5. On shipbuilding see p. 133. Adam Smith wrote in a somewhat similar vein, but he added that abundance of provision makes its price low and so attracts manufacturing workers (see Wealth of Nations, Book III, chap. iii). There is no reference to Cantillon.

58. I, 10. A clear statement appears in Nicholas Barbon's A Discourse of Trade (1690), ed. J. H. Hollander (Baltimore, 1903), pp. 13–16. He observes, on the one hand, that the "Price or Value" of anything (which arises from its "Use") fluctuates, being low when it it plentiful and high when it is scarce; for supply varies with the goodness of the season and other circumstances, while demand varies as "the Mind Changeth" and a thing grows "out of Use." Hence "things are just worth so much, as they can be sold for." On the other hand, everything nearly has its cost, and the seller attempts to base his price thereon. "The Price that the Merchant sets upon his Wares, is by reckoning Prime Cost, Charges and Interest. The Price of the Artificer, is by reckoning the Cost of the Materials, with the time of working them," and with the time priced according "to the Value of the Art, and the Skill of the Artist." If the market value of what the seller sells descends sufficiently below his expected price, with the result that the realized price does "not pay the Merchant Interest, nor the Artificer for his Time, they both reckon they lose by their Trade." When this is the case, it is implied, supply is adjusted accordingly.

59. The Theory of Economic Development (Cambridge, 1934), p. 36.

60. Cantillon (II, 1) criticized Locke for supposing that "the Market Prices of things should be proportionable to their quantity and to that of the Silver actually circulating in one place, because the Products and Merchandise sent away to be sold elsewhere do not influence the Price of those which remain." Locke (Works, V, 46) said that the "natural value of money" depends on the ratio of a kingdom's money to its whole trade; and that "the natural value of money, in exchanging for any one commodity, is the quantity of the trading money of the kingdom, designed for that commodity, in proportion to that single commodity and its vent."

61. Cantillon must have been familiar

with "Gregory King's Law," in itself an implicit schedule, which appears in Davenant's *Essay* (cited in n. 40 [Part I, p. 290]), p. 83, and which was inspired if not set down by King (see G. E. Barnett's Introduction to *Two Tracts by Gregory King* [Baltimore, 1936]).

62. See esp. I, 4, 10; II, 2; and pp. 68, 85–86, 100; also II, 1, where the use of hard money is traced to difficulties attendant upon barter and to the need of a common denominator in terms of which divers goods could be compared and exchanged in markets and decisions to buy or sell could be made intelligently.

63. Petty referred to labor as "the Father and active principle of Wealth, as Lands are the Mother" (Hull ed., pp. 68, 377). In medieval eyes production consisted in man's appropriation, through his labor, of the bounty of God (which post-medieval writers called the "bounty of Nature"). Some writers placed major stress upon land: e.g., John Asgill, *Several Assertions Proved* (1696), p. 21, and writers like Davenant, who thought taxes in the last resort a charge upon land. Cantillon's rejection of Vauban's "royal tithe" may imply that he believed taxes tended to be incident on rent, for he also approved a proportional tax on net rent (p. 89). Others stressed labor. Thus Hobbes asserted that "plenty dependeth (next to God's favour) merely on the labour and industry of men" (*op. cit.*, chap. xxiv). Locke even went so far as to impute "ninety-nine hundredths . . . wholly to . . . the account of labour" (*Of Civil Government*, Book II, par. 40). See also Marx, *Capital* (Kerr ed.), I, 46 ff. On land and labor as factors see Johnson, *op. cit.*, chap. xii; also cf. Schumpeter, *op. cit.*, pp. 17, 23 ff.

64. "Labour makes up" all or "nearly all the value" of some articles (e.g., a steel spring, a delivered pitcher of water); land makes up nearly the whole of the value of some commodities (e.g., hay, wood). See I, 10.

65. Cantillon reasons, particularly when he is stressing the independence of the landowning class and the reducibility of everything to terms of organic materials, as though labor represents embodied maintenance (i.e., organic materials), and, therefore, since products represent embodied labor and raw materials, as though products ultimately represent embodied maintenance. But, when he expresses himself in price terms, he reasons rather more as if maintenance is a numeraire. For various expressions see pp. 1–2, 27, 33, 70, 77, 81, 97.

66. I, 11; p. 24; also II, 4; p. 81.

67. I, 10; III, 1. In his *Treatise of Taxes* (1662) Petty sought "a natural Par between Land and Labour, so as we might express the value by either of them alone as well or better than by both, and reduce

one into the other"; for he looked upon products as "creatures of Lands and mens Labours thereupon." He then estimated the value of land in England at about twenty-one times its true rent, which consisted of the residuum of products left after seed had been allowed for and the workers cultivating the land had been supplied with "Clothes, and other Natural necessaries." See Hull ed., pp. 43–45; and pp. 48–49, 286–87, where he said that net rent was positively associated with density of population. In *Verbum sapienti* (1691), Petty, having estimated at 15 million pounds the income of land and "stock" supposedly worth 250 million, and the income of the population at 25 million, concluded that the value of the population was five-thirds that of the land and "stock," or property, namely, 416.7 millions (Hull ed., p. 108). In *A Treatise of Ireland* (1687), Petty estimated the ratio of the value of the population to that of property (i.e., land and stock) at 1.41 and 2.83 to 1, respectively, in England and Ireland (computed from Hull ed., p. 574). Petty presents several versions of par in *The Political Anatomy of Ireland*, which is the only one of his works to which Cantillon specifically refers. Defining as rent the amount of food that unattended land will yield, and as wages the additional food that the same land will yield if attended, he states that both rent and wages have been expressed in the same terms, namely, food, or amount of food required per man per day. He values a cabin "at the number of days food, which the Maker spent in building of it," and "Art" at the number of days of "Simple Labour" that the introduction of the "Art" saves, or makes possible, beyond what would have been accomplished by "Simple Labour" unassisted by this "Art." Finally, he indicates that, if each of several kinds of labor is paid in money, it becomes possible to convert one kind of labor into another (see Hull ed., pp. 181–82; see also Gaëton Pirou, "La Théorie de la valeur et des prix chez W. Petty et chez R. Cantillon," *Revue d'histoire des doctrines économiques et sociales*, IV [1911], 271–78; Johnson, *op. cit.*, chaps. vi and xii–xiii).

68. According to Petty's estimates, these claims were not so minor. In his *Treatise of Ireland* (Hull ed., p. 574), he estimated at about 18 per cent the fraction of "the Expence" of the English people distributed as "the Interest of the Stock or Personal Estates"; the corresponding figure for Ireland he put at about 17 per cent. Similar figures are not given in Petty's *Political Economy of Ireland*, to which Cantillon specifically referred. Barbon (*op. cit.*, p. 20) described interest as the "Rent" of "Wrought . . . Stock," but did indicate how interest income compared in magnitude with rent income. Cf. North, *op. cit.*, p. 4.

69. I, 8, 17. Cantillon, concerned with

explaining the behavior of wages, does not urge, as did many mercantilists, that wages be held down in order that a larger amount of effort might be forthcoming. Concerning English wage theory prior to Cantillon's day see E. S. Furniss, *The Position of the Laborer in a System of Nationalism* (New York, 1920); also M. T. Wermel, *The Evolution of the Classical Wage Theory* (New York, 1939), chaps. i–ii.

70. Petty, who was alert to the importance of transfer relations, stated that the amount of rent, or surplus, was positively associated with goodness of location, population density, quality of land, and the skill with which men cultivated land (see Hull ed., pp. 43, 49, 78, 89–90, 249, 256, 268, 286–87, 564). He indicated that "almost all Commodities have their Substitutes or Succedanea" (*ibid.*, p. 90), but he did not employ the principle of factor substitution in his analysis of rent levels. Locke (*Works*, V, 33–34, 69–70) merely touched upon possible causes of declines in rent. Cantillon notes (p. 27) that rent is greater when population is greater.

71. Perhaps the first clear statement of the notion of three rents, one each for landlord, farmer, and farmer's "charges," is that of John Bellers in his *An Essay towards the Improvement of Physick, Etc.* (1714), who also noted that the value produced by a country's "labour amounts to near 8 or nine Times as much as the Rents of the Lands" and that "the Labour of one half of the People in the Nation, raise all Necessaries for themselves and the other half" (see S. Bauer, "Quesnay's Tableau économique," *Economic Journal*, V [1895], 5–6, and A. Ruth Frey, *John Bellers* [London, 1935], p. 126). Davenant (*op. cit.*, pp. 72–73) estimated the "Neat Produce" of various lands at from two to four times the rent charged; Petty (Hull ed., pp. 89, 268) put it at three-fourths. Locke (*Works*, V, 73), in an illustration, put the landholders' share at one-third of the amount of money required for carrying on the trade of England.

72. I, 12. Cantillon is careful to point out that he is assuming a closed economy, since, if it be open, some entrepreneurs and mechanics may live "at the Expense of Foreign Landowners." Cantillon makes use of his notion of three rents in I, 14, 15, 16; II, 3, 9. He remarks that in some countries (e.g., around Milan and in China) the landlord's share may exceed one-third but that, when this is the case, "the Farmers are generally very poor" and are not always able to pay. The proprietor is well advised to hold the rent at one-third, since then the farmer may have some capital wherewith to exploit the land more effectively. It is at this point also that Cantillon states (as did the Physiocrats later) that "the larger the Farm the better off the Farmer will be," probably because he had in mind that the capital/land ratio would

be better on large than on small farms (see II, 3).

73. The evidence showed that "there are in a State many classes and channels of Interest or Profit, that in the lowest classes Interest is always highest in proportion to the greater risk, and that it diminishes from class to class up to the highest which is that of Merchants who are rich and reputed solvent. The Interest demanded in this class is called the current rate of Interest in the State and differs little from interest on the Mortgage of Land." A solid and solvent merchant's short-term bill was as good as a lien upon land, since the danger of the former's bankruptcy was balanced by the possibility of a lawsuit respecting the lien (p. 116).

74. Sir Dudley North (*op. cit.*, pp. 4–7), who observed that in England consumer loans (e.g., of great landowners) made up nine-tenths of "the Moneys imployed at Interest," said that interest depended upon the ratio of lenders to borrowers. Whereas Cantillon (p. 97) considered "hoarded money, plate," etc., "of no present utility," North (*op. cit.*, p. 6 and "postscript") looked upon such hoards as satisfying what amounts to "liquidity preference" and as tending to become available for trade, lending, etc., as the interest rate rises. Petty (Hull ed., pp. 304, 446–48) attributed the fall of the interest rate in England to "the increase of Mony" and advocated creation of a bank in the event there was "too little Money." Locke believed "the natural interest of money" to vary inversely with the ratio of a country's money to the debts of its inhabitants and with the proportion of its money to its trade. Unlike Petty, he did not think the interest rate could be "effectually" reduced "by a law"; and, having noted that a country could obtain money (i.e., gold and silver) only through mining, conquest, or commerce, he indicated that a lessening of the interest rate would cause a diminution in the amount of money available for trade (see *Works*, V, 9–10, 13, 37, 44–46). Thus Locke recognized liquidity preference but not, Keynes remarks (*The General Theory of Employment, Interest and Money* [New York, 1936], pp. 342–44), fluctuations therein. John Law also held to the rather common view that money is borrowed more readily and at lower interest when it is "in greater Quantity" (e.g., *Money and Trade Considered* [2d ed.; London, 1720], p. 13). On French views see P. Harsin, *Les Doctrines monétaires et financières en France du XVIe au XVIIIe siècle* (Paris, 1928). Although Cantillon noted (p. 32) that outstanding loans "usually exceed all the money in the State," he did not relate this ratio to a state's monetary requirements.

75. Pp. 32–33, 43–44, 82, 89, 93–94, 113.

76. He supposed that individuals kept

cash on hand to meet "unforeseen emergencies"; at all events, this was not an important cause of borrowing (pp. 82–83).

77. II, 9–10. Seventeenth-century English opinion respecting interest was varied, ranging from those (e.g., Thomas Mun) who believed that a high rate was associated with prosperous trade through those (e.g., Josiah Child, Thomas Culpeper the elder) who, believing a low rate to be favorable to trade, favored the use of law to reduce the rate, to those who believed that the rate was determined naturally in the market (which reflected monetary conditions). Cantillon's opinion that the rate of return on land, being more secure (p. 32), would be lower than that on other types of investment was shared by (among others) Barbon (*op. cit.*, pp. 32–33), Petty (Hull ed., pp. 447–48), North (*op. cit.*, p. 4), and Locke (*Works*, V, 65–66). On French opinion see Harsin, *op. cit.*

78. III, 8. Cantillon added that speculation and corruption tended to accompany maneuvers of the sort described and that, while the "excess notes" would not normally enter goods markets, they would be presented to the bank for silver if fear of a crisis developed. The early operations of the Bank of England are touched upon in John Clapham, *The Bank of England* (2 vols.; Cambridge, 1944).

79. London brewers, who extended credit in kind to alehouse-keepers, grew "rich" so long as no more than half the alehouses went bankrupt each year (p. 15); and yet, because they could buy conveniently, alehouse as well as other customers at retail did not mind paying prices that allowed large profit and interest rates.

80. I, 13; also pp. 23, 112. Barbon (*op. cit.*, pp. 32, 82) had observed that among the "hazards" run by the trader (who expects "to get more than Interest by his Goods") was the impossibility "when he has Bought his Goods, To know what he shall Sell them for." Locke believed that it was pointless, given the existing "scarcity of money and bad security," to urge reducing the interest rate to 4 per cent, since at a 6 per cent rate "the borrowers already are far more than the lenders" (*Works*, V, 76–77).

81. I, 17; pp. 54–55; II, 7; pp. 97–98; also III, 4; pp. 146–48; III, 5; pp. 154–55. Copper coins, when they had a face value in excess of their intrinsic value, would pass in petty trade for more than their intrinsic value, at least so long as their number was limited and their use was confined to the facilitation of petty trade (III, 4; pp. 269–73). Earlier (I, 17; II, 1) he had explained how, because of their properties, gold and silver had superseded other articles as money in all areas of monetary use except that of the "smallest purchases." In sixteenth-century Spain goods and money had been brought within the scope of a single demand-oriented theory of value (see

Marjorie Grice-Hutchinson, *The School of Salamanca* [London, 1952], p. 50).

82. The ratio obtaining in England could differ very greatly from that obtaining in Japan, because the transfer of either metal from one country to the other was so risky and costly (III, 4; p. 151).

83. III, 5. Cantillon criticized Sir Isaac Newton for reducing the money value of gold instead of adjusting upward (as the market had already done) the price of silver coins, saying that it was more natural to adopt adjustments already made by the market and that the downward adjustment of the money value of gold had increased the metallic burden of England's debt to foreigners. Newton's reduction of the money value of gold, "devised only to prevent the disappearance of light and worn coins," had not brought the mint ratio in line with the market ratio; in consequence silver was not being brought to the mint, and only "worn" silver coins remained in circulation (*ibid.*). On the controversy (occasioned by William Lowndes's proposal that worn silver coins be called in at nominal value, reminted at the cost of the Exchequer, and then reissued at a 25 per cent increase in denominational value) which prompted Locke's economic writings (*Works*, V, 1–206) and his statement (in opposition to Lowndes and to views subsequently expressed by Barbon and other supporters of the land-bank scheme of 1696) of the thesis that money is essentially synonymous with bullion, and which eventuated in the policy Cantillon criticized, see G. F. Shirras and J. H. Craig, "Sir Isaac Newton and the Currency," *Economic Journal*, LV (1945), 217–41.

84. See pp. 62–63 and also pp. 145–46. Cantillon of course implies that the money commodity has utility. F. Galiani (*Della moneta* [1751], Book I, chaps. i–ii) expressed it better when he said that the value of monetary objects rests upon their "scarcity" and their "utility." John Law (*op. cit.*, pp. 6–9, 75–78, 83), in the course of his argument that paper money based on land was superior to silver, also took exception to Locke's (*Works*, V, 21–23) description of the value of money as imaginary, saying that money must be based upon something valuable.

85. Rist (*op. cit.*, pp. 33, 172, 203) describes Cantillon as the first writer to distinguish "clearly between credit instruments and money properly so-called." Cantillon's treatment of commercial credit and clearing operations is touched upon below. As Rist notes (p. 72), Cantillon, like his contemporaries, did not distinguish between bank notes and bank money or checks.

86. III, 6–8, and also p. 154. The capacity of "fictitious and imaginary money" to raise prices was the same as that of "real money" until it had become discredited (p. 167). Petty said (Hull ed., p.

446) that "a Bank . . . doth almost double the Effect of our coined Money."

87. II, 3–4. Should the landlords' share exceed one-third, "a greater quantity of actual money is needed for circulation, other things being equal" (pp. 82–83). It was best to base one's estimate upon the value of the landlords' share, since this value was "easily ascertainable" from tax returns, since the ratio of this share to the value of the total agricultural output was independent of the price level, and since it was difficult to estimate the value of the whole output from available price and yield data. He referred to Petty's estimate of one-tenth, "for which he gives no reason," given in the *Political Anatomy of Ireland*. Petty stated that "in most places . . . the Money of the whole Nation is but about 1/10 of the Expence of one Year"; but in this work he also put Ireland's monetary requirement at about one-seventh of her annual "expence" (Hull ed., pp. 192, 216). Petty arrived at the "sum of Money which will compleatly and plentifully drive the Trade" of a kingdom as follows: add to "half a Years Rent for all the Lands" a "Quarters Rent of the Houseing" and "a Weeks Expence of all the People"; if there be foreign trade, increase this sum by an amount approximating "a Quarter of the Value of all the exported Commodities" (*ibid.*, p. 446; also pp. 113, 216, 310). Underlying his method of estimating was the supposition that money used to pay land rents circulated twice a year, whereas that used to meet "expence" circulated fifty-two times a year. Locke (*Works*, V, 21–29, esp. p. 28), after reviewing the circumstances whereon depends "the quickness of . . . circulation" of money, concluded that "it cannot well be thought that less than one-fiftieth part of the labourer's wages, one-fourth part of the landholder's yearly revenue, and one-twentieth part of the broker's yearly returns in ready money, will be enough to drive the trade of any country"; and that under no circumstances could the required amount be "less than one moiety of this." North (*op. cit.*, "postscript") said that "there is required for carrying on the Trade of the Nation, a determinate Sum of Specifick Money, which varies, and is sometimes more, sometimes less, as the Circumstances we are in requires." This sum would become available "without any aid of Politicians," flowing in and out of hoards, foreign sources, and the mint as required. Physiocratic estimates that an economy required money in an amount approximating 50–100 per cent of the net product (which in turn approximated two-fifths of the gross agricultural output) reflects Cantillon's influence (see my "The Physiocrats and Say's Law of Markets," *op. cit.*, p. 323). Galiani (*op. cit.*, Book IV, chap. i) later said that in the Kingdom of Naples the amount of money required approximated one-eighth of the

annual payments. Adam Smith, observing that it was "perhaps, impossible to determine" the proportion circulating money bore to the "whole value of the annual produce," mentioned estimates of 3–20 per cent (*op. cit.*, p. 280).

88. II, 4; also III, 2, where he describes the use of "bills of exchange" and their clearing within France as the means whereby the transport of money is held fairly close to the minimums required to settle uncompensated residual amounts; p. 141, where he indicates that the credit of bankers may delay but cannot prevent sending "the balance of trade in specie to the place where it is due"; p. 168, where "the clearings at Lyons" fairs are put at eighty times the "ready money" used; and II, 5, on how the countryside and the provincial cities proceed to settle annually their "balance or debt to the Capital."

89. II, 3–4.

90. III, 2–3. Thomas Mun (*England's Treasure by Forraign Trade* [London, 1664], chap. iv) was explaining the credit-transfer operations of Italian banks at a time when these were not carried on in England (Clapham, *op. cit.*, I, 5).

91. This section is based upon II, 6–8; III, 1.

92. E.g., p. 104. Cantillon did not subscribe (as did James Steuart and others who lay stress upon the adequacy of a state's money supply) to an explicit employment theory, and he apparently supposed that the bulk of increments in money normally are spent rather than hoarded. Yet he seems to have recognized the need for balanced growth (p. 15), and his various accounts of the diffusion of new demands set in motion by new increments in money suggest that he supposed the existence of at least some concealed unemployment. It is probably correct to say, therefore, that an implicit employment theory is to be found in some of his arguments.

Cantillon did not attach so much importance to the availability of liquid assets as did Steuart, who seems to have foreseen that the ratio of intangible to tangible assets would increase as economic development progressed and to have felt that economic development would be facilitated by the increase of monetary and other liquid assets (see S. R. Sen, "Sir James Steuart's General Theory of Employment, Interest and Money," *Economica*, XIV [1947], 19–36; W. F. Stettner, "Sir James Steuart on the Public Debt," *Quarterly Journal of Economics*, LIX [1945], 451–76; and Steuart's *An Inquiry into the Principles of Political Economy* [1767], esp. Books II and IV). One does not sense in Cantillon's *Essai* a feeling for the dynamics of a long-run developmental process, a feeling which, though founded upon different principles, is present in the works of both Steuart and Smith. Nor is there in Cantillon that lively appreciation of the benefits of technological development which one encounters in Petty's writings.

93. Pp. 50–51, 87–88, 104, 128.

94. II, 6–8; III, 1.

95. Pp. 108–10, 169. Cf. Keynes, *Treatise*, II, 150–52; H. Michell, "The Edict of Diocletian: A Study of Price Fixing in the Roman Empire," *Canadian Journal of Economics and Political Science*, XIII (1947), 1 ff., and "The Impact of Sudden Accessions of Treasure upon Prices and Real Wages," *ibid.*, XII (1946), 1 ff.

96. Cantillon's analysis runs in terms of hard money and price and income changes. He does not indicate whether, in his opinion, the departure of an exchange rate from par tended to produce equilibrating effects or the use of short-term international loans significantly reduced the international flow of specie (cf. III, 3). Steuart (*An Inquiry into the Principles of Political Economy*, Book IV, Part II, chaps. viii ff.) favored the use of loans for this purpose.

97. On the development of the theory see Viner, *op. cit.*, chaps. i–ii, esp. pp. 74 ff. Cantillon does not seem to have known Gervaise's *The System or Theory of the Trade of the World* (London, 1720), several of whose views parallel Cantillon's (see J. M. Letiche, "Isaac Gervaise on the International Mechanism of Adjustment," *Journal of Political Economy*, LX [1952], 34–43). As noted earlier, Viner finds no evidence that Hume was influenced by Cantillon's work, which he could have read in manuscript form.

98. Cf. Rist, *op. cit.*, p. 287. The questions authors ask have much to do with what they see. For example, one gets from Nicole Oresme's *Traictie de la première invention des monnoies* (ca. 1360) the impression that, had his purpose been other than it was in his sixth chapter, on "Who is and should be the owner of this money?" he might have given expression to a theory that described the self-regulating character of international specie flow in his day. This chapter is included in a selection appearing in A. E. Monroe, *Early Economic Thought* (Cambridge, 1924), pp. 87–88.

99. On (iii) see H. G. Johnson, "Demand for Commodities Is *Not* Demand for Labor," *Economic Journal*, LIX (1949), 535–36, and P. A. Samuelson and W. F. Stolper, "Protection and Real Wages," *Review of Economic Studies*, IX (1941), 58–73; see also my "Aspects of the Economics of Population Growth," *Southern Economic Journal*, XIV (1947–48), 137–40, 144–47, 173.

100. He failed to indicate that whether there would be an increase in the aggregate number of hours worked depended on the elasticity of demand for income in terms of effort (see J. R. Hicks, *Value and Capital* [Oxford, 1939], pp. 36–37).

101. See Landry, "Une Théorie négligée," *op. cit.*, pp. 314, 364, 747, 773; al-so my *French Predecessors of Malthus*, esp. chaps. iv–v, and "Malthus's Total Population Theory: A Restatement and Reappraisal," *Canadian Journal of Economic and Political Science*, XI (1945), 234–44. The relevant literature is cited in these works. See also my "French Population Theory since 1800," *Journal of Political Economy*, XLIV (1936), 591–92.

102. See Ricardo, *Principles of Political Economy and Taxation*, chaps. xxxi and also xxvi; and cf. Mill, *op. cit.*, Book I, chap. vi. See Landry's comment upon Mill, "Une Théorie négligée," pp. 376–77.

103. Maunier, *op. cit.*, pp. 638–49.

104. *Op. cit.*, Book III, chap. iii.

105. See *The Wealth of Nations*, ed. E. Cannan ("Modern Library"), Book I, chaps. vii and x, and Cannan's notes. In his sole reference to Cantillon (*ibid.*, pp. 68–69) Smith pointed out that the wages of labor sometimes exceeded double their maintenance. Presumably Cantillon would have agreed, for he had implied (I, 11) that a worker's upkeep might appreciably exceed double his mere maintenance. See, on Cantillon's influence on wage and other theories, my two works cited in n. 3; cf. also Wermel, *op. cit.*

106. Cantillon's entrepreneur did not have much of Saint-Simon's "most essential producers," or of Schumpeter's innovator, in him. As has been noted, Cantillon did not appreciate, as Petty seems to have done, the importance of technological improvements; nor did he appreciate, as Petty did, that, since output per worker was higher in manufactures than in agriculture, the stimulation of manufacturing was indicated (e.g., see Hull ed., pp. 249, 289–90).

107. See Rist, *op. cit.*, p. 289; also pp. 314–15, on the modern character of Cantillon's account of open-market operations. Joseph Massie's able and empirical explanation of the relation between money and interest, *The Natural Rate of Interest* (1750) appeared two years before Hume's essay on interest but had not the same effect. Much of Cantillon's analysis was published anonymously by Postlethwayt, 1749–51 (Higgs, *Essai*, pp. 383–86 and Appendix A).

108. See, e.g., Marget, *op. cit.*, I, 307–10, 501; II, 25, 29, 125, 308, 353.

109. See Keynes, *Treatise*, chap. vii. Until Marx wrote, sight was lost also of Quesnay's theory of circular flow, which quite possibly was inspired by Cantillon's *Essai*.

110. On this point see Rist, *op. cit.*, p. 118; also his account (pp. 33, 172, 203) of the surrender, particularly by Ricardo, of the distinction, first made by Cantillon, between money and bank notes and other credit instruments.

111. See e.g., J. W. Angell, *The Theory of International Prices* (Cambridge, 1926), chap. viii; Harsin, *op. cit.*, pp. 234 and 251; Marget, *op. cit.*, II, 309.

6.

MARCUS ARKIN
University of Cape Town

The Economic Writings of David Hume— A Reassessment[1]

I

In almost all walks of life nowadays, there appears to be growing alarm over the danger inherent in our highly specialized world that the various branches of learning will become water-tight compartments, not only divorced from one another, but increasingly aloof from those underlying philosophical and scientific principles which traverse all frontiers of study, and — if given sufficient scope — should be constantly adding to our stock

Reprinted from *The South African Journal of Economics*, XXIV (September 1956), 204–20, slightly enlarged, by permission of the author and the publisher.

of knowledge through a cumulative process of cross-fertilization. This seems sufficient pretext for trying to momentarily divert attention from the live issues of the present to the more leisurely mid-18th century in order to reassess the economic contribution of one who looked upon the study of society as an indivisible entity.

"Hume has an eminent place among economists, and for one to whom the study of such phenomena was but a casual inquiry, it is marvelous how much he saw. He is free from the crude errors of mercantilism; and twenty years before Adam Smith hopes, 'as a British subject', for the prosperity of other countries".[2] With these words Professor Laski began one of the neatest eulogies ever penned on David Hume as economist; it is significant that the eulogist himself was not primarily a teacher of economics. The tendency on the part of the economists has been to adopt one of two conventional attitudes: either Hume has been regarded as an appendage of the mercantilists (although, admittedly, a "liberal" one), or, rather more frequently, he has been looked upon as a major precursor of Adam Smith and his essays have been considered as seeds from which some of the more important doctrines of the *Wealth of Nations* eventually germinated.

It was David Hume's misfortune that his penetrating essays were written during something of a twilight period in the development of economic thought. By the mid-18th century the vociferous controversies which had revolved around the "favourable balance of trade" doctrine had long since passed into limbo, while the problems of a mechanized factory civilization were still very much in their swaddling-cloths. An age of transition — that much overworked and misused phrase — can be legitimately applied to the era of Hume, when the British economy had become a hybrid of enclosures and open-fields, nascent factories and "putting-out" industries, and, in the sphere of commerce, enterprising one-man shows and privileged chartered companies; it was a period when individual initiative vied with entrenched vested interests as never before and seldom since and during which the traditional Puritan hankering after parsimony — which had played such a notable rôle in stimulating capital accumulation in the course of the previous century — was being engulfed by a wave of conspicuous consumption on the part of a new semi-leisured class. Moreover, these middle decades of the 18th century witnessed the emergence of a landless urban proletariat faced with problems vastly different from those which beset the traditional village labourer — problems which the country's legislators had little opportunity to deal with, even if they recognized their existence, since they were confronted with their own apparently insuperable dilemma of the exchequer's mounting public debt. In such an age it is not surprising that many students of economic affairs desperately searched for an overall panacea, and frequently failed to perceive that different problems called for a whole variety of policies. As a consequence, modern historians of economic thought, with their worldly-wise after-the-event perspectives, have chosen to look upon the whole period between Josiah Child and Adam Smith as a kind of Dark Age in the development of their science, scarcely worthy of their detailed attentions.[3]

During recent years the *Wealth of Nations* has come to be regarded increasingly as the product of a master synthesiser who expertly delved into a host of earlier treatises, instead of being treated as the brain-child of an omniscient Father of Political Economy. Yet this tendency has helped more than ever to relegate Hume to the status of a respectable predecessor deserving honourable mention, but hardly meriting recognition as an economist in his own right. But in part, too, it has been the fault of the book trade: while the printing presses have busily churned out innumerable monographs on almost every conceivable aspect of the subject — many of them of dubious permanent value — the essays of David Hume have been hard to come by, and most of them have rested undisturbed amid the numerous weighty editions of the writer's philosophical works which it was so fashionable to publish during the 19th century.[4]

Now, at long last, Hume's writings on economics have been conveniently brought together for the first time in a single volume,[5] with the texts of the various original editions expertly edited by a painstaking associate professor of a Mid-Western university, who has also provided a much-needed analytical introduction based on a doctoral dissertation prepared for the exacting mentors of the University of Chicago. In this introductory section, Professor Rotwein, after briefly describing something of the background of the age in which Hume wrote, proceeds to explain the relationship between Hume's economic ideas and his general philosophical principles, stressing especially the manner in which Hume the economist was influenced by Hume the psychologist and the student of natural history. These relationships are all-important if any adequate re-assessment is to be made of his place in the development of economic thought, since Hume was essentially an astute observer of contemporary economic life in its entirety rather than a critic of a number of specially chosen topics.

Hume's economic writings cover nine of the twelve essays in the *Political Discourses*, the first edition of which appeared as an octavo volume of a little more than 300 pages in 1752. Couched in an easy-going self-assured prose, the style of these papers is in marked contrast to the stilted and frequently self-conscious language of the commercially unsuccessful *Treatise of Human Nature,* of which they form an obvious appendage. Since Hume clearly recognized the multidimensional nature of human experience, it is not surprising that he attempted to follow-up his general survey with a series of less formal commentaries of behaviour in economic situations. As a supplement to these essays, Professor Rotwein has added a small collection of relevant passages extracted from Hume's private correspondence, including the replies of such diverse associates as the Baron Turgot and James Oswald of Dunnikier.

The book under review is not without its blemishes: an analytical table of contents for the long introductory section and a fuller index would have been valuable aids to the serious reader, while there are occasions when Professor Rotwein rather overstresses some of the more remotely abstract philosophical aspects of Hume's thought; moreover, by far the longest of the essays reprinted here — "Of the Populousness of Ancient Nations" — is summarily dismissed with one or two quite inadequate general comments. But these relatively minor defects are more than outweighed by the Editor's penetrating insight into the mind of his subject and by the pioneering service he has rendered in making these essays more easily accessible to a public which has long regarded Hume as one of the apostles of the Age of Enlightenment, but has as yet scarce looked upon him as an economist who in many respects was at least equal in stature to his close friend at the University of Glasgow.

II

The *Treatise* itself had a twofold purpose: (i) to consider the science of man, and (ii) to investigate the laws of behaviour;[6] thus, from the outset, Hume intended to employ his principles of human nature for exploring the moral sciences, including economics. And it is essentially because of this close relationship between his philosophical and economic thought, that almost all Hume's essays are permeated with historical and psychological elements.

Hume attempted to study and write history as a general science of human experience, and, in fact, his deep interest in the subject ante-dated work on the *Treatise* itself. Since laboratory research in the moral sciences was out of the question, he felt that investigations into the past might furnish sufficient "experiments" to form the basis of reasonably reliable propositions on the principles of human nature. This does not imply that Hume was unaware that the lack of adequate statistical data placed great difficulties in the way of formulating such generalizations; nor does it mean that he overlooked the tendency for human behaviour itself to vary in accordance with changes of environmental conditions. He recognized both of these problems, but felt, as Professor Rotwein puts it, "that the generalizations of his own economic analysis were at the very least respectable approximations to accurate descriptions of experience" (p. xxxi).[7]

The psychological foundation of Hume's economics is to be found in his treatment of the motives underlying economic activity, or, as he puts it, "the causes of labour."[8] There are, in his opinion, four such causes, bound up in the desires for "pleasure", "action", "gain", and "liveliness". The first of these — the desire for "pleasure" — is used throughout the essays in a very general sense to signify those passions (such as pride) which are gratified through the consumption of wealth. Secondly, Hume believed that lucrative employment is one aspect of a universal desire for action, akin to hunting or the pursuit of knowledge, since it has a practical usefulness and offers a physical or mental stimulus.[9] In the third place, although various interpretations of avarice — or the desire for "gain" — are to be found scattered about Hume's writings, his general inclination is to approach an embryo "acquisitive instinct" concept; under conditions of lucrative employment, "especially if the profit be attached to every particular exertion of industry", then a person "has gain so often in his eye, that he acquires, by degrees, a passion for it, and knows no such pleasure as that of seeing the daily increase of his fortune".[10] Finally, there is the invigorating influence of lively sensations in stimulating economic activity — even disagreeable or painful experiences will be preferred to absolute repose; on the other hand, a want of liveliness leads to idleness or to a perpetual search for pleasure as forms of compensation. Consequently, Hume tended to look upon the "debauchery" of the poorer classes as a symptom of social frustration.[11]

Hume's economic psychology, therefore, constantly stresses the divers forces which motivate action; "What is man but a heap of contradictions!" he once asserted. Professor Rotwein neatly sums-up the conflicting instincts on which, in Hume's opinion, economic behaviour rests: "man produces in order to attain 'pleasures'; enjoying the difficulties encountered in the activity itself, however, he not only delights in those pursuits which show genuine promise of thwarting his desire to consume but, in the course of the 'game', conceives a passion to withhold and preserve his acquisitions from use. He wishes his wants gratified, but, likewise enjoying the emotional excitement of having wants, he desires his wants unsatisfied, and finding himself too heavily taxed with 'tranquility' will seek refuge if necessary even in the bitter-sweet pleasure of pain" (p. lii). Thus, in spite of his own scientific disposition, Hume retained a sharp awareness of the variety and contrariness to be found in the economic and social behaviour of mankind.

III

Most of Hume's essays are brief by modern standards. They take the form of a series of loosely inter-connected running commentaries bound together by the underlying theme of whether or not economic principles remain valid when analysed in the light of history and other related subjects.[12]

The main outlines of Hume's explanation for the rise and development of economic activity through the impact of changing environmental conditions appear in the first of the nine essays reproduced in this collection, "Of Commerce". In the course of his argument, Hume develops the thesis that commercial expansion not only enhances the welfare of the individual but also promotes the power of the state. "Trade and industry", he asserts, "are really nothing but a stock of labour, which, in times of peace and tranquility, is employed for the ease and satisfaction of individuals; but in the exigencies of state, may, in part, be turned to public advantage" (p. 12). In the concluding pages of this essay he demonstrates that foreign commerce — which, he argues, usually precedes the expansion of internal trade — is of particular importance in the process of economic growth: it furnishes raw materials for new industries, widens the scope of employment, extends the activities and increases the size of the merchant class, and satisfies the demand for luxuries and novelties. "In short, a kingdom, that has a large import and export, must abound more with industry, and that employed upon delicacies and luxuries, than a kingdom which rests contented with its native commodities. It is, therefore, more powerful, as well as richer and happier" (p. 13).[13]

The whole problem of "luxury" receives detailed attention in the essay which follows, "Of Refinement in the Arts", and here historical analysis plays a major rôle in the unfolding of the discussion and in helping to frame conclusions. Hume attempts to steer a middle course between the opposing views which, on the one hand, looked upon even "innocent" luxury as an evil,[14] and, on the other, regarded "excessive" refinement as a social blessing. The whole question, he argues, must be judged in terms of its influence on human welfare: an era of "innocent" luxury is usually a happy, well-bred age, whereas material excesses can become the source of many ills, but are nevertheless preferable to a condition of society without any refinements at all; in any case, he sensibly adds, there is no hard and fast line of demarcation between "innocent" and "vicious" luxury — the concepts are elastic and depend on the time, people, and particular circumstances under consideration. Moreover, material refinement invariably encourages artistic and intellectual pursuits: "Thus *industry, knowledge,* and *humanity,* are linked together by an indissoluble chain, and are found, from experience as well as reason, to be peculiar to the more polished, and, what are commonly denominated, the more luxurious ages" (p. 23).[15] The second part of this essay (pp. 25–32) is taken up with a series of excursions into history in order to demonstrate the relationship between economic progress and individual liberty: far from undermining political freedom, Hume asserts, a highly-developed economy promotes parliamentary government, since it leads to the appearance of an influential middle-class whose main concern is not to tyrannize over others but to gain security of property through equitable laws.[16]

It is probably in the sphere of pure monetary theory that Hume the economist is best remembered nowadays. The monetary literature of the mid-18th century was a mixture of mercantilist and classical elements: while most writers still tended to stress the desirability of money because of its intrinsic worth and its stimulating effects on trade, by Hume's time the basic elements of the quantity theory were also generally appreciated. The essay "Of Money" begins with a clear distinction between money and wealth — a distinction towards which the mercantilist pamphleteers themselves had been groping ever since the days of Thomas Mun. This is followed by a discussion (pp. 34–35) of the relationship between the level of money and the international aspect of economic development: Hume, in attempting to discredit the mercantilists, maintains that an upswing in the quantity of money may prove harmful to a nation in its foreign commercial dealings; in this connection, however, he tends to overlook the fact that an influx of treasure may not be due to a windfall or to restrictive trade practices, but to an increase in the productivity of export industries, so that prices need not necessarily rise. The "two observations" which comprise the bulk of the essay are much more constructive than this initial argument: the first (pp. 36–40) concerns the relationship between money and the wealth of a community, where — by using the historical evidence of the influx of American silver into Europe — he demonstrates the benefits that flow from a slowly increasing quantity of money and, as a consequence, a gently rising price-level; "The good policy of the magistrate consists only in keeping it [i.e., the quantity of money], if possible, still encreasing; because, by that means, he keeps alive a spirit of industry in the nation, and encreases the stock of labour, in which consists all real power and riches"(pp. 39–40). Here, then, for the first time in English economic literature, is a succinctly worded theory of controlled inflation, with all its unresolved ambiguities. The second observation (pp. 40–46) deals with the relationship between money and the wealth (and power) of the state: after emphasising the transformation which takes place in a country under the impact of growing specialization, Hume contrasts the weakness of most administrations where primitive barter still prevails with the efficiency and vigour of governments in more advanced exchange-economies, where the sovereign "may draw money by his taxes from every part of the state; and what he receives, goes farther in every purchase and payment" (p. 45). Such pointed emphasis on the economic implications of the growth of a money economy was most unusual for the mid-18th century.[17]

This general discussion of monetary theory is followed by the famous essay "Of Interest", which was "in some respects far in advance of much that was written afterwards".[18] In Hume's time interest was still generally regarded as a purely monetary phenomenon, and an increase in the quantity of money so as to reduce the cost of borrowing was being repeatedly advocated. Such an increase, Hume asserted, would only raise prices and would not affect the amount of wealth available for loans, since rates of interest alter only in accordance with changes in the supply of and the demand for real savings, which, in their turn, are conditioned by the pace of economic progress and "changes in manners and customs" (p. 46).[19] This he demonstrates by contrasting conditions in a self-sufficing agrarian economy, where the prevailing rigid class-structure helps to create a scarcity of capital so that high interest rates prevail, with a competitive exchange economy, where trade promotes frugality and the accumulation of large net additions to the supply of real wealth, so that further investment and industrial growth are encouraged, leading eventually to a fall in rates of interest (pp. 49–56). Nor, in his opinion, is this analysis weakened by the historical accounts of great treasure inflows, for example, into ancient Rome or 16th century Spain: although interest rates admittedly fell immediately after the Roman and Spanish conquests, that was due to the new money being concentrated in a few hands which had the same effect as an increase in economic activity by raising the level of loanable funds; but the habits of those societies had not really altered and thus, as the previous relationships were restored between the supply and demand for loans, so also did the rates start to rise again. Hume's survey, therefore, of the phenomenon of interest, while it does not conform to any single doctrinal school of thought, contains socio-economic reasoning of the first order.

The most important element in the doctrinal defeat of the mercantilist creed of foreign trade control was the formulation of what Viner has labelled "the theory of the self-regulating mechanism of international specie distribution",[20] of which the fullest exposition before the 19th century in

England is to be found in Hume's essay "Of the Balance of Trade". The substance of Hume's argument is well known, and, in essence, consists of applying the quantity theory of money to foreign trade and in distinguishing between short- and long-period trends. If a country increases its supplies of precious metals by pursuing a favourable trade-balance, prices in that land rise and foreigners buy less from it. After a time, the value of the country's exports fall below the value of its imports and treasure moves out to make up the difference. Then, as internal stocks of money dwindle, prices fall and the export trade recovers. Thus, since trade and treasure are akin to water in two connected vessels, constantly seeking their natural levels, a favourable balance cannot continue indefinitely and government intervention towards that end is at best futile. A country's supply of precious metals is inevitably in proportion to its actual needs in business and industry, so that "a government has great reason to preserve with care its people and its manufactures. Its money, it may safely trust to the course of human affairs, without fear or jealousy" (p. 77).[21]

Hume's views on foreign trade were elaborated further in the short essay "Of the Jealousy of Trade",[22] in which he is primarily concerned with the dangers inherent in the mercantilist assumption that protection is essential if economic expansion elsewhere is not to undermine the domestic level of employment and industry. He rejects such a parochial attitude out of hand and points to international division of labour as the natural foundation of economic prosperity — progress in one country is not a hindrance but beneficial to others: "I shall therefore venture to acknowledge that, not only as a man, but as a British subject, I pray for the flourishing commerce of Germany, Spain, Italy, and even France itself. I am at least certain, that Great Britain, and all those nations, would flourish more, did their sovereigns and ministers adopt such enlarged and benevolent sentiments towards each other" (p. 82). Such cosmopolitan reflections were to have a pronounced impact on British public opinion and, in the sphere of practical policy, paved the way towards the Anglo-French commercial treaty of 1786.[23]

In the first part of his essay "Of Taxes" (pp. 83–86), Hume reconciled the "utility of poverty" views of his mercantilist predecessors with the subsequent arguments of the classical school that any tax affecting labour will reduce its effective supply, by emphasizing the potential stimulating results of *moderate* taxes and the possible dangers flowing from excessive impositions. Writers like John Law and William Temple were fond of suggesting that every additional tax creates a new ability on the part of the taxpayer to bear it. Hume readily admits that, since natural difficulties often stimulate "the spirit of industry", artificial burdens (like taxes) may also have the same result; but the stimulating effect of difficulty operates only within certain limits, and continually rising taxes must eventually "destroy industry, by producing despair".[24] The second part of this essay (pp. 86–89) consists of a criticism of the physiocratic contention that all taxes fall ultimately upon land, so that "it were better to lay them originally there, and abolish every duty upon consumptions". Hume develops, instead,

148

a diffusion theory of incidence and points out that, although "every man . . . is desirous of pushing off from himself the burden of any tax, which is imposed, and of laying it upon others: But as every man has the same inclination, and is upon the defensive; no set of men can be supposed to prevail altogether in this contest" (p. 87).

The essay "Of Public Credit" is a sociological and political tract as well as a study of fiscal policy. The opening section (pp. 90–96) summarises the merits and drawbacks of public credit: on the positive side, by providing a profitable outlet for idle funds, it encourages economic development; instead of investing their surplus resources in the land, "More men . . . with large stocks and incomes, may naturally be supposed to continue in trade, where there are public debts; and this, it must be owned, is of some advantage to commerce, by diminishing its profits, promoting circulation, and encouraging industry" (p. 94). On the negative side, however, public debts lead to a migration of people towards the capital (a trend which may result in political instability and civil disorders), have a dangerous inflationary effect, encourage foreign control of domestic assets, and promote the growth of an idle class of rentiers. The larger part of the essay (pp. 97–107) is concerned with the specific problem of Britain's continually rising national debt: the dishonest behaviour of politicians and the public's gullibility and forgetfulness are coupled together as the main reason why this deficit is likely to go on growing until the repudiation stage is reached; not only are there many political and social dangers inherent in such a situation, but the inevitable repercussions on economic life must also prove detrimental. Hume's estimate of the national debt's future progress proved fairly accurate, yet, in predicting ultimate bankruptcy — although, cautiously, assigning no precise date! — he seriously underrated the country's capacity to continue bearing such a massive financial burden.

IV

Very much more detailed in treatment than any of the other essays reproduced in this collection, is Hume's tract "Of the Populousness of Ancient Nations," which ranks as an important milestone in the empirical treatment of population questions prior to Malthus. Hume's main purpose in this study is to refute the widespread belief that there had been a steady fall in the world's population since ancient times,[25] by examining a variety of theoretical considerations and stressing, especially, the close relationship between population growth and economic progress.

Hume was clearly aware of the tremendous difficulties in the way of making such an historical comparison because of the very imperfect demographic data available even in his own day, while "the facts delivered by ancient authors, are either so uncertain or so imperfect as to afford us nothing positive in this matter" (p. 147). All that he wished to demonstrate was that the prevalent view about the greater populousness of the ancient world should be regarded with a considerable degree of scepticism. Yet, although he was able to make little or no use of vital statistics, his commentary is based on a very thorough study of all the classical texts he could lay his hands on in the Advocates' Library, Edinburgh; the whole essay, in fact, is a monument to its author's painstaking delvings into "the realms of gold".

The first major difference in the domestic situations of the two periods, as far as Hume could see, was the widespread prevalence of slavery in ancient times and its absence from modern Europe. He finds sufficient evidence in the writings of Plutarch and Seneca to infer that there was only a negligible amount of reproduction among the slave communities of Greece and Rome, and that the institution was, therefore, a factor limiting "the populousness of mankind and that its place is much better supplied by the practice of hired servants" (p. 124). Moreover, the influence of modern monasticism and vows of chastity seem less harmful to propagation than the ancient habit of exposing children during infancy; and, although Hume adds a damning note on the drawbacks of foundling hospitals, he feels justified in coming to the general conclusion that, as far as domestic life and manners are concerned, the 18th century is superior to the ancient world.

The political customs and institutions of both ages are then examined in order to "weigh their influence in retarding and forwarding the propagation of mankind" (p. 128). Since Hume believed that "small commonwealths" and "equality of fortune" were closely related factors stimulating population growth, it seemed at first sight that the city-state arrangements of ancient Greece and the early Roman Republic were conducive to that end, while in modern times similar circumstances were to be found only in Holland and Switzerland, where, in spite of unfavourable geographical conditions, relatively large populations prevailed. On the other hand, the perpetual wars and constant civil disturbances of the ancient city-states more than neutralized these advantages: "In those days there was no medium between a severe, jealous Aristocracy, ruling over discontented subjects; and a turbulent, factious, tyrannical Democracy" (pp. 142–143).

In addition, economic life in the ancient world was never in such a flourishing state as in mid-18th century Europe. In this connection, Hume mentions the very limited variety of garments available to the ancient peoples, the negligible flow of long-distance trade — indicated by the many examples of high interest rates and profits —, the imperfections of navigational techniques, and the absence of any marked degree of urban specialization or large scale commercial farming on a systematic basis; in contrast, he lists the positive influence of modern developments, such as mechanical innovations, instruments of credit, effective postal arrangements, the oceanic discoveries, and — most important of all — the far greater security of persons and property, which enables capital to accumulate and industrial and commercial populations to flourish.

"Thus, upon comparing the whole, it seems impossible to assign any just reason, why the world should have been more populous in ancient than in modern times. The equality of property among the ancients, liberty, and the small divisions of their states, were indeed circumstances favourable to the propagation of mankind: But their wars were more bloody and destructive, their governments more factious and unsettled, commerce and manufactures more feeble and languishing, and the general police more loose and irregular. These latter disadvantages seem to form a sufficient counterbalance to the former advantages; and rather favour the opposite opinion to that which commonly prevails with regard to this subject" (p. 147).

In the second half of the essay Hume examines the unreliability of ancient reports and statistics. He shows how all numbers in the classical manuscripts have been subjected to much corruption, while too few enumerations were made of any significant tract of country to afford a large enough view for purposes of comparison; but even in the estimates of city-republics, the slave populations were seldom included, leaving "as great uncertainty as ever with regard to the populousness even of single cities" (p. 148). He has an easy task in revealing the contradictions of ancient authorities quite apart from the uncertain readings of manuscripts. He finds rampant exaggeration, and he deduces, for example, that Greece in the days of the small republics, maintained no more than 1,290,000, "no mighty number, nor exceeding what may be found at present in Scotland, a country of not much greater extent, and very indifferently peopled" (p. 161). A detailed examination follows of the figures assigned to particular cities in antiquity, with Athens and Rome receiving special attention.[26]

There follows a rather ingenious argument (pp. 171–173) in which Hume suggests that, while climatic changes may not be essential for population growth, on the other hand, a larger concentration of people in any given area may lead to significant improvements in the weather. Several ancient and modern authors are quoted to support the view that Europe had become more temperate since classical times, for, with closer settlement and a more intensive use of resources, many of the forest-belts had been cleared, "which formerly threw a shade upon the earth, and kept the rays of the sun from penetrating to it".[27]

The essay concludes (pp. 174–183) with comparisons of the estimated populations of "all the countries which are the scene of ancient and modern history", and a detailed examination of a celebrated passage from Plutarch[28] which helps to reinforce the impression that there is little "foundation for the complaint of the present emptiness and desolation of the world" and suggests that "The humour of blaming the present, and admiring the past, is strongly rooted in human nature, and has an influence even on persons endued with the profoundest judgment and most extensive learning" (p. 183).

There are many comments scattered about this essay which have a distinct Malthusian flavour.[29] Not only does it abound in remarks such as "Wherever there are most happiness and virtue, and the wisest institutions, there will also be most people" (p. 112), but the restraining influences of "poverty and necessity" are frequently stressed — otherwise, "Almost every man who thinks he can maintain a family will have one; and the human species, at this rate of propagation, would more than double every generation" (p. 111). Yet, although Hume only deals with one aspect of the subject, his attitude towards the population problem is both broader and somewhat less Utopian than Malthus' analysis, while many of his inferences are thoroughly un-Malthusian, such as the following suggestion favouring direct intervention to stimulate an upswing in numbers: ". . . as there is in all men, both male and female, a desire and power of generation, more active than is ever universally exerted, the restraints, which they lie under, must proceed from some difficulties in their situation, which it belongs to a wise legislature carefully to observe and remove" (p. 111).

This essay, then, "Of the Populousness of Ancient Nations," represents one of the first serious excursions into the field of economic history, and, as a consequence, Hume himself becomes the forerunner of a whole series of economists who, ever since his day, have been repeatedly urging their historian colleagues to place strict limits on the dependability of their research materials.

V

By 18th century standards David Hume was not a prolific letter-writer. Nevertheless, he maintained a lively correspondence with a host of friends and disciples, both in Britain and across the Channel. Posterity is greatly indebted to his executors who, for some inexplicable reason, failed to carry out the express wish that his private papers were to be destroyed. The extant letters not only shed valuable light on the various facets of Hume's personality, but also help to clarify many aspects of his more formal writings and to show how some of his economic ideas evolved and were subsequently modified. In the section of the work under review devoted to relevant extracts from Hume's correspondence, the passages have been placed in their proper chronological sequence and coupled with the appropriate replies, while the Editor has gone one step further than Professor Greig by translating the letters which Hume wrote to and received from his physiocrat and other French associates.[30]

The opening item comes from a letter to Montesquieu written in April, 1749, which contains the first statement of Hume's quantity-theory specie-flow doctrine,[31] while, in the same letter he also counters Montesquieu's arguments against the creation of public debts by suggesting that the practice may have some advantages;[32] both of these points, as has been already noticed, were to be subsequently elaborated in the economic essays.

The second letter, written some six months later, is a lengthy one from James Oswald criticizing the manuscript of the "Balance of Trade" essay and showing that the price-effects postulated in the quantity-theory specie-flow doctrine are not as inevitable as Hume suggests if account is also taken of possible income-effects.[33] In the reply to Oswald, which follows, Hume admits the validity of this assertion and was to incorporate it into his own analysis of the mechanism of adjustment.[34]

There follows an exchange of views between Hume and that energetic pamphleteer Josiah Tucker (1758) on commercial relations between "poor" and "rich" countries. Hume defends the stand he had previously taken in the essay "Of Money": although a country with an extensive trade enjoys numerous advantages over a relatively undeveloped area, yet, with a rising price-level, it may eventually lose its leadership to such a poor country where relatively low commodity and labour costs prevail; in this manner, Hume asserted, a general law of growth and decay may be said to operate between nations. Tucker, on the other hand, using an embryo theory of comparative costs as the basis for his reply, suggests that, although in nature things undermine themselves by growing over-large, no such law prevails among trading countries. Hume, he insists, has overstressed the importance of low prices, but these "will advance in price, in proportion to the advancement of every thing else. And therefore the grand advantage which . . . the poor country [is supposed] to have over the rich, in point of cheapness of wages, and of raw materials, will grow less and less every day. In short, though both countries may still go on in their respective improvements, the poor country, according to my apprehension, can never overtake the rich, unless it be through the fault and mismanagement of the latter" (pp. 204–205). This exchange induced Hume to abandon some of his earlier views on the relationship between poor and rich countries and to insert a significant paragraph in his essay "Of the Jealousy of Trade" — published a few months later — in which he points out that, owing to the "diversity of geniuses, climates, and soils", no country, so long as it remains industrious, need fear that its "neighbours will improve to such a degree in every art and manufacture, as to have no demand from them" (p. 79).[35]

In many respects the most interesting and important item in this collection consists of an interchange of arguments between Hume and Turgot (1766–67). Although Turgot by no means accepted all the implications attached to the concept of a *produit net* which Quesnay had formulated in his *Tableau Economique*,[36] he was an ardent exponent of the physiocratic view that all taxes are ultimately shifted to land. Thus, this correspondence gave Hume an opportunity to clarify the case he had already made against this notion in his essays, and, especially, to counter the assertion that entrepreneurial activity in commerce and manufacturing does not yield a taxable surplus.[37] Turgot, however, neatly side-stepped the issue and never conceded the cogency of Hume's reasoning. As Professor Rotwein remarks, "In view of the fundamental differences in perspective between Hume and the physiocrats, it is not surprising to find that the exchange scarcely provided a basis for a clear joining, much less a resolution, of the issue" (p. lxxxii).

Hume's growing exasperation with the French school is clearly reflected in a letter to the Abbé Morellet (July, 1769). The Abbé had sent him a prospectus of a proposed *Dictionnaire du Commerce*, and, after praising its scope and offering some additional information on types of currency in use in the American colonies, Hume adds: "I see that, in your prospectus, you take care not to disoblige your economists [i.e., Quesnay and the physiocrats] by any declaration of your sentiments; in which I commend your prudence. But I hope that in your work you will thunder them, and crush them, and pound them, and reduce them to dust and ashes! They are, indeed, the set of men the most chimerical and most arrogant that now exist . . . . I wonder what could engage our friend, M. Turgot, to herd among them" (pp. 215–216).

The correspondence between Hume and Adam Smith is generally well known,[38] although, in view of their close friendship and high regard for each other, there is surprisingly little discussion in it on specifically economic problems. However, to round off this collection, a letter dated 1st April, 1776, to Adam Smith is included, in which Hume expresses obvious pleasure at the publication of the *Wealth of Nations*, but adds one or two cautionary remarks on Smith's theory of rent.[39]

VI

There can be little doubt that, although Hume's economic writings, unlike Adam Smith's, comprise only a small portion of his published works and are much more informally presented, in a number of respects their treatment is more subtle and successful than what is to be found in the *Wealth of Nations*. By regarding history and psychology as the focal points of his analysis, Hume was able to contribute a great deal towards an awareness of the significance of these subjects in all studies of economic activity. Quantitatively, Smith's work contains much more historical and psychological material, yet he seldom looks upon the subjective aspects of human behaviour as being historical variables, while the psychological elements usually play a subsidiary rôle.

In the details of their work, Hume, in many particulars, was also the more penetrating of the two writers. Thus, while Adam Smith's constant stress on humanity's innate disposition to "truck and barter" is comparable with Hume's account of "the progress of opulence", yet the former's treatment is much more static in approach, especially when he discusses the development of international specialization; moreover, he regards the early progress of commerce as sometimes having a dislocating effect on an economy,[40] whereas Hume looked upon the advance of trade as being essential to both industrial and agricultural expansion. Similarly, Smith's theory of money[41] is inferior to that of Hume's; it admittedly contains much valuable descriptive material, but is largely analytical in character and never closely linked to the earlier account of the evolution of an exchange economy;[42] Hume, on the other hand, in his essay "Of Money", never loses sight of the general problem of economic growth and continually relates his analysis to a firm historical context.

Perhaps the strangest omission from the *Wealth of Nations* is Adam Smith's failure to recapitulate Hume's theory of the self-regulating mechanism of specie distribution in international trade, although he closely followed Hume's reasoning on most other aspects of the subject. This neglect by Smith of Hume's most valuable contribution to foreign trade analysis is all the more puzzling in view of the fact that in his university lectures he expounded with obvious approval a synopsis of his friend's observations on this very point.[43]

The sharpest distinction between Hume and Smith is to be found in their respective treatments of the question of capital accumulation. To Hume, the effective desire to save depends both on the opportunities which people have to improve their positions and on the means whereby they can earn their incomes; but, as far as Adam Smith was concerned, an intense desire to improve one's lot was universal, so that there seemed to be no reason whatsoever why all groups at all times should not be equally frugal.[44] In proceeding to discuss "stock lent at interest",[45] although Smith freely acknowledges his debt to "Mr. Hume", he takes over only the purely mechanical aspects of the latter's doctrine — i.e., that rates of interest are determined by the supply and demand for real capital — but does not adequately emphasize the importance of differentiating between ephemeral monetary influences on rates and those that reflect the long-term effects of economic progress.

Since it was Adam Smith who formulated the habit of abstracting theoretical issues from historical influences — a habit which was to become even more pronounced in the work of Ricardo and the later classical exponents — it is probably much easier to become doctrinaire through reading the *Wealth of Nations* than from a study of Hume's essays.

VII

While it is not difficult to appreciate the sheer intellectual brilliance of Hume's work — he was, indeed, the first distinguished man of letters to make a fortune from literature alone and still preserve his independence — the modern significance of his economic thought, particularly, goes very much further than that. Within recent years there has been an increasing tendency for economists to broaden the scope of their inquiries: the growing importance of problems connected with full employment and trade unionism, the contemporary concern about underdeveloped areas, the expanding activities of the state, and even the doctrines of imperfect competition, have all encouraged the use of concepts which go far beyond the orthodox classical treatment of value and distribution. Since all these questions are closely bound up with the ideological pressures of social change, the desirability of alternative systems, and the measurement of economic growth, they have resulted in a revived interest in history and psychology on the part of modern theorists. Consequently, because of their fundamental attempt to incorporate economics into a broader study of human experience, Hume's essays can still be re-read today with great profit.

His writings retain their freshness even on purely monetary issues — that most sophisticated branch of modern studies. His observations on the relationship between money and the wealth of a community are, in fact, an extremely clear analysis of the multiplier process,[46] while he fully anticipated the modern distinction between transient and long-run influences on capital returns.[47] Nor should his pertinent remarks be forgotten on the evils of a continually rising public debt, to which a gullible community can readily be made to acquiesce by the skilful manipulations of unprincipled politicians.[48]

Such gullibility, in Hume's opinion, stems directly from a strong irrational element frequently present in economic behaviour. Men often, he insisted, "act knowingly against their interest: For which reason the view of the greatest possible good does not always influence them".[49] This awareness that people may repeatedly adopt courses of action harmful to themselves is in refreshing contrast to the unrealistic psychological hedonism formulated by Jeremy Bentham and elaborated by Stanley Jevons and others; in fact, Hume's economic psychology is much more "modern" in its approach to the problem of utility than that of most British writers of the 19th and early 20th centuries, Alfred Marshall included.[50]

On the other hand, because of his belief that economic activity may prove intrinsically rewarding[51] and his assumption that possibilities exist for the economic advancement of all members of society, Hume was able to argue that the need to overcome difficulties serves as a spur to effort and thus is conducive ultimately to the raising of living standards.[52] Here again, therefore, Hume's attitude is akin to the modern view that economic activity may well embrace a conscious seeking out of difficulties, whereas the "disutility of effort" doctrine developed by Smith, Ricardo, and the classical school suggests that by nature man finds such activity irksome and disagreeable.[53]

In connection with the present deep interest in the problems of underdeveloped areas, Hume's views on international trading relationships have a particularly modern flavour. No nation need fear such competition from "poorer" areas since the heterogeneity of factor-endowments enables resources to be diverted to other branches of production; in fact, the progress of more backward regions — by promoting a wider spread of resources — creates a buffer which helps to insulate the domestic economy from sudden external shocks.[54]

In many directions, therefore, Hume's writings penetrate deeper than those of some of his more oft-quoted successors. The day may well come when teachers and students instinctively set back their time-charts from 1776 to 1752 and divide the history of economic thought into two main periods — before and after the work of David Hume.

NOTES

1. Address given to the Economic Society of South Africa, Cape Town Branch, on Friday, 1st June, 1956, and suggested by the appearance of *David Hume: Writings on Economics*, edited by Eugene Rotwein; Edinburgh: Thomas Nelson and Sons, 1955. Pp. cxi + 224. Price 30s. (Page references in the body of this paper allude to this publication.)

2. Harold J. Laski, *Political Thought in England from Locke to Bentham*, p. 118.

3. For instance, except for Hume himself, whom he tolerates rather than admires, Erich Roll, in his *History of Economic Thought*, has much more to say about economic thought in the Old Testament than in England during the first half of the 18th century; two other popular texts, L. H. Haney's *History of Economic Thought* and W. A. Scott's *The Development of Economics*, tend to skip the period altogether.

4. Even the excellent standard edition of the *Essays, Moral, Political and Literary* (edited by T. H. Green and T. H. Grose), first issued in 1875, has been apparently out of print since 1898.

5. See note 1.

6. cf. Mary Shaw Kuypers, *Studies in the Eighteenth Century Background of Hume's Empiricism*, Pt. II, chs. iv and v, and Gladys Bryson, *Man and Society: The Scottish Inquiry of the Eighteenth Century*, ch. v.

7. Incidentally, Hume's monumental and controversial *History of England* (1757–62) contains numerous discussions on economic issues, including strong arguments in favour of an unrestricted domestic trade and against government controls over wages and prices; references to relevant passages are given by Rotwein, pp. lxxix-lxxxi. See, also, Kuypers, *op. cit.*, Pt. II, ch. vii.

8. "Of Refinement in the Arts", p. 21 ff.

9. Hume modelled this argument on his chapter "Of Curiosity, or the Love of Truth" in the *Treatise*, Bk. II, Part III.

10. "Of Interest", p. 53.

11. His attitude towards the "labouring poor" and the vexed problem of idleness was in strong contrast to that of most other mid-18th century commentators (such as Josiah Tucker and Henry Fielding), who saw in the prevalence of such "idle pleasures" the fulfillment of an inborn craving.

12. " . . . notwithstanding the unconnected form of these little treatises, there runs through them a profound unity of thought, so that they indeed compose in a certain sense an economic system. They exhibit in full measure Hume's wonderful acuteness and subtlety . . . in combination with the breadth, the absence of prejudice, and the social sympathies which so eminently distinguish him; and they offer, besides, the charm of his easy and natural style and his rare power of lucid exposition"—J. K. Ingram, article "Political Economy", *Encyclopaedia Britannica*, 9th edition, Vol. XIX, p. 364.

"Written in essay form in a pellucid style, these discourses turned the searchlight of rational and historical inquiry upon problems of vast interest to an age that was slowly sloughing itself out of the moribund skin of mercantilism"—E. C. Mossner, *The Life of David Hume* (Nelson, 1954), p. 269. But, although Professor Mossner goes on to describe Hume as "a shrewd anticipator of Adam Smith", he can spare no more than two pages out of nearly 700 for an assessment of the economic writings in a work which purports to be a biographical consideration of Hume's intellectual activities.

13. In part, the tone of this section resembles the chapter "Of the Use and Benefit of Trade" in Nicholas Barbon's *A Discourse of Trade* (1690), although Hume does not fall into the mercantilist trap of suggesting "That Trade may be Assistant to the Inlarging of Empire" (pp. 23–24, Hollander ed.).

14. Sir Josiah Child and Bishop Berkeley were typical exponents of this attitude, while Bernard de Mandeville in *The Fable of the Bees* (1714), although he argued that wasteful expenditure was economically necessary, insisted on stressing the essential vileness of human nature.

15. This theme that there exists a startling correlation between economic development and cultural achievement, has been recently traced along historical lines by S. B. Clough, *The Rise and Fall of Civilization*, McGraw-Hill, N.Y., 1951, whose conclusions are at sharp variance with the theory of "challenge and response" put forward by Toynbee in *A Study of History*.

16. Some gaps and contradictions in this section of the essay are discussed by Prof. Rotwein (p. ciii); useful commentaries on Hume's treatment of the luxury issue as a whole are to be found in E. A. J. Johnson's *Predecessors of Adam Smith*, pp. 168–170, 295–297.

17. The most surprising omission from these economic essays is Hume's failure to develop anything approaching a comprehensive theory of value; nevertheless, some significant reflections on this subject are to be found scattered about, and one passage in the essay "Of Money", especially, displays a clear awareness of the relationship between supply and demand, and the influence of relative scarcity on prices—"It seems a maxim almost self-evident, that the prices of every thing depend on the proportion between commodities and money, and that any considerable alteration on either has the same effect, either of heightening or lowering the price. Encrease the commodities, they become cheaper; encrease the money, they rise in their value. As, on the other hand, a diminution of the former, and that of the latter, have contrary tendencies" (pp. 41–42).

18. Edmund Whittaker, *A History of Economic Ideas*, p. 534. See the paper by J. M. Low, "The Rate of Interest: British Opinion in the Eighteenth Century," *The Manchester School of Economic and Social Studies*, Vol. XXII, No. 2 (May, 1954).

19. The concept of interest as a consequence rather than as a cause of economic growth, had been suggested by Sir Dudley North in his *Discourses Upon Trade* as early as 1691: "it is not low Interest makes Trade, but Trade increasing, the Stock of the Nation makes Interest low" (p. 18. Hollander ed.); it is extremely unlikely, however, that Hume ever read North (see McCulloch's remarks in the Preface to *Early English Tracts on Commerce*, p. xii).

20. *Studies in the Theory of International Trade*, p. 74.

21. For an estimate of the significance of Hume's quantity theory specie-flow doctrine in the ideological transition from mercantilism to "classical capitalism", see E. O. Golob, *The "Isms"—A History and Evaluation*, Harper, N.Y., 1954, ch. i.

22. Published in 1758—i.e., six years after the other economic essays—in *Essays and Treatises on Several Subjects*, 2nd edn. It reflects Hume's final position on the free-trade issue; see section V, below, on the correspondence with Tucker.

23. Nearly two centuries before Hume wrote this essay, Jean Bodin in France

had also reflected on the heterogeneity of factor-endowments among nations—

> " . . . God with admirable foresight has arranged things well: for he has so divided his favours that there is no country in the world so fruitful that it does not lack many things. Which God seems to have done to keep all the subjects of his republic in friendship, or at least to prevent them from making war on each other for very long, being always dependent one upon another"— *Reply to the Paradoxes of Malestroit* (1569), in *Early Economic Thought* (ed. Monroe), p. 140.

But Bodin's voice had been drowned under a wave of restrictive mercantilist legislation. In England, in 1701, the anonymous author of *Considerations on the East-India Trade* had used international specialization as the basis for his arguments favouring a more liberal commercial policy; see the present writer's article on "A Neglected Forerunner of Adam Smith", *South African Journal of Economics,* December, 1955, pp. 299–314.

24. In his remarks here Hume also foreshadows Adam Smith's four canons that any tax should conform to the standards of justice, certainty, convenience, and economy.

25. In France, this argument had been popularized by Montesquieu, *L'Esprit des Lois* (1748), Bk. xxiii, whose views were being spread in Britain by the Rev. Robert Wallace; the latter had sent Hume a manuscript copy of his *Dissertation on the Numbers of Mankind in Antient and Modern Times,* and the printing of Hume's essay led the clergyman to have his own work published in 1753. For background material pertinent to the writing of this essay, see Hume's letters to John Clephane (April, 1750) and Gilbert Eliot (February, 1751), in J. Y. T. Greig (ed.), *Letters of David Hume,* Vol. I, p. 140, 152–153; in E. C. Mossner, *The Forgotten Hume,* pp. 105 ff., there is an account of the friendly spirit in which the debate with Wallace was conducted.

26. Hume apparently believed that the degree of urbanization at any period is limited to a maximum concentration of about 700,000 inhabitants; cities of that size, he argued, automatically check their own growth by stimulating expensive ways of living and extravagant luxuries, thereby "raising the price of all labour and commodities" and ultimately driving enterprise to smaller and cheaper places (cf. pp. 169–170).

27. He also points to a parallel trend in "our northern colonies in America" which "become more temperate, in proportion as the woods are felled" (p. 173).

28. Taken from one of the Pythian dialogues, *De defectu oraculorum,* which deals with prophecy and demonology and links the decline of the oracle with that of the population.

29. cf. James Bonar, *Theories of Population from Raleigh to Arthur Young,* pp. 165–177.

30. There remains the danger that future students of Hume's economic thought will tend to rely solely on these selections, ignoring the many discussions on economic topics in Hume's other letters —discussions which, though perhaps briefer and less compact than the ones reprinted here, remain important adjuncts to any balanced estimate of his contribution.

31. "It is difficult for a loss of balance to reach the point where it will do considerable harm to a nation . . . It does not seem that money, any more than water, can be raised or lowered anywhere much beyond the level it has in places where communication is open, but that it must rise and fall in proportion to the goods and labour contained in each state" (pp. 188–189).

32. "The merchants who have capital in the public funds keep but little money in their coffers for the needs of their business: they can dispose of this capital whenever they please to meet any demand. Consequently, this capital serves two ends: first, to yield them a fixed revenue: secondly, to advance their business; consequently the merchant is able to conduct his business with smaller profits on his goods, which is advantageous for trade" (p. 189).

33. "The increased quantity of money" (wrote Oswald) "would not necessarily increase the price of all labour and commoditys; because the increased quantity, not being confined to the home labour and commoditys, might, and certainly would, be sent to purchase both from foreign countreys, which importation, unless obstructed by arbitrary and absurd laws, would keep down the price of commoditys to the level of foreign countreys" (pp. 191–192).

34. This problem had been recognized as early as 1720 by Isaac Gervaise in his pamphlet, *The System or Theory of the Trade of the World* (reprinted by The Johns Hopkins Press, Baltimore, 1954; for a useful interpretation of the theoretical merits of Gervaise's *System,* see J. M. Letiche, "Isaac Gervaise on the International Mechanism of Adjustment", *Journal of Political Economy,* Vol. LX, No. 1, February, 1952, pp. 34–44); yet, it was not until the publication of Bertil Ohlin's *Inter-regional and International Trade* in 1931, that the income-effects on the pattern of foreign trade received detailed attention (see Ohlin, Part IV). On the Hume-Oswald correspondence, see the article by J. M. Low, "An Eighteenth Century Controversy in the Theory of Economic Progress", *The Manchester School of Economic and Social Studies,* Vol. XX, No. 3 (Sept., 1952), pp. 312–317.

35. Hume's complete renunciation of

protective tariffs in this essay also stems directly from his correspondence with Tucker. He had previously expressed the belief that, since a law of growth and decay operated between countries, their long-term interests must be opposed; and, on this basis, he had in fact made a concession to the tariff argument (cf. "Of the Balance of Trade" p. 76). Tucker, on the other hand, "never succeeded in seeing clearly or in absorbing Hume's exposure of the fallacies underlying his own system of economic thought."—Jacob Viner, reviewing R. L. Schuyler (ed.), *Josiah Tucker: a Selection from His Economic and Political Writings*, in *Journal of Political Economy*, Vol. 40 (June, 1932), pp. 416–418.

36. See Schumpeter's comments on the relationship between Turgot and the physiocrats, *History of Economic Analysis*, pp. 243–247, and, for a rather different interpretation, Gide and Rist, *A History of Economic Doctrines*, ch. i.

37. "I beg you also to consider, that, besides the Proprietors of Land and the labouring Poor, there is in every civilised Community a very large and a very opulent Body who employ their Stocks in Commerce and who enjoy a great Revenue from their giving Labour to the poorer sort. I am perswaded that in France and England the Revenue of this kind is much greater than that which arises from Land: For besides Merchants, properly speaking, I comprehend in this Class all Shop-Keepers and Master-Tradesmen of every Species. Now it is very just, that these should pay for the Support of the Community, which can only be where Taxes are lay'd on Consumptions. There seems to me no Pretence for saying that this order of Men are necessitated to throw their Taxes on the Proprietors of Land, since their Profits and Income can surely bear Retrenchment" (p. 209).

38. See W. R. Scott, *Adam Smith as Student and Professor*, section P, and Greig's edition of Hume's *Letters*, esp. Vol. II.

39. On Hume's criticism of Smith's ideas about rent, see Leo Rogin's comment, *The Meaning and Validity of Economic Theory*, p. 83. According to Hume, Smith was a "lazy correspondent" with a strong aversion to writing letters; cf. Keynes' review-article of *Adam Smith as Student and Professor*, *Economic History*, Vol. III, No. 13 (Feb., 1938), p. 45.

40. *Wealth of Nations*, ed. Cannan, Modern Library edn., p. 392.

41. *Ibid.*, Bk. II, ch. ii.

42. *Ibid.*, Bk. I, ch. iv.

43. "Mr. Hume published some essays showing the absurdity of these and other such doctrines. He proves very ingeniously that money must always bear a certain proportion to the quantity of commodities in every country; that whenever money is accumulated beyond the proportion of commodities in any country, the price of goods will necessarily rise; that this country will be undersold at the foreign market, and consequently the money must depart into other nations; but on the contrary whenever the quantity of money falls below the proportion of goods, the price of goods diminishes, the country undersells others in foreign markets, and consequently money returns in great plenty. Thus money and goods will keep near about a certain level in every country. Mr. Hume's reasoning is exceedingly ingenious"—*Lectures of Adam Smith*, ed. Cannan, p. 197. Jacob Viner, *op. cit.*, p. 87, declares the omission of this theory from Smith's published work to be "one of the mysteries of the history of economic thought".

I am greatly indebted to my colleague, Mr. W. L. Taylor, for bringing this point to my notice and for enabling me to study his thesis, prepared for the London School of Economics, on "Francis Hutcheson and David Hume as Predecessors of Adam Smith".

44. " . . . the principle which prompts to save, is the desire of bettering our condition, a desire which, though generally calm and dispassionate, comes with us from the womb, and never leaves us till we go into the grave. In the whole interval which separates those two moments, there is scarce perhaps a single instant in which any man is so perfectly and completely satisfied with his situation, as to be without any wish of alteration or improvement of any kind . . . in the greater part of men, taking the whole course of their life at an average, the principle of frugality seems not only to predominate, but to predominate very greatly"—*Wealth of Nations*, pp. 324–325.

45. *Ibid.*, Bk. II, ch. iv.

46. "Of Money", pp. 36–40; an even more detailed treatment of the multiplier process is to be found in Richard Cantillon's *Essai sur la Nature du Commerce en Général* (1755), ed. Higgs, pp. 163–167.

47. "Of Interest", pp. 55–58.

48. "Of Public Credit", pp. 103–107.

49. *A Treatise of Human Nature*, Everyman's Ed., Vol. II, p. 129.

50. It was not until 1913 that any theorist of prominence returned to Hume's argument that the notion of utility need not imply a hedonistic theory of desire; writing in *The Economics of Enterprise*, which he published that year, H. J. Davenport roundly asserted that "The utility of an object need mean nothing more, and should be taken to mean nothing more, than one way of expressing the simple fact that the object is desired" (p. 99). For a considerable time thereafter, however, this was a solitary cry from the other side of the Atlantic.

51. "There is no craving or demand of the human mind more constant and insatiable than that for exercise and employment; and this desire seems the foundation of most of our passions and pursuits. De-

prive a man of all business and serious occupation, he runs restless from one amusement to another"—"Of Interest", p. 53.

52. In this connection, Hume contrasted the attitude towards economic activity on the part of peoples living in tropical and temperate zones: "What is the reason", he asks, "why no people, living between the tropics, could ever yet attain to any art or civility, or reach even any police in their government, and any military discipline; while few nations in the temperate climates have been altogether deprived of these advantages? It is probable that one cause of this phenomenon is the warmth and equality of weather in the torrid zone, which render clothes and houses less requisite for the inhabitants, and thereby remove, in part, that necessity, which is the great spur to industry and invention"—"Of Commerce", pp. 17–18.

53. Of course, they went a step further and applied this argument to their theory of value: "The real price of every thing", Adam Smith asserted, "what every thing really costs to the man who wants to acquire it, is the toil and trouble of acquiring it"—*Wealth of Nations,* p. 30.

54. cf. "Of the Jealousy of Trade", pp. 79–80.

7.

JOSEPH J. SPENGLER

Duke University

The Physiocrats

and Say's

Law of Markets

It has ever been man's custom, when a new gospel appears, to discover foretokenings of this gospel in the works of prophets who have gone before. In compliance with this custom, economists have discovered inklings of Lord Keynes's "general theory" in the writings of Veblen, Marx, Proudhon, Malthus, and others. It is not my intention to add to this list of prophets. It is my purpose, rather, to describe in some detail the physiocratic theory of consumption or expenditure and to indicate how this theory, together with the associated theory of production, both anticipated and contributed to the formulation of the Say-Mill "Law of Markets." This so-called law, in turn, gave a direction to economic analysis, one unintended outcome of which was Lord Keynes's "general theory." In a sense, therefore, it is in the physiocratic conception of circular flow that Say's law and Lord Keynes's theory had their origin, even as did Marx's scheme of "simple reproduction."

Discussion of consumption is probably as ancient as the art of articulation. Classic and medieval treatments of this subject ran largely in terms of the normative and the (closely associated) political, in terms of what was hurtful and what was beneficial and in terms anticipatory of the later distinction between "productive" and "unproductive." Such change in emphasis

Reprinted from *The Journal of Political Economy*, LIII (September, December 1945), 193–211, 314–47, slightly enlarged, by permission of The University of Chicago Press.

as the early modern period witnessed was essentially toward the political rather than toward the economic. Not until the close of the seventeenth century was attention focused upon the essentially economic aspects of consumption and not until the latter half of the eighteenth century was consumption examined in terms of circuit flow.

Prior to the nineteenth century, most of the discussion of consumption had to do with "luxury," with its role, its effects, and its control. The development of the town economy and the expansion of commerce, however, thrust two questions to the fore in the eighteenth century, if not earlier. Is the prospect of consumption and enjoyment, especially of comforts and luxuries, essential to the exercise of effort, skill, and ingenuity by the working and the undertaking classes? Is the expansion of production contingent upon the development of consumption, particularly of mass consumption? Or does the creation of goods and services proceed apace in essential independence of their distribution and consumption?

These questions were raised by a number of writers who antedated the physiocrats and were later considered by both their critics and their defenders. It is true that many seventeenth- and eighteenth-century English writers emphasized the virtuousness of frugality, thrift, saving, and accumulation, those who condemned hoarding doing so chiefly because of its supposed adverse effect upon trade; and that many also subscribed to the opinion that low wages are more favorable to industry than are high wages.[1] Yet free spending and consumption had advocates, especially in the eighteenth century. Consumption was described both as the real end of, and as a principal stimulus to, economic activity. By providing a market for goods and services, consumption quickened trade and economic activity in general; and by furnishing the prospect of enjoyment and pleasure, it prompted men to work and otherwise to augment production. Most of these writers therefore opposed sumptuary controls.[2]

Of the French writers who antedated the physiocrats, none emphasized the economic role of consumption more than did Boisguillebert (1646–1714), precursor of Adam Smith, anticipator of Quesnay, and exponent of laissez faire, who traced most of the economic ills of the French masses to underconsumption, which (he believed) had its origin in extreme economic inequality.[3] Consumption, he said, is prerequisite to production in two ways: (a) unless men are amply rewarded with goods and services, they will not be disposed to exercise much effort and skill; (b) unless there is adequate (i.e., mass) consumption, unless the vast majority are "placed in a condition . . . . to be able to procure all their necessities, and even superfluities," there will not be a sufficient market to absorb all products at prices high enough to encourage their production. "Consumption and revenue are one and the same thing." And it is by "persons of small means," who constitute the "greatest number," that the "greatest consumption" is and must be provided. The poor man spends his écu "a hundred times," while the rich man, who hoards his money for months and years and thus commits a "theft" against "king and . . . . State," spends it once or not at all. Whence, if there is to be sufficient consumption to assure a maximum of prosperity, the poor must be relieved of their taxes and provided with a much greater share of "true wealth" (i.e., "a full enjoyment . . . . of the necessaries . . . . [and] all the superfluities").[4]

Less humanitarian, less infused with the economic importance of mass consumption, and more centered about the question of luxury were the views of J. F. Melon, Montesquieu, and Cantillon regarding the role of consumption. Melon opposed sumptuary legislation and described luxury as an inevitable concomitant of progress, as a necessary stimulus to the exercise of productive effort and ingenuity, and as an essential source of employment.[5] Montesquieu expressed a common opinion when he described luxurious expenditure as essential to the maintenance of the poor wherever, as in monarchies and aristocracies, inequality prevailed; for under these circumstances many would be without livelihood if they could not minister to the wants of the wealthy. "Were the rich not to spend their money freely, the poor would starve."[6] He also characterized the production and sale of superfluities as essential to the development of agriculture and to the stimulation of population growth in countries where the land was not divided into small and equal portions. For the cultivators of land will not produce above their own needs unless they "have a desire of enjoying superfluities," which "they can receive only from the artificer."[7]

According to Cantillon, the landed proprietors "alone are independent"; theirs alone is the power of the purse. Upon them are dependent both the "hired" workers and the "undertakers," by whom all "exchange and circulation" are conducted. He did not emphasize the role of consumption in general, but he insisted, in consistence with his theory of the economic dominance of the landowners, that upon their fancies, fashions, and modes of living depended both the use to which land was put and the amount of subsistence available for the support of others than landowners.[8] He drew attention, also, to the circulatory character of the economic process[9] and to the role of the "entrepreneur." Cantillon's views reappear in part in the works of (among others) Condillac,[10] whom several of the physiocrats (Le Trosne and Baudeau) criticized, and G. Garnier, who, although the translator of Adam Smith, long upheld certain opinions of the physiocrats.[11] In one respect, however, Garnier's opinion resembled Montesquieu's rather than Cantillon's or Quesnay's; for he made the extension of cultivation depend upon the landowners' feeling a need for more of the products and services of other classes.[12] Cantillon did not emphasize this point, whereas Quesnay supposed that the landed proprietors automatically increased their disbursements as their revenues expanded.

None of the prephysiocratic writers developed what may properly be called a rounded theory of consumption, for none had a sufficiently clear conception of the essentially circular and continuous character of the economic process. Because none of these writers resolved economic life into its two component streams — that of goods and that of money, each moving in an opposite direction, none devoted adequate attention to the determinants of the behavior of these two streams. This the physiocrats attempted, only to fail in part — largely because of their angleworm theory of production and their disregard of the entrepreneurial function. Even so, their analysis revealed the circularity of the economic process and posed problems which led to the formulation of Say's law of markets and prepared the way for both Marx's scheme of flow and that now associated with the name of Lord Keynes.

A. QUESNAY'S THEORY OF PRODUCTION [13]

The physiocratic theory of production is important because of the restrictions which it imposes upon the physiocratic theory of consumption. This theory of production consists of three parts: (*a*) that relating to agriculture, fishing, and mining, which alone are described as reproductive (or productive),[14] i.e. capable of yielding a *net product;* (*b*) that relating to *sterile* employments, which are incapable of yielding a net product; and (*c*) that relating to the activities of those who are supported out of the net product of the extractive industries.

Quesnay incorporated the physiocratic theory of production, together with the associated theory of commodity circulation, in the *Tableau économique*, one of the three great inventions, declared Mirabeau, which give stability to political societies and bind them together. Writing and money are the other two. Though in after years the *Tableau* was ridiculed, Marx judged it "the most brilliant idea of which political economy had hitherto been guilty," and he evolved out of it an improved version to facilitate analysis of the structure of capitalism.[15]

Quesnay's abbreviated *Tableau*[16] summarizes, in terms of annual aggregates, reproduction and distribution in an extensive agricultural kingdom (i.e., France) with a fully developed agriculture and a population of 30 million, who subsist "avec aisance, conformément à leur état." This population is divided into three classes: the *productive*, which includes those engaged in agriculture, fishing, and mining; the *sterile*, which includes manufacturers, artisans, distributors of commodities, artists, and members of the liberal professions, together with the servants of this class; the *proprietary*, which includes landed proprietors and others paid or supported immediately out of proprietary revenue (e.g., religious personnel; the sovereign, together with the administrative, military, and other personnel in the service of the state).[17] The productive class comprises half the population, and the sterile and proprietary classes, one-fourth each.[18] The population is equipped with 130 million arpents of land of varying quality fitted for cultivation, in so far as possible, by past *avances foncières*. Agricultural equipment (*avances primitives*) worth 10 billion livres is at the disposal of the agricultural class. This equipment, together with annual advances of 2 billion livres, enables the farming population to maintain agricultural output (i.e., reproduction) at a maximum level of 5 billion livres and to supply the proprietary and sterile classes with a sufficiency of subsistence and raw materials. The components of the *Tableau* and their significance are treated in greater detail below.[19]

Gross and net reproduction (i.e., production) in agriculture is governed by three kinds of advances, the productive effect of any one of which is conditioned by the state of the others:[20] *avances annuelles, avances primitives,* and *avances foncières.* The annual advances include outlays for the preparation of the soil, for seed, planting, cultivation, and harvesting, for the shelter of domestic animals,[21] and for the support of workers engaged in agriculture. The primitive advances consist of the durable instruments of production required in agriculture — tools, machinery, cattle, work-animals, etc. The *avances foncières* represent the various outlays that have been made in the past by the proprietor of the landed property, or by its previous owners, to suit the land for cultivation, e.g., clearing, leveling, drainage, plantations, hedges, buildings. While there can be practically no reproduction unless annual advances are made, their effectiveness in evoking crops with exchange value is conditioned by the amount of past primitive advances, for these, if adequate, permit economy in the use of annual advances (especially of those for labor), augment and conserve annual output, and improve its quality. The productive effectiveness of both annual and primitive advances is governed, in turn, by the degree to which the land has been fitted for agriculture by past *avances foncières;* if these have been deficient or not maintained, crop yields suffer accordingly.[22]

The ratio of annual advances to primitive advances and (presumably) to *avances foncières* varies with type of crop and condition of soil, the mode of cultivation being given. Normally and on the average in a well-developed agricultural economy, such as is described in the *Tableau,* the ratio of primitive to annual advances is 5 to 1. It is supposed, furthermore, that the cultivator must recover each year, besides his annual advances, a 10 per cent[23] gross return on his primitive advances; otherwise primitive advances will not be kept up, and annual reproduction will shrink in volume. The physiocrats did not indicate with equal precision the relative magnitude of the *avances foncières* or the return expected thereon. As a rule, however, they supposed that two-fifths of the annual reproduction is normally distributed to the landed proprietor, of which return not much more than one-third may safely by appropriated for the support of state and church. Baudeau fixed at one-third the proportion of the revenue (= net product) which must be devoted to the maintenance, renewal, and amelioration of the *avances foncières.*[24] The continuance of reproduction at a level of 5, therefore, calls each year for annual advances of 2, and outlays of 1 and about 0.67, respectively, in the form of *avances primitives* and *avances foncières.*

Given annual advances of 2 billion and primitive advances of 10 billion livres, Quesnay, in the abbreviated *Tableau,* supposes an annual reproduction of 5 billion livres is normally achieved.[25] Of these 5 billion, 3 constitute *reprises,* or the return of expenses incurred by the cultivators (i.e., 2 billion in the form of annual advances, and 1 billion in the form of the 10 per cent return on the primitive advances which is required to keep the latter intact). These 3 billion must, therefore, be restored to the cultivators and reinvested in agriculture; for otherwise annual and primitive advances will fall short of the amounts required to maintain agricultural reproduction at a level of 5 billion. The remaining 2 billion constitute the *net product,* the monetary equivalent of which passes, in consequence of the competition of farmers (i.e., agricultural undertakers) for the use of land, to the landed proprietors who share it with the sovereign and others supported out of the net product and who must employ something like one-third of it to maintain and improve the *avances foncières.*[26] It is because the sale of agricultural products returns to cultivators a gross income which covers all expenses of production comparable to those incurred in the "sterile" occupations and provides, in addition, a surplus or *net product,* imputable to land (or to the bounty of nature) and available in part for the general needs of society, that the agricultural class is described as the productive class.

The sterile class is characterized as unproductive because it does not produce a net surplus. The goods and services which it sells command, in competitive markets, prices that return, and only return, the necessary expenses of production. Among these expenses the physiocrats included the remuneration of labor,[27] outlays for materials, and a return, corresponding to "interest" and/or "profits" on advances.[28] But there is included no return corresponding to the imputed contribution (i.e., "net product") of agricultural land. Whence the sterile class, since it does not bring such a "net product" into being, is unproductive.

Although the sterile class is "unproductive," it is useful and necessary; it creates goods and services with a money value sufficient to provide it with food, shelter, etc., with raw materials for working up, and (presumably) with a return on its advances. In nonphysiocratic terms, the sterile class produces goods and services with a net value equal to two-fifths of the annual reproduction of the productive class. According to the abbreviated *Tableau,* the sterile class purchases from the productive class raw materials and subsistence valued at 2 billion livres, of which it consumes one half as subsistence. The other half it fashions into goods and services with an exchange value of 3 billion livres, of which 2 billion are delivered to the productive and the proprietary classes in exchange for the 2 billion of money wherewith it purchases raw materials and subsistence; it consumes the remaining billion. The sterile class therefore nets 2 billion annually.[29]

The proprietary class, though very useful, is not "productive" in the physiocratic sense of the term.[30] Rather it is *disposable.* The landed proprietors are not forced, by the need of subsistence, to perform particular work or tasks; nor are the services of the disposable class required in agriculture and the sterile employments, for they are supported out of the net product. Hence they can provide the general needs of society — administration, defense, education, religious ministration, etc. — either by their personal efforts or by turning over to the state a part of their revenue (i.e., net product) for the employment of men to provide these general needs.[31]

The physiocrats were exponents of efficiency in agriculture, in sterile employments, and in governmental activities. They exhibited some familiarity with the circumstances governing output, especially in agriculture; but they devoted little attention to the laws of returns as such. They emphasized the importance of the use of capital, particularly in agriculture,[32] the need for skilled agricultural undertakers (i.e., *fermiers*) possessed of capital, and the superiority of *grande culture* to *petite culture*, with its small gross product and relatively smaller net product.[33] Were *grande culture* everywhere substituted for *petite culture* in those branches of agriculture devoted to grains and small crops, and were productive expenditures increased by 125 per cent, Quesnay wrote in 1757,[34] total product would increase by 105 per cent, and the surplus above productive expenditures by nearly 400 per cent. Evidently, French agriculture was far less productive than it might have been. The smallness of agricultural output Quesnay and his followers attributed to a shortage of agricultural capital and of well-to-do and skilled agricultural undertakers, a shortage which was traceable, in turn, to a number of remediable conditions (e.g., lack of foreign markets for agricultural products, restrictions upon agricultural entrepreneurs, fetters upon competition, favoritism toward nonagricultural branches of the economy, undeveloped internal transportation system, defective fiscal system, heavy and uneconomic taxes). Were these conditions remedied, their argument ran, capital and undertaking ability would flow into agriculture and gradually carry its output to the *economic* maximum of which the country was capable.[35]

While the physiocrats recognized that, even under a system of *grande culture*, a country's capacity to produce foodstuffs and agricultural raw materials is limited,[36] they did not, as a rule, indicate whether "average returns" would decline before this limit was reached. They observed that returns fall at the extensive margin, but they did not usually make the same observation with respect to the intensive margin. For their objective was not the development of laws of returns but the formulation of the case for investment in agriculture and for the replacement of *petite* by *grande culture*. Quesnay's abbreviated *Tableau* suggests that, so long as reproduction can be augmented, an increase of 1 unit in annual advances is accompanied by an increase of 2½ units in total reproduction and 1 unit in net product.[37] In many of the discussions these, or similar, constant ratios are assumed. Baudeau, in his analysis of what constituted harmful luxury, postulated a stage of "increasing" returns — i.e., a stage in which an increase in annual advances is accompanied by a relatively greater increase in net product — and implied a subsequent stage in which returns thus defined decrease.[38] Turgot alone clearly formulated the problem, when he took exception to Saint-Péravy's supposition, derived from Quesnay's works, that the ratio of total production to annual advances is constant at 5 to 2. Not only is this ratio higher, other things equal, on superior than on inferior land, Turgot reasoned; but even on a given piece of land it rises as advances are increased, reaches a peak, and thereafter declines until a point is reached at which further advances add nothing to total product. Net product is affected accordingly; at first it increases faster than annual advances, then less rapidly, until a point is reached at which further advances add nothing to net product, returning only the expenses of production.[39] Turgot's observations regarding variation in the productive effectiveness of advances were not, however, incorporated into the physiocratic theory of production.[40]

Annual production and its circulation in Year 1, as summarized in the *Tableau*, may now be described as follows. Let m_1 and m_2 each equal 1 billion livres in money. Let M_{n1} and M_{n2} each equal 1 billion livres of raw produce set aside as the net product. Let M_i equal 1 billion livres raw produce corresponding to the 10 per cent return on primitive advances totaling 10 billions. Let M_{a1} and M_{a2} each equal 1 billion livres of raw produce destined to serve as annual advances. Let F_0 equal 1 billion livres of wrought goods and services carried over by the sterile class from Year 0. Let F_1, F_2, and F_3 each equal 1 billion livres of wrought goods and services, produced in Year 1, of which F_1 and F_2 are destined for consumption in Year 1, while F_3 is destined to be carried over into Year 2. At the commencement of Year 1 the productive class possesses m_1 and m_2; and in the course of the year it harvests, as the result of 2 billion annual advances, a reproduction of 5 billion: $M_{n1} + M_{n2} + M_i + M_{a1} + M_{a2}$. It transfers m_1 and m_2 to the proprietary class in acquittal of the annual rent determined on the basis of the past net product. The proprietary class restores m_1 to the productive class, receiving in return M_{n1}, and exchanges m_2 for F_0, the carry-over inventory of the sterile class. With m_2 the sterile class purchases M_{n2} from the productive class. The productive class, in need of wrought goods and services, exchanges 1 billion livres $(m_1 + m_2)/2$ for the sterile class's F_1; and the latter restores this money to the productive class, receiving in exchange M_i. The results are summarized in Table 1. The proprietary class obtains for consumption M_{n1} and F_0. The productive class retains M_{a1} and M_{a2} for annual advances, secures F_1 as a return on its primitive advances, and recovers m_1 and m_2 in anticipation of Year 2 rent. The sterile class comes into possession of 1 billion raw produce for subsistence, provides itself with F_2, and fabricates F_3 for sale in Year 2.

The preceding account of the circulation of money and output, with reproduction and expenditure patterns assumed as given, runs in terms of annual aggregates. The physiocrats, however, conceived of the interclass circulation of money, goods, and services as an unending process, the continuity of which they sought to suggest by zigzag lines in their unabbreviated "economic" tables.[41] Output and money flowed continually through the circuits connecting each class with each other class. For example, the proprietary class and its dependents do not specifically exchange m_1 for M_{n1}, or m_2 for F_0; rather they continue throughout the year to purchase raw produce from the productive class and wrought goods and services from the sterile class, their purchases per year from each class aggregating 1 billion livres, and their total purchases, 2 billion (equals revenue, or net product). The sterile class continues throughout the year to sell to, and to buy from, the productive class, its annual purchases, however, exceeding its annual sales by the amount (1 billion livres) which it obtains in the course of the year from the proprietary class.[42] It is, as will be indicated, upon the con-

TABLE 1

Summary of Circulation in *Tableau économique*

Productive Class (Prod. Cl.)	Proprietary Class (Prop. Cl.)	Sterile Class (St. Cl.)
Money: $m_1\rightarrow$Prop. Cl. $m_2\rightarrow$Prop. Cl. and thence to St. Cl.	Exchanges claim to revenue ($=$net product) for m_1 and m_2, and then exchanges m_1 for M_{n1} and m_2 for F_0.	$F_0\rightarrow$Prop. Cl. (for m_2) $m_2\rightarrow$Prod. Cl. (for M_{n2}) $F_1\rightarrow$Prod. Cl. $\left(\text{for } \dfrac{m_1+m_2}{2}\right)$
Reproduction: $M_{n1}\rightarrow$Prop. Cl. (for m_1) $M_{n2}\rightarrow$St. Cl. (for m_2) $M_i\rightarrow$St. Cl. $\left(\text{for } \dfrac{m_1+m_2}{2}\text{, or } F_1\right)$ $M_{a1}\left\{\text{retained as subsistence}\right.$ $M_{a2}\left.(\text{or annual advances})\right.$		$\dfrac{m_1+m_2}{2}\rightarrow$Prod. Cl. (for M_i) $\left.\begin{array}{l}F_2\\F_3\end{array}\right\}\begin{array}{l}\text{retained for}\\\text{consumption}\\\text{and future sale}\end{array}$
Consumption: F_1 M_{a1} M_{a2}	Consumption: M_{n1} F_0	Consumption: $\dfrac{M_i+M_{n2}}{2}$ F_2
Carry-over into Year 2: m_1 m_2		Carry-over into Year 2: F_3

tinuity of this circulation and upon the pattern of national expenditure or consumption (i.e., distribution of expenditures between the sterile and the productive classes) that, in physiocratic theory, economic health, prosperity, and progress depend.

Quesnay's analysis of the *Tableau* suggests that the fully developed agricultural economy described in his abbreviated *Tableau* remains in a state of self-perpetuating equilibrium so long as the ratios given by him are adhered to, and that consequently the appropriate proportional distribution of the population among the three socioeconomic classes persists. This suggestion implies either that the economy is essentially static or that the circumstances regulating its growth operate with equal force in all its branches. Quesnay's various discussions, however, imply that he did not rule out dynamic forces making for progress and that the physiocrats did not suppose that the values of the determinants of equilibrium, or the manner in which the population is distributed, must necessarily continue unchanged. For example, given improvement in agricultural techniques, the fraction of the population required by agriculture might fall below one-half. The physiocrats, however, did not carefully appraise and weigh the forces making for change in methods of production or in the standard of life and habits of consumption and incorporate such findings into the fundamental body of their theory. Their theory, therefore, remained essentially static, in part, perhaps, because they considered a static formula better suited to demonstrate their principles.

The physiocrats always expressed their theory of circular flow in interclass, rather than in interindividual, terms. Notwithstanding, their theory of circular flow forced upon them several conclusions of importance. They looked upon money as an instrument whose essential function it is to facilitate the circulation of goods and services, to serve as a medium of exchange. In consequence, they recognized that commerce consists, not in buying and selling, but in the exchange of goods and services for goods and services. They thus laid the groundwork for the formulation of Say's law of markets and evoked its actual statement by their treatment of consumption and expenditure. They recognized, too, that if money ceases to perform its function, the nexus between potential purchasers and potential sellers is broken, thus anticipating Keynes; but they did not develop this theory, for they supposed that in a *healthy* economy founded upon their principles money would always perform its proper function.

B. THE PHYSIOCRATIC PATTERN OF EXPENDITURE, OR CONSUMPTION

The physiocratic theory of net product imposed definite restrictions upon the physiocratic theory of expenditure, or consumption. The physiocrats could emphasize, as they did, the dependence of economic prosperity and progress upon the continuity of expenditure, or consumption — upon the continuity of circular flow. But they could not, as can exponents of an unqualified theory of productivity, find continuity of expenditure to be sufficient in itself. Consumption and expenditure must be according to pattern — according to the pattern imposed by the principle that only agriculture, fishing, and mining are capable of yielding a "net product." If this pattern is not conformed to, economic degradation sets in; whereas if it is conformed to, economic expansion ensues, other circumstances permitting. The physiocratic pattern of expenditure was later condemned by Say and others as a makework pattern. This it was not; for, given the physiocratic theory of net productivity, the physiocratic pattern of expenditure was essential to expansion just as, given the modern theory of production, a pattern of expenditure must include an allowance for capital formation to permit expansion.

Prosperity and progress required, the physiocrats believed, that a sufficient fraction of the national income be spent upon raw produce. In an economy whose agriculture is fully developed and whose revenue (equals net product) has been maximized,[43] the proprietary class must spend half its revenue with the productive class and half with the sterile class; the sterile class must spend with the productive class the money, equal in the aggregate to the annual revenue, which it receives from the latter and from the proprietary class; and the productive class must consume in the form of agricultural products two-thirds of its *reprises*,[44] limiting to one-third the fraction utilized in the form of goods and services supplied by the sterile class.[45] If the several classes spend lesser amounts with the productive class, annual reproduction and net product must decline; if they spend more, annual reproduction will not expand enough to increase net product and revenue, inasmuch as cultivation has already been intensified and extended as much as circumstances permit.

It is not clear whether or not the physiocrats anticipated an end to progress and the advent of a stationary state. Baudeau and Dupont and some of the others seem to have supposed that technological progress would postpone, if not prevent, the arrival of such a state. Quesnay, on the contrary, as his discussion of China suggests, may have expected eventual stationariness.[46] The postulating of a stationary economy in the economic tables supports this inference.

Given an economy that is fully developed and in equilibrium, as implicitly defined by the physiocrats, an increase in the rate of consumption of goods and services supplied by the sterile class must precipitate a decline in the rate of consumption of agricultural products and therefore in the rate of annual advances and annual reproduction. Given an underdeveloped economy, an even greater relative decline may result. Suppose, for example, that in Year 1 the proprietary class in a fully developed economy decreases by 100 livres its annual purchases from the productive class and increases by this 100 its annual spendings with the sterile class. The effect of this shift in consumption, physiocratic reasoning suggests, would be as follows: The productive class suffers a 67 (i.e., $100 - 33$) livre decrease in income, for the sterile class returns to the productive class in exchange for necessary raw materials only one-third of the additional 100 livres spent with the sterile class by the proprietary class. As a result, the capacity of the productive class to make annual advances declines by 67 livres. Whence the productive class reduces by 67 the annual advances it makes in Year 2,[47] and annual reproduction in Year 2 falls by 167 (i.e., $2\frac{1}{2} \times 67$), and net product by 67.[48] Furthermore, if in Year 2, the proprietors again spend an extra 100 livres with the sterile class, agricultural income will fall another 67. Accordingly, if, under these circumstances, the proprietors exact an undiminished rent in Year 2, the income of the agricultural class will be 234 livres less than in the last normal Year 0. The productive class therefore will reduce its annual advances in year 3 by 234 below normal, and annual reproduction will decline by 585 (i.e., $2\frac{1}{2} \times 234$), and net product by 234. Persistence, on the part of the proprietary class, in this heightened rate of expenditure with the sterile class thus produces a cumulative diminution in annual reproduction. Primitive advances come to be neglected; and the cultivators' capacity to pay rent (revenue) diminishes with the decline in net product. *Grande culture* gradually gives place to *petite culture*, and population begins to decline in number and well-being. If the sterile class and/or the productive class attempts in like manner to increase their consumption of the products of the sterile class, the tendencies unloosed by the initial change in the consumption pattern of the proprietary class are accentuated.

A shift of purchasing-power, such as has been postulated, from the productive to the sterile class must, according to physiocratic theory, soon injure the proprietary and the sterile classes; for the well-being of both is founded upon that of the productive class. Net product declines as annual reproduction falls; whence the rent (revenue) which the proprietary class can exact must diminish. The demand for the goods and services of the sterile class is governed by the revenue passing to the proprietary class and the returns (*reprises*) flowing to the productive class; as annual reproduction falls, therefore, this demand must diminish and with it the prosperity of the sterile class.[49]

Even as the physiocrats condemned the diversion of purchasing-power to the sterile class, so did they defend its diversion to the productive class, circumstances permitting. Suppose, for example, that the proprietary class increases by 100 livres its consumption of agricultural products and diminishes by 100 its expenditure with the sterile class. The income of the productive class increases by 67. The following year the productive class augments its annual advances by 67. Whence annual reproduction increases by 167; net product, by 67; and the return (*reprises*) to the productive class, by 100. Again, suppose foreign purchases of French agricultural products increase by 100 livres. Annual advances will be increased by 100 in the ensuing year and augment reproduction by 250, net product by 100, and returns (*reprises*) to cultivators by 150. In fact, so long as a nation's agriculture is underdeveloped and suffering from a shortage of capital and annual reproduction falls short of the amount consistent with the maximization of net product, an increase in the rate of expenditure upon agricultural products, even if at the immediate expense of the sterile class, will augment annual reproduction and net product. In the course of time, therefore, the demand for goods and services supplied by the sterile class will increase, and population will grow and provide a still greater market for the outputs of both "producing" classes.[50]

The physiocratic conception of the pattern of consumption was expressed most firmly in their theory of luxury, to which Baudeau gave the greatest precision. Even in 1758, Quesnay had observed that a diversion of expenditure from the productive to the sterile class operated to reduce annual reproduction and net product.[51] Subsequently, he warned that it is *luxe de décoration* (i.e., excessive expenditure with the sterile class), and not great or ostentatious consumption of subsistence (*luxe de subsistance*),[52] that is to be feared; but he did not indicate with precision when expenditure upon sterile products becomes excessive and harmful, merely observing that if agriculture was short of capital or if the internal transportation system was defective, less than half of the revenue of the proprietor class should be spent upon superfluities supplied by the sterile class.[53] Mirabeau declared that when a nation's agriculture is degraded, the proprietary class must spend more than half its revenue with the productive class and so build up agricultural productivity.[54] Baudeau defined *luxe* as "harmful expenditure" and included thereunder any increase in unproductive expenditure which was prejudicial to productive expenditure and to production itself. For example, if a landowning cultivator, who has been obtaining an output of 6,000 with advances of 3,000, is able, in consequence of improved methods, to obtain the same output with advances of 2,500, he may spend the 500 saved with the sterile class and yet not be guilty of harmful expenditure. But if this same cultivator, his property having deteriorated, finds it necessary for a time to advance 4,000 a year in order to obtain an output of 6,000, he is guilty of harmful expenditure if he advances less than 4,000 and thereby holds output below 6,000 and net product below what it should be.[55] Baudeau thus makes both cultivator and proprietor morally responsible, each within his own sphere, for the maintenance of annual reproduction and net product.[56] Whether Baudeau meant also to say that cultivator and proprietor are responsible for the *continued augmentation* of advances until net product has been raised to the attainable maximum is not clear; but it is plain that both he and other physiocrats considered such conduct and expenditure most meritorious.[57]

The physiocratic view of the pattern of consumption permeated also their discussions of price fluctuations and of taxation. Given an economy whose agriculture is underdeveloped or whose farmers are receiving less than a *bon prix* (i.e., a competitive equilibrium price) for their products,[58] an increase in the level of prices received by farmers for agricultural produce will result in increased investment in agriculture and in an augmentation of annual reproduction and net product. Quesnay, for example, considers an economy such as the French, whose agriculture is both burdened with indirect taxes and suffering from a shortage of capital. Suppose, he says, that the establishment of completely free trade in agricultural products raises by one-fifth the price of all French agricultural products other than those consumed in kind by cultivators and their families and that money wages and the sale value of embodied raw materials are increased enough to compensate for this price increase. Even so, net product will increase. For the terms of foreign trade will become more favorable to France; only five-sixths as much raw produce will be required for the payment of indirect taxes; and the spread between what the farmers receive and what the final consumers pay will be reduced, the saving in costs of distribution passing initially to the farmers.[59] Moreover, while competition will eventually transfer this increase in net product to the proprietors, both the sterile and the productive classes benefit from the advance in price, and the population capacity of the nation increases. The *real* income of the sterile class increases in consequence of the increase in annual reproduction and the resultant increase in purchases from this class. Until existing leases expire and competition adjusts land rents upward in consistence with the increase in net product, farmers retain the increase in net product and invest it in primitive advances and improvements, which augment the productivity of their farms and provide them with greater returns, even after rents have been adjusted upward. A decrease in the price of agricultural produce, Quesnay observed, would set in motion an opposite chain of effects.[60]

In their discussions of taxation the physiocrats insisted, first, that all taxes except those directly and immediately incident upon landed proprietors be removed and, second, that the aggregate amount of revenue collected from the proprietors for the support of state and church functions do not exceed a determined fraction of the income of the landed proprietors. Ultimately, irrespective of what kinds of taxes and burdens a state imposes, the income finally received by the state, together with the costs of collecting this income, comes out of the net product, or revenue, which passes, or otherwise would pass, to the landed proprietors. The state, therefore, should collect its income directly from the proprietors; for by so doing it minimizes the cost of collecting taxes, as well as the uncertainties, opportunities for graft, and other psychic and financial burdens incident to tax collection;[61] and it prevents the multiplication, in cities far removed from farming areas,[62] of rich and parasitic financiers and tax farmers. When, on the contrary, a state relies upon indirect taxes, it imposes these avoidable burdens and expenses upon agriculture, the ultimate source of all tax revenue; it establishes conditions unfavorable to the consumption of raw produce; and it tends to overestimate the amount of tax revenue that can be collected without depressing annual reproduction.[63]

With respect to the second point — that a state cannot *continually* collect in taxes more than a determinable amount — the physiocrats declared that only about one-third of the net product may be appropriated by the state for the support of functions properly performable by state or church.[64] It is this one-third which, in physiocratic terms, is completely *disposable* — i.e., if it is divided properly between the productive and sterile classes, it is unnecessary to the maintenance or even augmentation of net product and, therefore, appropriable and utilizable for state and church functions.[65] Out of this third there must be provided remuneration of public servants, for their troubles and cares, funds for the support and perfection of social institutions, and other advances essential to the public good.[66] Were the state to appropriate more than one-third of the net product, investment in agriculture would be neglected, and annual reproduction and net product would decline. For the proprietor required a third of his net product merely to repair and improve his property, and a second third to compensate him for his *avances foncières,* for his pain and care, and for his risks; presumably, if these two-thirds were not forthcoming, the proprietor would allow his property to deteriorate.[67]

C. CONTINUITY OF EXPENDITURE, OR CONSUMPTION

The continuity of economic activity was contingent, as was its expansion, the physiocrats held, upon the continuity and the expansion of the effective demand (*i.e.,* consumption), at prices satisfactory to farmers, for agricultural produce and raw materials. For, given such demand, investment in agriculture, together with agricultural output, would expand; and, given such expansion of agriculture, industry and commerce would progress in proper measure.[68] Because they believed that continuity of consumption presupposed continuity of the circular flow of money and goods, the physiocrats insisted, in substance, that income received be promptly restored to the income stream — i.e., spent — and made to maintain the demand for agricultural produce and, if possible, to facilitate the expansion of both output and consumption; and they opposed practices which delayed the restoration of money received to the income stream.

Each producer is the creator of a surplus beyond his own requirements, of which he must dispose if he is to continue its supply; for to him this surplus is a superfluity which he would exchange for something he deems necessary. If he cannot exchange it on satisfactory terms for goods and services which he wants; if, because satisfactory markets are denied to him, he is compelled to sell his superfluity dirt cheap, he will curtail its output and cease investing in its production. Yet he cannot sell unless others stand ready to buy, and others cannot sell unless he stands ready to buy. Whence commerce is essential to transmute that which is superfluous into that which is necessary and thus stimulate production; and consumption, *by consumers able to purchase at prices satisfactory to producers,* regulates reproduction. Mercier represented the physiocratic view well when he wrote:

> *La consommation est la mesure de la reproduction,* car des productions qui resteraient sans consommation, dégénéraient en superflu sans utilité, sans valeur; et dès-lors on cesserait de faire les avances de leur culture. . . .
>
> Ainsi, en considérant le commerce comme une multitude de ventes et d'achats faits en argent, *personne n'est acheteur qu'autant qu'il est vendeur;* et comme acheter c'est payer, *personne ne peut acheter qu'en raison de ce qu'il vend,* parce que ce n'est qu'en vendant qu'il se procure l'argent pour payer ce qu'il achète.
>
> De ce que tout acheteur doit être vendeur, et ne peut acheter qu'autant qu'il vend, il résulte évidemment un deuxième axiome: c'est que *tout vendeur doit être acheteur, et ne peut vendre qu'autant qu'il achète;* qu'ainsi *chaque vendeur doit, par les achats qu'il fait à son tour, fournir aux autres l'argent pour acheter les marchandises qu'il veut leur vendre.*[69]

"In the order prescribed by the Author of Nature," wrote Mirabeau, "the expenditure of wealth must necessarily precede the reproduction of wealth." And he added that poverty is born of frugality; and national ruin of the cessation of productive expenditures.[70]

Aggregate consumption of raw produce at satisfactory prices was governed by the size and the comfort (i.e., purchasing-power) of the domestic population and by the extent of export demand. So long as aggregate domestic consumption fell short of aggregate output, given efficient cultivation and diversified crops,[71] it was essential that the surplus be sold abroad, the creations of foreign sterile classes being accepted in exchange.[72] Under conditions of free trade such necessary exportation[73] would always take place, and prosperity would therefore persist. Meanwhile, if economic activity at home remained unfettered and unobstructed and a satisfactory pattern of consumption continued, the domestic market would expand, and the need to export would diminish. For then provisions would be abundant, advances would be expanding, and employment would be available; whence population would increase in number and comfort until, the economy having become fully developed and peopled, there would be little production available for exportation.[74] To bring about this desirable course of development it was both unnecessary and inadvisable that population growth be

175

encouraged;[75] it was essential merely that competition be untrammeled, that internal and external commerce be free, and that the common man be allowed to improve his moral and physical condition, his productive effectiveness, and his mode of living.

The physiocrats took it for granted that, given economic liberty and no obstructions to the circular flow of money and products, the demand for agricultural products, at satisfactory prices,[76] would keep pace with output and that the nonagricultural branches of the economy would prosper accordingly.

C'est ainsi que la société se perpétue par ce cercle non interrompu de reproduction & de consommation, entretenu par la fécondité inépuisable de la terre, aidée du travail de l'homme & des avances.[77]

They supposed, moreover, that, so long as the "loix de l'ordre" were observed and the economy therefore remained healthy, this circular flow would not be interrupted, and the "value" of raw produce would remain at a satisfactory level.[78] Turgot, in an earlier work, had implicitly denied that unemployment would persist so long as interoccupational movement was possible, thus anticipating Say's law. A given occupation is surcharged with workers when there are too many workers in this occupation in relation to the number engaged in other occupations. But there is a full-employment equilibrium, he implies, and this is restored through the redistribution among other occupations of the surplus of workers in the overcrowded occupation. Such redistribution, moreover, is accomplished through the voluntary interoccupational movement of workers when obstacles are not put in the way of such movements; for workers tend to transfer from occupations where wages are relatively low to those where they are relatively high.[79]

The physiocrats, it has been noted, found the economic *primum mobile* in the realm of agriculture; upon its expansion depended that of everything else. They denied, therefore, that manufactures and commerce *must* be developed in order either (*a*) to provide employment and (therefore) consumers to absorb agricultural raw produce and thus support its price[80] or (*b*) to provide varied and tempting products calculated to prompt proprietors and cultivators to expand agricultural production more than they otherwise would.[81] For, given economic liberty and a suitable fiscal system, they supposed, proprietors and cultivators would have adequate access to markets and sufficient incentive to augment production, while nonagricultural branches of the economy would naturally expand sufficiently to absorb a proper amount of agricultural produce and to provide in exchange a suitable amount of nonagricultural goods and services. The physiocrats thus solved the problem in question by denying its existence in an economy that conformed to the laws of the natural order, by ignoring sociopsychological barriers to the growth of consumption, and by asserting that desire would keep pace with production.[82]

The physiocrats — especially Quesnay and Mirabeau — urged that the common man be provided with opportunity to secure some education, to

176

increase his productive capacity and social usefulness, and to augment his consuming-power. It was barbarous to suppose, as many did, that poverty was the enemy of sloth and that a society must be well supplied with igno-rant poor to perform its painful tasks. The peasant would work the harder by virtue of his opportunity to win more than a bare existence. The comfort that "commerce gives excites the common people to work."[83] More impor-tant, it was upon the comfort — upon the mass purchasing-power — of the common people that the demand for raw produce and, therefore, the pros-perity of agriculture and of the nation depended. This part of the popula-tion was "incomparably more numerous" than the wealthy, and its actual and potential capacity to consume was correspondingly greater.[84] "It was neces-sary above all," declared Mirabeau, "that the common people be in a posi-tion to consume products of good value."[85] Quesnay had even remarked in an early paper that, although domestics and workers engaged in the fabrication of luxuries were unproductively employed, they did not hoard any of the money income they received from the rich but spent it for food, clothing, etc., and thus sustained consumption and production.[86]

While the physiocrats considered its service as a medium of exchange to be almost the sole function[87] performable by money and practically antici-pated Say in treating the demand for goods as issuing from their supply, they did not suppose the circular flow of money and commodities to be immune to interruption. And they condemned a number of practices which operated, in the admittedly unhealthy French economy, to interrupt this flow. For, given such interruption, a downward spiral is initiated:

> Dès que l'argent devient le moyen unique dont on peut se servir pour acheter, tout serait perdu s'il cessait circuler; il est d'une nécessité absolue qu'il ne fasse que passer dans chaque main.[88]

Moreover, if the conditions making for this interruption continue, "the equilibrium of prosperity is broken, and replaced by the equilibrium of misery and of degradation."[89]

In Section B we considered two conditions — decorative luxury and burdensome and uneconomic taxes — which, according to the physiocrats, interrupted the circular flow of money and commodities. Excessive expendi-ture upon nonagricultural goods and services, it was noted, diverted money income away from agriculture, reduced net product, and eventually con-tracted the income of both the sterile class and the sovereign. It is not always clear whether the diminution in agricultural income is traceable, in physiocratic opinion, to a diversion of money into circuits with which agriculture is not fully connected or whether there has occurred an over-all shrinkage in monetary purchasing power, immediately traceable to a de-cline in velocity, to hoarding, to a leakage abroad, or to a diminution in the effectiveness of the substitutes for hard money; for the process of decline is not carefully described.[90] A similar effect is produced, said the physiocrats, when the tax burden is excessive, whether because the government seeks too much revenue or because the government has recourse to indirect taxes and so imposes upon agriculture a burden several times the amount of the revenue which the government actually receives. Not only did indirect taxation check consumption directly;[91] it also operated, because of the manner in which it was administered, to accumulate pecuniary riches in the hands of a few who did not and could not provide a market for products as advantageous and extensive as otherwise would have been provided by those whose incomes were reduced by the taxes in question.[92] Effects similar to the ones occasioned by indirect taxation and decorative luxury were produced by obstructions of economic liberty and the extension of favors to industry and commerce.[93]

Most important of the obstructions (other than those already mentioned) to the production-sustaining circular flow of money, according to Quesnay, were its removal from circulation through unbalanced external trade,[94] its diversion into idle hoards, and its passage into circuits where it no longer had reproduction for its object.[95] In general, Quesnay reasoned, when money was withdrawn from production-stimulating circulation, where it facilitated the exchange of value for value and thus served to perpetuate wealth,[96] both the demand for agricultural products and their prices fell;[97] whence profits, reproduction, and other economic activity declined. He urged, therefore, that money income not be hoarded by any class and that savings be promptly invested, inasmuch as capital formation and the increase of advances depended upon *wisdom* in expenditure, even as the maintenance of agricultural income depended upon the continuance of expenditure.[98] He urged further:

> *Que la totalité des sommes du revenu rentre dans la circulation annuelle et la parcoure dans toute son étendue:* qu'il ne se forme point de fortunes pécuniaires, ou du moins qu'il y ait compensation entre celles qui se forment et celles qui reviennent dans la circulation; car autrement ces fortunes pécuniaires arrêteraient la distribution d'une partie du revenu annuel de la nation et retiendraient le pécule du royaume au préjudice de la rentrée des avances de la culture, de la rétribution du salaire des artisans et de la consommation que doivent faire les différentes classes d'hommes qui exercent des professions lucratives: cette interception du pécule diminuerait la reproduction des revenus et de l'impôt.[99]

Quesnay condemned a number of practices which, he believed, made for the formation of "sterile" pecuniary fortunes and thus operated to deprive agriculture of income and of funds necessary for its pursuit and development. He referred in particular to the manner of collecting indirect taxes, to tax-farming, to the sale of *rentes* and to other governmental borrowing, and to traffic in securities and funds.[100] He recommended:

> *Que l'administration des finances, soit dans la perception des impôts, soit dans les dépenses du gouvernment, n'occasionne pas de fortunes* pécuniaires qui dérobent une partie des revenus à la circulation, à la distribution et à la reproduction.[101]

Quesnay and Mirabeau objected to prevailing fiscal practices because they allegedly gave rise to sterile pecuniary fortunes and fostered expenditure upon ornamental luxuries. They also objected to these practices because (*a*) they diverted capital from agriculture and augmented the price of agricultural capital and (*b*) they operated to increase interest costs of the state and of the nonagricultural branches of the economy, thus burdening agriculture, out of whose annual reproduction all interest had ultimately to be paid, inasmuch as capital was unproductive.[102] Quesnay therefore proposed that the interest rate on agricultural loans be not permitted to rise above the natural and proper rate — i.e., the rate of return which landowners could realize on the purchase price of land; for if the latter rate were exceeded by the interest rate, land values would fall, capital would not flow into agriculture, and agriculture would not be ruined.[103] Mirabeau went beyond Quesnay in proposing policies based upon the principle that all interest comes out of the annual reproduction. He disapproved of most methods of financing industry and commerce and advocated restricting the rate of interest on agricultural loans and the limitation of such loans to the provision of capital for agriculture.[104]

Other leading members and friends of the physiocratic school looked upon regulation of interest rates as inconsistent with the principle of economic liberty. Turgot, for example, opposed all legal fixation of the interest rate, saying that its determination must be left to competition, to supply and demand, and that it was moving downward in consequence of the growing abundance of capital.[105] Dupont, Le Trosne, Saint-Péravy, and others shared Turgot's opinion that the determination of the interest rate must be left to competition; they supposed that it would settle at the proper level if the principles of the natural order were complied with.[106]

In his comments upon several of Turgot's papers relating to saving and capital formation, Dupont presented what he supposed to be Quesnay's views on this matter. Dupont's account suggests that, whereas Turgot emphasized the role of saving, taking investment for granted, the physiocrats emphasized investment and product-increasing expenditure, taking for granted such temporary nonspending, or saving, as was essential.[107] Dupont's analysis, while physiocratic in character, also anticipates Say's distinction between productive and unproductive consumption.[108]

Before men had discovered the use of money, said Dupont, they had made savings in kind, even as livestock farmers still did. With the introduction of metallic money, however, saving was facilitated; for it was now possible for men to accumulate very small amounts, adding to their cumulating total until it was sufficient for the purchase of desired commodities, properties, improvements, etc., or for the extension of loans to undertakers. The introduction of money made possible also the hoarding of that which was intended to serve as a medium of exchange. Such nonspending — i.e., *thésaurisation* or hoarding — of money income received was not capital formation; its effect, in fact, was quite the opposite. For capital formation consisted in, or issued out of, the intelligent *expenditure* of money income received and of sums which had been built up out of petty savings.[109]

Dupont admitted that small sums must be cumulated into amounts sufficiently large for profitable investment by the saver or for the extension of loans to those engaged in agriculture and industry.[110] But he insisted that these necessary amounts, once cumulated, must be promptly employed to form capital; for their sequestration in stagnant hoards necessarily restricted reproduction. Producers and fabricators could sell their products at satisfactory prices only if the recipients of money income purchased these products and thus restored their money receipts to circulation; when this was not done, undertakers found it impossible to move their products at prices high enough to justify their continuation of production at existing levels. Suppose, said Dupont, that proprietors, whose rental incomes are paid in money, do not spend all of it, saving (i.e., withholding from circulation) part of it instead.[111] A corresponding part of the harvest will consequently lack purchasers at satisfactory prices, and agricultural income and revenue therefore will decline. Furthermore, if the "parsimonious proprietors," whose saving has precipitated the decline in agricultural income and revenue, attempt to meet the situation by additional saving, they will further depress both agricultural income and their own revenues. And should they persist in this course, they will steadily worsen their situation until "they are come to the point where absolute poverty will make saving by them impossible" and force them into the working classes.[112]

Dupont's argument, he indicates, is intended to show not that men should spend all that they receive without regard to the objects of their expenditure but that they form capital through intelligent expenditure rather than through saving.[113] For purposes of discussion he distinguished four types of expediture: (1) *dépense folle,* or the extraordinary and unnecessary expenditure of "capital"; (2) *dépense sterile,* or outlay for daily consumption, which neither increases nor decreases capital; (3) *dépense conservatrice,* or outlays for durable goods (or durable sources of satisfaction), which, although they are not productive of wealth, serve important uses — e.g., houses, machines, furniture, etc.; (4) *dépense productive,* or expenditures which increase both the mass of products required for the satisfaction of daily needs and the raw materials out of which are fabricated the durable sources of satisfaction for which type 3 — *conservatrice* — expenditure is made. Of these four types of expenditure, the greatest contribution to capital formation is made by type 4, with type 3 next in order of general desirability. Nations tended to accumulate capital, therefore, as they concentrated their expenditures upon "productive" and "conservative" objects.

Dupont's analysis, if truly representative of the opinions of Quesnay and his school[114] regarding saving, expenditure, and capital formation, indicate that the physiocrats believed that money received must promptly be restored to the income stream and that a sufficient proportion of this stream must be continually channeled into agriculture, in the form of demands for raw produce at satisfactory prices and in the form of advances intended to augment agricultural productivity and output.[115] Under these circumstances reproduction and economic activity tend to expand, and all is well.

It is evident that the physiocrats anticipated both Say's observation that commerce consists in the exchange of goods and services for goods and services and his inference that an increase in output always generates an increase in demand. The physiocrats did not, however, suppose this inference to be valid at all times and for all economies. It was descriptive only of a balanced and *healthy* economy — that is, balanced and healthy in a physiocratic sense; it was not descriptive of the French economy in which they lived, for this economy was neither balanced nor healthy. The physiocrats therefore found it necessary, as did Keynes later, to stress the importance of consumption. While they did not conceive of anything like the multiplier effect, they did infer, in consequence of their peculiar theory of production, that an economy might be in equilibrium either at a prosperity or at a depression level.

Because the physiocrats supposed their peculiar pattern of expenditure to be necessary to the health of the French economy and because they denied that money received always is promptly restored to the income stream, Say directed against them his law of markets, a law which must have been suggested to him by their analysis of circulation and the role of money in a healthy economy. Say, however, unlike the physiocrats, supposed this law to hold under nearly all conditions. His law, despite its inherent defectiveness and its failure to correspond with the facts, gave a direction to economic thought regarding consumption and expenditure out of which the Keynesian theory evolved as a kind of antithesis.

D. PHYSIOCRATIC CONTRADICTIONS

In preceding sections it has been indicated that the physiocrats' theory of productivity imposed severe limitations upon their theory of consumption and circulation, and it has been implied that the physiocrats, while indirectly critical of the vested interests of their day, were essentially spokesmen for the landed interests. It has been implied also that contradictory principles infused the physiocratic philosophy. To these contradictions we shall give but passing attention, however, inasmuch as they bear in but small measure upon the theme of this paper.[116]

Among the economic principles to which the physiocrats subscribed were these three: (*a*) the institution of private property is essential, at all times and in all places, to the well-being and development of societies; (*b*) complete economic liberty — freedom of exchange, of entry, and of competition — is prerequisite to the maximization of effort and conducive to the private and the public interest; (*c*) activity and policy directed to the maximization of the net product are necessary to, and consistent with, the maximization of the collective welfare.

Critics of the physiocratic philosophy have pointed out that principle *c* is not universally consistent with principle *b*; that pursuit of principle *c* must eventually involve conflict with, and sacrifice of, principle *b* and its corollary, principle *a*. Quesnay's liberalism, it is said, was narrow and negative — contingent upon its serving, as it did at the time it was enunciated, the interests of agriculture and upon its favoring the increase of the net product. Were the pursuit of principle *b* to run counter to that of principle *c*, it is said, Quesnay would have sacrificed principle *b* to principle *c*, even to the extent of supporting state intervention in favor of agriculture. In support of this interpretation, Quesnay's critics adduce citations from his writings and point, by way of illustration, to his advocacy of regulation of the interest rate.[117] A. Dubois has denied this interpretation, pointing to Quesnay's rejection of mercantilist opinions regarding money, to his failure to demand favoritism for agriculture, to his discovering support for economic liberty in the natural order and the natural laws established by Providence, and to the inconsistency of export bounties and indirect taxation with his theory of tax incidence.[118] Yet Dubois admits that if it could have been proved to Quesnay that legislation (e.g., tariffs) would increase the net product, he might have found such intervention to conform to the natural order.[119]

Quesnay's critics agree in supposing that the leading members of the school, other than Mirabeau, who subscribed without qualification to Quesnay's views, assigned primacy to principles a and b. These disciples of Quesnay, in event of conflict between principles c and b, would have subordinated the pursuit of principle c to that of the overriding principle b, it is inferred.

The inconsistency of principles c and b is not significant for the purposes of the present discussion. At most, supposing principle b were subordinated to principle c, consumer sovereignty would be more restricted. There is present in the physiocratic treatment of consumption, however, a contradiction which was not resolved. It has been pointed out that the physiocrats, in particular Le Trosne and Mercier, counted upon the growth of mass demand to provide a great and expanding domestic market for agricultural produce. It is evident that, other things being equal, the magnitude of the mass demand depends upon the level of wages and that the magnitude of the net product varies inversely with the level of agricultural expenses, of which wages are the major component. If, then, primacy is assigned to the maximization of net product, a limit necessarily is imposed upon the permissible augmentation of wages, which affect, directly or indirectly, the magnitude of the net product and which influence the extent of mass purchasing-power. This conflict Quesnay and Mirabeau did not resolve. Le Trosne and others resolved it implicitly by assigning primacy to the principle of economic liberty; for, if the determination of both wages and net product is left to the forces of competition, the conflict between augmentation of purchasing-power and augmentation of net product disappears. The physiocrats, who appear to have accepted this solution, did not, however, inquire carefully into the circumstances which channelize the play of competition; nor did they advance such arguments for greater equality as are to be found in the writings of Lauderdale and James Mill.

E. SMITH AND "PARSIMONY"

Adam Smith thought well of the physiocratic system, despite "its imperfections." Of this we have evidence in his characterizing it as "the nearest approximation to the truth . . . . yet . . . . published . . . . upon political economy." He singled out for praise their representing wealth "as consisting . . . . in the consumable goods annually reproduced by the labour of the society" and their describing "perfect liberty as the only efficient expedient" for maximizing "this annual reproduction."[120] We have further evidence in the fact that only after his visit with the physiocrats did Smith distinguish between productive and unproductive labor, incorporate a scheme of distribution in his body of economic doctrine, and develop the thesis that productive labor is set in motion by the laying-out of capital stock.[121] Smith seems to have placed less stress upon the essential circularity of the process of production and distribution than did the physiocrats.

While Smith believed that agricultural capital put in motion more productive labor than an equal capital employed in manufactures,[122] he did not subscribe to the physiocrats' "representing the class of artificers, manufacturers and merchants, as altogether barren and unproductive,"[123] or to their corollary theses regarding the role of manufacturers and commerce and the effect of the circulation of proprietary revenue upon the annual produce. Moreover — and this point is of primary importance for the present discussion — Smith took exception to the physiocratic depreciation of what he called "parsimony."[124] For he apprehended no boundary to the desire of men for products other than food and no consolidated indisposition on the part of men, living in an advanced state,[125] to spend or invest whatever income was received. Necessity forced the masses to spend what they earned, while good sense impelled the well-to-do to disburse what they received:

> In all countries where there is tolerable security, every man of common understanding will endeavor to employ whatever stock he can command, in procuring either present enjoyment or future profit. . . . . A man must be perfectly crazy who . . . . does not.[126]

Although Smith declared consumption to be "sole end and purpose of all production,"[127] he dwelt upon the importance of "parsimony." His work may be said to usher in that emphasis upon the accumulation of material wealth — an emphasis which drew support from the fear of population growth and (later) from the acceptance of Say's law — which dominated economic thinking until the period of World War I. Upon parsimony depended the augmentation of "capitals" and the annual produce; for it increased the funds "destined for the maintenance of productive hands" and thus tended to add "value to the annual produce." Hence he lauded frugality, condemned public and private prodigality, and expressed alarm at the growth of public debt.[128] He took it for granted that what was saved would shortly be expended and so conceived "parsimony" to comprehend both the act of saving and the succeeding act of investment.

> What is annually saved is as regularly consumed as what is annually spent, and nearly in the same time too; but it is consumed by a different set of people.[129]

The undertaker of some great manufactory [who cuts his operating expenses by 500] will naturally employ [this saved amount] in purchasing an additional quantity of materials to be wrought by an additional number of workmen.[130]

Smith was not alarmed lest there be more saved than could be invested, for capital accumulation tended to increase production and to cheapen consumption. Specifically, as "stock" increased, the supply of food and other products increased, while the funds destined for the maintenance of labor expanded; in consequence, the population grew, and, as a result, the opportunity to employ "stock" again improved.[131] If "stock" increased more rapidly than population and "capital" had to be directed into less lucrative employments, profits fell.[132] Yet the carrying trade, though the least lucrative of these employments open to capital, was capable of setting a very large amount of "stock" to work.[133] Smith apparently believed that if geographic, technological, and other forms of progress came to an end, wages and profits would fall to a very low level and capital formation and population growth would practically come to a standstill. He did not suggest, however, that in such a hypothetical stationary state there would be underconsumption and underproduction because of oversaving.[134]

Smith's discussion of parsimony, while not formulated precisely in the same terms as Say's law, is permeated by its spirit; for he looked upon money as essentially a facilitator of exchange and upon exchange as essentially barter.[135] He emphasized, as had a number of mercantilists, but for somewhat different reasons, the importance of frugality and thrift; yet he did not share their or the physiocrats' fear of hoarding.[136] Saving did not tend to reduce the demand for goods and services; rather it eventuated in capital formation and in an enlargement of both supply and demand. Presumably he was thinking of an economy in a healthy state. Say's law may be derived from Smith's, even as it may be inferred from the physiocratic writings, and it would have been deduced from one or the other had Say never written.

F. LAUDERDALE

While the doctrines of the physiocrats did not win many adherents in England, the views of Smith predominating, their opinions received occasional support even in the early nineteenth century. Most important for the present discussion was John Gray's criticism, based upon physiocratic principles, of Smith's views, since Gray's work[137] must have influenced Spence. Dugald Stewart commented favorably upon the opinions of the physiocrats, having been assisted in their study by Lord Lauderdale,[138] but he did not, as did Godwin,[139] share their dislike of "parsimony."[140]

Although Lord Lauderdale was critical of the basic tenets of physiocracy,[141] he marshaled their views on circulation and expenditure against both Smith's views on "parsimony" and popular notions regarding the effects of indulging what Lauderdale called "this baneful passion for accumulation"; for "consumption, most undoubtedly, must always precede production."[142] And just as the "effectual demand" for a given commodity regulates its supply, so must the totality of demand for commodities regulate the totality of their supply.[143] Whence it follows that "abstinence from expenditure, and consequent accumulation," if not counteracted by private prodigality or governmental disbursements, must diminish total demand and therefore the total output. Parsimony per se cannot, therefore, as "popular prejudice" would have it, increase public weath; for it cannot enlarge or improve the effectiveness of the sources of wealth. Rather, because it operates to discourage production, it must tend to diminish wealth:

> Deprivation of expenditure, and consequent accumulation, far from being a means of increasing the wealth of the nation, must, . . . by discouraging production, inevitably tend to its diminution.[144]

Lauderdale made three applications of his thesis, each consistent only in part with physiocratic theory — to capital formation, to fiscal policy, and to the distribution of wealth:

> There must be, at all times, a point determined by the existing state of knowledge in the art of supplanting and performing labour with capital, beyond which capital cannot profitably be increased, and beyond which it will not naturally increase.[145]

If revenues are diverted to the formation of unneeded capital, such diversion diminishes demand and discourages production in the areas from which the funds are removed. Moreover, this discouragement is not completely offset by the encouragement given to the makers of capital instruments, whose value, besides, is presently depressed by their overproduction. The net effect of such diversion, therefore, is a diminution of total production.[146]

In his comments on the proposal to set aside £15 million annually for sinking-fund purposes, Lauderdale developed his thesis further. If these funds were not spent, both the demand for goods and the opportunity to employ capital would be diminished correspondingly. If this sum were used to take up securities, those to whom it was paid in exchange for these securities would not spend it for goods, since they would regard it "as capital"; nor could they on short notice and in an economy already depressed by the initial withdrawal of this sum invest more than a fraction of it in capital instruments.[147] Lauderdale concluded, therefore, that too rapid debt retirement would depress demand and discourage production and capital formation.[148] He observed, furthermore:

> Parsimony, when pushed beyond a certain extent, whether private, or public, whether the effect of the depraved taste of individuals, or of an erroneous system of legislation must be fatal to the progress of public wealth.[149]

Lauderdale made no use of anything like a multiplier principle, however; nor did Spence.

The "distribution of wealth" not only regulated "the portion of demand for different descriptions of commodities" and influenced population growth[150] but also affected the rate at which a nation could accumulate wealth. Where there was greater equality, agriculture flourished, there were more men with *both* the incentive and the means to introduce new and more efficient instruments of production, and there was a more extensive and more rapidly growing mass demand to absorb the greater output made possible by the introduction of better methods of production. Where, on the contrary, there was "great inequality," these favorable conditions did not exist.[151]

A proper distribution of wealth insures the increase of opulence, by sustaining a regular progressive demand in the home market, and still more effectually, by affording to those whose habits are likely to create a desire of supplanting labour, the power of executing it.[152]

G. WILLIAM SPENCE

Napoleon's "continental system" inspired two works, both intended to show that, should Napoleon succeed, "he would only lop off superfluous branches, not hew down the main trunk" of Britain's economy.[153] Both works were founded in part upon physiocratic principles, and both were designed to demonstrate that Britain was not dependent upon commerce, as Napoleon's policy assumed. Thomas Chalmers, the author of one of these works, later evolved out of certain of its principles the thesis that a general glut was possible[154] and an argument against undue parsimony. The author of the other, William Spence (1783–1860), condemned parsimony and asserted the primacy of consumption.[155]

Unlike Quesnay, Spence attached great importance to manufacturing and its development, saying that the expansion of agriculture depended upon that of manufacturing, which, directly and indirectly, provided a market for agricultural produce and a stimulus to its extension; yet, like Cantillon and Quesnay, he emphasized the spending and consuming role of the landed proprietor. "Agriculture and manufactures are the two chief wheels in the machine which creates national wealth; . . . [and] it is the latter which communicates motion to the former"; but the power which sets these wheels in motion "is the class of land proprietors."[156]

Every civilized society, said Spence, combining the views of Smith and Quesnay, comprises four classes: (*a*) landowners; (*b*) cultivators; (*c*) manufacturers, who, while unproductive in the physiocratic sense of the term, convert raw produce into manufactures; and (*d*) the unproductive class proper, consisting of all who do not fall within the first three classes and whose services perish at the instant of their performance. Class *b* derives revenue from the land and transfers it to class *a*, whence it passes, in exchange for goods and services, to classes *c* and *d*, who, in turn, spend it with class *b* for produce. This production-stimulating circulation is contingent, however, upon prompt and sufficient spending by the landed proprietors.[157]

It is a condition, then, essential to the creation of national wealth, that the class of land proprietors, expend the greater part of the revenue which they derive from the soil. They are the agents, through whose hands the revenue of the society passes, but in order that wealth and prosperity should accrue to the community, it is absolutely necessary, that they should spend this revenue. So long as they perform this duty, everything goes on in its proper train. With the funds which the manufacturing and unproductive classes appropriate to themselves, from the expenditure of the class of land owners, from supplying the members of this class with various objects of necessity, or of luxury, which their desires, whether natural or factitious, require, they are enabled to purchase the food which the farmer offers to them. The farmer being enabled to dispose of his produce, acquires the funds necessary for the payment of his rent, and thus, the revenue again reverts to the land proprietor, from whom it was in the first instance derived, again to be expended, and again to perform the same duty of circulation.[158]

Spence therefore condemned Smith's defense of parsimony, saying that "expenditure, not parsimony, is the province" and the "duty" of the landed proprietors and that the expansion of manufactures, of agriculture, and of population is contingent upon the progressive increase of this expenditure. Suppose the landed proprietors "save" 1 million of their revenue. The market for the products and services of classes c and d will be reduced correspondingly, and they, in turn, will have that much less to spend on agricultural products; whence the income of the cultivators will fall in like measure, and they will be unable to requite their rental obligation to the proprietors. Nor, says Spence, is the outcome otherwise, if the million is lent at interest. For then it is "employed as capital" — at the very time that the diminution in expenditure "decreases the means of the profitable employment of capital"; and, while it may "give employment to manufacturers," it cannot "diminish the hardships of those" who have been "deprived of the revenue derived from its expenditure."[159]

It followed, since agricultural expansion and economic expansion in general are contingent upon the expansion of expenditure by the landed proprietors, that "the increase of *luxury* is absolutely essential to [the] well being" of England and Europe. For since a proprietor can "procure all the necessaries and comforts of life" by the expenditure of a "few hundred a year," he must, if he is to disburse the remainder of his revenue, exchange it for luxuries, in especial for "luxuries *fabricated at home*,"[160] and these must therefore be available. Unlike Quesnay, Spence did not distinguish between decorative luxury and *luxe de subsistence*, for he believed that, so long as the proprietor spent his revenue with classes c and d, no difficulties would arise.[161] It made no initial difference, in fact, whether a proprietor employed 500 men to construct "a splendid palace" or "to blow glass bubbles, to be broken as soon as possible," for in either case the workers required as much agricultural produce.[162] It was preferable in the longer run, however, that men purchase "permanent" (i.e., durable) luxuries, which added to a nation's "wealth," rather than "luxuries . . . of a transitory nature." And it was "highly" desirable, "in a moral point of view," that the members of the "unproductive" class "be occupied in ministering to the wisdom, rather than the follies, of society, in contributing to its instruction, rather than its amusement."[163]

Spence's general position on luxury and manufactures and on their relation to agriculture was much closer to that of Germain Garnier than to that of Quesnay. In reply to critics who pointed to the evils (occupational diseases, depraved morals, etc.) attendant upon the development of urban manufactures, Spence said: "I have contended for the increase of luxury, because I can see no other way by which the poor of Europe can draw the produce of the soil out of the hands of its possessors."[164]

In his discussion of fiscal policy, Spence followed Lauderdale rather than Quesnay and defended debt-creation and taxation. Man is "much more inclined to save and to hoard, than to spend," while proprietors do not tend to disburse all their revenue. Whence offsets to this tendency to save are required, and these are supplied by debt-creation and taxation. Debt-creation by the government converts "what was destined for capital, into consumable revenue," thus stimulating agriculture. Since he believed that the establishment of a sinking fund would reverse this process, Spence opposed it, citing Lauderdale's arguments. Taxes, while ultimately incident upon land, transferred to the government revenue which the proprietors might otherwise have saved but which the government spent, thus benefiting agriculture:

> Expenditure, in short, is the very essence of a system like ours, and what difference can it make to the prosperity of the country whether it is indebted for this expenditure to the government or its subjects.[165]

H. JAMES MILL'S REPLY

One, and possibly two, of the critical replies which Spence's pamphlet provoked[166] were inspired by Say's *Traité*, a pamphlet by James Mill in which Say's law of markets was clearly formulated, and a review, possibly by Henry Brougham, in the *Edinburgh Review*,[167] in which Say's principle was hinted at. The author of the latter wrote:

> We are perfectly ready to admit, that consumption must exist somewhere, or there could be no production; and that there are limits to the accumulation of capital, though we do not know where to place them: but we are strongly inclined to believe, that *production generates consumption*, as well as consumption production; and that an increasing capital naturally produces an increased use of consumable commodities, from the greater cheapness of manufactures, the comparative higher price of labour, the improved cultivation of the soil, the more rapid increase of population, and the constant growth of an important class of consumers living upon profits of stock, and the interest of money. . . . . Each manufacturer and artificer becomes a consumer to his brother manufacturers and artificers in different lines.[168]

Brougham, if it was he who reviewed Spence's pamphlet, did not, in his other works, avail himself of the principle that "production generates consumption." Charles Bosanquet's pamphlet on commerce, for example, provided Brougham with an excellent opportunity to apply Say's law. But Brougham missed it. Bosanquet had declared that, since England was in need of more people than her agriculture could support, she must further develop her commerce and manufactures and exchange wrought goods for raw produce; she must, in short, develop "a balance of labour" rather than a "balance of trade."[169] And he had added: "But manufacture is only a second cause; it has no intrinsic momentum; the *primum mobile* is consumption." Of these opinions Brougham said only that he was "unable to admire" them. But he did remark, following his comment that "a general glut" of sugar was the cause of the West Indian trouble, that in all "ordinary lines of employment" supply always approaches but never quite catches up with demand, inasmuch as "the capital which is accumulated from profits, can only be reinvested, so as to augment the stock yielding annual increase, slowly and with difficulty. . . . ."[170]

In his review of Lauderdale's work, Brougham approved the substance of the former's broadened definition of what is productive but criticized his opinions on capital accumulation.

It is because new capital, *i.e.*, stock not consumed but saved, gives employment to new men, and sustenance to increased numbers of inhabitants, and because it exercises the inventive powers of its possessors, that its accumulation may fairly be said to have no definable bounds.[171]

Nonetheless, he observed that when a nation's economy had become fully developed, "parsimony must then be unnecessary, as no new channels of employment can be opened." Holland had nearly reached this stage of development, and England soon would, unless she improved her agriculture and developed her colonies.[172] He noted, moreover, that a mere increase of the food supply would not augment the population and thus provide a market for this food, inasmuch as the growth of population was regulated by the growth of the supply of *both* food *and* comforts and luxuries.[173]

In his reply to Spence, James Mill, apparently following Say, distinguished between productive and unproductive consumption, "between the commodities which are destined to serve for immediate and unproductive consumption, and the commodities which are destined to operate as the instruments or means of production,"[174] and he stated that what is annually produced is annually consumed in one form or another. Mill emphasized the importance of parsimony and, while admitting that an individual commodity might be overproduced because another was underproduced, denied the possibility of general overproduction or a glut.[175] He charged Spence with repeating Lauderdale's untenable opinions on fiscal policy and with building upon Mercier's "remarkable" principle — "La consommation est la mesure de la reproduction" — instead of upon the valid principle — "Consumption is posterior to production."[176]

Parsimony, says Mill, following Smith and Say, is essential to a nation's progress in wealth and well-being, for only that part of the "annual produce" which is consumed (i.e., employed) "for the sake of reproduction" serves to augment the "whole annual produce" and thus to increase comfort. Moreover, given peace and a suitable distribution[177] of wealth, together with competition and a curb on the inclination of governments to spend rather than to save, "the disposition of mankind to save and to better their condition" would probably provide enough capital formation to permit progress.[178]

Parsimony did not imply hoarding and underexpenditure, or underconsumption, inasmuch as that which was saved was promptly expended, either by the saver himself or by a borrower:

> Of the two parts of the annual produce, that which is destined for reproduction and that which is destined for consumption, the one is as completely expended as the other, and that part which is destined for reproduction, is that which is probably all expended in the shortest time.[179]

> The self interest of men, ever has impelled and ever will impell them, with some very trifling exceptions, to use every particle of property which accrues to them, either to the purpose of immediate gratification, or of future profit. That part, however, which is destined for future profit, is just as completely consumed, as that which is destined for immediate gratification.[180]

It was absurd, therefore, to say that government borrowing or taxation served to increase expenditure, consumption, and production; for the money taken over by the government and employed in "dead consumption" would "have been as certainly laid out in the purchase of commodities, had it remained as [private] capital."[181]

In general, Mill declared, saving eventuates promptly in investment, and production automatically generates the purchasing-power necessary to remove itself from the market. Hence the underexpenditure and underconsumption, which Spence, Lauderdale, and the physiocrats feared, cannot be. Mill thus gave full and explicit expression to what later was called Say's law:

> Every country will infallibly consume to the full amount of its production. . . . . The production of commodities creates, and is the one and universal cause which creates a market for the commodities produced. . . . . The collective means of payment of the whole nation . . . . consist in its annual produce. . . . . A nation can never be naturally overstocked either with capital or with commodities; as the very operation of capital makes a vent for its produce. . . . . When money is laid out of the question, is it not in reality the different commodities of the country, that is to say, the different articles of the annual produce, which are annually exchanged against one another? . . . . The demand of a nation is exactly its power of purchasing. But what is its power of purchasing? The extent undoubtedly of its annual produce. . . . . How great soever the annual produce may be it always creates a market to itself. . . . . [A nation's] power of purchasing is always equivalent to its power of producing, or at least to its annual produce.[182]

I. SAY'S LAW OF MARKETS

Whereas Mill's law of demand originated in his attempt to demolish specific opinions of Spence, Lauderdale, and Mercier, Say's law of markets grew out of his effort to overthrow finally the supposedly untenable but lingering doctrines of the physiocrats and to substitute in their place a somewhat modified Smithianism. For the physiocratic theory of the unique productivity of land he substituted the principle that whatever creates utility is productive;[183] for the physiocratic theory of *luxe*, the doctrine of productive and unproductive consumption; for the physiocratic theory of interclass exchange, the theory of interindividual exchange; for the physiocratic stress upon agriculture, stress upon manufactures and their growing importance; for the physiocratic emphasis upon the landed proprietor as the center of the economic scheme of things, emphasis upon the active entrepreneur as the principal animator and organizer of economic life; and for the peculiar and circumscribed physiocratic doctrine of circular flow and the primacy of consumption, his generalized law of markets and the primacy of production. This law of markets he directed, at first, against those who did not believe that consumption readily and necessarily adjusts itself to increases in production and, later, against the theory of general glut identified with the names of Malthus and Sismondi.

Say developed the thesis, especially in his chapter on "Des débouchés," that "c'est la production qui ouvre des débouchés aux produits," money serving as a mere agent of transfer, which performs a "momentary function"; that, while the supply of some one commodity may temporarily outrun the demand for it, the supply of all commodities cannot outrun the demand for all commodities, inasmuch as an excess of one product presupposes an offsetting deficit of something else and as it is supply which gives rise to demand. He concluded, therefore, that, the more numerous are producers and the more varied are productions, the more numerous and extensive are markets for productions; that the success of one branch of industry promotes that of all others; that the vent abroad for a nation's productions is determined by its purchases abroad; and that the encouragement of "unproductive" consumption is of no benefit to commerce or production, since the difficulty always lies, not in stimulating the desire of consumption, but in supplying the means of consumption.[184]

Although Say's *Traité* did not assume substantially final form until the second edition (1814), the essence of his views regarding the importance of capital formation, the need of curbing unnecessary unproductive consumption, and the origin of demand in production is already to be found in the 1803 edition. If this be true — and it is contrary to Hollander's opinion — it may be inferred from the similarity of Mill's to Say's analysis that the distinction of having first formulated Say's law belongs to Say alone.[185]

There is not much of the law of markets in Say's chapter on "Des débouchés" in the first edition; but the spirit of the law underlies many of his observations in other chapters, and its essence is stated. In this chapter, after noting that each producer creates a surplus which he desires to exchange for portions of the surpluses of other producers, Say declares that one pays "for products with products," money serving only as a medium of exchange, and that if a nation has too much of one type of product it may provide for its sale by creating more of another type. He describes as "one of the most important truths of political economy" the fact that it is not an abundance of money but an abundance of products in general which makes for "facile markets."[186] In a later chapter Say denies that demand depends upon consumption, saying that consumption is an effect of production and that supply equals demand, since each equals the sum of what is unproductively consumed and what is accumulated.

> Pour consommer il faut acheter; or on n'achète qu'avec ce qu'on a produit. La quantité de produits demandés est-elle donc déterminée par la quantité de produits créés? Sans aucun doute. Chaque peut à son gré consommer ce qu'il a produit; ou bien avec son produit en acheter un autre. La demande des produits en général est donc toujours égale à la somme des produits . . . le meilleur moyen d'ouvrir des débouchés aux produits est de les multiplier et non de les détruire . . . les bornes de la production . . . sont dans les moyens de produire.[187]

To Garnier's suggestion of the possibility of a general congestion of markets, Say replies that, while for a short time too much of some one product may be produced, too much of *all* products cannot be produced, since the total demand for products is nothing but the whole mass of products which have been produced.

> Je ne conçois pas que les produits de l'industrie d'une nation en général, puissent jamais être trop abondans, car l'un donne les moyens d'acheter l'autre. . . .
> La demande des moyens de production en général . . . tient à l'étendue de la production. Et comme l'étendue de la production dépend de l'étendue des moyens de production, la demande des moyens de production s'étend dans le même proportion que les moyens de production euxmêmes; c'est-à-dire en résultat, qu'une nation a toujours les moyens d'acheter tout ce qu'elle produit.[188]

Say made use of this law of markets in his analysis of saving, capital formation, and consumption and directed it specifically against those who asserted that "parsimony" gave rise to underconsumption and overproduction. Consumption, he said, involves the "destruction of utility." Consumption is of two kinds: (*a*) *productive*, which, while it satisfies no wants, results in the creation of a new value, and (*b*) *unproductive*, which, while it creates no new value, usually gratifies a want. Capital formation causes no diminution of expenditure or consumption; for, although it presupposes frugality and saving, it consists in essence in the substitution of productive for unproductive consumption. Say therefore dismissed as unfounded the fear that frugality might lead to a diminution in expenditure and output, because he took it for granted that, as a rule, what was saved was not hoarded but was promptly consumed productively. And he praised frugality as necessary to progress in industry, opulence, and civilization.[189]

The same distinctions and arguments appear in the 1803 edition, where he stresses the importance of economy, frugality, saving, and capital formation. A nation cannot have too much capital, he suggests; nor is it likely to have a supply even approximately sufficient in view of man's propensity to multiply and his avidity for pleasures. Savings are not withdrawn from circulation so long as there is order and security. For neither a saver nor a borrower wants to forego interest on his funds; and there are a "thousand ways of placing savings." Savings therefore are consumed, but productively;

they furnish markets for products which are "useful and capable of engendering others, in place of evaporating in frivolous consumption." Suppose, says Say, that a wealthy man cuts his unproductive consumption by 20,000 francs and lends these to a manufacturer. The latter promptly invests them and furnishes employment to as many workers as are thrown out of work by the wealthy lender's discontinuance of a portion of his unproductive consumption. What is more important, since the 20,000 francs are spent *productively*, the revenues of the lender, the manufacturer, and the workers increase and the market for products expands accordingly.[190]

Say singled out for criticism the views of those who, in his opinion, had alleged the primacy of (unproductive) consumption and had described spending as preferable to frugality (especially Mercier and the physiocrats); of those who had declared free spending by the wealthy to be essential to the support of the poor (e.g., Fontaine, Voltaire, Montesquieu); and of those who had advocated extensive spending by governments and had found public debt to be advantageous:

> How great, then, must be the mistake of those, who, on observing the obvious fact, that the production always equals the consumption, as it must necessarily do, since a thing cannot be consumed before it is produced, have confounded the cause with the effect, and laid it down as a maxim, that consumption originates production; therefore that frugality is directly adverse to public prosperity, and that the most useful citizen is the one who spends the most.[191]

Say did not object to *necessary* unproductive consumption, indicating that, because of the lowness of income and the urgency of human wants, the bulk of human consumption always had been and always must be of this character. But he did object to unproductive consumption, whether by individuals or by governments, which was unnecessary and which had the destruction of utility as its sole object; for it served merely to destroy resources which might otherwise be put to productive use. Of this sort, Say believed, was the consumption recommended by the physiocrats.[192]

It was unnecessary, Say observed further, to excite mankind to consume and thus, by subjecting them to the urgings of unsated wants, to endeavor to impel them to produce more. Such prompting assumed that it was as easy to increase production as to augment consumption; moreover, it tended to substitute unproductive for productive consumption. It was equally unnecessary to hold down wage rates in order to actuate men to work longer hours, in order to satisfy a given budget of wants; for, since human wants multiply as fast as they can be satisfied, men are constantly pressed by them to maximize their efforts, output, and earnings.[193]

J. CONCLUSION

The physiocrats concerned themselves with what are now considered the two major objects of economic analysis — resource allocation and the level of economic activity — indicating that these two economic categories are interconnected. The maximization of output, in their opinion, depended upon the pattern and the continuity of consumption and upon the employment of a sufficient proportion of a nation's mobile resources in agriculture and other extractive industries capable of yielding a net product. The nineteenth- and early twentieth-century writers, in consequence of their subscription to Say's law of markets, practically removed one of these objects — the level of economic activity — from consideration and concentrated attention upon the other — resource allocation and pricing.

The physiocrats were responsible, in several respects, for the formulation of Say's law, which could have been inferred from their writings and which is substantially present in the work of Smith, who apparently was influenced by the physiocrats' notions of circulation. The physiocrats looked upon money as essentially an intermediary, particularly in a healthy economy, and they emphasized the fundamental role of goods and services in the circulatory scheme of the *Tableau économique*, thereby pointing to the real and nonpecuniary character of exchange, which was later stressed by Say. Second, the physiocrats emphasized the primacy of the consumption of agricultural produce, a thesis that was generalized into the primacy of all consumption by Lauderdale and Spence, and thus provoked Say and Mill to enunciate their law which assigns primacy to production. The physiocrats' emphasis upon the primacy of the consumption of agricultural produce issued out of their theory of net production, with its playing-down of nonagricultural economic activities, and out of the fact that the physiocrats lived in an unhealthy economy, in which, in their opinion, fiscal practices were depriving agriculture of loan capital, causing hoarding, depressing the level of demand for both agricultural and other products, and interrupting the circular flow of money and goods and services.[194]

Although Smith distinguished between productive and unproductive labor and indicated a preference for durable goods, he gave expression to the essence of Say's law; for he viewed exchange as essentially barter and money as an instrument employed to facilitate exchange. He did not, therefore, apprehend the possibility of a general glut. Yet he failed to put Say's law in terms of a simple formula, perhaps because he missed the full import of the physiocratic theory of circular flow.

Lauderdale substituted for the restricted productivity theories of Quesnay and Smith a generalized theory of productivity and for the physiocratic emphasis upon the primacy of the consumption of agricultural produce, emphasis upon the primacy of consumption in general. Somewhat after the manner of the physiocrats and more explicitly, Lauderdale indicated that whatever part of the national income could not be invested must be spent upon consumer goods and services; else the level of economic activity would fall. He observed, furthermore, that the rate at which savings could be absorbed, while not invariable, was limited; hence, like some of the physiocrats, he noted the supposed danger of too great frugality. Lauderdale assigned greater importance to money as such than did Quesnay and Smith, and he drew attention in much greater measure than had his predecessors to the adverse effect of marked economic inequality upon the level of economic activity and the rate of economic progress.

194

Spence differed from the physiocrats in a number of respects, among them the following: (*a*) he looked upon manufacturing as an expansive — albeit unproductive — force; (*b*) he did not declare that a definite fraction of the national income must be spent upon agricultural products; and (*c*) he attached greater importance to the pecuniary aspects of fiscal policy. But he accepted much of the circulatory scheme of the physiocrats and made the level of economic activity depend upon spending by the landed proprietors.

Say's formulation of his law of markets appears to have issued out of his desire to bring physiocracy to term and out of suggestions in the writings of Smith and the physiocrats. For the restricted physiocratic and Smithian theories of productivity he substituted a generalized theory of utility creation; but he distinguished between unproductive and productive consumption, and he emphasized the importance of wealth accumulation, to which productive consumption alone gave rise. From Smith he took over the principle that all income received is promptly expended, productively or unproductively. From the physiocrats and possibly from Smith he adopted the idea that money performs only a momentary function in each exchange. From the physiocrats, too, he must have got a notion of circular flow. Perhaps as a result of Smith's inspiration, Say generalized the physiocratic thesis — that men need not be spurred to produce by the prospect of obtaining manufactures — into the thesis that men need not be excited by luxuries, since wants multiply at least as fast as they can be supplied. Say was able, therefore, to direct two counter-principles against both the physiocratic thesis that consumption is primary and Lauderdale's thesis that there could be too much saving: (*a*) since exchange consists essentially in bartering goods and services, the demand for goods is equivalent to their supply and increases with their supply; (*b*) consumption is always commensurate with production, since that portion of income received which is not devoted to unproductive consumption is expended upon productive consumption. Say thus supposed what the physiocrats had implicitly denied: that an economy is always in a healthy state. The physiocrats had evolved their theory to rehabilitate an economically sick France. They probably would not have denied the essential truth of Say's principles, given appropriate conditions, but they would have denied that these conditions were to be found in Bourbon France.

Although Mill gave fuller expression in 1808 to the law of markets than did Say in 1803, Mill seems to have built his law around the principle to which Say gave expression in 1803. Had Mill not become acquainted with Say's principle, he might have developed the view he got from Smith — that men always spend, in one way or another, the income which they receive. As it was, Mill apparently took over from Say the distinction between productive and unproductive consumption and expanded somewhat Say's fundamental thesis that, since exchange is resolvable into barter, demand is commensurate with supply. For Say's views on these matters were such as would appeal to a disciple of Smith, and they were well suited to serve as a basis for a reply to the opinions of Spence and Lauderdale.

Whence Mill incorporated Say's views in his reply to Spence. What is important for the present discussion, however, is that the physiocratic thesis — that consumption is primary — provoked both Say and Mill to formulate the counterthesis.

In after years the law of markets became dominant, for not only did it possess validity under appropriate circumstances and serve to describe what was taking place, but it was also congenial to a climate of opinion which played down state interventionism and played up the sufficiency of economic individualism, the self-adjusting character of the economic system, and the capacity of that system to provide and absorb vast amounts of capital and improvements. The physiocratic contribution to the formulation of this law was forgotten at a time when it was directed against Malthus, Sismondi, Chalmers, and others who asserted that the circular flow of goods, services, and money is susceptible of interruption. Forgotten too, except by Marx, was the more important discovery by Quesnay that economic relations are resolvable into a circular flow, whose continuity is contingent upon the presence of certain conditions. To these conditions — not, of course, the specific conditions which Quesnay would have enumerated — the Keynesian analysis drew attention at the same time that it revealed, as several physiocrats had hinted, that an economy may come to rest at a prosperity level, or at a depression level, or at some intermediate level.

NOTES

1. E. A. J. Johnson, *Predecessors of Adam Smith* (New York, 1937), esp. pp. 168, 287 ff., 289 ff.; J. Viner, *Studies in the Theory of International Trade* (New York, 1937), pp. 26–30, 32–33, 45–50, 90.

2. Hume, who contributed much to the synthesis of these views, drew upon the opinions of Mandeville, particularly upon those relating to psychology (see Johnson, *op. cit.*, pp. 169 ff., 292 ff.; Viner, *op. cit.*, pp. 33, 90–91; F. B. Kaye's Introduction to his edition of Mandeville's *The Fable of the Bees* [Oxford, 1924]). Some of Mandeville's comments anticipate some of Veblen's opinions.

3. See Hazel Van Dyke Roberts, *Boisguilbert, Economist of the Reign of Louis XIV* (New York, 1935). For the sake of convenience, our brief references will be to this study rather than to Boisguilbert's own works. On his relations to the physiocrats see G. Weulersse, *Le Mouvement physiocratique en France* (Paris, 1910), and "Notes inédites sur Boisguilbert par le Marquis de Mirabeau," *Revue d'histoire de doctrines économiques*, III (1910), 113–51; H. Higgs, *The Physiocrats* (London, 1897); Dupont's remarks, reprinted in Auguste Oncken, *Oeuvres économiques et philosophiques de F. Quesnay* (Frankfort, 1888), pp. 146 ff. This work is hereinafter referred to as "Quesnay, *Oeuvres.*" Ques-

nay (*ibid.*, p. 357) refers to Boisguillebert's work.

4. For these citations and the works from which they are taken see Roberts, *op. cit.*, pp. 148, 168–71, 204–5, 285–89.

5. J. F. Melon, *Essai politique sur le commerce* (1734), in E. Daire (ed.), *Economistes financiers du XVIIIᵉ siècle* (Paris, 1851), chap. ix. Melon was influenced by Mandeville and others and, in turn, gave direction to Voltaire's defense of luxury (see A. Morize, *L'Apologie du luxe au XVIIIᵉ siècle et "Le Mondain" de Voltaire* [Paris, 1909]). The views of various French writers upon luxury are touched upon in my *French Predecessors of Malthus* (Durham, 1942), and in A. Lichtenberger, *Le Socialisme au XVIIIᵉ siècle* (Paris, 1895).

6. Montesquieu, *De l'esprit des lois* (1748), Book VII, chaps. i.–v. While this statement relates to monarchies, it is also applicable to aristocracies; for in the latter, his argument suggests, expenditure is equally necessary to counterbalance the effects of inequality (*ibid.*, chap. iii).

7. Ibid., Book XXXIII, chap. xv. Consumption and luxury are treated also in other parts of *De l'esprit des lois*. In this work the influence of Mandeville, not present in Montesquieu's *Lettres persanes* (1721), is very evident. For the later his-

tory of the doctrine that manufactures must be developed to stimulate agriculture, see my *French Predecessors*, esp. chap. iv, and my "Malthus' Total Population Theory: A Restatement and Reappraisal," *Canadian Journal of Economics and Political Science*, February–May, 1945.

8. Cantillon, *Essai sur la nature du commerce en général* (1755), translated and edited by Henry Higgs (London, 1931), Part I, chaps. xii–xv; see also pp. 364 ff. for Higgs's account of Cantillon, the *Essai*, and its influence (cf. Ricardo, *Principles of Political Economy and Taxation* [3d. ed.], chap. xxxi, par. 142).

9. "After reading well over a thousand economic writings of earlier date than 1734," writes Higgs (*Essai*, p. 388), "I would put Cantillon's analysis of the circulation of wealth, trite as it may now appear, on the same level of priority as Harvey's study of the circulation of the blood."

10. See A. Lebeau, *Condillac économiste* (Paris, 1903), and my *French Predecessors*, pp. 136–44. While Condillac supposed that the landowning class exercised great influence on production in consequence of the relative magnitude of its income, he observed that the demands of other classes also influenced the pattern of production (see A. Landry, "Une Théorie néglegée . . . ," *Revue d'économie politique*, XXIV [1910], 314, 364, 747, 773; see also n. 183, below).

11. Quesnay (art. "Grains"), Mirabeau (*L'Ami des hommes*), Morellet, Graslin, A. Smith, and Sir James Steuart are among those who referred to Cantillon. On Cantillon's influence see F. A. von Hayek, "Richard Cantillon, sa vie, son oeuvre," *Revue des sciences économiques*, X (1936), 92 ff., 160 ff., 206 ff.

12. See Garnier's *Abrégé élémentaire des principes de l'économie politique* (Paris, 1796); see also E. Allix, "L'Oeuvre economique de Germaine Garnier," *Revue d'histoire des doctrines économiques et sociales*, V (1912), 317–42; R. Maunier, "Un Economiste oublié: Peuchet (1758–1830)," *Revue d'histoire des doctrines économiques et sociales*, IV (1911), 247–63. Peuchet followed Garnier in part.

13. The works, other than those of Quesnay already cited, to which there will be frequent reference in Sections A–C are: Mirabeau, *L'Ami des hommes*, Part VII (Hamburg, 1760), and *Philosophie rurale* (Amsterdam, 1763); E. Daire (ed.), *Oeuvres de Turgot* (Paris, 1844), and *Physiocrates* (Paris, 1846). Use has been made of the following works in Daire's *Physiocrates*: Dupont de Nemours, *De l'origine et des progrès d'une science nouvelle* (1768), and *Abrégé des principes de l'économie politique* (1772); Mercier de la Rivière, *L'Ordre natural et essentiel des sociétés politiques* (1767); N. Baudeau, *Première introduction à la philosophie économique* (1771), *Explication du Tab-*

leau économique (1768–70), and *Explication sur le vrai sens du mot stérile appliqué à l'industrie* (1767). Dupont edited the *Abrégé*, which he attributed to Charles-Frederick, Margrave of Baden. Daire's collection includes only the 18 economic chapters of Mercier's 44-chapter work. Use has been made also of Le Trosne, *De l'ordre social*, and *De l'intérêt social*, published in one volume (Paris, 1777); N. Baudeau, *Principes de la science morale et politique sur le luxe et les loix somptuaires* [1767], ed. A. Dubois (Paris, 1912); Quesnay's unpublished articles, "Hommes" and "Impôts," *Revue d'histoire des doctrines économiques et sociales*, I (1908), 3–88, 137–86; Turgot, *Reflections on the Formation and the Distribution of Riches* [1770], translated by W. Ashley (London, 1899). Ashley's translation is based upon Turgot's original work and therefore is free of the several modifications made in the text by Dupont, modifications which are retained in the Daire edition. Our references are sometimes to the Ashley, sometimes to the Daire, edition. Turgot shared some, but not all, of the opinions of the physiocrats. His writings, however, contribute appreciably to our understanding of physiocracy. Inasmuch as the present paper deals with only one aspect of physiocracy, the philosophical basis and the ethical precept ("let nature rule") of physiocratic doctrine are not examined.

14. The physiocrats do not always make it clear whether fishing and mining yield a net product as does agriculture, for their primary concern was agriculture. In this paper we shall refer only to agriculture; for what is said of agriculture is applicable in principle to fishing and mining, if these branches of extractive industry are considered productive, as they were by Quesnay and Baudeau (see Quesnay, *Tableau économique* [1758] [see n. 16 below] and Oncken, pp. 384 ff., 444 ff., 516 ff., 526 ff., Baudeau, in Daire, *Physiocrates*, pp. 713–39, 823, 868–73; Mercier, *op. cit.*, pp. 585–606; Le Trosne, *De l'intérêt*, chaps. v–vii; Weulersse, *op. cit.*, I, 244–315, esp. 277–80).

15. See P. M. Sweezy, *The Theory of Capitalist Development* (New York, 1942), p. 75 and Appen. A; K. Marx, *Capital* (Chicago, 1906), I, 647–48, II, 414 ff.; Mirabeau, *Philosophie rurale*, I, 19, 52–53; cf. also W. Leontief, *The Structure of American Economy, 1919–1929* (Cambridge, Mass., 1941), p. 9; and J. Schumpeter's analysis of circular flow in his *Theory of Economic Development* (Cambridge, 1934), chap. i.

16. See "Analyse du Tableau économique" (1766), *Oeuvres*, pp. 305 ff., and Oncken's notes on pp. 125, 305, 328, 662. The summary or abbreviated table apparently grew out of Quesnay's article, "Grains" (see n. 19 and text below); it relates to a whole kingdom, whereas the

earliest (1758) table relates primarily to the productive activities and exchange of a single farmer. The earliest table appeared in Quesnay's privately printed *Tableau économique* (1758), of which a facsimile edition was brought out in 1894 by the British Economic Association. For a summary account of this table see S. Bauer, "Quesnay's *Tableau économique*," *Economic Journal*, V (1895), 1–21. A number of economic tables, designed to illustrate the theories of production and distribution underlying Quesnay's *Tableau*, are presented by Mirabeau in *L'Ami des hommes*, Part VII, and in *Philosophie rurale*. The most lucid explanation of the *Tableau* is to be found in Baudeau's *Explication du Tableau économique* (1767 ff., 1776), which had Quesnay's approval (see *ibid.*, in Daire, *op. cit.*, p. 867). The unabbreviated tables are intended to provide a complete picture of the circulation of products and of the effects of changes in circulation (see Weulersse, *op. cit.*, I, 68–72, 129–30; A. Voelcker, "Der Tableau économique Quesnays und seine Erklärung," *Schmollers Jahrbuch*, LV [1931], 841–53; also n. 41 below).

17. For accounts of these three classes and their functions, see Mercier, *op. cit.* (1767 ed.); Baudeau, *Introduction;* Le Trosne, *De l'intérêt.*

18. The physiocratic scheme resembles somewhat that of Cantillon, who looked upon land as the source of all wealth, upon the proprietors as the center of the distributive system, and upon large-scale agriculture as superior to small scale. Normally, he said, one-half of the population, including many proprietors, lived in towns and cities, and the remainder in the country. The urban population consumed at least one-half the annual produce, two-thirds of this half being purchased with money income received from the landed proprietors, and about one-third with money received from the agricultural population in exchange for goods and services supplied by the urban population. The farmers (i.e., agricultural undertakers) turned over to the proprietors as rent the monetary equivalent of one-third of the annual agricultural produce, and this the proprietors spent in the city. The farmers retained one-third of the annual produce as profit and utilized the remaining third for the support of their help and animals. At least one-sixth of the annual produce was turned over, directly or indirectly, by the farmers to the urban population for merchandise (see *Essai*, pp. 3, 43, 45, 121, 123, 125, 127; also my *French Predecessors*, chap. iv. S. Bauer (*op. cit.*, pp. 5–6, n.) finds Cantillon's notion of "three rents" expressed at least as early as 1714, in John Bellers' *An Essay towards the Improvement of Physick, etc.* (1714).

19. In the article "Fermiers," which first appeared in the *Encyclopédie* in 1756, Quesnay estimates the territory of France at 100 million arpents, and the cultivatable portion at half. Of the 50 million cultivatable arpents, about 36 million are cultivated, 30 million by *petite culture*, and 6–7 million by *grande culture* (see n. 33, below). The editors of the *Encyclopédie* reported the territory of France as about 125 million arpents, of which about 60 million were cultivatable (see Quesnay, *Oeuvres*, pp. 171–72 and n.). In "Grains" (1757) Quesnay apparently accepts the 60-million estimate. He concluded that, given an efficient agriculture, France could produce 4 billion livres of products (chiefly grains, livestock, vinicultural products, and small crops) per year at a minimum (see *Oeuvres*, pp. 214–15). If one allows for such products (e.g., forestry, hemp) as are not included in the 4 billion minimum and supposes the minimum is exceeded, one approximates the 5 billion given in the *Tableau*.

20. Other conditions, the analysis implies, remain constant, e.g., the quantity and quality of the land under cultivation, the methods of cultivation. It also is assumed that the cultivator is free to produce those crops which offer the best return and that output can be sold at a satisfactory price. This and the following paragraphs are based largely upon Baudeau's *Explication du Tableau* and in part upon Quesnay's "Analyse . . . " and "Maximes," in *Oeuvres*, pp. 305 ff., 329 ff.

21. Baudeau (*Explication du Tableau*, p. 823) includes at least part of the subsistence of domestic animals. Quesnay, however, does not include in the 5 milliards of reproduction assumed in his abbreviated *Tableau* such expenses as those of commerce and the subsistence of animals employed in cultivation; were these included, the gross value of annual reproduction would total 6.37 milliards (*Oeuvres*, p. 320; also Mirabeau, *Philosophie rurale*, chap. vii, to which Quesnay refers).

22. See Baudeau, *Introduction*, p. 759.

23. This return provides interest on capital advanced by the cultivator, replacement of the durable instruments, and compensation for risks and losses; it returns each year a sum equal to one-half the annual advances (i.e., $0.1 \times 5 \div 1$).

24. *Introduction*, pp. 759–60; see Sec. B below.

25. See n. 21, above, for expenses not included in the 5 billion gross output. The revenue (i.e., the monetary equivalent of the net product) of the proprietors, Quesnay also notes, will be equal in value to the annual advances, or to two-fifths of the annual reproduction, only on condition that liberty in commerce (i.e., freedom of trade) sustains the sale value of agricultural products "à un bon prix" (e.g., 18 livres per septier for *blé*), and that cultivators pay no taxes or impositions, directly or indirectly (see "Analyse . . . ,"

Oeuvres, pp. 311 ff.; see also below, nn. 58, 61, and 63 on *bon prix* and on taxes). Elsewhere (*Oeuvres*, p. 700) Quesnay stated that at one time in France annual advances of 100 reproduced 300.

26. Competition on part of farmers for the use of agricultural land, the physiocrats held, distributes the monetary equivalent of the net product to the landowning proprietors (e.g., see Le Trosne, *De l'intérêt*, p. 514). Turgot noted that only when competition for the use of land is keen does the entire surplus pass to the proprietors (*Réflexions*, par. lxiv, which Dupont apparently approves). Quesnay observed that when leases were renewed, competition forced farmers to pay for the use of land a rent equivalent to the net product and that rich and skilled farmers, since they could wrest a greater net product from the land, could and did pay higher rents than farmers who were short of capital. While he admitted that poor farmers might offer more for the use of land than they could afford to pay, he said that only a rental contract which was to the mutual advantage of both farmer and landowner was "solide et heureux" (see *Oeuvres*, pp. 508 and n., and 515; also Baudeau, *Introduction*, pp. 766–69).

27. Wages and salaries tend to cover familial living expenses and the costs (if any) of education and training. The familial living budget includes sometimes only subsistence and sometimes allowances for additional elements. In essence, the physiocratic wage theory runs in terms of standard life and labor supply rather than in terms of productivity (see my *French Predecessors*, pp. 202 ff.).

28. The physiocratic treatment of interest, profits, rents, and quasi-rents is obscure. The clearest discussion is to be found in Turgot, who differed from the physiocrats in a number of respects. Turgot stated that investment in every undertaking is conditioned on the receipt of a return over and above allowances for replacement of advances, risks, and compensation for care and labor involved and that gross returns on advances (i.e., capital) in different employments tend to remain in line, one with another, preserving "a kind of equilibrium" (see *Réflexions, Oeuvres*, I, 36–44, 56–59, 63; also 450–51). Dupont, who criticized other views of Turgot (e.g., on capital formation, see below, n. 107 and text), did not take exception to these statements. The sale price of land, moreover, Turgot notes (e.g., *ibid.*, p. 64), tends to equal the capitalized value of the return to land less taxes; this statement Dupont approved. Quesnay and Mirabeau believed that interest charges fall ultimately upon the land (see below, n. 103 and text). On interest see also Le Trosne, *De l'intérêt*, p. 600; and Weulersse, *op. cit.*, I, 310–15.

29. This interpretation is based upon Baudeau's *Explication du Tableau*, which

Quesnay approved; it is consistent with the expositions of Quesnay and others.

30. If production is defined in modern terms and if it is supposed that the proprietary class behaves as Baudeau would have it behave, it may be said that the proprietary class "produces" services with a value of not more than 2 billion. If we add this sum to the 2 billion created by the sterile class and the 5 billion reproduction supposed in the *Tableau*, we get a total product, somewhat short in nonphysiocratic terms, of 9 billion. If we appraise the net contribution of the proprietary class at zero, the total annual product (= disbursed income) approximates 7 billion. Léon Walras, who criticized the physiocrats' treatment of price formation and immaterial production, fixed this annual product at 7 billion (see *Eléments d'économie politique* [Paris, 1926], pp. 386–89).

31. Only a part of the revenue, or net product, is, strictly speaking, disposable. For the proprietors must devote a part of their revenue and a part of their efforts to the maintenance and amelioration of their agricultural property; otherwise it will deteriorate, and with it the productiveness of annual and primitive advances (see Sec. B).

32. They observed that even in the nonagricultural branches of the economy the introduction of large-scale enterprise and of labor-saving machinery increased output per worker, decreased cost, and increased the supply of goods at the disposal of the community (e.g., see Baudeau, *Introduction*, pp. 714–15, 717, 720–21; also Weulersse, *op. cit.*, I, 602–5). I have followed Baudeau and designated as *avances foncières* the expenditures which Quesnay designated as *dépenses foncières*. Baudeau also used the term *avances souveraines* to designate social and economic overhead capital (i.e., highways, canals, rivers, ports, etc.); these expenditures came ultimately out of the sovereign's share of the national product, the magnitude of which was ultimately conditioned by the degree to which there was investment in the form of overhead capital. *Ibid.*, p. 666.

33. Quesnay's discussion suggests that by *petite culture* he meant cultivation carried on by means of oxen and under the métayer system, and by *grande culture* that carried on with horses by well-to-do farmers. While Turgot is more explicit, he but expresses what Quesnay meant. Turgot described as areas of *petite culture* those where the peasant cultivator was without capital of his own and made use only of such equipment, etc., as the proprietor could provide, giving in exchange a share of the crop as under the métayer system; and as areas of *grande culture*, those where well-to-do undertakers (*fermiers*), well supplied with capital, cultivated the land of proprietors under a lease arrangement, paying a money rent for the use of the land and retaining the profits. Under

grande culture, in contrast with *petite culture,* therefore, much more capital was used, cultivation was directed by skilled undertakers (*fermiers*), and producing units were larger as a rule (see Quesnay, *Oeuvres,* articles "Fermiers" and "Grains," also "Maximes . . . ," pp. 334, 346–52; Turgot, *Oeuvres,* I, 20–22, 544 ff.; also Weulersse, *op. cit.,* I, 333–66).

34. See "Grains," *Oeuvres,* p. 214; many of the principles of physiocracy are fore-shadowed in this article, originally published in the famous French *Encyclopédie.*

35. The abbreviated *Tableau* is descriptive of a state in which this maximum has been achieved, Quesnay's discussion suggests: "Dans l'état de prospérité d'un royaume dont le territoire serait porté à son plus haut degré possible de culture, de liberté et de facilité de commerce, et où par conséquent le revenue des *propriétaires* ne pourrait plus s'accroître, ceux-ci pourraient en dépenser *la moitié* en achats à la *classe sterile*" (see *Oeuvres,* p. 318; his italics).

36. This limit is not fixed, said Baudeau, but is continually extensible through progress in the state of the arts (see *Principes économiques de Louis XII et du cardinal d'Amboise,* pp. 43–44, cited by A. Dubois, in his Introduction to Baudeau's *Principes de la science morale,* p. xv). Dupont also was optimistic concerning the prospect of technological progress (see my *French Predecessors,* pp. 198–99).

37. However, see Maxim VI (*Oeuvres,* p. 332), where Quesnay notes that net product may increase more rapidly than advances.

38. *Principes,* pp. 13 ff.

39. Turgot, *Oeuvres,* I, 418–23.

40. Although Quesnay suggests, in his remarks on his abbreviated *Tableau,* that the volume of annual advances has been carried to as high a level as is advisable in the agricultural economy therein described, he does not specifically say that a further increment of advances would add nothing to net product. He indicates only that *total* net product equals *total* annual advances. It must be inferred, however, that net product has been maximized.

41. The unabbreviated tables are defective in that they do not include enough transactions to complete the annual circulation. It is essential, as has been shown, that the productive class sell 3 billions of produce, 1 to the proprietary class and 2 to the sterile class, receiving in exchange 2 billions in money and 1 billion in the products of the sterile class. In the unabbreviated table, however, the sterile class appears to spend with the productive class only 1 of the 2 billions in money it receives from the other two classes. Accordingly, the year seems to end with the sterile class in possession of 1 billion unwanted money and in need of an additional billion of raw produce, and the productive class in pos-

session of 1 billion unwanted raw produce and short 1 billion of the money required to pay the proprietors. Whence, to complete annual circulation, the productive class must deliver this billion of raw produce to the sterile class in exchange for 1 billion of money. This transaction must be assumed to take place; it cannot readily be fitted into the fifty-fifty distributional scheme of the unabbreviated table. Voelcker (*op. cit.,* pp. 82–86) considers possible solutions to the problem. For the purposes of this paper, the complete solution we have postulated, following Baudeau, is adequate.

42. Although the physiocrats supposed, as a rule, that the amount of money required to circulate the annual reproduction approximated 50–100 per cent of the net product (see n. 94, below), they did not specifically build their estimates upon the size and frequency of the rental payments. For example, if the farmers pay their annual rent in twelve monthly allotments, the economy requires a much smaller amount of money than if the farmers requite their annual rent with one payment at the close of the economic year. Cantillon, with whose doctrines Mirabeau and Quesnay were familiar, had dealt with this problem (*op. cit.,* Part II, chaps. iii–iv); he indicated that the amount of money needed depended upon the magnitude of the landlords' rents, the extent to which credit was employed, and the saving and other practices upon which velocity of circulation depended (*ibid.,* pp. 147, 149).

43. As we have already indicated, Quesnay and his school did not make use of the marginal concept. Whence the reader must infer from his wording that the net product is maximized and that, therefore, annual advances have been increased to the point where an additional increment yields only enough to cover expenses of production (i.e., annual advances and the indispensable return on primitive advances) (e.g., see Quesnay, *Oeuvres,* p. 318).

44. Given an annual reproduction of 5, it will be recalled, net product or revenue aggregates 2, and the *reprises* (or return of the productive class) 3.

45. E.g., see Quesnay, *Oeuvres,* pp. 314 ff.; Mirabeau, *Philosophie rurale,* Vol. I, chap. iii.

46. "Despotisme de la Chine," *Oeuvres,* p. 660.

47. For the sake of simplicity it is assumed that primitive advances continue intact, and that the proprietary class does not neglect *avances foncières.*

48. In accordance with physiocratic practice, it is assumed that returns are constant, i.e., that an increase or decrease of 1 unit in annual advances always results in an increase or decrease of 2½ in annual reproduction, and of 1 in net product. This assumption is tenable only on condition that, so long as net product falls short of

the attainable maximum, annual advances, annual reproduction, and net product increase at the same rate. The physiocrats did not, as a rule, when applying the theory of the *Tableau*, recognize or express this condition; yet in their discussion of agricultural productivity in general they did not always assume constant returns. However, see n. 39 and text, above.

49. Much of the physiocratic literature deals with the consequences of a decline in the demand for, and hence in the volume and exchange value of, agricultural production. The above discussion, while not founded upon any specific physiocratic example, is consistent with physiocratic theory (for specific examples see Mirabeau, *L'Amie des hommes*, Part VII, and *Philosophie rurale;* see below, n. 60, on falling prices).

50. It is taken for granted above that the additional agricultural output can be sold at satisfactory prices and that, if necessary and advisable, an expanded foreign demand for agricultural products can be met in part through the transfer to agriculture of some of the workers in sterile employments, sterile products being supplied in greater measure from abroad. If agricultural prices are too low initially, they will move upward in consequence of the increased demand (see below, n. 60 and text.)

51. *Tableau économique* (1758).

52. *Oeuvres*, p. 317. He not only approved but advocated the consumption, especially on the part of the proprietors, of agricultural products that were of good quality or fancy; for the sale of these brought better returns to cultivators than did the sale of cheap foodstuffs and helped to sustain the prices of the latter (*ibid.*, pp. 317 ff.; also Mirabeau, *Philosophie rurale*, II, chap. viii, 45 ff.).

53. *Oeuvres*, pp. 316–20, 335. In a fully developed economy, as has been noted, Quesnay and Mirabeau allow the proprietary class to spend half its revenue with the sterile class.

54. *Philosophie rurale*, I, 210. In both this work and in *L'Ami des hommes* (Part VII) Mirabeau devoted much space to demonstrating how excessive expenditure with the sterile class reduces annual reproduction and visits ruin upon nations.

55. Baudeau, *Principes*, pp. 14–15, 19, 25, 27, 32. In a later work he declared that while a proprietor should keep up and improve his landed property, so doing, while meritorious, was not obligatory (cited by Dubois in his Introduction to *Principes*, p. xvi). Baudeau, of course, condemned, as did all physiocrats, sumptuary legislation of every sort.

56. To this opinion other physiocrats subscribed in spirit at least.

57. See Baudeau, *Principes*, pp. 13–14, 31–32; Dupont, *Abrégé*, pp. 379 ff.; Quesnay, *Oeuvres*, pp. 347–50.

58. Free competition conciliates all

interests, insures justice, reduces the role of government to a minimum, establishes *le bon prix*, and thus maximizes satisfaction (Le Trosne, *De l'intérêt*, pp. 557–59, 603–5, 624–27). Mercier wrote: "Le *bon prix* est tout l'opposé de la *cherté*: il est précisément le prix qui naturellement et *nécessairement* se trouve attribué par la concurrence à chaque marchandise, et en raison de ceux des autres marchandises. Ainsi, quel qu'il soit, il est toujours proportionné, et jamais démesuré; il est enfin ce qu'il doit être pour l'intérêt commun des vendeurs et des acheteurs" (see *op. cit.*, p. 570). The *bon prix*, it should be noted, was also a *stable* price, making for general economic stability (see also Quesnay, *Oeuvres*, pp. 246–48, 335–36 [Maxims XVIII, XIX, XXV], 670–74; Weulersse, *op. cit.*, I, 479 ff.). Quesnay pointed out that even commercial reprisals against foreign nations affected adversely the nation enacting such measures (*Oeuvres*, p. 489).

59. On the relation of the level and the stability of prices to the spread between what the consumer pays and what the farmer receives, see Quesnay, *Oeuvres*, p. 197 n.; Dupont, *De l'exportation et de l'importation des grains*, ed. E. Depitre (Paris, 1911), chaps. iv–v; Weulersse, *op. cit.*, I, 519–20.

60. See "Premier problème économique" (1766), *Oeuvres*, pp. 496–515. He employs a *tableau* to illustrate the effects. He indicates, moreover, that while the supposed price increase produces the effects outlined, it does not follow that a further price increase would produce similar beneficial effects, because the consequences of a price increase depend upon the condition, or state of development, of an economy at the time the price increase occurs (*ibid.*, p. 510). He attached much importance, however, to fluctuations in the price of agricultural products and preferred increases to decreases. "L'augmentation ou la diminution des prix des productions sont donc des causes principales de la prospérité ou de dépérissement des empires. . . . Mais toujours trouvera-t-on, selon les différents cas, hors celui de disette, un advantage plus ou moins grand dans les augmentations des prix, et un dommage plus ou moins grand dans les diminutions" (see *ibid.*, p. 508 n.). See also Saint-Péravy (*Principes du commerce opposé au trafic*, Part I [1786], pp. 80–83), who shows how an increase in the supply of metallic money initially leads to higher prices, forced saving, and increased investment (cited by J. Viner, *op. cit.*, p. 187 n.).

61. It will be recalled that, according to the physiocrats, neither the sterile class nor the productive class receives and retains any income that is appropriable or *disposable;* that the returns (*reprises*) of the productive class and the income of the sterile class consist only of necessary expenses, on the restoration of which the continuation at former levels of both repro-

duction and sterile activities is contingent. Any tax or burden, therefore, which is imposed on these expenses (e.g., a tax upon cultivators or merchants or workers or provisions) will continue to be shifted until it falls upon that part of the national income (i.e., annual reproduction)—namely, the disposable portion of the net product—whence it cannot be shifted, inasmuch as retention of this part is not essential to the continuation of productive and sterile employments (see Quesnay, "Impôts," *op. cit.; Oeuvres*, pp. 332, 337–41, 696 ff.; Le Trosne, *De l'ordre social*, Discours IV; Mercier, *op. cit.*, pp. 465–523).

62. The more distantly removed the nonproductive consumers of agricultural commodities are from farming areas, the greater is the cost of transporting farm products to markets and the smaller is the percentage that farmers receive of the prices final consumers pay for these products (e.g., see Quesnay, *Oeuvres*, p. 323, also pp. 298, 302; Mercier, *op. cit.*, p. 548; Dupont, *Abrégé*, p. 380). The wealthy inhabitants of cities, moreover, tended to spend their incomes largely upon *luxe de décoration* rather than for agricultural produce (see e.g., Quesnay, *Oeuvres*, pp. 302 ff.; Mirabeau, *Philosophie rurale*, I, 284 ff.).

63. E.g., see Quesnay, on indirect taxes (*Oeuvres*, pp. 696–716; also pp. 332 ff., 337 ff.); Mirabeau, *Philosophie rurale*, chap. ix, and *L'Ami des hommes*, Part VII, pp. 42 ff., 155 ff.; Mercier, *op. cit.*, pp. 463–524; Le Trosne, *De l'intérêt*, chap. viii; see also Turgot, *Oeuvres*, I, 392 ff.

64. As we have already indicated, the proprietary class as a whole must spend, in a fully developed economy, one-half its income with the productive class; and in an economy with an underdeveloped agriculture, more than half. This limitation pertains to the *disposition* of the income of the proprietary class, of which state and church income is a part. We are concerned above with the *amount* of income appropriable for state and church.

65. Baudeau put the disposable portion at one-third (see n. 67, below). Quesnay fixed the tithe at one-seventh, the sovereign's share at two-sevenths, and the sovereign's whole portion (including about 27 per cent of the tithe) at about 32½ per cent, of the net product (see "Analyse . . . ," *Oeuvres*, pp. 311 ff. and n.). Dupont (*Origine*, pp. 355 ff.; *Abrégé*, pp. 377 ff.) and Mercier (*op. cit.*, pp. 469 ff., 473 ff., 477 ff.) did not specifically fix the disposable portion, but they did discuss some of the circumstances which govern how much the state may take. Dupont, for example, said that the state must not take so much of the net product that "le sort des propriétaires fonciers cesse d'être le meilleur sort dont on puisse jouir dans la société" (*Origine*, pp. 356, 364). The proprietors had originally agreed, the phys-

iocrats held, to support the sovereign, particularly for security reasons. He thus became and was a co-proprietor. What was transferred to the sovereign, consistently with the principles of the natural order, was not really a tax, therefore, but only his share. Moreover, this share had not really been the possession of the existing landowning class; it had not been bequeathed (e.g., see Mercier, *op. cit.*, pp. 450–53, 477 ff.; Dupont, *Origine*, pp. 356–58; *Abrégé*, pp. 377–78; Quesnay, *Oeuvres*, p. 338).

66. The sovereign, of course, was not free to dispose as he would of tax revenue. It was obligatory upon him to provide not only education and defense but also, for example, to support and ameliorate the public patrimony (highways, waterways, quays, harbors, public buildings, etc.) (see Baudeau, *Introduction*, chaps. iii and vi; Dupont, *Abrégé*, pp. 377–78).

67. "La loi de la justice et celle de la sagesse se réunissent donc pour attribuer au moins les deux grands tiers du produit net, ou revenu clair et liquide, à chaque propriétaire foncier; un premier tiers non disponible, mais confié comme un dépôt sacré, dont la destination nécessaire est l'entretien, la réparation, la rénovation periodique et l'amélioration continuellement indispensable des avances foncières ci-devant faites; un second, comme juste récompense des dépenses, des travaux et des soins du propriétaire (Baudeau, *Introduction*, pp. 759–60).

"Reste un peu moins du tiers de ce produit quitte et net que peuvent revendiquer en corps les mandataires quelconques de la souveraineté, et cette réclamation est fondée de leur part sur les deux mêmes titres que celle des cultivateurs et des propriétaires fonciers" (*ibid.*, p. 760).

68. Industry and commerce naturally expanded in proper proportion to territorial revenue when their progress was not subjected to governmental interference (see Mirabeau, *Philosophie rurale*, III, chaps. x–xi; also *ibid.*, II, 28 ff., where he says, in substance, that nonagricultural economic activities and societies are but dependencies of agriculture, capable of expanding only as the latter expands; see also Quesnay, *Oeuvres*, pp. 333, 343–44, 391 ff.; and n. 115, below).

69. *Op. cit.*, pp. 537, 540–41, 493, 545 (his italics); see also Le Trosne, *De l'intérêt*, pp. 511–13, 553, 603–4, and *De l'ordre*, pp. 200 ff. n.; Mirabeau, *Philosophie rurale*, I, 44–48; Dupont, "Maximes . . . ," in Daire, *op. cit.*, pp. 390–92; Quesnay, *Oeuvres*, pp. 475, 478, and "Hommes," *op. cit.*, p. 19.

70. *Philosophie Rurale*, II, 55; III, 41; I, 208. Mirabeau had in mind an agricultural kingdom, not a commercial state.

71. Given crop diversification, the aggregate domestic demand for raw produce was necessarily greater than when crops were undiversified and there was less

variety to tempt consumers. For this reason, among others, the physiocrats opposed restrictions upon the farmer's freedom to cultivate what he believed to be marketable and profitable (e.g., see Quesnay, *Oeuvres*, pp. 333–34, 346–47, 391).

72. E.g., see Le Trosne, *De l'intérêt*, pp. 510 ff., 618 ff. According to Mercier, since foreign commerce provides an outlet for all surplus production, "consumption no longer has known limits"; the products of a nation can be sold at "the best possible price," and abundance cannot depress agriculture (see *op. cit.*, pp. 545–46; also Quesnay, "Du commerce," *Oeuvres*, pp. 446–94). Mirabeau, who emphasized the dependence of consumption upon the level of income received (*Philosophie rurale*, II, chap. viii), indicated three conditions, given which, a large agricultural output operated to depress net product: (1) lack of foreign markets; (2) inefficient methods of production; and (3) reduction of farm income through taxes on provisions (*ibid.*, I, 301). The physiocrats did not look with approval upon exportation that resulted from the fact that the domestic population was poverty-ridden and incapable of buying enough raw produce at satisfactory prices (e.g., see Le Trosne, *De l'intérêt*, pp. 620–24).

73. The physiocrats held, consistently with their general theory of circular flow, that a nation must purchase abroad in the same amount as it sells abroad. Inasmuch as precious metals are not wealth but merely materials out of which money and certain products may be made, a nation must accept practically all payments in the form of goods; it must not strive for a "favorable balance" and precious-metal imports. An exporting agricultural nation should accept in payment for its raw produce such foreign manufactures—namely, those consisting at most in small measure of primary raw materials produced in that nation —as can be obtained more cheaply abroad than at home. An agricultural nation, Quesnay's analysis suggests, derives a double advantage from agricultural exportation: (1) expansion of agricultural income and net product and (2) freedom from dependence upon foreign sources for indispensable raw produce and freedom from the fluctuations in demand to which luxury exports are subject (e.g., see Quesnay, *Oeuvres*, pp. 236–37, 240, 324 ff., 333–34, 344–45, 352–53, 446 ff., Mirabeau, *Philosophie rurale*, I, 211 ff., II, 141–42, III, chaps. x–xi; see also A. I. Bloomfield, "Foreign-Trade Doctrines of the Physiocrats," *American Economic Review*, XXVIII [1938], 716–35; and n. 74).

74. External commerce, wrote Mercier, is only a *pis-aller*; it is necessary when domestic consumers are unable to provide a sufficient demand for raw produce at a *bon prix*. It is necessary also when a state, because of climatic or other conditions, is unable to supply all the raw products of which it has need; then it is "a necessary evil" (see *op. cit.*, pp. 547–48; also Quesnay, "Du commerce," *Oeuvres*, pp. 483–85, and "Analyse . . . ," pp. 320 ff.). While the physiocrats defended freedom of trade on philosophical grounds, they were not fully alert to the advantages of international specialization. They advocated the establishment of free trade in grain largely because they believed that such trade would augment the price of grain and raw produce, increase net product, and thus make for economic prosperity. They favored the exportation of raw produce rather than that of wrought goods because only the former contributed appreciably to the expansion of net product. They preferred domestic to foreign markets, other things being equal, because the former entailed less transportation and handling costs and therefore returned a larger proportion of selling price to the cultivator. On their trade theory see Bloomfield, *op. cit.*, esp. pp. 731 ff.; on the grain question see E. Depitre's Introduction to Dupont's *L'Exportation . . . des grains* (Paris, 1911).

75. Population necessarily grew fast enough when economic conditions were good, the physiocrats asserted with one voice. "Population . . . proportions itself always to the means of subsistence," wrote Le Trosne (*De l'intérêt*, p. 510). "Augmentez les revenus, la population s'étendra à mesure: sortez de cette règle, vous ne tenez rein," declared Mirabeau (*Philosophie rurale*, II, p. 70). See also Dupont, *Origine*, pp. 346, 353–54; Quesnay, "Hommes," *op. cit.*, pp. 13, 38 ff., 53, 64, and *Oeuvres*, pp. 509 ff., where he traces the effect upon population growth of an increase in revenue; and my *French Predecessors*, pp. 176 ff. The physiocrats took exception to the view that a state such as France might increase its population capacity and population by exchanging wrought goods for raw produce, arguing in essence that, since France's agriculture was so underdeveloped, it was necessary to do everything consistent with free competition that would expand French agriculture and with it the subsistence and opportunity for productive employment on which population growth depended (see Mirabeau, *Philosophie rurale*, II, 141 ff.; Mercier, *op. cit.*, pp. 595–96; my *French Predecessors*, pp. 118–19, 126 ff., 186).

76. See n. 58, above, on *bon prix*.

77. Le Trosne, *De l'intérêt*, p. 553. The *Tableau économique* was contrived in part to describe the circular flow.

78. *Ibid.*, pp. 512–13.

79. See Turgot, *Oeuvres*, I, 330–31, notes to his translation (1755) of Josiah Tucker's *Reflections on the Expediency of a Law for the Naturalization of Foreign Protestants* (London, 1751–52). In this paper Tucker discussed unemployment in terms of reciprocal employment and of obstacles to the "circulation of labor," de-

claring that "le travail d'un homme donne de l'ouvrage à un autre homme" (see Turgot's translation, *op. cit.*, pp. 327–32). Quesnay was familiar with these and other of Tucker's views, and his notion of circulation may have been inspired by him as well as by Cantillon. The importance of the laborer as a consumer was commented upon by several English writers before 1750 (see E. S. Furniss, *The Position of the Laborer in a System of Nationalism* [New York, 1920], pp. 140–43).

80. See Quesnay, *Oeuvres*, pp. 393–94.

81. *Ibid.*, pp. 674–79; Baudeau, *Explication du Tableau*, pp. 850–52. However, see nn. 83 and 86, below, for a partial exception.

82. "Le besoin seul est le père de l'industrie, il sollicite l'artisan à s'y livrer pour gagner sa subsistance, il sollicite aussi tous ceux qui peuvent acheter à se procurer ses ouvrages. La politique peut se dispenser de se joindre au besoin pour exciter les hommes à y satisfaire, parce que la classe stérile s'étendra toujours à proportion des richesses du pays . . . [the more expenditures are diverted to agriculture] plus il y aurait de productions consommables et surtout de productions comestibles. Il y aurait donc dans ce cas une plus grande consommation, puisqu'il y aurait plus de productions à consommer. Les consommateurs, par conséquent, qui n'aspirent qu'après une plus grande faculté de consommer, se multiplieraient et consommeraient" (see Quesnay, *Oeuvres*, pp. 391, 393).

83. *Ibid.*, pp. 345, 354; "Hommes," *op. cit.*, pp. 46, 86. Quesnay's discussion of mass purchasing-power raises two questions. Was mass purchasing-power to be increased, even at the expense of the net product? Did he include under "common people" all wage-earning classes? In response to the latter question it may be said that apparently he did have in mind all the common people, even though he referred most frequently to those living in rural areas and noted that their lot was worse, as a rule, than that of those living in cities (see *Oeuvres*, pp. 345, 354, 391–92; also Mercier, *op. cit.*, pp. 499 ff.). Regarding the first question, see Sec. D, below.

84. Quesnay, *Oeuvres*, pp. 264, 335 (Maxim XX), 393–94; "Hommes," *op. cit.*, p. 46. Quesnay was at pains to show that the real income of the common people was greater when the price of provisions was high than when it was low (Maxim XIX and n., *Oeuvres*, pp. 335, 353–54). Le Trosne also notes the greater potential consuming-power of the underlying population (*De l'intérêt*, pp. 589, 620–21).

85. *Philosophie rurale*, II, chap. viii, p. 64, also pp. 45, 81 ff. Historians, Mirabeau noted, concerned themselves with the revolutions of thrones but not with those of wealth (*ibid.*, p. 53). Cf. this statement with Malthus' remark that the history of

the common man was ignored (*Essay* [1st ed.], p. 32). Chapter viii of *Philosophie rurale* is attributed to Quesnay (G. Schelle, *Dupont de Nemours* [Paris, 1888], p. 23).

86. "Hommes," *op. cit.*, pp. 78–79. Workers engaged in the creation of luxuries are useful also, in so far as "they provoke the wealthy" to spend (*ibid.*, p. 79). In his later works Quesnay apparently takes it for granted that in a *healthy* economy the wealthy spend or invest their incomes promptly.

87. "L'argent est reçu comme gage intermédiaire entre les ventes & les achats, & il sert de mesure commune, de valeur pour valeur," states Le Trosne (*De l'intérêt*, p. 531); see also Quesnay, *Oeuvres*, pp. 288 ff., 348 ff.; Mercier, *op. cit.*, pp. 542–43; Dupont, *Abrégé*, p. 373. By implication at least, the physiocrats recognized money's passive role as standard of value and unit of account (e.g., see Le Trosne, *De l'intérêt*, p. 531). In April, 1815, Dupont wrote to Say in defense of the physiocratic tenets: ". . . car il n'y a pour payer les récoltes que les récoltes elles-mêmes, ou directement par échanges, ou indirectement par leur métamorphose en travail et en objets que le travail a fabriqués, dont les *récolteurs* ont fourni les consommations auxquelles elles ont ainsi prêté ou avancé leur valeur. Tous les acheteurs sont vendeurs; tous les vendeurs sont acheteurs" (see Daire, *Physiocrates*, p. 402); cf. Dupont's summary of Quesnay's maxims (*ibid.*, pp. 391–92).

88. Mercier, *op. cit.*, p. 541. He adds that it is not each individual's buying and selling that must balance but rather "the general mass of sales and purchases"; and he indicates that this dictum applies to both intranational and international commerce (*ibid.*, pp. 541, 544–45). Turgot remarked, however, that it is only in the long run that sales and purchases abroad tend to balance (letter to Dupont [1766], cited by Bloomfield, *op. cit.*, p. 721).

89. Le Trosne, *De l'intérêt*, p. 513; see below, n. 112 and text. See Mercier, *op. cit.*, pp. 498 ff., for description of the process of decline.

90. See, however, Mirabeau, *L'Ami*, Part VII, and *Philosophie rurale*, Vol. I, chap. vii, and Vol. III, chap. x; also n. 97 below. One may make various assumptions and apply physiocratic principles accordingly.

91. Quesnay wrote with reference to an indirect tax, such as one on merchandise, that this "insidious resource is a surcharge which reduces the people to a forced saving in consumption, which arrests work, which extinguishes reproduction, and which ends by ruining subjects and sovereign" (*Oeuvres*, p. 339). See Mercier's account (*op. cit.*, pp. 492–504) of the progressive degradation occasioned by a defective tax system.

92. Le Trosne, *De l'intérêt*, pp. 589, 620–21. The "ignorant cupidity" of the

landed proprietors prevented their perceiving that all the indirect taxes fall upon the revenue of the land, Quesnay observed (*Oeuvres*, p. 704).

93. See citations given by Weulersse, *op. cit.*, Vol. I, Book II, chaps. iii–iv.

94. He warned against a nation's allowing part of its revenues to pass abroad unless offset by an influx of merchandise or silver (*argent*), and he indicated that the gain of merchants, when a nation is suffering loss in its reciprocal foreign commerce, is won at the expense of circulation, distribution, and reproduction. He pointed out, however, that a nation derived no advantage from a "favorable balance" and the consequent inflow of precious metals unless it had need of these in industry or as money (see *Oeuvres*, pp. 288 ff., 324 ff., 333 [Maxim X], 336 [Maxim XXIII], 482 ff.; and "Hommes," *op. cit.*, pp. 25–27). Several of the physiocrats understood the price-specie flow mechanism and dealt with the favorable balance theory accordingly (e.g., see Le Trosne, *De l'intérêt*, pp. 546 ff.; Mercier, *op. cit.*, p. 576; Bloomfield, *op. cit.*, pp. 726–28; see also n. 97, below).

95. Quesnay characterized as sterile the investment of funds in unproductive loans, the acquisition of useless commissions, privileges, etc.: "Leur circulation stérile ne les empêche point d'être fortunes rongeantes et onéreuses *à* la nation" (*Oeuvres*, pp 342–43).

96. *Ibid.*, p. 349. "La circulation de l'argent doit avoir tout à la fois un objet et un effet, qui est la REPRODUCTION," declared Dupont (*Abrégé*, p. 373). Le Trosne (*De l'intérêt*, p. 540) wrote: "L'argent n'est pas l'objet de la circulation; ce sont les productions qui le font mouvoir."

97. See "Du commerce" (Oeuvres, p. 481 and n.), where Quesnay says that the withdrawal of money from circulation for purposes of accumulation causes the price of agricultural produce, together with profits and reproduction, to fall. The physiocrats took it for granted that agricultural income would fall in consequence of the withdrawal of money from circulation; yet, while they subscribed to a quantity theory of money and prices, they did not trouble to trace out in detail the effect upon demand and upon prices of such a withdrawal. As a rule, they fixed at between 50 and 100 per cent of the value of the annual revenue (equals net product) the amount of money required to circulate the annual reproduction; and they supposed that this amount would be available so long as the economy was in a healthy condition. They indicated, moreover, that the amount of money required varied inversely with its velocity and that the amount of hard money required depended upon the use made of book credit and money substitutes (see Quesnay, *Oeuvres*, pp. 325, 348 ff.; Mirabeau, *L'Ami des hommes*, Part VII, pp. 53 ff.; 120 ff.; Le Trosne, *De l'intérêt*, chaps. iii–iv; Dupont, in Turgot, *Oeuvres*, I, 152; Bloomfield, *op. cit.*, pp. 720–26; see also above, n. 42).

98. See *Oeuvres*, pp. 304, 335 (Maxim XXI), 336 (Maxim XXVII), 475, 481–82 and n.

99. Maxim VII (*Oeuvres*, pp. 332–33 [his italics]). He included among the fortunes which re-enter into circulation and offset withdrawals those which, having been "stériles ou oisives," are employed to form advances in agriculture, commerce, or profitable manufactures (*ibid.*, p. 342).

100. *Ibid.*, pp. 337 (Maxims XXVIII–XXX), 401 ff., 714–15; "Hommes," *op. cit.*, pp. 75–76, 78–79, 87; see also Mirabeau, *Philosophie rurale*, I, 284–85, II, 331–33, III, 53–54. The fiscal operations described, said Quesnay, congregated people in the capital city and thus stimulated destructive luxury and increased transportation costs.

101. *Oeuvres*, p. 337 (Maxim XXVIII [his italics]).

102. Fishing and mining are here ignored. On the interest problem see Weulersse, *op. cit.*, I, 310–15, 389–91, 395–96; also n. 103.

103. Quesnay, *Oeuvres*, pp. 399–406, also 190, 257; A. Rougon, *Les Physiocrates et la réglementation du taux de l'intérêt* (Paris, 1906), chap. i. Quesnay proposed fixing only the rates of perpetual *rentes* but not the rates on loans, which were recallable at maturity or at the pleasure of the lender and which were used in industry and commerce but not in agriculture. Practical considerations, together with the belief that competition and the loan arrangements open to industry and commerce served to hold down their interest charges, led Quesnay to limit his proposal to fix the interest rate to perpetual *rentes* (see Rougon, *op. cit.*, esp. pp. 24 ff., 41–75). Elsewhere (*Oeuvres*, p. 481 n.), Quesnay attributed the comparative lowness of urban interest rates to the accumulation of pecuniary fortunes in cities—fortunes which did not flow into agriculture; whence he observed that the level of the interest rate was not an index of a nation's wealth.

104. Rougon, *op. cit.*, chap. ii. Several minor writers followed Mirabeau in part (Weulersse, *op. cit.*, I, 397–400). The physiocrats rejected the monetary theories of the mercantilists and monetary schemes to ease interest rates.

105. *Reflections*, pp. 67–74, 76, 78–86; also *Oeuvres*, I, 106 ff. Turgot's opinions regarding saving and the productivity of capital differed somewhat from those of the physiocrats.

106. See Oncken's notes in Quesnay, *Oeuvres*, pp. 399–400; Weulersse, *op. cit.*, I, 397–402; Rougon, *op. cit.*, chap. iii; see also Sec. D, below.

107. Turgot in 1770 charged Dupont with supposing that "saving and hoarding

are synonymous" in order "to cover certain mistaken expressions" of Quesnay in his earlier writings (see Appen. to *Reflections*, p. 112). Turgot stated that the introduction of gold and silver had facilitated saving, lending, and capital formation and had made possible the development of nonagricultural activities and specialization generally (*ibid.*, pp. 64–65). He described as "the circulation of money" the continual return, with profit, to undertakers of their advances, and the continual reinvestment of at least the returned advances; and he indicated that if, because of disorder in expenditures, the undertakers ceased to get back their advances with necessary profit, production, consumption, and revenue would decline (*ibid.*, pp. 62–63). Inasmuch as revenues and other incomes are received in the form of money, almost all savings are made in this form; whence money, though an infinitesimal part of a nation's capital, "plays a great part in the formation of capitals." But "none of the undertakers make any other use of" the money they save "than to convert it *immediately* into the different kinds of effects upon which their undertaking depends; and thus this money returns to circulation . . . ." (*ibid.*, pp. 98–99 [his italics]). Turgot observed also that while money, when employed in advances, is not sterile, inasmuch as it "procures a definite profit," this profit comes, as do capital and revenue generally, from the land (*ibid.*, pp. 69, 98).

108. See Sec. I below, Society, Dupont observed, benefited in greater measure from productive, than from unproductive, expenditure; for it cost no more to support a productive worker than an idle or an unproductive worker; it cost no more to subsist a cultivator than a musician (see Dupont's notes to Turgot's *Oeuvres*, I, 52–53).

109. The interest rate depended, other things being equal, said Turgot, upon the degree to which money was placed in reserve for lending. Accordingly, if the rate of current expenditure was increased at the expense of saving, capital accumulation would decline, while both prices and the interest rate would rise. Dupont objected, not to Turgot's view as such, but to his emphasis upon *saving*. "In general," said Dupont, "it is much less *from saving out of the expenditure of revenues* than from the wise employment of this expenditure, that capital formation arises" (see *Réflexions*, pp. 49 ff. and n. [Dupont's italics]).

110. Sometimes a saver must await an opportunity to employ his cumulated fund profitably (*ibid.*, p. 53).

111. Compare this account (*ibid.*, p. 52) with Quesnay's (*Oeuvres*, p. 475).

112. See Dupont's note in Turgot, *Oeuvres*, p. 52; cf. also n. 86 and text, above. Dupont describes avarice (i.e., hoarding or nonspending) as a "mortal sin," inasmuch as it brings death to those who depend for subsistence upon the expenditures of others.

113. "Ce ne sont pas réellement des épargnes, mais des dépenses bien dirigées, qui sont la source de l'augmentation de leurs capitaux, et de l'amélioration de leur fortune" (*ibid.*, p. 53; also p. 51). With respect to Turgot's observation that "the spirit of economy" augments capital, Dupont remarked that the word "economy" meant "good administration," which proscribed *dépenses folles* and prescribed *dépenses conservatrices et productives* (*ibid.*, p. 55).

114. The essence of Dupont's comments is to be found in his notes to the *Réflexions* (Turgot, *Oeuvres*, I, 50–53, 55; but see also 33, 68, 152–53, 427). When Dupont published Turgot's *Réflexions* in the *Ephémérides* in 1770, he amended Turgot's views on property and slavery to make them completely consistent with physiocratic philosophy. Because of Turgot's objections to modification of his views, Dupont put his own opinions on saving in commentary notes and included these almost unchanged in his edition of Turgot's works published in 1808–11 (see G. Schelle, "Les Réflexions de Turgot," *Journal des économistes*, XLIII [4th ser., 1888], 3–16; also Oncken, *op. cit.*, pp. 802–5, on Dupont's later views). Dupont states specifically (Turgot, *Oeuvres*, I, 427) that Quesnay approved small savings, on condition that they were invested or loaned as soon as possible and that he opposed *thésaurisation* because it deranged the "natural order of distribution," depressed agricultural prices and income, checked cultivation, and made necessary the importation of precious metals to reestablish circulation.

115. The physiocrats apparently intended their theory of saving, expenditure, and capital formation to apply only to an agricultural state, such as they conceived France to be, but not to a mercantile state whose population depended predominantly upon industry and commerce rather than upon agriculture. Such a commercial state was essentially the commercial agent of large agricultural states and could continue in this capacity in the face of competition from other commercial states only by holding down its costs and required profits. It could derive no benefit from internal expenditure upon agricultural activities because it had little or no agriculture to fructify in this manner. Accordingly, since it could not benefit from internal expenditure and since it needed to cut its operating expenses and required profit rates to the minimum, it stood to benefit from the accumulation of funds which served to reduce the interest rate and to make possible the enlargement of its activities. "Mais on doit penser autrement des petites nations commerçantes qui n'ont pas de territoire; car leur intérêt les oblige

d'épargner en tout genre de dépenses pour conserver et accroître le fonds des richesses nécessaires à leur commerce, et pour commercer à moins de frais que les autres nations afin de pouvoir s'assurer les avantages de la concurrence dans les achats et dans les ventes chez l'étranger" (see Quesnay, *Oeuvres*, p. 355, also 236–37; Le Trosne, *De l'intérêt*, pp. 541–52, 642–45; also Mercier, *op. cit.*, pp. 566–68; cf. also n. 68 and text, above).

116. Interpretations of physiocracy differ. N. J. Ware concludes that the physiocrats developed their theory simply to serve the "special needs of a new land-owning class" and, the better to accomplish their purpose, assimilated into their doctrine the concepts and shibboleths then in vogue (see "The Physiocrats: A Study in Economic Rationalization," *American Economic Review*, XXI [1931], 607–19). Moreover, as E. Allix has shown, those who, during and after the French Revolution, supported the interests of the landed class and advocated the creation of a state to be managed by and for this class, drew their main inspiration from the physiocrats and, in some measure, from Cantillon, the principal anticipator of certain of their doctrines. Against this group was pitted a new school, which eventually became consolidated under the leadership of Say (see Allix, "La Rivalité entre la propriéte foncière et la fortune mobilière sous la Revolution," *Revue d'histoire économique et sociale*, VI [1913], 297–348, and "L'Oeuvre économique de Germain Garnier, *ibid.*, V [1912], 317–42; see also Weulersse, *op. cit.*, II, 717 ff.; and M. Palyi, "The Introduction of Adam Smith on the Continent," in *Adam Smith, 1776–1926* [Chicago, 1928], pp. 199–208). A different interpretation is presented by Max Beer. He concludes that Quesnay's main purpose was the re-creation of "a medieval society which should be of greater permanency and excellence than the old one had been." This society was to be headed by a pious king, subject to the laws of nature, which were to be interpreted for him by a council of jurists in the same manner as the laws of God were interpreted for medieval kings by the spiritual lords and canon lawyers. This society was to consist of three estates: (*a*) the nobility and the clergy, to be charged with secular and religious administration and to be supported out of the net product; (*b*) the cultivators of the land, to be responsible for the support of the state and the subsistence of the population, and to be entitled only to their own sustenance; (*c*) the unproductive tradespeople and merchants, whose moderate reward was to be fixed, not by statutory control, but by the more effective device of free competition. While Quesnay's purpose probably was at variance with that of the more liberal members of his sect, several circumstances prevented the development of

diversity of opinion and the resultant decomposition of the school into conflicting groups. Quesnay did not try to build up a "neo-feudal realm"; hence he did not reveal his real purpose. Furthermore, since the sect was not provided with an opportunity to translate its theoretical principles into action, it never got out of the vague-principle stage, and the differences in meaning and interpretation implicit in the system did not become manifest to its votaries (see Max Beer, *An Inqury into Physiocracy* [London, 1939], pp. 167–70, 178–83).

117. See Rougon, *op. cit.*, pp. 21 ff., 137 ff.; H. Truchy, "Le Libéralisme économique dans les oeuvres de Quesnay," *Revue d'économie politique*, XIII (1890), 925–54; M. Sauvaire-Jourdan, "Isaac de Bacalan et les idées libre-échangistes en France," *Revue d'économie politique*, XVII (1903), 589 ff., 698 ff.

118. A. Dubois, "Quesnay anti-mercantiliste et libre-échangiste," *Revue d'économie politique*, XVIII (1904), 213–29; also E. Depitre, Introd. to his edition of Dupont's *De l'exportation et de l'importation des grains*, etc. (Paris, 1911), pp. xv ff.

119. Dubois, "Quesnay anti-mercantiliste . . . ," *op. cit.*, p. 224.

120. *The Wealth of Nations* ("Modern Library," ed. E. Cannan), p. 642.

121. See E. Cannan's Introd. to Smith's (1763) *Lectures on Justice, Police, Revenue and Arms* (Oxford, 1896), pp. xxviii–xxxi, and his own *Theories of Production and Distribution* (3d ed.; London, 1924), pp. 183 ff.

122. *Wealth of Nations*, Book II, chap. v. Ricardo (*op. cit.*, chap. xxvi) and J. S. Mill (*Principles of Political Economy* [Ashley ed.], Book I, chap. i, par. 3) criticized Smith on this score. Because Smith did not, as did Ricardo, reason from the scarcity of land, he did not present a determinate stationary state; and because he overlooked certain dynamic elements, the implications of his theory were more pessimistic than those of Ricardo and Mill (see V. Edelberg, "The Ricardian Theory of Profits," *Economica*, XIII [1933], 70–71 and n.; L. Robbins, "The Concept of Stationary Equilibrium," *Economic Journal*, XL [1930], 195–200). Whether or not Smith's formulation of the notion of a stationary state was influenced by Quesnay's views (see n. 46 and text, above) is not evident. To arrive at the conception of a stationary state, one needs only to postulate (*a*) that the supply of a significant productive factor is fixed and (*b*) that this fixity cannot be overcome through technological progress or through the substitution for the factor in fixed supply of other factors whose supply is increasable.

123. "Labour which adds to the value of the subject upon which it is bestowed" is "productive"; labor which does not have

this effect, however useful it may otherwise be, is "unproductive." Unproductive work "perishes in the very instance of its production," whereas productive labor fixes and realizes itself in some particular subject or vendible commodity" (see *Wealth of Nations*, pp. 314 ff.). Smith did not distinguish between productive and unproductive consumption, except to say (*ibid.*, pp. 321 ff.) that what is saved is consumed. His conception of productivity and his insistence upon the importance of accumulation also led him to describe (*ibid.*, pp. 329–32) spending on durable goods as more conducive to public opulence than spending on perishable goods and services. Pre-Smithian writers had sometimes distinguished between productive and unproductive labor (Johnson, *op. cit.*, pp. 215–16, 245–46, 282) and expressed a preference for durable goods.

124. *Wealth of Nations*, pp. 638–42.

125. In a "rude" state of society, however, men (especially the great landholders) could do little else but "hoard whatever money they saved"; for in such a state there was little commerce and manufacturing to absorb savings or prompt expenditure; gentlemen could not with propriety lend or engage in trade; and, because of the political insecurity prevailing, men sought protection against the future in hoards (*ibid.*, pp. 268, 385–86, 859–60).

126. *Ibid.*, p. 268, also pp. 69, 164.

127. *Ibid.*, p. 625. Consumption, he noted elsewhere, affects both human happiness and effort; for he described improvements in the "circumstances of the lower ranks" as essential to their happiness and as conducive to the increase of their industry (*ibid.*, pp. 79, 81, 82–83).

128. *Ibid.*, pp. 321–25, 863, 872–73. He was far more concerned at public than at private prodigality, observing that in the past "private frugality and prudence" had counteracted the prodigality of the spendthrift ruling classes (*ibid.*, pp. 325, 328–29).

129. *Ibid.*, p. 321. Concerning Smith's theory of capital and peculiar use of terms, see Cannan, *Theories of Production and Distribution*, pp. 18 ff. and 55 ff. See below, n. 182, for James Mill's use of above passage.

130. Smith, *Wealth of Nations*, p. 272.

131. *Ibid.*, pp. 79 ff., 87, 146, 164. Although he did not make use of Hume's self-regulating mechanism in his later work, Smith supposed that the amount of circulating medium tended to adjust itself to the "annual produce" (*ibid.*, pp. 277 ff., 323–24, 409). In his *Lectures* (p. 197) Smith had given a summary of Hume's analysis.

132. *Wealth of Nations*, pp. 87, 339, 341–55, 593 ff.

133. *Ibid.*, pp. 354, 593 ff.; see n. 122 and text, above.

134. *Ibid.*, pp. 93–97; see n. 122, above; cf. also J. S. Mill, *op. cit.*, p. 732.

135. *Wealth of Nations*, pp. 22 ff.

136. See Viner, *op. cit.*, pp. 24, 26–33, 45–51, 86, 89–91, for the English mercantilists' views on thrift, hoarding, etc.

137. [John Gray], *The Essential Principles of the Wealth of Nations Illustrated, in Opposition to Some False Doctrines of Dr. Adam Smith and Others* (1797). E. R. A. Seligman touches upon Gray's work his *Essays in Economics* (New York, 1925), pp. 65–67. Gray's book was reviewed favorably in the *Gentleman's Magazine*, LXVII, Part II (October, 1797), 858–59. See Sec. G, below, for Gray's influence on Spence.

138. See Stewart's "Lectures on Political Economy," first published in Sir William Hamilton's edition of Stewart's *Collected Works* (Edinburgh, 1877), VIII, 253–332. Stewart expresses indebtedness "for much important information" to Lauderdale's "researches and speculations concerning the history and principles of the Economical system" (*ibid.*, pp. 300–301). Stewart refers to Gray's work (*ibid.*, p. 275) and to proposals of a tax on net rent, made by Vanderlint and Asgill (*ibid.*, pp. 299–300). Unlike the physiocrats, Stewart found in the expansion of manufactures the principal stimulus to agriculture (*ibid.*, pp. 153, 169–70, 201 ff.). Stewart's lectures were attended by Lauderdale, Brougham, James Mill, Thomas Chalmers, Sydney Smith, Francis Jeffrey, and others who subsequently became distinguished. As late as 1803, Francis Horner was trying to complete his set of physiocratic writings (see L. Horner, *Memories and Correspondence of Francis Horner* [London, 1843], I, 230).

139. See Godwin's essay on avarice and profusion, in the *Enquirer* (Philadelphia, 1797), pp. 135–48. Malthus criticized this essay (*Essay* [1st ed.], chap. xv).

140. E.g., see Stewart, *op. cit.*, VIII, 194 ff.; IX, 320 ff. Doctrines opposed to parsimony were several times criticized by Stewart's students. Francis Jeffrey condemned Herrenschwand's proposal to insure progressive consumption and production by means of government spending (*Edinburgh Review*, I [October, 1802], 98–106). Francis Horner (*Edinburgh Review*, I [January, 1803], 409) criticized Canard's assertion that England's debt expansion had saved her from the evils attendant upon a superabundance of wealth. Canard had said that, if a nation acquires a surplus of wealth above what can be employed as capital, the national spirit of accumulation and the national prosperity are undermined. In these circumstances, government borrowing absorbs the "superfluity" and retards "the commencement of national decline. Every loan, therefore . . . is a wholesome bleeding, which relieves the political body from a plethoric malady." There is no suggestion of Say's

law in Horner's review, however. J. R. McCulloch cites an anonymous work (*Sketch of the Advance and Decline of Nations* [London, 1795], p. 82), in which it is said: "To suppose that there may be a production of commodities without a demand, provided these commodities be of the right species, is . . . absurd . . ." (See his *The Literature of Political Economy* [1845], p. 22). McCulloch believed (*ibid.*, p. 21 n.) that Say's principle had been enunciated also by J. Tucker (see n. 79, above) and by F. Mengotti (*Il Colbertismo* [1791]).

141. *An Inquiry into the Nature and Origin of Public Wealth and into the Means and Causes of Its Increase* (Edinburgh, 1804). Having defined "wealth" to include "all that man desires, as useful or delightful to him" and "individual riches" to consist of that portion of wealth "which exists in a degree of scarcity," Lauderdale indicated that a change in the latter rarely reflected a commensurate change in the former and that emphasis upon venal value (e.g., by the physiocrats) led to untenable conclusions (see *ibid.*, pp. 7, 49–50, 56–57, 105, 133, and chap. ii generally). He rejected both the Smithian and physiocratic notions of productivity, saying that land, labor, and capital were sources of wealth and therefore productive. Of Smith's distinction between productive and unproductive labor he said that, whether production be defined in terms of wealth or of exchange value, the creator of a perishable service was no less productive than the fabricator of a more durable commodity. Of the physiocratic doctrine of net product he said that it overlooked the fact that the *reprises* were as much wealth as the *produit net* and made the magnitude of a nation's wealth turn, in part, on holding down the maintenance of the agricultural producers and that it ignored the productive power of labor and capital (see *ibid.*, chap. iii, esp. pp. 120–53, 205). Smith had overdone the case for the division of labor, failing to observe that its effects are largely confined to the realm of the refined arts. The main reason for mankind's great increase in opulence was "the power man possesses, of directing his labor to the objects of increasing the quantity, and meliorating the quality, of the productions of nature;—and . . . . the power of supplanting and performing labor by capital" (*ibid.*, pp. 303–4).

142. *Ibid.*, pp. 218, 121.

143. *Ibid.*, pp. 246 ff. He cites Quesnay's Maxim VII (see n. 99, above) and a quotation to the same effect from Mirabeau.

144. *Ibid.*, pp. 222, and 208–10, 229–30.

145. *Ibid.*, p. 228; see also pp. 214–15.

146. *Ibid.*, pp. 217–22.

147. Lauderdale cited Robert Walpole to the effect that public creditors could afford to receive only 1 million a year (*ibid.*, p. 254).

148. *Ibid.*, pp. 230, 244–62, 265–67. Were the government to raise a large sum and disburse it promptly, said Lauderdale, the resulting shifts in demand would temporarily disorganize the economy, even though there was no "parsimony" (see *ibid.*, pp. 244–45; see also Viner, *op. cit.*, pp. 189–94, for the opinions of Lauderdale and others who shared his opinions on fiscal policy and its bearing upon production in the deflationist post-Napoleonic period).

149. *Op. cit.*, p. 271.

150. *Ibid.*, pp. 306, 311, 314, 339–42, 349–50, 364.

151. *Ibid.*, pp. 344–49, 351–53. Lauderdale cites Bacon, Berkeley, and Voltaire as observing that "the opulence of the lower orders tends to accelerate the growth of national wealth" (*ibid.*, pp. 350–51 and n.). While Lauderdale refused to say what distribution of wealth was most favorable to production, he believed that the distribution in Britain was more favorable than that in France (*ibid.*, pp. 344–47). He was, far more than the physiocrats, an exponent of mass demand. For the views of Malthus and others on this question see my paper cited in n. 7. See also F. A. Fetter, "Lauderdale's Oversaving Theory," *American Economic Review*, XXXV (1945), 263–83, which appeared after the present paper was completed.

152. Lauderdale, *op. cit.*, pp. 349–50. Even the distribution of wealth in foreign countries with which a given nation traded was of significance, inasmuch as it affected the foreign demand (*ibid.*, pp. 355–65). Commerce, said Lauderdale, while not a means of increasing wealth, served to set these means in motion (*ibid.*, pp. 355–56, 359–60; see also pp. 353–55 for his criticism of Quesnay's views on commerce).

153. L. Stephen, *The English Utilitarians* (London, 1912), II, 243.

154. Thomas Chalmers, *Political Economy* (New York, 1832), chap. v; also chaps. vi–vii, in which he re-examines the relation between foreign trade and employment and maintenance. His first work, *An Enquiry into the Extent and Stability of National Resources* (Edinburgh, 1808), was more than half-completed when Spence's pamphlet came to his attention. Chalmers divided the population into three classes: (*a*) the producers of *first* necessaries, or subsistence; (*b*) the producers of *second* necessaries, such as clothing and lodging; and (*c*) the remainder, or *disposable* part, of the population. Since Britain produced about 97 per cent of her food supply, she needed only to increase *a* slightly to become self-sufficient. The bulk of her disposable population, many of whom were engaged in producing exports to exchange for luxury imports, could be diverted to her

military and naval establishments, and yet her supply of *necessaries* would remain adequate. Napoleon's policy would but empty Britain's shops to fill her armies. On the composition of Chalmers' work see W. Hanna, *Memoirs of the Life and Writings of Thomas Chalmers* (New York, 1853), Vol. I, chap. vi. Chalmers' work was severely criticized by a reviewer who said that Chalmers' proposals would destroy liberty and substitute the "powerful principle of sloth" for that "great spring of human movement, the desire and hope of bettering their condition," and that Chalmers mistook "fluency of expression for fertility of thought" (see *Eclectic Review*, IV, Part II [1808], 575–89). The reviewer agreed (*ibid.*, p. 578) with Chalmers' principle, stated also by Spence, that, since imports equal exports, the total demand for a nation's output originates at home.

155. William Spence, *Britain Independent of Commerce* (London, 1807) (my page references are to the first edition). Spence later achieved some distinction as an entomologist. He is not to be confused with Thomas Spence, an English forerunner of Henry George. Spence repeated many of his opinions in *Agriculture the Source of the Wealth of Britain* (London, 1808). To the "Monthly Reviewers," who had remarked that the physiocratic theory of the nonproductivity of manufactures had never won support in England, Spence recalled a favorable notice of Gray's work (see n. 137, above); and to all his critics he exhibited many supposedly physiocratic remarks of G. Garnier and Malthus (see *Agriculture*, etc.). Of Spence's pamphlet a reviewer in the *Monthly Magazine*, which some years earlier had carried both a favorable comment on Gray's work (IX [1800], 621) and a criticism of it by a follower of Smith (*ibid.*, pp. 332–34), said (XXV [1808], 304); "The Soil is a very prolific lady, and so often in the straw, that her family must inevitably be got rid of, by foreign and other commerce, or they will reduce her to beggary."

156. *Britain*, pp. 16, 20, 24–25. To the growth and spread of manufactures he traced the dissolution of the inefficient feudal order of society and the release of the profit motive and the forces of production therewith associated (*ibid.*, pp. 16–25, 65). Hume and Smith had given forcible expression to this view. The above citation from Spence may have been suggested by Gray (*op. cit.*, p. 118; see Seligman, *op. cit.*, pp. 66–67), who declared that "the rise of rents [i.e., the increase of net product] enlarges the power of the main wheel that moves every other wheel in Society, and is itself set in motion by nature and the industry of man."

157. *Britain*, pp. 7–12, 15–16, 25. One-sixth of Britain's population sufficed to provide food, he estimates (*ibid.*, p.

67). Of the quantity of money "necessary" for "circulation," Spence remarked only that a nation's imports and exports would balance after it had acquired "so much of the precious metals as is necessary for the purpose of circulation, and of supplying the demand of its inhabitants for articles of plate" (*ibid.*, p. 46; also pp. 14–15, where he says that the type of circulating medium in use has no bearing upon the laws of production).

158. *Ibid.*, pp. 26–27; also pp. 7–12. Spence points out that the farmer, too, receives revenue—a return above the subsistence of his family and helpers and the rent he pays to the proprietor—which, under certain circumstances (e.g., when the land has been let on long lease, or when the proprietor has not exacted so high a rent as he might), includes part of the *true* rent. "With respect to this profit," the cultivators "stand in the place of the class of land proprietors, and . . . . the reasoning applied to the latter class . . . . will equally apply to them." Because "it greatly simplifies the argument," Spence supposes that the whole of the revenue passes to the proprietors (see *ibid.*, p. 26 n.).

159. *Ibid.*, pp. 27–30; also *Agriculture*, pp. 66, 68.

160. *Britain*, pp. 29–32, 59. Foreign commerce, as the physiocrats had shown, could not add to wealth, since, as a rule, equal values were exchanged and the demand for domestic manufactures originated, directly or indirectly, in the domestic economy. Accordingly, even though imports and exports ceased, the domestic market could absorb all domestically produced goods and services—goods which were usually preferable, on moral grounds to imports (e.g., tobacco, wine, perishables) (see *ibid.*, pp. 34–69). He characterized the arguments in support of commerce as "sweepings of Colbert's shop" (*ibid.*, p. 42). Chalmers, too, had reasoned that the demand for exports, as well as for domestically consumed products, originated at home.

161. He did not square this opinion with his statement (see n. 159 and text, above) regarding the use of revenue for capital formation.

162. *Britain*, p. 42.

163. *Ibid.*, p. 33. Luxury would not hurt a nation whose wealth, unlike that of ancient Rome, was derived from its "own internal resources." Nor would it enervate "that class, from which the army of the state must be chiefly supplied," inasmuch as the "bulk of that class . . . . will never enjoy more than the bare necessaries of life" (*ibid.*, p. 31; cf. pp. 23–24). Whereas William Paley favored limiting luxury to the few, Spence supposed that it would be so restricted by the scheme of things (cf. n. 164, below). On Paley and Malthus see my paper cited in n. 7, above.

164. *Agriculture*, pp. 69–70, Spence cites in support of this view Edmund

Burke's statement: "I am sure that no consideration, except the necessity of submitting to the yoke of luxury, and the despotism of fancy, who in their own imperious way will distribute the surplus product of the soil, can justify the toleration of such trades and employments in a well-regulated state. But for this purpose of distribution, it seems to me, that the idle expenses of monks are quite as well directed as the idle expenses of us layloiterers." Burke had also said, regarding the "income of the landed capitalist," that "the only concern of the state is, that the capital taken in rent from the land, should be returned again to the industry from whence it came," and with the "least possible detriment to the morals" of all concerned (see his "Reflections on the Revolution in France" [1790], in *Works* [London, 1803], V, 290–92). In 1769 Burke had defended luxury—largely "decency and convenience"—saying that it "excites industry, nourishes emulation, and inspires some sense of personal value into all ranks of people" (*Works*, II, 203–4). Burke, unlike Lauderdale and Mill, at times supposed that great inequality was especially favorable to the permanence of the institution of property (see A. Cobban, *Edmund Burke* [London, 1929], p. 195).

165. *Britain*, p. 71 n. Spence was not wholly consistent with others of his opinions when, in this note, he said that the receivers of interest on government loans spent all this interest; that taxes, though ultimately incident on land, oppressed those in the middle ranks who lived on fixed income; and that, while the country had enough productive laborers, the government ought to spend more of its revenues on national improvements (see also *Agriculture*, p. 70 n.).

166. It was also criticized by Robert Torrens and by an anonymous reviewer for the *Eclectic Review* (III, Part II [December, 1807], 1052–58), who subsequently (*ibid.*, IV, Part I [June, 1808], 554–59) praised Mill's pamphlet and formulation of Say's law. It was approved by William Cobbett and by the anonymous author of *Sketches on Political Economy* (1809), whose publication, Seligman states (*op. cit.*, p. 68), brought to an end the attempt to popularize physiocracy in England, except for its partial support by Thomas Chalmers. *Sketches* is attributed, on what grounds I am unaware, to Granville Sharp (1735–1813).

167. XI (January, 1808), 429–48. The anonymous author of this review also reviewed Spence's reply (*Agriculture*) critically (see *Edinburgh Review*, XIV [April, 1809], 50–60, esp. 54, where the earlier review is referred to). The author of this review treated production much as did Say (see n. 183, below): "Man never creates. The quantity of matter in the universe is always the same. All that he does, is . . . . to arrange or to mould it in

such a way as to make it more subservient to his use or gratification than it was before" (see *Edinburgh Review*, XIV [April, 1809], 54). Brougham, in his review of Lauderdale's work (see *ibid.*, IV [July, 1804], 358–59), had written in similar vein: "There is no essential difference between the powers of man over matter, in agriculture, and in other employments. It is a vulgar error, to suppose that, in the operations of husbandry, any portion is added to the stock of matter formerly in existence." The farmer, like the manufacturer, merely "works up [the] raw material." To this statement and article Spence's critic refers (see *ibid.*, XIV [April, 1809], 54) the reader who desires further information. It is quite possible, therefore, since Brougham here treated production as did Say, that he may have read Say's *Traité* before writing the review of Lauderdale's work. If this be the case and if Brougham were the author (see n. 168) of the two reviews of Spence's pamphlets, it is likely that the criticism of Spence's views was inspired by Say's *Traité*. The author of these two reviews, even if he were not Brougham, may have derived his inspiration from Say's work.

168. *Edinburgh Review*, XI (January, 1808), 434, 435 (my italics). This reviewer also pointed out that in Britain the landed proprietors controlled only a small portion of the nation's purchasing-power (*ibid.*, pp. 434–35). The author of this review is not identified by W. A. Copinger in his *On the Authorship of the First Hundred Numbers of the "Edinburgh Review"* (Manchester, 1895); nor is he identified as Brougham in a recent study of the latter's contributions (see E. Schneider *et al.*, "Brougham's Early Contributions to the *Edinburgh Review*: A New List," *Modern Philology*, XLII [1945], 152–73). That Brougham may have been the author of this review of Spence's work is suggested, however, by several facts. We have already indicated (see n. 167) that Brougham and the anonymous reviewer treated production in the same manner. The reviewer of Spence's *Britain* pamphlet also referred approvingly (see *Edinburgh Review*, XI [January, 1808], 440) to Brougham's "able" *Inquiry into Colonial Policy*. Furthermore, Brougham himself, in a laudatory review of a pamphlet by Spence (see n. 170, below) on West Indian affairs (see *Edinburgh Review*, XIII [January, 1809], 382 ff., esp. 383), remarks that "we had the fortune to dissent from the doctrines" of Spence's *Britain Independent*. Against the view that Brougham did the review of Spence's *Britain* pamphlet may be set the fact, supported in the text, that he did not make much use of the proposition that production begets consumption. F. W. Fetter rejects the view that Brougham reviewed Spence's initial work (*Edinburgh Review*, XI [1808], 429–48) as well as his reply to critics

211

(*ibid.*, XIV [1809], 50–60). The former, thought A. Trollope, might have been written by T. R. Malthus; the latter, Henry Cockburn surmised, by Buchanan and Jeffrey. See "The Authorship of Economic Articles in the *Edinburgh Review*, 1802–47," *Journal of Political Economy*, LXI [1953], 243–46. The attribution to Malthus is quite open to question, even though the author of the review (*loc. cit.*, pp. 446–48) declares himself no "blind" admirer of foreign trade.

169. Bosanquet's views were those of the eighteenth century (e.g., see Johnson, *op. cit.*, pp. 230 ff., 301 ff.).

170. *Edinburgh Review*, XI (October, 1807), 148–49, 156–57, 169. Bosanquet's work (*Thoughts on the Value to Great Britain of Commerce in General, and of the Colonial Trade in Particular* [1807]), one of several reviewed by Brougham, inspired William Spence's *Radical Cause of the Present Distress of the West India Planters Pointed Out* (1807), which was favorably reviewed by Brougham in the *Edinburgh Review*, XIII [1809], 382 ff.

171. *Edinburgh Review*, IV [1804], 373.

172. *Ibid.*, p. 373. Brougham employs the term "parsimony" in the same manner as Smith (*ibid.*, pp. 373–74) and defends the sinking-fund scheme on the ground that it restores funds gradually to their former owners and so facilitates their investment (*ibid.*, p. 375). In earlier articles he had defended the sinking-fund arrangement (*ibid.*, III [1804], 480 ff.); described borrowing from merchants and manufacturers as a better means than increased taxation for financing war, inasmuch as it did not tend to diminish "the revenue of the nation" (*ibid.*, V [1804], 117–18); and commented on the difficulty, in the absence of war, of finding sufficient "vent for capital" (*ibid.*, pp. 115–16, 119).

173. *Ibid.*, IV (1804), 361–62. He is criticizing the thesis, which he attributes to Quesnay, that an increase in the food supply produces an increase in population and thus provides a market for itself. Later Malthus (*Principles of Political Economy* [1st ed.; London, 1820], chap. iii, sec. i), in his discussion of rent, said that necessaries, "when properly distributed," create their own demand by facilitating population growth. See also n. 184, below.

174. James Mill, *Commerce Defended* (London, 1808), pp. 46–49. Mill is criticizing Spence's assertion that durable commodities are preferable to nondurable commodities. Pyramid-building cannot enrich a country. Mill appears to accept Smith's distinction between productive and unproductive labor, however. Mill's arguments reappear in chap. iv of his *Elements of Political Economy*, first published in 1821.

175. *Commerce Defended*, pp. 85–87. Mill criticized in detail Spence's views on productivity, agriculture, commerce, exchange, and fiscal policy.

176. *Ibid.*, pp. 76 n., 79, 96 n. While Mill purports to quote from Mercier's *L'Ordre* (II, 138), he actually misquotes from Say (see n. 191, below), who paraphrases Mercier. Mill also repeats Say's anecdote (*Traité* [1st ed.], II, 367 n.).

177. War, said Mill, is the great devourer of capital and the great source of human misery (*Commerce Defended*, pp. 118–20). Great inequality is unfavorable to parsimony and conducive to unproductive consumption, for then the number of persons is great "who have no occasion to devote themselves to any useful pursuit." He attributed England's lack of agricultural progress to the largeness of the landholdings (*ibid.*, pp. 74, 115). He indicated, too, that, from the pressure of circumstances and competition, merchants and manufacturers dealt more liberally with their workmen than did landlords (*ibid.*, p. 114).

178. *Ibid.*, pp. 69–71, 85–89.

179. *Ibid.*, p. 76; also pp. 77–78.

180. *Ibid.*, pp. 71–72.

181. *Ibid.*, pp. 91–94.

182. *Ibid.*, pp. 79, 80, 81, 81–82, 83, 84, 86.

Mill's early views on "parsimony" are expressed in a review of Lauderdale's work (see "Lord Lauderdale on Public Wealth," *Literary Journal*, IV [July, 1804], 2–18, esp. 12–15, 16–17). Mill does not yet give expression to Say's principle; but he treats Lauderdale's views on "accumulation" and sinking funds much as Smith would have done and cites Smith to the effect that what is produced is consumed (see *Wealth of Nations*, pp. 321–22; also n. 129 above). The wealth and productive powers of nations are increased through additions to "the active stock of society." Man does not think "of accumulating dead stock"; he saves only that part of his income which he can employ or lend with advantage. It is virtually impossible for parsimony to "accumulate faster than employment can be procured for active stock in any country." There is no basis in theory or in recent British experience for supposing that debt repayment will be significantly conducive to oversaving and underconsumption. "All the fears . . . . with regard to the failure of consumption are groundless." Mill cites several passages from Lauderdale having to do with the ill effects of marked inequality, but he does not appraise them. Presumably he viewed them sympathetically (see n. 177 above).

183. Condillac had said: "Produire, en effet, c'est donner de nouvelles formes à la matière" (*Le Commerce et le gouvernement* [Paris, 1798 ed.], Part I, chap. ix, p. 79). Say directed against the physiocratic theory of production the argument that, since the mass of matter is constant, man cannot create material objects; he can only change the form of matter and give it utility (see *Traité* [2d and later

eds.], Book I, chap. i; [1st ed.], Book I, pp. 23–30). While Say therefore rejects the physiocratic and Smithian theories of productivity in the first edition, he does not reject Smith's view that some employments of capital are inherently more advantageous to a society than others (see *ibid.*, Book I, chaps. vi, xviii, xlii–xliii; Book IV, chap. xviii; [6th ed.], pp. 402–4; cf. nn. 132–33 and text, above).

Of production, both Brougham and Spence's anonymous critic (see n. 167) wrote much as did Say. Whence it is possible that they knew Say's *Traité*. If this be true, it illuminates the *Edinburgh Review's* criticism of Spence. Cursory investigation suggests that the first edition of Say's *Traité* was slow to become known in England. It is not evident from Lauderdale's work whether he had seen Say's work prior to completing his *Inquiry;* his criticism of Smith's theory of productivity differs from that of Say. Dugald Stewart does not refer to Say's work. It received little or no attention in the reviews.

184. *Traité* (6th ed.; Paris, 1841), Book I, chap. xv; *Cours complet d'économie politique* (Paris, 1840), I, 340–47; *Catéchisme d'économie politique,* in *Oeuvres diverses* (Paris, 1848), pp. 41 ff. In one place (*Cours,* I, 340–41) Say reasons much as did the physiocrats at times, suggesting that an increase of production gives rise to population growth and thus provides a market for itself. (cf. n. 173, above). For technical formulations and appraisals of Say's law, see O. Lange's "Say's Law: A Restatement and Criticism," in Lange *et al., Studies in Mathematical Economics and Econometrics* (Chicago, 1942), pp. 49–68; H. Neisser, "General Overproduction: A Study of Say's Law of Markets," *Journal of Political Economy,* XLII (1934), 433–65.

185. Hollander concluded, following a careful analysis of the epistolary and other communications between Mill and Say and an examination of the writings of Mill and Say, that Mill was the first to publish the substance of the law and that Say, who merely anticipated it in his 1803 edition, subsequently developed it more fully than Mill and independently of Mill. Say's 1803 edition, Hollander observed, "contained practically nothing of the doctrine commonly ascribed to him"; its passages relating to markets "at best suggest a state of mind." Mill therefore got only the germ of the law from Say (see Hollander's Introd. to Ricardo's *Notes on Malthus* [Baltimore, 1928], pp. lxxix–lxxxv). C. Gide and C. Rist (*A History of Economic Doctrines* [2d rev. ed.; New York, 1915], p. 116 n.) wrote of Say's statements regarding overproduction that they "vary from one edition to another, and anything more unstable . . . . would be difficult to imagine." McCulloch (*op. cit.,* p. 21) found the first edition "nearly as good as the last." Say changed the organi-

zation of his work between 1803 and 1814, reducing the number of books from five to three, and modified the verbal content appreciably. The last edition includes two chapters not in the second; otherwise the arrangement is essentially the same, but the verbal content differs somewhat. The first and second editions are in two volumes; the sixth is in one.

186. *Traité* (1st ed.), I, Book I, chap. xxii, 152–55. Say still looks upon foreign markets as less advantageous than the domestic market and as a supplement to the latter (*ibid.,* pp. 154–55). But he denies that any one nation's prosperity is obtained at the expense of other nations (*ibid.,* chap. xli); and in his criticism of the balance-of-trade theory he indicates that purchasing-power originates in production (*ibid.,* pp. 157, 179). In his criticism of the physiocratic thesis that a high price level for provisions is generally advantageous, Say observes that national real income, production, and employment are independent of the level of prices (*ibid.,* Vol. II, Book III, chap. iv).

187. *Ibid.,* II, Book IV, 175–77.

188. *Ibid.,* pp. 177–80, also p. 548, under "Débouchés."

189. *Traité* (6th ed.), pp. 59 ff., 112–22, 435, 440–43, 453–55. Lauderdale's views are specifically criticized (*ibid.,* p. 115 n). See also *Cours,* I, 150, 153; II, 204–5, 237, 240, 511 n.; *Catéchisme,* pp. 32–35.

190. *Traité* (1st ed.), I, 17, 89–91, 94–96, 102, 129; II, 135–36, 182–84, 346–47, 360–67, 376, 380–81. On types of consumption see *ibid.,* II, 340–42, 346–55; on the importance of "economy," pp. 368, 386–88.

191. *Traité* (6th ed.), p. 459 (Prinsep's trans.); (1st ed.), II, 358. In the first edition this quotation appears in a chapter (Book V, chap. iii) entitled, "Si un état s'enrichit par ses consommations." Citing Mercier (*op. cit.,* II, 138), Say remarked with respect to the physiocrats: "*La consommation est la mesure de la reproduction,* disaient-ils; c'est-à-dire: *plus il se consomme, plus il se produit.* Et, comme la production enrichit, on en a conclu qu'un état s'enrichissait par ses consommations, que l'épargne était directement contraire à la prosperité publique, et que le plus utile citoyen, était celui qui dépensait le plus" (see *Traité* [1st ed.], II, 358–59). Say, who was hypercritical of Mercier and Mirabeau (*ibid.,* I, xvi ff.; [6th ed.], pp. 24–27), distorts Mercier's thesis which was merely the orthodox physiocratic theory of consumption and reproduction (see n. 176, above, on Mill's use of Say's citation). Say describes war as one of the worst forms of unproductive consumption (*Traité* [1st ed.], II, 357, 427).

192. *Traité* (6th ed.), pp. 459–60, 469–70, 543–44; (1st ed.), II, 356–57, 359–60, 366–67, 379–80, 395–407, 522;

Cours, II, 206–15, 248 ff., 517 n., 558 n.; *Catéchisme,* pp. 93–94. Say opposed sumptuary laws (*Traité* [1st. ed.], II, 384–85).

193. The above argument appeared in the 1803 and later editions (see *Traité* [1st ed.] II, 376–78, 381–83; [6th ed.], pp. 462, 464; *Cours,* II, 210–11, 212).

194. It is likely that had the physiocrats lived at a time when banking facilities were better developed than in mid-eighteenth-century France, they would have put less stress upon their theory of hoarding and have emphasized, instead, factors causing fluctuations in monetary velocity and in the quantity of other than "hard" mediums of exchange.

8.

ARTHUR I. BLOOMFIELD

University of Pennsylvania

The Foreign-Trade

Doctrines of

the Physiocrats[1]

Although the Physiocrats were not primarily interested in the subject of foreign trade, they did devote some discussion to the matter which has hitherto been neglected. The bulk of their foreign-trade theorizing was concerned with the negative task of demonstrating the fallacies of the balance-of-trade doctrine of the Mercantilists. On the positive side, while they argued for free trade, based largely upon their "natural-order" philosophy and upon an incomplete realization of the benefits of international specialization, in practice they were primarily concerned with achieving the free exportation of grain. In the course of their discussions, attention was devoted to the quantity theory, the price-specie flow mechanism, the velocity of circulation of money, the "terms of trade," the law of markets and the foreign exchanges. Most of their ideas on these matters were borrowed from other writers, notably Hume, Cantillon and Boisguilbert. Moreover, inasmuch as they held fast to a narrow conception of the real nature and gains of foreign trade, and viewed it disdainfully as a necessary evil, the Physiocrats' positive contributions to the subject were at best meager and unsatisfactory.

I. INTRODUCTION

During the past decade there has been a considerable growth of interest in the theory of international trade, and valuable contributions have been

Reprinted from *The American Economic Review,* XXVIII (December 1938), 716–35, by permission of the author and the American Economic Association. At the time of original publication, the author was living in Chicago.

made to the literature in this field. Although most of the work has been concerned with modifying and extending various aspects of the "Classical" doctrine, much attention has also been devoted to a more careful and intensive examination of the earlier literature. In addition to Angell's comprehensive treatise,[2] illuminating studies have been made of the foreign-trade doctrines of earlier writers and schools of thought, notably the English and French Mercantilists.

It is significant to notice, however, that very little attention has been specifically devoted to the foreign-trade theories of the first "school" of economists, the Physiocrats. Although there is a large and valuable literature on the Physiocratic movement,[3] this aspect of their system has been conspicuously neglected. The only comprehensive analyses in this field are the earlier studies of Permézel[4] and Savatier.[5] These works are concerned more with the practical side of the Physiocratic views on foreign trade than with the theoretical aspects, which have as yet not received analysis and evaluation in the light of modern international trade and monetary theory.

Systematic discussions of the monetary aspects of their foreign-trade theories especially have been lacking. Angell devotes but a few pages to the matter, and most books on the Physiocrats make only passing reference to it. The various historians of monetary theory, notably Hoffmann,[6] Monroe,[7] Loria[8] and Zuckerkandl,[9] as well as other writers on historical phases of monetary doctrines, make little mention, if any, of the Physiocrats. The only exception here appears to be Gonnard.[10]

The reason for this almost general neglect is not difficult to determine, for the Physiocrats had comparatively little interest in foreign trade and monetary matters. Such views as they had on the subject were seldom presented in systematic or comprehensive fashion, and evidenced, in general, a lack of originality. They did write sufficiently on these topics, however, to warrant a study of this aspect of their system. The purpose of this paper is not to demonstrate that they made particularly valuable or original contributions to foreign-trade and monetary theory, but rather to fill a minor, though noticeable, gap in the history of the literature. An attempt will be made herein to present a systematic digest of their more significant discussions in this field.

The Physiocrats were largely indebted, in their discussions of money and foreign trade, to the ideas of other writers. Three men, especially, seem to have shaped their general doctrinal position — namely, Hume, Cantillon and Boisguilbert.[11] To Hume they were indebted for one of the earliest scientific analyses of the nature of foreign trade, and from him they derived many of their liberal ideas. Between 1753 and 1759 some three different French translations were made of Hume's economic essays, originally published in 1752 under the title of *Political Discourses*,[12] and these exerted considerable influence on them.[13] Hume himself spent some time in France and was intimately acquainted with different members of the School. Since the "discovery" of Cantillon by Jevons in 1881,[14] the many similarities between his doctrines and those of the Physiocrats have become abundantly clear. Their discussions of wealth, value, money and monetary circulation have much in common. The indebtedness to Boisguilbert is perhaps even more striking. Although the Physiocrats made very few references to him, the remarkable similarity between their doctrines becomes inexplicable unless one is prepared to admit this indebtedness. In their writings we find a similar disdain for money and the balance of trade, a similar preoccupation with agriculture, and similar arguments for freer trade.[15]

II. THE CRITICISM OF MERCANTILISM

A. *Monetary Doctrines before the Physiocrats*

The greater part of the foreign-trade and monetary doctrines of the Physiocrats can be fully understood and appreciated only if it is remembered that the movement arose primarily as a reaction to Mercantilism, which had laid exaggerated stress on the necessity of accumulating a large stock of the precious metals by means of an export surplus. This philosophy, which for long had dominated both government policy and economic literature, had by the time of the Physiocrats showed definite signs of disintegration. The period immediately antedating the movement was one of transition to more liberal ideas, and although most of the writers were still Mercantilistic in outlook, we find in their writings an increasing realization of the weaknesses of trade restriction and bullionism.

The earliest attacks on Mercantilism were on the monetary side. For one thing, it was argued that money was *not* wealth and could not satisfy human wants. This anti-Mercantilist notion, hinted at in the earlier literature,[16] found definite expression in the writings of Boisguilbert, Vauban, Law, Mélon, Forbonnais, d'Argenson and others.[17] Coupled with this notion was also specific recognition of simpler forms of the quantity theory of money, the realization that the accumulation of the precious metals would merely increase prices, without an increase of the community's real wealth. Its earliest formulation in England is usually credited to Locke, but as Viner has shown,[18] it had been earlier stated by Malynes, Mun, Cotton, Robinson and others. The connection between an influx of the precious metals and rising prices was recognized in France at an early date by Bodin.

The most effective single weapon in the doctrinal defeat of Mercantilism was the theory of the self-regulating mechanism of the international distribution of specie. The purpose of this doctrine was to demonstrate that under an international metallic currency the supply of the precious metals would automatically take care of itself. Any excess, or deficiency, of the amount required by a country to maintain international equilibrium would be corrected by the influence of changes in price levels, shifts in trade balances, and specie flows. Although Hume systematized and popularized the doctrine by his precise formulation of it in 1752,[19] North (1691), Gervaise (1720), Cantillon (1730), Vanderlint (1734) and others had earlier stated it with varying degrees of completeness and correctness.[20]

217

In France, especially, the period preceding the Physiocratic movement was productive of many monetary discussions. Most important were the writings of Law, Daguesseau, Mélon, Dutot, Forbonnais, Paris-Duverney and Cantillon.[21] It was a period of intense monetary controversy which arose largely as a result of depressed economic conditions and the disordered state of the French finances. Although Mercantilistic in outlook, these writers, Cantillon above all, offered some penetrating suggestions as to the nature of monetary fluctuations, prices and the foreign exchanges.

The Physiocrats were not, however, primarily interested in these matters which had so engaged the attention of their predecessors, and consequently, monetary discussions form but a small part of their writings. To establish their own point of view as to the sole productivity of agriculture and the necessity of free trade, it was essential for them, however, first to demolish the preconceptions of the Mercantilists. Thus the greater part of their monetary discussions consists of attempts to demonstrate the fallacies of the balance-of-trade doctrine. Here a variety of arguments was used, most of which had been stated in various forms by earlier writers.

B. Money as "un Gage"

The first Mercantilist notion attacked by the Physiocrats, and the one on which they probably lavished the most attention, was the identification of money and wealth. It was made clear that a country's wealth consisted not in its stock of money but in its resources and its goods destined for consumption. As Quesnay expressed it,

> ... l'argent n'est pas la richesse dont les hommes ont besoin pour leur jouissance. Ce sont les biens nécessaires à la vie et à la production annuelle de ces biens mêmes qu'il faut obtenir.[22]

In the Physiocratic scheme, money is considered solely as a medium of exchange, a "gage" and a mere "signe représentatif."[23] A sharp and clear-cut distinction is thus drawn between *real* wealth (la richesse primaire, réelle, véritable, naturelle), and *pecuniary* wealth (la richesse sécondaire, rélative, représentative). Money is a means, not an end, nor has it any "dynamic" function such as that attributed to it by the Mercantilists.[24] It is of benefit only to the extent that it is exchanged for "primary" wealth.

Closely allied with this is the notion that a country does not "gain" by the acquisition of the precious metals through trade, for this necessitates giving up in exchange an amount of real wealth equal in value. Speaking of a country which endeavors to sell more than it buys, Le Trosne argues that

> ... elle augmenteroit la masse de l'argent chez alle, & non ses richesses, car elle auroit payé cet argent tout ce qu'il vaut. Elle auroit acquis de l'argent, mais elle n'auroit plus les richesses qu'elle auroit données pour l'avoir; il n'y a donc point-là d'augmentation de richesses.[25]

Consequently, the Physiocrats contended that a policy of trying continually to accumulate precious metals by forcing exports and retarding imports is unwise, for the country concerned is parting with more real wealth than it is acquiring. The surplus of metals obtained is of benefit only to the extent that it is reconverted into real wealth. A continuing "favorable" balance of trade (if such were possible) is therefore undesirable, and in itself gives no indication of the real "gain" from trade.[26]

C. The Law of Markets and the Sterility of Trade

The Physiocrats were among the first to see that all trade reduces itself to an exchange of commodities against commodities, money merely serving an intermediate rôle. This notion, subsequently elaborated upon and popularized by J. B. Say as the "loi des debouchés," formed an integral part of the Physiocratic critique of Mercantilism. Throughout the writings of the Physiocrats we find frequent references to the fact that "acheter, c'est vendre, et vendre, c'est acheter";[27] "personne n'est acheteur qu'autant qu'il est vendeur";[28] "pour vendre beaucoup il faut acheter beaucoup, et *vice versa*";[29] and "il en est des nations comme des particuliers; la somme de leurs ventes est égale à la somme de leurs achats."[30] The notion here, of course, is that a nation can buy only to the extent that it sells, and can sell only to the extent that it buys. It cannot continually attempt to sell and never to buy; for by failing to buy it does not give other nations the wherewithal to buy from it. It was for this reason among others that the Physiocrats considered the balance-of-trade doctrine as nothing more than "un phantôme,"[31] "une chimère,"[32] and "aveugle et cupide politique."[33]

It is clear that this "law" gives no adequate explanation of the mechanism of international trade inasmuch as it omits reference to such an essential element as specie-flows, and the causes underlying them.[34] Then, again, there is no reason why there should be any necessary equality between a nation's commodity exports and imports, even if its total debits and credits do balance. The doctrine, moreover, if it is to have any significance at all, is a long-run affair. Turgot seems to have been the only one to recognize this. In a letter to Dupont de Nemours he wrote:

Je sais bien que tous les achats et les ventes sont toujours au pair à la longue; mais prenez-y garde, cette proposition est susceptible dans le fait des limitations. Tout tend au niveau, mais rien n'y est . . . malgré la liberté des communications, dans l'état actuel, il y a des nations qui s'enrichissent et d'autres qui s'appauvrissent, des nations qui achètent plus qu'elles ne vendent.[35]

Another argument used by the Physiocrats against the balance of trade doctrine was that all trade was "sterile," and that there was no possibility of "gain" involved in it. This "sterility" was argued from several different points of view,[36] the most common being that trade was merely an exchange of equal values, with no addition to the sum total of wealth of either of the traders.[37] This doctrine, which was applied both to domestic and foreign trade, does not, however, preclude the notion of "gain" in its usual sense as gain in utility. Although it is correct to say that trade is an "exchange of equal values," nevertheless each party increases his utility by the act, and this in itself constitutes the real "gain" derivable from trade. The Physiocrats merely used the word "gain" in a different way: to them it meant a clear surplus of *value*, which from their point of view trade does not afford.[38] Quesnay, Le Trosne and Mercier did, however, grasp the concept of an increase in utility resulting from trade, but they did not look upon this as a "gain."[39]

D. *The Quantity Theory*

It was pointed out above that by the time of the Physiocrats simpler forms of the quantity theory had gained substantial acceptance in the literature. Although most treatises on the history of monetary doctrines neglect to mention the Physiocrats as adherents to this theory,[40] an examination of their writings reveals that, following their predecessors, they had clear recognition of the influence of the quantity of money on prices. This was used as another weapon in the attack on Mercantilism.

In the following quotations are presented statements of the quantity theory in its most elementary form:

La valeur de l'argent, rélativement à celle des denrées, était alors au moins le double de ce qu'elle est aujourd'hui, l'argent étant beaucoup moins rare depuis la decouverte des mines d'Amérique.[41]

. . . le prix de toutes sortes d'ouvrages augmente journellement à Paris . . . une des causes de cette augmentation est le rengorgement des métaux qui arrivent . . . des mines du Perou et du Potose.[42]

À mésure que la masse de l'argent s'accrôit, il perd de son prix.[43]

. . . plus d'argent rendra tout plus cher s'il entre dans la circulation.[44]

Here the relationship is of the simple form $P = f (M)$, the "goods side of the equation" being ignored. No *precise* relationship between M and P is specified. Other writers took account of the "goods side," and presented more advanced statements of the theory. For example:

La proportion entre la masse des gages pécuniaires, & celles des denrées diminuant continuellement, il se trouveroit chaque année moins de ceux-la pour obtenir la livraison de celles-ci, dont la valeur vénale diminueroit.[45]

On dit que les assignats vaudront l'argent et serviront aussi bien que l'argent; si cela est, comme il n'y aura ni plus de pain ni plus de vin qu'auparavant, ceux qui voudraient avoir du pain . . . seront donc obligés de donner plus d'assignats ou plus d'argent pour la même quantité de pain ou de vin . . . s'il y avait le double d'argent, il faudrait acheter le double plus cher.[46]

S'il (Law) avait lu et medité Locke . . . il aurait su que toutes les denrées d'un État se balancent toujours entre elles et avec l'or et l'argent, suivant la proportion de leur quantité et de leur débit . . . que, quand il y a plus d'or, il est moins cher, et qu'on en donne plus pour une quantité déterminée des marchandises. . . ."[47]

Here the influence of the amount of goods in circulation is recognized, and in several cases,[48] a precise relationship between money, goods and prices is specified. It was also seen that paper money affected prices in the same manner as metallic money. None of these writers, however, discussed the question of *how* an increase in the quantity of money leads to higher prices. Unlike Cantillon, who carefully explained how this was effected by an increased expenditure on the part of those receiving the new money,[49] the Physiocrats seemed to look upon the relationship between money and prices as purely automatic.[50]

E. The Velocity of Circulation of Money

Toward the end of the seventeenth century, discussions of the velocity of circulation of money began to appear in the literature. Sir William Petty and John Locke were among the first to refer specifically to it.[51] Its rôle was generally misunderstood at first, being tied up with the prevailing notion that a definite amount of money was needed to carry on trade (some definite level of prices being assumed). In France, Boisguilbert seems to have been the first to refer to the velocity of circulation of money. He considered it higher among the poorer than the wealthier classes.[52] Cantillon devoted an elaborate discussion to the matter, and was the first to recognize the influence of velocity on prices.[53]

Holtrop, in his brief reference to the Physiocrats, contends that they did not concern themselves at all with the question of monetary circulation,[54] and he gives no indication that they discussed the velocity concept. This is not correct, for considerable discussion was devoted to these matters.

The rôle of monetary circulation formed an integral part of Quesnay's *Tableaux Économiques*,[55] and his ideas on the subject were echoed by other Physiocrats. Production was considered as taking place in an annual cycle, and money was looked upon as annually circulating between the three "classes" of the community. The flow would commence with the activities of the peasant class at the beginning of the crop season and pass successively through the hands of the other classes, returning at the end of a year to the point from which it started.[56] There was thus an annual cycle, or circular flow of money, by means of which the annual production of the country was exchanged among the different groups. At the beginning of the crop season the cycle would recommence.[57]

There is also specific recognition of the velocity concept. It was clearly pointed out that money, by changing hands several times, is equivalent to a larger supply of money:

. . . l'argent, sans augmenter en masse, suffira à tous les echanges, *la celerité de son mouvement* supplée à sa quantité[58] . . . *une plus grande rapidité dans la circulation* de ces espèces péceniaires suppléent aisément à la dimunition de leur quantité[59] . . . la masse des richesses pécuniaires . . . sont toujours éffectives dans un État par leur quantité ou par *la celerité de leur circulation*.[60] (Italics mine.)

It is unfortunate that the Physiocrats merely presented the concept without elaborating upon it in the manner, for example, of Cantillon. In general, they seemed to regard velocity as a means of supplementing any possible "deficiency" of metallic money, and thus used the concept as a further criticism of the Mercantilist stress on "treasure." The implication here was, of course, that some definite amount of means of payment was needed to circulate the annual production, and that the actual amount of metallic money needed would vary with the velocity of circulation. This amount of money was never made very clear, but was usually looked upon as bearing a more or less definite relationship to the annual revenue of the country.[61] Saint-Peravy, for example, estimated that a rich country could easily get along with an amount equal to one-quarter of the annual revenue.[62] Quesnay stated that an amount equal to the annual revenue would normally be more than sufficient,[63] and elsewhere argued that rarely did it exceed one-half of this quantity.[64]

One effective argument frequently used by English writers against Mercantilism was that since paper money can serve as a substitute for metallic money, there was no need to lay stress on the necessity of an accumulation of the precious metals.[65] There is abundant recognition of this same point in the Physiocratic literature.[66] Closely allied with it is the notion that the wealthier a country is, the less proportionately will be its need for the precious metals, because the credit standing of individuals will generally be better, and their promissory notes can circulate from hand to hand as money.[67] Paper money was looked upon as performing a rôle analogous to that of an increased velocity of circulation — namely, that of supplementing the stock of metallic money. The exact amount of money "needed" by a country would therefore be dependent upon the state of the velocity of circulation, and upon the quantity of paper money in circulation.

F. The Price-Specie Flow Mechanism

Very little systematic discussion has been devoted to the doctrine of the self-regulating mechanism of the international distribution of specie as found in the Physiocratic literature. Angell devotes a few paragraphs to the matter and concludes that

> . . . it is apparent that while Hume's practical policies in international exchange had exerted a considerable influence upon Physiocratic doctrine, his theories themselves had wholly failed to take root . . . the price-specie mechanism (was) presented . . . to some extent by the Physiocrats . . . it is presented and then simply neglected.[68]

He argues that it was not the Physiocrats, but rather their contemporary, Isaac de Bacalan, who during this period presented the best discussion of the Hume doctrine, a discussion which

> presents the only explicit statement in the French literature until less than a hundred years ago of the equilibrium tendency inherent in the working of the price-gold flow mechanism.[69]

In this section it will be shown that the Physiocrats had more to say about the doctrine than Angell assumes, that the statements of Le Trosne and Turgot are in every respect as satisfactory as that of de Bacalan, and that an equilibrium tendency is clearly stated in the writings of these latter men.

The best statement of the price-specie flow mechanism that I have been able to find in the Physiocratic literature, and one that seems to have been overlooked entirely, is that of Le Trosne:

Quel avantage trouverait donc une nation à amasser ainsi beaucoup d'argent, et à en recevoir beaucoup plus qu'elle n'en donnerait? . . . Les nations voisines ne pourraient plus consommer ses productions, parce que l'argent devenu rare chez elles aurait augmenté de valeur par rapport aux productions, comme il a baissé chez cette nation à raison de son abondance. Loin donc de pouvoir lui acheter en argent, elles reviendraient lui vendre leurs productions, *et ferait ainsi refluer chez elles ce même argent qui leur a été enlevé, jusqu'à ce que le niveau fut rétabli.*[70] (Italics mine.)

This clear-cut statement has all the essentials of the Hume doctrine. There is the recognition that a specie flow to one country from neighboring countries causes a rise of prices in the former and a fall of prices in the latter (this *opposite* movement of prices was not explicitly recognized by de Bacalan[71]), leading to such a shift in trade balances as to cause the specie to flow out again until an equilibrium level is reëstablished. This level is presumably understood to be that at which the imports and exports of each country balance.

Turgot, in a long passage,[72] carefully describes how the precious metals from the mines of one country are distributed throughout all the trading nations of the world. The first effect of the introduction of the new supply will be to raise prices above the level prevailing elsewhere, with the result that the surplus will be drained off, by means of unfavorable trade balances, to those countries with which it trades. Prices will rise similarly in these countries, and specie flows will continue from nation to nation until, on the cessation of the output of the mines, an international equilibrium will be established. At this point, the total exports and imports of each nation will be equalized.

Mercier de la Rivière discusses the self-regulating mechanism briefly, but in a less effective manner than Le Trosne and Turgot. An inflow of the metals, he argues, will cause prices to rise, leading to an adverse trade balance and a specie outflow, which he figuratively compares to a river overflowing its banks.[73] No mention is made of any resulting equilibrium adjustment. Baudeau gives an exceptionally good statement, and comes very close to a complete account of the mechanism.[74] Saint-Peravy does not carry the argument very far. He recognizes that a specie inflow will raise prices and cause exports to fall off, but failing to refer to the counter-flow of specie, he concludes that the result will be an accumulation of unsold surpluses of goods.[25] Mirabeau, in his earlier work, states that an attempt to accumulate the precious metals will be unsuccessful, for the specie will flow out to other nations, as if through "un sac percé."[76] No explanation is given, however.

From the above references it should be clear that most of the Physiocrats had some recognition of the self-adjusting mechanism. Only Le Trosne and Turgot carried it to its logical conclusion; the others were content to state but one-half of the mechanism. More often the argument was presented merely in the form that each country would, under an international metallic standard, get its "necessary" supply of the precious metals, no explanation being specified. One cannot always be certain, however, whether or not by the term "necessary" amount, the Physiocrats had in mind at all times that amount needed to maintain an international equilibrium of price levels. In one interesting passage describing the international distribution of specie, Mercier contends that the quantity each country will "get" will be proportional to the volume and price of its commodities.[77] Abstracting for the moment from velocity, this is an unobjectionable statement, and is especially true in the case of a small country. Here the price level is first determined for it by international conditions, and such an amount of specie will flow in as is necessary to maintain that equilibrium level. That is, T and P are determined firstly, and M secondly, V assumed to be given.[78] Although they did not explicitly state it, the Physiocrats, given their general recognition of the rôle of velocity, would no doubt have granted that an increase in velocity would correspondingly diminish the amount of specie inflow necessary for the maintenance of equilibrium.[79]

G. The "Balance of Trade" and the Foreign Exchanges

In their frequent discussions of the balance of trade, the Physiocrats, with a few exceptions, never seem to have recognized the existence of any "invisible" items.[80] According to them, the "balance" meant merely the difference between commodity exports and imports. Nowhere is a distinction drawn between the balance of trade and the balance of indebtedness. The only clear-cut statement of the different constituent items in the balance which I have been able to find in the Physiocratic literature is that of Dupont de Nemours. He cautions against drawing inferences from the state of the foreign exchanges as to the relative flow of commodity exports and imports because

> toute autre manière . . . de faire passer des fonds d'un pays dans un autre, les emprunts publics ou privés, les remboursemens, les rentes, les subsides, les operations sur les monnoies, les avances mêmes de marchandises faites par spéculation d'une nation à l'autre . . . influent sur le *cours de change*.[81]

Other isolated references to invisible items are made. Mirabeau discusses the question of inter-government lending,[82] and in another passage refers to short-term borrowing between nations and the possibility of a sudden repatriation of the funds.[83] Quesnay recognizes rent payments,[84] and Mercier mentions the outflow of money resulting from the movement of businessmen from one country to another.[85] Frequent reference is made to freight charges levied by one nation on another for shipping services,[86] and to payments to foreign middlemen engaging in international trade. With the exception of Dupont, however, none of these writers seemed to

recognize the possible influence of these invisible items in offsetting or re-
inforcing the balance of trade and consequently in affecting exchange rates
and specie flows.

Very few references can be found in the Physiocratic literature to the
foreign exchanges. This is somewhat surprising in view of the fact that there
had already been considerable discussion on the subject both in
England[87] and in France.[88] I have been able to find systematic discussions
only in the writings of Dupont[89] and Saint-Peravy.[90] Both recognized clearly
the general rôle, under an international metallic standard, of exchange
fluctuations, gold movements and the gold points. Both defined the par of
exchange in the conventional way, and explained that deviations from equilibrium depended upon the state of the balance of trade. The position of the
gold points was correctly stated as depending upon the cost (including insurance) of transporting specie from one country to another.[91] Dupont
offers some interesting suggestions as to the different effects resulting from
the settlement of debts in the currency of the debtor, and of the creditor,
country. Neither he nor Saint-Peravy, however, seem to have recognized the
fact, earlier stressed by Hume, that exchange fluctuations within the gold
points play a rôle in the mechanism of adjustment, by stimulating or deterring commodity flows. Both men gave excellent discussions of arbitrage and
speculation in the exchanges. In general, however, they added little, if anything, to what had already been developed before them on foreign-exchange
theory.

H. The Physiocratic Concept of Wealth

It has been shown above that the Physiocrats employed a variety of verbal
weapons in their attack on Mercantilism. Not only did they argue that
money was *not* wealth, but they contended that its accumulation was
undesirable, unnecessary and even impossible. Their own concept of wealth
was, however, of a peculiar sort. They believed that not only must there
be an abundance of consumable goods, but these must sell at a high price.
The greatest wealth and prosperity consisted in the greatest amount of
exchange values. Quesnay expresses this point of view concisely:

> Plus le blé, le vin, les laines, les bestiaux sont chers et abondants, plus il y a
> des richesses dans l'État. *La non-valeur avec abondance n'est point richesse; la
> cherté avec pénurie est misère; l'abondance avec cherté est opulence.*[92]

To many observers this appears at once as a contradiction in terms.
Sauvaire-Jourdan,[93] and following him, Permézel,[94] both argue that this
could be possible only if the quantity of money were equally abundant,
which is, at bottom, a Mercantilist notion.

By "cherté," however, the Physiocrats did not have in mind a price that
was necessarily excessive. They were referring to a "bon prix," a world
price as established under a free trade régime, and which it was believed
would be remunerative to the producer. This was explicitly stated by
Quesnay and Mercier:

... nous n'entendons pas ici, par le mot de *cherté*, un prix qui puisse jamais être excessif, mais seulement un prix commun entre nous et l'étranger.[95]

Le bon prix est tout l'opposé de la cherté.[96]

This being so, the so-called paradox of "cherté" and "abondance" disappears. For if all that is meant by "cherté" is an international price, the assumption of an abundant quantity of money is not necessary.[97]

III. THE FREE-TRADE VIEWS OF THE PHYSIOCRATS

A. Introduction

Although the Physiocrats are commonly referred to as the "first school of free traders," most of their ideas on the subject were anticipated by earlier writers. The period preceding the Physiocratic movement witnessed the gradual diffusion of more liberal notions on the subject of foreign trade, and many of the elements of the free-trade doctrine as subsequently developed were prevalent in the literature.[98]

An understanding of the Physiocratic views on the subject necessitates first an examination of their attitude toward foreign trade in general. In reaction to the Mercantilist stress on foreign trade, the Physiocrats were led to belittle its importance and to view it with disdain. Both Quesnay[99] and Mercier[100] considered it a "pis-aller," resulting from the fact that the domestic market was not sufficiently large to absorb the annual output of certain goods, which had consequently to be shipped abroad. Foreign trade was considered as "sterile"; such "gains" as were made were appropriated by middlemen and constituted a deduction from the country's revenue.[101] There is even the hint that foreign trade is destined ultimately to disappear altogether.[102] The Physiocrats argued, moreover, that a large volume of trade might be an indication, not of prosperity, but of impoverishment. It might either represent a narrow domestic market, resulting in large exports, a scarcity of domestic wealth necessitating large imports, or regional shortages due, for example, to crop failures.[103]

In addition to the "sterility" argument, the Physiocrats laid considerable stress on *distance,* and the resulting transport charges as one of the main factors making for the inconvenience of foreign trade. They argued that since the burden of transport charges became greater as trade increased, it was to a nation's advantage to reduce its foreign commerce as much as possible.[104] This argument reveals their relative lack of understanding of the real gains of trade.

B. Elements of Free-Trade Doctrine

Despite their general disdainful attitude toward foreign trade, the Physiocrats laid much stress on the necessity of free trade. On closer examination, however, it is not surprising to find the nature of their free trade views somewhat different from that of the modern doctrine.

226

In keeping with their general philosophical position, the Physiocrats supported free trade on the ground of the natural order, as being in harmony with justice and constituting an inalienable right of mankind. Several also made use of the old argument that differences in natural conditions and variations in harvests in different countries are indications of a divine will that nations trade freely with each other.[105] Others contended that the prosperity of one nation is dependent upon the prosperity of all others, and that due to this international economic solidarity, it is a short-sighted policy to try to gain in trade at the expense of a neighboring state.[106] On this point, however, Turgot differed somewhat from other members of the school.[107]

References are also made to the international division of labor, but this was never made an integral part of the Physiocratic free-trade doctrine. Each country was considered as endowed with "produits privilegiées" which, because of natural conditions or national aptitudes, it could produce more "cheaply"[108] than other countries. The implication here was that it would be to the advantage of each country to specialize in the production of these commodities, and to exchange them for goods which could not be so advantageously produced at home. It was also implied that under free trade this state of affairs would be achieved.[109] Dupont criticized the English for putting duties on the import of hats, and stated that it would have been better for them to buy their hats abroad where they could be had more cheaply, and to divert their resources to the production of other commodities.[110] Quesnay argued that

La France . . . ne doit pas pretendre à un commerce général, elle doit en sacrifier quelques branches, les moins importantes, à l'avantage des autres parties qui lui sont plus profitables. . . .[111]

These ideas were, however, exceptions to the general rule, and found but scant recognition in the literature. The Physiocratic disdain for foreign trade precluded them from presenting a comprehensive case for free trade on the basis of international specialization. In general, foreign trade was considered as a last resort which should be avoided as far as possible.[112] Free trade was recognized as indispensable, however, in the case of those goods which could not possibly be produced at home, or only at a prohibitive cost.[113] It was repeated time and again that a large foreign trade was neither essential nor desirable. Because of this, it is not surprising that so little discussion was devoted to the advantages of international specialization.[114]

C. The Free Exportation of Grain

The real nature of the "free trade" views of the Physiocrats is made clearer on turning to a brief examination of their views on the grain trade. The grain problem had long been an important one in the French economy, and had engaged the special attention of successive governments and writers of the day. The chief controversial issue at stake was the question of the free exportation of grain, which up to 1764 had generally not been permitted.[115] The Physiocrats opposed the ban strenuously, and wrote innumerable tracts to prove the advantages of a free exportation policy, which they argued was necessary to prevent a depression of grain prices in France resulting from good harvests. If the unwelcome surplus could be drained off, domestic prices would be sustained. Under such a regime a "bon prix" would be established, this being a uniform and competitive price as determined in world markets, any price differences being eliminated by the movement of grain from low-price to high-price areas. It was believed that not only would this price be a uniform one, but also relatively constant from year to year, and sufficiently remunerative to producers to enable them to continue operations. By thus acquiring "un prix constamment avantageux"[116] and "une valeur soutenue, constante et uniforme,"[117] producers would extend operations, hire more men and increase the "produit net" and the general prosperity of the nation. But as long as prices were low, production would slow down and the national income diminish. A cardinal tenet in the Physiocratic doctrine was thus the belief that freedom of exportation would lead to higher prices for the domestic producer; and higher prices, as seen above, were associated with greater national prosperity.

Although the logic of this argument equally involves the free *importation* of grain, the Physiocrats generally neglected this aspect of the problem, especially before 1768.[118]

IV. CONCLUSION

This brief survey should serve to make it clear that the "free trade" doctrines of the Physiocrats were of a very narrow sort. Despite their frequent affirmations of the necessity of complete freedom of trade,[119] the Physiocrats were primarily interested in achieving the free *exportation* of *grain,* and the bulk of their foreign-trade theorizing was oriented about this objective. Relatively little attention was devoted to the importation side of the problem, or to the question of foreign trade in manufactured goods. Many have contended that their arguments have much in common with those of modern agrarian *protectionists,*[120] although this is generally denied. Their prime interest was, above all, to free *internal* trade from the many restrictions imposed upon it, because they believed that if this were achieved, and other methods taken to stimulate consumption,[121] the domestic market would normally be sufficiently broad to absorb the total annual output. As an interim measure, free exportation of grain was supported as a means of disposing of burdensome surpluses and of maintaining the domestic price. They did not want to further foreign trade, but rather to see it shrink as far as possible from "natural" causes. They even looked forward to the time when foreign trade would disappear altogether. Such "free trade" views as they had were merely part of a wider program for the furtherance of the interests of the agricultural classes, which were identified with those of the nation as a whole.

In conclusion, it may be stated that the Physiocrats were not innovators in the field of international trade and monetary theory. Their chief accomplishment here — if one may attribute any to them — was their criticism of the balance-of-trade doctrine. But even in this respect they added little to what had already been developed before them, most of their ideas being culled from the body of anti-Mercantilist doctrine prevalent at the time. They lacked the scientific precision of Hume, and the ability to integrate their scattered notions on the subject of foreign trade[122] into a comprehensive whole. Nevertheless, they did much to popularize the ideal of freer trade relations, as well as the shortcomings of the balance-of-trade doctrine, and must be considered, therefore, as having contributed to the doctrinal defeat of Mercantilism. Their general disdainful attitude toward foreign trade, however, and their distorted conception of the real gains derivable from it, make such "free trade" views as they had of a peculiarly narrow sort. For these reasons, the contributions of the Physiocrats to international trade theory must be considered as meager and unsatisfactory.[123]

NOTES

1. The writer is especially indebted, in the preparation of this paper, to Professor Jacob Viner for the benefit of his advice and criticism. The assistance of Professor J. U. Nef and Dr. G. Meyer is also acknowledged. These men are not responsible, of course, for any errors of fact or interpretation that may be contained herein.

2. J. W. Angell, *The Theory of International Prices*, Cambridge, 1926.

3. The most complete study of the Physiocrats is G. Weulersse, *Le Mouvement Physiocratique en France*, Paris, 1910. Other scholarly general accounts are A. Oncken, *Geschichte der Nationaloekonomie*, Leipzig, 1902, pp. 314–481, and H. Higgs, *The Physiocrats*, London, 1897. The best short survey is J. Schumpeter, "Epochen der Dogmen- und Methodengeschichte," *Grundriss der Sozialökonomik*, i, pp. 39–53. There is also a host of monographic studies on various aspects of their system.

4. P. Permézel, *Les Idées des Physiocrats en Matière de Commerce Internationale*, Lyon, 1907.

5. R. Savatier, *La Théorie du Commerce Chez les Physiocrates*, Paris, 1918.

6. F. Hoffmann, *Kritische Dogmengeschichte der Geldwerttheorien*, Leipzig, 1907.

7. A. E. Monroe, *Monetary Theory before Adam Smith*, Cambridge, 1923.

8. A. Loria, *Studi sul Valore della Moneta*, Turin, 1891.

9. R. Zuckerkandl, *Zur Theorie des Preises*, Leipzig, 1889.

10. R. Gonnard, *Histoire des Doctrines Monétaires*, ii, Paris, 1936, pp. 106–49.

11. By the term "Physiocrats," I refer in this essay specifically to Quesnay, Mercier de la Rivière, Marquis de Mirabeau, Dupont de Nemours, Abbé Baudeau, Le Trosne, Saint-Peravy and Turgot. The writings of such minor Physiocrats as Roubaud and Abeille are omitted from this discussion. It should be remembered that the views of later Physiocrats like Le Trosne and Turgot differed somewhat from those of the other members of the School.

12. F. Sauvaire-Jourdan, *Isaac de Bacalan et les Idées Libre-Échangistes en France*, Paris, 1903, p. 33.

13. For example, J. Pallard: "En France, l'influence de Hume is certaine . . . quant à ses oeuvres, certainement tous ceux qui s'intéressent aux sciences sociales dans la seconde moitié du XVIIIᵉ siècle . . . les étudierent . . . on sait que Quesnay a lu les essais de Hume, et que cette lecture . . . fut l'origine du libéralisme tout spécial du chef des Physiocrates." *La Liberté du Commerce Extérieur au XVIIIᵉ Siècle*, Rennes, 1904, pp. 151–53. See also Sauvaire-Jourdan, *op. cit.*, p. 36; Weulersse, *op. cit.*, ii, p. 26; W. Bickel, *Die Okonomische Begrundung der Freihandelspolitik*, Zurich, 1926, p. 22; S. Bauer, "Zur Entstehung der Physiocratie," *Jahrbucher für Nationalökonomie und Statistik*, N.F., xxi (1890), p. 146. G. Schelle has argued, however, that the influence of Hume on the Physiocrats has been greatly exaggerated. See his *L'Économie Politique et Les Économistes*, Paris, 1917, pp. 122–23, and his "Sur les Physiocrates," *Journal des Économistes*, xxxi (1911), pp. 240–42. See also A. Schatz, *L'Oeuvre Économique de David*

Hume, Paris, 1902, pp. 233–43. It is interesting to note that Hume himself considered the Physiocrats "the set of men the most chimerical and most arrogant that now exist." See his letter to the Abbé Morellet, July 10, 1769, in *The Letters of David Hume*, edited by J. Y. T. Greig, Oxford, 1932, ii, p. 205.

14. W. S. Jevons, "Richard Cantillon and the Nationality of Political Economy," *Contemporary Review*, 1881. Reprinted with the text of Cantillon's "Essai sur la Nature du Commerce en Général" in Higgs's edition, London, 1931. For studies specifically tracing the relationship between Cantillon and the Physiocrats, see P. Legrand, *Richard Cantillon, un Mercantiliste Précurseur des Physiocrates*, Paris, 1900, and W. Rouxel, "Un Précurseur des Physiocrates: Cantillon," *Journal des Économistes*, 5th ser., vii (1891). For a recent estimate of Cantillon's life and work, rich in bibliographical material, see F. A. von Hayek, "Richard Cantillon, Sa Vie, Son Oeuvre," *Revue des Sciences Économiques*, April, June, and October, 1936.

15. The most comprehensive account of the influence of Boisguilbert on the Physiocrats is found in F. Cadet, *Pierre de Boisguilbert, Précurseur des Économistes*, Paris, 1870, especially pp. 358–92.

16. For example, by North and Bodin.

17. For a short discussion, see A. Dubois, *Précis de l'Histoire des Doctrines Économiques*, i, Paris, 1903, pp. 282–84.

18. Jacob Viner, *Studies in the Theory of International Trade*, New York, 1937, pp. 40–41.

19. "Political Discourses," in *Essays Moral, Political and Literary*, 1875 ed., i, pp. 330–345.

20. Viner, *op. cit.*, pp. 74–87.

21. The best discussion of this whole period is to be found in P. Harsin, *Les Doctrines Monétaires et Financières en France*, Paris, 1936. See also J-M. Pascal, *Manipulations Monétaires et Commerce Internationale*, part i, Paris, 1936; Gonnard, *op. cit.*, ii, pp. 17–105.

22. Francois Quesnay, *Analyse du Tableau Économique*, 1766, in *Oeuvres Économiques et Philosophiques de F. Quesnay*, edited by A. Oncken, Paris, 1888, p. 324. All further references below, by pages, to the different writings of Quesnay, will be to this edition.

23. "Dans l'argent, ils ne virent plus qu'un organe ayant pour fonction de faire circuler les richesses commerçables." H. Denis, *Histoire des Doctrines Économiques et Socialistes*, i, Paris, 1904, p. 76.

24. Money is also considered "sterile." *Cf.* Quesnay's dictum, "L'argent n'engendre pas l'argent." For this reason the Physiocrats considered interest on loans as a burdensome deduction from the country's revenue. For a careful study of this aspect of their doctrines, see A. Rougon,

Les Physiocrates et la Règlementation du Taux de l'Intérêt, Paris, 1906.

25. "Discussions sur l'Argent et le Commerce," in his *Recueil de Plusieurs Morceaux Économiques*, Amsterdam, 1768, p. 205. *Cf.* also Mirabeau, *Philosophie Rurale*, ii, Amsterdam, 1763, p. 278. Quesnay argues that this is true even in the case where a country obtains the precious metals from its own mines; it must here "give up" an equivalent amount of real wealth in the form of wages to those working the mines. *Questions Intéressantes sur la Population, l'Agriculture et le Commerce*, 1758, p. 290 n.

26. A similar notion was expressed by Boisguilbert. *Cf.* Cadet, *op. cit.*, p. 247.

27. Mirabeau, *op. cit.*, iii, p. 249.

28. Mercier de la Rivière, *L'Ordre Naturel et Éssentiel des Sociétés Politiques*, 1767, reprinted in E. Daire, *Physiocrates*, Paris, 1846, p. 540.

29. Guérineau de Saint-Peravy, *Principes du Commerce Opposé au Trafic*, Paris, 1786–87, i, p. 8.

30. G-F. Le Trosne, *De l'Intérêt Social*, 1777, in Daire, *op. cit.*, p. 919.

31. *Ibid.*, p. 919.

32. Saint-Peravy, *op. cit.*, ii, p. 103; Quesnay, *Du Commerce: Premier Dialogue entre M. H. et M. N.*, 1766, p. 478.

33. Mercier, *op. cit.*, p. 575.

34. Angell, *op. cit.*, p. 229 n.

35. Feb. 20, 1766, in *Oeuvres de Turgot*, edited by G. Schelle, Paris, 1914, ii, p. 150. Dionnet has argued that the Physiocrats exaggerated the importance of this law. *Le Neomercantilisme*, Paris, 1910, pp. 211–13.

36. Trade was also regarded as "sterile" because it resulted in no "produit net," and because it did not increase the quantity of material goods. *Cf.* Savatier, *op. cit.*, pp. 82–87.

37. Quesnay, *Analyse*, p. 321; Mercier, *op. cit.*, p. 544; Le Trosne, *Discussions*, pp. 211–12.

38. *Cf.* Gide et Rist, *History of Economic Doctrines*, New York, p. 27.

39. Quesnay, *Réponse au Mémoire de M. H.*, 1766, p. 395; Le Trosne, *op. cit.*, pp. 211–12; Mercier, *op. cit.*, p. 544.

40. The same comment is applicable to studies dealing specifically with the history of the quantity theory. *E.g.*, H. P. Willis, *Journal of Political Economy*, iv (1896), J. L. Laughlin, *The Principles of Money*, New York, 1911, ch. 7, and others. Permézel goes so far as to state that the Physiocrats had nothing whatsoever to say of the quantity theory, *op. cit.*, p. 241.

41. Quesnay, *Du Commerce*, p. 462 n.

42. Mirabeau, *L'Ami des Hommes*, quoted in L. Brocard, *Les Doctrines Économiques et Sociales du Marquis de Mirabeau*, Paris, 1902, p. 156.

43. Mercier, *op. cit.*, pp. 584–85.

44. Baudeau, *Avis au Peuple sur Son*

Premier Besoin, Paris, 1774, p. 70. For a much fuller statement see his *Principes de la Science Morale et Politique,* 1767 (Collection des Économistes, Paris, 1912), pp. 16–18.

45. Saint-Peravy, *Mémoire sur les Effets de l'Impôt Indirect,* London, 1768, p. 112.

46. Dupont de Nemours, *Effet des Assignats sur le Prix du Pain,* 1790, in Daire, *op. cit.,* p. 386.

47. Turgot, "Deuxième Lettre à l'Abbé de Cicé," in his *Oeuvres,* i, p. 146. See also *La Formation et la Distribution des Richesses,* 1766, *op. cit.,* ii, p. 582.

48. See also Dupont, *De l'Exportation et de l'Importation des Grains,* 1764 (Collection des Économistes, Paris, 1911), pp. 15–16 n.

49. *Essai,* Higgs ed., ch. 6.

50. Exception must be made for Saint-Peravy, who in a notable passage discovered by Viner, *Studies,* p. 187, does devote some discussion to tracing out the effects of an increase of money. He argues that the first effect will be to raise prices, but costs will lag behind. This will increase profits and give a spur to production. Consumers will be forced, however, to undergo a "privation momantanée" (forced saving) until costs gradually rise to the new level of prices. *Du Commerce,* i, pp. 80–83.

51. A. E. Monroe, *op. cit.,* pp. 136–38; M. W. Holtrop, "Theories of the Velocity of Circulation of Money in Earlier Economic Literature," *Economic History,* No. 4 (1929), p. 503.

52. Holtrop, *op. cit.,* p. 512.

53. Monroe, *op. cit.,* p. 256; Holtrop, *op. cit.,* p. 508.

54. *Ibid.,* p. 513.

55. The plural is used here because actually two different Economic Tableaus can be distinguished in the Physiocratic literature; the "Tableau Fondamental" and the "Tableau Abrégé." For an elaboration of these the reader is referred to A. Voelcker, "Der Tableau Economique Quesnay's und Seine Erklärung," *Schmollers Jahrbuch,* lv (1931), pp. 841–54.

56. Baudeau gave some attention to what he called a "circulation incomplète," the case where part of the monetary flow only passes through the hands of two, instead of three, classes. *Cf.* "L'Explication du Tableau Économique," 1776, in Daire, *op. cit.,* pp. 856–64, especially p. 858.

57. On this idea see especially Quesnay, *Analyse,* pp. 305–17, Baudeau, *op. cit.,* pp. 856–64, Saint-Peravy, *op. cit.,* i, pp. 77–87, especially pp. 77–78; Le Trosne, *De l'Intérêt Social,* p. 924, and the references listed below in this note. The prime concern of the Physiocrats was that these annual monetary circulations should be unimpeded and their "natural" course undisturbed. This was one of the main reasons why they were antagonistic to

hoarding ("thesaurisation"). In this respect their views were very similar to those of the bulk of the Mercantilist writers. (Viner, *op. cit.,* pp. 45–49.) Quesnay considered it a maxim of government policy "que la totalité des sommes du revenu rentre dans la circulation annuelle et la parcoure dans toute son étendue; qu'il ne se forme point de fortunes pécuniaires . . . ." *Maximes Générales du Gouvernement,* 1758, p. 332. Mirabeau compared the circulation of money to that of the blood, and argued that "il faut que tout circule sans rélâche; le moindre arrêt feroit depôt." *Philosophie Rurale,* i, p. 66 and p. 117; and elsewhere he considered a complete and unimpeded circuit as "la première condition pour que l'état de la société soit favorable." *Les Économiques,* Amsterdam, 1771, iii, p. 294. Not only was it argued that hoarding was detrimental, but the same was applied to "unproductive" expenditures of all sorts, the effect of which was to alter the quantity and "natural" course of the monetary flow.

58. Le Trosne, *De l'Intérêt Social,* p. 916; also *Discussions,* p. 203.

59. Saint-Peravy, *op. cit.,* ii, p. 102.

60. Quesnay, *Grains,* 1757, p. 238; *cf.* also *Grains,* p. 220, and *Analyse,* p. 315 n. for a remarkably clear statement. See the brief reference to Quesnay in E. Kellenberger, *Geldumlauf und Thesaurierung,* Zurich, 1920, pp. 27–28, and Marget's comments, "Zur Dogmengeschichte des Begriffes 'Umlaufsgeschwindigkeit der Guter,'" *Zeitschrift für Nationalökonomie,* iv (1933), p. 201 n. *Cf.* also Mercier, "Un seul écu qui change de main 100 fois, équivaut à 100 écus et rend les mêmes services." *Op. cit.,* p. 572. Mirabeau also contends that "on attribue à sa quantité ce qui ne provient que de sa rapidité." *Philosophie Rurale,* i, p. 115, and refers to a case where "la circulation est ralentie." *Ibid.,* p. 115. Elsewhere he talks of "le plus ou le moins de rapidité de ce cercle complet," *Les Économiques,* iii, p. 294, and "la longueur des circuits," *ibid.,* p. 43.

In general, the Physiocratic concept of velocity would seem to correspond to what Holtrop has called the "motion-theory" of the velocity of circulation concept. *Op. cit.,* p. 508.

61. This notion is an old one, being found in the writings of North, Petty, Barbon, Locke, Cantillon, and Berkeley. *Cf.* Jacob Hollander, "The Development of the Theory of Money from Adam Smith to David Ricardo," *Quart. Jour. Econ.,* xxv (1911), p. 438.

62. *Op. cit.,* i, p. 80.

63. *Analyse,* p. 325.

64. *Maximes Générales,* note to Maxim 13.

65. Viner, *op. cit.,* ch. 2, *passim. Cf.* also Adam Smith, *The Wealth of Nations,* 1776, Cannan ed., London 1904, i, p. 403.

66. Le Trosne, *De l'Intérêt Social,* p. 916; Saint-Peravy, *op. cit.,* i, p. 80; Quesnay, *Sur les Travaux des Artisans,* 1766, p. 543.

67. Quesnay, *Analyse,* p. 325; Le Trosne, *Discussions,* p. 203; Mirabeau, *Philosophie Rurale,* iii, p. 280. This general idea seems to have been first stated by Davenant. *Cf.* W. Roscher, *Principles of Political Economy,* Lalor translation, Chicago, 1878, i, p. 373.

68. *Op. cit.,* pp. 223–26.

69. *Ibid.,* p. 225.

70. *De l'Intérêt Social,* pp. 919–20; see also p. 916. Viner, in criticism of the above passage of Angell, has also shown that the notion of an equilibrium tendency was clearly stated by Sismondi in 1803. See his article, "Angell's 'Theory of International Prices'," *Jour. Pol. Econ.,* xxxiv (1926), p. 601.

71. *Cf.* Angell, *op. cit.,* p. 224.

72. "Sur le Mémoire de Saint-Peravy," 1767, in *Oeuvres,* ii, pp. 652–54.

73. *Op. cit.,* p. 576; see also p. 583.

74. *Principes de la Science Morale et Politique,* pp. 16–19. Note the phrase, "Voilà donc votre balance retournée," p. 19.

75. *Op. cit.,* ii, pp. 101–2.

76. *L'Ami des Hommes,* quoted in Brocard, *op. cit.,* p. 154.

77. *Op. cit.,* p. 585 *Cf.* also Quesnay, *Questions Intéressantes,* p. 288.

78. *Cf.* for a discussion of these matters, Viner, *op. cit.,* pp. 365–77.

79. I have been unable to find any reference to the rôle of changes in demand in one or both of the countries as an equilibrating factor in the mechanism of adjustment, such as was presented, for example, by de Bacalan about this time.

80. For discussions in England of invisible items in the balance before Adam Smith, see Viner, *op. cit.,* pp. 13–15.

81. *Lettre à la Chambre de Commerce de Normandie,* Paris, 1788, p. 120. This little-known work is an excellent study of the course of the balance of trade and the foreign exchange rates between England and France. For a similar list of items in the balance, see Cantillon, *op. cit.,* p. 263.

82. *L'Ami des Hommes,* quoted in Brocard, *op. cit.,* pp. 375–77.

83. *L'Ami des Hommes,* Avignon, 1758–60, part ii, p. 217.

84. *Répétition de la Question au Sujet de Bénéfice . . . ,* 1766, p. 417.

85. *Op. cit.,* p. 580. Also Quesnay, *Maximes,* p. 333.

86. *E.g.,* Le Trosne, *De la Concurrence des Étrangers dans la Navigation,* in his *Recueil,* pp. 95–195.

87. *Cf.* Eli Heckscher, *Mercantilism,* London, 1935, ii, pp. 243–51.

88. Notably by Law, Daguesseau, Forbonnais and Cantillon. See the references in note 21.

89. *Op. cit.,* pp. 110 *et seq.*

90. *Op. cit.,* ii, pp. 111–118.

91. Recognition of the specie points dates back to Gresham (1558), Petty (1662) and Clement (1695). Viner, *op. cit.,* p. 78.

92. *Grains,* p. 246. *Cf.* also his *Hommes,* published by Bauer in *Revue d'Histoire des Doctrines Économiques et Sociales,* i (1908), p. 25.

93. *Op. cit.,* p. 24.

94. *Op. cit.,* p. 79.

95. Quesnay, *Grains,* p. 248.

96. Mercier, *op. cit.,* p. 570.

97. *Cf.* for this same point, A. Dubois, "Quesnay Anti-Mercantiliste et Libre-Échangiste," *Rev. D'Écon. Pol.,* xviii (1904), pp. 228–29.

98. For the best discussion of this whole period, see Oncken, *Geschichte der Nationaloekonomie,* pp. 247–313. For shorter accounts see Sauvaire-Jourdan, *op. cit.,* pp. 12–17; Permézel, *op. cit.,* pp. 15–35; Bickel, *op. cit.,* pp. 12–29 and 52–78; Pallard, *op. cit.,* pp. 15–36; Dubois, *Précis,* book iii, chapter 7.

99. *Du Commerce,* p. 484. Quesnay also considered foreign trade as "dispendieux . . . onéreux . . . bon à éviter," *ibid.,* p. 449.

100. *Op. cit.,* p. 547. Le Trosne considered it an "inconvenient necéssaire," *op. cit.,* p. 968.

101. Quesnay, *Analyse,* p. 321.

102. Mercier, *op. cit.,* p. 605.

103. Le Trosne, *op. cit.,* pp. 965–68; also Baudeau, *Introduction à la Philosophie Économique,* 1771, in Daire, *op. cit.,* p. 738.

104. Le Trosne, *op. cit.,* p. 968; Mercier, *op. cit.,* pp. 547–48; Quesnay, *Répétition de la Question,* p. 419 n. This stress on transport charges is in contrast to the approach of modern international trade theorists, who tend to abstract from them in their reasoning. Exception must be made here, however for Sidgwick, *The Principles of Political Economy,* London, 1901, pp. 209–23, and Knut Wicksell, "International Freights and Prices," *Quart. Jour. Econ.,* xxxii, (1918).

105. *E.g.,* Saint-Peravy, *op. cit.,* i, p. 4.

106. Quesnay, *Grains,* p. 239; Mirabeau, *Philosophie Rurale,* iii, p. 151. For a prominent statement of this argument, see Hume "Essay on the Jealousy of Trade," in *Essays Moral Literary and Political,* 1875 ed., i, p. 345.

107. He supported free trade, not on the grounds of the natural order and international economic solidarity, but on the assumption that every man knew his interests better than anyone else, and if left alone, would best serve his own interests and those of society. T. Lafont, *Les Idées Économiques de Turgot,* Bordeaux, 1912, p. 80, p. 180. A similar notion can be found in Mirabeau, *cf.* Savatier, *op. cit.,* p. 160. Quesnay also had some recognition of the "economic man."

108. Presumably in terms of "real

costs," although this is not explicitly stated.

109. The Physiocrats' case for free trade, as well as that of Adam Smith, did not advance beyond this point. *Cf.* Jacob Viner, "The Doctrine of Comparative Costs," *Weltwirtschaftliches Archiv,* xxxvi (1932, ii), p. 359. There seems to have been no recognition at all in the Physiocratic literature of comparative advantage.

110. Quoted in G. Schelle, *Dupont de Nemours et L'École Physiocratique,* Paris, 1888, p. 36. Turgot comes close to the proposition recently stressed by Ohlin to the effect that the main factor determining international specialization is the difference as between countries in the relative abundance and hence in the relative prices of the different productive factors. *Cf.* "La Marque des Fers," 1773, in his *Oeuvres,* pp. 624–25.

111. *Grains,* pp. 240–41.

112. Mirabeau, for example, believed that imports should only be allowed after all the possibilities of local sources of supply had been exhausted. *Cf.* Brocard, *op. cit.,* p. 185.

113. Mercier, *op. cit.,* p. 547.

114. It might be in order, at this point, to mention that the Physiocrats, despite their denial of any "gain" in trade, believed that it was to a country's advantage to sell its exports at a high price, and to buy its imports at a low price. This was, of course, recognition of the "commodity terms of trade" concept. It was elaborated upon in arithmetical examples by Quesnay, *Maximes,* pp. 335, 353; Dupont, *De l'Exportation,* p. 42, and Mirabeau, *Philosophie Rurale,* i, p. 229, and *ibid.,* iii, p. 250. This idea was an old one. *Cf.* Viner, *Studies,* p. 555.

115. The best account of the historical background is to be found in G. Afanassiev, *Le Commerce des Céréales en France au Dix-Huitième Siècle,* Paris, 1894. The chief reason for the ban on the exportation of grain was to assure cheap bread, both for the purpose of keeping wages low, and for warding off internal disorder.

116. Dupont, *op. cit.,* p. 45.

117. Le Trosne, *La Liberté du Commerce des Grains, Toujours Utile et Jamais Nuisible,* Paris, 1765, p. 38. While it is true that the price of an international commodity will tend to be the same in all countries, it is, of course, false to infer that such a price will be necessarily either constant or remunerative.

118. Weulersse, *op. cit.,* ii, p. 475. In ridiculing the prevalent fear that free exportation would expose France to the dangers of famine, they did admit, however, that free importation could be permitted in case of shortage. In the case of manufactured goods, it was said that free importation could be permitted here in order that, in turn, France would be able to dispose of her agricultural products abroad.

119. *Cf.,* for example, Quesnay's famous maxim: "Qu'on maintienne l'entière liberté du commerce; car la police du commerce intérieur et extérieur la plus sure, la plus exacte, la plus profitable à la nation et à l'État, consiste dans la pleine liberté de la concurrence." *Maximes,* p. 336. Similarly, Turgot: ". . . la verité est que toutes les branches de commerce doivent être libres, également libres, entièrement libres . . ." *La Marque des Fers,* in *Oeuvres,* p. 621.

120. *Cf.* H. Truchy, "Le Libéralisme Économique dans les Oeuvres de Quesnay," *Revue D'Économie Politique,* 1899, p. 926.

121. *I.e.,* by restricting hoarding and "unproductive" expenditures. See note 57 *supra.*

122. Due to lack of space, I am unable to discuss certain minor aspects of the Physiocrats' foreign-trade doctrines, such as the incidence of import and export duties, the distinction drawn between "legitimate" commerce and "trafficking," government policy in relation to shipping, trade regulation, etc.

123. Professor N. J. Ware, in an interesting article, has contended that the Physiocratic doctrine was merely a rationalization of the special interests of the new class of commoner landowners which emerged from the French bureaucracy during the reign of Louis XIV. These new landowners, unlike those they succeeded, were interested in making agriculture a remunerative occupation, and this necessitated the abolition of the many restrictions upon it. This explains the "propagandistic" nature of the Physiocratic writings, and the stress laid upon the sole productivity of agriculture, the "impôt unique" and the freedom of exportation of grain. "The Physiocrats: A Study in Economic Rationalization," *Am. Econ. Rev.,* 1931.

9.

BERT F. HOSELITZ
University of Chicago

The Early

History of

Entrepreneurial Theory

Words have their history which reflects the history of institutions and customs. When a new word appears in a language or when an old word assumes a new meaning it is proof that social development has made this new meaning necessary, in order to find a designation for the new reality.[1]

I. THE CONCEPT "ENTREPRENEUR" IN FRANCE BEFORE CANTILLON

For a long time economists commonly assumed that the concept "entrepreneur" was introduced into economic literature by J. B. Say. This view was supported by a short passage in the popular and widely-read book by Gide and Rist on the history of economic doctrines. Although they were chiefly interested in emphasizing the fact that Smith had neglected to develop the concept, they clearly implied that it cannot be found in earlier works in economic literature. In the seventh edition of their work they added that the role of the entrepreneur had already been underlined by Cantillon.[2] On the authority of Gide and Rist, the problem was apparently settled and economists turned to other matters. Although Henry Higgs had noted in

Reprinted from *Explorations in Entrepreneurial History*, III (April 15, 1951), 193–220, by permission of the author and the publisher.

1897 that Quesnay used the word "entrepreneur,"[3] this was regarded apparently as a *curiosum* in terminology and duly forgotten. Nobody thought of looking for earlier usage of the concept or its occurrence in the economic literature before Cantillon. Doctor Redlich, therefore, deserves our gratitude for having opened up the matter again and for having drawn attention to the fact that this problem deserves further investigation.[4]

I have been unable to find any evidence that there existed an economic theory of entrepreneurship prior to Cantillon, but the history of the concept entrepreneur, as well as some of its English equivalents sheds light on some interesting aspects of the organization and performance of large-scale undertakings.

The first step in the attempt to determine the earliest use and meaning of the word entrepreneur was a search in historical dictionaries of the French language. The standard work in this field, the *Dictionnaire de la langue française* by E. Littré, gives three definitions of the word *entrepreneur*.[5] The most general and probably earliest meaning of the term is "celui qui entreprend quelque chose." In other words, it simply refers to a person who is active, who gets things done. This meaning was formed during the Middle Ages in the normal course of development of the French language. In this period many nouns designating an actor were derived from the corresponding verbs. *Entreprendre* (with the connotation to do something) was in use as early as the twelfth century and in the course of the fifteenth century the corresponding noun developed.[6] The word entrepreneur in this meaning of a person who assumes some task, was not too uncommon during the late middle ages and it was used by such men as François Villon, and the author of *La belle dame sans merci*, Alain Chartier, and even in the form "entrependreur" as early as the fourteenth century.[7] It apparently is used not infrequently also by Lemaire de Belges (ca. 1473–ca. 1525), and other authors of the sixteenth century, but by that time it tends to change in meaning somewhat. The enterprise in which the typical entrepreneur of the sixteenth century participates is usually some violent warlike action. Lemaire de Belges calls Hector and other Trojan warriors entrepreneurs, and other French authors of the sixteenth century describe them as hardy, usurping, and intent to risk their lives and fortunes.[8] We are here in the presence of a development looking towards the later connotations of the word *entrepreneur*. By the beginning of the seventeenth century an *entrepreneur* was considered to be a person whose activity definitely implied risk-bearing (which at that time was equivalent with uncertainty-bearing). But not anyone who bore risks was an *entrepreneur*. Above all, the term was not applied to manufacturers or merchants, but only to that relatively small group of men who charged themselves with really large-scale undertakings. The most common enterprises on a large scale were contracts between the crown or some other public or semipublic body and a wealthy or skilled person for the erection of a building, the furnishing of supplies for the army, or similar tasks. Typically, an entrepreneur was thus a person who entered into a contractual relationship with the government for the performance of a service, or the supply of goods. The price at which the contract was valued was fixed and the entrepreneur bore the risks of profit and loss from the bargain.

This meaning of the word is very frequent in French legal and economic literature of the seventeenth and early eighteenth centuries and this is reflected in the dictionaries of the time. Furetière, for example, defines entrepreneur as "celuy qui entreprend. Il se dit premierement des Architectes qui entreprennent les batimens à forfait." And he adds the following example: "*L'Entrepreneur* de la jonction des mers s'y est enrichi. On le dit aussi des autres marchez à pris fait. On a traité avec un *Entrepreneur* pour fournir l'armée de vivres, de munitions."[9] The first edition of the Dictionary of the French Academy defines the word even more narrowly: "*Entrepreneur*, qui entreprend un bastiment, pour un certain prix," that is, an *entrepreneur* is a contractor of public works.[10]

Turning now from dictionary definitions and literary usage to occurrences of the word *entrepreneur* in the legal and economic literature, we find the concept used throughout the sixteenth and seventeenth centuries primarily with the connotation of contractor to the government. From the numerous occurrences in the laws of France, I quote only a few instances. In the last years of the sixteenth century Henry IV attempted to promote the drainage of land in southwestern France. He invited a Dutch engineer Humphrey Bradley to supervise this work and on April 8, 1599 issued an edict appointing Bradley as *maître de digues*. The edict provides among other things for the partition of the drained land between the proprietors of the soil and Bradley and his associates, who are in one place referred to as *iceux entrepreneurs*. In January, 1607, a new edict for the drainage of bogs was issued, confirming the earlier one of 1599, but here the contractor and his associates are not referred to any more as "ledit Bradléij et ses associez," but "lesdits entrepreneurs."[11] In similar fashion the term *entrepreneur* was applied to contractors who undertook to build and repair roads, bridges, harbors and fortifications.[12]

What may be of particular interest to economists is that Montchrétien uses the term *entrepreneur*. Writing about the failure to establish French settlements in Florida by Jean Ribaud and Dominique de Gourgues between 1562 and 1567, Montchrétien says: "Voicy le bout des entreprises françoises en la Floride, lesquelles furent destourbées en partie par le peu d'industrie et par la mauvaise conduite des entrepreneurs . . ."[13] The appearance of the term is of particular interest since the earlier sixteenth century meaning of a person who participates in quasi-warlike exploits and the later meaning of contractor are fused. For the French captains who attempted to establish colonial settlements in Florida, were not just conquistadors on their own; they had been commissioned to this task by Admiral Coligny, and quite apart from what the true relationship was, Montchrétien regarded them as contractors for the King.

An examination of the changing role of the technical and managerial personnel directing the execution of large scale public works throws considerable light on the development of the new meaning of the term *entre-*

preneur, and also helps to understand why the concept could be adopted by Cantillon and his contemporaries to designate the person who bore the risks of any enterprise, not merely in the field of public construction, but also in farming or manufacturing.

The typical entrepreneur — in the Schumpeterian sense — of the Middle Ages was the man in charge of the great architectural works: castles and fortifications, public buildings, abbeys, and cathedrals. Most numerous, most important and most extensive in scope were buildings for religious purposes. Up to the end of the twelfth century, the men in charge of the planning and execution of these works were usually clerics. They were the inventors and planners of the work, they performed the functions of architect, builder, and manager, and, in addition, they usually also hired and supervised the laborers, procured the materials and transacted the business necessary for the execution of the construction project. It is important to note, however, that they bore no risks, since they did not contract for the execution of a finished piece of work, but rather carried forward their building until the resources on hand were exhausted.

Beginning with the thirteenth century the monk or abbot as builder tended gradually to become replaced by lay master-builders. These *maîtres de l'oeuvre* may be regarded as the earliest contractors, but their function was not too clearly determined, since they seem sometimes to have undertaken the entire execution of a project and sometimes to have served purely in the capacity of expert adviser. In the latter case, which apparently was not too uncommon, some cleric (or group of clerics) performed the entrepreneurial functions (that is, over-all planning and supervision of the work) while the expert architect submitted his plans and estimates, and was paid a fee for this work. The architect often lived in another city and visited the construction project at intervals in order to check on the progress of the work or solve especially thorny problems which had arisen during the building.[14]

With the decline of the Middle Ages and the increase of secular power, the importance of clerics as creative entrepreneurs and builders tended to decrease, and finally almost to disappear. The chief construction works were no longer cathedrals and abbeys, but fortifications, roads, bridges, canals, harbors, palaces, and other secular public buildings. Under the impact of nascent capitalism the procedures employed in the planning and execution of public works became progressively more rationalized, and entrepreneurial and managerial functions more specialized. Still, the division of labor was often not pushed very far. For example, a man like Bradley was a creative entrepreneur who also managed the routine business arising in his drainage projects. The same may be said of many of the builders of the extensive canal system in central and southern France during the seventeenth century, for example, Guillaume Boutheroue, the *entrepreneur* of the canal of Briare, and Riquet, the first builder of the canal of Languedoc. Similar evidence comes from England. The drainage of the great fen country in Lincolnshire, Huntingdonshire, and neighboring counties in the early seventeenth century was carried through sometimes by "undertakers" or "adventurers" who often handled the business and technical side of the work. The harassing experiences of Vanbrugh, the architect of Blenheim (1705–1712), with his laborers, suppliers of stone and other materials — and incidentally also his patroness, the duchess of Marlborough — have been admirably described by Mr. Dobrée.[15]

But if we have numerous examples from the seventeenth and later centuries of many public and quasi-public works for which the artistic, engineering, and commercial aspects of the enterprise were performed by one and the same person, it is nevertheless true that a division of labor begins to set in and a progressively clearer distinction is made between the architect or engineer (who specializes in the artistic or technical work) and the entrepreneur or contractor (who takes on the commercial aspects of the task). The architects especially felt that their services were of a higher quality than those of ordinary master-masons or contractors. This sentiment was enhanced in France by the formation of an Academy of Architecture, and in 1676 *entrepreneurs*, master-masons in the building trade, were prohibited from adopting the designation *"Architecte du Roi,"* an appellation which was reserved to those men whom the King had chosen to compose his Academy of Architecture, to which only outstanding artists were admitted.[16] With the growing importance of secular public buildings and with the progressive division of labor between the technical or artistic creator of a new construction on the one hand and the contractor on the other, the contractor became an entrepreneur who performed a twofold role. He executed the economic functions in achieving the completion of a work, that is, he was responsible for bringing together the factors, labor, materials, machines, and so on, which were necessary to complete the physical production of a work. In this role he appears like the modern entrepreneur in the economic theory of the nineteenth century, who combines the factors of production in the required proportions for the attainment of some output. But, in addition, he does this on his own account. He bears the risk, he is held to his bid by the public authority with which he contracted, and he has the task of seeing to it that his costs not only do not exceed, but remain as much as possible below the price for which he has contracted to perform the work. Although this entrepreneur was not the object — so far as I am aware — of investigation by economic writers before Cantillon, his function is, nevertheless, essentially identical with the description given by J. B. Say.[17]

The final stage of development of the entrepreneur as government contractor can most clearly be seen in the work by Bernard F. de Belidor, *La science des ingénieurs*. This book was first published in 1729, and is thus contemporary in conception with the dictionary of Savary and the *Essai* of Cantillon. Belidor's book was considered the most authoritative text of its kind in its day. It was found worthy of special approbation by Vauban, and the author himself became director of the *Ecole des Ponts et Chausées* when it was founded in 1752. Although the bulk of Belidor's work is concerned with the technical aspects of various kinds of public construction, he discusses in several places the role of the *entrepreneur* and his relation to the *ingénieur* in the planning and execution of public works. Although Belidor's statements on the functions of entrepreneurs are intended merely as a description of actual relations, his discussion of this topic might be regarded as a theory of entrepreneurship, since it clearly exhibits the social role and the motivations of the entrepreneur as commonly understood in the early eighteenth century.

Belidor describes the procedure by which public works (for example, the construction of a fortress) are contracted for. The technical designs are made known by public advertisement and a date is fixed at which entrepreneurs are to gather in order to extend competitive bids for the execution of the work. The contract is awarded to that entrepreneur "qui a fait la condition du Roi la meilleure." This contract obligates the entrepreneur to meet the following conditions: the entrepreneurs must furnish all materials, funds for wages, vehicles, scaffolds, bridges, boards, tools, machines, ropes, and generally all things necessary to the accomplishment of the work. They undertake to finish the work within a given time and according to the exact specifications made by the *ingénieurs*. The work is to be executed with all possible care and is subject to inspection and certification, in accordance with custom, by the *ingénieur* in charge. The contract price is to be paid in installments in accordance with the progress of the work and the various "advances" have to be countersigned by the principal *ingénieur* in charge of the technical aspect of the work. The entrepreneur was, thus, confronted with a situation where he knew the total revenue he could expect, and where he could maximize his profit by minimizing costs. He therefore clearly bore the risk of profit or loss, and of the magnitude of that profit or loss.

After having stated the formal legal aspects of the matter Belidor gives advice to the *ingénieur* on his conduct in the matter. He starts with the assertion that the entrepreneur is interested in the work only "en vue du gain," and the *ingénieur* thus must always observe that everything is done in good order and that all "malfaçons ou de la négligence dans le travail" be avoided. There follows a long list of possibilities of cutting corners, which must be most carefully observed. At the same time the *ingénieur* should bear in mind that the entrepreneur wants to make a profit. He should therefore advise him of how he can reduce his costs, if possible, but if the entrepreneur "a fait un mauvais marché, ou qu'il lui arrive dans le cours du travail des contre-temps fâcheux et inévitables, ce n'est point à l'ingénieur à y entrer." Finally Belidor warns the *ingénieur* to remain untouched by the "tons plaintifs qui sont assez ordinnaires à ces Messieurs."

In conclusion Belidor asks whether it is more advantageous to have one contractor for the entire work or several for the various parts of it. He favors a single entrepreneur, because there is less mutual recrimination and faultfinding; because it is easier to locate responsibility; because a more consistent time schedule can be maintained; and because in case of need a large entrepreneur can always find sub-contractors. Hence even if the various parts of the work have been contracted for by different entrepreneurs, Belidor prefers that one of them be placed in the position of ultimate command and responsibility.[18]

We see, therefore, that Belidor's theory of entrepreneurship is the exact counterpart of Cantillon's theory which originated at about the same time. In Cantillon's theory an entrepreneur is someone who buys at a certain cost price and sells at an uncertain price; according to Belidor the entrepreneur sells at a certain price, but his costs are uncertain. The net effect is the same in both cases, since the gains or losses of each transaction, and hence the total income of the entrepreneur are uncertain.

II. ENGLISH CONCEPTS DESIGNATING ENTREPRENEURIAL ACTIVITY BEFORE ADAM SMITH

Before entering into a discussion of entrepreneurial theory after Cantillon, I wish to draw attention to some English equivalents of the word *entrepreneur* as it was understood in the seventeenth and early eighteenth centuries. The most common English equivalent for the French entrepreneur was the word "undertaker," and sometimes "adventurer." The second term was used, as is well known, from the fifteenth century on in the name "Merchant Adventurers"; the term was also applied to Irish land speculators and other entrepreneurs in farming, drainage projects, and similar occupations throughout the seventeenth century. But the term tended to become obsolete in this special meaning during the eighteenth century. In Dr. Johnson's dictionary (1755) the term adventurer is defined: "He that seeks occasion of hazard; he that puts himself in the hands of chance."[19] It is curious to note that the word adventurer enjoyed a short revival in the translation of Say's *Traité* by C. R. Prinsep. He justifies this practice by saying that "the word *entrepreneur* is difficult to render in English; the corresponding word, *undertaker,* being already appropriated to a limited sense."[20]

The word undertaker was hardier and appears to have been used more frequently and in more varied meanings. In general, its history was parallel to the French word *entrepreneur.* At first (in the fourteenth and fifteenth centuries) it chiefly designated simply a person who took upon himself the doing of some task. Very soon, however, it acquired the meaning of someone who executed on his own risk a task imposed on him by the government. For example, Robert Payne, discussing in 1590 the establishment of landed estates by Englishmen in Ireland under Queen Elizabeth, talks of "the worsser sorte of vndertakers which haue seignories of her Maiestie." These he criticizes for not having attracted English "seruants," because they "find such profite from the Irish tenantes . . . So that they care not although they neuer place any English man there." He contrasts them with the "better sorte of vndertakers" who "do seeke by all meanes possible to plant their landes with English mē according to the meaning of her Maiesties graūt."[21] Payne refers to the so-called Munster undertakers who were given, by an Act of 1586, estates in fee at low rents in the counties of Cork and Waterford with the condition of settling on an average estate from 75 to 85 English farmers, freeholders, copyholders, and cottagers. The name "under-takers" was applied to the settlers, because they undertook to observe these and other conditions enjoined by the Queen. It is plain that the word under-taker in this context was equivalent to contractor rather than to the later meaning of entrepreneur, for Payne chides those who act rationally in the desire to make maximum profits as "bad" and praises those who regardless of their own profit interests scrupulously fulfil the conditions of the grant as "good" undertakers. The same criticism is again voiced about ten years later by Fynes Moryson, who makes the undertakers partly responsible for the rebellion under Tyrone in 1598. From Moryson's account it appears that there were few "good" undertakers, for after listing the conditions of settle-ment, he continues "these and like covenants were in no part performed by them. Of whom the men of best qualitie never came over, but made profit of the land."[22]

But Moryson's work is evidence that the word undertaker was more generally used to designate a government contractor. He paraphrases a letter received on September 27, 1602, by the Lord Deputy at Dublin from the Lords of England dealing with abuses in the supplying of the English army in Ireland with victuals and remedies therefor. Food was dispatched from English ports, but instead of arriving at its proper destination, it was suspected that it had been sold freely upon arrival and had even fallen into the hands of the rebels. The Lords of England therefore proposed that "so soone as any contract is made with the undertakers, wee send an abstract thereof unto your Lordship" so that on the basis of this information the ship-ments could be checked upon arrival. The Lords of England moreover dis-claimed belief that irregularities occurred at the English end, since ship-ments were checked there by the Surveyor and "the undertakers absolutely denie the sending of any victuals thither, but such as is to serve the Souldier, and to performe the Contracts."[23] Here again the word undertaker is used in a context in which the contract relation with the government is empha-sized, but the meaning is clearly extended to apply not merely to a small group of settlers, but to any person standing in this relationship with the public power.

Gradually the meaning of the term undertaker came to be extended. I found in a letter of 1612 from Paris a reference to a "french-man called Moisett, otherwise Montauban heeretofore a taylour, but one y^t that hath inrichted himselfe to ye valewe of three or foure hundred thousand crownes, by having been one of the principall undertakers of ye great farme of salte."[24] The term was also used to designate those men who obtained grants from the crown — and later from Parliament — to drain the fens. Here (as well as in the case of the farming of the French salt tax), the notion that the undertaker was to make a profit was already clearly implied. Sir William Dugdale quotes an order of the Lords of the Council, dated 12 July, 1620, which reads in part: "that . . . good security should be given to the undertakers for a moiety of the clear profits, which by the draining should be improved upon every man's ground."[25]

Gradually the emphasis on the contract or quasi-contract relationship with the government in which an undertaker found himself lost ground and more weight was placed on the circumstance that an undertaker was involved in a risky project from which an uncertain profit may be derived. In this sense the word undertaker was in competition with the word projector. Although there are instances, chiefly from the eighteenth century, showing that a projector was thought of as an innovator, the usual distinction made between the undertaker and the projector was that the former was thought to be an honest man engaged in a business the outcome of which was uncertain, whereas the other was usually thought of as a schemer, cheat, or speculator. This distinction is expressed quite clearly in a passage from a rather curious work by S. Primatt, which first appeared in 1667. Writing about the advisability of opening coal mines in various parts of England, the author says:

There are divers other sorts of Collieries in Inland Countries in *England*, whose profit consists in an Inland Market; and they do produce in many places great profit to the Undertakers, but are as uncertain as others . . . There are as many Projectors (who have more of fancy and imagination in their Designs, than of any real operation) that do undertake in the dreining these and other sorts of Mines.[26]

This passage displays very plainly the special connotation of the two words, the meaning of which was never very far apart.[27] Another characteristic of the word undertaker also seems to have been that it generally referred to the entrepreneur of sizeable enterprises such as coal mines, drainage operations and the like. In fact, the earliest use of word undertaker, designating an entrepreneur of a business involving risks, that I have found occurs in a document of the town council of Nottingham of 13 September, 1630. This document is a grant of monopoly to a group of Nottingham burghers, headed by "maister Maior" to "sincke a pitt or pitts in the townes woods and wasts." The document specifies conditions under which persons who want to "adventure a partt or proporcion of monie" shall participate in the profits and concludes that "this companie [i.e., town council] are from tyme to tyme to assist theise Vndertakers as theire shalbe cawse" to ensure the profitability of the enterprise.[28]

Additional evidence that an undertaker was thought of as a large entrepreneur could easily be adduced. One or two more examples must suffice. In a letter written around 1701 to Robert Harley, William Penn talks about the depletion of British timber owing to the extension of mines, and adds: "If great undertakers there would fall upon it here we might supply England and give her woods time to recover, and convert these countries to arable pasture, into the bargain."[29] Here the undertaker is depicted almost in terms reminiscent of Veblen's Captain of Industry. He is really a creative entrepreneur who not only engages in profitable projects but makes the desert bloom. The socially beneficial effect of private interest, the very epitome of what Sombart understood by the effect of the spirit of capitalism, cannot be expressed more clearly and concisely.

By the time this letter was written, the old meaning of the word undertaker, in the sense of government contractor, had almost entirely passed out

242

of use. Nevertheless it still appears occasionally, especially in official documents. For example, the *London Gazette* of 9–11 February, 1709, contains a despatch from The Hague in which it is reported that "an Agreement is concluded with Undertakers for furnishing the Magazines on the Frontier with Forage, as they have before done for as much Bread as shall be requisite for the Subsistence of the Troops, and as many Waggons as shall be needed for the Publick Service. It is now under Deliberation how a sufficient Fund, or the necessary Credit, may be settled, for enabling the Undertakers to perform their Contract."[30] Here the emphasis on the undertaker as government contractor is quite plain, but this meaning tends to disappear completely, at any rate in non-official language, during the next two decades. By the middle of the eighteenth century an undertaker was quite simply a big business man, and more often an ordinary business man. In this sense Adam Smith writes, as if in passing, of the "undertaker of a great manufacture,"[31] and Postlethwayt, whose *Dictionary* contains in translation a good part of Cantillon's *Essai*, uses the word "undertaker" as the straight translation of the French word *entrepreneur*.[32] But by the time of Postlethwayt and Smith the more general meaning of the word tended to become obsolete and only the special meaning of an arranger of funerals survived. The undertaker in English economics was replaced by the capitalist who only toward the end of the nineteenth century again gave way to the entrepreneur.

III. THE THEORY OF ENTREPRENEURSHIP OF THE PHYSIOCRATS

If the word undertaker disappeared from the arsenal of English political economy after the middle of the eighteenth century and with it a proper theory of entrepreneurship, the same was not true in France. Cantillon's work enjoyed considerable popularity after its publication and the writers of the Physiocratic school were thoroughly familiar with it. Indeed, it has been surmised that the marquis de Mirabeau, the father of the famous orator of the Revolution, intended to plagiarize it and publish it as a work of his own.[33] More important than this episode is the fact that François Quesnay seems to have been influenced to some extent by Cantillon. Although the claim cannot be made that Quesnay's views on entrepreneurship are directly derived from Cantillon, there is no doubt that in Quesnay's earliest economic writings in the great *Encyclopédie*, in which the rudiments of his views on the social organization underlying a modern economy are outlined, the aspects relating to the norms of agricultural production are reminiscent of Cantillon's discussion of the same topic. For in his article "Grains" Quesnay cites with approval a passage by Cantillon in which the latter mentions the advantages of large farms. In the same context Quesnay then continues to describe the operator of a large farm as an *entrepreneur* "who guides and turns to account his enterprise by his intelligence and his wealth."[34] We shall see a little later how this tersely expressed idea was developed into a new theory of entrepreneurship by Quesnay's disciples.

But first we must turn to a somewhat fuller account of Quesnay's system in order to determine more exactly the proper place of the entrepreneur in the socio-economic structure.

The most appropriate designation which can be given to Quesnay's system is that of agrarian capitalism. The outstanding feature of it is that the part played by the various classes is related to, and, in fact, determined by the economic function the members of each fulfil. Analysts of the system of Quesnay have commonly been interested in following up his division of society into the productive, sterile, and proprietary classes. In examining the real basis for this division they have come to conclude that Quesnay erred, above all, in his evaluation of the sterile class. They have thus rejected the system outright as contradictory with reality, or have spent much time and effort in the attempt to elucidate the reasons why Quesnay and his disciples did not assign productive powers to industrial occupations.

I propose to follow another and, for our purpose, more fruitful course. We are not interested primarily in relating Quesnay's system to the real world of his day, but in finding whether it was possible for him within his system to develop a theory of entrepreneurship which is an advance over that of Cantillon. We will, therefore, leave out of consideration at first the sterile class, and concern ourselves only with the relations of the proprietary and the productive classes. Each of these classes is really composed of two groups of persons. The first includes the sovereign (and his associates exercising political power) and the landowners; the second includes the farmers and the farm laborers. Quesnay himself regards the first class as homogeneous and makes the right of the sovereign for part of the *produit net* contingent upon his being a landowner, deriving his prerogative to levy taxes upon the historical role of the monarch, who once "owned" all the land in the state. Only his disciples, particularly Le Mercier de la Rivière and Baudeau, sharpened the distinction between the sovereign and the rest of the proprietors. But since we are concerned here not with the political theory of the Physiocrats, but with their explanation of the social structure in terms of economic factors, we may regard the King as the biggest landowner. The proprietors have a right to the *produit net*, not because of their power to exploit the rest of society, nor (with the possible exception of the sovereign) because of political privilege, but as an outflow of their contribution toward the attainment of a gross product (*produit brut*). Their income is justified on the basis that they made the "*avances foncières,*" that is, that they contributed their property to the productive process. This is the basis on which they derive a title to income and that income is the *produit net*.[35] Rent, in Quesnay's system is thus the income of landowners, purely as a consequence of the fact that they are owners of the only productive agent apart from labor. But whereas the net product of labor is zero (in agriculture and industry), because the laborer consumes (in equilibrium) values equal to that produced by his efforts, the net product of land may be, and in a "well-regulated kingdom" ordinarily is positive.

The difference between the gross product and the net product constitutes the income of the farmer and other persons engaged in agricultural production. We now have to analyze more closely the components of this part of the income of society. The outlay of the farmers is composed of two parts, the *"avances primitives"* and the *"avances annuelles."* The former are roughly speaking expenditures on the maintenance and replacement of the fixed capital of the farm, the latter are composed of expenditures on raw materials used up annually in the production process and wages for agricultural laborers. The total national product is thus equal to the sum of the *avances annuelles, avances primitives* and *produit net (avances foncières)*.[36]

Quesnay has represented in his *Tableau économique* the picture of a static society in which no accumulation of capital occurs and where no uncertainty is present. The same gross product is produced year after year and the same shares of it are distributed among the various classes. Hence it follows that the *avances primitives* are equal and certain every year and that consequently the income of the tenant farmer, who performs the entrepreneurial role is also certain and fixed. It appears, therefore, that in Quesnay's system the theory of Cantillon, who regarded the bearing of uncertainty on the entrepreneurial function, has been given up. The entrepreneurial theory appears to have become colorless; an entrepreneur is simply a tenant farmer who rents a property at a fixed rent and produces a given output with given factors at given prices.

This view is lent added support by the fact that Quesnay has nowhere provided a definition of the term entrepreneur or a description of entrepreneurial activity. I have found three places in his writings where the word *entrepreneur* is mentioned. One was mentioned earlier: Quesnay's remark that the operator of a large farm is an entrepreneur. The second time the word is used occurs also in the article "Grains" where Quesnay employs it to designate businessmen (members of the sterile class) whose large income he explains because others make equivalent expenditures.[37] Here the word is treated as a common term which needs no special definition or explanation. The third occurrence is in a letter to the Intendant of Soissons, which was written in 1760. Quesnay is here again emphasizing the advantages of large farms over small ones and says: "Vous dites encore que les trop gros laboureurs ne peuvent pas satisfaire au travail de leurs grandes entreprises. Le fermier ne doit pas être le travailleur. Un gros fermier est un habitant notable, un riche entrepreneur qui est continuellement à cheval, pour se porter ponctuellement à toutes les parties de son entreprise."[38]

Here again the word is used in a colorless meaning. The entrepreneur is simply the *patron* who does not participate in the regular labor process, but supervises it. Quesnay thus does not use the term *entrepreneur* in a technical sense, he simply employs it in a connotation which it has generally acquired in the second half of the eighteenth century. The *Encyclopédie* defines *entrepreneur* simply as "il se dit en général de celui qui se charge d'un ouvrage: on dit un *entrepreneur* de manufactures, un *entrepreneur* de bâtimens."[39] And Ferdinand Brunot who has written the most elaborate and erudite history of the French language concludes that in the later eighteenth century the term is applied to anyone at the head of an enterprise in the most general sense.[40]

But although Quesnay and his disciples did not employ the term entrepreneur in a technical sense, they nevertheless elaborated a full theory of entrepreneurship which contains many modern elements. In a nutshell it is contained in the passage from Quesnay cited earlier, but it was more fully and systematically stated by Baudeau. I have mentioned before that the seeming absence of such a theory in the writings of Quesnay is due primarily to the fact that the *Tableau économique* contains only a static analysis. As soon as this assumption is relinquished, the entrepreneurial function takes on full life.

Although the *produit net* has been regarded by some critics of physiocracy as a surplus, this view is only partially correct. In a purely physical sense it is the surplus over the necessary costs of production, but within the nexus of a monetary economy, the Physiocrats assumed that rents were a cost, determined in advance of production. In fact, they favored stabilizing rent payments as much as possible by advocating long leases.[41] Thus in practice, they envisaged a system in which the tenant farmer would be confronted with a very rigid cost structure. His rent payments are fairly fixed and similarly the wage rates are fixed (and correspond to the value of the maintenance of a laborer). But the actual outcome of the harvest is indeterminate, since it depends upon weather and other factors which the tenant farmer cannot foresee. Similarly, the price of the crop is uncertain. The entrepreneur is thus in the position which Cantillon has posited, his expenses are certain while his revenue is uncertain; his net income is thus subject to "risk." This is clearly expressed by Baudeau when he says: "Le *Cultivateur en chef* est celui qui fait à ses depens, à ses risques, périls et fortunes les avances . . . qui conduit enfin *pour son propre compte* tout l'ensemble de l'exploitation."[42]

But more than that. Since the agricultural entrepreneur carries on production on his own risk and his own account he must have the capacity of economically combining the appropriate goods and services to the end of his greatest profit. Here again Baudeau is quite explicit. He says: "Tel est le but des grandes exploitations productives; premièrement de doubler, tripler, quadrupler, décupler s'il est possible la récolte . . .; secondement d'épargner le nombre des hommes employés à ce travail, en les réduisant à la moitié, au tiers, au quart, au dixième, s'il est possible."[43] But in order to do this, the *cultivateur en chef* must be a truly innovating entrepreneur. Baudeau is fully aware of the forward steps that invention makes possible. He never tires of pointing out that cultivating is an art, and that the progressive state of cultivation is dependent upon the fact that the entrepreneurs be "*habiles*," that they "aient acquis les connoissances de leur art, . . . soient animés par une grande emulation à mettre leur savoir en usage."[44] And if the cultivators are often ignorant of the most advanced methods, they need to be instructed. The writings of the Physiocrats are full of proposals to improve agricultural techniques. They propose the translation of English texts on agriculture; they propose the nationwide distribution of handbooks and guides describing new tools, new crops, and new procedures; they propose prizes, honors, agricultural research, model farms, and pilot plants. They have no doubt that, if all this knowledge becomes available, the innovations will be adopted, and they rely upon laissez-faire and the force of self-interest (and the prevalence of large farms, which can economically adopt the new techniques and other innovations) to attain this end.[45]

It can be seen that the concise phrase of Quesnay describing the entrepreneur as a person "qui gouverne et fair valoir son entreprise par son intelligence et par ses richesses" is pregnant of a wealth of hidden meaning if interpreted in the light of the entire system of Physiocratic doctrine. The entrepreneur bears uncertainty, organizes and supervises production, introduces new methods and new products, and searches for new markets. In order to do this properly he must gain free access to a wide variety of markets, and he must be able to rely on the government to provide for him the utmost freedom of action in his undertakings. Although essentially devoid of political power the large tenant farmer, that is, the agricultural entrepreneur, is in the very center of the economy. All else turns about him. Baudeau and the more orthodox members of the Physiocratic school, though not unmindful of the requirement that a successful entrepreneur must be wealthy, stress primarily his cleverness, knowledge and willingness to operate rationally by using the most productive methods. Turgot, the one member of the school who stood with one foot outside it and was anything but orthodox, stresses more the wealth which the entrepreneur must have in order to succeed.

It would be wrong to exaggerate the differences between Baudeau and Turgot, for in the last resort they participated in the same intellectual current and were, on the whole, in the same camp. They both derive their economic theorizing from Quesnay and on the basis of his teaching an entrepreneur must be endowed with and put to account both his intelligence and his wealth. The difference between Turgot and Baudeau is thus primarily one of emphasis, but as such it is unmistakable. Baudeau's entrepreneur is a farm operator who plans, organizes, risks, and happens to be a wealthy man. Turgot's entrepreneur is a rich industrialist or merchant, who, in order to accumulate more wealth, engages in certain risky operations or plans and supervises productive activity.[46]

This new emphasis given by Turgot to the entrepreneurial concept also comes out in the terminology he uses. He usually does not employ the term *entrepreneur*, but speaks of *"entrepreneur manufacturier"* or *"entrepreneur capitaliste."* In reality this last expression is pleonastic since Turgot regards the designations *capitaliste* and *entrepreneur* as synonymous.[47]

The difference in emphasis between Baudeau and Turgot seems to derive from the fact that each paid primary attention to a different branch of production. Baudeau was concerned, above all, with agriculture. Under the technological conditions prevailing in eighteenth century French agriculture the major non-human factor of production was land. Compared with it, capital was of relatively minor proportions. The most expensive factor in this branch of production need not be bought, but could be leased by the entrepreneur. At the same time the problem of increasing agricultural output by means of better techniques and better organization of farm labor was imperative. The English had shown the way and were known to experiment with and actually use superior methods.[48] Hence Baudeau rightly emphasized the need for knowledge and information ("intelligence") of the agricultural entrepreneur. In contrast, Turgot was primarily concerned with relations in the industrial sector of the economy. Although he grants that the *fermier* is an entrepreneur, he considers primarily the *entrepreneur-manufacturier*. But the industrial entrepreneur could lease only a small part of the assets used in his productive enterprise. In industry new capital had to be created constantly. Here the process of capital accumulation was much more obvious and visible than in agriculture, although it was not completely absent there either. Thus the function of the entrepreneur as the supplier of capital (or, what is the same thing, funds for accumulation) receives primary attention.

Turgot's views of entrepreneurship are thus midway between the traditional French view which sees in the entrepreneur chiefly a risk-bearer (Cantillon and to a certain extent Baudeau) or planner of production (Say and to a certain extent Baudeau) and the view of classical British economists who saw in him chiefly a supplier and accumulator of capital. That this latter view tended to predominate in British political economy during the last quarter of the eighteenth and the first half of the nineteenth century is not surprising in view of the rapid growth of industry which ostensibly set the pace for economic development. Even in France, whose industrial revolution did not really get under way until the end of the first quarter of the nineteenth century, Chaptal estimates that coal output more than tripled in the thirty years between the French revolution and the appearance of his book and that other industries showed equivalent increase.[49] In view of this it is not surprising to see that in the English economic literature the entrepreneur was identified with the capitalist and that the latter concept tended to supersede the former. Only with the more refined analysis of economic functions in a complex society which began after the middle of the nineteenth century and culminated in the Marshallian system was the entrepreneur rediscovered by English economists.

IV. THE LINKS BETWEEN CANTILLON AND SAY

If the analysis at the end of the preceding section is accepted, then it is at once clear that Say's insistence on the entrepreneurial function as distinct from that of the capitalist is a distinctive mark of his work. Is it possible that this trend of thought was instilled in him by the experiences of his life? None of the notable British economists of that period, Smith, Lauderdale, Malthus, Ricardo, James Mill, Senior, had had any practical experience as entrepreneurs. They were professors or men whose means had been acquired by inheritance or on the stock exchange. But Say had been an industrial entrepreneur. From 1804 to 1812 he was running a spinning factory, which he had established first at Maubuisson and transferred in 1806 to the village of Aulchy-les-Moines (Pas-de-Calais) and which he could maintain only by constant efforts in combatting the negligence, indifference, and listlessness of his workers and by braving adverse conditions imposed by nature as well as the concealed hostility of many of the inhabitants of Aulchy and environs. It is not unlikely that these experiences impressed upon him the peculiar role played by the entrepreneur who must be a real leader of men, who must be capable to plan productive operations under his guidance and who must be willing to supervise constantly the execution of his plans. It should be noted that the full fledged theory of entrepreneurship was elaborated by Say only in the later editions of his *Traité* and in his *Cours,* which both appeared after his return from Aulchy to Paris.[50]

However, this leaves the question still open whether any intellectual connection between Cantillon and Say can be established. That there existed a purely linguistic bridge in the fact that the word *entrepreneur* was quite commonly used can hardly be considered as conclusive. Another link would be through the works of the Physiocrats. It has been shown that Cantillon's work was known to them, and Say knew, of course, the work of Quesnay and Turgot. But the evidence is too tenuous to provide us with any tangible data which would indicate that Say was influenced through them, even indirectly, by Cantillon. A third possible link is through Say's correspondence with Dupont de Nemours. But these letters deal with the more general methodological question of economics and do not descend to such special questions as entrepreneurial theory.[51] Finally, there exists another possible link through Germain Garnier, the translator of Smith's *Wealth of Nations.* Garnier published (anonymously) a small book in 1796, entitled *Abrégé élémentaire des principes de l'économie politique,* which was strongly influenced by Cantillon and which in some places repeats passages from Cantillon verbatim. Say was familiar with Garnier's work, but since he regarded Garnier chiefly as a belated representative of Physiocracy, his reaction against him was primarily negative. It is not likely, therefore, that Say would have adopted Cantillon's views on entrepreneurship from this source. Moreover, if we consult the references in Say's work to Garnier, we find that they are concerned exclusively with questions of economic conditions in antiquity, Say's refutation of the Physiocratic views of Garnier, and a few minor points on the value of labor, taxes and the computation of national wealth, which all are a consequence of Garnier's adherence and Say's opposition to the economic theories of Quesnay and his school.[52]

There do not seem to be any other more or less direct intellectual links between the theories of entrepreneurship of Cantillon and Say. But we must ask whether there is much sense in looking for such links. Are the two theories so similar or so closely related that one would suspect one to be descended from the other? On the whole, the answer must be negative. Although Cantillon and Say both elaborated a theory of entrepreneurship, they have little more in common than the word entrepreneur (and this had been used, as we have seen, also by Quesnay, Turgot, and others) and certain obvious externals. But these facts alone do not permit us to suspect that the study of the history of ideas would adduce evidence which might establish an intellectual relationship between the two theories. Marx and Marshall, who were only one generation apart, and who might also have known one another personally, both have a theory of capital, but I am not aware of anyone having suggested that the two theories are related, even as contradictions of one another. And yet both men use the same term and certain externals in their theories are identical.

Cantillon's theory of entrepreneurship is very simple. The function of the entrepreneur is to bear uncertainty. Cantillon explicitly excludes from his theory the notion that the entrepreneur must also be in a position to supply capital, and he even says explicitly that "All the rest are Undertakers, whether they set up with a capital to conduct their enterprise, or are Undertakers of their own labour without capital, and they may be regarded as living at uncertainty; the Beggars even and the Robbers are Undertakers of this class."[53] Finally there is no indication in Cantillon's work that the entrepreneur was also a planner, organizer, and supervisor of the factors of production which he employed. We have seen that the Physiocrats and Turgot developed a much more elaborate set of theories of entrepreneurship in which entrepreneurial activity is described as embracing more than one type of behavior and in which different writers have variously stressed the planning and organizing function, the innovating function, or the capital supply function of the entrepreneur. Say's theory of entrepreneurship is much closer to that of the Physiocrats than to that of Cantillon. And yet it may justly be doubted whether the works of Turgot or Quesnay should be regarded as a source of Say's inspiration, precisely because of his fundamental opposition to their theories. True, Say had admiration for their advocacy of laissez-faire and, in particular, the economic policy of Turgot. But while he considered Turgot to have been a great statesman he approved of his statesmanship only because he regarded Turgot's views as not having been derived from the "secte économiste," an interpretation which is, on the whole, certainly wrong.[54] All this leads me to believe that Say developed his theory of entrepreneurship independently, and that his experiences as a master cotton spinner rather than any intellectual forbears should be made responsible for his ingenious contribution to classical economic theory.

In analyzing Say's ideas on entrepreneurship two views must be strictly separated: the pure theory of entrepreneurship which emerges if one considers the function of the entrepreneur in economic equilibrium and the empirical descriptions of what modern capitalistic entrepreneurs typically do. I shall attempt in conclusion to state and examine these views briefly.

Say's theory of the entrepreneur begins with his tripartite division of functions which must be met in any process of production. These functions are exhibited by operations of three kinds, the research of the scientist, the "applications" of the entrepreneur, and the performance of the laborer. (*Cours*, vol. I, p. 97). Although all three operations may be performed by one and the same person they can be isolated analytically. The entrepreneur is therefore not a member of a distinct social class (as with the

Physiocrats) but must be regarded as the performer of a social function, which does not necessarily correspond with a special position in the structure of society.[55] But what are the "applications of the entrepreneur"? The entrepreneur is the principal agent of production. For although the other functions are admitted to be indispensable for the creation of any good or service, the entrepreneur puts them to work. "It is he who estimates needs and above all the means to satisfy them, who compares the end with these means. Hence this principal quality is to have good judgment. He can lack personal knowledge of science, by judiciously employing that of others, he can avoid dirtying his own hands by using the hands of others, but he must not lack judgment; for then he might produce at great expense something which has no value." (*Cours*, vol. I, p. 100). The function of the entrepreneur is thus that of mediator. He combines the means (factors of production) in order to achieve as an end the production of a good and his function consists precisely in performing this combination. He is, as Say says in another place, "L'intermediaire entre toutes les classes de producteurs, et entre ceux-ci et le consommateur. Il administre l'oeuvre de la production; il est le *centre de plusieurs rapports*." (*Traité*, p. 371. Italics not in original).

But these "applications of the entrepreneur" are not random. As can be seen from the quotation in the last paragraph, they must lead to the creation of an object or service possessing value. The combinatory activity of the entrepreneur thus attains its full meaning only if the proper relationship between means and end, that is, between the using up of factors of production and the expected product yielded by the production process, is observed. This is where the entrepreneur's judgment of values becomes important. But it should be noted that this judgment is confined strictly to the relationship arising within a particular production process and does not extend to consideration of economic relations beyond this process, not to speak of relations that are ultimately determined by changes in the social structure. Moreover Say does not discuss the entrepreneurial function in a dynamic environment, but in purely stationary equilibrium which is characterized by the equality of prices of products with their costs of production. In particular, he sees no relationship between entrepreneurial activity and capital accumulation or investment.[56] Thus in the last resort his theory of entrepreneurship is in full contrast to that of Schumpeter who maintains that in equilibrium entrepreneurial profits are necessarily zero and who thus finds a place for the exercise of entrepreneurial functions only in a dynamic process. In other words, whereas for Schumpeter the characteristic of entrepreneurial activity is the introduction of innovations, for Say it is the organization and combination of productive factors for a given task. At the same time Say has stressed explicitly the notion, which we found to have already been present in Physiocratic thought, that the entrepreneur is the central figure in the economy. He is the universal mediator. He mediates between landlord and capitalist, between scientist and manual laborer, between the various suppliers of productive services among one another, and between producers and consumers. If seen in this light, Say's theory of entrepreneurship is not only fundamentally different from the later theory of entrepreneurship but also from the earlier ones of Cantillon, Baudeau and Turgot.

However, we must still consider one additional point. In one place in the *Cours* Say extends his description of entrepreneur from one who merely combines factors for the production of a good that has value, to that of a person who works on his own account. His argument runs as follows: in a market economy the entrepreneur acquires productive services by purchase or hire. To the extent to which he has contracted for them he either acquires property rights in them or obtains them under conditions where he is able to dispose of them freely and at his will. (*Cours*, vol. I, p. 510). Hence he uses them in his own productive activities and becomes the owner of the finished products. Production is therefore carried through on the account of and at the risks of the entrepreneur. (*Cours*, vol. II, p. 34). The sentence, 'Il n'en est pas moins entrepreneur puisqu'il produit pour son compte, et que son profit dépend de la valeur du produit qui results de ses soins," (*ibid.*) thus is the core of a second view of entrepreneurship on the part of Say.

No one has expressed the view more firmly and consistently that economics must base its generalizations on empirical evidence rather than on abstract axioms than Say. His chief objection to the Physiocrats was that he considered them to start from such abstract axioms rather than from careful investigation of the real world around them.[57] It might, therefore, be said that Say's double characterization of entrepreneurship is an outflow of his empirical method. It would be easy to show that the entrepreneur of the early nineteenth century engaged in the organisatory activity which Say attributes to him and that he usually was a man who ran a business on his own account. This would, however, be irrelevant for the evaluation of Say's theory of entrepreneurship, because we are not concerned with how entrepreneurs actually behaved, but which aspects of their behavior Say selected for his theory.

We are here confronted with a problem of scientific method which is crucial for any empirical science, and for empirical social science, in particular. The actual behavior patterns of entrepreneurs, their motives and objectives may display a considerable degree of variation, both as between persons or industries, as well as between countries and geographical areas. The task of developing a theory of entrepreneurship consists in selecting those aspects of entrepreneurial behavior which are most significant and in determining the degree of generality with which they are found. In other words out of the manifold and different acts which entrepreneurs have performed or may be expected to perform one has to eliminate all those which are "accidental" or which are the result of special circumstances of the person, the time, the locality, the industry, or other factors. Those acts which are left constitute then the most typical forms of entrepreneurial behavior and we can then indicate how commonly they are found. This procedure results not only in an entrepreneurial theory, but indicates at the same time whether, and to what extent entrepreneurial activity is dependent upon certain institutional relations. Say has quite properly carried through such an analysis, and has come to the result that the most significant aspect of the entrepreneur is his position as mediator or co-ordinator in production, and that the entrepreneurial function so defined is found in all situations in which men have to meet potentially unlimited needs with scarce means, in other words, in all situations in which economic activity, a choice between the alternative use of productive resources, must be exercised. We have seen earlier that Say explicitly states that entrepreneurial activity of this kind is found also in savage society, and, by logical extension, it is part of the daily labor of Robinson Crusoe.[58]

If this is recognized then the fact that the entrepreneur produces for his own account is not part of the general theory of entrepreneurship, but is an observation of a peculiar historical relationship, which was quite common in the period in which Say wrote, but which had been absent in earlier periods, and which tended to disappear later with the growth of corporate enterprise. Say's entrepreneur — and this is also a point of difference between him and Schumpeter on the one hand, and Cantillon and the Physiocrats and the other — is not confined to a capitalist society. He appears wherever production is carried on, where this production results in the creation of values, and where not all the goods and services used in production are free goods.[59]

We thus come to the conclusion that Say has two theories of entrepreneurship. One is general and independent of a particular social framework. The second is the theory of the capitalist entrepreneur, not in the sense which Turgot gave to the phrase, but of an entrepreneur in a competitive capitalist society where the individually owned firm predominates. This entrepreneur is not only characterized by being the organizer and planner of production, but he also carried on this activity on his own account.[60] As a consequence he may be bearing certain risks, or, in other words his income may be uncertain. His income is thus determined by two factors. The first is the price established by the forces of supply and of demand for any particular kind of entrepreneurial labor. Thus Say arrives at stipulating a gradation of entrepreneurial labor depending upon the scarcity of the capacities and knowledge required in each class of entrepreneurial activity. This was already referred to earlier in note 56. Say lists in his *Cours* (Vol. II, pp. 35–38) the major causes which determine the supply of entrepreneurial labor. They are (1) the necessity of having the moral qualifications which this kind of work requires, (2) the necessity of attaching to the enterprise a sufficient capital, and (3) the uncertainty of whether and what profits will be made. Only men who have the necessary moral qualifications, who can either supply their own capital, or induce others to provide them with it in sufficient magnitude and who are willing to bear the risks involved can become entrepreneurs; and depending upon the magnitude of the capital or risks involved and the complexity of the business the supply of entrepreneurial labor will vary. In the ordinary one-family-farm little capital is involved, risks are not great, and the only "moral qualifications" needed are that common amount of judgment which Say thinks is found quite frequently. It is different with men who operate institutions of high finance or big commercial enterprises. The primary source of entrepreneurial income even under this system is not profit as a premium for risk, but a wage as compensation for a highly skilled type of labor, which is scarce. (*Cours*, Vol. II, p. 38–39).

Only as a second consideration does Say acknowledge that entrepreneurial income may be derived from the exploitation of an innovation. This is at least implicit in Say's discussion of the introduction of a new product or the establishment of a new firm, and in his advice that a good entrepreneur must follow, and, if possible, precede his competitors in the application of new methods. (*Cours*, Vol. I, pp. 298–301). Pursuing his thought along these lines Say finally arrives at stipulating the necessary qualifications for the entrepreneur. He lists among others a "judicious courage which can envisage all manner of risks and an imperturbable *sang-froid* which permits one to choose all means of escaping them." (*Ibid.*, p. 303.). Thus the entrepreneur turns out to be the hardy and courageous innovator who plants his standard in new and unknown country.

It should be noted that these considerations are not part of Say's theory of entrepreneurship but descriptions of the socio-psychological and institutional framework determining the exercise of entrepreneurial activity in a system of competitive free enterprise capitalism. Although Say arrives at a stipulating special qualification for the entrepreneur, his theoretical scheme envisages entrepreneurial activity as an economic function and not as a social role performed by a particular class of men. From the point of view of economic theory his views of entrepreneurship constitute an important advance since they neatly distinguish the contribution to production made by personal services of businessmen as distinct from services of nonhuman agents of production owned or controlled by them. But although Say himself did not always fully satisfy his own rigorous demand that theoretical economic matters should be kept strictly apart from the wider social problems with which they are associated, his emphasis on the former induced him to develop a theory of entrepreneurship which is singularly barren for the explanation of the entrepreneurial function in a dynamic capitalist society. In this sense his work is a step backward from the insights gained by the Physiocrats. Only after it had been shown by Schumpeter that the entrepreneur was not the guardian of economic equilibrium but the disturber of equilibrium was a new and fruitful development of entrepreneurial theory possible.

NOTES

1. Henri Hauser, *Les débuts du capitalisme*, p. 309.

2. Compare Charles Gide & Charles Rist, *Histoire des doctrines économiques*, 2nd ed. (Paris, 1913), p. 132 with 7th ed. (Paris, 1947), p. 123.

3. See Henry Higgs, *The Physiocrats*, (London, 1897) p. 31, note 1.

4. See Fritz Redlich, "On the Origin of the Concepts of 'Entrepreneur' and 'Creative Entrepreneur'," *Explorations in Entrepreneurial History*, Vol. I, No. 2 (February, 1949), pp. 1–7.

5. This dictionary was published in four volumes in 1889. The references to *entrepreneur* appear on p. 1437 of volume II.

6. See K. Nyrop, *Grammaire historique de la langue française*, (Copenhagen, 1908) vol. 3, pp. 116–117.

7. Littré, *op. cit.*, p. 1437, and Frederic Godefroy, *Dictionnaire de l'ancienne langue française*, (Paris, 1884), vol. III, p. 297.

8. See the large number of quotations from sixteenth century literature in Edmond Huguet, *Dictionnaire de la langue française du seizième siècle*, (Paris, 1946), vol. III, p. 531. See also Littré, *op. cit.*, vol. II, p. 1437.

9. Antoine Furetière, *Dictionnaire universel*, (The Hague, 1690), Vol. I, p. 951.

10. *Le Dictionnaire de l'Académie Française*, [First edition], (Paris, 1694), Vol. II, p. 314. It is interesting to note that this definition, although enlarged, never entirely disappears from the dictionary and that even the 6th (1835), 7th (1878), and 8th (1932) editions do not contain a definition of the word *entrepreneur* corresponding to its technical meaning in economics.

11. Cf. F. A. Isambert et al., (ed.), *Recueil général des anciennes lois françaises*, (Paris, 1829), Vol. XV, pp. 217 and 315–322.

12. A number of Arrêts du Conseil d'Etat and Ordonnances exhibiting this terminology and dating from 1667, 1669, 1670, 1672, 1685, 1700, and 1706 are reprinted in P. Gallotti, *L'entrepreneur à travers les âges*, (Paris, 1921), pp. 415–418, and 428–433.

13. Antoyne de Montchrétien, *Traicté de l'oeconomie politique*, (ed. by Th. Funck-Brentano) (Paris, n.d. [1924]), p. 297. It is perhaps not without interest to note that similar enterprises by Englishmen were called "projects" and their leaders "projectors," as is evidenced, for example, in a passage in Robert Beverly, *The History and Present State of Virginia*, first published in London, 1705, reprinted under the editorship of Louis B. Wright, Chapel Hill, 1947, p. 23. Here Sir *Walter Raleigh* is called "the great Projector and Furtherer of these Discoveries and Settlements". As will be shown later, the term projector had an invidious flavor and was applied to either fraudulent or highly speculative enterprisers. This attests the risky nature of the early colonization schemes.

14. See E. Viollet-le-Duc, *Dictionnaire raisonné de l'architecture française du XIe au XVIe siècle*, (Paris, 1875), Vol. I, pp. 107–116.

15. On the construction of French canals see A. Debauve, *Les travaux publics et les ingénieurs des ponts et chaussées depuis le XVIIe siècle*, (Paris, 1893) pp. 173–191; on the drainage of fens see Margaret James, *Social Problems and Policy During the Puritan Revolution: 1640–1660* (London, 1930) pp. 125–128; on the building of Blenheim see Bonamy Dobrée, *Essays in Biography: 1680–1726* (London, 1925) pp. 99–128.

16. Gallotti, *op. cit.*, pp. 25–26.

17. See, among numerous instances, the very clear example given by Say when he says, in talking of an agricultural entrepreneur: "il a dû se livrer à quelques combinaisons pour réunir les moyens nécessaires pour obtenir un produit quelconque; il a dû mettre en balance ce que ces moyens lui coûteraient, avec l'avantage qu'il retirerait du produit. Il a dû s'instruire des procédés d'agriculture au moyen desquels on le fait arriver à bien; et enfin il a fallu qu'il s'occupât de l'exécution de ces procédés." *Cours complet d'économie politique pratique*, (Paris, 1840), Vol. I, pp. 97–98. On Say's general theory of entrepreneurship see below, Part IV of this essay.

18. For this and the preceding three paragraphs see [Bernard F. de] Belidor, *La science des ingénieurs dans la conduite des travaux de fortification et d'architecture civile* (Paris, 1729), book VI, pp. 46–50. See also the discussion of the same problem in book III, pp. 29–31.

19. Samuel Johnson, *A Dictionary of the English Language*, (London, printed by W. Strahan, 1755), Vol. I, sub "Adventurer".

20. See Jean-Baptiste Say, *A Treatise on Political Economy*, transl. by C. R. Prinsep, M. A. (Philadelphia, 1827) p. 18 note. John Stuart Mill, when confronted with the same problem, uses the word "undertaker", but he adds in a footnote: "It is to be regretted that this word, in this sense, is not familiar to an English ear. French political economists enjoy a great advantage in being able to speak currently of *les profits de l'entrepreneur*" (*Principles of Political Economy*, ed. by Sir W. J. Ashley, (London, 1909), p. 406).

21. Robert Payne, *A Brife description of Ireland*, ed. by Aquilla Smith, reprinted in Irish Archaeological Society, *Tracts Relating to Ireland*, (Dublin, 1841) Vol. I, pp. 7–8.

22. Fynes Moryson, *An Itinerary Containing His Ten Yeeres Travell*, etc. (first published 1602, reprinted Glasgow, 1907), Vol. II, p. 219.

23. *Ibid.*, Vol. III, p. 219.

24. See the letter by Sir T. Edmondes to Sir D. Carleton, of September 16, 1612, reprinted in Historical Manuscripts Commission, *Tenth Report*, App. I (Manuscripts of the Earl of Eglinton . . . and G. Wingfield Digby, Esq.), (London, 1885) p. 604.

25. William Dugdale, *The History of Imbanking and Draining of divers Fens and Marshes, etc.* (first published 1662, reprinted London, 1772) p. 406. This book abounds in references to the operations of "undertakers" in draining and land reclamations in the seventeenth century. See also the petition of the inhabitants of East Holland and Sibsey of December 11, 1640, requesting that they be indemnified against the damage they suffered since "this Sir Anthony Thomas, pretending the fens were hurtfully surrounded about 10 years since, procured himself to be chief undertaker for draining the drowned grounds in those parts." *Calendar of State Papers, Domestic Series, 1640–41*, (London, 1882) Vol. 17, p. 308.

26. S[tephen] P[rimatt], *The City and Country Purchaser and Builder*, (second ed. by William Leybourne, London, 1680) pp. 30–31.

27. As late as 1755, Dr. Johnson gives as a definition of *Undertaker* "one who engages in projects and affairs" and as one of *projector* "one who performs schemes or designs." Although for both words additional, more special meanings are given, the two definitions just quoted show the closeness of the two concepts. See Samuel Johnson, *op. cit.*, Vol. II, sub. "Projector" and "undertaker".

28. W. T. Baker, ed., *Records of the Borough of Nottingham* (London, 1900), Vol. 5, p. 144.

29. Historical Manuscripts Commission, *Fifteenth Report*, App. IV (Manuscripts of the Duke of Portland), (London, 1897) p. 31.

30. *The London Gazette*, No. 4651 of February 9—February 11, 1709, col. 2 of p. 1.

31. See *The Wealth of Nations*, ed. by Edwin Cannan (New York: Modern Library, 1937) p. 438.

32. See Malachy Postlethwayt, *The Universal Dictionary of Trade and Commerce*, (Second ed., London, 1757) Vol. I, p. 498 (Article CIRCULATION). This article is virtually a translation of chapter XIII of book I of Cantillon's *Essai*. See on this point Edwin Cannan's "Communication", *Economic Journal*, VI (1896), p. 165.

33. See on this point the interesting researches by Henry Higgs, "Richard Cantillon", *Economic Journal*, I (1891), p. 266.

34. See François Quesnay, *Oeuvres économiques et philosophiques*, (ed. by Auguste Oncken, Frankfurt & Paris, 1888), pp. 218–219.

35. The actual term *"avances foncières"* is, I believe, not used by Quesnay, but stems from Baudeau (cf. his *Premiere introduction à la philosophie économique*, (ed. by A. Dubois, Paris, 1910) p. 12). Quesnay himself speaks of *"dépenses foncières"* (*op. cit.*, p. 471) and explains them as the "premières avances pour mettre leurs [the proprietors'] terres en état d'étre cultivées" (*ibid.*, p. 529). It is interesting to note that both passages occur in articles contributed in 1766 to the *Journal de l'Agriculture* which at that time was the "house organ" of the Physiocrats, and that the notion of *avances foncières* had not been developed when Quesnay devised the *Tableau économique*. The notion of the *avances foncières* appears to be an afterthought rounding out the logic of the system and providing at the same time a reason for the rent income, as based on the contribution of a productive service. The matter has been taken up in an extended form by Baudeau in the work cited earlier, which appeared first in 1767. Baudeau also makes the additional distinction between *avances foncières* and *avances souveraines* (*op. cit.*, p. 12), the latter consisting in the development of roads, canals, and other utilities, as well as the administration of law which makes property secure. In this extended system every claim to income (or revenue) is thus justified by the contribution of some productive service; here an apotheosis of rational capitalist calculation is at the basis of a treatise on economic principles.

36. See Quesnay, *op. cit.*, p. 316.

37. *Ibid.*, p. 234.

38. This letter is reprinted in Othmar Thiele, "François Quesnay und die Agrarkrise im Ancien Régime", *Vierteliahrschrift für Social- und Wirtschaftsgeschichte*, IV (1906), pp. 644–52. The quoted passage is on p. 646.

39. D'Alembert and Diderot, eds., *Encyclopédie*, (Paris, 1755), Vol. V, p. 732.

40. See F. Brunot, *Histoire de la langue française des origines à 1900*, (Paris, 1905), Vol. VI, 1. partie, pp. 386–7.

41. See Quesnay's letter to the Intendant of Soissons, in Thiele, *op. cit.*, p. 647. Mercier de la Rivière moreover shows that if free competition prevails in the market for leases on farms uniform rents for land of homogeneous quality will be established and the rents form then a cost factor for the tenant operator. *L'ordre naturel et essential des sociétés politiques* in E. Daire, ed., *Physiocrates*, (Paris, 1846), p. 460.

42. Nicholas Baudeau, *op. cit.*, p. 48.

43. *Ibid.*, p. 46.

44. *Ibid.*, p. 51.

45. On the many proposals by the Physiocrats toward the introduction of innovations of all sorts into agriculture, see Georges Weulersse, *Le mouvement physiocratique en France*, (Paris, 1910) Vol. I, pp. 374–378. As an example of the fact that the Physiocrats were ready to practice what they preached may serve the establishment by the marquis de Mirabeau of a technically advanced flour mill and bakery which enabled him to produce bread more cheaply than was possible with traditional methods. See Louis de Lomenie, *Les Mirabeau*, (Paris, 1889) Vol. II, pp. 276–278.

46. See Anne Robert Jacques Turgot, *Réflexions sur la formation et la distribution des richesses*, in Gustave Schelle, ed., *Oeuvres de Turgot*, (Paris, 1913–23) Vol. II, pp. 569–570.

47. See *ibid.*, pp. 572, 569, 570. There exist two English translations of Turgot's *Réflexions*, one by an anonymous author, first published in 1793 and later incorporated in J. R. McCulloch, *A Select Collection of Scarce and Valuable Economical Tracts*, (London, 1859); the other by Sir W. J. Ashley, published under the title *Reflections on the Formation and the Distribution of Riches*, (New York, 1898). In both translations Turgot's *"entrepreneur capitaliste"* is rendered by "capitalist

undertaker", a fact which does not surprise us with regard to the anonymous writer of 1793, but which seems a somewhat stilted antiquarianism in the translation of Professor Ashley. Certainly by 1898 the word undertaker had been superseded in English economic language by the word entrepreneur.

Another curious circumstance relating to Turgot's treatment of capitalist entrepreneur is the fact that it has been completely ignored. This is particularly surprising of Gide and Rist, who have not failed to point out other divergences between Turgot and the more orthodox members of the "Physiocrat sect". Certainly Turgot was considered important enough to be studied carefully and, for a short period, the claim was not uncommon in France that he was the true founder of modern economics rather than Adam Smith. As concerns his theory of entrepreneurship, he is clearly superior to Smith, and yet this fact seems not to have been noted heretofore.

48. On the technological superiority of British to French agriculture at the time, see Arthur Young, *Political Arithmetic,* (London, 1774), pp. 158–166.

49. See Chaptal de Chanteloup, *De l'industrie française,* (Paris, 1819) Vol. II, pp. 112–113 and ff.

50. On the details of Say's biography see Ernest Teilhac, *L'oeuvre économique de Jean-Baptiste Say* (Paris, 1927) esp. pp. 24–26. Teilhac also notes that the second edition of the *Traité,* published in 1814, seems to show the influence of Say's experiences at Aulchy and he singles out as evidence for this Say's notion of the entrepreneur, among other things. See *ibid.,* p. 29.

51. This correspondence has been reprinted in *Oeuvres diverses de J. B. Say* (ed. by Ch. Comte, E. Daire, & Horace Say, Paris, 1848) pp. 361–397.

52. See the following references to Germain Garnier in Say's major works: *Traité d'économie politique* (6th ed., Paris 1841) pp. 245, 257, 288, 334, 338; *Cours complet d'économie politique pratique* (2nd ed., Paris, 1840) vol. I, pp. 214, 424, 534; vol. II, pp. 428, 558. See especially the footnote on p. 214 of volume I of the *Cours* for Say's general evaluation of Garnier's work and the aspects of it which he regarded as important. (All citations hereinafter will be to these editions of the two works.) On the social background of the opposition between Garnier and Say, see the stimulating essay by E. Allix, "La rivalité entre la propriéte foncière et la fortune mobilière sous la Révolution," *Revue d'histoire économique et sociale,* VI (1913), pp. 297–348, esp. 336–346.

53. Richard Cantillon, *Essai sur la nature du commerce en général,* (ed. with an English transl. by Henry Higgs, London, 1931) p. 55.

54. See Say, *Traité,* pp. 24–25, and esp. on Turgot's *Réflexions,* p. 34, note 1.

55. It should be noted that the Physiocrats were, of course, aware that one and the same person could be proprietor, farmer, and agricultural laborer. But they regarded such a state of affairs as an indication of stagnation and decline, or of barbarism. (See, for example, Baudeau, *op. cit.,* pp. 45–46). Say, on the contrary, stipulates that the entrepreneurial function is found in any culture in which production is carried on, regardless of the structure of that society. (*Cours,* vol. I, pp. 98–99).

56. See, for example, *Traité,* p. 323. Say's fundamentally static view of entrepreneurial income is perhaps nowhere better exhibited than in a passage in his *Traité,* pp. 370–371, where he discusses the causes for differences in the profits in different industries. He says there: "All kinds of industry do not require the same amount of skill and knowledge on the part of the entrepreneur. A farmer, who is an agricultural entrepreneur, need not know so many things as a merchant who trades with faraway countries . . . If the knowledge which makes a good farmer is more common than that which makes a good merchant, need we be surprised if the labor of the first receives a lower pay than that of the second?"

57. See, for example, *Cours,* vol. II, p. 556; *Traité,* p. 24; and especially Say's letter to Dupont de Nemours of November 15, 1815, in *Oeuvres diverses de J.-B. Say,* pp. 389 ff.

58. See note 55 above.

59. That this was Say's own view of the essential nature of his concept of entrepreneur—and that such factors as risk bearing and production on his own account were not considered essential elements of the concept—is attested by his *Epitome des principes fondamentaux de l'économie politique,* a list of definitions and basic theoretical relations which was appended to the later editions of the *Traité.* Since this is a very condensed statement, I take the liberty to quote the essential parts: "Ils (les entrepreneurs) concourent à la *production* en applicant les connaissances acquises, le service des capitaux et celui des *agens naturels,* à la confection des produits auxquels les hommes attachent une valeur . . . Ce qui fait la difficulté de la tâche de l'entrepreneur, c'est de créer des produits qui vaillent autant ou plus que leurs frais de production . . . Si les produits valent plus que les frais de production, c'est un surcroît de profit pour l'entrepreneur, surcroît qui lui est ordinairement enlevé par la concurrence." *Traité,* pp. 579–580.

60. As soon as he has reached this insight Say comes to agree with Cantillon that "un peintre, un statuaire du premier ordre, . . . peuvent etre consideres comme entrepreneurs, puisqu'ils agissent pour leur propre compte." *Cours,* Vol. II, p. 40.

PART FOUR

THE CLASSICAL

SCHOOL

AND MARX

THE SIGNIFICANCE OF the classical school is not that it "invented" the economic problem or that it initiated study of it. Economics is concerned with scarcity and the consequent necessity of somehow administering economic resources (and the desirability of increasing economic resources), and scarcity is not a phenomenon of only the last two centuries. Furthermore, there were significant attempts before Adam Smith to comprehend both the nature of the economic problem and how a genuine economic organization can exist in the absence of all-pervasive central political direction. The classical economists, however, together with some of their eighteenth-century predecessors, posed an objective which was quite unique, they indicated fairly clearly a mode of economic-social organization conducive to the attainment of the objective, and they suggested, albeit inadequately, how the operation of such an organization might be fruitfully analyzed.

"While the medieval conception of the object of human effort was the salvation of human souls," Heckscher summarizes, and "mercantilist statesmen and writers saw in the subjects of the state means to an end, . . . [viz.] the power of the state itself," "economic liberalism, or laissez faire, aimed at the temporal welfare of individuals."[1] The "temporal welfare of individuals" could, in general, be enhanced by an economy based upon private property and the allocation of resources through use of market forces generated by, and reflective of, decisions of individual consumers and resource owners. Although the objective and the requisite economic organization were coherent, the scope and boldness of the conceptions of the classical economists were not matched by the refinement of their analytic tools. Still, many of the essential elements of later theory are contained or at least adumbrated in the classical writings. More important is the perspective of an efficiently and impersonally price-directed and expanding economy which the classical economists bequeathed.[2]

1. Eli F. Heckscher, "Mercantilism," *Encyclopaedia of the Social Sciences* (New York: The Macmillan Co., 1933), vol. 10, p. 335.
2. "If we ask ourselves what, in the last analysis, was the main contribution of Classical Political Economy to the understanding of social relationships, there can surely be only one answer: the theory of the division of labour and the market. . . . That all societies of any complexity involved division of labour, that the division was in a very ultimate sense perhaps the major ingredient of the social bond—these were truths that had been recognized in greater or less degree since Plato and Aristotle. But the understanding of the dependence of the division upon the extent of the market and of the way in which, given law and order, strong spontaneous forces working through the market were ceaselessly in operation tending to adapt the organization of production to the influence of pecuniary demand—this was an insight which is due chiefly to the Classical writers." Lionel Robbins, *Robert Torrens and The Evolution of Classical Economics* (London: Macmillan & Co., Ltd., and New York: St. Martin's Press, 1958), p. 234. According to the interpretation of Myint (Selection 17), the classical emphasis was directed more to expansion of the economy, *i.e.*, augmenting aggregate output, than to efficiency in allocating any given total of resources.

259

The essays of Part Four will be introduced by short reviews of Adam Smith (1723–1790) and David Ricardo (1772–1823) on value theory, Ricardo on income distribution, the classical theory of international trade, and the position of John Stuart Mill (1806–1873).

THE THEORY OF VALUE: SMITH AND RICARDO

It is not to be supposed that the value theories of Smith and Ricardo exhaust the entire classical discussion. Not only were there variations, some more harmonious than others, on the themes presented by these two central figures; one finds in the classical literature antecedents of the marginal utility approach, as in the writings of Nassau Senior (1790–1864). But the views of Smith and Ricardo are the most representative of the classical approach.

Smith

We are to distinguish "value in use," which is the utility, or capacity to satisfy wants, of an object, from "value in exchange," which is the power of an object to purchase other goods. Utility neither determines nor measures price. "The things which have the greatest value in use [*e.g.*, water] have frequently little or no value in exchange; and, on the contrary, those which have the greatest value in exchange [*e.g.*, diamonds] have frequently little or no value in use."[3] While Smith does speak of "utility," resolution of the water-diamond paradox called for the concept of *marginal* utility, but this concept was to wait another century for general adoption.

Putting aside, as the other dominant members of the classical school were to do, the utility approach to value theory, Smith presents, first, a pure labor theory. Or rather he entangles two labor theories. The *labor-embodied* version holds that the exchange value of a commodity is *determined* by the amount of labor required to produce it. "The real price of everything, what everything really costs to the man who wants to acquire it, is the toil and trouble of acquiring it" (p. 30). And thus (in primitive society), "the proportion between the quantities of labour necessary for acquiring different objects seems to be the only circumstance which can afford any rule for exchanging them for one another" (p. 47). The *labor-commanding* interpretation emphasizes that the value of an object is *measured* by the amount of labor which the object can purchase. With an economy organized around division of labor, a person consumes little or none of his own physical product, and he is rich or poor depending on the amount of others' outputs which he can acquire. "The value of any commodity, therefore, to the person who possesses it, and who means not to use or consume it himself, . . . is equal to the quantity of labour which it en-

3. Adam Smith, *An Inquiry into the Nature and Causes of the Wealth of Nations* (1776), ed. Edwin Cannan (New York: Random House, Inc., 1937), p. 28. All quotations of Smith are from this source. An excellent secondary source is Paul H. Douglas, "Smith's Theory of Value and Distribution," in *Adam Smith, 1776–1926* (Chicago: University of Chicago Press, 1928), pp. 77–115.

ables him to purchase or command. Labour, therefore, is the real measure of the exchangeable value of all commodities" (p. 30). The two approaches can be merged in a single sentence: ". . . [first] the quantity of labour commonly employed in acquiring or producing any commodity, is the only circumstance which can regulate [second] the quantity of labor which it ought commonly to purchase, command, or exchange for" (pp. 47–48).

If labor were the only input and if all labor were homogeneous, the labor-embodied and the labor-commanding results would be the same. With regard to the latter qualification, "it is often difficult to ascertain the proportion between two different quantities of labour. The time spent in two different sorts of work will not always alone determine this proportion. The different degrees of hardship endured, and of ingenuity exercised must likewise be taken into account." Allowance is commonly made for such considerations; "it is adjusted, however, not by any accurate measure, but by the higgling and bargaining of the market" (p. 31).

Consider an economy in which labor is the only input. "If among a nation of hunters, for example, it usually costs twice the labour to kill a beaver which it does to kill a deer, one beaver should naturally exchange for or be worth two deer" (p. 47). With competitive markets, constant returns to scale, and labor which is both homogeneous and mobile, in long-run equilibrium either commodity, a beaver or a deer, will sell for its constant alternative cost in terms of the other commodity — although Smith did not thus pursue the analysis and simply asserted that the exchange ratio of one beaver equal to two deer is "natural" (p. 47). (Nor did Smith explain that the proportions of the total labor force devoted to beaver- and to deer-production would be determined by demand conditions.)

There is, it appears, no incompatability between the two labor approaches when the entire social output is produced and received by labor alone. But perhaps a portion of the output of a particular commodity, say, one-third, goes to "capital." Then we may suppose that five units of labor ($5L$) combine with capital to produce a commodity with a (labor-commanding) value of $7\frac{1}{2}L$, and the labor embodied in the commodity thereby differs from the amount of labor which the commodity commands. This is not crucial *if* labor and capital are combined in the same proportion in all commodities: two commodities each embodying $5L$ of labor (plus amounts of capital equal in the two cases) will exchange exactly for each other, just as would be the case when labor is the only input — and the amount of labor actually embodied in the commodity given in an exchange equals the amount in the commodity received. The serious problem arises when two commodities of different labor-capital ratios exchange, notably when labor itself is one of the commodities. In the resources market, $5L$ of labor are sold for commodities worth $5L$, but these commodities paid for labor would include only ($5 \times \frac{2}{3} =$) $3\frac{1}{3}L$; and the $5L$ of labor sold would be then embodied in products with a market value of $7\frac{1}{2}L$.[4]

4. Ricardo later perceived that a distinction must be drawn between the "embodied" and "commanding" approaches to the labor theory. "It was Karl Marx, however—who, as a value theorist, was indeed the last great figure in the classical school—who most

A pure labor theory is applicable only "in that early and rude state of society which precedes both the accumulation of stock and the appropriation of land" (p. 47). In more advanced economies, the price of a commodity is composed partly of profit and of rent, in addition to wages, and the aggregate output is divided among capitalists, landowners, and workers. "Wages, profit, and rent, are the three original sources of all revenue as well as of all exchangeable value" (p. 52).

At a given place and time, there is "an ordinary or average rate" of wages, profit, and rent "in every different employment," and "these ordinary or average rates may be called the natural rates" (p. 55). "When the price of any commodity is neither more nor less than what is sufficient to pay the rent of the land, the wages of the labour, and the profits of the stock employed . . . , according to their natural rates, the commodity is then sold for what may be called its natural price. The commodity is then sold precisely for what it is worth, or for what it really costs the person who brings it to market" (p. 55).

The actual, or market, price is "regulated" by the "proportion" of the quantity of the commodity "actually brought to market" and the "effectual" demand of those "willing to pay the natural price" (p. 56). The (short-run) market price may fluctuate above or below the (long-run) natural price, but powerful market forces tend to bring it to the natural level.

When the quantity of any commodity which is brought to market falls short of the effectual demand, all those who are willing to pay the whole value of the rent, wages, and profit, which must be paid in order to bring it thither, cannot be supplied with the quantity which they want. Rather than want it altogether, some of them will be willing to give more. A competition will immediately begin among them, and the market price will rise more or less above the natural price . . . .

When the quantity brought to market exceeds the effectual demand, it cannot be all sold to those who are willing to pay the whole value . . . . Some part must be sold to those who are willing to pay less, and the low price which they give for it must reduce the price of the whole. The market price will sink . . . .

When the quantity brought to market is just sufficient to supply the effectual demand and no more, the market price naturally comes to be either exactly, or as nearly as can be judged of, the same with the natural price. . . .

If . . . it exceeds the effectual demand, some of the component parts of its price must be paid below their natural rate. If it is rent, the interest of the landlords will immediately prompt them to withdraw a part of their land . . . . The quantity brought to market will soon be no more than sufficient to supply the effectual demand. All the different parts of its price will rise to their natural rate, and the whole price to its natural price (pp. 56–57).

---

clearly pointed out the economic contradictions involved. He tried to restore the labor theory of value by making the value of laboring power (i.e., human effort expended in production) that of the commodities required to support and maintain the laborers and those who were to replace them. . . . Since, however, the laborers expended more units of labor than were embodied in the commodities which they consumed, the balance appropriated by the recipients of rent, interest, and profits was termed by Marx 'surplus value.' The most distinctive feature of Marxian economics comes directly therefore from Smith's confusion between labor-cost and labor-command." Douglas, op. cit., p. 91.

Ricardo

Like Smith, Ricardo distinguishes "value in use" from "value in exchange." Nothing has exchange value unless it is useful, but exchange value is not necessarily in proportion to utility. "Utility then is not the measure of exchangeable value, although it is absolutely essential to it."[5]

While there is a small proportion of commodities which is available only in fixed supply, the value of which "varies with the varying wealth and inclinations" of possible buyers (p. 12), Ricardo is concerned only with commodities which "can be increased in quantity by the exertion of human industry, and on the production of which competition operates without restraint" (p. 12).

Smith had held that prior to capital accumulation and land appropriation, "the proportion between the quantities of labour necessary for acquiring different objects seems to be the only circumstances which can afford any rule for exchanging them." Ricardo agrees that "this is really the foundation of the exchangeable value of all things, excepting those which cannot be increased by human industry" (p. 13). ". . . it is the comparative quantity of commodities which labour will produce that determines their present or past relative value" (p. 17). Thus, as a first approximation, Smith's labor-embodied (but not labor-commanding) theory is accepted.

There is again the question of "different qualities of labour, and the difficulty of comparing an hour's or a day's labour, in one employment, with the same duration of labour in another" (p. 20). But in a manner reminiscent of Smith and presaging Marx, the problem is easily dismissed: "The estimation in which different qualities of labour are held, comes soon to be adjusted in the market with sufficient precision for all practical purposes, and depends much on the comparative skill of the labourer, and intensity of the labour performed. The scale, when once formed, is liable to little variation" (p. 20).

The introduction of capital is not necessarily a complicating factor. For "still the same principle would hold true, that the exchangeable value of the commodities produced would be in proportion to the labour bestowed on their production; not on their immediate production only, but on all those implements or machines required to give effect to the particular labour to which they were applied" (p. 24). Consider two occupations employing the same number of workers. *If* the capitals used require equal amounts of labor to produce, *i.e.*, the ratios of "fixed" capital to labor are the same, and the capitals are equal in durability, changes in the wage rate (which would change equally in both occupations) would not affect relative values — although profits would vary inversely with wages.

---

5. David Ricardo, *On the Principles of Political Economy, and Taxation* (1817; 3rd ed., 1821), in *The Works and Correspondence of David Ricardo*, ed. Piero Sraffa (Cambridge: Cambridge University Press, 1951), I, 11. Unless otherwise indicated, all citations of Ricardo are from this source. Useful reviews are given by Oswald St. Clair, *A Key to Ricardo* (London: Routledge & Kegan Paul, 1957), and by Mark Blaug, *Ricardian Economics: A Historical Study* (New Haven: Yale University Press, 1958).

However, the ratio of fixed capital to the "circulating" capital paid to labor may differ among occupations, fixed capital may differ in durability, and the rates of turnover of circulating capital may differ. These possibilities considerably modify, Ricardo says, the simple labor-embodied theory, for a time element has been thereby introduced into the productive process.

The price of a commodity will be greater, "the greater the length of time which must elapse before it can be brought to market" (p. 34), whether — to review two cases — because (a) of the introduction of fixed capital into the production of the more expensive commodity or (b) of spreading the production process over a longer period.

(a) Suppose that two men each employ 100 laborers each year, but with one in the second year using machines produced in the first year. In the second year, the machine-user must make not only the regular return on the capital used to employ labor, but "a further sum . . . for the profit on" the money "invested in machinery," and consequently his goods must sell for more (p. 34).

Year I: One man employs 100 @ £50 = £5000 to construct a machine; the other employs 100 @ £50 = £5000 to grow corn. At the end of the year, the value of the machine = the value of the corn = £5000 + 10% profit = £5500.

Year II: One employs 100 = £5000 to grow corn, as before; the value of the corn = £5000 + £500 = £5500. The other employs 100 = £5000 plus capital worth £5500 to produce cloth; the value of the cloth = £5000 + £500 + 10% of £5500 = £6050.

"Here then are capitalists employing precisely the same quantity of labour annually on the production of their commodities, and yet the goods they produce differ in value on account of the different quantities of fixed capital, or accumulated labour, employed by each respectively" (p. 34). Thus Ricardo includes the current rate of profit in the costs that price must cover: value is proportionate to the cost of production, including the remuneration of capital as well as of labor.

(b) Goods produced by the same quantity of capital will differ in value if the capital is engaged longer in one case than the other. Suppose that two commodities each require 40 man-years to produce; in one case, 20 men are employed for two years, and in the other 40 men for one year.

Alternative I: Employ 20 @ £50 = £1000 for one year; output = £1000 + £100 = £1100. In the second year, employ 20 = £1000; output = £1100. But in the second year, 10% must be earned also on the investment made in the first year. Total value of output for the two years = £1100 + £1100 + £110 = £2310.

Alternative II: Employ 40 @ £50 = £2000; output = £2000 + £200 = £2200.

Thus "one commodity is more valuable than the other, although no more labour was employed on its production" (p. 37). "In both cases the superior price of one commodity is owing to the greater length of time which must elapse before it can be brought to market. . . . The difference in value arises

264

in both cases from the profits being accumulated as capital, and is only a just compensation for the time that the profits were withheld" (p. 37).

If the rate of profit falls (because of a rise in wages), it will lower the relative values of "all commodities which are produced by very valuable machinery . . . or which require a great length of time before they can be brought to market . . . ." (p. 35). Suppose, in case (a) above, that profits fall from 10 per cent to 9 per cent, thereby making the Year II cloth output equal to £5500 + 9% of £5500 = £5995, while corn still sells for £5500.[6] Here, a rise in wages lowers, absolutely as well as relatively, the value of cloth.

But in analyzing changing relative values, "although it would be wrong wholly to omit the consideration of the effect produced by a rise or fall of labour, it would be equally incorrect to attach much importance to it; and consequently . . . I shall consider all the great variations which take place in the relative value of commodities to be produced by the greater or less quantity of labour which may be required from time to time to produce them" (pp. 36–37). Indeed, "the greatest effects which could be produced on . . . relative prices . . . from a rise of wages, could not exceed 6 or 7 per cent; for profits could not, probably, under any circumstances, admit of a greater general and permanent depression than to that amount" (p. 36).[7]

RICARDO'S DISTRIBUTION MODEL

Ricardo directed his major attention to "the natural course of rent, profit, and wages." "To determine the laws which regulate this distribution, is the

6. The value of corn in both years and the value of the machine constructed in the first year remain at £5500. The amount of labor and of capital employed has not changed, so these values remain the same; the rise in wages is matched by the fall in profits. Since the wage bill plus a variable percentage of the wage bill equals a constant £5500, it is implied that if the profit rate falls from 10 per cent to 9 per cent, then the wage bill rises from £5000 to £5045.9, and profit falls to £454.1. Ricardo does not present all these calculations, and St. Clair's illustration of the point (op. cit., p. 34) appears to be slightly in error.

7. The last passage has inspired Stigler to dub Ricardo's theory as a "93 per cent labor theory of value." But it "is of course a cost-of-production theory." There appears "no basis for the belief that Ricardo had an analytical labor theory of value, for quantities of labor are not the only determinants of relative values. Such a theory would have to reduce all obstacles to production to expenditures of labor or assert the irrelevance or nonexistence of nonlabor obstacles, and Ricardo does not embrace either view. On the other hand, there is no doubt that he held what may be called an empirical labor theory of value, that is, a theory that the relevant quantities of labor required in production are the dominant determinants of relative values. . . . This is not to say that Ricardo's analytical theory was correct, for it contained several important deficiencies. It excluded rent from costs, and even if the supply of land were fixed the rent a piece of land could yield in one use would be a cost to other uses. (Ricardo's practice of assuming that land was used to grow only corn obscured this point.) His theory was wrong in reducing all capital to previously expended labor plus interest; except in some irrelevant day of Genesis all capital has been made by the cooperation of earlier capital and labor and land. This view may have fostered his empirical judgment that labor quantities were decisive, but one could have adopted (wisely or not) the empirical proposition even if he had a correct concept of capital. And of course if all commodities are not produced subject to constant costs, an explanation of relative values that ignores demand is simply inadequate." George J. Stigler, "Ricardo and the 93% Labor Theory of Value," American Economic Review, XLVIII (June 1958), 360, 361–62.

principal problem in Political Economy" (p. 5). But neither Ricardo nor other writers until the "marginalist revolution" beginning in the 1870's looked upon distribution theory as an integral part of price theory, with the determination of the value of productive services being an aspect of the over-all pricing procedure, with the input prices being essential variables in the scheme of market organization and rational production operations, and with the distributive payments in a generalized price system being both costs which must be covered and incomes which are earned when services are sold. Ricardo makes explicit his dichotomy between "value" theory and "distribution" theory: "After all, the great questions of Rent, Wages and Profits must be explained by the proportions in which the whole produce is divided between landlords, capitalists and labourers, and which are not essentially connected with the doctrine of value."[8]

Inadequate and, indeed, peculiar as this approach was, it still is true that Ricardo's analysis of distribution can be presented as a coherent, even if incomplete, model.[9] In its broadest outline, the model first disposes of rent as a differential surplus and then divides the remaining product between wages and profit by calculating wages and treating profit as a residual.

Rent. Land is scarce and nonhomogeneous. "If all land had the same properties, if it were unlimited in quantity, and uniform in quality, no charge could be made for its use, unless where it possessed peculiar advantages of situation" (p. 70). Because of soil differences in fertility and in location relative to the market, the cost of producing a given quantity of agricultural commodities (which is also a given value, for a single market price is assumed to prevail) will vary from place to place. The single price will be just at the level required to cover the greatest cost of production.

The exchangeable value of all commodities . . . is always regulated, not by the less quantity of labour that will suffice for their production under circumstances highly favorable . . . but by the greater quantity of labour necessarily bestowed . . . by those who continue to produce them under the most unfavorable circumstances; meaning — by the most unfavorable circumstances, the most un-

---

8. Letter from Ricardo to J. R. McCulloch, June 13, 1820, in Sraffa, *op. cit.*, 1952, VIII, 194.

In the classical works, "what we find . . . is that the discussions of value theory give, in connection with natural price, a fair indication of the general nature of the organization mechanism and process under price competition, but that the chapters on distribution ignore this reasoning and approach the subject from an entirely different point of view. In other words, the discussion of cost of production in relation to price is in general realistic, even if seriously incomplete, but the writers had little or no comprehension of the fact that the costs of production are identical with the distributive payments— that the two are simply the prices of productive services under different names. In the chapters dealing with distribution, i.e., with the various 'shares,' there is no approach to the subject in terms of competitive pricing or of supply and demand; also, there is little explicit theory of organization, while such organizational theory as is stated or most clearly implied is of another sort than the analysis of allocation and co-ordination of resources through price competition." Frank H. Knight, "The Ricardian Theory of Production and Distribution," *Canadian Journal of Economics and Political Science*, I (May 1935), 173, reprinted in *On the History and Method of Economics* (Chicago: University of Chicago Press, 1956), pp. 63–64.

9. *Cf.* William J. Baumol, *Economic Dynamics* (2nd ed.; New York: The Macmillan Co., 1959), pp. 14–21, and Gerald M. Meier and Robert E. Baldwin, *Economic Development* (New York: John Wiley & Sons, Inc., 1957), pp. 25–39.

TABLE I

Labor-and-	Equal-sized land grades			
capital doses	A	B	C	D
1	40	35	30	25
2	35	30	25	20
3	30	25	20	15
4	25	20	15	10

favorable under which the quantity of produce required, renders it necessary to carry on the production (p. 73).

No rent is paid at the margins of production, but on intramarginal lands rent appears as the price-determined surplus of revenue over cost.

Since price is determined by cost at the margins of cultivation and rent is a pure surplus, "rent is not a component part of the price of commodities" (p. 78). "The value of corn is regulated by the quantity of labour bestowed on its production on that quality of land, or with that portion of capital, which pays no rent. Corn is not high because a rent is paid, but a rent is paid because corn is high" (p. 74).

Figures in Table I are the marginal products (which, of course, is not Ricardo's term) of labor-and-capital, *i.e.*, the additions to total output of one-unit increases in labor-and-capital. Suppose that each input costs $40. If the price of corn is $1, it is feasible to put a dose on land A. If the price rises to $40/35 = $1 1/7, a dose can be put on B (and another dose on A, but Ricardo puts more emphasis on the "extensive" than on the "intensive" margin). But if the price rises to $1 1/7, revenue from the dose on A rises to $45 5/7, giving a rent of $5 5/7. If the price rises to $40/30 = $1 1/3, a dose is put on C; then rent on A rises to $13 1/3, and rent on B appears equal to $6 2/3.

As an economy expands and extends the margins of cultivation, production costs and prices rise, thereby generating additional rent. "The rise in rent is always the effect of the increasing wealth of the country, and of the difficulty of providing food for its augmented population. It is a symptom, but it is never a cause of wealth" (p. 77).

Wages. The long-run "natural" price of labor is "that price which is necessary to enable the labourers, one with another, to subsist and to perpetuate their race, without either increase or diminution" (p. 93). The fluctuating "market" price, which tends to gravitate toward the natural level, is "the price which is really paid for it, from the natural operation of the proportion of the supply to the demand" (p. 94). If the market price exceeds the natural price, the laborers' standard of living rises; population and the number of laborers increase; and wages fall to their natural level. If the market price is below the natural, "the condition of the labourers is most wretched" (p. 94); "privations" reduce their number; thus market price rises.

However, the "market rate may, in an improving society, for an indefinite period, be constantly above" the natural rate (pp. 94–95). The demand for labor is determined by the amount of capital, for "capital is that part of the wealth of a country which is employed in production, and consists of food, clothing, tools, raw materials, machinery, etc., necessary to give effect to labour" (p. 95). Since capital, "the means of employing labour" (p. 98), may for a time increase more rapidly than the supply of laborers, market wages may temporarily rise above the natural level.

The size and the degree of permanence of the differential between market and natural wages is determined in large part by whether more labor is required to produce the consumption goods demanded by the workers.

> In proportion as . . . countries become populous, and land of a worse quality is taken into cultivation, the tendency to an increase of capital diminishes; for the surplus produce remaining, after satisfying the wants of the existing population, must necessarily be in proportion to the facility of production. . . . the land being limited in quantity, and differing in quality, with every increased portion of capital employed on it, there will be a decreased rate of production, whilst the power of population continues always the same (p. 98).

As the demand for labor falls with the declining rate of capital accumulation, wages tend to fall; also, prices of necessaries bought by labor tend to rise, "because more labour will be necessary to produce them" (p. 101). ". . . the labourer would be doubly affected, and would be soon totally deprived of subsistence. Instead, therefore, of the money wages of labour falling, they would rise; but they would not rise sufficiently to enable the labourer to purchase as many comforts and necessaries as he did before the rise in the price of those commodities" (pp. 101–2). (But while real wages would fall, the increase in money wages "would necessarily diminish the profits of the manufacturer; for his goods would sell at no higher price, and yet the expense of producing them would be increased" [p. 102].)

For illustration, assume that the laborer originally spends half of his income on corn and half on other things. Assume that as the price of corn rises, money income rises by an amount enabling the laborer to continue to buy the same quantity of all commodities.[10]

"In proportion as corn became dear, he would receive less corn wages, but his money wages would always increase, whilst his enjoyments, on the above supposition, would be precisely the same. But as other commodities would be raised in price in proportion as raw produce entered in their composition, he would have more to pay for some of them. . . . and there-

---

10. Summarized algebraically, if
a = (constant) amount spent on things other than corn,
P_c = price of corn,
b = (constant) amount of corn purchased,
W = wages,
then
$$W = a + P_c b.$$

TABLE II

With corn at $2.00, he would spend for 5 of corn	$10
and on other things	10
Income (total expenditure)	20
With corn at $2.25, he would spend for 5 of corn	$11.25
and on other things	10
Income	21.25
With corn at $2.50, he would spend for 5 of corn	$12.50
and on other things	10
Income	22.50

fore, even with the above increase of wages, his situation would be comparatively worse" (pp. 103–4).

Profit. The capitalist is a residual claimant: profits are not determined independently, but are equal to total product minus rent and wages. Farms on the no-rent margin always receive the same total receipts as cultivation expands, regardless of diminishing returns to inputs on land. And for intra-marginal farms, since wages and profits are everywhere the same at any given time, total receipts net of rent (*i.e.*, wages plus profits) remain constant: the price of corn rises as the margin is extended, but the addition to gross receipts is siphoned off into rent.

Since total receipts net of rent remain constant and are divided into wages and profits, it follows that an increase in money wages must mean a fall in profits. ". . . profits depend on the quantity of labour requisite to provide necessaries for the labourers [*i.e.*, wages], on that land or with that capital which yields no rent" (p. 126).

Summary of the model. The productivity data of Table III are different from those used in Table I, and they are given for only the extensive margin.

It is assumed, as before, that the worker consumes 5 corn and that at the outset his income is divided equally between corn and other things. If it is assumed further that $P_c = \$2$ and $O = 15$ on Plot I, then T and W follow directly. And since it is assumed still further that $R = 0$ at this price, P also can be deduced, for $P = T - W$ when $R = 0$.

As P_c rises, $P + W$ remains constant, and $R = T - (P + W)$. $P + W$ remains constant not only for Plot I irrespective of P_c, but also for all other plots, for at any given level of P_c, P and W must be uniform for all plots.

The constant $P + W$ can be applied to any plot. Thus, given $P + W$ and O for Plot II, the minimum P_c required to bring II under cultivation equals $(P + W)/O$. Given outputs of 15 and of 12 for Plots I and II, and given the price of $2 initially on I, the price must rise to $2.50 to make feasible the cultivation of II — but, of course, the price rising to $2.50 will increase rent on I. Ricardo's alternative exposition runs: on Plot I, 12 units of output could be produced with $12/15 = .8$ "dose" of input; on II, 12 are produced with 1 dose; the ratio of inputs is $.8/1$, so the price (value) ratio should be the same, *i.e.*, $.8/1 = 2/2.5$.

Suppose, instead, that we are given the new P_c but not O for Plot II. At a price of \$2.50, wages and profits are determined for Plot II (equal at the same price to those on I), and rent is zero on II. These together give T and imply O (*i.e.*, $O = T/P_c$).

The "net" T is always \$30, which also is "total" in no-rent cases, *i.e.*, net $T = $ total $T - $ rent. As cultivation is extended and the price of corn rises, the level of money wages (but not real income) rises, profits therefore progressively fall, and aggregate rent increases. ". . . profits depend on high or low wages, wages on the price of necessaries, and the price of necessaries chiefly on the price of food . . . . The natural tendency of profits then is to fall; for, in the progress of society and wealth, the additional quantity of food required is obtained by the sacrifice of more and more labour" (pp. 119, 120).

In our illustration, by the time that the price of corn reaches \$4, all of the "net" receipts go into wages, and "there must be an end of accumulation; for no capital can then yield any profit whatever, and no additional labour can be demanded, and consequently population will have reached its highest point. Long indeed before this period, the very low rate of profits will have arrested all accumulation . . . ." (p. 120).

THE CLASSICAL THEORY OF INTERNATIONAL TRADE

The classical economists were perhaps at their best in international trade theory. In the century since John Stuart Mill, the labor (or 93 per cent labor) theory of value has been abandoned, as has the classical approach to distribution. But international trade theory as left by Mill remained essentially untouched until after World War I, and even during the past forty years developments in this area have been more supplemental than destructive: the classical structure, modified a bit and elaborated considerably, still stands.[11]

Smith

Adam Smith did not advance formal international trade theory, but his was a powerful voice in opposition to mercantilism and in preparing the way for more liberal commercial policies.

In criticism of what he deemed to be the view of the mercantilists, Smith asserts that "it would be too ridiculous to go about seriously to prove, that wealth does not consist in money, or in gold and silver; but in what money purchases, and is valuable only for purchasing" (p. 406).

Consumable commodities, it is said, are soon destroyed; whereas gold and silver are of a more durable nature, and, were it not for this continual exportation,

---

11. See James W. Angell, *The Theory of International Prices* (Cambridge: Harvard University Press, 1926); Jacob Viner, *Studies in the Theory of International Trade* (New York: Harper & Brothers, 1937); Chi-yuen Wu, *An Outline of International Price Theories* (London: G. Routledge & Sons, Ltd., 1939).

TABLE III

Plot	Price (Pc)	Output (O)	Receipts (T)	Profit (P)	Wages (W)	Rent (R)
I	$2.00	15	$30.00	$10.00	$20.00	$ —
	2.50		37.50	7.50	22.50	7.50
	3.00		45.00	5.00	25.00	15.00
	3.50		52.50	2.50	27.50	22.50
	4.00		60.00	—	30.00	30.00
II	2.50	12	30.00	7.50	22.50	—
	3.00		36.00	5.00	25.00	6.00
	3.50		42.00	2.50	27.50	12.00
	4.00		48.00	—	30.00	18.00
III	3.00	10	30.00	5.00	25.00	—
	3.50		35.00	2.50	27.50	5.00
	4.00		40.00	—	30.00	10.00
IV	3.50	8.57	30.00	2.50	27.50	—
	4.00		34.28	—	30.00	4.28
V	4.00	7.5	30.00	—	30.00	—
Total	2.00	15	30.00	10.00	20.00	—
I–V	2.50	27	67.50	15.00	45.00	7.50
	3.00	37	111.00	15.00	75.00	21.00
	3.50	45.57	159.50	10.00	110.00	39.50
	4.00	53.07	212.28	—	150.00	62.28

might be accumulated for ages together, to the incredible augmentation of the real wealth of the country. . . . We do not, however, reckon that trade disadvantageous which consists in the exchange of the hard-ware of England for the wines of France; and yet hardware is a very durable commodity, and were it not for this continual exportation, might too be accumulated for ages together, to the in-credible augmentation of the pots and pans of the country (pp. 407–8).

He agrees with Hume's position (but does not improve upon Hume's exposition) that a nation in the ordinary operations of the market gets the amount of money, like other commodities, that it requires, and it cannot retain a greater amount. Whether a country grows richer or poorer depends not on the balance of trade, but on "the balance of the annual produce and consumption." A favorable balance of production over consumption can exist in a country entirely separated from the rest of the world or it "may be constantly in favor of a nation, though what is called the balance of trade be generally against it" (p. 464).

Smith recognized possible reasonable exceptions to the free trade rule: there is the national defense argument for protection of key industries, com-pensatory import duties may avoid penalizing domestic producers, possibly retaliation against high foreign tariffs can be an effective bargaining device, and difficulties can arise if existing duties are reduced too rapidly. But the emphasis of Smith is on the advantages of unfettered commerce. Extension of the market through foreign trade permits greater productivity: "the nar-rowness of the home market does not hinder the division of labour in any particular branch of art or manufacture from being carried to the highest perfection" (p. 415). All nations would "find it for their interest to employ their whole industry in a way in which they have some advantage over their neighbors" and import from each other (p. 424). "If a foreign country can supply us with a commodity cheaper than we ourselves can make it, better buy it of them with some part of the produce of our own industry, employed in a way in which we have some advantage" (p. 424).

The principal benefit from foreign trade, Smith concludes, is that "it carries out that surplus part of the produce of their land and labour for which there is no demand among them, and brings back in return for it something else for which there is a demand. It gives a value to their super-fluities, by exchanging them for something else, which may satisfy a part of their wants, and increase their enjoyments" (p. 415).

Ricardo

Prior to the nineteenth century, significant answers had not been given to the questions of what goods a nation opening international trade would find it advantageous to export and to import and on what terms it would ex-change its exports for the goods imported. Robert Torrens (1780–1864) early contributed to the discussion of both questions, but the writers gener-ally and properly associated with these issues are Ricardo and John Stuart Mill.

The flow of trade, *i.e.*, the international pattern of specialization, is determined by *comparative* costs, according to Ricardo, not by *absolute* costs, as suggested by Smith: a nation may profitably import goods which it could itself produce with a lower labor cost than can the exporting nation if its efficiency in making exportable goods, with which the imports are bought, is relatively greater still.

Suppose, Ricardo wrote, that it requires the labor of 100 men for one year to produce a given amount of cloth and the labor of 120 for the same period to produce a certain quantity of wine in England, whereas in Portu-gal it requires 90 man-years to produce the same amount of cloth and 80 man-years to produce an equal quantity of wine. Portugal produces more output per laborer of both cloth and wine, but it is mutually advantageous to the two countries for Portugal to specialize production on, and export, wine, receiving cloth from England. Portugal would thereby benefit by getting for the labor of 80 men what it would have cost her the labor of 90 to produce domestically; and England, giving cloth for wine, would obtain for the labor of 100 men what it would cost her 120 to produce domestically.

Since Ricardo assumed a 1:1 trading ratio, or terms of trade, between the respective quantities of cloth and of wine, his position on the proximate basis of trade is that a country will export that commodity (*a*) in which it has a comparative advantage, (*b*) provided that it can produce that com-modity more cheaply than it could produce its import good. If, for example, cloth still cost 100 man-years and wine 120 in England but cloth cost 80 and wine 90 in Portugal, *i.e.*, if *each* country could produce cloth at less cost than it could produce wine, trade would not be mutually beneficial. If England got the product of 120 men at a cost of 100, Portugal would get at a cost of 90 what she could have produced domestically at a cost of only 80; or if Portugal got the product of 90 men at a cost of 80, England would have to pay 120 for what she herself could produce for 100.

Mill

Mill follows Ricardo in adopting the principle of comparative advantage, from the consideration of which "we perceive in what consists the benefit of international exchange."[12]

Setting aside its enabling countries to obtain commodities which they could not themselves produce at all; its advantage consists in a more efficient employment of the productive forces of the world. . . . The produce of the whole world would be greater, or the labour less, than it is, if everything were produced where there is the greatest absolute facility for its production. But . . . while the labour and capital of a country remain in the country, they are most beneficially employed in producing . . . the things in which it lies under the least disadvantage, if there be none in which it possesses an advantage (p. 578).

The gains of a more efficient use of resources lie immediately in the gaining of imports, not in the disposing of "surpluses."

The only direct advantage of foreign commerce consists in the imports. A country obtains things which it either could not have produced at all, or which it must have produced at a greater expense. . . . Adam Smith's theory . . . was that it afforded an outlet for the surplus produce of a country. . . . The expression, surplus produce, seems to imply that a country is under some kind of necessity of producing the corn or cloth which it exports; so that the portion which it does not itself consume, if not wanted and consumed elsewhere, would either be produced in sheer waste, or if it were not produced, the corresponding portion of capital would remain idle. . . . Exportation ceasing, importation to an equal value would cease also, and all that part of the income of the country which had been expended in imported commodities, would be ready to expend itself on the same things produced at home, or on others instead of them (pp. 579–80).

Mill's illustration of comparative advantage runs in terms of differential outputs obtained with given labor inputs. Suppose that 10 yards of broadcloth cost in England as much labor as do 15 yards of linen, and in Germany a certain amount of labor can produce either 10 yards of broadcloth or 20 yards of linen. As in Smith's beaver-deer example, in long-run competitive equilibrium the physical transformation, or substitution, ratios in the two countries give the respective domestic exchange ratios: without for-

12. John Stuart Mill, *Principles of Political Economy* (1848; 7th ed. 1871), ed. Sir W. J. Ashley (London and New York: Longmans, Green & Co., 1929), p. 578. Unless otherwise indicated, all citations of Mill are from this source.

eign trade, in England 10 yards of broadcloth trade for 15 yards of linen, and in Germany 10 yards of broadcloth exchange for 20 of linen.

If trade is opened, England will export broadcloth, and Germany will export linen. The terms of trade will lie within the limits of the respective domestic ratios, for England has no incentive to trade unless she receives at least 15 yards of linen in exchange for 10 of broadcloth, and Germany will pay no more than 20 of linen. Instead of *a* particular terms of trade, as Ricardo assumed, there is a *range* of possible terms.

The terms of trade, which will be common to both countries, will be determined by "the Equation of International Demand," which is "but an extension of the more general law of value, which we called the Equation of Supply and Demand" (p. 592). The market-clearing principle is stated: "The produce of a country exchanges for the produce of other countries, at such values as are required in order that the whole of her imports may exactly pay for the whole of her imports" (p. 592; see also p. 587).

. . . all trade, either between nations or individuals, is an interchange of commodities, in which the things that they respectively have to sell constitute also their means of purchase: the supply brought by the one constitutes his demand for what is brought by the other. So that supply and demand are but another expression for reciprocal demand: and to say that value will adjust itself so as to equalize demand with supply, is in fact to say that it will adjust itself so as to equalize the demand on one side with the demand on the other (p. 593).[13]

THE CLOSE OF THE CLASSICAL PERIOD: JOHN STUART MILL

It is not quite correct to say that the classical system of economic analysis came to term with John Stuart Mill, since J. E. Cairnes (1823–1875) endeavored to strengthen weak points in the system, and since the stamp of the classical approach remained on economic science, particularly prior to the 1930's. Mill was, however, the last great expositor of the system, though of one sufficiently modified to lead some incorrectly to infer that Mill was not a classical economist, or of one sufficiently unmodified in essentials to prompt others to conclude that Mill had made no contributions. Suffice it to say that Mill, in his *Principles of Political Economy* (1848), undertook to take account of newer developments in economics and sociology and bring the work of Smith and of Ricardo up to date. In the course of this undertaking he made a number of specific contributions, several of which appeared in his earliest writings.[14] These were incorporated into economic science, even though the period succeeding his death saw the ascension of

13. The equilibrium terms of trade at a given time are determined by the relative positions of the "reciprocal demand" schedules; changes in the terms are determined by the shifts and elasticities (or "extensibilities," in Mill's term) of the schedules. Mill's laborious exposition was put forth geometrically later by Alfred Marshall (1842–1924) and by Francis Y. Edgeworth (1845–1926). For a more recent discussion, see William R. Allen, "The Effects on Trade of Shifting Reciprocal Demand Schedules," *American Economic Review*, XLII (March 1952), 135–40.

14. George J. Stigler identifies a half-dozen in "The Nature and Role of Originality in Scientific Progress," *Economica*, XXII (November 1955), 296–99.

marginal analysis which he little appreciated, believing the theory of value settled.

Here we may point to the main contributions that Mill made in addition to giving a somewhat new and more systematic form to the economics of Smith and Ricardo. (1) Mill's treatment of reciprocal demand has already been noted. (2) Mill expressed demand and supply in substantially functional terms (though less precisely than did Cournot) and in his analysis of price formation took account of elasticity (pp. 446–48, 594–96). (3) He improved the theory of value, translating it into money terms (p. 488) and taking into account both the fact that rent is a cost of production when land can be put to alternative use (pp. 475, 479) and the fact that the prices of jointly produced products, though dominated by demand, must in combination cover the joint costs of these products (p. 570). (4) He improved the treatment of economic mobility, showing with his theory of noncompeting groups how intergroup barriers generate wage differences (p. 393), and demonstrating in his treatment of external trade and capital movement, that some of this traffic was town-country in character whereas some of it was not (pp. 685–86). (5) Mill was alert to the presence of economies of scale, to their manifestation in terms of interfirm differences in fortune, and to the significance of these economies for the future of joint-stock and other forms of business organization suited to the needs of firms or industries in which these economies obtained (Bk. I, Chap. 9). (6) Mill drew attention to the fact that functional distribution might not be governed entirely by the forces of competition, as when custom affected rents (pp. 242–45), and the fact that, even in the absence of complete monopoly, retail and possibly other prices might be partly dominated by custom and hence be only imperfectly governed by competition (pp. 245–48, 415–16, 440–41). What Mill described as the impact of custom upon pricing was in part, however, only the impact of what has since been connoted by such expressions as "monopolistic competition."

(7) While Mill underestimated the utilizability of capital and exaggerated the tendency of the return on capital to fall toward a zero-saving level, he did recognize, more clearly than had his classical forebears, the extent to which migration, capital exports, and commodity imports might increase the income-producing and population-supporting capacity of an advanced country like England (Bk. IV, Chap. 4). (8) In the theory of economic development that runs through his *Principles*, Mill stresses the importance of noneconomic as well as of economic factors (*e.g.*, pp. 189–90), assesses the role government might play, and gives contingent support to infant-industry protectionism whilst emphasizing its possibly bad effect (p. 922).

(9) Mill's treatment of Say's Law illustrates the care with which he endeavored to reason. Thus, he distinguished between barter and "interchange by means of money" and pointed out, much as did careful neoclassical writers,[15] that in the latter situation the sale of a good for money may not

15. See, *e.g.*, F. M. Taylor, *Principles of Economics* (New York: The Ronald Press Co., 1925), Chap. 15.

be succeeded immediately by the exchange of this money for a good, with the result that sales and purchases may not immediately balance unless money itself is "considered as a commodity."[16] Mill indicated, however, that the outcome depended in part on whether commodity money or credit was envisaged by the analyst. If the money in use were a commodity, with its value governed by the forces which govern the value of other commodities, a general oversupply of commodities could not develop. If, however, credit money were used, there might result a temporary excess of commodities in terms of money.[17]

16. John Stuart Mill, *Essays on Some Unsettled Questions of Political Economy* (London: John W. Parker, 1844), pp. 68–71; also *Principles,* Bk. III, Chap. 14.
17. See Bela A. Balassa's detailed paper, "Mill and the Law of Markets," *Quarterly Journal of Economics,* LXXIII (May 1959), 263–74.

10.

EMIL KAUDER
Illinois Wesleyan University

Genesis of the

Marginal Utility Theory

From Aristotle to the

End of the

Eighteenth Century

Several times the history of the marginal utility theory had to be re-written. The triumvirate Jevons, Menger, Walras knew only Gossen as their forerunner. To-day we recognise that the analysis of subjective elements in economic valuation starts with Aristotle. He begins a trend of thought whose traces abound in the writings of the Middle Ages, the Renaissance and the enlightenment. French, Italian and Swiss authors of the enlighten-ment have so perfected this analysis, that it might have been possible dur-ing the time of Adam Smith to base a system of political economy entirely on marginal utility calculation. To prove this claim a short history of the utility theory from Aristotle to Galiani and Bernoulli is presented on the following pages.[1]

It is generally accepted that Aristotle was the first who created the con-

Reprinted from *The Economic Journal*, LXIII (September 1953), 638–50, by permission of the author and The Royal Economic Society.

cept of the value in use. That he had a far-reaching knowledge of this field is generally unknown. Only Oskar Kraus of Prague, who was a student of Aristotle and of the Austrian school of economics, presented a complete picture of the Aristotelian thoughts, which show similarities with the Austrian theories of much later date.[2] Economic goods, as Aristotle pointed out, derive their value from individual utility, scarcity and costs. If the amount of goods is increasing the value decreases and can even become negative.[3] Aristotle had at least some knowledge of the law of diminishing utility.[4] Even Menger's theory of imputation based on loss calculation (Verlustgedanke) can be found in Aristotle, as Oskar Kraus has pointed out. Aristotle claimed in the *Topics* — a work not often read by economists — that the value of one good can be judged best if we lose or add it to a given group of commodities. The greater the loss which we suffer from a destruction of this good, the "more desirable" is this commodity. Also, the more we gain by the addition of a thing, the higher is its value. The context makes it quite clear that Aristotle applies his argument to economic goods (example of the pruning-hook and the saw in the *Topics*). Menger and Böhm-Bawerk used the same reasoning. Whether they read the *Topics* could not be found out.[5]

So Aristotle's economic thinking already contained a number of concepts which have since become important elements in the marginal utility theory. Yet for the next 1,600 years these thoughts were not used. It was not before A.D. 1200 that growing complications of market forms and the discussion of the just price forced the medieval doctors to handle, at least partly, the Aristotelian instruments. The philosophers in the thirteenth and fourteenth centuries, Thomas Aquinas, Henry of Ghant, Johannes Buridanus, two great theologians of the counter-reformation in the sixteenth and seventeenth centuries, Louis de Molina and Leonardus de Lessius (de Leys) and even the two Protestant authorities of natural law during the seventeenth century, Hugo de Groot (Grotius) and Samuel von Pufendorf claim often with the same words that the value of a commodity is determined by utility and scarcity.[6] They all follow their master, Aristotle, and they do not present any essential new ideas. They are not interested primarily in a more exact explanation of economic valuation but in the presentation of a very complicated casuistry of the just price, for which their value discussion forms a preface. Their value theories are a mixture of costs and subjective values, of objective prices and valuations. Utility is more often than not the general welfare of a community and not the specific pleasure of an individual. The medieval doctors had not improved the utility concept, but it was their great merit to keep alive the Aristotelian theory and his discussion about value. Their works and those of their teacher, Aristotle, were read by the Italian and French economists of the seventeenth and eighteenth centuries, who presented the first essential progress since Aristotle.

Between the schoolmen and this new group stands Gian Francesco Lottini (fl. 1548), who was discovered by Augusto Graziani.[7] Lottini, an Aristotelian scholar, shady politician and gang leader of a Venetian murder ring to boot,[8] writes at the end of his colorful life a vade-mecum for a prince.

Lottini's work "Avvedimenti civili," inspired by Machiavelli's "I Principe," contains a number of shrewd political observations which are loosely strung together by the social philosophy of his great Greek teacher.[9] Lottini writes as an elderly statesman, not as an economist; he touches economic subjects only incidentally. But even so, he mentions economic principles of great importance. Lottini's point of departure is the traditional Aristotelian dichotomy between the common good (il ben publico) and the goods serving individual needs (bene in particulare).[10] Common welfare and individual well-being, so explains Lottini, are not identical, but are related to each other. The common good is the foundation of the citizen's personal welfare; e.g., if the citizen loses his property he can get it back with the help of the state.[11] Private needs are satisfied with goods; these goods produce pleasure. His explanation of pleasures is typical for the transition between medieval and modern thinking. He moralises like a schoolman and he analyses like a modern scientist at the same time. We feel pleasure by satisfying our needs, which are wants of food and of sex.[12] In satisfying our appetites, moderation, regulated by reason, is advisable. Reason should make men different from beasts.[13] Unfortunately too many people do not find a limit for their insatiable appetite.[14] Man does not even pay enough attention to his future, *he overrates his present needs,* because he follows his senses which reveal his present wants, and not his reason with which he may plan for the future.[15] Behind the moralist Lottini is the shrewd observer of human foibles who almost discovers the infinity of wants and who knows about the underestimation of future wants.[16] Like Molière's Monsieur Jourdan, who did not know that he was speaking prose, Lottini apparently was not aware of the fact that he was dealing with economic subjects; neither was this seen by his many readers. So it is understandable that not he but his younger contemporary Davanzatti started the Italian school of economists.

Davanzatti and his followers, especially Montanari and Galiani, formed a school, because they had a common principle (the Aristotelian value in use) and a common program (the application of this principle to other economic subjects). Davanzatti[17] and, following him almost verbatim, Montanari[18] explain the value of money on a completely subjective basis. Money reflects the value of commodities. ". . . tant' altre cose vale, tant oro vale . . ."[19] (Davanzatti). The young Abbé Galiani, one hundred years after Montanari, finds a new formulation of the value theory, and presents a subjective theory of distribution.[20] Value is defined as a ratio between utility and scarcity. With the decrease of scarcity, utility falls and vice versa. The ratio between utility and scarcity does not only explain the value of consumer goods but also the value of productive factors, especially labor. The value of labor is determined by the peculiar utility and scarcity of the special kind of labor in demand. Talents and geniuses are much higher paid than the common laborer, because Nature produces and matures only a small number of able men. Generally speaking, according to Galiani, it is not labor costs which determine value, but rather value which determines labor costs. 150 years after Galiani, Böhm-Bawerk reached a very similar conclusion. Galiani's theory of interest has a strong resemblance to the explanation presented by the Austrian economist. Interest, so the young abbé claims, is the difference between present and future money. Galiani must have found this theory independently, he knew some of his forerunners, especially Davanzatti, but he had not read Lottini.[21]

Galiani developed an economic theory based entirely on subjective estimation. The outlines of his system are still valid to-day. Yet one problem is only touched and not satisfactorily explained, price.[22] The French economist and statesman, Anne Robert Turgot, who accepted Galiani's value theory, filled this empty spot in an unfinished paper: "Valeurs et Monnaies."[23] Turgot uses a simplified model for the explanation of the exchange mechanism. Two men are living on an isolated island, one, A, has maize, the other, B, owns kindling wood.[24] A freezes to death if he has no kindling wood, and B is starving if he has only wood, but no food.[25] A is willing to barter his maize for kindling wood and B likes to exchange his wood for maize. Both plan to keep a maximum of their own commodity and to get a maximum of the other's good.[26] A wants to give 3 measures of maize for 6 armfuls of wood and B wants to exchange 6 armfuls of wood for 9 measures of maize. Since these personal estimations cannot be realised in exchange, A and B have to give more of their own product and/or to demand less from the other. Eventually a point of agreement is reached, where the individual value of the offered good is still lower than the value of the commodity received. If the exchange rate is 4 measures of maize to 5 armfuls of kindling wood, A prefers 5 armfuls of kindling wood to 4 measures of maize, and B prefers 4 measures of maize to 5 armfuls of kindling wood.[27] If we have two wood-collectors instead of one and two maize-owners instead of one the situation will be essentially not different from the isolated exchange between two persons. If one maize-owner tries to undersell the other, the two who stored up wood will turn to him and raise his price. As in the case of an isolated exchange, the result will be one rate for all barters between the four partners.[28] According to Turgot, both exchange models prove that barter leads to a higher total utility for each partner than isolated production of one single commodity.[29] Any reader acquainted with our literature knows that Turgot's explanation is almost identical with the theory of isolated exchange presented by Menger and by Wicksell.[30]

With Galiani and Turgot subjective valuation becomes the keystone for a method of thinking. This theory had to be defended against the new classical system, which was based on labor costs. The defense of Galiani, his followers, and his friends was taken over by Condillac.[31] According to him, costs are not the cause of value, but the value is the cause of costs.[32] Condillac's counter-attack against the classical cost theory is the parting shot of an army falling back. Before 1800 Italian and French writers were already drawn into the orbit of British classical thinking. An attempted synthesis of utility value and cost theory was the main object of later Italian writers.[33] Yet before decadence set in they had thoroughly explored the utility concept and its consequences, although they were still not able to explain the value of a concrete unity. Galiani can easily show why gold is normally more

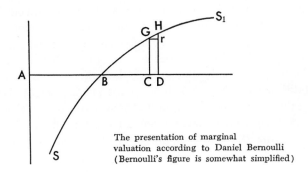

The presentation of marginal
valuation according to Daniel Bernoulli
(Bernoulli's figure is somewhat simplified)

valuable than bread. Yet why one slice of bread has the same value as another slice, why one ounce of gold has the same value as another ounce
cannot be calculated with the help of Galiani's instruments.

No doubt the Italian economists were often near the correct solution,
but they did not reach it.[34] They cannot grasp it, because they lack the
marginal method.

The first step in the exploration of the marginal value had been taken
outside the camp of the economists proper. In 1738, twelve years before
Galiani's work was published, the mathematician Daniel Bernoulli, writing
mainly about games of chance, isolated the theory of marginal value, especially the value of money.[35] In exploring marginal value Bernoulli assumes
that a fortune will be increased by successive small increments.[36] Given
these conditions, it is very likely, so he continues, that the value of an additional amount is inversely proportional to the pecuniary possessions which
a person already owns.[37] Consider that one person, so Bernoulli continues,
has a fortune of 100,000 ducats and draws from it an income of 5,000
ducats, and another poorer person has a fortune of 100,000 half-ducats, and
draws from it an income of 5,000 half-ducats, then for the wealthier person
one ducat is worth as much as one half-ducat for the poorer person.[38] This
is indeed a bold conclusion, which can be drawn only if an interpersonal
measure for the utility reaction of different persons can be discovered.
Whether such a common standard can be found is still an open question.

Obviously the law of diminishing utility[39] is not only basic to this interpersonal comparison but also to Bernoulli's very important mathematical
analysis, which explains individual estimations. In Bernoulli's chart, the
fortune of a person is represented on the abscissa starting in A; the value
of gains is represented by the ordinate. A person starts with the fortune
AB. To this fortune will be added the amount BC; the utility of this additional amount is presented by the segment BG of the curve SS. Now an
infinitely small amount of money is added, CD. The additional value of CD
is Hr. Hr is the marginal utility of CD.[40] So Daniel Bernoulli combines the law of decreasing utility with the higher calculus and discovers
the marginal utility.[41] Similar ideas can be found in Buffon[42] and Laplace.[43]

Neither Buffon nor Laplace, during the end of the eighteenth century and the beginning of the nineteenth century, essentially improved Bernoulli's discovery. The most important author in this group is undoubtedly Bernoulli. But even he cannot offer a complete analysis of marginalism; he finds the marginal value, but he does not see that the marginal value is identical with the individual values of all the other pieces in a group of equal commodities. Even so, his achievements are important. He, like his French and Italian contemporaries, added new parts to the slowly emerging structure of a subjective value theory. How far all these writers had progressed in solving the riddle of marginal utility can be seen from the following table:

1. Value is dependent on utility and scarcity. (Adopted from Aristotelism and Thomism by Davanzatti, Montanari, Galiani, etc.)

2. Essential for economic valuation is the concrete and not the abstract utility. (Galiani in opposition to the Doctors.)

3. Concrete utility is determined by the law of diminishing utility. (Mentioned earlier by Aristotle but much more clearly expressed by Davanzatti, Montanari, Galiani, etc.)

4. The value of the last piece is the marginal utility. (Bernoulli.)

5. Utility and scarcity decide not only the value of consumer goods but also the value of the factors of production. The consumer's choice is the final factor of economic action. (Galiani, Condillac.)

6. Prices are the outcome of individual comparison between goods. (Turgot.)

So the Italo-French school has gone a long way from the teaching of the Doctors, and even Aristotle is surpassed at least in some respects. Yet it was the tragedy of these writers that they wrote in vain, they were soon forgotten. No scholar appeared to make out of these thoughts the new science of political economy. Instead, the father of our economic science wrote that water has a great utility and a small value. With these few words Adam Smith had made waste and rubbish out of the thinking of 2,000 years. The chance to start in 1776 instead of 1870 with a more correct knowledge of value principles had been missed.

NOTES

1. Main publications about the prehistory in chronological sequence:

Achille Loria, *La Teoria del Valore negli economisti Italiani*, Bologna, Garagni, 1882. (Reprint from *Archivo Giuridico*.) This short paper has an outspoken Marxian bias.

Augusto Graziani, *Storia critica della teoria del valore in Italia*, Milano, U. Hoepli, 1889. The best collection of material concerning the Italian period. (Quoted *Storia critica*.)

Idem, "Le idee economiche degli scrittori Emiliani e Romagnoli sino al 1848," *Memorie della Regia Academia de Scienze, Lettere ed Arti in Modena*, Serie IIme, Volume X, pp. 431 *et seq.* Modena, 1893. (Quoted *Le idee economiche . . .*)

Hannah Robie Sewall, "The Theory of Value before Adam Smith," *Publications of the American Economic Association*, Third Series, Vol. II, no. 3, August 1901.

Rudolf Kaulla, *Die geschichtliche Entwicklung der modernen Werttheorien*,

Tübingen, Lauppsche Buchhandlung, 1906.

Otto Weinberger, *Die Grenznutzenschule*, Halberstadt, Meyer's Buchdruckerei, 1926.

2. See Dr. Oskar Kraus, "Die Aristotelische Werttheorie in ihren Beziehungen zu den Lehren der modernen Psychologenschule," *Zeitschrift für die gesamte Staatswissenschaft*, Tübingen, Lauppsche Buchhandlung, Volume 61, 1905, pp. 573 *et seq.* As late as 1940 Kraus' investigations were neglected by Edmund Whittaker, *A History of Economic Ideas*, New York, Longmans, Green & Co., 1940, p. 65. Whittaker apparently read only the *Politics* and the *Nicomachean Ethics*, but he did not pay any attention to the other works, especially the *Topics*, one of the main sources of Kraus' information.

3. "External goods, like all other instruments, have a necessary limit of size. Indeed, all things of utility (including the goods of the body as well as external goods) are of this character; and any excessive amount of such things must either cause its possessor some injury, or, at any rate bring him no benefit." Aristotle, *Politics*, VII, I, p. 1323, b. 7 (Sir Ernest Barker's translation), quoted in Kraus, *op. cit.*, p. 582.

4. Kraus, *ibid.*, and Whittaker, *op. cit.*, p. 65.

5. To justify his claim Kraus quotes from Aristotle, Menger, and Böhm-Bawerk (Kraus, *op. cit.*, pp. 584, 585). A complete English version of these quotations is given here.

"Moreover, judge by the destruction and losses and generations and acquisitions and contraries of things: for things whose destruction is more objectionable are themselves more desirable. Likewise also with the losses and contraries of things; for a thing whose loss or whose contrary is more objectionable is itself more desirable. With the generations or acquisitions of things the opposite is the case: for things whose acquisition or generation is more desirable are themselves desirable." Aristotle, *Liber Topicorum*, Book III, ch. 2, ¶8, p. 117 a (translation W. A. Pickard-Cambridge; from the works of Aristotle, Ross ed., Oxford).

"Again, a thing is more desirable if, when added to a lesser good, it makes the whole a greater good. Likewise, also you should judge by means of subtraction: for the thing upon whose subtraction the remainder is a lesser good may be taken to be a greater good, whichever it be whose subtraction makes the remainder a lesser good." Aristotle, *op. cit.*, Book III, ch. 3, ¶ 11, 12, p. 118 b.

"The value of one concrete commodity of higher order [producers' goods—E. K.] is identical with a difference of valuation, in which the higher value is determined by the want satisfaction created by a combination of goods of higher order including the concrete good in question and the lower value by the want satisfaction created by the same combination of goods of higher order without this concrete good." Carl Menger, *Grundsätze der Volkswirtschaftslehre*, Second edition, Vienna, Hölder-Pichler-Tempsky, 1923, p. 157.

"Value judgements take place mainly at two occasions: first if we dismiss a commodity from our fortune, *e.g.*, either by making a present or by bartering or by consumption; second if we acquire a commodity to increase our fortune. . . . A commodity which is already in our hands will be appraised according to the *loss* which we suffer by giving it away. . . . A commodity which is still in our hands will be valued in the opposite way according to the *increase of utility* which its acquisition brings." Eugen von Böhm-Bawerk, "Grundzüge der Theorie des wirtschaftlichen Güterwerts," *London School of Economics and Political Science. Series of Reprints of Scarce Tracts in Economic and Political Science*, reprinted from "Jahrbücher für Nationalökonomie und Statistik," *Neue Folge*, Vol. 13, p. 33, footnote 2.

Kraus, *op. cit.*, compares this Böhm-Bawerk quotation with his first quotation from the *Topics*. The resemblance is rather far-reaching.

6. For this period the following works have been used:

Hugo de Groot, *De Jure Belli ac Pacis libri tres*, Reproduction of the edition of 1646, Carnegie Institute of Washington, 1913, especially liber II, ch. 12, ¶ XIV, pp. 232, 233.

Samuel Pufendorf, *De Jure Naturae et Gentium*, Vol. I, Frankfurt and Leipzig, 1769, 5th book, ch. I, ¶ 4.

V. Brants, "L'économie politique et sociale dans les écrits de L. Lessius," *Revue d'histoire ecclésiastique*, Vol. XIII, No. 1, Louvain, January 1912.

Dr. Edmund Schreiber, "Die volkswirtschaftlichen Anschauungen der Scholastik seit Thomas v. Aquin," *Beiträge zur Geschichte der Nationalökonomie*, Vol. I, Jena, Fischer, 1913, pp. 69, 70 *et passim*.

George O'Brien, *An Essay on Medieval Economic Thinking*, London, Longmans, Green & Co., 1920.

Selma Hagenauer, "Das 'justum pretium' bei Thomas von Aquino. Ein Beitrag zur Geschichte der objektiven Werttheorie," Beiheft 24 zur *Vierteljahrsschrift für Sozial- und Wirtschaftsgeschichte*, Stuttgart, Kohlhammer, 1931. The author is of the opinion that Aquinas has only an objective theory of value. According to my thinking this is a rather one sided opinion.

W. Seavey Joice, S. J., *The Economics of Louis de Molina* (Doctoral thesis, typescript), Harvard, November 1948. The thesis contains in the appendix a translation of Molina's value theory.

All the writers mentioned in the text and in this footnote use often the same words for the determination of the value in use: *Buridanus:* "Valor rerum aestimatur secundum humanam indigentiam. . . . " "Nihil est bonum nisi propter causas finales; . . . Sed supplementum videtur mensurari per indigentiam; majoris enim valoris est supplementum quod majorem supplet indigentiam." George O'Brien, *op. cit.,* pp. 109, 110.

Antonius of Florence determines value by three factors, virtuositas, raritas and placibilitas. George O'Brien, *ibid.*

Thomas Aquinas explains subjective value from the working together of "indigentia" and the "diversitas copiae et inopiae." Edmund Schreiber, *op. cit.,* pp. 43, 57.

Leonardus Lessius. "Indigentia humana" and "necessitas" or "inopia" determine economic value. V. Brants, *op. cit.,* p. 85.

Hugo de Groot: "Indigentia" and "copia." Hugo de Groot, *op. cit.,* Grotius does not quote here the schoolmen, but it is very likely that he knew them.

Samuel Pufendorf, op. cit., explains value in the same way as Hugo de Groot.

7. Graziani, *Storia critica,* pp. 29, 30.

8. About Lottini's somewhat unsavory character see Cecily Booth, *Cosimo I, Duke of Florence,* Cambridge, England, at the University Press, 1921, pp. 131, 132, 199. Despite his reputation, he was known to the great historian Francesco Guicciardini. Exact dates about Lottini's life could not be acquired. He was secretary to Cosimo I, de Medici, Duke of Florence in 1548.

See also *La Bibliofilia,* Rivista dell'-arte, Firenze, 1909, Vol. 10, 1908–9, p. 368. About his style see Bartolomeo Gamba da Bassano, S*erie dei Testi di Lingua,* Venezia, Gondoliere, 1839, Sec. xvi, p. 441, first column.

9. Shortly after Lottini's death several editions of his work were printed.

Gian Francesco Lottini da Volterra, *Avvedimenti Civili,* Al Serenissimo D. Francesco Medici Gran Duca di Toscana, In Firenze, Nella stamperia di Bartolomeo Sermatelli, 1574. (In Houghton library, Cambridge, Mass., quoted *Avvedimenti,* edition Florence.)

PROPOSITIONI OVERO CON- SIDERATIONI in materia di cope di stato sotto titolo di Auuertimenti, Auuedimenti, Civili & Concetti Politici, di M. Francesco Guiccardini, M. Gio [sic E. K.] Francesco Lottini M. Francesco Sansovini, In Vinegia, Presso Altobello Salicato, 1588, Alla Libraria della Fortezza. (Also in Houghton library quoted *Avvedimenti,* edition Vinegia.) This copy belonged once to the English poet and theologian John Donne (1573–1631), whose marginal notes in ink stressed the connection between Lottini and Aristotle. The Houghton library also has an edition of 1583, of which the edition of 1588 is a reprint.

Lottini . . . *Avvedimenti Civili* . . . In Venetia, Fabio & Agostino Zopini, 1582.

(Rare book-room University library of the University of Illinois, Urbana-Champaign, quoted *Avvedimenti Civili,* edition Venice.)

All editions are identical in text and in paragraphs, but not in spelling and in pagination. The pagination is in folio.

10. Folio 17, v, ¶ 60, edition Venetia. Folio 82, ¶ 178, edition Florence. For full quotation see next footnote.

11. "Il vero bene di ciascuna cosa, la quale sia parte d'un altra, non consiste in se stessa, ma hà il fondamento, in quell'altra, di cui essa è parte." (If a thing is a part of another thing, it has no true value in itself, but its value is established by that other thing of which it is a part (*my translation*) —i.e., the individual good is a part of the common welfare and has therefore no value in itself.) The personal or individual good "sta posto, e fondato nel ben publico della Città. . . " (is based and founded on the common welfare of the state (*my translation*). If anything dangerous happens to the private goods. . . "possono tutta via sperare di potersi con l'aiuto del publico ageuolmente riauere." (There is hope that one can regain these goods easily with the help of the state (*my translation*). All quotations from edition Florence, Folio 82, ¶ 178.

12. ". . . il mangiare & le cose de Venere. . . " (Folio 128, ¶ 278).

13. ". . . il piacere in ciò non dee passar la misura, . . ." (Folio 87, ¶ 188, edition Florence)—pleasure ought to be moderate (*my translation*). In pleasure-seeking ". . . se non da colore, che non sanno far differenza dell'essere huomo all essere bestia. . . " (Folio 43, v, ¶ 187, edition Vinegia)—do not pretend that there is no difference between man and animal.

14. "Jo ho conosciuti molti, che sono stati insaziabili nel domàdaré . . ." (Folio 70 r, ¶ 195, edition Venice)—I have known many whose demand could not be satisfied.

15. "Ben che le cose future da gl'-huomini saui antiuedute habbiano chiari ssime ragione da douer succedere nel modo, che s'antiueggono, tutta via, perche le presenti sono dinàzi à gl'occhi, esi tocanno quasi cõ mano, ell haño hauuto nõ poche volte forza di tirarei medisimi huomini saui à pigliar piùtosto la più uicina sodisfazzione, che aspettare la lõtana, . . ." Folio 91 r, ¶ 260, edition Venice)—Future things, as far as they can be foreseen by wise men, have the clearest reason to happen all the time in the way in which they have been foreseen. In spite of it the present, which is before our eyes and which can, so to speak, be grasped with our hands, has forced, more often than not, even wise men to pay more attention to the nearest satisfaction than to hope for the far future.

The reason, according to Lottini, is that one pays more attention ". . . di ciò che il senso uede, che di quanto può far conoscere per uia di ragione, . . ." (Folio 91, v, ¶ 260, edition Venice)—to those things which one sees with his senses than to those which one can learn by reason.

See also "Di maniera, che pochi son quelli che delle deliberazione lunghe, e pericolose vogliano ostenatemēte vederne il fine" (Folio 70, v, ¶ 196, edition Venice) —Only a few people follow a long-lasting and risky project stubbornly to its end.

16. Graziani's valuable discovery of the *Avvedimenti* is somewhat marred by misunderstandings. Graziani claims that Lottini made all economic actions dependent from needs. ". . . Che i bisogne sono il primo motore delle azione economiche . . ." (Graziani, *Storia critica*, p. 29). This is not quite correct because, as an Aristotelian, Lottini believes that pleasure-seeking should be restrained by moderation and reason, which, according to the author of the *Avvedimenti*, are the final rules of human action. Furthermore, Graziani asserts that Lottini has discovered the infinite character of needs. "Egli afferma che la soddisfazione d'un bisogno determina tosto il sogerne d'un altro. . ." (Graziani, *ibid.*)—He [Lottini] claims that after one want is satisfied another soon will come into existence (*my translation*). As I had pointed out before, Lottini had never characterized the interplay of want and satisfaction exactly in such a way. Lottini is rather inclined to consider the infinite character of needs as a moral aberration.

17. Bernardo Davanzatti (1529–1606) was a merchant, an economist, a famous translator of Tacitus, an historian of the English reformation, he became, when seventeen years of age (1547), a member of the Florentine Academy. He is a typical representative of the Counter-reformation, a man of great classical erudition and at the same time a stern Catholic. This religious attitude is strongly expressed in his *Dello Schisma d'Inghilterra* (About the English Reformation). See Enrico Bindi ed., *Le opere di Bernardo Davanzatti*, Florence, Monnier, 2 vols., 1852. Besides Bindi the following works about Davanzatti were used:

Gino Arias, "Les précurseurs de l'économie monétaire en Italie: Davanzatti et Montanari," *Revue d'économie politique*, 1922, p. 733 *et seq.*, especially p. 736.

18. Geminiano Montanari (1633–87), Professor at Bologna and later at Padua. See Gino Arias, "Les précurseurs," *op. cit.* The following work of Montanari was used: Geminiano Montanari, "Della Moneta," Trattato Mercantile, *Scrittori Classici Italiani de Economia Politica*, Parte antica, Vol. III, Milano, Destefanis, pp. 43–5, 58 *et seq.* The work was originally published in 1683 under the title: LA ZECCA IN CONSULTA DI STATO (Money in the Affairs of Government). It was republished with the original title in *Economisti del Cinque e Seicento*, Augusto Graziani, ed. Bari, Laterza, 1913.

19. As much as other things are worth, as much value has gold. Davanzatti, *op. cit.*, p. 33. Gold is here used figuratively in the sense of money.

20. Ferdinando Galiani (1728–87), *Della Moneta*. (First anonymous edition of 1750 or 1751 was not in my hands.) I used the edition of Fausto Nicolini, Bari, Laterza, 1915, and the English translation of Arthur Eli Monroe, *Early Economic Thought*, Cambridge, Harvard Press, 1945, pp. 281 *et seq.* (quoted Monroe). The outstanding economist Galiani was in his younger days, when he wrote his treatise on money, a fervent Catholic. Later in Paris he became a Voltairian wit and free-thinker. He has attracted the attention of many writers. From the abundant literature the following papers were used:

S. G. Tallentyre, *The Friends of Voltaire*, New York, G. P. Putnam's Sons, 1907. See especially "Galiani the Wit," pp. 62 *et seq.* Fausto Nicolini, editor, *Il Pensiero del Abate Galiani*, Bari, Laterza, 1909, pp. 3 *et seq.*

Wilhelm Eduard Biermann, "Der Abbé Galiani als Nationalökonom, Politiker und Philosoph nach seinem Briefwechsel," *Volkswirtschaftliche und Wirtschaftsgeschichtliche Abhandlungen* (Essays in honour to the 60th birthday of Wilhelm Stieda), Leipzig, Veit, 1912, pp. 168 *et seq.*

Fausto Nicolini, "Giambattista Vico e Ferdinando Galiani," *Ricerca Storica. Giornale Storico Della Letteratura Italiana*, Vol. LXXI (10 semestre 1918), pp. 142 *et seq.*

Gino Arias, "Ferdinando Galiani et les Physiocrates," *Revue des sciences politiques*, Vol. XLV (1922), pp. 346 *et seq.*

Louise Sommer, "Abbé Galiani und das physiokratische System," *Zeitschrift für Volkswirtschaft und Sozialpolitik*, Neue Folge, Vol. V, p. 341.

Graziani, *Storia Critica*, pp. 100 *et seq.*

21. "Value, then, is a ratio; and this is compounded of two ratios, expressed by the names UTILITY and SCARCITY." Galiani, *Moneta, op. cit.*, translation Monroe, p. 283.

"I believe that the value of human talents is determined in the very same way as that of inanimate things, and that it is regulated by the same principles of scarcity and utility combined." Galiani, *Moneta*, translation Monroe, p. 292.

"Be it noted, however, that scarcity is not to be reckoned according to the proportion in which talents are produced, but according to the numbers that reach maturity; hence the greater difficulty of developing a talent to a high degree worthy of it, the greater is the price." Galiani, *Moneta*, translation Monroe, *ibid.*

"Hence arose exchange and interest, which are brothers. One is the equalizing of present money and money distant in space, made by an apparent premium, which is sometimes added to the present money, and sometimes to the distant money, to make the intrinsic value of both equal, diminished by the less convenience or the greater risk. Interest is the same thing done between present money and money that is distant in time, time having the same effect as space; and the basis of the one contract, as of the other, is the equality of the true intrinsic value." Galiani, *Moneta*, translation Monroe, p. 302.

22. Galiani only says that "price follows scarcity." Monroe, p. 297.

23. Anne Robert Jacques Turgot, Baron de L'Aulnes (1727–81), "Valeurs et Monnaies," *Oeuvres de Turgot*, ed. Daire, Vol. I, Paris, Guillaumin, 1844, pp. 72 *et seq.* See also *Oeuvres de Turgot*, ed. Gustave Schelle, Paris, Alcan, 1919, "Valeurs et Monnaies," Vol. III, pp. 79 *et seq.* The following quotations are all from the Schelle edition. R. Schelle considers it possible that Turgot wrote the paper about 1769. It should be published in Abbé Morellet's dictionary: *Dictionnaire du Commerce*. A prospectus of this dictionary was published in 1769. The dictionary itself was never finished. See Schelle, p. 79 footnote (*a*).

24. Turgot, ed. Schelle, pp. 89 *et seq.* I have added the letters A and B for the sake of simplification and clarification.

25. ". . . mais le bois que l'un pourra consommer dans un mois lui deviendra fort inutile si, dans cet intervalle, il meurt de faim faute de maïs, et le possesseur du maïs ne sera plus avancé, s'il est exposé à périr faute de bois; . . ." Turgot, ed. Schelle, p. 90.

26. "c'est l'intérêt de garder chacun le plus qu'il peut de sa denrée, et d'acquérir le plus qu'il peut de celle d'autrui." Turgot, *ibid.*

27. "Au moment où l'échange se fait, celui qui donne, par exemple, quatre mesures de maïs pour cinq brasses de bois, préfère sans doute ses cinq bras aux quatres mesures de maïs; il leur donne une valeur estimative superieure; mais, de son côté, celui qui reçoit les quatre mesures de maïs les préfère aux cinq brasses de bois." Turgot, *ibid.*, p. 91.

28. Turgot, ed. Schelle, pp. 97, 98.

29. "Il est bon d'observer ici que l'introduction de l'échange entre nos deux hommes augmente la richesses de l'un et de l'autre, c'est-à-dire leur donne une plus grande quantité de jouissances avec les mêmes facultés. Je suppose, dans l'exemple de nos deux sauvages, que la plage qui produit le maïs et celle qui produit le bois soient éloignées l'une de l'autre. Un sauvage seul serait obligé de faire deux voyages pour avoir sa provision de maïs et celle de bois; il perdrait, par conséquent, beaucoup de temps et de fatigue à naviguer. Si, au contraire, ils sont deux, ils emploieront, l'un à couper du bois, l'autre à se procurer du maïs, le temps et le travail qu'ils auraient mis à faire le second voyage. La somme totale du maïs et du bois recueilli sera plus forte et, par conséquent, la part de chacun." Turgot, ed. Schelle, p. 93.

30. Carl Menger, *op. cit.*, pp. 186 *et seq.* Knut Wicksell, *Lectures on Political Economy*, translated by E. Classen, London, Routledge, 1946, Vol. I, p. 49.

31. Etienne Bonnot de Condillac, Abbé de Mureaux (1714–80), "Le commerce et le gouvernement," *Oeuvres complètes de Condillac*, Vol. IV, Paris, Houel, Year VI (1798). Condillac, *Oeuvres philosophiques*, Vol. I, Texte établi et représenté par George Le Roy. Corpus Général des Philosophes Français, Publié sous la direction de Raymond Bayer, Paris, Presse Universitaire de France, 1947, "Traité des sensations" (1754), pp. 221 *et seq.*

32. "Une chose n'a pas une valeur, parce qu'elle coûte, comme on le suppose; mais elle coûte parce qu'elle a une valeur." Condillac, *Oeuvres complètes, op. cit.*, pp. 14, 22.

33. Graziani, in his *Le idee economiche*, mentions the following Italian economists of the beginning of the nineteenth century: Francesco Isola, Melchiorre Gioia, Adeodati Ressi, Carlo Bosselini and Giovanni Romagnosi, who try to combine, in one way or another, utility value with cost theory.

34. Very clearly expressed by A. Carino Canina, who praises the clearness and exactness of Montanari's thinking, yet Canina knows very well that Montanari never touches the marginal principle. ". . . senza pero, che si acceni al principio marginalista." A. C. Canina, "Valore e rarita nel pensiero di G. Montanari," *Istituto Lombardo di Scienza e Lettere*, Milano, Vol. LXXVII, 1943–44, p. 166, footnote 1.

35. Daniel Bernoulli, *Versuch einer neuen Theorie der Wertbestimmung von Glücksfällen*. Edited by A. Pringsheim under the title "Die Grundlage der modernen Wertlehre," Brentano und Leser, *Sammlung älterer und neuerer staatswissenschaftlicher Schriften des In- und Auslandes*, No. 9, Leipzig, 1896. (Original edition and title "Specimen Theoriae Novae de Mensura Sortis" 1738, not used.) About Daniel Bernoulli see *Allgemeine Deutsche Biographie*, Vol. II, Leipzig, 1875, p. 478, Daniel Bernoulli (N. Cantor.)

36. Bernoulli, *Versuch, op. cit.*, p. 27, ¶5.

37. "Valde probabile est lucrulum quodvis semper emolumentum afferre summae bonorum reciproce proportionale," Bernoulli, ¶5, see "Die Grundlage," *op. cit.*, p. 13.

38. Bernoulli, ¶6, "Die Grundlage," *op. cit.*, p. 30.

39. It is probable, but it cannot be proven, that his residence and studies in Italy brought him in contact with econo-

mists who taught him the elements of economic value.

40. Bernoulli, ¶7, "Die Grundlage," *op. cit.*, p. 32.

41. For this reason I cannot agree with Schumpeter's remark that Thünen was the first who used "the calculus as a form of economic reasoning." Joseph A. Schumpeter, "Review of the Troops," *Quarterly Journal of Economics*, Vol. LXV, May 1951, p. 151.

42. Buffon, "Essai d'arithmétique morale," *Oeuvres complètes*, 12th vol., Paris, s.d., pp. 155 *et. seq.*, especially pp. 168–9. Buffon discussed the problem apparently about the same time that Daniel Bernoulli wrote his essay, *ibid.*, p. 170, and footnote p. 171.

43. Pierre Simon, le Marquis de Laplace, *Essai philosophique sur les probabilités*, Paris, 1825.

11.

H. M. ROBERTSON
University of Cape Town

W. L. TAYLOR
University College of Rhodesia and Nyasaland

Adam Smith's

Approach to

the Theory

of Value[1]

I

It has been powerfully argued by Dr. Emil Kauder that "the analysis of subjective elements in economic valuation starts with Aristotle," and that "French, Italian and Swiss authors of the enlightenment have so perfected this analysis, that it might have been possible during the time of Adam Smith to base a system of political economy entirely on marginal utility calculation."[2] We are not, of course, attempting any kind of assessment of Dr. Kauder's learned case, but aim only at calling attention to two points of contrast concerning Adam Smith's treatment of value. These points come at such a vital turning-point in the history of economic thought that they deserve more emphasis and examination in the many discussions of Smith's fundamental ideas than they have hitherto received.

First, there is the contrast between Smith's treatment of value and that of his Scottish predecessors, Gershom Carmichael and his teacher Francis Hutcheson; and secondly, there is the contrast between Smith's own treatment in his *Lectures* of 1762–63 and that in the *Wealth of Nations*. The

Reprinted from *The Economic Journal*, LXVII (June 1957), 181–98, by permission of the authors and The Royal Economic Society. At the time of original publication, Professor Taylor was with the University of Cape Town.

doctrines on value taught by "the never-to-be-forgotten Dr. Hutcheson" had come from Puffendorf via Gershom Carmichael. Before Puffendorf these ideas can be traced back through Grotius to the Aristotelian tradition. Hutcheson's treatment of value anticipates not so much the more one-sided utility theory of Jevons and Menger, but rather the well-balanced, dual, "both-blades-of-the-scissors" analysis of Marshall. Whether or not Smith did know, or could have reasonably been expected to explore, much of the relevant writings of Davanzatti, Montanari, Galiani, Turgot, Condillac and Bernoulli (set out so illuminatingly by Dr. Kauder), the ideas of Puffendorf, Carmichael and Hutcheson were fully at his disposal to build on had he wished. It is interesting to see to what extent Smith, in the *Wealth of Nations,* chose to alter decisively the emphasis of his approach to value at the expense of the ideas of scarcity and usefulness stressed by Hutcheson (and to some extent by Smith himself in his *Lectures* in 1762–63) in the direction of a one-sided, almost exclusive emphasis on labour and cost of production.

Puffendorf's brief discussion of value lays direct emphasis on the two basic elements of usefulness and scarcity,[3] fundamental concepts which were clearly indicated and transmitted by Puffendorf and his Scottish followers to Adam Smith.

Puffendorf's ideas on value came to Hutcheson via Gershom Carmichael (1672(?)–1729), Hutcheson's teacher and immediate predecessor in the Glasgow Chair of Moral Philosophy, and the first professorial occupant of that most celebrated of chairs. Carmichael translated Puffendorf's *De Officio* into Latin and added a critical expository commentary in footnotes. Hutcheson himself said that Carmichael was "by far the best commentator" on Puffendorf and that "the notes are of much more value than the text."[4] To the brief chapter on value Carmichael adds some half-dozen notes, including some of the greatest acuteness, which show a clear and masterly grasp of the various fundamental elements of the value problem, as, for example, in the following summary:

"In general we may say that the value of goods depends on these two elements, their *scarcity* and the *difficulty of acquiring them.* . . . Furthermore, scarcity is to be regarded as combining two elements, the number of those demanding (the good) and the usefulness thought to inhere in the good or service and which can add to the utility or pleasure of human life."[5]

In another note Carmichael lays further emphasis on the subjective element by pointing out that the usefulness or "aptitude," which is an essential constituent of value, may be real or imagined (p. 249).

Hutcheson's teachings on value follow very closely those of Puffendorf, as further sharpened and developed by his almost forgotten teacher, Carmichael. These ideas have not been completely neglected, since Edwin Cannan quoted two or three paragraphs on the subject from the *Introduction to Moral Philosophy* (1747).[6] But Hutcheson's brief treatment deserves considerably more attention than it has yet received, both for its own sake and as a contrast to the treatment of Adam Smith in the *Wealth of Nations.*

Hutcheson's fullest discussion comes on pp. 53–5 of Volume II of his *System of Moral Philosophy* (1755):

"The natural ground of all value or price is some sort of *use* which goods afford in life; this is prerequisite to all estimation. But the prices or values in commerce do not at all follow the real use or importance of goods for the support, or natural pleasure of life. . . . When some aptitude to human life is presupposed, we shall find that the prices of goods depend on these two jointly, the *demand* on account of some *use* or other which many desire, and the *difficulty* of acquiring, or cultivating for human use."

"Use" is defined by Hutcheson as:

"Not only a natural subserviency to our support, or to some natural pleasure, but any tendency to give any satisfaction, by prevailing custom or fancy, as a matter of ornament or distinction."

"Difficulty of acquiring" is explained in terms of scarcity as:

Not only a great labour, or toil, but all other circumstances which prevent a great plenty of the goods or performances demanded. . . . Price is increased by the rarity or scarcity of the materials in nature, or such accidents as prevent plentiful crops of certain fruits of the earth; and the great ingenuity and nice taste requisite in the artists to finish well some works of art, as men of such genius are rare. The value is also raised, by the dignity of station in which according to the custom of a country, the men must live who provide us with certain goods, or works of art."

Hutcheson summarised as follows:

"When there is no *demand*, there is no price, were the *difficulty* of acquiring never so great; and were there no *difficulty* of labour requisite to acquire, the most universal *demand* will not cause a price; as we see in fresh water in these climates. Where the demand for these two sorts of goods is equal, the prices are as the difficulty. Where the difficulty is equal, the prices are as the demand" (italics supplied).

This discussion aims at drawing attention to some significant contrasts with Smith's treatment of value in the *Wealth of Nations*. The famous explicit treatment of utility and value, consisting of the single paragraph on "value-in-use" and "value-in-exchange," appears in Book I, Chapter IV. This brief discussion is rounded off by a lengthy elaboration of a labour and cost of production analysis and of a labour standard of value ("utility" or "value-in-use" having been dismissed from the scene). Various other aspects of value theory are touched on in passing, for example, in Book I, Chapters V, VI and VII. Again in Chapter II, Part II, in discussing the prices of the precious metals, Smith states that the demand for them arises partly from their utility, and partly from their beauty, and mentions that the qualities of utility, beauty and scarcity are the basis of the high prices of the precious metals. But unlike his immediate Scottish predecessors, who placed the term and concept of scarcity in a central and dominant position in their treatment of value, Smith, in these few digressions from his definitive treatment of value, includes the idea of scarcity implicitly, but not explicitly.

(*a*) In contrast with Hutcheson's emphasis on "some sort of use" being "a natural ground of all value or price," Smith lays it down (Book I, Chapter 4) that "utility" or "value-in-use" is *not* a necessary ingredient of exchange value, since things "which have the greatest value in exchange have frequently little or no value in use" (or "utility"), *e.g.*, diamonds.[7]

(*b*) Whereas Carmichael and Hutcheson by "use" or "usefulness" meant something closely similar to the concept of utility as required and employed in modern value theory (*i.e.*, power to satisfy any kind of want, "real" or "imagined," basic or ornamental), Smith, in the *Wealth of Nations*, resorts to a narrower ethically tinged sense of "utility" (according to which diamonds have little or no utility).

(*c*) While Smith makes only passing reference to the fundamental term "scarcity" and makes no reference to it at any critical point in his discussion of value, both the term and the concept of scarcity (or "difficulty") had a very central place in the chapters of Puffendorf and Hutcheson and had been very clearly emphasised in the two sentences of Carmichael.[8]

The broad general influence of Hutcheson on Smith seems generally to have been assumed, or even sometimes explicitly stated, to cover their ideas on value, as for example, when Smith's distinguished biographer, John Rae, wrote that Hutcheson's "remarks on value contain what reads like a first draft of Smith's famous passage on value in use and value in exchange."[9] It is suggested, on the contrary, that the texts justify us in suggesting that the differences, as they stand, have far more fundamental implications than any similarities, and that these differences are all the more crucial considering that we are surely here at a major turning point in the history of economic thought.

II

In the light of this first contrast between Hutcheson's ideas on value and those of the *Wealth of Nations* some further examination and emphasis may be appropriate regarding the contrast between Smith's treatment of value in the *Lectures* of 1762–63 and his definitive treatment in the *Wealth of Nations*.[10] The second contrast is based on two passages in the *Lectures:*

(*a*) The two opening sections of the division of the *Lectures* devoted to political economy are entitled (by Cannan) *Of the Natural Wants of Mankind* and *That all the Arts are subservient to the Natural Wants of Mankind.* Cannan points out that there is nothing corresponding to these two sections at the beginning of, or later on in, the *Wealth of Nations*, though almost all the other important sections of this part of the *Lectures* match up with the opening chapters in the *Wealth of Nations*. He wrote —

"It is not easy to explain why the first two sections were omitted from the *Wealth of Nations,* and the fact will be regretted by those who ask for a theory of consumption as a preliminary to the other parts of political economy."[11]

From the opening sentences Smith links his general subject of *Cheapness* and *Plenty* ("or, which is the same theory, the most proper way of procuring wealth and abundance"), directly with the ideas of plenty and scarcity; and like Puffendorf and Hutcheson, and unlike his own later positive treatment in the *Wealth of Nations,* Smith introduces this fundamental concept into his explanation of the water-and-diamonds paradox.

"It is only on account of the plenty of water that it is so cheap as to be got for the lifting; and on account of the scarcity of diamonds (for their real use seems not yet to be discovered) that they are so dear."[12]

Moreover, Smith in this opening section is mainly concerned to point out that most of the production of a community, when any considerable division of labour has developed, is for meeting not basic "natural" wants but those springing from the love of variety or delicacy of taste, on account of which gems of diamonds, for example, are "much esteemed by us," though iron is far "more useful."

Certainly these two opening sections in the *Lectures* are, at most, general discussions of "wants and their satisfactions," yet surely their presence marks a most significant contrast with what has often not unreasonably been construed to be the one-sided general emphasis on labour and production in the *Wealth of Nations.*

(*b*) The second point of contrast relates to Section 7 (in this division of the *Lectures*), *What Circumstances regulate the Price of Commodities,* as compared with the corresponding Chapter VII in the *Wealth of Nations* on natural and market price. In this chapter we are simply told about market price that it —

"is regulated by the proportion between the quantity which is actually brought to the market, and the demand of those who are willing to pay the natural price."[13]

We are given no further word of explanation or analysis of "demand" beyond that we are to understand by "demand," "effectual demand" and not the "absolute" demand which a poor man might have for a coach and six (*ibid.*). While Puffendorf, Carmichael and Hutcheson explicitly put the term and concept of scarcity in a crucial and vital place in their analysis Smith makes no direct reference to "use" or usefulness, and only includes the concept of scarcity in an implicit fashion, *e.g.* —

"A competition will immediately begin among them, [buyers] and the market price will rise more or less above the natural price, according as either the greatness of the *deficiency,* or the wealth . . . of the competitors happened to animate more or less the eagerness of the competition. Among competitors of equal wealth and luxury the same *deficiency* will generally occasion a more or less eager competition, according as the acquisition of the commodity happens to be of more or less importance to them."[14]

These ideas of scarcity and utility are basically essential for any satisfactory treatment of value theory; yet Smith tended to turn away from them and emphasise the role of labour.

In the *Lectures* we are given three determinants of market price:

"First, the demand, or need for the commodity. There is no demand for a thing of little use; it is not a rational object of desire.

Secondly, the abundance or scarcity of the commodity in proportion to the need of it. If the commodity be scarce, the price is raised, but if the quantity be more than is sufficient to supply the demand, the price falls. Thus it is that diamonds and other precious stones are dear, while iron, which is more useful, is so many times cheaper, though this depends principally on the last cause, viz.: —

Thirdly, the riches or poverty of those who demand" (p. 176).

The *Lectures* do not go further on this subject than these headings. But the explicit presence of these ideas, the perceptive connection and lucid linking together in a basic and fundamental explanation of utility, scarcity and demand (in the manner of Hutcheson and Carmichael) may be held to mark a certain contrast with the treatment devoted to this problem in the *Wealth of Nations*.

In direct contradiction with the famous statement in the *Wealth of Nations*, it is noteworthy in the above passage that diamonds in fact have, and must have, considerable "use" from the fact of their being demanded, and very much demanded, since their price is raised thereby above the price of iron, in spite of the latter being "more useful" (*i.e.*, having a greater total utility). It has been noted above that Smith had previously held that no "real use" had yet been discovered for diamonds, so his treatment of use and utility appears somewhat inconsistent in the *Lectures*. But Smith here is inconsistently *right*, and we prefer economists who are inconsistently right to those who are consistently wrong.

It would be dangerous to lay much much store on the precise wording of the ideas presented in the *Lectures*, and it is quite impossible (as Scott argued against Cannan) to conclude from the omission of a subject or idea from the *Lectures* that it had not occurred to, or been treated by, Smith in 1762–63. But the approach to and ideas on value of the Aristotle-Puffendorf-Carmichael-Hutcheson tradition are all explicitly, if not so very compactly and consistently, set out in the *Lectures*, and it can at least be safely assumed that they are not the invention of a note-taker. In fact, according to Scott,[15] it can be assumed that Smith probably gave them a much fuller treatment than is apparent from the text of the notes.[16]

Referring to Smith's treatment in the *Wealth of Nations*, Dr. Kauder concludes his review of seventeenth- and eighteenth-century utility theorists with the following judgment on Smith:

"Yet it was the tragedy of these writers that they wrote in vain, they were soon forgotten. . . . Instead, the father of our economic science wrote that water has a great utility and small value. With these few words Adam Smith had made waste and rubbish out of the thinking of 2,000 years. The chance to start in 1776 instead of 1870 with a more correct knowledge of value principles had been missed" (p. 650).

These are rather strong words, and in spite of the tantalising anticipations before 1776 of modern utility theory to which Dr. Kauder (from post-1870 hindsight) has been able to refer, it may still appear an unreasonably harsh judgment. But Smith certainly did know the ideas on value of Hutcheson and Carmichael, which also had roots two thousand years old in Aristotle, and had, in fact, expounded them in his *Lectures*.

If the above quotation from the *Lectures* (p. 176) on demand, use and scarcity had appeared in the text of the *Wealth of Nations*, and if, on the other hand, the famous paragraph in the *Wealth of Nations* on value-in-use and value-in-exchange (where it is suggested that utility is *not* a necessary prerequisite of value-in-exchange) had occurred in the *Lectures*, then it could be undoubtedly claimed that, at this point, the *Lectures* give a garbled and incomplete account of Smith's ideas. It could also be pointed out that the correct and definitive account could be found, where one would expect to find it, in the *magnum opus* which took him so long to write. But as it is, the "correct and definitive" treatment comes second-hand from much abbreviated notes of earlier lectures, and the garbled and incomplete version in the finished *magnum opus*. It seems that there may always remain a certain rather fascinating aura of mystery as to why the most crucial elements in these ideas were hidden in the background of the *Wealth of Nations* almost as though by some deliberate process of censorship.

If one is an upholder of the labour theory of value one can wholeheartedly applaud the new and different emphasis Smith adopted in the *Wealth of Nations* in his treatment of the fundamentals of value. But if one considers that the ideas of scarcity and "usefulness" are basic and essential for any satisfactory treatment, or if one even defines the subject-matter of economic science in terms of the scarcity concept, then there can be only regret for Smith's new emphasis given with such vastly influential consequences in the *Wealth of Nations*, which led on to at least a serious underemphasis on, and, at times, to the almost complete eclipse of, these ideas in British political economy for nearly a hundred years.[17] Smith's treatment of value appears as a profoundly consequential divagation from the main path of European thinking, a divagation very many of the steps in which had subsequently to be retraced.

III

It is one thing to pose a problem in the transmission of ideas; but it is another and most unsatisfactory thing to leave it as an unsolved problem. Dr. Kauder attempts no solution of the problem of why Adam Smith "made waste and rubbish out of the thinking of two thousand years" — if one excludes the cheap corollary that it must be because Adam Smith was neither as learned nor as perceptive as Dr. Kauder himself. But, as has been shown above, the pupil of Francis Hutcheson and the lecturer of 1762–63 could hardly make use of the bluff Johnsonian *riposte*, "Sir, it was pure ignorance."

It is, of course, rather hard to saddle so unoriginal and derivative a writer as the Adam Smith of this Schumpeterian age with making waste of so many years of effective thought with these few words: "water has a great utility and a small value."[18] For these few words are indeed even more than second-hand. The contrast also goes backwards almost 2,000 years in the history of thought; the very phrasing is an echo of the same illustration given by John Law in 1705,[19] and the same way of putting it is shared not only by Francis Hutcheson, who taught him, but even by Samuel Puffendorf, who was put forward by Dr. Kauder as a model whom Adam Smith would have done well to follow.

"Those things are of the least account or Value [remarked Puffendorf] without which Human Life is least able to subsist; and therefore not without the most singular Providence of Almighty God, *Nature* has been very *bountiful* in providing *plentiful* store of those things. [But] the wanton Luxury of Mankind has set *extravagant Rates* upon many things . . . which Humane life might very well be without, for instance upon *Pearls* and *Jewels*."[20]

Admitting all the myopia with which Smith may have viewed the proposition, it is difficult to sustain that by adopting it he was discarding the valuable traditions of 2,000 years. He used few words because he was merely echoing something he regarded as traditional, trite and obvious, and, in doing so, can hardly be accused of drawing a fresh curtain of his own devising over a long tradition of price theory based on utility.

It might be remembered that Von Wieser himself treated this "paradox of value" with considerably more respect. Indeed, he started his great work on *Natural Value* by pointing out that it would appear obvious to any intelligent business-man, as it did to the early theorists, that the value of things was derived from their utility. But facts, including the paradox that "things which have a great deal of use have often a smaller value than those which have little use," showed that this conclusion was not so obvious, after all, but on the contrary, "as often and as strikingly, that value is in agreement with the exact antithesis of use — namely with costs."

As a result, Von Wieser pointed out, for a long time many of the best writers on value refused to consider utility as the source of value, but asserted that the value of goods comes from the difficulty of their attainment and is proportionate to it. On the other hand, most of those who have based their theory on utility have been manifestly unsatisfactory:

"They have either placed themselves in contradiction to the facts . . . without explaining away the contradiction, or laid so much stress on these facts that, in the end, they can scarcely be distinguished from those writers who have rejected the principle of utility, except by their express avowal of that principle."[21]

One could hardly deny that Daniel Bernoulli, as early as 1738, had made an attempt — in the diagram and accompanying explanation given by Dr. Kauder — to give geometrical representation to the use of the differential calculus to represent the diminishing marginal utility of additions to a man's fortune. But it is done upon the basis of an assumption concerning the relationship between this marginal utility and the size of the man's existing fortune which is purely arbitrary (viz., inverse proportionality), and his geometry does no more than illustrate the assumption. Adam Smith would not have flinched from the interpersonal comparison or from the assumption that the marginal utility of an addition to (or, at any rate, subtraction from) the greater fortune was less than that of a similar addition to the smaller fortune.[22] But he was certainly suspicious enough of the Political Arithmetician to distrust the spurious trick of pretending to give precise measurement to what was mere assumption.

It is not immediately apparent from Bernoulli's explanation (as there given) that the relative curve SS_1 in the diagram (SS in the text) represents, as it must, the total utility derived from additions to a basic fortune; its shape depends upon the particular — and unconvincing — assumption made, and it surely postulates a good deal of post-1870 hindsight to read into this apparently rather inadequately explained diagram what we are told Adam Smith might have built upon in 1776.

The marginal-utility analysis which was developed after 1870 was an analysis applied to the problem of individual values, on the basis of different quantities of individual commodities already possessed or different rates of acquisition of commodities. There is no hint that Bernoulli's purely formal illustration of what can be interpreted as a particular rate of diminishing marginal utility of money can be applied to the problem of individual prices. Moreover, on a straightforward interpretation of the wording given, Bernoulli's discovery would seem to have taken place in the course of a piece of reasoning which assumes implicitly that the total utility of 100,000 ducats is the same as the total utility of 50,000 ducats![23] It is true that, with post-1870 hindsight we can interpret otherwise the statement "then for the wealthier person one ducat is worth as much as one half ducat for the poorer person." But the obvious pre-1870 reading would have been that Bernoulli's "worth" of each ducat or half-ducat was something capable of addition to give this surprising result; only since 1870 could the more sophisticated reading be generally adopted, that it means only "marginal utility" and that summation is impossible.

When Adam Smith is blamed for not building out of these thoughts the new science of political economy, the question surely arises whether one could have expected him to build upon a foundation of such arrant nonsense as this last supposition must at the time have appeared to be. But why did he not, in the *Wealth of Nations*, build upon his own earlier propositions that the market price of a commodity was based on:

"First, the demand, or need for the commodity. . . . Secondly, the abundance or scarceness of the commodity in proportion to the need of it. . . . Thirdly, the riches or poverty of those who demand. . . ."?[24]

The answer would appear to be, in the first place, that Adam Smith felt that this sort of subjective analysis was leading nowhere. It had not so far proved capable of being employed in any actual quantitative measurement, while even had he been aware of Bernoulli's illustration, since this posited equal utilities derived from the possession of two very different fortunes, it might not have proved very encouraging to pursue it further.

That Adam Smith turned his back upon utility largely because it did not seem to provide more than vague generalisations is not difficult to imagine. Yet perhaps he did not turn his back upon it so decisively as is usually supposed.

Two fundamental ideas running through the *Wealth of Nations* may be regarded as evidence of this. The first is the stress which Adam Smith laid upon men's propensity to barter as the origin of a socio-economic organisation based on the division of labour. It would seem doubtful that Adam Smith had really abandoned the primacy of subjective estimates of utility as a determinant of value, when his whole system is bound up with the existence of a society in which the different individuals implicitly offer: "Give me that which I want, and you shall have this which you want," in which "every man thus lives by exchanging, or becomes in some measure a merchant, and the society itself grows to be what is properly a commercial society."[25] Clearly this depends upon different subjective valuations of the objects of exchange.

The second lies, of course, in his stress on there being a necessary connection between the apparently independent sets of prices comprised under his classification of "natural price" and "market price." This was already formulated in the *Lectures* (p. 173), but it formed a more important feature of the *Wealth of Nations*. The "Early Draft" published by Professor Scott is clearly a link between Adam Smith's earliest formulation and his final one, for it sets out both elements of which only one apiece (and that a different one each time) is stressed almost to the exclusion of the other in the *Lectures* and in the *Wealth of Nations*.[26]

What is the essential difference between the *Lectures* and the *Wealth of Nations* in this respect? Surely that, although in the *Lectures*, Adam Smith asserts that:

"Of every commodity there are two different prices, which though apparently independent, will be found to have a necessary connection, viz. the natural price and the market price."[27]

it there remains little more than an assertion.

His supply-and-demand formula refers only to market price. His natural price formula is applied only to the natural price of labour, and hardly goes beyond — if indeed it goes as far as — Cantillon. But in the *Wealth of Nations*, on the other hand, new stress is given to the determinants of natural price, by way of the model, designed to explain at one and the same time both value and distribution, for which he may have been indebted either to the Physiocrats[28] or to James Oswald of Dunnikier.[29] The component parts of the price of every commodity can be resolved into the shares of wages, profits and rent, and —

"as the price or exchangeable value of every particular commodity, taken separately, resolves itself into some one or other, or all of those three parts; so that of all the commodities which compose the whole annual produce of the labour of every country, taken complexly, must resolve itself into the same three parts, and be parcelled out amongst different inhabitants of the country, either as the wages of their labour, the profits of their stock, or the rent of their land. . . . Wages, profit and rent are the three original sources of all revenue as well as of all exchangeable value."[30]

Thus the unifying analysis is that there is everywhere an "ordinary," "average" or "natural" rate of wages, profit and rent which determine "natural" prices of commodities. National output (= income) is equivalent to the total contribution of the three factors of production co-operating through the division of labour. National income (= output) is distributed as the payment for the services of these factors. Individual "natural" prices are determined by this distribution, though they also determine the distribution, just as in Marshall's analogy, "when several balls are lying in a bowl, they mutually govern one another's positions."

Just in the same way as, in the *Lectures*, Adam Smith virtually confined himself to a rather superficial supply-and-demand theory of natural price, though asserting a connection with market price and mentioning quite incidentally that "labour . . . is the true measure of value" (p. 190), so now in the *Wealth of Nations*, without abandoning the explanation of market price *via* utility and scarcity inherited through Hutcheson, Puffendorf and the Scholastics, he concentrated upon what now appeared to him to be the more important phenomenon of "natural price" or normal value, for which the traditional utility approach appeared inadequate.

The explanation must be that, in the *Wealth of Nations*, Adam Smith had cast his thought in a more ambitious role. His eyes were set, not on the transient determination of market values but on a long-term demonstration of the causes of the variations in the *Wealth of Nations* in which alone could he make clear:

"That there is in every country what may be called a natural balance of industry, or a disposition in the people to apply to each species of work precisely in proportion to the demand for that work."[31]

In the *Wealth of Nations* Adam Smith was studying the influence of society and social institutions upon material welfare, leaving aside the various technical considerations which previous authors had always mixed up with these. In his *Introduction and Plan of the Work* he made the main points of his analysis quite clear. He was interested in the social causes which determine real national income per head. The first major influence of social organisation upon economic welfare, as thus conceived, is exerted through the division of labour. Hence Adam Smith first devoted attention to the reasons why the division of labour leads to an increased produce (Book I, Chapter I) and next considered the principle from which the division of labour draws its force, namely, mutual exchange (Chapter II). Then he discussed the limits which determine how far the division of labour may proceed (Chapter III).

The division of labour is, on the one hand, derived from a human propensity to exchange, and on the other hand, it gives rise to the importance of exchange in developed communities. Exchange, in turn, is facilitated by the use of money, discussed in Chapter IV, and gives rise to the problems of value discussed in Chapters V–VII. He shows that the acts of production and valuation proceed *pari passu* with the distribution of the National Product amongst the owners of the co-operant factors of production. And so he goes on to discuss wages (Chapter VIII) and profits (Chapter IX), connecting them in Chapter X by discussing the principles which give rise to differences in earnings for different employments of labour and capital — which, incidentally, throws further light upon the share of those two components of the natural price of commodities. Chapter XI completes the general picture (and Book I) by discussing rent and the influence of the progress of the economy upon the distribution of the product between landlords, wage-earners, merchants and master-manufacturers: It contains a long digression upon a practical question, to which further reference will have to be made, viz., the complications introduced by variations in the value of silver itself (the standard measure of value as price) during the past four centuries.

With increasing division of labour, the economic and social importance of capital is enhanced, hence in Book II Adam Smith discussed capital in greater detail in five separate chapters, whose inter-relationship was explained in a short introduction. In Book III he discussed, with a wealth of comparative historical illustration, the "different progress of opulence in different nations." This is bound up with differences of economic policy, such as are discussed in Book IV, which is in the main a discussion of and an attack upon mercantilistic principles of regulation which have hindered the achievement of a greater national product through the more effective division of labour. Having thus, in Books III and IV, examined the influence of the state upon economic welfare, in Book V he discussed what expenditure the state ought to undertake and how it ought to raise the necessary revenue if it was to promote the general welfare at least cost.[32]

It is evident that the *magnum opus* was cast in the mould of a powerful unifying conception. Now within this framework it is clear that the measurement, in real terms, of the "wealth" of nations, and in particular of its progress, would seem to call for some unvarying standard of value which would enable valid comparisons to be made through time. For this purpose, market values which depended on momentary whims and fashions on the market, on temporary relationships between supply and demand, did not appear satisfactory. For this reason, if for no other, it does not appear inexplicable that Adam Smith no longer paid so much attention to the lines of argument taken over from Hutcheson, which had served well enough in the *Lectures*.

He now made much more of the distinction between natural (*i.e.*, normal or long-run) price and market price. He showed that over a long enough period, market price must be sufficient to cover all costs included in the natural price, *i.e.*, the sum of the normal wages, profit and rent of the co-operant factors of production. He elucidated the relationship further by demonstrating that owing to immobilities (*e.g.*, monopolies, lack of knowledge of alternatives, etc.), market price might be kept for quite long periods above the natural rate. Incidentally, in discussing the case of the market price falling below the natural price, he brought in the concept of a margin at which the market price for the whole supply is fixed, *i.e.*, a concept of a marginal demand price falling in much the same category as that implied in Ricardo's remarks quoted in note 25.

"When the quantity brought to market exceeds the effectual demand, it cannot all be sold to those who are willing to pay the whole value of the rent, wages and profit, which must be paid in order to bring it thither. Some part must be sold to those who are willing to pay less, and the low price which they give for it must reduce the price of the whole."[33]

In the *Wealth of Nations* also, he made very much more of the distinction between the "real" and the "nominal" price of commodities. He discussed the advantages of making long-term calculations in corn rather than money, on the grounds that corn was more likely to maintain stability of its own value. But, as a solution to the problem of finding an invariable standard of value, he plumped for labour.

It is worth while to look at Smith's own statement of the reasons for his choice:

"But as a measure of quantity, such as the natural foot, fathom or handful, which is continually varying in its own quantity, can never be an accurate measure of the quantity of other things; so a commodity which is itself continually varying in its own value, can never be an accurate measure of the value of other commodities. Equal quantities of labour, at all times and places, may be said to be of equal value to the labourer, in his ordinary state of health, strength and spirits; in the ordinary degree of his skill and dexterity, he must always lay down the same portion of his ease, his liberty and his happiness. The price which he pays must always be the same, whatever may be the quantity of goods which he receives in return for it. Of these, indeed, it may sometimes purchase a greater and sometimes a smaller quantity; but it is their value which varies, not that of the labour which purchases them. At all times and places that is dear which it is difficult to come at, or which it costs much labour to acquire; and that cheap which is to be had easily, or with very little labour. Labour alone, therefore, never varying in its own value, is alone the ultimate and real standard by which the value of all commodities can at all times and places be estimated and compared. It is their real price; money is their nominal price only."[34]

This is clearly based upon a definite psychological assumption regarding the disutility or real cost of labour. The assumption is surely erroneous; but the problem involved is of such fundamental importance that there is little mystery about the reasons why Adam Smith, once having set his mind to this problem of inter-temporal comparisons, should have put aside his earlier approach to problems of value based on the ideas of scarcity and usefulness in favour of "a one-sided, almost exclusive emphasis on labour and cost of production." (see p. 289 above). Nor, indeed, are the ideas of scarcity and usefulness abandoned; they are merely taken for granted. When Adam Smith, in the passage just quoted, or in the succeeding one, plumped not merely for labour but for the amount of labour commanded in the market, as providing the measure of the real price of everything, he was not excluding those inevitable market forces; he was merely tackling a different problem:

"The real price of every thing, what every thing really costs to the man who wants to acquire it, is the toil and trouble of acquiring it. . . . That money or those goods . . . contain the value of a certain quantity of labour which we exchange for *what is supposed at the time to contain* the value of an equal quantity . . . it was not by gold or by silver but by labour, that all the wealth of the world was originally purchased; and its value, to those who possess it, and who want to exchange it for new productions, is precisely equal to the quantity of labour which it can enable them to purchase or command."[35]

As Malthus put it, accepting Samuel Bailey's view that "value, in its ultimate sense, appears to mean the esteem in which any object is held," he would on that very basis choose the amount of labour commanded by the commodity at two different periods as providing the most certain measure of changes in the esteem in which it was held.[36]

Unfortunately, while upon Adam Smith's assumptions regarding the real cost of his labour always remaining the same to the labourer, the amount of labour commanded would provide a standard measure of value, this must be regarded as irrelevant to the problems of what determine values, since no satisfactory explanation is offered as to why the price of any article should be such as to *command* any given quantity of labour. The different nature of the problems was obscured by an attempt to link "labour" in another way with the problem of normal or "natural" values, in which an illegitimate transference was attempted from a simplified model of a primitive society to a realistic model of a more developed one.

In assessing the component parts of "natural" prices of commodities, which are equivalent to the total factor payments necessary to ensure continuity of supplies to the market, Adam Smith made the amount of labour *expended* or *embodied* in production the sole source of the particular value of commodities in primitive communities, to which "natural" profit and "natural" rent had to be added in the case of more developed communities.[37] But he gave no satisfactory explanation of these added elements; and he left a confusion here which Ricardo (who seems to have had a different view from the one put forward here regarding Adam Smith's intentions) confounded still further in his attempt to bring in logical consistency.[38]

If a true explanation is given here of the reasons for Adam Smith turning from "scarcity and utility" to a labour theory of value, did he not, in fact, do more for the progress of economics by a grand failure in an impossible but fundamental task, than he would have done, had he been content to add a seventh rung or even to strengthen some of the existing steps in the rickety ladder of subjective-value theory such as, according to Dr. Kauder, it appeared in 1776? Economics has remained less than a science because, in spite of all efforts, no firm basis has yet been discovered for the measurement of real national income or for relating changes in the product with changes in welfare. But it would have remained mere *dilettantism* had the attempt to make a genuine *Inquiry into the Nature and the Causes of the Wealth of Nations* not been undertaken.[39] If Adam Smith committed some folly in his attempt to forge a labour theory of value into a tool for use in this great task, perhaps it was because —

"At that period of history this theory was worth being taken up by any gifted genius who could make it throw a first ray of light into the dark mass of economic phenomena. . . . A great thought may in the long run turn into a childish error."[40]

Finally, even upon the assumption that the marginal-utility revolution of the 1870s at last illumined all, and that costs can be firmly put in their place as opportunity costs or displaced alternatives, what is the fundamental-factor scarcity that makes it necessary for alternative uses of factors to be foregone? Could it be that in his ordinary state of health, strength and spirits, in the ordinary degree of his skill and dexterity, the output of a man's labour is limited by his finding labour irksome?

NOTES

1. It is a pleasure for one of the authors (W. L. Taylor) to record the helpfulness, counsel and stimulating suggestions, and to acknowledge the valuable co-operation he received, from Mr. T. W. Hutchison of the London School of Economics in the preparation of an earlier draft of a part of this paper.

2. E. Kauder, "Genesis of the Marginal Utility Theory," *Economic Journal*, Vol. LXIII, September 1953, pp. 638 ff.

3. Here is an English version of some of the relevant passages in Puffendorf's *De Officio*, Chapter XIV: "The natural Ground of the *Common Value*, is that Fitness which any Thing or Action has for supplying, either mediately or immediately, the *Necessities* of Humane Life, and rendring the same more *easie* or more comfortable. Hence it is we call those things which are not of any *Use* to us, *Things of no value*. There are nevertheless some *things most useful* to Humane Life, which are not understood to fall under any *determinate Price or Value*; (e.g., the upper Regions of the *Air*, the *Sky*, and the *Heavnly Bodies*, the clear Light of the *Sun*, the serene and pure *Air*) . . . the *necessity* of the thing or its extraordinary *Usefulness* is not always regarded; but on the contrary we see those things are of the least account or Value, without which Human Life is least able to subsist; and therefore not without the singular Providence of Almighty God, *Nature* has been very *bountiful* in providing *plentiful* store of those things. But the *rarity* or *Scarceness* of Things conduces chiefly to the enhancing their Value. . . ." *The Whole Duty of Man According to the Law of Nature*, by that famous Civilian Samuel Puffendorf. Translated by F. C. (London, M DC XCI), pp. 165-7.

4. F. Hutcheson, *Introduction to Moral Philosophy*, 1747, p. i.

5. See p. 247 n. of Carmichael's edition of Puffendorf's *De Officio* (2nd ed., Edinburgh, 1724): "In genere hic dici potest. Pretium rerum ex his duobus capitibus pendere, *Indigentia*, et *Adquirendi difficultate* . . . . Indigentia, sc., porro ex duobus aestimatur, numero sc. amientium, et aptitudine, quam isti rei vel operae inesse putant, qua ad vitae humanae usum aut voluptatem aliquid conferre possit." Very little seems to have come down about Carmichael, though he was the founder of the Glasgow school of moral philosophy. For further details of his life and career, see W. L. Taylor, "Gershom Carmichael, a Neglected Figure in British Political Economy," *The South African Journal of Economics*, Vol. 23, September 1955, pp. 251 ff.

6. See E. Cannan, *Review of Economic Theory* (London, 1929), p. 160.

7. L. H. Haney, *History of Economic Thought* (New York, 1936), p. 217, points out that Smith's distinction between value-in-use and value-in-exchange seems to correspond with the idea of *valeur usuelle* and *valeur vénale* as held by Quesnay and the Physiocrats.

Paul H. Douglas, in his lecture

"Smith's Theory of Value and Distribution" in *Adam Smith, 1776–1926; Lectures to Commemorate the Sesquicentennial of the Publication of the "Wealth of Nations,"* edited by J. M. Clark (Chicago: The University of Chicago Press, 1928), p. 78, goes so far as to say of Smith's treatment of "utility" in the *Wealth of Nations:* "Not only is utility not a determinant of exchange value, but—and here Smith goes farther than Ricardo and later exponents of the labour theory of value—it is not even a necessary prerequisite."

8. Halévy remarks on Hutcheson's discussion of "use" and value, that his language is "more exact than Smith's on two points: By 'use' Hutcheson, differing from Adam Smith, means not only natural or reasonable utility, but also any aptitude to produce a pleasure which is founded on custom or fashion: and, above all, by 'difficulty of acquiring,' he means not only the amount of work necessary in order to produce or to obtain the object, but, in a more general way, the scarcity of which this difficulty is only a particular instance." Elie Halévy, *The Growth of Philosophic Radicalism,* translated by Mary Morris, with a Preface by A. D. Lindsay (London, 1928), p. 96. According to Halévy, Smith "had the choice between two perfectly distinct traditional doctrines" on value: that represented by Puffendorf and Hutcheson, who based value on utility and scarcity, and that represented by Locke, who based value on labour. Halévy suggests that "it is a curious question" why Smith and subsequent economists chose to follow what he describes as the tradition of Locke. Whether or not this is a fully satisfactory description of Locke's ideas on value, it seems quite clear that Smith *could* have chosen, but in the *Wealth of Nations* all but completely discarded, the most important elements in the doctrines of Puffendorf and Hutcheson.

9. See J. Rae, *Life of Adam Smith* (London, 1895), p. 14. This passage is quoted approvingly by W. R. Scott, *Francis Hutcheson* (Cambridge, 1900), p. 237, who adds, however: "It should be noted that while Hutcheson emphasises the position of labour he does not make it the sole distinguishing characteristic of wealth, for he also adds the limitation of supply and appropriation—as for instance, 'the rarity or scarcity of the materials in nature, etc.'" Surely this is an absolutely fundamental addition by Hutcheson, particularly as Hutcheson, as in one of the quotations above, relates scarcity to demand.

10. See E. Cannan, *Review of Economic Theory,* p. 164, and Marian Bowley, *Nassau Senior and Classical Economics* (reprinted New York, 1949), pp. 67–9, who have also touched on the differing treatments of value in Smith's *Lectures* and the *Wealth of Nations.*

11. E. Cannan, *Lectures of Adam Smith* (Oxford, 1896), Editor's "Introduction," p. xxvii.

12. *Ibid.,* p. 157.

13. A. Smith, *Wealth of Nations,* Cannan Edition (London, 1950), Vol. I, p. 58.

14. *Ibid.,* pp. 58–9.

15. W. R. Scott, "The Manuscript of An Early Draft of Part of *The Wealth of Nations,*" *Economic Journal,* Vol. XLV, September 1935, p. 431.

16. The manuscript of the opening chapters of *An Early Draft of the Wealth of Nations,* (c. 1763) (printed by W. R. Scott in his *Adam Smith as Student and Professor,* pp. 322 ff.) dates apparently from 1763, just after the *Lectures,* but may already be said to mark a transition towards the *Wealth of Nations.* The manuscript volume begins with a chapter headed "Chapter 2," the substance of which was to become Chapters I and II in the *Wealth of Nations.* The Chapter I still apparently intended, but not in fact included in the 1763 manuscript, would presumably have covered the subject of wants and their satisfaction, discussed in the first two sections of the *Lectures,* but finally omitted from the *Wealth of Nations.* The chapter on price in the manuscript (Chapter 3) is simply an outline of headings which follows the *Lectures* in setting out three determinants of market price and specifically mentions needs and scarcity, but even more briefly than in the *Lectures.*

17. The eloquent comments of Paul H. Douglas may be recalled: "By failing to follow up the hints which these writers (Locke and Harris) had developed, Smith helped to divert the writers of the English Classical School into a cul-de-sac from which they did not emerge, in so far as their value theory was concerned, for nearly a century, while he also helped . . . to give rise to the economic doctrines of nineteenth-century socialism. . . . There are, it seems to me, few more unfair instances in economic thought than the almost complete unanimity with which the English-speaking economists of the chair have heaped condemnation upon the over-worked and poverty-stricken Marx, who worked under such great difficulties, and, save for the comments of Jevons and a few others, have heaped praises upon Smith and Ricardo. The failure was the failure not of one man but of a philosophy of value, and the roots of the ultimate contradiction made manifest to the world in the third volume of *Das Kapital* lie embedded in the first volume of the *Wealth of Nations,*" (*op. cit.,* pp. 80 and 95).

18. E. Kauder, *op. cit.,* p. 650. Adam Smith's "few words," in fact, have a homelier ring than those ascribed to him. "Nothing is more useful than water; but it will purchase scarce any thing; scarce any thing can be had in exchange for it. A diamond, on the contrary, has scarce

any value in use; but a very great quantity of other goods may frequently be had in exchange for it" (*Wealth of Nations*, Cannan edition (London, 1950), Vol. I, p. 30).

19. Conveniently reproduced in E. Cannan, *Review of Economic Theory* (London, 1929), p. 159.

20. Samuel Puffendorf, *op. cit.*, pp. 167–8.

21. F. Von Wieser, *Natural Value*, English Translation by Mrs. C. Malloch, ed. W. Smart (London, 1893), pp. 3–5.

22. Adam Smith: *Theory of Moral Sentiments* (1759), Bohn Standard Library Edition (London, 1853), Pt. III, Ch. 3, p. 195. "The poor man must neither defraud nor steal from the rich, though the acquisition might be much more beneficial to the one than the loss could be hurtful to the other."

23. E. Kauder, *op. cit.*, p. 648.

24. *Lectures*, pp. 176–7 (see above p. 293).

25. *Wealth of Nations*, Cannan Edition (London, 1950), Vol. I, pp. 16 and 24. One is tempted to bring in collateral evidence from the still more uncompromising exponent of a labour-theory-of-value, David Ricardo. In his chapters on the incidence of taxes, Ricardo shows his awareness of a theory of consumer's demand in such characteristic passages as this: "Whatever habit has rendered delightful will be relinquished with reluctance . . . but this reluctance has its limits. . . . One man will continue to drink the same quantity of wine, though the price of every bottle should be raised three shillings, who would yet relinquish the use of wine rather than pay four. Another, will be content to pay four, yet refuse to pay five shillings. . . . Every man has some standard in his own mind by which he estimates the value of his enjoyments, but that standard is as various as the human character," (D. Ricardo, *On the Principles of Political Economy and Taxation*, Ch. XVI (ed. P. Sraffa and M. H. Dobb) (Cambridge University Press, 1951), Vol. 1, p. 241).

26. W. R. Scott, *Adam Smith as Student and Professor* (Glasgow, 1937), pp. 345–6.

27. *Lectures*, p. 173.

28. *Ibid.*, Cannan's introduction, pp. xxx–xxxi.

29. W. R. Scott, *Adam Smith as Student and Professor*, pp. 117–18, 320–1.

30. *Wealth of Nations* (Cannan edition), Vol. I, p. 54.

31. W. R. Scott, *Adam Smith as Student and Professor*, p. 346.

32. While this analysis of the leading features of the *Wealth of Nations* is based essentially on Adam Smith's own account of his intentions in the *Wealth of Nations* itself and on an assessment of how far he succeeded in carrying them out, based upon the book as a whole, its formulation has undoubtedly been influenced by the similar one of N. G. Pierson in "Het begrip van volksrijkdom," *Verspreide Economische Geschriften, Dl.I. De methode en theorie der Staathuishoudkunde* (Haarlem, 1910), pp. 52–3.

33. *Wealth of Nations* (Cannan Edition), Vol. I, p. 59.

34. *Wealth of Nations* (Cannan Edition), Vol. I, p. 35.

35. *Ibid.*, Vol. I, pp. 32–3.

36. T. R. Malthus, *Definitions in Political Economy*, 1827 (reprinted New York, 1954), pp. 126, 165. In fact, Malthus went further, and while rejecting the "labour embodied" as the measure of the value of a commodity, still asked "whether the labour required to produce a commodity does not, beyond all comparison, express more nearly the esteem in which the commodity is held than a reference to some other commodity, the producing labour of which is utterly unknown, and may therefore be one day or one thousand years?" Malthus was the economist amongst Smith's immediate successors to whom the importance of the problem of making valid comparisons through time was most apparent, and his remarks therefore form a valuable commentary upon Adam Smith's intentions. See also his *Principles of Political Economy*, 2nd edition, 1836 (reprinted New York, 1951); especially the "Advertisement," pp. vii–xi, and Chapter II, especially Sections V–VI, pp. 93–122.

37. *Wealth of Nations*, Bk. I, Ch. VI.

38. Although this is a rather lengthy survey, it is doubtful if, in fact, it adds anything to the sympathetically critical analysis in Marian Bowley, *op. cit.*, pp. 67–74.

39. Some ingenious attempts to measure relative economic welfare per head in different countries may turn out to be mere sophistications of Adam Smith's measuring rod of "labour commanded." Thus if one tries to measure comparative real earnings in terms of Colin Clark's "International Units," the result will be to price the earnings of labour in terms of a basket of commodities valued at constant dollar prices based on the years 1925–34. This is merely an inverse relationship linking commodities and the amount of labour exchangeable for it, to the one put forward by Adam Smith. But one can sympathise with Clark's impatience with those who are content to take up a mere *non possumus* attitude. See Colin Clark, *The Conditions of Economic Progress* (London, 1951), Ch. 2.

40. F. Von Wieser, *op. cit.* p. 202.

12.

JACOB VINER
Princeton University

Adam Smith

and

Laissez Faire[1*]

I. THE HARMONIOUS ORDER OF NATURE

An endeavor to make a just appraisal of Adam Smith's original contributions to economic doctrine would even today be a task of extraordinary difficulty. On the one hand, what was serviceable in his doctrines has become so thoroughly incorporated in our modern thinking that we discover it upon the slightest provocation in whatever we may read that was written before his day, and we are especially prone to make a virtue of obscurity in his predecessors by taking it for granted that it conceals premature insight rather than unduly prolonged lack of it. On the other hand, there is always great danger lest what we credit to a writer as priority of doctrine may not in reality be merely an indecent exposure of our own ignorance concerning his predecessors. There is much weight of authority and of evidence, however, that Smith's major claim to originality, in English economic thought at least, was his detailed and elaborate application to the wilderness of economic phenomena of the unifying concept of a co-ordinated and mutually interdependent system of cause and effect relationships which philosophers and

Reprinted from *The Journal of Political Economy*, XXXV (April 1927), 198–232, by permission of the author and The University of Chicago Press. This article forms Chapter 5 of *Adam Smith, 1776–1926* (Chicago: The University of Chicago Press, 1928), and it is reprinted in Jacob Viner, *The Long View and the Short* (Glencoe, Ill.: The Free Press, 1958), pp. 213–45. At the time of original publication, the author was with The University of Chicago.

theologians had already applied to the world in general. Smith's doctrine that economic phenomena were manifestations of an underlying order in nature, governed by natural forces, gave to English economics for the first time a definite trend toward logically consistent synthesis of economic relationships, toward "system-building." Smith's further doctrine that this underlying natural order required, for its most beneficent operation, a system of natural liberty, and that in the main public regulation and private monopoly were corruptions of that natural order, at once gave to economics a bond of union with the prevailing philosophy and theology, and to economists and statesmen a program of practical reform.

Smith was *the* great eclectic. He drew upon all previous knowledge in developing his doctrine of a harmonious order in nature manifesting itself through the instincts of the individual man. The oldest source in which he expressly finds an approach to his own views is in the science of the classical philosophers: "In the first ages of the world . . . . the idea of a universal mind, of a God of all, who originally formed the whole, and who governs the whole by general laws, directed to the conservation and prosperity of the whole, without regard to that of any private individual, was a notion to which [the Ancients] were utterly strangers . . . . [but] as ignorance begot superstition, science gave birth to the first theism that arose among those nations, who were not enlightened by divine Revelation."[2]

The Roman *jus naturale,* through Grotius and Pufendorf, strongly influenced Smith's thinking. The Renaissance emphasis on the individual, the naturalistic philosophy of Shaftesbury, Locke, Hume, Hutcheson, the optimistic theism of the Scotch philosophers, the empiricism of Montesquieu, were more immediate and more powerful influences. Science, philosophy, theology, psychology, history, contemporary observation of facts — all of them were made to produce, under Smith's capable management, an abundance of evidence of the existence of an order in nature in which beneficent intentions toward mankind could be discerned. If Smith at times showed more catholicity than scientific discrimination in what he accepted as supporting evidence, if some of this evidence appeared upon close scrutiny to be conjectural, contradictory, irrelevant, or inconclusive, the richness of argument, the power of his exposition, the attractiveness of his conclusions served to overwhelm the captious critic and to postpone closer scrutiny to a later day.

Smith's major claim to fame, as I have said, seems to rest on his elaborate and detailed application to the economic world of the concept of a unified natural order, operating according to natural law, and if left to its own course producing results beneficial to mankind. On every detail, taken by itself, Smith appears to have had predecessors in plenty. On few details was Smith as penetrating as the best of his predecessors. There had been earlier pleas for freedom of internal trade, freedom of foreign trade, free trade in land, free choice of occupations, free choice of place of residence. Some philosophers, notably Shaftesbury and Smith's own teacher, Hutcheson, had already extended to economic phenomena, though sketchily, the concept of an underlying natural order manifesting itself through the operation of physical forces and individual psychology. But Smith made an original forward step when he seriously applied himself to the task of analyzing the whole range of economic process with the purpose of discovering the nature of the order which underlay its surface chaos. Claims have been made for the Physiocrats, but the evidence indicates that Smith had already formulated his central doctrine before he came into contact with them or their writings. As early as 1755 Smith had publicly asserted his claim to priority, as against some unnamed rival, in applying to the economic order the system of natural liberty. In doing so, he cited a lecture, delivered in 1749, which even in the fragment which has survived contains the essence of his fully developed doctrine, as expounded in the *Wealth of Nations*. It even uses an English equivalent of the very phrase "laissez faire," which the Physiocrats were soon to make the war cry of the system of natural liberty.

Projectors disturb nature in the course of her operations on human affairs, and it requires no more than to *leave her alone* and give her fair play in the pursuit of her ends that she may establish her own designs. . . . Little else is required to carry a state to the highest degree of affluence from the lowest barbarism but peace, easy taxes, and a tolerable administration of justice; all the rest being brought about by the natural course of things. All governments which thwart this natural course, which force things into another channel, or which endeavor to arrest the progress of society at a particular point, are unnatural, and, to support themselves, are obliged to be oppressive and tyrannical.[3]

In his *Theory of Moral Sentiments,* Smith develops his system of ethics on the basis of a doctrine of a harmonious order in nature guided by God, and in an incidental manner applies his general doctrine with strict consistency to the economic order. In his later work, the *Wealth of Nations,* Smith devotes himself to a specialized inquiry into the nature of the economic order. It is a commonplace among the authorities on Adam Smith that it is impossible fully to understand the *Wealth of Nations* without recourse to the *Theory of Moral Sentiments.* The vast bulk of economists, however, who have read the *Wealth of Nations* without reading the *Theory of Moral Sentiments,* have not regarded Smith's masterpiece as an obscure book, as one especially hard to understand. On the other hand, the very authorities who are most emphatic in asserting the need of reference to the *Theory of Moral Sentiments* to understand the *Wealth of Nations,* once they embark upon their self-imposed task of interpreting the latter in the light of the former, become immersed in difficult problems of interpretation for which scarcely any two writers offer the same solution. The system of individual liberty is much in evidence among the interpreters of Smith, but that natural harmony which should also result is strikingly lacking. The Germans, who, it seems, in their methodical manner commonly read both the *Theory of Moral Sentiments* and the *Wealth of Nations,* have coined a pretty term, *Das Adam Smith Problem,* to denote the failure to understand either which results from the attempt to use the one in the interpretation of the other. I will endeavor to show that the difficulties of the authorities result mainly from their determination to find a basis for complete concordance of the two books, and that there are divergences between them which are impossible of reconciliation even by such heroic means as one writer has adopted of appeal to the existence in Smith's thought of a Kantian dualism. I will further endeavor to show that the *Wealth of Nations* was a better book because of its partial breach with the *Theory of Moral Sentiments,* and that it could not have remained, as it has, a living book were it not that in its methods of analysis, its basic assumptions, and its conclusions it abandoned the absolutism, the rigidity, the romanticism which characterize the earlier book.

II. THE "THEORY OF MORAL SENTIMENTS"

In the *Theory of Moral Sentiments,* Smith develops the doctrine of a beneficent order in nature, manifesting itself through the operation of the forces of external nature and the innate propensities implanted in man by nature. The moral sentiments, self-interest, regulated by natural justice and tempered by sympathy or benevolence, operate in conjunction with the physical forces of nature to achieve the beneficent purposes of Nature. Underlying the matter-of-fact phenomena of human and physical nature is benign Nature, a guiding providence, which is concerned that natural processes shall operate to produce the "happiness and perfection of the species." Smith is unfortunately far from explicit as to just how Nature makes certain that nature shall not betray the former's intentions, though he does say that Nature dictates to man the laws which he shall follow.[4] It seems, however, that the essence of Smith's doctrine is that Providence has so fashioned the constitution of external nature as to make its processes favorable to man, and has implanted *ab initio* in human nature such sentiments as would bring about, through their ordinary working, the happiness and welfare of mankind. The many titles by which this beneficent Nature is designated must have taxed severely the terminological resources of the Scotch optimistic theism. Among them are: "the great Director of Nature,"[5] "the final cause,"[6] "the Author of Nature,"[7] "the great judge of hearts,"[8] "an invisible hand,"[9] "Providence,"[10] "the divine Being,"[11] and, in rare instances, "God."[12] Smith definitely commits himself to the theism of his time. The harmony and beneficence to be perceived in the matter-of-fact processes of nature are the results of the design and intervention of a benevolent God.

The idea of that divine Being, whose benevolence and wisdom have, from all eternity, contrived and conducted the immense machine of the universe, so as at all times to produce the greatest quantity of happiness, is certainly of all the objects of human contemplation by far the most sublime. . . . . The administration of the great system of the universe, ... the care of the universal happiness of all rational and sensible beings, is the business of God and not of man. To man is allotted a much humbler department, but one much more suitable to the weakness of his powers, and to the narrowness of his comprehension; the care of his own happiness, of that of his family, his friends, his country.[13]

Thus self-preservation, and the propagation of the species, are the great ends which Nature seems to have proposed in the formation of all animals. . . . . But though we are . . . . endowed with a very strong desire of those ends, it has not been intrusted to the slow and uncertain determinations of our reason to find out the proper means of bringing them about. Nature has directed us to the greater part of these by original and immediate instincts. Hunger, thirst, the passion which unites the two sexes, the love of pleasure, and the dread of pain, prompt us to apply those means for their own sakes, and without any consideration of their tendency to those beneficent ends which the great Director of nature intended to produce by them.[14]

Society can get along tolerably well even though beneficence is absent and self-interest and justice alone operate. "Society may subsist among different men, as among different merchants, from a sense of its utility, without any mutual love or affection; and though no man in it should owe any obligation, or be bound in gratitude to any other, it may still be upheld by a mercenary exchange of good offices according to an agreed valuation." Beneficence "is the ornament which embellishes, not the foundation which supports, the building. . . . Justice, on the contrary, is the main pillar that upholds the whole edifice." "Society may subsist, though not in the most comfortable state, without beneficence; but the prevalence of injustice must utterly destroy it."[15]

There are no serious flaws in the harmonious operation of natural forces, even in the economic order, where self-interest, which is ordinarily a virtue, but if not regulated by justice may degenerate into vice, is the most powerful of the impulses to action:

If we consider the general rules by which external prosperity and adversity are commonly distributed in this life, we shall find, that notwithstanding the disorder in which all things appear to be in this world, yet even here every virtue naturally meets with its proper reward, with the recompense which is most fit to encourage and promote it; and this too so surely, that it requires a very extraordinary concurrence of circumstances entirely to disappoint it.

What is the reward most proper for encouraging industry, prudence, and circumspection? Success in every sort of business. And is it possible that in the whole of life these virtues should fail of attaining it? Wealth and external honours are their proper recompense, and the recompense which they can seldom fail of acquiring.[16]

The poorer classes have little if any ground for complaint as to their lot in life, and no reason to seek to improve it except by methods which contribute to the general welfare of society. "In the middling and inferior stations of life, the road to virtue and that to fortune . . . are, happily, in most cases, very nearly the same. . . . The good old proverb, therefore, that honesty is the best policy, holds, in such situations, almost always perfectly true."[17] Beneficent Nature so operates the machinery behind the scenes that even inequality in the distribution of happiness is more apparent than real:

[The rich] are led by an invisible hand to make nearly the same distribution of the necessaries of life which would have been made had the earth been divided into equal portions among all its inhabitants, and thus without intending it, without knowing it, advance the interest of the society, and afford means to the multiplication of the species. When Providence divided the earth among a few lordly masters, it neither forgot nor abandoned those who seemed to have been left out in the partition. These last, too, enjoy their share of all that it produces. In what constitutes the real happiness of human life, they are in no respect inferior to those who would seem so much above them. In ease of the body and peace of the mind, all the different ranks of life are nearly upon a level, and the beggar, who suns himself by the side of the highway, possesses that security which kings are fighting for.[18]

Smith concedes that the processes of nature operate at times with what, by man's standards, are results so unjust that they arouse our indignation:

Fraud, falsehood, brutality, and violence, ... excite in every human breast such scorn and abhorrence, that our indignation rouses to see them possess those advantages which they may in some sense be said to have merited, by the diligence and industry with which they are sometimes attended. The industrious knave cultivates the soil, the indolent man leaves it uncultivated. Who ought to reap the harvest? Who starve, and who live in plenty? The natural course of things decides it in favour of the knave; the natural sentiments of mankind in favour of the man of virtue.[19]

This is a familiar dilemma of the optimistic theology, but Smith is precluded from adopting the familiar solution that "the ways of the Lord are inscrutable" by the fact that he is at the moment engaged in the task of formulating with great precision and assurance just what the ways of the Lord are. A contemporary economist of Adam Smith, Josiah Tucker, who was also by the necessity of his profession a theologian, when faced with an apparent conflict between the processes of nature and the "fundamental Principle of Universal Benevolence" found an ingenious solution in the conclusion a priori that there must be something wrong in the appearance of things: "I conclude *a priori*, that there must be some flaw or other in the preceding Arguments, plausible as they seem, and great as they are upon the foot of human Authority. For though the Appearance of Things makes for this Conclusion . . . . the Fact, itself, cannot be so."[20] Smith also succeeded in keeping his theory alive when the force of conflicting fact seemed to threaten to destroy it, but his method was more gentle to the facts. Man has been given by nature one standard by which to judge it, but nature has retained another and different standard for itself. "Both are calculated to promote the same great end, the order of the world, and the perfection and happiness of human nature."[21] Only an inordinately exacting critic would suggest that this solution is not wholly satisfactory, since Smith can have logically reached it only by applying to nature its own standard, which it was not appropriate for man to use. But if this solution does not satisfy, Smith has another one. If we despair of finding any force upon earth which can check the triumph of injustice, we "naturally appeal to heaven, and hope that the great Author of our nature will himself execute hereafter what all the principles which he has given us for the direction of our conduct prompt us to attempt even here; that he will complete the plan which he himself has thus taught us to begin; and will, in a life to come, render to every one according to the works which he has performed in this world."[22]

310

If, judged by men's standards, the order of nature does not result in perfect justice on earth, we apparently have two alternative explanations: either that man's standards are an inadequate basis for appraisal, or that there is opportunity in a future state for redress of the injustices of the present one.

What we have, therefore, in the *Theory of Moral Sentiments* is an unqualified doctrine of a harmonious order of nature, under divine guidance, which promotes the welfare of man through the operation of his individual propensities. Of these, self-interest is the most important one, in so far as economic life is concerned, though it is subject to the regulations of natural justice, to which it must conform. "In the race for wealth, for honours, and preferments, he may run as hard as he can, and strain every nerve and every muscle, in order to outstrip all his competitors. But if he should jostle, or throw down any of them, the indulgence of the spectator is entirely at an end. It is a violation of fair play, which they cannot admit of."[23] In economic matters, benevolence plays but a minor rôle. There is no express formulation of a principle of laissez faire, and no explicit condemnation of governmental interference with individual initiative; but it is quite clearly implied that self-interest, if regulated by justice, which may be natural justice, but is likely to be more effective if it is administered by a magistrate, is sufficient to attain the ends of Nature in the economic world. There is convincing evidence from other sources that Smith was already an exponent of the system of natural liberty.

III. THE SYSTEM OF NATURAL LIBERTY IN THE "WEALTH OF NATIONS"

Traces of the general doctrine expounded in the *Theory of Moral Sentiments,* that there is a beneficent order in nature which, if left to take its own course, will bring to mankind maximum happiness and prosperity, are undoubtedly to be discovered in the *Wealth of Nations.* Traces of every conceivable sort of doctrine are to be found in that most catholic book, and an economist must have peculiar theories indeed who cannot quote from the *Wealth of Nations* to support his special purposes. But it can be convincingly demonstrated, I believe, that on the points at which they come into contact there is a substantial measure of irreconcilable divergence between the *Theory of Moral Sentiments* and the *Wealth of Nations,* with respect to the character of the natural order.

In the first case, the emphasis in the *Theory of Moral Sentiments* upon a benevolent deity as the author and guide of nature is almost, though not quite, completely absent in the *Wealth of Nations.* There are only a few minor passages in the later work which can be adduced as supporting evidence of the survival in Smith's thought of the concept of a divinity who has so shaped economic process that it operates necessarily to promote human welfare: an incidental allusion to "the wisdom of nature";[24] a remark that with respect to smuggling the laws of the country had "made that a crime which nature never meant to be so";[25] and a more famous passage, the main reliance of those who would completely reconcile the doctrines ex-

311

pounded in the two works, in which Smith repeats the phrase "the invisible hand" which he had used in the *Theory of Moral Sentiments*.[26] The only explicit reference to God is one which could have given but scant comfort to the natural theology of his time: "Superstition first attempted to satisfy this curiosity [about natural phenomena] by referring all those wonderful appearances to the immediate agency of the gods. Philosophy afterward endeavored to account for them from more familiar causes, or from such as mankind were better acquainted with, than the agency of the gods."[27] To the extent that Smith in the *Wealth of Nations* does expound a doctrine of a harmonious order in nature, he accounts for it, as a rule, and perhaps even invariably, by reference to "more familiar causes [and] to such as mankind were better acquainted with, than the agency of the gods." The significance for our purposes of this virtual disappearance from the *Wealth of Nations* of the doctrine of an order of nature designed and guided by a benevolent God is that it leaves Smith free to find defects in the order of nature without casting reflections on the workmanship of its Author.

To some extent Smith makes use of this freedom. In both works he finds an inherent harmony in the order of nature, whereby man, in following his own interests, at the same time and without necessarily intending it serves also the general interests of mankind. In the *Theory of Moral Sentiments*, this harmony, as I have shown, is represented as universal and perfect. In the *Wealth of Nations*, this harmony is represented as not extending to all elements of the economic order, and often as partial and imperfect where it does extend. Where harmony does prevail, it is as a rule a sort of average or statistical harmony, revealing itself only in the general mass of phenomena and leaving scope for the possibility that natural processes whose general effect is beneficial may work disadvantageously in individual cases or at particular moments of time. As a rule, though not invariably, Smith qualifies his assertions of harmony by such phrases as "in most cases," "the majority," "in general," "frequently." For example, the exercise of common prudence is a prerequisite if the system of natural liberty is to operate harmoniously, and "though the principles of common prudence do not always govern the conduct of every individual, they always influence that of *the majority* of every class or order."[28] "It is advantageous to the great body of workmen . . . that all these trades should be free, though this freedom may be abused in all of them, and is more likely to be so, perhaps, in some than in others."[29] Drawbacks "tend not to destroy, but to preserve, what it is *in most cases* advantageous to preserve, the natural division and distribution of labour in the society."[30]

There are a number of well-known passages in the *Wealth of Nations* in which Smith asserts the existence of a more-or-less complete harmony between the general interests of society and the particular interests of individuals.

It is not from the benevolence of the butcher, the brewer, or the baker, that we expect our dinner, but from their regard to their own interest. We address ourselves, not to their humanity but to their self-love, and never talk to them of our own necessities but of their advantages. . . . .[31] Every individual is continually exerting himself to find out the most advantageous employment for whatever capital he can command. It is his own advantage, indeed, and not that of the society, which he has in view. But the study of his own advantage naturally, or rather necessarily leads him to prefer that employment which is most advantageous to the society. . . . .[32] As every individual, therefore, endeavors as much as he can both to employ his capital in the support of domestic industry, and so to direct that industry that its produce may be of the greatest value; every individual necessarily labours to render the annual revenue of the society as great as he can. He generally, indeed, neither intends to promote the public interest, nor knows how much he is promoting it. By preferring the support of domestic to that of foreign industry he intends only his own security; and by directing that industry in such a manner as its produce may be of the greatest value, he intends only his own gain, and he is in this, as in many other cases, led by an invisible hand to promote an end which was no part of his intention. . . . .[33] The natural effort of every individual to better his own condition, when suffered to exert itself with freedom and security, is so powerful a principle, that it is alone, and without any assistance, not only capable of carrying on the society to wealth and prosperity, but of surmounting a hundred impertinent obstructions with which the folly of human laws too often incumbers its operations; though the effect of these obstructions is always more or less either to encroach upon its freedom, or to diminish its security.[34]

But whereas in the *Theory of Moral Sentiments* such general statements as these comprise the main substance of the doctrine of a harmonious order in the economic world, in the *Wealth of Nations* they play a much more modest rôle. Though Smith in the *Wealth of Nations* frequently makes general statements intended apparently to apply to the entire universe, he has always before him for consideration some concrete problem, or some finite section of the universe. In no instance does Smith rely heavily upon his assertions as to the existence of harmony in the natural order at large to establish his immediate point that such harmony exists within the specific range of economic phenomena which he is at the moment examining. Such demonstration he accomplishes primarily by means of reference to the nature of these specific phenomena, by appeal to some self-evident principles of human psychology, by citation of historical object lessons, or by inference from contemporary experience. The general statements, though they may, as has been asserted, reveal the secret basis of Smith's conclusions, are given the appearance of mere obiter dicta, thrown in as supernumerary reinforcements to an argument already sufficiently fortified by more specific and immediate data. Smith's argument for the existence of a natural harmony in the economic order, to be preserved by following the system of natural liberty, is, in form at least, built up by detailed inference from specific data and by examination of specific problems, and is not deduced from wide-sweeping generalizations concerning the universe in general. What were the secret mental processes of Adam Smith whereby he really reached his conclusions it seems at this late date somewhat difficult to talk about with any degree of assurance.

Nowhere in the *Wealth of Nations* does Smith place any reliance for the proper working of the economic order upon the operation of benevolence or sympathy, the emphasis upon which was the novel feature in the account of human nature presented in the *Theory of Moral Sentiments*. In the *Wealth of Nations,* benevolence is not merely as a rule left out of the picture of the economic order; when mentioned, it is with the implication that it is a weak reed upon which to depend. "By pursuing his own interest he frequently promotes that of the society more effectually than when he really intends to promote it. I have never known much good done by those who affected to trade for the public good. It is an affectation, indeed, not very common among merchants, and very few words need be employed in dissuading them from it."[35] The only other instance in which Smith concedes the possible operation of benevolence in the economic world he also does not take too seriously:

> Whatever part of the produce . . . . is over and above this share, he [i.e., the landlord] naturally endeavors to reserve to himself as the rent of his land, which is evidently the highest the tenant can afford to pay in the actual circumstances of the land. Sometimes, indeed, the liberality, more frequently the ignorance, of the landlord, makes him accept of somewhat less than this portion. . . . . This portion, however, may still be considered as the natural rent of land, or the rent for which it is naturally meant that land should for the most part be let.[36]

The consequences of the intervention of liberality apparently are not "natural," are not in accordance with the intent of nature! Smith shows little faith in the prevalence of benevolence in the economic sphere. "Man has almost constant occasion for the help of his brethren, and it is in vain for him to expect it from their benevolence only. . . . . It is not from the benevolence of the butcher, the brewer, or the baker, that we expect our dinner, but from their regard to their own interest."[37] "The late resolution of the Quakers in Pennsylvania to set at liberty all their negro slaves, may satisfy us that their number cannot be very great. Had they made any considerable part of their property, such a resolution could never have been agreed to."[38] Even the college professor cannot be expected to expend much energy in teaching effectively, cannot even be depended upon to teach at all, if it is not made to his interest to do so.[39] In the case of the clergy, the situation seems even more desperate. If they are endowed, they become indolent, and their zeal and industry become impaired. If, on the other hand, they are dependent upon voluntary contributions for their support, they become too zealous. He quotes from his skeptical friend Hume:

> . . . . This interested diligence of the clergy is what every wise legislator will study to prevent; because, in every religion except the true, it is highly pernicious. . . . . Each ghostly practitioner, in order to render himself more precious and sacred in the eyes of his retainers, will inspire them with the most violent abhorrence of all other sects, and continually endeavor, by some novelty, to excite the languid devotion of his audience. No regard will be paid to truth, morals, or decency in the doctrines inculcated. Every tenet will be adopted that best suits the disorderly affections of the human frame. Customers will be drawn to each conventicle by new industry and address in practising on the passions and credulity of the populace.[40]

Smith laid little stress even in the *Theory of Moral Sentiments* upon the importance of benevolence in the economic order. But writers who have labored under a sense of obligation to find a basis for reconciliation of the *Wealth of Nations* with the *Theory of Moral Sentiments* have nevertheless discovered a problem in the insignificant rôle assigned to benevolence in the *Wealth of Nations*. Buckle's solution of the problem was that in the *Wealth of Nations* Smith was deliberately abstracting from all principles of human nature except self-interest, whereas in the *Theory of Moral Sentiments* he aimed at a complete picture of human nature. Not a trace of evidence is discoverable, however, that Smith in the *Wealth of Nations* was aware that he was abstracting selected elements from the totality of human nature. It awaited a later and keener mind, Ricardo, to discover the possibilities of the technique of deliberate abstraction in the field of economics. A more ingenious attempt at reconciliation rests, in part, on the identification of self-interest as used in the *Wealth of Nations* with rational pecuniary interest, with a desire for more wealth, and by demonstrating that Smith takes into account other motives than the rational desire for more wealth, claims to demonstrate that Smith did not exclude all principles but self-interest from the economic sphere. But self-interest meant to Smith not only the desire for wealth, but self-love in all its possible manifestations. "It is the interest of every man to live as much at his ease as he can."[41] "Avarice and ambition in the rich, in the poor the hatred of labour and the love of present ease and enjoyment," envy, malice and resentment,[42] all of these are manifestations of self-interest; the agreeableness, the ease or hardship, the cleanliness or dirtiness, the honorableness or dishonorableness, of the different employments are all factors affecting the attractiveness to labor of different occupations, as well as the wages paid: "Honour makes a great part of the reward of all honourable professions."[43] Smith distinguishes also between what a man is interested in and what is to his interest. Man is sometimes ignorant of the latter. "But though the interest of the labourer is strictly connected with that of the society, he is incapable either of comprehending that interest, or of understanding its connexion with his own."[44] It is what a man regards as his interest, even though mistakenly, that controls his actions. But every possible impulse and motive to action is included under self-interest except a deliberate intention to promote the welfare of others than one's self.

From his examination of the operation of self-interest in specific phases of the economic order and of the consequences of government interference with the free operation of self-interest, Smith arrives at an extensive program for the extension of the system of natural liberty through the abolition of existing systems of governmental regulation, though he nowhere brings the several items in that program together. Four main reforms are advocated. Free choice of occupations is to be established through the abolition of the apprenticeship regulations and settlement laws; free trade in land, through the repeal of laws establishing entails, primogenitures, and other restrictions on the free transfer of land by gift, devise, or sale; internal free trade, where such does not already prevail, by the abolition of local customs taxes;

315

and most important of all, free trade in foreign commerce, through the abolition of the duties, bounties, and prohibitions of the mercantilistic régime and the trading monopolies of the chartered companies. These various restrictions and regulations are objectionable either because they operate to keep commerce, labor, or capital from following the channels in which they would otherwise go, or because they attract to a particular species of industry a greater share of the factors than would ordinarily be employed in it. In all of these cases there is close harmony, under the system of natural liberty, between the interests of individuals and the public interest, and interference by government, instead of promoting, hinders, though it does not necessarily prevent, the attainment of prosperity.

In England all of this program has been achieved, and in so far as such things can be traced to their source, the influence of the *Wealth of Nations* was an important factor in bringing about the reforms. That they were genuine reforms most economists will admit, though even in England there is no longer the unanimity there once was on these matters. It is a somewhat ironical coincidence that the least important plank in Smith's program, the reform of the English law of property, should be in process of achievement only as the permanence of the greatest of his victories, the establishment of free trade in foreign commerce, faces its first serious threat in sixty years.

IV. FLAWS IN THE NATURAL ORDER

The foregoing is familiar matter. What is not so familiar, however, is the extent to which Smith acknowledged exceptions to the doctrine of a natural harmony in the economic order even when left to take its natural course. Smith, himself, never brought these together; but if this is done, they make a surprisingly comprehensive list and they demonstrate beyond dispute the existence of a wide divergence between the perfectly harmonious, completely beneficent natural order of the *Theory of Moral Sentiments* and the partial and limited harmony in the economic order of the *Wealth of Nations*. Masters and workmen have a conflict of interest with respect to wages, and the weakness in bargaining power of the latter ordinarily gives the advantage in any dispute to the former.[45] Masters, traders, and apprentices, on the one hand, and the public on the other, have divergent interests with respect to apprenticeship rules.[46] The interest of merchants and manufacturers is in high profits, which are disadvantageous to the public.[47] Merchants and manufacturers have interests opposed to those of the farmers and landlords,[48] and of the general public.[49] "People of the same trade seldom meet together, even for merriment and diversion, but the conversation ends in a conspiracy against the public, or in some contrivance to raise prices. It is impossible indeed to prevent such meetings, by any law which either could be executed, or would be consistent with liberty and justice."[50] The corn-dealer, on the whole, performs a useful service, but because of his "excess of avarice he does not perform it perfectly."[51] The merchant exporter sometimes finds it to his interest, when dearth prevails both at home and abroad, "very much to aggravate the calamities of the dearth" at home by exporting corn.[52] Men commonly overestimate their chances of success in risky ventures, with the consequence that too great a share of the nation's stock of capital goes into such ventures.[53] It being the custom to pay attorneys and clerks according to the number of pages they had occasion to write, their self-interest led them "to multiply words beyond all necessity, to the corruption of the law language of, I believe, every court of justice in Europe."[54] Private initiative cannot be trusted to take proper care of the roads.[55] Division of labor operates to impair the intelligence, enterprise, martial courage, and moral character of the laborers,[56] though division of labor is itself "the necessary, though very slow and gradual, consequence of a certain propensity in human nature . . . the propensity to truck, barter, and exchange one thing for another."[57] In old countries, "rent and profit eat up wages, and the two superior orders of people oppress the inferior one."[58] This is only a partial list of the defects in the natural order, even when left to take its own course, which Smith points out, though it would suffice to provide ammunition for several socialist orations. This is a far cry from the account given in the *Theory of Moral Sentiments* of a perfectly harmonious order of nature, operating under divine guidance, to promote its "great end, the order of the world, and the perfection and happiness of human nature."

In the *Theory of Moral Sentiments* Smith started out with a few general propositions about the nature of the universe which any educated Scotchman of his day would have vouched for as self-evident truths; and following them wherever they led him, he picked up en route a few more self-evident truths about the nature of human nature, and finally reached conclusions of the sort we have examined. Failing to compare his conclusions with the facts, he saw no necessity for qualifying them, and no reason for re-examining his premises. Unfortunately, these premises were in special need of careful scrutiny, for they were all drawn from a peculiar class of axioms which urgently require, but are incapable of, proof. In his earlier work Smith was a purely speculative philosopher, reasoning from notions masquerading as self-evident verities. In the *Wealth of Nations* Smith made use of a rich harvest of facts gathered by personal observation at home and abroad, by conversation and correspondence with many keen and intelligent observers of the current scene, by wide reading in a miscellany of sources, from law books to travelers' tales. With this factual material Smith kept close contact, and he never departed from it for long. He still, it is true, retained his flair for resounding generalizations of heroic range. There is a long-standing feud between sweeping generalization and run-of-the-mill factual data, and when Smith brought them together he did not always succeed in inducing altogether harmonious relations. But Smith's strength lay in other directions than exactly logical thinking, and he displayed a fine tolerance for a generous measure of inconsistency. It is to his credit that when there was sharp conflict between his generalization and his data, he usually abandoned his generalization.

There would be little ground for insistence upon reconciliation between the *Theory of Moral Sentiments* and the *Wealth of Nations* if it were simply a case of comparing one book written in 1757 with another written in 1776. It may not be as common as it should be for a man in his full maturity to advance beyond the level of his first book; but it surely is not a rare phenomenon requiring to be explained out of existence. In every respect which is of concern to the economist as such, with the possible exception of his treatment of benevolence, the apparent discrepancies between the *Theory of Moral Sentiments* and the *Wealth of Nations* mark distinct advances of the latter over the former in realism and in application of the saving grace of common sense. But in the last year of his life Smith made extensive revisions and additions to the *Theory of Moral Sentiments,* without diminishing in any particular the points of conflict between the two books. This would make it seem that in Smith's mind, at least, there was to the last no consciousness of any difference in the doctrines expounded in the two books. Though we grant this, however, are we obliged to accept his judgment and to strain interpretations in order to find consistency prevailing where inconsistency appeareth to reign supreme? I think not. There persisted within the *Wealth of Nations,* through five successive editions, many, and to later eyes obvious, inconsistencies. When Smith revised his *Theory of Moral Sentiments* he was elderly and unwell. It is not altogether unreasonable to suppose that he had lost the capacity to make drastic changes in his philosophy, but had retained his capacity to overlook the absence of complete co-ordination and unity in that philosophy.

V.   THE FUNCTIONS OF GOVERNMENT

Adam Smith, as has been shown, recognized that the economic order, when left to its natural course, was marked by serious conflicts between private interests and the interests of the general public. This would seem to suggest that there was an important sphere in which government interference with private interests might promote the general welfare. In his one deliberate and comprehensive generalization dealing with the proper functions of the state, Smith made it clear, however, that he would narrowly restrict the activities of government. "According to the system of natural liberty, the sovereign has only three duties to attend to; . . . . first, the duty of protecting the society from the violence and invasion of other independent societies; secondly, ... the duty of establishing an exact administration of justice; and, thirdly, the duty of erecting and maintaining certain public institutions and certain public works."[59] Even here, however, he grants to government a somewhat more extensive range of proper activities than in many scattered dicta throughout the remainder of the book, where he was primarily condemning some specific governmental activity and was not really giving serious consideration to the wider problem of the proper range of governmental activity. Smith had himself undermined what is ordinarily regarded as his principal argument for laissez faire, by demonstrating that the natural order, when left to take its own course, in many respects works against, instead of for, the general welfare. How can his adherence, notwithstanding, to a policy of narrow limitation of the functions of government be explained?

The *Wealth of Nations*, though it was from one point of view only a segment of a larger and systematic treatise on social philosophy, was at the same time a tract for the times, a specific attack on certain types of government activity which Smith was convinced, on both a priori and empirical grounds, operated against national prosperity, namely, bounties, duties, and prohibitions in foreign trade; apprenticeship and settlement laws; legal monopolies; laws of succession hindering free trade in land. Smith's primary objective was to secure the termination of *these* activities of government. His wider generalizations were invoked to support the attack on *these* political institutions. Everything else was to a large degree secondary. Smith made many exceptions to his general argument for laissez faire. But his interest as a reformer and a propagandist was not in these exceptions. He nowhere gathered together in orderly fashion the exceptions which he would have made to his general restriction of government activity to protection, justice, and the maintenance of a few types of public works and public institutions. When considering in general terms the proper functions of government, he forgot all about these exceptions. If he had been brought face to face with a complete list of the modifications to the principle of laissez faire to which he at one place or another had granted his approval, I have no doubt that he would have been astounded at his own moderation. I once heard a president of a state bankers' association at the afternoon session of its annual convention make the theme of his presidential address the unmitigated iniquity of government interference with business and the necessity of more business men in government in order that they should see to it that there was less government in business. In the evening of the same day he introduced to the audience the state commissioner of banking as one to whom the bankers were deeply indebted, because by promoting the enactment of sound regulations governing the entrance into the banking field and the practice of banking he had secured the suppression of irresponsible and fraudulent banking, to the benefit of the solid and respectable bankers there assembled and of the general public. He was as sincere in the evening as he had been that afternoon. Not only was Smith fully capable of this type of inconsistency, but there is in the *Wealth of Nations* an almost exact parallel of this modern instance.[60]

There is no possible room for doubt, however, that Smith in general believed that there was, to say the least, a strong presumption against government activity beyond its fundamental duties of protection against its foreign foes and maintenance of justice. In his *Lectures*, Smith had said: "Till there be property, there can be no government, the very end of which is to secure wealth [i.e., to make wealth secure] and to defend the rich from the poor,"[61] following closely Locke's dictum that "Government has no other end but the preservation of property." In the *Wealth of Nations* he was more guarded: "Civil government, so far as it is instituted for the security of property, is in reality instituted for the defence of the rich against the poor, or of those who have some property against those who have none at all."[62] What were the considerations which brought Smith to his laissez faire conclusions? His philosophical speculations about a harmonious order in nature undoubtedly made it easier for him to reach a laissez faire policy, though I believe that the significance of the natural order in Smith's economic doctrines has been grossly exaggerated. But was not government itself a part of the order of nature, and its activities as "natural" as those of the individuals whom it governed? Smith is obscure on this point, and an adequate answer to this question, if possible at all, would require a detailed examination of Smith's position in the evolution of political theory, especially with respect to the origin of government and the character of the state of nature in the absence of government. It is clear, however, that to Smith the activities of government in the maintenance of justice are an essential part of the order of nature in its full development, and that such activities are not interferences with the system of natural liberty.

In the *Theory of Moral Sentiments* there is a vague passage which seems to suggest that government itself is an agency of the order of nature, and to imply that all of its activities may, therefore, be as "natural" as those of individuals.[63] In the *Wealth of Nations*, Smith is a little more precise. He draws a definite line between those activities of government which are, and those which are not, in accord with the natural order, on the basis of empirical data. Government activity is natural and therefore good where it promotes the general welfare, and is an interference with nature and therefore bad when it injures the general interests of society. Whether in particular circumstances it works well or ill is to be determined only by examination of the character of those circumstances, though in most cases such examination may be expected a priori to reveal that it works badly.

This general presumption against government intervention in the affairs of mankind was itself largely the product of direct inference from experience. Against those particular activities of government which he subjected to special attack, viz., mercantilistic regulations, settlement and apprenticeship laws, legal monopolies, Smith thought he had specific objections, drawn from the results of their operation, sufficient to condemn them. Aside from protection and justice, these were the important activities of the governments of his day. In condemning them he was not far from condemning all the main types of government activity, aside from justice and protection, which were prominently in the public view. To justify these activities, it was necessary, Smith believed, to credit government with better knowledge of what was to a man's interest than the ordinary man himself was endowed with. This Smith could not concede. The standards of honesty and competence of the governments of his day with which Smith was acquainted were unbelievably low, moreover, not only in comparison with what they are today in England, Germany, and the Scandinavian countries, but apparently even in comparison with earlier periods in English political history. Smith had encountered few instances in which government was rendering intelligent and efficient service to the public welfare outside of the fields of protection and justice. The English government of his day was in the hands of an aristocratic clique, the place-jobbing, corrupt, cynical, and class-biased flower of the British gentry, who clung to the traditional mercantilism not so much because of a strong faith that it met the problems of a growing trade struggling to burst its fetters, but because they did not know anything else to do. Even when Smith was prepared to admit that the system of natural liberty would not serve the public welfare with optimum effectiveness, he did not feel driven necessarily to the conclusion that government intervention was preferable to laissez faire. The evils of unrestrained selfishness might be better than the evils of incompetent and corrupt government.

In this connection, Smith has, indeed, a lesson to teach the "new economics" of the present day, which is peddling antique nostrums under new trademarks, and which has substituted for the answer to all economic problems of the classically trained parrot, "demand and supply," the equally magical phrase, "social control." If the standards of public administration are low, progress from a life regulated by the law of demand and supply to a life under the realm of social control may be progress from the discomforts of the frying-pan to the agonies of the fire.

It is the highest impertinence and presumption, therefore, in kings and ministers, to pretend to watch over the economy of private people, and to restrain their expense, either by sumptuary laws, or by prohibiting the importation of foreign luxuries. They are themselves always, and without any exception, the greatest spendthrifts in the society. Let them look well after their own expence, and they may safely trust private people with theirs. If their own extravagance does not ruin the state, that of their subjects never will.[64] . . . The violence and injustice of the rulers of mankind is an ancient evil, for which, I am afraid, the nature of human affairs can scarce admit of a remedy.[65]

Where, by exception, good government made its appearance, Smith was ready to grant it a wider range of activities.

The orderly, vigilant, and parsimonious administration of such aristocracies as those of Venice and Amsterdam, is extremely proper, it appears from experience, for the management of a mercantile project of this kind. But whether such a government as that of England; which, whatever may be its virtues, has never been famous for good economy; which, in time of peace, has generally conducted itself with the slothful and negligent profusion that is perhaps natural to monarchies; and in time of war has constantly acted with all the thoughtless extravagance that democracies are apt to fall into; could be safely trusted with the management of such a project, must at least be a good deal more doubtful.[66]

Smith believed, moreover, that there were evils involved in the economic order which it was beyond the competence of even good government to remedy. To repeat a useful quotation: "People of the same trade seldom meet together, even for merriment and diversion, but the conversation ends in a conspiracy against the public, or in some contrivance to raise prices. It is impossible indeed to prevent such meetings, by any law which could be executed, or would be consistent with liberty and justice."[67] We have tried, in this country, to abolish Gary dinners by law. Whether we have succeeded seems still to be open to argument.

So much for the negative aspects of Smith's theory of the functions of the state. Let us examine now what concessions he made to the possibilities of the promotion of human welfare through governmental action. Smith conceded that it was the duty of the government to provide protection against external foes, and on the ground of their necessity for defense, he approved of commercial regulations which on purely economic grounds he would condemn. "The act of navigation is not favourable to foreign commerce, or to the growth of that opulence which can arise from it. . . . As defence, however, is of much more importance than opulence, the act of navigation is, perhaps, the wisest of all the commercial regulations of England."[68] In the same spirit, Smith mildly supported bounties on manufactures necessary for defense, which would not otherwise be produced at home.[69]

Smith assigned to government also "the duty of establishing an exact administration of justice." Unfortunately, Smith never succeeded in carrying out his original plan of writing a treatise on jurisprudence, and the scattered materials in the *Wealth of Nations* and the meager outline in the *Lectures* are insufficient to give us a trustworthy judgment as to what he would include under "justice." His own definition in the *Wealth of Nations*, "the duty of protecting, as far as possible, every member of the society from the injustice or oppression of every other member of it,"[70] if broadly interpreted, would assign to government the task of a major reconstruction of the economic order, since Smith, as has been shown, recited many phases of it in which injustice and oppression prevailed. It seems clear, however, that Smith, like later and more doctrinaire exponents of laissez faire, took for granted the inevitability of private property and class conflict, and understood by justice the whole legal and customary code of his time dealing with individual rights, privileges, and obligations under that system of economic organization. It is also likely that Smith failed to see how far acceptance of even the prevailing code of justice carried him from a simple order of nature in which natural justice automatically emerges from the harmony of individual interests, independently of governmental machinery and sanctions. Punishment and enforcement of redress after the act in case of dishonesty, violence, fraud, clearly would be included under the "administration of justice." Smith would, perhaps, include as a proper phase of this function such preventive measures as would tend to give security against the perpetration of dishonesty, extortion, and violence. In any case, he does not oppose such regulations, though his *Lectures* indicate that he would include them under "police" rather than "justice."[71] "The institution of long apprenticeships can give no security that insufficient workmanship shall not frequently be exposed to public sale. When this is done it is generally the effect of fraud, and not of inability; and the longest apprenticeship can give no security against fraud. Quite different regulations are necessary to prevent this abuse. The sterling mark upon plate, and the stamps upon linen and woollen cloth, give the purchaser much greater security than any statute of apprenticeship."[72] Unqualified adherence to the principle of *caveat emptor* was apparently not a necessary implication of Smith's laissez faire doctrines. Enforcement of contracts is specified as an important function of government,[73] and a law obliging masters to pay wages in money rather than in kind is justifiable as a protection to the workers against fraud. "It imposes no real hardship upon the masters. It only obliges them to pay that value in money, which they pretended to pay but did not always really pay, in goods."[74] "Where there is an exclusive corporation, it may perhaps be proper to regulate the price of the first necessary of life."[75] Protection of slaves against violence by their masters is approved of both as in accord with common humanity and as promoting the productivity of slave labor.[76] Smith recognized the existence of a higher social justice, which may override the "natural liberty" of the individual, but he would invoke it sparingly. Regulations of paper money banking "may, no doubt, be considered as in some respect a violation of natural liberty. But those exertions of the natural liberty of a few individuals, which might endanger the security of the whole society, are, and ought to be, restrained by the laws of all governments; of the most free, as well as of the most despotical. The obligation of building party walls, in order to prevent the communication of fire, is a violation of natural liberty, exactly of the same kind with the regulations of the banking trade which are here proposed."[77] But "To hinder . . . . the farmer from sending his goods at all times to the best market, is evidently to sacrifice the ordinary laws of justice to an idea of public utility, to a sort of reasons of state; an act of legislative authority which ought to be exercised only, which can be pardoned only in cases of the most urgent necessity."[78] We have here, perhaps, the germ of that later maxim of convenient vagueness, that every individual should be protected in his natural rights, but only to the extent to which they do not interfere with the natural rights of others. There is no evidence that Smith would include as a proper phase of the administration of justice any drastic revision of the content of these rights.

There remains to be considered the third government function: "erecting and maintaining certain public works and certain public institutions, which it can never be for the interest of any individual, or small number of individuals, to erect and maintain; because the profit could never repay the expence to any individual or small number of individuals, though it may frequently do much more than repay it to a great society."[79] Smith here clearly assigns to the government a duty of promoting the general welfare other than in connection with protection and justice, if the means to do so are within the power of the government, but not within the power of individuals. What the relationship of this function is to the natural order Smith does not discuss in the *Wealth of Nations*. The attention given to it by Smith has been attributed to the influence of the Physiocrats. In the *Theory of Moral Sentiments* there is one passage which appears to praise such institutions, but may have been intended in a satirical sense:

The same principle, the same love of system, the same regard to the beauty of order, of art and contrivance, frequently serves to recommend those institutions which tend to promote the public welfare. . . . . It is not commonly from a fellow-feeling with carriers and waggoners that a public-spirited man encourages the mending of high roads. When the legislature establishes premiums and other encouragements to advance the linen or woollen manufactures, its conduct seldom proceeds from pure sympathy with the wearer of cheap or fine cloth, and much less from that with the manufacturer or merchant. The perfection of police, the extension of trade and manufactures, are noble and magnificent objects. . . . . They make part of the great system of government, and the wheels of the political machine seem to move with more harmony and ease by means of them. . . . . All constitutions of government, however, are [ought to be?] valued only in proportion as they tend to promote the happiness of those who live under them.[80]

In the *Lectures,* the only relevant passage is a passing reference under the general heading of "Police" to what may be regarded as a detailed phase of this function of government, the promotion of cleanliness, presumably of the streets.[81]

In the *Wealth of Nations* the discussion lacks somewhat in breadth, perhaps because it is merely incidental to Smith's discussion of the financial aspects of government. The public works and public institutions in this class, says Smith, "are chiefly those for facilitating the commerce of the society, and those for promoting the instruction of the people."[82] He nowhere purports to give a complete list of the public works proper to government, but he mentions highways, bridges, canals, and harbors. In discussing the propriety of particular projects, however, he completely ignores the criterion he had laid down at the beginning of his discussion, namely, the impossibility of their being conducted profitably as private enterprises. The only reason he gives for his approval of government maintenance of the highways is that private management would not have a sufficient incentive to maintain them properly, and therefore could not be trusted to do so.[83] He apparently approves of government operation of canals, though he grants that they can be left safely in private hands,[84] and that they can be profitably managed by joint-stock companies.[85]

The modern issue of the propriety of government participation in commerce and industry is dealt with by Adam Smith almost solely from the viewpoint: Can the government make a net revenue out of it? He takes coinage for granted as a government function without considering any possible alternative. He apparently approves of government operation of the post-office, but if so, the only ground given is the ability of the government to manage it with successful financial results.[86] He in general disapproves of government ventures into business, but solely on the ground that the government is a poor trader and a poor manager. The public domain, except what may be needed for parks, should be disposed of, because the sovereign is a poor farmer and forester. Smith apparently could not read German, and makes no references to German literature. Knowledge of the success of some of the German principalities in managing the public domain, and in other phases of public administration, would perhaps have lessened Smith's opposition to government ventures into industry. The modern advocate of laissez faire who objects to government participation in business on the ground that it is an encroachment upon a field reserved by nature for private enterprise cannot find support for this argument in the *Wealth of Nations.*

Of government "institutions," other than public works, intended to facilitate commerce, Smith opposes legal monopolies in general, though he concedes the validity of a temporary monopoly when a trading company undertakes, at its own risk and expense, to establish a new trade with some remote and barbarous nation, and he indicates that he approves for the same reason of the institutions of patent and copyright.[87]

Smith supports the participation of the government in the general education of the people, because it will help prepare them for industry, will make them better citizens and better soldiers, and happier and healthier men in mind and body. Public education is made necessary to check as far as may be the evil effects on the standards, mentality, and character of the working classes of the division of labor and the inequality in the distribution of wealth.[88] Here once more Smith draws a picture of the economic order under the system of natural liberty which is quite different from that beatific state which he dreamed about in the *Theory of Moral Sentiments.*

It is quite probable that Smith overlooked some current activities of government to which he would have given his approval if they had been called to his attention. The absence, for instance, in the *Wealth of Nations* of any discussion of poor relief as a public function has often been commented upon, and is generally regarded as having been due to oversight. But we have not yet revealed the full extent to which Smith showed himself prepared to depart from a rigid policy of laissez faire. The one personal characteristic which all of his biographers agree in attributing to him is absent-mindedness, and his general principle of natural liberty seems to have been one of the things he was most absent-minded about. We have already seen that in his more systematic discussion of the functions of government, Smith made important concessions to the possibility of government promotion of the general welfare through public works and institutions. In stray but frequent moments of intimate contact with facts apparently hostile to the principle of natural liberty, Smith conveniently forgot the principle and went beyond the limits set in his formal discussion to the proper activities of government. In arguing for the duty of government to support educational institutions which promote the martial spirit of the people, Smith incidentally concedes that "it would deserve its most serious attention to prevent a leprosy or any other loathsome and offensive disease, though neither mortal nor dangerous, from spreading itself among them,"[89] from which it may reasonably be inferred that he would even more strongly support public action taken to prevent the spread of dangerous diseases, and thus would include public hygiene among the proper functions of government. In many instances Smith supported government restrictions on private initiative where neither justice nor defense was involved, and where the sole aim was to improve upon the direction which private initiative gave to the investment of capital, the course of commerce, and the employment of labor. He supported the compulsory registration of mortgages,[90] and he wrote approvingly of colonial laws which promoted agricultural progress by checking the engrossing of land.[91]

To the great indignation of Jeremy Bentham, he approved of the prevailing restriction of the maximum rate of interest to 5 per cent, on the ground that if a higher rate were current, "the greater part of the money which was to be lent, would be lent to prodigals and projectors, who alone would be willing to give this high interest. . . . . A great part of the capital of the country would thus be kept out of the hands which were most likely to make a profitable and advantageous use of it, and thrown into those which were most likely to waste and destroy it."[92] We may be inclined to agree with Bentham that this is an inadequate defense of the usury laws, but what makes it significant for our purposes is that it involves an admission on Smith's part that the majority of investors could not be relied upon to invest their funds prudently and safely, and that government regulation was a good corrective for individual stupidity.

Smith also makes several concessions to the mercantilistic policy of regulation of the foreign trade. He admits that there are circumstances under which export restrictions on corn may be warranted;[93] he approves of a moderate export tax on wool on the ground that it would produce revenue for the government and at the same time would afford an advantage over their foreign competitors to the British manufacturer of woolens;[94] he favors moderate taxes on foreign manufactures, which would still give to domestic workmen "a considerable advantage in the home market."[95]

Smith recommended that rents in kind should be taxed more heavily than money rents, because "such rents are always more hurtful to the tenant than beneficial to the landlord."[96] He would tax rent from leases which prescribe to the tenant a certain mode of cultivation more heavily than other rent, in order to discourage the practice of making such leases, "which is generally a foolish one."[97] He would tax at more favorable rates the landlord who cultivates a part of his own land, because it is of importance that the landlord, with his greater command of capital and his greater willingness and capacity to try experiments, should be encouraged to take an active part in agriculture.[98] He would penalize by heavier taxation the landlord who capitalizes a part of the future rent, because this is usually the expedient of a spendthrift, is frequently hurtful to landlord and tenant, is always hurtful to the community.[99] Shortly thereafter, however, Smith returns to laissez faire: "The principal attention of the sovereign ought to be to encourage, by every means in his power, the attention both of the landlord and of the farmer; by allowing both to pursue their own interest in their own way, and according to their own judgment."[100]

Smith gives a little support to the use of the taxing power as what would now be called "an instrument of social reform." He approves of a tax on the retail sale of liquor so adjusted as to discourage the multiplication of little alehouses,[101] and of a heavy tax on distilleries as a sumptuary measure against spirituous liquors, especially if accompanied by a reduction in the tax on "the wholesome and invigorating liquors of beer and ale."[102] He supports heavier highway tolls upon luxury carriages than upon freight wagons, in order that "the indolence and vanity of the rich [be] made to contribute in a very easy manner to the relief of the poor."[103] He asserts that "the gains of monopolists, whenever they can be come at [are] certainly of all subjects the most proper" for taxation.[104] The modern single-taxer finds support for his cause in Smith's argument for the special taxation of land values. "Ground-rents, so far as they exceed the ordinary rent of land, are altogether owing to the good government of the sovereign. . . . . Nothing can be more reasonable than that a fund which owes its existence to the good government of the state, should be taxed peculiarly, or should contribute something more than the greater part of other funds, towards the support of the government."[105] He lends mild support to the principle of progressive taxation: "It is not very unreasonable that the rich should contribute to the public expence, not only in proportion to their revenue, but something more than in that proportion."[106]

Though there is nowhere in Smith's writings a general discussion of the possibilities of voluntary co-operation, he makes clear that he did not hope for much good from it. Making a reasonable inference from past experience, but a bad forecast of the subsequent trend, he saw in the joint-stock company very limited promise even for money-making purposes.[107] It was his verdict that the corporate guilds had failed to promote good workmanship.[108] Exception being made for the Presbyterian church, he saw even in religious associations much to blame.[109] About the only types of voluntary association in which Smith saw a high degree of effectiveness in accomplishing their purposes were associations of merchants and manufacturers to exploit the consumer and of masters to exploit the worker.

Adam Smith was not a doctrinaire advocate of laissez faire. He saw a wide and elastic range of activity for government, and he was prepared to extend it even farther if government, by improving its standards of competence, honesty, and public spirit, showed itself entitled to wider responsibilities. He attributed great capacity to serve the general welfare to individual initiative applied in competitive ways to promote individual ends. He devoted more effort to the presentation of his case for individual freedom than to exploring the possibilities of service through government. He helped greatly to free England from the bonds of a set of regulatory measures which had always been ill advised and based on fallacious economic notions, but he did not foresee that England would soon need a new set of regulations to protect her laboring masses against new, and to them dangerous, methods of industrial organization and industrial technique. Smith was endowed with more than the ordinary allotment of common sense, but he was not a prophet. But even in his own day, when it was not so easy to see, Smith saw that self-interest and competition were sometimes treacherous to the public interest they were supposed to serve, and he was prepared to have government exercise some measure of control over them where the need could be shown and the competence of government for the task demonstrated. His sympathy with the humble and the lowly, with the farmer and the laborer, was made plain for all to see. He had not succeeded in completely freeing himself from mercantilistic delusions, and he had his own peculiar doctrinal and class prejudices. But his prejudices, such as they were, were against the powerful and the grasping, and it was the interests of the general masses that he wished above all to promote, in an age when even philosophers rarely condescended to deal sympathetically with their needs. He had little trust in the competence or good faith of government. He knew who controlled it, and whose purposes they tried to serve, though against the local magistrate his indictment was probably unduly harsh. He saw, nevertheless, that it was necessary, in the absence of a better instrument, to rely upon government for the performance of many tasks which individuals as such would not do, or could not do, or could do only badly. He did not believe that laissez faire was always good, or always bad. It depended on circumstances; and as best he could, Adam Smith took into account all of the circumstances he could find. In these days of contending schools, each of them with the deep, though momentary, conviction that it, and it alone, knows the one and only path to economic truth, how refreshing it is to return to the *Wealth of Nations* with its eclecticism, its good temper, its common sense, and its willingness to grant that those who saw things differently from itself were only partly wrong.

NOTES

* Lecture delivered at the University of Chicago on January 21, 1927, in a series commemorative of the one hundred and fiftieth anniversary of the publication of the *Wealth of Nations*.

1. References to Adam Smith's writings are to the following editions: *History of Ancient Physics*, and *Theory of Moral Sentiments*, in "Essays Philosophical and Literary by Adam Smith" (Ward, Lock & Co., London, n.d.); *Wealth of Nations*, Cannan edition; *Lectures*, Cannan, editor.

2. *History of Ancient Physics*, pp. 391, 392.

3. Rae, *Life of Adam Smith*, p. 62. Italics mine.

4. *Theory of Moral Sentiments*, p. 75.

5. *Ibid.*, p. 71 n.

6. *Ibid.*, p. 80.

7. *Ibid.*, p. 96.

8. *Ibid.*

9. *Ibid.*, p. 163.

10. *Ibid.*, p. 163.

11. *Ibid.*, p. 210.

12. *Ibid.*, pp. 80, 97.

13. *Ibid.*, p. 210.

14. *Ibid.*, p. 71 n.

15. *Ibid.*, p. 79.

16. *Ibid.*, p. 146.

17. *Ibid.*, p. 58.

18. *Ibid.*, p. 163.

19. *Ibid.*, pp. 147, 148.

20. *Four Tracts* (Gloucester, 1774), p. 12.

21. *Theory of Moral Sentiments*, p. 148.

22. *Ibid.*, p. 149.

23. *Ibid.*, p. 76.

24. *Wealth of Nations*, II, 174.

25. *Ibid.*, II, 381.

26. *Ibid.*, I, 421.

27. *Ibid.*, II, 256.

28. *Ibid.*, I, 278. Italics mine.

29. *Ibid.*, I, 456.

30. *Ibid.*, II, 1. Italics mine.

31. *Ibid.*, I, 16.

32. *Ibid.*, I, 419.

33. *Ibid.*, I, 421.

34. *Ibid.*, II, 43.

35. *Ibid.*, I, 421.

36. *Ibid.*, I, 145.

37. *Ibid.*, I, 16.

38. *Ibid.*, I, 365.

39. *Ibid.*, II, 250 ff.

40. *Ibid.*, II, 273 ff.

41. *Ibid.*, II, 250.

42. *Ibid.*, II, 203.

43. *Ibid.*, I, 102.

44. *Ibid.*, I, 249.

45. *Ibid.*, I, 68–69.

46. *Ibid.*, I, 125.

47. *Ibid.*, I, 100; II, 112 ff.

48. *Ibid.*, I, 129.

49. *Ibid.*, I, 250, 428.

50. *Ibid.*, I, 130.

51. *Ibid.*, II, 26.

52. *Ibid.*, II, 40.

53. *Ibid.*, II, 64–65.

54. *Ibid.*, II, 213.

55. *Ibid.*, II, 217.

56. *Ibid.*, II, 267.

57. *Ibid.*, I, 15.

58. *Ibid.,* II, 67.
59. *Ibid.,* II, 185.
60. Cf. *ibid.,* II, 307.
61. *Lectures,* p. 15.
62. *Wealth of Nations,* II, 207.
63. *Theory of Moral Sentiments,* pp. 163–64.
64. *Wealth of Nations,* I, 328.
65. *Ibid.,* I, 457.
66. *Ibid.,* II, 303.
67. *Ibid.,* I, 130.
68. *Ibid.,* I, 429.
69. *Ibid.,* II, 23.
70. *Ibid.,* II, 185.
71. *Lectures,* 154 ff.
72. *Wealth of Nations,* I, 123.
73. *Ibid.,* I, 97.
74. *Ibid.,* I, 143.
75. *Ibid.,* I, 144.
76. *Ibid.,* II, 88.
77. *Ibid.,* I, 307.
78. *Ibid.,* II, 41–42.
79. *Ibid.,* II, 185.
80. *Theory of Moral Sentiments,* pp. 163–64.
81. *Lectures,* p. 154.
82. *Wealth of Nations,* II, 214.
83. *Ibid.,* II, 217.
84. *Ibid.,* II, 217.
85. *Ibid.,* II, 247.
86. *Ibid.,* II, 303.
87. *Ibid.,* II, 245.
88. *Ibid.,* II, 267 ff.
89. *Ibid.,* II, 272.
90. *Ibid.,* II, 347.
91. *Ibid.,* II, 73.
92. *Ibid.,* I, 338.
93. *Ibid.,* II, 41.
94. *Ibid.,* II, 152.
95. *Ibid.,* II, 367. Smith may, however, have supported such taxes as an alternative to the existing higher taxes and prohibitions of import, and not as preferable to free import.
96. *Ibid.,* II, 316.
97. *Ibid.*
98. *Ibid.*
99. *Ibid.,* II, 315.
100. *Ibid.,* II, 318.
101. *Ibid.,* II, 337.
102. *Ibid.,* II, 375.
103. *Ibid.,* II, 216.
104. *Ibid.,* II, 377.
105. *Ibid.,* II, 329.
106. *Ibid.,* II, 327.
107. *Ibid.,* II, 246.
108. *Ibid.,* I, 131.
109. *Ibid.,* II, 273 ff.

13.

T. W. HUTCHISON
University of Birmingham

Bentham

as an

Economist[1]

I

In the spring of 1941, at the original suggestion of J. M. Keynes, the Royal Economic Society commissioned Dr. Stark to prepare a comprehensive edition of Bentham's economic writings. Dr. Stark's task did not include the tracking down of long-vanished documents as had that of Ricardo's editor, but rather lay primarily in deciphering, sorting, selecting from and piecing together the masses of manuscript material at University College, the British Museum and Geneva. These vast heaps of papers were only legible with great difficulty, and were shuffled about in a state of complete confusion, which such pagination as Bentham had provided only aggravated rather than alleviated. Everyone interested in the history of economic thought, and in Bentham in particular, is very deeply indebted to Dr. Stark for the devotion and skill with which he has produced these three volumes and for the great interest and illumination they afford.

Dr. Stark's problems have inevitably, in the nature of the case, been those of continual selection and arrangement. The more or less insoluble problems of selection were on two fronts: that of selecting "economic" from "non-economic" writings — necessitated by modern specialism — and that of selecting those worth including from the masses of notes and fragments.

Reprinted from *The Economic Journal*, LXVI (June 1956), 288–306, slightly enlarged, by permission of the author and The Royal Economic Society. At the time of original publication, the author was with The London School of Economics.

Since, almost by definition, a "scholar" is one who never trusts, if he can possibly help it, any other selection or arrangement than his own, one might run the risk of appearing "unscholarly" unless, at least formally, certain reservations were expressed. (Not that we wish to press such reservations, because Dr. Stark has the obvious and valid reply that if one does not like *his* selection and arrangement, then one can go and bury oneself in the Bentham manuscripts for ten years, as he did, and produce one's own.)

However, unexhausted by the myriad problems of selection and arrangement posed by the manuscripts, Dr. Stark went on to select and arrange for this edition two anthologies, at the start of Vol. I and at the end of Vol. III, of passages from Bentham's already published non-economic writings, designed to illustrate or unfold his conception first of the Philosophy of Economic Science and, at the end, of the Psychology of Economic Man. But helpful and instructive though these passages are — extending from single sentences to several pages — one would like to feel certain that their inclusion has not taken up space which might have gone to material of interest to economists, still unpublished. Perhaps one *should* feel certain about this, in view of the extreme care and competence of Dr. Stark's work. Nevertheless, there is in fact the example of an extremely interesting fragment on the moral calculus, published for the first time in 1952, which would certainly have been a most suitable and valuable item for this edition.[2] We trust that this is an isolated example. Dr. Stark informs us that before the publication of this edition only "at best the tenth part" of Bentham's economic writings had been available in print (I, p. 11). It is difficult to estimate the percentages of new and previously published material in these three volumes, since some of the texts have been re-arranged or expanded as compared with the versions already available. But it does not seem that very much more than a half, or two-thirds at the most, can be new, and therefore very large quantities of Bentham's economic writings must still remain in manuscript, being presumably too repetitive, fragmentary or incoherent to do anything with.

The great services which these volumes afford might be briefly described as follows. First, they enable us to consider for the first time Bentham's contribution to political economy, which though it certainly does not take the form of a carefully finished, well-rounded achievement, easy to weigh up, is nevertheless chock-full of powerful, fertile and independent ideas on some of the perennial and fundamental problems of economic analysis and policy. At least some of the misconceptions about Bentham's standing as a political economist ought now to be removed (at any rate, for example, the statement Keynes once made that Bentham "was not an economist at all").[3] More particularly, these volumes put before us in all their profusion and variety Bentham's ideas on the theory of money, investment and employment,[4] and they tell a deeply interesting story of the development and the fundamental changes in his ideas on this subject. Bentham devoted about eighteen years to political economy (*c.* 1786–1804), and in that time moved from a thorough-going acceptance of the "classical" Smithian doctrines on saving and investing and their implications for policy, to what amounts to a thorough-going rejection. After 1804 he never actively returned to the subject or showed much interest in the great new developments of the Ricardo era, except for a minor pamphlet in 1821. This story provides us with another of those ironies in the history of economic thought — all the more ironical in this case in view of the tremendous fame and influence of our author — where good original ideas, fundamentally acceptable to most economists of a subsequent period, were left buried and suppressed while the stage was dominated by doctrines now mainly and fundamentally rejected.

These volumes add little or nothing to the analysis of utility and diminishing utility available in Bentham's already published writings. It has often been pointed out, obviously with much truth, that Bentham's development of, and emphasis on, the two concepts of maximisation and utility make him above all the ancestor of neo-classical economic theorising, and especially of Jevons and Edgeworth. But these ideas were developed in Bentham's political, legal and philosophical writings. As an *economist,* as to-day defined, Bentham made no attempt to develop an economic calculus or a theory of relative values and prices. His economic theorising, in fact, is of an exactly opposite pattern to that typical of the neo-classicals. It is *not* mainly abstract, deductive and "micro-economic," tightly organised around the assumption of a maximising individual; but on the contrary, is rather practical, "macro-economic," concerned with aggregate monetary problems, and if not statistical, at any rate concerned to exploit such crude statistics as were available, while being ready for and calling for more.[5]

Finally, these volumes make it possible to reassess, as seems rather badly needed, Bentham's theory of economic policy, or his views on the role of the state in economic life. Our next three sections will refer briefly to some comments of Bentham on utility and value, will go on to tell in more detail of the development of some of his ideas on money, investment and employment, and will then discuss his doctrines on the role of the state.

II

As we have said, these volumes add very little that is new of the felicific calculus or the analysis of utility, to which Bentham had made such original contributions, mainly in his already published non-economic writings. Nor does Bentham attempt a systematic analysis of value and price. The most important new passage on this subject in these volumes takes the form of an interesting criticism of Adam Smith's treatment of utility. This comes in *The True Alarm* (1801), the opening sections of which are the nearest we get in Bentham's writings to a systematic account of economic principles. After emphasising that "all value is founded on utility . . . where there is no use, there cannot be any value" (III, p. 83), Bentham goes on to Smith's distinction between value in use and value in exchange, complaining that Smith "has not attached to it clear conceptions." Bentham is referring, of course, to the famous fatal sentences in *The Wealth of Nations,* almost the only ones throughout the book where value in use or utility gets any explicit mention, where Smith says, quite definitely, that value in use is in no way necessary for value in exchange, and vice versa, and that the two are in fact "frequently" quite separate. Bentham criticises Smith not for the distinction itself but for the way in which he formulates it, and for illustrating it by the paradox of water and diamonds. Bentham himself resolves this paradox on lines which clearly point in the direction of the marginal utility theory, that is, by invoking the plenty or scarcity of the supply, though he does not, of course, actually introduce the marginal concept:

"*Water* is the example he has chosen of that sort of article which has great value with a view to use but none with a view to exchange. In order to realize how erroneous the latter assertion is, he would only have had to consult in London the New River Board, and to remember that at Paris he had seen it sold retail by those who carry it into the houses.

"He gives *diamonds* as an example of that sort of article which has great value with a view to exchange and none with a view to use. This example is as ill chosen as the other. . . . The value of diamonds is . . . a value in use. . . .

"The reason why water is found not to have any value with a view to exchange is that it is equally devoid of value with a view to use. If the whole quantity required is available, the surplus has no kind of value. It would be the same in the case of wine, grain, and everything else. Water, furnished as it is by nature without any human exertion, is more likely to be found in that abundance which renders it superfluous: but there are many circumstances in which it has a value in exchange superior to that of wine" (III, pp. 87–8).

It is clear that if Bentham had ever got down to formulating precisely a general theory of value his approach would have differed fundamentally from the "classical" analysis of Smith and Ricardo. He would have continued in the tradition of Galiani, Pufendorf and the Schoolmen.[6]

III

Bentham's economic writings deal mainly with macro-economic questions arising, in several cases, out of topical issues of war finance and inflation, or "how to pay for the war," and his theoretical analysis is centred around questions of capital, saving, investment, money and employment. His starting point was that of a thorough-going, but even then by no means uncritical, disciple of Adam Smith. He accepted, to start with, the Turgot-Smith analysis of saving and investment[7] (the cornerstone of "classical" economics in the Keynesian sense) and, what went logically with it, the unqualified approval of "parsimony" and saving, and what came to be the Ricardo-Treasury view of the uselessness and waste of public works and public investment. On the other hand, in his later economic writings we find Bentham completely and fundamentally rejecting this self-same set of ideas, putting his finger very precisely on the limitations in its assumptions and applicability, and advocating in consequence completely different policies and a very different attitude to the role of the state in economic life. The trend of Bentham's thinking on these subjects is perfectly clear, though in writings that are often unfinished and dashed off in a completely unrevised note form, there are numerous deviations and inconsistencies around the trend.[8] If he had devoted a certain amount of time and patience to the task of working his ideas up into a finished, balanced treatise, or if he had found some understanding disciple to help him in this task — instead of Dumont, Mill and Ricardo — it is clear that Bentham could have produced a work as outstanding as Thornton's *Paper Credit.*

Bentham's first economic work, the well-known *Defence of Usury,* is primarily a policy pamphlet containing little in the way of theoretical analysis. Though devoted to criticising Smith from a more-Smithian-than-Smith point of view, it is entirely under the influence of Smith. We have now an hitherto unpublished postscript to the *Defence* which shows how his theoretical interests were developing. Here Bentham gives us a restatement of the Turgot-Smith theory of saving and investing and draws from it the logical implication that voluntary "parsimony" or saving always must result in, and is unconditionally necessary for, capital accumulation. He writes: "Whoever saves money, as the phrase is, adds proportionately to the general mass of capital. . . . The world can augment its capital only in one way: viz by parsimony" (I, pp. 196–8), and "parsimony" here means voluntary private individual saving. This leads on, as Bentham puts it, to "the development of the Principle 'No more trade than capital' or 'capital limits trade' " (I, p. 201). In the *Manual* Bentham actually complains that Smith had not been explicit enough in proclaiming this principle, though he adds, with more justification, that Smith "conforms to it in every recommendation he gives, and writes almost throughout as if it were constantly uppermost in his thoughts" (I, p. 233).[9]

The principle, Bentham tells us, "that the trade of every nation is limited by the quantity of capital, is so plainly and obviously true as to challenge a place among self-evident propositions" (I, p. 212). As we know, propositions in economics laid down as plainly and obviously true and self-evident very often, when one begins to dig into them, fold up into definitions, tautologies or, at best, trivialities. So rather than argue over what Bentham "really meant," in the abstract, by this principle, it may be more fruitful to consider what in practice it implied for him by observing the lively political rabbits which he conjures out of this collapsible opera-hat. The first political rabbit to emerge from this proposition "No more trade than capital" has *"laissez-faire"* written all over it. It is the same animal (or at any rate one of a very similar species) as the Ricardo-Treasury view. As Bentham puts it:

"Therefore no regulations nor any efforts whatsoever, either on the part of subjects or governors, can raise the quantity of wealth produced during a given period to an amount beyond what the productive powers of the quantity of capital in hand at the commencement of that period are capable of producing" (I, p. 201).

Hence government action can only *divert* investment resources from one line to another, not raise the level of investment.

The *second* important political rabbit — perhaps a rather surprising one — which Bentham conjures from his principle of "No more trade than capital" is that it would pay Great Britain to give up her colonies — or at any rate

334

that there are no economic advantages, in the form of the investment opportunities they provide, to outweigh the burdens and expenses of their upkeep.

The chain of argument is that there is only a fixed fund of capital; there are always just as profitable outlets for this at home, which do not require the extra military and administrative expenses that colonial investment necessitates. This assumption, that there are always just as profitable investment outlets at home — which incidentally seems possibly to conflict with Bentham's often-repeated generalisations about the falling rate of profit — is based on a sort of Say's market analysis applied to agriculture, to the effect that the supply of savings-investment will always create its own profitable demand — which is really implicit in the Turgot-Smith analysis.[10]

After *The Defence of Usury* and a brief essay on *Colonies and Navy* (1790), Bentham's next main economic work is the *Manual of Political Economy* (1793–95), from which we have already inserted some quotations.[11] In this treatise on the principles of economic policy Bentham is still to be found emphasising most strongly the *laissez-faire* conclusion which he takes to follow from his doctrine of "No more trade than capital": government can only *divert* investment funds, not raise the total level of investment.

"Whatever is given to any one branch, is so much taken from the rest. . . . If the government money had not taken that direction, private money would if the government would have given it leave. . . . Every statesman who thinks by regulation to increase the sum of trade, is the child whose eye is bigger than his belly" (I, pp. 234, 241 and 252).

However, though continually repeating such sweeping categorical assertions, Bentham does for the first time introduce a qualification, which was to grow later into an extensive body of monetary analysis. This qualification comes in a note at the end of the *Manual* headed "Connection of the Paper Money Question with the Rest of the *Manual*." Though "forced accumulation" by means of taxation is first referred to in the main part of this work, the proper concept of "forced saving" (though not, of course, the *term*), appears first in this addition on paper money.

Bentham writes, Government "can't increase wealth because they can't increase capital. Is there anything it can and ought to do to increase capital? Does paper money, for instance, increase capital?" (I, pp. 269–70). Bentham's answer in equally brief note form is:

"If all were fully employed it [the issue of paper money] could not increase industry. If any were unemployed, or not fully employed, it might increase industry *pro tanto*. . . . It actually is productive of an addition to the mass of national wealth, in as far as it gets extra hands, or sets them to work at extra hours" (I, pp. 270–1).

However, at this point, in contrast with his later views, Bentham simply mentions this possibility as an abstract theoretical *curiosum*, and considers that in practice attempts by governments to act on it would be dangerous.

This is the last that we have from Bentham on the subject for several years. But it was a turning-point. For when he returns to the subject Bentham advances straight through the cleft he had thus opened in the Turgot-Smith saving-investment analysis and in the Principle based on it, of "No more trade than capital." In fact, he completely abandons that Principle and the particular assumptions on which it rests, as well as the policy conclusions he drew from it.

His lengthy work on *Circulating Annuities* (1800) — unfinished like so many of the others — is concerned with his scheme for interest-bearing government notes which would serve both as paper money and small savings certificates. Here Bentham strenuously analyses the effects of changes in the quantity of money on the level of economic activity. An increase in the quantity of money may, Bentham repeatedly tells us, either or both raise prices or raise output — if initially there is unemployed or misemployed labour available. He observes:

> "In political economy as in chemistry, results are scarce ever obtained pure: while part of the new influx [of money] is employing in producing the beneficial result of an increase of real wealth through the medium of profitable labour, other part will be employing itself in the raising of prices of labour here and there, and thence of this and that class of goods: and, indeed, it is scarce possible that a new mass of dormant labour should be called forth into act without making some addition to the recompence given to the mass already in employment" (II, p. 313).

Above all, Bentham notes, monetary inflation may be a serviceable policy in *"war time* — a time in which money having to be raised in large quantities for the service of government, must for a time be diverted from other channels" (II, p. 315).

The effects of monetary expansion depend on how or where the new money initially enters the system and on the propensity to consume or save of those who initially receive it. It is not too anachronistic to use the modern terms, for Bentham quite clearly understands something of the significance of the consumption function and even attempted a very rough calculation of its order of magnitude. For example he notes: "It cannot be supposed that upon the mass of income from labour — most of it . . . being the labour of the poorest classes, — the ratio of savings to income can amount to anything like what it does in the case of income from profit of stock: to anything like $\frac{10}{15} = \frac{2}{3}$ of the amount of income: one should scarcely expect to find it amount to $\frac{2}{30}$" (II, p. 324n). Bentham also notes that a higher percentage of the new money paid out to highly-salaried officers will be saved than of that paid out to the lower-salaried (II, p. 322).

At one point Bentham rejects the possibility of deflationary cures for unemployment and is led into some most "mercantilistic"-sounding statements, in direct contradiction to his earlier principle of the fixed relation between voluntary saving and capital formation:

> "No addition is ever made to the quantity of labour in any place, but by an addition made to the quantity of money in that place. . . . In this point of view,

then, money, it should seem, is the cause, and the cause *sine qua non,* of labour and general wealth" (II, p. 326).

He adds: "This and a great deal more that might be added, is not in Adam Smith — but it belongs not the less to the science so well taught by Adam Smith" (II, p. 330).

In fact, in a remarkable footnote Bentham proceeds to criticise Smith for at least one of the main themes of his attack on mercantilism:

"Though 2 millions' worth of gold and silver is not worth a farthing more than 2 millions' worth of anything else, there is not on that account any absurdity in the exultation testified by public men at observing how [great] a degree what is called the balance of trade is in favour of this country. . . . Seduced by the pride of discovery, Adam Smith, by taking his words from the kitchen, has attempted to throw an ill-grounded ridicule on the preference given to gold and silver" (II, p. 337n).

In fact, Bentham claims that he has indicated the way in which "an answer may be found to a question for which I have in vain endeavoured to find an answer in Adam Smith and other books" (II, p. 339) — that question is by what process and with what chain of causation new money enters the economic system. He complains that "for my own part, I must confess, I never was able to obtain what to me appeared a clear insight into this part of the subject from the instructions of Adam Smith. Metaphors taken from wheels and water seemed to take the place too often of definition and exemplification" (II, p. 342n).

In his different works Bentham alternates, superficially somewhat confusingly, between warnings against the damage done by *de*flation and forebodings as to the injustices of *in*flation — long and short term (as in *The True Alarm*). But whether he is concerned with the one or the other Bentham constantly emphasises the crucial importance of whether the initial situation is one of full employment or one where there are unemployed resources, that is, there is no question for Bentham of full employment, or something near it, constituting some sort of realistic norm or equilibrium towards which the system actually "tends." Bentham fully appreciated the distinctions implied between *in*flation and *re*flation, and *de*flation and *dis*inflation. For example, at the end of his pamphlet *Paper Mischief Exposed* (1800–1) Bentham examines the effects of what he calls "the money-hoarding system," or "the system of laying up hoards of money on the part of government, in reserve for casual exigencies" by some kind of budget surplus (II, p. 453). (Incidentally the "Paper-Mischief" is not that of paper money as such, which Bentham approves, but that of the unregulated issue of paper-money by numerous private banks.) In a period of full employment, or over-full employment, with prices rising, such "government hoarding" will not lower output but will damp down the rise of prices. But on the other hand, "let us suppose that there exists in the country a quantity of unemployed capacity for labour. . . . In this case the defalcation from the mass of money is really productive of a correspondent, though not equal, defalcation from the mass of wealth. The money hoarded by government, and hence defalcated from the stock of money in circulation, is parcel of the money raised by taxes: the taxes are imposts laid, for the most part at least, if not exclusively, on expenditure" (II, p. 454).

Bentham's next work is called *The True Alarm* (1801), its subject being the long-term and short-term dangers and injustices of inflation (especially with an unregulated private note-issuing system). Bentham wavered between writing a formal treatise and a polemical pamphlet and in the end — as usual — abandons the work unfinished. However, he turned the manuscript over to his editor Dumont, who ten years later (in 1811) consulted J. Mill and Ricardo about preparing it for publication, and we have the Notes on this work which Ricardo then made (*v*. Vol. III of Sraffa's edition p. 259).

Here Bentham attacks the Turgot-Smith savings-investment analysis at its roots, by setting out the different ways in which the individual can use his money income. Bentham explicitly includes what he calls "laying it up" — a possibility omitted in Smith's analysis of saving and investing. He also very precisely puts his finger on the two vulnerable points in that analysis — which nevertheless, as Schumpeter has shown, remained so extremely influential right through the nineteenth and into the twentieth century. These two vulnerable points are, first, analysis in real terms applied with no (or no adequate) qualification to a monetary economy; and, second, exclusion of the possibility of what Bentham calls "laying up" or the possibility of "hoarding."

Later on Bentham examines the effects of an increase in frugality or decrease in consumption (III, p. 120). The first effect of a decrease in consumption, if it is not offset, is a fall in prices and then of production. But, of course, the fall in consumption may be offset by an increase in investment either on the part of the savers themselves or of others who have borrowed from the savers, directly or through a banker, either to invest or consume. In this case only frictional adjustments will be necessary. But if the income saved "instead of being put into circulation, is for an indefinite time put into a chest and kept there" then the "case is the opposite of the preceding one." The fall in consumption is followed by a fall in prices, production, profits and investment. Thus frugality is now, for Bentham, by no means unconditionally beneficial as it had been in his earlier writings and in Smith. In fact, Bentham goes on to extol the benefits of luxury expenditure in the manner of Mandeville:

"Let the rich and those in power spend all their revenue, as far as is possible, on superfluities, they cannot deprive the merchant of his profit on their expenditure: and as for the merchant, . . . he will not be able to rid himself of that disposition to accumulate which, to a greater or less degree, seems to be inseparable from his mode of life. Hence whatever the manner of expenditure . . . the merchant will not fail to levy a tax on prodigality for the encouragement and the increase of industry and wealth" (III, p. 124).

Bentham also takes up in *The True Alarm* his doctrine that an expansive monetary policy can raise the level of economic activity without voluntary saving. The effects of such a policy will, of course, turn on whether or not there are unemployed resources. Here Bentham emphasises how very difficult it is to define or perceive in practice when this exact point of "full employment" has been reached. As to this Bentham makes a statistical estimate that would seem to require some upward revision for the period since 1800:

"A thousand politicians have ventured predictions, and a thousand politicians have been wrong. Everybody wishes to decide the question in order to declaim about the actual state of affairs and to say with emphasis that we have reached the highest possible degree of prosperity and that that prosperity is no more than a dream which is going to vanish. To me it seems that something is gained if the difficulty of pronouncing on this point is shown. It amounts to a refutation of all the positive assertions of the two parties, to giving both of them a lesson in moderation and toleration. In the eyes of impassioned ignorance there exists no difficult question" (III, p. 148).

It is interesting to turn to Ricardo's notes on *The True Alarm* and find him expressing his complete *dis*agreement with Bentham's doctrine as to the possible beneficial effects of an increase in the money supply — he does so as repetitiously as Bentham states his doctrine.

We find Ricardo asking: "Why should the mere increase of money have any other effect than to lower its value? How would it cause any increase in the production of commodities. . . . Money cannot call forth goods — but goods can call forth money" (reminiscent of a passage in Smith). In fact, Bentham's doctrine is for Ricardo "a stumbling block . . . that money is the cause of riches has been supported throughout the work and has in my view completely spoiled it."[12]

Ricardo, in fact, could see nothing at all in Bentham's doctrine, just as he could see nothing at all in Malthus' ideas on effective demand, and J. B. Say's ideas on utility and value. He was, of course, holding with the strictest logic to the Turgot-Smith theory of saving and investing — to what he called "Mr. Mill's Principle," or the Say-Mill analysis of markets.

There is just one more point to add by way of illustrating the development of Bentham's ideas, and this is from his next work *The Defence of a Maximum* (1801) (*i.e.,* a maximum price for bread). Bentham here referred back to his arguments in the *Defence of Usury,* fourteen years before, where he had *attacked* a *minimum* legal rate of interest. He is at pains, in defending a maximum price of bread, to point out that he did not attribute to the market rate of interest any automatic self-adjusting equilibrating tendencies — a view which supporters of his attack on the control of the rate of interest had ascribed to him. This passage is of considerable general interest from the point of view of Bentham's attitude to the principles of economic policy, and his scepticism as to the methodology of equilibrium theorising and the economic harmonies. His particular point is that the rate of interest does not adjust (or optimally adjust) saving and investment:

"Gentlemen, when they have done me the honour to join with me, as it seemed to them, in opinion on this subject, have sometimes, whether for shortness or for ornament, referred in this way to a law of hydrostatics as the ground for it. Money, according to my opinion, I mean according to their edition of it, was a sort of thing that would find its own level, or that ought to be left to find it. Between what does naturally take place, and what ought to take place, there is indeed some difference: but it is a difference which moralists are apt enough to overlook, which they constantly overlook as often as they talk of the law of nature. . . . Neither on that or any other occasion have I ever given, or shall I ever give, serpents for fish, sentiment or metaphor for argument. I have not, I never had, nor ever shall have, any horror, sentimental or anarchical, of the hand of government. I leave it to Adam Smith, and the champions of the rights of man (for confusion of ideas will jumble together the best subjects and the worst citizens upon the same ground) to talk of invasions of natural liberty, and to give as a special argument against this or that law, an argument the effect of which would be to put a negative upon all laws. The interference of government, as often as in my humble view of the matter the smallest balance on the side of advantage is the result, is an event I witness with altogether as much satisfaction as I should its forbearance, and with much more than I should its negligence. Neither in that book [*The Defence*] nor in any other book of mine will any expression be found by which any such association is attempted to be made between the idea of money and that of a level, *i.e.* between rates of interest and levels. I choose rather to remain unread than feed the reader with such arguments. The particles of a mass of fluid, the particles of a mass of water, have a propensity, when left to themselves, to range themselves upon the same level: human creatures have on their part a propensity to save their own lives: and when water in the search after a level is making its way too fast into a ship, pumps are employed by men to prevail on it to get the better of that propensity, and betake itself to a higher level, and this may serve as an argument in favour of a maximum to any gentleman who finds himself disposed to consider it as such" (III, pp. 257–8).

In comparatively a very few years Bentham had moved a very long way from his earlier wholehearted acceptance of the Turgot-Smith analysis of saving and investment and his dictum that "every statesman who thinks by regulation to increase the sum of trade, is the child whose eye is bigger than his belly."

IV

Our last quotation brings us to Bentham's views on the respective roles of state regulation and the free price mechanism, or his theory of economic policy — a subject which is now one on which widely diverging and even diametrically opposite views are authoritatively advanced. For a long time the consensus of opinion held that Bentham was a representative of thorough-going *laissez-faire* doctrines or, at least — which *may* be rather different — was typical of "classical" nineteenth-century economic liberalism. Dicey and Leslie Stephen must have had much to do with establishing this view of Bentham. Dicey used "Benthamism" and "Individualism" as alternative terms, and held that "faith in *laissez-faire* . . . is the very essence of legislative Benthamism."[13] Keynes claimed that in Bentham "we discover the rule of *laissez-faire,* in the shape in which our grandfathers knew it."[14] Alternatively, Bentham and Adam Smith are linked together as the two great joint patriarchs of economic liberalism.[15] Dr. Stark's editorial comments are, with some qualifications, in tune with this conception. He writes of Bentham's "fundamental liberalism" (III, p. 32), noting that he was "a liberal of the socially progressive variety, not a doctrinaire who would have sacrificed everything on the altar of the dead and deadening principle of *laissez-faire*" (III, p. 52). However, Dr. Stark also tells us that Bentham was "a typical 19th-century liberal in economic matters," and "in his heart of hearts a confirmed votary of *laissez-faire*" (II, p. 8). Presumably there is no direct contradiction here, but the category of "a confirmed votary" who nevertheless "would not have sacrificed everything on the altar" seems to introduce an extremely difficult theological subtlety.

However, in contrast with this view of Bentham as a representative of *laissez-faire* or, alternatively, as a leading fellow-"classical" alongside Smith, Ricardo and Senior, a diametrically opposite view has been gaining ground in recent years. For example, in his Centenary lecture C. K. Ogden, the *doyen* of Bentham-*forschung* referred to him as "the greatest social engineer in history bristling with Five-Year Plans."[16] Sir G. M. Trevelyan "concludes generally that Benthamism was 'in many respects the exact opposite of *laissez-faire.*'"[17] Professor J. B. Brebner goes so far as to argue (criticising Dicey) that "in using Bentham as the archetype of British individualism he [Dicey] was conveying the exact opposite of the truth. Jeremy Bentham was the archetype of British collectivism . . . Bentham and Smith were fundamentally contradictory of each other in their ideas of how to secure the general good."[18] Finally, a very recent study has concluded that "thanks to the efforts of many current scholars it is at last becoming clear that Bentham may with more truth be called the patriarch of British collectivism than the father of individualism."[19]

We are prepared to take the risk of opining that at least these more recent views are considerably less misleading than the opposite picture of Bentham as a representative of *laissez-faire* or, alternatively, as a classical liberal. But the one moral which clearly emerges from this rather confusing intellectual situation is that any attempt to pigeon-hole or classify (or "classicalise") Bentham is bound to be particularly misleading, and any attempt at a precise and concise generalisation about his views on the role of the State especially hazardous.[20] In the first place, much important evidence has not been available, and even now we may not have all that is relevant. Secondly, the writings themselves were often dashed off unrevised, with the author never attempting to reconcile inevitable contrasts, or strike an explicit and clear balance of emphasis. Thirdly, Bentham's own views were constantly changing, sometimes according to a steady long-termed trend, while sometimes simply fluctuating around the trend or according to no discernible trend. Any attempt at a concise generalisation would at least have to distinguish between Bentham's earlier and later positions.

With these volumes before us it can now be much more safely said that whatever *laissez-faire* maxims Bentham may have emitted from time to time — more frequently in the earlier phases of his economic work (*c.* 1786–95)

— as the years went on, he is to be found suggesting more and more economic functions for the State, some of them very fundamental and pervasive. His injunction to the State to "Be Quiet" ("without some special reason"), cannot signify much when one finds him going on to find enough "special reasons" for "noise" to satisfy a whole series of Fabian Summer Schools. But although it seems much less misleading to regard Bentham rather as a prophet of the Welfare State than of the Gladstonian Budget, we do not want to try here to categorise or classify him. We simply wish to contrast his views on the role of the State with those of Smith, Ricardo and Senior and to suggest that he cannot be regarded as one of the "classicals," if this term is to preserve any doctrinal significance.

The contrast between what Bentham had to say on the role of the State in the economic field and the views of any economist reasonably describable as a classical liberal may be summarised under five heads:

(1) We have just seen how Bentham came to reject the Turgot-Smith theory of saving and investing and the idea of the rate of interest as a beneficial automatic regulator of saving and investment. His change of view on this subject obviously has quite fundamental implications for his view of the role of the State in the economic field. None of those regarded as typical "classical" economists argued in the manner of Bentham that the State either could or should beneficently act on the aggregate level of investment and employment, or be responsible for maintaining these at a high level. Even Malthus is hardly a genuine and complete exception.

(2) No "classical" economist sets out with such explicitness and detail so many varied economic functions for the State: the Bank of England should be nationalised and the issue of paper money should be a monopoly of the Government; there should be governmental licensing and participation in all banking and some government control of speculation; there should be government activity in everything connected with the propagation of knowledge — universities, schools, agricultural and scientific research and the collection of statistics; the Government should also be responsible for hospitals, health services, transport and means of communication. A newly-published paper (*Plan for Augmentation of the Revenue*, 1794–95) suggests that the superior security and longevity of the State, as compared with private enterprise, suits it for the taking over of insurance business on a large scale, in particular life annuities, life insurance, lotteries and the various activities of friendly societies.

(3) Bentham approaches the problem of the agenda of the State by laying down four overriding ends of economic policy, subject only to — (or which are in fact the constituents of) — the supreme end of maximum happiness. The four ends are, in order of importance: subsistence, security, opulence and equality. The fulfilment of these four ends justifies any amount of State action, and three of them in their very nature — subsistence for all, security and equality — are bound to

call for far-reaching intervention. This prior specification of overriding ends surely amounts to an approach to the problems of economic policy from a direction diametrically opposite to that of Smith and Ricardo. Smith, at any rate, rather starts from the fundamental benefi- cence of the free-market mechanism and then traces around this the framework of State activity necessary to maintain, and at exceptional points correct or supplement, this mechanism.[21]

What was really implied for Bentham in his four different ends of policy is brought out in a remarkable outline draft (or *"brouillon"*) dated October 22, 1800, and headed "National Prospects or a Picture of Futurity" (Vol. III, pp. 481–3). "Opulence" includes "maximum opulence of the lower classes. . . . The higher the wages of labour, the better consistent with national security." Nevertheless, Bentham does not believe that government can raise wages above "what is sufficient for bare subsistence to a family of average size." But he *does* believe that government could and should be "giving security to that measure of subsistence." Bentham goes on to note the "Insufficiency of the general propensity to accumulation to ensure a sufficiency of the prin- cipal subsistence for man, *i.e.*, corn. Necessity of the interference of government for that purpose." Furthermore government could and should promote opulence "so far as concerns the increase of capital: by forcing *savings* from pleasurable expenditure and applying the amount in the shape of capital."

(4) Though repeatedly urging that the individual is the best judge of his own interests, Bentham explicitly rejects the general principle that the hidden hand can be relied upon to work adequately towards the end or ends he lays down: "That the uncoerced and un- enlightened propensities and powers of individuals are not adequate to the end without the control and guidance of the legislator is a matter of fact of which the evidence of history, the nature of man, and the existence of political society are so many proofs" (III, p. 311).

In particular, the primary end of subsistence for all (or for as many as possible) required, according to Bentham, a policy of "magazining," or of the wholesale storage by the state of food supplies, and the fixing of maximum prices: "Insurance against scarcity cannot be left with safety to individual exertion." On the subject of price-fixing he writes:

"As I have all along suspected, the horror in which it has been held by the best opinions, has nothing but prejudice, and a too indiscrimi- nate attachment to general principles for its foundation" (III, p. 262). It is not simply that Smith, James Mill, Ricardo or Senior did not hap- pen to put forward such far-reaching proposals, it is rather that one cannot conceivably imagine them doing anything but oppose schemes like Bentham's to the uttermost, as did Burke.[22]

(5) Bentham's explicit mention of equality as an end of policy (although he puts it last), along with the analysis of diminishing utility on which he based it, has no important parallel in the writings of other classical liberals. Certainly at other points Bentham emphasises,

in direct contrast with his egalitarianism, the importance of preserving established expectations. But this also runs counter to the principle of leaving distribution to the free market, or to Ricardo's dictum, for example, that "like all other contracts, wages should be left to the fair and free competition of the market and should never be controlled by the interference of the legislator."[23] Professor Stigler has emphasised "the relative unimportance of the distribution of income to the classical economists" — a justifiable generalisation so long as Bentham is not included.[24] Bentham's recognition of the egalitarian argument which might be deducible from the principle of diminishing utility, and his multifarious taxation proposals, especially that for limiting inheritance, foreshadow the whole recent trend of British tax policy. At what stage, if any, on the road to our present position Bentham would have wanted to get off the bus, it is impossible to say. But Bentham was unquestionably one of the major influences in favour of getting the bus started on its present route, and this distinguishes him essentially — for better or for worse — from "classical" liberals like Smith, Ricardo and Senior.

V

The greater part of this account of Bentham's economic ideas rests on material published for the first time in these volumes. Thus, as an economic theorist this most celebrated and influential of Englishmen is something of a Cournot or a Gossen, that is, one whose work as an economist was largely unknown and of virtually no influence in his own day. In contrast with his political and legislative ideas, his writings on monetary theory found no disciples to follow them up, while what *was* published of his economic writings somehow gave rise to most misleading and confusing accounts of his position on the principles of economic policy.

We have already noted that when Dumont consulted Ricardo and James Mill on preparing for publication *The True Alarm* — perhaps the most important work in these volumes — they were in complete disagreement with its central theories and did not consider it worth proceeding with, or its ideas worth exploring further — in spite of the almost superhuman prestige which Bentham is supposed to have had in their eyes. Nor, for his part, did Bentham ever seem to have shown any interest in or agreement with Ricardo's *Principles*, his sole recorded comments thereon being: "In Ricardo's book on Rent there is a want of logic. . . . He confounded cost with value." As regards economic ideas, therefore, there seems to be no more misleading claim than Bentham's to the effect that Ricardo was (through James Mill) "my spiritual grandson."[25] This could only apply to some of Ricardo's political and parliamentary activities. Bentham's economic ideas, both as regards theory and policy, run on fundamentally different lines from those of Ricardo. There are no grounds for supposing that a single sentence of Ricardo's *Principles* would have been different if Bentham had never existed.[26] The questions Ricardo formulated, the assumptions he reasoned from and the method he used are sharply distinguishable from those of

Bentham. In Bentham's economic writings there are no long chains of deductive reasoning. His approach is far more empirical and statistical, and he would have rejected the idea of political economy as a mainly deductive science based on a very few fundamental and more or less self-evident assumptions — as classically described, for example, by Senior. Though J. S. Mill's general approach to economic policy diverges less from Bentham's than does his father's or Ricardo's, the theoretical differences remain fundamental; and there is no sign of the younger Mill ever having read, much less marked and digested, Bentham's unpublished economic writings.

On the two central questions of economic theory, that of the determination of relative values and that of the determination of the main economic aggregates, Bentham in his later and more definitive writings differed from the classical approach of Smith and Ricardo, all along the line. So although, like Ricardo, Bentham started from the *Wealth of Nations,* and even in *The True Alarm* writes that the work of Smith "still is and deserves to be the textbook of political economy," this cannot bridge the quite fundamental differences in approach which Bentham had opened up. Bentham himself could not realise or foresee how important and fundamental the differences between his ideas and those of Smith and Ricardo were to become, when the lop-sided classical emphasis on labour and cost of production in value, and on the rate of interest as a smooth and beneficent regulator of saving, investing and aggregate employment were to harden into dominant and largely unquestioned orthodoxies. On the one hand, Bentham's ideas, both on value and on saving-investment and employment, follow the lines of pre-Smithian "mercantilist" writers such as John Law, Berkeley and Sir James Steuart. On the other hand, they point forward to Jevons, Edgeworth and Marshall in one direction, and to Keynes in another. Only as a rather mild and elastic type of Malthusian does Bentham share in any of the main "classical" doctrines. If Bentham is still to be described as a "classical" economist, along with Smith and Ricardo, then this much-controverted adjective is virtually emptied of any doctrinal significance.

NOTES

1. *Jeremy Bentham's Economic Writings. Critical edition based on his printed works and unprinted manuscripts,* by W. STARK, in three volumes (London: Allen & Unwin. Vol. I, 1952, pp. 412, 30s.; Vol. II, 1952, pp. 458, 40s.; Vol. III, 1954, pp. 600, 45s. Obtainable by Fellows of the Royal Economic Society at the following special prices: Vol. I, 20s.; Vol. II, 27s.; Vol. III, 30s.; application, including remittance, should be made to the Secretary, The Royal Economic Society, The Marshall Library, Downing Street, Cambridge.) Physically, these volumes, in particular in the spacing and margins, are in marked contrast with the Ricardo edition, and provide a not entirely welcome reminder of the austere years in which they were conceived.

2. See Appendix IV of D. Baumgardt's *Bentham and the Ethics of Today,* 1952, pp. 554–66. It might, on the other hand, have been useful and relevant to have included the *Tracts on Poor Laws and Pauper Management* printed in Vol. VIII of Bowring's edition, which contain, among other things, an interesting criticism of minimum-wage legislation, and also *Emancipate Your Colonies.*

3. *The End of Laissez-faire,* p. 21.

4. The importance of Bentham as a monetary theorist had been suggested by F. A. Hayek in his "Note on the Development of the Doctrine of Forced Saving,"

Quarterly Journal of Economics, 1932, pp. 123–33. See also J. Viner, *Studies in the Theory of International Trade,* p. 188.

5. M. P. Mack in a recent study refers to Bentham "spending at least 10 years of futile effort trying to ferret out correct statistics for the gross national income, tax revenues, agricultural production, etc." See "The Fabians and Utilitarianism," *Journal of the History of Ideas,* January 1955, p. 82. Bentham showed much interest in and reliance on the contemporary attempts at Political Arithmetic of Dr. Henry Beeke, who, in his *Observations on the Produce of the Income Tax* (1800), attempted to estimate the national income. Bentham also refers to the pioneer attempt at a price index-number of Sir George Evelyn Shuckburgh (1798). One may guess that Bentham was far more interested in this practical statistical attempt to measure changes in the value of money than in some of the near-metaphysical arguments over labour as a measure of value.

6. On the subject of the water and diamonds paradox, which had, of course, been satisfactorily resolved by a number of writers before Smith (*e.g.,* Davanzatti, Law and Galiani), Schumpeter writes of "the astounding fact that Smith and Ricardo thought that this alleged paradox barred the way to a theory of value based on value in use" and refers to Smith "thereby barring, for the next two or three generations, the door so auspiciously opened by his French and Italian predecessors" (*History of Economic Analysis,* pp. 300 and 309). Bentham's remarks, if they had had any influence, might have helped to re-open this door. Ricardo, however, when he read this criticism of Smith by Bentham, noted emphatically in favour of Smith (cf. his comments in *Works,* ed. Sraffa, Vol. III, p. 284).

Incidentally, Schumpeter's "astounding fact" becomes all the more astounding when one recalls that Smith's main general statement in the *Wealth of Nations* on utility and value, at any rate at some points, directly contradicts his own statements as reported in the Lecture Notes of 1763 on the relations of "use," demand and value, and also the indications given in the Lecture Notes of the way in which the water and diamonds paradox is to be resolved in terms of scarcities (*v. Lectures,* ed. Cannan, pp. 157 and 176–7). Smith's famous statement in the *Wealth of Nations* also contrasts at some critical points with the treatments of utility, scarcity and value by his predecessors at Glasgow, Hutcheson and Carmichael (who has a very acute note on the subject). I am indebted on this question to an unpublished essay by Mr. W. L. Taylor.

7. On the Turgot-Smith analysis of saving and investment, on the sharp break it marks with preceding doctrines and on its dominating influence right down into the twentieth century, see Schumpeter, *History of Economic Analysis,* in particular pp. 191–3 and 282–8. This theory of saving and investment (rather than what is called "Say's Law") might well be considered the cornerstone of "classical" economics in the Keynesian sense. And, in emphasising the immense influence and wide unquestioned acceptance of the theory in orthodox circles for 150 years, Schumpeter can be said to be offering considerable confirmation of Keynes' generalisation about the history of economic thought.

8. We must regard as outside the trend of Bentham's thought, as set out in these volumes, such passages as are to be found in his early letters expounding the desirability of public works for the relief of unemployment (1776), and suggesting that with a suitable monetary and investment policy "those commercial distresses which beget distrust and produce ruin to many respectable individuals, while they distrust the beneficial intercourse of commerce *could rarely happen*" (1779, Bentham's italics). See *Works,* ed. Bowring, Vol. X, pp. 85 and 338–9. The throwing out of these ideas could be regarded as a significant foretaste of Bentham's later position, but they come a decade before he began to devote himself regularly to political economy, before he had temporarily adopted the Smithian analysis of saving, investment and capital, and, of course, before any of the writings included in this edition.

9. Bentham's "Principle" is suggested, as follows, by Smith: "No regulation of commerce can increase the quantity of industry in any society beyond what its capital can maintain. It can only divert a part of it into a direction into which it might not otherwise have gone" (*Wealth of Nations,* Everyman ed., I, p. 398).

This principle of "No more trade than capital" is, of course, highly reminiscent, or rather anticipatory, of the Wages Fund doctrine. Indeed, Bentham is described as the originator of that doctrine by Marx: "The classical economists have always been fond of considering social capital as a fixed magnitude possessing a fixed degree of efficiency. But this prejudice does not harden into a dogma until we come to the arch-philistine, Jeremy Bentham, the insipid pedantic leathertongued oracle of the commonplace bourgeois intelligence of the 19th century . . . . I should call Mr. Jeremy a genius in the way of bourgeois stupidity," etc., etc., etc. (*Capital,* Everyman ed., Vol. II, p. 671).

10. Bentham's hypothesis of unlimited investment opportunities in agriculture at home is based on the assumption that the British labouring class provides an ever-expanding market for beer: "In England, the lowest wages of labour will always find a man more bread that he can eat: therefore considerably more wheat than is produced at present, would, if not exported, not find purchasers. But the lowest wages of labour, nor wages much above the lowest, will not find a man as much

strong beer as he can drink, nor even as he can drink without hurting himself. Therefore, even independently of exportation, there is no danger of the nation's being overstocked with such of the productions of agriculture as are fit for making beer . . . . Agriculture then will always find a sufficient market for itself: it is impossible it should ever fail to do so" (I, p. 206).

It would be most interesting to follow further Bentham's views on the economics of colonial development. Like those of other economists of the classical period, they tie in very closely with his analysis of saving, investment-opportunities and the falling rate of profit. By and large there seems to be a considerable change in Bentham's attitude to colonial development very broadly—though far from precisely —in tune with the change we are describing in his economic ideas. But the divergencies in Bentham's views on colonies seem very wide and erratic: contrast the vision with which the *Defence of a Maximum* (1801) ends and the preceding argument: "Men spreading in distant climes, through distant ages, from the best stock, the earth covered with British population, rich with British wealth, tranquil with British security, the fruit of British law" (III, p. 302), with Bentham's argument that if the two sides had acted rationally in 1776 the Americans would have sought to remain in the British Empire, and the British would have sought to get rid of the Americans (III, p. 357). The concluding paragraphs of *The Defence* cast some doubt on E. G. Wakefield's claim to have converted Bentham in his last years (1829-31) from his earlier view that colonisation was a waste of capital, to Wakefield's own strongly favourable views. Bentham had at least half-converted himself thirty years before. See *England and America*, p. 252 n., and R. C. Mills, *The Colonization of Australia*, pp. 94 and 152. For the latter reference I am indebted to Professor L. C. Robbins. As a further example of Bentham's vagaries one may cite his attack on the Navigation Laws at one point, and his justification of them at another (Contrast I, p. 211, and III, p. 340). Similarly with the infant industries argument for protection.

11. What appears as *The Manual of Political Economy* in Bowring's edition is, according to Dr. Stark, concocted from a mixture of manuscripts of two very different dates. Dr. Stark has sorted out the two works. Much of what appears as *The Manual* in this edition is published for the first time and dates from 1793-95, while much of what Bowring published as *The Manual* is now to be found in a work now called *The Institute*, dated 1801-4—the last important work in this edition.

12. See Ricardo, *Works*, ed. Sraffa, Vol. III, pp. 298, 301, 317-18 and 333. See also Ricardo's extensive comments in his first letter to James Mill in 1811 (Vol.

VI, p. 14). In 1822, when Ricardo visited Geneva, he further discussed with Dumont Bentham's economic ideas: "There were few of his doctrines, to which Ricardo did not object" (see Sraffa's note, Vol. III, p. 261 n.).

13. See A. V. Dicey, *Law and Opinion in England*, 2nd ed., p. 44. Apparently Dicey had some doubts later about his equation of Benthamism and individualism. In the preface to the 2nd edition he writes: "It is a curious question how far Bentham's own beliefs were logically opposed to the doctrine of sane collectivism" (p. XXX). On Bentham and the rule of *laissez-faire* Leslie Stephen wrote: "In purely economical questions scarcely an exception was admitted to the rule" (*The English Utilitarians*, Vol. I, p. 310). See also J. Bonar, *Philosophy and Political Economy*, p. 189, and R. F. Harrod, *Economic Journal*, 1946, p. 438, who writes: "We cannot really have a definition of individualism that excludes Bentham."

14. *The End of Laissez-faire*, p. 21.

15. See H. Simons, *Economic Policy for a Free Society*, pp. 104-5: writes of "Adam Smith and Jeremy Bentham and the tradition of thought identified with them." W. H. Hutt actually describes Bentham as "holding even more unwaveringly the *laissez-faire* doctrine" [than Smith], *Economists and the Public*, p. 137.

16. Cf. *Jeremy Bentham*, p. 14.

17. See the quotation by D. H. Macgregor, *Economic Thought and Policy*, p. 68.

18. See J. B. Brebner, "*Laissez-faire* and State Intervention in Nineteenth-century Britain," *Journal of Economic History*, Supplement VIII, 1948, pp. 59 ff. Brebner refers to the Constitutional Code of Bentham as "that forbidding detailed blueprint for a collectivist state." Professor L. Robbins, on the other hand, refers to the Code as "this great project for a practical Utopia" or "the good society" (*The Theory of Economic Policy in English Classical Political Economy*, p. 42). We are not concerned here with whether the society Bentham was trying to outline was "forbidding" or "good," but simply that it is extremely different from that argued for by Smith, Ricardo, Senior and other "classical" liberals.

19. Cf. M. P. Mack, *op. cit.*, p. 88.

20. Of the leading authorities on Bentham's view of the role of the state, Professor J. Viner seems alone to be beyond all criticism. He reminds us of the very wide range of state activities supported by Bentham without trying to categorise, classify or "classicalise" him. See *American Economic Review*, March 1949, "Bentham and J. S. Mill: the Utilitarian Background."

21. F. A. Hayek in his essay on *Individualism True and False* classifies Bentham as a "false" individualist, that is as a rationalistic, in a sense *a priori*, individualist (who is really a precursor of totalitarian dictatorship), rather than a

"true," cautious, empirical one. There certainly are some strains of "false individualism" to be found in Bentham's writings, and this laying down of comparatively precise over-riding "ends" of policy is the most dangerous of them, because, of course, the laying down of over-riding ends suggests the justification of *any* means; but there are also still more pervasive strains of "true" (*i.e.*, empirical) individualism and "true" collectivism (if on Hayek's definition collectivism can be "true," and, if it cannot, such arbitrariness would, perhaps, itself be an example of "false" individualism) (see *Individualism and Economic Order*, pp. 4 ff.).

22. Contrast with Bentham's statement, Burke's: "To provide for us in our necessities is not in the power of government. It would be a vain presumption in statesmen to think they can do it" (*Thoughts on Scarcity, Works*, Vol. III, World's Classics, p. 3). James Mill, though not exactly deficient in "presumption," and supposed to be a disciple of Bentham rather than Burke, in fact was explicitly on Burke's side on this issue. In discussing a somewhat scheme for "buffer stocks," put forward by Sir James Steuart, to counter extreme price fluctuations, Mill writes: "The author, it is evident, had never reflected with any accuracy, upon the operation of free trade, and therefore sees not the equalizing results which it is calculated to produce. He proposes, accordingly to do that very imperfectly, by a great number of very troublesome regulations, which perfect freedom of trade would do completely of its own accord. Nothing more is wanting than to leave the farmer at perfect liberty to sell his corn wherever he can get the best price for it, and the consumer to buy it wherever he can get it cheapest, without any restriction, without either burthen or encouragement. The necessary effects of this are to secure to the farmer and to the people at all times those exact prices which are best adapted to their mutual interests. To depart from this course is only to disturb the laws of nature, to gratify the freaks or the interests of particular men" (*Literary Journal*, 1806, p. 234). One cannot tell how Professor Hayek would classify this passage by Mill, but it *may* seem a clear case of "false" rationalistic individualism, with the "true" empiricism on the side of Steuart and Bentham. Certainly Bentham would have exploded at this appeal to "the laws of nature" if it had come to his notice. It is also reasonable to guess that Smith, Ricardo and Senior would have been on the side of Burke and James Mill, and not on that of Steuart and Bentham. (The above quotation from Mill may be contrasted with Bentham's discussion of the rate of interest quoted at length at the end of Section III above.)

23. *Principles*, Sraffa ed., p. 105. Or compare Ricardo's statement to Trower (*Letters*, Sraffa edition, Vol. VIII, p. 133): "Political Economy, when the simple principles of it are once understood, is only useful, if it draws governments to right measures in taxation. We very soon arrive at the knowledge that Agriculture, Commerce, and Manufactures flourish best when left without interference on the part of Government, and that, the necessity which the state has for money to defray the expenses of its functions, imposes on it the obligation to raise taxes, and thus interference becomes absolutely necessary."

24. See *Five Lectures on Economic Problems*, pp. 1–2. Professor Stigler himself notes differences between Bentham and "Classical" economists on this subject. Moreover, though he refers to it rather distastefully, Bentham recognises what might be called "dog-in-the-manger egalitarianism" as a force which policy-makers must take into account from the point of view of social peace and cohesion (and which so many over-simplified theories of economic policy of classical descent do *not* take into account). That is, Bentham did not hold to the facile and far-reaching assumption that the satisfaction an individual gets from his income is a function simply of *its* size alone, while the size of his neighbours' incomes is entirely irrelevant: "If on any occasion the interest of the public and the interest of the individual happened to be so combined and tied together, that on condition of seeing an individual reap a profit to the amount of a hundred thousand, the public might reap a profit to the amount of a million, the plan would be turned aside from or rejected. Whatever satisfaction might be excited by the idea of the million gained by everybody and nobody, would be sowered and turned to regret by a glance of the hundred thousand pound gathered into a store of which the owner was in view" (III, p. 297).

25. See Bowring's edition of the *Works*, Vol. X, p. 498. We have noted above a practical issue—that of price control of basic foodstuffs—where Bentham and J. Mill were on diametrically opposite sides. The example, surely, has some significance in terms of general principles. J. S. Mill noted the wide differences in cast of mind between his father and Bentham: "His mind and Bentham's were essentially of different construction" (*Autobiography*, World's Classics, p. 172). On the other hand, there is certainly a very close intellectual affinity between Mill and Ricardo; see "James Mill and the Political Education of Ricardo," *Cambridge Journal*, November 1953.

26. Elie Halévy, *The Growth of Philosophic Radicalism*, p. 281, concludes that it was the very different influence of James Mill that shaped Ricardo, *not* Bentham: "The idea of political economy as a science of laws—laws of equilibrium and laws of progress—static laws and dynamic laws—does not come from Bentham." G. J. Stigler states bluntly "Ricardo . . . was not a Benthamite." ("The Development of Utility Theory," *Journal of Political Economy*, 1950, p. 311.)

14.

JOSEPH J. SPENGLER
Duke University

Malthus's Total

Population Theory:

A Restatement

and Reappraisal[1]

Commentators on Malthus's population theory have generally based their remarks upon the *Essay*, particularly upon his observation that "population invariably increases where the means of subsistence increase, unless prevented by some very powerful and obvious checks" which are resolvable into "moral restraint, vice, and misery."[2] They have overlooked important passages in the *Essay*, having to do with the circumstances on which depend the increase and the *availability* of subsistence, and, therefore, the growth of population.[3] They have overlooked his extended consideration of the question of population in the *Principles* where his primary concern was the increase of the supplies on which population growth depends.[4] They have, therefore, missed his *total* population theory, and the manner in which it developed.

It is our purpose, in this essay, to discover the *whole* of Malthus's population theory, and to indicate, in some measure, the views of earlier and contemporary writers regarding elements of which this theory is composed.[5] In section I we discuss Malthus's theory of economic progress and the "effec-

Reprinted from *The Canadian Journal of Economics and Political Science*, XI (February, May 1945), 83–110, 234–64, by permission of the publisher.

tual demand" for labour, as it relates to the population question. While this discussion is based upon the *Principles* much more than upon the *Essay* and other writings, it is evident, as we state in the conclusion, that Malthus's theory of demand probably evolved out of his consideration of the population question. In section II, we examine Malthus's treatment of industrialization, in which he apparently found a workable solution to both the problem of economic progress and the question of population. In section III we examine his views on luxury, on the exportation of "work," and on the encouragement of population growth, together with his conception of optimum population and his supposed role as a counter-revolutionary. Consideration of these topics serves to illuminate his social philosophy and to bring into sharper focus aspects of his theory treated in sections I and II.

I

It is in Malthus's *Principles* that we find most fully developed the thesis that the progress of population in number and well-being depends upon the maintenance and expansion of the "effectual demand" for labour.[6] True, a number of writers anticipated Malthus in making population growth dependent upon the state of employment, but none developed, as he did, the importance and pre-conditions of an "effective demand" for labour. In several papers, written in 1751–60, Benjamin Franklin reasons that population growth depends upon employment, "room," the ease with which families may be supported, and habits of consumption.[7] His arguments, advanced in support of freedom on the part of the American colonists, to expand geographically and industrially, were echoed by several English writers. "So that one of our Countrymen established in *America,* finds full Employment for several Hands here; and as full Employment will always draw people, it plainly follows from thence, that our Settlements abroad must increase the Number of People at home."[8] Arthur Young asked: "Is it not evident that demand for hands, that is employment, must regulate the numbers of the people?"[9] Steuart declared that mankind "must ever be, in proportion to the food produced"; but he added that "provided there be a demand for man, whatever use he be put to, the species will multiply" as long as "food is to be found."[10] Adam Smith observed that marriage and multiplication are encouraged when the demand for labour "is continually increasing."[11] Howlett, in a criticism of Price's view that England had suffered a decline in population, mentions "room," urban markets for agricultural products, and the prospect of employment, as conducive to population growth.[12] From his "fundamental proposition" Paley deduced, among other things, that: "Employment affects population 'directly,' as it affords the only medium of distribution, by which individuals can obtain from the common stock a supply for the wants of their families: it affects population 'indirectly,' as it augments the stock itself of provision, in the only way by which the production of it can be effectually encouraged, by furnishing purchasers."[13]

Malthus's thesis appears in the *Essay,* especially in the later editions, but does not stand out; because he was not there greatly concerned, as in the *Principles*, with what makes for progress in "supplies." Nor is it evident, in the *Essay*, by what writers, if any, he was influenced with respect to the effect of the state of employment upon population growth. His thesis appears to be vaguely foreshadowed in the first edition; and in the second, a number of its elements are discussed. In the fifth edition, finally, he achieved a greater integration of his earlier and narrower treatment of demographic matter with his developed analysis of the dependence of population growth upon employment, and with his discussion of the circumstances upon which progress in wealth and employment rests. Yet his *total* population theory is hardly to be gleaned from the *Essay* alone; it must be discovered in both the *Essay* and the *Principles*.

Malthus's primary concern in the last chapter of the *Principles* is "the progress of Wealth" and what conditions this progress. It is taken for granted that what makes for progress in wealth makes for progress in number and well-being. This is not quite his view in the first and second editions of the *Essay* where he makes the progress of the "labouring poor" (i.e., the vast majority) in number and well-being depend predominantly upon "the increase of the funds destined for the maintenance of labour" — i.e., upon the food supply made available to the masses; and where he points out that these funds do not tend to keep pace with wealth[14] as defined by Adam Smith. In the fifth edition, however, he writes: "A rapid increase of wealth indeed, whether it consists principally in additions to the means of subsistence or to the stock of conveniences and comforts, will always *ceteris paribus*, have a favourable effect on the poor." But he adds that it will have this effect only if "individual prudence" is joined with the skill and industry that produce wealth.[15]

In the first *Essay*, in reply to Godwin, Malthus commented briefly on the demand for labour, and justified expenditure by the wealthy, but he gave no prominence to the demand factor and its determinants.[16] The frugal man, he declared after Adam Smith, saves from his income to add to his capital; and this he uses to maintain "productive labour," or to lend to others "who will probably employ it in this way." Godwin's "avaricious man," on the contrary, "locks up his wealth in a chest, and sets in motion no labour of any kind, either productive or unproductive"; he "locks up the power of producing" wealth and denies to workers a market for their labour.[17] Malthus remarked also that whereas several centuries earlier there was "much less labour in England, in proportion to the population," and more "dependence," there was now more work and less dependence because the introduction of manufactures had enabled the poor "to give something in exchange for the provisions of the great Lords, instead of being dependent upon their bounty."[18] He indicated, moreover, that an "increasing demand for labour," together with an "increasing produce," ameliorates the condition of the labourer and thus encourages marriage.[19]

"What is mainly necessary to a rapid increase of population, is a great and continued demand for labour," he wrote in 1820.[20] If the demand for labour is not sufficient to convert "supplies" into consumable provisions[21] and channel these goods to the labouring masses, the growth of the latter in number and well-being is retarded.[22] Accordingly, assuming that subsistence is obtainable, the measure of population is the quantity of employment. For employment regulates "the wages of labour, on which the power of the lower classes of people to procure food depends; and according as the employment of the country is increasing, whether slowly or rapidly, these wages will be such, as either to check or encourage early marriages; such as to enable a labourer to support only two or three, or as many as five or six children."[23]

The continuation of an effective demand for labour is necessary, in the short as well as in the long run, to the continuation of population growth, well-being and nuptiality fluctuating with the short-run demand for labour. Population growth oscillates because a population cannot immediately adjust the supply of labour to oscillations in the demand for it. "But though the progress of population is mainly regulated by the effective demand for labour, it is obvious that the number of people cannot conform itself immediately to the state of this demand. Some time is required to bring more labour into the market when it is wanted; and some time to check the supply when it is flowing in with too great rapidity."[24] When the demand for labour declines sharply, population growth falls off even though provisions are plentiful, because marriages are less frequent when the prospect of employment is poor. "If the general demand for labour fail, particularly if the failure be sudden, the labouring classes will be wretched in the midst of cheapness; if the demand for labour be considerable, they will be comparatively rich in the midst of dearness."[25]

A country's population may fall far short of its capacity to support numbers at the same time that it is redundant in relation to employment opportunities. For while the potential population capacity of a country is fixed by its resources,[26] the progress of a country's population in number and well-being depends upon the growth of the "effectual demand" for labour. If this demand does not continue to increase, the population will not be actuated to increase,[27] and cannot increase, whatever be the country's resource equipment. This demand "is proportioned to the rate of increase in the quantity and value of those funds, whether arising from capital or revenue, which are actually employed in the maintenance of labour."[28] If, for any reason, these funds do not increase and flow to labour, the demand for labour will be checked,[29] even though there "be a great deficiency of population compared with the territory and powers of the country"; and while "it might be very desirable that it should be greater," efforts to encourage the growth of the population will prove futile until an effectual demand for labour develops and wages rise in consequence. Until such demand develops, labour and population will be redundant in relation to demand, however deficient they may be in relation to resources.[30]

But supposing that an effective demand for labour continues, how far will population growth proceed in a country? The answer, Malthus's discussion suggests, depends ultimately upon the habits of consumption of the population and upon the skill and industry with which they develop and utilize their resource equipment.[31] Population will come to a stand when cultivation has been pushed to the point where "the labour of a man upon the last land taken into cultivation will scarcely do more than support such a family as is necessary to maintain a stationary population," and when, in consequence, profits sink "to the lowest rate required to maintain the actual capital."[32] Habits of consumption being given, how far cultivation can be pushed depends upon its efficiency. How low wages may fall, and therefore how far cultivation may be pushed, depend upon the habits of the lower classes, or upon "the amount of those necessaries and conveniences, without which they would not consent to keep up their numbers to the required point."[33] He pointed out that population growth never dropped precipitately, but tapered off gradually, the falling off in the rate of increase in the funds destined for labour generating the necessary habits and feelings.[34]

It is worth noting that when Malthus states that population is regulated by wages,[35] he does not mean wage rates; he means family earnings and the purchasing power of the masses. It is the "average earnings of the families of the labouring classes throughout the year on which the encouragement to marriage, and the power of supporting children, will depend, and not merely the wages of day-labour estimated in food."[36] The highest rate of population growth, therefore, did not necessarily coincide with the highest real wage rate;[37] in fact "some increase of prices generally accompanies the most effective demand for produce and population."[38] For when prices (including that of "corn") rise, or are rising somewhat, in relation to the money wage rate, there is "fuller employment" (including "task work" and other employment for women and children[39]): and both the money and the real income of the family rises. When, on the contrary, the price of "corn" falls in relation to the money wage rate and employment diminishes, the "command of the labouring classes over the necessaries of life" declines, and with it the stimulus to population growth.[40]

It was commonly assumed, said Malthus, that progress in wealth, and therefore in number and well-being, necessarily accompanies population growth, saving, the introduction of labour-saving inventions, and soil fertility.

This assumption was invalid, he reasoned; it took for granted both that mankind produce and consume at the maximum possible rate, and that every increment in productive power generates an offsetting increment of consumption.

Progress in wealth, without which a continuing increase in numbers cannot take place, is not begotten of the hard pressure of numbers upon subsistence, or of "want alone." Neither "encouragements to population," nor even the "natural tendency of population to increase beyond the funds for its maintenance," furnishes an "effective stimulus" to the continued increase of wealth. If the desire of the labouring classes for "necessaries and conveniences" were a sufficient stimulus to production, Europe would be peopled to the limit of "its power to produce," and the earth would probably contain "at the very least, ten times as many inhabitants as are supported on its surface at present"; and yet, "almost universally," the wealth of states "is very far short of their powers of production. The desire of the labourer for goods and services will avail towards their production only if there is a "reciprocal demand" for his labour. This demand he cannot provide himself; it is forthcoming only when the employers of labour can dispose of its product at a profit. "An increase of population, when an additional quantity of labour is not required, will soon be checked by want of employment and the scanty support of those employed, and will not furnish the required stimulus to an increase of wealth proportioned to the power of production."[41] Here, by his emphasis upon the importance of demand, Malthus is setting limits to the capacity of the principle of population to generate progress, limits not so clearly indicated in the *Essay*.[42]

Of saving he wrote in like vein, even though he esteemed the eighteenth-century virtues, frugality and thrift, and accepted the current opinion that growth of capital depends primarily, not upon science and technology, but upon accumulation which, like labour, is accompanied by "spiritual anguish."[43] Wealth can be increased only through the "conversion of revenue into capital."[44] But saving from revenue "to add to capital" can augment capital and thus facilitate population growth only on condition that it does not diminish the "effectual demand" for commodities and labour. Suppose the productive power of farmers and manufacturers to grow as the result of an increase in the output per worker. If each group is disposed to consume the added increment of output of the other, all will be well. But if one or both parties "were disposed to save largely, with a view of bettering their condition, and providing for their families in future, the state of things would be very different." The demand for labour would diminish; for the manufacturer, "owing to the parsimony of the farmers and the want of demand for manufactures," would be unable to absorb the additional output of the farmer; while the farmer, because of the inability of the manufacturer to buy, would lack a market for his added output. Hence Malthus concluded that the adoption of too "parsimonious habits" might be accompanied "by a marked depression of wealth and population."[45]

The "laws that regulate the increase of capital" resemble those which regulate the increase of population. When there is an "effectual demand for commodities . . . a demand by those who are able and willing to pay an adequate price for them" — and in consequence wages and profits are high enough, population and capital tend to increase; if such demand is lacking, they do not increase. Malthus inferred, therefore, that a population might be "greatly redundant, compared with the demand for it and the actual means of supporting it, although it might most properly be considered as deficient, and greatly deficient, compared with the extent of territory, and the powers of such territory to produce additional means of subsistence." In like manner capital might be redundant in relation to a country's demand for it at the same time that such country was under-equipped with capital. In the former situation the encouragement of births would not finally add to population, while in the latter case saving from revenue would add little to the capital supply.[46]

Malthus dealt with soil fertility and invention much as he had dealt with saving; but he emphasized in greater measure the psychological barriers to the expansion of demand upon which he had touched in his discussion of savings. He emphasized, in keeping with his conception of human behavior tendencies,[47] that the demand for income in terms of effort is such as to yield a backward falling supply curve for effort.[48] "An efficient taste for luxuries and conveniences, . . . such . . . as will properly stimulate industry, . . . is a plant of slow growth"; for the "luxury of indolence" tends always to swamp the luxury of goods.[49] It may be true, Malthus states, that those who possess "fixed monied revenues, obtained by inheritance, or with little or no trouble," stand ready to spend such income and thereby create employment for the labour and capital that satisfies the resulting demand. "But where the amount of the revenues of a country depend[s], in a considerable degree, upon the exertion of labour, activity and attention, there must be something in the commodities to be obtained sufficiently desirable to balance this exertion, or the exertion will cease. . . . Most men place some limits, however variable, to the quantity of conveniences and luxuries which they will labour for."[50] For example, unless cultivators have a taste for conveniences and luxuries which they wish to satisfy out of greater profits, they tend to employ less labour in cultivation when output per unit of labour input increases; and under similar circumstances receivers of profits and rents behave in like manner. The disposition of workers to offer their services is similarly conditioned.[51] Love of indolence, therefore, operates to check progress in wealth, numbers, and well-being.[52] For this reason, in part, Malthus came to look with greater favour upon industrialization, which tends to expand tastes and move the curve of supply of effort downward and to the right.

In view of the shape of the supply curve of effort, a continued increase of wealth and population is not necessarily assured when the soil is fertile and production is easy; these conditions, in fact, may permit and foster indolence and so check progress in number and well-being. Fertility of the soil conduces to production only if there is an effective demand for work and product, for income in terms of effort; only if the owners of land are incited by the prospect of conveniences and luxuries to evoke its productive powers, and the labouring classes are pressed by "the want of necessaries" to create conveniences and luxuries.[53] If these conditions do not prevail, labourers will be disposed to put forth only enough effort to win an easy subsistence; landowners, content with little luxury other than retainers, will call forth small agricultural output; and few persons will engage in the production of conveniences and necessities. Whence there may at once be overpopulation in relation to the demand for labour and underpopulation in relation to resources. These unpropitious circumstances are found when, as under feudalism, the ownership of land is concentrated in the hands of the few, and "caprice and indolence . . . prevent many from cultivating their lands." He pointed, by way of extreme illustration, to Ireland and New Spain. "The power of supporting [or "employing"] labour may exist to a much greater extent than the will . . . . The necessity on the part of labourers of employing only a small portion of time in producing food does not always occasion the employment of a greater portion of time in procuring conveniences and luxuries . . . . The deficiency of wealth in a fertile country may be more owing to want of demand than to want of capital . . . . The fertility of soil alone is not an adequate stimulus to the permanent increase of wealth."[54]

Malthus approved all saving of labour and inventions because "their tendency is to increase the gross produce and to make room for a larger population and a larger capital."[55] But of the introduction of labour-saving inventions, which are "the natural consequence of improvement and civilization," he wrote as of the fertility of land.

> The pre-eminent advantages derived from the substitution of machinery for manual labour, depend upon the extension of the market for the commodities produced, and the increased stimulus given to consumption; . . . without this extension of market and increase of consumption, they must be in a considerable degree diminished. Like the fertility of land, the invention of good machinery confers a prodigious power of production. But neither of these great powers can be called fully into action, if the situation and circumstances, or the habits and tastes of the society prevent the opening of a sufficient market, and an adequate increase of consumption.[56]

Unless the power to produce is united in proper proportion with the "means of distribution," Malthus concluded, it will not beget wealth and population.

> The powers of production, to whatever extent they may exist, are not alone sufficient to secure the creation of a proportionate degree of wealth. Something else seems to be necessary in order to call these powers fully into action. This is an effectual and unchecked demand for all that is produced. And what appears to contribute most to the attainment of this object, is, such a distribution of produce, and such an adaptation of this produce to the wants of those who are to consume it, as constantly to increase the exchangeable value of the whole mass.[57]

Of this thesis Malthus had found support in the increase of the English population in 1800–10, which he attributed to a greatly increased demand for labour, combined with increased powers of production in both agriculture and manufactures. "What has taken place is a striking illustration of the principle of population, and a proof that in spite of great towns, manufacturing occupations, and the gradually-acquired habits of an opulent and luxuriant people, if the resources of a country will admit of rapid increase, and if these resources are so advantageously distributed as to occasion a constantly-increasing demand for labour, the population will not fail to keep pace with them."[58] Production and general wealth, "like particular portions of it," always proceed in the wake of "effectual demand," — savings generally issuing out of the "increase in the value of the national revenue" without diminishing demand and consumption; and population follows. But when the "two grand elements of wealth," production and distribution, are not conjoined in proper proportions, and distribution cannot therefore satisfactorily circulate produce and give adequate value to it, they do not carry riches and population "to the utmost limits" of the available resources; they "produce only, after the lapse of many thousand years, the scanty riches and scanty population, which are at present scattered over the face of the globe."[59]

In the *Principles*, as in the *Essay*, Malthus described as "most important" with respect to progress in wealth and numbers those elements "which come under the head of politics and morals": e.g., security of property which depends upon the "political constitution of a country," upon its laws, and upon their administration; "those habits" which make for "regular exertions" and "general rectitude of character."[60] But he devoted most attention to conditions which join the will with the power to consume and generate a demand to evoke and offset the power to produce, and which favour "that increase of value which depends upon distribution." These conditions are three in number: division of landed property; internal and external commerce; maintenance of "an adequate proportion" of society in personal services and situations enabling them "to make a demand for material products without contributing directly to their supply."[61]

Writing, as he did, at a time when the feudal land economy still blanketed much of the world, Malthus stressed the fact that the non-division of land was retarding progress in number and well-being. Only if land is sufficiently subdivided to permit an effective demand for produce and labour can wealth and population increase appreciably. Laws and customs which perpetuate, as they did in Europe during feudal times, "a most unequal and vicious division of landed property," retard the growth of wealth and cause countries to "remain for ages very scantily peopled, in spite of the principle of population." This is especially true of inland countries unfavourably situated for foreign and domestic commerce. Great proprietors, as Adam Smith observed, are commonly bad cultivators. Furthermore, even if they are animated by a passion for the consumption of manufactures, they are too few in number to supply a demand sufficient to actuate the production of "any important mass" of manufactured products. "The excessive wealth of the few is in no respect equivalent, with regard to effectual demand, to the more moderate wealth of the many." Natural resources will not be fully exploited, and manufacturing will not flourish, so long as immense landed properties are not broken down and there has not been created "a greater number of demanders in the middle ranks of life who [are] able and willing to purchase the results of productive labour." The judicious division of landed property was essential, therefore, to the maintenance and augmentation of the "exchangeable value" of wealth, to the stimulation of production, and to the increase of the population in number and well-being.[62]

To commerce Malthus now attached much greater importance than in his early writings. Internal and external commerce — the "exchange of what is wanted less for what is wanted more" — distributes the produce of a country in a manner consonant with the wants and tastes of the population and thereby increases the "exchangeable value of our possessions, our means of enjoyment, and our wealth." It facilitates the "formation of those wants and tastes, and that desire to consume, which are absolutely necessary to keep up the market prices of commodities, and prevent the fall of profits." It serves to join the will to employ with the ability to employ, and thus to set labour in motion in so far as the available "funds for the maintenance of labour" permit. It operates, in short, to supply that "effectual demand," lack of which occasions stagnation. But since exchange is mediated by money, commerce will help keep labour employed only if the prices of commodities sufficiently exceed the price of the labour embodied therein to allow adequate profits to producers; and this condition is more likely to be met when money wages and prices are stable or rising than when they are falling.[63]

In every society there must be "a considerable class of persons who have both the will and power to *consume more material wealth* than they produce."[64] For in every society there are many who produce more material wealth than they consume. Those engaged in the production of the "necessaries of life," or funds for the maintenance of labour, produce a "neat surplus above what is required for the maintenance of the persons so employed."[65] Those engaged in other lines of material production likewise produce more than they consume. Accordingly, unless there exist persons who can and will absorb these material surpluses, "effectual demand" will be deficient, producers will no longer create a great deal more than they consume, and wealth and population will cease to grow long before they reach the limit "which bounds the power of maintaining population." More specifically, the master producers and capitalists, their workmen, and the landlords cannot together supply a demand sufficient "to keep up and increase the value of that which is produced." The first may have the power, but they lack the will. The workmen may have the will, but they lack the power; for their employers cannot pay them enough to supply this power and at the same time realize the profit necessary to induce undertaking and production. Landlords are too few in number. The deficiency in consumption must be made up, therefore, by Adam Smith's "unproductive labourers,"[66] by that "body of persons engaged in personal services of various kinds"; these (i.e., menials, soldiers, statesmen, judges and lawyers, physicians, clergy, and teachers, etc.) provide necessary services and "call forth those exertions which are required to give full play to [the] physical resources" of a country.

> The specific use of a body of unproductive consumers, is to give encouragement to wealth by maintaining such a balance between produce and consumption as will give the greatest exchangeable value to the results of the national industry. If such consumers were to predominate, the comparatively small quantity of material products brought to market would keep down the value of the whole produce, from the deficiency of quantity. If, on the other hand, the productive classes were in excess, the value of the whole produce would fall from excess of supply. There is therefore a certain proportion between the two which will yield the greatest value, and command for a continuance the greatest quantity of labour."[67]

Malthus laid down several qualifications with respect to the manner in which "unproductive consumers" were to be employed and paid. The number of menials must not be disproportionately large in relation to the "neat revenue" of the society; because if too many persons are so employed the augmentation of subsistence and wealth is checked. Furthermore, while it is possible to spend the whole of the "neat surplus" upon menials, soldiers, sailors, and other suppliers of personal service, it is preferable that part of this surplus be used to maintain those engaged in the production of conveniences and luxuries. For the latter form of employment provides a more stable source of income and a greater "stimulus to production" and cultivation "in modern states" than does diversion of the whole "neat revenue" to the sustenance of menials, soldiers, and sailors. But not all that can be spent will be spent upon "material luxuries and conveniences" because, the demand for these soon abating, the "owners of land and capital would have very slender motives to employ them in the most productive manner." Hence some of the "neat surplus" must be spent for personal services; and the "most effective encouragement even to the production of necessaries" results when the two "stimulants," material luxuries and conveniences and personal services, operate "under the most favorable proportions."[68] In so far as practicable, those engaged in personal services should be "paid voluntarily by individuals," for then they are "most likely to be useful in exciting industry, and . . . least likely to be prejudicial by interfering with the costs of production"; and while it is desirable and necessary that some be paid out of public revenues, it is important that these not be supported through "injudicious" taxation which is a deterrent to progress.[69]

To summarize: Malthus always looked upon the available and accessible means of subsistence as setting the upper limit to population growth and capacity, and upon "the increase of the means of subsistence" as the "only true criterion of a real and permanent increase in the population of any country," the "habits of living" being given.[70] The food supply became the sole and sufficient limiting agency, however, only when the population of a country had been carried to the maximum of whose support that country was capable, "habits of living" and external trading relations being given. Until this point was reached population growth was conditioned by the amount of employment available and in prospect: for upon employment depended the stimulus to agricultural production, access, on part of the masses, to the means of subsistence, and their disposition to marry. If, for any reason, employment failed to expand, population failed to grow, whatever the food producing potentialities of a country. Population growth, therefore, depended upon the growth in the "effective demand" for labour, by which actual and prospective employment was fixed; it did not depend upon the mere power to produce, for the power to produce did not necessarily generate an offsetting power to consume, and did not, therefore, necessarily bring into being a corresponding and growing "effective demand" for labour. Such a demand, in fact, tended to be realized only when proper moral and political conditions prevailed, when the social structure was elastic, when agricultural land holdings were adequately broken up, when commerce was active, when there were enough persons willing and able to consume more material wealth than they produced, and when human wants were multiplying sufficiently to overcome the inelasticity of the demand for goods and services in terms of effort.

As we state in the conclusion, Malthus apparently came to recognize the importance of the role of the effectual demand for labour in consequence of his initial concern with the checks to population growth, and with the less immediate origins of some of these checks. For this reason too he considered the long-run as well as the short-run determinants of the effectual demand for labour and population. These considerations, in turn, led him to note the importance of industrialization as a means of dissolving obstacles to the expansion of the demand for labour and to the progress of population in number and well-being. This we examine in section II.

II

Industrialization has commonly been advanced by twentieth-century economists as the means whereby population pressure may eventually be reduced in areas which at present are relatively overpopulated. For industrialization, it is supposed, provides employment for the excess agrarian population, supplies purchasing power wherewith deficiencies in the domestic food supply may be made up, and brings about urbanization and the adoption of a cultural pattern suited eventually to bring population growth to a stand. For much the same reasons Malthus too favoured industrialization: a nation's economy should be sufficiently industrialized to establish a working balance between its agricultural and its non-agricultural branches, but not so industrialized as to make it partly dependent upon foreign sources for foodstuffs and therefore insecure with respect to provision.[71] In such an economy, Malthus's argument suggests, an adequate "effectual demand" for labour tends to be maintained, and the inhabitants tend to utilize their resources effectively and to make provision for growth in number and well-being at the same time that they acquire habits of work and consumption appropriate to guard the nation against the evils of undue multiplication.

In the First Essay Malthus did not fully appreciate the significance of industrialization, in part because he was impressed by the seeming importance of subsistence and concerned lest English economic policies restrain agricultural progress. He carried these views over into the second edition in which, none the less, especially in his discussion of the checks, he dwelt upon the importance of industrialization. His final and more integrated views appear already in the fifth edition, which reflects his consideration of the problems subsequently treated in the *Principles*. To the end he stressed the primacy of agriculture in economic expansion, and the principle that food must precede population.[72]

In the first edition, in criticism of Adam Smith's view that an increase in national wealth necessarily redounds to the advantage of the common man, Malthus stated that "every accession to the food of a country" immediately benefits the whole society in greater measure than a corresponding accession to manufactures; that "ornamental luxuries" add little to "the mass of happiness"; that the expansion of manufactures had enticed labour from agriculture and checked the augmentation of the food supply; and that foreign commerce can contribute little to the maintenance of labour. In Europe, urban industry had been unduly encouraged and the "natural order of things" had been inverted, agricultural expansion having been founded upon the surplus capital of manufactures instead of manufactures upon the surplus capital of agriculture; had the natural order been followed, Europe would have "been much more populous, . . . and yet not more incumbered by its population."[73] He proposed, as a means of aiding the poor, premiums for turning up fresh land and "all possible encouragements held out to agriculture above manufactures."[74]

In the second edition Malthus was much more friendly to industry.[75] He observed that although "agriculture cannot flourish without a vent for its commodities," which may be furnished by commerce and manufactures, it is the "disposable produce" of agriculture which sets, or at least should set, the limits to the development of commerce and manufactures within a country. For if these two branches of the economy are overdeveloped, and the population of a state comes to subsist in part upon imported provision, it is "exposed to all the accidents of time and chance." When things are "left to take their natural course, . . . the commercial part of the society" does not tend to increase "beyond the surplus produce of the cultivators." But — and here his discussion relates primarily to England — things had not been left to take their natural course in England. Commerce and manufactures had been stimulated, and agriculture checked, by the navigation acts and colonial trade monopolies; hence "the body politick" was in a somewhat diseased state, and threatened with a scarcity of provision. For this reason, and because adequacy of the food supply was "a matter of the very highest importance," Malthus concluded that agriculture must be restored to its proper proportions, and that a bounty would be justified if necessary to re-establish balance.[76] In his discussion of great landed areas, such as Siberia, and of countries with little manufacturing and commerce, however, he dwelt upon the need to develop these branches of the economy, if agriculture was to expand and population to grow as it might and ought.[77]

A number of reasons apparently acted in combination to lead Malthus to attach greater importance, in his later writings, to manufactures and commerce. First, his consideration of the role of private property and of the views of the Physiocrats and others led him to note that the agriculturalist must have a vent for the surplus which, under a system of private property, he normally produces, and which he would exchange for non-agricultural goods and services and for the contributions of the state.[78] Although in theory all effort might be directed into agriculture until it was fully developed, in practice, with men constituted as they are and with society founded (as it must be) upon private property, agriculture cannot expand in the absence of a growing demand for its products. Second, "the condition of the lower classes certainly does not depend exclusively upon the increase of

funds for the maintenance of labour, or the means of supporting more labourers." For while the growth of population depends principally upon the
increase of the food supply, the lower classes "cannot be considered as in a
good state" unless they enjoy, in addition to "strict necessaries" and food,
"some conveniences and even luxuries." And they cannot command these
conveniences and luxuries unless, instead of allowing their numbers to
keep pace with the means of subsistence (i.e., "means of supporting more
labourers"), they exercise prudential restraint. Nor are they likely to "acquire a decided taste for conveniences and comforts" and, therefore, a strong
disposition to practise moral restraint, until conveniences and comforts have
"become plentiful compared with food, which they never do till food has
become in some degree scarce," as in economies that are not predominantly
agricultural.[79] Third, in so far as the well-being of the lower classes depends
upon non-agricultural goods and services, Malthus's reasoning suggests, it is
in order to encourage their production, for "the powers of the earth in the
production of food have narrower limits than the skill and tastes of mankind
in giving value to raw materials."[80]

The condition of the labouring classes in an agricultural country may be
good, but it is not likely to be good, even though there the evils attendant
upon urban employments are necessarily at a minimum. It will be good if,
even though the price of manuufactures expressed in corn is high, corn
wages suffice to provide workers with both food and an adequate residuum
of purchasing power with which to obtain the relatively expensive conveniences and luxuries — relatively expensive because they are imported, or produced at high cost by undeveloped domestic industries. Such a favourable
situation was enjoyed by labour in America. The "condition of the labouring
classes must be the worst possible," however, if "the wages of labour estimated in food are low" and, because the country lacks manufactures, the
prices of manufactures, in terms of food, are high, as they must inevitably
be. This unfortunate condition, moreover, will tend to persist. For the labouring classes will not have the opportunity to acquire "the custom of
enjoying conveniences and comforts" and hence will not develop "those
habits of prudential restraint" which operate to push wages above the subsistence level; and the owners of landed property, or those who determine
the uses to which it is put, will not be actuated to employ it in a manner
suited to evoke large yields.[81]

It was not the predominance of agriculture as such which accounted for
the tendency, in agricultural systems, of the growth of capital and the demand for labour to suffer a "premature check," and of the progress of the
population in number and well-being thereby to be retarded. This tendency
originated in the "vices of the government and the structure of society,
which prevents its full and fair development" of agriculture. He pointed to
America as "perhaps the only modern instance of the fair operation of the
agricultural system,"[82] and to the feudal system of land tenure, together
with the complex of tastes and practices joined thereto, as the social arrangement most unfavourable to the progress of agriculture and the improvement
of the condition of the labouring masses. The "remains" of this system con-

tinued to impede cultivation "in every country of Europe, and in most of its colonies in other parts of the world"; at the same time they did not "proportionably" encourage commerce and manufactures. Under the feudal system there was no mass demand for agricultural products, no disposition on the part of the land-owning class to maximize agricultural production, and no body of satisfiable but unsated wants to prompt members of all classes to exert themselves. It operated, therefore, to check the augmentation of "the surplus produce of the cultivators [which], taken in its most enlarged sense measures and limits the growth of that part of the society which is not employed upon the land; . . . [of] the number of manufacturers, of merchants, of proprietors, and of persons engaged in the various civil and military professions . . . ." And, because it operated to check the augmentation of surplus produce, it restrained the progress of population in number and well-being.[83]

When, for whatever cause, land was undivided, and there existed little or no commerce and manufactures to supply a market for the surplus produce of agriculture, to stimulate its extension and improvement, and to provide all classes with incentives to work, population growth came to a premature stop, and the masses languished in indolence and misery. "If in the best cultivated and most populous countries of Europe the present divisions of land and farms had taken place, and had not been followed by the introduction of commerce and manufactures, population would long since have come to a stand from the total want of motive to further cultivation, and the consequent want of demand for labour."[84]

Malthus pointed, by way of illustration, to Poland, Russia, Siberia, and Turkey where, "under the agricultural system, the condition of the lower classes . . . is very wretched." In Poland, for example, misery was widespread, not because the country was agricultural, but because landed property was not divided, the inhabitants were in a servile situation, and consequently, urban industry was without encouragement.

> While the land is cultivated by boors, the produce of whose exertions belongs entirely to their masters, and the whole society consists mainly of these degraded beings and the lords and owners of great tracts of territory, there will evidently be no class of persons possessed of the means either of furnishing an adequate demand at home for the surplus produce of the soil, or of accumulating fresh capital and increasing the demand for labour. In this miserable state of things, the best remedy would unquestionably be the introduction of manufactures and commerce; because the introduction of manufactures and commerce could alone liberate the mass of people from slavery and give the necessary stimulus to industry and accumulation.

He adds that if the Polish people were already free and industrious and the land was easily divisible and alienable, Poland might still for many years exchange raw products for the finer manufactures of foreign countries; but that under these circumstances, "the condition of the people would more resemble that of the inhabitants of the United States of America than of the inhabitants of the unimproved countries of Europe."[85]

Undoubtedly Malthus was led, by his study of the checks to population, to recognize the importance of industrialization and the expansibility of employment. Already in the 1803 edition, in consequence of his analysis of population growth in economies founded upon slavery, or upon concentrated ownership of property in land,[86] he observed that "the distribution of the means of subsistence" is as essential to the growth of population as is their production; that their distribution is necessary to evoke their production; and that their distribution is contingent upon there being an effectual demand for labour to distribute these means to the masses.[87] In the ancient world, so long as landed property was divided into small shares, this "division itself" provided "distribution." But when the system of small property gave place to one of inequality and concentration, distribution had to be provided in other ways.[88] This the Romans had failed to do. Instead of setting the landless free citizens to work in agriculture and manufactures, they had filled these employments with slaves, thereby denying work and support (other than gratuities) to the free population. For this reason, and because Italian agriculture was permitted to decay, the free population had declined.[89]

Defective distribution operated also in the modern world to put the population under a "moral impossibility of increasing,"[90] when, though a plentiful subsistence might be procured with facility, conditions were not favourable to the division and improvement of land, and few or no manufactures existed. In these circumstances there was little demand for labour at a wage sufficient to provide support for a family; for there was little employment to be had off the farms, while farmers, able to provide their own subsistence, were without the prospect of manufactured goods to excite them to overcome their "natural indolence" and engage labour to produce an agricultural surplus. What is wanted in these countries, in order to increase population, Malthus declared, is not mere immigration, or a direct encouragement to procreation, "but the creation of an effectual demand for the produce of the soil, by promoting the means of distribution. This can only be effected by the introduction of manufactures, and by inspiring the cultivator with a taste for them, and thus enlarging the internal market."[91]

In light of his analysis, Malthus concluded that wealth had increased, and with it the number and well-being of the population, as the feudal system had given way, a mercantile and manufacturing middle class supplied with capital had come into being, a taste for material conveniences and luxuries had developed, a mass demand for goods and services and therefore for labour had evolved, and agriculture had received the stimulus of an expanding market.

If a taste for idle retainers, and a profusion of menial servants, had continued among the great landholders of Europe from the feudal times to the present, the wealth of its different kingdoms would have been very different from what it is now . . . . The growing taste of our ancestors for material conveniences and luxuries, instead of personal services, was the main cause of the change. While the latter continue to be the predominant taste, few comparatively will be living on the profits of capital. The great mass of society will be divided chiefly into two classes, the rich and the poor, one of which will be in a state of abject dependence upon the other. But a taste for material objects, however frivolous, almost always requires for its gratification the accumulation of capital, and the existence of a much greater number of manufacturers, merchants, wholesale dealers, and retail dealers. The face of society is thus wholly changed. A middle class of persons, living upon the profits of stock, rises into wealth and consequence; and an increasing accumulation of capital, almost exclusively derived from the industry of the mercantile and manufacturing classes, affects to a considerable extent the division and alienation of those immense landed properties, which, if the fashion of personal services had continued, might have remained to this time nearly in their former state, and have prevented the increase of wealth on the land, as well as elsewhere.[92]

In the feudal times . . . the landlords could in no other way spend their incomes than by maintaining a great number of idle followers; and it was by the growth of capital in all the employments to which it is directed, that the pernicious power of the landlords was destroyed, and their dependent followers were turned into merchants, manufacturers, tradesmen, farmers, and independent labourers — a change of prodigious advantage to the great body of society, including the labouring classes.[93]

Malthus concluded, furthermore, that a country is best off when it unites "great landed resources with a prosperous state of commerce and manufactures," and is free, therefore, of the evils peculiar either to a commercial or to an agricultural economy.[94] Such a country is free of the evils of feudalism; it is free of dependence, for markets and foodstuffs and raw materials, upon foreign countries; it is free to distribute its capital between agricultural and non-agricultural enterprise, to equalize profits in both branches, and to preserve economic balance between them; and it is more than compensated for the evils ("diminished power of supporting children"; increased employment in "occupations less favourable to health, and more exposed to fluctuations of demand and unsteadiness of wages") attendant upon industrialization.

Under these circumstances, it is scarcely possible that it should ever experience that premature stagnation in the demand for labour, and the produce of the soil, which at times has marked the history of most of the nations of Europe. In a country in which manufactures and commerce flourish, the produce of the soil will always find a ready market at home; and such a market is peculiarly favorable to the progressive increase of capital. But the progressive increase of capital, and particularly of the quantity and value of the funds for the maintenance of labour, is the great cause of a demand for labour, and of good corn wages, while the high relative price of corn, occasioned by the improved machinery and extended capital employed in manufactures, together with the prosperity of foreign commerce, enables the labourer to exchange any given portion of his earnings in corn for a large proportion both of domestic and foreign conveniences and luxuries.

Even when the demand for labour begins to slacken, and corn wages to fall, and the increase of labour to be checked, "the high relative value of corn" wages keeps up "comparatively the condition of the labouring classes"; they cannot be reduced to the miserable state of agricultural countries where the demand for labour is stationary and wages supply only necessities.[95]

In sum, a population seldom can be well off and increasing until considerable progress has been made in industrialization. For industrialization is an important component of the complex of elements favourable to an effective and expanding demand for labour, and to the increase of "supplies" generally. It acts as a solvent upon inelastic feudal structures. It helps to offset the check to the demand for luxuries and conveniences arising from the "general desire of mankind to better their condition, and make provision for a family." It inspires people with wants "calculated to excite their exertions in the production of wealth," and, therefore, overcomes in part the "luxury of indolence," always a weighty obstacle to progress in wealth, number, and well-being.[96] Manufactures and commerce

infuse fresh life and activity into all classes of the state, afford opportunities for the inferior orders to rise by personal merit and exertion, and stimulate the higher orders to depend for distinction upon other grounds than mere rank and riches. They excite invention, encourage science and the useful arts, spread intelligence and spirit, inspire a taste for conveniences and comforts among the labouring classes; and, above all, give a new and happier structure to society, by increasing the proportion of the middle classes, that body on which the liberty, public spirit, and good government of every country must mainly depend.[97]

While Malthus's analysis here runs in terms of commerce and manufactures, he foresaw, as had Petty in some measure as early as 1691, that with economic progress the working population moves "from agriculture to manufacture, and from manufacture to commerce and services."[98] Were the powers of production in a rich and well-peopled country trebled, he supposed by way of illustration, the potentially available output would be called forth only on condition that it could be distributed. And it would be distributed, he argues in substance, only on condition that intelligent members in lower occupational classes were moved upward, and, if necessary, new occupations and situations were created.[99] At the time Malthus was writing, expansion of employment in manufactures and commerce and, in a lesser measure, in the professions and services, gave promise of bringing about sufficient distribution to release the growing powers of production.

Industrialization, Malthus's argument runs, also makes for the growth and spread of habits suited to prevent undue natural increase and so to guard the economic and social gains of the poor, — of habits, the lack of which unleashes population pressure and visits poverty upon populations, whatever be their "supplies."[100] A "permanent and general improvement in the condition of the poor" is contingent upon the generation of "prudential habits" among the lower classes; it cannot be effected "without an increase in the preventive check." Nothing is more likely to generate prudential habits than civil liberty; and nothing is more calculated to induce deferment of marriage without endangering virtue than the diffusion of luxury, of a taste for the comforts and conveniences of life, among the mass of the people.[101] But civil liberty flourishes, as a rule, where the growth of commerce and manufactures has brought feudalism to term;[102] and a taste for conveniences and comforts tends to become diffused where industrialization provides both these classes of goods and services and the opportunity, on the part of the labourer, to purchase them with that portion of his income not absorbed by food and other necessaries.[103]

Industrialization is favourable also to the generation of habits of industry and prudential restraint, in that it tends to push up the relative price of food and to reduce the relative price of the remaining elements in the worker's budget.[104] "The desirable thing, with a view to the happiness of the common people, seems to be that their habitual food should be dear, and their wages regulated by it."[105] For then habits of industry and prudence tend to prevail, and the overall purchasing power of the worker's wages is favourable. If the labourer can satisfy his food requirements with little effort, he tends to prefer leisure to giving up additional time in exchange for conveniences and comforts; and he acquires neither a higher standard of life nor habits of industry. If, on the contrary, the price of food is relatively high, and the labourer finds it necessary to devote the "main part" of his time to procuring food, his behaviour undergoes modification. He develops habits of industry and, as a rule, acquires "a decided taste for the conveniences and comforts of life"; for since he already has given up most of his time in exchange for food, he "seldom" grudges working his "remaining time, which is but inconsiderable compared with the commodities it will purchase." With the progress of a country in wealth, industry, and cultivation, the cost and price of corn rise in relation to the cost and price of other goods. Hence, while the labourer's "power of maintaining a large family" declines, his opportunity and desire to "command" decencies, comforts, and better lodging and clothing increase, and his disposition to unite "individual prudence" with skill and industry acquires strength.[106]

Industrialization operates in still another manner to strengthen the overall inclination to exercise prudential restraint; because it serves, as has already been noted, to increase the relative number in the middle part of society.[107] For an increase in the relative number in the middle part of society, and a decrease in the relative number in the inferior part of society, is "most favourable to virtuous and industrious habits, . . . to the growth of all kinds of talents," to the improvement of the prospects of the lower classes, and to the diffusion and animation of the desire to better one's condition.[108]

Malthus did not emphasize the retention of a taste for conveniences and luxuries. For, following Hume in part, he supposed that a nation, like an individual, having acquired a given scale of living, would not easily relinquish it. When a nation has acquired the "tastes necessary to give value to a great quantity of labour not employed upon actual necessaries . . . a considerable resistance will be made to any essential fall in its value."[109] In the first as well as in later editions of the *Essay* he indicated that he believed it very difficult to reduce a standard of living that had been acquired.[110]

Malthus's heightened approval of industrialism and commerce brought his opinions more into line with those of Hume and others, who, however, were less concerned with the population problem. Where manufactures and "mechanic arts" do not flourish, Hume declared, agriculturalists are without markets and, therefore, without temptation "to encrease their skill and industry . . . . A habit of indolence naturally prevails." And much land remains uncultivated. Whence commerce and awakened wants are necessary to rouse men and release the forces of production.[111] Men multiply when agriculture prospers, Steuart observed; and agriculture prospers most when wants are many and complex, there is vent for its products, and agriculturalists feel need for non-agricultural goods.[112] Adam Smith traced the dissolution of the comparatively static feudal economy and the expansion of agriculture to the rise of commerce and manufactures and the development of the town economy.[113] Young emphasized the dependence of prosperity in agriculture upon the adequacy of outlets for its products, and the dependence of population growth upon the state of agriculture and employment generally. [114] Paley wrote that "The business of one half of mankind is to set the other half at work; that is, to provide articles, which, by tempting the desires, may stimulate the industry, and call forth the activity of those, upon the exertion of whose industry, and the application of whose faculties, the production of human provision depends."[115] These writers, in short, found in an expanding market for agricultural products a stimulus to agriculture and to the production of provision, on which population growth depends; but they did not apparently seek in industrialization the source of a cultural barrier to undue multiplication.

III

In this section, consisting of five parts, we examine: (i) Malthus's views on "luxury"; (ii) his appraisal of the frequently expressed "export of work" argument; (iii) in what sense his doctrine was counter-revolutionary; (iv) his stand on measures to encourage marriage and natality; and (v) his position on optimum population.

(i) Luxury

Luxury has ever been the subject of controversy, and in the course of this controversy many arguments have been advanced both against and in support of luxury. Some of these, present in the writings of his day, and relating to the population problem, were touched upon by Malthus,[116] and will be considered here.

(1) Young expressed an ancient opinion when he wrote that "on the soft beds of luxury most kingdoms have expired";[117] and so did those who supposed luxury to be a deterrent to marriage and the disposition to procreate.[118] Malthus did not say much of the possible evil effects of luxury, in part because he considered the deterring influence exercised upon marriage by luxury to be necessary and salutary, and in part because he supposed that luxury would not unduly check population growth so long as it did not operate to restrict the augmentation of the food supply.[119] He did not approve of luxury when compounded with vice,[120] nor of great luxury on the part of the opulent few at the expense of the labouring majority. He apparently agreed with those who supposed that a "prodigious quantity of

human exertion wasted upon trivial, useless, and sometimes pernicious objects . . . might be wholly saved or more effectively employed," but he rejected the egalitarian correctives usually proposed.[121]

In 1803 Malthus observed that luxury, "when it falls short of actual vice," stimulates agriculture, commerce, and manufactures, but he added that "there seems to be a point, beyond which it must necessarily become prejudicial to a state, and bring with it the seeds of weakness and decay." He did not refer, as did Paley, to the tendency of luxury to diminish the "frequency of marriage among the poor," or to its supposed enervating effects. Rather, luxury becomes "prejudicial" when those employed "in preparing or procuring luxuries" become too numerous in relation to "the funds which are to support them"; when "it is pushed so far, as to trench on the funds necessary for its support, and to become an impediment instead of an encouragement to agriculture"; when, because too few people are employed in agriculture, food imports become necessary. For he did not believe that those engaged outside agriculture "can be sufficiently secure of this food, if they depend for it principally on other countries." No large nation, become dependent in part upon foreign food supplies, had continued "with undiminished vigour," nor would England, or any other large nation, prove an exception to this rule in the future. Whence he inferred that English agriculture, which, he believed, had suffered in consequence of undue stimulation of commerce and manufactures, needed to be encouraged and developed so it could supply the nation's food requirements. This thesis appears in modified form in the fifth and later editions where he emphasizes the superiority of the agricultural-commercial system over both the agricultural and the commercial systems.[122]

(2) Goods and services, Richard Cantillon had observed, vary in respect to their coefficients of production; they may embody much land and little labour, or much labour and little land. If they embody relatively large amounts of land, the labour requirement of an economy will be less than if they embody relatively large amounts of labour; and if the labour requirement is less, either wages will be lower, or (annual wages being assumed constant) employment will be less, or both wages and employment will be less, than if the labour requirement is great. Population, the scale of living being given, will vary with the labour requirement. And the labour requirement will depend upon the "Taste, Humours and Manner of Living of the Proprietors of Land," who, as the principal property owners and leading consumers in an economy, largely determine the volume of goods and services called for, and the extent to which these goods and services will consist predominantly of labour rather than of land. Upon the tastes of the proprietors, therefore, depend the means allotted for the support of population and, consequently, population growth itself. If, for example, proprietors prefer horses to goods and services composed largely of labour, numbers will be less, for there will not be so much subsistence for their support, and its relative price may be higher.[123]

Of the writers with whose views on population Malthus was acquainted, none emphasized the point that it is through the media of coefficients of production that tastes influence both the demand for labour and the wage level; but several touched upon whether or not population growth is checked when resources are utilized in the production of goods and services other than subsistence. Thus Hume observed that were the land of a convent bestowed upon a nobleman, not many more citizens would be furnished; that the conversion of fertile land into vineyards checked population growth; and that "great equality of fortune" was favourable to propagation.[124] And Wallace, an exponent of the virtues of small landownership and simplicity of tastes, declared that, so long as the earth is not fully cultivated, the employment of men upon "works of ornament" and many other non-agricultural tasks instead of upon "multiplying food," operates to restrain world population growth.[125] Mirabeau when still a disciple of Cantillon, contended, among other things, that one horse, *ceteris paribus*, displaced four men.[126] Steuart remarked that numbers become greater when a people live on a cereal rather than on an animal food diet; but he denied Mirabeau's thesis that, in France, the "unnecessary consumption of the earth's productions" and the use of land for gardens, highways, etc., reduced the food supply available to man and thus "hurt population." For France was not fully cultivated; and so long as a state was not fully cultivated, men did not want for subsistence, and an increase in the demand for agricultural products, whatever their destination, served to stimulate agriculture and therefore to favour population growth.[127]

Although Paley did not assign to landed proprietors the important role allowed them by Cantillon, he did indicate that both the amount of subsistence and the volume of employment were conditioned by tastes. He noted that the adoption of an animal food diet by the English had restrained their population growth, inasmuch as a country could not support so many people on an animal food as on a cereal diet; and he observed that manufactures and commerce might divert resources from the production of subsistence. But he did not believe that the development of commerce and manufactures had checked population, saying, on the contrary, that it had favoured propagation; for it had augmented employment and, by expanding the demand for agricultural produce, had absorbed and distributed the surplus production of agriculture and stimulated its increase. Some branches of commerce and manufactures, he noted, however, promoted employment, and therefore population, in greater measure than others; namely, those which embodied relatively large amounts of labour and relatively small amounts of land suited for the cultivation of subsistence. Whence he concluded that a nation would reach "its proper extent of population" only if its soil were "applied solely to the raising of provision" for its inhabitants, and if its commerce and manufactures were devoted primarily to the creation and sale of labour-embodying wrought goods.[128]

Malthus did not treat of the "horses versus men" thesis as such, nor did he evaluate the views expressed on this matter by his predecessors, or consider Cantillon's analysis of the demand for labour. But he gave expression to this thesis in the First Essay, only to reject it, and the inferences drawn from it, in later editions. In the 1798 edition he observed, apparently following Paley in part, that a country would not support as many inhabitants on a meat as on a corn diet; and that the new system of grazing, under which cattle were fattened on good land instead of on waste land as formerly, "together with the great number of horses at present kept for pleasure," were the "chief causes, that have prevented the quantity of human food . . . from keeping pace with the increased fertility of the soil." He added that the English population would experience greater growth were these two conditions modified, but he did not recommend such modification.[129] Furthermore, he esteemed the production of food above that of luxuries, because it contributed more to the "mass of happiness in the society"; and he expressed alarm that manufactures were expanding at the expense of agriculture and diverting resources from farming. But he considered impractical proposals to shunt into agriculture either the idle rich, or those employed in "the labours of luxuries."[130]

In the second and later editions of the *Essay* Malthus modified his earlier evaluation of the "horses versus men" thesis. He admitted that the shunting of resources from the production of subsistence for men to other uses tended to make the population of a country, or its actual capacity to support numbers, less than it otherwise would be; but he rejected the inferences that were commonly drawn from this fact, and pointed out that under a system of private property it was impossible to produce as large a volume of foodstuffs as the land, in conjunction with a nation's labour power, was capable of producing.

The lot of the lower classes would not be better were no foodstuffs and no resources diverted to non-food uses; in fact, such diversion in good times served to cushion the population against failing crops and bad times. The "real effect" of "waste among the rich," of "land remaining uncultivated," of keeping horses "for pleasure," "is merely to narrow the limit of the actual population; but they have little or no influence on what may be called the average pressure of distress on the poorer members of society."[131] These circumstances serve, as does "the consumption of grain in distilleries" in China, to prevent the arrival of population at the "utmost limits of subsistence" and to provide a disposable reserve in bad times.

> On the supposition that the food consumed in this manner may be withdrawn, on the occasion of a scarcity, and be applied to the relief of the poor, they operate certainly, as far as they go, like granaries, which are only opened at the time that they are most wanted, and must therefore tend rather to benefit than to injure the lower classes of society.[132]
>
> China, without her distilleries, would certainly be more populous; but on a failure of the seasons, would have still less resource than she has at present; and, as far as the magnitude of the cause would operate, would in consequence be more subject to famines, and those famines would be more severe.[133]

Malthus reasoned in like manner that a relatively expensive diet tended to cushion the impact of "scarcity."

When the common people of a country live principally upon the dearest grain, as they do in England on wheat, they have great resources in a scarcity [in the form of cheaper but nourishing food] . . . ; but when their habitual food is the lowest in this scale, they appear to be absolutely without resource, except in the bark of trees, like the poor Swedes; and a great portion of them must necessarily be starved.[134]

Already in the First Essay he had observed, following comment upon population pressure in China, "It is probable that the very frugal manner in which the Gentoos are in the habit of living, contributes in some degree to the famines of Indostan."[135] Malthus therefore opposed, as had Necker by implication, the substitution, in times other than of scarcity, of cheap for relatively expensive diets; he looked upon cheap foods merely as means of easing the impact of occasional scarcity and distress.[136]

To those who would do away with horses and cattle and substitute spade culture, Malthus replied that such a policy would reduce agricultural output, the demand for labour, and population. English soil could not produce much without dressing, and the best dressing was provided by cattle.[137] Horses were necessary to transport produce and manure; without their help in the fields it would be impossible to cultivate effectively land of poor quality.[138]

To those who inferred from "the appearance of uncultivated heaths" that the "internal economy" of a country was necessarily unsound, Malthus replied that it did not and could not pay to dress and cultivate all land, poor, middling, and good alike: — this would constitute a "palpable misdirection and waste both of individual and national resources." For since the supply of soil dressing was almost always limited, and the supply of labour was sometimes limited, the maximization of agricultural production was contingent upon putting these productive agents where they would do the most good.[139]

Under the system of private property — which Malthus supposed would always prevail — "the practical limits of population . . . must be always very far short of the utmost power of the earth to produce food"; because land is cultivated only up to the point where "the last employed labourers" can produce enough to replace themselves (i.e., support a wife and rear two children). "And it is happy for mankind that such are the laws of nature." For under this arrangement the excess produce (above maintenance) of the cultivating class serves to support the non-cultivating population whose efforts supply the non-food components of the family budget; and a suprasubsistence scale of living is attainable by most. Were the system of private property, and the limit set by it to population growth, removed, incessant labour and degradation would soon become the lot of most if not all.

But what statesman or rational government could propose that all animal food should be prohibited, that no horses should be used for business or pleasure, that all the people should live upon potatoes, and that the whole industry of the nation should be exerted in the production of them, except what was required for the mere necessaries of clothing and houses? Could such a revolution be effected, would it be desirable? particularly as in a few years, notwithstanding all these exertions, want, with less resource than ever, would inevitably recur.[140]

(3) The production and consumption of luxuries and conveniences, as was shown in part in sections I and II, served three major purposes, in Malthus's opinion. They overcame indolence and called forth effort in general;[141] they stimulated agriculture by providing a market for its products, and helped to sustain an effective demand for labour; and they operated to establish a suitable barrier in the way of too great population growth. But luxuries and conveniences could not serve these three purposes unless the taste and demand for them were widely diffused through the population; then only would the vast majority acquire habits of industry and be able to provide a necessary mass demand. Malthus, therefore, differed from such writers as Paley, who believed that the vast majority should toil incessantly and live frugally "in order to minister to the excessive luxuries" of the opulent few.[142]

It is by no means necessary that the rich should be excessively luxurious, in order to support the manufactures of a country; or that the poor should be deprived of all luxuries, in order to make them sufficiently numerous. The best, and in every point of view the most advantageous manufactures in this country, are those which are consumed by the great body of the people. The manufactures which are confined exclusively to the rich are not only trivial, on account of the comparative smallness of their quantity, but are further liable to the great disadvantage of producing much occasional misery among these employed in them, from changes of fashion. It is the diffusion of luxury therefore among the mass of the people, and not an excess of it in a few, that seems to be most advantageous, both with regard to national wealth and national happiness.[143]

He differed from Paley, furthermore, in that he considered the widespread diffusion of a taste for luxuries among the mass of people to be the condition best calculated to actuate restriction of number. For if it be allowed that "some powerful check to population must prevail," and that "a taste for the comforts and conveniences of life will prevent people from marrying, under the certainty of being deprived of these advantages," then it must be allowed that the extension of this taste is both "little prejudicial to the happiness and virtue of society" and well suited to raise "that standard of wretchedness" or point below which the lower classes "will not continue to marry and propagate their species."[144] Finally, it is among peoples through whom a taste for luxuries and decencies has become diffused, that the master-springs of industry, the hope of betterment and the fear of want, exercise the most salutary influence.[145]

(ii) Exportation of Work

Long before Malthus wrote, English mercantilists were contending that the greater the exports, and the smaller the imports, the greater was the employment of English labour.[146] It followed that insomuch as population growth depended upon employment, it found a stimulus in an excess of exports over imports. Steuart, who looked upon employment as the primary stimulus to multiplication,[147] declared:

> If the value of the matter imported be greater than the value of what is exported, the country gains. If a greater value of labour be imported, than exported, the country loses. Why? Because in the first case, strangers must have paid, *in matter*, the surplus of labour exported; and, in the second case, because the country must have paid to strangers, *in matter* the surplus of labour imported.
>
> It is therefore a general maxim, to discourage the importation of work, and to encourage the exportation of it.[148]

Yet he apparently did not look with great favour upon a people's carrying "their numbers far beyond the proportion of their own growth" and becoming dependent, in part, upon potentially transient foreign sources for provisions.[149] Wallace remarked that a given country could, by exchanging goods and services for foodstuffs, support more people than the produce of its lands could subsist; but he added that such commerce, by diverting labour from agriculture, tended to diminish the number of mankind in the world as a whole.[150] Paley described the exchange of domestic wrought goods for foreign raw produce as conducive to the augmentation of employment and population, and the exchange of domestic raw produce for foreign wrought goods as "unfavourable to population, because it leaves no . . . demand for employment"; and he characterized the exportation of corn, except by new countries or in years of great plenty, as "noxious to population," or as indicative of "a defect of population."[151]

Malthus did not specifically evaluate the "export of work" thesis, as formulated by its exponents. He admitted, of course, that a nation might add to its food supply by importation. But, in 1803, he rejected a Smithian variant of this thesis, and warned against England's becoming dependent upon foreign-produced foodstuffs. A nation which exchanges wrought goods for rude produce, said Adam Smith, "exports what can subsist and accommodate but a very few, and imports the subsistence and accommodation of a great number."[152] To such exportation Malthus took exception. He pointed to the relatively great "clear national profit" yielded by the exportation of raw produce; to the fact that a nation must produce more than enough food in good years if it is to have enough in bad years; and to the industrial disadvantage of high wages which tend to accompany a domestic scarcity of provision. And he remarked, much as in the first edition, that a country which, for a time, "exported its raw produce, would be able" in the end "to subsist and accommodate a much greater population than" a country which relied appreciably upon imported raw produce. He therefore opposed a large country's becoming dependent upon foreign-produced provision.[153]

Malthus's principal concern remained the difficulty of making the food supply keep pace with a continually growing population, and the necessity of rendering this food supply secure.[154] In the 1817 and 1826 editions, however, his main thesis was that a nation, particularly if it was large, could not safely and judiciously exchange labour embodied in commerce and manufactures for foreign-produced foodstuffs, and thus support a part of its population at the expense of foreign-owned food funds. For it could not safely be supposed that a country with a "commercial system" — i.e., an economy founded predominantly upon manufacturing and foreign commerce — could export a continually expanding volume of manufactures, receiving in exchange a correspondingly expanding volume of food and raw materials, and so support a continually expanding population at a level of living consistent with the "existing habits of the people"; this supposition held true at best only so long as those in control of the foreign sources of food and raw materials were both willing and able to go on increasing their exports of these commodities to importing "commercial" countries.

A number of circumstances may operate individually or jointly to cause a "commercial" country to suffer difficulty in the procuring of subsistence even "while the means of raising food in the surrounding countries may still be comparatively abundant." The absolute and/or comparative advantages of an exporting country, which depend on "capital and skill," and the present possession of commercial channels, "cannot in their nature be permanent" and secure against the competition of other producing areas. Moreover, the countries which supply food and raw materials may, in the course of their "natural progress," also come to supply their own requirement of manufactures. Furthermore, an exporting commercial country may, while it still retains its comparative advantage in production and exportation, glut its foreign markets, suffer an adverse turn in the terms of trade, and depress the profitability of its own manufacturing industries. Finally, if the customer countries which furnish raw materials and food are, "from indolence and want of accumulation," not progressive, they will fail to provide an *expanding* market or to constitute an *expanding* source of supplies. The situation of a food importing country is, therefore, somewhat precarious at best; "it could not longer exist" if food and raw materials were denied to it, and it would begin to decline if its commercial transactions furnished it with a diminishing volume of food imports. "Though it be most readily admitted that, in a large landed nation, the evils which belong to the manufacturing and commercial system are much more than counterbalanced by its advantages, as long as it is supported by agriculture, yet, in reference to the effect of the excess which is not so supported, it may fairly be doubted whether the evils do not decidedly predominate."[155]

Malthus's attitude toward import restrictions and export bounties derived from his belief that a nation should provide its own foodstuffs in adequate quantity.[156] It would not do for Europe to become dependent upon America for "corn," giving manufactures in exchange; for when "America began to withdraw its corn from Europe and the agricultural exertions of Europe were inadequate to make up for this deficiency, it would certainly be felt that the temporary advantages of a greater degree of wealth and population (supposing them to have been really attained) had been very dearly purchased by a long period of retrograde movements and misery."[157] It was advantageous, on balance, to facilitate population growth through the de-

375

velopment of an agricultural-commercial system that furnished adequate foodstuffs from domestic sources. But it was not advantageous to found the support of part of the population upon imported corn, purchased at the expense of industrial and urban evils and a present and future precariousness of the food supply. "I should have no hesitation in considering such wealth and population as much too dearly purchased. The happiness of a society is, after all, the legitimate end even of its wealth, power, and population."[158] While Malthus did not continue to favour export bounties on corn,[159] his concern over the security of the food supply, together with his scepticism regarding the adequacy of foreign trade as a guard against "scarcity," led him to conclude that large countries, capable of producing a sufficient and not too variable supply of corn, might with advantage impose restrictions upon the importation of corn. Such a system of restrictions, provided that it allowed for the importation of corn in years of scarcity, would prevent the evils peculiar to a "commercial system," and, by assuring an adequate domestic food supply, would render a country secure in the possession of such improvements in manufactures as it developed.[160] Malthus's conclusion therefore resembled that of the nineteenth-century German writers who favoured measures to make that nation self-sufficient in terms of provision.

(iii) Was Malthusianism Counter-revolutionary?

Malthus's population theory, as set down in the *Essay*, has commonly been looked upon, by both right wing and left wing writers, as part of the counter-revolutionary answer to the rational movement which culminated in the French Revolution.[161] It was so viewed by Godwin. Marx, having declared that the principle of population "was greeted with jubilance by the English oligarchy as the great destroyer of all hankerings after human development," sought to refute it.[162] Godwin and William Thompson had already made the attempt, as had Proudhon and others. So varied a group of writers as Henry George, August Bebel, and G. B. Shaw, were to respond in like manner. In early nineteenth-century France certain Catholic writers discovered in Malthus support for their social philosophy, while liberal economists found in the *Essay* a complete answer to the arguments of the exponents of revolution.[163] In England and in America his work met a similar reception.[164] In fact, not until the twentieth century and the widespread diffusion of contraceptive practice, did the Malthusian argument against social revolution cease to be urged

Three doctrines, or sets of beliefs, were converging in the latter part of the eighteenth century, and Malthus's *Essay* is a product of this convergence. It had been noted that man was making progress, technological and social; and that, since progress is cultural in character and culture is cumulative, progress must, *ceteris paribus*, be cumulating and unending. Of this view Godwin and Condorcet were enthusiastic exponents.[165] Secondly the common man, once looked upon as a creature of little dignity placed in the world for the service of the master classes, was coming into his own. A beneficiary, primary and secondary, of the redistribution of economic and political power under way, he was held in greater esteem than formerly; his wants, rights, and potentialities were receiving more attention than ever, and they would receive even greater attention as the democratic movement, and the values it stood for, gained in scope. It had been remarked, thirdly, that man does not live in a *boundless* physical, social, and psychological universe; that limitations are imposed upon his behaviour, and upon the outcome of this behaviour, by this circumscribed physical milieu, by his restricted physiological and psychological makeup, and by the social and institutional controls which issue out of these physical and personal conditions. Efforts to resolve and synthesize acceptably these three somewhat inconsistent sets of beliefs were brought to a head by the French Revolution and the principles it posed, and by consideration of proposals for the relief of the poor made as a result of the economic crisis occasioned in England by war with France and by bad harvests.[166]

The social philosophies of those who, before Malthus, concerned themselves with aspects of the problem to whose solution he addressed himself, were compounded in varying proportions of the three sets of beliefs which converged in Malthus's *Essay*. At one extreme is Hobbes who, supposing limited that for which men strive, and practically unbounded the appetites which actuate men to strive, concluded that men could live together in peace only if there was "a common power to keep them all in awe" and establish a maintainable balance between want and want-satisfaction.[167] Wallace, though not a disciple of Hobbes, reasoned in a like manner when he concluded that man's passions must eventually "involve . . . in universal confusion" even those living under the most perfect of governments. For under such governments "the inconveniences of having a family" would be removed, and the limited "earth would at last be overstocked" with inhabitants, with the result that force and fraud, war, cruel and unnatural customs, inequality, and other impediments to human happiness and population growth would be restored.[168] So also reasoned Townsend when, premising that fear of want impels men to work and that population growth is desirable only insofar as it is the consequence of industry and frugality, he condemned both communism and the poor laws.[169] Hobbes, Wallace, and Townsend, in short, supposed that progress, however great, would never free men of the necessity of resolving, albeit most imperfectly, the problems arising out of the pressure of unrestrained appetites against limited resources, or establish among men an essential identity of interests.

At the other extreme are Locke and, more particularly, Godwin and Condorcet. For Locke postulated a natural identity of interests, a state of nature that was peaceful and virtuous, a theory of nature essentially optimistic, and a comparatively easy solution — peaceful competition and exchange — for the problem of distribution and order Hobbes saw issuing out of scarcity.[170] Godwin, believing that self-love is incompatible with virtue, that a fusion of interests is attainable, that benevolence may be substituted for self-love as the primary motive to action, that labour could be changed "from a burthen into an amusement," and that progress, which is cumulative in character, was being retarded by the existing institutional framework of

377

society, found in the abolition of this framework the key to the augmentation of human happiness. He proposed substituting for the system of property a system of equality, and for the existing institution of marriage — a "system of fraud" and the "worst of monopolies" — a system of free and flexible unions, it being "a question of no importance" in a "state of equality . . . to know who is the parent of each individual child"; and he looked forward to a time when every "species of public institution, may be laid aside as unnecessary."[171] Among the objections to the establishment and perpetuation of a system of equality considered by Godwin was that arising from the "principle of population" and developed by Wallace in 1761. To this Godwin replied that "myriads of centuries" might pass before the "habitable globe," as yet only one-fourth cultivated and badly at that, would be fully stocked; and that "when the earth shall refuse itself to a more extended population," men, their minds having established empire over matter, "will probably cease to propagate."[172] Condorcet, in contradistinction to Godwin, emphasized the cumulative and progressive character of cultural and institutional change, suggesting that, if population pressure ever threatened, mankind would subject it to rational control.[173] Godwin and Condorcet, in short, discovering in mental, moral, and cultural progress an easy means of escape from the limitations recognized by Hobbes and stressed by Wallace, were not alarmed lest the democratic scheme of values be threatened by the free play of men's passions in a circumscribed universe.

While the form which Malthus's reply to Godwin took was largely determined by the latter's argument, its substance reflected Malthus's conception of the ends of man, his estimate of man's behaviour tendencies, and his expectations regarding cultural progress. That Malthus subscribed to the democratic scheme of values, is evident in his views on education, on the extension of the right of suffrage,[174] and on the happiness of men. Accepting, as he did, the Christian view, which "places our present as well as our future happiness in the exercise of those virtues which tend to fit us for a state of superior enjoyment," and the principle of utility, in his opinion the surest natural "criterion of moral rules," and deeming good that which makes for virtue and happiness, he urged men to subject their passions to the guidance of reason and so avoid pain and evil, or having suffered these, to profit thereby and direct themselves back into the path of virtue.[175] Evidently, therefore, Malthus differed from Godwin and Condorcet regarding values and ends, democratic and otherwise, in terms of detail far more than in terms of generality.

But Malthus did not believe these values and ends so easy of realization as did Godwin and Condorcet, and he considered it better that men be alert to the difficulties that might beset their ventures than that they remain ignorant.[176] While he anticipated a "brilliant career of physical discovery," and "confidently" hoped that in consequence mankind would progress in virtue and happiness "to no unimportant extent,"[177] he looked upon resources as fixed by the niggardliness of nature far more than by the state of the industrial arts; and he always remained less optimistic than Godwin and Condorcet with respect to the prospective rate of technological progress and its effect upon production, particularly in agriculture where the augmentation of output on land under tillage and at the extensive margin was attended with much and increasing difficulty.[178] He pointed, moreover, to the limitedness of space, which would restrict increase as surely as would lack of food.[179]

Of greater practical importance, in Malthus's opinion, than the inability of progressing technology to overcome the limits to the augmentation of production set by a comparatively fixed physical milieu, were the obstacles interposed, in the way of the improvement of the human lot, by man's passions, of which that between the sexes was but one. For, while the human passions are either necessary to human welfare, or capable of being made conducive thereto, and, in accordance with the apparent intent of the Creator, should be directed to this purpose,[180] they cannot be subjected completely to appropriate discipline by human reason and institutions, and, therefore, because of their over-pursuit and misdirection, produce pain and evil as well as happiness and welfare.[181] In short, because he attached greater weight than did Godwin to the impelling power of the "corporeal propensities" and lesser weight to the ordering power of "reason," Malthus was forced to substitute for Godwin's expectation of indefinite improvement in human affairs the expectation of only limited improvement,[182] and for Godwin's proposal that institutions be removed, the counter-recommendation that institutional restrictions and self-control be strengthened through appropriate education.[183]

The passion between the sexes, out of which issued the principle of population, was good and necessary in Malthus's scheme, for he looked upon this principle as "best suited to the nature and situation of man"[184] and as the main motive behind social progress.[185] Hence, whereas earlier writers had been content to recount almost every supposed advantage of population growth except that which Marlowe put in the mouth of Mephistophilis, Malthus pointed to both the necessary and the salutary character of the tendency of numbers to increase faster than supplies, emphasizing, however, its influence upon man's individual motivation rather than its possible effect upon the division of labour. For man is unsuited to profit by unearned leisure, indolent and torpid by nature, "inert, sluggish, and averse from labour, unless compelled by necessity." The principle of population — its effort "to increase with greater rapidity than its supplies" — provides this necessity. It excites man to action, "to further the gracious designs of Providence," and, operating in conjunction with the pressure of his wants, awakens his mind and sharpens his faculties. It presses man to extend cultivation and fulfil the "end of nature," namely, the peopling of the earth. It overcomes that *vis inertiae,* which, as Nieboer has remarked, has played so great a part in the history of mankind.[186] In fact, were control of numbers easy, population would not "reach its natural and proper extent," a "necessary stimulus to industry" would be removed, and the improvement of man's mundane lot would be retarded.[187] For this reason, far more than because of any immediate theological prejudice,[188] he approved only of "moral restraint," at which he had at least hinted in the First Essay, as a preventive

379

check; he ignored the question of post-marital control; and he opposed the practice of contraception.[189]

It was essential, however, that the passion between the sexes be subjected to proper restraint; for the principle of population could not, if its multiplicative effects were insufficiently contained, efficiently generate social progress. When the pressure of numbers became so great as virtually to universalize misery and poverty and to check capital formation, stimulants to industry were dulled, and despotism and ignorance, so fatal to the improvement of the standard of living, tended to flourish.[190] When, on the contrary, men were alert to the imminence of intensified population pressure and to the evils that accompanied it, they tended to develop habits of prudence, thrift, and industry, and in consequence, to conduct themselves in a manner conducive to progress in well-being.

Institutions and customs, Malthus's argument runs in substance, develop largely out of the underlying nature of man and his physical environment. If they are both to survive and to contribute to man's welfare, they must consist with his nature and impose direction and restraint upon his passions. And they must be consonant with the principle of population, serving at the same time to promote industry and thrift and to favour the more salutary and less objectionable of the checks whose function it is to repress the superior power of population.[191] Malthus, therefore, found untenable both Godwin's conception of the nature of man and his complete oversight of the regulatory function of existing institutions. The socio-economic organization of mankind could not be built around the principle of benevolence;[192] it had to be founded upon self-love, upon the "principle of self-interest" and those institutions which gave expression to this principle — namely, marriage and the family, private property and inheritance, and a form of government calculated to preserve these institutions. It was to this principle and to these institutions that men owed whatever progress they had made and whatever capacity they had shown for curbing the principle of population.[193] These institutions served to channelize properly the passions of men, to make each person of discretionary age and status dependent predominantly upon himself, and to visit upon each the fruits, good or bad, of his behaviour and practice.[194] Where these circumstances prevailed, the "master spring of industry, the desire of bettering our condition," together with the fear of making it worse, had freest play, and man was most prone, *ceteris paribus*, to practice prudential restraint;[195] there too and there alone competition and competitive individualism could flourish without degenerating into war.[196]

Were existing institutions abolished and a system of equality established in their place, man would no longer feel those "stimulants to exertion which can alone" overcome his natural indolence and prompt him to cultivate the earth and fabricate the conveniences and comforts necessary to his happiness. This argument Malthus considered decisive. But he added a second and supposedly as decisive argument, which followed from the tendency of the human race to increase faster than the means of subsistence. In a system of equality no one is or feels himself to be under constraint not to marry; nor is marriage in any wise rationed; nor is the tendency to multiply too rapidly restricted by those means "which result from the laws of private property, and the moral obligation imposed on every man by the commands of God and nature to support his own children." It followed, Malthus concluded, either that this tendency must be restrained by means "infinitely more cruel," or that a system of equality must, soon after having been established, terminate in poverty and misery.[197] He rejected as unworkable, therefore, the systems of Godwin, Condorcet, Owen, and the Spenceans, together with Raynal's view that man had a right to subsistence and Paine's opinion that man's want of happiness originated in his governmental institutions.[198]

Suppose a state of equality were established, free of all those institutions to which many attributed man's want of happiness. Could such a state persist, Malthus asked, in the face of the fact that it did not consist with the laws of nature and the passions of men? His answer was in the negative. Upon the establishment of such a state of equality, numbers would grow until want again made itself generally felt and the spirit of benevolence gave place once more to "self-love." Thereupon private property and marriage would be restored and with them inequality; all without property would be under the necessity of working; and numbers would be restrained by the checks growing out of the re-established parental responsibility for offspring. Attempts to set up systems of equality, therefore, were doomed to failure; because they generated population pressure which, in turn, brought about the return of the institutions of property and family and the restoration of inequality and of a society divided into classes. Even so, attempts to establish a system of equality could visit much misery upon men before such a system finally gave way to a set of institutions consistent with the laws of nature and the passions of men.[199]

Malthus's several views on charity and public relief have the appearance of inconsistency; in his opinion, however, they were consistent, one with another, and with his conception of man's proclivities. When a prosperity-inducing stimulus to wealth and population is suddenly removed, and as a result, "produce" and "consumption" get out of balance, it is better to employ those thrown out of work by the decline in the demand for labour than to expose them to the "bad moral effects of idleness" and the "evil habits" which come with extended dependence upon alms. The employment provided, however, should be of the sort whose results "do not come for sale into the market," or "interfere with existing capitals," and thus worsen the actual state of affairs; it should add to consumption without adding to the output of immediately salable produce. Employment on public works of all kinds — e.g., the making and repairing of roads, bridges, railways, canals, etc. — and on the improvement of the land met this requirement, in Malthus's opinion.[200] Even so there was some danger that the provision of such employment through the expenditure of revenues raised by taxation or public subscription might "have the effect of concealing too much the failure of the national demand for labour, and prevent the population from gradually accommodating itself to a reduced demand."[201]

Malthus observed also that, under circumstances such as Great Britain then (1816–17) found itself — a sharply contracted demand for labour and much unemployment — "emigration is most useful as a temporary relief," serving to shorten the interval required by a population to "conform itself to the state of demand for labour." Emigration would not, however, provide permanent relief of population pressure.[202]

Because Malthus was a utilitarian he could not subscribe to the doctrine of natural rights, or admit that the indigent had a natural right to relief as some writers maintained;[203] because he supposed the principal cause of poverty to be undue population growth, he entertained no hope of permanent relief from redivision of wealth and similar measures,[204] and because he believed that man should depend upon "his own exertions, his own industry and foresight," he approved of work-relief only under the conditions indicated and of charity only when men were the victims of "unmerited calamities."[205] Were the idle and the negligent assured public support, the tendency on the part of men to exert themselves in order to better their condition and win security would be weakened, and population growth would be unduly stimulated.[206] The English poor laws operated to generate idleness and dissipation and "to create the poor which they maintain," to lower wages, to divert resources from the more industrious to the less valuable members of society, and to diminish the general resources of a country; therefore they defeated their benevolent purpose.[207] The determination of the proper rate of population growth, Malthus implied, should be left to the price of labour, which, if "left to find its natural level . . . expresses clearly the wants of society respecting population";[208] and each should be made to depend upon his own resources and efforts for the support of himself and his family. Malthus therefore advocated that the poor laws be gradually abolished; that each be made solely responsible for the support of himself and his family; that by means of a suitable educational programme, such as Adam Smith had proposed, the poor be acquainted with the true cause of their poverty and with the necessity of practising moral restraint; and that maximum possible effect be given to "the desire of bettering our condition, . . . the true mode of improving the state of the lower classes."[209]

Malthus was a counter-revolutionary in that he opposed certain principles associated with the French Revolution and condemned revolution in general. He was a conservative in that he attached great weight to the essentially constant, and less weight to the essentially variable, elements in nature, man, and social relations; in that he stressed the regulatory function of institutions in general, and not only opposed but also considered very improbable any important change in the fundamental institutional and social structure of English society; and in that he held, and believed it necessary to hold, the individual almost completely responsible for his actions and for his failure to act. He was a conservative too in that, while he advocated the education of the masses, he did not suppose man to be so plastic as Helvetius had assumed, and therefore readily transformable, by law and training, into a virtuous being. He was a conservative, finally, in that he could find no grounds for easy optimism and an easy harmonizing of interests: man's road had been hard and it would probably continue hard. But he was not a counter-revolutionary in that he opposed all changes in government and in institutional structure; for he estimated their value in terms of their utility and not in terms of their mere preservation. Hence his opposition, for example, to feudalism. Neither did he oppose improvement of the condition of the common man. This he always sought, and this, together with the strengthening of democratic values, the implementation of his doctrines was intended to accomplish. He supplied, in the form of his concept of effective demand (which implicitly denied a natural identity of the interests of men), an instrument of analysis conducive to the amelioration of the condition of the common man, the full potentialities of which were not grasped until a century after his death.[210]

(iv) Pro-marriage and Pro-natality Measures

Many writers, in the eighteenth and preceding centuries, had advocated the adoption, by the state, of measures intended to multiply marriage and to stimulate natality.[211] Moreover, the second half of the eighteenth century had witnessed, in England, both controversy over whether the ancient or the modern nations were the more populous, and expression of apprehension at the seeming non-growth of the English population.

Malthus took the side of Hume against Wallace on the question of the comparative populousness of ancient and modern nations,[212] and the side of those who said that England's population had grown since the revolution (1688),[213] inasmuch as he believed that the means of subsistence had increased, and in consequence, population. Furthermore, he opposed both measures designed directly to encourage marriage and natality, and institutional arrangements which, though not established for this purpose, tended to exercise the same effect; because he supposed that, when food was available and accessible to the masses, men needed no additional stimulus to multiply, and because he disapproved certain of the objectives of the populationists. He did not, of course, oppose economic improvements which, by making for the increase of wealth and employment, operated also to increase numbers.[214]

The disposition on the part of men to marry and multiply, Malthus always supposed, is sufficiently strong to provide whatever numbers the prevailing prices of labour, the habits of consumption of the population, and the resources and available food supply of a country call for.[215] It would suffice to do this if the produce of the earth were unlimited; it has sufficed and does suffice to do this in the face of many obstacles;[216] it suffices, and often more than suffices, to do this when, as is almost always the case, a population's economic universe is limited, its food supply is susceptible of only slow augmentation, and it can obtain little relief through emigration or through importation of provision.[217] It is futile, therefore, to encourage early marriage, to disgrace celibacy, or otherwise to force natality and population growth. For when the available food supply and resources can accommodate only a given rate of growth, an increase in natality above the level required to supply this rate merely brings about an offsetting increase in mortality,[218] and it may produce a state of misery unfavourable to the augmentation of production, and, therefore, to population growth.[219] A nation can no more load population upon its agricultural resources beyond their capacity to support than a grazier can crowd stock upon his pastures beyond their capacity to subsist.[220]

If numbers fail to increase, or if they decline, Malthus's argument continues, it is not for want of a disposition on the part of men to marry and multiply; it is for want of food.[221] The underlying causes of the non-growth or decline of population must be sought, therefore, in the conditions which prevent the augmentation of the food supply or its being made available to the lower classes.[222] Efforts to stimulate natality, as distinguished from successful efforts to augment the food supply, are doomed to failure. For this reason, and because they tended to worsen the condition of the lower classes, Malthus opposed encouragements to natality, the poor laws, and all other arrangements that transferred from the individual to the community responsibility for the support of his offspring. But he did not oppose allowances for children above six and he did not condemn measures such as Colbert's, because these schemes for relief, while they provided help to occasional very large families, did not encourage marriage.[223]

Malthus did approve, however, as was shown earlier, of changes in the economic structure of society which, while consistent with the sentiments and passions of men and conducive to the improvement of the state of the lower classes, served to augment the output of goods and services, to increase the effective demand for labour, and to facilitate population growth. For he looked upon population growth, if it took place under proper conditions, as good, and upon the usual pro-natality measures as bad, not because they might induce an increase in births, but because they could not evoke both an increase in births *and* the other conditions prerequisite to the support and happiness of the population.[224]

Malthus was always at pains to show that population normally tends to increase when the food supply accessible to the masses expands; for much of his social theory rested upon this assumption. He denied that "the passion between the sexes, or the natural prolifickness of women, diminishes in the progress of society."[225] And while he admitted of a "very few instances, such as the negroes in the West Indies, and one or two others, where population does not keep up to the level of the means of subsistence," he insisted upon their unimportance and unrepresentativeness.[226] "Under every form of government, however unjust and tyrannical, in every climate of the known world, however apparently unfavourable to health, it has been found that population, almost with the sole exception above alluded to, has been able to keep itself up to the level of the means of subsistence."[227] Had Malthus assigned considerable weight to checks of the sort he here has in mind, or had he anticipated the subsequent widespread diffusion of effective contraceptive practices, he would not only have had to modify his evaluation of measures intended to encourage marriage and natality; he would also have had to reformulate his theory of social progress.

(v) Optimum Population

Although the notion of an optimum population is not recent, it was not until the nineteenth century that this concept was rather carefully formulated in terms of per-capita income, or per-capita welfare.[228] Many pre-nineteenth century writers observed that power, national strength, happiness, etc., are conditioned by population density and population growth. These writers differed, however, with respect to what they wanted maximized, for they differed in social philosophy and value attitudes; and while every social philosophy and set of value attitudes emphasizes a maximum of some sort, not all emphasize the same maximum. These writers differed, therefore, regarding what constitutes an optimum population. Some of the mercantilists, for example, favoured population densities and growth rates suited to maximize national power. Others favoured a population condition designed to maximize the income of the dominant minority. Still others favoured a population situation somewhat consistent with the welfare of the common man. In general, late eighteenth-century writers, who attached importance to the happiness of the many, and who shared the new emphasis upon the dignity of the human personality and the right of the common man to participate significantly in the fruits of economic and political progress, had begun to think in terms of population densities and growth rates consistent with the improvement of the economic lot of the lower classes; and in their writings are foreshadowed the later income and welfare optimum concepts. These eighteenth-century foreshadowings of the optimum concept, unlike the late nineteenth- and twentieth-century notion, ran in essentially static rather than in dynamic terms. Furthermore, the late eighteenth-century writers, unlike those of earlier periods, did not suppose that population growth could be stepped up or down in accordance with the requirements of their optima; for it had come generally to be accepted that population growth adjusts itself to the food supply and the prevailing patterns of consumption.

Malthus, as has already been indicated, looked upon the principle of population as good and necessary to social progress, and he stressed the advantages associated with population growth. A country's power to increase its resources and defend its possessions depends upon its having a population that is efficient — i.e., almost "constantly employed." It is the Creator's intention that the earth be replenished. There is nothing "more desirable than the most rapid increase of population, unaccompanied by vice and misery."[229] "There is not a truer criterion of the happiness and innocence of a people than the rapidity of their increase."[230] Malthus did not, however, educe an argument for population growth from the principle of division of labour, presumably because he took this for granted, preferring instead to consider barriers to the extension of specialization.[231]

At the same time Malthus was interested primarily in the prevention of poverty, in the amelioration of the condition of the underlying population, and in democratic values generally. Hence, while he favoured the growth of population, he insisted upon its being "healthy, virtuous, and happy"; and he declared himself "an enemy to vice and misery, and consequently to that unfavourable proportion between population and food, which produces these evils."[232] He did not admit the opinion that numbers should be sufficiently great to make manpower continually available to recruiting sergeants and employers at very low wages; for then the lower classes could experience neither the personal respectability nor the improved economic situation that might otherwise be theirs, and war, because of the redundancy of popula·tion, would be more probable.[233] "The wealth and power of nations," Malthus wrote, in consistence with his utilitarian philosophy, "are, after all, only desirable as they contribute to happiness."[234] And nations are "happy according to the liberality with which" the food they can produce or acquire "is divided, or the quantity which a day's labour will purchase."[235] Hence he said that the object of those who would better the condition of the lower classes "must be . . . to enable the labourer to command a larger share of the necessaries and comforts of life."[236] And he pointed to the undesirability as well as to the practical and institutional impossibility of utilizing land and resources in such manner as to carry population to a theoretical maximum.[237]

In his treatment of the significance of low mortality, and of the superiority of death-control to birth-increase as a means of augmenting population, Malthus anticipated modern writers. Death-control necessarily presupposed birth-control; it could not be realized in the absence of the latter. A diminished proportion of births, he said, means reduced mortality, a saving of that which otherwise would be expended upon those who die prematurely, and a population composed more largely of adults and therefore more efficient and productive. Hence he advocated "such a price of labour, combined with such habits" as would reduce natality and mortality and eventuate in an efficient population.[238] He pointed to low mortality, furthermore, as an index of civilization and happiness. "A decrease of mortality at all ages is what we ought chiefly to aim at; and as the best criterion of happiness and good government, instead of the largeness of the proportion of births, which was the usual mode of judging, I have proposed the smallness of the proportion dying under the age of puberty."[239] This end — a necessary result of a diminished proportion of births — was to be sought, not through the practice of birth control which Malthus condemned, but through the practice of moral restraint.[240]

It is evident, in view of what has been said, that Malthus did not conceive of an income optimum, or maximum per capita income, population. He favoured both numbers and the abolition of poverty. He insisted upon uniting in a compatible manner "the two grand *desiderata,* a great actual population, and a state of society, in which abject poverty and dependence are comparatively but little known."[241] He had in mind a society in which the vast majority could enjoy an income sufficient to provide some conveniences and comforts, and as many could marry as the resources of a country and an economic system founded upon private property and individual responsibility would permit. It was his wish apparently that the principle of population continue to challenge men, but under such circumstances that they might meet this challenge effectively.[242] Specifically, he conceived of a society whose members would consider themselves duty-bound not to marry and have families until they could support them, and in which women could "look forward with just confidence to marriage at twenty-seven or twenty-eight."[243] Accordingly, since he supposed that prior to marriage moral restraint would rule, and presumably that after marriage neither moral restraint nor contraception would be practised, he had also to suppose that under normal conditions population would grow, and that, if welfare were not to be endangered, the supply of food and other goods would at least keep pace with population growth. But he blunted these suppositions by making marriage contingent upon the ability of those marrying to support their families, and by thus making the age at which men and women might actually marry with propriety conditional upon the augmentability of the food supply.[244] In theory, therefore, he made sufficient provision, in his "ideal" society, for the exorcising of the devil he had raised, and for the avoidance of the evils associated with a too great ratio of population to resources.

Malthus did not concern himself with what many present-day writers consider to be the real Devil of Population — a continuing deficiency of births. This possible source of underpopulation did not alarm him since he assumed that, given sufficient industry and sufficient emphasis upon agriculture, there would be no persisting deficiency of births or population.[245] He recognized, however, that a country, even though overpopulated in relation to the available food supply, might nonetheless be very much underpopulated in relation to its resources, because these resources were being improperly developed and utilized. The remedy, in these circumstances, was not the encouragement of marriage and natality, but the augmentation of productive power and employment.

In sum, it may be said that while Malthus did not have in mind the modern population optimum, he did have in mind optimum densities and optimum growth rates. These depended upon circumstances. They were intended to be consistent with his underlying philosophy. They were sometimes exceeded, and sometimes fallen short of. They were, if not consonant with the maximization of welfare in the modern meaning of the term, in keeping with his notions of welfare and his anticipations regarding the future.

CONCLUSION

Malthus lived in what, for a section of the European sphere, was the latter part of a period of transition; in a period when the industrial revolution was still transforming the productive basis of society from one in which land predominated to one in which the instruments of industry and commerce would predominate; in a period when the comparatively unlimited demand of the masses was beginning to outstrip the limited demand of the opulent few; in a period when the feudal polity and economy was being dissolved and converted into a polity that was more democratic, and an economy that was more non-agricultural, urban and free-enterprise, in character. In this new scheme of things the common man was far more important than in the erstwhile pattern of society. Upon his efforts depended the output of goods and services, upon his purse depended the opportunity to sell, and upon his soldierly skill depended the national security; he was, therefore, invested with more dignity and significance than in times past. Malthus, in his demographic and economic analysis, in his condemnation of feudal values, in his opposition to sumptuary and other controls upon the common man's right to consume, and in his emphasis upon the fact that the wants of the labouring many are far more important than those of the strategically situated few, recognized the new and growing role of the common man and gave expression to it.

Malthus's demographic and economic doctrines were influenced in their development, of course, by the climate of opinion in which he found himself, and by the views of those who preceded him or were contemporary with him. For example, his moral philosophy, as Bonar observed, "starts from a teleology. Nature makes nothing in vain."[246] Nature affords manifold evidence of the existence and the "goodness" of the Deity Who is anterior to her, and Whose instrument she is; her contrivances, even when they appear to produce evil, are directed to beneficial purposes, and, on the whole, allow more pleasure than is necessary to the fulfilment of the purposes of Nature and the Deity.[247] Malthus's teleological interpretation of the role of the "principle of population" reflects this philosophy. From the theodicy of the eighteenth-century as well as from contemporary moral and economic philosophy came the real cost elements in Malthus's theory of production. From his teleological conception of the principle of population and from his real cost theory of production flowed his defence, if not the emotional basis of this defence, of state, family, and property. In his rejection of the principle of the natural identity of interests, except insofar as landlord and state were concerned, originated in part at least his refusal to admit that a large country might, with safety, import provision and enjoy, in this respect, the advantage of international division of labour.

Far more striking is the seeming fact that Malthus's fundamental economic and demographic doctrine evolved almost naturally and necessarily out of the principles laid down and the problems recognized in the First Essay. There he showed that the "principle of population" — so named but differently analyzed by Godwin — arising out of the passion between the sexes, is at once the main generator of social progress and the sufficient source of the institutions of state, family, and private property. This principle is necessary to force man out of his torpor. Yet, if it is allowed too free play in a circumscribed Nahrungsspielraum, it inevitably produces widespread and at times almost universal misery. Whence its operation must be

388

restrained. And it can be restrained, consistently with the precepts of virtue and morality and the surety of human happiness, only under a regime of individual responsibility founded upon private property and the family and guarded by the state; — under a regime which, were it temporarily abolished, would of necessity be restored. It follows, from the necessity and inevitability of private property, that the population of a country cannot permanently be forced above the level consonant with the system of private property.

Malthus's consideration of the checks which hold down the inhabitants of a country to the number that it can subsist led him to conclude that numbers are regulated by subsistence. It also led him to observe that in many, if not in most countries, there were fewer inhabitants than these countries were capable of supporting in comfort, and that despite their comparative fewness, many of these inhabitants were living in poverty. His attention was directed, therefore, to the obstacles to the increase of subsistence, to which both the fewness and the misery of the inhabitants were to be traced — to the impediments, in short, to the salutary operation of the principle of population. These impediments, he found, assumed various forms: bad government, insecurity of property, concentration of the ownership of land, slavery, and so on. Yet, they were reducible to a common denominator, lack of an effective demand for labour. Between the resources (or "supplies"), actual and potential, of countries, and their inhabitants, stood institutional barriers which prevented these resources from supporting as great a demand for labour as they were capable of supporting, and from calling forth as great a growth of numbers as the principle of population could supply in consistence with human happiness and the preservation of the institutions of the family and private property. It was in consequence of his analysis of the checks to the growth of population and to the augmentation of "supplies," in short, and not to the influence of the Physiocrats and others who recognized the importance of consumption and glimpsed the circuit flow inherent in economies, that Malthus discovered the importance of the effective demand for labour, to the treatment of which the second part of the *Principles* was devoted. [248]

Malthus's analysis of the circumstances which governed the effective demand for labour directed his attention to the importance of what we have called industrialization. For he was concerned not so much with temporary interruptions of the economic circuit flow as with the conditions that regulated the expansion through time of the total effective demand for labour; and he thought not so much in terms of employment maxima and minima, as of a given time, as in terms of population maxima and minima. He found in industrialization, therefore, and in the associated development of what Fisher and Clark have called "tertiary" employments, the means of providing an effective and expanding demand for labour, and, consequently, for population. He found in industrialization, furthermore, the most satisfactory means of denying too free a play to the principle of population. For industrialization made for the development of civil liberty, for the diffusion of a taste for comforts and luxuries, and for the generation of habits of industry and prudence. It tended, therefore, to give effect to the principle of population and to insure population growth in consistence with the intent of the Creator and the happiness of men,[249] and yet to contain population growth sufficiently to guard this happiness.

NOTES

1. Our references are generally to first (1798), second (1803), and last (sixth, 1826) editions of the *Essay on the Principle of Population.* We have used the 1926 reprint of the first edition and the edition published, with introduction by G. T. Bettany, in 1890 (London), as a reedition of the sixth. When the last edition differs from the second, the difference is noted; and when otherwise advisable, reference is made to both editions. Our references are to the second edition of the *Principles of Political Economy* (London, 1836; reprinted in 1936) except when the second edition differs significantly from the first (1820), which is rarely for the purposes of the present study. Use has been made of several of Malthus's pamphlets, cited in the text; of articles by Malthus in the *Edinburgh Review* (July, 1808, vol. VII, pp. 336–55; July, 1821, vol. XXXV, pp. 362–77) and in the *Quarterly Review* (January, 1824, vol. XXIV, pp. 297–334); of an article attributed to Malthus (*Edinburgh Review*, Aug., 1810, vol. XVI, pp. 464–76); of G. W. Zinke, "Six Letters from Malthus to Pierre Prevost" (*Journal of Economic History,* vol. II, 1942, pp. 174–89); of Malthus's letters (1829) to N. W. Senior, printed in the latter's *Two Lectures on Population* (London, 1829); and of *A Summary View of the Principle of Population* (London, 1830), an abridgment of the article on population done by Malthus, apparently in late 1822, for the 1824 Supplement to the *Encyclopaedia Britannica.* Malthus's opinions, expressed in *A Summary View,* are the same as those expressed in the last editions of the *Essay* and the *Principles.* Aspects of Malthus's work have been well treated by, among others, J. Bonar, *Malthus and His Work* (London, 1924), and J. H. Hollander, in his introduction to David Ricardo's *Notes on Malthus* (Baltimore, 1928), edited by Hollander and T. E. Gregory. The population situation in England in Malthus's lifetime has been treated by T. H. Marshall in "The Population Problem during the Industrial Revolution" (*Economic History* [Supplement to *Economic Journal*], vol. I, 1929, pp. 429–56) and "The Population of England and Wales from the Industrial Revolution to the World War" (*Economic History Review,* vol. V, 1935, pp. 65–78); M. C. Buer, *Health, Wealth, and Population, 1760–1815* (London, 1926); G. T. Griffith, *Population Problems of the Age of Malthus* (London, 1926).

2. *Essay,* p. 14; cf. 1st ed., pp. 140–1.

3. E.g., his qualifying footnote (*Essay,* p. 14, also p. 295; first added in the 1817 edition): "It should be observed that, by an increase in the means of subsistence, is here meant such an increase as will enable the mass of the society to command more food. An increase might certainly take place, which in the actual state of a particular society would not be distributed to the lower classes, and consequently would give no stimulus to population."

4. In the *Essay,* well described by Bonar (*Malthus,* p. 5) as an inquiry "into the nature and causes of poverty," Malthus "endeavoured to trace the causes which practically keep down the population of a country to the level of its actual supplies"; while in the *Principles* his object was "to shew what are the causes which influence these supplies, or call the powers of production forth into the shape of increasing wealth." See *ibid.,* p. 309; 1st ed., p. 345.

5. In the second edition (preface) Malthus states that he deduced the main argument of the first essay from the writings of Hume, Wallace, Adam Smith, and R. Price. The writings of Condorcet and Godwin, of course, gave form and direction to his argument. He both rejected and adopted views set forth in William Paley's widely read *Principles of Moral and Political Philosophy* (London, 1785). Among the writers who saw that poverty arises from "a too rapid increase of population" Malthus numbered Plato, Aristotle, Montesquieu, Benjamin Franklin, James Steuart, Arthur Young, Joseph Townsend, and some of the Physiocrats. The editions of the *Essay* of most significance are the first, the second, and the fifth. He gave final form to most of what he had to say in the fifth (1817). Our references, of course, are usually to the sixth, which, for the purposes of the present discussion, is virtually identical with the fifth.

6. This thesis is set forth most fully in the last chapter of the *Principles* where

he treats of "the immediate causes of the progress of wealth"; it appears in substantially the same form in the 1836 as in the 1820 edition.

7. On Franklin's views see my "Malthusianism in Eighteenth Century America" (*American Economic Review*, vol. XXV, 1935, pp. 691–8). Franklin's *Observations . . . etc.*, written in 1751 and published in 1755, were printed in Burke's *Annual Register* (London) in 1760. Franklin's recommendation that Canada be annexed by Britain, a recommendation based in part upon his population thesis, was followed. Malthus refers to Franklin in the second and later editions of the *Essay* (I, i). Malthus got from a pamphlet by Styles and cited by Price evidence that the American population was doubling in twenty-five years (*Essay*, 1st ed., pp. 105, 185). Adam Smith, too, stated that population doubled in twenty to twenty-five years in the British colonies in North America. See *Wealth of Nations* (Cannan edition, Modern Library), pp. 70, 392.

8. John Campbell, *The Present State of Europe* (London, 1753, 4th ed.), p. 508. Arthur Young cites this passage with approval in his *Political Arithmetic* (London, 1774), pp. 107–9. A similar argument appeared in *An Account of the European Settlements in America* (London, 1758), vol. II, pp. 293 ff., attributed to Edmund Burke. Adam Smith (*Wealth of Nations*, p. 416) observed that the discovery of America opened new markets, intensified divisions of labour and improvements, and augmented wealth and income; it must, therefore, on his principles, have facilitated population growth in Europe and England.

9. *Political Arithmetic*, p. 86; also pp. 61–2, 68–9, 91, 107 ff., 319–20. Franklin is cited on p. 68. Young took exception to James Steuart's making population depend immediately upon the quantity of food instead of upon employment which gives man the "value of food." Malthus later criticized opinions such as Young's "Increase your people as much as you please, food will increase with them" (*ibid.*, p. 69).

10. *An Inquiry into the Principles of Political Economy* (1767) (*Works*, London, 1805, vol. I, pp. 31, 49; also pp. 30, 49, 73, 191, 193). On p. 154 he speaks of "the *effectual* demand . . . which makes the husbandman labour. . . ." His italics.

11. *Wealth of Nations*, p. 80, also pp. 68–9, 79, 81.

12. John Howlett, *Examination of Dr. Price's Essays on the Population of England and Wales*, etc. (1781). See J. Bonar, *Theories of Population from Raleigh to Arthur Young* (New York, 1931), pp. 210–11; C. E. Stangeland, *Pre-Malthusian Doctrines of Population* (New York, 1904), p. 348; sec. III (iv) of this article.

13. *Principles of Moral and Political Philosophy*, p. 453. His fundamental proposition was (p. 443): "Wherever the commerce between the sexes is regulated by marriage, and a provision for that mode of subsistence, to which each class of the community is accustomed, can be procured with ease and certainty, there the number of people will increase; and the rapidity, as well as the extent of the increase will be proportioned to the degree in which the causes exist."

14. 1st ed., chap. XVI; 2d ed., III, vii. He repeats the proposition that the funds for the maintenance of labour do not bear a fixed relation to wealth and capital in the last edition (III, xiii) and in the *Principles* (2d ed., pp. 234–5). See also below, sections II and III. Adam Smith had said that it is not the actual greatness of national wealth (i.e., "revenue" and "stock") "but its continual increase, which occasions a rise in the wages of labour"; that "the progressive state is the best for the labouring poor"; and that wages are low in a stationary state and inadequate in a declining state. The "demand for labour, according as it happens to be increasing, stationary, or declining" requires an "increasing, stationary, or declining population" (*Wealth of Nations*, pp. 69, 73, 81, 85). With this statement Malthus would agree in so far as the "demand for labour" is resolvable into "funds . . . for the maintenance of labour." See note 27, below.

15. 5th ed., III, xiii, last paragraph; 6th ed., *ibid.*

16. In his essay, "Of Avarice and Profusion," William Godwin sought to refute the "currently established" maxim that "it is the duty of the rich man to live up to his fortune," and to demonstrate that the "profuse" man injures the mass of mankind in much greater measure than does the "avaricious" man. The avaricious man lives a life of self-denial; he does not burden the labouring poor, and yet he does not lock up physical goods against use by his contemporaries. The many wants of the profuse man, on the contrary, but increase the burden of work upon the poor and deprive them of the leisure and means necessary to "intellectual cultivation"; whence, whoever invents a new dish or creates a new luxury, adds to the hardship and drudgery of the lower orders but not to their wages and comfort. See *The Enquirer* (Philadelphia, 1797), pp. 135–48; also *Enquiry Concerning Political Justice* (Philadelphia, 1796), vol. II, bk. VIII, chap. II, pp. 316 ff.

17. *Essay*, 1st ed., pp. 282–5, 295–8. Even supposing production were not checked, how could the unemployed establish title to "a proper share of the food and raiment produced by the society?" (*ibid.*, pp. 298–300). See also sec. III (iii) of this article.

18. *Ibid.*, pp. 293–4. This statement was obviously inspired by Godwin's comment (*Enquirer*, p. 140) that several cen-

turies earlier, when there "was little of manufacture," the great proprietors could not, together with their families, consume all the foodstuffs to which they had title.

19. *Essay*, 1st ed., p. 119. Wages are made to depend, in the first edition, upon the ratio of workers to "the fund appropriated to the maintenance of labour, . . . the aggregate quantity of food possessed by the owners of land beyond their own consumption" (*ibid.*, pp. 205, 305–6). It followed that population pressure was the real cause of low wages (*ibid.*, pp. 30–6, 82–3); that it was better to increase agricultural than non-agricultural production (e.g., 324–6); that an increase in the ratio of proprietors to labourers would benefit the latter and facilitate population growth (*ibid.*, pp. 344–5). He was still thinking predominantly, as did so many eighteenth-century writers (e.g., see my *French Predecessors of Malthus*, Durham, 1942) in terms of an essentially cereal or provision standard of life.

20. *Principles*, 1st ed., p. 261. In the second edition, p. 234, he writes "essentially necessary"; see also *ibid.*, p. 224.

21. The term "wage goods," as used by modern writers, does not quite represent Malthus's later view inasmuch as he looked upon provisions as the limitational factor (see note 26, below). Following F. M. Eden, Malthus supposed that in a labourer's family of average size two-fifths of the expenditures went for bread or meal, one for meat and dairy products and potatoes, and two for house-rent, fuel, soap, candles, tea, sugar and clothing. It followed that the price of corn, while it exerted a powerful influence upon the price of labour, did not regulate it "wholly"; and that corn and labour rarely kept "an even pace together." See *Observations on the Effects of the Corn Laws* (1814), edited by J. H. Hollander (Baltimore, 1932), pp. 9–11, 15, 20; also *Inquiry into the Nature and Progress of Rent* (1815), edited by J. H. Hollander (Baltimore, 1903), pp. 39–42.

22. "An increase in the means of subsistence . . . which in the actual state of a particular society would not be distributed to the lower classes, . . . would give no stimulus to population" (*Essay*, p. 14, n. added in 1817; also p. 295, cf. 2d ed., p. 421). See also below on family earnings.

23. *Essay*, p. 426; 2d ed., p. 471. See also *Essay*, pp. 93–4, 127, 138–9, 172; 2d ed., pp. 119–20, 162, 178, 221.

24. *Essay*, p. 331; also pp. 428–9 (2d ed., p. 471). On oscillation of population growth see sec. iii (iii) of this article. In a small country, with little variety of employment and a snug fit of population to available employment, nuptiality is more sensitive to conditions of employment than where numbers are great and the employment situation is obscure (*Essay*, pp. 144–6; 2d ed., pp. 186–8).

25. *Principles*, pp. 436–7; also p. 437

n. (not in 1st ed.) where he says that when there is no demand for labour, "charity" is their only source of food. See also *Essay*, pp. 331, 429; 2d ed., pp. 471–2; *Quarterly Review*, 1824, pp. 326–7. Malthus's concern above is with the decline in the demand for labour that developed upon the termination of the Napoleonic wars. See *Principles*, ii, i, 10; J. J. O'Leary, "Malthus's General Theory of Employment and the Post-Napoleonic Depressions" (*Journal of Economic History*, vol. III, 1943, pp. 185–200). See sec. iii (iii) of this article, on public works and emigration. Malthus's attitude toward manufacturing was conditioned in part by his belief that employment therein was uncertain and unstable (*Essay*, pp. 420–3; 2d ed., iii, vii).

26. He uses the term "resources" at times; e.g., see *Essay*, pp. 547–50 (written in 1807). The *limitational* group of resources, however, appears to be food; for he nowhere suggests that some lack other than food fixes the potential maximum. Furthermore, he described "want of food" as the "ultimate check" and as the "most efficient cause of the three immediate checks"; and "increase in the means of subsistence" as the "only true criterion of a real and permanent increase in the population." See *Essay*, pp. 7, 288, 294; 2d ed., pp. 336, 340, 347. He nowhere observed that what constitutes the *limitational* resource, or group of resources, depends upon the consumption habits of the population, presumably because he supposed this limitational resource to be food. He anticipated that the situation of the labouring classes would improve, if they exercised moral restraint, even though subsistence had come nearly to a stand (Senior, *Two Lectures on Population*, p. 71).

27. "When the demand for labour is either stationary, or increasing very slowly, people not seeing any employment open by which they can support a family, or the wages of common labour being inadequate to this purpose, will of course be deterred from marrying. But if a demand for labour continue increasing with some rapidity, although the supply of food be uncertain, on account of variable seasons and a dependence on other countries, the population will evidently go on, till it is positively checked by famine or the diseases arising from severe want." See *Essay*, p. 429; 2d ed., pp. 471–2. Cf. Adam Smith, note 14 above.

28. *Principles*, p. 234. "These funds consist principally in the necessaries of life, or in the means of commanding the food, clothing, lodging, and firing of the labouring classes of society" (*ibid.*, p. 234); "luxuries" are not included in the "funds . . . for . . . ordinary labour" (*ibid.*, p. 365). This statement does not appear in the first edition (cf. pp. 261, 418–19) where he sometimes uses the term "re-

sources" as he uses the term "funds etc." in the second (cf. 1st ed., p. 246 with 2d ed., p. 223). He had already employed the concept of "funds" (which, as Taussig observes [*Wages and Capital*, New York, 1898, p. 160], he apparently derived from Adam Smith [*Wealth of Nations*, bk. I, cap. viii]) in the *Essay* (1st ed., p. 305; 2d ed., p. 420). Adam Smith (*ibid.*, p. 421) had made employment depend upon a society's "whole capital." See also note 21 above.

29. Elsewhere (*Quarterly Review*, 1824, pp. 326–7) he said that if the elasticity of demand for produce were less than unity, an increase in the supply of the funds destined for the maintenance of labour would be accompanied by a diminution in the quantity of labour employed. He was thinking in terms of the demand for labour and had in mind a situation in which the demand for produce was slack and the money price of labour apparently was high and sticky in relation to the money price of corn (cf. below, note 48). See also *Principles*, pp. 231–3.

30. *Principles*, II, i, 10, pp. 414–15, 424. See also *Essay*, pp. 96, 367–8, 428–30; 2d ed., pp. 122, 472. Malthus reasoned in like manner with respect to capital whose law of increase he compared to that of population. If an effectual demand for capital is lacking, and in consequence the rate of return on it is too low, saving from revenue to add to capital will merely aggravate the distress of the capitalists just as an increase of births augments misery and mortality when an effective demand for labour is lacking (*Principles*, pp. 404, 414–15, 433–5).

31. On the effect of trading relations, here supposed given, see below, sections II and III (ii). The increase of the funds destined for the maintenance of labour depends "upon the degree of industry, intelligence and activity" with which a country's physical powers of production are called forth (*Edinburgh Review*, 1810, p. 467).

32. *Essay*, pp. 400, 420, 428; *Principles*, pp. 281–2, also pp. 114–15, 158–9, 275–6, 278–9, 297–8. Under these circumstances, rent too would come to a stand (*ibid.*, I, iii, pp. 140–3, 146, 154, 160–1, 199, 211). On Malthus's views on rent see Bonar, *Malthus*, pp. 237 ff.; Hollander, *Notes*, pp. xxxiv–lxvii. Between interest of landlord and that of state Malthus found the "strictest union," at least so long as a country did not import food; but between other classes (e.g., labour, capitalists) and the state there existed no such close identity of interest (*ibid.*, pp. lxi ff.; *Principles*, p. 206). See also sec. III (iii) of this article.

33. *Essay*, pp. 400, 428; *Principles*, I, iv, 2, pp. 224–6, also p. 279. See his discussion of the forces that might bring population growth in Ireland to a stop (*Edinburgh Review*, 1808, pp. 343, 353). Also *Essay*, 2d ed., p. 427, where he refers to Steuart's statement (*Works*, vol. I, chap. XVIII) of the limit to population growth in a commercial state.

34. E.g., see *Edinburgh Review*, 1808, p. 345.

35. Population is "regulated by the real wages of labour" and comes to "a stand when the necessaries which these wages . . . command [are] not sufficient, under the actual habits of the people, to encourage an increase of numbers" (*Essay*, p. 400, not in 2d ed.; also pp. 420, 428; also *Summary View*, pp. 35, 64).

36. *Essay*, p. 427; also pp. 426–8; not in 2d ed. See also *Edinburgh Review*, 1821, p. 373.

37. The standard of life, differences in which also account for differences in the effect of given real wage rates, is here implicitly supposed constant (*Essay*, p. 428).

38. *Principles*, p. 240, also p. 252; also p. 387, where he suggests that when prices fall, wages lag, and consequently, production and employment decline. An influx of money, occasioned by a favourable balance of trade, Paley had said, encourages population growth: indirectly, by stimulating employment; directly, but only for a time, by increasing money wages faster than the price of provisions (*Principles of Moral and Political Philosophy*, pp. 462–5).

39. Of the extension of the practice of task work, with its long hours and low rates of pay, Malthus disapproved; it was prejudicial to health and happiness, even though it provided temporary relief in times of scarcity. See *Inquiry*, p. 40 n.; and cf. *Principles*, p. 279.

40. *Essay*, pp. 426–8; *Principles*, I, iv, 3, 5, pp. 232–4, 239–40, 258–60. Population grew at a higher rate in 1790–1811 than in 1735–55; corn wages were lower in 1790–1811 than in the earlier period, but, because of fuller employment and greater parish allowances, the real income of the lower classes was greater. See *Essay*, p. 428; also *Principles*, I, iv, 4–5, and p. 234. When prices are rising, entrepreneurial prospects improve, together with the demand for labour. E.g., see Zinke, "Six letters from Malthus to Pierre Prevost," pp. 185–7. Malthus attributed the lack of demand for labour and capital at the close of the Napoleonic wars to a diminution of "home revenues" aggravated by "contraction of the currency"; but he rejected proposals to issue paper money, saying that what was wanted was higher prices and lower wages in terms of bullion (*Principles*, I, ii, 10, pp. 416, 424–6, 480–2).

41. *Principles*, II, i, 2, especially p. 313.

42. See sec. III of this article.

43. C. E. Ayres, *The Theory of Economic Progress* (Chapel Hill, 1944), pp. 52–61. The progress of a country in capital equipment, population, and/or well-being,

Malthus observed as had Adam Smith (*Wealth of Nations*, p. 464), depends upon "the produce of a country" exceeding "the consumption of those employed in its production" (*Principles*, p. 41).

44. *Principles*, p. 314. Malthus criticized (*ibid.*, p. 314 n.) Lauderdale (*Nature and Origin of Public Wealth*, Edinburgh, 1804) for going "much too far in deprecating capital accumulation." Lauderdale (*ibid.*, pp. 339–42) cites Malthus (*Essay*, 2d ed., pp. 9–10) and declares that the distribution of wealth to which the preventive check is to be traced, "in a great degree determines the progress of population throughout the world." Lauderdale quoted with approval (pp. 247–8) Quesnay's attack upon hoarding and emphasis upon consumption, in which view Hollander (*Notes*, p. lxxix) finds the beginning of the doctrine against which Say's law was directed. In his *Letters to Malthus* ([1821], London, 1936) Say did not examine critically Malthus's views on population as enunciated in the *Principles*.

45. *Principles*, II, i, 3, pp. 320–6; cf. *Essay*, pp. 94–6, 127; 2d ed., pp. 120–2, 162.

46. *Ibid.*, pp. 328, 326–30, 414–15; also *Essay*, pp. 430–1 (2d ed., pp. 473–4) and sec. III (iv) of this article.

47. See sec. III of this article.

48. Cf. L. Robbins, "On the Elasticity of Demand for Income in Terms of Effort" (*Economica*, vol. X, 1930, pp. 123–9); J. R. Hicks, *Value and Capital* (London, 1939), pp. 36–7; P. H. Douglas, *The Theory of Wages* (New York, 1934), chap. XII. Malthus did not apply this type of analysis in his discussion of saving. See also note 29, above.

49. *Principles*, pp. 320–2, 402–4. The "general desire of mankind to better their condition, and make provision for a family" re-enforced and intensified the limit imposed on the demand for luxuries and conveniences by the "luxury of indolence" (*ibid.*, p. 402). Edward Gibbon, having noted that luxury prompts the landowner to improve his estate and distributes to non-landowners that which they otherwise would not receive, declared that "in the present imperfect condition of society, luxury, though it may proceed from vice or folly, seems to be the only means that can correct the unequal distribution of property" (*The Decline and Fall of the Roman Empire*, Modern Library Edition, vol. I, p. 48). Wallace considered simplicity of tastes most favourable to propagation when lands were evenly divided. Yet he supposed that when many or most men have more land than they need to maintain themselves, they "must be lazy and indolent" and less populous than they would be if arts and manufactures were introduced among them, their tastes were refined, their wants were increased, and their desires were excited by alluring objects: "this awakens ambition, kindles emulation, quickens industry, and engages men to labour, that they may procure the tempting objects they desire"; and it facilitates progress in wealth and number (*A Dissertation on the Numbers of Mankind in Ancient and Modern Times*, Edinburgh, 1753, pp. 27–9; but see sec. III (i)–(iii) of this article. See also C. Montesquieu, *De l'esprit des lois* (1748), XXIII, xv, IV, iv.

50. *Principles*, p. 355.

51. *Ibid.*, pp. 320–1. This thesis is well developed in the *Essay*. "If the labourer can obtain the full support of himself and family by two or three days labour," he will usually prefer leisure rather than work the remainder of the week "to furnish himself with conveniences and comforts" (*Essay*, pp. 424–5). In the first edition (pp. 77–8) Malthus suggests that an increase in money wages alone would cause workers to fancy themselves richer and therefore to reduce the number of hours of labour they stood ready to supply.

52. E.g., see *Principles*, pp. 337, 340; *Essay*, pp. 424–5. Adam Smith did not estimate the demand for income in terms of effort as did Malthus. "The desire of food is limited in every man by the narrow capacity of the human stomach; but the desire of the conveniences and ornaments of building, dress, equipage, and household furniture seems to have no limit or certain boundary" (*Wealth of Nations*, p. 164). Plenty did not cause men, as a rule, to relax their industry. "Some workmen, indeed, when they can earn in four days what will maintain them through the week, will be idle the other three. This, however, is by no means the case with the greater part. Workmen, on the contrary, when they are liberally paid by the piece, are very apt to overwork themselves . . ." (*ibid.*, p. 81, also pp. 82–3). Steuart (*Works*, vol. I, p. 193) had remarked that "the most delicate liver in Paris will not put more of the earth's productions into his belly, than another"; but he added that "there are no bounds to the consumption of *work*." Steuart believed, however, that where men are lazy, or tastes and manners are simple, cultivation tends to be restrained and with it multiplication; he considered such nations "in a *moral incapacity* of multiplying" (*ibid.*, pp. 38–40, 44, 47, 157). Human happiness, observed Hume, consists in "action, pleasure, indolence." When the "mechanical arts" are undeveloped, there is left to men only indolence, and it loses much of its relish because it does not succeed to labour. Where there is no taste and no demand for "superfluities, men sink into indolence, lose all enjoyment of life, and are useless to the public." See "Of Luxury" (*Essays Moral, Political, and Literary*, edited by T. H. Green and T.

H. Grose, New York, 1898, vol. I, pp. 300–3). Hume later entitled this essay, "Of Refinement in the Arts."

53. Among the three causes of rent Malthus numbered "that quality peculiar to the necessaries of life being able, *when properly distributed,* to create their own demand, or to raise up . . . demanders in proportion to . . . necessaries produced." See *Principles,* 1st ed., pp. 139–40, 541; 2d ed., p. 140; *Inquiry,* p. 18; Hollander, *Notes,* pp. xlvi ff.; my italics. While an increase in raw produce alone cannot occasion a proportionate increase in populations, Malthus noted, it should be recollected that land produces besides food the materials for clothing, lodging, and firing —the means, in short, by which people are brought into being and supported. Land thus differs from every other kind of machine. See *Principles,* 1st ed., pp. 141–2; 2d ed., p. 142. Malthus's discussion here is not well integrated with that in the text above.

54. *Principles,* II, i, 4, especially pp. 344, 351, 331–5, 342–3, also *Essay,* e.g., I, ix (in 2d ed.). Cf. Malthus's views (e.g., *Principles,* pp. 342–3) with those of Cantillon and Garnier (in *French Predecessors,* chap. IV). Hume ("Of Commerce," *Essays,* vol. I, pp. 298–9) remarked that favourable agricultural conditions sometimes make for poverty. In Ireland, Malthus observed (*Edinburgh Review,* 1808, p. 341), indolence and holidays restricted the supply of labour and thus prevented wage rates from falling as much as they otherwise would; in this instance the effect was beneficial.

55. *Principles,* p. 370, note on Ricardo's treatment of "gross and net revenue." See also Hollander, *Notes,* pp. xcii–xcvi.

56. *Principles,* II, i, 5, p. 360; also 355–7.

57. *Principles,* II, i, 6, p. 361. Distribution, as Malthus used the term, adapts products, "in quantity and quality, to the actual tastes and wants of the consumers, and creates new tastes and wants by means of greater facilities of intercourse" (*ibid.,* p. 371; not in 1st ed.). Paley (*Principles of Moral and Political Philosophy,* pp. 451 ff.) had described "distribution" as "of equal consequence with the production" of provision. On the idea of distribution, see E. Cannan, *History of the Theories of Production and Distribution,* 3rd ed., London, 1924, chaps. VI–VIII. Malthus's thesis, stated above, appears in the *Essay,* pp. 93 ff., 127, 138–9; 2d ed., pp. 119 ff., 162, 178. Malthus criticized both Sismondi's reply to the *Essay* and his assertion that the "free-contract" wages system was responsible for unemployment, poverty, and population pressure (*Principles,* p. 366 n.; Zinke, "Six Letters from Malthus to Pierre Prevost," pp. 182 ff.).

58. *Essay,* p. 244, 5th ed., II, pp. 103–4.

59. *Principles,* p. 371, also pp. 363–7, 415, 424. Cf. *Essay,* pp. 95, 428; *Summary View,* pp. 6, 18, 27, 37–40.

60. *Principles,* pp. 309–10; also note 86 below.

61. *Ibid.,* p. 372.

62. *Principles,* II, i, 7; *Essay,* pp. 93 ff., 127, 134 ff. (2d ed., pp. 119 ff., 162, 172 ff.); also *Principles* (p. 154; cf. p. 199) where he states that improperly conceived taxes upon the produce of land check cultivation and bring population to a premature stop. Although Malthus observed, as had Adam Smith (*Wealth of Nations,* p. 392), that primogeniture checks cultivation (*Essay,* p. 286; 1st ed., p. 344), and that in America "easy division of landed property" had facilitated cultivation and population growth (*Principles,* p. 373), he opposed extreme subdivision, because it prevented efficient cultivation, discouraged "prudence in marriage," and undermined civil liberty. Unlike Ricardo (*Notes,* p. 211), he was alarmed lest the French law of succession bring about a minute subdivision of agricultural property, and, within a century, visit "extraordinary poverty and distress" upon the French people and destroy their republican form of government. See *Principles,* pp. 375–9; *Essay,* pp. 204, 210, 214, 511. On later interpretations of the effect of this law see my *France Faces Depopulation* (Durham, 1938), pp. 146–56. In the British Empire primogeniture and entail did not prevent the breaking up of landed property; and their usual effects were offset by the fact that England was industrially developed and possessed a great consuming middle class. Furthermore, in England the landed aristocracy counterbalanced the mercantile class, thus making the constitution more secure; while the opportunity "to contend in wealth with the great landlords" stimulated merchants and manufacturers to exercise their skills. See *Principles,* pp. 379–81. Paley (*Principles of Moral and Political Philosophy,* pp. 450–1, 474–5) had described "the right of *common*" and "*manorial claims*" as condemning the land "to perpetual sterility," and tithes as retarding cultivation, and all these conditions as unfavorable to population growth.

63. *Principles,* II, i, 8, especially pp. 384–8, 393–7, also pp. 240, 403. Earlier (p. 324 n.) Malthus states that economists "from the rear or appearing to attach too much importance to money, have perhaps been too apt to throw it out of their consideration in their reasonings." On Malthus's role in the development of the theory of trade see J. Viner, *Studies in the Theory of International Trade* (New York, 1937); Hollander, *Notes,* pp. c–cvi.

64. *Principles,* p. 400, my italics.

65. *Ibid.,* p. 234. It was frequently

noted that agriculturalists produce a surplus above their own maintenance for which they must find vent, and upon which depends the size of the non-agricultural population. E.g., see Hume, "Of Commerce" in *Essays*, vol. I, p. 289; Steuart, *Works*, vol. 1, pp. 40, 46, 117; Adam Smith, *Wealth of Nations*, bk. III, cap. i, iv; my *French Predecessors*.

66. Malthus included under "productive" labour, that which is "directly productive of material wealth"; and under "personal services," that which does not directly create material wealth, and which Adam Smith called "unproductive" (*Principles*, pp. 35, 49; cf. 1st ed., pp. 30 ff.).

67. *Principles*, II, i, 9, especially pp. 412–13, 404–12. Malthus noted that since menials are complements to unproductive forms of wealth such as houses, the demand for the latter depends in part upon the availability of the former (*ibid.*, pp. 408–9).

68. *Ibid.*, I, iv, 3, pp. 234–6, 239; cf. *Essay*, pp. 416–17.

69. *Principles*, II, i, 9, especially pp. 404–13.

70. *Essay*, pp. 294–5.

71. On this point, see sec. III (i) and (ii) of this article.

72. E.g., *Essay*, III, xiv; 2d ed., III, xi; also Bonar's comments, *Malthus*, pp. 136 ff. On agriculture, see *ibid.*, 1st ed., chaps. xvi–xvii and pp. 95–7; 2d ed., III, vii–x; 5th ed., III, viii–xiii. Our discussion is based largely on his final views.

73. Essay, 1st ed., chaps. xvi–xvii, especially pp. 301–2, 308–10, 312–15, 320–6, 329, 332–7, 344; cf. Adam Smith, *Wealth of Nations*, pp. 391 ff. Malthus apparently was not too friendly to industry (*Essay*, 1st ed., p. 293); but he considered it as reasonable to expect to prevent a "mistress from growing old by never exposing her to the sun or air" as to expect to prevent the development of manufactures and luxury in new countries (*ibid.*, pp. 343–4).

74. *Ibid.*, pp. 96–7, 300–1.

75. He now looked upon "commerce and manufactures" as "the most distinguishing characteristics of civilization, the most obvious and striking marks of the improvement of society, and calculated to enlarge our enjoyments, and add to the sum of human happiness. No great surplus produce of agriculture could exist without them. . . ." (*Essay*, 2d ed., pp. 467–8, n.).

76. *Essay*, 2d ed., pp. 422, 426–9, 436–40, 450–1, 465–6; also sec. III (ii) of this article. Malthus's concern at the supposed neglect of agriculture is remindful of the Physiocrats. He was careful to point out, however, that in the absence of moral restraint, no measures could make the food supply keep pace with an unchecked population (*ibid.*, pp. 467–9; also 1st ed., pp. 27–9, 346–7, where he is more pessimistic than in the second).

77. *Essay*, 2d ed., pp. 120 ff., 162, 193–4, 205–6, 221–2.

78. E.g., *Essay*, p. 369; 2d ed., pp. 433–9.

79. *Essay*, III, xiii, pp. 416, 419, 424–5. Here Malthus is taking exception to Adam Smith's (*Wealth of Nations*, bk. I, cap. viii) manner of reasoning that every increase in wealth makes for the improvement of the condition of the lower classes. In the second edition (pp. 420–9, 435; cf. 1st ed., pp. 305–21) Malthus said: "The comforts of the labouring poor must necessarily depend upon the funds destined for the maintenance of labour; and will generally be in proportion to the rapidity of their increase." These funds do not tend to keep pace with wealth. If wealth increases at the expense of agriculture, workers tend to suffer a decrease in real wages, and some of their number are shunted into relatively unhealthful urban occupations. "Unless the increase of the riches of a country from manufactures give the lower classes of the society, on an average, a decidedly greater command over the necessaries and conveniences of life, it will not appear that their condition is improved." In the last editions he states that although an increase of wealth "does not imply a proportionate increase of the funds for the maintenance of labour, yet it brings with it advantages to the lower classes of society which may fully counterbalance the disadvantages with which it is attended" (*Essay*, p. 425).

80. *Essay*, p. 419. Malthus's point here is that the supply of food is less elastic (cf. p. 310 in 1st ed.) than that of non-agricultural products; but he remarks (*Essay*, p. 424; not in 2d ed.) that, with the labourer converting less of his wages into food, "he will not indeed have the same power of maintaining a large family; but with a small family he may be better lodged and clothed, and better able to command the decencies and comforts of life." Cf. Senior, *Two Lectures on Population*, p. 71. See above, note 21, for composition of worker's budget.

81. *Essay*, III, viii, especially pp. 360–8; also *Principles*, pp. 364–5. This argument does not appear in first and second editions; but there (1st ed., pp. 293–4; 2d ed., pp. 221–2, 438, 593) Malthus notes the evils peculiar to a feudal agricultural economy and indicates that agriculture, to be prosperous, must have vent for its products.

82. *Essay*, pp. 364, 368; also *Principles*, p. 373, where he notes the stimulus to American agriculture supplied by "foreign commerce" and the "easy division of landed property."

83. *Essay*, pp. 173, 368–9, 423–5; 2d ed., pp. 221–2; *Principles*, pp. 374–5. Griffith (*Population Problems of the Age of Malthus*, pp. 255–6) attributed the fact, that before the Industrial Revolution the

English population was practically stationary, to the localized character of markets and demands and to "the general water-tight structure of society." Before 1860 American pro-slavery writers defended the slave economy on the ground, among others, that, being less elastic than free-labour economies, it was more immune to population pressure. See my "Population Theory in the Ante-Bellum South" (*Journal of Southern History*, vol. II, 1936, pp. 360 ff.); "Malthusianism and the Debate on Slavery" (*South Atlantic Quarterly*, vol. XXXIV, 1935, pp. 170 ff.).

84. *Essay*, I, ix, p. 95 (not in 2d ed.). Excessive soil fertility merely aggravated the difficulty described. For similar opinions, see 2d ed., pp. 120–1, 162, and note 88, below.

85. *Essay*, p. 368, also pp. 93 ff., 173, 424–5; 2d ed., pp. 120 ff., 221–2; *Principles*, II, i, 4, on Ireland and New Spain.

86. Malthus noted, of course, such impediments to agriculture and population as bad government, tyranny, insecurity of person and property, lack of habits of industry, and localized institutional obstacles to effective cultivation. See *Essay*, pp. 72, 80, 83, 89, 100, 104–5, 148–9, 158, 428; 2d ed., pp. 92, 103, 106, 113–14, 126, 132, 190–1, 204–5; citations in Bonar, *Malthus*, pp. 78–9, 196, 198. See note 60 and text.

87. *Essay*, pp. 80, 93–4, 138–9, 150, 156, 159, 172; 2d ed., pp. 103, 119–20, 178, 193, 202, 205–6, 221.

88. "In countries where . . . land is divided into very large shares; . . . arts and manufacturers are absolutely necessary to the existence of any considerable population. Without them modern Europe would be unpeopled" (*Essay*, p. 127; 2d ed., p. 162). Cf. Hume, *Essays*, vol. I, p. 412, whom Malthus cites in the preceding paragraph. See also Wallace, note 49 above.

89. *Essay*, pp. 127, 134–9; 2d ed., pp. 162, 172–9. Malthus's emphasis is upon the defective distributive system which accompanied slavery in Rome rather than upon the acknowledged unfavourableness of slavery to propagation. Steuart (*Works*, vol. I, pp. 50, 52) had contended that so long as the wants of men were few, slavery was necessary to agricultural progress and multiplication. "Men were then forced to labour because they were slaves to others; men are now forced to labour because they are slaves to their own wants." Cf. Herrenschwand's analysis, summarized in my *French Predecessors*, pp. 291 ff.

90. Malthus here cites Steuart, *Works*, vol. I, pp. 38–40, 154–6. See note 52 above.

91. *Essay*, pp. 93–6; 2d ed., pp. 119–22. Because it is "most difficult" to change long-existing habits, Malthus added, the importation of industry and industrial workers may be advisable in these circumstances (*Essay*, p. 98; 2d ed., p. 124).

92. *Principles*, pp. 42–3, also pp. 115–16, 350 n.; *Essay*, pp. 367–70, and pp. 145–6 (2d ed., pp. 187–8), where he compares the composition of employment in Norway with that in England.

93. *Essay*, pp. 423–4; also pp. 534–5 (2d ed., p. 593).

94. *Essay*, III, ix; 2d ed., pp. 425–7, 467–9 n.; also sec. III (ii) of this article. The security of a nation's capital, Adam Smith wrote (*Wealth of Nations*, p. 395), is contingent on its being invested in part in domestic agriculture.

95. *Essay*, III, x, xiii, especially pp. 379, 372–3, 378–82, 387, 423–5.

96. *Principles*, pp. 402–3.

97. *Observations*, pp. 24–5.

98. See C. Clark, *The Conditions of Economic Progress* (London, 1940), p. 176. Clark substantiates this thesis stated several years earlier by A. G. B. Fisher (e.g., "The Economic Implications of Material Progress," *International Labor Review*, vol. XXXII, 1935, pp. 5 ff.).

99. *Principles*, 1st ed., pp. 482–3 (not in 2d ed.). The substance of this argument, however, appears in the second edition. See also O. Pancoast, "Malthus versus Ricardo . . ." (*Political Science Quarterly*, vol. LVIII, 1943, pp. 47–66).

100. "The condition of the labouring classes of society must evidently depend . . . partly on the habits of the people in respect to their food, clothing, and lodging"; upon the amount of necessaries and conveniences "without which they would not consent to keep up their numbers" (*Principles*, I, iv, 2, p. 224). See also *Essay*, pp. 536–7; 2d ed., pp. 595–6.

101. *Essay*, IV, xiii, pp. 534–5, also pp. 367, 471, 479–80, 491; *Principles*, pp. 226–7.

102. E.g., see *Essay*, pp. 368, 378–9, 424–5; 1st ed., pp. 123 n., 293–4; *Principles*, II, especially vii–viii. Adam Smith (*Wealth of Nations*, p. 385) had said: "Commerce and manufactures gradually introduced order and good government, and with them, the liberty and security of individuals." Hume, Adam Smith believed, was the first writer to note this. See Hume's essays, "Of Commerce" and "Of Luxury," in *Essays*.

103. *Principles*, I, iv, 2, pp. 224–5; *Essay*, pp. 378–9, 424–5. He noted, however, that in some Scottish parishes the introduction of manufactures had made possible the employment of very young children with the result that both marriages and child mortality had increased (*ibid.*, p. 251; 2d ed., p. 324). Malthus, of course, looked with disapproval upon the indiscriminate employment of children (*Essay*, p. 530; 2d ed., p. 586).

104. *Essay*, III, viii, pp. 364–7, also p. 379.

105. *Ibid.*, p. 515, also p. 379; 2d ed., p. 579. Here Malthus has in mind that if the price of food is high, and money wages and the supply of labour are largely regulated by it, the overall condition of the common people must improve for reasons indicated in the text. Malthus did not, however, say wages are regulated by the price of corn, or of food. He observed, rather, that they are influenced by the prices of both food and the other elements included in the worker's budget, and by changes in his habits of consumption (*Observations*, pp. 9–12, 15, 20; *Principles*, pp. 218 ff., 225–9). In another connection he said that a high price for raw produce signified a favourable state of economic affairs (*Inquiry*, pp. 39–42; Hollander, *Notes*, pp. xliii ff.); and even in the *Principles* (2d ed., pp. 184–9) he indicated that when a country was prosperous the price of its raw produce tended to be high.

106. *Essay*, pp. 364–7, 379, 423–5. Malthus's attitude toward the repeal of the corn laws may have been somewhat influenced by the above considerations, since repeal would lower the prices of corn and labour (*Principles*, p. 105). Were the ports opened to grain, the stimulus to population arising from the cheapness of grain would probably depress real wages in England (*Observations*, p. 26). His argument is similar to that he advanced against a cheapened diet (*Essay*, pp. 515–16).

107. E.g., see *Essay*, pp. 423–5; *Principles*, pp. 373–6.

108. *Essay*, IV, xiii, pp. 534–6, also p. 543; 2d ed., pp. 594–5, 603–4; cf. 1st ed. pp. 367–9. Industrialization intensified somewhat the operation of the positive checks because urban and manufacturing employments were less healthful than rural employments, and probably would always remain so (*Essay*, pp. 420–1, 538; cf. 2d., pp. 422, 597).

109. *Principles*, pp. 355–6.

110. *Essay*, p. 294; 1st ed., p. 132.

111. "Of Commerce" (*Essays*, vol. I, pp. 289–90, 293, 296).

112. *Works*, vol. I, chaps. V–VIII, XVIII, pp. 177, 203–4, 210–12.

113. *Wealth of Nations*, bk. III. Cf. Steuart's account (*Works*, vol. I, chap. x) of the decline of the feudal economy.

114. *Political Arithmetic*, chap. I, sec. vii.

115. *Principles of Moral and Political Philosophy*, p. 456. See also E. Burke, *Works* (London, 1803), vol. I, pp. 203–4, vol. V, pp. 290–2.

116. For an account of some of these arguments, see my *French Predecessors of Malthus;* E. A. J. Johnson, *Predecessors of Adam Smith* (New York, 1937); H. Baudrillart, *Histoire du luxe* (Paris, 1878–80); F. B. Kaye, introduction and notes to *The Fable of the Bees . . . Bernard Mandeville* (Oxford, 1924).

117. E. Young, *The Centaur, not Fabulous* (1755) (Philadelphia, 1795), p. 47.

118. Thus Paley, *Principles of Moral and Political Philosophy*, p. 444, having noted that "habitual superfluities become actual wants: opinion and fashion convert articles of ornament and luxury into necessaries," added that, "in the present relaxed state of morals and discipline," men will not "enter into marriages which degrade their condition, reduce their mode of living, deprive them of the accommodations to which they have been accustomed, or even of those ornaments or appendages of rank and station, which they have been taught to regard as belonging to their birth, or class, or profession, or place in society." See also Wallace, *Dissertation*, pp. 19, 26 ff., 160.

119. E.g., see *Essay*, pp. 429–31, on the causes of depopulation; and p. 11, where he says that, given access to the means of subsistence, population tends to increase "even in the most vicious societies." Cf. the views of Baron Grimm (*French Predecessors*, pp. 236 ff.) and Paley (*Principles of Moral and Political Philosophy*, pp. 445–6).

120. *Essay*, pp. 9–10, 134–7, 171; 1st ed., p. 100; 2d ed., p. 467 n. "The vices of mankind are active and able ministers of depopulation" (1st ed., p. 139).

121. *Essay*, III, iii, p. 318; not in early editions.

122. *Essay*, 2d ed., pp. 467–9 n., 592–4 n. See also sec. II and sec. III (ii) of this article. Steuart (*Works*, Vol. I, p. 117) had said: "That number of husbandmen, therefore, is the best, which can provide food for all the state; and that number of inhabitants is the best, which is compatible with the full employment of every one of them."

123. "The more Horses there are in a state the less food will remain for the People." On Cantillon's theory see my *French Predecessors*, chap. iv, and A. Landry's historical and analytical essay, "Une théorie, négligée. De l'influence de la direction de la demande sur la productivité du travail, les salaires et la population" (*Revue d'économie politique*, vol. XXIV, 1910, pp. 314, 364, 747, 773); also Douglas, *Theory of Wages*, pp. 266–7. Cantillon glimpsed but did not develop the point that since non-proprietors also are consumers, the number of non-proprietors depends in part upon the tastes of non-proprietors and the extent to which they prefer goods and services consisting predominantly of labour; or the corollary that the level of wages, if not fixed by a constant scale of living, depends in part upon the tastes of non-proprietors. Eubulus, said V. Pareto (*Cours d'économie politique*, Lausanne, 1896–7, vol. I, p. 139), criticized those who nourished beasts for pleasure rather than children.

124. "Of the Populousness of Ancient

Nations" (*Essays*, vol. I, pp. 395–6, 397–8, 430).

125. *Dissertation*, pp. 17, 20–30. He admitted, however, that where the "lands are very unequally divided . . . that country must be thinly peopled, unless elegance is studied, and proper encouragement given to the arts which conduce to it." *Ibid.*, pp. 17–18. Wallace did not assert, however, that the production of ornaments should be delayed until the earth was fully cultivated (*ibid.*, p. 21).

126. At this time (1756) Mirabeau had not yet joined the Physiocrats who reasoned that, in France at that time, luxury which eventuated in a demand for subsistence was more favourable to agriculture and population growth than was decorative luxury. See my *French Predecessors*, pp. 131, 182, 185 ff. Malthus referred to Mirabeau's observation that revenue was the source of population (*Essay*, p. 433; 2d ed., p. 477).

127. *Works*, vol. I, pp. 156–7, 189–99.

128. *Principles of Moral and Political Philosophy*, pp. 446, 449–50, 455–9. Those branches of "manufactory . . . are, in their nature, the most beneficial, in which the price of the wrought article exceeds in the highest proportion that of the raw material: for this excess measures the quantity of employment" (*ibid.*, p. 459). See also sec. III (ii) of this article. Paley did not consider "mechanical contrivances, which abridge labour," to be detrimental to population, inasmuch as they did not diminish "the quantity of employment" (*ibid.*, pp. 470–2).

129. *Essay*, 1st ed., pp. 76, 308–10, 314–21, 329. The new system of grazing, made profitable by the increased price of meat, he traced to "the present great demand for butchers meat of the best quality." *Ibid.*, pp. 316–19.

130. *Ibid.*, pp. 289–92, 298–9. Because the rich were few in number, their assistance would be "comparatively trifling"; and because of the principle of population, want would still exceed supply even if the creators of luxuries turned to the production of necessaries. Here Malthus is replying to Godwin (*Enquirer*, pp. 139–40).

131. *Essay*, III, xiv, p. 435; 2d ed., p. 477. Wretchedness, Malthus pointed out elsewhere, was the lot of a large proportion of the population in China where "no arable land lies fallow" and where relatively little labour and few vegetable and animal products were diverted to non-food uses. *Essay*, I, xii, pp. 116–17; 2d ed., pp. 148–9.

132. *Essay*, III, xiv, p. 435; 2d ed., p. 478.

133. *Essay*, I, xii, p. 126; 2d ed., p. 161. Pro-slavery writers in America defended the loose slave economy and the associated wasteful consumption on the ground that it permitted retrenchment when times were hard. See references in note 83 in sec. II of this article.

134. *Essay*, IV, xi, p. 514; 2d ed., pp. 577–8.

135. *Ibid.*, p. 131.

136. *Essay*, IV, xi, pp. 514–16; 2d ed., pp. 577–80. See also his discussion of the population-increasing effect of the introduction of the cheap potato diet into Ireland (*Essay*, pp. 259–60, 365–7; 2d ed., pp. 334–5, 579–81; *Principles*, pp. 211, 345 ff.; *Edinburgh Review*, 1808, pp. 339–40, 344). Adam Smith (*Wealth of Nations*, pp. 160–1) was more enthusiastic than Malthus about the potato.

137. *Essay*, III, ii, p. 311, also pp. 435–8; 2d ed., pp. 371, 466–9; 1st ed., p. 187. Malthus here is emphasizing the difficulties in the way of increasing the supply of subsistence and the impossibility, in a country like England, of living by vegetable cultivation alone.

138. *Principles*, I, iv, 3, pp. 237–8; 1st ed., p. 263.

139. *Essay*, III, xiv, pp. 435–8; 2d ed., pp. 466–9, 478–82. Malthus pointed to the "barren heaths" of China and to the error of the French in cultivating too much poor land.

140. *Essay*, III, vi, p. 346, x, pp. 382–4; 2d ed., pp. 414–15. Chap. x, in its final form, first appeared in the fifth edition (1817). In chap. vi, on the poor laws, Malthus's object is to show that the abolition of private property would greatly worsen the material lot of most men. See sec. III (iii) of this article.

141. It is their "passions" that cause men to labour, Hume had said; it is the "spirit of avarice and industry, art and luxury" that actuates men to work effectively; it is their "desires and wants" that determine how many hands the "proprietors and labourers" of land will employ. It is foreign commerce, which presents the more opulent with undreamed-of objects of luxury, that "rouses men from their indolence" and raises in the better-to-do "a desire of a more splendid way of life than what their ancestors enjoyed." See "Of Commerce" (*Essays*, vol. I, pp. 289–90, 293, 296). Mandeville and others, before Hume, had emphasized the role of the passions (Kaye, *The Fable of the Bees . . . by Bernard Mandeville*, Vol. I, Introduction, parts IV–V). Malthus would not have approved Mandeville's view that national wealth consists in "a Multitude of laborious Poor" (*ibid.*, vol. I, p. 287); and he did not approve Mandeville's "system of morals" (*Essay*, p. 553 n.); but he made use of the notion of "passions" (see note 180 below, and text).

142. "The condition most favourable to population is that of a laborious, frugal people, ministering to the demands of an opulent, luxurious nation; because this situation, whilst it leaves them every advantage of luxury, exempts them from the evils which naturally accompany its ad-

mission into any country." Under these circumstances much employment is provided by luxury manufacture; yet, since the vast majority are without a taste for these luxuries, they are not under pressure to support this taste by refraining from the "formation of families." See Paley, *Principles of Moral and Political Philosophy*, pp. 446–8.

143. *Essay*, IV, xiii, pp. 534–5; 2d ed., pp. 592–3; *Principles*, pp. 373 ff., where this view is developed more fully; also sec. I–II of this article. Hume had said that everyone should enjoy "all the necessaries and many of the conveniences of life." See "Of Commerce" (*Essays*, vol. I, pp. 296–7).

144. *Essay*, IV, ix, p. 498, xiii, pp. 534 n., 535; 2d ed., pp. 557, 593–4. See also *Essay*, pp. 471, 491; 2d ed., pp. 524, 545; *Principles*, I, iv, 2; Senior, *Two Lectures on Population*, pp. 85–6. Malthus may have got his "standard of wretchedness" (*Essay*, p. 498) from Paley who said (see Malthus, *ibid.*, p. 534 n.) that mankind will "breed up to a certain point of distress." See 2d ed., pp. 557, 592 n.

145. *Essay*, III, xiv, pp. 431–2, IV, xiii, pp. 535–6; 2d ed., pp. 475, 594–5, and notes, pp. 592, 593.

146. Viner, *Studies in the Theory of International Trade*, pp. 51 ff.; Johnson, *Predecessors of Adam Smith*, chap. xv.

147. *Works*, vol. I, p. 191.

148. *Ibid.*, vol. II, p. 2 (italics in text). Arthur Young (*Political essays*, 1772, p. 538; cited by Viner, *Studies in the Theory of International Trade*, p. 54) stated that a favourable balance of trade suggested that foreigners "employ more of our poor than we do of theirs." Cantillon, by whom Steuart was influenced, had indicated that a country could increase its population by exchanging products embodying labour for agricultural products, but he did not recommend a state's becoming dependent upon foreign-produced foodstuffs (*French Predecessors*, pp. 118 ff., 124 ff.)

149. *Works*, vol. I, pp. 117, 158–9, 212–14; vol. II, pp. 6–8.

150. *Dissertation*, pp. 18, 21–3, 148.

151. *Principles of Moral and Political Philosophy*, pp. 458–9, 469–70.

152. Adam Smith, *Wealth of Nations*, vol. IV, ix, p. 642.

153. It was worse for a country like England to become slightly dependent upon foreign sources than for small countries like Holland and Hamburg to become largely dependent. England "is in a much more precarious situation with regard to the constancy of its supplies, than such states as draw almost the whole of their provisions from other countries." *Essay*, 2d ed., p. 425. For reply to Adam Smith, not included in 1817 revision, see *ibid.*, pp. 448–51, and for general view, pp. 426, 429, 437–8, 467–9 n. See for his

similar but less developed position, 1st ed., pp. 311–13, 322–6, 336–7.

154. No policy, of course, could obviate the need to exercise moral restraint (e.g., *Essay*, 2d ed., pp. 467–9). On the differences between Malthus and Ricardo regarding criteria of national well-being and effects of trade, see Hollander, *Notes*, pp. xxxix ff., xliii, xcix ff.

155. *Essay*, III, ix, xii, p. 409; also *Observations*, pp. 22–4, 28–9. Malthus did not expect "perfect freedom of trade" ever to be realized (*Essay*, p. 415; cf. 2d ed., p. 466). He did not dwell upon the possible ill effects of naval or other forms of blockade except to suggest that a commanding navy gives an importing country surer access to foreign supplies (*Essay*, 2d ed., pp. 425, 468 n.; 1st ed., p. 311).

156. *Essay*, III, x–xii; 2d ed., III, vii–x; *Principles*, p. 427; Bonar, *Malthus*, pp. 217–29, 245–52. In his *Observations*, etc. (1814) Malthus, having considered the supposed advantages and disadvantages of export bounties and import restrictions, expressed himself in favour of a constant protective import duty on corn, and of continuation of the "old bounty" with a view to relieving a "glut" (*ibid.*, p. 34). British agriculture could not, in the face of foreign competition, grow enough corn to support the increasing population, Malthus noted, but he did not stress so much as later the risk of making a considerable part of the population dependent upon foreign supplies (*ibid.*, pp. 16–24, 28–9).

157. *Essay*, pp. 403–4; 2d ed., pp. 446–7.

158. *Essay*, III, xii, p. 409; also III, ix, pp. 376 ff. on the decline of Venice and other places. Malthus was not familiar with the population and economic theories of G. Ortes which reflected the situation of which Malthus wrote.

159. He wrote approvingly of bounties in the second edition of the *Essay* (pp. 451, 465–6), in view of the then state of English agriculture.

160. *Essay*, III, xi–xii, especially pp. 400–4, 412–15.

161. "The Age of Reason ended in the French Revolution. The Age of Stupidity began with Malthus." See J. R. Commons, *Institutional Economics* (New York, 1934), p. 244. "Malthus's book was anti-jacobin, expressly written to refute the equalitarian Utopia." Élie Halévy, *The Growth of Philosophic Radicalism*, translated by Mary Morris (London, 1928), p. 205. "Malthus was steeped in an inveterate Toryism as to social and economic organization." Hollander, *Notes*, p. xxiv, also p. xcvii. On replies to Malthus, see Bonar, *Malthus*, bk. IV.

162. *Capital* (Chicago, 1906), vol. I, p. 676 n. See also S. M. Levin, "Marx versus Malthus" (Papers of the *Michigan Academy of Science, Arts, and Letters*, vol.

XXII, 1936, pp. 243 ff.). Pareto (*Cours d'économie politique*, pp. 118–19) had contended that Malthus's philosophy weakened the argument against revolutionary change.

163. See my "French Population Theory since 1800" (*Journal of Political Economy*, vol. XLIV, 1936, pp. 585 ff., 743 ff.).

164. See my "Population Doctrines in the United States" (*Journal of Political Economy*, vol. XLI, 1933, pp. 433 ff., 639 ff.). Cursory examination of English materials supports the above opinion.

165. E.g., see J. B. Bury, *The Idea of Progress* (London, 1924); Halévy, *The Growth of Philosophic Radicalism*; my *French Predecessors*. On differences between views of Godwin and Condorcet, see note 172 and text.

166. On these precipitating circumstances see Halévy, *The Growth of Philosophic Radicalism*, pp. 230 ff.; Bonar, *Malthus*, pp. 27–31.

167. *Leviathan*, vol. I, xiii.

168. *Various Prospects of Mankind, Nature, and Providence* (London, 1761), pp. 113–25. Earlier he had said that "had it not been for the errors and vices of mankind, and the defects of government and education, the earth . . . perhaps might have been overstocked, many ages ago"; but he added that, with conditions as they were, there was no reason to fear that the earth would be fully cultivated, or that every country would be "plentifully stored with inhabitants." See *Dissertation*, pp. 13, 149.

169. *A Dissertation on the Poor Laws* (London, 1786). See Halévy, *The Growth of Philosophic Radicalism*, pp. 228–30.

170. On Hobbes and Locke, see T. Parsons, *The Structure of Social Action* (New York, 1937), pp. 87–106; Halévy, *The Growth of Philosophic Radicalism*. Locke's competitive solution was adopted by Adam Smith, Ricardo, and others.

171. *Political Justice*, vol. I, pp. 125–8, 330–42, vol. II, pp. 152–4, 170–1, 350 ff., 361 ff., 367–75. There is, Godwin believed, a natural tendency in men toward justice which, if allowed to develop, fuses the interest of men. On this point see Halévy, *The Growth of Philosophic Radicalism*, pp. 193 ff.

172. *Political Justice*, vol. II, bk. VIII, chap. IX. Godwin, referring to Condorcet's work on progress, said that Condorcet rested his hopes upon the "growing perfectibility of art" instead of "upon the immediate and unavoidable operation of an improved intellect," as did Godwin. *Ibid.*, p. 377 n. See note 182 below.

173. On Condorcet's views, see my *French Predecessors*, pp. 259–63.

174. Halévy, *The Growth of Philosophic Radicalism*, p. 244.

175. *Essay*, pp. 10 n., 440–1, 446, 448–9, 455, 543–4, 567–8; 2d ed., pp.

484–5, 490–1, 494–5, 502–3; 1st ed., chaps. XVIII–XIX; *Summary View*, pp. 76–7; Zinke, "Six Letters from Malthus to Pierre Prevost," p. 183; Bonar, *Malthus*, bk. III.

176. *Essay*, pp. 567–8 (1807). In this respect, and in his philosophy generally, Malthus reflected in some measure the philosophical "optimism" of the eighteenth century, with its emphasis upon the reality and the necessity of evils. See A. O. Lovejoy, *The Great Chain of Being* (Cambridge, 1936), chap. VII. Against this gloomy necessitarianism the philosophers of progress revolted; and in this revolt Malthus, despite his strictures upon the philosophy of indefinite progress, played no small part, being in some measure (see Bonar, *Malthus*, pp. 376 ff.) under the influence of the same ideas as affected Godwin and Condorcet.

177. *Essay*, pp. 543–4.

178. This is evident in his emphasis upon the two ratios (e.g., *ibid.*, I, i and p. 551); in his estimate (1817) that England might support two or three times as many people at a somewhat improved scale of living; and in his supposition that in America, which might support fifty times its then (1817) population, the rate of growth would fall appreciably and labourers would "in time be much less liberally rewarded" (*ibid.*, pp. 292–4, 360, 461, 551). Only in newly settled areas (*ibid.*, pp. 285 ff., 329–31, 439), and for a limited time, could food and numbers increase rapidly (cf. Adam Smith, *Wealth of Nations*, pp. 532 ff.). In the 1803 *Essay* (pp. 7, 473 and note), Malthus, who had merely implied a law of diminishing returns in agriculture in the 1798 edition, expressed such a law, and declared contrary to fact James Anderson's position that a law of increasing returns prevailed in intensive cultivation. See J. H. Hollander's introduction to Malthus's *Inquiry into the Nature and Progress of Rent* (1815) (Baltimore, 1903). In the Encyclopedia article (*Summary View*, pp. 4–6, 26–7, 31, 34), Malthus emphasized the "diminishing and limited power of increasing the produce of the soil," observing that the forces of improvement ("division of labour," "invention of machinery," "accumulation of capital") are less efficient in increasing food than in augmenting conveniences and luxuries.

179. *Summary View*, p. 5; *Principles*, pp. 208–9. See also Ricardo's comment upon Malthus's observation that the Creator did not ordain "unlimited facility of producing food" inasmuch as space was limited (*ibid.*, p. 209; Hollander, *Notes*, pp. 108–10).

180. *Essay*, pp. 444–8, 452–5 (also in 2d ed.); also Bonar, *Malthus*, pp. 324–35. Here Malthus follows Paley (*Natural Theology* [1802], Albany, 1803, chap. XXVI, pp. 344–45), who referred (*ibid.*, p. 340) to Malthus's first essay; and who

looked upon vice and misery as consequences, in part, of the excessive pursuit and the misdirected use of the passions, and who emphasized the need for their subjection to reason and self-government aided by religion. On the doctrine of passions see Kaye, *The Fable of the Bees . . . by Bernard Mandeville*, Introduction; Halévy, *The Growth of Philosophic Radicalism*, vol. I, i; J. Laird, *Hume's Philosophy of Human Nature* (London, 1932), chap. VII. See note 141 above.

181. *Essay*, IV, i; also pp. 10 n., 551-2.

182. *Essay*, 1st ed., chap. XIII; also *Edinburgh Review* (1810), pp. 472, 475. Of Godwin's remark that the passion between the sexes might be extinguished, Malthus said: "Men in the decline of life have, in all ages, declaimed against a passion which they have ceased to feel" (*Essay*, 1st ed., pp. 210-11). On the Malthusian versus the anti-Malthusian view of progress, see Halévy, *The Growth of Philosophic Radicalism*, pp. 242-4, 275-6, 363 ff.

183. On the important role of education in the later utilitarian scheme, see Halévy, *The Growth of Philosophic Radicalism*, pp. 20 ff., 282 ff. Malthus's faith in education, while not so marked as that of Helvetius, was great. See *Essay*, pp. 439-43, 531-40 (in 2d ed.). In 1807, having indicated that he had not intended by his opinion to alarm the prejudices of the poor, he said: "We have only to proceed in improving our civil polity, conferring the benefits of education upon all, and removing every obstacle to the general extension of all those privileges and advantages which may be enjoyed in common" (*ibid.*, p. 565).

184. *Principles*, p. 208.

185. "The principle of population, therefore, appears as the essential motive force behind social progress." See E. F. Penrose, *Population Theories and their Application* (Stanford, 1934), p. 24. Here (*Essay*, pp. 446-7) Malthus is thinking in terms of man's supposed psychological nature. Elsewhere (see secs. I and II of this article) Malthus noticed other determinants of progress when he observed that extreme misery checks progress, and that bad government and watertight institutional structures bring the growth of wealth and population to a premature stop. T. H. Marshall (*Economic History Review*, 1935, p. 76), having noted that population "must be regarded as a cause and not merely as an effect," concluded that in England "the rapid growth of the population may have been on the whole a stimulus to economic progress, but it was at times a cause of friction and distress."

186. *Slavery as an Industrial System* (The Hague, 1910), p. 414. While Paley looked upon the principle of population as good, he nonetheless described the *vis*

inertiae as making for tranquility and order (*Natural Theology*, pp. 340-1, 344-5).

187. *Essay*, pp. 445-52, 545-7, 572; 1st ed., pp. 354, 358-66, 370-1; *Principles*, pp. 208-9; also sec. III (iv) and (v) of this article.

188. This distinction is not important, for his interpretation of the role of the principle of population had a theological basis.

189. *Essay*, IV, i-ii, pp. 9, 301, 559-61, 572; 1st ed., p. 340; Penrose, *Population Theories and their Application*, pp. 21-30; S. M. Levin "Malthus' Conception of the Checks to Population" (*Human Biology*, vol. X, 1938, pp. 214-34). Malthus referred to prolongation of lactation, considered by Petty to be a hindrance to speedy propagation, (cited by R. R. Kuczynski, in L. Hogben, *Political Arithmetic* [New York, 1938], p. 293) but did not suggest it, as did certain nineteenth-century writers, as an effective preventive check, either because he considered it *per se* ineffective (*Essay*, pp. 23, 81), or because he considered it too powerful and otherwise unsanctionable.

190. *Essay*, pp. 431-2, 434-5, 471-3, 498; also in 2d ed. "Even poverty itself, . . . the great spur to industry, when it has once passed certain limits, almost ceases to operate"; and hopeless indigence "destroys all vigorous exertion." *Essay*, p. 432.

191. *Essay*, III, i-iii, also pp. 21, 24, 571-3; *Summary View*, pp. 35-6, 41-2, 72. Although men tend to blame their troubles upon institutions, the effects of institutions are "superficial" in comparison with the effects of "those deeper-seated causes of evil which result from the laws of nature and the passions of mankind." *Essay*, pp. 307-8, 457-8; also in 2d ed. On the checks, the conception of which Malthus got (*Essay*, 1st ed., pp. 339 ff.) from a consideration of Price's untenable conclusion, see Levin, cited in note 189 above.

192. *Essay*, III, ii, p. 317, also p. 573; 2d ed., pp. 378-9. In the Encyclopedia article, Malthus states that the alternatives are Godwin's system of common property and that of private property, of which the latter is by far the more productive and the more conducive to the generation of desirable habits and moral qualities; and that popular education cannot fit men for a system of common property. See *Summary View*, pp. 35-7, 72-4; Bonar, *Malthus*, pp. 76-7.

193. *Essay*, III, ii-iii, p. 543; 2d ed., pp. 366 ff., 604; 1st ed., pp. 286 ff.; *Principles*, pp. 208-9. The passion of self-love, however, if "pushed to excess" becomes the vice of selfishness (*Essay*, p. 554 n.). That egoism is the predominating, if not the exclusive, inclination of human nature, was commonly accepted in the eighteenth century (Halévy, *The Growth of Philosophic Radicalism*, p. 14).

194. He attributed the improved condition of the lower classes in France after the revolution to the diminished proportion of births which he traced to the fact that everyone now depended "more upon himself and less upon others." *Essay*, p. 361; this was written in 1817. See note 62 in sec. I of this article.

195. *Essay*, pp. 347, 529, 535, 539, 543; in 2d ed. "The desire of bettering our condition, and the fear of making it worse, . . . is the *vis medicatrix reipublicae* in politics, and is continually counteracting the disorders arising from narrow institutions" (*ibid.*, p. 347). Cf. also Bonar, *Malthus*, pp. 120–2.

196. Parsons, *The Structure of Social Action*, p. 106.

197. *Essay*, III, iii, pp. 320, 323, also, pp. 49 n., 479. Although chap. III in bk. III was not added until 1817, the substance of the above argument appears in both the first and second editions.

198. *Essay*, III, i–iii, IV, vi, pp. 475–7; Malthus expressed substantially the same opinion in the first and second editions.

199. *Essay*, III, ii–iii. Hume, noting that property was inconsistent with both "profuse abundance" and extreme scarcity, associated its origin with relative scarcity. See Commons, *Institutional Economics*, pp. 140 ff.; Laird, *Hume's Philosophy of Human Nature*, pp. 227 ff.

200. *Essay*, pp. 352–3; *Principles*, II, i, 10, pp. 429–30. These views were first published in the 1817 *Essay* and the 1820 *Principles*. Malthus is dealing here with the problem of post-war unemployment—an extreme instance of the oscillatory nature of population growth; of the tendency of numbers, in response to the stimulus of increased employment, to grow temporarily beyond the capacity of the labour market to absorb them. See *Essay*, pp. 11–14, 141, 411, 481–2; *Principles*, pp. 279–80, 416–17, 435–6. In the First Essay (pp. 30–5), Malthus, already alert to the time factor, commented upon the oscillatory character of population growth, saying that this vibration had escaped notice because the histories of mankind "are histories only of the upper classes." Steuart (*Works*, vol. I, p. 193) remarked that agricultural production and therefore population growth oscillate; he proposed that, when the demand for labour falls short of the supply, balance be restored by diminishing hands through their employment as soldiers, in colonies, and on public works (*ibid.*, p. 310). Condorcet was somewhat aware of this oscillation, Malthus (*Essay*, 1st ed., p. 152) noted.

201. *Principles*, pp. 429–30. Malthus opposed proposals to supply the deficiency in demand for labour through an issue of paper money (*ibid.*, pp. 431–2), or through a reduction in taxes (*Essay*, pp. 354–5); he supposed, rather, that a public works programme would divert purchasing power to those employed thereon and so spread unemployment "over a larger surface" (*ibid.*, pp. 353–4).

202. *Essay*, III, iv, pp. 331–2 (1817), 573–4; also Bonar, *Malthus*, pp. 195–9, for Malthus's evidence before the Emigration Committee in 1827. "A certain degree of emigration is . . . favourable to the population of the mother country," he remarked (*Essay*, p. 287; 2d ed., p. 340), as had Franklin and others (see notes 7–8 and text in sec. I of this article).

203. *Summary View*, pp. 71–4; *Essay*, pp. 552–8; also pp. 475–7, for criticism of views of Paine and Raynal on rights, pp. 541–2, where he denies right of the poor to demand employment and maintenance; also 2d ed., pp. 531, for the famous feast passage expunged from later editions. Malthus looked upon man's rights as not unconditional (Halévy, *The Growth of Philosophic Radicalism*, pp. 242 ff.). On Malthus's idea of utility, which he may have gotten from Paley, see *Essay*, pp. 500–1, and Bonar, *Malthus*, pp. 39, 213, 331–3, 346–8. The principle of utility, which Bentham and others apparently took from Hume (Halévy, *The Growth of Philosophic Radicalism*, pp. 11 ff.), was employed by Burke to attack the theory of the Rights of Man (*ibid.*, pp. 156–7). From Burke Malthus may have learned the suitability of this principle to the defence of necessary institutions.

204. *Essay*, pp. 541–2, 580, 582–3; also sec. III (v) of this article. "No desire, however great, of increasing our subsistence can keep us out of the reach of the most miserable poverty, if we do not, at the same time, exercise the more efficient power we possess of restraining the progress of population by prudential habits." Senior, *Two Lectures on Population*, p. 70, also p. 84. The poor alone are "the arbiters of their own destiny" (*Principles*, p. 279).

205. *Essay*, IV, x, especially pp. 503–4; also chaps. XI–XIII. Most of the cited material appeared in the second edition. In his unpublished *The Crisis* he had advocated outdoor relief and commended Pitt's proposal to accord special relief to fathers of more than three children (Halévy, *The Growth of Philosophic Radicalism*, p. 235). Malthus opposed public housing, the use of cash reserve subsidies to encourage deferment of marriage, more than limited application of the cow system, and assured assistance for the aged and for widows and orphans. See *Essay*, III, i; IV, xi; pp. 556–64; Zinke, "Six Letters from Malthus to Pierre Prevost," p. 184.

206. *Essay*, III, i, pp. 299 ff.; 1st ed., pp. 149 ff. Here Malthus is criticizing Condorcet.

207. *Principles*, pp. 72–3; *Essay*, III, v–vii, pp. 342 ff.; iv, ix, p. 493; most of this material is also in the second edition. Elsewhere he expressed "doubt of the effect of our poor laws in encouraging an increase of population. Their direct effects are certainly to do this"; but their indirect

effects upon housing may counterbalance their direct effects (Zinke, "Six Letters from Malthus to Pierre Prevost," p. 184). Young (*Political Arithmetic*, pp. 93 ff.) had said that the poor law, by causing the supply of cottages to be restricted, checked marriage and population (cf. Malthus, *Essay*, p. 532). Griffith (*Population Problems of the Age of Malthus*, chap. vi, pp. 165, 169) concludes that the effect of the poor laws upon marriage and natural increase was slight, but Marshall ("The Population Problem during the Industrial Revolution," *Economic History*, pp. 431 ff.) believes that only by a comparative study of local figures may the Malthusian view, if invalid, be disproved.

208. *Essay*, iii, v, pp. 339–40, also pp. 172, 506 (also in 2d ed.); *Principles*, pp. 72–3.

209. *Essay*, iv, iii, vi–ix, xii; most of this material is already in the second edition; see also 1st ed., chap. v. Hume (*Essays*, vol. I, p. 439) had said that the parish-rates tended to produce "idleness, debauchery, and a continual decay" even as had the ancient Roman *sportula*. Charity, wrote Steuart (*Works*, vol. I, pp. 118–23, 210–11) with especial reference to Spain, because it gives food, stimulates multiplication that is not of advantage to society; it does not cure misery. Adam Smith (*Wealth of Nations*, pp. 135 ff.) declared that the poor laws obstructed "the circulation of labour." Townsend, looking upon the poor laws as the beginning of communism, condemned them on the same ground he condemned communism (see note 169 and text above). Although Malthus did not at first know Townsend's work, he was criticizing, in his discussion of Condorcet, what appears to be the latter's reply to Townsend (Halévy, *The Growth of Philosophic Radicalism*, pp. 228–30; also Malthus's comments on Townsend, *Essay*, pp. 502, 506–8). Already in the late seventeenth century, at which time a large population was considered desirable because it meant a large labour supply, the poor law was condemned on the ground that it reduced the available supply of labour. See T. E. Gregory, "The Economics of Employment in England, 1660–1713" (*Economica*, vol. I, 1921, pp. 37, 40, 41).

210. See J. J. O'Leary, "Malthus and Keynes" (*Journal of Political Economy*, vol. L, 1942, pp. 901–19). Malthus was not a reactionary, concludes Bonar (*Malthus*, pp. 298–9, 336), and "would have been much amazed to hear that his doctrines were . . . a vindication of things as they are."

211. E.g., see Stangeland, *Pre-Malthusian Doctrines of Population*; E. A. J. Johnson, *Predecessors of Adam Smith*; A. Small, *The Cameralists* (Chicago, 1909); my *French Predecessors*.

212. Wallace had said that ancient nations were more populous in his *A Dissertation on the Numbers of Mankind in Ancient and Modern Times* (1753); Hume had said the modern nations were more populous ("Of the Populousness of Ancient Nations," *Essays*, vol. I, pp. 381–442). See Malthus, *Essay*, pp. 59 ff., pp. 136 ff., 158; 1st ed., pp. 55–9. This controversy engaged the attention of many eighteenth-century writers.

213. Price had said that England's population had decreased since 1688; and John Brown in *An Estimate of the Manners and Principles of the Times* (London, 1757), pp. 186 ff. had found "great Reason to believe . . . the Nation is less populous than it was fifty years ago," inasmuch as "Vanity and Effeminacy" had lessened the "Desire of Marriage," and "Intemperance and Disease" had increased mortality and occasioned, "among the *lower Ranks* . . . in some Degree an Impotence of Propagation." That Price was mistaken, and that England's population had increased had been asserted by Young (*Political Arithmetic*, pp. 64 ff., 96 ff., 322 ff.), by Wales (1781), and by Howlett (*Examination of Dr. Price's Essays on the Population of England and Wales*, etc.) who supposed a one-third increase since 1688. In the first *Essay* (pp. 314–15) Malthus supposed that the truth "lies between" the estimates of Price and Howlett. On Malthus's later views see Essay, ii, viii–ix, and p. 428; *Principles*, i, iv, 5. Concerning population growth in eighteenth-century England, see Griffith, *Population Problems of the Age of Malthus*, chap. i; Marshall, "The Population Problem during the Industrial Revolution"; Buer, *Health, Wealth and Population*; E. C. K. Gonner "The Population of England in the Eighteenth Century" (*Journal of the Royal Statistical Society*, vol. LXXVI, 1913, pp. 261–303). On the views of Price, Howlett, and others see *ibid*.; also Bonar, *Theories*, chap. vii, and *Malthus*, pp. 108–9, 171–9.

214. See sec. iii (v) of this article, on optimum population. He did not generally evaluate the theses of populationist writers; but he criticized Montesquieu and Süssmilch for advocating encouragement to marriage (*Essay*, pp. 181–2), and Young for supporting the cow system and a potato diet (*ibid*., iv, xi); and he approved the views of Townsend and the French Committee of Mendicity (see my *French Predecessors*, pp. 307 ff.) on the poor laws (*Essay*, pp. 485, 506 ff., in 2d ed.). Of earlier populationist doctrine he wrote: "In the earlier ages of the world, when war was the great business of mankind, . . . legislators and statesmen . . . encouraged an increase of people in every possible way." Popular religions had supported this view. The consequent rapid procreation had conduced to incessant war and so to the perpetuation of these pronatalist moral sentiments. The Christian religion, however, had subordi-

nated marriage to higher duties and had imposed on man the obligation not to marry until he could support his children; it thus operated to prevent a redundancy of population and resultant offensive war, and to bring about widely diffused well-being which made for effective defence against aggression. *Essay*, pp. 453–5 (in 2d ed.); also 5th edition (preface), where he comments on the demand, now (1817) at an end, for men, occasioned by the Napoleonic wars.

215. *Essay*, pp. 156, 227, 339–40, 363, 377–8, 433–4, 547–8, 578–9; Senior, *Two Lectures on Population*, pp. 61–4; Bonar, *Malthus*, pp. 114–16, 329. Prudence would never win "too great a mastery over the natural passions and affections." See *Edinburgh Review*, 1810, pp. 472, 475.

216. *Essay*, II, xiii, also pp. 429–30; also in 2d ed.

217. *Ibid.*, pp. 324, 438–9 (in 2d ed.). Malthus was not disposed, as were some of the perfectibilians, to look upon the source of provision as an almost inexhaustible widow's cruse (2 Kings 4.4).

218. *Ibid.*, pp. 181, 432–5, 547–51; also bks. I–II; also Bonar, *Malthus*, pp. 139–42. A similar argument appears in Steuart, *Works*, vol. I, pp. 104–7, 207–9; cf. Adam Smith, *Wealth of Nations*, p. 79.

219. *Essay*, pp. 431–5.

220. *Ibid.*, pp. 360–1, 546–7.

221. "There never has been, nor probably ever will be, any other cause than want of food, which makes the population of a country permanently decline," *Ibid.*, p. 429.

222. *Ibid.*, e.g., pp. 136, 138–9, 428–30.

223. *Ibid.*, pp. 453–5, 536–7; also IV, xi. Malthus criticized Pitt's poor bill on the ground that it might tend to increase population (*ibid.*, 1st ed., pp. 94–5, 134–5).

224. Even Paley, a populationist, emphasized only indirect stimulants such as encouragement of agriculture and employment (*Moral Philosophy*, pp. 472–4).

225. *Essay*, p. 575 (1817); *Summary View*, pp. 58–62. Had he pursued his line of thought regarding the effect of European contact upon natives (*Essay*, pp. 36–7; cf. also p. 46), or the desire-weakening effect of overindulgence, and licentiousness (e.g., *Essay*, pp. 56, 103, 139 n., 171–2), he might have hit upon John Rae's theory of the decline in the "effective desire of offspring." Because he was intent upon demonstrating the existence of the principle of population, he overlooked this possibility. See also Levin's discussion, "Malthus' Conception of the Checks to Population" (*Human Biology*, vol. X, pp. 230 ff.).

226. *Essay*, 3rd ed., vol. I, i, ii, p. 28. In the fifth and sixth editions he wrote "some instances" and described them as "extreme cases." Slaves in the West Indies would be able "by procreation fully to supply the effective demand for labour,"

were their condition raised to that of the masses in the "worst governed countries of the world" (*Essay*, p. 569 [1807], also p. 137). He supposed that "depravity of morals" checked marriage "at least among the upper classes" in ancient Rome, but he attributed the lack of population growth in the other classes to slavery and other institutions unfavourable to industry (*ibid.*, I, xiv).

227. *Essay*, p. 569. The word "almost" was not included in this passage when it first appeared in 1807.

228. See A. B. Wolfe, "The Optimum Size of Population," in L. I. Dublin, *Population Problems* (New York, 1926); L. Robbins, "The Optimum Theory of Population," in *London Essays in Economics in Honour of E. Cannan* (London, 1927); S. S. Cohn, *Die Theorie des Bevolkerungsoptimums* (Marburg, 1934); my "Pareto on Population, II" (Section VII, *Quarterly Journal of Economics*, November, 1944).

229. *Essay*, pp. 546–50 (1817); also p. 460.

230. *Essay*, 1st ed., p. 108, also p. 137.

231. The checks in operation, he implied, reflect in some measure the prevailing division of labour (*Essay*, p. 176).

232. *Essay*, pp. 546, 547.

233. *Essay*, pp. 453–4, 461–2, 546, 549, 565, 582–3. The same view appears in the second edition. On military aspects of population growth, see also *Edinburgh Review*, 1808, pp. 350–1, 1810, pp. 474–5. He declared himself "an enemy to large standing armies" (*Essay*, p. 473; 2d ed., p. 526).

234. *Essay*, p. 516 (in 2d ed.); Zinke, "Six Letters from Malthus to Pierre Prevost," p. 183.

235. *Essay*, p. 295; 1st ed., p. 136. In *Principles* (pp. 33–4) he said that "the people will be rich or poor, according to the abundance or scarcity with which they are supplied," in comparison with their population, with "wealth" (i.e., "material objects, necessary, useful, or agreeable to man").

236. *Essay*, pp. 459, 535 (in 2d ed.). This was his object (*Edinburgh Review*, 1821, p. 374).

237. See sec. III (i) (2) of this article.

238. *Essay*, pp. 181, 533–4, 537, 566 and note.

239. *Essay*, p. 549; first published in 1807.

240. *Ibid.*, pp. 559–61, 572. On this point see also Norman Himes, Appendix A in the reprint of Francis Place's *Illustrations and Proofs of the Principle of Population* (London, 1930); and Penrose, *Population Theories and their Application*, pp. 28–30.

241. *Essay*, p. 460; in 2d ed.

242. "I have always considered the principle of population as a law peculiarly suited to a state of discipline and trial" and as confirming the scriptural view of

man's state on earth (*Essay*, p. 585; published in 1817). A. J. Toynbee (*A Study of History*, London, 1939, vol. IV, pp. 207 ff.), in his discussion of the Solonian solution of the Hellenic population problem, provides us with a kind of illustration of what might be called the demographic "challenge and response" theory implicit in Malthus's writings. Malthus did not note this outcome, commenting only upon Solon's sanctioning of child exposure (*Essay*, pp. 128–9).

243. *Essay*, pp. 451–2, 493–5; 2d ed., pp. 497–9, 549, 552–3; Penrose, *Population Theories and their Application*, pp. 27–8. Malthus condemned as unjust and immoral positive laws limiting the age of marriage; it was up to the individual to decide whether he was in a position to marry or not (*Essay*, p. 357; published in 1817). Malthus's view regarding moral restraint and deferment of marriage was substantially the same as the medieval view that a man should not marry until he had a living. Malthus observed that in America the rigours of existence tended to eliminate the physically unfit (*ibid.*, p. 24), but he ignored questions relating to selection and eugenic values, adverting, in his treatment of the views of Plato and Aristotle (*ibid.*, I, xiii), only to the quantitative problem. He did not anticipate the argument Galton was later to direct, on grounds of selection, against the mischievous results of "prudential" postponement of marriage (*Inquiries into Human Faculty and its Development*, Everyman ed., pp. 207 ff.).

244. *Essay*, pp. 3–4, 285–8, 439; in 2d ed. He noted that the age at marriage cannot be so low in old and settled as in new countries.

245. *Ibid.*, pp. 461–4; sec. III (iv) in this article.

246. *Malthus*, p. 319.

247. This view, which is so evident in Malthus's works, is well expressed by Paley in both his *Moral Philosophy* and his *Natural Theology*.

248. It is not our intention to deny the existence of striking parallelisms between the doctrine of Lord Keynes, for example, which embodies elements found also in Malthus's theories, and the doctrine of Quesnay: viz., emphasis upon consumption, treatment of circuit flow, widespread popularity and appeal, etc. It is our intention rather to indicate that Malthus's analysis of the role of demand and consumption originated largely in his study of the operation of the principle of population.

249. It must be kept in mind that Malthus did not sanction contraception or anticipate the vital revolution it has brought about.

15.

GEORGE J. STIGLER
University of Chicago

The Ricardian

Theory of

Value and

Distribution

January 22, 1821

To David Ricardo
MY DEAR SIR:

I hope you will have the goodness to state to me your opinion on this point [the effect of changes in wages on values of goods], for it is one on which of all others I most wish to have sound opinions.

Yours most faithfully,
J. R. McCulloch

English economics was in a state of ferment at the beginning of the nineteenth century; Adam Smith had founded no cult. The period teemed with able economists; yet David Ricardo, within a decade of his debut, was the acknowledged leader of the young science of economics. Within this decade, indeed, his chief work was done; and it was sufficient to make him the most influential economist of his century. This was an extraordinary achievement of an extraordinary man.

Reprinted from *The Journal of Political Economy*, LX (June 1952), 187–207, by permission of the author and The University of Chicago Press. At the time of original publication, the author was with Columbia University.

I propose to set forth in this essay my understanding of Ricardo's basic contributions to the theory of value and distribution. In order to provide a sketch of the setting in which Ricardo wrote, I shall first trace the development of two main strands of his theory, the theories of population and rent.[1]

I. THE THEORY OF POPULATION

If we put aside Smith's principles of the workings of competitive markets, the first pillar of the Ricardian system to be erected was the theory of population. Although this theory has an extensive pre-Malthusian history and gave rise to an enormous early nineteenth-century literature, we shall begin with a sketch of the immediate setting in which Malthus presented the theory and shall trace its development in Malthus' and Ricardo's hands.

William Godwin, an exponent of an intellectual naturalism which did not quite extend to anarchism, achieved considerable fame in the closing years of the eighteenth century. He proposed the abolition of property, almost all government and law, marriage, the division of labor, and diverse other social institutions—but by peaceful means. It was inseparable from his thought that such "reforms" were meritorious only in the measure that they were freely embraced by all men; for example:

> If, in any society, wealth be estimated at its true value, and accumulation and monopoly be regarded as the seals of mischief, injustice, and dishonour, instead of being treated as titles to attention and deference, in that society the accommodations of human life will tend to their level, and the inequality of conditions will be destroyed. A revolution of opinions is the only means of attaining this inestimable benefit. Every attempt to effect this purpose by means of regulation, will probably be found ill conceived and abortive. Be this as it will, every attempt to correct the distribution of wealth by individual violence, is certainly to be regarded as hostile to the first principles of public security.[2]

Godwin accordingly not only opposed violence and revolution but explicitly stated that "the equality for which we are pleading, is an equality which would succeed to a state of great intellectual improvement."[3]

The rationale of this philosophy is that social systems mold the characters of their members and that most or all of the vices of man are therefore attributable to social institutions: "What is born into the world is an unfinished sketch, without character or distinctive feature impressed upon it."[4] The gradual elimination of institutions such as property, together with the irresistible triumph of truth, would eliminate unsocial ambitions, avarice, sloth, and other imperfections of man. Godwin's vision was noble and his arguments candid and often ingenious. If he was inexcusably neglectful of the influence of men on institutions, he was right in stressing the influence of institutions on men.

In the penultimate chapter of *Political Justice*, we should note, Godwin discussed Robert Wallace's earlier rejection of equality because of "the principle of population." Godwin disputed this pessimistic view on two scores. The first was a brief allusion to the efficacy of moral restraint: "It is impossible where the price of labour is greatly reduced, and an added population threatens a still further reduction, that men should not be considerably under the influence of fear, respecting an early marriage, and a numerous family."[5] The second was that the problem was of no immediate concern: three-quarters of the globe was uncultivated, men wasted most of their productive efforts (under existing institutions) on meretricious objects, and "myriads of centuries" would pass before overpopulation was a real problem.[6]

By a different route Condorcet reached a similar view of the good society — which, however, allowed a much larger place to the sciences.[7] He believed also in the perfectibility of man and the inevitability of progress, less on moral grounds than because a historical survey emphasized to him the cumulative character of knowledge and liberty. He, too, noticed the population problem in a regime of equality:

It may, however, be demanded, whether, amidst this improvement in industry and happiness, where the wants and faculties of men will continually become better proportioned, each successive generation possess more various stores, and of consequence in each generation the number of individuals be greatly increased; it may, I say, be demanded, whether these principles of improvement and increase may not, by their continual operation, ultimately lead to degeneracy and destruction? Whether the number of inhabitants in the universe at length exceeding the means of existence, there will not result a continual decay of happiness and population, and a progress towards barbarism, or at least a sort of oscillation between good and evil?[8]

This problem, however, lay far in the future because of the prospective great advances of technology, and, should it ever threaten to become real, Condorcet alluded to the possible development of contraceptives:

. . . prior to this period [of overpopulation] the progress of reason will walk in hand with that of the sciences; that the absurd prejudices of superstition will have ceased to infuse into morality a harshness that corrupts and degrades, instead of purifying and exalting it; that men will then know, that the duties they may be under relative to propagation will consist not in the question of giving *existence* to a greater number of beings, but *happiness;* will have for their object, the general welfare of the human species; of the society in which they live; of the family to which they are attached; and not the puerile idea of encumbering the earth with useless and wretched mortals.[9]

Among the admirers of Godwin and Condorcet, as we know, there was a Daniel Malthus, and his advocacy of their doctrines led his son, Thomas Robert, to devise the counterarguments soon published as *An Essay on the Principle of Population* (1798). The *Essay* sought to demonstrate the impossibility of all such schemes for the major improvement of mankind because they violated natural (biological) laws. We may summarize the argument briefly in Malthus' own words. Two postulates are stated to be sufficient for this vast demonstration:

First, That food is necessary to the existence of man.

Secondly, That the passion between the sexes is necessary, and will remain nearly in its present state.[10]

Actually, several further assumptions are required, and they are implied in the basic statement of the theory:

Assuming then, my postulata as granted, I say, that the power of population is indefinitely greater than the power in the earth to produce subsistence for man.

Population, when unchecked, increases in a geometrical ratio. Subsistence increases only in an arithmetical ratio. A slight acquaintance with numbers will show the immensity of the first power in comparison of the second.

By that law of our nature which makes food necessary to the life of man, the effects of these two unequal powers must be kept equal.

This implies a strong and constantly operating check on population from the difficulty of subsistence. This difficulty must fall some where; and must necessarily be severely felt by a large portion of mankind.[11]

Thus the argument moves rapidly; by page 37, Malthus feels "at a loss to conjecture what part of it can be denied."

The ratios are supported with a parsimony of evidence. Only one example was necessary to show the power of population to grow at a geometrical rate — it doubled every twenty-five years in the United States.[12] The law of growth of subsistence is supported by assertions of incredulity:

Let us now take any spot of earth, this Island for instance, and see in what ratio the subsistence it affords can be supposed to increase. We will begin with it under its present state of cultivation.

If I allow that by the best possible policy, by breaking up more land, and by great encouragements to agriculture, the produce of this Island may be doubled in the first twenty-five years, I think it will be allowing as much as any person can well demand.

In the next twenty-five years, it is impossible to suppose that the produce could be quadrupled. It would be contrary to all our knowledge of the qualities of land. The very utmost that we can conceive, is, that the increase in the second twenty-five years might equal the present produce. Let us then take this for our rule, though certainly far beyond the truth; . . . The most enthusiastic speculator cannot suppose a greater increase than this. In a few centuries it would make every acre of land in the Island like a garden.

Yet this ratio of increase is evidently arithmetical.[13]

The contradiction between the ratios is solved by the checks to population, all of which may be classified under two heads. The basic, inevitable check is misery, operating through all the channels that malnutrition may find. A second, highly probable, check is vice, under which Malthus includes not only sexual promiscuity but at times also war. Still another check — postponement of marriage because of prudence — is mentioned, but it is given little attention, because in Malthus' opinion it is almost always accompanied by vice.[14] Condorcet's suggestion of contraception is dismissed with a reprimand.[15]

Let us now probe more deeply. Are the two ratios to be taken literally? One cannot be too sure of Malthus' intention; certainly he used these ratios frequently enough to the end of his life. But one can say that they were often taken literally and that to them the *Essay* owed its powerful impact. It would have been enough for Malthus' position if he had merely asserted that the rate of growth of population, unless repressed by the checks, *far* exceeded the rate of growth of subsistence. Yet, from the viewpoint of persuasion, the ratios probably had to be of different mathematical forms. Although an annual increase of population by 2 per cent would as surely overwhelm an annual increase of 1 per cent in the means of subsistence — the former doubles in thirty-five years, the latter in seventy years — it would have reduced the argument to the question of the facts of growth, and here no man's voice was loud.

No explicit trace of the law of diminishing returns was present; yet Malthus' ratios implicitly assumed sharply diminishing returns, for his numbers define the production function,

$$L = 2^{P-1},$$

where L is labor (proportional to population) and P is produce. With this production function, indeed, if workers received a wage equal to their marginal product, the aggregate wage bill would be independent of the size of the labor force, and population simply could not grow.[16]

Finally, was the level of subsistence of the masses some biological minimum or was it culturally determined? Malthus is reasonably clear that usually it is a cultural minimum, well above the biological minimum. For he admits of "some variation for the prevalence of luxury, or of frugal habits," and agrees with Adam Smith that the population would increase greatly if Englishmen were to adopt a potato diet.[17] We should notice that this cultural minimum impairs some of the arguments against perfectibility, for men can presumably be taught to insist upon a high minimum. It does not affect the law as an economic generalization, however, if the minimum is fairly stable.

Godwin replied to Malthus (and to other less temperate critics) with courtesy and cogency.[18] The principle of population was greeted as a major contribution to political economy and to the understanding of society. But, Godwin properly argued, this principle denied all possibility of large progress and had no special relevance to Godwin's proposals.[19] Nevertheless, it did bear also on Godwin's hopes; and against it he had two defenses. First, infanticide, abortion, and similar practices, though "painful and repulsive," are preferable to Malthus' checks of misery and vice: "If the alternative were complete, I had rather such a child should perish in the first hour of its existence, than that a man should spend seventy years of life in a state of misery and vice."[20] Second, men of the more enlightened classes already postpone marriage to avoid the poverty resulting from a great family, and in Godwin's society this prudence will be characteristic of the entire population.[21] Surely Godwin was right, judged not only by the historical fact that this was the one objection to his system that the nineteenth century removed but also by contemporary evidence of widespread postponement

411

of marriage, which indicated that this sort of behavior was not beyond mortal man.

Malthus capitulated, while still claiming victory, when in the second editions of the *Essay* (1803) he gave special prominence to a new preventive check (in addition to vice) to population — moral restraint:

> The preventive check, is peculiar to man, and arises from that distinctive superiority in his reasoning faculties, which enables him to calculate distant consequences. . . . These considerations are calculated to prevent, and certainly do prevent, a great number of persons in all civilized nations from pursuing the dictate of nature in an early attachment to one woman.
>
> If this restraint does not produce vice, as in many instances is the case, and very generally so among the middle and higher classes of men, it is undoubtedly the least evil that can arise from the principle of population.[22]

Given the possible — although in Malthus' opinion the improbable — efficacy of the moral restraint, Godwin had carried this issue; and, with the steady decline of his popularity and influence, he was also losing the argument for perfectibility. Henceforth, however, population received more attention, and Godwin's schemes less. Yet this origin left a permanent imprint on the formulation of Malthus' doctrine, and it explains in part why he was content to leave the economics of population at a very preliminary stage.

Aside from the addition of the check by moral restraint, only one substantially new factor was introduced in the later editions of the *Essay*, and this was diminishing returns:

> When acre has been added to acre till all the fertile land is occupied, the yearly increase of food must depend upon the melioration of the land already in possession. This is a stream, which, from the nature of all soils, instead of increasing, must be gradually diminishing.
>
> The improvements of the barren parts [of a nation] would be a work of time and labour; and it must be evident to those who have the slightest acquaintance with agricultural subjects, that in proportion as cultivation extended, the additions that could yearly be made to the former average produce, must be gradually and regularly diminishing.[23]

This concept of diminishing returns — if anything so muddy can be called a concept — was not elaborated or given much emphasis, and Malthus was quite willing to deny diminishing returns when a particular point might be served.[24]

Indeed, one is impressed by Malthus' lack of interest in the economics of population. The concept of a subsistence level is not analyzed, nor are the factors which determine its height and changes isolated. The time necessary for population to respond to changes in the means of subsistence is left vague: Is it two years,[25] or is it the generations during which social customs respecting marriage are slowly modified?

Most important of all, there is no analysis of the factors which govern the rate of growth of output and hence (on his theory) of population. Some elements of such a theory are implicit in Malthus' defense of the mixed

412

agricultural-commercial (industrial) economy.[26] Malthus was a forerunner of the current writers on the "industrialization of backward areas"; his variation, however, was the equally desirable "agriculturalization of industrial areas."

Malthus assumed that the welfare of the masses of population depended chiefly on the supply of bread; so agriculture was the basic industry. The chief role of manufactures — and this only in a society with an unequal ("feudal") distribution of property — was to entice the landlords to cultivate the land intensively to procure luxuries. In his own words:

> Agriculture is not only, as Hume states, that species of industry, which is chiefly requisite to the subsistence of multitudes, but it is in fact the *sole* species by which multitudes can exist; and all the numerous arts and manufactures of the modern world, by which such numbers appear to be supported, have no tendency whatever to increase population, except so far as they tend to increase the quantity and facilitate the distribution of the products of agriculture.[27]

This would suggest that a nation ought to be agricultural; and Malthus skirts this view but rejects it because — a characteristic irrelevance — some agricultural nations have poor governments or a poor distribution of ownership of property and because manufactures provide a market for labor that undermines feudalism.[28]

Yet he rejects the commercial nation even more completely. Foreign competition will eventually eliminate large profits from manufacturing, and so also will domestic competition. (Malthus seems to have had the peculiar notion that the competitive rate of return in manufactures must soon fall to low levels, with the accumulation of capital, but that in agriculture it remains high.) The industrial nation may suffer if its agricultural customers suffer from indolence or misgovernment, and more certainly it must decline when eventually the agricultural nations develop their own manufactures. The mixed economy somehow avoids all these objections and reaps all the advantages of both systems.

Here, as elsewhere, Malthus purveyed a strange mixture of occasional insights and drab fallacies. His belief in the essentially developmental role of a nation's specialization clashed with his belief that a balanced economy represented an optimum and stable policy. He was able to dismiss the prosperity flowing from trade and industry only by shrinking generations into hours, and England would never have risen to its pinnacle if it had followed his advice.

The *Essay* became much longer and vastly duller, when Malthus added long accounts of population in ancient, primitive, and modern agricultural and industrial states. These descriptive accounts did not demonstrate the principle of population, as he claimed; rather, they demonstrated that death comes in many forms and that births are influenced by social customs. Malthus simply had no canons of evidence. He recited — and embroidered — travelers' accounts of primitive societies, seizing like a gossip columnist upon every reference to misery and vice and ignoring those to prosperity or virtue. He found the principle of population confirmed in the prosperity of

413

England during the twenty years before 1811 and also by the depression after the Napoleonic wars.[29]

What evidence could have been used to test the theory? If the subsistence level has any stability, and hence any significance, Malthus' theory was wrong if the standard of living of the masses rose for any considerable period of time. He did not investigate this possibility (but see below) and ignored the opinions of such authorities as Sir Frederick Eden that it had been rising for a century.[30] His theory was also contradicted if population grew at a constant geometrical rate in an "old" country, for then the means of subsistence were also growing at this rate, since population never precedes food.[31] Despite the rapid increase of population in almost all western European nations at the time, which he duly noted, he persisted in considering this as only a confirmation of his fecundity hypothesis.[32]

Malthus kept his *Political Economy* in a separate compartment from his *Essay*. Though there were many uses of, and many deferential references to, the principle of population in the *Political Economy*, in the discussion of wages the principle was substantially ignored. For example:

This great increase of command over the first necessary of life [from 1720 to 1750] did not, however, produce a proportionate increase of population. It found the people of this country living under a good government, and enjoying all the advantages of civil and political liberty in an unusual degree. The lower classes of people had been in the habit of being respected, both by the laws and the higher orders of their fellow citizens, and had learned in consequence to respect themselves. The result was, that their increased corn wages, instead of occasioning an increase of population exclusively, were so expended as to occasion a decided elevation in the standard of their comforts and conveniences.[33]

In a historical survey of wages, he finds them rising from the mid-fourteenth to the sixteenth century, then falling for a century — hardly a clear example of a strong tendency of wages to approach a subsistence level.[34] Indeed, Malthus goes so far as to investigate the factors (liberty and education) which lead workers to increase their standard of comfort rather than their numbers when income rises. Like a successful general, Malthus occupied all the positions.

Ricardo accepted the simple version of the first edition of the *Essay*, in which wages were always equal to some fixed ("subsistence") level in the long run:

. . . No point is better established, than that the supply of labourers will always ultimately be in proportion to the means of supporting them.

. . . So great are the delights of domestic society, that in practice it is invariably found that an increase of population follows the amended condition of the labourer.[35]

This was Ricardo's general assumption; but, when he came to analyze wages, the Malthusian theory was virtually ignored:

Notwithstanding the tendency of wages to conform to their natural rate, their market rate may, in an improving society, for an indefinite period, be constantly above it; for no sooner may the impulse, which an increased capital gives to a new demand for labour be obeyed, than another increase of capital may produce the same effect; and thus, if the increase of capital be gradual and constant, the demand for labour may give a continued stimulus to an increase of people.

It is not to be understood that the natural price of labor, estimated even in food and necessaries, is absolutely fixed and constant. It varies at different times in the same country, and very materially differs in different countries.[36]

Even the arithmetic rate of growth of subsistence is questioned:

It has been calculated, that under favourable circumstances population may be doubled in twenty-five years; but under the same favourable circumstances, the whole capital of a country might possibly be doubled in a shorter period.[37]

One can disregard the last passage, as pertaining only to new countries, but the indefinitely prolonged excess of the market over the natural wage rate and the possibility of a steady upward movement of the natural rate must simply be recorded as correct views which Ricardo did not know how to incorporate into his theoretical system.

The later history of the Malthusian theory is beyond our province, but we should notice that it was not popular among the best economists. Longfield rejected the theory,[38] and Senior proposed, in an ironical letter to Malthus, an alternative "nomenclature": "I should still say, that, in the absence of disturbing causes, food has a tendency to increase faster than population, because, in fact, it has generally done so. . . ."[39] Had not John Stuart Mill lent to it his great authority, it would have been declining rapidly in importance by mid-century.

The "principle of population" had the dubious honor of receiving from history one of the most emphatic refutations any prominent economic theory has ever received. It is now fashionable to defend Malthus by saying that his theory applies to other places and times than those to which he and his readers applied it. This may be true, but it is tantamount to scientific nihilism to deduce from it any defense of Malthus. It is an odd theory that may not some day and somewhere find a role; for every answer one can find a correct question.

And yet Malthus deserves commendation for two important services that rise above the quality of his work. The first is that he gave population an important role in economic theory. The very failure of his theory was a large cause for the near-abandonment of population studies by later economists, and this seriously reduces his contribution to economics but does not eliminate it. The second service was the recognition that it is possible to deal fruitfully with population in terms of conventional economic theory. The identification of cost of subsistence with cost of production was illegitimate, but the explanation of birth-rate differentials through differentials in costs may well prove to be an important avenue through which economists may make contributions to the study of population.

415

II. THE THEORY OF RENT

England began its era of continuous importation of wheat — sporadic importation began a generation earlier — in the same year that it embarked upon the Napoleonic Wars, 1793. In June of this year, wheat was 51s. a quarter. It rose to 80s. in 1796, and after a drop rose again to 128s. in 1801, fell again up to 1804, and then began to rise and finally reached 152s. in August, 1812. Thereafter it fell sharply but irregularly, until it had fallen to 41s. by 1822.[40] The law of 1804 provided for export bounties if the price fell below 54s. and high import duties (30s.) when the price was less than 60s., but low duties (7½d.) when the price was above 66s. The wartime inflation had wholly outmoded this act, and moves for new protection began in 1813, as prices began to fall; and in 1814 both Lords and Commons appointed committees to report on the question. Their reports were the apparent stimulus to the publication of the pamphlets of West and Malthus. (At least West's pamphlet, however, was no stimulus to Lords and Commons; in 1815 they enacted a prohibition on importation when the price fell below 80s. and free importation at higher levels.)

The hearings before these committees emphasized the relationship between the high corn prices and the more intensive and extensive cultivation of the soil in the years up to 1812. Indeed, even the questions before the Lords' committee were sufficiently emphatic on the relationship:

> If the prices continue as low as at present, even if you were to pay no rent for such a farm as yours is, could you continue to raise grain and cultivate it in the same expensive manner you have recently cultivated it? (Reply: "Certainly not; . . . I must certainly discharge one third of my hands.")
>
> Supposing that wheat was to fall to 3l. 10s. permanently upon an average, . . . could the farmer continue to cultivate that species of land which you have mentioned as being poor cold land? (Reply: "I think not; that would be the lowest price; he could scarcely get any profit upon that.")[41]

Although there were ample clues for the development of the classical rent theory, it would be unjust to treat the inventors of the theory as mere codifiers of generally accepted and realized truth. These hearings had their full share of irrelevancies and inconsistencies — as hearings usually do — and the outlines of the theory in the facts of the time are undoubtedly much clearer to modern than to contemporary eyes.[42]

Had Sir Edward West been less successful in the law, he might have been a leading economist of the era. His pamphlet displays a mind that was inventive and logically bent, and he had a rare talent for marshaling evidence to bear on a theory.[43] He immediately sets forth "a principle in political economy":

> The principle is simply this, that in the progress of the improvement of cultivation the raising of rude produce becomes progressively more expensive, or, in other words, the ratio of the net produce of land to its gross produce is continually diminishing. . . .

416

Each equal additional quantity of work bestowed on agriculture, yields an actually diminished return, and of course if each equal additional quantity of work yields an actually diminished return, the whole of the work bestowed on agriculture in the progress of improvement, yields an actually diminished proportionate return. Whereas it is obvious that an equal quantity of work will always fabricate the same quantity of manufactures.[44]

The "progress of improvement" must be interpreted to mean the growth of output; West, like Malthus and Ricardo, gave little thought to technological improvements. The mistaken identification of diminishing average and diminishing marginal products also continued throughout the Ricardian literature. West found diminishing returns to be due to the necessity for resort to inferior lands,[45] but more fundamentally it was due to the diminishing returns from more intensive cultivation. This was proved by what was essentially an inference from the fact that simultaneous cultivation of different grades of soil existed in stable equilibrium:

And the very fact that in the progress of society new land is brought into cultivation, proves that additional work cannot be bestowed with the same advantage as before on the old land. For 100 acres of the rich land will, of course, yield a larger return to the work of 10 men, than 100 acres of inferior land will do, and if this same rich land would continue to yield the same proportionate return to the work of 20 and 30 and 100 as it did to that of 10 labourers, the inferior land would never be cultivated at all.[46]

West contributed two additional lines of demonstration of the law, and both were ingenious, although unconvincing. The first is summarized in his own words:

The division of labour and application of machinery render labour more and more productive in manufactures, in the progress of improvement; the same causes *tend* also to make labour more and more productive in agriculture in the progress of improvement. But another cause, namely, the necessity of having recourse to land inferior to that already in tillage, or of cultivating the same land more expensively, *tends* to make labour in agriculture less productive in the progress of improvement. And the latter cause more than counteracts the effects of machinery and the division of labour in agriculture; because, otherwise agricultural labour would neither become more productive, or remain equally productive, in the progress of improvement.

In either of which cases, since labour in manufactures becomes more productive, *all* labour would become more productive, and the profits of stock, which are the net reproduction, would, of course, rise in the progress of improvement. But the profits of stock are known to fall in the progress of improvement, and, therefore, neither of the first two first suppositions is the fact, and labour in agriculture must, in the progress of improvement, become actually less productive. It is then shewn that this effect cannot be produced by a rise in the real wages of labour.[47]

Unfortunately, the last sentence claims too much: he was not able to show that the fall in the rate of profits could not be due to a rise of wages.[48] This elegantly contrived analysis is very similar to Ricardo's theory, except that the fall of profits is a historical generalization rather than (as with Ricardo) an analytical theorem.

The second proof was that, as a matter of historical fact, rent was a declining share of the total product of agriculture, and this was equivalent to diminishing returns — an equivalence so complete that this was an alternative way of stating the law of diminishing returns. But a decline of rent relative to total produce does not rigorously imply either diminishing average product or diminishing marginal product of labor; wage rates may be rising enough to cause the decline in the share of rent.[49] The argument is perverse, in that if rent were a rising share of total product, then one could deduce the existence of diminishing marginal returns.[50] The whole analysis, however, is dependent on a constant state of technology.

From the theory of diminishing returns, West succinctly developed the classical rent theory:

> If in case of any increased demand for corn, capital could be laid out to the same advantage as before, the growing price of the increased quantity would be the same as before, and competition would, of course, soon reduce the actual price to the growing price, and there could be no increase of rent. But on any increased demand for corn, the capital I have shewn which is laid out to meet this increased demand is laid out to less advantage. The growing price, therefore, of the additional quantity wanted is increased, and the actual price of that quantity must also be increased. But the corn that is raised at the least expense will, of course, sell for the same price as that raised at the greatest, and consequently the price of all corn is raised by the increased demand. But the farmer gets only the common profits of stock on his growth, which is afforded even on that corn which is raised at the greatest expense; all the additional profit, therefore, on that part of the produce which is raised at a less expense, goes to the landlord in the shape of rent.[51]

The theory is deftly used to refute the arguments of Sir Henry Parnell that the prohibition of importation of grain will lower the domestic price, and to estimate the price of wheat under such a prohibition (at least 90s.) and in the absence of all import duties (perhaps 60s.). West also makes an elegant analysis of the effects of the 1688 export bounty on grain. His pamphlet contains a quality of economics that is not exceeded in his generation.

Almost simultaneously Malthus proposed much the same theory, but with much less incisiveness and clarity.[52] He managed to invent two errors for each truth, and some of Ricardo's analysis can be viewed as a reaction to Malthus' peculiar approach. Three causes of the high price of raw produce (relative to the cost of production) were found:

> First, and mainly, That quality of the earth, by which it can be made to yield a greater portion of the necessaries of life than is required for the maintenance of the persons employed on the land.
>
> 2dly, That quality peculiar to the necessaries of life being able to create their own demand, or to raise up a number of demanders in proportion to the quantity of necessaries produced.
>
> And, 3dly, The comparative scarcity of the most fertile land.[53]

The first cause of rent may charitably be read as a clumsy statement that land must be productive.[54] The second cause is formally irrelevant: rent could appear in a society in which the demand for corn was forever constant.[55] Yet the statement contains an important element of truth: rents will be higher, the more rapidly the demand for agricultural produce grows. The third cause is, of course, a sufficient, although not a necessary, condition for the existence of rent.[56]

The existence of diminishing returns on superior land was demonstrated by Malthus, as by West, by the resort to inferior land.[57] The determination of rent was also substantively identical with West's theory: rent was the excess of produce over the return on the capital (wage advances) of the farmer (tenant), which equaled the marginal product of labor times the amount of labor. Aside from this one contribution, however, the pamphlet was an undistinguished performance. It had many erroneous dicta, such as that improvements in agriculture always increase rent[58] and that the theory of rent for corn lands differs from the theory for vineyards, because the products of the latter have no influence on population! A tortured defense of a high price of corn and large rents was his chief theme (it was dictated by Malthus' protectionism), and it was argued on such grounds as that it is a sign of wealth for a nation to pay a high price for corn[59] and that laborers are not injured by a high price of corn if wages rise even more than corn prices.[60]

It follows, then, that the interest of the landlord is always opposed to the interest of every other class in the community.

I shall greatly regret that considerations for any particular class, are allowed to check the progress of the wealth and population of the country. If the interests of the landlord be of sufficient consequence, to determine us not to avail ourselves of all the benefits which would follow from importing corn at a cheap price, they should also influence us in rejecting all improvements in agriculture, and in the implements of husbandry . . . .[62]

In his own formulation of the rent doctrine, Ricardo went beyond West at one point: the analysis of the effects of improvements on rent.[63] Improvements were classified in two types: those which increase the output from given land and those which reduce the amount of labor necessary to produce a given product from given land.[64] These classes are not mutually exclusive, although Ricardo so implies.

In dealing with the first, or land-saving, improvements, Ricardo assumed (i) that the quantity of corn demanded was independent of its price — his customary assumption — and (ii) that the marginal product curve of labor on land was shifted upward a constant amount by the improvement. It then follows, as he argues from numerical examples, that rent will be reduced.[65] In the second class of improvements (which is surely vacuous under his definition), the effect on rent depends on the changes in the shape of the marginal product of labor curve.

Ricardo was prone to exaggerate the conflict of interests between land-lords and other economic classes, and his discussions of improvements in agricultural techniques is an important example of this. Under his usual assumptions his conclusion should have been that improvements always benefit the landlords: the marginal product curve of capital-and-labor is higher relative to the cost of capital-and-labor,[66] and, since the supply of labor is infinitely elastic at a given real wage, rents must rise in the long run. It cannot be said that he wholly ignored this implication,[67] but he chose, for a change, to emphasize only the short-run effects, and then only in the adverse case.[68]

The theory of rent as these men used it could be properly applied only to a resource whose commercial supply was rigidly fixed and which could be used for only one purpose — the raising of corn. It is astonishing how easily and implicitly they identified this resource with British agricultural land, although the supply of land was being increased, and hardly without cost, and although this land was improved by investments of infinitely varied durability. Ricardo may be interpreted as attempting to avoid this identification by his definition of rent as the payment for the use of "the original and indestructible powers of the soil."[69] Yet, after this preliminary gesture — which is inadequate — he usually identified rent with the contemporary payments to landlords. The aggregation of all uses of land into "raising corn" is noticed rather than questioned by Malthus.[70]

This *Anschauung* may not have been particularly objectionable with respect to the problems in which Ricardo was interested. Grain formed a very large part of the standard of living of the working classes (perhaps one-third of total expenditures), and the elasticity of supply of land was doubtless relatively small in the moderately short run. But it is illuminating to see what an astonishingly narrow range of problems Ricardo could be interested in if he found this theory adequate. The structure and trend of individual prices, which had called forth some of Smith's best analysis[71] and which became the central concern of neoclassical economics, were simply outside his domain.

At the level of technical analysis, the theory of rent marked a large advance over Smith's looser formulations. Yet it is noteworthy that Ricardo did not have that instinct for symmetry and generality which we now associate with the formal theorist. The law of diminishing returns was never applied outside agriculture, and the assumption of fixity of supply was not viewed as a limiting case of the infinite array of possible supply elasticities. Despite his penchant for abstract analysis, Ricardo was not a formalist: he was a theorist who wished to answer definite questions (presented by economic problems), and he made his theory no more general than these questions required.

III. THE RICARDIAN THEORY

In the theories of population and rent, as we have seen, Ricardo was chiefly a borrower, and he did not improve upon either theory in any basic respect. In the synthesis of these theories into a general theory of value and distribution, he struck out on his own. The peculiar combination of doctrines that makes up his system is truly original.

The outlines of his theory were beginning to emerge in his *Essay on the Influence of a Low Price of Corn on the Profits of Stock* (1815). We shall sketch the main elements of this theory before we turn to the *Principles*. The argument rested upon four propositions:

First, in the (domestic) production of corn, there is diminishing returns to composite dose of capital-and-labor. What is the dose of capital-and-labor? Strictly speaking, it is a dose of capital, and this capital consists of fixed capital (buildings, machinery, etc.) and circulating capital (the advances to laborers). The amount of circulating capital is set by the amount of labor (which is in fixed proportion to the fixed capital), and the wage rate.[72]

Second, the return to this dose of capital (and labor) is equal to the marginal product — cost of production equals price.

Third, the return on capital in agriculture fixes the rate of return that must also be obtained in other industries.[73]

Ricardo defended this amazing proposition as follows: Given the population, the demand for food is fixed in amount. Unless population changes, the output of corn will not change, and therefore — in the absence of technological improvements in agriculture — the investment in agriculture is fixed. Competition will not allow two profit rates; hence the profit rate in nonagricultural industries must equal that in agriculture.

This is a violent sequence. If new inventions raise the profit rate in manufactures, how is it restored to the agricultural rate? The internally consistent reply for Ricardo to make would have been: With an absolutely inelastic demand for corn, the attempt of capital to leave agriculture would force up the price of corn and hence the profit rate in agriculture until it equaled the profit rate in manufactures. But this is the reverse of Ricardo's conclusion; he argued, instead, that the profit rate in manufactures would fall back to the agricultural rate, as capital flowed into manufactures.[74]

A somewhat more comprehensible explanation can be inferred from his letters to Malthus. Innovations in nonagricultural industries will have no effect upon the cost of subsistence and hence upon wages (Ricardo temporarily forgot that other things besides food enter the worker's budget). Profits can be high for a short time (say five years), but soon the effects of the innovations will be overcome by the accumulation of capital. The only persistent force, working to lower profits, is diminishing returns in agriculture.[75] This proposition was not advanced in the *Principles*.

Fourth, the rent of land will be equal to the total product minus the amount of agricultural capital times its profit rate.

This is not a complete system because, in the absence of more explicit theories of population and capital accumulation, the aggregate output of the economy is not determined. The system does determine the division of product between landlords and others, but not between capitalists and laborers. Ricardo avoided this latter problem (although the subsistence

421

wage theory lurked in the background). He denied, in fact, that the division between wages and profits was determinate:

> As experience demonstrates that capital and population alternately take the lead, and wages in consequence are liberal or scanty, nothing can be positively laid down, respecting profits, as far as wages are concerned.[76]

The *Essay* thus contained two main elements of the Ricardian system: the theory of rent and the dominant influence of diminishing returns in agriculture upon the rate of profits. The completed system required two further elements: the subsistence theory of wages and the measure of value. These were presented in the *Principles,* to which we now turn. Neither the organization nor the exposition is very felicitous, and I shall restate the central argument in my own words.

The competitive firm sells its product at a price which, on the average, equals its cost of production.[77] These costs of production are the various outlays of the entrepreneur on productive services; but from the social viewpoint one class of costs is pure transfer payments, which are unnecessary to call forth the (fixed quantity of) productive services. These transfer payments are the rents paid for the use of land, and they can be eliminated from consideration by discussing costs at the extensive or intensive no-rent margins.

The various outlays of the entrepreneur are bewilderingly numerous, and they must be aggregated into fewer classes if useful generalizations are to be made. Let us classify all expenditures in two classes: fixed capital and circulating capital. Circulating capital is used up in a short time — say a year or less; fixed capital is the remainder.[78] The chief employment of circulating capital is advances of wages to laborers.[79]

The wages of labor are also diverse, varying with skill, cost of education, and the like. Yet the occupational wage structure is very stable, so we may treat a skilled laborer as (say) three unskilled laborers if the former's wage is three times that of unskilled labor. Thus the expenditure on wages may be taken as proportional to the number of "equivalent unskilled" laborers.[80] (Ricardo should also have specified that the occupational structure of laborers is stable.)

Let us turn now to fixed capital — machines, buildings, and other durable equipment. Here we face a double problem: the machines are of very different durabilities; and the value of machines per worker varies widely among industries. Therefore, a rise in wages relative to interest (profits) will raise the prices of goods made with little fixed capital or with capital of short life, relative to the prices of goods in which more, and more durable, fixed capital is used.[81] But for broad purposes this refinement is not important: "The reader . . . should remark, that this cause of the variation of [relative values of] commodities is comparatively slight in its effects."[82] It is unimportant because the relative prices of labor and capital can vary little, whereas the quantities of labor necessary to produce various commodities can undergo large changes. (He should also have specified that the ratio of fixed capital to wage payments cannot undergo large changes.)

TABLE 1

Value of product = 180 × \$1 =	\$180
Wage rate = 5 × \$1 + \$5 =	10
Wage bill = 10 × \$10 =	100
Total profits = \$180 − \$100 =	80
Rent =	0

As a corollary of this theory of value, there exists no perfect measure of value, i.e., a measure of value independent of the fluctuations of wage and profit rates. The varying proportions of fixed to circulating capital and the varying durability of fixed capital imply that, given a change in the ratio of wage rates to profit rates, the values of goods will change differently, depending on the choice of the commodity used to measure their values.[83] But find a commodity which is produced with an average ratio of labor to capital (and this of average durability), then the ideal measure will be approximated.[84] Assume we have found such a near-ideal measure of value — the amount of labor (and corresponding amount of fixed capital) necessary to produce, say, gold.

Ricardo can now solve his basic problem: the distribution of the total produce among the various productive factors. Let us begin with the situation where 10 men on a given farm produce 180 bushels of corn.[85] This corn sells for \$1 in terms of the measure of value, that is, the production of a bushel of corn requires the same quantity of capital and labor as the production of the quantity of gold designated as \$1. Moreover, let each worker receive a subsistence wage of 5 bushels plus \$5 of other necessaries. (We quote these other necessaries in value terms because their production is subject to constant costs.) We may summarize the situation (Table 1).

Now, with the progress of capital and population, resort must be had to Grade II land, on which 10 men (and corresponding capital) produce 170 bushels. The price of wheat must rise to $18/17 = \$1.0588$ per bushel, because the quantity of labor (and capital) per bushel has risen in this proportion relative to the ideal standard. The new situation is as shown in Table 2. (Recall that the rate of profits on marginal land sets the rate obtainable on superior land.) We could continue the arithmetic, but we have already reached the great conclusion: With the growth of population, the rate of wages rises, the rate of profit falls, and aggregate rents rise — all in terms of the measure of value.

Ricardo's basic theorem on distribution — "a rise of wages . . . would invariably lower profits"[86] — is thus strictly dependent on his measure of value. The product of a given quantity of capital and labor, be it large or small, always has the same value; hence the larger the value of labor (wages), the smaller will be the value of capital (profits). This is not equivalent to the proposition that a rise in wages will lead to a fall in the share of total income received by capitalists, for Ricardo had no theory of the share of total income going as rent.

Ricardo argues, almost parenthetically, that under certain conditions the inverse relationship between wages and profits holds also when they are expressed in terms of ordinary money rather than in an ideal standard. If a country is on the gold standard, its price level cannot vary (much) because of changes in domestic factor prices; gold flows will soon restore its former level. If, further, the productivity of capital and labor do not change, a rise in money wages will lead to a fall of money profits — in no other way can international monetary equilibrium be restored.[87]

One could criticize Ricardo's theory on many grounds. The population was not at a subsistence level, the occupational structure of the labor force and the relative wage structure were not stable, improvements in agricultural technology were neither negligible nor sporadic, technological progress in nonagricultural industries could offset diminishing returns in agriculture, etc. Malthus, however, concentrated his criticisms chiefly on one point: the ratio of circulating to fixed capital varies greatly among industries, and this fact vitiates Ricardo's measure of value. Extreme examples were adduced to demonstrate this: wine (and oak trees) increase in value without any direct labor expenditures (circulating capital); shrimp may be collected on the seashore without any fixed capital.[88]

This was a serious ambiguity, as Ricardo frankly recognized. Suppose corn is produced with much labor and little fixed capital, whereas the ideal commodity used to measure value is produced with a lower ratio of labor to fixed capital. Then diminishing returns in agriculture no longer entail a proportional rise in the value of corn (in terms of the ideal commodity), and, in fact, there is no method of determining how much the value of corn will rise. Ricardo would have had to introduce variable proportions between labor and fixed capital in each industry in order to cope with this problem, and this modification would have had radical consequences for his general system.

Ricardo summed up the general historical implications of this theory as follows:

> The natural tendency of profits then is to fall; for, in the progress of society and wealth, the additional quantity of food required is obtained by the sacrifice of more and more labour. This tendency, this gravitation as it were of profits, is happily checked at repeated intervals by the improvements in machinery, connected with the production of necessaries, as well as by discoveries in the science of agriculture which enable us to relinquish a portion of labour before required, and therefore to lower the price of the prime necessary of the labourer. The rise in the price of necessaries and in the wages of labour is however limited; for as soon as wages should be equal . . . to the whole receipts of the farmer, there must be an end to accumulation; for no capital can then yield any profit whatever, and no additional labour can be demanded, and consequently population will have reached its highest point. Long indeed before this period, the very low rate of profits will have arrested all accumulation, and almost the whole produce of the country, after paying the labourers, will be the property of the owners of land and the receivers of tithes and taxes.[89]

Depending on the relative strengths of technological progress and diminishing returns, the dismal stationary state lies near or far in the future — but in any case, it lies farther in the future with free trade in corn! Ricardo

TABLE 2

	Grade I Land	Grade II Land
Value of product	180×$1.0588 = $190.58	170×$1.0588 = $180.00
Wage bill*	102.94	102.94
Profit	77.06	77.06
Rents	10.58	0

* The wage rate is
5 × $1.0588 + $5 = $10.294.

pays little attention to this final, historical equilibrium, so we are entitled to infer that he did not believe that it was near.

Although both Adam Smith and Ricardo had cost theories of value, there were important differences even in the basic principles, of which four may be noted here. First, Smith believed that population changes lagged behind changes in the quantity of capital; therefore, wages were indefinitely above the subsistence level in an advancing society.[90] Second, the tenor of Smith's theory of rent, which was not given a coherent statement, was that aggregate rents are a residual but that the rent of any one use of land is a cost determined by the alternative uses of the land.[91] Ricardo ignored the multiplicity of uses of land. Third, Smith believed that the accumulation of capital led to a fall in the rate of profits,[92] whereas Ricardo — arguing from Say's law — denied that capital accumulation had any effect upon the rate of profits (unless the cost of food increased).[93] Finally, Smith's measure of value (ideally, money wages; as an approximation, corn prices) was designed to answer the same question as modern index numbers: how to eliminate differences in the value of money and thus ascertain the "real" changes. Ricardo's measure, on the other hand, was not a price deflator; it was designed to locate the source of changes in value in order to connect wages and profits to labor's and capital's shares in the national income minus rents.

Modern economics is closer to Smith's position than to Ricardo's on each of these differences, although in the case of rent we use Ricardo's technique to analyze Smith's problem. This is not surprising: Ricardo had neither Smith's genius for isolating fundamental empirical relationships nor his supreme common sense. Yet Ricardo was, in his own terrain of technical analysis, superior to Smith. We may illustrate this superiority by comparing the two men's analyses of the effects of a tax on agricultural profits.

Smith, after describing and criticizing the French *taille*, makes the following analysis:

When a tax is imposed upon the profits of stock in a particular branch of trade, the traders are all careful to bring no more goods to market than what they can sell at a price sufficient to reimburse them for advancing the tax. Some of them withdraw a part of their stocks from the trade, and the market is more sparingly supplied than before. The price of the goods rises, and the final payment of the tax falls upon the consumer. But when a tax is imposed upon the profits of stock employed in agriculture, it is not the interest of the farmers to withdraw any part

425

of their stock from that employment. Each farmer occupies a certain quantity of land, for which he pays rent. For the proper cultivation of this land a certain quantity of stock is necessary; and by withdrawing any part of this necessary quantity, the farmer is not likely to be more able to pay either the rent or the tax. . . . The farmer, however, must have his reasonable profit as well as every other dealer, otherwise he must give up the trade. After the imposition of a tax of this kind, he can get this reasonable profit only by paying less rent to the landlord.[94]

Smith does not explain why less land cannot be tilled; he does not explain how the threat of farmers to abandon farming will lower rents; nor does he explain why, if some farmers do leave the industry, the price of the product will not rise at the same time that rents fall.

Ricardo begins in a similar fashion:

A partial tax on profits will raise the price of the commodity on which it falls: a tax, for example, on the profits of the hatter, would raise the price of hats; for if his profits were taxed, and not those of any other trade, his profits, unless he raised the price of his hats, would be below the general rate of profits, and he would quit his employment for another.[95]

The conclusion is generalized:

If it be agreed, that by taxing the profits of one manufacturer only, the price of his goods would rise, to put him on an equality with all other manufacturers; and that by taxing the profits of two manufacturers, the prices of two descriptions of goods must rise, I do not see how it can be disputed, that by taxing the profits of all manufacturers, the prices of all goods would rise, provided the mine which supplied us with money, were in this country, and continued untaxed.[96]

Prices will rise in varying proportions because of the varying ratios of fixed capital to circulating capital, the varying durability of fixed capital, etc. Now consider the effect upon landlords of a tax on profits (1) in every industry except corn, (2) in every industry, and (3) in the industry growing corn only.[97] In the first case every price except that of corn would rise. The landlord's corn and money rents being unchanged, he would suffer a fall in real income. In the second case corn would also rise in price, and, since its output was constant (on the customary assumption of zero demand elasticity), money rents would rise correspondingly; so the landlord's rent would retain its full purchasing power. In the third case money rents would rise, and real rents would therefore also rise.

Ricardo's analysis is perhaps little more rigorous than Smith's — for example, in the first case it is difficult to believe that profits in agriculture would not fall. Yet Ricardo's analysis is more consistent with his general theoretical system, and it is more subtle and systematic. It is perhaps worth adding, however, that the landlord who accepted Smith's opinion in preference to Ricardo's and opposed a tax on (and especially a tax only on) agricultural profits would be taking better care of his interests.

I shall not go further with the applications that Ricardo makes of his theory to taxation, currency, international trade, and in his polemics with other economists. These applications are not impeccable — for example, the celebrated chapter on machinery rests upon a logical error[98] — but they were made with rare consistency. Much of the appeal of the Ricardian system must have come from these demonstrations of the certainty, almost the routine, with which it seemed to dispose of troublesome problems and opinions. The age of formulas had begun.

IV. CONCLUSION

The legendary figure of Ricardo as a stern logician and a powerful debater is, I think, correct in essentials. I should prefer to say that his logic was severe in its simplifications rather than superlative in its rigor, but the dominant characteristic of the man was undoubtedly his perseverance and consistency in dealing with a few basic ideas.

Economics is the body of substantive generalizations on the workings of economic systems. Ricardo did not enlarge much this body of knowledge: his one addition to Smith's work was the systematic, though only partial, recognition of diminishing returns. Perhaps no other economist has ever fully shared Smith's immense understanding of the forces that govern the structure and development of economies; certainly Ricardo was not distinguished for his ability to discover great inductive generalizations.

Economics is also an engine of analysis, and Ricardo, with his great powers of abstraction and synthesis, was a master-analyst. Population, natural resources, capital accumulation, and the distribution of income — these were woven into a sweeping theoretical system. Measured by the significance of the variables and the manageability of the system, he fashioned what is probably the most impressive of all models in economic analysis.

It is here that Ricardo's service to economics lies. His naked logic and pseudologic helped to establish a professional frame of mind which did much to reduce promiscuous fact-gathering and *ad hoc* theorizing and to incite order and precision. This was the basic "Ricardo effect"; and, even with our modern knowledge of the painful extremes to which it can be carried, we must thank him for it.

NOTES

1. A draft of this paper was completed before the magnificent edition of Ricardo's works edited by Sraffa and Dobb began to appear. I have decided to leave for another occasion the discussion of the new information which this edition contains.

2. *Enquiry concerning Political Justice* (3d ed.; London, 1798), II, 441.

3. *Ibid.*, p. 480.

4. *Ibid.*, I, 37.

5. *Ibid.*, II, 517.

6. *Ibid.*, p. 518.

7. *Outlines of a Historical View of the Progress of the Human Mind* (London: J. Johnson, 1795); the original French edition appeared in 1793.

8. *Ibid.*, pp. 344–45.

9. *Ibid.*, pp. 346–47.

10. *Essay* ("Reprints of the Royal Economic Society" [London, 1926]), p. 11.

11. *Ibid.*, pp. 13–14.

12. *Ibid.*, p. 20. This fact came from Richard Price's *Observations on Reversionary Payments* (4th ed.; London, 1783), I, 282, where it is restricted to the "northern colonies." It represents the estimate of a Dr. Styles, and the role of immigration is not discussed by Price or by Malthus.

13. *Essay*, pp. 21–22.

14. *Ibid.*, pp. 28–29, 62–70.

15. "He alludes, either to a promis-

cuous concubinage, which would prevent breeding, or to something else as unnatural. To remove the difficulty in this way, will, surely, in the opinion of most men, be, to destroy that virtue, and purity of manners, which the advocates of equality, and of the perfectibility of man, profess to be the end and object of their views" (*ibid.*, p. 154).

16. For

$$L\frac{dP}{dL} = \frac{1}{\log_e 2}.$$

17. *Essay*, pp. 55, 130–37.

18. *Thoughts Occasioned by the Perusal of Dr. Parr's Spital Sermon* (London, 1801).

19. "The reasonings of the *Essay on Population* did not bear with any particular stress upon my hypothesis . . ." (*ibid.*, p. 55).

20. *Ibid.*, p. 65.

21. *Ibid.*, pp. 72–73.

22. *Parallel Chapters from the First and Second Editions of an Essay on Population*, ed. W. J. Ashley (New York, 1895), pp. 87, 88. Moral restraint is formally defined as the preventive check "which is not followed by irregular gratifications" (*ibid.*, p. 90). It is apparent that only on strained meanings will misery, vice, and moral restraint embrace all checks to population, as Malthus repeatedly claims. He is forced to discuss emigration as a short-lived palliative and alludes to contraceptives as a form of vice.

23. *Ibid.*, pp. 82, 84.

24. For example, he asserts that in England diminishing returns did not hold in the twenty years before 1814 (*Essay* [8th ed.; London, 1878], pp. 360–61). Here Malthus was arguing for import duties on corn.

25. *Ibid.*, p. 373.

26. *Ibid.*, Book III, chaps. viii–x. His proagricultural bias diminished but did not disappear with time (see J. Bonar, *Malthus and His Work* [London, 1924], pp. 245 ff.).

27. *Essay* (8th ed.), p. 112.

28. Another advantage claimed for manufacturers is that wages are in proportion to corn prices, so the nonfood component of the standard of living of the masses will be larger with cheap manufactures. This is simply inconsistent with the principle of population.

29. *Essay* (8th ed.), p. 425.

30. *The State of the Poor* (London, 1797), I, 560 ff.

31. *Essay* (8th ed.), p. 384 n.

32. In the first edition of the *Essay*, Malthus conjectured that the population of England was almost stable: "It is difficult, however, to conceive that the population of England has been declining since the revolution; although every testimony concurs to prove that its increase, if it has increased, has been very slow" (p. 314).

33. *Principles of Political Economy*

(2d ed.; "London School Reprints," 1936), p. 228.

34. *Ibid.*, Book I, chap. iv. The investigation was tenuous in the extreme, however; only the prices of corn and labor were compared, on his customary assumption that grain was the basic element of the standard of living of the workers. If it ever had this role, it had probably lost it by the seventeenth century.

35. *Principles of Political Economy and Taxation*, ed. P. Sraffa and M. Dobb, (Cambridge, England, 1951), pp. 292, 407; also pp. 219, 398.

36. *Ibid.*, pp. 94–95, 96.

37. *Ibid.*, p. 98.

38. *Lectures on Political Economy* ("London School Reprints" [London, 1931]), Appendix.

39. *Two Lectures on Population* (London, 1829), p. 58.

40. See C. R. Fay, *The Corn Laws and Social England* (Cambridge, England, 1932); and Thomas Tooke, *A History of Prices* (London, 1838), II, 390.

41. *Reports Respecting Grain, and the Corn Laws* ("Sessional Papers, 1814–15"), V, 18, 30.

42. Thus Arthur Young listed the rise of population, taxes, and foreign trade (as a measure of wealth) as the sufficient explanations for the rising price of corn, and he attributed the rise of rents chiefly to investments of landlords (*Report from the Select Committee on Petitions Relating to the Corn Laws of This Kingdom* ["Sessional Papers, 1813–14"], III, 82, 86).

43. *The Application of Capital to Land* (1815), reprinted with an Introduction by J. H. Hollander (Baltimore, 1903).

44. *Ibid.*, pp. 9, 12. The mistaken equivalence of the first two parts of the first sentence will be noticed later.

45. "Consider the case of a new colony; the first occupiers have their choice of the land, and of course cultivate the richest spots in the country: the next comers must take the second in quality, which will return less to their labour, and so each successive additional set of cultivators must necessarily produce less than their predecessors" (*ibid.*, p. 13).

46. *Ibid.*, p. 14.

47. *Ibid.*, pp. 23–24.

48. West used three lines of argument to show this. First, he asserted that the rate of population increase diminishes in the progress of improvement, so that, on Malthusian grounds, real wages must be diminishing (*ibid.*, p. 20). He was factually wrong on population growth, and it seems inconsistent to employ Malthus' theory, which assumes constant real wages, to disprove the existence of rising real wages. Second, he argued that high wages are always accompanied by a high rate of profits. In substance he held a wage-fund doctrine and believed that high profit rates would lead to a high rate of increases of the wages fund (the degree of parsi-

mony being given) and thus to a more rapid rise of wage rates (*ibid.*, pp. 22–23). Third, he argued that wages and profits are both high in America, so that high wages are not the cause of low profits (*ibid.*, pp. 21–22). But at most this shows that profits depend upon other variables as well as on wage rates.

49. Let P be product, N, the number of laborers, and P' the marginal product of labor. Then the proportion of rent to total product is

$$\frac{P - NP'}{P},$$

and its derivative with respect to N is negative if

$$NPP'' + PP' > N(P')^2,$$

or

$$PP'' > P'\left(P' - \frac{P}{N}\right).$$

One cannot deduce from this either a decreasing average product—which requires $(P' - P/N)$ to be negative—or a decreasing marginal product, $P'' < 0$.

50. In the notation of the previous footnote, then $NPP'' + PP' < N(P')^2$ and, since $-P'(P - NP')$ must be negative if rents are positive, P'' must be negative.

51. *The Application of Capital to Land*, p. 39.

52. *An Inquiry into the Nature and Progress of Rent*, reprinted with an Introduction by J. H. Hollander (Baltimore, 1903).

53. *Ibid.*, p. 15.

54. Actually, Malthus means it as a requirement that the total produce be in excess of the subsistence level of the worker. This is a condition necessary for the continuous *payment* of rent by tenants to landlords but not for the existence of a surplus over the quantity of labor times its marginal product.

55. Malthus states the contrary: that, if population is constant, an abundant produce "might reduce the price of raw produce, like the price of manufactures, to the cost of production" (*Nature and Progress of Rent*, p. 16). The trivial condition under which this is true is excluded by the third cause.

56. Ricardo wrote to Malthus that "your first and third causes of high price appear to me to be directly at variance with each other. The first is the fertility of land, the third the scarcity of fertile land" (January 24, 1817, *Letters of David Ricardo to Thomas Robert Malthus* [Oxford, 1887], p. 127). The paradox is verbal: fertility in this realm of discourse is an economic property of land and is measured by its price; hence scarcity and fertility represent the same forces.

57. *Nature and Progress of Rent*, p. 27. It may be remarked that no one stated the law correctly with reference to this point. All these writers applied equal quantities of capital and labor to equal areas of land to measure differential rent. This violated the "best technology" assumption: equal quantities of capital-and-labor on different lands would not reveal the full difference in their productivity and might even reverse it. One should apply equal quantities of capital-and-labor to such quantities of each quality of land that the optimum technology is used on each quality of land.

58. *Ibid.*, p. 24.

59. *Ibid.*, p. 39.

60. Even for Malthus the argument is extraordinarily imprecise; consider the relations between these three statements:

"There is nothing so absolutely unavoidable in the progress of society as the fall of wages . . ." (*ibid.*, p. 22).

"We see in consequence, that in spite of continued improvements in agriculture, the money price of corn is *caeteris paribus* the highest in the richest countries . . ." (*ibid.*, p. 38).

"With the regard to the labouring classes of society, it is a very short-sighted view of the subject, which contemplates, with alarm, the high price of corn as certainly injurious to them . . . . And I do not scruple distinctly to affirm, that under similar [prudential] habits, and a similar demand for labour, the high price of corn, when it has time to produce its natural effects, so far from being a disadvantage to them, is a positive and unquestionable advantage" (*ibid.*, pp. 39–40).

The last view is based on the belief, already encountered in the *Essay*, that population follows food supply, not real wages.

61. See esp. *Principles*, chap. xxxii.

62. *An Essay on the Influence of a Low Price of Corn on the Profits of Stock* (*Works*, ed. Sraffa and Dobb, IV, 21, 41); also *Principles*, pp. 335–36, 400.

63. Ricardo was independently approaching the theory of rent before the pamphlets of West and Malthus appeared (see his letters to Malthus in 1814).

64. *Principles*, p. 80.

65. For a geometrical illustration see A. Marshall, *Principles of Economics* (8th ed.; London, 1920), p. 835. In effect, Ricardo defined the production function as $\emptyset(N)$ where N is the number of laborers, before the improvement, and as $\emptyset(N) + aN$ after the improvement. With diminishing marginal returns, rent varies with the number of workers; and fewer workers are now needed to produce the same product.

66. He believed that improvements had little effect on the shape of the marginal product curve (*Principles*, pp. 412–13).

67. *Ibid.*, pp. 79–80, 412.

68. Clearer notice of long-run effects was taken in the third edition, in answer to Malthus' criticisms (*ibid.*, pp. 81 n., 335–36).

69. *Ibid.,* p. 44; see, however, p. 261 n.

70. *Nature and Progress of Rent,* p. 17.

71. *Wealth of Nations,* Book I, chap. xi.

72. *The Works and Correspondence of David Ricardo,* ed. Sraffa and Dobb (Cambridge, 1951), IV, 10–11.

73. *Ibid.,* pp. 13 n., 23–24.

74. *Works,* IV, 24.

75. *Letters,* pp. 43, 46, 52, 57.

76. *Works,* IV, 23.

77. ". . . We mean always such commodities . . . on the production of which competition operates without restraint" (*Principles,* p. 12).

78. *Ibid.,* p. 31.

79. "In one trade very little capital may be employed as circulating capital, that is to say in the support of labour . . ." (*ibid.,* p. 32). The other use of circulating capital is presumably to purchase raw materials, whose costs are, in turn, resolvable into rent or payments for fixed or circulating capital.

80. *Ibid.,* chap. i, sec. 2.

81. *Ibid.,* secs. 4 and 5. The period of turnover of circulating capital is also recognized as a factor in the effects of wage changes.

82. *Ibid.,* p. 29; *Letters to Malthus,* p. 176.

83. Commodities made with relatively much labor will rise in relative price when wage rates rise relative to profit rates.

84. *Principles,* pp. 44–45. For a discussion of the measure of value in the first edition, see *ibid.,* pp. xlii ff.

85. *Ibid.,* pp. 112 ff.

86. *Ibid.,* p. 127.

87. See *ibid.,* pp. 104–5, 126–27, 213–14; and *Works,* IV, 213–16.

88. *Letters to Malthus,* pp. 179, 222.

89. *Principles,* pp. 120–21.

90. *Wealth of Nations* ("Modern Library" ed. [New York, 1937], p. 69.

91. *Ibid.,* Book I, chap. xi, esp. pp. 144–46, 149, 152, 159.

92. *Ibid.,* pp. 87 ff.

93. *Principles,* pp. 289–93.

94. *Wealth of Nations,* p. 807.

95. *Principles,* p. 205.

96. *Ibid.,* p. 213.

97. *Ibid.,* pp. 210–13.

98. Ricardo tacitly assumes that workers displaced by a technological advance cannot be employed elsewhere; for a good analysis see K. Wicksell, *Lectures on Political Economy* (London, 1934), I, 133–41.

16.

JOHN M. CASSELS
Washington, D.C.

A Re-Interpretation

of Ricardo

on Value

For over a century now Ricardo's views on value have been very commonly misunderstood. It is the purpose of the present paper to show that, altho his work did undoubtedly contribute in a very important way to the subsequent development of the labor theory of value, it is a complete mistake to regard Ricardo himself as either an adherent or an exponent of that theory. There are, it is true, many passages in his chapter on value which seem at first sight to indicate an acceptance of the labor theory. But on closer examination it will be found that most of them refer not to values but to variations in values, that almost all the others refer to special simplified cases, and that the few remaining statements which do relate to the actual valuation process are merely survivals from the earlier stages of his thinking and are entirely contradicted by what he wrote later in the amended editions of his book and in his letters. It is a curious anomaly that Ricardo, whose rare intellectual honesty and keen discernment are nowhere more admirably displayed than in his critical rejection of this theory, should have come to be regarded as one of its most distinguished exponents.

In what follows it will be shown that his famous chapter on value was

Reprinted from *The Quarterly Journal of Economics*, XLIX (May 1935), 518–32, by permission of the author and The Harvard University Press. Copyright, 1935, by the President and Fellows of Harvard College. At the time of original publication, the author was with Harvard University.

never intended as an exposition of any theory of value in the accepted sense of the term but was written for the special purpose of providing him with a particular logical link that was required in his elaborate chain of reasoning about the dynamics of distribution; that, since in his analysis of distribution he was primarily concerned to show how the Corn Laws would benefit the landlord class at the expense of the capitalist class, it was sufficient for his purpose to demonstrate how the value of corn would be *changed* by a *change* in the amount of labor required for its production, without the necessity of his explaining how the actual value of corn was determined at any particular time either in the presence or in the absence of the duties; that the theory of value which Ricardo quite evidently regarded as axiomatic was an expenses of production theory in which profits are included among the necessary costs; and finally, that, altho he undoubtedly began by basing his deductions on a labor theory of value suggested by his reading of The Wealth of Nations, he subsequently discarded this theory as invalid and developed in its place a demonstration, based directly on his own money cost theory, to prove merely that *variations* in the quantities of labor expended in producing different commodities must of necessity produce approximately proportionate *variations* in their relative values.

The difficulties which have been encountered all along in finding a satisfactory interpretation of Ricardo's Principles have been due not only to the intricacy of his reasoning and the obscurity of his writing but also to the preconceived ideas with which his readers have invariably approached his work. We have naturally expected to find in the chapter on value in a book entitled The Principles of Political Economy an explanation of *how* values are determined. We have looked for a discussion of the forces which determine how much of one good shall be given, at any particular time, in exchange for another; we have looked for a discussion of the principles according to which, at any one time, the ratios of exchange for various commodities are established. This is what we have found in the corresponding chapters of other books and this is what we have insisted on finding in the first chapter of Ricardo.

This, however, was certainly not what Ricardo meant to give us. Altho in his chapters "on natural and market price," "on profits," "on the influence of supply and demand on prices" and elsewhere in his writings he shows that he understood very well the operation of the forces of supply and demand, in his chapter "on value" they receive no more than a passing reference. Again, altho he regarded "cost of production including profits" as the "ultimate" determinant of exchange values for all goods that are freely reproducible by human effort, the only account we are given of *how* costs are related to values was added as an afterthought in chapter XXX, almost at the end of the book. When Ricardo wrote his chapter on value he was concerned not with the ratios of exchange which might exist at any one time but with the changes in those ratios which might take place between two periods of time. He was not interested in the fact that one piece of cloth might be exchanged, at any particular time, for two quarters of corn but he was intensely interested in the possibility that, ten years later, one piece of cloth might be exchanging for only one quarter of corn. Ricardo stated his own position as follows: "The inquiry to which I wish to draw the reader's attention relates to the effects of variations in the relative value of commodities." So engrossing, indeed, was his interest in this question of the *"variations in relative value"* that those very words or their equivalents occur no less than 200 times in this one short chapter, an average of 7 times on every page.

Why was Ricardo so interested in these variations in value? Because they affected the distribution of the national income among the landlords, the capitalists and the laborers. He says in his preface that "to determine the laws which regulate this distribution is the principal problem of Political Economy." What was uppermost in his mind was undoubtedly the effect of the Corn Laws on the relative prosperity of the landlords and the capitalists. His Principles developed out of earlier papers which dealt more explicitly with this particular problem. He realized, as did many others of his class, that the protective duties so beneficial to the rent-receivers were distinctly disadvantageous to those who drew their income in the form of profits. To prove this by incontrovertible logic was the ultimate object of Ricardo's endeavor. The result, as we shall see, was a remarkable intellectual structure, at the foundation of which was his celebrated principle of diminishing returns, and for which the keystone was found in the close relationship between the changes in the quantity of labor embodied in commodities and the variations that take place in their relative values.

More specifically, what he undertook to show was that the operation of the principle of diminishing returns enforced by restrictions on the importation of corn would inevitably result in a decrease in the *proportion* of the total national income going to the capitalist class. The steps in his reasoning were as follows:

1. As society advances population increases and the number of laborers increases proportionately.

2. If we measure quantity of labor simply by working time it follows that the total quantity of labor employed in producing the national income increases in the same proportion.

3. Since corn is the staple food of the people and its consumption per capita cannot be materially reduced the total corn crop (if importation is prevented) must also be increased in about the same proportion.

4. Because of "the laws of nature which have limited the productive powers of the land" the production of each additional quarter involves a greater expenditure of labor, and the amount of labor embodied in the corn crop as a whole increases in greater proportion than the total quantity of labor available for the production of the national income.

5. Since the quantity of labor embodied in the corn crop has increased relatively to the quantity embodied in all other commodities it follows that, if the variation in exchange values is proportionate to the changes in the quantities of labor embodied, the corn crop now represents a larger share than formerly of the total income of the community measured in terms of general purchasing power.

6. As the margin of production is pushed farther and farther beyond the point of diminishing returns the *landlords* receive as rent (according to Ricardo's fig-

433

ures) a larger and larger share of the corn crop and consequently a share of the total income which is increased in even greater proportion.

7. Since the *laborers'* per capita consumption of corn cannot be reduced the total physical quantity necessarily going to that class must increase in proportion as the corn crop itself. Assuming then, as Ricardo does, that the other elements in their subsistence are produced under the same conditions as before (i.e. at the same labor cost) it follows that the wage-earnings' share of the total income measured in terms of general purchasing power is substantially increased.

8. Thus we arrive at the conclusion that, since each of the other classes gets a larger share of the national income, the *capitalists,* as the residual legatees, are left with a smaller proportion than they formerly obtained.[1]

From the foregoing outline it is evident that Ricardo's discussion of value was subsidiary to his discussion of distribution. It is only when this is realized that the peculiarities of the opening chapter can be satisfactorily accounted for. His whole analysis of distribution depends for its validity upon his ability to establish at least an approximate correspondence between the variations in the exchange values of commodities and the changes in the quantities of labor time necessary to produce them (see step 5). It was in order to establish this vital point that he wrote his chapter "on value."

The reason that these fundamental steps in Ricardo's demonstration do not stand out more clearly in the text itself is that he stated them there in a curiously cryptic way. Instead of dealing directly with the distribution of the whole national income he based his analysis on the distribution of agricultural produce from a single farm between the farmer, his landlord and his hired laborers. The link between the distribution on an individual farm and distribution in the community as a whole is to be found in his concept of an ideal invariable standard of value. If we succeed in keeping its significance constantly in mind as we study the chapters dealing with distribution (especially the chapter on profits) we discover that the underlying logic of his argument is essentially the same as that outlined above. The difficulty is that this is the most elusive link in the whole chain of his reasoning — so elusive indeed that it is commonly supposed to be missing entirely. Even Professor Cannan has written that Ricardo "always appears to treat *a farm* as a kind of type of the industry of the whole country and to *suppose* that the division of the whole produce can be easily inferred from the distribution on the farm." (The italics are mine.)

The employment of the idea of an invariable standard of value was the most natural thing in the world for an economist of the early nineteenth century. It was one of the central concepts of economic theory in Ricardo's day and no doubt imposed itself upon his thought without any conscious choice on his part. We may be pretty sure, moreover, that it added to the difficulty of his own thinking in much the same way that it has added since to the difficulties of those who have tried to understand him. In spite of the complications introduced by this troublesome concept the logic of his deductions appears to be perfectly sound. The particular standard of value which he set up was a purely hypothetical one and was specially designed to suit the purpose he had in hand. "To facilitate the object of this enquiry," he says, "altho I fully allow that money made of gold is subject to most of the variations of other things *I shall suppose* it to be invariable."[2] (The italics are mine.)

This imaginary ideal money of which he assumed himself to be possessed was designed to measure the variations in the quantity of labor embodied in different commodities. It follows from this assumption that total national income measured in terms of price (ideal) can only vary in proportion to the changes in the total amount of labor expended in producing it. That being so it is clear that, since the amount of corn produced is always proportionate to the total labor of the community, a rise in its price (ideal) per quarter must mean that the crop as a whole has come to represent a larger proportion than formerly of the total national income measured in terms of this ideal money. It follows further from the nature of this arbitrary standard, and from the relations established between the variations in quantities of labor expended and the variations in value, that the corn crop represents a larger proportion of the national income in terms of general purchasing power. From this point on his analysis follows closely the outline given above.[3]

In the light of the foregoing discussion of Ricardo's methods and objectives his perplexing chapter on value becomes intelligible. Striking verbal inconsistencies remain because of his failure to rewrite the text completely as his thinking of the subject progressed, but the real significance of these contradictory statements and the underlying meaning of the chapter as a whole become perfectly clear. It will help us in reëxamining this chapter if we recognize three different stages in the development of his thought: first, the stage in which he based his conclusions about the variations in values on Adam Smith's theory that actual values correspond to the quantities of labor embodied in the products; second, the transitional stage in which, altho he had renounced the labor theory as such because it was inconsistent with his own money cost theory, he was still inclined to argue that the exchange values of goods would be *proportionate* to the amounts of labor bestowed on their production; and finally, the stage in which he gave up even this claim that values would be proportionate and derived directly from the money cost theory itself the relations he required to establish between the *variations* in values and the *variations* in the quantities of labor expended in producing the goods.

Of the first stage only a few traces remain, at the very beginning of the chapter on value. There can be little doubt that the idea of a fundamental relation between labor and value was suggested to him by an early reading of The Wealth of Nations. Being a hard-headed business man rather than a philosopher he did not share Adam Smith's interest in the ethical significance of a labor theory of value, but when he came to work out the principles of his own economic system he was naturally attracted to an idea which fitted into it so nicely. Thus we find him quoting with approval near the beginning of the chapter Smith's statement that "labor was the first price . . . the original purchase money paid for all things." A little later he himself says that the labor expended in producing commodities "is really the foundation of the exchangeable value of all things, excepting those which cannot be increased by human industry." There follows immediately after this a statement which is highly significant because it indicates the real nature of his interest in the labor theory of value. He writes "*if* the quantities of labor realized in commodities regulate their exchangeable value, every *increase* in the quantity of labor must *augment* the value of that commodity on which it is exercised, as every *diminution* must *lower* it." (The italics are mine.)

Several passages representative of the second stage in the development of Ricardo's thought are to be found in the third edition of the Principles. From a comparison of this edition with the earlier ones it is clear that his views had undergone considerable modification between the time that these passages were originally written and the time that the final edition was published. Ricardo's objective during the transitional stage in which these passages were written was, it will be remembered, to show that on the basis of a money cost theory values would be *proportionate* to the quantities of labor expended on the commodities. His first step was to eliminate rent from among the costs. This he did by pointing out that it is the marginal cost of a commodity that affects its price — the cost on no-rent land. That being so the costs of production which affect value are reduced to two, wages and profits. His adherence to a cost of production theory in this form is explicitly avowed in a footnote as follows: "Mr. Malthus appears to think that it is part of my doctrine that the cost and value of a thing should be the same; it is, if he means by cost, 'cost of production' including profits." He explains in this connection that in measuring the quantity of labor embodied in commodities we must include not only the labor expended "on their immediate production" but also that which was bestowed "on all those implements and machines" which contributed to their manufacture. Having thus eliminated rent and reduced capital to past labor the temptation to treat profits merely as a percentage of wages and to suppose that total costs would, therefore, always be proportionate to the wage-bills paid must have been almost irresistible. Ricardo did for a time succumb to this temptation and wrote in a well-known passage: "I have not said, because one commodity has so much labor bestowed upon it as will cost £1,000, and another so much as will cost £2,000, that therefore one would be of the value of £1,000, and the other of the value of £2,000; but I have said that their value will be to each other as two to one." He did not identify costs with wages. He made no attempt to eliminate profits as he had eliminated rent. He was content with his claim that the inclusion of profits would not disturb the proportional relationship between wages and costs.

A further step was necessary in order to reach the conclusion required for the main purpose of his investigation. He had to slip from the use of the term "wages" to the use of the term "quantity of labor" (measured by time). This was an entirely illogical step but Ricardo took it. We find in more than one place the statement that the relative values of commodities are "regulated" or "governed" by the "relative quantities of labor bestowed on their production."

436

It is to Ricardo's credit that he himself perceived later the error into which he had fallen. In a letter to McCulloch in the summer of 1820 he wrote, "I sometimes think that if I were to write the chapter on value again which is in my book, I should acknowledge that the relative value of commodities was regulated by two causes instead of one, namely, by the relative quantity of labor necessary to produce the commodities in question, and by the rate of profit for the time that the capital remained dormant, and until the commodities were brought to market."

About the same time in a letter to Malthus he admitted the weakness of this step in his proof but defended the validity of his final conclusions about the effects of the increasing cost of corn on the distribution of the national income among the different classes of society. He recognized that his proposition about quantity of labor regulating value was "not rigidly true." "But," he says, "the doctrine is less liable to objections when employed not to measure the whole absolute value of the commodities compared, but the *variations* which from time to time take place in relative value." (The italics are mine.)

This statement in his letter to Malthus was characteristic of the third phase in the development of his thought on the subject of values and value relations. The essential elements of the direct proof which he used to relate *variations* in values to *variations* in labor inputs measured by time, while present in the first and second editions of the work, were given the greatest prominence in the final edition. The superiority of this proof over that which we have just been examining lies in the fact that whereas no logical link was found between wage-bills and quantities of labor (time), such a link was discovered between *variations* in the wage-bills and the *variations* in quantities of labor (time). In section II of the chapter on value Ricardo explains why in dealing with the variations in the relative values of commodities between two different periods he is justified in ignoring differences in the qualities of labor altho these differences in quality admittedly affect the relative values themselves. "The estimation," he says, "in which different qualities of labor are held comes soon to be adjusted in the market with sufficient precision for all practical purposes and . . . The scale, when once formed, is liable to little variation. If a day's labor of a working jeweller be more valuable than a day's labor of a common laborer, it has long ago been adjusted and placed in its proper position in the scale of value. In comparing, therefore, the value of the same commodity at different periods of time, the consideration of the comparative skill and intensity of labor required for that particular commodity needs scarcely to be attended to, as it operates equally in both periods."

Wage-bills depend, of course, on two factors, the length of time worked and the rate of pay per unit of time. The first of these is, according to Ricardian terminology, the "*quantity*" of labor. It is evident then that if the rates of pay remain the same (or change proportionately through some common cause) the changes in the wage-bills will correspond exactly with the changes in the quantity of labor expended. This was the link in his reasoning that Ricardo required and the subsequent steps in his deductions are logically supported by it, altho the connection between this step and the later ones is obscured by the particular method of exposition he adopted. What he did from this point on in his discussion was to treat labor as if it were all of the same quality. In all the numerical illustrations which are introduced the rates of remuneration for labor are uniform regardless of the nature of the work which is being done. While this procedure is logically valid it is obviously liable to be misleading. There can be no doubt that the treacherous step in Ricardo's transitional deductions referred to above resulted, in part at least, from his adoption of this dangerous procedure and that many of his readers have been misled in exactly the same way into the belief that he had demonstrated a correspondence between actual values and the quantities of labor expended.

Before leaving this particular subject we may well consider for a moment why Ricardo should have attached to the term "quantity of labor" the meaning that he did. By defining it as a quantity measurable purely by time he made it impossible to relate it to value and difficult to relate it even to variations in value. Why should he not have made it a quantity measurable by wages? The answer is simple. From an earlier part of our study we discovered how important it was for him to bring into as direct relationship as possible the total food supply and the total quantity of labor. The fact that the amount of subsistence required and the amount of work done are both dependent on time provided him with the necessary link between them and determined immediately the meaning that should be attached to the term "quantity of labor."

In the development of his argument Ricardo proceeds from the consideration of a hypothetical case in which no capital at all is employed in production to the consideration of an exceptional case in which it happens that labor and waiting (to use the term now familiar) are combined in the same proportions in all industries and finally to the consideration of more realistic cases in which labor and waiting are combined in different proportions in different industries. The first case is dismissed almost without discussion; the second is dealt with in the latter part of section III; and the realistic cases are dealt with in sections IV and V.

Unfortunately for his readers Ricardo, a pioneer in this field of investigation, did not have at his disposal the precise concepts and the carefully considered terminology which are available to economists today. He was obliged to struggle along with such cumbersome concepts as "the proportions of fixed and circulating capital," "the degree of durability of fixed capital," "the time which must elapse before it (the product) can be brought to market," "the rapidity with which it (the capital) is returned to its employer," and so on. We naturally have some difficulty in grasping the significance of this unfamiliar language but a careful study of his explanations and his illustrations enables us to see that the idea he had in mind was what Jevons would have referred to as "the amount of investment of capital." This "amount of investment of capital" or this "amount of waiting" is a quantity of two dimensions, value and time, obtained by multiplying together the amount of money invested and the length of time that elapses before it is returned to the investor.

Stated in modern terms, then, Ricardo's conclusions were: (1) that where the proportions of labor and waiting (both measured by money) are the same in the different industries concerned, the variations in the values of the products will be exactly proportionate to the changes in the quantity of labor (time) expended on them; (2) that even where labor and waiting enter in unequal proportions the correspondence, altho not exact, will be sufficiently close to afford a basis for the deductions he wished to make about the dynamics of distribution. Referring to the effects on values of a change in the rate of profits he wrote, "The reader should remark that this cause of the variation of commodities is comparatively slight in its effects." This factor he believed to be limited in the range of its effect to 6 or 7 per cent. "Not so," he says, in contrast, "with the other great cause of variation in the value of commodities, namely the increase or diminution in the quantity of labor necessary to produce them. If to produce the corn eighty instead of one hundred men should be required, the value of the corn would fall 20 per cent . . . An alteration in the permanent rate of profits, to any great amount, is the effect of causes which do not operate but in the course of years, whereas alterations in the quantity of labor necessary to produce commodities are of daily occurrence." Therefore, he declares, "*I shall consider all the great variations which take place in the relative value of commodities to be produced by the greater or less quantity of labor which may be required from time to time to produce them.*"

This arbitrary disregard of the minor variations may appear at first sight to be a rather high-handed method of dealing with a troublesome discrepancy. But it involves no relaxation in the logic of his analysis. Since he was concerned with the variations in the value of corn, a commodity "chiefly produced by labor," the recognition of the effects of changes in the rate of profits would have strengthened rather than weakened his case. The falling rate of profits found (according to Ricardo) in an advancing society would affect the value of corn in exactly the same way as the increase in the quantity of labor necessary for its production and would contribute in like manner to the redistribution of the national income with which we are here concerned. In making the above assumption Ricardo's object was not to gain any dialectic advantage but merely to simplify the presentation of his argument.

A more important assumption than this, however, is made in these sections without any explicit mention whatever. In all the reasoning involved in his direct proof he has taken for granted that the proportions in which labor and waiting are combined in the different industries remain constant between the two periods under consideration. It was not necessary for him to assume, as is sometimes supposed, that the proportions are the same in all industries but it was necessary to assume that they were constant. This means, in the language of Bohm-Bawerk, that "the period of production" for each commodity must remain unaltered, i.e., that the "roundaboutness" of the process in each industry must remain the same. It allows for no fundamental changes in the methods of production. Altho this assumption is only made implicitly we have no reason to doubt Ricardo's willingness to accept the conditions implied. The case is closely parallel to that in which he assumed that the qualities of labor would remain the same in different industries. Both of these assumptions seem more reasonable when we realize that, in spite of his references to the gradual advance of society, he really had in mind the effects which would be brought about in a relatively short time by the imposition of a high tariff on corn. In speaking of the qualities of labor he says, "the variation is very inconsiderable from year to year, and therefore can have little effect, for short periods, on the relative value of commodities." The same might well have been said of the arts of production.

The reinterpretation here suggested of Ricardo's chapter on value is not only logically consistent with all he wrote but is also psychologically consistent with what we know of his own character and background. He was a retired business man, actively engaged in politics, and keenly interested in the practical economic problems of his day, who had a remarkably penetrating and logical mind but was absolutely untrained in the arts of academic men and was persuaded to write his book only by the insistent pressure of his friends. He undertook this task only a few years before his death and he continued to reconsider his views to the very end. He was not interested in expounding any theory of value for its own sake — least of all a labor theory. He took over the idea of a labor theory from Adam Smith but he can never have believed himself that labor "created" value directly by its embodiment in commodities. He was not even interested in the "real costs" of production. His deductions are all based on money costs and the farthest that he ever went in the direction of a labor theory was to say (carelessly) that costs would be proportionate to labor expended. Even in this relation he had no direct interest; he used it merely as a means of reaching his conclusions about variations in value; and recognizing in the end the error in this step of his reasoning he eliminated it from the main chain of his deductions. The real significance of Ricardo's chapter on value lies not in the fact that occasional passages seem to support a labor theory but rather in the evidence it gives us that he had examined this theory critically and was finally led to reject it entirely.

NOTES

1. There is one additional step to which we may refer, altho it really carries us beyond the field of distribution as Ricardo had defined it. Having satisfied himself that the proportion of the national income going to the capitalist class must inevitably decline, he goes on to speak as if the rate (%) of return on capital must also fall. He uses the term "fall in profits" ambiguously to refer to either of these changes and his language suggests that the one follows necessarily from the other, whereas in fact the validity of this final step depends not so much on his analysis of distribution as upon his belief that saving is only slightly affected by a reduction in the rate of return on investment. He seems to have been misled here partly

because he had based his analysis on an individual farm instead of dealing with the community as a whole.

2. It is true, as Professor Hollander has pointed out, that Ricardo was later drawn into the current controversy about the best practical measure of value, but as far as this book is concerned the idea of an invariable standard served merely as a form in which to express his thought and contributed nothing itself to the logic of his argument. It was essential to the presentation of his case in the form he chose but was quite unessential to its fundamental logic. His whole chain of reasoning was independent of this concept and he realized quite clearly that the existence or nonexistence of such a standard in actual fact did not matter to him in the least. "Of such a measure," he says, "it is impossible to be possessed, because there is no commodity which is not itself exposed to the same variations as the things the value of which is to be ascertained."

3. The ideal standard is no more essential to the logic of the chapter on value than it is to the discussion of distribution. The prominent position it is given in section I of the Principles is unwarranted and our understanding of Ricardo's reasoning is greatly facilitated if we skip from the end of the tenth paragraph in section I to the beginning of section II.

17.

HLA MYINT
University of Rangoon

The Classical

View of the

Economic Problem

There seems to be a fundamental inconsistency in the currently accepted opinions concerning the classical economists. We have been brought up on the belief that their main concern is to show that the equilibrium process of the free market will lead to a more efficient allocation of resources among different industries than state interference.[1] On the other hand, we have been frequently told that the classical analysis is vitiated by the Labour theory which conceives the economic problem as the struggle of man to transform resources given by nature into material wealth. It has been said that the classical economists confuse the "economic problem," which consists in the choice between alternative methods of using given resources to maximise the satisfaction of given consumers' wants, with the "technical problem" of physical productivity; and that consequently they are guilty of a "materialist bias" (Cf., Robbins, *Nature and Significance of Economic Science*, chs. 1–3).

These two opinions are held simultaneously and implicitly by many economists and it will be seen that they are inconsistent with each other. The first credits the classical economists with an essentially correct, if rather

Reprinted from *Economica*, n.s. XIII (May 1946), 119–30, by permission of the author and the publisher. This article forms Chapter 1 of Hla Myint, *Theories of Welfare Economics* (Cambridge: Harvard University Press, 1948). At the time of original publication, the author was with Oxford University.

rough, solution of the problem of allocating scarce resources which, according to the second, they understand only imperfectly.

This inconsistency is fundamental, for the two opinions attribute to the classical economists two entirely different outlooks on the nature of the central economic problem.

When we say that the central problem of the classical economists is to allocate resources efficiently among different industries, we imply (i) that they start from the assumption of a given quantity of resources and (ii) that they are mainly concerned with the maximisation of consumers' wants as expressed by their market demands for different commodities. In short we attribute to them what is known as the "scarcity" concept of the economic problem. The efficiency of the allocation of resources among competing uses cannot be judged except on the assumption of a given quantity of scarce resources and in terms of quantities of consumers' satisfaction.

On the other hand, the Labour theory suggests an entirely different outlook on the economic problem. It starts from a fundamental contrast between land or natural resources, given once for all, and labour which is augmentable. Further, the problem of equilibrium adjustments to the consumers' demand is faded out and the analysis is largely confined to the physical level. Thus the amount of material wealth can be increased, either by raising the physical productivity of labour or by increasing the supply of labour.

The problem now is to determine which of the two view-points, the "scarcity" concept of the economic problem or the labour-theory outlook, should be regarded as the central principle which unifies the different aspects of classical economic thought into a coherent whole. In what follows it will be argued that the method of regarding the problem of allocating resources as the main concern of the classical economists fails to provide such a central unifying principle, as it fails to explain a formidable array of things which are undoubtedly characteristic features of classical thought. It fails to explain, for instance, the classical "materialist bias" as typified by J. S. Mill's concept of the "economic man" and also the classical economists' preoccupation with the problem of capital accumulation which developed into the celebrated controversy over Malthus's Glut theory. It will be argued further that once we have learnt to steep ourselves in the labour theory outlook and to regard the "allocative" problem as a subsidiary theme, all these apparently puzzling features sort themselves out into a coherent pattern and that this pattern is very different from what we normally understand by the "familiar tenets of the classical school."

I

What then is the outlook on the economic problem suggested by the labour theory? In its simplest form, the labour theory depicts a primitive agricultural community, self sufficient, and having only a rudimentary system of exchange. In this setting it is natural to look upon production as the struggle of man against nature and to measure wealth in terms of the physical product of labour. This is the starting point of Adam Smith's analysis; from it he proceeded on the assumption that the more complicated structure of a developed economy may be reduced in its essential features to this basic model of the "early and rude state of society." Thus he tried to show that behind the "veil of money" and complex relations of trade and industry, the essential nature of economic life remained the same; that it consisted in the physical process in which commodities were annually produced and consumed. From this he derived his basic criterion of economic policy: it must be favourable to the greatness of the annual produce of labour.

In the "Introduction and Plan" to the *Wealth of Nations* Smith laid down two major determinants of the size of the annual produce or the national dividend: (i) "the skill, dexterity and judgment with which its labour is generally applied" and (ii) "the proportion between the number of those who are employed in useful (or productive) labour and those who are not so employed." Smith's conception of the economic problem in a developed economy may be best understood by following up these two determinants.

(i) The first way in which the primitive economy may develop is by opening itself up for trade; by extending the area of the market and division of labour either within its own national boundary or beyond it. Starting from a technical concept of production as the tranformation of natural resources into physical products, Smith was impressed by the striking possibilities of increasing productivity by the division of labour. He put it down as the most potent method of increasing the size of the national dividend (*Op. cit.*, Cannan ed., vol. I, p. 5).

At this point it may be pointed out that one of the most powerful considerations behind Smith's desire for free trade is not the purely subjective consumers' gains from free exchange. He desired free trade mainly because it increases physical productivity by widening the scope of the division of labour and by bringing in fresh natural resources into the framework of production. Thus subjective gains apart, free trade is desired because it increases the annual produce of a country's labour even when considered at the purely physical level. In other words, free trade is a method of expanding the economic system horizontally so as to reap the advantages of increasing physical returns brought about by overcoming the technical indivisibilities of production (Cf., Allyn Young, "Increasing Returns and Economic Progress," *Economic Journal*, 1928). Perhaps one may say that the difference between the modern concept of free competition and Smith's is that the former is a method of "tightening up" the allocative efficiency within a given productive framework while the latter is a method of "widening" the area of the economy.

This does not, however, mean that Smith did not know of the existence of the subjective consumers' gains in the modern sense. In analysing the mechanism of exchange which accompanies the division of labour, he became aware of the fact that on top of the increase in physical productivity there was a further class of gains: "It gives a value to their superfluities by exchanging them for something else which may satisfy a part of their wants and increase their enjoyments" (*Ibid.*, p. 413). But this transition to the subjective level of analysis is neither clear-cut nor sustained and some of the modern interpreters are going too far when they would have us believe that Smith's central problem was to maximise the satisfaction of consumers' wants as expressed by their market demands for different commodities (e.g., M. Bowley, *Nassau Senior and the Classical Economists*, p. 67).

Perhaps a more balanced assessment of Smith's opinions on this point may be stated as follows. He would of course agree that the final aim of all production is consumption and that in the ultimate analysis wealth must consist in quantities of consumers' satisfaction. But he seems to assume implicitly that under normal conditions, i.e., in the absence of shortage or glut, the consumers' satisfaction from a commodity may be regarded as depending on its "value-in-use" as determined by its intrinsic physical properties. This amounts to assuming that quantities of satisfaction are roughly proportional to quantities of physical products. Granted this first approximation, he went on to develop the bulk of his analysis on the assumption that more substantial additions to the wealth of a nation could be made by increasing the volume of physical output rather than by making refined adjustments to the consumers' preference positions on the basis of a given volume of products. Thus, the allocative problem became a subsidiary theme and however far Smith might have leant towards the demand approach, he could confine himself to the physical level of analysis suggested by his initial labour-theory outlook. In the exchange economy, as in the primitive economy, the first major determinant of the size of the annual produce is the technical conditions governing the physical productivity of labour.

(ii) The second major determinant of the wealth of the nation, according to Smith, is the proportion in which its labour is used between "productive" and "unproductive" purposes. Without entering into a detailed discussion of the meaning of "productive" labour, we may broadly define it as that labour used for investment purposes.[2] Now, in Smith's time, fixed or durable capital played only a very small part in economic life and the bulk of investment was in the form of circulating capital or "advances to labour." Thus broadly speaking, "productive" labour may be regarded as that labour which produces material necessities or wage goods which enable society to maintain a greater quantity of labour for future production. An increase in saving thus increases the size of the wage fund which raises wages above the subsistence level and stimulates the growth of population. Thus the greater the proportion of resources used in "productive" purposes, the greater will be the supply of labour available to society.

This again accords with the labour-theory outlook, which starts from a fundamental contrast between land, the passive and nonaugmentable factor, and labour the active and augmentable factor. Given the natural resources and average productivity of labour, the size of the national dividend may be regarded as being determined by the major variable, the supply of labour. Thus the second way in which our initial model of the primitive economy may develop is to expand itself vertically, by increasing its capital accumulation and population.

The two methods of increasing the size of the national dividend, horizontally by widening the area of the market and the division of labour and vertically by increasing the supply of labour, are complementary and not competitive. However, Smith seems to think capital accumulation is the more important mainspring of economic progress. Without capital accumulation, division of labour cannot be carried out to any considerable extent and the new investment opportunities offered by a greater freedom of trade cannot be fully utilised. On the other hand, a mere increase in capital accumulation resulting in an increase in population by itself can open up enormous scope for increasing returns for labour, not only due to the "abridging of labour" by machinery, but also due to the overcoming of technical indivisibilities. Here, not having a clear idea of the principle of diminishing returns from land, Smith appears to think that a mere increase in population will increase the productivity of labour. Comparing society to a private workshop, Smith wrote: "The greater their number, the more they naturally divide themselves into the different classes and sub-divisions of employment" (*Ibid.*, p. 88).

To sum up: the labour-theory outlook systematically shifted Smith's focus of attention from the problem of allocating *given* resources among different industries to maximise the consumers' satisfaction to the problems of increasing the physical productivity of labour and the total volume of economic activity. The subjective level of analysis was pushed to the background by the broad assumption that quantities of consumers' satisfaction are roughly proportional to the quantity of physical product. The assumption of a given quantity of resources was undermined by Smith's interest in the possibilities of increasing the national dividend by increasing the degree of the division of labour and the total supply of labour.

II

After Adam Smith, the classical outlook on the economic problem moved further and further away from the problem of allocating given resources efficiently among different industries. It is true that J. B. Say, a notable disciple of Smith, made important advances in the demand approach and even initiated a minor tradition of the marginal utility and productivity analysis which included such considerable figures as Montifort Longfield and Nassau Senior (Cf., M. Bowley, *op. cit.*, ch. 2, secs. v and vi). But these economists exerted little influence on the main stream of classical economic thought. Malthus also might be regarded as a demand economist. But again his interest was centred on the influence of the total Effective Demand on the volume of employment and not on the allocative mechanism of relative demand for particular products in different markets. To him the wastages due to the collapse of general economic activity and the "glut" were overwhelmingly more important than wastages due to the mal-distribution of resources. When however we come to the main stream of classical economic thought dominated by the Ricardian tradition we find the physical output approach of the labour theory firmly established almost to a complete neglect of the allocative problem. It continued to be so until the "marginal revolution."

It is significant that the development of economic thought after Adam Smith should be given its initial impetus by a simultaneous discovery of the principle of diminishing returns from land by many economists, notably by West, Anderson and Malthus. This discovery was brought to a head by government enquiries into the state of British agriculture. But even without that external stimulus, it would probably have been discovered since it is the next step of generalisation to be arrived at by the logic of the man-against-nature view of the economic problem. It laid down a basic relation between the constant factor, land, and the variable factor, labour, and set a determinate limit to the process in which additional doses of labour can be applied to a given quantity of natural resources.

Perhaps the way in which this development affected the classical analysis can be illustrated by adopting the expositionary device suggested by Smith, viz., to regard society as one giant firm, employing one main type of variable factor, labour, and producing a single "commodity," which we may call "corn" after Ricardo, meaning by it a more or less homogeneous physical mass of "material necessities" or wage goods. Smith had pictured this giant firm as working under increasing returns; as being capable of almost unlimited expansion either by free trade or capital accumulation.

What the Ricardian theory of Distribution in fact did was to curb this expansive optimism by showing that society as a giant firm would be working, on the contrary, under conditions of diminishing returns and that there would be a determinate limit to which population could expand, marked by the stationary state. Ricardo argued that the increase in population brought about by progressive capital accumulation would extend the margin of cultivation to poorer lands where a greater quantity of labour would be required to produce a standard unit of "corn." The price of "corn" would then rise and a higher rent would be claimed by the owners of the better grade land. Since real wages could not fall below the minimum subsistence level, money wages would rise which would in turn lower the rate of profit. Expansion would come to a stop when the marginal product of labour had fallen so low as to leave nothing for the capitalists after wages and rents had been paid off; for at this point, there would be no further incentive to accumulate capital and expand economic activity. Thus the emphasis was shifted from the absolute scale of social production to the social net product or the "Net Revenue" which increases at a diminishing rate as the scale of production is expanded. Thus Ricardo argued that it was not enough to infer the wealth of society from the Gross Revenue as Smith had done; we must further examine the balance sheet of the giant firm to find out how much net product in terms of "corn" has been left, after the wages of labour have been paid off. "Provided its net real income, its rents and profits be the same, it is of no importance whether the nation

447

consists of ten or twelve millions of inhabitants" (Ricardo, *Principles of Political Economy*, Everyman's edition, pp. 234–235). The aim of economic policy was thus to increase the net social output rather than the absolute scale of social production.

Malthus's contribution consisted in showing that it was not sufficient to regard society merely as a giant producing unit; and that it should also be studied as a giant consuming unit. He believed that there was no automatic synchronisation of society's capacity to produce and its capacity to consume; and that an attempt to expand economic activity by capital accumulation would result in a breakdown and a glut, long before the extreme limit of Ricardo's stationary equilibrium was reached.

We have not simplified the essential features of the classical analysis by suggesting the analogy of a giant firm producing a single commodity, "corn," with a single variable factor, labour. In the light of economic conditions existing at that time, there is much to be said for such a method of abstraction. In those days, wage goods in fact consisted of a few primary products which could be lumped together under the head of a single commodity, "corn," and the output of "corn" could then be used as a convenient index of the output of consumers' goods in general. At the subsistence level of real wages, "determined by the habits and customs of the people," a given output of "corn" could maintain a determinate quantity of labour. Labour, being a versatile factor, could then be turned to the production of all sorts of articles, both "necessities" and "luxuries," particularly so when the bulk of the luxury consumption was in the form of direct personal services. The concept of labour as the single variable factor is again a justifiable assumption. As we have pointed out, fixed capital played a relatively unimportant part in the economic life of that time and investment was mainly in the form of "advances to labour." Since land was assumed to be fixed in supply, social output could then be treated as the function of a single major variable, the quantity of labour.

It might at first sight be thought that an economic system supposed to produce a single "commodity" with a single variable factor could not give rise to any economic problems as we understand them nowadays; that once it is assumed that quantities of satisfaction are proportionate to the quantities of physical products, all problems of production would be of a purely technical nature. This however, is not true. For even when we have completely faded out the problem of allocating given resources among competing industries (and this extreme measure is not adopted by the classical economists), there still remains a major problem of choice: the choice between using labour directly for present consumption, or using it indirectly or "productively" so as to increase its own supply and thus increase future consumption. Here, the modern economist, working at the subjective level of analysis, would say resources should be allocated between present and future consumption, according to the time preferences of the consumers. The classical economists, however, were working at the physical level of analysis. Since they believed that quantities of satisfaction are proportional to quantities of physical product, they arrived at the following interesting conclusion: optimum allocation between present and future would be attained when the physical product of direct labour is equal to that of indirect or "stored up" labour. That is to say, so long as the "round-about-method" of production yields a greater physical product than direct labour, additional investment would increase the economic welfare of society. Thus, the stationary equilibrium at which the rate of profits is reduced to zero may be regarded as the point of optimum investment according to Ricardo, although he was far from being cheered by its prospect.

Thus again we have a shift of the centre of attention from the problem of allocating *given* resources among different consumers' goods industries to the broader problem of distributing the resources between the consumers' goods and the producers' goods sectors of the economic system with a view to expanding the total volume of economic activity. Ricardo and Malthus might not be able to agree on the ideal "balance of production and consumption"; but they did agree that the key to economic prosperity depended on this balance. Malthus, with his Effective Demand approach, might not be able to accept the physical output approach of Ricardo, but he devoted the whole Book II of his *Principles of Political Economy* to the problem of Economic Progress and not to the problem of Economic Equilibrium. The fact that the "glut controversy" became the foremost issue of those times is a sufficient indication how far the centre of attention had shifted away from the equilibrium adjustments of relative consumers' demand in different industries to the savings-investment nexus.

III

The triumph of the Ricardians in the "glut" controversy was such that even that fragment of subjective element contained in Malthus's Effective Demand theory disappeared from classical economic thought. With J. S. Mill, technological considerations became predominant and the physical output approach was completely systematised.

This is apparent from the celebrated arrangement of the contents of his *Principles* which set the tradition of dividing the subject-matter of economics into Production, Distribution and Exchange. In Book I, under the heading of Production were considered those topics, later on to be repeated *ad nauseam* by the old-fashioned textbooks, e.g., advantages of division of labour, different laws of returns in agriculture and industry, relative merits of the large- and small-scale production, etc., all bearing on the technical efficiency of the producing unit in the best tradition of scientific factory organisation. The underlying idea of this Book is that the size of the national dividend is determined entirely by technology and the laws of changes in the supply of factors, almost independently of the equilibrium process of the market.

When Distribution and Exchange were introduced in Books II and III, they merely played a secondary role of parcelling out this predetermined block of wealth, national dividend, among different individuals according to the prevailing system of economic organisation. It was not thought that

449

Distribution and Exchange could directly affect the size of the national dividend.

Hence followed Mill's famous distinction between the laws of Production which are immutable physical laws and the laws of Distribution and Exchange which pertain to existing social institutions.

"The laws and conditions of Production of wealth partake of the character of physical truths. There is nothing optional or arbitrary in them. Whatever mankind produces must be produced in the modes and conditions imposed by the constitution of external things and by the inherent properties of their bodily and mental structure. — The opinions and wishes which may exist in these matters do not control the things themselves." (J. S. Mill, *Principles of Political Economy*, Ashley ed., pp. 199–200.)

Having absorbed Rae's theory of saving as the choice between the present and future consumption, Mill appears to be rather uneasy about the fact that the quantity of capital accumulation, a major determinant of the physical output, would depend on human choice. But he heroically stuck to his deterministic theory of production by arguing that the "excess of production above the physical necessaries of the producers" not only offered the upper limit to savings, but also partly contributed to "determine how much would be saved." (*Ibid.*, p. 164, cf. p. 175).

With this deterministic theory of production there was a shift of emphasis from Adam Smith's concept of wealth as a flow of "annual produce," or the national dividend, to the concept of wealth as a stock, the national capital. Since the size of the physical output was supposed to follow as a determinate technical function from a given stock of resources and technique, the wealth of society could simply be measured by measuring the physical magnitude of its capital stock. Hence, more than any other classical economist, Mill made it a principle to exclude immaterial services from his "philosophically correct" definition of wealth as "instruments, meaning not only tools and machinery alone, but the whole accumulation possessed by individuals and communities" for the attainment of their ends. (*Ibid.*, pp. 8–9).

"It is essential to the idea of wealth to be susceptible to accumulation; things which cannot, after being produced, be kept for some time before being used are never regarded as wealth, since however much of them may be produced or enjoyed, the person benefited by them is no wise richer, is no wise improved in circumstances" (*Ibid.*, p. 47).

Thus the tendency of the nineteenth-century statisticians like Giffen to give pride of place to the calculation of the national capital rather than that of national income was in line with the economic theory of their time (Cf. Giffen, *The Growth of National Capital*).

Finally, it may be noted that once wealth was defined in a thoroughgoing materialistic fashion, Mill's much maligned concept of the "economic man" became the necessary logical prop to support the whole approach. It was merely a more explicit and courageous formulation of the idea which was implicit in the minds of most of the classical economists, viz., quantities of consumers' satisfaction might be assumed as being roughly proportional to quantities of physical product and that therefore a greater quantity of physical product or material wealth would be normally more preferable than a lesser quantity.

IV

Our interpretation of the classical outlook on the economic problem, if accepted, seems to cast a serious doubt on the practice of taking it for granted that the central problem of the classical economists was to demonstrate the "allocative efficiency" of the equilibrium adjustments to consumers' demand in the free market. We have seen that they were concerned, not so much with the problem of maximising consumers' satisfaction in the modern sense, as with the problem of increasing the total physical output. The central principle, which successfully unifies the various classical economic doctrines from Adam Smith to J. S. Mill, embodies the following fundamental proposition: viz., the economic welfare of society can be more effectively promoted (i) by increasing the physical productivity of labour and (ii) by increasing the total volume of economic activity,[3] rather than by tamely accepting the given quantity of productive resources and making refined adjustments in allocating them among different industries. From this follow the two major canons of classical economic policy: (i) free trade which extends the scope of division of labour and brings fresh resources into the productive framework and (ii) capital accumulation which enables society to maintain a greater quantity of labour.

What we have said above does not, of course, mean that none of the classical economists were ever concerned with the "allocative" problem. This would be going to the other extreme. A careful reading of the *Wealth of Nations* would reveal that Smith's analysis of this problem was on the whole confined to two odd chapters, chs. 7 and 9, Bk. I; but that within this narrow compass Smith succeeded in showing that the equilibrium process of the competitive market will lead to an optimum allocation of resources among different industries whether or not we share his metaphysical optimism concerning the working of the "invisible hand." Again, Ricardo's theory of Comparative Cost (as distinct from Smith's theory of increasing returns from expansion of international trade) might be regarded as a classic piece of optimum reasoning, although Ricardo confined himself to the physical level of analysis and was concerned only with the technical optimum and not with the subjective optimum.[4] Finally, we might consider J. S. Mill's theory of reciprocal demand in international trade as opening up the whole avenue of demand approach.

All these points should be admitted. But even so, it is a far cry from this to the belief that the "allocative" problem was the *central* preoccupation of the classical economists. As we have tried to show, the truth of the matter was that taking classical literature as a whole, considerations concerning "allocative" efficiency were eclipsed by broader considerations concerning the means of raising the physical productivity of labour and expanding the total volume of economic activity. Once this is admitted, to exalt the "allocative" problem into the central problem of classical economics seems to be nothing short of reading our present-day preoccupation with the "allocative" problem into the classics through the distorting spectacles provided by the General Equilibrium economists of the Marginal Utility school. It is time we learnt to cure ourselves of this theoretical anthropomorphism and to approach the classical economists in the context of their own intellectual climate.

Were the classical economists, then, guilty of a confusion between the "technical" and the "economic" problem? If we accept their method of analysis at the physical level, the answer on the whole is no. It is true that the less gifted followers of the classical economists frequently got themselves lost in the niggling details of technological efficiency. But none of the major classical economists, with the possible exception of J. S. Mill, seems to be guilty of the "confusion between the technical and the economic problem," at least in the sense in which the present writer understands the phrase. That is to say, unlike the full-blooded technocrats they were not bemused by the purely technological or engineering possibilities of increasing output divorced from the economic calculus based on the relation between cost and output. If they get different results from us (e.g., they would advocate saving beyond the time-preferences of the savers so long as indirect labour yields a higher physical product than direct labour), it is because they were applying the economic calculus to physical quantities of labour and physical quantities of output. Perhaps Henry Sidgwick restated the classical position most clearly when he explained that:

"The use of a more efficient machinery would not always result in the efficiency of labour as a whole: since the better instrument might require more labour to make and to keep in repair, and it is possible that this extra labour might be more productive if applied in some other way. Thus an invention *technically* successful may fail *economically*" (*Principles of Political Economy*, 3rd ed., pp. 124–5).

Of course it is quite true that a full distinction between the "technical" and the "economic" problem is not possible unless we can take into account the consumers' wants; unless we can choose among the many technically efficient ways of production a particular method which maximises the consumers' satisfaction according to the existing relative prices of the factors and the products. But may we not start with the physical level of analysis as a first approximation, always remembering that a second and more close approximation can be attained only by a further analysis at the subjective level?

After all, even when the economic welfare of society is regarded as consisting in the satisfaction of individuals' wants, it cannot be denied that this subjective economic welfare is as much quantitatively affected by the techno-institutional factors as by the equilibrium process of the market. Or perhaps even more. Therefore, it is not surprising that after decades of work on the "allocative" problem many modern economists should have turned their attention to such problems as output per man-hour, the extent of unused capacity, the socially desirable rate of investment, etc., problems having a distinctly classical flavour.

NOTES

1. For recent examples of this belief see A. P. Lerner's *Economics of Control*, p. 67, and T. de Scitovszky "A Note on Welfare Propositions in Economics," *Review of Economic Studies*, November 1941, pp. 77–8.

2. Cf. my article "The Welfare Significance of Productive Labour," *Review of Economic Studies*, Winter, 1943.

3. This is quite compatible with Ricardo's emphasis on Net Revenue since expansion in total economic activity will increase the absolute size of the Net Revenue, although at a diminishing rate.

4. I.e., Ricardo was concerned with getting maximum physical output out of a given quantity of labour and not with getting maximum consumers' satisfaction out of a given quantity of product. Thus foreign trade "will very powerfully contribute to increase the mass of commodities and *therefore* the sum of enjoyments." *Principles*, Everyman's edition, p. 77 (Italics mine); also *ibid.*, p. 81. Quantities of satisfaction are still implicitly assumed to be proportional to quantities of physical products.

18.

BERNICE SHOUL
Bard College

Karl Marx

and

Say's Law

I. INTRODUCTION

A. The Need for Systematizing Marx's Position on Say's Law

For one hundred and fifty years economic theory has built on the corner-stone of classical economics — Say's Law of Markets.[1] In one or more of its various meanings and implications this "law" has been involved in all economic analysis, and has been the source of much needless controversy. This includes the long and inconclusive controversy concerning Karl Marx's position on Say's Law and his related theories of crises and evolution.

The reason for the present article on Marx and Say's Law is that it still appears that Marx's position has not been clarified, any more than the meanings and implications of Say's Law have been agreed upon. What follows is an attempt to show that differences of opinion on Marx's position on Say's Law arise both from differences of emphasis on the various meanings and uses of the "law" per se, and from differing views as to which arguments of Marx were directed toward these various interpretations of Say's Law. It is hoped that this discussion will show (1) that Marx's position on Say's Law was not a self-contradictory one, as has been alleged; and (2) that although

Reprinted from *The Quarterly Journal of Economics*, LXXI (November 1957), 611–29, slightly enlarged, by permission of the author and The Harvard University Press. Copyright, 1957, by the President and Fellows of Harvard College.

his position was a complicated one, it can be systematized from an examination of his theoretical structures, some of which assume certain aspects of Say's Law and some of which do not.[2]

Inasmuch as Marx did develop several models of the capitalist system in order to analyze different essential features of this system, and inasmuch as Say's Law has several meanings, it is important to know in which of his models and for what reasons Marx accepted or rejected the different aspects of the law. The Marxian models to be considered are the following: (1) the circular flow model which postulates Say's Law; (2) the model of monetary exchange which denies Say's Law; and (3) the dynamic model which provisionally assumes Say's Law only as a means for demonstrating a tendency to breakdown and the inevitability of crises and cycles in spite of the operation of Say's Law.

Differences of opinion are found among recent experts on Marx as to the very existence, as well as to the nature, of his theory of crises and cycles. All are agreed that Marx denied the validity of Say's Law; that is, that he argued against its central proposition that there could be no endogenously created crises.

But on more than this there is no agreement and the debate continues as to "what Marx really meant." Schumpeter contended that although in Marx's work there are valuable insights into the nature of crises, and that Marx was, in fact, the first economist to see the cycle as a whole, no single cycle theory can be found in, or reconstructed from, his work without many additional hypotheses.[3] Maurice Dobb, on the other hand, argued that, "Undoubtedly, for Marx the most important application of his theory was in the analysis of the character of economic crises,"[4] and that Marx's cycle theory was specifically based on the interaction of the falling tendency of the rate of profit and the countertendencies to this law.[5] Paul Sweezy wrote that in Marx there are elements of two cycle theories; one, somewhat inconclusive and unconvincing, based on the falling tendency of the rate of profit, and the other, more important, but not systematized by Marx himself, based on a disproportion between the growth in output and demand for consumption goods.[6] Joan Robinson argued that this disproportion between the output of consumption goods and effective demand is the cycle theory that Marx *would* have developed had he not been taken up by the "false scent" of the falling rate of profit which, she argued, explains nothing at all.[7]

The conclusions of the present essay on Marx are (1) that he was indeed "opposed" to Say's Law for the reasons (primarily monetary) generally adduced; (2) but that his position was more complicated than that of simple opposition, since some of his models postulate Say's Law; and (3) that the theory of crises and cycles for which there seems the best evidence in Marx is one of inadequate profits, *independent* of any shortage of demand, a consequence of more fundamental contradictions than those arising from the nonfulfillment of Say's Law. In other words, according to the present writer, Marx rejected Say's Law in so far as it generalized both the essential nature of the capitalist system and the mechanisms of its equilibration, but he accepted Say's Law merely as a formal statement of the logic of the economic circular flow, and also used it in the initial development of his own theory of "breakdown." Thus, Marx rejected the premises and implications of Say's Law as concealing the essential nature of the capitalist system. Yet, at the same time, he built an economic model himself in which crises and cycles would occur *in spite of the operation of Say's Law,* in spite of the assumption of equilibrium between supply and demand.

B. The "Duality" of Marx's Position on Say's Law

The duality of Marx's position on Say's Law has been noted by Joan Robinson as follows:

> Marx evidently failed to realize how much the orthodox theory stands or falls with Say's Law and set himself the task of discovering a theory of crises which would apply to a world in which Say's Law was fulfilled, as well as the theory which arises when Say's Law is exploded. This dualism implants confusion in Marx's own argument, and, still more, in the arguments of his successors.[8]

Could it not be the case that the confusion to which Mrs. Robinson refers arises from a failure to see that for Marx the world dominated by Say's Law and the world in which it is exploded are, in fact, two models of the capitalist system, each constructed for a different purpose? Marx's theoretical world in which Say's Law dominates is an abstract model of pure, competitive capitalism. This ideal capitalism is so "pure," in fact, that all but industrial capital is excluded, commodities exchange at their normal labor values without price deviation, there are no problems of lags, frictions, or monetary difficulties. The theoretical world in which Say's Law is exploded is a closer approximation to reality but it is still a theoretical model which assumes away any "faulty distribution of social labor among the individual spheres of production."[9]

The contradiction in the two models is no accident, although it is unfortunate that Marx did not make his method clear. The purpose of establishing the first model, the world in which Say's Law dominates, was to demonstrate that the "law of motion" of capitalist society produces not only a *tendency* to ultimate stagnation, or breakdown, but crises and business cycles as well, *even when the equilibrium conditions of Say's Law are fulfilled.* The purpose of establishing the second model was to point out the ever-present *possibility* of crises occasioned by the fact that the capitalist economy is one of *monetary exchange,* not of *barter.* In the world dominated by Say's Law, the drive for profits produces cycles endogenously in spite of the fulfillment of the equilibrium conditions postulated by the law. In the world where Say's Law is exploded crises occur *because of the very nature of commodity exchange.*

II. THE FOUR MEANINGS OF SAY'S LAW

It is possible that much of the confusion about Marx's position on Say's Law arises from the failure to specify the various meanings and implications of Say's Law, on which Marx did take different but not contradictory positions. It may be useful to recall the four essential meanings of Say's Law, as developed by Say and, more fully, by Mill and Ricardo. These are as follows. (1) Supply creates its own demand; hence, aggregate overproduction or a "general glut" is impossible. (2) Since goods exchange against goods, money is but a "veil" and plays no independent role. (3) In the case of partial overproduction, which necessarily implies a balancing underproduction elsewhere, equilibrium is restored by competition, that is, by the price mechanism and the mobility of capital. (4) Because aggregate demand and supply are necessarily equal, and because of the equilibrating mechanisms, output can be increased indefinitely and the accumulation of capital proceed without limit.

It was Ricardo's explicit formulation of Say's Law to which Marx's primary criticism was directed. In Ricardo all four meanings of the law are clearly stated. In regard to the first two meanings of the law, those relating to aggregate demand and the role of money, Ricardo asserted,

Productions are always bought by productions, or by services; money is only the medium by which the exchange is effected. Too much of a particular commodity may be produced, of which there may be such a glut in the market as not to repay the capital expended on it; but this cannot be the case with respect to all commodities; . . .[10]

Of the third meaning of the law, relating to partial overproduction, he wrote,

Mistakes may be made, and commodities not suited to the demand may be produced — of these there may be a glut; they may not sell at their usual price; but then this is owing to the mistake and not to the want of demand for production.[11]

Ricardo's view on the fourth meaning of the law regarding accumulation was that,

There cannot, then, be accumulated in a country any amount of capital which cannot be employed productively until wages rise so high in consequence of the rise of necessaries, and so little consequently remains for the profits of stock, that the motive for accumulation ceases.[12]

Ricardo's explicit limit to capital accumulation, the adequacy of profits, is not a contradiction of Say's Law, in so far as the law concerns the adequacy of *demand* at any level of output and assumes an adequate motive for continued supply. The tendency to stagnation which Ricardo indicated is theoretically possible even while Say's Law in its other aspects is fulfilled. This tendency to stagnation was deduced by appealing to additional postulates, those relating to population growth and the physical productivity of land. Say's Law in itself implies the possibility of equilibrium at all levels of output and the unlimited development of an inherently adaptive economy.[13]

Marx's position, as distinct from that of Ricardo, essentially was that (1) general overproduction *becomes* possible precisely because (2) money, while a "veil" only in the sense that it is a medium of exchange, is also a store of value in commodity exchange, and that this exchange is a dual one whose parts may be separated in time and place. As a consequence, (3) partial overproduction is almost inevitable and easily can produce a cumulative downward spiral. And, most important, (4) even if Say's Law were fulfilled, unlimited accumulation is impossible because of (for reasons other than those advanced by Ricardo) the fall in the rate of profit.

III.   MARX ON SAY'S LAW AS THE CIRCULAR FLOW

Marx's reproduction models[14] postulate the operation of Say's Law. What is involved is his explicit recognition of the economic circular flow. In these models, aggregate output is divided into two departments, Department I representing producers' goods and Department II representing consumers' goods. The output of each department equals the inputs of "constant" capital (machinery and raw materials) and "variable" capital (wages) plus the "surplus value" (profit) created.

The equilibrium conditions for "simple reproduction" and for accumulation are that in each case the constant capital of the *second* (consumers' goods) department is equal to the variable capital plus the surplus value of the *first* department (producers' goods).

Marx's reproduction models express the same tautologies as are contained in Say's Law, that aggregate demand is elicited by and is identically equal to aggregate supply, that consumption equals production, and that revenues equal sales. The equilibrium conditions are met via the exchanges within and between the two departments. So far Marx used a familiar tool, although his was the first (and more elaborate) exposition of the circular flow since Quesnay.

In setting up his formal reproduction schemes and their conditions of equilibrium, Marx thus followed in the classical tradition. His criticism of classical economists, particularly of Say, is entirely different from that of the classical critics of Say's Law — Malthus especially — and some of Marx's own successors, notably Rosa Luxembourg, who tried to negate Say's Law by proving an error in the logic of Marx's own reproduction models.

It might seem unnecessary to deal with the economic logic behind both Say's Law as a model of the circular flow and Marx's own reproduction schemes, in view of the fact that Schumpeter's analyses of the circular flow and Leontief's input-output analyses have once more made the "tableau economique" a basic instrument of economic reasoning. However, it was the central issue in the old classical controversy on Say's Law, notably in the debates between Malthus and Ricardo, and in the controversies among Marx's followers.

Malthus believed he negated Say's Law and proved the possibility (and likelihood) of general gluts with his arguments concerning (1) the exchange of commodities against money and labor, as different from exchange against other commodities,[15] and (2) the limits to accumulation arising from the falling rate of profit.[16] However, the inadequacy of effective demand which, in Malthus' view, made for the general glut, was funda-

mentally an inadequacy *built into his own theoretical system.* This is because of his very definition of value, which he measured by the labor which
commodities could *command,* not as with Ricardo, by the labor which commodities *embodied.* According to Malthus' definition, aggregate demand
(subsistence wages, or labor "commanded") is defined in terms of the labor
contained in commodities, and aggregate supply in terms of this quantity
plus the surplus, or profit, created in production. Thus, given Malthus' particular theory of value, Say's Law *could* not hold, and, as Ricardo finally
pointed out, Malthus' debates with Ricardo could lead nowhere because
they started from different premises.[17]

In the case of Rosa Luxembourg who believed Marx should have been
completely opposed to Say's Law, the argument (although based on the
labor-embodied theory of value) also concerns difficulties in the "realization" of aggregate output, not in the case of simple reproduction, but only
of expanded reproduction, or accumulation.[18] However, in Marx, accumulation itself furnishes the demand for these additional commodities although
Luxembourg did not see this. Hence her own logically impossible solution —
the noncapitalist market which somehow buys without ever selling anything.

Thus Luxembourg's "correction" of Marx's reproduction model, which
itself formally expresses one aspect of Say's Law, rests on misunderstanding,[19] rather than on a logically alternative economic model. On the level
of abstract economic logic, both Say's Law and Marx's reproduction models
are but tautological expressions of the necessary equality of aggregate supply and demand. On this level a logically alternative model is not possible.
It is in this sense that, as a first approximation, Marx constructed a theoretical world where Say's Law dominates.

IV. THE EQUALITY OF AGGREGATE DEMAND AND SUPPLY
AND THE "MONEY VEIL"; MARX'S ANSWER
TO SAY'S LAW

In a different model from that discussed above, however, Marx argued
that Say's Law *could not* operate. This is precisely because, while in the
circular flow model it appears that commodities do exchange against commodities, in a model concentrating on the *monetary* exchange of commodities, it becomes clear that commodities must first exchange against money
before they can exchange against each other. Marx's contention was that it
is this dual exchange that gives the ever-present possibility of crises.

The fundamental theorem of Say's Law that, because commodities really
exchange against each other, money is merely an instrument of exchange,
represented for Marx a complete misapprehension of the fundamental
nature of the capitalist economy. He believed that it is the specific peculiarity of the capitalist system that commodity exchange is a dual one, an
exchange of qualitatively different use values which are at the same time
quantitatively equal exchange values. It is this duality, he argued, that gives
rise to problems unknown in a barter economy, where use values are ex-

459

changed directly without being transformed and circulated as exchange values via the instrument of money. It is this dual nature of the commodity (as use value and as exchange value), which he called the key to the capitalist system, the "pivot on which a clear comprehension of political economy turns."[20] According to Marx it was because the classical economists worked only within a model suitable for a barter economy that they failed to see this duality and thus failed to see the possibilities of endogenous crises. Marx's critique of the classical model, contained in his analysis of Ricardo, is as follows:

In order to prove that capitalist production cannot lead to general crises, all conditions and determining forms, all principles and *differentiae specificae*, in short, capitalist production itself, is denied. In fact, it is proven that if the capitalist form of production, instead of a specifically developed, particular form of social production, were rather a form of production more elementary than its earliest beginnings, then its particular oppositions and contradictions, and, therefore, their eruption in crisis, would not exist.

According to Ricardo, following Say, products are always bought by products or services; money is only the medium through which the exchange is accomplished.

Thus, in the first place, the commodity, in which there is an opposition between use value and exchange value, is transformed into a mere product (use value), therefore, the exchange of commodities into mere exchange of products, that is, mere use values. That means not only going back to a stage before capitalist production, but even before the mere production of commodities; and it means assuming away the most complicated phenomenon of capitalist production — the world market crisis — by denying the first condition of capitalist production, namely, that the product must be a commodity, must therefore appear in the form of money, and must go through the process of metamorphosis. Instead of speaking of wage-labor, he speaks of "services," a word in which the specific characteristics of wage-labor, and its use — namely, to increase the value of the commodities against which it is exchanged and thus to generate surplus value — is again omitted, and thereby, also, the specific relationship through which money and commodity are transformed into capital. . . . Money . . . is considered only as a means of exchange, not as an essential and necessary form of existence of the commodity, which must present itself as exchange value, namely as general social labor. By striking out the essence of exchange value through transforming the commodity into a mere use value (product) one can easily deny, and, in fact, must deny, an essential, independent form which also has an independent existence, as against the original form of the commodity, in the process of the metamorphosis. Here the crises are reasoned away by forgetting or denying the first prerequisites of capitalist production, the existence of the product as a commodity, the duplication of the commodity in commodity and money, the resulting separation in the exchange of commodities, and, finally, the relationship of money or the commodity to wage labor.[21]

Instead of the classical picture Marx's second model is of a world in which crises are always possible precisely because of the dual nature of the commodity and the "metamorphosis" of its exchange value from commodity to money and back again to commodity. Marx claimed that it is this necessary transformation of value which gives rise to what he called the two *abstract forms of crises.*

Underlying the metamorphosis of the commodity there was, for Marx (and in his view not understood by the classical economists), the metamorphosis of "social labor." This is the abstract, undifferentiated labor whose quantitative equality in the exchange process is what transforms qualitatively different use values, produced by labor of specific skills, into *quantitatively equivalent* exchange values. Thus, the dual nature of the commodity was traced to the dual nature of labor in capitalist society, and, consequently, the dual nature of exchange to the dual nature of the commodity form itself. Marx explained this theoretical foundation of his system in great detail in the first two chapters of *Capital*, I. It is the very basis of his critique of Say's Law and classical economics in *Theorien über den Mehrwert.*

This foundation deserves emphasis lest it be concluded that Marx's opposition to Say's Law was a purely monetary one, and that he considered the structure and disruptions of the monetary system, or the "behavior of money" to be an independent cause of crises. Marx's criticism of Say's Law may be called "monetary criticism" only to the extent that it stresses the difficulties inherent in monetary exchange. But it must be made clear that this "monetary criticism" refers not simply to "unneutral money" (as opposed to the classical "money veil") but arises from Marx's theory of the dual nature of labor and of the commodity in the capitalist economy.

In his most succinct analysis of the possibilities of crises, Marx did not give details but presented rather a purely formal case. The analysis specifies the two essential features of the exchange of commodities that make crises possible. These are (1) the separation of purchase and sale, inevitable in any money economy, and (2) the fact that money, the universal store of value, is used as a means of payment to bridge this separation. It is a specification of the "formal possibilities" of crises rather than a theory of the causes of crises, as sometimes has been inferred. Marx's argument is as follows.

The most abstract form of the crisis, and, therefore, the formal possibility of crisis, is, thus, the metamorphosis of the commodity itself, which . . . contains the contradictions between use value and exchange value included in the unity of the commodity, and between money and commodity. . .[22]

The crisis in its second form arises from the function of money as a means of payment, whereby money figures in two different moments separated in time, and in two different functions. . . . Both of these forms are entirely abstract although the second is more concrete than the first.[23]

(1) *The Separation of Purchase and Sale.* The metamorphosis of commodities, the transformation of exchange value from commodity to money to commodity, means that sale and purchase are distinct in both time and place. Commodity exchange, unlike barter, the direct exchange of use values, presents the ever-present possibility that the commodity, which exists *actually* as a use value, and only *ideally* as an exchange value, may

not be *realized* as an exchange value. "No one can sell unless some one else purchases. But no one is forthwith bound to purchase because he has just sold."[24]

The metamorphosis of commodity-capital, C-M-C, presupposes the inverse metamorphosis of money-capital, M-C-M. A disturbance of the latter metamorphosis thus means a disturbance of the former.

If the interval in time between the two complementary phases of the complete metamorphosis of a commodity becomes too great, if the split between the sale and the purchase becomes too pronounced, the intimate connection between them, their oneness, asserts itself by producing — a crisis.[25]

And, according to Marx, the crisis is nothing more than the process by which the unity of production and circulation, of purchase and sale, is forcibly restored.[26]

(2) *Money as Means of Payment.* The fact that money serves not only as the means of circulation, but also as a means of payment (since it is a store of value), gives rise to the second possibility of crises. Thus if any commodity cannot be sold in a given period of time, whether because of changes in tastes or savings habits, money can no longer fulfill its function as a means of payment. A single producer cannot pay his debts or realize the value of his commodities. This means that the whole network of mutual debts and obligations is disturbed. According to Marx, this second possibility of crises is always accompanied by the first, the separation of purchase and sale. But the first possibility may exist without the second, that is, independently of the fact that money serves as a means of payment (which *may* be hoarded) and independently of the use of credit. This second possibility of crises is realized not because commodities are unsaleable as such, but because they are unsaleable within a given period. Marx asserted that all monetary crises are, in fact, the realization of this second abstract form of crisis.[27]

Marx's summary discussion of the possibilities of crises is useful not simply as a summary, but also because it contains a warning against confusing the *formal possibilities* of crises with their *cause*.

The general possibility of crises is the formal metamorphosis of capital itself, the separation of purchase and sale in time and space. But this is not the cause of crises. It is nothing more than the most general form of crises, thus of the crisis in its most general expression. *One cannot say that the most abstract form of the crisis is the cause of crises.* If one seeks the cause, it is precisely to understand why the form of its possibility becomes a reality.

The general conditions of crisis . . . must be developed from the general conditions of capitalist production.[28]

In his specific discussion of Say's Law and of the formal possibilities and realization of crises, Marx did *not* develop the cycle theory that would indicate the fundamental "cause" of crises. This can be found in *Capital*, III, although it requires considerable reconstruction to make Marx's meaning clear.

Marx held that in the crises of reality the "formal possibilities of crises" become realized in a variety of ways. As a consequence, the precipitating factor which actually sets off any given crisis thus *appears* to be causal. But, according to Marx, such a precipitating factor is more superficial and should not be confused with the more fundamental "cause" of crises, the "general conditions of capitalist production." He gave numerous examples of such disturbances of equilibrium. For instance, the crisis can be set off by a monetary stringency. Or it might be precipitated by an inequality of depreciation reserves and the replacement needs of fixed capital. Or changes in the period of capital turnover, or of consumers' tastes, or of savings habits — all these can precipitate a crisis, make a formal possibility a reality, and by so doing give the crisis its unique historical features. Marx did not develop his argument to deal with the details of the concrete and varying disturbances of equilibrium. This is because he was more concerned with showing that, contrary to Say's Law, the very nature of the system makes crises always possible. However, Marx noted that the real crisis, when it did appear, whatever its precipitating factors, always seems to be due to partial overproduction somewhere in the system which is not corrected according to Say's Law, but spreads and cumulates into general overproduction.

V. MARX'S VIEW OF PARTIAL OVERPRODUCTION AND THE GENERAL GLUT

The theorem that partial gluts cannot lead to a general glut is central to Say's Law. The general acceptance of this theorem among nineteenth century economists, despite its blatant contradiction by reality, can be explained only by the facts that at the time when classical economics was in full flower the business cycle was in its infancy and that early crises were, in fact, associated with monetary and trade difficulties, which, it could be argued, arose from exogenous sources, from wars, politics, and errors in banking and trade policy.[29] In logic the theorem follows directly from the postulate that aggregate supply and demand are equal and from the theorems of competitive price adaptations and of factor mobility. Thus in theory no endogenously created crises are possible.

The inadequacy of the explanation brought forth criticism at the time, long before that of Marx. One of the chief critics was Malthus. Another was Sismondi, who, writing at the same time (1819) as Malthus, denied the self-regulating feature of the classical model. His arguments are based on various grounds, including the inadequacy of mass purchasing power and, more specifically, on the time lag between production and consumption and on frictions which prevent the equalization of supply and demand for specific commodities.[30]

Marx's view of the general glut differs from that of Sismondi in so far as he considered the "contradictions" of capitalism to be more fundamental than those of lags and frictions, and further disagreed with the assumption, implicit in Sismondi, more explicit in Rodbertus,[31] that crises could be

463

avoided by a different distribution of purchasing power within the capitalist economy. Because his interest in capitalism was in its fundamental tendencies, Marx had little to say about the failure of the competitive mechanism to adjust the malallocation of resources responsible for partial overproduction. What he did say was that, by its very nature, an unplanned economy would produce too much or too little of specific commodities, and that price adjustments and factor mobility were inadequate to prevent such errors from leading to a general glut. Moreover, Marx argued that not only was there continual price deviation from value, but there was also an additional difficulty in the fact that changes in productivity continually alter values themselves.[32] In any case, if overproduction appears in a sector of some importance and it becomes necessary to sell commodities at prices which do not cover costs, the difficulty multiplies and the result is — the general glut.

Marx's description of what happens is classic:

> But under all circumstances the equilibrium is restored by making more or less capital unproductive or destroying it. This would affect to some extent the material substance of capital, that is, a part of the means of production, fixed and circulating capital, would not perform any service as capital; a portion of the running establishments would then close down. Of course, time would corrode and depreciate all means of production (except land), but this particular stagnation would cause a far more serious destruction of means of production. However, the main effect in this case would be to suspend the functions of some means of production and prevent them for a shorter or longer time from serving as means of production.
>
> The principal work of destruction would show its most dire effects in a slaughtering of the *values* of capitals. That portion of the value of capital which exists only in the form of claims on future shares of surplus-value or profit, which consists in fact of creditor's notes on production in its various forms, would be immediately depreciated by the reduction of the receipts on which it is calculated. One portion of the gold and silver money is rendered unproductive, cannot serve as capital. One portion of the commodities on the market can complete its process of circulation and reproduction only by means of an immense contraction of its prices, which means a depreciation of the capital represented by it. In the same way the elements of fixed capital are more or less depreciated. Then there is the added complication that the process of reproduction is based on definite assumptions as to prices, so that a general fall in prices checks and disturbs the process of reproduction. This interference and stagnation paralyses the function of money as a medium of payment, which is conditioned on the development of capital and the resulting price relations. The chain of payments due at certain times is broken in a hundred places, and the disaster is intensified by the collapse of the credit-system. Thus violent and acute crises are brought about, sudden and forcible depreciations, and actual stagnation and collapse of the process of reproduction, and finally a real falling off in reproduction.[33]

Marx followed this description of the crisis and downswing phases of the cycle with an equally vivid description of the recovery and upswing phases. He referred to the work of "other agencies," to wage, cost, and price reductions, to the "new combinations" which raise productivity, restore profitability, and pave the way for a new cycle under "expanded conditions of production in an expanded market, and with increased productive forces."[34]

Obviously, Marx saw that crises *appeared* as a state of general overproduction, the very state which Say's Law denied to be a consequence of endogenous economic forces. What *caused* the periodic appearance of this state of general overproduction is another question which can be dealt with only in considering Marx's theory of capital accumulation and capitalist evolution.

VI. ACCUMULATION OF CAPITAL AND ECONOMIC DEVELOPMENT; MARX'S ALTERNATIVE TO SAY'S LAW AND THE CLASSICAL SYSTEM

Marx's theory of economic development is the core of his work, and in that theory capital accumulation plays the central role. This theory is a large subject, beyond the scope of the present article. What is of interest here, however, is the fact that this theory is developed initially within a model which postulates Say's Law. In the previously discussed model emphasizing monetary exchange Marx argued that, contrary to Say's Law, endogenous crises are always *possible*. In the model emphasizing capital accumulation Marx argued that even if Say's Law *could* operate, crises and ultimate breakdown would be inevitable.

There are three points to be emphasized concerning the relation between Marx's theory of economic development and Say's Law. (1) Marx's model does not contradict the "law" in any of its meanings in so far as it postulates Say's Law in assuming that demand and supply are everywhere equal and that equilibrium prevails in the value system. (2) Marx's theory of evolution, while an *alternative* to the Ricardian theory of stagnation (itself no contradiction to Say's Law), is also an alternative to the stagnation theory adumbrated by such critics of Ricardo and Say as Malthus and Sismondi. (3) The limit to capital accumulation deduced in Marx's model, like that indicated by Ricardo, is no contradiction to Say's Law, in so far as this limit in each case arises from the side of capital *supply*, whereas Say's Law asserts the existence of adequate *demand* at any level of output.

Marx's dynamic model postulates Say's Law for an obvious methodological reason — to examine the fundamental tendencies of the system underlying the disturbances of the market. It is as if Marx were determined to show, by ruling out of the model the difficulties which he elsewhere acknowledged to be inherent in exchange, that his basic disagreement was on a much deeper level. Thus, with the assumptions of Say's Law, Marx deduced what he considered the inevitability of capitalist breakdown.[35]

In so far as Marx's dynamic model starts with the assumptions of Say's Law and ends with a theory of cycles and stagnation, it is entirely distinct from the models of other critics of the classical system. In Malthus (if we ignore the fact that disequilibrium is almost built into the system because of his definition of value), the general glut emerges because of oversaving.

In Sismondi, the general glut is a consequence of lags and frictions. In Marx, it follows from the conditions of accumulation even when there are no disturbances in the savings-investment process and no other lags or frictions. Marx's own analyses of the systems of Malthus and of Sismondi[36] make it clear that while he too shared their disapproval of the classical refusal to see the effects of capitalist income distribution, of monetary disturbances, of lags and frictions, his explanation of crises and ultimate breakdown is based on entirely different considerations. It is important to recognize this, since two of the three leading interpretations of Marx's theory of economic development see in it as basic the very factors stressed by earlier critics of the classical system — "disproportionality" and underconsumption,[37] recognized by Marx, but not considered causal.

In Marx, as in Ricardo, the fundamental causal element in economic development is the rate of profit, whose long-run tendency is to fall. However, the falling tendency of the rate of profit was attributed by Marx not to the decline in the fertility of land and consequent rise in rents and wages but instead to technological improvement of the labor-saving kind. The motivation for such improvement is the drive for profit, but its consequence defeats the profit motive through the reduction, within the total means of production, of the proportion of labor — the only value and surplus value, or profit, creating element. The increasing ratio of nonwage or *constant* capital (machinery and raw materials) to *variable* capital (wages), or the increase in the "organic composition of capital," was, according to Marx, the inevitable consequence of the drive for profit, but also the reason for the fall in the rate of profit.[38]

Marx considered his development of the law of the falling tendency of the rate of profit to be of paramount importance and his special contribution to political economy. He wrote:

Simple as this law appears . . . all of political economy has so far tried in vain to discover it. . . . Since this law is of great importance for capitalist production, it may be said to be that mystery whose solution has been the goal of the entire political economy since Adam Smith. The difference between the various schools since Adam Smith consists in their different attempts to solve this riddle.[39]

The riddle to which Marx referred is that the law of the falling tendency of the rate of profit is a "two-faced law" which explains both the *fall* in the *rate* of profit and the *rise* in the *mass* of profit.

The falling rate of profit is a long-run *tendency* in Marx's view, a tendency which the accumulation process restrains with various "counteracting causes."[40] Their effect is chiefly to cheapen the elements of capital, that is, to reduce the costs both of subsistence goods and material means of production, whether through increasing productivity at home or the advantages of foreign trade.

However, the long-run tendency of the rate of profit to fall was seen by Marx as a fundamental law, the source of periodic crises, themselves overcome by the effects of the counteracting causes, and hence of cyclical development.[41] Moreover, although Marx did not develop this analysis very far, the implication is clear that the falling rate of profit is inexorable, because the accumulation process develops on the basis of an ever increasing proportion of nonwage (and nonvalue creating) capital, and because the countertendencies to the falling rate of profit become less effective.[42] Thus the logical development of the Marxian model would be that the capitalist system is one of cycles induced by this tendency of the rate of profit to fall and of ultimate stagnation as the tendency of the falling rate of profit becomes stronger and the countertendencies weaker.[43]

The Marxian model of evolution is thus quite different from that of Ricardo. Like the latter it postulates Say's Law and deduces a tendency to stagnation due to the falling rate of profit. Unlike Ricardo's model, however, it deduces the falling rate of profit directly from the labor theory of value alone, with no additional postulates but that capitalists seek to maximize their profits. Also, unlike Ricardo's model, Marx's model offers an explanation of crises and cycles as well as a theory of secular trend.

From this discussion of Marx's different models it thus appears that his position on Say's Law was indeed complicated. In some models he used Say's Law for specific analytic reasons. In another model he directly opposed it. The difference between the models arises from the intention to isolate and emphasize specific features of the economy. Hence the complicated "position" on Say's Law is not one of inconsistency but the consequence of deliberate methodology.

NOTES

1. This "law" bearing Say's name and attributed to him by Ricardo is generally credited to James Mill. Mill expounded the doctrine in his *Commerce Defended* (1808), which appeared between the first edition of Say's *Traité d'Economie Politique* (1803), where the doctrine is barely outlined, and the second edition (1814) where it is more fully developed. For this view as to priority, see the Introduction by Jacob W. Hollander and T. E. Gregory (ed.) to Ricardo's *Notes on Malthus* (Baltimore, 1928). That Say deserves priority is the view taken by Joseph Spengler in "The Physiocrats and Say's Law of Markets, II," *Journal of Political Economy*, LIII (Dec. 1945), 341–42. The latter opinion seems reasonable since in Say's first edition it is already stated that when a nation has too many products of one kind the means of selling them is to create another kind (*Traité*, I, 153–54), that "The demand of products in general is thus equal to the sum of the products" (*ibid.*, II, 176), and that "A nation always has the means of buying all it produces" (*ibid.*, II, 180). It was Mill, however, who developed Say's Law, especially in asserting the possibility of unlimited accumulation and the impossibility of general overproduction. (*Commerce Defended*, London, 1808, p. 85.) It was Ricardo who fully developed Say's Law and made of it the core of classical economics. His role will be discussed further in this article.

2. Unfortunately Marx's own economic system was left in such an unfinished state and with so many apparent contradictions that until the last fifteen years or so reconstruction of this system generally has seemed insufficiently rewarding to attract the interest of professional economists. Only the first volume of *Capital* was prepared for publication by Marx himself, the remaining incompleted two volumes having been edited by Friedrich Engels. The standard English edition is the Kerr edition (Chicago, 1909). Marx's monumental work on the history of economic thought from Sir William Petty to his own day, originally planned as a fourth volume to *Capital*, was edited by Karl Kautsky, and published in three volumes as *Theorien über den Mehrwert* (Stuttgart, 1905–10).

Two partial English translations of this latter work are available. The first volume has been translated from the French (Molitor) edition by Terence

McCarthy as *A History of Economic Theories; From the Physiocrats to Adam Smith* (New York, 1952). Selections from the first two volumes have been translated from the original German by G. A. Bonner and Emile Burns as *Theories of Surplus Value* (London, 1951).

Marx's theory of evolution and of cycles, although nowhere stated in full, is developed in part in Volume I, more specifically in Volume III of *Capital* (especially in chap. 15). His most explicit treatment of Say and the classical economists is in *Theorien über den Mehwert*, II (2) and III.

3. Joseph A. Schumpeter, *Capitalism, Socialism, and Democracy* (New York, 1942), pp. 38–42.

4. Maurice Dobb, *Political Economy and Capitalism* (New York, 1945), p. 79.

5. *Ibid.*, chap. 4.

6. Paul M. Sweezy, *The Theory of Capitalist Development* (New York, 1942), chaps. 8–10, esp. pp. 179–84.

7. Joan Robinson, *An Essay on Marxian Economics* (London, 1947), p. 42.

8. *Ibid.*, p. 51.

9. *Theorien über den Mehrwert*, II (2), 301.

10. David Ricardo, *Principles of Political Economy and Taxation* (Everyman ed., New York, 1943), p. 194.

11. Ricardo, *Notes on Malthus* (Baltimore, 1928), p. 160.

12. Ricardo, *Principles*, p. 193.

13. In the final formulation of Say's Law by John Stuart Mill, there was considerable modification, since, according to Mill, "This argument is evidently founded on the supposition of a state of barter; . . . If, however, we suppose that money is used, these propositions cease to be exactly true." (*Essays on Some Unsettled Questions of Political Economy*, 2d ed., London, 1874, p. 69.)

14. *Capital*, II, chaps. 20, 21.

15. T. R. Malthus, *Principles of Political Economy* (London, 1819), pp. 353–54. Say removed part of this objection by admitting that labor is a commodity. (J. B. Say, *Letters to Malthus*, London, 1821, pp. 22–23.) Malthus' argument against the idea of money as a veil was not answered, and he is rightly regarded as a contributor to monetary analysis and the theory of liquidity preference.

16. Malthus, *op. cit.*, pp. 9, 370. Malthus developed a concept of an optimum rate of accumulation defined by the acceptable rate of profit. It should be pointed out that this argument about the rate of profit concerns lack of profitability *due to a shortage of demand*. Ricardo admitted a falling rate of profit could lead to eventual stagnation, but with him the only reason for a falling rate of profit was the increase in wages occasioned by the increased costs of producing subsistence goods. Marx, like Malthus, stressed the fall in the rate of profit, but for entirely

different reasons than those adduced by Malthus and Ricardo. For Marx's critique of Malthus, see *Theorien über den Mehrwert*, III, 9–10; 43–49.

17. "Allowing you your premises, I see very few instances in which I can quarrel with your conclusions. I agree with all you say concerning the glut of commodities; allow to you your measure, and it is impossible to differ in the result." (*Letters of David Ricardo to Thomas Robert Malthus*, ed. James Bonar, Oxford, 1887, p. 216.)

18. Rosa Luxembourg, *Die Akumulation des Kapitals* (Leipzig, 1921), pp. 60–75. Luxembourg objected in addition that the reproduction schemes do not correspond to reality, where proportional accumulation does not prevail, and further objected to Marx's giving the impetus to accumulation to Department I (means of production) to whose scale of accumulation Department II adapts. (*Ibid.*, pp. 102–3.) Her fundamental objection to Marx's model of expanded reproduction is that a necessary shortage of demand would make accumulation impossible.

19. Luxembourg's misunderstanding of the whole concept of the circular flow is illustrated by her criticism of Marx's model of expanded reproduction of which she wrote, "Obviously, we turn in a circle." (*Ibid.*, p. 104.)

20. *Capital*, I, 48.

21. *Theorien über den Mehrwert*, II (2), 275–76 (my translation).

22. *Ibid.*, II (2), 282.

23. *Ibid.*, II (2), 283.

24. *Capital*, I, 127.

25. *Ibid.*, I, 128.

26. *Theorien über den Mehrwert*, II (2), 282.

27. *Ibid.*, II (2), 288.

28. *Ibid.*, II (2), 289 (my emphasis). This passage is of key importance. Study of the chapter on crises in the *Theorien über den Mehrwert*, and especially of this passage avoids misunderstanding of Marx's cycle theory. The popular theories of crises and cycles attributed to Marx, which are based on "disproportions" or "realization" difficulties, rest on the very confusion Marx warned against, the confusion between the abstract form, and the cause, of crises.

29. From the French Revolution until the 1820's the English economy was disturbed by wars, blockade, and consequent inflation. These events could rightly be regarded as exogenous as could the monetary crises of later years be considered a consequence of currency mismanagement. It should be recalled that Ricardo, the abstract theorist, was also deeply concerned with practical matters, as in *The High Price of Bullion* (1810). Ricardo's theories of money and of international trade ultimately became the basis for Bank of England policy.

30. Jean Charles Leonard Simonde

de Sismondi, *Nouveaux principes de l'économie politique*, I (Paris, 1819), esp. 303–11, 374–81. It should be recalled that Sismondi was primarily an historian rather than an economist. As such his contribution to economics was not one of logical analysis, but rather of a broad historico-economic vision which led him to see the capitalist economy as but one of several historical stages of economic progress and to be highly critical of capitalism.

31. Karl Rodbertus, *Overproduction and Crises* (New York, 1898), pp. 123–32. The first German edition with which Marx was familiar appeared in 1850–51. Marx countered Rodbertus' underconsumption idea by pointing out that the working class enjoys its greatest prosperity just before the outbreak of the crisis and that "advocates of the theory of crises of Rodbertus are requested to make a note of this." (*Capital*, II, 476n.)

32. *Theorien über den Mehrwert*, II (2), 300–14.

33. *Capital*, III, 297–98.

34. *Ibid.*, III, 299.

35. Marx's model does not specify the exact conditioning or timing of capitalist breakdown. It deduces only a tendency to breakdown, expressed in periodic crises, due to the increasing contradictions of the economic system. Apparently, Marx expected crises to become more severe. However, crises alone would not bring the end of capitalist production. The transformation from capitalism to socialism, like that from feudalism to capitalism, was expected to be a prolonged social transformation made necessary by the inability of capitalism to continue to develop the "productive forces," and made possible by the action of the working class.

Although Marx did not work out his theory of specifically economic breakdown, except in the most general terms, such a theory can be reconstructed from his work. Most of the controversy on Marxian economics from the end of the nineteenth century on was concerned with just this problem. Unfortunately for economic

analysis, however, most of the discussions confused theoretically deduced tendencies with historical prediction. Moreover, in much of the literature "breakdown" seems to suggest some very specific moment of economic chaos and the crumbling of bank walls. A more reasonable interpretation would be that the breakdown of the system would mean stagnation, since a stagnant capitalist system is a contradiction in terms.

36. *Theorien über den Mehrwert*, III, 43–55.

37. An excellent survey of the crisis and breakdown theories ascribed to Marx appears in Sweezy, *op. cit.*, chaps. 9–11.

38. *Capital*, III, 247–49.

39. *Ibid.*, III, 249–50.

40. These are discussed in *Capital*, III, chap. 14.

41. Marx referred to a "decennial cycle (interrupted by smaller oscillations)." (*Ibid.*, I, 694.) His view was that the system automatically responds to crises in a cyclical pattern. "Effects, in their turn, become causes, and the varying accidents of the whole process, which always reproduces its own conditions, take on the form of periodicity." (*Ibid.*, I, 695.)

42. As examples, cost minimization has limits, particularly in the case of wages. Similar limits prevail in the possible gains from foreign trade, particularly as several countries compete for gains in trade with, or capital export to, backward areas, and as these areas are themselves industrialized. Marx did not develop this argument but it is implied. On the other hand, he did not consider the effects of other countertendencies which had not made their appearance historically and would not fit into his abstract model of pure, competitive capitalism, such as the effects of trade unions, monopolies, and government stimulation and support of the economy.

43. An elaborate reconstruction of the Marxian model along similar lines appears in Henryk Grossman, *Das Akkumulations- und Zusammenbruchs-gesetz des Kapitalistischen Systems* (Leipzig, 1929).

19.

RONALD L. MEEK
University of Glasgow

Some Notes

on the

"Transformation

Problem"[1]

The debate initiated by Böhm-Bawerk on the alleged "great contradiction" between Volume I and Volume III of Marx's *Capital* has by no means been resolved to the satisfaction of all parties. In one form or another, and with various degrees of sophistication, a number of aspects of the question continue to be hotly disputed to-day. In particular, literature on the so-called "transformation problem" has multiplied considerably since Paul Sweezy drew the attention of English-speaking readers to it in 1946 in his *Theory of Capitalist Development.*[2]

The present article sets out to do three things. First, it examines Marx's own discussion of the transformation of "values" into "prices of production," dealing in particular with the meaning which ought properly to be ascribed to his famous statement that "total values equal total prices of production." Second, it reviews two solutions of the "transformation problem" which have recently been put forward, and suggests an alternative method of solution which (it is submitted) illustrates more effectively than the others the essential point which Marx was trying to make. Third, it says something

Reprinted from *The Economic Journal*, LXVI (March 1956), 94–107, by permission of the author and The Royal Economic Society.

about an important gap in Marx's argument which still remains after the "transformation problem" has been solved.

"Profit," wrote Marx, "is . . . that disguise of surplus-value which must be removed before the real nature of surplus-value can be discovered. In the surplus-value, the relation between capital and labour is laid bare."[3] In Volume I of *Capital,* therefore, Marx presents us with an analysis of surplus value stripped of its disguise. In this first stage of his argument the surplus value produced in each branch of industry is assumed to accrue to the capitalists *in that branch* in the form of a net gain. Now, since the only possible source of this surplus value, according to Marx's account, is the surplus labour performed by the labourers actually employed on the job, it follows that the ratio of net gain to capital must be unequal in cases where the organic composition[4] of the capitals concerned is unequal.[5] In actual fact, however, the rates of profit in the different branches tend towards equality under developed capitalism, and the organic compositions of capital tend if anything towards greater inequality. It is evidently necessary, therefore, that the Volume I assumptions should be removed at a later stage in the proceedings, and the effect of their removal upon the Volume I conclusions duly examined.

The assumptions are removed in Parts 1 and 2 of Volume III, where the question of the relations between surplus value and profit is considered. In actual fact, Marx argues, the amount of profit which the capitalists in each branch of industry receive must be sufficient to yield them the average rate of profit on the *total* quantity of capital which they employ, so that in the majority of cases the amount of profit they receive will differ from the amount of surplus value actually generated in their own branch of industry. But this does not mean that the Volume I analysis is vitiated. On the contrary, Marx believed that without this analysis political economy would be left "without a rational basis."[6] For, according to him, the profit which the capitalists in each branch of industry receive must be conceived as accruing to them by virtue of a sort of redivision of the aggregate surplus value produced over the economy as a whole. This aggregate surplus value is, as it were, reallocated among the different branches of industry so that the capitalists in each branch share in it not in accordance with the amount of capital they have spent on wages but in accordance with the total amounts of capital they have severally employed. Without the Volume I analysis to determine the magnitude of this aggregate, Marx maintained, the average rate of profit would be, as he put it, "an average of *nothing.*"[7]

In his analysis of surplus value in Volume I, Marx had assumed that the commodities in which the capitalist producers dealt were bought and sold "at their values" in the Marxian sense — *i.e.,* at equilibrium prices which were proportionate to the quantities of socially necessary simple labour required to produce them. So long as it is taken for granted that the net gain received by the capitalists in each branch of industry consists of the surplus value generated in that branch, this is a reasonable enough assumption. But the conversion of surplus value into average profit necessarily implies the transformation of values into what Marx called "prices of production."[8] It implies, in other words, that the majority of commodities do *not* tend to sell "at their values," but at "prices of production" which normally diverge to some extent from their values. The question immediately arises, therefore, whether Marx's Volume III analysis of exchange ratios in terms of prices of production can be regarded merely as a modification of his Volume I analysis in terms of values (as Marx himself argued), or whether it should be regarded as being in contradiction to it (as Böhm-Bawerk and his followers have insisted).

The basic point in Marx's answer to this question is as follows. The transformation of values into prices is brought about as a result of the conversion of surplus value into profit. Now the volume and rate of surplus value[9] are evidently determined by the ratio $\frac{\Sigma a}{\Sigma v}$ (where a is the total value, in the Marxist sense, of a given finished commodity); and the volume and rate of profit are determined by the ratio $\frac{\Sigma a_p}{\Sigma v_p}$ (where the subscript p indicates that a and v have been transformed from values into prices).[10] Marx argues, in effect, that $\frac{\Sigma a}{\Sigma v} = \frac{\Sigma a_p}{\Sigma v_p}$. (This, as we shall see, was what Marx had in mind when he said that "total values equal total prices."[11]) In other words, he argues that the ratio between the value of commodities in general and the value of the commodity labour power, upon which he had in Volume I conceived surplus value to depend,[12] remains unchanged when it is expressed in terms of prices rather than values, so that profit can be said to be determined in accordance with the Volume I analysis. If this is so, it can be plausibly argued that the very degree to which individual prices of production diverge from values is ultimately determined according to the Volume I analysis. Thus the disturbance introduced into the operation of the law of value as described in Volume I is a *calculable* disturbance, and "in the exact sciences it is not the custom to regard a calculable disturbance as a refutation of a certain law."[13]

Marx's discussion of this problem is developed in two stages, the first of which has received much more attention than the second. In the first stage he takes "five different spheres of production," deliberately assuming that none of the commodities concerned enters into the production of any of the others. Thus capitals I to V in the accompanying table[14] can be considered as the component parts of one single capital of 500. Each of the constituent capitals shown in column 1 totals 100, but the cost price of each of the outputs is less than 100, since it is assumed that only a portion of the value of the constant capital is transferred to the commodity in the period we are considering.[15] The amount so transferred is shown in column 2, and the cost price, which is the sum of v and used-up c, is shown in column 3. It is assumed that the working day is everywhere equally divided between necessary and surplus labour, so that surplus value (shown in column 4) is equal to v. The total *value* of each of the outputs being considered (shown in column 5) represents the sum of the cost price and the surplus

(1)	(2)	(3)	(4)	(5)	(6)	(7)	(8)
Capitals	Used-up c	Cost price	Surplus value	Value	Profit	Price of produc-tion	Devia-tion of price from value
I. 80c+20v	50	70	20	90	22	92	+ 2
II. 70c+30v	51	81	30	111	22	103	− 8
III. 60c+40v	51	91	40	131	22	113	−18
IV. 85c+15v	40	55	15	70	22	77	+ 7
V. 95c+ 5v	10	15	5	20	22	37	+17
			110	422	110	422	

value. Now it is evident that the sale of these commodities at their values would result in very unequal rates of profit on each of the capitals. In actual fact, however, Marx maintains, the total pool of surplus value, amounting to 110, is allotted ("by means of competition"[16]) to the individual capitals in accordance with the total size of each — in this case uniformly so that each receives a profit of 22 (column 6). The "price of production" (column 7), then, at which each output actually tends to sell, is the sum of the cost price and the profit, and differs in each case from the value. But since the total profit is by definition equal to the total surplus value, it naturally follows that in the present case the sum of the prices of production is equal to the sum of the values, or, to put the same thing in another way, that the deviations of prices from values (column 8) cancel one another out.[17]

Marx's statement that the sum of the prices is equal to the sum of the values has come in for considerable criticism. From Böhm-Bawerk onwards, critics have questioned whether this statement can be held to be meaningful, whether it embodies a tautology and so on, and have generally concluded that Marx's "argument" is quite untenable. Some of the difficulty no doubt arises from the fact that Marx, having illustrated this equality arithmetically in the particular case just described (the case where mutual interdependence is abstracted from), immediately went on, rather rashly perhaps, to say that "in the same way the sum of all the prices of production of all commodities in society, comprising the totality of all lines of production, is equal to the sum of all their values."[18] The implication of this statement, read in its context, might seem to be that when the assumption that none of the commodities concerned enters into the production of any of the others is dropped, so that the values of input as well as those of output have to be transformed into prices of production, a transformation carried out on the basis of a redistribution of the pool of surplus value will bring out total prices equal to total values in the arithmetical sense. This is in fact not so. On any plausible set of assumptions regarding the manner in which the different branches of the economy are inter-related, it will soon be found upon experimenting with various sets of figures that if the values of input as well as those of output are to be transformed into prices of production, it is normally impossible to effect a simultaneous transformation which will make total profit equal to total surplus value and at the same time make total prices of production equal to total values. In all but very exceptional cases, we may preserve one of these equalities, but not both.[19]

473

If Marx's attention had been drawn to this fact, he might well have reformulated some of his expressions regarding the equality of total prices and total values, while still insisting on the essential point they were designed to express — viz., that after the transformation of values into prices of production the fundamental ratio upon which profit depended[20] could still be said to be determined in accordance with the Volume I analysis. In the special case where none of the commodities concerned enters into the production of any of the others, he might have said, the ratio remains the same for the simple reason that the relevant quantities remain the same — the denominator remains the same by hypothesis, and the numerator remains the same because *in this case* the sum of the prices necessarily equals the sum of the values. In the more difficult case where the various branches of production are mutually interdependent, he might have said, the sum of the prices does not necessarily "come out" equal to the sum of the values, but the fundamental ratio can still be said to be determined in accordance with the Volume I analysis. And it would have been possible for him to illustrate this, as I shall show below, by an arithmetical example rather similar in character to that described above.

However, it would be wrong to suggest that Marx simply ignored this more difficult case. On the contrary, his examination of it, although by no means detailed, was sufficiently well organised to be said to constitute that second stage in his argument of which I have spoken above. He begins by dropping the assumption that none of the commodities concerned enters into the production of any of the others. In actual fact, he writes, "the elements of productive capital are, as a rule, bought on the market," so that "the price of production of one line of production passes, with the profit contained in it, over into the cost-price of another line of production." At first sight it might seem as if this would mean that the profit accruing to each capitalist might be counted several times in a calculation such as that which has just been described, but Marx has little difficulty in disposing of this superficial objection. The dropping of the assumption, however, does indeed make one "essential difference," which Marx describes as follows:

"Aside from the fact that the price of a certain product, for instance the product of capital B, differs from its value, because the surplus-value realized in B may be greater or smaller than the profit of others contained in the product of B, the same fact applies also to those commodities which form the constant part of its capital, and which indirectly, as necessities of life for the labourers, form its variable part. So far as the constant part is concerned, it is itself equal to the cost-price plus surplus-value, which now means cost-price plus profit, and this profit may again be greater or smaller than the surplus-value in whose place it stands. And so far as the variable capital is concerned, it is true that the average daily wage is equal to the values produced by the labourers in the time which they must work in order to produce their necessities of life. But this time is in its turn modified by the deviation of the prices of production of the necessities of life from their values. However, this always amounts in the end to saying that one commodity receives too little of the surplus-value while another receives too much, so that the deviations from the value shown by the prices of production mutually compensate one another. In short, under capitalist production, the general law of value enforces itself merely as the prevailing tendency, in a very complicated and approximate manner, as a never ascertainable average of ceaseless fluctuations."[21]

Marx returned to the same point a few pages later, emphasising that the transformation process involves a modification of the Volume I assumption that "the cost-price of a commodity is equal to the value of the commodities consumed in its production." The price of production of a given commodity, he writes —

"is its cost-price for the buyer, and this price may pass into other commodities and become an element of their prices. Since the price of production may vary from the value of a commodity, it follows that the cost-price of a commodity containing this price of production may also stand above or below that portion of its total value which is formed by the value of the means of production consumed by it. It is necessary to remember this modified significance of the cost-price, and to bear in mind that there is always the possibility of an error, if we assume that the cost-price of the commodities of any particular sphere is equal to the value of the means of production consumed by it. Our present analysis does not necessitate a closer examination of this point."[22]

And in a later passage, repeating the same point once more, Marx argues that "this possibility does not alter the correctness of the rules laid down for commodities of average composition."[23]

This is where the so-called "transformation problem" comes into the picture. Marx's "method of transforming values into prices," it is said, meaning by this his original calculation outlined in the table above, contains an "error," since it does not take account of the fact that the values of elements of input as well as those of elements of output have to be transformed into prices.[24] It is then claimed that Marx can be rescued from this "error" simply by showing the *formal possibility* of a consistent derivation of prices from values in the case of mutual interdependence. When values are transformed into prices, the ratio of price to value must be the same when a given commodity is considered as input as when it is considered as output; and after the transformation the rate of profit must come out equal in the case of each capital concerned. These ratios of price to value, and the rate of profit, are regarded as the main unknowns. The "transformation problem" then reduces itself to this: can the relations between the various branches of production, and the various conditions which are to be fulfilled as a result of the transformation, be expressed in the form of an equational system which is "determinate" in the mathematical sense — *i.e.*, in which the number of equations is equal to the number of unknowns? The assumption lying behind these researches is that if the relations and conditions can in fact be so expressed, Marx's "method of transforming values into prices" is itself transformed from an invalid to a valid one.

The best-known solution, that of Bortkiewicz, commences with the particular set of value relationships postulated by Marx as existing between the three main Departments of the economy (I = means of production;

II = workers' consumption goods; III = capitalists' consumption goods) under conditions of simple reproduction. Employing the usual notation, these value relationships can be expressed in the form of three equations:

$$\text{I.} \quad c_1 + v_1 + s_1 = c_1 + c_2 + c_3$$
$$\text{II.} \quad c_2 + v_2 + s_2 = v_1 + v_2 + v_3$$
$$\text{III.} \quad c_3 + v_3 + s_3 = s_1 + s_2 + s_3$$

If we take the ratio of price to value to be x in the case of means of production, y in the case of workers' consumption goods and z in the case of capitalists' consumption goods; if we further call the average rate of profit r; and if we state as a condition of the problem that the relations appropriate to simple reproduction should continue to obtain after the transformation of values into prices as before it, then the following equalities must hold:

$$\text{I.} \quad c_1 x + v_1 y + r(c_1 x + v_1 y) = (c_1 + c_2 + c_3)x$$
$$\text{II.} \quad c_2 x + v_2 y + r(c_2 x + v_2 y) = (v_1 + v_2 + v_3)y$$
$$\text{III.} \quad c_3 x + v_3 y + r(c_3 x + v_3 y) = (s_1 + s_2 + s_3)z$$

Here there are four unknowns (x, y, z and r), and only three equations. Bortkiewicz reduces the unknowns to three by the ingenious expedient of assuming: (a) that the value scheme was expressed in terms of money, and (b) that gold is the money commodity, and is produced in Department III, in which case z may reasonably be taken as $= 1$. The equational system thereupon becomes determinate, and solutions for x, y and r can be fairly readily derived. Upon applying these solutions to various sets of figures, it is seen that total profit comes out equal to total surplus value, but that total prices normally diverge from total values. Neither the equality nor the inequality, however, has anything more than formal significance. As Bortkiewicz says, in relation to a particular set of figures,

"That the total price exceeds the total value arises from the fact that Department III, from which the good serving as value and price measure is taken, has a relatively low organic composition of capital. But the fact that total profit is numerically identical with total surplus value is a consequence of the fact that the good used as value and price measure belongs to Department III."[25]

It is only in the special case where the organic composition of the capital employed in Department III is equal to the social average that the sum of the prices will come out equal to the sum of the values.

Winternitz adopts the same general attitude towards the problem as Bortkiewicz, but clears the Bortkiewicz solution of certain redundancies and unnecessary artificialities. He commences with the usual value scheme in the three Departments:

$$\text{I.} \quad c_1 + v_1 + s_1 = a_1$$
$$\text{II.} \quad c_2 + v_2 + s_2 = a_2$$
$$\text{III.} \quad c_3 + v_3 + s_3 = a_3$$

But instead of assuming the equilibrium conditions appropriate to Marx's reproduction schemes, he assumes merely that when a_1 varies by x (the price–value ratio for means of production), then c_1, c_2 and c_3 also vary by x; and that when a_2 varies by y (the price–value ratio for workers' consumption goods), then v_1, v_2 and v_3 also vary by y. Thus he arrives at the following simple equational system:

$$\text{I.} \quad c_1x + v_1y + S_1 = a_1x$$
$$\text{II.} \quad c_2x + v_2y + S_2 = a_2y$$
$$\text{III.} \quad c_3x + v_3y + S_3 = a_3z$$

By putting $\dfrac{a_1x}{c_1x + v_1y} = \dfrac{a_2y}{c_2x + v_2y}$ (each of these expressions being equal to

$1 + r$), solutions for $x : y$ and for r are easily obtained. A further set of relationships between x, y and z must then be postulated in order to determine the price level for the system as a whole. From a purely logical point of view, it obviously does not matter what relationships are postulated, but Winternitz puts

$$a_1x + a_2y + a_3z = a_1 + a_2 + a_3$$

(*i.e.*, sum of prices = sum of values) because in his opinion this is "the obvious proposition in the spirit of the Marxian system."[26] Solutions for x, y and z are then yielded immediately without any special difficulty. When applied to various sets of figures, these solutions naturally bring out the sum of prices equal to the sum of values, but total profit normally diverges from total surplus value.

Winternitz's solution, although in essence very similar to Bortkiewicz's, is evidently simpler and therefore more acceptable from a purely mathematical point of view. Indeed, it is the special merit of Winternitz to have exposed the triviality of the whole problem as so posed — a triviality which tended to be hidden by Bortkiewicz's over-elaborate and confusing method. The Winternitz solution is an effective reply to those who said that it was not formally possible to transform values into prices when elements of input as well as output were involved. But it seems to me that something more is required before a tranformation of the Bortkiewicz-Winternitz type can properly be used to *illustrate* the second stage of Marx's Volume III argument.[27] The essential point for Marx, as we have seen, was that after aggregate surplus value had been converted into profit, and values consequently transformed into prices, the ratio $\dfrac{\Sigma a}{\Sigma v}$ should be equal to the ratio $\dfrac{\Sigma a_p}{\Sigma v_p}$. Is it possible to effect a transformation which brings these ratios out equal, and if so under what conditions?

This problem can be dealt with as follows. Select three sets of quantities for c, v and s in Departments I, II and III, such that the rate of surplus value in the Marxist sense $\left(\dfrac{s}{v}\right)$ is equal in each case, and that the organic composition of capital in Department II is equal to the social average[28] — for example:

$$c_1 + v_1 + s_1 = a_1$$
$$\text{I.} \quad 3 + 4 + 4 = 11$$

$$c_2 + v_2 + s_2 = a_2$$
$$\text{II.} \quad 18 + 15 + 15 = 48$$

$$c_3 + v_3 + s_3 = a_3$$
$$\text{III.} \quad 9 + 6 + 6 = 21$$

Proceed now to transform these expressions into the following:

$$\text{I.} \quad c_1 x + v_1 y + S_1 = a_1 x$$
$$\text{II.} \quad c_2 x + v_2 y + S_2 = a_2 y$$
$$\text{III.} \quad c_3 x + v_3 y + S_3 = a_3 z$$

on the basis of the following equalities:[29]

$$\frac{S_1}{c_1 x + v_1 y} = \frac{S_2}{c_2 x + v_2 y} = \frac{S_3}{c_3 x + v_3 y}$$

and

$$S_1 + S_2 + S_3 = s_1 + s_2 + s_3$$

The result of this calculation in the given case is as follows:

$$\begin{array}{ccccc} & c_1 x & v_1 y & S_1 & a_1 x \\ \text{I.} & 2{\cdot}592 + & 3{\cdot}710 + & 3{\cdot}202 = & 9{\cdot}504 \end{array}$$

$$\begin{array}{ccccc} & c_2 x & v_2 y & S_2 & a_2 y \\ \text{II.} & 15{\cdot}552 + & 13{\cdot}911 + & 15{\cdot}052 = & 44{\cdot}515 \end{array}$$

$$\begin{array}{ccccc} & c_3 x & v_3 y & S_3 & a_3 z \\ \text{III.} & 7{\cdot}776 + & 5{\cdot}564 + & 6{\cdot}784 = & 20{\cdot}124 \end{array}$$

This calculation, like Marx's original one in the case where mutual inter-dependence was abstracted from, shows the result when a fixed aggregate of surplus value is re-allocated in the form of profit at the average rate among the various capitals concerned. The sum of prices diverges from the sum of values, but the real point to which Marx wished to draw attention when he emphasised the equality between total prices and total values in the original case — i.e., that after the transformation of values into prices the fundamental ratio upon which profit depended[30] could still be said to be determined in accordance with the Volume I analysis — is illustrated in this case too. It is no longer true that the numerator and the denominator of the ratio remain unchanged as a result of the transformation, but under the assumed conditions *both will always change in the same proportion*, so that $\dfrac{a_1 x + a_2 y + a_3 z}{v_1 y + v_2 y + v_3 y}$ remains equal to $\dfrac{a_1 + a_2 + a_3}{v_1 + v_2 + v_3}$. The achievement of this result is dependent (in the great majority of cases) upon the equality initially postulated between $\dfrac{c_2}{c_2 + v_2}$ and $\dfrac{\Sigma c}{\Sigma c + \Sigma v}$ — i.e., upon the assumption that the organic composition of capital in the wage-goods industries is equal to the social average. [31, 32]

478

Such an illustration, however, would fill only part of the gap in Marx's analysis. To fill the rest of it, one must turn to economic history rather than to mathematics. The "derivation of prices from values," according to Marx's general economic method,[33] must be regarded as a historical as well as a logical process. In "deriving prices from values" we are really reproducing in our minds, in logical and simplified form, a process which has actually happened in history. Marx began with the assumption that goods sold "at their values" under capitalism (so that profit rates in the various branches of production were often very different), not only because this appeared to be the proper starting-point from the logical point of view but also because he believed that it had "originally"[34] been so. He proceeded on this basis to transform values into prices, not only because this course appeared to be logically necessary but also because he believed that history itself had effected such a transformation. The exchange of commodities at their values, or approximately at their values, Marx wrote —

"requires . . . a much lower stage than their exchange at their prices of production, which requires a relatively high development of capitalist production. . . .

"Aside from the fact that prices and their movements are dominated by the law of value, it is quite appropriate, under these circumstances, to regard the value of commodities not only theoretically, but also historically, as existing prior to the prices of production. This applies to conditions, in which the labourer owns his means of production, and this is the condition of the land-owning farmer and of the craftsman in the old world as the new. This agrees also with the view formerly expressed by me that the development of product into commodities arises through the exchange between different communes, not through that between the members of the same commune. It applies not only to this primitive condition, but also to subsequent conditions based on slavery or serfdom, and to the guild organisation of handicrafts, so long as the means of production installed in one line of production cannot be transferred to another line except under difficulties, so that the various lines of production maintain, to a certain degree, the same mutual relations as foreign countries or communistic groups."[35]

But Marx did not pursue the historical aspects of the problem of the transformation of values into prices very much further than this, and his critics have taken full advantage of the fact that a number of problems still remain unsolved.[36] Böhm-Bawerk, for example, argued that if the derivation of prices from values had in fact proceeded in the manner which Marx's analysis suggests, "there must be traces of the actual fact that *before* the equalization of the rates of profit the branches of production with the relatively greater amounts of constant capital have won and do win the smallest rates of profit, while those branches with the smaller amounts of constant capital win the largest rates of profit"; and he went on to assert (following Sombart) that there are in fact "no traces of this to be found anywhere, either in the historical past or in the present."[37] Engels attempted to deal with this and other related problems in his important "Supplement" to Volume III of *Capital*,[38] giving a suggestive account of the manner in which, in the formative years of the development of capitalism, the prices of commodities were adjusted above or below their values in order to bring the surplus value into equality with the average rate of profit. This essay is certainly the most ambitious attempt to bridge the gap in Marx's argument which we possess. But even this is really little more than a preliminary sketch, and many details still remain to be filled in.

It is, of course, quite open to the Marxist, if he wishes, to by-pass this question by characterising the view expressed by Marx in the passage just quoted as a sort of "Robinsonade." Marx, it might be argued, was really doing little more than take over the traditional Classical idea that exchange ratios were proportional to embodied labour ratios only in that "early and rude state of society" of which Adam Smith spoke. Such a characterisation would not affect the utility of the labour theory of value as a tool for the analysis of *capitalist* society — given a satisfactory solution to the logical problem of the transformation of values into prices; but on the other hand it does not seem likely that Marx himself would have been prepared to accept it. Marx and Engels always insisted very strongly that the logical method of treatment which they adopted in their work on political economy was "nothing else than the historical method, only divested of its historical form and disturbing fortuities." The chain of thought, said Engels,

"must begin with the same thing that this history begins with and its further course will be nothing but the mirror-image of the historical course in abstract and theoretically consistent form, a corrected mirror-image but corrected according to laws furnished by the real course of history itself, in that each factor can be considered at its ripest point of development, in its classic form."[39]

Given this approach, it seems probable that Marx would have continued to take the view that his *logical* transformation of values into prices was the "corrected-image" of some actual *historical* transformation.

Engels, in the "Supplement" referred to above, tried to solve the problem by suggesting that up to the time when the capitalist form of production came upon the scene, commodity prices in actual fact normally tended to "gravitate towards the values fixed by the Marxian law and oscillate around these values."[40] This suggestion does not on the whole seem very plausible, for fairly obvious reasons connected with the prevalence of various forms of monopoly, the low degree of factor mobility, etc., in most pre-capitalist societies. Fortunately, however, it is not necessary to follow Engels all the way in this matter: it is quite sufficient to show that history has in fact effected a transformation of one type of *supply price* into another.[41] Broadly speaking, there are two main types of supply price to be found in the history of commodity exchange — first, that of the producer who thinks of his net receipts as a reward for his labour, and, second, that of the producer who thinks of his net receipts as a profit on his capital. What Marx did, in effect, was to assume that the first type of supply price was characteristic of all pre-capitalist forms of society (abstracting here from those specific features differentiating pre-capitalist societies from one another which in other contexts he was especially concerned to emphasise), and to concentrate on the task of showing how the coming of capitalism, with its conversion of labour power into a commodity, accomplished the actual transformation of the first type of supply price into the second.[42] This, I think, is the historical transformation of which the logical transformation considered above must be regarded as the counterpart.

NOTES

1. I acknowledge with thanks valuable criticisms of the original draft of this article made by Mr. M. H. Dobb, Mr. A. L. Wright and Dr. G. A. P. Wyllie. None of these, however, must be held responsible for any errors which remain.

2. See Sweezy, *The Theory of Capitalist Development* (London, 1946), pp. 109 ff.; Ladislaus von Bortkiewicz, *Value and Price in the Marxian System* (reprinted in *International Economic Papers*, no. 2, 1952); Bortkiewicz, *On the Correction of Marx's Fundamental Theoretical Construction in the Third Volume of "Capital"* (reprinted as an appendix to Sweezy's edn. of Böhm-Bawerk's *Karl Marx and the Close of his System* and Hilferding's *Böhm-Bawerk's Criticism of Marx* (New York, 1949)); J. Winternitz, "Values and Prices: A Solution of the So-called Transformation Problem" (*Economic Journal*, June 1948, p. 276); K. May, "Value and Price of Production: A Note on Winternitz's Solution" (*Economic Journal*, December 1948, p. 596); Joan Robinson, in a review in *Economic Journal*, June 1950, p. 358; Rudolf Schlesinger, *Marx: His Time and Ours* (London 1950), pp. 139 ff.; and M. H. Dobb, *A Note on the Transformation Problem*, in *On Economic Theory and Socialism* (London, 1955), p. 273.

3. *Capital*, Vol. III (Kerr edn.), p. 62.

4. The organic composition of capital is the ratio between the part of capital spent on equipment, raw materials, etc., which Marx calls *constant* capital (c), and the part spent on wages, which he calls *variable* capital (v).

5. Marx assumes here that the ratio of surplus values (s) to v is the same in all branches of industry.

6. *Capital*, Vol. III, pp. 176–7.

7. *Theories of Surplus Value* (*Selections*) (London, 1951), p. 231.

8. "The price of production", wrote Marx, "includes the average profit. We call it price of production. It is, as a matter of fact, the same thing which Adam Smith calls *natural price*, Ricardo *price of production*, or *cost of production*, and the physiocrats *prix nécessaire*, because it is in the long run a prerequisite of supply, of the reproduction of commodities in every individual sphere" (*Capital*, Vol. III, p. 233).

9. I am using the expression "rate of surplus value" here to mean the ratio of surplus value to *total* capital. Marx normally used it to mean the ratio of surplus value to *variable* capital.

10. It is, of course, assumed here that the national income resolves itself only into wages and profits.

11. Cf. M. H. Dobb, *Political Economy and Capitalism*, pp. 46 and 72–3.

12. Marx starts in Vol. I with the fundamental exploitation ratio

$$\frac{s}{v} \left(= \frac{\text{Surplus labour}}{\text{Necessary labour}} \right);$$ adding unity to this ratio, we get

$$\frac{v + s}{v} \left(= \frac{\text{Working day}}{\text{Necessary labour}} \right).$$

When the latter expression is applied to the totality of commodities, it becomes

$$\frac{\Sigma (v + s)}{v} \left(= \frac{\text{Total labour force}}{\begin{array}{c}\text{Labour required to} \\ \text{produce wage-goods}\end{array}} \right):$$

and, given conditions of equilibrium between the different branches of the economy, this ratio

$$\frac{\text{Total labour force}}{\text{Labour required to produce wage-goods}}$$

is equal to the ratio

$$\frac{\text{Value of finished commodities}}{\text{Value of wage-goods}} \left(= \frac{\Sigma a}{\Sigma v} \right).$$

For example, in the following case Department I produces means of production and Department II consumers' goods; the

ratio $\frac{s}{v}$ is the same for both Departments;

and the equilibrium conditions appropriate to simple reproduction prevail between them (*i.e.*, $c_2 = v_1 + s_1$):

	c_1	v_1	s_1	a_1
I.	80	60	40	180
	c_2	v_2	s_2	a_2
II.	100	90	60	250

It will be seen that the ratios

$$\frac{\text{Working day}}{\text{Necessary labour}} \left(= \frac{5}{3} \right),$$

$$\frac{\text{Total labour force}}{\begin{array}{c}\text{Labour required to} \\ \text{produce wage-goods}\end{array}} \left(= \frac{250}{150} \right),$$

and

481

$$\frac{\text{Value of finished commodities}}{\text{Value of wage-goods}} \left(= \frac{250}{150} \right)$$

are all equal.

13. P. Fireman, quoted by Engels in his preface to Volume III of *Capital*, p. 25.

14. This table is an amalgamation of those on pp. 183 and 185 of *Capital*, Vol. III, with some of the figures re-arranged.

15. The turnover periods of v are assumed to be the same in each case.

16. *Capital*, Vol. III, p. 186.

17. It is evident that the only case in which price and value would coincide would be one in which the composition of the capital concerned coincided with the "social average."

18. *Capital*, Vol. III, p. 188.

19. For an example of one of these exceptional cases, see the transformation exhibited in Tables II and IIIb on pp. 111 and 120 of Sweezy's *Theory of Capitalist Development*.

20. There is a slight technical difficulty here. When Marx said that "total values equal total prices" it is fairly clear that what he had in mind was the equality of the ratios $\frac{\Sigma a}{\Sigma v}$ and $\frac{\Sigma a_p}{\Sigma v_p}$, each calculated over the economy as a whole. (Cf. Dobb, *loc. cit.*). Given conditions of equilibrium between the different Departments, these ratios will be equal to the basic exploitation ratio $\frac{\Sigma(v+s)}{\Sigma v}$. In the case we have just considered, however, where the information which we are given covers only a part of the economy, it is obvious that the numerical value of the ratio $\frac{\Sigma a}{\Sigma v}$ derived from this information alone (assuming that we are able to derive it at all) is likely to differ from the numerical value of $\frac{\Sigma a}{\Sigma v}$ which we could derive from complete information regarding the economy as a whole. (For example, if we assume that the table gives us complete information regarding the output of finished goods, but of no other branches of production, Σa will be the same but Σv will be under-estimated.) A similar sort of difficulty arises in the second stage of the argument (to be considered shortly), where we have full information concerning the economy, but where it is not desirable to postulate equilibrium conditions. In both these cases our calculation of $\frac{\Sigma a}{\Sigma v}$ from the information which we are given is likely to differ from that of the basic exploitation ratio $\frac{\Sigma(v+s)}{\Sigma v}$. In such cases, then, if we want

to illustrate by an arithmetical example what Marx had in mind when he said that "total values equal total prices," the best we can do is to start with a ratio whose numerator is the sum of the total values of all the commodities (whether finished or otherwise) about which we are given information, and whose denominator is the sum of all the v's which we are given; and then to show that the numerical value of this ratio remains the same when those values which the particular problem requires to be transformed into prices are so transformed. The numerical value of this ratio will not normally be identical with that of $\frac{\Sigma a}{\Sigma v}$ calculated for the economy as a whole, but it will express the same underlying idea. In what follows the symbol a will be used for the total value of any commodity, whether finished or not.

21. Quotations from *Capital*, Vol. III, pp. 188–90. There is a similar passage at the end of Marx's comments on Bailey in the *Theories of Surplus Value* (not included in the English edn.) which shows that the point had occurred to Marx several years before the publication of the first volume of *Capital*.

22. *Capital*, Vol. III, pp. 194–5.

23. *Ibid.*, Vol. III, pp. 241–3.

24. As will be clear from what has been said above, it was not intended to take account of this fact, since mutual interdependence was specifically abstracted from.

25. Bortkiewicz, in Sweezy's edn. of Böhm-Bawerk's *Karl Marx and the Close of his System*, etc., p. 205.

26. *Economic Journal*, June 1948, p. 279.

27. The Bortkiewicz-Winternitz solutions can certainly be used to *prove* the proposition that a consistent transformation of values into prices is formally possible, but they cannot be used to do any more than *illustrate* Marx's own argument. To suggest that any argument in *Capital* stands or falls by Marx's arithmetical illustrations is to betray a serious misunderstanding of his method, and it would be equally wrong-headed, I think, to set out to "rescue" Marx from his errors with the aid of mathematical formulae. As May has said (*op. cit.*, p. 598): "Marx . . . used calculations primarily as illustrations to accompany verbal arguments which combined process and cross-section analysis in a way which could hardly be fitted to the mathematical techniques available even to-day."

28. *I.e.*, that $\frac{c_2}{c_2 + v_2} = \frac{\Sigma c}{\Sigma c + \Sigma v}$.

29. These two equalities express, of course, the equality of profit rates, and the equality of the sum of profits with the sum of surplus values.

30. See footnote 4 above, p. 481.

31. I am indebted to Dr. Wyllie for a mathematical proof both of this general result and of its dependence in normal cases upon the condition $\dfrac{c_2}{c_2 + v_2} = \dfrac{\Sigma c}{\Sigma c + \Sigma v}$. While the result will always be reached when this condition is satisfied, there may be a few special cases in which it could be reached without the condition being satisfied.

32. In Marx's arithmetical illustration to the first stage of his argument, the conditions laid down do not require that the values of the elements of input should be transformed into prices. It is possible to re-interpret his figures, however, so that they illustrate a situation in which the values of v (but not of c), as well as those of a, have to be transformed into prices, and in which the organic composition of capital in the wage-goods industries is equal to the social average, so that v is the same whether expressed in price or in value terms (i.e., that $y = 1$). In the present case, where c, v, and a have all to be transformed into prices, the fact that the organic composition of capital in the wage-goods industries is equal to the social average no longer necessarily means that $y = 1$.

33. The best short description of Marx's general economic method is that given by Engels in a review of Marx's *Critique of Political Economy* which appears as an appendix in the English edn. of Engels's *Ludwig Feuerbach*, pp. 98–101.

34. *Capital*, Vol. III, p. 186.

35. *Ibid.*, Vol. III, pp. 208–9. Cf. p. 212: "Competition first brings about, in a certain individual sphere, the establishment of an equal market-value and market-price by averaging the various individual values of the commodities. The competition of the capitals in the different spheres then results in the price of production which equalises the rates of profit between the different spheres. *This last process requires a higher development of capitalist production than the previous process.*" (My italics.) Cf. also pp. 207–8.

36. Engels, referring to the passage just quoted, said that "if Marx had had an opportunity to work over the third volume once more, he would doubtless have extended this passage considerably. As it stands it gives only the sketchy outline of what is to be said on the point in question" (*Engels on "Capital,"* p. 102).

37. *Karl Marx and the Close of his System* (Sweezy's edn.), p. 49. See also Hilferding's reply on pp. 169–72.

38. Reprinted in *Engels on "Capital,"* pp. 94 ff.

39. Engels, appendix to *Ludwig Feuerbach*, p. 99.

40. *Engels on "Capital,"* p. 106.

41. The labour theory of value, like all cost theories, approaches the value problem via the supply price, and can afford a determinate explanation of actual prices only in so far as these are equal to or tend towards supply prices.

42. See on this point *Capital*, Vol. I (Allen & Unwin edn.), pp. 148–9.

PART FIVE

THE HISTORICAL SCHOOL

AND

INSTITUTIONALISM

CRITICAL DOCTRINES SELDOM ASSUME organized form until the object analyzed has itself taken on a stable and viable shape. It was not until the eighteenth century that the science of economics took on a relatively stable form as a result of the writings of Quesnay, Hume, possibly Cantillon, and, above all, Adam Smith. It was not until the nineteenth century that this still evolving science — now recognized to be an engine of analysis — was delineated quite sharply and explicitly, at first by Ricardo and others essentially in the Smithian tradition, then by Menger and his disciples, with their insistence upon the importance of choice and demand, and finally by Marshall and his mathematically oriented contemporaries, with their emphasis upon the role of the price system and the centrality of the behavior of private price-making and price-taking decision-makers (*i.e.*, individuals, households, firms, coalitions). As the shape of this new science, together with its formal and its empirical implications, became well marked, however, the supposed tenets of its expounders — by now looked upon as exponents of orthodox principles and as essentially defenders of the politico-economic order found in northwest Europe and the United States — became subject to criticism of various sorts and from various quarters. These criticisms varied greatly in range, intensity, and underlying assumptions. Some were mild though effective (*e.g.*, those of F. List and American nationalists who favored temporary protectionism); others were innocuous (*e.g.*, those of the utopian or associative socialists and the anarchists), or devoid of much influence (*e.g.*, the Christian "socialists," the solidarists). Some proved quite influential (*e.g.*, those of Sismondi, the Saint-Simonians, A. Comte, and K. J. Rodbertus, all quite historically oriented).

Three sets of criticisms stand out in the works of authors opposed to the classical or the neoclassical system of economics: the body of ideas formulated by Karl Marx, which after the 1860's displaced or dominated other schools of socialist theory; the collection of views advanced by nineteenth-century proponents of a historical approach to the study of economic behavior; and the somewhat heterogeneous assembly of opinions advanced in the United States between 1900 and 1940 by "the institutionalists," in particular by Thorstein Veblen and his followers and later by J. R. Commons.

Some of Marx's essentially economic ideas were dealt with in Part Four. In the present part, Grossman (Selection 20) describes Marx's use of evolutionary concepts, of concepts that had been adumbrated already by the historian and socio-economic theorist, Simonde de Sismondi (1773–1842), as well as anticipated by Richard Jones, who criticized his English classical contemporaries on historical and sociological grounds and who is also a forerunner of the twentieth-century institutionalists. The views of these institutionalists are summarized in Homan's essay (Selection 21). The opinions of members of the historical school are dealt with only cursorily in the selection from Grossman's essay, in which it is argued that Hegel was not responsible for the "historicizing" of economics. Credit for this accomplishment, Grossman believes, belongs primarily to Condorcet (1743–1794), who supposed that every nation tended to progress similarly, though at different times and rates; and to Saint-Simon (1760–1825), who emphasized the growing importance of science and administration and the rising industrial class, who described the course of social progress in terms of a series of progressive and retrogressive periods, and who helped to inspire the view that economies move through a more or less ordered sequence of developmental stages. In this introduction, therefore, the role of the historical school is examined further and related to that of the American institutionalist school.

ANTECEDENTS OF THE HISTORICAL SCHOOL

The eighteenth century witnessed more than the rise of economics as a science; it witnessed also efforts to extend to the field of human affairs that rigorous method of inquiry and explanation which had been responsible for the revolutionary advance made in physical science in the seventeenth century. Men now supposed that it was unnecessary to search for additional and better methods. A suitable one was at hand. It was but necessary to recognize that all problems are factual in character and hence susceptible of unique solution when reduced to terms of their elements. It was "no longer utopian," therefore, to suppose that "a wholly just, wholly virtuous, wholly satisfied society" might be created.[1] It was against this way of thinking that many nineteenth-century thinkers protested, though only some on the Smithian premise that unconscious and spontaneous interindividual cooperation is far more important than conscious design. Some were disturbed at the French Revolution and its aftermath. Some protested against various of the themes of apostles of the Enlightenment: against their secularism and rationalism; against their depreciation of established institutions, the accomplishments of past ages, and the role of man's will; against their supposition that progress might be achieved everywhere through recourse to science under enlightened leadership; against their reduction of man and society (as of the physical world) to mechanical instead of to organic terms; against their emphasis upon the individual rather than upon the Folk or the Nation; and so on. They thus expressed and reinforced a new *Weltanschauung*, which in turn affected how many thinkers defined and studied economics and economic problems. The eighteenth-century belief in the economic efficacy of applied science and centralized planning remained strong, however, in some circles, especially among the followe.s of Comte and Saint-Simon.

1. Isaiah Berlin, *The Age of Enlightenment* (New York: New American Library, 1956), p. 28.

There resulted, for many, a shift in the focus of attention, especially in Germany. The object of this attention became man, now conceived of as a being who varied in space and time, and who, as a member of his nation or folk or other community, underwent cultural evolution. It became "fashionable," especially after Schelling's and Hegel's views on the philosophy of history had become known, "to think not only of human nature generally, but also of reason itself, as something developing within history, and hence as something continually affected by changing conditions of individual and social life."[2] At the same time the individuality of epochs and nations was coming to be stressed by L. von Ranke; the influence of the *Volksgeist*, by F. C. von Savigny, founder of German historical jurisprudence; and the advantage of comparative method, by students of philology. Man's motives and character, together with his institutions and aspirations, came to be looked upon as variable and evolving, especially as evidence of evolution, cultural as well as biological, was accumulated. The method of inquiry which eighteenth-century social scientists had found adequate was no longer deemed sufficient, therefore, and as good as was to be had; nor was pursuit of self-interest still considered to be the unique key to man's behavior. Use must be made of historical principles and preconceptions.

The impact of this new historical and sociological emphasis was felt by economical writers in Germany earlier and in much greater measure than elsewhere. For here historical methods were early employed in many disciplines. Nationalist aspirations were strong and growing. Moreover, for a number of reasons, the economics of Smith and Say (in which natural and conjectural rather than philosophical or purely empirical history played a part) did not become so ascendant in Germany as in England and France. Among these reasons may be included the persistence of cameralistic influence and a concern with detailed policy, Germany's partial intellectual isolation, the presence of feudal interests and of a Romantic "economic" literature favorable thereto (*e.g.*, Adam Müller's works), and a variety of economic problems which had been at least partially solved in England.

There came into being three essentially historical types of approach, each in some measure hostile to that of the classical economists. First, emphasis might be placed upon the accumulation of factual data, upon the disclosure of the diversity and variegatedness of man's behavior, and upon showing his economic tendencies to be not universal in character but quite sensitive to differences in his cultural situation. Second, concern might be manifested primarily in the discovery of tendencies or laws of economic development, or of the stages through which an economy must evolve, together with the susceptibility of economic evolution to acceleration through conscious, collectivistic intervention. Third, it might be taken for granted that an economy would progress in accordance with the principles of dialectical materialism and hence more or less independently of conscious human intervention; this approach reflects, even more than does the second,

2. See H. D. Aiken, *The Age of Ideology* (New York: New American Library, 1956), p. 16; also Geoffrey Barraclough, *History in a Changing World* (Oxford: Basil Blackwell, 1956), p. 2.

the influence of Hegel. Each of the first two approaches was employed by members of the historical school, especially in Germany. The third was that given classic form by Marx and Engels; it provided a basis for socialist policy until, in and after the 1880's, Marxian socialism was given a more proletarian-revolutionary turn by N. Lenin and his associates.

While the nature of the approach of proponents of the historical method may be induced largely from a survey of the views of German members of the historical school, it should be noted that in each country in which this method had adherents (*e.g.*, England, the United States, France, Scandinavia), their work took on a somewhat unique form, since both economic problems and the state of social science and education varied from country to country. However, it is the German views that will be used here to exemplify the tenets of the historical economists.

Three professional economists, W. G. F. Roscher (1817–1894), follower of Ranke and Savigny, K. G. A. Knies (1821–1898), under the influence of Hegel, and Bruno Hildebrand (1812–1878), student of comparative philology, are usually described as the founders of the German Historical School, though Friedrich List (1789–1846), publicist and disciple of the Romanticist Adam Müller is sometimes grouped with them. List made use of comparative method and advanced a theory of economic stages; moreover, believing economic objectives to be subordinate to national objectives and alert to the marked dependence of a nation's strength upon its industry and transport, he advocated temporary protection of manufacture as a means of accelerating a country's passage through the earlier stages of economic development. The leading later representatives of the school include, besides its major spokesman, Gustav von Schmoller (1838–1917), G. F. Knapp (1842–1926) and Karl Bücher (1847–1930). Representative of a still later and final period are Werner Sombart (1863–1941) and Max Weber (1864–1920).

VIEWS OF THE GERMAN HISTORICAL SCHOOL

The views of the German historical economists may be set down under three headings, their criticism of the classical school, their positive themes, and their conception of economic policy and the role of the state. Of course, no one member of the school subscribed entirely to this summary, or to all the principles endorsed by any other particular member. There was never achieved within the school as much homogeneity of opinion as was to be found in the classical school or among the physiocrats. This comparative lack of homogeneity is attributable in part to the fact that the historical economists never highly conceptualized their views, preferring to formulate their opinions in quite empirical or in loosely defined terms.

The attitude of the historical economists to the tenets of the classical school and (later) of the Austrian school was always critical, though it varied from the position that the historical approach complemented that of these schools to the position that it must supersede it. Ricardo's method was found most unacceptable, as later was Menger's; to that of J. S. Mill, as to that of Smith, less objection was expressed. For Ricardo's approach was considered deductive and founded upon the premise that man's institutions and behavioral tendencies were essentially invariant and hence of the sort to permit one to infer universally valid and invariant economic principles and economic-policy indicators. Such an approach violated the basic injunction of the historical economists that one must eschew recourse to abstract methods, analytical models, and untested hypotheses. One must instead describe man's economic behavior and institutions as these are actually encountered in various times and places and (when possible) induce therefrom generalizations which are inconstant, variable, and (usually) of quite restricted applicability. One must conceive of man's motives and behavioral tendencies in psychologically realistic instead of in restrictedly suppositious terms. Man was not a mechanical, hedonistic atom, and his economic behavior could no more be described in purely individualistic terms than could that of a business enterprise. Man was always a member of diverse communities and groups, of "social organisms," and what he did was governed accordingly, being affected by noneconomic considerations as well as by those which the classical writers stressed. In sum, the historical economists objected to the classical model, in part because they found it empirically wanting, in part because they did not understand the analytical role performed by abstract models, in part because they did not appreciate the dependence even of the historian upon a variety of hypotheses, and in part because they thought of economics as serving a much broader range of values and purposes than did the classical economists.

Among the positive themes of the historical economists we may include their notions of economic development; their supposition that economic behavior and economic thought are cultural in character and hence time- and space-bound, with the result that the economic component of a societal system may not be looked upon as being so autonomous as the classical and the Austrian economists implied; and their inference, treated below, that since political considerations are of primary importance, the economic role of the state is necessarily great. Among the generalizations which detailed empirical and sometimes quantitative analysis might yield, the historical economists set most store by laws of economic development, though they differed in respect of the specificity, the variability, and the content to be assigned these "laws." One expression of this interest was the theory of economic stages, a theory (present already in Smithian and eighteenth-century thought) which, although never adequately reduced to terms of "ideal" types or constructs, was intended to facilitate comparison of national economies, to summarize or explain the course of economic development, and (especially as employed by List, who found manufacturing essential to cultural and political progress) to lend ideological support to development-accelerating policy. Thus Hildebrand, having criticized List's scheme, described barter, money economy, and credit economy as successive stages of economic organization; Bücher identified the successive stages as household, town, and national economy; and Schmoller, reasoning from German history, listed five stages of economy — village, town, territorial, national, and world. The usefulness of a theory of stages, though much criticized (*e.g.*, by Walter Eucken), had defenders inside and outside Germany even as late as the 1930's (*e.g.*, N. S. B. Gras). Recent utilizers of a stage approach (*e.g.*, C. Clark, W. G. Hoffman) have sought, however, to define each stage in purely economic terms.

The historical economists defined their stages in social and economic terms. In so doing, they were influenced in part by the view that economic activities cannot be completely sequestered, analytically or empirically, from noneconomic activities, since these several activities are interrelated, with each more or less dependent on others. Hence the methods appropriate to economics were those of cultural science rather than those of physical or of mental science. There was a role both for theory and for limited generalizations, however, even as Roscher had suggested when he sought to combine theory and description, and this role received expression especially in the method of ideal types, utilized by Bücher in his theory of stages and subsequently given theoretical form and practical application by Max Weber. This method explicitly recognized that specific stages in time or collections in space do not *per se* have meaningful and discernible concrete existence. But it recognized also that leading and relevant features of a period in time or a location in space can be abstracted and conceptualized and then used to analyze and explain events which empirical inquiry has disclosed. Undoubtedly awareness of the usefulness of abstractions of this sort eventually made for awareness of the usefulness of other abstractions, among them some of the models employed by the Austrian and the neoclassical economists.

Policy considerations and the economic role of the state were stressed by the historical economists, especially in Germany. The state was more than a political instrument designed to preserve law and order, maintain a milieu within which private enterprise could function, and undertake tasks that private enterprise could not accomplish effectively. The state, at least as conceived by many German writers, approximated a community or social organism that helped to define the ends of nations and individuals and assisted them in realizing these ends. These writers were not sympathetic, therefore, to so great an emphasis upon individual freedom and initiative as was found in Britain and America and as had become associated with classical economics. Egotism needed to be restrained. The ethical implications of economic activities needed to be assessed. The state needed to intervene in economic life not only to serve communal ends but also to overcome current economic weaknesses by fomenting industrial and transport development, undertaking needed agrarian reforms, and providing social insurance and greater equity in distribution so that the forces making for socialism might be weakened. There was need, therefore, for detailed study of particular economic problems and their possible solutions, so that appropriate policies might be adopted. In consequence, interest in particular kinds of economic problems (*e.g.*, agricultural, transport, monetary) and in the application of their findings became a major concern of the historical school.

While it is not easy to pinpoint the effects produced by the historical economists, since some of the effects in question are attributable in part also to changes in the climate of opinion and to the response made by other social scientists to changing circumstances, the nature of these effects may be indicated. The emphasis of the historical economists upon empirical inquiry, whether to discover coexisting facts or to infer causal relationships and trends, focused attention upon various concrete factors and changes which had been insufficiently taken into account by many writers in the classical tradition. They drew attention, for example, as in a number of instances did their Marxist contemporaries, to the existence of classes and often intense class conflict and to the need for mitigating arrangements; to implications of the rise of large firms and industrial combinations; to the growing and necessary role of trade unions; to the need for suitable social legislation and collective intervention if revolutionary socialism were to be held in check; and so on. They made more clear and concrete not only the great importance of the economic role of the state but also the need for economic policy to be formulated only after careful inquiry and in the light of relevant historical, institutional, and other factual circumstances. Their concern with the nature of social and cultural science helped give currency and shape to analysis of methodological and related issues. Representative of these issues were the nature of the difference between descriptive or idiographic science and nomothetic or law-formulating science (a distinction formulated by W. Windelband and criticized by H. Rickert); the effect of a social scientist's values and degree of ethical neutrality upon his conduct of economic or other social inquiry; the nature of objectivity and logic as manifested in the social sciences; the interrelations of economics and politics; and so on. Weber contributed importantly (as did Durkheim and Pareto), in part perhaps because of the influence of other historical-economic writers, to the growing recognition of the fact that relations based solely upon contract, mutual advantage, and the like were insufficient to bind men together and preserve a stable society; there was need also for social cement in the form of common and collective values, aspirations, etc.[3] This list suggests both the nature of the contributions made by the historical economists and the fact that they lay far more stress in the areas of economic applications and of sociology than in that of economic theory.

The historical economists also made negative contributions. Illustrative of the worst of these at the policy level was their endorsement of protectionism even in countries such as Britain and their failure to appreciate the extent to which international commerce could and did serve to free countries of the impact of comparative economic disadvantages. Far more important, of course, was the great slowing down of progress in economic theory in the Germany that had produced von Thünen, though not in other countries where the number of historical economists was too small to dominate the content of economics. This stagnating influence had its origin in the anti-

3. See Talcott Parsons, *The Structure of Social Action* (New York: McGraw-Hill Book Co., 1937).

theoretical bias of the historical economists and in their failure to conceptualize historical economics significantly and make sufficient use of abstract models, ideal types, etc. In consequence, the historical economists sometimes endorsed policies on economically untenable grounds (*e.g.*, some of their protectionism) or proved incapable of effectively criticizing ideologies (*e.g.*, the Marxian) whose value-premises were at variance with their own. Perhaps representative of this antitheoretical bias was the polemical attack Schmoller made upon Menger, his method of analysis, and the usefulness and theoretically unifying role of the marginal-utility principle, though this attack was sharper and less balanced than were the critiques of classical economics made by Schmoller's predecessors or by non-German historical economists.

By the turn of the century, however, this methodological conflict had been largely composed; economists were becoming alert to the complementary roles of theory, statistical and historical inquiry, and the use of mathematical and nonmathematical models, as well as to the restrictions to which economic generalizations become subject when they are given empirical content. Somewhat typical of the attitude of those subjected to criticism at the hands of the historical economists is that of Böhm-Bawerk who, while admitting the importance of historical and statistical inquiry and its usefulness in facilitating needed social reform, defended the contribution of the classical school and emphasized the fundamental importance of the "abstract-deductive" or "isolating" method employed by the Austrians. He noted in particular that in a number of spheres of investigation enough empirical data had been gathered for the time being, with the result that the current need was for the "effectual 'distillation'" of these data; whereas in others the primary need was always for theoretical analysis, since an economist's ordinary experience normally equipped him with the requisite empirical knowledge. There was much "the outward eye . . . unaided" could not see; the "mind" must therefore construct that which was lacking, "by means of a series of abstract speculations" such as had produced "the theory of final utility." This injunction was pertinent to historical economics. It, too, had need of "general theory" and "abstract deduction" even as economics based upon the "abstract-deductive method" had need (as was clearly recognized) to start with hypotheses that correspond "with the fact."[4]

The views of the German historical economists exercised considerable influence in other countries. In England, for example, they reinforced an indigenous and somewhat historist attack (inspired in part by Henry Maine and A. Comte) upon classical political economy. English historical economists (*e.g.*, Cliffe Leslie, J. K. Ingram, W. Cunningham) advocated enlarging the scope of economics, making it a more historical and evolutionary science, and resting its findings on relatively narrow premises induced from

4. See Eugen von Böhm-Bawerk, "The Historical *vs.* the Deductive Method in Political Economy," *Annals* of the American Academy of Political and Social Science, I (October 1890), 244–71.

reality. Their influence, though overrated, "was undoubtedly significant."[5] The American historists owed their inspiration largely to Germany, where a number of leading American economists (*e.g.*, J. B. Clark, E. J. James, R. T. Ely, H. C. Adams, E. R. A. Seligman) studied. Making discriminating use of German historist practice, they greatly modified current American economics and made it more empirical, more problem-oriented, more statistical, and less narrow in scope. They developed research interest in public finance, railroads, agriculture, labor questions, technology, the impact of economic legislation, the trade cycle, and other practical subjects.[6]

THE MARXIAN SCHOOL

Turning to the Marxian school, with its emphasis upon the materialistic rather than the cultural base of society, we encounter a similar, though differently focused, emphasis upon the inconstant, changing, and evolutionary character of the ingredients of society and their interrelations. The elements composing cultures are interrelated and form wholes or *Gestalten* which develop through time, largely because of changes that take place in the most dynamic of the components of this cultural whole. That component, Marx and his followers believed, was "the relations of production," property and otherwise, which fixed the social status and the economic role of individuals and governed their aspirations, motives, mental outlook, and degree of participation in the fruits of economic activity. At no time in history had their own degree of participation been generally acceptable or looked upon as equitable by all members of a society. Some were favored, others were exploited. Society therefore was divided into classes, into a beneficiary ruling class and an exploited class, with the former standing to gain from the maintenance of property relations.

Each class, it was held, had its own ideology, its own set of ideas respecting what was right and wrong, what the future held in store, what was to be done, and so on. Each class made use of this ideology, as of other instruments, in its struggle with the opposing class, man's history having long been a sequence of class struggles, sometimes hidden and sometimes open, but always between "exploiting and exploited, ruling and oppressed classes," between "freeman and slave, patrician and plebeian, lord and serf, guildmaster and journeyman, in a word, oppressor and oppressed." In Marx's day, the struggle was between the "Bourgeoisie," or capitalist class which owned the instruments of production, and the "Proletariat," which was without this equipment; and it would finally end in the supersession of the bourgeoisie by the proletariat and in a revolutionary reconstitution of society into a stable, classless, equitable, and generally acceptable form. This end would come about because the proletariat stood to gain by the change

5. See A. W. Coats, "The Historist Reaction in English Political Economy, 1870–90," *Economica*, XXI (May 1954), 143–53.
6. See Joseph Dorfman, "The Role of the German Historical School in American Economic Thought," *American Economic Review, Papers and Proceedings*, XLV (2) (May 1955), 17–28.

and was becoming increasingly aware of its prospective advantage, and because modifications in the mode of production were inevitable and suited, as a rule, to intensify or generate contradictions within the economy, to modify property relations, and to augment the potential power of the proletariat. Marx's forecast thus ran in terms of dialectical materialism which he constructed by standing Hegel's dialectic "on its head." The dialectical process of change was retained, but it was translated from idealistic and mental terms into realistic and material terms; and somewhat corresponding alterations were made in Hegel's treatment of such matters as the nature of determinism and the source of variation and change, the time- and space-boundness of ideas and motives, the nature and role of human consciousness, the relation of theory and practice, and so on. Marx's approach thus flowed in considerable degree out of the same general climate of opinion and philosophical interpretation as did that of the historical school. The two schools shared above all a belief in the persistence of evolution and change, in the elements of society as well as in their interrelations.

In his major work, *Capital*, the last two volumes of which were put together by F. Engels, Marx sought to describe rather precisely the laws of economic motion that permeate a capitalistic society and to demonstrate how these laws, operating in accordance with the tenets of dialectical materialism, must bring about the termination of capitalism and its replacement by a classless system, the operating rules of which he did not anticipate or describe in any detail. He seems to have counted predominantly on a comparatively persisting decline in the rate of profit rather than upon underconsumption or persisting internal economic imbalance. This decline would flow out of a steady increase in the amount of fixed capital used per worker, which tended, on balance, to reduce the relative amount of surplus or profit that could be gotten out of the working class even though its wages were kept very low by the presence of an industrial reserve army of unemployed recruited through population growth and the introduction of labor-displacing machinery. In consequence of this decline in the rate of profit, marginal firms would continue to fail and many of their owners would be converted into proletarians, with the result that this class would form an increasing fraction of the total labor force until in the end it would have enough strength to seize political power, establish a dictatorship of the proletariat, and eventually wipe out the vestiges of capitalism and establish a classless society.

About this process there was an automaticity remindful of the automaticity stressed by the classical and the Austrian economists, though in substance dissimilar thereto. In the end, however, the left-wing Marxists, under Lenin's leadership, lost faith in comparatively unassisted automaticity, condemned the exponents of evolutionary and gradualist socialism, and stressed the need of recourse to revolutionary methods if the advent of a finally socialist state were to be accelerated as it might. Needless to say, Marx's algebra could not substantiate his hopes and forecasts unless its elements were defined in unique ways not warranted even by his own

494

discussion; the denouement he sought was thus but one of a set of diverse possibilities implicit in his account. His most valuable scientific contributions consisted, therefore, not in his forecasts, but in his analysis of the trade cycle, of economic and related change generally, and of historical processes. His major influence consisted, of course, in the gigantic impetus he gave to an ideology that has already won sway over more than a third of the world's population.

THE AMERICAN INSTITUTIONALISTS

Some but not all of the American institutionalists subscribed to a critique of neoclassical and marginalist economics that resembled the historical and Marxian critiques in emphasizing the evolutionary character of economic society and its elements and their interrelations. This was the approach of Veblen and some of his followers, but not that of J. R. Commons, who focused attention less upon the impact of dynamic change through time than upon economic transactions and the role of collective action in resolving conflicts of interest involved in or arising out of transactions.

Veblen, under the influence of both Marx and the Darwinians, was highly critical of neoclassical and Austrian economic theory on the ground that economics was not, in its preconceptions or its analytical techniques, or in its problem-orientation, an evolutionary science, and was not, therefore, alert to the attitudinal, scientific, and institutional changes flowing out of the ascendancy of a "matter-of-fact" point of view and the emergence of an economy dominated by modern technology and the "machine process." Economics remained "substantially a taxonomic science," having been given its current form at an earlier period when modern technological conditions and the modern scientific point of view had not yet come into being. It was essential, therefore, that economic science be reconstituted and adapted to the analysis and solution of current problems, in particular the process of cumulative change and its determinants. "Under the stress of modern technological exigencies, men's everyday habits of thought are falling into the lines that in the sciences constitute the evolutionary method; and knowledge which proceeds on a higher, more archaic plane is becoming alien and meaningless to them. The social and political sciences must follow the drift, for they are already caught in it."[7] Changing circumstances would compel changes in the content of economics even as it would compel changes in the content of man's institutions which were no longer adapted to the needs of the day. Presumably, such subjects as the trade cycle, the behavior of prices, the impact of combinations and modern finance, the circumstances fixing the level of employment and output, institutional

7. See "Why is Economics not an Evolutionary Science?" *Quarterly Journal of Economics*, XII (July 1898), 373–97, esp. 397. Veblen's argument was further developed in a number of essays, some of which were later assembled in *The Place of Science in Modern Civilisation* (New York: B. W. Huebsch, 1919). Most of Veblen's views are succinctly summarized in Joseph Dorfman's *Thorstein Veblen and His America* (New York: Viking Press, 1935).

determinants of tastes and distribution, and the process of economic change as such would be far more suitable for inquiry than would marginal analysis, static firm theory, allocation, etc.

A satisfactory solution was not to be found in the methods of the historical school or in the Marxian approach. He was highly critical of the historical school in general and quite critical even of Schmoller's work. The historical school had produced history, not economics; it was innocent of the theory requisite to translate its accumulation of data and narratives into "a consistent body of knowledge." It lacked what every evolutionary science must have, "a theory of a process, of an unfolding sequence." Its earlier "romantic-historical line of inquiry and speculation," so un-Darwinian and un-Spencerian, had yielded "aphoristic wisdom," but "no cultural laws of the kind aimed at," since they apparently did not exist. Schmoller's work was superior in that he had come to rely upon a Darwinian rather than upon a Hegelian approach. Yet even he had failed to develop a genetic theory suitable to economics and the interpretation of his materials; nor had he freed his work of personal predilection, taste, and normative leanings, and grounded his findings solely upon "scientifically determinable cause and effect." He had not realized that "empirical generalisations" are not a substitute for an adequate account of "incessant cumulative change," of the "cumulative process of development, and its complex and unstable outcome." Some of his criticisms of Marx's analysis of economic change, by which Veblen had been somewhat influenced, are of the order of those which he directed against the historical school, which was, in his opinion, representative of the Hegelian right even as Marxism was representative of the Hegelian left. Marxian development theory was weak in general, since it rested upon Hegelian instead of upon Darwinian postulates, with the results that it could not accommodate a theory of impersonal, cumulative process, and that it overlooked the fact that "every improvement in working-class conditions is to be counted as a gain for the revolutionary forces." Marxian theory was sometimes wrong in detail as well as weak. Its supposition that worsening labor conditions and industrial crises, together with an inevitable class struggle, would bring about the downfall of capitalism was not in keeping with the facts. Its doctrine of an industrial reserve army was "fragile." It neglected trade-union and similar movements and overlooked the role of such psychological factors as the tendency to emulate. It even failed to anticipate the nature of the socialist government it forecast.[8]

Veblen, as Homan shows, did not convert economics or any branch of it into an evolutionary science. His own method was perhaps best exemplified in his studies of business enterprise and ownership and in his analysis of the rise of imperial Germany and Japan and of the conditions essential to the establishment of a permanent peace at the close of World War I. Yet his approach, as interpreted by others, though influential, especially outside the environs of economics, did not really produce a school. It resulted in a greater emphasis upon phenomena of change, upon descriptive economics,

8. This paragraph is based on Veblen's essay cited in the preceding note and on *The Place of Science . . .* , pp. 252–78, 387–456.

and upon the role of noneconomic factors which condition economic events. At the same time it affected the development of economic theory adversely in that some of Veblen's disciples, lacking his own grasp of theory, were comparatively hostile to it and to methodology and sometimes even depreciated the role of the rational in human affairs. Its major deposit may well be in the new orientations given economic inquiry by some of Veblen's abler disciples and perhaps also in the present-day recognition of the limitations of economics as such and the need, when some kinds of inquiry are undertaken, to supplement the tools of the economist with those that have been devised by sister disciplines. Today many economists are congenial, by training and conception of social science, to giving weight to at least some of the considerations stressed by Veblen. But this was not so true in his day when the training of most economists was not suited to make them appreciate his approach, nor were they likely to be interested in the sorts of problems to which his methods were adapted. In short, what he had to say was not found relevant by many economists; hence the limitedness of his impact.

Homan deals with the diverse views of the American economists whose qualities of dissidence and of congeniality to some of Veblen's views have caused them to be grouped together as a school — the institutional economists. While only some of these shared the strong interest of Marx, Veblen, and the historical economists in a developmental approach to economics, most of them gave attention to the institutional contexts within which economic activities are carried on and economic rationality is manifested, though few defined these contexts and their impact with care.

John R. Commons is an exception to much of what has been said and is included here because he looked upon himself, not as a creator or a proponent of institutional economics, but as an economist strongly interested both in economic theory and in giving "to collective action, in all its varieties, its due place in economic theory." He was not especially concerned, therefore, with developmental theory, though alert to the historical dimensions of problems. Economic action and pricing or distribution are at the bottom of that in which he was interested, the *transaction*, but the action in question is collective rather than individual, and the quantitative solution arises out of negotiation and arbitration instead of out of a balancing of the forces of supply and demand within a determinating market. Commons' main concern is thus the set of mechanisms, customs, and processes — legal and otherwise — through which order is brought out of a conflict of interests associated with a transaction, the parties to which are or may be mutually dependent; it is a mode of "creating a new harmony of interests — or at least order, if harmony is impossible." In his analysis of these mechanisms, etc., he found it necessary to deal with such concepts as property, futurity, volition, causation, and he was able to connect his inquiries with those made by earlier generations of economists.

It is not easy to discover the extent of Commons' specific influence even though his analytical unit, the transaction, usually involves the determination of a price. The general subject of his inquiry, however, conflict resolution, has been commanding increasing attention (*e.g.*, in the writings of C. I. Barnard and H. A. Simon), particularly when organization theory is employed to supplement firm theory, and a journal has been established to deal with the subject. Comparison of Commons' approach with those of these later writers may serve to illustrate the increase in the extent to which problems are conceptualized and put into theoretical terms today as compared with a quarter-century ago.[9]

COMPARISON

Comparison of the several approaches treated in this introduction with those of the writers discussed in Parts Four and Six reveals that the historical economists, together with Marx and Veblen, had a quite different conception of the scope of economics than did the classical economists and their marginalist and neoclassical successors. The neoclassical and Austrian economists were concerned primarily with the allocative mechanisms utilized in a society and with the circumstances that governed the functioning of these mechanisms; so also were the classical economists, though in a lesser degree, since they had not equipped themselves with an adequate conception of the role of marginal quantities and marginal individuals and firms. These economists were not interested in making comparisons across great reaches of time or cultural space. They could, therefore, treat as essentially constant and invariant such matters as man's behavioral tendencies and the institutions which governed his economically oriented interactions with his fellows. They could suppose man to behave in an economically rational manner within the social context and specific situations in which he found himself. They could even allow for changes in this context, usually by taking small changes and one at a time, just as they usually examined the effect of only one purely economic change (*e.g.*, in a price) at a time. Furthermore, they could abstract relevant features from reality and transform them into models designed to facilitate analysis, since other features of reality excluded from the model would exercise little influence upon the outcome. Their concern was essentially with economic statics; and they sought to limit this concern to what was highly relevant in particular cases and thereby to infer much from little. Longer-run development was of minor analytical concern to the marginalists, of greater concern to the neoclassical economists, and of yet greater concern to the classical economists; yet even these last confined their attention to such matters as population and capital growth while holding man's economic-behavior tendencies and institutions essentially constant.

In contrast, the historical economists and (in greater measure) Marx and Veblen were interested primarily in the process of change and in the effects of change in factors treated as constant by the economists whom they criticized; they were not greatly interested in such matters as allocative mechanisms. It is not possible to assess their performance nicely in

9. The best statement of Commons' approach is his *Institutional Economics* (New York: The Macmillan Co., 1934).

terms of the standards of those they criticized; it must be assessed in terms of their accomplishments, given their objectives. These accomplishments were not outstanding in most instances, above all on the part of Veblen's institutionalist followers. It is possible to infer, however, that this weakness of performance was highly correlated with a neglect of theoretical considerations, concern with which makes present-day recourse to interdisciplinary approaches so much more effective than were the approaches dealt with in Part Five.

20.

HENRYK GROSSMAN

The Evolutionist

Revolt Against

Classical Economics

Any theoretical analysis of a contemporary economic system must lead to the formulation of a standard with which to evaluate the existing level of development. To have any validity such a standard must be worked out of the developmental process itself and not merely from the level attained at the moment of analysis. It will therefore be useful to the present-day theorist to look back and see how dynamic or evolutionary thinking actually entered the field of economic theory.

The problem has not been adequately or at all accurately presented in our economic literature. Thus, Richard T. Ely writes: "It is probably due to Herbert Spencer more than to any other person that we have come to recognize the applicability of evolution to the various departments of the social life of man."[1] But the essay of Spencer to which he refers did not appear until 1857,[2] decades after others were already using evolutionary notions in the social sciences. J. B. Bury, to cite a more recent example, wrote a whole book on the idea of progress[3] without even mentioning Sismondi or Richard Jones — the two men who first worked out the idea of the historical succession of ever more advanced economic stages. In German economic literature either the problem is not discussed at all, as in Bücher's widely known

Excerpt reprinted by permission of The University of Chicago Press from "The Evolutionist Revolt Against Classical Economics," *The Journal of Political Economy*, LI (October, December 1943), 381–96, 506–22; pp. 381–86, 506–22 excerpted. At the time of original publication, the author, now deceased, lived in New York City.

study of the rise of national economy,[4] which does not once mention feudalism or capitalism; or else the sole responsibility for what they call the "sociologizing" of economics is falsely attributed to Hegel and his school.[5] Whittaker, too, in a recent book, makes the mistake of overestimating the German representatives of historicism — the German historical school and Hegel. At the same time, speaking of the French and English, he mentions the economic views of Saint-Simon, Sismondi, James Steuart, and Richard Jones, but not their ideas on evolution. Condorcet is not mentioned at all.[6]

The purpose of the present study is to show the decisive role of French and English economists in laying the basis for modern evolutionary theories of economics, and particularly for the work of Karl Marx. It is fully consistent with the general neglect of our problem that Marx's contribution to the "sociologizing" of economics is also widely misconstrued. According to Sombart, for example, the importance of Marx lies not so much in the field of economic theory as in the field of sociology. "Marx," he writes, "applied evolutionary thinking to the social process."[7] He gives us "an insight into the historical character of the economy, into *its constant changeability in the course of history*. He first created the *concept of the economic system* and made it the subject of economic science."[8] Sombart thus arbitrarily gives Marx credit for accomplishments he never claimed and thereby conceals and distorts the picture of Marx's real work.[9] Unfortunately, Sombart's view has been widely echoed, even in Socialist circles. Eduard Heimann, for example, repeats that Marx's decisive contribution to the growth of economics, his truly "Copernican significance," does not lie in specific theories, such as the theory of surplus value, the theory of concentration, or the theory of crisis, but in his having for the first time "historicized" or "sociologized" economics. It was Marx, he writes, who "first conceived [capitalism] to be historical, and therefore timebound, transformable and transitory." Marx was able to discover this insight because he was the "heir and executor of Hegel's thinking" and because he possessed the "political will" to attack static capitalism.[10]

We can easily dispose of the allegedly Hegelian basis for the "historicizing" of economics. All the great theorists of the French Enlightenment, with the exception of Rousseau, held the philosophic view that history was an endless progress marking man's path to reason.[11] Endless progress necessarily implies that the existing reality, the given state of affairs, will be negated and will not continue to exist indefinitely. Hegel, on the other hand, thought that history had reached its goal in his own day, that the idea and reality had found their common ground.[12] On this point, Marx was closer to the French tradition than to Hegel.

In the *Philosophy of Right*, Hegel patterns the notion of freedom after the free ownership of property. The historical process thus becomes a glorification of the history of the middle class; and Hegel's *Philosophy of History* ends with the consolidation of middle-class society. Here was a social system no longer to be transcended. We shall see that the French tradition from Condorcet through Saint-Simon and his disciples to Sismondi and Pecqueur was very different. For them the idea of historical progress ruled by reason tended to turn away from the possessing classes in favor of "the great mass of those who live by their work" (Condorcet). They stood opposed to the existing oppressive social system. Progress does not end with middle-class society. Quite the contrary, it will continue to unfold in the future in new social structures. Whereas one trend in eighteenth-century thought, influenced by the religious tradition of the Garden of Eden, placed the Golden Age in the past, at the beginning of man's history, Saint-Simon turned the sequence around. "The golden age," he wrote, following an idea of Condorcet's, "which a blind tradition had always placed in the past, lies ahead of us." Here, too, Marx is linked to French thought, not to Hegel.

We must remember that Hegel's *Philosophy of History* was a relatively late work, published posthumously in 1837, four years after Richard Jones had already appeared with his historical study of economics.[13] Hegel, furthermore, as we shall see later, expressly rejected the concept that must lie at the base of any genetic theory of development, namely, that a higher, more developed phase proceeds from the preceding, lower phase.

On the other hand, a genuinely powerful influence on evolutionary thinking must be assigned to the revolution in astrophysics brought about by the publication of Laplace's *Exposition du système du monde* in 1796. Laplace denied the unchanging character of "eternal" nature and offered his famous theory of the evolution of the planetary system, through purely mechanical phenomena of the attraction and repulsion of atoms, from a rotating ball of gas which, by cooling and contraction, threw off segments of its surface. These segments in turn united to become the planets. Both the earth and the entire solar system were formerly nonexistent, and the time will come when the sun will be extinguished and the universe will break apart.[14] At one time the earth was an uninhabited and unformed mass of gas. It required millions of years for the cooling of the earth's crust to create the conditions which brought into existence the lower organic forms and eventually man himself.

This evolutionary theory of astrophysics had already appeared in 1755 in an anonymous publication by Immanuel Kant.[15] It had failed to make headway against the biblical tradition of Genesis, however, and had passed unnoticed. Kant himself knew that he had "travelled on a dangerous journey" and went to great pains in his Introduction to ward off the charge of atheism. It required the intellectual atmosphere of the French Revolution to obtain recognition for such a work as Laplace's *Exposition*.

Finally, it must be noted that the "sociologizing" of economics is not and cannot be regarded as a purely intellectual development flowing from Hegel's dialectics or any other book. While the thinkers of the Enlightenment strove to deduce the eternal laws of a rational "natural order" from nature and from the properties of the human individual, the advocates of the evolutionary idea whom we are dealing with here based their universal laws and predictions on *history*, on actually observed *evolutionary tendencies*. Their ideas are the theoretical reflection of such great historical phenomena as the French and American revolutions[16] and the industrial revolution in England. Above all, it was the outbreak of the French Revolution which, like the eruption of a volcano, exposed the weaknesses of eighteenth-century rationalism. What caused such an eruption? To answer that question, man turned to history.[17]

The classical economists had also made some investigations of the past. Adam Smith, for example, revealed considerable historical knowledge, as in chapter iv of Book I, "Of the Origin and Use of Money," or chapter xi, "Digression concerning the Variation in the Value of Silver during the Course of the Four Last Centuries," and, above all, in Book III on the "Progress of Opulence in Different Nations."

The classical economists never reached the point, however, of permitting the idea of development to bring order out of the chaos of economic facts. Adam Smith distinguished between advancing, stationary, or declining conditions of society,[18] and Ricardo talked about the "progress" or "natural advance of society," of "an improving society" advancing from poverty to a flourishing condition.[19] But neither one knew of phases of development, only of datable conditions of one and the same capitalist society — conditions that varied in size of population, extent of capital accumulation, or knowledge of agricultural techniques[20] and not in their fundamental structure.[21] In his chapter entitled "On the Accumulation of Capital," Adam Smith's account of the historical development of England from the invasion of Julius Caesar is characteristic. He writes:

> When we compare the state of a nation at two different periods and find that the annual produce of its land and labor is evidently greater at the latter than at the former, that its lands are better cultivated, its manufactures more numerous and more flourishing, we may be assured that its capital must have increased during the interval between the two periods.[22]

"In different stages of society," wrote Ricardo in a similar vein, "the accumulation of capital. . . . is more or less rapid," so that in new settlements with little capital, for example, it is very slow. The "different stages" are thus nothing but levels of the same capitalist system of economy. Marx commented sarcastically that "Ricardo considers the capitalist form of labor as the eternal, natural form of social labor. He makes the primitive fisherman and the primitive hunter straightway exchange their fish and game as owners of commodities, in proportion to the labor-time embodied in these exchange values."[23]

The classical economists lacked an understanding of the real developmental sequence and changes of economic systems. Just as Rousseau in the *Social Contract* explained the origin of social institutions rationalistically, the classicists took a rationalistic rather than a genetic approach to the past. All previous societies were measured with the rational yardstick of free trade. That is why they knew of only two ideal states: the "original state of things," occurring before the fall from grace, as it were, and the bourgeois state in their own days, of more or less free trade and competition. All intervening epochs, with their severe limitations upon trade and industry, were condemned as unfit and erroneous. They were never discussed in terms of the limitations and conditions of their own time.[24]

We have become so accustomed to the idea of historical development that it is difficult for us to imagine such a lack of historicism. How did the change in our thinking come about? It must be stressed that we are not concerned with individual, isolated representatives of the evolutionary idea; such representatives appeared as early as the Middle Ages[25] and the Renaissance (Vico). The subject of our analysis is a current of thinking which emerged in the social sciences during the last third of the eighteenth century and became triumphant during the first half of the nineteenth century: the concept of the evolution of human society through a succession of economic stages, each superior to the preceding one. Six men are the main representatives of this current: Condorcet, Saint-Simon, and Sismondi in France; Sir James Steuart and Richard Jones in England; and, finally, Karl Marx, who synthesized and completed the whole development. Thereafter the theory of evolution through succession of definite economic structures was not further developed and fell into discredit with the dominant school.[26]

The great revolution in thought brought about by the French Revolution was most notable in the handling of social problems. Ever since Descartes, the notion of the unity of all knowledge had been generally prevalent. All phenomena, it was believed, no matter how complicated, can ultimately be understood by the same method — the mathematical method of the natural sciences. With the French Revolution, however, the idea arose that social phenomena constitute a special class, requiring special treatment and a special methodology. Eternally unchanging laws may be valid for the natural sciences, because nature is eternal and unchanging, but human society undergoes constant change (progress) from epoch to epoch. The particular task of the social sciences is therefore not to seek for eternal laws but to find the law of change itself.

It is true that the application of eternal natural laws to human society was still given formal recognition; but, in actual practice, men like Condorcet, Saint-Simon, and Richard Jones began to make sharp differentiations. Eventually, with the further spread of new sciences, such as chemistry and biology, in which mathematical analysis played no role, an open revolt set in against the applications of the methods of natural science to the study of society. Auguste Comte waged a bitter struggle against the "metaphysical prejudice that no real certainty can exist outside mathematics" and the "empty scientific overlordship temporarily granted the mathematical spirit." In the last "lesson" of his *Course*, Comte wrote: "Instead of seeking blindly for a sterile scientific unity, as oppressive as it is chimerical, in the reduction of all phenomena to a single order of laws, the human mind will eventually consider the different classes of events as having their special laws." He went on to say that "the laws of organic phenomena or social phenomena are established by the predominance of specific methods: the comparative method in biology, the historical method in sociology."[27]

504

Alongside the trend of thought linked with the French Revolution, another important movement grew out of the industrial revolution in England. Every year new technical processes were increasing the productivity of industry. The equilibrium of society was overthrown, to the detriment of the country districts and to the advantage of the towns, which were rapidly increasing both in number and in size. The workmen affected by the rapid introduction of machinery were in revolt against the novel conditions.[28] England was steadily moving away from the Continental type of agricultural nations, and this rapid process of differentiation demanded an explanation of its historical roots. "Why have not all civilized societies," wrote Lord Lauderdale, "derived equal benefit from them [i.e., from new technical inventions] — and what are the circumstances that retard the progress of industry in some countries, and that guide its direction in all?"[29]

The tremendous leap in production, on the other hand, particularly during and after the Napoleonic Wars, resulted in a marked increase in trade and extension of the world market. One of the consequences was the establishment of close economic and cultural contact between western European capitalism and the more backward economies of southern and eastern Europe, South America, and, above all, Asia. A clear understanding by means of historical comparison was thus afforded of the different economic systems still existing in different parts of the world and of the changeability of specific economic institutions, such as property. These new insights, together with the influence of the French Revolution previously discussed,[30] inevitably led to a better understanding of the historical development of all social institutions and to the formulation of the inductive method in the field of history and economics, which in the field of history is associated with the name of Auguste Comte.[31]

The chief representative of evolutionary ideas in the field of economics in England is the Reverend Richard Jones; but the way was prepared for Jones by the work of Sir James Steuart (1712–80), whose *Inquiry into the Principles of Political Economy*[32] reveals an evolutionary approach to economic problems. He argues that the "speculative person" or theorist must use not only deduction but also the inductive method grounded on observation. On the one hand, he must consider the universal factors — he must "become a citizen of the world."[33] In analyzing individual branches of the economy — population, agriculture, trade, industry, interest, or money — he cannot remain satisfied with mere description, "the nature of his work being a deduction of principles, not a collection of institutions."[34]

On the other hand, Steuart warns against too easy generalizations that are not properly based on experience, against

the habit of running into what the French call *Systèmes*. These are no more than a chain of contingent consequences, drawn from a few fundamental maxims, adopted perhaps . . . . rashly. . . . .[35] If one considers the variety . . . . in different countries, in the distribution of property . . . . of classes, [etc.] . . . . one may conclude, that . . . . principles, however, universally true, may become quite ineffectual in practice.[36]

505

Political economy must be adjusted to these differences. That is why, in approaching political economy, Steuart conducts "himself through the great avenues of this extensive labyrinth" of facts "by this kind of historical clue";[37] and he promises to treat the subject "in that order which the revolutions of the last centuries have pointed out as the most natural."[38]

In the second chapter of Book I, entitled "Of the Spirit of a People," Steuart offers a sketch of the historical development of Europe "from the experience of what has happened."[39] The "great alteration in the affairs of Europe within these . . . . centuries, by the discovery of America and the Indies," namely, the rise of industry and learning and the introduction of trade, led to the "dissolution of the feudal form of government" and the introduction of "civil and domestic liberty."[40] These, in turn, "produced wealth and credit, these again debts and taxes; and all together established a perfectly new system of political economy."[41] All these factors "have entirely altered the plan of government everywhere. From feudal and military, it is become free and commercial."[42]

The social transformation has led, in turn, to corresponding changes in "the manners of Europe";[43] and the two together are changing the spirit of the people, slowly to be sure, but nonetheless unmistakably, when we compare any two succeeding generations.[44]

The "sociologizing" of economic categories and institutions was carried through still more penetratingly and systematically by the Reverend Richard Jones (1790–1855), a man who has not been properly appreciated except by Marx.[45] Jones was the first Englishman to criticize the classical economists from the standpoint of the historical school. He sharply attacked their attempts to deduce economic laws valid for all times and all countries. He wrote:

We must get comprehensive views of facts, that we may arrive at principles which are truly comprehensive. . . . . [If] we determine to know as much as we can of the world as it has been, and of the world as it is, before we lay down general laws as to the economical habits and fortunes of mankind or of classes of men: there are open to us two sources of knowledge, — history and statistics, the story of the past, and a detail of the present condition of the nations of the earth. [On the other hand,] if we take a different method, if we snatch at general principles, and content ourselves with confined observations, two things will happen to us. First, what we call general principles will often be found to have no generality . . . . at every step of our further progress, we shall be obliged to confess [that they] are frequently false; and secondly, ...[46]

Jones was especially sharp in his criticism of the supposed universality of Ricardo's laws. He held that they have but limited historical validity, specifically only where Ricardo's presuppositions agree with the actual conditions. They are valid neither for the past nor for the future, because in different epochs the conditions change and no longer coincide with Ricardo's premises.[47]

This approach is genuinely epoch-making when contrasted with the "eternal" laws of the classicists. Just before the publication of Jones's major work,[48] his friend William Whewell hailed him as the founder of the inductive system of political economy, in contrast to Ricardo, the master of the deductive method, and expected that Jones's book would *faire époque*. Actually, the work received scant notice. Among the classical economists, only McCulloch gave it some attention, and he dismissed it as "superficial" and unimportant. John Stuart Mill describes Jones's *Essay on Distribution* as a "copious repertory of valuable facts on the landed tenures of different countries"; Jones's evolutionary ideas are not mentioned.[49] Much more recently Böhm-Bawerk, in his history of economic theory, the third German edition of which appeared in 1914, that is, after the publication of Marx's study of Jones in his *Theorien ueber den Mehrwert*, could not say more than that Jones "adds nothing important to our knowledge."[50] Marian Bowley disposes of him briefly by saying that he "looked upon sociology as a branch of economics, thus revising Comte's treatment of economics as a branch of sociology," and that he "criticized the classics for ignoring the relativity of economic laws."[51]

Though Jones's influence on his immediate contemporaries was thus slight, he exercised a powerful indirect influence through Marx. He is one of the few economists of whom Marx speaks with deep acknowledgment, despite the fact that Jones, a friend of Malthus, was very conservative in his political thinking and rejected Ricardo's doctrine of the opposition of class interests in favor of a faith in class harmony.[52] Marx recognized the limited bourgeois character of Jones's horizon but called him the last representative of the "true science of political economy"[53] and made a special analysis of each of his major works; we find in this analysis frequent references to Jones's superiority over the classical economists.[54]

Jones was not a theorist in the classical sense of developing categorical concepts by sharp, logical deduction from a given set of presuppositions. He was a historian. But, unlike the discredited school of Roscher, who substituted for theoretical laws an unthinking, chronological accumulation of unanalyzed descriptive material, Jones considered it his function to test and correct the prevalent theories against actual historical developments and to formulate concrete experience into new theoretical viewpoints and categories. With Thomas Hodgskin, for example, he was one of the earliest opponents of McCulloch's wage-fund theory, which held that there is a special fund of fixed magnitude for the employment of workers. Unlike Hodgskin, however, whose critique (1825) of this theory was a beautiful exercise in logic, Jones went to history to show that such a wage fund never really existed in fact. Quite the contrary, given a fixed amount of capital, there is continual fluctuation between its constant (for machines and raw material) and its variable (for wages) elements.[55] To this important theoretical conclusion Marx appended the gloss: "This is an important point";[56] and he developed it still further in critical opposition to the classical school in a chapter on "The So-called Labor Fund."[57]

Jones went still further. Whereas the wage-fund theory held that there is a rigid law of wages, that is, that wages can rise only if the number of workers decreases or if the amount of capital increases,[58] Jones showed by historical evidence that it is possible — and at given historical moments it actually occurs — that "great fluctuations in the amount of employment, and great consequent suffering, may sometimes be observed to become more frequent as capital becomes more plentiful."[59] This happens in the "periods of transitions of the laborers from dependence on one fund to dependence on another,"[60] that is to say, in the period of the transition from an economy of independent peasants and handicraftsmen to a system in which those groups become a propertyless proletariat. Such a "transfer" — the loss of economic independence through the loss of ownership of the means of production — obviously cannot be accomplished without serious disturbances.[61] Marx commented that Jones had here hit upon the germ of the idea of "primary accumulation," that is, the antecedent of capital formation, and had thus begun the necessary process of replacing the "absurd" and rationalistic notion of capital formation through "savings" by a more realistic and historically correct view.[62]

Even more important insights into the historical roots of the capitalist system are to be found in Jones's discussion of various systems of production. He was well aware of the fact that different systems have succeeded one another in the past; and he sought to work out their essential characteristics. The decisive factor in differentiating these various systems is *the way in which human labor is organized*. As this factor changes, the whole economic system changes. That is why Jones does not follow a chronological arrangement in describing the succession of economies but begins with the capitalist system as a yardstick with which to measure and differentiate earlier systems.

Like Sismondi, he considered the "transfer," i.e., the separation of the once independent producers (peasants and craftsmen) from their means of production, to be the necessary historical precondition for capitalism. Through the "transfer" process they became wage-workers dependent on the capitalist. "The first capitalist employers," he wrote, "those who first advance the wages of labor from accumulated stock, and seek . . . . profits . . . . have been ordinarily a class distinct from the laborers themselves."[63] This development had so far been limited pretty much to England,[64] and even there it was historically a late phenomenon.[65] In the previous centuries the hand-workers were supported not by the advances from capital but by land revenue, "the surplus produce" of the land.[66] This surplus produce "may be handed over to individual landowners" or it "may be paid to the State."[67] In the latter case "the wages of such workmen were derived directly from the revenue of their great customer, and not from an intermediate class of capitalists," and it "is in Asia that we observe this particular fund . . . . in full and continued. . . . predominance."[68] In Europe the number of workers paid out of land revenues is still large, but no longer predominant, and "in England itself, ... the body is comparatively small."[69]

Jones shows the superiority of the capitalist system over preceding forms. In China and throughout the East, for example, tailors and other artisans wander all over the city, day in and day out, seeking work in their customers' homes, and thus waste a great deal of time, while under capitalism the workers became sedentary and "can now labor continuously." Finally, on this basis, where one capitalist employs many workers, an organized division of labor becomes possible.[70]

It is on the basis of such concrete historical material that Jones developed his idea of the *sequence of economies through which every nation must pass, though at different tempos* according to their varying conditions. After a given economy becomes dominant, it begins to lose that position while still remaining very widespread, and it slowly becomes more and more subordinate to a new form. When Jones says that "England is much in advance of other nations," he does not mean that English conditions are better but merely that, "in arriving at our present position, we have passed through and gone beyond those at which we see other nations. . . . . *The future of all other people will, however, at some time, be like our present.*" This succession theory has exceedingly broad implications, as he himself recognized: "The prophecy is bold."[71] Following Condorcet, he sees an easier road ahead for the younger nations. They have "better hopes for the future" because, "if they assume our economic organization and power, [they] may escape many of the evils that have afflicted our progress, or from which we suffer now."[72]

Jones goes still further. Not only does he predict that every nation must ultimately attain the highest economic form so far developed — capitalism — but he sees the possibility of still further development in the future to a socialized form of production in which the separation of the wage-worker from the means of production will be ended. Capitalism is thus a historical and transitory, though necessary, stage on the road to a more advanced economy of the future.

> . . . . a state of things may hereafter exist, and parts of the world may be approaching to it, under which the laborers and the owners of accumulated stock, may be identical; but in the progress of nations, which we are now observing, this has never yet been the case. . . . . [The present system in which a body of employers pay the workers by advances of capital] . . . . may not be as desirable a state of things as that in which laborers and capitalist are identified; but we must still accept it as constituting a stage in the march of industry, which has hitherto marked the progress of advancing nations.[73]

Having shown the way in which historical economies succeed one another, Jones then tried to differentiate those elements in the economy which are particularly active and decisive in the process of transformation from the more passive and secondary ones. He was not interested in the traditional categories of political economy — profit, rent, wages, etc. — but in the changes in production in so far as they influence the growth of productive power and the character of the economy itself. His study of history led him to the conclusion that "changes in the economical structure of nations" teach us to understand the secrets of ancient and of modern history;[74] on the other hand, that changes in the structure of the economy are closely linked with

changes in the institution of property and that the differing property relations correspond to different stages in the development of productive
power.[75] For Jones, therefore, the

economical structure of nations [is made up of] the relations between the different classes which are established in the first instance by the institution of property
in the soil, and by the distribution of its surplus produce; afterwards modified
and changed (to a greater or lesser extent) by the introduction of capitalists, as
agents in . . . . feeding and employing the laboring population. An accurate
knowledge of that structure can alone give us the key to the past fortunes of the
different people of the earth, by displaying their economical anatomy, and showing thus, the most deeply-seated sources of their strength, the elements of their
institutions, and causes of their habits and character. It is thus we must learn
the circumstances which divide them into classes.[76]

In other words, the economic structure, as thus defined, is the key to
social relationships:

There is a close connection between the economical and social organization
of nations. . . . . Great political, social, moral, and intellectual changes, accompany
changes in the economical organization of communities. . . . . These changes
necessarily exercise a commanding influence over the different political and social
elements to be found in the populations where they take place: that influence
extends to the intellectual character, to the habits, manners, morals, and happiness
of nations.[77]

As communities change their powers of production, they necessarily change
their habits too. During their progress in advance, all the different classes of the
community find that they are connected with other classes by new relations, are
assuming new positions, and are surrounded by new moral and social dangers, and
new conditions of social and political excellence.[78]

This superstructure, in turn, "reacts on the productive capacities of the
body."[79]

Only after he has shown the historical relationship of capitalism to earlier
systems does Jones turn to the problem of modern land rent. Here, too, he
resorts to historical study and shows how modern ground rent developed
out of earlier forms. Rent takes on a completely different character within
each economy. In one case it is the dominant institution; in another it becomes subordinate to capital, and the landowning class no longer participates directly in production. Jones differentiates five historical types of rent:
(1) labor rent, i.e., slave and serf rent; (2) intermediate form of rent, which
is the transition from type 1 to type 3; (3) rent in kind; (4) money rent of
the precapitalist period; and, finally, (5) in the capitalist period, farmer's
rent (in the Ricardian sense). The latter differs from all others and can
exist only in a society based on the capitalist mode of production, because
rent, as a surplus above the average profit, requires as its precondition the
development of the industrial average-profit rate. In sum, every specific
form of property has its corresponding form of labor and of rent.[80]

Jones rejected Ricardo's theory of a "continuous diminution in the returns to agriculture and of its supposed effects on the progress of accumu-

lation."[81] By historical illustrations he showed that rents were actually highest in countries where agriculture was very productive, and he thus destroyed the *historical* basis of Ricardo's theory of rent. As the classical theory of profits and wages was closely connected with the theory of rent, the collapse of the latter endangered the classical theory as a whole.

It is not hard to see why Jones earned the enmity of the classical school and, on the other hand, the strong approbation of Marx. Jones, the latter wrote, is characterized

by that which all English economists since Sir James Steuart have lacked, namely, a sense for the historical differences in modes of production. . . . .[82]

What distinguishes Jones from the other economists, except for Sismondi, is that he emphasized the social determination [*Formgestimmtheit*] of capital as the essential factor.[83]

Probably the highest praise Marx could give Jones was to contrast his presentation of genetic developments with Ricardo, who "developed nothing."[84]

It is worth noting here the emphasis placed by John Stuart Mill on the intellectual backwardness of England — the country which in his judgment was "usually the last to enter the general movement of the European mind."[85] Mill underscored the charge that, whereas "the doctrine that . . . . the course of history is subject to general laws . . . . has been familiar for generations to the scientific thinkers of the Continent" [France], it was opposed in England well into the second half of the nineteenth century because it "conflicted with the doctrine of Free Will."[86] The fate of the new science of geology is particularly revealing in this context. The foundation for a rational evolutionary system of geology was laid in Italy by Generelli (a Carmelite friar) in 1749; in France by Desmaret (1777) and Lamarck (1802); in England by Hutton (1785). Hutton, however, was accused of heresy; evolutionary ideas were condemned as incompatible with the biblical account of Genesis.

It was in such an antievolutionary atmosphere that Jones, like Sismondi before him, had the courage to attack the whole structure of the classical economists, not merely specific doctrines, and to cast doubts upon the permanence of the capitalist system. Their critique of the existing economic order, their emphasis upon its historical, transitory character was considered a heresy, which could not be forgiven. As *theorists*, both men were ignored by the representatives of the dominant school and left in oblivion for nearly a century.

It is apparent that by the time Karl Marx (1818–83) began his work, in the forties of the last century, the application of evolutionary concepts to economic institutions and the formulation of the doctrine that economic systems are historical in character had been basically accomplished. Marx himself pointed that out repeatedly, though it was left to him to complete and sharpen the analysis. He took over the heritage of Saint-Simon and Sismondi in France, of James Steuart and Richard Jones in England, and of certain elements in Hegel's philosophy of history and, introducing certain new ideas of his own, created an integrated, original theory.

We need not underline the point and we assume it as well known that, for Marx, the Hegelian "development" meant something quite different from what the eighteenth-century Enlightenment, the Saint-Simonians, or even Sismondi, Jones, and positivists like Auguste Comte understood by this term. To men oriented to the natural sciences of their day, development meant nothing more than the generalization of an empirically and inductively constructed series of particular observations,[87] whereas Marx, like Hegel, understood the relationship between the particular and the universal quite differently, viewing the historical "object" as made up not of individual observations but of the *"cultural whole"* of social-collective unities.[88] Using the genetic method of the dialectic, with its constant creation and synthesis of opposites, Marx sought to grasp the evolution of these collective unities in their historical necessity. Every present moment contains both the past, which has led to it logically and historically, and the elements of further development in the future.

At the same time there is a fundamental point at which Marx is joined with Sismondi and Jones against Hegel — one which must not be overlooked in ascribing the "historicizing" of economics to Hegelian influence. For the former, the historical development, occurring in the external world in time, is a succession of objective economic stages of different economic structures, whereby the higher stage develops out of the lower. In other words, history has not a relativistic character, it does not depend on the accident of the observer's point of view, ideals, or standards. What Marx did was to remove the study of history from that subjective level to a higher one, where objective, measurable stages of development are perceived. He fulfilled Saint-Simon's hope of making history a science.

Hegel was flatly opposed to such a doctrine. The German word *Entwicklung* has two different meanings, translated into English (and French) by two distinct words — "development" and "evolution." Hegel always used the term in the first sense, meaning the unfolding and dissection of the various component elements (*Gedankenbestimmungen*) contained in the *Begriff* ("notion of the essentials of a thing"). Development is possible only under the rule of the *Begriff* and *hence takes place in the sphere of logic.* "The metamorphosis," Hegel wrote, "only occurs to the Begriff as such [i.e., to the notion of essential as in contrast to the notion of phenomenal], for only its change is development."[89] Hegel therefore attacked the concept of the natural philosophers (and thus also of the sociologists) that evolution as an objective process in history is the "external real production" of a higher stage from a lower one. He insisted, on the contrary, that "the dialectical Begriff, which leads the way for the stages, is *the inner one* itself."[90] That is why in the *Philosophy of History* he saw the various stages in world history, not as an objective process in the *sphere of real History*, but as a process within the *sphere of logic*.[91] World history is to Hegel the progress within man's *consciousness* of the idea of freedom, and it is this development of consciousness which determines the four principal levels achieved by the various peoples: the oriental world, the Greek, the Roman, and the Germanic world.[92]

Marx, on the contrary, uses the term *Entwicklung* mostly in the second sense, meaning not the development within the sphere of *logic* but, like Sismondi and Richard Jones, evolution as an objective process in the sphere of *real History*.[93]

With such a point of view, writes Lasson, "Hegel *must* reject the theory of [biological] evolution. Long before Darwin he had discarded all of Darwinism as an unclear confusion of the *notion* and external *existence*."[94] Hegel himself said of the idea of evolution as an objective process in the external world: "Such nebulous . . . . conceptions; and especially . . . . the idea of the rise of more developed animal organisms from the lower, etc., must be avoided by thinking analysis."[95]

Marx, on the contrary, accepts the idea of the rise of more developed structures from the lower, and for this reason he was one of the first to acknowledge the importance of Darwin's work. In a similar way, as Darwin uses nature's technology, i.e., the formation of the organs of plants and animals, as instruments to explain the origin and development of species, Marx wishes to use the history of human technology as an instrument which "enables us *to distinguish different economical epochs*,"[96] as the "productive organs of man are the material basis of all social organization"[97] and the "instruments of labour . . . . supply a *standard of the degree of development* which human labour has attained."[98]

In sum, Marx refuses to follow Hegel on the basic question of the concept of development but works rather from the conception of Sismondi and Richard Jones. For Marx, evolution is an objective process of history, whereby each historical period or social structure is *marked by specific objective tendencies*,[99] which can be discovered from the nature of the technological instruments and from the social organization of labor in the use of those instruments.[100]

From the basic point of view, Marx saw that the history of economic organization is a series of economies, each more advanced than its predecessor because of changes in the method of production: "In broad outline, we can designate the Asiatic, the antique classical, the feudal, and the modern bourgeois methods of production as so many epochs in the progress of the economic formation of society."[101]

Throughout Marx's writings there are scattered, but nonetheless profound, characterizations of each of these epochs.[102] His main efforts, however, were not directed to the precapitalist forms but to a systematic analysis of the genesis and development of the specific historical phases of capitalism[103] and to the transition from capitalism to socialism.[104] Marx views "the evolution of the economic formation of society as a process of natural history,"[105] and his aim "lies in the disclosing of the laws that regulate the origin, existence, development, and death of a given social organism and its replacement by another and higher one,"[106] whereby society "can neither clear by bold leaps, nor remove by legal enactments, the obstacles offered by the successive phases of its normal development. But it can shorten and lessen the birth-pangs."[107]

Marx showed, for instance, that industrial capitalism did not develop out of handicraft or out of accumulated rent from landed property (as Max Weber and Sombart later taught) but from the merchant. The latter, by progressively subordinating the production of the craftsman and transforming him into a proletarian, brought about the transition from mercantile to industrial capitalism. Starting with the decentralized workshop under command of the merchant-capitalist (domestic system), production moved into the various phases of the period of manufacture (co-operative, heterogeneous, and organic manufactures), and finally into modern large-scale industry based on the machine. Marx did not stop with the delineation of the broad lines of historical development, however. He continued the application of the genetic method to the individual organs, institutions, and functions of the capitalist mechanism.

We cannot go into the details of Marx's historical analysis. The important point to emphasize is that Marx never remained within the narrow framework of historical description but always made use of historical insights to deepen his theoretical understanding of the laws of development. *This close link between history and theory* is one of the factors that differentiates Marx from all his predecessors. An example will serve to illustrate this point. A study of the demography of antiquity, the Middle Ages, and the modern world led Marx to the insight that there is no universally valid law of population, as Malthus had taught, but that the modern trend toward the creation of a relatively surplus population "is a law of population peculiar to the capitalist mode of production; and in fact every special historic mode of production has its own special laws of population, historically valid within its limits alone."[108]

This type of historical analysis also led to important conclusions in economic theory. When Sombart raises the accusation that Marx "hardly ever *defines* . . . . his concepts . . . . such as capital, factory, plant, accumulation,"[109] he shows that he misses the true sense of Marx's historicism and even of Marxist terminology: he uses the word *Begriff* in the sense of "definition"; the word "concept" or "notion" (*Begriff*), however, is used by Marx in the specifically Hegelian sense, as notion of essence of a thing, as contrasted with the definition as merely notion of the phenomena.

Marx rejects the view that knowledge consists in classifying and defining and that the task of science is simply to discover a rational criterion for classification. This is the static approach of the classicists, looking upon social phenomena as unchangeable structures. Marx, on the other hand, is a spokesman of the new, dynamic approach. That is why social phenomena, in his judgment, are actually indefinable. They have no "fixed" or "eternal" elements or character but are subject to constant change. A definition fixes the superficial attributes of a thing at any given moment or period, and thus transforms these attributes into something permanent and unchanging.[110] To understand things it is necessary to grasp them genetically, in their successive transformations, and thus to discover their essence, their "notion" (*Begriff*). It is only a pseudo-science that is satisfied with definitions and the phenomenal aspects of things.[111] Without devoting more space to a characterization of Marx's analysis, we turn to an examination of the fruits of his analysis. By attributing to Marx the first application of evolutionary thinking to economics, critics have obliterated the original contribution that Marx really did make to our understanding of history and the specific differences between Marx and his predecessors. They have reduced his historical conceptions to a level that does not go beyond the horizon of bourgeois liberalism, that is, beyond the idea of evolution in the direction of constant progress "from the incomplete to the complete" — to quote Hegel.

The fundamental characteristic of Marx's historicism and the mark that distinguishes it from his predecessors are not the doctrine of the historical succession of economic systems but a special theory which, in addition to evolutionary changes *within* a given system, explains the objective and subjective conditions necessary for the *transition from one system to another*. Briefly stated, it is that within the existing economy a new economic form arises and grows, that the two enter into ever sharper conflict with each other, and that through the violent resolution of the conflict the new economy finally takes over.

Within this general theory there are three special theories: (1) a doctrine of a "universal social dynamic" of structural changes in society, valid for all "antagonistic" societies; (2) the theory of the *objective developmental tendencies of capitalism;* and (3) the theory of the subjective bearer of change, that is, the class-struggle theory. Obviously the second, unlike the two others, deals only with the special historical phenomenon of the transformation from capitalism to socialism. Like Condorcet and Saint-Simon, Marx teaches that the idea of evolution must be applied to the future as well as to the past, for one must seek in the perceptible structural changes of the present the lines of future development.[112]

. . . Saint-Simon and his school knew that the industrial system grew up within, and as a bitter enemy of, the feudal system of the later Middle Ages. For the Saint-Simonians, however, this insight was no more than a singular historical observation. Marx developed this observation into what we might call a universal birth story of a social system. Every new economic system, he taught, is born directly within the old and goes through a long process of maturation before it can displace its predecessor and become dominant. "New higher relations of production never appear before the material conditions of their existence have matured in the womb of the old society."[113] The displacement of the old system by the new is not an arbitrary process, to be accomplished at any chance moment. It requires the existence and slow maturation of certain necessary subjective and objective factors.[114]

For the first time in the history of ideas we encounter a theory which combines the evolutionary and revolutionary elements in an original manner to form a meaningful unit. Gradual changes in the productive forces lead at some point in the process to sudden changes in the social relations of production, that is to say, to political revolution. By underlining the evolutionary aspects, Marxism sharply distinguishes itself from the voluntarism of the utopian Socialists as well as from the pseudo-revolutionarism of putschists or partisans of the *coup d'état*. At the same time, Marxism does not give up the idea of revolution, but regards it as the necessary conclusion of the evolutionary process and as the instrument for achieving the transition to a new economic structure. This theory rests primarily on the fact that productive forces, legal property relations, and political power are subject to the law of uneven development.

Changes in the productive forces release a relatively rapid and dynamic element, out of which grows the assault against the structure of the old society as a whole. Legal property relations, on the other hand, and political power, which rests upon them, constitute the passive, conservative, static element, guarding the existing society against change. The latter element changes slowly, long after the changes in the productive forces and as the result of those changes. The new economic forces thus clash with the antiquated political and property relations, which no longer correspond to the new needs and fetter further progress. "Then comes the period of social revolution,"[115] in which the antiquated legal and political relations are broken and replaced by new ones that are appropriate to the new economic forces. Since the antiquated laws express only the vested interests of their creators and since these will never voluntarily renounce their privileges, the disappearance of the old laws entails the disappearance of their creators, the former ruling classes.

In his second special theory, dealing with *the objective developmental trends within capitalism,* "the natural laws of its movement,"[116] Marx tries to show that there is a limit to the development of capitalism, that it must reach a peak after which a *declining phase* will set in and that at a certain point the further functioning of the system will become impossible and its collapse inevitable. The system must be transformed not only because the working people reject it but also because the ruling classes cannot find any way out. During this critical period, despite progress in restricted sectors (technology, chemistry), the system as a whole loses its progressive character, and the symptoms of its disintegration grow more and more numerous; the system becomes a fetter on further development and can preserve itself only by violence and increasingly severe repression of the newly emerging social forces. In the end, however, it must be defeated in the conflict with these forces and yield to them. Thus progress is achieved only at the price of the misery and humiliation of individuals and entire peoples.

No predecessor of Marx had a similar theory. It is true that the Saint-Simonians wanted to make history an exact science and conceived the future to be a necessary product of the past; but they never got beyond the mere postulate and never attempted to work out a theory of the future tendencies of capitalism. Nor did Sismondi or Richard Jones. Their prediction that capitalism would be replaced by a higher form of economy did not rest upon theoretical arguments but merely on historical analogy: since all previous economic systems were transitory, they argued, we must assume the same to be true of capitalism.

Marx undertook to demonstrate the historical necessity of the decline and final disintegration of capitalism. When the process of accumulation reaches a certain point, he shows, there will be a transformation of quantity into quality. A condition of oversaturation with capital will arise, and no adequate new possibility for capital investment will be available. All further accumulation of capital will become impossible, and society will enter a permanent period of growing accumulation of idle capital, on the one hand, and of large-scale permanent unemployment, on the other. Thus the process of disintegration will begin. The property-owners' fear of losing their privileges gives the spiritual and political life of this period a reactionary character. In short, the whole structure of capitalism will be shaken to its roots, and the basis will have been laid for great political and economic transformations.[117] It is true, of course, that Bazard and later Pecqueur, following Sismondi, foresaw the crises, the misery, and the uncertainty of the working class. These insights remained mere particular observations with them, however, and not, as with Marx, elements of a steadily worsening disease of the system from epoch to epoch that would lead to ultimate paralysis.

The third element in Marx's general theory is that no economic system, no matter how weakened, collapses by itself in automatic fashion. It must be "overthrown." The theoretical analysis of the objective trends leading to a paralysis of the system serves to discover the "weak links" and to fix them in time as a sort of barometer indicating when the system becomes ripe for change. Even when that point is reached, change will come about only through active operation of the subjective factors. This part of the theory Marx developed in his study of the class struggle. Marx has frequently been charged with a "fatalistic" theory of the "historical necessity" of social development in some given direction. Such a charge rests on a serious misunderstanding of the theory of the class struggle. In all his writings Marx characteristically emphasizes the unity of theory and practice. This so-called "historical necessity" does not operate automatically but requires the active participation of the working class in the historical process. This participation, however, is itself not something arbitrary but follows from the pressure of the objective factors. The student of history and the forward-looking practical politician must therefore consider this subjective factor as in fact another objective condition of the historical process.[118]

While, for instance, Saint-Simon and his school do not give the working class any political role in the transformation of society, the main result of Marx's doctrine is the clarification of the historical role of the proletariat as the carrier of the transformative principle and the creator of the socialist society. To Marx, activity is an integral part of thinking, and truth cannot be discovered by a merely contemplative attitude, but only by action. This is the meaning of Marx's first thesis on Feuerbach: "Until now philosophers have only interpreted the world differently: the point is to change it." If philosophers from Montesquieu to Feuerbach taught that man is a product of natural and social environment, Marx observes that to an even greater extent man is influenced by his action on his environment. In changing the historical *object*, the *subject* changes himself.[119] Thus the education of the working class to its historical mission must be achieved not by theories brought from outside but by the everyday practice of the class struggle. This is not a doctrine but a practical process of existing conflicts of interests, in which doctrines are tested and accepted or discarded. Only through these struggles does the working class change and re-educate itself and become conscious of itself. Marx's attack on the "fatalistic economists"[120] is only an illustration of the fact that his dialectical concept of history has a twofold significance. In this he follows Hegel, for whom history has both an objective and a subjective meaning, the history of human activity (*historia rerum gestarum*) and human activity itself (*res gestas*).[121] The dialectical concept of history is not merely an instrument with which to explain history but also an instrument with which to make history. "Men make their own history, but . . . . they do not make it . . . . under circumstances chosen by themselves, but under circumstances found and transmitted from the past."[122]

It is in this double sense that the Marxist theory of the class struggle is to be understood. On the one hand, it is an expression of the existing conflict of interests between classes. At the same time, it transcends the mere statement of an existing factual condition, not as a fatalistic expectation of evolution, but as a guide to the active participation of the working class in the historical process. By this activity the objective tendencies can be realized and the forces of a reactionary but powerful minority that stand in the way of further development and progress overcome. In this latter sense the class struggle has always been a decisive subjective factor in history.[123]

It is worth repeating that no one before Marx understood history in this way. It is true that in the first third of the nineteenth century the ideologists of the victorious revolutionary French bourgeoisie — the historians Augustin Thierry, Mignet, and, above all, François Guizot — clearly recognized that the past centuries were dominated by class interests and class struggles. But they never went beyond the description of actual conditions, i.e., the struggles of the rising bourgeoisie against the landowning feudal class. They recognized class struggles only in the past and failed to see their continuation in their own time, in the existing relations between the working class and the bourgeoisie. In Marx the class struggle is not merely a description of actual facts but a part of an elaborated historical theory: he explains genetically the necessary emergence of class conflicts in various historical epochs and explains their origin, form, and intensity by the development of the productive forces in each period and by the position individuals and classes occupy in the productive process. This endows the doctrine of the class struggle with a concrete and profound meaning.[124]

On the other hand, Saint-Simon and his school, . . . had also recognized past class struggles only in a factual sense and did not admit them for their own time. The Saint-Simonians feared to arouse the hopes of the proletariat; and, convinced that progress must come through the élite of the upper classes, they wanted above all to win these upper classes over to their views.[125] Though the writings of Bazard, Enfantin, and later Pecqueur contain references to the struggle of the working class against the dehumanizing effects of capitalism,[126] these remain isolated statements of fact. In principle, the Saint-Simonians accepted the idea that

518

progress was a continuous transition from antagonism to peaceful association. Thus Pecqueur regards class struggle as an evil, like every other form of struggle, and compares it to war. He expects that in the future all forms of struggle will be less violent and that peaceful methods of production and distribution will develop. There is a wide gap between this view and the overpowering generalization of the *Communist Manifesto:* "The history of all hitherto existing society is the history of class struggles." Here, class struggle is not regarded as an evil but as a dynamic force, the lever of history. By fighting for its rights against the ruling class, the exploited and oppressed class creates a new historical situation. New rights are wrested from the ruling class, and the whole of society is thereby raised to a new and higher level. In this conception, class struggle does not end with the abolition of feudalism by the bourgeoisie; it is also typical of the relations between the bourgeoisie and the working class. According to Marx, the process of history on the road of progress, far from becoming increasingly peaceful, increases in violence with the development of capitalism, and class conflicts become the decisive instrument in the transition from capitalism to collectivism.

NOTES

1. "The Idea of Evolution in Society," in *Studies in the Evolution of Industrial Society* (New York, 1903), pp. 6–7.

2. Herbert Spencer, "Progress: Its Law and Causes," reprinted in *Illustration of Universal Progress* (New York, 1874).

3. *The Idea of Progress* (London, 1924).

4. Karl Bücher, *Die Entstehung der Volkswirtschaft* (5th ed.; Tübingen, 1906).

5. Thus Rudolf Kötschke (*Grundzüge der deutschen Wirtschaftsgeschichte bis zum 17. Jahrhundert* [Leipzig, 1923], pp. 12–15) has a section on the history of the idea of stages in economic development in which the names of Saint-Simon, Sismondi, James Steuart, and Richard Jones never appear. Kötschke, furthermore, follows Bücher's precedent in discussing the sequence not of complete economic structures, such as feudalism or capitalism, but only of partial units: village economy, town economy, territorial economy. Similarly, Sombart speaks of individual economy, transition economy, social economy; and, according to Richard T. Ely, the various stages are not characterized by the different types of social organization, but various occupational activities, such as hunting or fishing, agriculture or cattle-raising, are just different historical "stages" (hunting stage, fishing stage, etc. [*op. cit.*, pp. 26, 39]).

6. See Edmund Whittaker, *A History of Economic Ideas* (New York, 1940).

7. Werner Sombart, *Das Lebenswerk von Karl Marx* (Jena, 1909), p. 16.

8. *Ibid.*, pp. 53–54. Italics are mine.

9. It has frequently been pointed out that Sombart's historical statements simply do not stand up under close scrutiny. See, for example, Adolf Schaube's criticism of Sombart's account of certain early English developments, "Die Wollausfuhr Englands vom Jahre 1273," *Vierteljahrsschrift für Sozial- und Wirtschaftsgeschichte*, Vol. VII (1908).

10. "Karl Marx' Bedeutung für die Entwicklung der Nationalökonomie," *Kapitalismus und Sozialismus* (Potsdam, 1931), pp. 165, 168.

11. Turgot, for example, in his second Sorbonne discourse, "Sur les progrès successifs de l'esprit humain" (December, 1750), spoke of the "total mass of the human species, who, by alternations . . . . of goods and of evils, marches steadily, though with slow steps, to an ever greater perfection" (*Oeuvres de Turgot*, ed. Dupont de Nemours, II, 53–54).

12. Herbert Marcuse, *Reason and Revolution: Hegel and the Rise of Social Theory* (New York, 1941), p. 226.

13. Fifty years before Hegel, G. E. Lessing, the most prominent figure of the German Enlightenment, advanced certain evolutionist ideas in his essay *The Education of the Human Species* (1780); these ideas were strongly influenced by Adam Ferguson's *Essay on the History of Civil Society* (1767). Later on, Lessing's essay, translated into French (1829), belonged to the Saint-Simonian propagandist literature.

14. The influence of these views on Saint-Simon is clearly seen in his *Mémoires sur la science de l'homme* (1813) (*Oeuvres*, XL, 294).

15. *Allgemeine Naturgeschichte und Theorie des Himmels oder von dem mechanischen Ursprung des ganzen Weltgebäudes* (1755).

16. Contemporaries were astounded at the rapid post-Revolutionary progress of the United States, both in size of population and in development of agriculture, as contrasted with its "stagnation" under British rule. As one analyst phrased the problem, the United States was a country "where from a few adventurers, a power is now rising." And he continued: "The history of the world has furnished few instances of so great a tract of country undergoing a change, from an uncultivated and barbarous, to a civilized state; and it will well merit the attention of mankind to observe the different steps and the progress upon so large a scale" (William Playfair, *The Commercial and Political Atlas Representing the Progress of the Commerce of England during the Whole Eighteenth Century* [3d ed.; London, 1801], pp. 29–30).

17. The so-called German historical school of law, which received its programmatic statement in Savigny's *Vom Beruf unserer Zeit zur Gesetzgebung und Rechtswissenschaft* (Heidelberg, 1814), was itself only a by-product of the French Revolution. It was the answer of the conservative elements in Germany to the revolutionary method of lawgiving. Against the latter they insisted upon the slow method of historical, organic evolution. They thus condemned progress in the name of continuity. Marx's article "Das philosophische Manifest der historischen Rechtsschule" (*Literarischer Nachlass von Marx* [Stuttgart, 1902], I, 268 ff.) against Hugo is a most penetrating criticism of the methodological presuppositions of the historical school of law (see Sidney Hook, *From Hegel to Marx* [New York, 1936], pp. 141–44).

18. *Wealth of Nations*, Book I, chap. vii.

19. *The Principles of Political Economy and Taxation*, chap. v.

20. *Ibid.*, chap. i.

21. Richard Schueller (*Die Klassische Nationalökonomie und ihre Gegner* [Berlin, 1895]) did not succeed in clearing the classics of the charge of unhistoricism. All he shows is that Adam Smith and Ricardo emphasize the temporal, local, or cultural differentiations (p. 16), which result in modifications of the general laws of prices, average profits, rents and wages. But such differentiations can occur *within* a given economic system regarded as permanent and have nothing in common with the fundamental idea of the theory of evolution, that is to say, with the theory

of successive and different economic structures—an idea which is entirely absent from the classics and which Schueller does not discuss at all.

22. *Op. cit.*, Book II, chap. iii.

23. Karl Marx, *A Contribution to the Critique of Political Economy*, trans. N. J. Stone (Chicago, 1904), p. 69.

24. It was this attitude which Marx had in mind when he wrote: "Hence forms of social production that preceded the bourgeois form are treated by the bourgeoisie in much the same way as the Fathers of the Church treated pre-Christian religions." From such a point of view, feudal institutions are "artificial," bourgeois institutions "natural" (*Capital* ["Modern Library" ed.], I, 93).

25. Ibn Khaldun (1332–1406) in his work *Moccademat* [Prolegomena].

26. Whittaker approvingly quotes the opinion of the English historian, F. W. Maitland, directed against "architects of stage-systems," who are "prescribing a normal programme for the human race in decreeing that every portion of mankind must move through one fated series of stages" (*op. cit.*, p. 3).

27. Auguste Comte, *Cours de philosophie positive*, VI (Paris, 1842), 845 ff.

28. Élie Halévy, *A History of the English People* ("Pelican Books," 1937), II, 79–80.

29. James Lauderdale, *An Inquiry into the Nature and Origin of Public Wealth* (Edinburgh, 1804), p. 304.

30. Cf. p. 504.

31. We need not spend any more time on Comte, because he made no contribution to the particular problem under discussion. In his remarks on the method of historical comparison he assumes the validity of the same law of evolution for all peoples, since he holds that they all go through the same successive stages. His "three-stage" theory, however, has nothing to do with the succession of constantly higher, objective economic systems but deals only with intellectual advances. Man's interpretation of facts advanced from the attribution of all phenomena to supernatural agencies to the use of metaphysical abstractions and finally to scientific laws of succession and similitude. The "law" of the three stages is thus no historical law at all. It offers no causal, genetic explanation of development but merely a schematic description of historical sequences (see Comte's *Cours*, Vol. IV, Lesson 48; Roger Maudit, *Auguste Comte et la science économique* [Paris, 1928], p. 89; Salomea Krynska, *Entwicklung und Fortschritt nach Condorcet und A. Comte* [Berne, 1908], p. 78).

32. London, 1767.

33. *Inquiry into the Principles of Political Economy*, I, 3.

34. *Ibid.*, Preface, p. viii.

35. *Ibid.*, p. ix.

36. *Ibid.*, p. 3.
37. *Ibid.*, p. 16.
38. *Ibid.*, p. 150.
39. *Ibid.*, p. 16.
40. *Ibid.*, p. 150.
41. *Ibid.*
42. *Ibid.*, p. 10.
43. *Ibid.*, p. 11.
44. *Ibid.*
45. Marx's evaluation is restated by R. Hilferding, "Aus der Vorgeschichte der Marxschen Oekonomik: Richard Jones," *Die neue Zeit*, XXX, Part I (1900), 434–54; and by Erich Roll, *A History of Economic Thought* (London, 1938), pp. 309–16. We have already noted that Marx never claimed credit for having first introduced the historical factor into political economy. He pointed, besides Sismondi, to two men: James Steuart (1767) and, even more important, Richard Jones (1831), who, though ignorant of the Hegelian dialectic, was thoroughly familiar with the historical conditions of earlier epochs and with the economic conditions of the backward spheres of eastern Europe and Asia. Richard Jones, a friend of Malthus and his successor as a professor of economics at East India College, Haileybury, was an expert on Asiatic conditions, particularly in India, Persia, and Turkey. In his *Essay on the Distribution of Wealth* (London, 1831), Book I, "Rent," Jones lists as source of his historical analysis in an appendix a copious literature about Asiatic and South American countries. Particularly amazing is the knowledge of Asiatic economic conditions that Jones revealed in a work published twenty years later, *Textbook of Lectures on the Political Economy of Nations* (Hertford, 1852).
46. Richard Jones, *An Introductory Lecture on Political Economy* [1833], cited from *Literary Remains Consisting of Lectures and Tracts on Political Economy*, ed. William Whewell (London, 1859), pp. 569–70. The extracts given above have been rearranged somewhat.
47. A theory of rent, for instance, based on the English type of land system, which assumes individual ownership and free competition, cannot be applied to oriental societies, in which joint ownership and absence of competition are the rule.
48. *Essay on the Distribution of Wealth and the Sources of Taxation* (London, 1831).
49. *Principles of Political Economy* (Ashley ed., 1909), p. 252.
50. Böhm-Bawerk, *Geschichte und Kritik der Kapitalzinstheorien* (Innsbruck, 1914), I, 123; see also the recent monograph of Hans Weber, *Richard Jones, ein frueher englischer Abtruenniger der klassischen Schule der Nationaloekonomie*, ed. M. Saitzew (Zurich, 1939); and Karl Marx, *Theorien über den Mehrwert*, Vol. III. (3d ed.; Stuttgart, 1919), cited below as *Mehrwerttheorien*.

51. *Nassau Senior and Classical Economics* (London, 1937), p. 40. We have already called attention to Erich Roll's discussion of Jones, which does benefit from Marx's analysis but does not discuss Jones's position with respect to our particular problem. Mr. Nai-Tuan Chao's thoroughgoing thesis, *Richard Jones: An Early English Institutionalist* (New York: Columbia University, 1930), deals only with Jones's *system* of political economy: his theory of production and distribution, theory of rent, wages, and profit (pp. 45ff.). Jones's evolutionary theories, particularly his theory of the succession of economic stages, are not mentioned.
52. Jones, *Essay on the Distribution of Wealth*, p. 328.
53. Marx, *Mehrwerttheorien*, III, 489 and 491.
54. E.g., "Jones represents a fundamental advance over Ricardo" (p. 454); "Here is where Jones' superiority is strikingly brought out" (p. 453); "We see what a great leap it is from Ramsay to Jones" (p. 490). Altogether, Marx devoted seventy pages to the discussion of Jones (see *ibid.*, pp. 450–520).
55. Jones, *Introductory Lecture on Political Economy* (London, 1833), p. 52: "The amount of capital devoted to the maintenance of labor may vary, independently of any changes in the whole amount of capital." Here, and in nn. 59 and 64, I cite from the rare first edition because the chapter involved is not reprinted in the *Literary Remains*.
56. *Mehrwerttheorien*, III, 476.
57. *Capital* ("Modern Library" ed.), I, 667: "It has been shown in the course of this inquiry that the capital is not a fixed magnitude."
58. McCulloch, *Discourse on Political Economy* (Edinburgh, 1825), pp. 61–62.
59. *Introductory Lecture on Political Economy* (London, 1833), p. 52.
60. "Transfer of the laboring cultivators to the pay of capitalists. . . . transfer of non-agricultural classes to the employ of capitalists" (*ibid.*, pp. 52–53).
61. *Ibid.* The uprising of propertyless peasants in Norfolk, in the middle of the sixteenth century, when enclosures were made on a tremendous scale, is well known. This uprising was crushed, and "multitudes of dispossessed and impoverished villagers flocked to the towns" (H. de B. Gibbins, *The Industrial History of England* [London, 1910], pp. 88–89). It is not hard to see why just in this period occurs for the first time in history the application of the word "proletarii" in the modern sense, to denote propertyless day laborers, wage-workers, and "poore husbandmen" as a "fourth sort or classe" of society (see Sir Thomas Smith, *De republica Anglorum, a Discourse of the Common-wealth of England* (first published 1583; written about 1565), ed. L. Alston, with a Preface

by F. W. Maitland (Cambridge, 1906), Book I, chap. xxiv.

62. "What Jones calls 'Transfer' is what I call 'primary accumulation'" (Marx, *Mehrwerttheorien*, III, 477).

63. Jones, *Textbook of Lectures on the Political Economy of Nations* (*Literary Remains*, p. 444).

64. Jones, *Introductory Lecture* (London, 1833), p. 52.

65. *Textbook*, p. 454.

66. *Ibid.*, p. 440.

67. *Ibid.*, p. 440.

68. *Ibid.*, pp. 442, 444.

69. *Ibid.*, p. 443.

70. *Ibid.*, pp. 395, 396, 397, 455.

71. *Introductory Lecture*, pp. 558–59. Italics are mine.

72. *Textbook*, p. 412.

73. *Ibid.*, p. 445.

74. *Introductory Lecture*, p. 561.

75. Marx, *Mehrwerttheorien*, III, 452.

76. *Introductory Lecture*, p. 560. With the expression "economical anatomy" Jones foreshadows the famous phrase of Marx in the Preface to the *Critique of Political Economy* (1859) that legal relations and forms of state cannot be understood by themselves and that they are rooted in material conditions of life, that "the anatomy of the civic society is to be sought in political economy." It was Sir William Petty who first (1672) introduced the expression "political anatomy" to denote the knowledge of the economic structure of a country its "Symmetry, Fabrick and Proportion," as the basis for understanding the "Body Politick" (see "Political Anatomy of Ireland," in *The Economic Writings of Sir William Petty*, ed. Charles H. Hull [Cambridge, 1899], I, 129).

77. *Textbook*, pp. 405–6. Rearranged.

78. *Ibid.*, pp. 410–11.

79. *Ibid.*, p. 406.

80. *Essay on the Distribution of Wealth*, pp. 185, 188. Marx (*Mehrwerttheorien*, III, 452) points out that in Jones's work *On Rent* (1831) he starts with the different forms of real property, whereas two years later in his *Syllabus* (1833) he analyzes the different forms of labor that correspond to those types of property.

81. Jones, *Essay on the Distribution of Wealth*, p. xiii.

82. *Mehrwerttheorien*, III, 450.

83. *Ibid.*, p. 484.

84. *Ibid.*, pp. 451, 26, and *passim*.

85. *A System of Logic Ratiocinative and Inductive* (8th ed.; New York, 1900), p. 643.

86. *Ibid.*, p. 644.

87. See Ernst Troeltsch, *Die Dynamik der Geschichte nach der Geschichtsphilosophie des Positivismus* (Berlin, 1919), p. 67. From the antipositivists' viewpoint the relationship between the particular and the universal is presented in the excellent

book by Morris R. Cohen, *Reason and Nature* (New York, 1931), p. 161.

88. "In the study of economic categories, as in the case of every historical and social science, it must be borne in mind that . . . . the subject [is] the modern bourgeois society . . . ." (Karl Marx, *A Contribution to the Critique*, p. 302).

89. *Encyclopaedie der philosophischen Wissenschaften* (2d ed.; Leipzig, 1905), § 249.

90. *Ibid.* Italics are mine.

91. Hegel, *Vorlesungen ueber die Philosophie der Geschichte*, ed. Edw. Gans (Berlin, 1848), p. 70.

92. *Ibid.*, pp. 129–35; and Kuno Fischer, *Hegels Leben, Werke und Lehre* (Heidelberg, 1901), II, 748.

93. For that very reason Marx directs his criticism against Proudhon's notion of "evolution": Proudhon, he says, has accepted the "Hegelian Vieillerie" and is "incapable of following the real movement of history . . . . . The 'evolutions' of which Proudhon speaks are understood to be evolutions such as are accomplished within the mystic womb of the Absolute Idea" (Marx to Annenkov, 1846; see *Poverty of Philosophy* [New York, n.d.], p. 154).

94. G. Lasson, *Preface to Hegel's Encyclopaedie*, p. xvii.

95. *Encyclopaedie*, §249; see also Charles Renouvier, "L'Evolutionisme de Hegel," *Les Principes de la nature* (Paris, 1912), p. 271.

96. *Capital*, I, 200. Long before the publication of Darwin's work, in one of his earliest works—the critique of Proudhon (1847)—Marx had already emphasized the fundamental significance of human technology for the characteristics of a given society.

97. *Ibid.*, p. 406.

98. *Ibid.*, p. 200. Alongside this technological factor, the social factor is equally significant for the distinction of economic epochs from one another, namely, "the special manner in which this union [between laborers and means of production] is accomplished" (*ibid.*, II, 44).

99. As early as 1847 Marx wrote, against Proudhon: "The handmill gives you society with feudal lord; the steammill, society with the industrial capitalist" (*Poverty of Philosophy*, p. 92).

100. Elsewhere, in the section "On the Capitalistic Character of Manufacture," Marx differentiates the specific tendencies of the manufacturing period from the trends under industrial capitalism and lays the basis for the differences in the fact that "in the manufacture, the revolution in the mode of production begins with the *labor*-power, in modern industry it begins with the *instruments* of labor" (*Capital*, I, 405).

101. *Critique*, p. 13.

102. Thus he contrasted the unceasing technical revolutionizing of our economy

with the *static economic structure of Asiatic societies*, notably India, and saw the explanation in the fact that production was there organized in self-sufficing communities "based on possession in common of land, and on the blending of agriculture and handicraft and on an unalterable division of labor" (*Capital*, I, 392–94). In this connection the form of taxes, namely, taxes in kind, played an important role (*ibid.*, pp. 157, 158). In countries where central governments, by the use of artificial irrigation, made it possible to transform deserts into fertile fields, "one single war of devastation could depopulate a country for centuries, and strip it of all its civilization" (see Marx's article, "On the British Rule in India," *New York Daily Tribune*, June 25, 1853, reprinted in *Handbook of Marxism*, ed. Emile Burns [New York, 1935], p. 183).

103. For a good historical application of Marx's theory of the earlier stages of capitalism see Henri Pirenne, "The Stages in the Social History of Capitalism," *American Historical Review*, XIX (1913–14), 494–515.

104. Marx, *Criticism of the Gotha Programme* (1875) (New York, 1938).

105. *Capital*, I, 15.

106. *Ibid.*, p. 24.

107. *Ibid.*, pp. 14–15.

108. *Ibid.*, pp. 692–93.

109. W. Sombart, *Das Lebenswerk von K. Marx* (Jena, 1905), p. 52.

110. Marx made his point of view quite clear in his polemic against Cherbuliez: "First the notion of profit should have been *developed*, but nothing came out except the definition and that corresponds merely to its phenomenal aspects . . . . so that its existence is *stated* but nothing is said about its essence" (Marx, *Mehrwerttheorien*, III, 437–38). Elsewhere, in speaking of the economists, Marx says that their "definitions flatten out into shallow tautologies"; whereas the task of science is not the construction of abstract definitions but "the *reproduction of the concrete* subject in the course of reasoning" (*Critique*, pp. 271 and 293). There are, therefore, no "eternal" economic categories; every category is only "the theoretical expression of historical relations of production, corresponding to a particular stage of development in material production" (Marx to Schweitzer, January, 1865 [see *Poverty of Philosophy*, p. 167]).

111. ". . . . Which . . . . confines itself to systematizing [the phenomena] in a pedantic way, and proclaiming them for everlasting truth" (Marx, *Capital*, I, 93).

112. As early as 1843, Marx wrote to Arnold Ruge that we must not project "a construction of the future" or dogmatically anticipate the world, "but rather discover the new world out of the critique of the old" (*Literarischer Nachlass von Marx* [Stuttgart, 1902], I, 380). Twenty years later Marx wrote to Schweitzer that Proudhon and the Utopians were hunting for a "science" by which the social question was to be solved a priori "instead of deriving their science from a *critical knowledge of the historical movement*, a movement which itself produces material conditions of emancipation" (*Poverty of Philosophy*, p. 167).

113. *Critique*, p. 12. Elsewhere Marx emphasized (May, 1871) that the working class can expect no "ready-made utopias . . . . . They have no ideals to realize, but to set free elements of the new society with which the old collapsing bourgeois society itself is pregnant" (*The Civil War in France* [New York, 1940], pp. 61–62).

114. "They [the working class] know that in order to work out their own emancipation . . . . they will have to pass through long struggles, through a series of historic processes, transforming completely circumstances and men" (*The Civil War in France*, pp. 61ff.).

115. Marx, *Critique*, p. 12.

116. *Capital*, I, 14. It must be stressed that Marx does not use the word "trend" or "tendencies" in the usual sense of the term; by "trend" he means "tendencies working *with iron necessity* toward *inevitable* results" (*ibid.*, p. 13). The other factors and countertrends can weaken or slow up the dominant trend but not prevent it from asserting itself. Elsewhere Marx speaks about "that higher form to which present society is *irresistibly tending* by its own economical agencies" (*The Civil War in France*, p. 61).

117. For a detailed study of this theoretical analysis see Henryk Grossman, *Das Akkumulations und Zusammenbruchsgesetz* (Leipzig, 1929).

118. Of course, "class struggle" is not to be understood in the primitive sense that the workers must blindly attack the entrepreneur class wherever the two come into contact. Both the content and the form of the class conflicts are themselves determined by the attained level of historical development and by the concrete historical situation.

119. *Capital*, I, 198.

120. *Poverty of Philosophy*, p. 105.

121. Hegel, *Philosophie der Geschichte*, p. 75; Kuno Fischer, *op. cit.*, II, 739.

122. Marx, *The Eighteenth Brumaire of Louis Bonaparte*, in *Handbook of Marxism*, p. 116.

123. Sismondi, for instance, says that "the freedom of the Occident results from the rebellion of the non-owners" (against a small minority of landowers) . . . . "Between the tenth and the twelfth centuries, people without land reconquered freedom for the future generations" (*Histoire des républiques italiennes du moyen âge*

[Paris, 1840], III, 499, 107).

124. See G. Plekhanov, "The Beginnings of the Doctrine of the Class Struggle," *Die neue Zeit,* XXI (1903), 298, 304; and A. T. Tiumeniev, "Marxism and bourgeois historical science," in *Marxism and Historical Thought* (New York, 1935), pp. 235–319.

125. G. Weill, *L'Ecole saint-simonienne* (Paris, 1896), pp. 56, 293–94.

126. Constantin Pecqueur, *Economie sociale des intérêts du commerce et de l'industrie* (2d ed.; Paris, 1839), II, 125: "One fact is certain, general . . . . it is the silent but very decisive struggle of the workers against their masters with a view to forcing the captains of industry to raise their wages. . . ."

"How can one not see that to leave [the wage-earners] dependent on the insufficiency of a fluctuating wage is to wish to find oneself surrounded in times of crisis and general unemployment by a famished multitude, to create riot and civil war, and perhaps to arm new Spartans . . . ." (p. 108).

21.

PAUL T. HOMAN
Southern Methodist University

The Institutional School

The form assumed by the dissent from orthodox economics has differed from country to country and from period to period. In the United States such dissent has come in the twentieth century to be increasingly and indeed almost exclusively associated with what has been called the institutional school. Yet the numerous proponents of the institutional approach to economics differ so markedly in their views concerning the purpose, content and methodology of institutional economics and the bonds of spiritual unity among them, engaged as they are in diverse and vaguely related tasks, are so intangible that the use of the term school is justified only if the loosest possible meaning is attached to it. Nor is it to be inferred that the institutional approach to economic theory is exemplified only in the work of American economists or that before the twentieth century an institutional emphasis in economics was unknown.

Institutional studies have always held an important place in economics. While the classical doctrine and its derivatives have tended to make them a subordinate category of description, they have occupied a position of great importance in the explanatory scheme of most dissenting individuals and schools. Thus the work of Sismondi and Richard Jones may be described as primarily institutional. The German historical school of necessity was deeply concerned with the changing structure of economic institutions and the progressive adaptation of life and thought to such change. Karl Marx's attention was centered upon the evolution of economic institutions in their relation to the distribution of economic power. Other socialist thinkers

Reprinted from *The Encyclopaedia of the Social Sciences* (New York: The Macmillan Company, 1931), V. 387–92, by permission of the author and the publisher. This essay is the concluding section of a long article, "Economics." At the time of original publication, the author was with Cornell University.

also examined the origin and effects of economic institutions as a preliminary to devising ways and means of reconstruction. In general the institutional interest has been tied to reform movements of one sort or another and has been antipathetic to economic explanations running in terms of uniform self-interest, static economic relationships and a stable institutional structure.

While institutionalism is a word applied specifically to a phase of economic thought in the United States, it stands in a close spiritual relationship to certain developments in all the social sciences both in America and Europe. Thus, to take American examples, the work of Roscoe Pound and R. L. Hale in jurisprudence, of Charles A. Beard and J. H. Robinson in history and government and of W. F. Ogburn in sociology is based upon a set of similar presuppositions. Among economists in both England and France the closest alliance with institutional theory is found among groups primarily interested in projects of reform, such as the French solidarists and the English Fabians. Even in the relatively orthodox precincts of the University of Cambridge the influence of Marshall has stimulated an institutional interest, while Cannan at the London School of Economics has quite directly been responsible for a series of institutional studies, although not in the Veblenian terminology of American institutionalism. In Germany more than elsewhere may be found a rich development of ideas and activities like those in the United States. They are in part derivatives of the earlier historical and Marxian schools of economics, in part aspects of more recent sociological thought.

The institutional movement in American economics is peculiarly a derivative from the work of Veblen, although with his name should be linked that of C. H. Cooley and the pragmatic philosophical trend represented by William James and John Dewey. Much of Veblen's thought is compounded from the ideology of Marx and the historical school. What is most distinctive in it, however, is an introduction into economics of ideas derived from the evolutionary sciences, particularly biology, anthropology and psychology. Thus the central theses of Veblen are that human activity, including economic activity, may be most profitably approached from the angle of an evolutionary process; that institutions are decisive factors in shaping human behavior; that social science must deal with real human beings, not with a rationalized human nature, with the run of facts rather than with a normalized picture of them.

Stated in somewhat greater detail, the cardinal tenet of institutionalism is that contemporary society is a complex of institutions or habitual forms for organizing and regulating the behavior of individuals. Social institutions, including the economic, defined as those which bear on the behavior of individuals in providing the community with its complement of useful goods and which determine the manner of the control and use of these goods, are subject to change because of the impact of human nature, changes in technology and the general development of knowledge and ideas. In a certain sense the development of institutions is a competitive process, and its outcome determines what forms of behavior are acceptable and sanctioned. At any given time the behavior of individuals or groups is restricted within limits set by such formal or informal sanctions. Since in the view of psychologists "original human nature" is remarkably stable, most overt behavior must be explained by reference to the prevailing institutional structure, and this in its turn is intelligible only if viewed as a result of cumulative change.

The bearing of this general ideology on economics is in the first place critical. Institutionalism impugns the credibility of orthodox economic theory on the following counts: it asserts that orthodox economics depends upon a discredited hedonic theory of human behavior; that its basic institutional postulate of individualistic competition is inadequate and inaccurate; and that its central problem of determining the conditions of economic equilibrium rests on an untenable analogy to physical science and implies a static view of economic organization at variance with the actual processes of development. The institutionalists believe that while the equilibrium concept and the marginal method may be found useful for some subordinate purposes of analysis fundamentally correct explanations of economic phenomena are possible only by reference to the nature and prescriptive force of social institutions.

While the critical position which constitutes an essential ingredient of institutional economics is definite and clear cut, the positive content of institutionalism is not so well defined. In the nature of the case it is difficult to draw the boundaries of an economic science based upon institutional postulates. Since economic institutions, such as competition, the wage system, the credit system, the property system and the like, are but isolated aspects of a much more complex general structure of social institutions, the specific scientific boundaries between economics on the one hand and sociology, politics and jurisprudence on the other tend to become very indistinct. Moreover, since the raw materials of an institutional economics are of necessity a vast accretion of factual data, the institutional approach tends to realize itself in an unorganized and vaguely related congeries of separate studies, quantitative, descriptive or historical. In consequence there has been developed no technique of analysis, or methodology, of a uniquely institutional character. In fact, the common institutionalist attitude is that each economic study justifies itself on other grounds than those of method and that, methods being but instruments, each study may proceed with the aid of any extant methods of economic analysis or call into existence new methods. Thus is achieved a certain methodological elasticity in the treatment of social data, which are so complex that they must be subject to varied "approaches." In this there is striking contrast with orthodox economics, the peculiar strength of which is that it provides concepts and analytical procedure applicable to an unlimited number of detailed situations.

In discussions of methodology one rather commonly hears of the descriptive method, the quantitative method and the genetic method as adjuncts of institutional economics. This mode of speech involves some inaccuracy. Description, for example, can hardly be spoken of as a method, since realistic description of concrete data raises a host of problems of method with respect to categories, concepts and generalized results. The influence of the institutional approach in the field of description is, however, real and far reaching, not merely through promoting it but through attacking its problems in an experimental frame of mind. Thus institutionalism may alter the categorical framework of description; illustrations of this may be found in Hoxie's studies of labor organization, in studies of corporate organization and in other fields.

Quantitative analysis may be regarded as a specialized method of description, although a more ambitious theoretical destiny is held out for it. It has no particular affinity with institutional economics but has been linked to it as providing a type of institutional knowledge and perhaps a type of theoretical conclusion different in kind from the generalizations of orthodox economic theory. In this connection it is significant that the institutionalists regard W. C. Mitchell's treatise on *Business Cycles* (1913) as a positive contribution to their critical attack upon orthodox theory. Although quantitative analysis is no more allied to one type of theory than to another, quantitative studies have a very special interest for institutionalists and a special bearing on their system of thought, because they afford an opportunity and a justification on the grounds of expediency for arranging data in other categories and concepts than those crystallized in orthodox economic usage. In particular, quantitative-descriptive studies tend to present data in the categories in which they appear to those technically trained for, and actually engaged in, the various practical pursuits of life. For example, treatments of interest which deal with call money, commercial paper, bank loans, farm mortgages, public credit and the like are different in kind from systematic theories of interest but not an alternative to them. Another example is offered by studies of corporate organization and profits, a field in which the assumptions of general theory seem to have lagged behind the current facts. Such studies may be properly regarded as having an importance beyond the immediate end which induced them and as collectively furnishing data for extensive emendation of general economic theory.

The so-called genetic method, the explanation in terms of cumulative causation, may perhaps be regarded as a distinctive institutionalist method, although it has also been championed by such representatives of the German historical school as Karl Bücher. If contemporary phenomena are the outcome of a cumulation of causes in past time, they cannot be properly or accurately analyzed on causal lines without recourse to the genetic principle. In pressing this point home, in suggesting that orthodox theory is rationalized description and sometimes an apologetic rationalization of the economic institutions of a limited area and period, institutionalists have made orthodox theorists self-conscious and are in part responsible for the recent careful and modest statements of the functions of orthodox theory.

Unfortunately, in their enthusiasm for the genetic principle the institutionalists have overlooked its inadequacies as the sole method and the dangers often implicit in it. In its usual form of a translation of a limited number of historical sequences into terms of cause and effect it is of doubtful scientific accuracy. Nor is it capable, except when used in conjunction with deductive logic, of providing precise answers to many if not most of the analytical problems with which economists are faced. Institutionalist thought, which seems at times to regard the genetic method as an alternative to the allegedly invalid deductive method of generalizing on economic causation, seems not to have grasped the exact significance of the genetic principle.

On such methodological questions American institutionalism has not been as penetrating as might be wished. The methodological writings of Max Weber, who may be regarded as the champion of institutionalist economics in Germany, present the problem of "understanding the phenomena of life in their cultural significance" with more illumination. Having decided to eliminate analogies to the natural sciences as inapplicable, having discussed the objective and subjective aspects of the social scientist's work and the impossibility of creating a direct nexus between scientific knowledge and social policy, he adopted "ideal types" as his chief methodological instrument for the attainment of the necessary degree of abstraction in dealing with complex social data. This device, which isolates and synthesizes into a logically consistent picture factors deemed relevant to the historical development of the process under investigation, is a particular application of the genetic principle. It is, however, also open to the objections that rigid "ideal types" will command no consensus of support and that their very construction is a highly personal performance permitting the penetration of bias.

American institutionalist writing on methodological questions has taken the form of sections and chapters in books devoted to other subjects and of occasional articles in periodical publications. It has been on the whole of a very inferior or else very fragmentary character; it has not attempted, as J. R. Commons justly observes, "to go at the fundamental concepts upon which the institutional school should be constructed." American institutionalism is far from having thought through its problems when it criticizes economic doctrines so stated as to be unamenable to empirical verification and praises the quantitative method of analysis for the connection of its data with concrete reality, at the same time that it places reliance upon something yielding such vague and highly personal interpretative results as those of the genetic method. Actually, the institutional interest is for things in flux, and it has stood ready to approve whatever methods are applicable for the presentation or interpretation of processes of economic change. One cannot quarrel with this interest, but one may doubt whether it need carry with it an exaggerated dissent from the methods of presenting and interpreting the elements of economic stability and order which are the stock in trade of orthodox economic theory.

The tendency has been for institutional economics to make a virtue of its shortcomings. It has not regretted its inability to construct economic laws; on the contrary, it has neglected and tended to deride studies largely dependent upon a formal economic logic. It has applauded studies of the derivation of the contemporary institutional structure on the one hand and statistical or other accounts of observed behavior on the other; it has favored the multiplication of monographic studies. But it has achieved no synthesis of its data, no general plan wherein its parts will fit, no alternative

methods or concepts of general applicability. In fact, it has found a source
of gratification in changing economics into a collection of diverse types of
study, so long as these offer a concrete body of knowledge relevant to understanding the economic order. In much of this it appears to be repeating the
experience of the historical school, which it so greatly resembles and from
which it in part derives.

One reason for the lack of interest on the part of institutionalists in questions of method and system is that the thought and work of most institutional economists actually center less upon problems of scientific explanation
than upon those of public policy. Their orientation is primarily a welfare
and reform orientation. Centering their attention upon the mutability of
institutional structure, they quite generally regard their function as that of
bringing disinterested human intelligence to the guidance of social change.

It has been suggested that institutional economics consists of studies of
three types: genetic studies, studies of the economic significance of single
institutions and studies of typical economic structures in terms of economic
functions and types of organization. While this classification indicates the
emphases which are common to institutional studies, it offers no clue to the
positive content of institutionalist economics. In the absence of a consensus
as to the concepts and categories which should govern such studies, of
homogeneity in plan and method and of a unitary framework the content of
institutional economics can only be described as the aggregate result of all
these studies irrespective of the methods by which they have been pursued.
Another difficulty in this connection arises from the fact that many notable
studies of economic institutions have been made by persons who do not ally
themselves with a dogmatic acceptance of the institutionalist approach to
economic theory. Such studies cannot, however, be excluded from the range
of institutional economics.

Of the branches of economic inquiry in which the institutional approach
has proved most fruitful the field of business organization stands out prominently. In this field belong on the one hand studies such as W. H. Hamilton's *The Case of Bituminous Coal* (1925), which combine description with
theoretical analysis, and on the other theoretical and interpretative writing
like that of Veblen in *The Theory of Business Enterprise* (1904) and *Ab-
sentee Ownership* (1923) and of J. M. Clark in his *Studies on the Economics of Overhead Costs* (1923) and the *Social Control of Business*
(1926). Recent studies of corporation law in an institutionalist setting, such
as those of A. A. Berle, may also be properly considered as an investigation
into the genesis and functioning of an important form of business organization.

In the field of labor organization one finds also a mass of writing, descriptive and interpretative, much of which partakes of the institutionalist
spirit. At the head of such works must of course be placed the Webbs' *The
History of Trade Unionism* (1894) and *Industrial Democracy* (2 vols.,
1897). Hoxie was perhaps the most conspicuous American figure giving an
institutionalist interpretation of the labor movement. Other works, such as
Carter Goodrich's *The Miner's Freedom* (1925) and Solomon Blum's *Labor

Economics (1925) and the statistical and other writings of Leo Wolman and Isidor Lubin, are similarly related to the movement. One cannot of course overlook the important work of Commons in the labor field, but his interest in relating this work to a new theoretical orientation is a relatively late development.

As in other fields of inquiry, no type of theoretical orientation has any peculiar affinity with research in the field of business fluctuations. It is perhaps an accidental circumstance that one of the most distinguished American proponents of the institutional point of view, W. C. Mitchell, is also the author of the outstanding study in this field. Yet it is undoubtedly true that cyclical studies have not only attracted persons of institutional leanings but have strongly reenforced the effort to study economic phenomena in process, as opposed to analysis of the normal operation of economic forces, and to restate economic theory in these terms. They have impregnated with new meaning the distinction between statics and dynamics current in orthodox economics. In the work of J. M. Clark in the United States and of the German economists who differentiate between structure and conjuncture and attempt the establishment of a dynamic methodology there is promise that the study of business cycles will eventually lead to the formulation of a new theory of dynamic economics. Nevertheless, it is doubtful that quantitative cyclical analysis has the close affinity to institutionalism which is sometimes attributed to it.

The genesis and development of such complex sets of institutions as capitalism in its various aspects constitute a subject peculiarly attractive to the institutionalist. In this field one must notice particularly Werner Sombart's *Der moderne Kapitalismus* (3 vols., 1902–27). In distinguishing the three elements of spirit, form and technology and carrying them through the evolution of economic institutions Sombart has not merely added vastly to the factual knowledge of the past but has developed an interpretative scheme representing an example of that economic theory which Veblen has called "the theory of a process." In his sociological writings Max Weber has dwelt at length upon spiritual elements which underlie social institutions; his studies of the relation between the Protestant ethic and the spirit of capitalism offer a particularly penetrating contribution to the literature of economic institutions. A somewhat comparable contribution in this field is R. H. Tawney's *Religion and the Rise of Capitalism* (1926). Veblen is the only recent American economist to attempt historical analysis of a theoretical and interpretative sort, but what he did (e.g. in *The Instinct of Workmanship*, 1914) stands almost as the foundation of institutional economics and furnishes the basis for classing such men as Sombart and Weber with institutional economists. Commons' *Legal Foundations of Capitalism* (1924) must be added to the list of important works in this field. Although it cover a relatively short period and was preceded by a number of studies on the economic significance of property and contract it may be said to open a new branch of inquiry because it represents a peculiarly skilful handling of legal material for the purposes of well considered and thoroughly grounded economic generalization.

This brief survey of the institutionalist contributions may not be concluded without mention of the work of C. H. Cooley (*Social Process*, 1918; *Social Organization*, 1909) and of B. M. Anderson, Jr. (*Social Value*, 1911). The former is second only to Veblen in his general influence in establishing the institutional point of view, while the latter is the only American writer except Commons to attack the problems of economic value from the angle of institutionalist preconceptions.

It is impossible at present to give a definitive evaluation to institutionalism in the context of the historical development of economic thought. The institutionalists constitute one of the most active groups of economists today, and it is impossible to anticipate what will be the final impact of their thought upon the general body of economics. So far one effect of the movement has been to wear down the entrenched authority of the orthodox discipline, until it no longer can be regarded as providing the exclusively correct explanation of economic phenomena or the exclusively accredited instruments of economic analysis. Besides stimulating a large amount of useful research and analysis, oriented with reference to a postulated evolution of institutional structure, the movement has fertilized economic thinking at large by the infusion of new and relevant ideas. Having failed, however, to create a complete alternative organon of economic thought and seeming unlikely to do so, its separate and controversial existence appears due to be ephemeral. In the synthetic and creative construction of an adequate organon, which is the present task of economic theorists, the influence of the institutional movement will be large; but the outcome should be something larger, something better equipped methodologically than the institutional approach alone appears able to achieve.

PART SIX

MARGINALISM

AND

NEOCLASSICISM

THE WRITINGS OF W. Stanley Jevons, an Englishman, Carl Menger, an Austrian, and Leon Walras, a Frenchman, in the early 1870's inaugurated what may reasonably be termed "the marginalist revolution."[1] By the time — some two to three decades later — that the innovations were well established, economic theory was quite different from what it was as left by, say, John Stuart Mill.

The analytic tools which were forged, adapted, and popularized in the revolution promoted, first, a shift in attention and emphasis, a shift which brought gains, but not without costs. In general, economists appeared rather less daring in the breadth and sweep of their constructs, and their purposes and applications of analysis tended to be more restricted. The "magnificent dynamics" of the philosophers, clergymen, and stockbrokers who wrote economics in the classical period was replaced in large measure by the more formalized and rigorous statics of the professional economists beginning near the end of the nineteenth century.[2] If this may be deemed a cost, surely there were gains in the treatment of demand theory and of the theory of the firm. More important than the greater attention to, and the more adequate handling of, such specific areas of theory was the fact that the conscious and explicit adoption of marginalist techniques of analysis, accompanied by a flowering of interest in utility theory, made feasible — and well nigh inevitable — the curiously long delayed completion of the conception of a general *system* of interrelated prices.

The great gap in the classical presentation could now be filled: the theory of distribution could finally be integrated into price theory in general. In partial equilibrium theory, it was found that the determination of factor prices could be approached in the same manner as the determination of output prices, with marginal productivity the analytic companion of marginal utility. In more general equilibrium theory, the circle could be closed by demonstrating with some elegance that factor prices and output prices were simultaneously and mutually determined. It may well be an exaggeration to say, with Knight, that the classical writers were lacking any theory of a "system of prices."[3] And perhaps Schumpeter is overly gen-

1. There were scattered marginalist writings, some of high quality, prior to the revolution proper. For references with respect to utility, see Selections 24 and 25. For analyses of two other pioneers, von Thünen and Cournot, see Selections 22 and 23.
2. See William J. Baumol, *Economic Dynamics* (2nd ed.; New York: The Macmillan Co., 1959), Chap. 2, esp. pp. 13–15.
3. "The [economic] organization as a whole is worked out through two interacting systems of markets and prices, one for products, in which individuals are buyers and enterprises sellers, and one for productive services, in which the relation is reversed. The classical economists give no picture of a system of prices and practically no hint of a system of economic organization worked out and directed by price forces. . . . they failed to see the *relativity* of all values and of all costs; still less did they grasp

erous in holding that the early Austrians really understood, even if they did not exposit, perfectly well the co-ordinate and thoroughly intertwined roles of demand and of cost of production.[4] But the classical deficiency was critical, and the marginalist contribution was fruitful. The 1870's did, indeed, see the start of an intellectual revolution.

To supplement the essays which follow, we shall briefly review Jevons (1835–1882) and Alfred Marshall (1842–1924) on value theory and Eugen von Böhm-Bawerk (1851–1914) and Irving Fisher (1867–1947) on interest theory.

THE THEORY OF VALUE: JEVONS AND MARSHALL

Jevons died in 1882 and Marshall in 1924; the first edition of Jevons' *Theory of Political Economy* was published in 1871, and Marshall's *Principles of Economics* appeared originally in 1890. Small wonder that Marshall is generally considered a member of the "second generation" of marginalists. But Marshall was born only seven years after Jevons, and he had the main body of his theory completed by the end of the 1860's.

Knight takes exception to the opinion of Stigler (Selection 26) that "Menger's theory was greatly superior to that of Jevons." He feels that the work of Walras as well as that of Jevons and of Menger "shows such profound merits along with such glaring defects that a general rating is a matter of dubious balancing, if not quite presumptuous." But he considers Jevons to be "the under-rated one of the three; I find in his book more of

---

the identity of costs with distributive payments and the functional role of the two interacting sets of prices." Frank H. Knight, "The Ricardian Theory of Production and Distribution," *Canadian Journal of Economics and Political Science*, I (February 1935), 7, reprinted in *On the History and Method of Economics* (Chicago: University of Chicago Press, 1956), pp. 41–42. Lionel Robbins (review of Knight's *History and Method* in *American Economic Review*, XLVII [June 1957], 308) doubts that the second sentence quoted above is "even approximately correct." *Cf.* Footnote 2 in the Introduction to Part Four.

4. The "essential achievement" of the marginalist analysis "was precisely the new theory of *supply and cost* that it yielded. It is in this sense only that Jevons' saying should be understood: '*Value depends entirely upon utility.*' . . . They stood in no need of being told about the two blades [utility and cost of production] of Marshall's pair of scissors. What they aimed at showing was that *both* blades consist of the same material—that both demand and supply (no matter whether the case is one of exchanging existing commodities or one of producing them) may be explained in terms of 'utility.' . . . Both Jevons and the Austrians were in the habit of expressing themselves in terms of causal chains, which ran from the value of consumable goods to the value of resources as if the utility of a quantity of a consumers' good were first determined independently and then, in turn, determined causally the value of the producers' goods that went into its production. It was child's play for a superior technician to point out that this was inadmissible since the utility of the consumers' good depends upon its quantity and the latter upon its cost. . . . But Marshall of all men should have realized that this criticism takes advantage of deficiencies in technique, in particular of a glaring inability to understand the logic of interdependence, and entirely fails to do justice to the substance of the position criticized." Joseph A. Schumpeter, *History of Economic Analysis* (New York: Oxford University Press, 1954), p. 922. Marshall may have been too harsh with Jevons and the Austrians, but there is generally a temptation to believe that an author means what he says, and there is often a fine and nebulous line between verbal and technical inelegance, on the one hand, and conceptual inadequacy and confusion, on the other.

the essential 'pieces' of a sound theoretical system than I do in Menger's. And 'perhaps' more in Walras than in either — looking at his final version."[5]

Marshall spoke of the great originality of Jevons. But he considered Jevons' statement that "value depends entirely upon utility" to be "no less one-sided and fragmentary, and much more misleading, than that into which Ricardo often glided with careless brevity, as to the dependence of value on cost of production."[6] Marshall's value theory was designed to correct the "careless brevity" of Ricardo and recast classical doctrine in a mold giving proper weight to demand and making appropriate use of marginal analysis.

Jevons

Jevons "attempted to treat Economy as a Calculus of Pleasure and Pain,"[7] developing a theory which "may be described as *the mechanics of utility and self-interest*" (2nd ed., p. 23). The core of the theory is "the somewhat novel opinion" that *"value depends entirely upon utility"* (p. 2). Study of the "nature and conditions of utility . . . doubtless furnishes the true key to the problem of Economy" (p. 57; see also p. 46). In a volume of 267 pages, most of the first 161 pages are devoted to the "theory of pleasure and pain" (Chapter II), the "theory of utility" (Chapter III), and the "theory of exchange" (Chapter IV).

In this "calculus of pleasure and pain," "the object of Economy is to maximize happiness by purchasing pleasure, as it were, at the lowest cost of pain" (p. 27; see also p. 44). Since "pain is the opposite of pleasure," we may treat them as negative and positive quantities, and "our object will always be to maximize" the algebraic sum "in the direction of pleasure" (p. 38).

Since "it is surely obvious that Political Economy does rest upon the laws of human enjoyment" (p. 47), then "we must necessarily examine the character of the wants and desires of man" (p. 46), and "the whole theory of Economy depends upon a correct theory of consumption" (p. 47). A *commodity* is thus appropriately defined as "any object, or, it may be, any action or service, which can afford pleasure or ward off pain," and *utility* denotes "the abstract quality whereby an object serves our purposes, and becomes entitled to rank as a commodity" (p. 45).

Two general characteristics of utility are to be noted. First, "utility, though a quality of things, is *no inherent quality*. It might be more accurately described, perhaps, as *a circumstance of things* arising out of their relation to man's requirements" (p. 53). Under differing circumstances, a given article may possess *actual* utility (in which case it "is at the present

---

5. Frank H. Knight, "Introduction," in Carl Menger, *Principles of Economics* (1871) (Glencoe, Ill.: The Free Press, 1950), pp. 11–12, n.

6. Alfred Marshall, *Principles of Economics* (8th ed.; London: Macmillan & Co., Ltd., 1920, reprinted 1947), p. 817.

7. W. Stanley Jevons, *The Theory of Political Economy* (London and New York: Macmillan & Co., 1871), p. vii; see also p. 27. A second edition appeared in 1879, and two posthumous editions were brought out in 1888 and 1911. All quotations are from the first edition except where indicated.

moment actually useful to some person") or *prospective* utility ("although not actually useful, it is expected to be useful at a future time") or *potential* utility ("it would be useful if it were in the possession of some person needing it" [p. 72]), and only the first two types are of significance for economics. Second, "*utility is not proportional to commodity:* the very same articles vary in utility as we already possess more or less" (p. 53).

Since the utility of even food or water "beyond a certain point . . . appears to cease" (p. 53), it is essential to "discriminate between the *total utility* belonging to any commodity and the utility belonging to any particular portion of it" (p. 54). The "degree of utility" is the addition to total utility derived from possessing one additional unit of the commodity, total utility being the sum of the degrees of utility, and the "final degree of utility" — "that function upon which the whole Theory of Economy will be found to turn" (pp. 61–62) — is "the degree of utility of the last addition, or the next possible addition of a very small, or infinitely small, quantity to the existing stock" (p. 61). The importance of "the function expressing the final degree of utility" stems from "the general law" that "*it varies with the quantity of commodity, and ultimately decreases as that quantity increases.* No commodity can be named which we continue to desire with the same force, whatever be the quantity already in use or possession" (p. 62).

The law of diminishing final degree of utility solves the classical water-diamond paradox: "we cannot live a day without water, and yet in ordinary circumstances we set no value on it . . . simply because we usually have so much of it that its final degree of utility is reduced nearly to zero" (p. 62). It also indicates the criterion of rational allocation of a commodity capable of different uses: the commodity should be distributed in such fashion that "no alteration would yield . . . more pleasure; which amounts to saying that an increment of commodity would yield exactly as much utility in one use as in another" (p. 69).

The major application of the law of diminishing final degree of utility is in the theory of exchange. There is no "intrinsic value." "There are, doubtless, qualities inherent in such a substance as gold or iron which influence its value; but the word Value, so far as it can be correctly used, merely expresses *the circumstance of its exchanging in a certain ratio for some other substance*" (p. 82).

In the theory of exchange, essentially Jevons considers the case of two traders, each initially holding a different commodity, free to exchange at a ratio which will allow each trader to benefit, and the problem is to state the condition of exchange equilibrium, *i.e.*, the condition which will lead the voluntary exchange to cease. Suppose that one trader begins with a stock of corn and the other with beef, and suppose further that the ratio of exchange, which each trader takes as given, is 10 pounds of corn = 1 pound of beef. If at the outset the trader with corn is *willing* to give more than ten pounds of it for one pound of beef, and if the beef-holder is *willing* to accept less than ten pounds of corn for one of beef, each can gain by exchange at the going ratio. But as trade proceeds, the first trader will value corn more and more highly relative to beef, and the second will alter his relative valuation in favor of beef. Finally, Jevons assumes, there is an equilibrium in which the final degree of utility of beef is exactly ten times that of corn for both traders.

Exchange will thus go on till each party has obtained all the benefit that is possible. . . . This point of equilibrium will be known by the criterion, that an infinitely small amount of commodity exchanged in addition, at the same rate, will bring neither gain nor loss of utility. In other words, if increments of commodities be exchanged at the established ratio, their utilities will be equal for both parties (pp. 96–97).

The ratio of exchange of any two commodities will be the reciprocal of the ratio of the final degrees of utility of the quantities of commodity available for consumption after the exchange is completed (2nd ed., p. 103).

Useful as is this general line of analysis for the limited problem of the behavior of consumers as price-takers, it is scarcely a theory of general price determination, and even within its restricted scope, difficulties exist. For one thing, Jevons speaks of collective "trading bodies" rather than individual traders, and it is not made clear what can be meant by the final degree of utility of a commodity for a group of people. Furthermore, the equilibrium rate of exchange is not determined in Jevons' analysis; it is assumed as given, which means that an obvious question in the theory of exchange is left unasked, as well as unanswered.

Difficulties and omissions aside, Jevons concludes that "the Theory of Exchange . . . rests entirely on the consideration of quantities of utility, and no reference to labour or cost of production has been made" (p. 130).

The mere fact [which Ricardo conceded] that there are many things, such as rare ancient books, coins, antiquities, which have high values, and which are absolutely incapable of production now, disperses the notion that value depends on labour. Even those things which are producible in any quantities by labour seldom exchange exactly at the corresponding values. . . . The fact is, that *labour once spent has no influence on the future value of any article*: it is gone and lost for ever. In commerce, by-gones are for ever by-gones; and we are always starting clear at each moment, judging the values of things with a view to future utility (pp. 158–59).

But Jevons immediately adds that while "labour is never the *cause* of value, it is in a large proportion of cases the *determining* circumstance" (pp. 159–60; emphasis added):

Value depends solely on the final degree of utility. How can we vary this degree of utility? — By having more or less of the commodity to consume. And how shall we get more or less of it? — By spending more or less labour in obtaining a supply. According to this view, then, there are two steps between labour and value. Labour affects supply, and supply affects the degree of utility, which governs value, or the ratio of exchange (p. 160).

And "in order that there may be no possible mistake about this all-important series of relations" (2nd ed., p. 179), in his later edition Jevons restates:

Cost of production determines supply.
Supply determines final degree of utility.
Final degree of utility determines value (2nd ed., p. 179).

Marshall

Marshall's value theory is presented as a lengthy exercise in demand-and-supply analysis. "The nominal value of everything, whether it be a particular kind of labor or capital or anything else, rests, like the keystone of an arch, balanced in equilibrium between the contending pressures of its two opposing sides; the forces of demand press on the one side, and those of supply on the other. The production of everything, whether an agent of production or a commodity ready for immediate consumption, is carried forward up to that limit or margin at which there is equilibrium between the forces of demand and supply."[8]

Marshall felt that "until recently the subject of demand or consumption has been somewhat neglected." It now has "a greater prominence in economic discussions," largely because of "the growing belief that harm was done by Ricardo's habit of laying disproportionate stress on the side of cost of production, when analyzing the causes that determine exchange value" (p. 84). He gives a statement of "the law of satiable wants or of diminishing utility":

The *total utility* of a thing to anyone . . . increases with every increase in his stock of it, but not as fast as his stock increases. . . . In other words, the additional benefit which a person derives from a given increase of his stock of a thing, diminishes with every increase in the stock that he already has. That part of the thing which he is only just induced to purchase may be called his *marginal purchase*, because he is on the margin of doubt whether it is worth his while to incur the outlay required to obtain it. And the utility of his marginal purchase may be called the *marginal utility* of the thing to him (p. 93).

If we "translate this law of diminishing utility into terms of price" (p. 94), we acquire a falling "marginal demand price" (p. 95), *i.e.*, the price the buyer is willing to pay for an additional unit of the commodity. "There is then one general *law of demand:* — The greater the amount to be sold, the smaller must be the price at which it is offered in order that it may find purchasers; or, in other words, the amount demanded increases with a fall in price, and diminishes with a rise in price" (p. 99; see also p. 342). "The *elasticity* (or *responsiveness*) of demand in a market is great or small ac-

8. Marshall, *op. cit.*, p. 526. All other citations in this section are from the same source. For an analysis emphasizing the theory of the firm, see Ragnar Frisch, "Alfred Marshall's Theory of Value," *Quarterly Journal of Economics*, LXIV (November 1950), 495–524.

cording as the amount demanded increases much or little for a given fall in price, and diminishes much or little for a given rise in price" (p. 102).

Although each of two purchasers of a good tends to extend his purchases until their marginal demand prices are equal to the market price, it does not follow that the marginal utility of the article is the same for both purchasers, for "the marginal utility of money is greater for the poor than the rich" (p. 95, marginal note). "For each of them the marginal utility is measured by" the market price, "but this marginal utility is greater in the case of the poorer man . . . ." (p. 95). In order to maximize the utility of an article capable of several uses, a person "will distribute it among these uses in such a way that it has the same marginal utility in all" (p. 117). "And in a money-economy, good management is shown by so adjusting the margins of suspense on each line of expenditure that the marginal utility of a shilling's worth of goods on each line shall be the same" (p. 118).

While we may state the conditions of consumer equilibrium in terms of *marginal* utilities and prices, "how far [does] the price which is actually paid for a thing [represent] the benefit that arises from its possession"? (p. 124). The consumer receives "a surplus consisting of the excess of the *total* utility to him of the commodity over the real value to him of what he paid for it" (p. 830; emphasis added).

. . . the price which a person pays for a thing can never exceed, and seldom comes up to that which he would be willing to pay rather than go without it: so that the satisfaction which he gets from its purchase generally exceeds that which he gives up in paying away its price; and he thus derives from the purchase a surplus of satisfaction. The excess of the price which he would be willing to pay rather than go without the thing, over that which he actually does pay, is the economic measure of this surplus satisfaction. It may be called *consumer's surplus* (p. 124).

"While demand is based on the desire to obtain commodities, supply depends mainly on the overcoming of the unwillingness to undergo 'discommodities'" (p. 140). Thus there is a supply price as well as a demand price:

As the price required to attract purchasers for any given amount of a commodity, was called the demand price for that amount during a year or any other given time; so the price required to call forth the exertion for producing any given amount of a commodity, may be called the *supply price* for that amount during the same time (p. 142). The exertions of all the different kinds of labour . . . together with the abstinences or rather the waitings required for saving the capital used . . . will be called the *real cost of production* of the commodity. The sums of money that have to be paid for these efforts and sacrifices will be called either its money cost of production, or for shortness, its *expenses of production* (pp. 338–39).

Money costs, then, are payments required "to call forth an adequate supply of the efforts and waitings" (p. 339). Under certain assumptions (which

Marshall did not fully specify), "the money measure of costs corresponds to the real costs" (p. 350).

In considering the determinants of the supply price of a commodity, it is necessary to analyze "the normal cost of producing a commodity, relatively to a given aggregate volume of production; and for this purpose we shall have to study *the expenses of a representative producer* for that aggregate volume" (p. 317). The "representative firm" is one "which has had a fairly long life, and fair success, which is managed with normal ability, and which has normal access to the economies, external and internal, which belong to that aggregate volume of production . . . ." (p. 317).

Typically, the firm has available to it numerous different combinations of inputs which can produce any given volume of output of the commodity. It behooves the firm to choose that input combination of which the sum of the supply prices of the "factors of production" is "less than the sum of the supply prices of any other set of factors which could be substituted" (p. 341), replacing a less expensive method of production for more expensive methods. The entrepreneur strives so to adjust "the employment of each agent that, in its marginal application, its cost is proportionate to the additional net product resulting from its use" (p. 515), and thus he obtains "better results with a given expenditure, or equal results with a less expenditure" (p. 355).

The "dominant principle of substitution" (p. 435) applies not only to the optimum production of a given commodity, but also to the choice of employment of a given resource: the entrepreneur "will push the investment of capital in his business in each several direction until what appears in his judgment to be the outer limit, or margin, of profitableness is reached; that is, until there seems to him no good reason for thinking that the gains resulting from any further investment in that particular direction would compensate him for his outlay" (p. 356).

Finally, "when the demand price is equal to the supply price, the amount produced has no tendency either to be increased or to be diminished; it is in equilibrium" (p. 345). If the demand price for a thing is, say, greater than its supply price, "sellers receive more than is sufficient to make it worth their while to bring goods to market to that amount" (p. 345), and the amount produced tends to increase. Equilibrium prices, both short run and long run, are determined by the co-ordinate pressures of demand and of supply.

The "cost of production principle" and the "final utility" principle are undoubtedly component parts of the one all-ruling law of supply and demand; each may be compared to one blade of a pair of scissors. When one blade is held still, and the cutting is effected by moving the other, we may say with careless brevity that the cutting is done by the second; but the statement is not one to be made formally, and defended deliberately (p. 820; see also p. 348).

But the time element gives a greater significance to one "blade" than to the other under different circumstances. We may distinguish different periods over which price-determining forces operate:

Four classes stand out. In each, price is governed by the relations between demand and supply. As regards *market* prices, Supply is taken to mean the stock of the commodity in question which is on hand, or at all events "in sight." As regards *normal* prices, when the term Normal is taken to relate to *short* periods of a few months or a year, Supply means broadly what can be produced for the price in question with the existing stock of plant, personal and impersonal, in the given time. As regards *normal* prices, when the term Normal is to refer to *long* periods of several years, Supply means what can be produced by plant, which itself can be remuneratively produced and applied within the given time; while lastly, there are very gradual or *Secular* movements of normal price, caused by the gradual growth of knowledge, of population and of capital, and the changing conditions of demand and supply from one generation to another (pp. 378–79).

He is concerned chiefly with "the normal relations of wages, profits, prices, etc., for rather long periods" (p. 380).

Marshall concludes that "*as a general rule,* the shorter the period which we are considering, the greater must be the share of our attention which is given to the influence of demand on value; and the longer the period the more important will be the influence of cost of production on value. For the influence of changes in cost of production takes as a rule a longer time to work itself out than does the influence on changes in demand" (p. 349).

THE THEORY OF INTEREST: BÖHM-BAWERK AND FISHER

Böhm-Bawerk held that "as a rule present goods have a higher subjective value than future goods of like kind and number,"[9] and allegedly "this proposition is the kernel and centre" of his interest theory (p. 237). Three bases for the discounted valuation of future goods were presented. First, there are "different circumstances of want and provision in present and future" (p. 249). Those with "reason to hope" that in the future they will be better off will value immediately available goods relatively highly; those who anticipate worsening fortunes in the future can acquire present goods (including money) and generally store them until propitious times of consumption. Second, there is underestimation of the future: "it is one of the most pregnant facts of experience that we attach a less importance to future pleasures and pains simply because they are future, and in the measure that they are future" (p. 253). This irrationality stems from "incompleteness of the imaginations . . . of our future wants" (p. 254), "a defect in will" in failure to resist present cravings (p. 254), and "the shortness and uncertainty of life" (p. 255). Third, "the technical superiority of present

---

9. Eugen von Böhm-Bawerk, *The Positive Theory of Capital* (1888), trans. William Smart (New York: G. E. Stechert and Co., 1923), pp. 247–48. All quotations of Böhm-Bawerk are from this source. The most useful secondary source is George J. Stigler, *Production and Distribution Theories* (New York: The Macmillan Co., 1941), Chap. VIII; see also the exposition of Robert Dorfman, "A Graphical Exposition of Böhm-Bawerk's Interest Theory," *Review of Economic Studies,* XXVI (2) (February 1959), 153–58.

goods," for present goods permit the adoption of long processes of production, and "it is an elementary fact of experience that methods of production which take time are more productive" (p. 260).

In the later analysis of the determination of the rate of interest, Böhm-Bawerk's third point is central, but the first two considerations are dropped. Indeed, the later discussion provides an alternative explanation for the existence of interest. In short, his *subjective future-discounting* approach gives way to an *objective productivity* theory.[10]

Fisher magnanimously announced that Böhm-Bawerk and John Rae (1786–1873) laid the foundations of his interest theory, a theory incorporating intimately *both* time preference and productivity, or "impatience and opportunity."[11] In his "first approximation," incomes are assumed given and can be modified only by borrowing and lending. Under these hypothetical conditions, "time preference would cause interest without help from any rate of return over cost" (pp. 468–69). But "in real life men have the *opportunity* of choosing among many optional income streams. When such opportunities exist, time preference alone does not and cannot explain the emergence of interest" (p. 469).

Böhm-Bawerk

"Capital in general," Böhm-Bawerk wrote, "we shall call a group of products which serve as means to the Acquisition of Goods. . . . Social Capital we shall call a group of productions . . . destined to serve towards further production; or, briefly, a group of Intermediate Products" (p. 38). Capital makes feasible "roundabout methods" of production which are more fruitful than are noncapitalistic methods. "The roundabout ways of capital are fruitful but long; they procure us more or better consumption goods, but only at a later period of time" (p. 82). And "because the labourers cannot wait till the roundabout process . . . delivers up its products ready for consumption, . . . they become economically dependent on the capitalists who already hold in their possession what we have called 'intermediate products'" (p. 83). Thus, in classical tradition, capital is conceived to be a subsistence and maintenance fund, from which advances can be made to laborers; at a given wage rate, the greater the amount of capital the longer the "period of

10. "The truly astonishing aspect of Böhm-Bawerk's labored discussion of the future is that it is virtually ignored in his own theory! In his sections on the determination of the interest rate, Böhm-Bawerk assumes that the supply of capital is owned by those who do not undervalue the future, and that the demand for capital comes primarily from entrepreneurs. The technical superiority of present goods becomes the direct determinant of interest. . . ." Stigler, *op. cit.*, p. 218.

11. Irving Fisher, *The Theory of Interest* (New York: The Macmillan Co., 1930; reprinted by Kelley and Millman, Inc., New York, 1954), p. ix. All quotations of Fisher are from this source. A brief exposition of Fisher's theory is included in J. Hirshleifer, "On the Theory of Optimal Investment Decision," *Journal of Political Economy*, LXVI (August 1958), 330–33.

Although the 1930 date for *The Theory of Interest* is post-Marshallian and puts the volume in the era of what may be considered "contemporary" economics, Fisher tells us, justifiably, that the theory which it presents is little different in essentials from that in his 1907 book, *The Rate of Interest* (New York: The Macmillan Co.).

production" can be;[12] if wisely chosen and organized, longer periods of production are more productive than are shorter periods, although the average productivity of labor rises at a decreasing rate as the production period is lengthened.

Given the capital supply, the wage rate, and the period of production, how many workers can the economy employ? Suppose that there are five lines of activity, and the period of production is five years in each. Suppose also that it requires c-amount of capital to sustain workers for one year in any one line of activity. Finally, suppose that the five lines of activity are "staggered" by one year intervals, as illustrated in Figure I.

As of the beginning of 1888, what is the necessary accumulation of capital to carry on the five lines of activity? The workers in Activity I are just beginning a period of production, and the fruits of their labor will not be available for five years; there must be sufficient accumulation (i.e., $5c$) to carry them through the entire production period. But there need be only $4c$ accumulated at this time to take care of the workers in Activity II; the output of III will be available after three years; etc. Thus, although there are five lines of activity and a production period of 5 years, and $5 \times 5 = 25$, since the activities are staggered, the accumulation at any one time required to keep the whole process going is only $5 + 4 + 3 + 2 + 1 = 15$, a little more than half of 25. To put it a bit differently, "to allow the entire body of labourers to embark on a five years' production process, all that is required is subsistence for $(5 + 4 + 3 + 2 + 1)/5 = 3$ years, or a little more than *half* the period of production" of five years (p. 327). The longer the production period, the closer we come to requiring exactly half the subsistence for the full period. In the calculations to follow, suppose that the ratio is exactly one-half.

In algebraic notation, we may say that approximately,
$$C = \tfrac{1}{2}Lwp,$$

when C = capital,
$\quad L$ = labor,
$\quad p$ = period of production (number of years),
$\quad w$ = annual wage rate.

Böhm-Bawerk assumes an economy with capital of $15,000,000 and 10,000 workers; let the wage rate be $300, and consider an entrepreneur with $10,000 capital. He could hire 66.67 laborers for one year, 33.33 with a production period of two years, etc., as indicated in Table I. With higher wage rates, the maximum number of employees is naturally smaller at any

---

12. ". . . the production period of a consumption good is, strictly speaking, to be reckoned from the moment on which the first hand was laid to the making of its first intermediate product, right down to the completion of the good itself. . . . the production period of almost any consumption good could in any strict calculation, trace its beginning back to early centuries. . . . Of course the finished product of to-day owes a quite infinitesimal fraction—not worth calculation even if that were possible—to the firstlings of labour in these far-off centuries . . . . It is more important and more correct to look at the period of time which elapses *on the average* between the expenditure of the original productive powers, labour and uses of land, as successively employed in any work, and the turning out of the finished consumption goods" (p. 88).

FIGURE I

	1885	1886	1887	1888	1889	1890	1891	1892	1893
I	c	c	c	c	c	c	c	c	c
II	c	c	c	c	c	c	c	c	c
III	c	c	c	c	c	c	c	c	c
IV	c	c	c	c	c	c	c	c	c
V	c	c	c	c	c	c	c	c	c

given length of production period. In his presumed endeavor to maximize profits, the entrepreneur must choose the appropriate combination of wage rate and period of production.

It may be helpful to plot the data of Table I in Figure II. Each of the dashed curves measures the number of laborers hired at the indicated wage rate and at alternative periods of production, the capital supply being given. Recalling that

$$C = \tfrac{1}{2}Lwp,$$

with C given throughout the analysis and with w given for any specified curve, it follows that

$$Lp = constant.$$

That is, each of the dashed curves is a rectangular hyperbola.

The solid curves plot the "total profit" columns of Table I, each again representing a different wage rate. Each curve shows the total profit at the indicated wage rate and at alternative periods of production.

Moving down a dashed curve, the number of workers hired falls as the period of production lengthens. Moving to the right on a solid curve, total profits rise, hit a maximum, and then decline as the period of production lengthens.

For exactly full employment of labor, 6.67 workers must be hired; a horizontal dotted line is drawn at this level. But such a line will intersect *all* of the rectangular hyperbolas: with *any* wage rate there will be *some* period of production which will give full employment of labor — the lower the wage rate, the longer is the necessary period of production. (All of the curves, dashed and solid, are constructed on the basis of full utilization of capital.)[13]

With given capital and labor supplies, which of the wage rates (and corresponding period of production) giving full employment of both labor and of capital is the unique equilibrium rate? The greatest total profit is $5111, with a period of production of *three* years and a wage rate of $300; but the dashed curve representing a wage rate of $300 gives exactly full employment of labor only with a period of production of *ten* years. If a period of three years is adopted with a $300 wage rate, there will tend to

13. Böhm-Bawerk does not note explicitly that there can be full employment of capital and of labor at any wage rate.

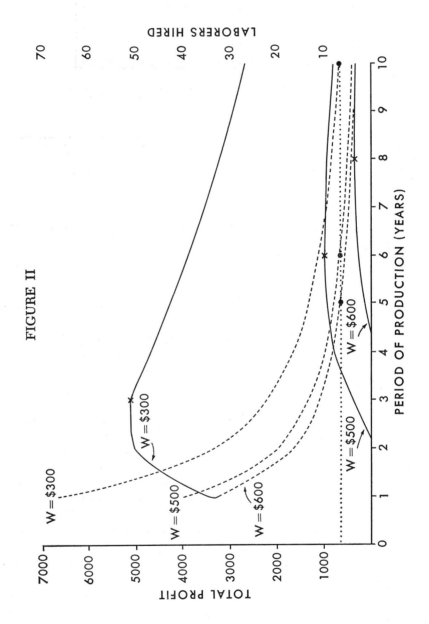

FIGURE II

TABLE I

Production period (years)	Annual product per worker	Annual wages $300			Annual wages $600			Annual wages $500		
		Profit per worker	Number of workers	Total profit	Profit per worker	Number of workers	Total profit	Profit per worker	Number of workers	Total profit
1	$350	$50	66.67	$3333	−$250	33.33	Loss	−$150	40	Loss
2	450	150	33.33	5000	− 150	16.67	Loss	− 50	20	Loss
3	530	230	22.22	5111*	− 70	11.11	Loss	30	13.33	$400
4	580	280	16.67	4666	− 20	8.33	Loss	80	10	800
5	620	320	13.33	4266	20	6.67	$133	120	8	960
6	650	350	11.11	3888	50	5.55	277	150	6.67	1000*
7	670	370	9.52	3522	70	4.76	333	170	5.71	970
8	685	385	8.33	3208	85	4.17	354*	185	5	925
9	695	395	7.41	2925	95	3.70	351	195	4.44	866
10	700	400	6.67	2666	100	3.33	333	200	4	800

be overemployment of labor, *i.e.*, entrepreneurs will desire to employ more laborers (33,333.33) than are available (10,000),[14] and the wage rate will be bid up. (Put somewhat differently, since no more workers can be hired than the number available, there would be underemployment of capital, the surplus capital then being used to bid up the price of labor.) Alternatively, if a period of production of ten years is used, we do not have a final equilibrium situation, for the individual entrepreneur would then have an incentive to move up the total-profit curve toward the maximum point by shortening the period of production and increasing his hiring of labor, again bidding up the wage rate.

Similarly, the period of production (eight years) which maximizes profit when the wage rate is $600 is not an equilibrium period, for fewer than 6.67 workers would be hired. And if, with a wage of $600, the period of production is shortened to five years in order to employ all labor, profits will not be maximized.

Obviously, the only equilibrium situation is that in which *a* maximum total profit and also full employment of labor are both attained with the same period of production. In our illustration, we achieve both objectives only with a wage rate of $500 and a period of production of six years.

To summarize, product per worker increases at a decreasing rate as the period of production is lengthened; product per worker minus wage per worker gives profit per worker; profit per worker times the number of workers gives total profit; total profit will be at a maximum at some period of production — the higher the wage, other things equal, the longer the period at which profits are maximized. We then have three conditions of equilibrium: (*a*) all capital is employed, (*b*) all labor is employed, and (*c*), for stability, conditions (*a*) and (*b*) must be met with a period of production which maximizes the rate of return consistent with the prevail-

14. That is, with a wage rate of $300 and a period of production of three years, the entrepreneur with $10,000 capital will wish to hire 22.22 workers, and a total capital of $15,000,000 could support 22.22 × 15,000,000/10,000 = 33,333.33 workers.

ing wage rate. Finally, this "rate of return," *i.e.*, total profits as a proportion of total capital, is the equilibrium rate of interest; in our illustration, the rate of interest is 1000/10,000 = 10 per cent. There is established an equilibrium among the quantity of capital, the number of laborers, the wage rate, and the period of production; the interest rate is a measure of the productiveness of the production process thereby established.

Böhm-Bawerk suggests that the foregoing is a rather negative demonstration that "the necessary equilibrium could have been reached at no other rate of interest" (pp. 391–92), given all the initial assumptions. A more positive approach helps to reveal the *origin* and the *function* of interest as well as the manner of *determination* of the interest rate.

Wise extensions of the period of production are remunerative to entrepreneurs, but they require more capital, *i.e.*, presently available goods to provide subsistence in time-consuming production processes. Capital is scarce, and the competitive bidding for capital will inevitably make it command a price, *i.e.*, interest or agio.[15] The interest rate, therefore, performs a rationing function: it makes uneconomic the adoption of production processes which, in the aggregate, would require more capital than the economy possesses, and it thereby allocates the limited capital supply among the different industries in a rational fashion.[16] The rationing function is performed because the rate of interest is "limited and determined by the productiveness of the last extension of process economically permissible, and of the further extension economically not permissible . . . . The rate is determined by the surplus return of the last permissible extension of production. This coincides almost to a word with Thünen's celebrated law which makes the rate of interest depend on the productiveness of the 'last applied dose of capital' " (pp. 393, 394).

Fisher

Suppose, with Fisher, that a man has a certain money income this year (Year I) and that he will receive a certain income next year (Year II). These two basic incomes are given, but, we shall suppose further, the man

---

15. "If the stock of wealth be sufficient to maintain the population during an average of one year's production period, every one will wish to engage in a two year's process with its great productiveness, and, the stock of wealth not being sufficient to advance subsistence to everybody for two years, there will be . . . bidding against each other . . . and the agio on present goods will appear" (pp. 332–33).

16. "Now the constant presence of the agio on present goods is like a self-acting drag on the tendency to extend the production period; without checking it all at once it makes it more difficult, and more difficult in proportion to the projected length of the process. Extensions which would be harmful as regards social provision are thus made economically impossible. Moderate extensions over the average process, however, are not absolutely prevented, but are limited to those branches where, from peculiar economic or technical circumstances, the productiveness that goes with the extension of the period is so great that they can bear the progressive burden of the agio. Branches, again, where longer processes are somewhat, but only a little, more productive, are tempted to escape the burden of agio by recurring to periods under the average. Thus, finally, under the influence of the agio, the total fund of subsistence is divided out automatically among the individual branches of production, in such amounts that each branch adopts that length of process which—in the condition of the fund—is most favourable to the total provision" (p. 335).

may modify the amounts of money coming available to him in each of the years by borrowing or by lending for one year. If, say, he borrows in Year I and repays in Year II, he will increase his "income" available in I and reduce his "income" in II; the lender is reducing his Year I's "income" and increasing his Year II's "income." But such trading by a person of "some of his income of one year for some of another man's income for the other year" (p. 235) will be done at a rate of interest. Normally, it will be a positive rate; thus the borrower gives up more dollars in Year II than he acquired from the lender in Year I. Fisher's first problem is to consider how an individual, possessing certain basic incomes in Years I and II and having access to a perfect capital, or loan, market in which he may either borrow or lend at a given market rate of interest, will rationally consider modifying his net income streams in the two years.

In Figure III, money incomes are measured on both axes, income for Year I horizontally and for II vertically. P_1 indicates the basic income position of the individual. This position can be altered, we assume for the moment, only by borrowing and lending at the given rate of interest.

The rate at which this year's dollars can be swapped against next year's is indicated by the slope of the straight dashed lines, labeled M. Starting from P_1, the person *can* go into the loan market and increase Year I's income and decrease Year II's (*i.e.*, borrow this year and repay next year) by moving down and to the right on curve M_1; or decrease Year I's income and increase II's by being a lender and moving up and to the left on M_1. If there were a zero rate of interest, dollars of Years I and II would exchange one-for-one, and the slope of M_1 would be $(-)1$, or $(-)100$ per cent, *i.e.*, 45 degrees to either axis. With a positive rate of interest, M_1 is steeper, the rate of interest being measured by the divergence of the actual slope of M_1 from a slope of 100 per cent.

While the person *can* move along the objective "market" line, M_1, will he wish to move from P_1, and, if so, in which direction, *i.e.*, as a borrower or a lender? Here we must incorporate into the analysis what Fisher calls the subjective "willingness" curves, labeled W. These are indifference curves: any given W-curve is a locus of alternative combinations of Year-I-income-plus-Year-II-income which are equally desired by the person; the farther from the origin is the curve, the greater the level of well-being. There is an infinite number of W-curves, so one of them must pass through P_1.[17] The individual is *willing* to have (*i.e.*, is indifferent to having) his incomes in the two years modified by moving up or down W_3.

Starting, then, at P_1 in Figure III, the person evidently *can* acquire

---

17. Fisher assumes that at any given ratio of Year II income and Year I income, the lower the W-curve (nearer the origin), the steeper it is: with a relatively small income, a person is willing to sacrifice (lend) a given amount of Year I income only for a relatively large addition to Year II income, or he is willing to give up a relatively large amount of Year II income in order to acquire (borrow) a given addition to Year I income. Similarly, any given W-curve becomes steeper as it moves upward and to the left: every successive reduction in Year I income must be compensated by ever-increasing increments in Year II income. Thus "a man's actual degree of impatience depends on" both "the whole contour of his whole family of Willingness curves" and "his particular income situation on the map" (p. 249).

FIGURE III

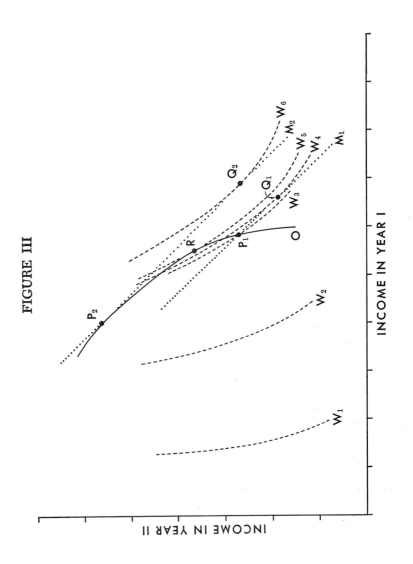

INCOME IN YEAR I

INCOME IN YEAR II

additional Year I income with a smaller sacrifice than, at the extreme, he is *willing* to suffer. In short, the rate of interest is smaller than the rate of time preference, and the person will be a borrower. If, in contrast, M_1 were steeper than W_3 at P_1, the person would have an incentive to lend: his market return would be greater than is required to keep him at the original indifference level.

In the case illustrated, as the individual borrows, he moves down M_1, leaving W_3 and moving continuously onto higher W-curves — until he reaches point Q_1, where M_1 and W_4 are tangent. Q_1 is the point of equilibrium, for there the interest rate equals the time preference rate; the individual currently borrows the horizontal distance from P_1 to Q_1 and next year repays the (greater) vertical distance from Q_1 to P_1.

Each person has his own indifference map of W-curves, but each is confronted, in the perfect loan market, by M-curves of given slope, *i.e.*, there is a single interest rate. The equilibrium rate "clears the market" by equating the aggregate sum which lenders wish to lend with the sum which borrowers wish to borrow.

If we imagine the market rate to be very high, say 25 per cent, then, the bulk of individuals would try to lend and few would want to borrow. The aggregate of loans thus offered would exceed the demand and the interest rate would fall. Conversely, if the rate were too low, demand would exceed supply and the rate would rise. Since the total sums actually lent must equal, in the aggregate, those borrowed, the horizontal displacements of all the Q's in one direction must equal that of all the other Q's in the other direction. . . . In short, the geometric "center of gravity" of all the Q's must coincide with that of all the P's, in order that the loan market may be cleared (p. 256).

In his "second approximation to the theory of interest," Fisher assumes that the individual is no longer confined to a single income position (P_1) except as modified by borrowing and lending, but rather "he now has the opportunity to choose any one of many income positions" (p. 264). He can have a basic income position any place in the area bounded by curve O, his objective "investment opportunity" line. He will confine his choice to points on the O-line itself: the points within the O-line "would never be chosen under any circumstances, since each inside point is excelled by some points on the boundary in respect to *both* years' incomes" (p. 264). The O-line "may be defined as the limiting line of a group of points which represent all the optional income situations available to an individual who neither borrows nor lends" (pp. 277–78). "It is simply a geometric picture of the technical limitations of an individual's income in the two years" (p. 265), and it is reasonable, but not necessary, to draw it as a smooth, continuous curve, concave to the origin, which "represents a law of decreasing returns in the sense that each succeeding dose of $100 invested out of this year's income will return less and less next year" (p. 279).

If the person now has an O-line and is initially at P_1 but does not have access to the loan market, he would do well to move up the income boundary. As he sacrifices income in Year I for income in Year II, he cuts across successively higher W-lines, until he reaches point R on W_5, the highest attainable indifference curve. The slope of the O-curve at any point gives the "marginal rate of return over cost," or "investment opportunity rate" (p. 270). At R, the rate of return is equal to the "marginal rate of time preference," or "degree of impatience" (p. 270).

If we assume again that the person can enter the loan market and borrow or lend at the going interest rate, he can shift not only along the O-curve but also along an M-curve. Therefore, he can move first to P_2 (not R) and then to Q_2. Assuming that the same interest rate still prevails, M_2 is parallel to M_1, and Q_2 is the point of tangency of M_2 with the highest possible W-curve while still touching (tangent to) the O-curve. In this equilibrium, the interest rate is equated to both the marginal rate of return over cost and the marginal rate of time preference.

Again, while each individual in the loan market considers the rate of interest as given, the rate will tend to settle at that level which will clear the market, with the aggregate funds being offered by lenders equated to the aggregate being demanded by borrowers.[18]

While Fisher overly generously credits Böhm-Bawerk with presenting the time preference theory "clearly and forcibly" (p. 473), he feels that in attempting to integrate the productivity factor (the so-called technical superiority of present over future goods), Böhm-Bawerk "erred greatly" (p. 474). But such integration is essential, for it is impossible "to determine the rate of interest from the subjective side alone, through time preference, or from the objective side alone, through investment opportunity, or 'productivity,' or 'technique of production'" (p. 496). Fisher achieved his purpose (and without use of Böhm-Bawerk's dubious concept, the average period of production) in a "masterpiece" which is "a wonderful performance, the peak achievement, so far as perfection within its own frame is concerned, of the literature of interest."[19]

---

18. In a briefly stated "third approximation," Fisher introduces uncertainty, and the risks which characterize the real world variously muddy the clear-cut conclusions of the first two approximations.

19. Joseph A. Schumpeter, "Irving Fisher's Econometrics," *Econometrica*, XVI (July 1948), 225, reprinted in *idem, Ten Great Economists* (New York: Oxford University Press, 1951), p. 230.

22.

ARTHUR H. LEIGH
Reed College

Von Thünen's Theory

of Distribution and

the Advent of

Marginal Analysis

The pioneer contributions of the nineteenth-century German economist Johann Heinrich von Thünen (1783–1850) to the development of the concept and technique of marginal analysis place him in a rank of first importance among economic thinkers. To the historian of economic thought his intricate theories and his distinctive approach to economic analysis hold peculiar interest. He is original in developing an explicit general application of the marginal productivity concept to the theory of distribution.[1] His deductive reasoning is supplemented by inductive analysis based in part upon extensive facts and figures gathered from his own experimental estate in Mecklenburg, and he combines surprisingly advanced modern concepts with orthodox Ricardian doctrines. Yet Thünen's single published economic treatise, *Der isolirte Staat*, has not been widely read, owing perhaps to its voluminous proportions, to its formidable array of algebraic symbols, and, in the case of English-speaking students of economics, to the fact that it has never been translated into English. John Bates Clark and Alfred Marshall have recognized and praised Thünen's contribution to economic

Reprinted from *The Journal of Political Economy*, LIV (December 1946), 481–502, by permission of the author and The University of Chicago Press.

theory,[2] and a number of historians of economic doctrine refer briefly to some of his ideas;[3] but there is to the knowledge of the present writer no adequate English summary and discussion of his more important theories.[4] Marshall comments as follows on Thünen's work:

> I have long ago forgotten Cournot; and I may be wrong. But my impression is that I did not derive so much of the substance of my opinions from him as from von Thünen. Cournot was a gymnastic master who directed the form of my thought. Von Thünen was a *bona fide* mathematician, but of less power: his blunder as to the natural wage is not of the same order as Cournot's little slips. But, to make up, he was a careful experimenter and student of facts and with a mind at least as fully developed on the inductive as on the deductive side. Above all he was an ardent philanthropist. . . . . And I loved von Thünen above all my masters. Professor Fisher has cared for Cournot. I would that someone would care for von Thünen. He should not, I think, be translated: but an abstract of his work should be given, with translations of a good deal of his second volume.[5]

In the pages which follow an attempt is made to reproduce as clearly and completely as possible within the confines of a single article the principal theories of Thünen relating to marginal analysis and the theory of distribution. After two brief sections dealing with Thünen's explanations of land rent, interest, and entrepreneurs' profit there follows a condensed exposition of his theory of wage and interest rate determination. The paper ends with an evaluation of Thünen's theories in the light of modern economic doctrines. It should be noted at the outset that Thünen's work deserves study less for the conclusions at which he arrives, some of which are absurd, than for its highly significant contribution to the development of new and more fruitful methods of analysis.

THE "ISOLATED STATE"

To simplify and clarify his analysis, Thünen sets up a hypothetical model which he calls the "isolated state." He describes this model as a state composed of a single large city located in the center of a broad plain which is all of equal fertility but void of navigable rivers and canals, the only means of transportation being the wagon. The inhabitants of the city supply the inhabitants of the surrounding country with manufactured articles in return for raw produce. Various kinds of agricultural products are grown in concentric circles around the city, the exact location at which each product is raised being determined by the cost of transporting it to the city. In the area nearest the city, for example, garden vegetables and fresh milk are produced, cultivation is intensive because of the high price of land, and soil fertility is maintained by the application of fertilizer rather than by allowing a part of it to lie fallow each year. Farther from the city, wheat is produced by the enclosure system; still farther wheat is produced by the three-field system; and in the outermost circles the land is used for grazing. Surrounding the cultivated plain lies an impenetrable wilderness which separates the state from the rest of the world. The soil in the wilderness is as fertile as any other, and the limit of cultivation is determined only by transportation cost. It is further assumed that the "isolated state" possesses mines near the city and that its population is constant.[6]

Thünen elaborates with minute and realistic detail upon the principles (including that of alternative cost) which govern the location of agricultural production, and with as much care he points out that his simplifying assumptions, like those of a controlled laboratory experiment in physics, are in many ways unrealistic and acknowledges the danger of generalizing the conclusions derived from such assumptions.[7] He is too much concerned with supporting his theory with realistic detail and actual statistics to confine himself rigidly to his hypothetical model, and he therefore changes his assumptions and compares his theory with observed fact at frequent intervals. Nevertheless, the concept of the isolated state forms the nucleus for most of his theoretical discussion.

THE THEORY OF LAND RENT

Thünen's theory of land rent is based upon the same fundamental principles as that of Ricardo — differences in the value product of different units of labor and capital due to nonuniformity in land fertility or convenience of location and to the effects of intensive cultivation. He criticizes Adam Smith's definition of land rent as that part of the value of the product of the estate which remains after the tenant farmer has paid wages and the other expenses of the farm and has taken the usual interest on his capital, on the ground that such a definition fails to distinguish between the rent of the land itself and the interest on capital invested in buildings, fences, and other improvements. Acknowledging that Ricardo had rectified Adam Smith's error by confining the term "rent" to payment for the use of the "original and indestructible powers of the soil," Thünen points out that the estate revenue (*Gutsrente*) must be subdivided into its two component parts — ground rent or land rent (*Bodenrente* or *Landrente*) and interest on all capital invested in improvements. This distinction is based upon long-run mobility. Capital will not be invested in the development of a new estate unless the prospective estate revenue is at least sufficient to yield a return on the invested capital at the current rate of interest, yet the estate may be brought into cultivation if the revenue is no more than this amount (i.e., if land rent proper is zero). If the revenue of an existing estate should fall, or if the current rate of interest should rise, the total estate revenue may fall short of the interest at the current rate on the capital invested in the estate. To the extent that estate revenue is less than interest on invested capital, the land rent is negative. In such circumstances the estate will continue under cultivation only until the capital invested in it can be withdrawn or disinvested through undermaintenance. In short, the concept of land rent as a residual can apply only to those qualities of the land itself which are strictly nontransferable, even in the long run.[8]

In the isolated state, where all land is of equal fertility, estates located in the inner circles of cultivation yield a land rent by virtue of their relatively advantageous position with respect to the central city and the consequent lower cost of getting their produce to market. The price of wheat[9] in the central city is determined by the production plus transportation cost of obtaining wheat from the most distant estates whose product is required to bring the city's supply of food to the necessary level. This cost depends upon the rates of wages and interest, which tend to maintain a uniform level throughout the state.[10] Since the wheat produced on estates near the city and brought to market at low transportation costs sells at the same price in the city as does wheat brought in from distant estates at high transportation costs, the saving in transportation costs enjoyed by the more favorably situated estates constitutes their land rent. Land rent is zero on the most distant estates and increases steadily with decreasing distance from the market city.[11] In the real world, differences in fertility as between estates give rise to land rent in the same manner as do differences in location advantages. Thus, as a general rule, the land rent of an estate originates in the advantages enjoyed by that estate with respect to convenience of location or to soil quality as compared with other estates which must be cultivated to supply the demand.[12]

Thünen recognizes a second origin of land rent in the phenomenon of diminishing returns which accompanies increasingly intensive cultivation of a given area of land. As additional laborers and capital are applied to the cultivation of a given estate, each successive laborer together with the capital with which he is equipped adds a smaller increment to the total product of the estate. Since the value of the last added worker, which equals the increment of product value he produces minus the interest on the capital he uses, determines the wage of all workers, there remains, in the case of each worker except the last employed, a surplus of product value over wages paid which forms the second basis for land rent. Rent arises from this source even though all land is equally well situated and of equal fertility, provided only that all such land is under cultivation.[13] In illustration of this point, Thünen assumes a plain of uniform fertility with a large number of small cities distributed evenly over it and surrounded by a sandy desert. Under these circumstances, land rent from the first cause — the differential advantage of some estates over others with respect to fertility or location — would be negligible, but rent from the second cause — the influence of increasing intensity of cultivation — would arise provided only that all the arable land has been taken into cultivation.[14]

Thünen's third component of land rent is the interest on capital invested in those improvements of the estate which once made can never be destroyed or separated from the soil.[15] His inclusion of this element which appears at first to be in conflict with his earlier strict definition of land rent seems to be based upon the assumption that the improvements the interest of which is to be classed as land rent are, like land, wholly nontransferable, and that capital once invested in them can therefore command only a residual share of the product which may fall short of (but presumably could not exceed) the current interest rate.

INTEREST AND ENTREPRENEURIAL PROFIT

Criticizing Adam Smith and most of the other English writers for lumping together as "profit" the interest on invested capital and the profit of the entrepreneur,[16] Thünen makes a careful distinction between the two.

He defines capital as the product of past human labor[17] used for the purpose of increasing the effectiveness of human labor, that is, used productively in such a way that it maintains itself permanently intact through replacement of consumed physical units and that it yields a revenue. It is distinct from natural or original forces, including land, and from commodities or "supplies" consumed without producing a substitute and without making labor more effective.[18] His definition and explanation of interest must be inferred from various statements and passages scattered through his discussion. He treats interest as the price or the payment for the use of capital arising from the fact that capital increases the effectiveness or productiveness of labor and from the fact that no free individual will accumulate capital at the sacrifices involved in exerting labor and in foregoing the luxuries which might otherwise have been enjoyed unless he receives a compensation in the form of interest which is worthy of his sacrifice.[19] In the rate of interest for loaned capital there are usually included two elements: (1) the compensation which the debtor pays for the temporary use of the capital under the condition that he will repay the sum loaned and (2) an insurance premium against the possible loss of the capital, a risk which often accompanies long period loans. He adds that what he calls interest in the present work includes only the first of these elements.[20]

The entrepreneur's trade profit in the strict sense consists only of that part of his revenue which remains after the deduction of (1) the interest on his invested capital; (2) an insurance premium against fire, hail, shipwreck, and all other insurable risk; and (3) his salary of management and administration. This surplus or trade profit remains to the entrepreneur in spite of the competition of other entrepreneurs because there is no insurance against each and every danger which is connected with enterprise. A common example of such a noninsurable risk is the movement of prices. Although the chances of gain are often fully as great as the chances of loss, the former do not compensate wholly for the latter, since to the individual entrepreneur who risks his entire fortune and reputation in his enterprise, the pleasure of doubling his fortune is far less intense than the suffering which would result from the complete loss of his fortune. A man of his capacity and training would have the opportunity of obtaining a lucrative and secure position in the civil service, and therefore some additional compensation must be offered him if he is to undergo the hazards of an enterprise.[21] In addition to receiving a compensation for noninsurable risk, the entrepreneur who manages his own business should receive a reward for his labor of direction and management which is something in excess of the salary received by a hired manager of equal knowledge and ability; for, when his own fortune and reputation are at stake, he will exercise far more energy and ingenuity than would a hired manager, even if the latter were trying to do his duty.[22]

After making these careful distinctions, however, Thünen places them in the background and concludes that in the theory of distribution we may treat the entrepreneur as a hired manager paid by his profit, and that we need therefore consider only the laborer, the capitalist, and the landowner in analyzing the distribution of the product of labor.[23]

THE MATHEMATICAL THEORY OF WAGE AND INTEREST-RATE DETERMINATION

It is Thünen's opinion that statements of his predecessors in explanation of the interest rate to the effect that the rate is determined by the supply and demand for capital or that it tends to vary inversely with the quantity of capital in the economy are mere descriptions of observed external facts and fail to offer any real and fundamental explanation of those facts.[24] Similarly, when natural wages are explained in terms of the supply and demand for labor, a fact is given as an explanation. Furthermore, the subsistence-level concept tends to lull the conscience of the observer so long as the worker is not actually suffering starvation. Since this problem involves conflict between social classes, a more definitive solution is needed.[25]

Thünen's own attempt to develop a more satisfactory explanation of interest and wage rates occupies the major part of his second volume. In a seemingly tireless effort to make his theory airtight, he leads the reader through several long series of calculations, each begun from a different point of view and all arriving eventually at the same set of conclusions. He first approaches the problem of wage and interest rates by assuming (1) a community of persons having the technological knowledge of civilized European nations but no capital and living in a large tropical country rich in natural resources and favored by climate. For further simplification, it is assumed (2) that the community is isolated from the rest of the world, (3) that it is large enough to take full advantage of the division of labor as soon as the requisite capital is present, (4) that the land is of equal fertility and of such vast expanse that everyone can take as much as he wants without cost, and (5) that all the inhabitants are workers, there being no employer-employee relationships.[26]

Under these circumstances one laboring family, working for one year without the aid of capital, can produce $110c$, where c is a unit of the major subsistence commodity equal to a hundredth part of the quantity necessary to maintain one laboring family for one year. Since each family can produce in one year a surplus of $10c$ over and above the $100c$ necessary for its subsistence, it can, in the course of ten years, accumulate sufficient subsistence (abstracting from storage problems) either to live for one year without working or to spend that year in the production of

558

useful tools such as bows and nets, i.e., capital. Working with the capital it can produce in one year, a family can produce a net product (after maintaining capital) of 150c. With a yearly surplus of 50c, it need devote only two years of labor to the production of subsistence before it is once more free to spend a year in capital production. But this particular family is already provided with sufficient bows, arrows, and nets, and it therefore lends this newly created capital to another family who has not as yet acquired any capital. Since this second family can, with the aid of the borrowed capital, produce a yearly product of 150c after maintaining the capital and returning it intact, and since there is not as yet sufficient capital in the country to provide each working family with as much capital as can be produced by one year of labor, the lender can demand as payment for the use of his capital the full difference between the 150c which the borrowing family can produce with the aid of the capital and the 110c which it could produce unassisted by capital, a payment which in this stage of development amounts to 40c and which will continue to accrue indefinitely to the capital-producing worker as interest on the capital he produced with one year of labor. The interest rate is calculated by dividing the yearly revenue (40c) by the wages of one year of labor (110c), and the result in this case is 36.4 per cent.[27] Thus, for the surplus of one year of labor, the worker has the choice of receiving 10c in perishable consumables or a perpetual revenue of 3.64c per year. Here, says Thünen, we discover the origin and basis of interest and its relation to capital.[28]

After every worker in the community has been supplied with as much capital as can be produced by the labor of one family working for one year, capital production will continue, though perhaps the new capital will take a different form, for example, spades and hatchets instead of bows and nets. Thus in the course of time, each worker will be supplied with capital amounting to the product of two, three, four, five, etc., years of labor. The product of each worker will rise with each increase in the quantity of capital with which he works. But the increase of revenue resulting from the use of increased quantities of capital does not keep pace with the increase of capital itself, so that each added unit of capital results in a smaller increment in revenue than had its predecessor. Different forms of capital enhance the efficiency of labor to different degrees. Capital-producing workers will at first produce those forms which are most effective in increasing the product of labor, but, when they have produced as many of such instruments as can be used to advantage, they must devote their efforts to the production of less efficient forms of capital. For this reason, therefore, the revenue of capital tends to decline as the quantity of capital increases.[29]

Thünen next divides his workers into two classes, one group which specializes in capital production and another which works with capital borrowed from the first group; but he retains the simplifying assumption that all workers are their own masters, none being hired by others. Each member of the latter class retains as his wages his total product minus the interest on the capital which he borrows from the capital-producing laborers. Thus when each worker is supplied with as much capital as is produced by one year of labor, his total yearly product is $150c$, the revenue of the capital which he uses is $40c$ as shown above, and his wages are $110c$. When capital produced by two years of labor is used by each worker, however, the additional capital adds only $36c$ to the laborer's product, bringing it to a total of $110c + 40c + 36c = 186c$. When the quantity of capital in the community has reached this level, the capital-producing workers, because of the free competition among them, can obtain only $36c$ per year as revenue for *all* units of their capital, even though the first units used add as much as $40c$ to the product of labor. Under competitive conditions capitals requiring equal quantities of labor for their production must receive equal revenue. Thus the revenue of all capital is determined by the revenue of the last added units of capital. Thünen stresses the importance of this law in the following words: "Die Rente, die das Kapital im Ganzen beim Ausleihen gewährt, wird bestimmt durch die Nutzung des zuletzt angelegten Kapitaltheilchens. Dies ist einer der wichtigsten Sätze in der Lehre von den Zinsen."[30]

The worker who, with the aid of two units of capital, can produce $186c$ must, therefore pay to the capital-producing worker only $2 \times 36c$ or $72c$ as interest on his borrowed capital and can retain $114c$ as his wages, which have thus risen by $4c$ as a result of his using the second unit of capital. Similarly, the revenue per unit of capital falls, and his wages rise as further additions are made to the capital with which he works.[31]

Since the rate of interest in Thünen's analysis is calculated by dividing the revenue of a unit of capital by the wages of the labor required to produce a unit of capital, that rate must fall with the increase of capital even more abruptly than does the absolute revenue per unit of capital. Thus, when wages equal $110c$ and revenue per unit of capital equals $40c$, the rate of interest equals $40c/110c$, or 36.4 per cent; but, when two units of capital are used by each worker and wages rise to $114c$ while revenue falls to $36c$, the interest rate falls to $36c/114c$, or 31.6 per cent. This decline in the interest rate continues as the quantity of capital used by each worker increases to three, four, five, etc., units.[32]

The capital-producing workers have no power to prevent this decline in the interest rate which works against their own interests, for they have no monopoly on capital production, every worker according to Thünen's assumptions being free to engage in capital production if this occupation appears more profitable to him than the production of current consumables.[33] What, then, motivates a continued production of capital in the face of declining interest rates, and what is the limit to capital increase? In answer to this question, Thünen reminds the reader that capital is the product of labor and that it is formed exclusively from the worker's surplus — the excess of his wages over his necessary subsistence. It follows that, the higher the wages, the larger will be the surplus, and the easier capital production will become. In other words, the larger the yearly surplus of each worker,[34] the smaller the number of years he must work in order to accumulate the equivalent of one unit of capital or the smaller the number of workers who must pool their surpluses during one year in order to save the equivalent of

TABLE 1*

(1)	(2)	(3)	(4)	(5)	(6)	(7)	(8)	(9)
Units of Capital per Worker	Labor Product	Total Revenue of Capital	Wage	Worker's Surplus	Rate of Interest	Revenue One Unit Capital	Workers NeededTo Save One Unit of Capital	Revenue for One Worker's Surplus
	(c)	(c)	(c)	(c)	(%)	(c)		(c)
0	110.0	0.0	110.0	10.0	—	—	—	—
1	150.0	40.0	110.0	10.0	36.4	40.0	11.00	3.64
2	186.0	72.0	114.0	14.0	31.6	36.0	8.14	4.42
3	218.4	97.2	121.2	21.2	26.7	32.4	5.72	5.66
4	247.6	116.8	130.8	30.8	22.3	29.2	4.25	6.87
5	273.9	131.5	142.4	42.4	18.5	26.3	3.36	7.83
6	297.6	142.2	155.4	55.4	15.2	23.7	2.80	8.46
7	318.9	149.1	169.8	69.8	12.6	21.3	2.43	8.76
8	338.1	153.6	184.5	84.5	10.4	19.2	2.18	8.81
9	355.4	155.7	199.7	99.7	8.8	17.3	2.00	8.65
10	371.0	156.0	215.0	115.0	7.25	15.6	1.87	8.34

* Der isolirte Staat, II, Part I, 113.
The unit c as defined on p. 558 above.

a unit of capital, and thus the smaller the number of laborers among which the yearly revenue of one unit of capital must be divided. An example from Thünen's figures may make this rather complex analysis clearer. When a quantity of capital amounting to the product of two years of labor is being used by each worker, the wage of one year of labor is 114c, the revenue of one unit of capital is 36c, and the worker's surplus (wage of 114c minus subsistence requirements of 100c) is 14c. Then the number of workers who must pool their surpluses in order to accumulate in one year the equivalent of one unit of capital is 114c/14c, or 8.14 workers; and the annual revenue which each worker will obtain through future time as a result of the investment of his surplus for the present year equals the revenue of one unit of capital, or 36c, divided by the number of participants in the investment of that unit of capital, or 8.14 workers, which equals 4.42c. When three units of capital are used by each worker, however, the wage becomes 121.2c, the revenue of one unit of capital is 32.4c, and the surplus is 21.2c. Then 121.2c/21.2c = 5.72 workers, and the revenue which each obtains for his invested surplus is 32.4c/5.72, or 5.66c, a higher revenue than before, even though the revenue of one unit of capital and the rate of interest have declined. In short, as capital accumulates, the rate of interest falls, wages rise, the revenue per unit of capital declines, but the cost of capital production decreases.[35] Thünen summarizes these trends in Table 1.

Column 7 in Table 1 is the marginal product of capital, derived from the increments in total product per worker resulting from the increase of the quantity of capital used by each worker as shown in column 2.[36] Column 8, the number of workers whose surpluses for one year must be pooled in order to accumulate the equivalent of one unit of capital, is obtained by dividing the yearly wage of one worker (col. 4), in terms of which Thünen expresses one unit of capital, by the yearly surplus of one worker (col. 5), obtained by deducting from the wage the necessary subsistence of one working family — 100c. Column 9, the revenue accruing to one worker from his investment of one year's surplus, is then derived by dividing the revenue of one whole unit of capital (col. 7) by the number of workers participating in it (col. 8). Finally, column 6, the rate of interest, is the quotient of the revenue of one unit of capital (col. 7) divided by the value in terms of wage cost of one unit of capital (col. 4).[37]

Thünen assumes that the workers' own interests will motivate them to produce just that amount of capital which will maximize the revenue obtainable from the investment of one year's surplus; that is, that they will seek to maximize the quantities expressed in column 9 of Table 1. He concludes that, under the circumstances assumed in the example, this revenue is maximized when the community possesses eight units of capital per worker, at which point the wage of one year's labor would be 184.5c, and the rate of interest would be 10.4 per cent.[38]

In keeping with his characteristic regard for realistic detail, Thünen carefully points out that the data in Table 1 depend upon the fertility of the soil and upon the other natural advantages of the particular country under discussion. He presents a second table in which the soil is assumed to be less fertile and the product of one laborer is less by one-fourth than that of a corresponding laborer (using an equal quantity of capital) in Table 1.[39] Here the condition of maximum revenue (as Thünen defines it) is reached when 10.5 units of capital are used by each worker, at which point the yearly wage of a worker is 167c and the rate of interest is 6.65 per cent. Thus, with decreasing soil fertility, a larger quantity of capital per worker will be used, but wages and the rate of interest will decline.[40]

For his second general approach to the problem of wage and interest-rate determination, Thünen returns to his original model of the isolated state, in which there are landowners, employers, and hired laborers. He takes the outer edge of the cultivated plain as the point at which the equilibrium levels of wages and the interest rate are determined and makes the following assumptions: (1) that land rent for estates located in this outer ring of cultivation is zero, or so near to zero that it can be neglected, and that consequently the entire product of such estates is divided between workers and owners of capital; (2) that wage-earning laborers now cultivating existing estates are free to leave their present employments to take up free new land at the outer rim of cultivation, which is as fertile and otherwise as advantageous as land already being cultivated at the border of the plain; (3) that the wages of such workers are something in excess of their subsistence needs, so that they have a surplus from which they may accumulate the capital required for the opening-up and development of a new estate (an assumption defended by the observation that, since the population of the European working class has recently been rising by about 1 per cent annually, their wages must have been more than sufficient to enable them to live and to perpetuate the population at a constant level); (4) that, because of the free mobility of workers, the real wages of workers throughout the isolated state are equal (abstracting, for the sake of simplicity, differences in skill and in the quality of workers) and that wages determined at the border of the plain therefore determine the wages for the entire state; and, finally, (5) that, because of the free mobility of capital within the isolated state, interest rates (meaning net interest remaining after the deduction of all risk premiums) are the same throughout the state, since rates determined at the border of the plain determine the rate throughout the isolated state.[41]

Since any worker possessing sufficient capital may discontinue working for wages and participate in the development of a new estate,[42] he can be persuaded to remain in the service of his employer on an old estate only if the amount of his annual wages plus the interest he can receive by loaning as much capital as he would require to develop new land is at least equal to the annual product which he and his capital could obtain by the cultivation of new land.[43] Upon the basis of this assumption Thünen continues his analysis with the use of the following algebraic symbols: the annual wages of a working family expressed in measures of wheat is $(a + y)$, where a is the amount necessary for the subsistence of the family and y is the surplus available for accumulation; q is the quantity of capital which a working family must possess in order to develop new land, expressed in units equal to the quantity of capital which can be produced by one family working for one year; p equals the annual product, expressed in measures of wheat, which one working family can produce when assisted by q units of capital;[44] and z is the rate of interest. Since Thünen expresses his unit of capital as the wages of one year of labor, the quantity of capital q may be expressed in terms of measures of wheat as $q(a + y)$. The above condition for the necessary wage at the boundary of the isolated state may then be expressed by the following equation

$$(a + y) + q(a + y)z = p ,$$

where a, q, and p are known magnitudes and y and z are unknown. By solving this equation for $(a + y)$, the wage may be expressed as $p/(1 + qz)$ and, by solving for z, the interest rate may be expressed as $[p - (a + y)]/q(a + y)$. The latter expression states merely that the interest rate in general equals the difference between the yearly product of one laborer and the yearly wage of that laborer divided by the capital which he uses, all quantities being expressed in terms of measures of wheat. But since there are two unknowns and only one independent equation, the problem is so far indeterminate, and we have obtained only an inverse functional relationship between y and z.[45]

To arrive at the equilibrium level of wages and the corresponding equilibrium rate of interest, Thünen presents an example in which a group of free workers agrees to establish a new estate which is to be equal in size to the previously existing estates, upon which n working families will be continuously employed and in which nq units of capital (q units per worker) will be invested. Since, by Thünen's definition of a unit of capital, one worker produces one unit in a year, the construction of the capital to be invested in the estate — the clearing, draining, fencing of the land, and the construction of buildings, etc. — will require the labor for one year of nq of the workers in the capital-producing group. The remainder of the group continues in the capacity of wage-earning laborers on the old estates. Each of these workers turns over the entire surplus of his wages for that year, amounting to y measures of wheat, to the members of the group who are engaged during that year in the construction of the new estate, each of whom requires as subsistence during the year a measures of wheat. It follows that for the nq workers so engaged a total of anq measures of wheat is necessary and that, therefore, the number of workers in the group who are earning subsistence as wage-earners during the year must be anq/y workers. Thus the total number of workers constituting the capital producing group amounts to $nq + (anq/y)$, or $nq(a + y)/y$ workers. Since each has, during the year of construction, lived upon the bare subsistence of a measures of wheat and has contributed his surplus of y measures to the creation of capital, each deserves to share equally in the revenue of the estate. Since the n cultivating workers thenceforth to be continuously employed on the new estate must be paid the same wage as all other workers including the capital-producing workers themselves — $(a + y)$ measures of wheat — and since each of these hired cultivating workers will produce a product of p units annually, then the annual revenue of the estate accruing to the group of $nq(a + y)/y$ capital producing workers will amount to $n[p - (a + y)]$. Thus the revenue of each member of the capital-producing group will be $n[p - (a + y)] \div nq (a + y)/y$, which reduces to the expression $[p - (a + y)]y/q(a + y)$. Substituting z for its equivalent $[p - (a + y)]/q(a + y)$, we obtain zy.[46]

Thünen now assumes that all workers will want to maximize not their total annual incomes, as might be expected, but this revenue zy which each can earn by investing one year's surplus. He also assumes that all workers, being free to move between the hired-worker status and the capital-producing status, will voluntarily establish a value for y and hence a value for the wage $(a + y)$ which will maximize the revenue zy, and that the wage so established will be the norm for the entire state. These assumptions he expresses in the following words:

Die Bestimmung des Arbeitslohns ist hier in die Hände der Arbeiter selbst gelegt, und der aus der Bestimmung der Arbeiter hervorgehende Lohn ist, wie vorhin nachgewiesen normirend für den ganzen isolirten Staat.

Die Willkühr der Arbeiter findet bei dieser Feststellung ihres Lohns keine andere Schranke als die des eigenen Interesses.

Bei der Kapitalerzeugung kann aber der Arbeiter kein anderes Ziel haben, als das, für seine Arbeit die höchst mögliche Rente zu erlangen.[47]

To find a value for y at which the revenue zy is at a maximum, he differentiates the expression for the revenue $[p - (a + y)]y/q(a + y)$ with respect to y and sets the derivative equal to zero. This equation he solves for the wage $(a + y)$ and obtains the equation

$$(a + y) = \sqrt{ap} .$$

Thus, he declares, a wage equal to $\sqrt{ap}$ is the natural or equilibrium wage, established neither by the requirements of the laborer nor by supply and demand, but by the free self-determination of the worker himself.[48] Expressed in words, Thünen's "equilibrium wage" is the geometric mean between the necessary subsistence of the working family and the average product of a working family, that is, the total product of an estate divided by the number of working families employed upon it.

Having thus found the "equilibrium" rate of wages, Thünen carries his calculations a step further to find the corresponding "equilibrium" interest rate. The revenue of that part of a new estate which is cultivated by one working family (or, in other words, the revenue contributed on the average by each of the permanent cultivators of the estate) equals annual product per family (p measures of wheat) minus annual wage per family ($a + y$ measures of wheat). The quantity of capital per family is q units, which can be expressed as $q(a + y)$ measures of wheat when wages are equal to $(a + y)$ measures. Since the rate of interest equals annual revenue divided by the capital from which it originates, the interest rate z equals

$$\frac{p - (a + y)}{q(a + y)}.$$

Solving this equation for the worker's yearly surplus (y), we obtain

$$y = \frac{p}{1 + qz} - a,$$

and the revenue (yz) which the worker received by investing his year's surplus is expressed by the equation

$$y z = \frac{pz}{1 + qz} - az.$$

To find the rate of interest (z) at which this revenue (yz) reaches a maximum, Thünen sets the first derivative of the above expression for yz equal to zero, solves for z, and obtains the equation

$$z = \frac{\sqrt{ap} - a}{aq}.$$

When this value for z is substituted in the equation for wages

$$a + y = \frac{p}{1 + qz},$$

the result may be reduced to the equation

$$a + y = \sqrt{ap},$$

which agrees with the maximizing value for wages obtained in the preceding paragraph. Thünen concludes that it is in the interest of both capital-producing workers who invest their surpluses in the construction of new estates or new capital and the hired workers who simply loan their surpluses at the prevailing rate of interest (z) to establish a wage rate equal to $\sqrt{ap}$ and an interest rate equal to $(\sqrt{ap} - a)/aq$.[49]

Having arrived at these expressions for the "equilibrium" rates of wages and interest, Thünen proceeds to check their accuracy by attacking the problem from other points of view. The most significant of these alternative calculations amounts to a refined version of the principle of marginal productivity. He reminds the reader that, as the quantity of invested capital increases, each successively added unit yields a smaller revenue than its predecessor and that competition among capital producers establishes the general level of the interest rate at the yield of the last added unit of capital. He points out, however, that in his tabulation of data illustrating this principle (Table 1) his increment of capital is very large, amounting to the quantity of capital produced by one year of labor, and that, in fact, the relative national capital does not increase by such large jumps but by a continuous growth which passes through all intervening points. To be accurate, therefore, we must assume the last increment of capital to be infinitesimally small.[50] Accordingly, he divides one of his units of capital into n parts, where n is some large number, and takes one of these parts as his marginal unit. Then if the yearly product of one laborer using q units of capital is equal to p measures of wheat, and if the same worker using a capital of $q + (1/n)$ units produces $p + \beta$ measures, we may conclude that $1/n$ units of capital yields a yearly revenue of β measures, and that one unit of capital yields $n\beta$ measures which may be expressed as α measures. The yearly revenue which must be paid for the q units of capital used by a laborer is therefore αq measures, and this quantity subtracted from his annual product of p measures equals his wage, which may be expressed as $p - \alpha q$ measures of wheat. With a wage of $p - \alpha q$, the capital of q units has the value $q(p - \alpha q)$ measures of wheat. It follows that the interest rate (revenue ÷ capital) may be expressed by the following equation

$$z = \frac{\alpha q}{q(p - \alpha q)} = \frac{\alpha}{p - \alpha q}.$$

Thünen now asks whether these expressions for wages and the interest rate are compatible with those found in the preceding analysis.[51]

In solving this problem, he points out that the wage $\sqrt{ap}$ maximizes the revenue of the capital-producing workers for any given values of p (yearly product of each laborer) and q (quantity of capital used by each laborer), and that this wage varies as p and q vary. Thus, by varying the quantity q, the capital-producing worker can vary the values of p, $\sqrt{ap}$, and α (the marginal product of a unit of capital); and it may be assumed that he will give q that value which will maximize his revenue, yz. That such a maximum exists may be deduced from the observed fact that the revenue does not increase with the value of q (the quantity of capital per worker) indefinitely.

Since the wage $(a + y)$ equals $p - \alpha q$, the surplus (y) equals $p - \alpha q - a$, and the interest rate (z) equals $\alpha/(p - \alpha q)$, the revenue (yz) may be expressed as

$$\frac{(p - \alpha q - a)\,\alpha}{p - \alpha q}.$$

Thünen now differentiates this expression with respect to α (which is a function of q) and finds that, when the resulting derivative is set equal to zero, the expression $p - \alpha q = \sqrt{ap}$. After testing these results with numerical examples, he offers the following conclusions: (1) When q is given that value which equates $p - \alpha q$ and $\sqrt{ap}$, the revenue (yz) reaches an unconditional maximum. (2) When q falls below that value, revenue declines, and the first formula gives a smaller value for wages than does the second. (3) When q rises above this value, revenue declines, and the first formula gives a higher value for wages than does the second. (4) The natural desire of capital-producing workers to maximize their revenue (yz) will lead them to increase the relative capital (q) to that point where $p - \alpha q = \sqrt{ap}$, or where $q = (p - \sqrt{ap})/\alpha$, and that therefore the level of wages thus established, together with the corresponding interest rate $\alpha/(p - \alpha q)$, is in equilibrium.[52]

According to that part of Thünen's analysis just described, interest is determined marginally, while wages are determined residually; that is, wages equal what is left of product (p) after interest (αq) has been deducted from it. To check his results, Thünen now reverses the process and seeks to determine wages marginally, stating that wages equal the increment of product produced by the last employed worker in a large enterprise.[53] He points out that the number of workers required to cultivate an estate, for example, is by no means a fixed number and that any estate may be cultivated more or less intensively within a very wide range. By the use of numerical examples he indicates clearly that, as the number of workers cultivating the estate increases, the increment of product resulting from the addition of one worker to the laboring force tends to diminish and that, if the owner of the estate is acting rationally, he will increase his labor force until the product value added by the last employed worker just equals his wage.[54] But, says Thünen, the wage which the last employed worker receives must be determining for all workers of equal skill and efficiency, because equal efforts cannot be rewarded with unequal wages. In the course of a rather lengthy discussion of the welfare of laborers, Thünen makes it clear that, in his opinion, the general level of wages in the state is determined by the increment in product value produced by the last added worker, for at a higher wage, employers, following their own interests, would discharge some of their workers, and the resulting competition of unemployed workers for jobs would reduce the general wage level until all were once more employed. Conversely, if wages were below this level, competition among employers would raise wages to the equilibrium level.[55]

To determine the share of the laborer in the product p (which is the joint product of a laborer and the capital he uses) on the basis of the marginal productivity of labor, Thünen assumes that the total quantity of capital in a large enterprise is held constant, while the number of laborers employed is allowed to change. At the outset, this enterprise employs n workers and nq units of capital. Each worker, using q units of capital, produces a product of p and receives a wage of A. Thus the revenue of the enterprise is equal to $n(p - A)$. If we now suppose one laborer to be discharged, each of the $n - 1$ remaining laborers would use a capital of $nq/(n - 1)$

units, and will produce a product equal to p', where $p' > p$, the difference between these two quantities being designated as v. Thus the total product of the enterprise will be $(n-1)p'$, or $(n-1)(p+v)$; the total wage bill for $n-1$ workers will be $(n-1)A$; and, hence, the revenue of the enterprise will equal $(n-1)(p+v) - (n-1)A$. If the owner of the enterprise, following his own interest, had previously employed just enough workers to equate the marginal product and the wage of the last employed worker, then the discharge of this worker would leave his revenue unchanged. We may therefore set the expression for the revenue of the enterprise before the change equal to that for the revenue after the change, as follows:

$$np - nA = (n-1)(p+v) - (n-1)A .$$

Solving this equation for the wage (A), we obtain[56]

$$A = p - (n-1)v .$$

Since n is assumed to be a very large number, the quantity 1 in this expression is so insignificant that it may be ignored, and the equation may be written simply as

$$A = p - nv .$$

Similarly, by approximation, the capital used by each worker $nq/(n-1)$ may be written $q + (1/n)q$. Thus, as a result of the discharge of one worker, each of the remaining workers uses an additional capital of $(1/n)q$ units and produces an additional product equal to v. But, in the example previously discussed, we found that, when the capital used by one worker increases by $1/n$ units, his product increases by an amount equal to β. Since in the present case the increase in capital used by each worker is q times $1/n$, the increase in his product is βq. Therefore $v = \beta q$, and, since $n\beta$ equals α (according to the previous example), nv is equal to αq. Substituting αq for nv in the above expression for wages $A = p - nv$, we obtain the expression $A = p - \alpha q$, which is the formula for wages developed in the preceding example. Having previously demonstrated that the wage $p - \alpha q$ must, under conditions of equilibrium, be equal to the wage $\sqrt{ap}$, Thünen concludes that he has further substantiated his original results by arriving at them through a different method.[57]

To obtain still another check upon his conclusions regarding the equilibrium level of wages and the interest rate, Thünen assumes that, since a given capital is the equivalent of a certain perpetual revenue, the two may be regarded as identical or interchangeable, and he then attempts to determine the condition (i.e., the rates of wages and interest) under which a given perpetual revenue can be produced at the smallest possible cost.[58] Believing that the origin and the effectiveness of capital is ultimately attributable to labor, he maintains that labor is the only correct unit in which to measure the cost of producing a capital or a permanent "revenue." But, in his own peculiar way, he measures the labor cost of producing such a revenue as the number of workers who must invest their wage surpluses

(y) for one year in order to produce the source of the given revenue. Thus the level of wages as well as the rate of interest have a direct influence, and the quantity of capital in the community has an indirect influence upon the result. With the growth of the social capital, labor becomes more productive, wages rise, and the production of capital becomes easier. But the same increase in social capital reduces the "utility" or the effectiveness of capital because further investment must resort to inferior tools, machines, land, etc.[59] There is, however, a certain rate of wages and interest at which the number of workers' surpluses required to produce the given revenue reaches a minimum. According to the above calculations, the rate of interest (z) when wages are expressed as $(a + y)$ is represented by the formula $[p - (a + y)]/q(a + y)$, and the revenue accruing from the investment of one worker's yearly surplus (yz) may be expressed as that formula multiplied by y. Thus the number of workers (or workers' surpluses) required to produce a given revenue, which may be designated as ar, will equal

$$ar \div \frac{[p - (a + y)]y}{q(a + y)} = \frac{arq(a + y)}{[p - (a + y)]y}.$$

To find the wage at which a capital capable of producing the revenue ar can be constructed in a year with a minimum number of workers, Thünen differentiates the above expression with respect to y (a being a constant equal to the subsistence of one worker for a year) and, setting the derivative equal to zero, finds that the expression reaches a minimum when y equals $\sqrt{ap} - a$ or when the wage $(a + y)$ equals $\sqrt{ap}$. For the corresponding rate of interest he substitutes $\sqrt{ap}$ for $(a + y)$ in the expression for the interest rate

$$z = \frac{p - (a + y)}{q(a + y)}$$

and obtains

$$z = \frac{\sqrt{ap} - a}{aq},$$

a conclusion which agrees with those obtained in previous examples.[60]

Finally, Thünen presents an analysis of the equilibrium relationship between the quantity of labor and the quantity of capital employed by an entrepreneur, which is important because it strongly suggests the modern concept of the marginal rate of substitution and because it brings out quite clearly the principle that aggregate revenue is maximized when the marginal expenditure on each agent employed equals its marginal value productivity. He observes that capital and labor are mutual substitutes and presents a number of examples in support of this observation. The drainage of a peat bog which had required the continuous labor of one man might be accomplished by a canal which could be dug by twenty men working for one year. Similarly, continuous labor may be replaced by the investment of capital by the clearing of stones from agricultural land or by the purchase of threshing machines and other farm implements. But not all these investments are equally effective in replacing labor. In some cases the continuous labor of one man may be replaced by the investment of the labor of only ten men for one year, while in other cases as many as twenty, thirty, or fifty man-years of labor would be necessary. It will be in the farmer's interest, says Thünen, to make all such investments in which the ratio of annual wages saved to cost of investment is greater than the rate of interest at which capital can be borrowed.[61] He then demonstrates by further detailed calculation that if z represents the interest rate and k represents the number of man-years of labor (units of capital) which must be invested to replace the continuous labor of one worker, then the ratio between the quantities of capital and labor employed is in equilibrium, and no increase in revenue can be obtained by the substitution of either for the other, when k equals $1/z$.[62]

Thünen presents the same concept even more clearly in another section of his second volume. Here he goes through one of his algebraic calculations to demonstrate that, when capital and labor are measured in the same units (i.e., when a unit of capital and a unit of labor are each expressed as the wages of one laborer for one year), the equilibrium ratio between the marginal product of a unit of labor and that of a unit of capital is as 1 is to z.[63] Since in the production of the common product of capital and labor the entrepreneur is free to substitute one factor for the other, he will, if he knows and is following his own interests, alter the proportion between the quantity of labor and the quantity of capital he employs until the ratio between the "effectiveness" (marginal productivity) of each equals the ratio between their respective unit costs; that is, until both ratios are as 1 is to z.[64] Thünen not only presents in an unmistakable form the principle that an entrepreneur maximizes his revenue by employing each agent to the point at which its marginal cost equals its marginal value productivity but also stresses the general applicability of this principle. It is the task of every rational farmer, he observes, to find that point in every branch of his operations at which increase in expenditures and increase in product are in equilibrium, for at this point his net revenue reaches a maximum.[65] There are numerous instances scattered through his own analysis in which he applies the principle that all forms of expenditure should be carried to the point where the product of the last added unit just equals its cost, for example, in the improvement and fertilization of land and the development of natural resources,[66] in the employment of workers,[67] in the purchase and use of machinery and other equipment,[68] and in the intensity of land cultivation.[69]

Throughout most of his discussion Thünen treats the isolated state as an existing entity of unchanging size, but in one very brief section he regards it as expanding and investigates the limits to its growth. He first points out that, as the state expands, poorer or less conveniently located land must be taken into cultivation and that, as a result, the joint product of labor and capital, and hence the level of wages and interest, must decline. But the formation of capital involves a cost to the capital-producing worker — the effort and industry necessary to construct it and the sacrifice of the luxuries which he might have obtained by the immediate consumption of his wage surplus. A free man can be induced to undergo this effort and sacrifice only if he can expect to receive adequate compensation in the revenue of his capital which he or his children can enjoy without further labor. Expansion of the state through new investment will therefore cease when the revenue of capital falls so low that, in the estimation of capital producers, the return obtainable from further investment is insufficient to compensate for the effort and sacrifice of capital formation.[70] Similarly, Thünen suggests (in a different section) a limit to the increase of population. When population increases in relation to the quantity of capital and the quantity of good agricultural land, the marginal productivity of labor, and hence the level of wages, tend to fall. The limit of this process is reached when the wage has fallen to a — the necessary subsistence of a laboring family. Thus, in the final analysis, he returns to the old subsistence theory of wages which he had attempted to supersede.[71]

CRITICISM AND CONCLUSION

Thünen is guilty of several rather obvious technical errors in his analysis of wage and interest-rate determination. The first of these is his use of the yearly wage of a laboring family (in measures of wheat) to express the unit of capital upon which his calculations are based. This blunder involves not only the erroneous assumption that capital is produced wholly by labor and that the whole cost of producing a unit of capital is the wages of the labor employed in its production but also a serious internal inconsistency in his reasoning. This inconsistency can be demonstrated most easily by refer- ence to Table 1. Thünen's unit of capital, which he describes as the quantity of capital produced by one working family laboring for one year, is ex- pressed by the figures in column 4 — the annual wage of a working family. This expression clearly increases as capital intensity (the quantity of capital used per worker) increases. Thünen explains this increase in the annual wage (and in the expression for a unit of capital) solely by the fact that each worker, *including each capital-producing worker,* is being assisted by an increasing number of units of capital. Thus, for example, when five units of capital are being used by each worker, the wage stands at $142.4c$ *only* because each worker is using five units of capital. But, in expressing his unit of capital in terms of its cost of production, he considers only the $142.4c$ paid as wages and forgets the $131.5c$ paid as interest on the capital used by the worker in producing the unit of capital in question. Thus Thünen could be correct even within the framework of his own system *only* if his unit of capital, as expressed in terms of its cost of production, included not only its wage cost but also its interest cost, an expression which may be found in column 2 of the table. He could hardly assume arbitrarily that the unit of capital is the product of a worker unaided by capital, while express- ing the unit of capital in terms of an annual wage which could prevail only if each and every worker employed a certain quantity of capital.

A second and equally serious error in Thünen's system is his assumption that the capital-producing worker finds it to his interest to maximize the yearly revenue to be obtained by investing the "surplus" of *one* year's wages; that is, to maximize the algebraic expression yz. Actually, if Thünen's capital-producing worker sought to maximize any current quantity, it would probably be the whole income derivable from his year's labor and from all the invested capital he owns — not yz, but something like the quantity $(a + y) + zC$, where C stands for all the capital he now possesses as a result of past accumulation. As for an equilibrium limit to further accumulation, there is no meaningful maximizing formula to define such a limit. It is difficult to imagine any set of conditions, however unrealistic, under which the quantity yz would be the object of maximization.[72]

In addition to these technical blunders, Thünen falls into the error of oversimplification and overabstraction, notwithstanding his great respect for and ample use of facts and figures. After criticizing the subsistence theory of wages as it was expounded by his English contemporaries, Thünen proceeds to adopt a subsistence concept as one of the fundamental bases of his calculations and to use it as though it were subject to precise quantitative measurement and formulation. The nebulous character of any such concept needs no elaboration here, and it need only be pointed out that if Thünen's expression a — the necessary subsistence of one working family for one year — has no precise meaning, then his expressions y, $\sqrt{ap}$, and all the other formulas and expressions based upon them also lose their meaning. Furthermore, the quantity p, which Thünen designates the "labor product," can have little analytical significance, for it is merely the annual product of an enterprise (abstracting from land rent and trade profit) divided by the number of workers employed in that enterprise, a quantity sometimes rightly referred to by Thünen as the joint product of labor and capital. The product of an enterprise is in nearly all cases the joint product of many agents, including, as a rule, many kinds of labor. The "product of labor," or of any other agent, can be distinguished and meaningfully expressed only as its marginal product and not as its "average product." Thünen's error in this connection is an illustration of his general, though not wholly consistent, acceptance of the classical belief that labor produces all product value and is only "assisted" by capital. Finally, Thünen's model in which all capital is produced and owned either individually or in groups or societies by laborers who work for wages at the common rate appears to be too extreme an abstraction from the conditions even of nineteenth-century Germany to serve as a basis for analyzing the "normal" rates of interest and wages supposed to prevail in the real world.

The errors and weaknesses just pointed out strike at the very foundation of Thünen's theoretical structure, at least with respect to wage and interest-rate determination, and are sufficient to invalidate his formal conclusions regarding the equilibrium rates of wages and interest. It is therefore not at all upon these formal conclusions that his real importance as a contributor to the theory of distribution rests. That contribution is to be found rather in the methods which he used in arriving at his conclusions.

The most outstanding feature of Thünen's analysis of wage and interest rate determination is his application to it of the principle of marginal productivity. He presents a far more precise and more refined statement of this theory than does any previous theorist known to the present writer. His insistence upon the infinitesimal increment, his use of the symbols of differential calculus to express marginal productivity, his clear statement of the principle of variable proportions and the mutual substitutability of labor and capital, and his rudimentary development of the concept of the marginal productivity concept to wages as well as to the revenue of capital in sufficient to insure him a place of first importance in any history of economic theory.

Thünen also deserves recognition for his broad application of the marginal productivity concept to wages as well as to the revenue of capital in all its forms. He is a pioneer in the use of marginal analysis to determine the proportions in which productive agents must be combined in a process to achieve maximum efficiency and maximum return; that is, to organize or to allocate scarce resources with a view to maximum value product.

Another significant aspect of Thünen's discussion is his refined subdivision of the entrepreneur's gross revenue into true interest as the contribution of capital, a wage for the personal services of the entrepreneur himself, an insurance premium as compensation for risk, and pure "trade profit" as a final residual arising from the noninsurable uncertainty of the future. It represents an improvement over the English classical concept of "profit" as the entire revenue of the capitalist-entrepreneur which remains after the payment of rent and wages.

Also worthy of note is Thünen's extensive use of mathematical symbols in developing his theories at a time when such precise formulation was all too little used in economic literature. Many of his complex notions would be practically unintelligible were they not stated precisely and unmistakably in mathematical terms. Yet Thünen's work demonstrates not only that mathematics can be a very effective aid, in many cases an indispensable aid to analysis and exposition, but also that it can magnify the consequences of small errors if it is misused. In Thünen's case, mathematical deduction from inappropriate premises led him into such absurdities as his equilibrium wage, $\sqrt{ap}$. In spite of his numerous mistakes, however, Thünen's high development of marginal analysis in conjunction with the mathematical formulation and exposition, which makes its application and use far easier and more effective, represents a contribution to economic theory of the first magnitude.

NOTES

1. In 1834, sixteen years before the publication of the second volume of Thünen's *Der isolirte Staat*, which contains the bulk of his theory of marginal productivity, the Irish economist Mountifort Longfield (1802–84) had applied a rough concept of marginal productivity to the theory of interest-rate determination, pointing out that the general rate of interest depends upon the effectiveness in assisting labor of "that portion of capital which is employed with the least efficiency" or the "last portion of capital brought into operation"; yet his version of the theory

was neither refined nor generally applied (*Lectures on Political Economy* [Dublin: William Curry, Jr., & Co., 1834], pp. 186–99). The present writer has found no conclusive evidence to indicate whether Thünen read and was influenced by the writings of Longfield or whether he developed his marginal concept independently.

2. Cf. J. B. Clark, *The Distribution of Wealth* (New York: Macmillan Co., 1914), pp. 321–24; Alfred Marshall, *Memorials,* ed. A. C. Pigou (London: Macmillan & Co., 1925), pp. 21–22, 99–100, 359–60, 412–13.

3. Cf. Eugen von Böhm-Bawerk, *Capital and Interest,* trans. William Smart (New York: Brentano's, 1922), pp. 164–73; L. H. Haney, *History of Economic Thought* (New York: Macmillan Co., 1913), pp. 279–90; Edmund Whittaker, *A History of Economic Ideas* (New York: Longmans, Green & Co., 1943), pp. 546–47, 592; Edwin Cannan, *A Review of Economic Theory* (London: P. S. King & Son, 1929), pp. 260–61.

4. In 1895 H. L. Moore published an article in the *Quarterly Journal of Economics* on Thünen's theory of wages which includes some detailed analysis of his premises and arguments and an evaluation of the opinions of some earlier critics of Thünen's work, most of whom were German. Moore's discussion is by no means a complete treatment of Thünen and fails either to bring out his real errors or to give due emphasis to his development of marginal analysis (Cf. H. L. Moore, "Von Thünen's Theory of Natural Wages," *Quarterly Journal of Economics,* IX [1895], 291–304, 388–408).

5. Marshall, *op. cit.,* pp. 359–60.

6. *Der isolirte Staat,* I, 1–8, 229–41; II, Part I, 7–9; II, Part II, 1–2.

7. *Ibid.,* I, 268–69; II, Part I, 7, 10.

8. *Ibid.,* I, 14–19.

9. Thünen uses wheat as a representative agricultural product in discussing his theory of rent, but it is very clear that he does not regard it as the only commodity to which the theory applies.

10. *Der isolirte Staat,* I, 223–27.

11. *Ibid.,* pp. 227–29; II, Part I, 7–9.

12. *Ibid.,* I, 40–45, 225, 228; II, Part I, 7.

13. *Ibid.,* I, 228–29; II, Part II, 67–71.

14. *Ibid.,* II, Part II, 115–18.

15. *Ibid.,* pp. 71–72.

16. *Ibid.,* Part I, p. 85.

17. In most of the cases in which he defines capital he treats it as the product of labor alone, although in one case he adds natural forces (*ibid.,* p. 82) and in another he observes that, since capital can substitute for human labor, it also serves in the production of more capital (*ibid.,* p. 201). In connection with the latter observation, however, he comments that, since the original capital was produced solely by labor and since the

effectiveness of capital can be traced to labor, human labor is the true creator of capital.

18. *Ibid.,* pp. 26, 82, 88, 107, 200–201; Part II, pp. 2–3.

19. *Ibid.,* Part I, p. 76, 193–94, 207–8; Part II, pp. 132–33.

20. *Ibid.,* Part I, p. 82.

21. *Ibid.,* pp. 83–86.

22. *Ibid.,* pp. 86–88.

23. *Ibid.,* pp. 88–89.

24. *Ibid.,* pp. 55–57, 70–77.

25. *Ibid.,* pp. 38–43, 51–54.

26. *Ibid.,* pp. 90–93.

27. The above calculation of the interest rate is expressed by Thünen as follows: "In dem vorliegenden Fall ist der Lohn für 1 Y.A. = 110c; die Rente, die das aus der Arbeit eines Jahrs hervorgegangene Kapital bringt, betragt 40c.

"Das Verhaltniss ist also wie 110c: 40c = 100 : 36.4, und der Zinsfuss ist 36.4 pCt" (*ibid.,* p. 95).

28. *Ibid.,* pp. 93–96.

29. *Ibid.,* pp. 96–101.

30. *Ibid.,* p. 103.

31. *Ibid.,* p. 104.

32. *Ibid.,* pp. 105–6. Thünen admits that invested capital is usually measured in terms of money rather than in terms of the wages or the value of the labor required for its production, but he asserts that, in the determination of the interest rate, the result would be the same either way. In support of this assertion he supposes that c equals $1.00, that wages of labor equal $110, that capital revenue equals $40, and that revenue divided by capital equals the interest rate. Then, he says, the interest rate would equal $40/$110, or 36.4 per cent, which is the same result as that obtained above. It is quite obvious that this example proves nothing, for he is still measuring his invested capital in terms of the wages of the labor which is required to produce it, the only change being that these wages are now expressed in dollars rather than units of the subsistence commodity. The errors into which this approach leads the author will become more apparent as the exposition progresses and will be pointed out and discussed in detail later in the present paper.

33. *Ibid.,* p. 111.

34. Thünen assumes that the capital-producing worker uses as much capital in the production of further capital as all other workers use in the production of consumables and that the capital-producing worker who owns the capital with which he works must deduct the interest on that capital from his total labor product in calculating his wages. The wages of all workers, capital-producing and non-capital-producing, are therefore the same, and Thünen's unit of capital—that amount which can be produced by one working family in one year of labor—is expressed

as the wages of a year of labor. For example, if the general level of wages at a given time is 114c, then one unit of capital is expressed as 114c, i.e., the wages which must be paid to a capital-producing worker during the year in which he is producing the unit of capital in question.

35. *Der isolirte Staat*, II, Part I, 107–10.

36. In a later part of his discussion Thünen brings out the necessity of calculating marginal product on the basis of infinitesimally small increments and admits that the conclusions derived from Table 1 are inaccurate because of the large marginal units there used.

37. *Der isolirte Staat*, II, Part, 1, 113.

38. *Ibid.*, p. 114.

39. *Ibid.*, p. 122.

40. *Ibid.*, pp. 114–23. Thünen believes that European conditions correspond to the assumptions underlying his second table of data, in which the product of one laboring family unassisted by capital is far below the necessary subsistence of such a family. Since the first capital must have been produced by human beings working without the aid of capital, and since human beings unaided by capital could not live under the natural conditions of Europe, he concludes that man and his first capital must have originated in tropical climates where coconut and banana trees grow wild, where neither clothing nor shelter is required, and where man, unaided by capital, could not only produce enough to live on but could produce a surplus from which capital could be accumulated. Man must then have migrated to less favored areas of the earth, taking with him sufficient capital to enable him to produce a living in those areas.

41. *Ibid.*, pp. 140–48. Thünen maintains that the above assumptions, particularly the last two, are not unrealistic, although he admits that, owing to limitations upon the mobility of workers and capital between countries and states and to differences in customs, habits, the security of capital, etc., wage and interest rates may in reality be higher in some states than in others.

42. To avoid complicating variables, Thünen assumes that a new estate would be equal in size to previously existing estates and that such a new estate would, therefore, be developed not by one working family plus its capital but by a group of such families who pool their labor and capital in a joint project. For simplicity, however, he divides the invested capital, the gross product, and the revenue of the new estate by the number of families participating in its development and ownership and thus obtains what amounts to a one-family farm as the basis of his analysis.

43. *Der isolirte Staat*, II, Part I, 141.

44. Thünen assumes that if the enterprise has expenses other than wages and interest, these expenses are deducted from the gross yearly revenue of the enterprise before the value of p is calculated. Thus p is defined as the gross annual revenue of the enterprise minus all expenses not classed as interest or wages, this quantity divided by the number of working families employed. It is the joint product of *one* of the homogeneous working families employed by the enterprise and the quantity of capital (q) which that family uses (*ibid.*, pp. 123–25).

45. *Ibid.*, pp. 141–42, 149–50.

46. *Ibid.*, pp. 150–54; cf. *ibid.*, p. 141.

47. *Ibid.*, p. 152.

48. *Ibid.*, p. 157.

49. *Ibid.*, pp. 159–61.

50. *Ibid.*, p. 166.

51. *Ibid.*, pp. 166–67.

52. *Ibid.*, pp. 168–78. Thünen's understanding of the principle of marginal productivity as it is applied to the revenue of capital is illustrated in a passage appearing in Vol. II, Part II, in which he expresses the marginal product of capital as the ratio between dp (an infinitesimal increment of product) and dk (an infinitesimal increment of capital giving rise to it). This approaches the most refined modern definition of marginal product as the partial derivative of the production function with respect to the variable agent under consideration: $\delta p / \delta a$ (*ibid.*, Part II, p. 51).

53. *Ibid.*, Part I, p. 178.

54. *Ibid.*, pp. 178–85. It is interesting to note in this connection that Thünen recognizes the fact that the smaller enterprise is at a disadvantage as compared to the larger enterprise because, owing to the indivisibility of such factor units as laborers, draft horses, tools, machines, etc., the smaller firm cannot adjust the marginal value product of each type of agent to its marginal cost as exactly as can the large enterprise. This condition is commonly known as "lumpiness" in modern economic literature.

55. *Ibid.*, pp. 185–93.

56. It may be noted that within Thünen's general approach the same result can be obtained in a somewhat more direct manner by setting up an equation in which the wage (A) equals the difference between total product of the enterprise before the discharge of the marginal worker and the total product of the enterprise after this event, thus

$$A = np - (n - 1)(p + v) = \\ p - (n - 1)v.$$

57. *Der isolirte Staat*, II, Part I, 193–96.

58. *Ibid.*, p. 200.

59. *Ibid.*, pp. 198–201.

60. *Ibid.*, pp. 201–3.

61. *Ibid.*, p. 161.

62. *Ibid.*, pp. 163–64.

63. To understand the logic of this statement, it must be remembered that Thünen's unit of labor is one man-year and that his unit of capital is the product of one man-year of labor, expressed in terms of the wages of one man-year of labor, i.e., $(a + y)$ measures of wheat. Thus the cost of a unit of labor is $(a + y)$ measures as wages, and the cost of a unit of capital is $z (a + y)$ measures as interest. The ratio between the cost of employing a unit of labor and the cost of employing a unit of capital is therefore as 1 is to z, and in equilibrium the ratio of their marginal productivities would also be as 1 is to z.

64. *Der isolirte Staat*, II, Part I, 123–28.

65. *Ibid.*, p. 183.

66. *Ibid.*, I, 13–15; II, Part I, 162.

67. *Ibid.*, I, 18–20; II, Part I, 181, 185–90.

68. *Ibid.*, pp. 181–82, 197–98.

69. *Ibid.*, pp. 178–80, 182–85.

70. *Ibid.*, pp. 130–34.

71. *Ibid.*, pp. 187–93. Thünen shows a lively interest in the welfare of the laboring classes and discusses the problem at some length in several sections of his work. He suggests that much of the misery of the working classes in the real world is due to their low marginal productivity resulting from their tendency toward over-rapid increase in numbers and to their lack of education and points out that, if the Socialists were enlightened by political economy, they would exert their efforts toward increasing labor's productivity. He also observes that under European conditions, where there is no free land to be had, the worker is not free, as he is in the isolated state, to take up and cultivate new land of his own when wages fall very low.

Under these conditions the worker has no protection against the exploitation of the employer, who increases his own profits by lowering wages to a minimum. The natural wage $\sqrt{ap}$ may therefore not be realized in European countries, where wages depend upon the competition of workers and reach their limit only at the standard of bare subsistence. Thünen's own remedy for the situation is a substantial improvement in the education of the working classes, aided by the state, not only to increase the productivity of those classes, but also make them eligible to become entrepreneurs and public officials and thus to break the monopoly of the educated few upon these opportunities (*ibid.*, pp. 43–51, 185–93, 206–212; Part II, pp. 140–45).

72. Moore attributes to J. V. Komorzynski a similar criticism of Thünen's assumption that the workers will seek to maximize the quantity zy. Komorzynski maintains that "the interests of laborers as to the relation of wages and interest vary according as they have saved during many or during few years," i.e., if they have saved much capital, they will wish high interest and low wages and vice versa. He concludes that "there is no definite relation of wages and interest that, under all circumstances, is the best relation for the laborers." Moore comments that "Komorzynski's argument does not prove an error in Thünen's work: it merely shows its incompleteness," and that "we cannot deny that the laborers who are just beginning to save will be interested in having the relation of wages and interest such that they will obtain a maximum income from their surplus when that surplus is placed at interest," i.e., that they will wish to maximize the quantity zy (Moore, *op. cit.*, pp. 399–402).

23.

A. J. NICHOL

A Re-Appraisal of

Cournot's Theory of

Duopoly Price[1]

Almost a hundred years ago, Antoine Augustin Cournot gave to an un-appreciative world his little volume entitled *Researches into the Mathematical Principles of the Theory of Wealth.*[2] Many of his ideas by this time have been absorbed in the everyday thought of economics;[3] but in spite of special attention in recent years,[4] it seems to the present writer that the strength and the weakness of one important feature of his work is not yet fully understood. The feature referred to is Cournot's treatment[5] of duopoly price, i.e., price when a few, particularly when *two*, are selling to many.

The long-prevailing disagreement[6] on this subject is regarded in this article as originating in an unrecognized disagreement regarding a certain "institution" of the market. (1) In some markets, e.g., a large security or commodity exchange, *prices are both bid and asked;* the prices of actual transactions are determined by bargaining between buyers and sellers. (2) In other markets, e.g., any retail market, *prices are almost always named by sellers;* buyers scarcely ever have the opportunity to suggest alternative prices. In a market of this kind, buyers decide how much is to be purchased at any price quoted by sellers — within the limit prescribed by the total quantity sellers are willing and able to sell at this price; in this manner buyers have an indirect influence on the price, but buyers do not have a

Reprinted from *The Journal of Political Economy*, XLII (February 1934), 80-105, by permission of The University of Chicago Press. At the time of original publication, the author, now deceased, was with Duke University.

direct voice in price determination. (3) In a third class of markets, *buyers name prices.* Sellers are left to determine — within the limit of maximum willingness and ability to purchase — the quantity to be sold at any particular price named by buyers. A North Carolina tobacco farmer, for example, bringing his product to market, is offered a price by a buyer representing one of the large tobacco companies. In most cases, it is useless for the farmer himself to suggest any other price. If he fails to receive any better offer from any other buyer, and is still dissatisfied with the price, his only alternative is to take his tobacco back to the farm.

In a freely competitive market, any equilibrium price — whether it is a temporary equilibrium between "short-run" supply and demand, or a "normal" equilibrium between "long-run" supply and demand — is unaffected by the particular way in which prices are named. When buyers and sellers are both extremely numerous, and each individual buyer or seller transacts only a very small part of the total business, an equilibrium price is determined by the intersection of a demand curve and a supply curve.[7] If the market price rises above this intersection, the total quantity offered is greater than the total quantity demanded. Then reductions in the price offers of sellers, or lower bidding on the part of buyers, or both, tend to bring the market price back to the intersection. If the market price falls below the intersection, the quantity demanded is greater than the quantity offered. Then, higher bidding on the part of buyers, or advances in the price offers of sellers, or both tend to bring the price back to the intersection. No matter whether prices are bid or asked, or both bid and asked, the market price tends toward the same equilibrium level in any particular case under consideration.

In a purely monopolistic market, the particular way in which prices are named is likewise of comparatively little significance from the viewpoint of general analysis. A monopoly may either directly name a price, or indirectly control the bidding of buyers by limitation of the quantity offered to them, or both. The price of any particular maximum of profits for which the monopoly may be striving in any particular situation is theoretically the same, regardless of the manner in which prices are announced.

In general analysis of the competitive dealings of *two* sellers with *many* buyers, it also seems at first sight a matter of slight consequence, *whether sellers or buyers name prices.*[8] This simple question, however, is *a key to interpretation* of Cournot's theory of duopoly. If it is assumed that *only buyers* name prices, his theory is easy to understand. Let it be assumed that in a given market, the highest price (p), bid among a large group of buyers for any particular quantity (D) of a given commodity (say mineral water), conforms with the following equation:

$$p = -\frac{1}{5000} D + 90.$$

In more familiar terms, the demand for the commodity may be represented as in Table I.

TABLE I

DEMAND SCHEDULE

Quantity Offered*	Highest Price Bid (Cents)
150,000	60
175,000	55
200,000	50
225,000	45
250,000	40
275,000	35
300,000	30
325,000	25
350,000	20
375,000	15
400,000	10

* Units of commodity *per interval of time*. All quantities in the following discussion are to be interpreted in the same sense.

Suppose it is the custom of the market that only buyers shall bid; to sellers is left the option of determining how much shall be offered. Then, in order to present a simple illustration of Cournot's theory, let it be assumed that there are only two producers, M and N, each capable of unlimited production under conditions of constant unit costs;[9] M's costs, 20 cents per unit; N's, only 10 cents. If M and N combine, and form an absolute monopoly, N's plant only will be operated. In order to make the greatest possible profit, M and N may be expected under these circumstances to offer 200,000 units, and to accept only the highest price bid for this quantity, namely 50 cents. On the other hand, if N's cheaper facilities are divided among a large number of smaller producers, 400,000 units will be offered, and the price bid by buyers is 10 cents, equal to the cost of production per unit. Suppose, however, that M and N retain their separate organizations, and independently try to make as much money as possible in competition with each other. Under these conditions, the price, according to Cournot, gravitates to an *intermediate* level between 50 cents, the pure monopoly price, and 10 cents, the price of unlimited competition.

In the market under consideration, neither seller has a direct opportunity to name a price; or else, both refrain from so doing. Each seller, however, has the power to influence the bidding of buyers by adjustment of the quantity he offers to them. Each seller independently may be expected to try to exert this influence to his own greatest advantage; but being unable to foresee the quantity which his rival may offer at any time in the future, each seller, according to Cournot, bases his *calculations* at any given time on the quantity which his competitor is offering *at that time*. A series of adjustments may be necessary to reach an equilibrium. In the course of this process, neither duopolist necessarily remains inactive, while his rival sways the markets; nor need the *immediate* results anticipated by either duopolist be actually realized at all times. If *M* and *N* *concurrently* adjust their offerings in the manner which has been described, the same ultimate result prevails as if *alternately* they make adjustments.[10]

At an initial stage, *M* and *N* respectively may be supposed to offer any two quantities — say *M*, 220,000; *N*, 110,000 units. The highest price bid for the total quantity of 330,000 units, as shown by substitution in the equation of demand, or by interpolation in the demand schedule, is 24 cents. Neither *M* nor *N* has reason to view this initial price with complete satisfaction. *M*, assuming his rival's offerings constant, may change his own to 120,000 units, expecting to raise the price to 44 cents, and realize a maximum profit. *At the same time*, however, *N*, assuming *M*'s offerings constant, may change his to 90,000 units, expecting a maximum profit at price 28 cents. If so, the price actually bid by buyers for the total amount of 210,000 units, is 48 cents, a price not expected by either of the sellers. If other similar adjustments are made, however, the price approaches more nearly to their respective expectations. The history of a series of steps toward an equilibrium may be tabulated as in Table II.

As a matter of mathematical calculation, it may seem that an unlimited number of delicate final adjustments are necessary before the final result shown in step (n) is reached. The two sellers, however, seeing this result before it is reached, may be expected to agree tacitly to it, without passing through the last petty stages of adjustment. From any initial position, there are many possible ways of attaining the same equilibrium at price 40 cents. When it is reached, each seller makes a maximum profit *in view of the quantity which his rival is selling.*[11]

The same solution is obtained quickly by applying Cournot's formulas[12] to this particular problem, viz.,

(1) $$f(D) + D_1 f'(D) - \phi'_1(D_1) = 0.$$
(2) $$f(D) + D_2 f'(D) - \phi'_2(D_2) = 0.$$
(3) $$D = D_1 + D_2.$$

The equivalent of $f(D)$ in this particular problem has already been given,

viz. $-\dfrac{1}{5000} D + 90$. In view of the assumptions of constant unit costs,

$\phi_1(D_1) = 20D_1; \phi_2(D_2) = 10D_2.$

Therefore,

(4) $$\phi'_1(D_1) = 20; \qquad \phi'_2(D_2) = 10.$$

Solving:

(5) $$D_1 = 100,000; \qquad D_2 = 150,000.$$

(6) $$p = 40.$$

Any reader not already familiar with Cournot's theory is requested to note the distinctive features of this solution. Price 40 cents is a stable price, but yet it is not the price toward which a large number of competitors tend

TABLE II

	Quantity Offered by M	Quantity Offered by N	Total Quantity Offered	Price Expected by M (Cents)	Price Expected by N (Cents)	Price Bid by Buyers (Cents)
(1)	220,000	110,000	330,000	—	—	24
(2)	120,000	90,000	210,000	44	28	48
(3)	130,000	140,000	270,000	46	38	36
(4)	105,000	135,000	240,000	41	37	42
(5)	107,500	147,500	255,000	41 ½	39 ½	39
(6)	101,250	146,250	247,500	40 ¼	39 ¼	40 ½
(n)	100,000	150,000	250,000	40	40	40

under the same general conditions; indeed, Cournot's duopoly price in this case is much higher. On the other hand, the price of 40 cents is lower than a pure monopoly price.

Professor Chamberlin advances a *new* theory of duopoly in which it is assumed that sellers always anticipate each other's actions.[13] His generalizations are based on a case where there are no costs of production. His conclusions may also apply to cases in which both sellers' cost schedules are exactly the same. In most cases, however, the present one being a very simple example, all producers do not operate under the same cost conditions. For this reason the new theory of duopoly price may not be entirely accurate. Cournot's theory is applicable, no matter how great the diversity in costs of production. It still stands, therefore, as *the best general analysis of limited competition when only buyers name prices.*

The question now arises: Did Cournot intend to limit his theory of duopoly to situations in which *only buyers* name prices? There is no evidence to support an affirmative answer. In Cournot's treatment of pure monopoly, the monopolist *seller* named prices, and buyers determined quantities.[14] Not a word in Cournot's chapter on limited competition suggests any conscious change in the general institutions of the market, nor is competitive bidding among buyers even mentioned. Many economic theorists, however, tend to speak of market price *as if it were so obedient to abstract principles, that it needed no human voice or hand to proclaim it.* Falling into this manner of speaking, Cournot, as the present writer interprets him, did make an unconscious change in his assumptions. There is an indication of the change in the form of his equation of demand. In treatment of monopoly,[15] he assumed $D = F(p)$; in treatment of duopoly,[16] the reverse notation, $p = f(D)$. These two equations may represent equivalent relations; but when one substitutes values of p in the right-hand side of $D = F(p)$, in order to determine corresponding values of D, it is an indication that the calculator is thinking of amounts which buyers will take at *given* prices, i.e., prices established by others than themselves, e.g., sellers. Cournot's verbal analysis of monopoly corroborates this indication. On the other hand, if one substitutes values of D in the right-hand side of $p = f(D)$, in order to determine values of p, it is an indication that one is thinking of prices which buyers will pay for *given quantities,* i.e., quantities determined by others than themselves. No conclusion ought to be based on such slender evidence alone; on this particular point, not all may agree, but it is significant in its relation to the major points of Cournot's discussion. It is clear that Cournot had in mind a situation in which *sellers determined quantities* — independently — but did not compete with each other by quoting *different prices.*

"In this case," said Cournot, "the price is necessarily the same for each producer."[17]

Proprietor (1) can have no direct influence on the determination of D_2: all that he can do, when D_2 has been determined by proprietor (2) is to choose for D_1 the value which is best for him. This he will be able to accomplish, *suitably modifying the price,* except as proprietor (2), who, seeing himself forced to accept this price and this value of D_1, may adopt a new value of D_2, more favorable to his interests than the preceding one.[18]

What price is it that the two seek to modify to their own respective interests? *It is not a price directly named by either seller:* for, if sellers name prices, the mere fact that one of them changes his price does not *compel* the other to make a like change; if sellers name prices, either one may maintain his price at any level, if he so chooses, in spite of a change in his rival's price, or a change in the volume of his rival's offerings. As Edgeworth showed in his problem, when sellers name prices, and sellers are few, a perfectly uniform price is not a logical necessity.[19] The perfect uniformity of price in Cournot's problem is not explained, *unless prices are directly determined by buyers.* An agreement between sellers may possibly be conceived to bring about the same result; but any agreement or understanding between sellers is carefully abstracted.[20] Cournot's discussion is intelligible only on the assumption that both sellers, in accordance with the custom of the market, accept *the highest price bid* for their combined offerings. Then, and only then, can one duopolist, influencing buyers by a change in the quantity he offers to them, "force" the price he desires upon his rival, unless the latter also changes the quantity which he offers. Cournot, however, was apparently unconscious of the underlying condition, and the limitations which it placed upon his theory.

Amoroso, Cournot's chief defender, also assumed price changes to be brought about by changes in quantity; and upon this basis Amoroso verified Cournot's theory, adding many new and interesting details.[21] Amoroso also, however, was unconscious of the implied assumption that *only buyers name prices.*[22] It is believed that other illustrations and expositions of Cournot's theory become clearer if an explicit statement of this essential condition is added.

Pareto's criticism of Cournot's mathematics is familiar to those acquainted with the literature of the subject; likewise, Pareto's remark that the problem is "over-determinate."[23] Pareto's own view of the *conditional validity* of Cournot's theory, however, has not been discussed by any other writer Pareto did not realize the underlying assumption that only buyers name prices. He therefore introduced another assumption which, as he saw it, was a departure from the spirit of pure competition, but was nevertheless necessary to the correctness of Cournot's problem.

In reality the problem which A. A. Cournot treats is not that of competition, but another problem which may be formulated as follows: Suppose we have two individuals who between them have a monopoly on the sale of a given commodity. Let us assume that one of them is able to determine arbitrarily the quantity which he will sell, viz., D_1. Suppose then the other one *lets him sell it,* and only under this condition does the second man calculate the quantity D_2 which he himself sells to make a maximum profit. . . . . Furthermore, let us suppose that when the second man has determined the quantity he will sell, the first one, *respecting the same condition,* recalculates the quantity D_1 which he will sell in order to realize a maximum profit.[24]

If Cournot's analysis is to be re-vamped, in order to make it applicable to markets in which *sellers* name prices, this suggestion of Pareto's may appear at first sight to be of some significance; but in a market where *only buyers* name prices, the added assumption is purely superfluous, and to a certain extent misleading.

If each competitor is to *let* his rival sell any particular quantity, it is pertinent to inquire how he may *prevent* him. For present purposes, it is necessary to extend this inquiry only to a market in which buyers name prices:

(1) Competitive "sales talk" is out of the question, for, according to Cournot, the products offered by the two competitors are known to be identical.

(2) No seller, by accepting lower *bids,* can prevent his rival from selling what he wills. If either seller departs from the implied custom of Cournot's market by accepting *less* than the highest price bid, the other seller can, if necessary, accept lower bids also, and still dispose of his intended offerings. Thus, although one injures the other, he does not prevent the sale of any given quantity; and he himself loses possible profits, or increases his losses. In the numerical example which has been discussed, it has been shown that the highest price bid for 120,000 units offered by M, and 90,000 units offered by N, is 48 cents. If M accepts less than 48 cents, say 45 cents, for his 120,000 units, N can also accept 45 cents for his offerings. The sale of N's 90,000 units is by no means prevented; nor is M in any way the gainer. It is to the interest of both sellers to accept only the highest price bid for their combined offerings.

The total quantity demanded at 45 cents is 225,000 units. Some one may perhaps suggest that *before* N agrees to accept 45 cents, M may sell all, or at least enough of the total quantity demanded at this price, to prevent N from selling his 90,000 units. If this is done, however, M's price ceases to be a price bid by buyers for a known and limited quantity. M's price becomes a price *named by himself* for a quantity larger than he originally offered. Thus the assumption that only buyers name prices is violated.

(3) Even if one seller "dumps" a large quantity of goods on the market,

forces the bidding down to a low level, and thus inflicts a loss on his rival, the latter may still — if he chooses — continue to sell the same quantity. If in the "long run," the financial resources necessary for production are exhausted, he must of course desist; but in Cournot's market, only immediate effects are considered in any particular phase of adjustment.

Therefore, it is false to say that either seller in Cournot's market "allows" the other to sell any particular quantity, *for he does not have the power to prevent it. Each seller is forced by the strength of the other to acquiesce in a division of sales.* Any attempt to monopolize the market by accepting a loss, or profits less than those immediately possible, is abstracted by the assumption that each seller seeks a maximum profit on his immediate transactions. Neither altruism nor "good fellowship" enter into the problem No special assumption is needed except that *only buyers name prices.*

If Cournot had had the advantage of competent criticism during his own lifetime, no doubt he would have set forth unmistakably all the assumptions of his own analysis. *Thus much useless controversy might have been avoided.* As it was, Bertrand, criticizing him after his death, thought of a situation in which sellers named prices, and tossed Cournot's conclusions carelessly aside. Edgeworth considered his discussion limited by "uniformity of price."[25] A uniform price was a logical necessity in the market which Cournot had in mind. Pareto, who understood Cournot in some ways best of all, still failed to grasp the masterly simplicity of his analysis, and added an unnecessary assumption.

On the other hand, some readers of Cournot, seeing an apparent confirmation of certain features of his analysis in actual business, are inclined to credit him with more than he really accomplished. Considerable ingenuity has been displayed in the effort to fit his theory, consciously or unconsciously, to markets in which *sellers* name prices. Indeed, a sort of replica of his theory can be created for this purpose by imagining a large number of artificial conditions. The trouble with most efforts in this direction is that a picture of the complete situation is not borne in mind; a detail here or there seems to be adjusted satisfactorily, but not the whole scheme. One purpose of this article is to show *how ridiculous the ensemble becomes, when Cournot's theory is applied to any market in which sellers name prices.*

Professor Zeuthen writes, "The characteristic feature of Cournot's solution is really that if it is to be correct, it must be based on the assumption that a price reduction on the part of one monopolist will attract the unsatisfied wants more easily and quickly than it would attract the customers of his competitor."[26]

Professor Zeuthen is hardly to be recommended as a faithful interpreter of Cournot. As one other writer has already pointed out, Zeuthen misses entirely one of the most fundamental features of Cournot's analysis. "Cournot does not consider price changes on the part of the monopolists as motivating influences. Initial causes in his problem are always variations in quantity, which automatically bring about changes in price."[27]

584

Another important point is also missed. Cournot was perfectly explicit in stating that both producers always sold *at the same price*. There is no tendency as in Edgeworth's market for buyers to drift *en masse* from one seller to another because of a difference in price.[28] Professor Zeuthen assumes differences in price,[29] and then endeavors to explain what in the original version of Cournot is already explained by perfect uniformity of price. Furthermore, changes in price in Cournot's market, as shown by any illustration or exposition, are not extremely small changes, except in certain theoretically possible, but practically negligible final adjustments. Professor Zeuthen considers only very small changes in price.[30] For this reason, if for no other, his treatment is inadequate. If changes in price are *very slight,* and one duopolist lags behind his competitor *for an appreciable length of time* in reducing his price, it may be that the price leader, as Professor Zeuthen suggests, gets all the new business, while the other duopolist retains only the business he has been doing. If changes in price are more pronounced, however, it becomes more and more improbable that the seller who is slow to reduce his price, will retain all his previous sales. Adhering more closely to Cournot's general outline, it may be assumed that the duopolists reduce prices *simultaneously* to the same level, or that one *immediately* follows a reduction by the other. Under these circumstances, it seems ridiculous to suppose that either one has any appreciable advantage over his rival in attracting "unsatisfied wants."

There is still another fault with this attempted revision of Cournot. The process of oscillation toward an equilibrium price involves not only reductions in price, but also *advances*. Professor Zeuthen does not consider at all half of his own problem. He introduces a very original assumption regarding the behavior of buyers when the price is lowered, but says nothing of their behavior when the price is raised.

The only way to test the applicability of Cournot's solution to a market in which sellers name prices is *to consider systematically all the necessary conditions*. These conditions become a preposterous maze; but since some admirers of Cournot insist upon seeing in his analysis more than is really there, it is well to examine every possibility with patience.

For purposes of illustration, the same numerical example which has been discussed may be reviewed with a few alterations. Let it be assumed that M's costs, as before, are 20 cents per unit; and N's, 10 cents per unit. The equation of demand, however, may be more conveniently expressed, for determination of quantities which buyers will take at sellers' prices, as follows:

$$D = -5000p + 450,000.$$

The corresponding demand schedule, with revised column headings, appears in Table III.

In the first place, both sellers must always be supposed to sell *at the same price;* otherwise, as already noted in criticism of Zeuthen's interpretation, a complication is introduced which is totally foreign to Cournot's problem. This assumption of one price in itself does not appear to be objectionable, for two competitors are often observed to compete with each other, charging the same price.

In the second place, however, *a very artificial method of changing prices* must be conceded. In Cournot's original version of the theory, the price bid by buyers changes automatically with changes in quantity; and at any given time the price bid for the offerings of both duopolists is always the same. If Cournot's theory, however, is to be re-stated, in order to apply to a market in which sellers name prices, how shall two sellers, who are bona fide competitors, always move their prices in the same direction at the same time and by the same amount? In step (3) of Table II, M is shown to expect and desire a price of 46 cents; N, a price of 38 cents. No actual difference in market price occurs, in accordance with Cournot's original implied assumption, because the issue is directly decided by the impartial bidding of buyers. If sellers name prices, however, and M directly announces a price of 46 cents, and N a price of 38 cents, two prices appear in the market. In the absence of competitive bidding among buyers, no third force is present to bring M's price and N's price immediately to any particular uniform level. The uniformity of price necessary in all steps toward Cournot's equilibrium, can be maintained then only by some sort of agreement or understanding between sellers.

1. It may be imagined that in each particular stage of adjustment, one seller leads in a price change, and the other immediately follows. Thus, in the illustration just given, N, although he may desire a price of 38 cents, may temporarily bow to the will of M, and accept M's price of 46 cents; or else, M may temporarily accept N's price of 38 cents. Then, in succeeding stages of adjustment it may be imagined that M and N alternate in accepting each other's prices, until an equilibrium is reached.

2. In each particular stage of adjustment it may be imagined that both sellers compromise with each other in the matter of price. Thus, if M desires a price of 46 cents, and N a price of 38 cents, it may be supposed that they quickly compromise on the price, say 36 cents, at which their intended offerings at 46 cents and 38 cents respectively can all be sold. An equality between total amount offered and total amount demanded is not ordinarily considered necessary in any market *except at an equilibrium price;* independent competitors do not usually name prices with the purpose of insuring the sale of each other's stock, but by a series of such agreements at *disequilibrium prices,* it may be imagined, an equilibrium price is reached.

3. A combination of steps from 1 and 2 may also be supposed to lead to Cournot's equilibrium.

Under any of these conditions, changes in price, instead of being automatically regulated by competitive bidding among buyers, are governed by a convention utterly foreign to the spirit of Cournot. Cournot carefully abstracted any agreement or understanding between sellers.[31] These conditions in themselves, moreover, are highly improbable. The amount of co-operation required would be more naturally and intelligently invested in a perfectly monopolistic combination.

In the opinion of the writer this difficulty alone is sufficient to invalidate

TABLE III

DEMAND SCHEDULE

Price Named by Seller (Cents)	Quantity Taken
60	150,000
55	175,000
50	200,000
45	225,000
40	250,000
35	275,000
30	300,000
25	325,000
20	350,000

Cournot's solution in any market in *which sellers name prices;* but ignoring this difficulty, or passing lightly over it with stereotyped phrases, some admirers of Cournot try to reconcile his theory with reality in other respects. Therefore, attention is invited to *a special system of limitation of sales* necessary to the correctness of Cournot's solution *when sellers name prices.* Vilfredo Pareto outlined this system. Pareto regarded Cournot's market as one in which sellers named prices; otherwise, he would scarcely have introduced his own new assumption. The last part of Pareto's discussion of Cournot's theory of duopoly in a footnote in *L'Encyclopédie des sciences mathématiques*[32] may seem to some readers a sympathetic review, and a possible description of actual conditions; but the present writer is convinced that it was intended as the climax of a *reductio ad absurdum.* Pareto first stated his technical mathematical objections to Cournot's theory, and then in simpler terms tried to show that Cournot had really solved only an artificial problem of no significance. The attempted exposé, as already shown, falls down completely in a market where only buyers name prices. Pareto deserves credit, however, for an outline of some of the conditions which have to be met when sellers name prices to make Cournot's solution applicable. Lest anyone believe that Pareto, in his efforts to reduce Cournot's theory to absurdity, unwittingly stumbled on a set of conditions which make Cournot's theory all the more significant, Pareto's analysis is again made the basis of a *reductio ad absurdum* in this article.

The essence of Pareto's idea is *mutual limitation of sales in deference to certain arbitrarily recognized "rights" of one's rival.* If Cournot's solution is to be correct, changes in the sales of either competitor, according to Pareto, are made alternately; and in each step toward the final equilibrium, each seller must be assumed to limit his own sales so *as not to interfere with the other's sales.* It is not sufficient, *when sellers name prices,* to assume, as Professor Chamberlin suggests, that the less active seller in any particular phase of adjustment "will hold his supply fixed";[33] if Cournot's solution is correct, under present conditions, the other seller also must take care not to take his rival's *momentarily recognized share of the business* away from him. If *M* is temporarily taking the more active part, and *N* is selling 110,000 units, *M* does not interfere with the sale of *N's* 110,000 units;

and N reciprocates by not interfering with the sale of any *new* quantity which M may decide to sell. An imaginary series of steps toward an equilibrium is shown in Table IV, subject to the following assumptions:[34]

1. Each duopolist *in turn* leads in changing the price.

2. The "other" duopolist in each step immediately follows the price change initiated by his rival.

3. In each new adjustment, the price leader takes up only the "slack" in the demand at the new price. He does not interfere with the continued sale of the quantity which his rival has been selling at the price immediately preceding.

4. In each new adjustment the less active duopolist makes no effort to sell more than he sold in the immediately preceding stage of adjustment. Thus he places no obstacle in the way of the sale of any new quantity which the price leader may offer.

5. Subject to these conditions, each duopolist in turn calculates a new price, so as to realize for himself a maximum profit.

Edgeworth assumed that each seller in turn would cut into the sales of his rival by quoting a slightly lower price; but disregarding this method of interference, the utter improbability of any series of events, such as illustrated in Table IV, may be made clear by contrast with a similar series of steps *without artificial limitation of sales.* Let us assume that the same prices are quoted, one after another, and that neither competitor at any time makes any effort to attract business away from his rival *by quoting a lower price,* but that each one sells at the price of the moment *the quantity which buyers ask of him.* Then buyers, being extremely numerous, having no preference for either seller, having equal access to both of them, buying in either case an identical product at the same price, may be expected as a group to divide their total purchases between the two sellers *equally* — just as when one tosses a large number of coins in the air approximately half of them may be expected to fall "heads up," and half "tails." By the law of large numbers the greater the number of coins, and in this case the greater the number of buyers, the less becomes the expectation of any significant variation from an equal division.

The fact that one seller may be a trifle slower than the other in changing his price does not appreciably alter this result. As a matter of reality, few buyers become immediately aware of differences in price. Since in this case differences in price are assumed to prevail for no appreciable length of time, this consideration may be entirely ignored.

Furthermore, if buyers act rationally (and it is assumed that they do), *the fact that one duopolist may offer buyers more than half the total quantity demanded* at the price of the moment *will not in itself cause buyers as a group to depart from an equal division of their total purchases.* The mere display of a larger stock of goods does not create any prejudice in its favor among rationally minded buyers, as long as an equally accessible smaller stock is known to consist of units of the same nature and quality. Therefore, neither duopolist can sell more than half the total quantity demanded at any price at which his rival also is selling, *unless his rival limits*

TABLE IV

	Price (Cents)	Announced by	Followed by	M's Sales	N's Sales
(1)	24	—	—	220,000	110,000
(2)	44	M	N	120,000	110,000
(3)	38	N	M	120,000	140,000
(4)	41	M	N	105,000	140,000
(5)	39 ½	N	M	105,000	147,500
(6)	40 ¼	M	N	101,250	147,500
(n)	40	?	?	100,000	150,000

his sales to less than half the total quantity demanded. *Either duopolist may prevent his rival from selling more than half, by offering fully half himself, as long as they both sell at the same price.*

In Cournot's original version of the problem, it was not necessary to use different symbols for quantity offered and quantity sold. If the price is determined by competitive bidding among buyers for quantities offered, it is to the interest of each seller to accept only the highest price which clears the market — even if the price of the moment is not an equilibrium price. All goods offered under these circumstances may be assumed to be sold, no matter what the immediate price. Thus, Cournot was justified in using D_1 and D_2 to represent quantities offered and quantities sold.

If Cournot's theory, however, is to be *re-stated* in order to apply to a market in which *sellers name prices,* the possibility must be considered of a discrepancy between quantities offered and quantities sold. As a general proposition, when sellers name prices, the total quantity offered is not necessarily equal to the total quantity sold, except at equilibrium. At a price other than that of equilibrium, the total quantity offered may be greater than the quantity actually sold. Thus, if O_1 and O_2 represent respectively quantities offered by M and N, at any price p not that of equilibrium, and if D_1 and D_2 represent respectively quantities actually sold by M and N, $p = f(D_1 + D_2)$; but unless some special explanation is given, it is not necessarily true when sellers name prices, that $p = f(O_1 + O_2)$, or that $D_1 = O_1$ and $D_2 = O_2$. As long as each seller is able and willing to sell *all that is asked of him* at the same price as his rival, *no matter how much more* either seller may offer *in addition,* the division of actual sales between the two sellers is equal in the present case. Under these conditions, any additional quantity offered by either duopolist remains *unsold.*

Suppose total sales are $D = F(p)$, or as in this particular case, $D = -5000p + 450,000$. Then in accordance with the conditions which have been specified, individual sales, D_1 and D_2, conform with the relation: $D_1 = D_2 = \frac{1}{2}F(p)$; or in this particular case, $D_1 = D_2 = -2500p + 225,000$. The peculiar system of limitation of sales necessary to the correctness of Cournot's solution, *when sellers name prices,* may be contrasted in detail with what is believed to be the more rational and realistic system outlined in the preceding symbols. For purposes of comparison, Table IV, by reference to the last equation, or the demand schedule in Table III, may be extended as in Table V.

When sellers name prices as in columns (*a*) and (*b*), sales may be assumed to be adjusted as in columns (*c*) and (*d*), if Cournot's solution is to be correct. No simpler series of adjustments can be imagined to lead to the same result. If this simple series, then, is shown to be irrational, any more complicated series of adjustments which may lead to the same result, appears irrational *a fortiori*. In columns (*e*) and (*f*), sales at the same prices are shown, subject to the condition that each duopolist sells all that is asked of him at the same price as his rival. In this particular case neither competitor is restrained from selling all that is asked of him at any of the prices in Table V, by any consideration of cost of production. The marginal cost of any quantity to each producer, like his average cost, is constant in this case, viz., *M*, 20 cents; *N*, 10 cents. The marginal and the average cost of any quantity to either *M* or *N* is much less than any of the prices under consideration.

Step 1 of Table V may be passed over without particular comment. It is only an initial position postulated for the sake of a concrete illustration. Let step 2 be taken as the first example of artificial limitation of sales necessary to the correctness of Cournot's solution under present conditions. *N* is assumed to have followed a price change initiated by *M*, as shown in columns (*a*) and (*b*). Thus, the price has been raised from 24 cents to 44 cents. *N*, by accepting the opportunity open to him to sell to half the market, may dispose of 115,000 units at 44 cents, as shown in column (*f*). He may thus prevent *M* from selling 120,000 units — column (*c*) — and cut *M*'s sales down to 115,000 units, the same quantity as his own. See columns (*e*) and (*f*). In actual business, no one turns customers away simply because his rival has surplus stock on hand to sell at the same price; but if Cournot's solution is to apply in this case, *N*, in ridiculous awe of *M*'s "rights," or in partial blindness to his own interests, must be supposed, in spite of his unlimited productive capacity, to limit his sales in step 2 to 110,000 units, the same amount he sold in step 1. See column (*d*). Only by this concession on *N*'s part is it possible for *M* to sell 120,000 units at price 44 cents.

In step 3 a similar absurdity appears in column (*c*). Here, however, the tables are reversed. This time it is *M* who suffers from a nonsensical convention. Since it is *M*'s turn to follow a price change made by *N*, *M* must, if the system is to be obeyed, restrict his sales in step 3 to 120,000 units, the same amount he sold supposedly in step 2. See column (*c*). By accepting the opportunity open to him, *M* can sell 130,000 units, as shown in column (*e*).

A slightly different kind of foolishness is exhibited in step 4. In this step it is the price leader, not the more passive actor in the farce, who suffers as a result of an artificial system. In step 4, *M* leads an advance in price from 38 cents to 41 cents, as shown in columns (*a*) and (*b*). *N* immediately follows this advance. *M* has consented, however, to "respect" the amount of business which *N* did in step 3, i.e., 140,000 units. See column (*d*). The fact that *N* may still offer 140,000 units in itself does not prevent *M* from selling 122,500 units. In so doing, *M* can reduce *N*'s sales to the same amount also,

TABLE V

Step	(a) Price (Cents)	(b) Price Named by	With Artificial Limitations		With No Artificial Limitations	
			(c) M's Sales	(d) N's Sales	(e) M's Sales	(f) N's Sales
(1)	24	—	220,000	110,000	—	—
(2)	44	M	120,000	110,000	115,000	115,000
(3)	38	N	120,000	140,000	130,000	130,000
(4)	41	M	105,000	140,000	122,500	122,500
(5)	39½	N	105,000	147,500	126,250	126,250
(6)	40¼	M	101,250	147,500	124,375	124,375
(n)	40	?	100,000	150,000	125,000	125,000

as shown in columns (e) and (f). In accordance with certain imaginary ethics of competition, however, N, as the less active participant in immediate adjustment, is granted certain immunities as well as duties. M, therefore, must refrain from encroaching on the sale of N's 140,000 units, and content himself with the sale of only 105,000 units, as shown in column (c).

When the final equilibrium is reached, M is still shown at a disadvantage as a result of this intricate, inconvenient, and utterly impossible system. By accepting his opportunity to sell to half the market, M can dispose of 125,000 units at 40 cents, the same price as N's; but being restrained by a mysterious agreement, M offers only 100,000 units.

In Cournot's original version of the theory, each seller determines the quantity he offers at any given time with the rational purpose of influencing the bidding of buyers to his own best advantage. If Cournot's theory is to be revised, however, in order to apply to a market in which sellers name prices, no matter whether the exact arrangement parallels the one just illustrated or not, determination of quantities must be conditioned by *arbitrary concessions* on the part of one or both the competitors. *When buyers name prices*, neither duopolist, as Cournot correctly insisted, has any direct influence on the quantity his rival may sell; neither duopolist can prevent the other from selling what he chooses: nor is it easy for either one to predict what the other will sell. Under these conditions, D_1 and D_2 are *independent variables*, Pareto's objections notwithstanding. *When sellers name prices*, however, each duopolist does have a direct and predictable influence on the sales of his rival, even when they both sell at a common price; for at any price at which they both may sell, either one may sell more than half the total quantity demanded, if his rival limits his offerings to less than half the total quantity demanded; but neither one can sell more than half, if his rival is able and willing to transact the full half of the business which chance tends to throw his way. It is incredible that two intelligent competitors, selling the same product in the same market, having power to name prices, or participate in a price agreement, should fail to perceive this tendency toward *an equal division of sales*. It is incredible that either one would, under these conditions, neglect his influence on his rival's sales, assume them constant, and thus magnify or diminish his own opportunities. If each duopolist can sell half the total quantity demanded at any common price, with a profit on each unit, neither one can be reasonably expected to limit his share of the business at this price to less than half, and thus allow his rival to transact more than half. Willingness to do so, however, is necessary, as Pareto somewhat vaguely indicated, if Cournot's solution is to apply *when sellers name prices*.

The only way to make sense out of nonsense in this case is to restore Cournot's original implied assumption. *If sellers leave the actual naming of prices to buyers*, the situation straightens itself out. Then, and only then, does it become worthy of the imagination of a great genius. As far as the present writer can see, *it is incorrect to apply Cournot's solution to any market in which sellers name prices*. Under these conditions, Cournot's solution is dependent upon (1) *a very improbable system of changing prices;* and (2) *a still more improbable system of limitation of sales*. Thus, the entire analysis has to be rewritten; the spirit of the original, in which no agreement or understanding between sellers appears, is violated, and the final result is exceedingly complicated without being realistic.

If sellers merely mention or suggest prices, there can be no objection to Cournot's solution. If either seller temporarily insists upon any price other than that bid by buyers, the process of price stabilization at Cournot's level may be only temporarily delayed. The final achievement of Cournot's equilibrium price, however, is not a reasonable expectation *unless, in accordance with the prevailing custom of the market, prices are directly determined by competitive bidding among buyers*.

For years economists in general accepted F. Y. Edgeworth's unfavorable judgment of Cournot's theory of duopoly. Edgeworth failed to recognize adequately the conditional validity of Cournot's conclusions.[35] Edgeworth's own conclusions have by this time been severely criticized.[36] In fact, with the swing of the pendulum of opinion in favor of Cournot, perhaps Edgeworth no longer receives due consideration. Any detailed study of his analysis is not within the scope of the present article. There is, however, at least one permanent virtue in his approach which stands out clearly in comparison with the earlier work of Cournot. Edgeworth — like Bertrand — was consistent in assuming *that sellers name prices, and buyers determine quantities.* In Edgeworth's discussion of duopoly,[37] one reads of this seller and then the other seller lowering or raising his price; nothing is said of buyers naming their prices; nor does any part of the reasoning depend upon competitive bidding among buyers. The choice between Cournot and Edgeworth involves something more important than *the supposition that one man's sales remain constant*, or *that his price remains constant*.[38] The main question is one of conformity with the actual institutions of buying and selling.

It is a matter of common observation that when a few are dealing with many, *the few almost always name prices*. None of the many expects any price offer of his to be taken seriously, except in rare instances. Lack of organization prevents the multitude from having any direct voice in price determination. Its only influence arises indirectly from the quantities it buys or sells. Bertrand and Edgeworth instinctively recognized this fact. Cournot perhaps did also. This may have been the reason why he failed to state one of the essential assumptions of his argument. He deserves all honor for having recognized, long before any one else, that duopoly was a problem distinct from monopoly or unlimited competition; but in spite of the valiant defense of Amoroso, and in view of the keen analysis of Pareto, it appears that Cournot actually got no further than a description of a sort of double or multiple *auction sale*.[39]

NOTES

1. The manuscript of this article has been read in more than one stage of revision by Professor Henry Schultz. To him the writer is indebted for many constructive criticisms, and references to important material which otherwise would have been neglected. The writer himself, however, assumes full responsibility for any errors which may still appear.

2. *Recherches sur les principes mathématiques de la théorie des richesses* (Paris, 1838). English translation by N. T. Bacon, with Introduction and Notes by Irving Fisher (Macmillan, 1897; reprinted 1927, 1929).

3. Cf. Alfred Marshall in the Preface to the First Edition of his *Principles of Economics*:

". . . . two kinds of influences have affected, more than any other, the substance of the views expressed in the present book; but their form has been most affected by mathematical conceptions of continuity, as represented in Cournot's *Principes mathématiques de la théorie des richesses*.

"Under the guidance of Cournot, ... I was led to attach great importance to the fact . . . . that . . . . the demand for a thing is a continuous function" (pp. ix–x).

4. Knut Wicksell, "Mathematische Nationalökonomie," *Archiv für Sozialwissenschaft und Sozialpolitik*, LVIII, Heft 2 (1927), 252–81, especially 267–75; Joseph Schumpeter, "The Instability of Capitalism," *Economic Journal*, XXXVIII (1928), 361–86, particularly 369–70n.; Harold Hotelling, "Stability of Competition," *Economic Journal*, XXXIX (1929), 41–57; E. H. Chamberlin, "Duopoly: Value When Sellers Are Few," *Quarterly Journal of Economics*, XLIV (1929), 81–100; Luigi Amoroso, "La curva statica di offerta," *Giornale degli economisti*, LXX (1930), 1–26, especially 11–20; Erich Schneider, "Zur Theorie des mehrfachen Monopols," *Archiv für Sozialwissenschaft und Sozialpolitik*, LXIII (1930), 541–46; Griffith C. Evans, *Mathematical Introduction to Economics* (McGraw-Hill, 1930), pp. 22–27; F. Zeuthen, *Problems of Monopoly and Economic Warfare* (London, 1930), pp. 24–62; Erich Schneider,

Reine Theorie monopolistischer Wirtschaftsformen (Tübingen, 1932), especially pp. 132–75; E. H. Chamberlain, *The Theory of Monopolistic Competition* (Harvard University Press, 1933), pp. 30–55.

5. Cournot, *Researches*, chap. vii, pp. 79–89.

6. Cf. J. Bertrand's review of Walras and Cournot in *Journal des Savants* (September, 1883) pp. 499–508; F. Y. Edgeworth, *Papers Relating to Political Economy* (1925), I, 111–42; Vilfredo Pareto, "Economie mathématique," *Encyclopédie des sciences mathématiques* (Paris-Leipzig, 1911), Tome I, Vol. IV, Fasc. 4, pp. 606–8n.; *Manuel d'économie politique* (Paris, 1927), pp. 595–602; F. Y. Edgeworth, "The Mathematical Economics of Professor Amoroso," *Economic Journal*, XXXII (1922), 400–407, particularly 402–5.

An earlier article by Pareto, "Di un errore del Cournot nel trattare l'economica politica colla matematica," *Giornale degli economisti*, IV, Series 2 (1892), 1–14 is a criticism of Cournot's theory of a protective tariff and related topics. *Vide Researches*, chap. xii.

7. In graphic representation of the situation, it is assumed that quantities are measured along the horizontal axis, and prices along the vertical axis, as is the custom in Great Britain and America. With very slight verbal changes, however, the discussion above may also apply when prices are measured along the horizontal axis, and quantities along the vertical axis.

8. A. L. Bowley, in analysis of the theory of bargaining between monopolies, shows that it makes considerable difference which monopoly names the price; and which the quantity to be exchanged. *Vide Economic Journal*, XXXVIII (1928), 651–59. In his brief consideration of duopoly price, however, no notice is taken of the parallel question. Cf. *Mathematical Groundwork of Economics* (Oxford, 1924), p. 38.

9. The special assumption of constant unit costs is not essential to Cournot's theory. It falls, however, within his more general treatment. A still simpler illustration of the theory is afforded by a situa-

tion in which there are no costs of production, or a situation in which both producers operate under the same cost conditions. It is desired, however, to avoid any general conclusions which may rest upon too narrow a basis.

10. For illustrations of alternating adjustments, see Knut Wicksell, *Archiv für Sozialwissenschaft und Sozialpolitik*, LVIII, Heft 2, 269–70; E. H. Chamberlin, *Quarterly Journal of Economics*, XLIV, 66–69; *Monopolistic Competition*, pp. 32–34; Luigi Amoroso, *Giornale degli economisti*, LXX, 12–15; F. Zeuthen, *Problems of Monopoly*, pp. 29–31.

11. The process of adjustment of quantities is graphically represented in the back of Cournot's *Researches* (Figure 2). An explanation of this diagram is found on page 81.

12. *Researches*, p. 85.

13. *Quarterly Journal of Economics*, XLIV, 83ff.; *Monopolistic Competition*, pp. 46ff.

14. *Researches*, pp. 56ff.

15. *Ibid.*, p. 56.

16. *Ibid.*, p. 80.

17. *Loc. cit.*, p. 79.

18. The quotation above follows Bacon's translation (p. 80), except in one phrase shown in italics. This phrase Bacon translated, "by properly adjusting his price." Cournot himself wrote: "Ce à quoi il parviendra en modifiant convenablement le prix" (original edition [1838], p. 89).
Two points in French grammar are involved:
(1) The use of the participial form in -*ant* (*modifiant*).
"As a gerund, it denotes either *simultaneous action* or 'means by which' . . . . en = while, in, on, when, as, by, etc., or *is untranslated*" (Frasier and Squair, *French Grammar* [1921], p. 219). (Italics inserted.)
(2) The use of the definite article (*le*).
"The definite article is commonly used with the force of a possessive adjective, *when no ambiguity arises from its use*" (Frasier and Squair, p. 319). (Italics inserted.)
Bacon's translation of the phrase, "en modifiant convenablement le prix," and the translation substituted above are both grammatically possible, as far as the phrase itself is concerned; but Bacon's translation in this particular does not harmonize with the context, explained in the paragraph above following the quotation.
See also A. A. Cournot, *Principes de la théorie des richesses* (Paris, 1863), pp. 109–11; *Revue sommaire des doctrines économiques* (Paris, 1876), pp. 172–74.

19. F. Y. Edgeworth, *Mathematical Psychics* (London, 1881), reprinted by London School of Economics and Political Science (1932), p. 47; *Papers Relating to Political Economy*, I, 119ff.

20. Cournot, *Researches*, pp. 79–80, 83.

21. Luigi Amoroso, *Lezioni di economica matematica* (Bologna, 1921), pp. 254ff.; *Giornale degli economisti*, LXX, 11–20.

22. Cf. Edgeworth, *Economic Journal*, XXXII, 402.

23. Cf. Chamberlin, *Quarterly Journal of Economics*, XLIV, 95–96; *Monopolistic Competition*, pp. 181–82; Erich Schneider, *Archiv für Sozialwissenschaft und Sozialpolitik*, LXIII, 539–55; LXIV, 380.

24. *Encyclopédie des sciences mathématiques*, Tome I, Vol. IV, Fasc. 4, p. 608 n. (Italics inserted.)

25. F. Y. Edgeworth, *Mathematical Psychics*, p. 47.

26. *Problems of Monopoly and Economic Warfare*, p. 29.

27. "Bei C o u r n o t sind nicht Preisänderungen der Monopolisten sondern Mengenvariationen das Primäre, die ihrerseits dann automatisch Preisänderungen nach sich ziehen" (Erich Schneider, *Reine Theorie monopolistischer Wirtschaftsformen*, p. 173).

28. Edgeworth, *Papers*, I, 119ff.; cf. Hotelling, *Economic Journal*, XXXIX, 41–57.

29. *Problems of Monopoly*, pp. 29–31.

30. *Ibid.*, pp. 30–31.

31. *Researches*, pp. 79–80, 83.

32. Tome I, Vol. IV, Fasc. 4, p. 608n.

33. *Quarterly Journal of Economics*, XLIV, 72; *Monopolistic Competition*, p. 37.

34. The assumptions stated above are not the only ones which may be imagined to lead to Cournot's solution, when sellers name prices. It may also be supposed that in each stage of adjustment, each seller independently determines *a* price and *a* quantity (cf. Table II) which he thinks to his best interest, assuming no change in his rival's sales. Then, if there are differences in *intended prices*, the two sellers may be supposed to compromise in each step on that price which allows them both to dispose of their *intended offerings*. This arrangement, however, may be shown subject to the same general weaknesses as the arrangement described above.

35. Edgeworth professed great admiration for Cournot in *Mathematical Psychics*, p. 47, but considered his discussion limited by *uniformity of price*. This statement, however, does not go to the heart of the matter. Uniformity of price in Cournot's problem is dependent on the more fundamental assumption that only buyers name prices.

36. Joseph Schumpeter, *Economic Journal*, XXXVIII, 369–70n.; E. H. Chamberlin, *Quarterly Journal of Economics*, XLIV, 72–79; *Monopolistic Competition*, pp. 37–43; Amoroso, *Giornale degli economisti*, LXX, 16–18.

37. Edgeworth, *Papers*, I, 119ff.

38. Cf. Chamberlin, *Quarterly Journal*

of Economics, XLIV, 72; *Monopolistic Competition,* p. 37.

39. Cf. Edgeworth in criticism of Amoroso: "This procedure appears to us inappropriate to pure monopoly. It might be appropriate to a kind of *kartel* in which each producer is free from time to time to alter the amount of commodity which he puts on the market, the price being allowed in the interval between such changes to accommodate itself to the total supply. But this convention appears unduly to limit the characteristic freedom of the monopolist to vary price" (*Economic Journal,* XXXII, 402).

24.

FRANK H. KNIGHT
University of Chicago

Marginal Utility Economics

The founders of modern utility theory are generally recognized to be W. Stanley Jevons, author of *The Theory of Political Economy* (1871), Karl Menger, author of *Grundsätze der Volkswirtschaftslehre* (1871), and Léon Walras, the first instalment of whose *Eléments d'économie politique pure* appeared in 1874. These three men, working independently and belonging to different branches of European culture, came practically at the same time to the same position. Yet the central doctrine of marginal utility, now one of the most familiar in economic theory, was not a new discovery made by them or by any other writer usually associated with the marginal utility or Austrian school. After the work of the founders received general recognition, numerous statements of similar doctrine, varying in clearness and elaboration, were found scattered through the earlier literature. Some were by men who had been recognized in their day on other grounds, others by men who had died unheard of. If the most pathetic case is that of Gossen, the strangest is that of the famous economist Senior. This thinker, characterized by brilliant insights and inability to build upon them, not only stated the utility principle but especially emphasized its main consequence, namely, that cost affects price only indirectly through supply; yet he worked out his value theory as a whole on the Ricardian principle of subjective cost, without incorporating this premise. The utility theory had apparently to wait for the "fulness of time" and to be stillborn many times before it could live.

At the present time marginal utility analysis, in one or another of its

Reprinted from *The Encyclopaedia of the Social Sciences* (New York: The Macmillan Company, 1931), V, 357–63, by permission of the author and the publisher. This essay is a section of a long article, "Economics," and it forms Chapter 5 of Frank H. Knight, *The Ethics of Competition* (New York: Harper & Brothers, 1935).

numerous variants, is firmly established in the economic thought of all important countries. The country where utility theory first rose to dominance is Austria, hence the identification of "Austrian school" with marginal utility doctrine. The great triumvirate of Vienna, Menger, Böhm-Bawerk, and Wieser, were the first to sketch in the main outlines of the new theory; they enlisted an imposing array of followers including Sax, Philippovich, and Zuckerkandl, and trained a number of younger economists of whom Schumpeter and Hans Mayer are probably the best known. In Germany utility theory encountered opposition from the historical school, which was rapidly attaining prominence after the middle of the nineteenth century. Menger found himself therefore fighting the battle not merely of marginal utility but of the "exact" deductive method in social science; and allied with him was Dietzel, an economist who was nearer to the classical theory than to the Austrian school. The opposition in Germany was overcome only very slowly; not until after the war did marginal utility receive its full share of academic recognition in that country. In France the ground for utility theory was prepared by the writings of Condillac and J. B. Say. Although the mathematical performances of Walras met with disfavour, the theory was not forced to fight for survival; yet except for Walras French economics made no significant contribution to the theoretical exploitation of the utility principle. Italian economists, led by Pantaleoni and Pareto, took up particularly the mathematical variant of the new theory. Among other continental writers of the marginal utility orientation must be specifically mentioned Wicksell in Sweden, Pierson in Holland, Birck in Denmark, and Bilimovič in Russia.

In the English-speaking countries the acceptance of marginal utility was a reaction from the theories of the classical school, which had dominated economic thought since the publication of Adam Smith's *Wealth of Nations* (1776). In England the new theory was popularized by William Smart, the translator of Wieser and Böhm-Bawerk, and P. H. Wicksteed, a follower of Jevons. Despite an obvious reverence for the classical tradition and no less pronounced coolness toward Jevons, Marshall was even more responsible for the acclimatization of a modified form of marginal analysis in England. In the United States, where classical doctrines were not as strongly entrenched, Carey's influence was on the wane when utility theory found a thoughtful and original exponent in J. B. Clark. The other American writers with marginal utility leanings are Patten, Fetter and Irving Fisher, all of whom made original contributions on the specific problems.

It has always been recognized — it could not fail to be, as soon as the phenomena came under scrutiny at all — that a thing must be desirable in order to have power to command value in exchange. But the Smith-Ricardo school considered desirability only a condition of exchange value; they rejected it as a determinant of value on the empirical ground that there seems to be the widest discrepancy in fact between the usefulness of commodities and their prices. Smith cited the example of water and diamonds, previously used by Locke and Law; Ricardo, that of gold and iron. Dismissing utility as a cause of price, they fell back upon cost, which likewise had necessarily been recognized as a factor from the beginning of speculation on the subject. Smith believed that in a primitive state commodities might be expected to exchange on the basis of labour costs, and that in a developed exchange economy the cost which determines price consists of the money payments made by producers for the labour, capital, and land necessary to produce a commodity. Ricardo's highly abstract mind disliked the pluralism of Smith's treatment and his failure to integrate arguments proceeding from different standpoints. He conceived the idea that the theory of value could be made simple and unitary on the basis of labour cost alone. Several difficulties stood in the way, of which the most important were the roles of land and capital in production. The surplus theory of land rent, which had been stated by Smith, Hume, and Anderson and was getting recognition through West and Malthus and according to which rent is the effect and not a cause of price, seemed to Ricardo to remove the difficulty in the matter of land and was therefore used by him as the corner stone of a new system. If Ricardo was dissatisfied with the assumption of uniform capital outlays in various branches of production, the device by which he got rid of capital as a major cause of price differences, Senior's concept of abstinence, reduced capital cost to homogeneity with labour cost in terms of subjective sacrifice. After him the formulation of value theory on the basis of sacrifice cost remained unshakable down to the "revolution" inaugurated by the marginal utility theorists. Yet the recognition of "noncompeting" strata of labourers by Mill and Cairnes made it impossible longer to take the labour cost theory literally. At the same time the classical theory of distribution, also built around the surplus theory of rent, was placing an increasing strain on every mind free from prepossession and was virtually abandoned in J. S. Mill's overhauling of the classical system. When Mill also recanted on the wages fund theory, the wreck was so complete that a new start became inevitable.

In formal statement the new doctrine of Jevons and Menger seemed revolutionary indeed. It explained price in terms of utility, summarily rejected by the writers of the old school, and squarely inverted the accepted relation between cost and price by holding cost to be derived from price and not its cause. The key to the change of view was the recognition of the homely fact that commodities are esteemed not in accordance with their significance in general, but with that of any small unit of the available supply. All the units of any commodity being alike, that unit which is employed for the most important use can be replaced by the unit in the least important employment, and an equal value must attach to both. Hence the effective use value of any good decreases rapidly as the supply increases, and the paradoxes seen by the earlier writers vanish. The use value of a unit of either water or iron is very small, because it is so abundant that it is available for trivial uses; but it would increase almost indefinitely if the supply were reduced, while gold and diamonds would be little esteemed if abundant.

This conception of the use value of the single unit of a commodity, determined by the importance of the "last" unit, or the unit in the least important use, is now generally called "marginal utility," Smart's rendering of the German *Grenznutzen* of Wieser (in his translation of Wieser's *Der natürliche Werth* in 1893). The term was not used by any of the founders of the theory. In his paper delivered before section F of the British Association in 1862 (reprinted in 4th ed. of the *Theory*, pp. 303–14) Jevons called it "coefficient of utility" and in the book of 1871 "final degree of utility." Menger's term was simply "importance," that of Walras, "rarity." Jevons and Walras defined the notion with quantitative precision, using the mathematical theory of infinitesimals; Menger spoke only of units or portions as understood in everyday usage.

In attempting to explain price in terms of marginal utility the Austrian theorists encountered considerable difficulty when they found that the utilities of articles of the same price must be very different to rich and poor buyers. The difficulty was really imaginary and was due to reasoning in terms of absolute rather than relative utilities. Jevons saw and emphasized the truth that the doctrine of utility determining price involves only comparisons by each individual buyer for himself of the different uses for his purchasing power large or small; no comparison as between one individual and another, whether of utilities or disutilities, is called for.

From explaining price on the basis of use value as in turn dependent on scarcity, it seemed a natural step to reason that where goods come into existence through production, as most of them do, the means of production, or cost goods, will be valued to the same extent as the products to which they give rise and on the same principles. Any one unit of a productive resource will be valued in accordance with the least important unit of product for which it is available, i.e., according to the satisfaction actually dependent on its use. It is due primarily to Menger that the foundation was laid for a new approach to the valuation of "indirect goods," "goods of higher order," or productive resources. Jevons had a deeper insight at some points but did not break away from the influence of the older British approach completely enough to develop his theory of supply systematically, and the later Austrian writers became confused over side issues. The values of production goods constitute at the same time the money costs of production and the incomes through which product is distributed. The fruits of the new viewpoint were ultimately greater in the field of distribution than in that of the explanation of price.

As regards price theory, critical reflection soon revealed that the revolution was by no means so great as it appeared to be from the change in form of statement. On the one hand, men found a great deal of utility theory implicit in the treatment of the classical economists; and, on the other, there was much cost theory in Jevons and Menger. Smith argued that if in a primitive community it costs twice as many days' labour to kill a beaver as to kill a deer, then one beaver will exchange for two deer. With reference to this statement two observations must be made. The first is that if the labour is not of the same kind, freely transferable from one occupation to the other, the reasoning loses all force and meaning. The second is that the reasoning is valid not only for labour but also for any other cost good, such as an acre of ground, which is freely transferable from one employment to another. If the society for any reason has its choice between definitely limited amounts of two commodities, the above reasoning will still hold without any cost being involved. The real argument, not stated by Smith but necessarily implied, is that value depends on amount produced, producers being supposed to employ the resources in the production of the more valuable product. Far from being opposed to the utility principle, the cost theory presupposes its operation at every moment of the adjustment. It is clear also that Ricardo and his successors were fully aware of the role of demand. On the other hand, both Menger and Jevons saw, the latter the more clearly, that if price depends on utility as determined by scarcity, then scarcity in turn is generally the result of the high cost of production. Jevons gave the utmost typographical prominence to the words (*Theory*, 2nd ed., p. 179):

> Cost of production determines supply;
> Supply determines final degree of utility;
> Final degree of utility determines value.

The essential achievement of marginal utility in price theory was that of forcing a new realistic approach to the problem as a whole, centring attention upon the behaviour of actual human beings in competitive relations, each attempting to make the best of his situation in the buying-and-selling economic system. In this marginal utility theory was really following the example set by Adam Smith. Ricardian economics ran in terms of a sort of metaphysical necessity; the actual workings of competitive processes in bringing about the results contended for were assumed rather than clearly expressed, and for this reason much error as well as misplaced emphasis crept into the statements.

The greatest improvement introduced by the marginal utility viewpoint came in the field of distribution theory as a by-product of the changed view of cost. The classical Ricardo-Senior-Mill theory of distribution was utterly unrealistic. It did not consider the problem as one of the valuation of services furnished to production, under competition or monopoly, but as a matter of the successive slicing off of the social income by the three main economic classes found in the society of post-feudal Europe. Smith and Malthus, basing themselves upon an entrepreneur cost theory of price, afforded clear intimations of a realistic approach, but the building of a pain-cost theory of value around the pillar of the residual theory of rent threw all into the discard. It was the truly revolutionary contribution of the utility approach to force consideration of costs and distributive payments as integral parts of one general valuation problem, which has been gradually recognized as that of explaining economic organization under the influence of price facts and motives of individual self-interest.

In the formulation of explicit laws of price the utility theorists were no nearer the truth than the classical economists. The case of the deer and the beaver itself proves that the classicists were wrong in so far as they held that pain-cost has anything essential to do with price fixing. But prices are no more determined by psychological utilities than psychological disutilities. The essential principle is that producers choose the larger return from any productive activity irrespective of its being painful, pleasant, or indifferent and that amount produced in relation to demand fixes prices. When any two commodities can be produced with the aid of the same resources of whatever sort, freely transferable from the one use to the other, the prices of those commodities must in equilibrium be such that the alternative products of the same or equal units of resources exchange for each other. Price is determined by cost rather than utility but by cost in a physical, technical sense, not that of pain or sacrifice.

Comparisons of sacrifice, however, may be and commonly are involved in greater or less degree, and the operation of the utility principle is the basis of the whole process of adjustment. This is the alternative cost theory which is definitely the product of the utility approach. But alternative cost requires much explanation and qualification to fit it accurately to the facts of economic life. The reasoning assumes that all productive resources are freely and continuously transferable from one use to another, so that, as more of one good and less of its alternative are produced, the amount of the latter given up in increasing the output of the former by one unit remains unchanged. But this condition of constant cost rarely describes the situation exactly. In general, some of the resources are freely transferable, others not; and frequently some factors are available only in very large blocks, so that the most efficient organization requires very large-scale production. The first condition will give rise to increasing cost, and the latter to decreasing cost in the earlier stages of expansion of an industry. Given an indefinitely long time for readjustment, including changes in form of capital, retraining of labour, and whatever else may be involved, the law of constant cost is not far from the truth. Under such circumstances utility determines quantities produced but cannot affect the final equilibrium price. On the other hand, the factors of production are hardly transferable instantly in any degree; for a very short period the condition approximates that of fixed supply. In so far as this is the case, price is determined by the relative utilities of the supplies as they stand, cost exerting no influence at all. Problems actually encountered fall between these two limits; the longer the period over which one looks ahead, the greater the extent to which prices at the end of it will correspond to physical cost conditions and the less the role of utility. For ordinary producers' calculations the role of cost is certainly far the greater, but the actual quoted price at any moment, the price at which consumers buy from dealers, reflects rather the demand conditions, supply being "given." The influence of relative utility as compared with that of relative cost depends on the comparative elasticities of the two curves. In the short run, supply is highly inelastic and demand conditions predominate; in the long run, supply generally has practically infinite elasticity and predominates over demand, the latter being always of intermediate elasticity.

Where increasing cost is due to the more intensive exploitation of the non-transferable factors with increasing proportions of factors drawn in from without, utility and cost work together in determining price, the relative influence of each depending on the elasticities of the two curves. Where increasing cost is due to the fact that production depends on cost goods of special qualities, the supply of which is actually an increasing function of price, the price may be said to depend on the effects of both utility and cost, the latter in the sense of disutility. In general, however, the supply of labour is little dependent on disutility considerations; nor is the supply of capital for short periods, since it is an accumulating good. Moreover, labour and capital are employed so generally over the field of production that changes in the supply of either have to be very extensive to exert much influence on the relative supply of different commodities and hence on their prices.

The Austrians admitted the effect of cost on price through control of amount produced but held that cost is finally measured by the value of cost goods, which is derived from the value of products, and hence that utility finally controls price. The premise may be accepted as true, but the conclusion is fallacious. In so far as the costs of two commodities consist of different quantities of the same cost goods, these costs are relative physical magnitudes and are not measured by utility; this condition is much more typical for costs generally than that of distinct factors producing distinct products.

Similarly in the field of distribution the utility theorists gave the correct approach but in formulating the general principle fell into confusion. It is true that the distributive shares are simply the values of the productive services and that these are derived from product values. But in the effort to make utility the sole explanation these writers tended to argue as though different cost goods have different products or groups of products. In so far as that is true, the values of the cost goods may be said to reflect the relative utilities of the products. But the general situation is rather that ultimately all the productive resources cooperate in making each product. Hence the relative "utilities" of units of different resources depend on the relative physical quantities which they respectively contribute to each product. This sets the problem of imputation (*Zurechnung*), the division of a joint effect among cooperating causes.

Imputation was discussed by the Austrians at great length, but they reached no agreement among themselves and did not arrive at a clear and sound analysis. Here the first attempt was the best. Menger gave a fairly clear, if brief, sketch of the process of competitive imputation based on the essential fact that, while the factors almost always have to cooperate in production, any single one being practically ineffective alone, the proportions in which they are employed are variable, this makes it possible to divide the product of their joint activity among them by finding the effect of substituting a small quantity of one factor for a small quantity of another. Most of the school failed to see that the proportions are in fact variable almost without physical limit and that the producer's problem is precisely that of deciding upon the correct proportions of factors along with the problem of fixing the output for the enterprise. The main difficulty was that

602

economists as a class had remained ignorant of the fundamental logic of quantitative variation applicable to problems of joint causation, which had been worked out in connection with physical mechanics a century or more before. The way out was pointed especially by Marshall in England and J. B. Clark in America. The purchase of productive services by entrepreneurs follows exactly the same principles as the purchase of final products by consumers. The complementary relationship may be present or absent in either case. Buyers substitute small quantities of one productive service (or commodity) for small quantities of any other until they arrive at such proportions — varying from buyer to buyer — that they obtain from the last unit of each productive service (or commodity) equal additions to the final product (or to "total satisfaction"); competition sets all the prices in such a way as to clear the market.

The problem of interest presents a special difficulty in distribution theory, because the payment takes the form of an abstract arithmetical rate and not of a specific sum for the use of a concrete productive instrument. Ricardian economics had discussed the share of capital in the social income but had done nothing significant toward explaining the return as a rate, and the problem became a favourite one with the utility school. While Jevons made a brilliant attack on it, which was never adequately appreciated, Menger's work was very weak at this point. Böhm-Bawerk made it his main life work (*Kapital und Kapitalzins*, 2 vols., 1884–9) and under his influence and stimulation notable work has been produced in America (Fetter, Fisher, and others). As Böhm-Bawerk interpreted the problem of developing a theory of interest in harmony with marginal utility principles, it involved refuting productivity and use theories as well as Senior's abstinence doctrine (which Senior unaccountably never employed to explain the rate of interest but only the role of capital in connection with the prices of goods) and explaining the phenomenon in terms of a difference in subjective appreciation of present and future goods. Some critical students think this is what Böhm-Bawerk actually achieved. Undoubtedly a more general view is that, after almost a thousand pages of prolix argumentation, he gave in a few pages a none too clear but reasonably correct statement of the productivity theory, somewhat vitiated by the admixture of the wages fund view of the relation between capital and wages. The utility approach does not necessarily call for a psychological explanation of interest, in such terms, for instance, as the discount of future satisfactions; the simple theory that interest is a ratio between the net value product of capital goods and their money cost, as held by Wieser, would seem to be quite adequate.

It is generally claimed that the marginal utility doctrine and movement is responsible for two contributions of great scientific value. First, it focused attention on demand, which had been passed over and taken for granted by the Ricardians. In this connection the importance of its contribution cannot be overestimated. Demand has ever since been recognized as the driving power behind economic activity and economic organization, although generally physical cost relations exercise a much greater control over the superficial fact of exchange ratios. In the second place, it is claimed that utility theory carries the analysis of demand beyond the surface facts of quantity and price, that it "explains" demand. On this issue there is wide disagreement and the keenest controversy. On the one hand, some form of marginal utility theory is almost universally presented in textbooks, and it seems impossible to discuss economic behaviour in a utilitarian civilization without using utility concepts. On the other hand, the theory is not merely rejected by able critics as unreal and preposterous; it is in fact a favourite point of attack for the enemies of abstract theoretical economics as such.

The issue involves all the philosophical problems connected with the concepts and methodology not merely of economics but of all the sciences dealing with man. The utility theory should be seen as the culmination, historically and logically, of the rationalistic and individualistic intellectual movement of which the competitive economic system itself is one aspect and modern science and technology are others. To its admirers it comes near to being the fulfilment of the eighteenth-century craving for a principle which would do for human conduct and society what Newton's mechanics had done for the solar system. It introduces simplicity and order, even to the extent of making it possible to state the problems in the form of mathematical functions dealt with by the methods of infinitesimal calculus. Moreover, in harmony with eighteenth-century cravings, it claims to furnish a guide for social policy; it can be harnessed to the very practical purpose of proving that if only the state will limit itself to the negative function of defence against violence and predation and leave men free to pursue their own interests, individual self-seeking directed by market competition will bring about a simultaneous maximum of want-satisfaction for all concerned, which in this world view is the desideratum back of all thought and activity. The utility theorists were contemporary with Herbert Spencer and were philosophically his comrades in arms.

The reaction against utility theory is in part the natural reaction against the view of the world and of man which it embodies, in favour either of a more spiritual or less mechanistic view or one less apologetic and more radical; but in part also it is a reaction in precisely the opposite direction, toward more "scientific" conceptions. Under the first banner march those critics to whom the "economic man" is a caricature or a calumny or both. Some insist on treatment in terms of organic social purpose, historical forces, or culture patterns. Others insist on a degree of freedom and spontaneity or of realism in detail that would exclude any treatment except the recording of events as they happen and their imaginative interpretation. Of some of these protesters it must be said briefly that they do not understand either the logic or the purpose of the utility analysis. As a matter of course, the utility description of behaviour as an affair of comparing and choosing is valid only in so far as men compare and choose; no one in his senses has thought of it as the exclusive form of all activity in all historic time. More specifically, the "patterning" of interests does not invalidate the principles of utility analysis at all, so long as substitution is possible through varying proportions; and that is clearly the fact over a considerable field, whatever its precise extent may be.

In the more rigorous versions of the theory, however, there is an element of paradox and unrealism. The notion of increments of satisfaction undoubtedly implies that the value of life as a whole is some definite increasing function of the quantities of the various means of satisfactions available, which hardly agrees with common sense. It also implies the well-known consumers' surplus a quantity of free satisfaction representing the difference between what is paid for goods at the uniform market price per unit and what an omniscient monopolist could theoretically make the consumer pay by selling to him successive small portions at the maximum price for each separately. It would be hard to locate this free satisfaction in the consciousness of a typical consumer. It is necessary at least to distinguish sharply between valuing goods as increments to a supply of goods and valuing them as increments to a total satisfaction. In fact, the entire theory is much more convincing in the loose, common-sense formulation of Menger than it is in the more refined mathematical version of Jevons and Walras.

Critics of utility theory from the opposite direction contend that it is subjective and unscientific and advocate a treatment of economic phenomena by statistical methods using only physical magnitudes, quantities, and prices. They deny that utility explains demand or adds anything to the demand curve or schedule taken as a fact. Logically, they can put up a strong case. The analogy of utility theory with Newtonian principles does not stand up well under examination. In mechanics, if the forces are not directly accessible, at least the conditions under which they act and the effects are measurable and do repeat themselves accurately from one case to another. In economic behaviour the opposite is the case. Under no real circumstances can the behaving subject himself, not to mention any outside observer, ever know even afterward whether or not he actually performed in such a way as to realize maximum possible total satisfaction; and it is even less possible to repeat the choice experimentally with controlled variations. Indeed, on the basis of knowledge gathered from one's own experience and intercourse with others it seems that men do not balance alternatives correctly. All that can be claimed is that there is an effort to do so, with more or less approximation to this result; but the introduction of error into the reaction puts the whole relation on a categorically different basis from cause and effect in nature. On the other hand, the advocates of a purely statistical science do not seem to realize that economics, if it is to have any relation to human problems of means and ends, must be concerned with goods and services not in themselves, but as representing values or sacrifices. These cannot be treated as physical things but must be defined in the same vague and shifting terms as the human impulses, successes, and failures which the scientific mind finds such unsatisfactory material.

25.

GEORGE J. STIGLER
University of Chicago

The Development

of Utility Theory

But I have planted the tree of utility. I have planted it deep, and spread it wide. — BENTHAM.

The history of economic thought can be studied with many purposes. One may trace the effects of contemporary economic and social conditions on economic theory or — rather more bravely — the effects of economic theories on economic and social developments. One may study the history to find the original discoverers of theories, spurred on by the dream of new Cantillons; or one may compare the economics of the great economists with that of the rank and file, as a contribution to the structure and process of intellectual change. Or one may, and most often does, simply set forth the major steps in the development of a branch of economic theory, hoping that it can be justified by its contribution to the understanding of modern economics. This history of utility theory is offered primarily with this last purpose, although in the final section I review the history to answer the question, "Why do economists change their theories?"

The scope of this study is limited in several respects. First, it covers primarily the period from Smith to Slutsky, that is, from 1776 to 1915. Second, the study is limited to certain important topics and to the treatment

Reprinted from *The Journal of Political Economy*, LVIII (August, October 1950), 307–27, 373–96, slightly enlarged, by permission of the author and The University of Chicago Press. At the time of original publication, the author was with Columbia University.

of these topics by economists of the first rank. The application of utility theory to welfare economics is the most important topic omitted. An estimate of the part played by utility theory in forming economists' views of desirable social policy is too large a task, in the complexity of issues and volume of literature involved, to be treated incidentally. The omission is justified by the fact that most economists of the period used utility theory primarily to explain economic behavior (particularly demand behavior) and only secondarily (when at all) to amend or justify economic policy.[1]

I. THE CLASSICAL BACKGROUND

Adam Smith

Drawing upon a long line of predecessors, Smith gave to his immediate successors, and they uncritically accepted, the distinction between value in use and value in exchange:

The word VALUE, it is to be observed, has two different meanings, and sometimes expresses the utility of some particular object, and sometimes the power of purchasing other goods which the possession of that object conveys. The one may be called "value in use"; the other, "value in exchange." The things which have the greatest value in use have frequently little or no value in exchange; and on the contrary, those which have the greatest value in exchange have frequently little or no value in use. Nothing is more useful than water: but it will purchase scarce any thing; scarce any thing can be had in exchange for it. A diamond, on the contrary, has scarce any value in use; but a very great quantity of other goods may frequently be had in exchange for it.[2]

The fame of this passage rivals its ambiguity.

The paradox — that value in exchange may exceed or fall short of value in use — was, strictly speaking, a meaningless statement, for Smith had no basis (i.e., no concept of marginal utility of income or marginal price of utility) on which he could compare such heterogeneous quantities. On any reasonable interpretation, moreover, Smith's statement that value in use could be less than value in exchange was clearly a moral judgment, not shared by the possessors of diamonds. To avoid the incomparability of money and utility, one may interpret Smith to mean that the ratio of values of two commodities is not equal to the ratio of their total utilities.[3] On such a reading, Smith's statement deserves neither criticism nor quotation.

This passage is not Smith's title to recognition in our history of utility. His role is different: it is to show that demand functions, as a set of empirical relationships, were already an established part of economic analysis. The negatively sloping demand curve was already axiomatic; for example, "A competition will immediately begin among [the buyers when an abnormally small supply is available], and the market price will rise more or less above the natural price."[4] The effect of income on consumption was not ignored:

The proportion of the expence of house-rent to the whole expence of living, is different in the different degrees of fortune. It is perhaps highest in the highest degree, and it diminishes gradually through the inferior degrees, so as in general to be lowest in the lowest degree. The necessaries of life occasion the great expence of the poor. They find it difficult to get food, and the greater part of their little revenue is spent in getting it. The luxuries and vanities of life occasion the principal expence of the rich; and a magnificent house embellishes and sets off to the best advantage all the other luxuries and vanities which they possess. A tax upon house-rents, therefore, would in general fall heaviest upon the rich; and in this sort of inequality there would not, perhaps, be any thing very unreasonable.[5]

This type of demand analysis was continued and improved by Smith's successors, but his example should suffice to remind us that a history of utility is not a history of demand theory.

Bentham

Jeremy Bentham brought the principle of utility (to be understood much more broadly than is customary in economics) to the forefront of discussion in England at the beginning of the nineteenth century. In his *Introduction to the Principles of Morals and Legislation* (1789) he suggested the measurement of quantities of pleasure and pain (primarily for the purpose of constructing a more rational system of civil and criminal law). Four dimensions of pleasure and pain were distinguished for the individual: (1) intensity, (2) duration, (3) certainty, and (4) propinquity.[6]

The first two dimensions are clearly relevant to the measurement of a pleasure, but the latter two are better treated as two of the factors which influence an individual's response to a particular pleasure or pain.[7] Bentham did not give explicit directions for calculating a given pleasure and indeed devoted a long chapter (vi) to "Circumstances Influencing Sensibility," which listed no less than thirty-two circumstances (such as age, sex, education, and firmness of mind) that must be taken into account in carrying out such a calculation.

The theory was much elaborated with respect to economic applications in *Traités de legislation* (1802), a lucid synthesis of many manuscripts made by his disciple, Étienne Dumont.[8] Bentham was particularly concerned with the problem of equality of income, and this raised the question of comparisons of the utilities of persons who might differ in thirty-two circumstances:

It is to be observed in general, that in speaking of the effect of a portion of wealth upon happiness, abstraction is always to be made of the particular sensibility of individuals, and of the exterior circumstances in which they may be placed. Differences of character are inscrutable; and such is the diversity of circumstances, that they are never the same for two individuals. Unless we begin by dropping these two considerations, it will be impossible to announce any general proposition. But though each of these propositions may prove false or inexact in a given individual case, that will furnish no argument against their speculative truth and practical utility. It is enough for the justification of these propositions — 1st, If they approach nearer the truth than any others which can be substituted

608

for them; 2nd, If with less inconvenience than any others they can be made the basis of legislation.[9]

Thus, he achieved interpersonal comparisons, not by calculation, but by assumption, justified by the desirability (somehow determined) of its corollaries. This resort to a question-begging assumption was a fundamental failure of his project to provide a scientific basis for social policy: the scientific basis was being justified by the policies to which it led. In one of his manuscripts he argued that this assumption was merely an abbreviation and that the conclusions he deduced could be reached (more laboriously) without it,[10] which is not in general true.

Having surmounted this obstacle no better than subsequent economists, Bentham proceeded to establish a set of propositions on the utility of income:[11]

1st. Each portion of wealth has a corresponding portion of happiness.
2nd. Of two individuals with unequal fortunes, he who has the most wealth has the most happiness.
3rd. The excess in happiness of the richer will not be so great as the excess of his wealth.[12]

Each of these propositions was elaborated, and the utility calculus was used to defend equality ("The nearer the actual proportion approaches to equality, the greater will be the total mass of happiness"), although equality was finally rejected in favor of security of property. As corollaries, gambling was utility-decreasing and insurance utility-increasing.[13]

In a manuscript written about 1782, Bentham attempted to set forth more clearly the precise measurement of utility.[14] We are given a definition of the unit of intensity:

The degree of intensity possessed by that pleasure which is the faintest of any that can be distinguished to be pleasure, may be represented by unity. Such a degree of intensity is in every day's experience: according as any pleasures are perceived to be more and more intense, they may be represented by higher and higher numbers: but there is no fixing upon any particular degree of intensity as being the highest of which a pleasure is susceptible.[15]

(This suggested measure will be discussed in connection with the Weber-Fechner literature.) Then, shifting ground, Bentham argues that, although utility does not increase as fast as income, for small changes the two move proportionately,[16] so we may measure pleasures through the prices they command:

If then between two pleasures the one produced by the possession of money, the other not, a man had as lief enjoy the one as the other, such pleasures are to be reputed equal. But the pleasure produced by the possession of money, is *as* the quantity of money that produces it: money is therefore the measure of this pleasure. But the other pleasure is equal to this; the other pleasure therefore is as the money that produces this: therefore money is also the measure of that other pleasure.[17]

Unfortunately, this procedure is illegitimate; we cannot use an equality (or, more strictly, a constancy of the marginal utility of money) that holds for small changes to measure total utilities.[18] These suggestions are important chiefly in revealing Bentham's awareness of the crucial problems in his calculus and his ingenuity in attempting to solve them.[19]

Bentham had indeed planted the tree of utility. No reader could overlook the concept of utility as a numerical magnitude; and the implications for economic analysis were not obscure. But they were overlooked.

The Ricardians

The economists of Bentham's time did not follow the approach he had opened. One may conjecture that this failure is due to the fact that Ricardo, who gave the economics of this period much of its slant and direction, was not a Benthamite. It is true that he was the friend of Bentham and the close friend of James Mill, Bentham's leading disciple. Yet there is no evidence that he was a devout utilitarian and much evidence that he was unphilosophical — essentially a pragmatic reformer.[20]

It is clear, in any event, that Ricardo did not apply the utility calculus to economics. He began his *Principles* with the quotation of Smith's distinction between value in use and value in exchange and ended the volume with the statement: "Value in use cannot be measured by any known standard; it is differently estimated by different persons."[21] I should be content to notice that he left the theory of utility as highly developed as he found it — as much cannot be said for the theory of value — were it not for a remarkable interpretation of Marshall's:

> Again, in a profound, though very incomplete, discussion of the difference between "Value and Riches" he seems to be feeling his way towards the distinction between marginal and total utility. For by Riches he means total utility, and he seems to be always on the point of stating that value corresponds to the increment of riches which results from that part of the commodity which it is only just worth the while of purchasers to buy; and that when the supply runs short, whether temporarily in consequence of a passing accident, or permanently in consequence of an increase in cost of production, there is a rise in that marginal increment of riches which is measured by value, at the same time that there is a diminution in the aggregate riches, the total utility, derived from the commodity. Throughout the whole discussion he is trying to say, though (being ignorant of the terse language of the differential calculus) he did not get hold of the right words in which to say it neatly, that marginal utility is raised and total utility is lessened by any check to supply.[22]

In the chapter (xx) referred to, Ricardo defines riches as "necessaries, conveniences, and amusements," and value, as usual, is measured by the amount of labor necessary to produce a commodity. The chapter is essentially an exercise in the paradoxes of this definition of value; for example, if the productivity of labor doubles, riches double, but value changes only if the number of laborers changes. We may properly identify "necessaries, conveniences, and amusements" with total utility; but what of marginal utility? Ricardo says that, if a person receives two sacks of corn where formerly he received one, "he gets, indeed double the quantity of riches — double the quantity of utility — double the quantity of what Adam Smith calls value in use."[23] Hence he did not believe that marginal utility diminishes as quantity increases. He continued:

When I give 2,000 times more cloth for a pound of gold than I give for a pound of iron, does it prove that I attach 2,000 times more utility to gold than I do to iron? certainly not; it proves only as admitted by M. Say, that the cost of production of gold is 2,000 times greater than the cost of production of iron . . . if utility were the measure of value, it is probable I should give more for the iron.[24]

The writer of this passage cannot be said to have been close to the notion of marginal utility. I cannot find a single sentence that gives support to Marshall's interpretation, and I think that it should be added to the list of examples of his peculiar documentation and interpretation of predecessors.

Ricardo's influence was such that James Mill, the logical person to apply Bentham's system to economics, was content to present a rigid simplification of Ricardo's *Principles*;[25] and his son — whose formative work in economics, we must remember, came chiefly in the 1820's — did little more with utility.[26] Only the French utilitarian, J. B. Say, attempted to give utility a substantial place in economic theory, and he was prevented from doing so effectively by his inability to arrive at a notion of marginal analysis. In order to support the thesis that prices are proportional to utilities, he was driven to invent the metaphysical distinction between natural and social wealth:

One pays 2,000 times as much for a pound of gold as for a pound of iron. Here is how, on my theory, this phenomenon is explained. I assume with you that a pound of iron has the same utility as a pound of gold, although it is worth only one-two-thousandth as much. I say that there are in the iron 1,999 degrees of utility that nature has given us without charge, and 1 degree that we create by work, at an expense that we will assume only if a consumer is willing to reimburse us; hence the pound of iron has 2,000 degrees of utility. The gold also has 2,000 degrees of utility (on your assumption), which however can be obtained only on exacting terms, that is to say, . . . by expenses of 2,000. The 1,999 degrees of utility for which we do not pay when we consume iron are part of our natural wealth. . . . The single degree of utility which must be paid for is part of our social wealth.[27]

II.   THE UNSUCCESSFUL DISCOVERERS

The principle that equal increments of utility-producing means (such as income or bread) yield diminishing increments of utility is a commonplace. The first statement in print of a commonplace is adventitious; it is of no importance in the development of economics, and it confers no intellectual stature on its author. The statement acquires interest only when it is logically developed or explicitly applied to economic problems, and it acquires importance only when a considerable number of economists are persuaded to incorporate it into their analyses. Interest and importance are of course matters of degree.

Some economists gave clear statements of the principle of diminishing marginal utility but did not apply it to economic problems; they include Lloyd (1833), Senior (1836), Jennings (1855), and Hearn (1864).[28] Others applied utility theory to economic events without explicitly developing the principle of diminishing marginal utility: A. Walras (1831) and Longfield (1834), for example.[29] At least two economists — in addition to Bentham — elaborated the principle or applied it to economic problems but failed to persuade other economists of its usefulness.[30] Their theories will be summarized briefly.

Dupuit (1844)

Jules Dupuit, a distinguished engineer, was led to the marginal utility theory by his attempt to construct a theory of prices that maximize utility.[31] He distinguished total and marginal utility with great clarity and discovered "une espèce de bénéfice" that we now call *consumers' surplus*. It was defined as the excess of total utility over marginal utility times the number of units of the commodity, but it was actually taken to be the area under the demand curve minus the expenditures on the commodity (i.e., Marshall's measure without his restrictions).[32]

Armed with this concept, he investigated the optimum toll on a bridge. His analysis was as follows. Let NP be the demand (and marginal utility) curve, Op the price (Fig. 1). Then $OrnP$ is the absolute utility consumers obtain from the use of the bridge, and pnP is the relative utility. If the toll is reduced by pp', there is a net gain of consumer utility of qnn' (equal to the area under the demand curve between r and r' minus the expenditure $rr'n'q$).

Dupuit's general conclusion is: "The utility of a means of communication, and in general of any product, is at a maximum when the toll or the price is zero."[33] This is little more than a tautology, and Dupuit did not draw the further and illegitimate conclusion that the optimum toll rate is zero:

It will not be our conclusion [that tolls should be small or zero], when we treat of tariffs; but we hope to have demonstrated that [tariff rates] must be studied, combined on rational principles to produce simultaneously the greatest possible utility and a revenue which will repay the expense of maintenance and the interest on the capital investment.[34]

We see that he was not afraid of interpersonal comparisons of utility, and in fact he argued that the effects of price changes on the distribution of income must be ignored because they were merely transfers.[35]

Dupuit could not reach a complete theory of optimum prices because he did not devise a coherent theory of cost.[36] One is impressed by the narrowness of his vision; the explicit formulation of the concept of consumer surplus is elegant, but there is no intuition of the difficulties in the concept,

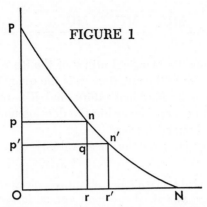

FIGURE 1

nor is there an attempt to construct the larger theoretical framework necessary to solve his problem.

Gossen (1854)

Heinrich Gossen is one of the most tragic figures in the history of economics. He was a profound, original, and untrained thinker who hid his
thoughts behind painfully complex arithmetical and algebraic exercises.[37]
He displayed every trait of the crank,[38] excepting only one: history has so
far believed that he was right. Only a few distinctive features of his work
will be commented upon.

First, Gossen's discussion of the laws of satisfaction is concerned only
with individual acts of consumption, such as the eating of slices of bread.[39]
Correspondingly, in his early diagrams marginal utility is a function of time
(duration of the act of consumption), and only after a considerable elaboration of this approach does he take quantity of a (perishable) commodity
as proportional to duration of consumption.[40] Yet he does not attempt to
work out a theory of the temporal pattern of consumption, and this portion
of his theory seems misdirected.

Second, he presents a theory of the marginal disutility of labor that is
completely symmetrical with that of the marginal utility of consumer goods.
Gossen's curve of the marginal disutility of income is essentially identical
with that which Jevons made famous: the early hours of work yield utility,
but, as the duration of labor increases, the marginal utility diminishes to
zero and then to negative values.[41] He defines the condition of maximum
utility as that in which the marginal utility of a unit of product is numerically equal to the marginal disutility of the labor necessary to produce
a unit of product.[42]

Third, Gossen was the first writer to formulate explicitly what I shall
call the fundamental principle of marginal utility theory:

> A person maximizes his utility when he distributes his available money among
> the various goods so that he obtains the same amount of satisfaction from the last
> unit of money (*Geldatom*) spent upon each commodity.[43]

We may translate this statement into semisymbolic form:

$$\frac{MU_1}{p_1} = \frac{MU_2}{p_2} = \frac{MU_3}{p_3} = \cdots,$$

where MU_i represents the marginal utility of the ith commodity and p_i its price. (We shall adhere to the notation: x_i is the quantity of commodity X_i, p_i is its price, MU_i is its marginal utility, and R is money income.) This equation marked a long step forward in the development of the relationship between utility and demand curves.

Finally, Gossen's views on the measurability of utility are vague but tantalizing:

> We can conceive of the magnitudes of various pleasures only by comparing them with one another, as, indeed, we must also do in measuring other objects. We can measure the magnitudes of various areas only by taking a particular area as the unit of measurement, or the weights of different bodies only by taking a particular weight as the unit. Similarly, we must fix on one pleasure as our unit, and hence an indefiniteness remains in the measurement of a pleasure. It is a matter of indifference which pleasure we choose as the unit. Perhaps the consequences will be most convenient if we choose the pleasure from the commodity which we use as money.[44]

He did not notice that there might be no unit of utility comparable with that of area or weight; and it is probably going too far to read into this passage the later position that it is sufficient to deal with the ratios of marginal utilities.

III. THE BEGINNINGS OF THE MODERN THEORY

The utility theory finally began to win a place in generally accepted economics in the 1870's, under the triple auspices of Jevons, Menger, and Walras. Independently these economists arrived at positions similar in the main and sometimes in detail.[45] I shall compare their treatments of certain basic problems of the theory, and henceforth our organization will be by subject.

A. Criticism of Received Doctrine

Each of these founders of utility theory criticized the Ricardian theory of value, but for each this was an incidental and minor point; they deemed the positive merits of the utility theory a sufficient basis for acceptance. Thus, only after completing the presentation of his utility theory did Jevons point out the deficiencies in Ricardo's labor value theory. These deficiencies were three: (1) Ricardo required a special theory for commodities with fixed supplies, such as rare statues. This proved that labor cost is not essential to value. (2) Large labor costs will not confer high value on a commodity if the future demand is erroneously forecast; "in commerce bygones are for ever bygones."[46] (3) Labor is heterogeneous, and the various types of labor can be compared only through the values of their products.[47] On the other hand, the cost of production theory of value fits in nicely as a special case of the utility theory, for it explains the relative quantities of commodities that will be supplied.[48]

Menger and Walras took fundamentally the same position. The former also gave the first two criticisms listed above and, in addition, made a parallel criticism to the Ricardian rent theory: if the value of land did not depend upon labor cost, this demonstrated a serious lack of generality in the classical theory of value.[49] Walras repeated the criticism that the classical theory lacked generality, emphasized the reciprocal effects of prices of products and of productive services on one another, and denied the existence of the class of commodities whose supplies could be infinitely increased, on the overly literal ground that no productive resource was available in infinite quantity.[50]

The task of elaborating and expounding the theory, and of exaggerating its merits and understating the usefulness of the classical theory — the inevitable accompaniments of intellectual innovations — fell largely to disciples, in particular Wieser and Böhm-Bawerk. These men did not improve on the substance of the theory — in fact, it deteriorated in their hands — so we shall pass them by.[51]

B. The Existence and Measurability of Utility

Without exception, the founders accepted the existence of utility as a fact of common experience, congruent with the most casual introspection. Jevons was most explicit:

> The science of Economics, however, is in some degree peculiar, owing to the fact . . . that its ultimate laws are known to us immediately by intuition, or, at any rate, they are furnished to us ready made by other mental or physical sciences.
> . . . The theory here given may be described as *the mechanics of utility and self-interest*. Oversights may have been committed in tracing out its details, but in its main features this theory must be the true one. Its method is as sure and demonstrative as that of kinematics or statics, nay, almost as self-evident as are the elements of Euclid. . . .[52]

I am inclined to interpret the silence of Menger and Walras on the existence of utility as indicative of an equally complete acceptance.

Menger glossed over the problem of measurability of utility. He represented marginal utilities by numbers and employed an equality of marginal utilities in various uses as the criterion of the optimum allocation of a good.[53] His word for utility — *Bedeutung* — was surely intentionally neutral, but probably it was chosen for its nonethical flavor.[54] Walras was equally vague; he simply assumed the existence of a unit of measure of intensity of utility and thereafter spoke of utility as an absolute magnitude.[55]

Jevons' attack on the problem of measurability was characteristically frank and confused. He denied that utility was measurable:

> There is no unit of labour, or suffering, or enjoyment.
> I have granted that we can hardly form the conception of a unit of pleasure

or pain, so that the numerical expression of quantities of feeling seems to be out of question.[56]

Yet he seemed also to argue that one cannot be sure that utility is not measurable but only that it could not presently be measured.[57] He was somewhat more skeptical of the measurability of utility in the first (1871) than in the second (1879) edition; for example, in the second edition he deleted the following passage:

> I confess that it seems to me difficult even to imagine how such estimations [of utility] and summations can be made with any approach to accuracy. Greatly though I admire the clear and precise notions of Bentham, I know not where his numerical data are to be found.[58]

With gallant inconsistency, he proceeded to devise a way to measure utility. It employed the familiar measuring rod of money:

> It is from the quantitative effects of the feelings that we must estimate their comparative amounts.
> I never attempt to estimate the whole pleasure gained by purchasing a commodity; the theory merely expressed that, when a man has purchased enough, he would derive equal pleasure from the possession of a small quantity more as he would from the money price of it.[59]

This position is elaborated ingeniously: We can construct a demand curve by observation (or possibly experiment), and then we can pass to the marginal utility curve by means of the equation,

$$MU_r p_i = MU_i \, ,$$

where MU_r is the marginal utility of income.[60]

> For the first approximation we may assume that the general utility of a person's income is not affected by the changes of price of the commodity. . . .
> The method of determining the function of utility explained above will hardly apply, however, to the main elements of expenditure. The price of bread, for instance, cannot be properly brought under the equation in question, because, when the price of bread rises much, the resources of poor persons are strained, money becomes scarcer with them, and $[MU_r]$, the [marginal] utility of money, rises.[61]

This procedure is so similar to Marshall's that we may defer comment until we discuss the latter's more elaborate version.

Unlike Walras and Menger, Jevons considered the question of the interpersonal comparison of utilities. He expressly argued that this was impossible[62] but made several such comparisons, as we shall notice later. Menger avoided the subject and did not engage in such comparisons; and Walras made only incidental interpersonal comparisons.[63]

C. Utility Maximization and the Demand Curve

Menger simply ignored the relationship between utility and demand. He was content to set some demand prices (he worked always with discontinuous schedules) which somehow represented marginal utilities[64] and proceeded to an elementary discussion of pricing under bilateral monopoly (the indeterminacy of which was recognized), duopoly (the complications of which were not recognized — a competitive solution was given), and competition (in which the absence of a theory of production had predictable effects).[65]

Jevons' attempt to construct a bridge between utility and demand was seriously hampered, I suspect, by his inability to translate any but simple thoughts into mathematics. His fundamental equation for the maximization of utility in exchanges was presented as a *fait accompli*:

$$\frac{MU_1}{MU_2} = \frac{p_1}{p_2}.$$

This equation was satisfactory for an individual confronted by fixed prices, but how to apply it to competitive markets?

Jevons devised two concepts to reach the market analysis: the trading body and the law of indifference. A trading body was the large group of buyers or sellers of a commodity in a competitive market.[66] The law of indifference was that there be only one price in a market.[67]

He proceeded in the following peculiar manner. Let the equation of exchange be applied to each trading body; for each group of competitive individuals the equation will determine the relationship between the quantity offered and the quantity demanded.[68] Hence we have two equations to determine the two unknowns: the quantities of x_1 and x_2 exchanged. Quite aside from the ambiguous concept of a trading body, this procedure was illicit on his own view that utilities of different individuals are not comparable.[69]

Walras succeeded in establishing the correct relationship between utility and demand. He first derived the equations of maximum satisfaction for an individual: if there are m commodities, and a unit of commodity x_1 is the *numéraire* in terms of which the prices of other commodities are expressed (so $p_1 = 1$), we have $(m - 1)$ equations:[70]

$$MU_1 = \frac{MU_2}{p_2} = \frac{MU_3}{p_3} = \ldots$$

Finally, the budget equation states the equality of values of the initial stocks of commodities (x_i^0) and the stocks held after exchange:

$$x_1 + x_2 p_2 + x_3 p_3 + \ldots = x_1^0 + x_2^0 p_2 + x_3^0 p_3 + \ldots.$$

We thus have m equations to determine the m quantities of the commodities demanded or supplied by the individual. We may solve the equations for the quantities demanded or supplied as functions of the prices:

$$x_2 = x_2 \, (p_2, p_3, \ldots)$$
$$x_3 = x_3 \, (p_2, p_3, \ldots)$$
$$\ldots\ldots\ldots\ldots\ldots$$
$$x_1 = (x_1^0 + x_2^0 p_2 + x_3^0 p_3 + \ldots) - (x_2 p_2 + x_3 p_3 + \ldots).$$

The $x_1, x_2, x_3, \ldots$, are the quantities held (demanded), and $(x_1^0 - x_1)$, $(x_2^0 - x_2)$, $(x_3^0 - x_3)$, $\ldots$, the quantities supplied.[71]

617

To determine the market prices, we simply add the demands of all n individuals in the market for each commodity

$$X_2 = \sum^n x_2 = \sum^n x_2 \, (p_2, p_3, \ldots)$$

$$X_3 = \sum^n x_3 = \sum^n x_3 \, (p_2, p_3, \ldots)$$

. . . .

and equate the quantities demanded to the quantities available (X_i^0)

$$X_2^0 = X_2$$
$$X_3^0 = X_3$$

. . . .

There are $(m-1)$ such equations with which to determine the $(m-1)$ prices of $x_2, x_3, \ldots$, in terms of x_1. It may appear that we have forgotten the budget equation, but it is not an independent relationship because it can be deduced from the other equations. If we multiply the last set of equations by the respective prices of the commodities and add, we obtain

$$p_2 \, (X_2^0 - X_2) + p_3 \, (X_3^0 - X_3) + \ldots = 0 \, .$$

But if we add the individual budget equations we obtain

$$\sum^n x_1 - X_1^0 = p_2 \, (X_2^0 - X_2) + p_3 \, (X_3^0 - X_3) + \ldots = 0 \, .$$

Hence if the quantity demanded equals the quantity available in $(m-1)$ markets, the equality must also hold in the mth market. This is equivalent to saying that if we know the amounts of $(m-1)$ commodities that have been exchanged for each other and an mth commodity, and the rates of exchange, we necessarily know the amount of the mth commodity exchanged.

The (Walrasian) demand function is thus the relationship between the quantity of a commodity and all prices, when the individual's (or individuals') money income and tastes (utility functions) are held constant. We shall adhere to this meaning of the demand function or "curve" (the two-dimensional illustration of course requiring that all prices except that of the commodity are held constant), and the relationship between quantity and money income (all prices and tastes being held constant) will be designated as the income curve.

D. The Applications of the Theory

Jevons gave only one application of his utility theory: a demonstration that both parties to an exchange gain satisfaction. The demonstration, as he gave it, was inconsistent with his denial of the possibility of comparing utilities of individuals, for it rested on the marginal utility curves of nations.[72]

Menger was even less specific but surely vastly more persuasive in his applications of the theory: he made it the basis of economic theory. The theory was given many everyday illustrations (mostly hypothetical, to be sure): it explained exchange, the wages of textile workers during the Civil

War cotton shortage, the shifts of goods between free and economic, etc. More important, the theory of production became simply an instance of the theory of marginal utility: productive services were distinguished from consumption services only in being goods of higher order. Menger's version had no predictive value, nor did he conjecture any new economic relationships. Indeed at least two of the founders of marginal utility theory — Jevons was the exception — knew much less about economic life than a dozen predecessors such as Smith and Babbage. Yet the theory served to systematize a variety of known facts of everyday observation and seemed to confer an air of generality and structural elegance upon price theory.

Walras also did a good deal of this reorientation of economic theory in terms of utility, whereby the value of productive services was determined by the values of products. But he also attempted a specific and natural application of the theory to demand-curve analysis.

This application was the derivation of the law that price reductions will increase the quantity demanded; price increases will decrease the quantity demanded.[73] Walras treated this as intuitively obvious, but it was a strict implication of his theory. Consider the equations of maximum satisfaction:

$$\frac{MU_1}{p_1} = \frac{MU_2}{p_2} = \frac{MU_3}{p_3} = \ldots$$

Assume p_2 falls by δp_2, and assume that the individual is deprived of his nominal increase in real income, $x_2 \delta p_2$. At the new price, $p_2 - \delta p_2$, the individual obtains a larger marginal utility per dollar from X_2 than from other commodities, hence he will substitute X_2 for other commodities. Restore now the increment of income $x_2 \delta p_2$, and it will be used to purchase more of every commodity, including x_2. The individual necessarily buys more X_2 at a lower price, and therefore all individuals buy more of X_2 at a lower price: the demand curve for each product must have a negative slope.[74]

A second application of utility theory was made in the theorem on the distribution of stocks: a redistribution of initial stocks of goods among the individuals in a market, such that each individual's holdings have the same market value before and after the redistribution, will not affect prices.[75] It is the amount of income, not its composition in terms of goods, that influences consumer behavior. The most interesting point with respect to this obvious theorem is that Walras stopped here on the threshold of the analysis of the effects of income upon consumption. One may conjecture that his penchant for analyzing what are essentially barter problems in his theory of exchange played a large role in this failure to analyze income effects.[76]

The theory of utility also led Walras to his theory of multiple equilibria.[77] This theory deals with the exchange of one commodity for another in a competitive market, when both commodities have utility to the individual.[78] The possessors of X_1 have a fixed stock — how much will they offer at various prices of X_1 (in terms of X_2)? When p_1 is zero (no X_2 is given in exchange for a unit of X_1), they will naturally supply no X_1; the supply curve begins at (or above) the origin. At higher p_1, they will offer more X_1 to obtain more X_2, but beyond a certain price, L, further increases in the price of X_1 will lead them to reduce the quantity of X_1 offered because they become relatively sated with X_2. Walras illustrates this with Figure 2, where D is the demand curve and S the supply curve. A' and A'' are points of stable equilibrium, because at higher prices the quantity supplied exceeds the quantity demanded and at lower prices the quantity demanded exceeds the quantity supplied. Point A, however, is an unstable equilibrium because at higher prices the quantity demanded exceeds the quantity supplied so the price rises even more, and conversely at lower prices. We shall not follow the history of multiple equilibria, in which economists have usually taken an apprehensive pride.

In the area of welfare economics, Walras' most important application was the theorem on maximum satisfaction:

> Production in a market governed by free competition is an operation by which the [productive] services may be combined in products of appropriate kind and quantity to give the greatest possible satisfaction of needs within the limits of the double condition that each service and each product have only one price in the market, at which supply and demand are equal, and that the prices of the products are equal to their costs of production.[79]

This theorem, which is not true unless qualified in several respects, gave rise to an extensive literature which lies outside our scope.[80]

IV.   THE FORM OF THE UTILITY FUNCTION

The three founders of the utility theory treated the utility of a commodity as a function only of the quantity of that commodity. If x_1, x_2, x_3, . . . , are the commodities, the individual's total utility was written (explicitly by Jevons and Walras, implicitly by Menger), as

$$f(x_1) + g(x_2) + h(x_3) + \dots .$$

They further assumed that each commodity yielded diminishing marginal utility. This form of utility function has the implication that the demand curve for each commodity has a negative slope, as I have already remarked. It has also the implication that an increase in income will lead to increased purchases of every commodity. This is easily shown with the fundamental equations,

$$MU_r = \frac{MU_1}{p_1} = \frac{MU_2}{p_2} = \frac{MU_3}{p_3} = \dots .$$

If income increases, the marginal utility of every commodity (and of income) must decrease, but the marginal utility of a commodity can be reduced only by increasing its quantity. This implication was not noticed.

Edgeworth destroyed this pleasant simplicity and specificity when he wrote the total utility function as $\varphi(x_1, x_2, x_3, \dots)$. He appears to have made this change partly because it was mathematically more general, partly because it was congruent with introspection.[81] The change had important implications for the measurability of utility that I shall discuss in Section V.

With the additive utility function, diminishing marginal utility was a

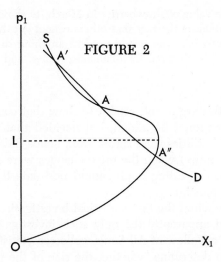

FIGURE 2

sufficient condition for convexity of the indifference curves;[82] with the generalized utility function, diminishing marginal utility was neither necessary nor sufficient for convex indifference curves.[83] Nevertheless, Edgeworth unnecessarily continued to assume diminishing marginal utility, but he also postulated the convexity of the indifference curves.[84]

Even with convexity, the generalized utility function no longer has the corollary that all income curves have positive slopes (or, therefore, that all demand curves have negative slopes). After a price reduction, δp_2, we may again segregate the effect of a change in relative prices by temporarily reducing the individual's income by $x_2 \delta p_2$. When we restore this increment of real income, we cannot be sure that each commodity will be consumed in larger quantity. Suppose an increase in X_1 reduces the marginal utility of X_2. Then when a portion of the increment of real income $x_2 \delta p_2$ is spent on X_1, MU_2 may diminish so much that the amount of X_2 must be reduced below its original quantity to fulfil the maximum satisfaction conditions.[85]

The only further generalization of the utility function (aside from questions of measurability) was the inclusion of the quantities consumed by other people in the utility function of the individual. Thus one's pleasure from diamonds is reduced if many other people have them (or if none do!), and one's pleasure from a given income is reduced if others' incomes rise. This line of thought is very old,[86] but it was first introduced explicitly into utility analysis in 1892. Fisher casually suggested it:

> Again we could treat [utility] as a function of the quantities of each commodity produced or consumed by *all persons* in the market. This becomes important when we consider a man in relation to the members of his family or consider articles of fashion as diamonds, also when we account for that (never thoroughly studied) interdependence, the division of labor.[87]

Henry Cunynghame made the same suggestion more emphatically in the same year:

Almost the whole value of strawberries in March, to those who like this taste-less mode of ostentation, is the fact that others cannot get them. As my landlady once remarked, "Surely, sir, you would not like anything so common and cheap as a fresh herring?" The demand for diamonds, rubies, and sapphires is another example of this.[88]

Pigou took up this argument, used it to show that consumer surpluses of various individuals cannot be added, but decided that these interrelation-ships of individuals' utilities were stable (and hence did not vitiate the con-sumer surplus apparatus) when the price changes were small.[89] It was only proper that Marshall's leading pupil should postulate the constancy of the marginal utility of prestige.

Pigou's article elicited the first statistical investigation designed to test a utility theory (and apparently the only such investigation during the pe-riod). Edgeworth, a Fellow of All Souls, collected statistics from "a certain Oxford College" to determine "whether the size of the party has any influ-ence upon the depth of the potations" — that is, upon the per capita con-sumption of wine. The data were presented in relative form lest they "should excite the envy of some and the contempt of others"; the conclusion was that the effect of the size of party was inappreciable.[90]

A few subsequent attempts have been made to revive this extension of the utility function to include the effect on one person's utility of other people's consumption, but the main tradition has ignored the extension. This neglect seems to have stemmed partly from a belief in the unimportance of the effect and partly from the obstacles it would put in the way of drawing specific inferences from utility analysis.

There remain three subordinate topics that may conveniently be dis-cussed here. They are (a) the graphical exposition of the theory of the gen-eralized utility function; (b) the attitude of contemporary economists toward Edgeworth's generalization; and (c) the Bernoulli hypothesis on the shape of the utility function.

A. Indifference Curves

With the introduction of the interrelationship of utilities of commodities, it was no longer possible to portray total utility graphically in two dimen-sions. Edgeworth devised indifference curves, or contour lines, to permit of a graphical analysis of utility in this case. In itself this was merely an exposi-tional advance, but it merits summarization because of its great popularity in modern times and because it later invited attention to questions relating to the measurability of utility.

We restrict ourselves to the case of two commodities, as Edgeworth and almost everyone since has done in graphical analysis.[91] We define the in-difference curve as the combinations of X_1 and X_2 yielding equal satisfac-tion, i.e., $\varphi(x_1,x_2) = $ constant. Edgeworth chose an asymmetrical graphical illustration of these curves that had a definite advantage for his purpose of

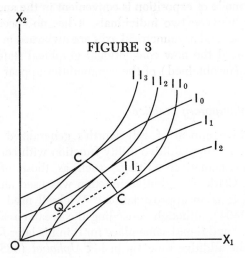

FIGURE 3

analyzing bilateral monopoly. He let the abscissa represent the quantity of X_1 obtained by the individual, and the ordinate represent the quantity of X_2 given up.

It is evident that such indifference curves have a positive slope (if both commodities are desirable), for the individual will require more X_1 to offset (in utility) the loss of more X_2. In fact, the slope of the indifference curve with respect to the X_1 axis will be

$$\frac{dx_2}{dx_1} = \frac{MU_1}{MU_2}.^{92}$$

In addition, Edgeworth postulated that the indifference curves are concave to the X_1 axis.

Edgeworth's pioneer demonstration of the indeterminacy of bilateral monopoly will illustrate the advantage of this formulation.[93] A trader possessing X_2 but no X_1 would be at the origin; his indifference curves are those labeled I in Figure 3. The second trader, who possesses X_1 but no X_2, will have the corresponding indifference curves (II), for he will be giving up X_1 and acquiring X_2 in exchange. The points where the two sets of indifference curves are tangent form a curve, CC, which Edgeworth christened the contract curve. The ends of the contract curve are determined by the condition that no trader be worse off after trading than before, i.e., by the indifference curves, I_0 and II_0. The final contract between the traders must take place on this contract curve, because if it occurred elsewhere, it would be to the gain of one party, and not to the loss of the other, to move to the curve. Thus point Q was not a tenable point of final contract because individual II can move from II_1 to the higher indifference curve II_2, while I remains on the same indifference curve, I_1. Any point on the contract curve is a position of possible equilibrium, and the precise position reached will be governed by "higgling dodges and designing obstinacy, and other incalculable and often disreputable accidents."[94]

623

Although this mode of exposition is convenient in the analysis of trade in two commodities between two individuals, it has no special advantage in the competitive case, and asymmetrical axes are awkward in algebraic analysis. Fisher introduced the now conventional graphical statement, in which the amounts held (or obtained) of the commodities appear on all axes.[95]

B. Contemporary Practice

Despite the intuitive appeal of Edgeworth's generalized utility function, economists adhered to the additive utility function with considerable tenacity. In the nonmathematical writings, such as those of Böhm-Bawerk, Wieser, and J. B. Clark, the additive function was used almost exclusively. Barone defended it as an approximation.[96] Wicksell used it exclusively in his *Über Wert* (1894), although conceding the greater realism of the generalized function,[97] and found some place for it in his later *Lectures*.[98] Wicksteed used only the additive function in his *Alphabet* (1888)[99] and also in the elementary exposition of the theory in his *Common Sense* (1910) but not in the "advanced" statement.[100] Finally, Marshall and Pareto were so influential as to require more extended discussion.

Marshall also started with the Jevons-Walras assumption, to which he had probably arrived independently. This assumption was not explicit in the first edition of the *Principles* (1890), but one can cite evidence of its presence.

First, in his mathematical characterization of the utility function Marshall ignores any interdependence of utilities.[101] Second, he asserts the law of negatively sloping demand curves in all generality: "There is then one law and only one law which is common to all demand schedules, viz. that the greater the amount to be sold the smaller will be the price at which it will find purchasers."[102] This is a corollary of diminishing marginal utility only if the utility function is additive. Third, he was prepared to measure the utility of all commodities as the sum of the individual utilities: "We may regard the aggregate of the money measures of the total utility of wealth as a fair measure of that part of happiness which is dependent on wealth."[103]

In the second edition (1891) the assumption became reasonably explicit:

> Prof. Edgeworth's plan of representing U and V as general functions of x and y has great attractions to the mathematician; but it seems less adapted to express the everyday facts of economic life than that of regarding, as Jevons did, the marginal utilities of apples as functions of x simply.[104]

The facts both of everyday life and of contemporary theory soon led Marshall to make serious qualifications of his theory but never to qualify this statement.

Even in the first edition Marshall had inconsistently recognized the existence of "rival" products, which were defined as products able to satisfy the same desires.[105] Fisher's discussion of competing and completing goods seems to have been the stimulus to Marshall to give more weight to interrelationships of utilities in the third edition of the *Principles* (1895).[106] Once persuaded, Marshall modified his theory on two points. The first was that he slightly modified his assertion of the universality of negatively sloping demand curves and in fact introduced the Giffen paradox as an exception.[107] The second alteration was in his treatment of consumers' surplus: "When the total utilities of two commodities which contribute to the same purpose are calculated on this plan, we cannot say that the total utility of the two together is equal to the sum of the total utilities of each separately."[108] No important changes were made thereafter.

These alterations were only patchwork repairs; Marshall did not rework his theory of utility. He retained to the last a theory constructed on the assumption of an additive utility function.

Pareto also conceded the validity of the Edgeworth generalization but continued to use chiefly the additive function in his early work.[109] Indeed, he offered the remarkable argument:

One sees now that instead of being able to use the indicated properties of the final degree of utility to demonstrate what laws demand and supply must obey, it is necessary to follow the opposite path, and use the knowledge of such laws one may obtain from experience to derive the properties of the final degree of utility. One cannot rigorously demonstrate the law of demand, but rather, from the directly observable fact that demand diminishes with the increase of price we deduce the consequence that the final degrees of utility may each be considered — as far as this phenomenon is concerned — as approximately dependent only on the quantity of the commodity to which it is related.[110]

In the *Manuel*, however, he showed that the additive utility function leads to conclusions which are contradicted by experience,[111] but defended it as an approximation which was permissible for large categories of expenditure and for small changes in the quantities of substitutes or complements.[112] There is no reason to believe that this is true.

C. The Bernoulli Hypothesis

The precise shape of the utility function received little attention in the main tradition of utility theory. Occasionally it was stated that the marginal utility of a necessity falls rapidly as its quantity increases and the like; and there were some mystical references to the infinite utility of subsistence. These were *ad hoc* remarks, however, and were not explicitly developed parts of the formal theory. Only one hypothesis about the marginal utility function ever achieved prominence: it was the Bernoulli hypothesis, which ultimately merged with the Weber-Fechner law, and to this literature we now turn.

In 1713 Nicholas Bernoulli proposed to a French mathematician, Montmort, five problems in probability theory,[113] one of which was equivalent to the following:

Peter tosses a coin in the air repeatedly until it falls heads up. If this occurs on the first throw, he pays Paul $1.00; if this occurs first on the second throw, he pays $2.00; on the third throw, $4.00; on the fourth throw, $8.00; and on the nth throw, 2.00^{n-1}. What is the maximum amount Paul should pay for this game?

Montmort replied, perhaps too easily, "Les deux derniers de vos cinq Problêmes n'ont aucune difficulté,"[114] for this was to become known as the St. Petersburg paradox.

Twenty-five years later Daniel Bernoulli introduced the paradox to fame.[115] Its paradoxical nature is easily explained: The probability of a head on the first throw is $\frac{1}{2}$, so the expected winning from the first throw is $\frac{1}{2}$ times $1.00, or $0.50. The probability of a first head on the second throw is $\frac{1}{4}$ ($\frac{1}{2}$ of tails on the first throw times $\frac{1}{2}$ of heads on the second), so the expected winning is $\frac{1}{4}$ times $2.00, or $0.50. The probability of a first head on the nth throw is $(\frac{1}{2})^n$, so the expected winnings are $(\frac{1}{2})^n$ times 2.00^{n-1}, or $0.50. Since these probabilities are exclusive, we add them to obtain the expected winnings from the game, which are $0.50 times the infinite possible number of throws. Thus the expected winnings of Paul are infinity — an excessive price for Paul to pay for the game, as even the mathematicians saw.

Bernoulli's solution was to take into account the diminishing marginal utility of money. In the later words of Laplace, he distinguished the mathematical from the moral expectation of a chance event upon which a sum of money depended: the moral expectation was defined as the sum of the products of the various advantages accruing from various sums of money times their respective probabilities.[116] To Bernoulli, "it appears in the highest degree probable" that each equal increment of gain yields an advantage which is inversely proportional to the individual's wealth,[117] i.e.,

$$dU = k\,\frac{dx}{x},$$

where dU is the increment of utility resulting from an increment dx of wealth and k is constant. It follows that total utility is a logarithmic function of wealth,

$$U = k \log \frac{x}{c},$$

where c is the amount of wealth necessary for existence.[118]

Bernoulli applied this formula to gambling, obtaining the now traditional result that mathematically fair bets are disadvantageous to both parties because the utility of the sum that may be gained is less than the utility of the sum that may be lost.[119] By a converse application, he calculated the maximum amount one should pay for insurance of specified risks.[120] Finally, he solved the paradox: a person with $1,000 should pay $6; etc.[121]

We should notice one further point in this beautiful memoir:

If [the initial wealth] appears to be infinitely large relative to the greatest possible gain, the arc [of the total utility curve from initial wealth to initial wealth plus the gain] may be considered an infinitely short straight line, and in this case the usual rule [for calculating mathematical expectations] is again applicable. This case is closely approximated in all games in which relatively small sums are at stake.[122]

Thus Bernoulli suggested the assumption of a constant marginal utility of wealth for small variations of wealth.

We cannot follow the immense literature of the paradox in mathematics, but a few views may be noticed.[123] Some mathematicians — the foremost was Laplace[124] — accepted Bernoulli's solution. Some, like Poisson, solved the problem by taking into account Peter's inability to pay if he had a sufficiently long run of tails, so Paul should pay an amount for the game determined by Peter's fortune.[125] Perhaps the most amusing solution was one by Buffon, which was based on the "lemma" that all probabilities smaller than .0001 are equal to zero (because this was the probability of dying during the day for a man of fifty-six, which was commonly treated as negligible).[126] Cournot, here as in demand theory, refused to look at utility and resorted to the market evaluation of the game.[127]

Perhaps the most surprising characteristic of this literature to the economist is the mathematicians' chief requisite of a solution: that a finite value be found for the value of the game. This is the only merit one can attach to the "limited-fortune" solution of Poisson and others, and even its spurious plausibility depends upon the particular formulation of the problem.[128] Bernoulli was right in seeking the explanation in utility (or alternatively, as Cournot did, in market appraisals), and he was wrong only in making a special assumption with respect to the shape of the utility curve for which there was no evidence and which he submitted to no tests.[129]

In 1860 this line of thought was joined by the independent series of researches that culminated in the Weber-Fechner law. E. H. Weber had proposed the hypothesis: the just noticeable increment to any stimulus is proportional to the stimulus (R — $Reiz$), or

$$\frac{dR}{R} = k \ .$$

Fechner made this constant of just noticeable differences the unit of sensation (S), to obtain

$$dS = C \, \frac{dR}{R} \, ,$$

or, integrating, $S = C \log R/R_0$, where R_0 is the threshold of sensation. Fechner performed a vast number of experiments on weight, temperature, tonal, and other types of discriminations which the formula fitted fairly well, and in the process he devised several methods of measurement (such as the constant method, in which Weber's k is determined by the proportion of [e.g.] "greater" to total responses in weight comparisons).[130] This was construed — by Fechner also — as proof of Bernoulli's hypothesis, with stimulus identified with income, sensation with pleasure.[131]

We need not follow the detailed evolution of psychologists' treatment of the Fechner law. For decades it was a lively topic of discussion,[132] but for a generation or more it has been declining in importance. Many exceptions have been found to Fechner's formula.[133] The concept of sensation has been severely restricted in meaning, and the form of response of a subject was found to affect his sensitivity.[134] At present Fechner's *Elemente* is important chiefly for the basic methods of measurement he invented and improved.

Many economists in this later period noticed the Bernoulli or Weber-Fechner "laws." The majority simply referred to the hypothesis, favorably or otherwise, and made no real use of the theory. In this group we may list Edgeworth,[135] Pareto,[136] and Wicksell,[137] as well as many lesser figures.[138]

Marshall took the Bernoulli hypothesis much more seriously than did any other leading economist. In 1890 he was prepared to apply it directly to whole income classes:

> If however it should appear that the class affected [by a particular event] in the one case is on the average, say, ten times as rich as in the other, then we shall probably not be far wrong in supposing that the increment of happiness measured by a given sum of money in the one case is, so far at least as its direct results go, about one-tenth as great as in the other.[139]

Whatever the reason, this use of the hypothesis disappeared in the second edition, but lesser evidences of Marshall's affection for the Bernoulli theory persisted.[140]

A group of writers on tax justice, mostly Dutch, made considerable use of the theory in discussions of the ideal rate of income-tax progression.[141] The enthusiasm for the Bernoulli hypothesis diminished when it was discovered that it led to proportional taxation under the equal sacrifice doctrine (each taxpayer to sacrifice an equal amount of utility).[142] Although the doctrine of proportional sacrifice (each taxpayer to sacrifice an equal proportion of his utility) leads to progressive taxation with the Bernoulli utility function,[143] the minimum sacrifice doctrine (which insured progression if the marginal utility of income diminished) soon triumphed.

Two Italian writers used the logarithmic law in quantitative work: Gini, in the analysis of demand;[144] del Vecchio, in the analysis of budgetary data.[145] These studies belong in the history of demand theory, however; and we shall not discuss them here.

Max Weber's famous essay on the Weber-Fechner law is commonly, and perhaps properly, interpreted as a final demonstration that economists can ignore this law. Weber had three main points. First, the law does not hold in all cases ("Tiffany-Vasen, Klosettpapier, Schlackwurst, Klassiker-Ausgaben, Prostituierten . . ."). Second, the law refers to psychical reactions to external stimuli, whereas economics deals with observable behavior in response to subjective needs. Third, economics can get along with the empirical fact that man has limited means to satisfy competing ends and can allocate these means rationally to maximize the fulfilment of the ends.[146] This pungently written essay is hardly conclusive, however, on whether economists should adopt the law. This turns on whether it yields fruitful hypotheses concerning economic behavior. Since it does not,[147] it should not be used.

V. THE MEASURABILITY OF UTILITY

The first careful examination of the measurability of the utility function and its relevance to demand theory was made by Fisher.[148] He solved the

TABLE 1

Symbol	Increment of Milk		
	Quantity (Cubic Inches)	Utility of Increment of Milk	Total Utility of Milk
Δm_1	3	1	1
Δm_2	4	1	2
Δm_3	5	1	3
Δm_4	6	1	4
Δm_5	7	1	5

measurability problem quite satisfactorily for the case in which the marginal utilities of the various quantities are independent of one another.[149] His procedure was as follows:

Select arbitrarily a quantity of any commodity, say, 100 loaves of bread. Let the marginal utility of this quantity of commodity be the unit of utility (or util). Grant the ability of the individual to order the utilities of specified amounts of two goods, i.e., to indicate a preference (if one exists) or indifference between the two quantities. Then it is possible to construct the utility schedule of (say) milk. Start with no milk, and find the increment of milk (Δm_1) equivalent to the hundredth loaf of bread, i.e., the minimum amount of milk the individual would accept in exchange for the hundredth loaf of bread. Find a second increment (Δm_2), given the possession of Δm_1, equivalent to the hundredth loaf, etc. We obtain thus a schedule (or function) such as that given in Table 1. This function gives the amounts of milk necessary to obtain equal increments of utility; by interpolation we determine the amounts of utility obtained from equal increments of milk (Table 2).

This initial choice of a unit is arbitrary, but this is not objectionable:

Any unit in mathematics is valuable only as a divisor for a second quantity and constant only in the sense that the quotient is constant, that is, independent of a third quantity. If we should awaken tomorrow with every line in the universe doubled, we should never detect the change, if indeed such can be called a change, nor would it disturb our sciences or formulae.[150]

Suppose now that the marginal utility of milk depends not only upon the quantity of milk but also upon the quantities of bread and beer — more generally, suppose the generalized utility function of Edgeworth holds. We could proceed as before in finding the quantities of milk, Δm_1, Δm_2, . . . , whose utilities equaled that of the hundredth loaf of bread. Let us now shift to the marginal utility of (say) 60 bottles of beer as our unit and proceed in identical fashion to find $\Delta m_1'$, $\Delta m_2'$ . . . , and thus measure the utility of milk in terms of beer. We shall find the new increments of milk, $\Delta m_1'$, $\Delta m_2'$, . . . , are not proportional to the old,[151] because the marginal utilities of beer and of bread will vary differently as the quantity of milk increases. Hence the total utility curve of milk will take on an entirely new shape, and not merely differ by a proportionality factor, when we change the commod-

TABLE 2

Milk (Cubic Inches)	Total Utility of Milk	Marginal Utility of Milk*
3	1.0000	—
6	1.7667	.7667
9	2.4333	.6667
12	3.0000	.5667
15	3.4667	.4667

* Per 3 cubic inches.

ity in terms of which it is measured. Thus we can no longer use this procedure to measure utility.[152]

Fisher concludes his brilliant dissertation with the argument that the total utility function cannot in general be deduced from the indifference curves and that, for purposes of explaining consumers' reactions to prices and income changes, there is no occasion to introduce total utility:

> Thus if we seek only the causation of the *objective facts of prices and commodity distribution* four attributes of utility as a quantity are entirely unessential, (1) that one man's utility can be compared to another's, (2) that for the same individual the marginal utilities at one consumption-combination can be compared with those at another, or at one time with another, (3) even if they could, total utility and gain might not be integratable, (4) even if they were, there would be no need of determining the constants of integration.[153]

Fisher's statement of the difficulty of constructing total utility functions from differential equations of the indifference curves was extremely concise,[154] and we shall elaborate it in connection with Pareto. We may note in passing that thirty-five years later Fisher qualified much of this argument. He was now willing to assume independence of utilities (at least for broad categories such as food and housing) and comparability of utilities of different persons — in order, apparently, to achieve concrete results applicable to income taxation.[155]

Pareto was the great proponent of doubts on the existence of unique utility functions and of the relevance of such functions to economic behavior. Apparently independently of Fisher, Pareto noticed the problem of the existence of a utility function as early as 1892.[156] Soon thereafter most of his basic mathematical theory was developed.[157] The import of the theory was realized only slowly, however: in the *Cours* (1896 and 1897) he was still willing to accept the interpersonal comparison of utilities for welfare purposes.[158] In the *Manuel* (1909), however, measurable utility had fallen into the background — of his theory, if not of his exposition. For Pareto, two questions on measurability were at issue.

The first, and to Pareto the major, problem is this: We can deduce the slopes of indifference curves at (in principle) all possible combinations of goods from budgetary data, because the slopes of the price lines equal the ratios of the marginal utilities (slopes of indifference curves). Thus we obtain empirically the differential equation of the indifference curves. Can we integrate it to obtain the equation of the indifference curves?

Before we look at the mathematics, we may present the problem verbally. Will the choices that an individual makes between combinations of goods differing by infinitesimal amounts be consistent with the choices he makes between combinations differing by finite amounts? For example, the individual starts with the combination $100X_1$, $100X_2$, $100X_3$. By infinitesimal steps we obtain an infinite number of combinations, each equivalent to the preceding, reaching ultimately the combination $90X_1$, $85X_2$, $120X_3$. Will the individual consider this last combination equivalent to the first? The intuitive answer usually is: Yes, he is consistent in his preferences. The mathematical answer is equivalent: If the preference system displays a proper continuity, the equation is integrable. If we postulate indifference surfaces, there is no problem: then by hypothesis the infinitesimal comparisons are consistent with discrete comparisons. Economists have usually been willing to admit that the individual can well display this type of consistency. Pareto at times did likewise.[159]

Mathematically, the issue is: Does the line integral of

$$f(x_1, x_2, x_3, \dots) \, dx_1 + g(x_1, x_2, x_3, \dots) \, dx_2$$
$$+ h(x_1, x_2, x_3, \dots) \, dx_3 + \dots = 0,$$

exist independently of the path between the beginning and end points? Pareto's first two answers are Fisher's: (1) Yes, if f is a function only of x_1, g only of x_2. . . .[160] (2) Yes, if there exists an integrating factor, that is, if the integrability conditions are fulfilled.[161] He adds: (3) If the integrability conditions are not fulfilled, the integral depends on the order of integration, and if this is known the equation can be integrated.[162]

Pareto displayed a peculiar literalness of mind when he tried to translate this third case into economic terms. He identified the order of integration with the order of consumption of the goods.[163] This was absurd for precisely the same reason that dinner-table demonstrations of diminishing marginal utility are objectionable; they do not bear on the problems economics is interested in. Acts of consumption are of little concern; the purpose of the theory of consumption is to explain the pattern of consumption, not its episodes. Economics is usually interested only in the time rates of purchase and consumption of goods, and it is not interested in whether the soup precedes the nuts, or whether the consumer drinks three cups of coffee at breakfast or one after each meal, or pours them down the sink. The correct translation of the integrability problem was in terms of the consistency of consumer preferences, not of the temporal sequence of consumption.[164] Pareto indicated elsewhere that economics is interested in repetitive patterns of behavior, and we may view this discussion as a minor aberration.[165]

Given the indifference curves, we come to the second issue: Can we deduce a unique total utility surface? In general, "No." There are in general an infinite number of total utility surfaces whose contours constitute these indifference curves. If we construct one utility surface, we can get another by squaring the amounts of utility, another by taking the logarithm of utility, etc. So far as observable behavior is concerned, one utility surface will do as well as another. We shall return to this, Pareto's basic answer.

He gave also an introspective reply. We can construct a unique total utility function if the consumer can tell us the magnitude of the utility gained by moving from one indifference curve (I_1) to a second (I_2) relative to the utility gained by a move from I_2 to I_3. If he can tell us that the move from I_1 to I_2 gains (say) three times as much utility as the move from I_2 to I_3, then utility is "measurable." That is, if we have one utility surface, we may no longer submit it to transformations such as squaring the amount of utility — then we should have increased the utility of the move from I_1 to I_2 to *nine* times the utility of the move from I_2 to I_3. We can still take the utility function (U) and write it as $(aU + b)$, but this merely says that the origin and unit of measurement are arbitrary for utility just as they are for length and other measurements.[166] But Pareto believed the consumer could not rank utility differences.

He did not adhere to these views with consistency. The *Manuel* is strewn with passages that are meaningful only if utility is measurable. Two examples will suffice: First, Pareto's definitions of complementary and competing goods were dependent on the measurability of utility.[167] Second, the marginal utility of income was discussed at length.[168]

Yet much of the foregoing discussion is a digression from the viewpoint of Pareto's mature theory of utility. This digression reflects the heavy hand of the past, and it is justified (rather weakly) chiefly on expository grounds.[169] Fundamentally, Pareto argued that the differential equation of the indifference surface is given by observation and that this is all that is necessary to derive the demand functions:

> The entire theory . . . rests only on a fact of experience, that is to say, on the determination of the quantities of goods which constitute combinations which are equivalent for the individual. The theory of economic science thus acquires the rigor of rational mechanics; it deduces its results from experience, without the intervention of any metaphysical entity.
>
> [Edgeworth] assumes the existence of utility (ophelimity) and from it he deduces the indifference curves; I instead consider as empirically given the curves of indifference, and I deduce from them all that is necessary for the theory of equilibrium, without having recourse to ophelimity.[170]

Observations on demand consistent with any utility function φ will also be consistent with an arbitrary utility index-function $F(\varphi)$ so long as the order of preference among the combinations is preserved $[F'(\varphi) > 0]$.[171]

Two mathematicians consolidated this position, that all notions of measurable utility could be eliminated from economics. W. E. Johnson demonstrated that the variation of quantity purchased with price and income was independent of the measurability of utility:

> This impossibility of measurement does not affect any economic problem. Neither does economics need to know the marginal (rate of) utility of a commodity. What is needed is a representation of the ratio of one marginal utility to another. In fact, this ratio is precisely represented by the *slope* of any point of the utility-curve [indifference curve].[172]

Johnson thereafter dealt only with ratios of marginal utilities.

Two years later E. E. Slutsky published his magnificent essay on the equilibrium of the consumer.[173] To put economics on a firm basis, "we must make it completely independent of psychological assumptions and philosophical hypotheses."[174] His utility function was accordingly an objective scale of preferences. Slutsky did not deny the interrelations of "economic" utility and "psychological" utility but sought to deduce empirical tests of any psychological hypotheses. If introspection suggests that the marginal utilities of commodities are independent, we can test the hypothesis by the equation it implies.[175] Slutsky assumes that the increment of utility obtained by moving from one combination to another is independent of the path of movement and offers an empirical test of its validity.[176] Conversely, he shows that a full knowledge of demand and expenditure functions is not sufficient in general to determine whether marginal utility diminishes.[177] The beauty and power of the essay are unique.

With Slutsky's development, introspection no longer plays a significant role in utility theory. There is postulated a function which the consumer seeks to maximize, and the function is given the characteristics necessary to permit a maximum. This is perhaps subjective in origin: the notion of maximizing behavior was probably derived from introspection, although it need not be. Slutsky posits such a function merely because it contains implications that observation can contradict, and hence yields hypotheses on observable behavior. We shall return later to the question whether this is an efficient method of obtaining hypotheses.

We have been marching with the vanguard; we retrace our steps now and examine the views of the other leading economists of the period on measurability.

Contemporary Practice

None of the other leading economists of this period rejected the measurability of utility; we may cite Wicksteed,[178] Wicksell,[179] Barone,[180] Edgeworth,[181] and Pigou.[182] It is true that by the end of the period the leading economists were realizing that measurability of utility was not essential to the derivation of demand curves, but they were loath to abandon the assumption. In part this reluctance was based on the desire to employ utility theory in welfare analysis; in part it was psychological theorizing. Yet with the passage of time, caution increased, as Marshall's evolution will illustrate.

Marshall was at first unqualified in his acceptance of the measurability of utility:

Thus then the desirability or utility of a thing to a person is commonly measured by the money price that he will pay for it. If at any time he is willing to pay a shilling, but no more, to obtain one gratification; and sixpence, but no more, to obtain another; then the utility of the first to him is measured by a shilling, that of the second by sixpence; and the utility of the first is exactly double that of the second.

The only measurement with which science can directly deal is that afforded by what a person is willing to sacrifice (whether money, or some other commodity, or his own labour) in order to obtain the aggregate of pleasures anticipated from the possession of the thing itself.[183]

Moreover, he fully accepted the intergroup comparisons of utility:

> Nevertheless, if we take averages sufficiently broad to cause the personal peculiarities of individuals to counterbalance one another, the money which people of equal incomes will give to obtain a pleasure or avoid a pain is an *extremely accurate* measure of the pleasure or the pain.[184]

Indeed, as we have already noticed, he believed that one can even compare the utilities of groups with different incomes, by using Bernoulli's hypothesis.

We need not trace in detail the growth of Marshall's caution and reticence in this area. He became unwilling to attribute precision to interpersonal comparisons.[185] The discussion of consumer surplus becomes increasingly defensive. Probably because of the growing criticism of hedonism, many terminological changes are made: "benefit" for "pleasure"; "satisfaction" for "utility"; etc. Bentham's dimensions of pleasure were approved at first;[186] they lose their sponsor and place in the text.[187] The distinction between desires and realized satisfactions becomes prominent.[188] Yet Marshall seems never to have been seriously skeptical of the measurability of utility, and the changes in his exposition were not accompanied by any change in the fundamentals of his theory.

VI. COMPLEMENTARITY

Jevons had noticed the case of "equivalent" (substitute) commodities and implicitly defined them by the constancy of the ratio of their marginal utilities.[189] In this he was inconsistent, for he treated the marginal utility of X_1 as dependent only on the quantity of X_1 in his general theory, whereas if X_1 and X_2 are "equivalent," the marginal utility of X_1 depends also on the quantity of X_2. One cannot define the usual relationships among the utilities of commodities with an additive utility function, so the utility theory of complementarity had to wait for Edgeworth's generalization of the utility function. In fact, it had to wait a little longer, for Edgeworth glossed over this problem in the *Mathematical Psychics*.

The first formal definition of the relationship between utilities of commodities was given by the remarkable Viennese bankers, Auspitz and Lieben:

The mixed differential quotient,

$$\frac{\partial^2 \phi}{\partial x_a \partial x_b},$$

indicates what influence (if any) an algebraic increase in x_b — a larger purchase or a smaller sale of B — has on the utility of the last unit of A purchased or not sold. If we consider the simplest case, in which only A and B are consumed,

$$\frac{\partial^2 \phi}{\partial x_a \partial x_b} = 0,$$

TABLE 3

		Total Utility Quantity of X_1		Marginal Utility of X_1
		1	2	
Quantity	1	3.0	5.4	2.4
of X_2	2	5.4	9.0	3.6

according as B complements the satisfaction derived from A, has no influence on it, or competes with A.[190]

Fisher repeated this definition and illustrated certain limiting cases by indifference curves. He defined two commodities to be perfect substitutes if the ratio of the marginal utilities of the amounts "actually consumed" was absolutely constant; they were perfect complements if the quantities consumed were in a constant ratio.[191] Edgeworth gave the same criterion in 1897.[192]

Let us illustrate the use of this criterion with a numerical example. We may construct a table of total utilities as a function of the quantities of X_1 and X_2 and from it calculate the marginal utilities of X_1 (Table 3). Our example has been so chosen that the marginal utility of a given quantity of X_1 increases when the quantity of X_2 increases, hence X_1 and X_2 are complements.

Now let us construct a new table, in which total utility is equal to the logarithm of the total utility in Table 3. This is the kind of transformation we may make if utility is not measurable; it does not preserve the relative differences between utilities, but it preserves their order. We now find (Table 4) that by the same criterion, X_1 and X_2 are substitutes. We have shown that the criterion is ambiguous if utility is not uniquely measurable.[193]

Perhaps Fisher was so casual on this point because he saw the dependence of the definition on the measurability of utility, and Edgeworth was unconcerned because he believed utility was measurable. But Pareto was inconsistent; he made extensive use of this definition at the same time that he was rejecting the measurability of utility.[194]

Marshall displayed greater inconsistency than Pareto, for he implicitly followed the Auspitz-Lieben definition even though he employed an additive utility function which did not permit of complementarity. Thus he speaks of "rival commodities, that is, of commodities which can be used as substitutes for it."[195] In the third edition this definition in terms of utility becomes reasonably explicit.[196] I suspect that Marshall was led into the inconsistency by his preoccupation with the role of rival and completing goods in production. That Pareto and Marshall adhered to the criterion is weighty testimony for its intuitive appeal.

W. E. Johnson supplied a definition of complementarity in terms of utility that was independent of the measurability of utility.[197] His criterion turned on the behavior of the slope of the indifference curve when one quantity was increased. That is to say, X_1 and X_2 are complements if the

TABLE 4

		Total Utility Quantity of X_1		Marginal Utility of X_1
		1	2	
Quantity	1	.4771	.7324	.2553
of X_2	2	.7324	.9542	.2218

more of X_1 the individual possesses, the larger the increment of X_1 he will give up to obtain a unit of X_2.[198] For the fairly broad classes of commodities usually dealt with in budget studies, all commodities are probably complements on the Johnson definition. Slutsky offered no definition of complementarity.[199]

It is difficult to see the purpose in Johnson's definition of complements, or, for that matter, in more recent versions such as that of Hicks and Allen. They cannot be applied introspectively to classify commodities (as the Auspitz-Lieben definition could be), so they offer no avenue to the utilization of introspection. Hence no assumption concerning their magnitude or frequency is introduced into the utility function — except for the condition that their frequency and magnitude be consistent with the assumption of stability.[200] As a result, such criteria can be applied concretely only if one has full knowledge of the demand functions. If one has this knowledge, they offer no important advantage over simple criteria such as the cross-elasticity of demand; if one does not have this knowledge, the simple criteria are still often applicable. The chief reason for presenting criteria in terms of utility, I suspect, is that, when familiar names are given to unknown possibilities, an illusion of definiteness of results is frequently conferred.

VII. THE DERIVATION OF DEMAND FUNCTIONS

Walras' derivation of the demand curves from utility functions was complete and correct for the generalized utility function of Edgeworth as well as for the additive utility function. But Walras passed from utility to demand intuitively and failed to demonstrate that any limitations on demand curves followed from the assumption of diminishing marginal utility.

Pareto was the first to make this logical extension of utility theory. Working with the simple additive utility function, he showed in 1892 that diminishing marginal utility rigorously implies that the demand curves have negative slopes.[201] A year later he partially solved the problem when the marginal utilities of the commodities are interdependent.[202] He could no longer deduce any meaningful limitation on the slope of the demand curve, and dropped the analysis. In the *Cours* he went further and argued that the demand curve for wheat may have a positive slope.[203]

A corresponding derivation of the effect of a change in income on the consumption of a commodity was presented in the *Manuel*, but Pareto gave no explicit mathematical proof and the analysis has generally been overlooked:

If we assume that the ophelimity of a commodity depends only on the quantity of that commodity that the individual consumes or has at his disposal, the theoretical conclusion is that, for such commodities, consumption increases when income increases; or, at the limit, that the consumption is constant when income exceeds a certain level. Consequently, if a peasant subsists only on corn, and if he becomes rich, he will eat more corn, or at least as much as when he was poor. He who has only one pair of sabots a year because they are too expensive, may when he becomes rich use a hundred pairs, but he will always use one pair. All this is in manifest contradiction to the facts: our hypothesis must therefore be rejected. . . .[204]

Despite this admirable test of the hypothesis of independent utilities, Pareto continued to find some use for the additive utility function.

Pareto also made a number of minor applications of utility theory to demand analysis. He showed that the demand and supply curves cannot be linear when there are three or more commodities and that the demand curve of a commodity cannot have constant elasticity when there are three or more commodities. Both demonstrations rested on the independence of the marginal utilities of the commodities.[205] We shall notice later his analysis of the constancy of the marginal utility of money.

Fisher had shown graphically in 1892 that if the utility function is not additive, an increase in income may lead to decreased consumption of a commodity.[206] The compatibility of negatively sloping income curves with convex indifference curves was first shown mathematically by W. E. Johnson.[207] Johnson also demonstrated that a rise in price may lead to an increase in the quantity of the commodity purchased.[208] Moreover, Johnson was first to carry through the explicit analysis of utility with the use only of the ratios of marginal utilities. His exposition was concise and peculiar, however, and was slow to receive attention.[209]

The complete and explicit analysis of the general case was given in lucid form by Slutsky.[210] We may illustrate his general logic with a numerical example. Let the individual consumer buy

100 units of X_1 at \$1.00, a cost of \$100,
60 units of X_2 at \$0.75, a cost of \$ 45,

exactly equaling his income of \$145. Let now the price of X_1 rise to \$1.10. Then the apparent deficiency of income, in Slutsky's language, is 100 times \$0.10 = \$10, for this is the amount that must be added to the individual's income to permit him to purchase the former quantities. If, simultaneously with the rise in the price of X_1, we give the individual \$10, Slutsky calls it a compensated variation of price. Although the individual experiencing a compensated rise in the price of X_1 can still buy the same quantities, he will always substitute X_2 for X_1, because X_2 is now relatively cheaper: Slutsky demonstrated that this is a consequence of the convexity of the indifference curves.[211] The individual will move to perhaps

86.36 units of X_1 at \$1.10, a cost of \$95,
80.00 units of X_2 at \$0.75, a cost of \$60.

The changes in quantities

$$86.36 - 100 = -13.64 \text{ units of } X_1,$$
$$80.00 - 60 = 20.00 \text{ units of } X_2,$$

were called the residual variabilities. If now we withdraw the $10 of income used to compensate for the variation in price, the individual may move to, say,

80 units of X_1 at $1.10, a cost of $88,
76 units of X_2 at $0.75, a cost of $57.

In our example the individual reduces the quantities of both goods when income falls; Slutsky calls such goods relatively indispensable. Had X_1 been relatively dispensable, the decline in income of $10 would have led to a rise in the quantity purchased, conceivably sufficient to offset the residual variation. We have thus the laws of demand:

1. The demand for a relatively indispensable good is necessarily normal, that is to say, it diminishes when its price increases and rises when the price diminishes.
2. The demand for a relatively dispensable good may in certain cases be abnormal, that is to say, it increases with the increase of price and diminishes with its decrease.[212]

In addition, he deduced the integrability equations connecting the effects of the price of X_1 on X_2 and the price of X_2 on X_1:

$$\frac{\partial x_1}{\partial p_2} + x_2 \frac{\partial x_1}{\partial R} = \frac{\partial x_2}{\partial p_1} + x_1 \frac{\partial x_2}{\partial R}. ^{[213]}$$

And so we have fulfilled the historian's wish: the best has come last.

Marshall

Marshall constructed a demand curve superior to Walras' for empirical use but related it to utility by an exposition less than masterly. This demand curve was of the form

$$x_i = f(p_i, R, I),$$

where I is an index number of all prices. Marshall assumed, of course, that tastes are fixed.[214] The constancy of the "purchasing power of money" (the reciprocal of our I) is an assumption governing the entire *Principles*, and it is specifically reaffirmed in the discussion of demand.[215] The role of money income is clearly recognized.[216]

I interpret I in Marshall's equation as an index number representing the average price of all commodities excluding X_i. Then his demand curve differs from the Walrasian demand curve in that he holds constant the average of other prices rather than each individual price. Changes in I may be measured by an index number embracing all commodities (including X_i), as in effect Marshall proposes, but only at the cost of inconsistency: when all prices except p_i are constant, I will vary with p_i. Unless the expenditure on X_i is large relative to income, and unless its price varies greatly, however, the quantitative error will be small.[217] We could eliminate this inconsistency (and certain ambiguities too) in Marshall's treatment by interpreting I as the average of all prices, so real income is held constant along the demand curve.[218] But then we should encounter new inconsistencies.[219]

Marshall insists that the prices of rival goods be held constant.[220] This proviso is troublesome to reconcile with the utility theory but not to explain. The reconciliation is troublesome because rival goods are defined in terms of utility and cannot exist with an additive utility function.[221] (We can of course eliminate this difficulty by generalizing the utility function or shifting to a definition of rival products in terms of demand cross-elasticities.) The purpose of the proviso is obvious, however; when p_i rises, consumers will shift to close rivals, and their prices will tend to rise even if the price level is stable, so the effect of changes only in p_i on purchases of X_i will be obscured.[222]

This Marshallian demand curve can be derived by the conventional Walrasian technique simply by grouping together all commodities except the one under consideration and identifying their price with the price level.[223] But then what is the role of that famous assumption, the constancy of the marginal utility of money (income)? The answer is that this additional assumption is quite indispensable to his textual instruction on how "to translate this Law of Diminishing Utility into terms of price."[224] Marshall moves directly and immediately from marginal utility to demand price by the (implicit) equation,

$$MU_i = \text{constant} \times p_i,$$

and adds, "so far we have taken no account of changes in the marginal utility to [the buyer] of money, or general purchasing power."[225] The assimption of constancy of the marginal utility of money is essential to his exposition of the relationship between utility and demand curves, and essential also to the substance of the apparatus of consumers' surplus. But it is not essential to the Marshallian demand curve if expositional simplicity is sacrificed.

Precisely what does Marshall mean by the constancy of the marginal utility of income? He tells us (in Book V!):

There is a latent assumption which is in accordance with the actual conditions of most markets; but which ought to be distinctly recognized in order to prevent its creeping into those cases in which it is not justifiable. We tacitly assumed that the sum which purchasers were willing to pay, and which sellers were willing to take for the seven hundredth bushel would not be affected by the question whether the earlier bargains had been made at a high or a low rate. We allowed for the diminution in the marginal utility of corn to the buyers as the amount bought increased. But we did not allow for any appreciable change in the marginal utility of money; we assumed that it would be practically the same whether the early payments had been at a high or a low rate.

This assumption is justifiable with regard to most of the market dealings with which we are practically concerned. When a person buys anything for his own consumption, he generally spends on it a small part of his total resources; while when he buys it for the purposes of trade, he looks to re-selling it, and therefore his potential resources are not diminished. In either case the marginal utility of money to him is not appreciably changed. But though this is the case as a rule, there are exceptions to the rule.[226]

It seems beyond doubt that Marshall treated the marginal utility of money as approximately, and not rigorously, constant, and fairly clear that it is constant with respect to variations in the price of a commodity whose total cost is not too large a part of the budget.

The large volume of writing on Marshall's assumption adds an ironical overtone to our phrase "expositional simplicity." Some of the studies have been concerned with the implications of strict constancy.[227] Pareto and Barone gave such interpretations in our period.[228] The approximate constancy of the marginal utility of income has also been discussed.[229] Pareto skirted such an interpretation;[230] it can be elaborated to show that approximate constancy has no implications beyond those already implicit in the additive utility function.[231] The assumption looms large in economic literature but marks a fruitless digression from the viewpoint of the progress of utility theory.

The Abandonment of Utility

Demand functions, as we have already noticed, had been treated as empirical data in the classical economics and in the work of economists such as Cournot.[232] Gustav Cassel was the first of the modern theorists to return to this approach. His theory was developed in 1899 and never changed thereafter in essentials.[233] He attacked the utility theory along two lines.

His first and constructive thesis was that one can employ demand functions directly, without a utility substructure:

> The individual has a value scale in terms of money, with which he can not only classify his needs but also express numerically their intensities. . . . If I adopt the fiction that the needs of individuals A and B are of the same intensity, if both value a given need at one mark, then I have extracted from the psychological assumptions everything that is relevant to the economic side of the matter.[234]
>
> The subjective element which we seek to isolate is the relationship between valuation and external factors [income and prices]. In order to discover this relationship, we must allow the external factors to vary; then the value the individual attributes to the good in question will also vary. This value is therefore a function of the external factors, and in this functional relationship we have the complete and pure expression of the subjective element, that is, of the nature of the individual so far as it affects the formation of prices.[235]

But Cassel made no studies of the properties of the demand functions.

No doubt it was psychologically inevitable that Cassel had also a second thesis: that the utility theory was full of error. This theory, he charged, required a unit of utility that no one could define;[236] it required unrealistic divisibility of commodities and continuity of utility functions;[237] it required, or at least always led to, meaningless interpersonal comparisons of utility;[238] the assumption of constancy of the marginal utility of money is meaningless or objectionable;[239] etc.

Wicksell quickly replied for the utility theorists and with sufficient vigor to estrange Cassel for life.[240] He properly pointed out the weaknesses in Cassel's criticisms of the marginal utility theory: that it did not require measurability of utility or interpersonal comparisons except for welfare analyses; that Cassel's discontinuity objections were unrealistic and in any event did not affect the substance of the theory; etc. Wicksell also properly pointed out the considerable use of utility language in Cassel's positive theory and his implicit use of utility to reach welfare conclusions. And, finally, Wicksell criticized Cassel for his rough treatment of predecessors on the rare occasion when he recognized them at all — a charge that was exaggerated but not unfounded.[241]

But Wicksell did not meet the substantive claim of Cassel that it was possible to start directly with demand functions and that the utility theory added no information on the nature of these functions. He seemed content at this point merely to argue that the utility theory incorporated reliable psychological information into economics.[242]

Barone employed the same empirical approach to demand in his famous article on collectivist planning:

> There is no need to have recourse to the concepts of *utility*, of the *final degree of utility*, and the like; and neither is it necessary to have recourse to Pareto's concept of the *Indifference Curve*. . . .
>
> . . . the *tastes* of the various individuals. On these last we will make no presupposition, no preliminary inquiry, limiting ourselves simply to assuming the fact that at every given series of prices of products and productive services, every single individual portions out the income from his services between consumption and saving in a certain manner (into the motives of which we will not inquire) by which, at a given series of prices, the individual makes certain demands and certain offers. These quantities demanded and offered vary when the series of prices vary.
>
> Thus we disengage ourselves from every metaphysical or subtle conception of utility and of the functions of indifference, and rely solely on the authenticity of a fact.[243]

Yet Barone is not an important figure in the movement to abandon utility. He employed this approach only in the one article,[244] and there perhaps chiefly to bring out the analogies between competitive and collectivist economies. What is more important, he did not discuss the crucial problem: Can one say more about the demand functions if they are derived from utility functions?

One final theorist of the period consistently ignored utility in his work on demand — Henry L. Moore. It was Moore's program to join economic theory with the then recent developments of statistical theory to quantify the important economic functions. In this lifelong task he has found no assistance in utility theory and paused only briefly to criticize it:

> In the closing quarter of the last century great hopes were entertained by economists with regard to the capacity of economics to be made an "exact science." According to the view of the foremost theorists, the development of the doctrines

of utility and value had laid the foundation of scientific economics in exact concepts, and it would soon be possible to erect upon the new foundation a firm structure of interrelated parts which, in definiteness and cogency, would be suggestive of the severe beauty of the mathematico-physical sciences. But this expectation has not been realized. . . .

The explanation is to be found in the prejudiced point of view from which economists regarded the possibilities of the science and in the radically wrong method which they pursued. . . . Economics was to be a "calculus of pleasure and pain," "a mechanics of utility," a "social mechanics," a "*physique sociale.*" . . . They seemed to identify the method of physical sciences with experimentation, and since, as they held, scientific experimentation is impossible in social life, a special method had to be devised. The invention was a disguised form of the classical *caeteris paribus*, the method of the static state.[245]

This is not the place to quarrel with certain aspects of Moore's methodological views, nor is it the place to discuss the deficiencies in his statistical work on demand, nor is it the place to give him his due as a major figure in the history of demand theory. It is a suitable place, however, to conclude our history of the theory of utility.

VIII. A THEORY OF ECONOMIC THEORIES

We have before us a fairly complete account of the major developments in one branch of economic analysis. I wish now to review this history with a view to isolating the characteristics of successful (and hence of unsuccessful) theories, where success is measured in terms of acceptance by leading economists. (It would require a different history to answer the interesting question: To what extent, and with what time interval, do the rank and file of economists follow the leaders?) The bases on which economists chose between theories may be summarized under the three headings of generality, manageability, and congruence with reality.

A. The Criterion of Generality

The successful theory was always more general than the theory it supplanted. The marginal utility theory was more general than the classical theory of value (with its special cases of producible and nonproducible goods); the generalized utility function was more general than the additive utility function; the nonmeasurable utility function was more general than the measurable utility function. On the other hand, the Bernoulli hypothesis was rejected as arbitrary (i.e., particularizing). There was no important instance in which a more specific theory supplanted a more general theory, unless it was Marshall's assumption of the constant marginal utility of money, and this assumption had little vogue outside Cambridge circles.

What does generality mean here? Occasionally it is simply an application of Occam's razor, of using a weaker assumption that is sufficient to reach the conclusion in which one is interested. The nonmeasurable utility function was the leading instance of this kind of generality, although I shall argue below that perhaps logical elegance was not the major reason for abandoning measurability. Very seldom has Occam's razor beautified the face of economic theory.

More often, generality meant the encompassing of a wider range of phenomena. The marginal utility theory enabled economists to analyze the values of nonproducible goods and the short-run values of producible goods. The generalized utility function allowed the analysis of interrelationships of the marginal utilities of commodities, which previously had been outside the domain of utility theory.

Yet we must note that generality is often only verbal, or at least ambiguous. The Walrasian theory was more general than the Ricardian theory in that the former applied to both producible and nonproducible goods, but it was less general in that it took the supply of labor as given. Cassel's empirical demand curves seemed more general in that they were valid even if every element of utility theory was banished;[246] but the utility theorist Wicksell could reply that the utility theory was more general because it permitted welfare judgments. Unless one theory encompasses all the variables of the others, their order of generality will vary with the question in hand.

Generality, whether formal-logical or substantive, is a loose criterion by which to choose among theories. It is always easy and usually sterile to introduce a new variable into a system, which then becomes more general. Yet a more general theory is obviously preferable to a more specific theory if other things are equal, because it permits of a wider range of prediction. We turn now to the other things.

B. The Criterion of Manageability

The second criterion employed in choosing between theories has been manageability. Economists long delayed in accepting the generalized utility function because of the complications in its mathematical analysis, although no one (except Marshall) questioned its realism. They refused to include in the individual's utility function the consumption of other individuals, although this extension was clearly unimportant only in the social life of Oxford. The nonintegrable differential equation of the indifference curves was similarly unpopular. In these cases manageability was the prime consideration: economists tacitly agreed that it is better to have a poor, useful theory than a rich, useless one.

Of course, this is true, although the choice is not really this simple as a rule. Manageability should mean the ability to bring the theory to bear on specific economic problems, not ease of manipulation. The economist has no right to expect of the universe he explores that its laws are discoverable by the indolent and the unlearned. The faithful adherence for so long to the additive utility function strikes one as showing at least a lack of enterprise. I think it showed also a lack of imagination; no economic problem has only one avenue of approach; and the non- and semimathematical utility theorists could have pursued inquiries suggested by theories beyond their powers of mathematical manipulation.[247] The investigator in his science is not wholly dissimilar to the child in his nursery, and every parent has marveled at how often unreasoning obstinacy has solved a problem.

C. The Criterion of Congruence with Reality

The criteria of generality and manageability are formal; the empirical element entered through the criterion of congruence with reality. It was required of a new theory that it systematize and "explain" a portion of the empirical knowledge of the times. It must perform tasks such as accounting for the fact that often goods sold for less than their costs of production (which the marginal utility theory did) or for liking bread more when there was butter on it (which the generalized utility function did).

The reality with which theories were required to agree was one of casual observation and general knowledge. It was composed of the facts and beliefs that the men of a time mostly share and partly dispute and of the observations of men who earned and spent incomes and watched others do so. Of course the type and amount of such information varied widely among economists. Some, like Marshall, had a deep knowledge of their economies; others, like Edgeworth and Pareto, were more worldly scholars; still others, like Walras and the young Fisher, kept the world at a distance.

This casual knowledge was loose and relatively timeless with respect to utility theory; these economists knew little more about utility and not a great deal more about demand than their ancestors. In this respect utility theory is not wholly representative of economic theory; in population theory, for example, casual knowledge changed radically with the times and exercised a decisive influence on the comparative acceptabilities of various population theories. The one changing element in the general knowledge was the growing skepticism of hedonism in academic circles. Economists were surely (if improperly) more susceptible to the proposal to abandon the measurability of utility when the psychologists chided them:

> Important as is the influence of pleasures and pains upon our movements, they are far from being our only stimuli. . . . Who smiles for the pleasure of smiling, or frowns for the pleasure of the frown? Who blushes to avoid the discomfort of not blushing?[248]

The sieve of casual knowledge was broad in its gauge. It could reject the notion (of Cassel) that consumers do not equate marginal utilities divided by prices because they do not know the prices, or the notion (of the abstemious Fisher) that the marginal utility of liquor increases with quantity. But it could not reject even the imaginary Giffen paradox. Casual knowledge is better calculated to detect new error than to enlarge old truth.

This third criterion of congruence with reality should have been sharpened — sharpened into the insistence that theories be examined for their implications for observable behavior, and these specific implications compared with observable behavior. The implication of the diminishing marginal utility of money, that people will not gamble, should have been used to test this assumption, not to reproach the individuals whose behavior the theory sought to describe.

Not only were such specific implications not sought and tested, but there was a tendency, when there appeared to be the threat of an empirical test, to reformulate the theory to make the test ineffective. Thus, when it was suggested that there might be increasing marginal utility from good music, as one acquired a taste for it, this was interpreted as a change in the utility function.[249] Yet if in the time periods relevant to economic analysis this phenomenon is important, it is a significant problem — the defenders had no right to rush to the dinner table. When it was suggested that the marginal utility of the last yard of carpet necessary to cover a floor was greater than that of fewer yards, the theory was modified to make the covering of the entire floor the unit of utility analysis.[250] They did not anxiously seek the challenge of the facts.

In this respect Pareto was the great and honorable exception. Despite much backsliding and digression, he displayed a constant and powerful instinct to derive the refutable empirical implications of economic hypotheses. He was the first person to derive the implications of the additive utility function with respect to demand and income curves. It was left for Slutsky to carry out this task for the generalized utility function, but Pareto — and he alone of the economists — constantly pressed in this direction.

But exception he was. The ruling attitude was much more that which Wieser formulated:

Any layman in economics knows the whole substance of the theory of value from his own experience, and is a layman only in so far as he does not grasp the matter theoretically, — i.e., independently, and for and by itself, — but only practically, — that is to say, in some given situation, and in connection with its working out in that situation. If this be true, how else shall be better proved our scientific statements than by appealing to the recollection which every one must have of his own economic actions and behavior?[251]

That this criterion was inadequate was demonstrated by the slowness with which utility theory progressed. The additive utility function was popularized in the 1870's; it was 1909 before the implication of positively sloping income curves was derived. The generalized utility function was proposed in 1881; it was 1915 before its implications were derived. The chief of these implications is that, if consumers do not buy less of a commodity when their incomes rise, they will surely buy less when the price of the commodity rises. This was the chief product — so far as hypotheses on economic behavior go — of the long labors of a very large number of able economists. These very able economists, and their predecessors, however, had known all along that demand curves have negative slopes, quite independently of their utility theorizing.

Had specific tests been made of the implications of theories, the unfruitfulness of the ruling utility theory as a source of hypotheses in demand would soon have become apparent. Had these economists sought to establish true economic theories of economic behavior — that is, to isolate uniformities of economic events that permitted prediction of the effects of given conditions — they would not long have been content with the knowledge that demand curves have negative slopes. They would have desired knowledge on the relative elasticities of demand of rich and poor, the effects of occupation and urbanization on demand, the role of income changes, the difference between short- and long-run reactions to price changes, and a whole host of problems which we are just beginning to study. They would have given us an economic theory which was richer and more precise.

These remarks shall have been completely misunderstood if they are read as a complaint against our predecessors' accomplishments. It would be purposeless as well as ungracious to deprecate their work. They improved economics substantially, and, until we are sure we have done as much, we should find gratitude more fitting than complaint. But we should be able to profit not only from their contributions to economics but also from their experiences in making these contributions. That such able economists were delayed and distracted by the lack of a criterion of refutable implications of theories should be a finding as useful to us as any of the fine theoretical advances they made.

NOTES

1. I have also omitted consideration of the criticisms raised by the antitheoretical writers, who played no constructive part in the development of the theory. For a discussion of some of their views see J. Viner, "The Utility Theory and Its Critics," *Journal of Political Economy*, XXXIII (1925), 369–87.

I wish to acknowledge the helpful suggestions of Arthur F. Burns, Milton Friedman, and Paul A. Samuelson.

2. *The Wealth of Nations* (New York: Modern Library, 1937), p. 28.

3. Or, alternatively, that the ratio of the prices of two commodities is not equal to the ratio of their total utilities; but this also requires an illegitimate selection of units: The price of what quantity of diamonds is to be compared with the price of one gallon of water? Smith makes such illegitimate statements; for example, "The whole quantity of a cheap commodity brought to market, is commonly not only greater, but of greater value, than the whole quantity of a dear one. The whole quantity of bread annually brought to market, is not only greater, but of greater value than the whole quantity of butcher's-meat; the whole quantity of butcher's meat, than the whole quantity of poultry; and the whole quantity of poultry, than the whole quantity of wild fowl. There are so many more purchases for the cheap than for the dear commodity, that, not only a greater quantity of it, but a greater value, can commonly be disposed of" (*ibid.*, p. 212; see also p. 838).

Nevertheless, this statement can be reformulated into a meaningful and interesting hypothesis: Order commodities by the income class of consumers, using the proportion of families in the income class that purchase the commodity as the basis for choosing the income class. Then does aggregate value of output fall as income class rises?

4. *Ibid.*, p. 56. Substitution is illustrated by the effects of a royal death on the prices of black and colored cloth (*ibid.*, p. 59).

5. *Ibid.*, pp. 793–94. This is of course the opposite of modern budgetary findings, but near-contemporary budget studies seem to me indirectly to support Smith.

6. *Op. cit.*, chap. iv. In addition, two further "dimensions" were added for the appraisal of the total satisfaction of an "act": the consumption of a loaf of bread might be the pleasure to which the first four dimensions refer; the theft of the loaf might be the act. These additional dimensions were fecundity and purity; respectively, the chance of one pleasure leading to another and the chance of a pleasure not being followed by a pain.

7. As Bentham indicated elsewhere (see *Works of Jeremy Bentham* [Edinburgh: Tait, 1843], I, 206; III, 214).

8. The reliability of the presentation of Bentham's views has been attested by Élie Halévy, *La Formation du radicalisme philosophique* (Paris: Germer Baillière, 1901), Vol. I, Appendix I. Here the Hild-

reth translation of the *Traités* is used (London: Trübner, 1871).

9. *Theory of Legislation*, p. 103.

10. "'Tis in vain to talk of adding quantities which after the addition will continue distinct as they were before, one man's happiness will never be another man's happiness; a gain to one man is no gain to another: you might as well pretend to add 20 apples to 20 pears, which after you had done that could not be 40 of any one thing but 20 of each just as there was before. This addibility of the happiness of different subjects, however, when considered rigorously it may appear fictitious, is a postulatum without the allowance of which all political reasoning is at a stand: nor is it more fictitious than that of the equality of chances to reality, on which that whole branch of the Mathematics which is called the doctrine of chances is established. The fictitious form of speech (expression) in both cases, which, fictitious as it is, can give birth to no false consequences or conclusions, is adopted from a necessity which induces the like expedient in so many other instances, merely for the sake of abbreviation: as it would be endless to repeat in every passage where it was used, what it was it wanted to be rigorously true" (Halevy, *op. cit.*, III, 481).

11. *Theory of Legislation*, pp. 103 ff.; all statements italicized by Bentham.

12. The use of marginal analysis was even more explicit in his *Pannomial Fragments*:

"But the quantity of happiness will not go on increasing in anything near the same proportion as the quantity of wealth:—ten thousand times the quantity of wealth will not bring with it ten thousand times the quantity of happiness. It will even be matter of doubt whether ten thousand times the wealth will in general bring with it twice the happiness.

". . . the quantity of happiness produced by a particle of wealth (each particle being of the same magnitude) will be less and less at every particle; . . ." (*Works*, III, 229; see also IV, 541).

13. *Theory of Legislation*, pp. 106–7.

14. Lengthy extracts are given by Halévy, *op. cit.*, Vol. I, Appendix II.

15. *Ibid.*, p. 398.

16. *Ibid.*, p. 408.

17. *Ibid.*, p. 410.

18. Bentham appears to have recognized this difficulty when, in a passage following a discussion of diminishing marginal utility, he wrote: "[Intensity] is not susceptible of precise expression: it *not* being susceptible of measurement" (*Codification Proposal* [1822], in *Works*, IV, 542).

19. For more general discussions of Bentham see W. C. Mitchell, "Bentham's Felicific Calculus," in *The Backward Art of Spending Money* (New York: McGraw-Hill Book Co., 1937); and J. Viner, "Bentham and J. S. Mill," *American Economic Review*, XXXIX (1949), 360–82.

20. See Bonar's Preface to *Letters of Ricardo to Malthus* (Oxford: Clarendon, 1887).

21. *Principles of Political Economy and Taxation* (Gonner ed.; London: Bell, 1932), p. 420.

22. *Principles of Economics* (8th ed.; London: Macmillan, 1920), p. 814.

23. *Principles*, p. 265.

24. *Ibid.*, pp. 267–68.

25. In his *Elements of Political Economy* (3d ed., 1827).

26. *Principles of Political Economy* (Ashley ed.; New York: Longmans, Green, 1929), pp. 442–44, 804.

27. Letter to Ricardo, July 19, 1821, in *Mélanges et correspondance* (Paris: Chamerot, 1833), pp. 116–17, 287–89; cf. also *Treatise on Political Economy* (Boston: Wells & Lilly, 1824), Book II, chap. i, and *Cours complet d'économie politique* (Paris: Guillaumin, 1840), I, 65–66, 71–72.

28. W. F. Lloyd, "The Notion of Value," reprinted in *Economic History, Economic Journal Supplement*, May, 1927, pp. 170–83; N. W. Senior, *Political Economy* (New York: Farrar & Rinehart, 1939), pp. 11–12; R. Jennings, *Natural Elements of Political Economy* (London: Longman, Brown, Green & Longmans, 1855), pp. 98–99, 119, 233 n.; W. E. Hearn, *Plutology* (London: Macmillan, 1864), p. 17. Lloyd, the third occupant of the Drummond chair in political economy at Oxford, gave much the most elaborate statement of the principle. Instead of applying it to contemporary economic problems, however, he emphasized the fact that marginal utility is not the same thing as exchange value and applied the theory to Robinson Crusoe to show this.

29. A. Walras, *De la nature de la richesse et de l'origine de la valeur* (Paris: Alcan, 1938), esp. chap. xi.; M. Longfield, *Lectures on Political Economy* ("London School Reprints" [London, 1931]), pp. 27–28, 45–46, 3 ff.

30. Daniel Bernoulli's much earlier discovery will be treated later.

31. His chief essays (published in 1844 and 1849) are reprinted in *De l'utilité et de sa mesure* (Torino: La Riforma Sociale, 1934).

32. Dupuit's instruction for measuring utility reveals the tacit identification of utility and demand curves: "Assume that all the like commodities whose general utility one wishes to determine are subjected to a tax which is increased by small steps. At each increase, a certain quantity of the commodity will no longer be purchased. The utility of this quantity in terms of money will be the quantity multiplied by the tax. By increasing the tax until all purchases cease, and adding the partial products, one will obtain the total utility of the commodity" (*ibid.*, p. 50; also p. 180).

33. *Ibid.*, p. 161. I have transposed the axes of Dupuit's diagram.

34. *Ibid.*, p. 51. Elsewhere he says that the ideal toll would be one proportional to the consumers' total utility, but this is impraticable because of "l'improbité universelle" (*ibid.*, p. 141); and the effects of alternative methods of financing public works (e.g., the incidence of taxes) must be studied before a practical recommendation can be made (*ibid.*, p. 161). Multiple price systems were also considered (*ibid.*, pp. 64–65, 140 ff.).

35. *Ibid.*, p. 52.

36. This is illustrated by the following quotation, in which price fluctuations are treated as exercises of arbitrary power:

"In order that there be an increase or decrease in utility, it is necessary that there be a decrease or increase in [a commodity's] cost of production—there being no change in its quality. When there are only variations in market price [prix vénal], the consumer gains what the producer loses, or conversely. Thus, when an article costing 20 francs to produce is sold for 50 francs, as a result of a monopoly or concession, the producer deprives every buyer of 30 francs of utility. If some circumstance forces him to lower his price by 10 francs, his income diminishes by 10 francs per unit and that of each buyer increases by 10 francs. There is a cancellation; no utility is produced" (*ibid.*, pp. 52–53).

37. Only a person who has labored through the volume can savor the magnificent understatement of Edgeworth: "He may seem somewhat deficient in the quality of mathematical elegance" ("Gossen," *Palgrave's Dictionary of Political Economy* [London: Macmillan, 1923], II, 232).

38. His *Entwickelung der Gesetze des menschlichen Verkehrs* (3d ed.; Berlin: Prager, 1927), which is not encumbered with chapters, begins with the famous sentences: "On the following pages I submit to public judgment the result of 20 years of meditation. What a Copernicus succeeded in explaining of the relationships of worlds in space, that I believe I have performed for the explanation of the relationships of men on earth."

39. For a good summary see M. Pantaleoni, *Pure Economics* (London: Macmillan, 1898), pp. 28 ff.

40. *Entwickelung*, p. 29; his treatment of durable goods is not sound (see pp. 25, 29–30).

41. *Ibid.*, p. 36.

42. *Ibid.*, p. 45.

43. *Ibid.*, pp. 93–94.

44. *Ibid.*, p. 123.

45. Marshall was a contemporary discoverer of the theory but did not publish it until later (*Memorials of Alfred Marshall* [London: Macmillan, 1925], p. 22). J. B. Clark was a somewhat later discoverer and never developed the theory to a level comparable with the best contemporary European analysis. He became preoccupied with a neglected problem to which he could not find a useful solution: how to apply marginal analysis to variations in the quality of goods (see *The Philosophy of Wealth* [Boston: Ginn & Co., 1892], Preface and p. 76 n.; *Distribution of Wealth* [New York: Macmillan, 1931], chaps. xiv–xvi).

46. *Theory of Political Economy* (4th ed.; London: Macmillan, 1911), p. 164.

47. *Ibid.*, p. 166.

48. *Ibid.*, p. 165.

49. *Grundsätze der Volkswirtschaftslehre* (Vienna: Braumüller, 1871), pp. 69, 120–21, 144–45.

50. *Éléments d'économie politique pure* (1926 ed.; Paris: Pichon & Durand-Auzias), Leçon 38. The first edition (Lausanne: Carbay, 1874) does not differ materially in substance on the subjects discussed here.

51. Wieser's paradox of value (that marginal utility times quantity may decrease when quantity increases) led to deep confusion (see *Natural Value* [New York: Stechert, 1930], Books I and II). Böhm-Bawerk's greatest polemic is *Grundzüge der Theorie des wirtschaftlichen Güterwerts* ("London School Reprints" [London, 1932]).

52. *Op. cit.*, pp. 18 and 21.

53. *Op. cit.*, p. 98 n.

54. On one occasion he states that his numbers represent only relative utilities and that numbers such as 80 and 40 indicate only that the former (marginal) utility is twice as large as the latter (*ibid.*, p. 163 n.).

55. *Éléments*, pp. 74, 102, 153.

56. *Op. cit.*, pp. 7 and 12.

57. *Ibid.*, pp. 7–9.

58. *Theory of Political Economy* (1st ed.; London: Macmillan, 1871), p. 12.

59. *Theory* (4th ed.), pp. 11 and 13.

60. *Ibid.*, pp. 146 ff. (Our notation.)

61. *Ibid.*, pp. 147 and 148.

62. *Ibid.*, p. 14.

63. See *Études d'économie politique appliquée* (Lausanne: Rouge, 1898), pp. 295 ff.; *Études d'économie sociale* (Lausanne: Rouge, 1896), pp. 209 ff.

64. "The value that a good has for an economizing individual is equal to the significance of that want-satisfaction" (*op. cit.*, p. 120; also chap. v).

65. *Ibid.*, pp. 177 ff., 208–9.

66. The requirement of competition was indirect: one characteristic of a perfect market was that "there must be no conspiracies for absorbing and holding supplies to produce unnatural ratios of exchange" (*Theory* [4th ed.], p. 86). It is evident that the trading body could not properly be used to explain prices, because its composition depended upon prices.

67. Jevons (*ibid.*, p. 95) stated the law of indifference as

$$\frac{dx_2}{dx_1} = \frac{x_2}{x_1}.$$

This notation is ambiguous (see Marshall, *Memorials*, p. 98; F. Y. Edgeworth, *Math-*

ematical Psychics [London: Paul, 1881], pp. 110 ff.).

68. Jevons seems to have introduced the trading bodies to get quickly to market prices, not because of an intuition that bilateral monopoly was indeterminate; at least he overlooked the difficulties in duopoly (*Theory* [4th ed.], p. 117).

69. "The reader will find, again, that there is never, in any single instance, an attempt made to compare the amount of feeling in one mind with that in another" (*ibid.*, p. 14).

70. *Éléments*, Leçon 8. Let total utility $= f(x_1) + g(x_2) + h(x_3) + \ldots$ In one of these utility functions, substitute the budget limitation,
$$x_1 + x_2 p_2 + x_3 p_3 + \ldots$$
$$= x_1^0 + x_2^0 p_2 + x_3^0 p_3 + \ldots,$$
where $x_1^0, x_2^0, x_3^0, \ldots$, are the initial stocks. Then maximize total utility to obtain the equations in the text.

71. This summary differs in notation and detail, but not in substance, from Walras' exposition (*ibid.*, pp. 123 ff.). The chief difference of detail is that Walras writes the utility as $f(x_i^0 + x_i)$, where I write it as $f(x_i)$, so his x_i can be negative.

72. *Theory* (4th ed.), pp. 142 ff. In the Preface to the second edition he proposed broader applications much closer to those of Menger and Walras but never worked out this position.

73. *Éléments*, pp. 131, 133.

74. The validity of this argument depends on the assumption that the marginal utility of a commodity is a (diminishing) function only of the quantity of that commodity (see Sec. IV).

75. *Ibid.*, pp. 145–49.

76. Perhaps mention should also be made of the applications of utility theory to labor. Jevons' theory of disutility was labored and at times confused (see my *Production and Distribution Theories* [New York: Macmillan, 1941], chap. ii). Walras' treatment was more elegant—he introduced the marginal utility of leisure in complete symmetry to the theory of consumption—but not much more instructive (*Éléments*, p. 209). Menger denied that labor was usually painful (*op. cit.*, p. 149 n.).

77. Marshall's theory of multiple equilibria is independent of utility analysis; it refers only to the long run, whereas Walras' theory is strictly short run. See Marshall, *Pure Theory of Domestic Values* ("London School Reprints" [London, 1930]).

78. *Éléments*, pp. 68–70; Wicksell restates the theory, *Lectures on Political Economy* (London: Macmillan, 1934), I, 55 ff.

79. *Éléments*, p. 231; Jevons also stated the theorem (*Theory* [4th ed.], p. 141).

80. Among the important writings during our period are: A. Marshall, *Principles of Economics* (1st ed.; London:

Macmillan, 1890), Book V, chap. vii; V. Pareto, "Il Massimo di utilità dato dalla libera concorrenza," *Giornale degli economisti*, Series 2, No. 9 (July, 1894), pp. 48–66; E. Barone, "The Ministry of Production in the Collectivist State," reprinted in F. A. Hayek, *Collectivist Economic Planning* (London: Routledge, 1938); K. Wicksell, *Lectures on Political Economy* (London: Macmillan, 1934), I, 72 ff.; L. Bortkewitch, "Die Grenznutzentheorie als Grundlage einer ultra-liberalen Wirtschaftspolitik," *Jahrbuch für Gesetzgebung, Verwaltung und Volkswirtschaft*, XXII (1898), 1177–1216; and A. C. Pigou, *Wealth and Welfare* (London: Macmillan, 1912).

81. *Mathematical Psychics*, pp. 20, 34, 104, 108.

82. Diminishing marginal utility for each commodity was not necessary, however: the indifference curves could be convex to the origin if every commodity except one yielded diminishing marginal utility, and the marginal utility of this exception commodity did not increase too rapidly. This exceptional case was first analyzed by Slutsky (see Sec. VII).

83. In the two commodity case
$$\frac{dx_2}{dx_1} = -\frac{\varphi_1}{\varphi_2}$$
is the slope of an indifference curve, and the condition for convexity is
$$\frac{d^2x_2}{dx_1^2} = -\frac{\varphi_2^2\varphi_{11} - 2\varphi_1\varphi_2\varphi_{12} + \varphi_1^2\varphi_{22}}{\varphi_2^3} > 0$$
where the subscripts to φ denote partial differentiation with respect to the indicated variables. It is clear that diminishing marginal utility (φ_{11} and φ_{22} negative) is not necessary for convexity, since φ_{12} can be positive and large, and it is not sufficient, since φ_{12} can be negative and large. In the additive case ($\varphi_{12} = 0$), at most one marginal utility can be increasing, as was pointed out in the previous footnote.

84. *Mathematical Psychics*, p. 36. He wrote the utility function as $\varphi(x_1, - x_2)$, in my notation, for reasons which will be pointed out below. He postulated that $\varphi_{12} < 0$, where $-x_2$ is work done by the person and x_1 is remuneration received. This is equivalent to assuming that an increase in remuneration increases the marginal utility of leisure, and would be represented by $\varphi_{12} > 0$ if we write the function as $\varphi(x_1, x_2)$, as is now customary. With diminishing marginal utility this condition leads to convexity (see previous note).

85. The conditions for maximum satisfaction are
$$\frac{\varphi_1}{\varphi_2} = \frac{p_1}{p_2},$$
$$x_1 p_1 + x_2 p_2 - R.$$
Differentiate these equations with respect to R (holding prices constant) and solve to obtain

$$\frac{\partial x_2}{\partial R} = \frac{p_2\varphi_{11} - p_1\varphi_{12}}{p_2^2\varphi_{11} - 2p_1p_2\varphi_{12} + p_1^2\varphi_{22}}.$$

The denominator of the right side is negative if the indifference curves are convex to the origin. The numerator, however, can be positive with $\varphi_{12} < 0$, so the whole expression may be negative (X_2 may be "inferior"). With the additive function, $\varphi_{12} = 0$ (and of course they assumed $\varphi_{ii} < 0$), so the expression must be positive (X_2 [and X_1] must be "normal"). Similarly, differentiate the equations with respect to p_2 holding p_1 and R constant) and solve to obtain

$$\frac{\partial x_2}{\partial p_2} = \frac{p_1\varphi_1 + x_2p_1\varphi_{12} - x_2p_2\varphi_{11}}{p_2^2\varphi_{11} - 2p_1p_2\varphi_{12} + p_1^2\varphi_{22}}.$$

Again the denominator is negative, and the numerator may be negative if φ_{12} is negative, so the whole expression may be positive. With the additive utility function and diminishing marginal utility, the expression must be negative.

86. E.g.: A. Smith, *Theory of Moral Sentiments* (Boston: Wells & Lilly, 1817), Part III, chap. iii; Part IV, chap. i; N. F. Canard, *Principes d'économie politique* (Paris: Buisson, 1801), chap. v; Senior, op. cit., p. 12.

87. *Mathematical Investigations in the Theory of Value and Prices* (New Haven: Yale University Press, 1937—reprint of 1892 ed.), p. 102. Fisher independently reached the generalized utility function of Edgeworth (*ibid.*, Preface).

88. "Some Improvements in Simple Geometrical Methods of Treating Exchange Value, Monopoly, and Rent," *Economic Journal*, II (1892), 37.

89. "Some Remarks on Utility," *Economic Journal*, XIII (1903), 60 ff. He wrote the utility function of the individual as

$$U = \phi\,[x,\,y,\,z,\,w,\,K\,(ab)],$$

where x, y, z, and w were quantities consumed by the individual, a_i was the quantity of x possessed by some other individual i, whose social distance was b_i, and K was a symbol "akin to, though not identical with, the ordinary Σ" (*ibid.*, p. 61).

90. *Papers Relating to Political Economy* (London: Macmillan, 1925), II, 323–24 n.

91. The three commodity indifference surfaces are of course the limit of literal graphical exposition, and even they have been deemed unappetizingly complex.

92. For dx_1MU_1 will be the gain of utility from an increment dx_1, and dx_2MU_2 will be the loss of utility from a decrement dx_2, and these must be equal if the movement is along an indifference curve.

93. *Mathematical Psychics*, pp. 20 ff.

94. *Ibid.*, p. 46.

95. *Op. cit.*, Part II.

96. *Le Opere economiche* (Bologna: Zanichelli, 1936), I, esp. pp. 22–23.

97. *Über Wert, Kapital und Rente* (Jena: Fischer, 1894), esp. p. 43.

98. *Lectures on Political Economy*, I,

46–47, 55 ff.; however, the generalized function is preferred (*ibid.*, pp. 41–42, 48–49, 79 ff.).

99. *Alphabet of Economic Science* (London: Macmillan, 1888).

100. *Common Sense of Political Economy* (London: Routledge, 1934), Vol I, chap. ii; Vol. II, chap. ii; the generalized function is used in Vol. II, chap. iii, esp. p. 479.

101. *Principles of Economics* (London: Macmillan, 1890), Mathematical Notes II, III, VII [I, II, VI]. References in brackets will be used for corresponding passages in the eighth edition.

102. *Ibid.*, pp. 159–60 [99].

103. *Ibid.*, pp. 179–80, also Mathematical Note VII. His Mathematical Note III [II] also implies an additive function if his p, "the price which [a person] is just willing to pay for an amount [x] of the commodity . . ." is interpreted as our x_1p_1 and the price to the person is treated as constant. See Sec. VII.

104. *Loc. cit.*, p. 756 [845]. See also the deduction of diminishing marginal utility from negatively sloping demand curves (*ibid.*, p. 159 [101 n.]).

105. See Sec. VI.

106. Reference is there made to Fisher's "brilliant" book, precisely on this point (*Principles* [3d ed.; London: Macmillan, 1895], p. 460 n. [390 n.]). For Fisher's discussion see Sec. VI below.

107. *Loc. cit.*, p. 208 [132]. See my "Notes on the History of the Giffen Paradox," *Journal of Political Economy*, LV (1947), 152–56.

108. He added the less than candid footnote: "Some ambiguous phrases in earlier editions appear to have suggested to some readers the opposite opinion (*loc. cit.*, p. 207 and n. [131 and n.]).

109. "Considerazioni sui principii fondamentali dell'economia politica pura," *Giornale degli economisti*, Series 2, Vol. V (August, 1892); *Cours d'économie politique* (Lausanne: Rouge, 1897), II, 332 ff.

110. "Considerazioni . . . ," op. cit., VII (1893), 307.

111. Below, Sec. VII.

112. *Manuel d'économie politique* (2d ed.; Paris: Giard, 1927), pp. 253 ff., 274.

113. P. R. de Montmort, *Essay d'analyse sur les jeux de hazard* (2d ed.; Paris: Quillau, 1713), p. 402.

114. *Ibid.*, p. 407.

115. In *Specimen theoriae novae de mensura sortis*; references are to the German translation, *Versuch einer neuen Theorie der Wertbestimmung von Glücksfällen* (Leipzig: Duncker & Humblot, 1896).

116. *Ibid.*, p. 27.

117. *Ibid.*, pp. 27–28. Marshall properly remarked on the difficulties raised by the use of wealth instead of income (*Principles* [8th ed.], p. 842).

118. On integrating the differential expression, we obtain

$$U = k \log x + \text{constant},$$

and the constant is determined by the condition that, when wealth is at the subsistence level c, $U = 0$.

119. *Op. cit.*, pp. 39–40.

120. *Ibid.*, pp. 42–44.

121. The moral expectation of the individual with initial wealth a is

$$U = \frac{1}{2} k \log \frac{a+1}{c} + \frac{1}{4} k \log \frac{a+2}{c}$$
$$+ \frac{1}{8} k \log \frac{a+4}{c} + \dots$$
$$= k \log \left(\frac{a+1}{c}\right)^{\frac{1}{2}} \left(\frac{a+2}{c}\right)^{\frac{1}{4}}$$
$$\times \left(\frac{a+4}{c}\right)^{\frac{1}{8}} \dots$$
$$= k \log \frac{v}{c},$$

where v is the sum of money whose utility equals the moral expectation. Hence

$$v = (a+1)^{\frac{1}{2}} (a+2)^{\frac{1}{4}} (a+4)^{\frac{1}{8}} \dots$$

and $(v - a)$ is the sum of money whose utility equals the expected gain of utility from playing the game.

122. *Op. cit.*, p. 33.

123. For the eighteenth century see I. Todhunter, *A History of the Mathematical Theory of Probability* (London: Macmillan, 1865).

124. *Théorie analytique des probabilités* (3d ed.; Paris: Gauthier-Villars, 1886), pp. xix–xx, chap. x.

125. S. D. Poisson, *Recherches sur la probabilité des jugements* (Paris: Bachelier, 1837), pp. 74–76. Thus if $F = 2^k$ is Peter's fortune, Paul's expected winnings are

$$\frac{1}{2} \cdot 1 + \frac{1}{4} \cdot 2 + \dots + \frac{1}{2^k} \cdot 2^{k-1} + 2^k$$
$$\times \left(\frac{1}{2^{k+1}} + \frac{1}{2^{k+2}} + \dots\right) = \frac{k}{2} + 1.$$

126. Todhunter, *op. cit.* At the present time the critical probability is .00005.

127. *Exposition de la théorie des chances* (Paris: L. Hachette, 1843), pp. 108–9, 334. He reformulated the problem: the state (chosen to avoid Poisson's solution) issues tickets: No. 1 pays $1.00 if the first throw is heads; No. 2 pays $2.00 if the first heads comes on the second throw; etc. He argued that no one would buy the high-numbered tickets.

128. J. Bertrand was surely right in this respect: "If one plays with centimes instead of francs, with grains of sand instead of centimes, with molecules of hydrogen instead of gains of sand, the fear of insolvency may be reduced without limit" (*Calcul des probabilités* [Paris: Gauthier-Villars, 1889], p. 64). Alternatively, one may alter the game, increasing the probability of longer runs and decreasing the rewards correspondingly.

129. The arbitrariness is illustrated by the fact that the Genevese mathematician, Cramer, had suggested that the utility of income be taken as proportional to the square root of income, in a letter to Nicholas Bernoulli, from which Daniel Bernoulli quotes an extract (*op. cit.*, pp. 55 ff.). It should be noted that, unless the utility of income has an upper bound, it is possible to devise some variant of the St. Petersburg paradox which will have an infinite moral expectation.

130. *Elemente der Psychophysik* (reprint; 2 vols.; Leipzig: Breitkopf & Härtel, 1889). See also E. G. Boring, *A History of Experimental Psychology* (New York: Appleton-Century, 1929), chap. xiii.

131. *Psychophysik*, I, 236 ff.

132. For a summary see E. B. Titchener, *Experimental Psychology* (New York: Macmillan, 1905), II, xiii–clxx.

133. J. P. Guilford, *Psychometric Methods* (New York: McGraw-Hill Book Co., 1936), chaps. iv and v.

134. H. M. Johnson, "Did Fechner Measure 'Introspectional' Sensations?" *Psychological Review*, XXXVI (1929), 257–84. Johnson reports a subject whose sensitivity was 18 per cent greater when distinguishing weights by voice than when distinguishing them by pushing the heavier weight toward the experimenter. It would be interesting to know the effect on sensitivity of pushing money.

135. *Mathematical Psychics*, pp. 7, 62; *Papers*, I, 210; II, 107 ff. Edgeworth flirted with the theory at first but later rejected it as arbitrary and accepted the equally arbitrary view that the marginal utility of income falls faster than the Bernoulli hypothesis suggests.

136. "Considerazioni . . . ," *Giornale degli economisti*, Series 2, VI (1893), 1–8. Pareto also deemed it arbitrary and pointed out that strictly it pertained to consumption, not to possessions.

137. "Zur Verteidigung der Grenznutzenlehre," *Zeitschrift für die gesamte Staatswissenschaft*, LVI (1900), 580. Wicksell thought the Weber-Fechner work might eventually permit interpersonal comparisons of utility.

138. E.g., O. Effertz, *Les Antagonismes économiques* (Paris: Giard & Bière, 1906), pp. 30–32; he encountered the theory first at a beer party where a professor of physiology made a "humorous and detailed application to the consumption of beer" (F. A. Lange, *Die Arbeiterfrage* [5th ed.; Winterthur: Ziegler, 1894], pp. 113 ff., 143 ff.; F. A. Fetter, *Economic Principles* [New York: Century, 1915], pp. 40–41).

139. *Principles* (1st ed., 1890), pp. 152–53; also p. 180.

140. *Principles* (8th ed., 1920), pp. 135, 717, 842–43.

141. For references and summaries see E. Sax, "Die Progressivsteuer," *Zeitschrift für Volkswirtschaft, Sozialpolitik und Verwaltung*, I (1892), 43 ff.

142. If $U = k \log R$, a tax of T involves a sacrifice of

$$k \log \frac{R}{R - T}.$$

On the equal sacrifice doctrine,

$$k \log \frac{R}{R-T} = \text{constant} = c$$

$$\frac{R}{R-T} = e^{c/k}$$

so

$$\frac{T}{R} = e^{-c/k} \, (e^{c/k} - 1) = \text{constant}.$$

143. Using the notation of the previous footnote, the doctrine requires that

$$\frac{k \log \dfrac{R}{R-T}}{k \log R} = \text{constant} = m,$$

or

$$\frac{R}{R-T} = R^m,$$

whence

$$\frac{T}{R} = 1 - R^{-m}$$

144. "Prezzi e consumi," *Giornale degli economisti*, Series 3, XL (1910), 99–114, 235–49.

145. "Relazioni fra entrata e consumo," *Giornale degli economisti*, Series 3, XLIV (1912), 111–42, 228–54, 389–439.

146. "Die Grenznutzlehre und das 'psychophysisches Grundsetz'" (1908), reprinted in *Gesammelte Aufsätze zur Wissenschaftslehre* (Tübingen: Mohr, 1922). The fundamental argument is in the third paragraph (pp. 361–68).

147. As applied to commodities, it puts unrealistic limitations on the income elasticities; as applied to income, it implies that there will be no gambling.

148. Walras had already pointed out that only the ratios of the marginal utilities enter into demand analysis: "What are v_a, v_b, v_c, . . . [the exchange values]? They are absolutely nothing but the indeterminate and arbitrary terms of which the ratios represent the common, identical ratios of the marginal utilities of all the commodities for all the exchangers in a state of general equilibrium of the market, and of which consequently only the ratios (taking the commodities two at a time)—equal to the ratios of the marginal utilities for every exchanger,—can be measured numerically. Thus value in exchange is essentially relative, being always based upon marginal utility, which alone is absolute" (*Éléments*, pp. 139–40). He dropped the discussion at this point.

G. B. Antonelli, an Italian engineer, anticipated some of the most important work, in his *Sulla Teoria Matematica della Economia Politica* (Pisa, 1886), which has been reprinted in the *Giornale degli Economisti*, X (N.S.), 1951, pp. 233–63, with expository articles by G. Demaria and G. Ricci. In this remarkable memoir, Antonelli investigates the possibility that if an individual is observed to consume various combinations of goods at various prices, there exists a (utility) function which is maximized for these quantities. He demonstrates that such a function can always be found by integration when there are only two commodities, and states the (integrability) conditions under which the function exists when there are three or more commodities. The sufficient conditions for a maximum are stated, but not exploited to derive conditions on the demand functions. The memoir apparently did not have the slightest contemporary influence.

149. *Op. cit.*, pp. 11 ff.

150. *Ibid.*, p. 18.

151. That is, $\Delta m_1: \Delta m_2: \Delta m_3: \ldots$ will not equal $\Delta m_1': \Delta m_2': \Delta m_3': \ldots$.

152. Fisher, *op. cit.*, p. 67.

153. *Ibid.*, p. 89.

154. *Ibid.*, pp. 74–75, 88–89.

155. See "A Statistical Method of Measuring 'Marginal Utility' and Testing the Justice of a Progressive Income Tax," in *Economic Essays Contributed in Honor of John Bates Clark* (New York: Macmillan, 1927), pp. 157 ff.

156. "Considerazioni . . . ," *Giornale degli economisti*, Series 2, IV (1892), 415. He refers casually to the fact that when the differential equation of the indifference curve is of the form

$$Q \, (x, y) \, dx + R \, (x, y) \, dy,$$

"it may happen the $P[R]$ and Q are not partial derivatives of the same function and then the function will not exist." This was not quite correct: in the two-commodity case there always exists an integrating factor.

157. "Considerazioni . . . ," *Giornale degli economisti*, Series 2, VII (1893). He introduces the index functions (p. 297), recognizes that it is always possible to integrate the differential equations when the marginal utilities are independent, and presents the integrability condition for the three-commodity case (p. 300). Let the differential equation of the indifference surface be

$$dx_1 + R dx_2 + S dx_3 = 0.$$

Then Pareto gives the integrability condition:

$$\frac{\partial R}{\partial x_3} = \frac{\partial S}{\partial x_2}.$$

He should have given,

$$\frac{\partial R}{\partial x_3} - \frac{\partial S}{\partial x_2} = S \frac{\partial R}{\partial x_1} - R \frac{\partial S}{\partial x_1}.$$

He also corrected the statement in the last footnote: "If there are only two economic goods, equation (52) is always integrable" (p. 299 n.). Subsequently he forgot this again (*Manuale di economia politica* [Milan: Piccola Biblioteca Scientifica, 1919—first published in 1906], pp. 499 ff.). He was gently reminded of it by V. Volterra, "L'Economia matematica," *Giornale degli economisti*, Series 2, XXXII (1906), 296–301.

158. *Cours d'économie politique* (Lausanne: Rouge, 1897), II, 47–48. The comparisons were limited to types or

classes of people to avoid personal idiosyncrasies. The measurability problem was referred to only incidentally (*ibid.*, I, 10 n.).

159. *Manuel*, pp. 169 n., 264.

160. *Ibid.*, pp. 545–46, 555; "Économie mathématique," *Encyclopédie des sciences mathématiques* (Paris: Gauthier-Villars, 1911), I, iv, 614.

161. *Manuel*, pp. 545 ff.; "Économie mathématique," *op. cit.*, pp. 598 ff. The equations are

$$f \left(\frac{\partial h}{\partial x_2} - \frac{\partial g}{\partial x_3} \right) + g \left(\frac{\partial f}{\partial x_3} - \frac{\partial h}{\partial x_1} \right)$$
$$+ h \left(\frac{\partial g}{\partial x_1} - \frac{\partial f}{\partial x_2} \right) = 0,$$

and similarly for all triplets of goods.

162. *Manuel*, pp. 553 ff.

163. *Ibid.*, pp. 251, 270, 539 ff.

164. Pareto might equally well have debated how one consumer can consume all goods at once, since the equality of marginal utilities divided by prices is a set of simultaneous equations.

165. *Manuel*, p. 262.

166. *Ibid.*, pp. 264–65.

167. See below, Sec. VI.

168. *Manuel*, pp. 579 ff.

169. *Ibid.*, p. 160.

170. *Ibid.*, pp. 160, 169 n.; see also pp. 539–44.

171. *Ibid.*, p. 542.

172. "The Pure Theory of Utility Curves," *Economic Journal*, XXIII (1913), 490. Of course the first sentence is too strong. See M. Friedman and L. J. Savage, "The Utility Analysis of Choices Involving Risk," *Journal of Political Economy*, LVI (1948), 279–304.

173. "Sulla teoria del bilancio del consumatore," *Giornale degli economisti*, Series 3, LI (1915), 1–26.

E. E. Slutsky was born in 1880 in Novom, Yiaroslavskoi Gubernii, and died in Moscow on March 10, 1948. As a student of mathematics at the University of Kiev in 1901, "because of his participation in an illegal meeting he was drafted as a soldier, and only a large wave of protests by students in the big cities of the country forced the government to return him to the University in the same year. At the beginning of the next year, 1902, E. E. was dismissed from the University without the right to study in any institution of higher education. Only after 1905 was he able to return to the University of Kiev, but this time he entered the law school. "This choice was dictated by E. E.'s desire to prepare himself for scientific work in the field of mathematical economics, an interest which he had developed from a thorough study of works of Ricardo, Marx, and Lenin. He finished at the law school in 1911, and received a gold medal for his final paper. However, because of his reputation for being 'unreliable' he was not asked to continue his academic career at the University." Thereafter he worked intensively in probability and mathematical statistics, teaching at the

Institute of Commerce at Kiev from 1912 to 1926, when he went to Moscow "to work in a number of scientific research institutions of the capital."

This information is from N. Smirnov's obituary notice, *Izvestiya Akademiia Nauk SSSR* ("Mathematical Series"), XII (1948), 417–20, a translation of which was kindly made for me by Dr. Avram Kisselgoff.

174. *Op. cit.*, p. 1.

175. *Ibid.*, p. 25.

176. *Ibid.*, pp. 3, 15–16. That is, the integrability condition is fulfilled.

177. *Ibid.*, pp. 19–23.

178. *Common Sense of Political Economy*, I, 148 ff.; II, 470, 473, 661.

179. *Lectures*, I, 29 ff., 221; he apparently did not fully understand the Pareto analysis (see his review of the *Manuel*, *Zeitschrift für Volkswirtschaft, Sozialpolitik, und Verwaltung*, XXII [1913], 136 ff.).

180. *Principi di economia politica* (Rome: Bertero, 1908), pp. 12–13, 22–24.

181. *Papers*, II, 473 n., 475.

182. *Wealth and Welfare* (London: Macmillan, 1912), *passim*.

183. *Principles* (1st ed.), pp. 151, 154 n.

184. *Ibid.*, p. 152. (My italics.) See also *ibid.*, p. 179.

185. The Bernoulli hypothesis is no longer applied to social classes. The "extremely accurate" comparison of groups with equal incomes becomes "there is not in general any very great difference between the amounts of the happiness in the two cases [two events with equal money measures]" (*Principles* [8th ed.], p. 131).

186. *Principles* (1st ed.), p. 153.

187. *Principles* (8th ed.), p. 122 n.

188. *Ibid.*, p. 92.

189. *Theory of Political Economy*, p. 134.

190. *Untersuchungen über die Theorie des Preises* (Leipzig: Duncker & Humblot, 1889), p. 482; see also pp. 154 ff., 170 ff.

191. *Mathematical Investigation*, pp. 65–66, 69, 70–71. The definitions of these limiting cases are independent of the existence of a unique utility function.

192. He was so punctilious in acknowledging predecessors that his tone suggests independence of discovery. See "The Pure Theory of Monopoly," reprinted in *Papers*, I, 117 n. His criterion differed in one detail—ϕ was the utility function in terms of money and hence involved the marginal utility of money (the complicating effects of which were not discussed). This was not inadvertent; he desired symmetry with the definition of complementarity of products in production (*ibid.*, I, 127; II, 123). The Auspitz and Lieben definition was given later (*ibid.*, II, 464).

193. Equivalently, let φ be a utility function, $F(\varphi)$ a transformation of it such that $F' > 0$. Then

$$U = F[\varphi(x_1, x_2)]$$
$$U_1 = F' \varphi_1$$
$$U_{12} = F' \varphi_{12} + F'' \varphi_1 \varphi_2$$

so F'' must be zero—the transformation must be linear—if the sense of the definition is to be preserved.

194. *Manuel*, chap. iv, pp. 576 ff.

195. *Principles* (1st ed.), p. 160; see also pp. 438 and 178 n., with its accompanying Mathematical Note VI referring to "several commodities which will satisfy the same imperative want. . . ."

196. "The loss that people would suffer from being deprived both of tea and coffee would be greater than the sum of their losses from being deprived of either alone: and therefore the total utility of tea and coffee is greater than the sum of the total utility of tea calculated on the supposition that people can have recourse to coffee, and that of coffee calculated on a like supposition as to tea" (*loc. cit.*, p. 207 n. [131–32 n.]).

197. *Op. cit.*, p. 495. See also Henry Schultz, *The Theory and Measurement of Demand* (Chicago: University of Chicago Press, 1938), pp. 608–14.

198. The commodities are complements if both of the following inequalities hold:

$$\frac{\partial \left(\dfrac{\varphi_1}{\varphi_2} \right)}{\partial x_1} < 0, \qquad \frac{\partial \left(-\dfrac{\varphi_1}{\varphi_2} \right)}{\partial x_2} < 0.$$

They are substitutes if one of the inequalities is reversed; the stability condition (convex indifference curves) inhibits the reversal of both inequalities.

199. His compensated variation of price is intimately related to the later definition of Hicks and Allen.

200. Thus, in the two-commodity case, both commodities cannot be substitutes on Johnson's definition; however, neither need be.

201. "Considerazioni . . . ," *Giornale degli economisti*, Series 2, V (1892), 119 ff. His demonstration is equivalent to ours (above, Sec. III). He also suggested the analysis of the problem of the simultaneous variation of all prices—which can be made equivalent to an income variation—but did not solve the problem explicitly (*ibid.*, p. 125). As we have noticed (Sec. IV), under the less stringent assumption of a convex utility function, one commodity can have a positively sloping demand curve.

202. "Considerazioni . . . ," *Giornale degli economisti*, Series 2, VII (1893), 304–6. This is equivalent to our illustration (Sec. IV).

203. *Cours*, II, 338. The discussion was hypothetical, employing the same argument that Marshall used for the Giffen case.

204. *Manuel*, pp. 273–74.

205. "Économie mathématique," *Encyclopédie*, I, iv, 616 ff.

206. *Mathematical Investigations*, pp. 73–74.

207. *Op. cit.*, p. 505.

208. *Ibid.*, p. 504.

209. A good discussion was given by Edgeworth, *Papers*, II, 451 ff.

210. It is summarized by Schultz, *op. cit.*, chap. i, xix; R. G. D. Allen, "Professor Slutsky's Theory of Consumers' Choice," *Review of Economic Studies*, February, 1936. Slutsky takes the equation,

$$d^2\varphi = \varphi_{11}\, dx_1^2 + \varphi_{22}\, dx_2^2 + \cdots$$
$$+ 2\, \varphi_{12}\, dx_1\, dx_2 + \cdots$$

and by a linear transformation puts it in the canonical form,

$$d^2\varphi = A_1 da^2 + A_2 db^2 + A_3 dc^2 + \cdots.$$

He carries through two analyses, one for all $A_i < 0$, called the normal case, and a second for one $A_i > 0$, called the abnormal case. If two or more A_i are positive, $d^2\varphi$ will not be negative along the budget constraint (*op. cit.*, pp. 4–5).

211. More precisely, he demonstrated that it is a consequence of the stability of the maximum the consumer has achieved (Slutsky, *op. cit.*, p. 14, Eq. 52).

212. *Ibid.*, p. 14.

213. *Ibid.*, p. 15.

214. *Principles* (1st ed.), p. 155 [94]: "If we take a man as he is, without allowing time for any change in his character. . . ."

215. "Throughout the earlier stages of our work it will be best . . . to assume that there is no change in the general purchasing power of money" (*ibid.*, p. 9 [62]).

216. In addition to a reference discussed below (*ibid.*, p. 155 [95]), we may cite Book III, chap. iii [iv], with its discussion of rich and poor buyers and the "disturbing cause." "Next come the changes in the general prosperity and in the total purchasing power at the disposal of the community at large" (*ibid.*, p. 170 [109]).

217. It is sufficient, Marshall says, to "ascertain with tolerable accuracy the broader changes in the purchasing power of money" (*ibid.*, p. 170 [109]); elsewhere he proposes to do this with an index number of wholesale prices (*Memorials*, pp. 207–10).

218. See M. Friedman, "The Marshallian Demand Curve," *Journal of Political Economy*, LVII (1949), 463–95.

219. Examples are the Giffen paradox and the statement that, in cases of multiple equilibria, consumers prefer to buy the quantity at the largest intersection of the supply and demand curves (*Principles* [1st ed.], p. 451 n. [472 n.]).

220. "One condition which it is especially important to watch is the price of rival commodities . . ." (*ibid.*, p. 160 [100]). Complements' prices were added in the second edition (*loc. cit.*, p. 158 [100 n.]).

221. See Sec. VII.

222. Marshall also assumes in effect that the anticipated future price equals the present price (*Principles* [1st ed.], p. 161).

223. No explicit derivation was given

along these lines, but one can be read into Mathematical Note III [II].

224. The phrase, but not the thought, dates from the second edition (*loc. cit.*, p. 151 [94]).

225. *Principles* (1st ed.), p. 155 [95]. In the first edition this was the only explicit statement of the assumption in the book on demand; but see also Mathematical Note VI with its cross-reference to pp. 392–93 [334–35]. After the quoted sentence, Marshall discusses the effect of income on the marginal utility of money but is eloquently silent on the effect of price changes.

226. *Ibid.*, pp. 392–93 [334–35]; see also [p. 132].

227. See M. Friedman, "Professor Pigou's Method for Measuring Elasticities of Demand from Budgetary Data," *Quarterly Journal of Economics*, L (1935), 151–63; P. A. Samuelson, "Constancy of the Marginal Utility of Income," in Oscar Lange *et al.* (eds.), *Studies in Mathematical Economics and Econometrics* (Chicago: University of Chicago Press, 1942), pp. 75–91.

228. In 1892 Pareto argued that the assumption implied that each demand curve has unitary elasticity; "Considerazioni . . . ," *Giornale degli economisti*, Series 2, IV (1892), 493. In 1894 Barone made a more elaborate analysis and reached a similar conclusion; *Le Opere*, I, 48. A few months later he offered a second interpretation: when p_i varies, money income varies by an amount equal to the change in expenditure on X_i (*ibid.*, pp. 59 ff.).

229. N. Georgescu-Roegen, "Marginal Utility of Money and Elasticities of Demand," *Quarterly Journal of Economics*, L (1936), 533–39.

230. *Manuel*, pp. 582 ff.; Économie mathématique," *op. cit.*, p. 631.

231. Let X_1 be the commodity, X_2 all other commodities. I interpret Marshall to mean that the rate of change of the marginal utility of X_2 is small relative to the rate of change of the marginal utility of X_1, or—introducing prices to eliminate the units in which commodities are measured—that

$$\frac{\varphi_{22}\, p_1^2}{\varphi_{11}\, p_2^2}$$

is approximately zero.

232. A. A. Cournot, *Mathematical Principles of the Theory of Wealth* (New York: Macmillan, 1929), esp. chap. iv.

233. "Grundriss einer elementaren Preislehre," *Zeitschrift für die gesamte Staatswissenschaft*, LV (1899), 395 ff.; cf. *The Theory of Social Economy* (New York: Harcourt, Brace, 1932), esp. pp. 80 ff., where the tone is much more gentle and conciliatory.

234. "Grundriss . . . ," pp. 398–99.

235. *Ibid.*, p. 436.

236. *Ibid.*, pp. 398 ff.

237. "The fact is, that every person who is even moderately well off buys the greater part of the articles he uses for much less than the value they have for him" (*ibid.*, p. 417).

238. *Ibid.*, p. 402.

239. *Ibid.*, pp. 428–29.

240. "Zur Verteidigung der Grenznutzenlehre," *Zeitschrift für die gesamte Staatswissenschaft*, LVI (1900), 577–91; amplified in some respects in "Professor Cassel's System of Economics," reprinted in *Lectures*, I, 219 ff. Cassel replied in an appendix to "Die Produktionskostentheorie Ricardos," *Zeitschrift für die gesamte Staatswissenschaft*, LVII (1901), 93–100.

241. Cassel was not the equal of Pareto in this respect (see especially the latter's "Économie mathématique").

242. "Zur Verteidigung . . . ," p. 580.

243. "The Ministry of Production in the Collectivist State" (1908), translated in F. A. Hayek, *Collectivist Economic Planning* (London: Routledge, 1938), pp. 246, 247.

244. Conventional utility analysis is used in his *Principi di economia politica*, Part I.

245. *Economic Cycles: Their Law and Cause* (New York: Macmillan, 1914), pp. 84–86.

246. Actually he put sufficient conditions on his demand functions to make them logically equivalent to those derived from indifference curves (see H. Wold, "A Synthesis of Pure Demand Analysis," *Skandinavisk Aktuarietidskrift*, XXVII [1944], 77 ff.).

247. E.g., the generalized utility function suggested studies of the interrelations of prices in demand; the effect of other people's consumption on one's utility suggested the use of relative income status rather than absolute income in demand analysis; etc.

248. William James, *Psychology* (New York: Holt, 1893), p. 445. William McDougall was more emphatic and pointed (as well as absurd and illogical): "Political economy suffered hardly less from the crude nature of the psychological assumptions from which it professed to deduce the explanations of its facts and its prescriptions for economic legislation. It would be a libel, not altogether devoid of truth, to say that the classical political economy was a tissue of false conclusions drawn from false psychological assumptions. And certainly the recent progress in economic science has largely consisted in, or resulted from, the recognition of the need for a less inadequate psychology" (*An Introduction to Social Psychology* [3d ed.; London: Methuen, 1910], pp. 10–11).

249. Marshall, *Principles* (8th ed.), p. 94; Wicksteed, *Common Sense*, I, 85.

250. Marshall, *Principles* (8th ed.), p. 94; Wicksteed, *Common Sense*, I, 83; Pareto, *Manuel*, p. 266.

251. *Op. cit.*, p. 5.

26.

GEORGE J. STIGLER
University of Chicago

The Economics

of Carl Menger

For a long generation Carl Menger has been in Anglo-Saxon countries a famous but seldom read economist. Historians of economic thought always give to him at least honorable mention as the man who, with Jevons and Walras, rediscovered and popularized the theory of subjective value. But the barriers of inaccessibility and language have served effectively to hide all but the barest outlines of his work from the bulk of English-speaking students of economics. None of Menger's writings has been translated, and his *magnum opus, Grundsätze der Volkswirtschaftslehre* (1871), has long been out of print. Menger's fame, in fact, has been largely a reflection of the achievements of his foremost disciples, Wieser and Böhm-Bawerk. This is a serious injustice; in important respects his theoretical structure was superior to that of his followers. Accordingly the London School of Economics deserves especial gratitude for having removed the barrier of inaccessibility, although not that of language, by fittingly closing its valuable series of "Reprints of Scarce Tracts" with his collected works.[1]

Menger's writings fall within three rather clearly defined fields: economic theory, methodology, and currency. The present essay is concerned only with his economic theory, which, with the exception of the long article, "Zur Theorie des Kapitals" (1888, in Vol. III of the reprint), is presented in the *Grundsätze*.[2] Full biographical details of Menger's life and an excellent

Reprinted from *The Journal of Political Economy*, XLV (April 1937), 229–50, by permission of the author and The University of Chicago Press. This article forms Chapter 6 of George J. Stigler, *Production and Distribution Theories* (New York: The Macmillan Company, 1941). At the time of original publication, the author was with Iowa State College.

discussion of his intellectual milieu are already available, and need not be repeated here.[3]

It will be interesting to begin by comparing Menger with Jevons, who published his *Theory of Political Economy* in the same year (1871) in which the *Grundsätze* appeared. Several parallels can be drawn between the two men. Each was, in contrast with Walras, essentially non-mathematical in method; each wrote on certain parts of economic theory but intended eventually to write a comprehensive treatise which never appeared;[4] each was in sharp revolt against the classical political economy. But Menger's theory was greatly superior to that of Jevons: It was systematic and profound; it avoided the clumsy and unnecessary use of mathematics; and in particular it generalized value theory to include a sound general theory of distribution.

The two men differed greatly in their influence on contemporary economic thought. Jevons had virtually no direct followers.[5] A strongly intrenched classical school, his repellent mathematics,[6] and the lacunae in his theoretical structure explain in part the fact that no "Jevonian" school emerged.

Menger was more fortunate. In his steps followed a group of able economists who, adhering closely to his general approach and frequently accepting even details and terminology of the *Grundsätze*, developed into the so-called "Austrian" school. Wieser and Böhm-Bawerk were outstanding among the nineteenth-century followers, but there were many others — among them Sax, Komorzynski, Mataja, Gross, and Meyer. Menger's success is clear in the light of Jevons' failure. The former faced no established theoretical tradition — what little theoretical German economics there was at the time possessed a strong anticlassical bias; Menger's treatment was lucid, systematic, and comprehensive; and, to mention a factor of ambiguous importance, his was good economic theory.

It is convenient to treat Menger's theory under four heads: "The Theory of Subjective Value," "Productive Organization: The Allocation of Resources," "The Theory of Imputation," and "The Distributive Shares: Classical Theory."

THE THEORY OF SUBJECTIVE VALUE

A thing secures *Güterqualität* (the quality of being a good), begins Menger, from the simultaneous fulfilment of four conditions (p. 3): (1) There must be a human want. (2) The thing must possess such properties as will satisfy this want. (3) Man must recognize this want-satisfying power of the thing. (4) Man must have such disposal over the thing that it can be used to satisfy the want. Things which fulfil the first two conditions are "useful things" (*Nützlichkeiten*); those fulfilling all four requirements are "goods" (*Güter*). The absence or loss of any one of these four conditions is sufficient to entail loss of a thing's *Güterqualität*. The last two of Menger's conditions are merely formal; the economic significance of the others deserves elaboration.

Human wants need not be rational; cosmetics(!) equally with food possess *Güterqualität* (pp. 4–5) — although Menger is optimistic enough to believe that irrational wants become less important as civilization progresses. Similarly, if the belief that a thing possesses want-satisfying power is mistaken (e.g., quack medicines), that again does not affect its *Güterqualität*. And, finally, the word "thing" is purposely vague: Menger argues strenuously that useful human activities, as well as useful material goods, belong in the category of goods (pp. 5–7).

This emphasis upon non-material goods — which is properly extended to include such things as monopolies, good-will, and patents (pp. 6–7) — is a genuine though neglected contribution to economic thought. Classical theory restricted economic analysis primarily to material goods (e.g., "productive" vs. "unproductive" labor), and this practice served — and still serves — to obscure some of the most fundamental concepts of economics, such as income, production, and capital. Menger follows the classicists, however, in failing to distinguish between *goods* and *services from goods*, as we shall presently see.

Menger immediately forestalls an obvious question: Do productive resources, which cannot be consumed directly, lack *Güterqualität?* Clearly not, for, although they cannot satisfy wants directly, they can be transformed into want-satisfying goods, and indeed most of man's economic activity is concerned with this transformation (pp. 8 ff.). Such productive resources are indeed goods; they are distinguished from directly consumable goods, "goods of first order," by the appellative "goods of higher order." If bread is a first-order good, flour, salt, fuel, and the baker's services are second-order goods, wheat is a third-order good, etc.

Menger's differentiation of productive resources from consumption goods solely on the basis of proximity to consumption led to a result important to economic theory. Why should not the same theory that is used to explain the value of consumption goods be applied to "unripened" consumption goods? Quite obviously it should be, and Menger's application of his value theory to production goods led to a correct if not wholly adequate statement of the marginal productivity theory of distribution.

The classification of goods into ranks was in itself, however, of dubious value. The same good, say coal, might be used both as a good of second order (in domestic heating) and perhaps as a good of ninth order (in smelting ore) in even a simple economy. And to attempt to trace in detail the stages in the production of even a simple commodity — a common pin, for instance — in the highly complex modern economy would amount to nothing less than a detailed description of economic life and its history! The concept of ranks is too precise, in other words, either for our analytical powers or for our analytical requirements. Menger himself makes no use of the concept of ranks other than to distinguish consumption goods from production goods; he says that the chief use of the concept is in providing an "insight into the causal relationship" between goods and want-satisfactions (p. 10).

One peculiarity of goods of higher order, Menger notes, is that they cannot produce goods of lower order without the co-operation of other, "complementary" goods of the same order (pp. 11 ff.).[7] It follows that, if the complementary goods of higher order are lacking,[8] the "good" in question cannot satisfy wants even indirectly, and is useless; it is no longer a good.

A second peculiarity of higher-order goods is the dependence of their own want-satisfying power on the want-satisfying power of their final, first-order products (pp. 17–21). This is the germ of the theory of distribution through "imputation" — i.e., the derivation of the value of productive agents from the value of their products.

It is now clear that the existence of unsatisfied human needs is the condition of each and every *Güterqualität*, and this substantiates the principle that goods lose their *Güterqualität* as soon as the needs whose satisfaction they previously served have disappeared. This is equally true whether the goods in question can be used directly in primary relationship to want-satisfaction or whether they secure their *Güterqualität* through a more or less mediate causal nexus leading to the satisfaction of human wants [p. 18].

. . . .

The requirements for goods of higher order are conditioned by our requirements for goods of first order . . . . [p. 35].

Human wants are thus the ultimate basis of all *Güterqualität*. Were people to lose their taste for tobacco, then cigars, cigarettes, and pipes, tobacco stocks, importers' technical services, factories and even tobacco plantations — all these would lose their *Güterqualität*.

The final peculiarity of goods of higher order to be noted at this point is the fact that their utilization always consumes time (pp. 21–26). Since, in the absence of complete knowledge and of complete control over nature, the future is not certain, the *anticipated* want which will be satisfied by a good of higher order at the end of its production process determines its *Güterqualität*. We may defer further consideration of higher-order goods to the section on Menger's theory of distribution.

So far Menger's theory has been presented only in its broad lines of qualitative causality; the quantitative aspects must now be sketched. Two preliminary concepts are of importance: (1) *Bedarf* (requirements), or the amount of each kind of good which an individual requires to satisfy all his wants within a given period of time (p. 34), and (2) supply, or the quantities of the various goods which are available to meet these needs during the same period of time (pp. 45 ff.). Menger's concept of *Bedarf* has no exact English equivalent. His definition and treatment suggest that the *Bedarf* of an individual is the quantity of goods necessary to bring about a complete satisfaction of that individual's needs (cf. pp. 34 and note, 38, 41).[9] He admits that human needs are indeed capable of indefinite development (*ins Unendliche entwicklungsfähig*), but this is a historical phenomenon; for sufficiently limited periods of time *Bedarf* is a fixed datum (p. 38).

An elaborate argument is presented (pp. 35–50) to prove that these two types of information, on *Bedarf* and on supplies, can legitimately be treated as known data in the analysis rather than analytical results (such as prices). This demonstration was highly essential, for the classical economists, whose analytical methods were even more advanced than those in contemporary German economics, did not assume productive resources to be given in amount.[10] Menger, on the other hand, clearly includes goods of higher order, or resources, among his fixed stocks (pp. 45–51). He must be considered one of the first economists to introduce the indispensable methodological tool of "static" assumptions into economic analysis. His treatment is, to be sure, primitive and oversimplified in the light of present-day accomplishments, but at the time it was a distinct innovation. In this respect, moreover, he was more influential, although less rigorous, than Walras, and distinctly superior to Jevons.[11]

One particular merit of Menger's treatment is his emphasis on the time dimension of these quantities — i.e., the fact that our requirements for and supplies of goods must be stated in terms of quantities per unit of time. This important point is obscure in Jevons and it is customarily ignored in modern textbooks on economics.[12]

With these two sets of data, supplies and requirements (each per unit of time), it is now possible to face the basic economic question: How should the given quantities be distributed to secure the greatest possible satisfaction of needs (pp. 51 ff.)?[13] Requirements (*Bedarf*) and available stocks stand in one of three possible relationships to each other: either may be greater than the other, or they may be equal.

Requirements, first, may exceed available quantities — the relationship which is to be observed "with the vast majority of goods." In this case the loss of a significant part of the stock will cause some known need to remain unsatisfied. Accordingly:

> People will endeavor . . . . to secure the greatest possible result by the intelligent application (*zweckmässige Verwendung*) of every given unit (*Teilquantität*) of the goods which stand in this quantitative relationship, and, similarly, to secure a given result with the least possible quantity of such goods . . . . (pp. 52–53).[14]

The individual will therefore devote such goods only to his "more important wants." Goods in this relation — i.e., smaller in quantity than the requirements for them — are "economic goods"; they will be kept, conserved, and used only according to the principle of economic behavior just quoted. Costs of any sort are per se irrelevant to the question of whether a good is economic or non-economic (p. 61 n.).

The second possible relationship holds when available stocks exceed requirements (pp. 57 ff.). Under this circumstance there is no inducement to husband the goods in question, to conserve their useful properties, to consider the relative importance of the wants they can satisfy, or, in general, to treat such goods in an economic manner. They are, in short, "non-economic" goods.

Changing times or circumstances may turn "non-economic" goods into "economic" goods, or vice versa (pp. 60 ff.). Factors contributing to a change in the relationship of supplies to requirements include changes in population, changes in human wants, the discovery of new want-satisfying powers of goods, and, of course, the depletion of resources. But this is historical change, external to Menger's theoretical corpus, and, need not be pursued. The third possible relationship between requirements and supplies, that of equality, is even less significant, and will be passed over.

We are now on the threshold of the quantitative determination of subjective value. One further preliminary step is necessary, the classification of wants according to their importance:

If we have indicated correctly the nature of the value of goods, so that it is established that in the last resort only the satisfaction of our wants has significance for us and that all goods clearly secure their value by a transfer to them of this significance, then the *differences* in value of various goods, which we can observe in actual life, can be based only on the differences in the significance of those want-satisfactions which depend on disposal over these goods [p. 87].

Obviously our different classes of wants are of widely differing importances to us: food, clothing, and shelter are indispensable; other goods, such as tobacco and chessboards, serve only to add comfort or pleasure (pp. 88 ff.). And not only do our specific kinds of wants, and accordingly their satisfactions, differ in importance, but our satisfaction of a particular want will be more or less complete as the quantity of goods available to meet it is greater or smaller (p. 90). A little food preserves life, more food insures health,[15] and additional quantities bring amenities, but to a decreasing extent,[16] until a point of satiation is reached (p. 91).

Menger illustrates by an arithmetical example the differences in the importance of the satisfaction of various kinds of wants and the decrease in the importance of the satisfaction of each kind of want as the quantity of the good satisfying that want is increased (p. 93). This table is reproduced here in a slightly condensed form:

I	II	III	IV	—	X
10	9	8	7	—	1
9	8	7	—	—	0
8	7	—	1		
7	—	1	0		
—	1	0			
1	0				
0					

The columns I–X represent different kinds of wants, in the order of their importance; the numbers in any column represent successive want-satisfactions from unit increases of the stock of goods satisfying that want — in modern terms, the "marginal" utilities. Column I may represent food; Column IV, tobacco. Ten units of "food" represent the individual's *Bedarf* for food.

Menger probably does not mean to say that the first unit of tobacco yields a satisfaction equal to that of the fourth unit of food, but only to indicate orders of importance; but unfortunately he is not precise as to the meaning of his magnitudes. He states that the "economizing" individual seeks to equalize all these margins in order to maximize his want-satisfaction: " . . . . The individual will endeavor . . . . to bring the satisfaction of his needs for tobacco and for means of sustenance into equilibrium" (p. 94). Indeed it is this " . . . . weighing of the different importances of wants, the choice between those which remain unsatisfied and those which, *according to the available means,* get satisfied, and the determination of the degree to which these latter wants get satisfied" that supplies the most consistent and influential motive in man's economic behavior (pp. 94–95 [my italics]).

This endeavor to maximize want-satisfaction by equating the "marginal" satisfactions of all wants can take place only through the allocation of income, and indeed Menger's theory of the distribution of "available means" seems to approach this.[17] Yet it is not clear that Menger sees the rôle of completely general purchasing power, for in the subsequent discussion he speaks of quantities of specific goods in relation to their limited possible uses — e.g., the farmer's corn may be used for food, seed, feeding cattle, etc. (pp. 95 ff.).

Elsewhere he notes that the ability to satisfy more than one want (or column) is a power possessed by "most goods" (p. 112 n.). He does not distinguish satisfactorily between goods which satisfy the one want and those which can satisfy qualitatively different wants.[18] But Menger's solution is, for the latter case, clear and correct:

> If a good is able to satisfy different types of wants, each of which has decreasing significance with the degree of completeness with which it has already been satisfied, the economic man will direct the quantity at his disposal first to the satisfaction of the most important wants regardless of what type they may be, and the remainder will be devoted to those concrete want-satisfactions which are next in importance, and so on with the filling of less important wants. This practice has the result that the most important of all those concrete wants which are not satisfied are of the same significance for all types of wants, and accordingly all concrete wants are satisfied to an equal level of importance [p. 98 n.].

Yet this is not a complete solution, since there are an infinite number of needs which any particular good cannot satisfy, and it is strange that one of the most important steps in the entire argument is found only in a footnote. Menger's failure to develop generally the method by which the individual maximizes his want-satisfaction is an outstanding weakness in his theory of value.

The valuation of a stock of goods follows directly from the principles of economic behavior and of variation in the qualitative and quantitative importance of wants. Assume that the individual has five units of the good capable of satisfying wants I and II. He will apply this stock to the three most important stages of I, with satisfactions 10, 9, and 8, respectively, and to the two most important stages of want II, with satisfactions 9 and 8, respectively. The last unit, the "marginal" application, will satisfy a want which has an importance of 8, and since by definition all units are identical, all will be valued at 8. We have then the principle of value: " . . . . The value of a unit of the available stock of a good is for every individual equal to the significance of the least important want-satisfaction which is brought about by a unit of the total quantity of the good" (p. 99 [italicized by Menger]; also pp. 107–8, etc.). Wants — equivalent to utility in Jevons — and supply are of correlative importance, so that although our need for air is great (represented by, say, Col. I), the supply is even greater and air is worthless. Diamonds are less needed (here perhaps Col. VIII), but the supply is so small that their value is high. The "paradox" of utility and value of the classicists is solved.

Menger elaborates this principle of value at considerable length by the use of examples (pp. 100–107), but only two aspects of the elaboration require attention here. He consistently adheres to a discussion in terms of a period of time, and this means in effect an individual's budget policy for that period. This mode of analysis properly avoids the unrealistic, misleading "dinner-table" examples of diminishing utility used by Jevons and, for that matter, most modern texts. A true understanding of diminishing utility cannot be secured by plying a person with successive oranges — "the desire of food is limited in every man by the narrow capacity of the human stomach." The important fact that every orange is the "marginal" orange is better shown by asking the same person to determine what portion of a limited budget for, say, a six-week camping trip would be devoted to oranges.

Second, there is litttle doubt but that Menger is discussing only relative utilities; the numerical examples are illustrative only of ordinal, not cardinal, relationships. These numbers serve to express "not the *absolute*, but rather the *relative* magnitudes of the significance of the want-satisfactions in question" (p. 163 n. [his italics]; cf. also pp. 92–93, 100–107). In this respect Menger's formulation of the theory of subjective value is a good deal closer to the modern tendency in the treatment of utility than are the expositions of Jevons and Walras. Here it should also be mentioned that although Menger is a thoroughgoing hedonist, he does not follow the later utilitarian practice of comparing the utilities of different individuals.[19] He explicitly denies the validity of such concepts as the "average man" and "average requirement" (p. 110 n.). It is a source of regret that this insight — which was shared by Jevons — was lost to his less gifted disciples. Böhm-Bawerk shamelessly compares the "utilities" of rich and poor,[20] and the purpose of Wieser's metaphysical concept of "natural value" is to overcome the nonexistent difficulty for the marginal utility theory of prices that the utility of a good varies between rich and poor individuals although the price is the same to all.[21]

The interesting question of the right to attribute a "marginal" or "incremental" utility theory of value to Menger may be considered briefly. His analysis is always in terms of the *Teilquantität* — literally the fraction or portion. Yet at numerous points the word is qualified: "practically significant portion"; "portion which is just observable."[22] It seems clear that Menger is thinking in terms of small, finite quantitative changes, and not of infinitesimals. He, unlike his co-discoverers of the utility principle, Walras and Jevons, probably had no mathematical training, and would therefore use such a common-sense approach rather than the convenient analytical concepts of continuity and derivatives. The concept of a small finite change is, of course, more realistic. In a mathematical treatment it yields a slightly indeterminate solution: the value found by withdrawal of a unit is larger than the value found by addition of a unit. But the realistic mathematician has the same problem if he postulates a limited power of discrimination on the part of the consumer, as with Edgeworth's "minimum sensibile."[23] Accordingly, Menger seems clearly to have formulated a "marginal" utility theory (although, as with Jevons, Menger devotes little attention to total utility).

The fundamental principles of Menger's theory of value have been presented in considerable detail, because it is on these important fundamentals that it is so strong. We must be content merely to suggest certain points which are developed in the later chapters on exchange and price. There is a good though simplified development of exchange equilibrium: the individual will equate the marginal utilities of different commodities in the special case of equal prices (esp. p. 168).[24] An anticipation of Edgeworth's contract curve (p. 178), a good statement of the principle of monopoly price (pp. 198 ff.), a reference to discriminating monopolies (pp. 196–97), a discussion of demand elasticity (p. 197 n.), are points which must be at least mentioned. In general it may be said that the analysis of demand is excellent, the analysis of supply factors distinctly less satisfactory.

PRODUCTIVE ORGANIZATION: THE ALLOCATION OF RESOURCES

Menger lays the groundwork for a correct theory of productive organization — i.e., for the determination of the allocation of resources. The final development, however, the theory of alternative cost, is left for Wieser to formulate.[25] This great hiatus in Menger's theoretical system is very hard to explain, especially since the correct allocation of resources is suggested in the footnote which has already been quoted in connection with his value theory (see above, p. 662). There, it will be recalled, Menger suggests that the most economic utilization of a good which satisfies several wants is to equalize its "marginal" significances for all wants. This pregnant suggestion, which contains the heart at once of the alternative-cost theory of value and of distribution theory, is never elaborated, nor is it applied directly to the problem of resource allocation.

Menger's preoccupation with directly consumable goods probably plays a part in the fundamental defect in his theory, the neglect of costs, but a more important explanation lies in his failure to realize the continuity of production — i.e., to realize that the price of a good must be sufficient to repay its costs (which are the products its resources could produce elsewhere) if the industry is to hold the productive resources used in it. This failure appears most clearly in his criticism of the cost theories of value (esp. pp. 119–22). As Menger says, historical costs are irrelevant to value;

a diamond is equally valuable whether it has been found or is the product "of a thousand days of labor." And it is true that

> experience also teaches that the value of the productive factors necessary to the reproduction of many goods [e.g., clothing which is no longer in fashion, obsolete machines, etc.] is much greater than the value of their product, and in many other cases their value is less than that of their product [p. 121].

But it is a *non sequitur* to argue from this, as Menger unfortunately does, that costs cannot influence value (pp. 119 ff.). He fails to consider the fact that although costs never have a direct effect on value, yet they are — "in the long run" — of at least co-ordinate importance in its determination, and in the limiting case of constant costs they are completely dominant. Only for very short periods of time is the supply curve of a commodity, assuming it to be perishable, so inelastic in comparison with its demand curve that the former may be ignored in price determination. And supply curves become more elastic as the time available for readjustments of scale of output increase, because resources become more mobile as between industries, and the influence of supply on price first becomes equal to and then typically exceeds that of demand. Under certain assumptions such as atomistic competition, non-specialization of resources, and unlimited time for full adjustment of the productive organization, constant costs tend to prevail and, in so far as that condition is approximated, demand determines only the quantity of a commodity sold, not its price. Menger's theory is therefore applicable only to very short-run "market" prices, and his failure to recognize the increasing mobility of resources through time vitiates, accordingly, his refutation of cost theories of value. This is also true of his criticism of classical theories of rent, wages, and interest (pp. 143–52), but this aspect may be deferred to a later point.

Menger does, however, make one specific contribution to production theory, a contribution the importance of which literally cannot be exaggerated. That contribution consists in the realization that the proportions in which productive agents may be combined to secure the same product are not fixed — the law of "proportionality" or "substitution":

> Now it is quite true that we have disposal over quantities of goods of lower order only by means of *complementary* quantities of goods of higher order, but it is equally certain that not only fixed quantities of the individual goods of higher order can be brought together in production, somewhat in the manner in which this is observed in chemical compounds. . . . . Rather we are taught by the most general experience that a definite quantity of any good of lower order can be secured from goods of higher order which stand in very different quantitative relationships to each other . . . . [p. 139, also p. 140].

This formulation of the principle of variation of proportions as a *general* rule governing *all* resources is one of Menger's greatest achievements, one which he is not required to share with either Jevons or Walras.[26] Classical theory recognized, of course, the possibility of varying the amount of capital-and-labor which could be applied to a given piece of land, and this was basic to the Ricardian theory of rent. But the proportion between labor and capital was generally assumed to be fixed; certainly variations in this proportion played no part in accepted classical theory.

The significance of the principle of variation of proportions is apparent. It leads directly to the marginal productivity theory of distribution (see next section). Until the principle of proportionality was fully developed, furthermore, no satisfactory solution of the problem of resource allocation was possible. Finally, as long as discussion ran in terms of fixed proportions between productive agents (or the question was ignored), the individual firm could not be used for purposes of analysis. A firm would require all factors in fixed relation to output; only socially — i.e., by general equilibrium analysis — would it be possible to fix the values of individual agents. It was a genuine retardation of economic advance that Wieser and Böhm-Bawerk (the latter in an incredibly crude manner) returned to the assumption of fixed-coefficients.

Quite surprisingly, Menger fails even to mention explicitly the technical principle of diminishing returns from an increasing proportion of any agent in a combination, and, accordingly, to realize its importance for his theory of distribution. The theory of marginal productivity leads to absurd results if any factor is assumed to be subject to increasing or even constant returns. But such an assumption is itself much more absurd, for no problem of resource allocation would arise. Nevertheless, opponents of the marginal productivity theory (e.g., Hobson) have occasionally used examples of increasing returns in "refutation."

One final point of excellence in Menger's brief treatment of production deserves notice: the absence of the classicists' "holy trinity" of land, labor, and capital. Productive factors are simply goods of higher order; the services of labor, land, and capital goods are on the same footing (p. 139). In Menger's treatment, in fact, specific productive agents are not grouped into arbitrary categories which lack economic significance. As a result, his theory of imputation, now to be considered, gains a symmetry difficult to secure so long as the classical trichotomy ruled economic discussion.

THE THEORY OF IMPUTATION

The greatest contribution of the theory of subjective value to theoretical economic analysis lies in the development of a sound theory of distribution — i.e., the view of distribution as the allocation of the total product among the resources which combine to produce it, through value imputation. Prior to Menger no satisfactory theory of distribution had emerged. The classical analysis was one of the division of income between social classes; Smith and his followers never confronted the problem of how a given product may be imputed to the resources which co-operate in its production or considered distribution as a value problem. Menger was the first economist to raise this question, and, moreover, to suggest the proper manner of answering it.

The outlines of the theory of imputation (*Zurechnung*)[27] — i.e., the valuation of productive goods on the basis of their contribution to the value of their products — have already been indicated.[28] Productive goods — goods of higher order — secure value only because they can satisfy wants indirectly, by producing consumption goods (pp. 67–70, 123–26, etc.). This leads to the general theorem of imputation: " . . . . The value of goods of higher order is always and without exception determined by the anticipated value of the goods of lower order in whose production they serve" (p. 124). The element of anticipation arises from the fact, previously noted, that production requires time.

The theory of the valuation of individual goods of higher order then follows from the theories of imputation and the theory of variation of proportions:

. . . . The value [of a quantity of a good of higher order] is equal to the difference between the significance of that want-satisfaction which would result if we had disposal over the quantity of the good of higher order whose value is in question and the significance, in the contrary case, of that satisfaction which would follow from the most economic application of the totality of goods of higher order in our possession [i.e., the remaining resources of this and other kinds] [p. 142].

The context (esp. pp. 139–40) makes it fairly clear (though not so clear as could be desired) that Menger is here, as elsewhere, speaking of the effect on the total product of the withdrawal of a *Teilquantität* — a unit — of a resource. This marginal product fixes the value of the resource.

Two cases are distinguished. When the withdrawal of one unit forces co-operating agents to seek employment in less profitable lines — the case of fixed proportions — the value of the variable factor equals the total loss of product minus the product secured by the complementary factors in other industries. But more commonly the proportions in which the factors may combine are variable, and then the withdrawal of one unit of one agent is accompanied by a rearrangement of the remaining factors,[29] and the diminution of quantity or quality of the product determines the value of the unit which has been withdrawn.

As far as this theory goes — and it is unquestionably superior to any preceding explanation of the determination of the value of productive agents, with the possible exception of that of von Thünen[30] — it is essentially correct. The only real criticism is to be leveled at its inadequacy: Menger has failed to develop the indispensable postulate of diminishing returns; and it is not clearly brought out that the units withdrawn must be small; and the question whether this method of valuation of agents exactly exhausts the total product is not raised.

One general weakness in Menger's exposition which clouds his value theory but is particularly deplorable in his distribution theory is the failure to differentiate between goods and their services. The value of a good, whether used in production or consumption, is less than the aggregate value of its services during its "lifetime" if this is of appreciable duration.

667

Nowhere does Menger clearly recognize this fact; its incidence on his theory of capital will be seen to be particularly heavy.

THE DISTRIBUTIVE SHARES: CLASSICAL THEORY

In a noteworthy section entitled, "On the Value of Land and Capital Uses and of Land Services in Particular" (pp. 142–52), Menger offers a trenchant criticism of the classical division of the "factors" of production. Ricardo had recognized (however rightly) that the value of land was not due to the labor expended upon it, and to reconcile this fact with his labor theory of value he established land as a separate category of goods. Menger's comment is brilliant but inconclusive:

> The methodological misconception which lies in this procedure is easily perceived. That a large and important group of phenomena cannot be reconciled with the general laws of a science which concerns itself with these phenomena, is clear proof of the need for reform of that science. It is not, however, a ground for the separation of one group of phenomena from the remaining objects of observation which are completely similar in their general nature — which would justify the most dubious methodological expedients —, and for erecting special highest principles for each of the two groups [pp. 144–45].

Menger's criticism is valid, but he fails to establish the fundamental economic identity of land and other forms of capital on which the criticism must rest. The recognition of this dualism in the classical theory of value had led some economists (Canard, Carey, Bastiat, Wirth, and Rösler are cited) to attempt to trace land values back to labor expenditures. Menger refutes this argument quite effectively in an emphatic statement that historical costs are irrelevant to present value (p. 145).

Ricardian rent theory is explicitly but inadequately contested as a special case of classical distribution theory. Menger fails to see that "the different qualities and locations of ground-plots" are not an essential feature of the classical doctrine; rent may equally well be measured from the intensive margin. As a consequence it is wrong to say that, "if all plots of ground were of equal quality and of equally favorable location, according to Ricardo they could not yield any rent . . . ." (p. 146). One must regret his too ready concessions that land is usually available only in a definite quantity, "not easily increased," and that immobility of land has the economic significance generally imputed to it. Under Menger's implicit static assumptions, capital and labor are also fixed in quantity; historically all three "factors" have experienced enormous increases. Immobility, again, is a technical attribute; the mobility of land as between different uses is much more important from the viewpoint of price theory (which, indeed, usually abstracts from transportation costs) than is spatial immobility.

Menger considers observable divergences of actual wages from those necessary to maintain a laborer to be a sufficient basis for a categorical denial of the subsistence theory of wages, and he suggests that wages depend, in fact, only on the value of the product of labor (pp. 150–51). This criticism of classical doctrine is also inconclusive, for, to the extent that wages govern population, the supply of labor may conceptually be so regulated that wages remain at a subsistence level. But again, as in the case of rent, he properly believes wages to be explicable by general value theory.

The greatest hiatus in Menger's system of distribution is unquestionably the virtual absence of any theory of capital.[31] Here the failure to distinguish between goods and services from goods is a fundamental weakness. Some beginning is made: It is asserted both that increases in capital can take place only through extensions of the (undefined) period of production (p. 127) and that all such extensions increase the productivity of capital (p. 136 n.). Menger thus sketches out what Böhm-Bawerk later developed.

Menger finds two limitations to increasing produce by extending the period of production: (1) the necessity for maintaining life (in a broad sense) in the immediate future and (2) an irrational preference for present over future satisfactions (pp. 126–28). This second factor, it may be noted, was deleted by Menger from the second edition, lest it be construed as supporting Böhm-Bawerk's theory of interest.[32]

Finally a vague and unsatisfactory definition of capital is presented:

.... The possibility of participating in the economic advantages which are bound up with production by goods of higher order .... is dependent for every individual on his disposal in the present over quantities of goods of higher order for the coming period of time, or, in other words, on possessing *capital* [p. 130, also pp. 127–33].

Capital, then, is defined as goods of higher order kept in possesion through a production period. This is clearly an inadequate definition, and provides no basis for a theory of interest, although such capital services (*Capitalnutzungen*) must, as Menger says, be compensated (pp. 133–36).

Other than the *Grundsätze*, Menger's only work in economic theory proper is the article already mentioned, "A Contribution to the Theory of Capital," which appeared in *Conrad's Jahrbücher* in 1888.[33] Here again no positive theory is presented, but the essay does contain two important principles. There is, first, an acute criticism of the classical emphasis on the technical, in contrast with the economic, character of capital. His comments on the validity of the practice of considering land and labor as "original" factors, capital as a secondary or derivative factor, really leave very little to be said on this subject.

The second theme of the article, which is in some respects even more important, is the necessity for conducting capital analysis in the monetary terms in which entrepreneurs deal with capital problems:

The real concept of capital includes the productive property, whatever technical nature it may have, so far as its money value [*Geldwert*] is the subject of our economic calculation, that is, if it appears in our accounting as a productive sum of money.[34]

These are profound truths; we can only lament that Menger does not build on them.

CONCLUSION

The foregoing condensation of Menger's economic theory need not be summarized, yet a word may be added with respect to the general impression left by the *Grundsätze*. Its caution — almost clairvoyant — in the development of basic economic concepts, the beautifully logical symmetry of its structure, its critical attitude toward received doctrine—these are impressions which can hardly fail to be left by a reading of the text. Certainly the most antagonistic cannot deny Menger a prominent place in the hall of economic fame, and the more enthusiastic, of whom the writer is one, will feel little hesitancy in acclaiming the *Grundsätze* as a treatise which is in fundamental respects unexcelled by any other between the *Wealth of Nations* and Marshall's *Principles*.

NOTES

1. Vol. I (Reprint No. 17): *Grundsätze der Volkswirtschaftslehre* (1871); Vol. II (Reprint No. 18): *Untersuchungen über die Methode der Sozialwissenschaften* (1883); Vol. III (Reprint No. 19): *Kleinere Schriften zur Methode und Geschichte der Volkswirtschaftslehre;* Vol. IV (Reprint No. 20): *Schriften über Geldtheorie und Währungspolitik.*

2. The methodological writings are in Vols. II and III; chap. viii of the *Grundsätze* and Vol. IV are on currency. All page references in the present essay will be to the *Grundsätze* (Vol. I) unless otherwise noted.

3. Consult F. A. von Hayek's Introduction to Vol. I for a general outline of Menger's life and work; his intellectual environment is finely treated by J. Schumpeter, "Carl Menger," *Zeitschrift für Volkswirtschaft und Politik* (N.F.), I (1921), 197–205.

4. Jevons' fragmentary *Principles of Economics*, which was published posthumously (1905) is well known; Menger added *erster, allgemeiner Teil* to the title-page of his first edition, very much as Marshall did twenty years later. Menger projected three additional parts to deal, respectively, with distribution, money, and credit; production and commerce; and general economic policy. Cf. Introduction to second edition (1923), p. vi. This second, posthumous edition was edited by Karl Menger, his son. It will not be considered here; cf. F. X. Weisz, "Zur zweiten Auflage von Carl Mengers 'Grundsätzen,'" *Zeitschrift für Volkswirtschaft und Politik* (N.F.), IV (1924), 134–54.

5. Wicksteed, the important exception, published his general, non-mathematical work, *The Common Sense of Political Economy*, only in 1910.

6. Thus Cairnes referred to his "abstruse mathematical symbols" (*Leading Principles*, p. 21 and note).

7. Menger saw what on occasion some of our modern theorists have failed to see: that where there is only one productive factor and one product that factor must be economically identical with its product, for no change could have taken place in the factor in the absence of another factor. Where this heroic construction is assumed it is nonsense to speak of costs, returns, or distribution.

8. The definition of complementary goods is extended (p. 14) beyond its original meaning to include all goods of higher orders needed to transform the higher good in question into a final product. This is done to avoid the situation where, for instance, all the necessary complementary goods of third order might produce a good of second order which, however, lacked the complementary goods of second order necessary to transform it into a final product.

9. *Bedarf* is therefore closely related to Walras' *utilité d'extension;* cf. *Eléments d'économie politique pure* (1926 ed.), 72 ff.

10. As Professor F. H. Knight has pointed out: "The stationary state of these classical writers was the *naturally* static or economic condition, which is the goal of progress . . . . not a state made static by arbitrary abstraction as a methodological device" (see *Risk, Uncertainty, and Profit*, p. 143 n.). Cf. also the penetrating analysis of L. Robbins, "On a Certain Ambiguity in the Conception of Stationary

Equilibrium," *Economic Journal,* XL (1930), 194–214.

11. Jevons had but a suggestion (*Theory of Political Economy* [4th ed.], p. 267); Walras' genuine advance was obscured from the view of most economists by its mathematical garb (*op. cit.,* esp. pp. 175 ff.).

12. In the numerous sections on dimensions of economic quantities which constitute the chief textual additions made in the second edition of the *Theory of Political Economy* (cf. 4th ed., esp. pp. 61 ff.), Jevons moved much closer to the conclusion that economic quantities must possess a time dimension. His treatment was naïve and unsatisfactory, however. Cf. P. H. Wicksteed, "On Certain Passages in Jevons' Theory of Political Economy," *Quarterly Journal of Economics,* III (1889), 293–314 (reprinted in *Common Sense of Political Economy* [1934], Vol. II).

13. The present discussion will be limited to goods of first order.

14. For the translation of *Teilquantität* as "unit" see below, p. 663.

15. But this additional food will be of a different type. Menger is speaking of broad classes of wants, not of the wants for specific goods. This ambiguity is never cleared up, unfortunately.

16. ". . . . die darüber hinausgehende Befriedigung aber eine immer geringere Bedeutung hat" (p. 92).

17. If the allocation of income is intended, then not marginal utilities but marginal utilities divided by prices, or in terms of units of equal value, are equated, of course. But we must not expect such refinement of statement from Menger.

18. Menger does not seem to realize the fundamental difficulties involved in making this distinction; difficulties which have manifested themselves so successfully in preventing the development of a satisfactory definition of a commodity. But although the basic problem is still unsolved (and probably will remain so), Menger's development is crude in comparison with modern statements.

19. There are minor lapses from this position in the later chapters on exchange and price, but they are infrequent and never affect the basic argument (cf. pp. 162 ff.).

20. "Grundzüge der Theorie des wirtschaftlichen Güterwerts," *Conrad's Jahrbücher* (1886), *London School Reprint No. 11,* p. 118.

21. *Natural Value* (1888), Book II, *passim.*

22. Thus, pp. 52, 77 (twice), 83, 102, 103, etc.

23. Cf. the remarks in *Mathematical Psychics, London School Reprint No. 10,* pp. 7, 60, 99–100.

24. Menger did not see that the units of all commodities could be so defined that they have equal prices.

25. Wieser's first publication, *Über den Ursprung und die Hauptgesetze des wirtschaftlichen Wertes* (1884), pp. 146–70, gives the essentials of the alternative cost theory. Wieser himself, however, never applied the theory correctly to the problem of distribution.

26. Walras recognized the principle as early as 1876 (*Théorie mathématique de la richesse sociale* [1883], pp. 65–66), but he did not add the marginal productivity theory to his original fixed-coefficients approach until, I believe, the third edition of the *Eléments* (1896).

27. The word *Zurechnung,* as well as the word "margin" (*Grenze*), is due to Wieser.

28. *Supra,* pp. 658 ff.

29. This necessary element of rearrangement is strongly implied (esp. p. 140) but not separately considered.

30. Menger appears not to have known of von Thünen, but his knowledge of the literature was great. The *Grundsätze* cites over one hundred and fifty economists, including apparently all the important names in the science down to his time except von Thünen, Gossen, and Cournot.

31. Menger denies the validity of the abstinence theory of interest on his usual grounds for dismissing subjective costs—i.e., capital value frequently appears without any self-denial on the part of the capitalist, as in the pre-emption of natural resources (p. 133 n.).

32. Cf. Introduction to second ed., p. xiv.

33. Reprinted in Vol. III of the *Collected Works,* pp. 133–83.

34. *Ibid.,* p. 174.

27.

MILTON FRIEDMAN
University of Chicago

Leon Walras

and His

Economic System

"Thus the system of the economic universe reveals itself, at last, in all its grandeur and complexity: a system at once vast and simple, which, for sheer beauty, resembles the astronomic universe." Leon Walras.[1]

The appearance of William Jaffé's loving translation of Leon Walras' *Elements of Pure Economics* offers an excuse for re-examining that great work some eighty odd years after its original publication. Though in so far as this is a review, it is a review of Walras and not of Jaffé, I cannot refrain from prefacing it with a word of thanks to Jaffé for his translation, which is a model of its kind: careful, accurate, and marked throughout by an unobtrusive attention to detail. His notes on the collation of editions are an important aid to research; his translator's notes illuminate many points of the text as well as directing the reader's attention to much recent writing that is relevant to its interpretation.

Though I regard as somewhat extravagant Schumpeter's judgment that, "so far as pure theory is concerned, Walras is . . . the greatest of all economists,"[2] there can be no doubt that the *Elements* is a great work which marked an important step forward in the development of economics as a science, and which still plays an important role in economic thinking. It is

Reprinted from *The American Economic Review,* XLV (December 1955), 900–909, by permission of the author and The American Economic Association.

well worth having a translation even at this late date in order to make it more readily accessible both to the profession at large and particularly to students learning to become economists: it belongs on their "five foot shelf." The comments that follow deal with the book in this context, as a piece of living literature, rather than with its role in the history of economic thought.

On the broadest level of generality, there are two main themes in the *Elements:* the analysis of *rareté,* or marginal utility; and the theory of general equilibrium. Walras regarded the two as fitting together in one harmonious whole, which is certainly tenable; he also viewed the marginal utility analysis as indispensable for the study of general equilibrium, which seems much more dubious. The marginal utility analysis impresses the modern reader as "dated," as important primarily in understanding the development of economic ideas rather than in directly extending his horizons as a scientist. For this reason I shall discuss the marginal utility analysis first, in order to clear the ground for the theory of general equilibrium.

I. RARETÉ

Walras essentially completes his analysis of the "Theory of Exchange of Two Commodities for Each Other," the title of Part 2 of the *Elements,* before he introduces utility analysis at all. Prior to that point, he has derived demand curves and offer curves, discussed their typical shapes, and considered the meaning of their points of intersection, distinguishing stable from unstable equilibria. These topics are described as revealing the "nature of exchange"; and utility curves are then introduced in order to examine "the cause" of exchange. Similarly, at each successive stage in the analysis — the extension of the theory of exchange of two commodities to several commodities, and the expansion of the system to include successively production, capital formation and credit,[3] and circulation and money — utility considerations strike the reader as something introduced rather artificially, as being on a different level from the rest of the analysis and capable of being extracted from it bodily without in any way altering its essence — a step that Cassel took in his reformulation of the Walrasian system.

Yet this is clearly not the way it seemed to Walras or to his contemporaries, Jevons and Menger. Today, Walras' primary contribution would surely be regarded as general equilibrium theory, of which at best only pale reflections can be found in Jevons or Menger; yet the three linked themselves together and were linked together by others as the pioneers of "marginal utility." Walras writes as an italicized theorem, "The exchange of two commodities for each other in a perfectly competitive market is an operation by which all holders of either one, or of both, of the two commodities can obtain the greatest possible satisfaction of their wants consistent with the condition that the two commodities are bought and sold at one and the same rate of exchange throughout the market," and goes on to say, "The main object of the theory of social wealth is to generalize this proposition. . . . We may say . . . that this proposition embraces the whole of pure and applied economics" (p. 143).

It is hard now for us to understand why this marginal utility analysis should have been regarded as so vital and revolutionary. We can repeat the formulae of the histories of economic thought that it gave a meaningful solution to the diamond-water paradox and so permitted demand to be assigned its proper role and the shackles of the cost of production or, even worse, labor theory of value to be overthrown. But I do not believe that such formulae carry real conviction or understanding. Partly, this is for the usual reason that an error, once pointed out, seems obvious to those who never held it, though it may have taken a real stroke of genius to discover the error and though simply pointing it out did not make it obvious to those who had the error imbedded in the fabric of their thought. But I suspect the main reason is quite different, namely, the change in our general philosophical and methodological outlook that has been wrought, though by no means directly, by the developments in physical science, in particular, by the replacement of the physics of Newton by the physics of Einstein. Surely this is why a chapter title like that of Lesson 10, "*Rareté*, the Cause of Value in Exchange," strikes us as an anachronism.

The almost purely metaphysical role of *rareté* in Walras is brought out very well by his discussion of measurement:

> The above analysis is incomplete; and it seems impossible, at first glance, to pursue it further, because intensive utility, considered absolutely, is so elusive, since it has no direct or measurable relation to space or time, as do extensive utility [the quantity that will be taken at a price zero] and the quantity of a commodity possessed. Still, this difficulty is not insurmountable. We need only assume that such a direct and measurable relationship does exist, and we shall find ourselves in a position to give an exact, mathematical account of the respective influences on prices of extensive utility, intensive utility and the initial stock possessed. I shall, therefore, assume the existence of a standard measure of intensity of wants or intensive utility . . . (p. 117).

In a modern writer, one would expect this to be followed by a statement that such an assumption, combined presumably with others, has observable implications of a kind that will enable utility, though "it has no direct or measurable relation to space or time," to be assigned numerical values that are inferred from what are regarded as its manifestations. Walras, of course, does not take this line. He says nothing more on the subject and simply proceeds to take for granted that there is something called *rareté* which has numerical values that can be plotted, averaged, and so on, and can be identified with "satisfaction" in a sense that is relevant for welfare purposes.

In a way, Walras' ready acceptance of the nonmeasurability by physical operations of his *rareté* is somewhat ironical. For, like the other pioneers of marginal utility, he made a subsidiary assumption about utility functions that, if accepted, gives a relatively straightforward method of assigning numbers to utility. Walras throughout assumes that the total utility of a collection of commodities can be written as the sum of functions, each containing as a variable the quantity of only one commodity. Indeed, one gets the impression that it may well have been this feature of his utility function that was to him the main justification for regarding *rareté* as *the* cause of value in exchange; for *rareté* was "absolute," depending only on the quantity of the one commodity itself, whereas value in exchange was "relative," the ratio of two such absolutes; and along the same lines, the utility curve for a particular commodity was more fundamental, because a function of only one variable, than the demand function which had to be regarded as depending on several. However, if a consumer's preferences can be validly represented by a sum of one-variable functions, a convenient measuring rod for utility is at hand; one need only take the utility added by some specified unit of one commodity, say the utility added by the tenth slice of bread, as the basic unit, and the utility of all other commodities can be expressed in terms of it — essentially the procedure that both Fisher and Frisch experimented with at a later date.

The reason why this method of measuring utility has not been adopted is, of course, because a utility function consisting of a sum of one-variable functions has implications for consumer behavior that are contradicted by observation, the most striking, perhaps, being the implication that the higher the income of a consumer, the more he will consume of every commodity separately, *i.e.*, that there are no inferior goods. Needless to say, Walras does not explore such implications, though he does record the corresponding implication that a demand curve for one commodity is always negatively sloped for given amounts possessed of other commodities (which is equivalent to given money income and other prices). However, he asserts this (on p. 91) prior to introducing his marginal utility analysis, giving little justification for it, apparently because he regarded it as obvious.

One must conclude, I think, that this part of Walras' book has interest almost solely for the student of economic thought. In so far as utility theory plays a role in modern economic analysis, it does so in a more sophisticated, albeit empirically emptier, form than in Walras, though it should perhaps be recorded that there is much current literature that has not advanced beyond Walras in its understanding of the meaning and role of the measurability of utility.

II.   THE THEORY OF GENERAL EQUILIBRIUM

Cournot writes in Chapter 11 of his *Researches*,

So far we have studied how, for each commodity by itself, the law of demand in connection with the conditions of production of that commodity, determines the price of it and regulates the incomes of its producers. We considered as given and invariable the prices of other commodities and the incomes of other producers; but in reality the economic system is a whole of which all the parts are connected and react on each other. An increase in the income of the producers of commodity A will affect the demand for commodities B, C, etc., and the incomes of their producers, and, by its reaction, will involve a change in the demand for commodity A. It seems, therefore, as if, for a complete and rigorous solution of the problems relative to some parts of the economic system, it were indispensable to take the entire system into consideration. But this would surpass the powers of

675

mathematical analysis and of our practical methods of calculation, even if the values of all the constants could be assigned to them numerically.[4]

It is Walras' great and living achievement to have constructed a mathematical system displaying in considerable detail precisely the interrelationships emphasized by Cournot. Did he thereby show Cournot to be wrong in supposing that the task surpassed the powers of mathematical analysis? I believe not. For there is a fundamental, if subtle, difference between the task Cournot outlined and the task Walras accomplished; an understanding of this difference is essential to an assessment of both the positive contribution of Walras and the limitations to that contribution; and failure to recognize the difference seems to me a primary source of methodological confusion in economics. It is clear from Cournot's references to "practical methods of calculation" and to the assignment of numerical values to constants that the "rigorous solution" he had in mind was not a solution "in principle," but a numerical solution to a specific problem. His goal was an analysis that would, given the relevant statistical material, yield specific answers to specific empirical questions, such as the effects of a specified tax on a specified product; answers that could be confronted by observation and confirmed or contradicted. And surely there can be little doubt that a "complete and rigorous solution" of this kind does "surpass the powers of mathematical analysis and of our practical methods of calculation" even today despite the enormous advances in methods of calculation. Cournot was quite right that *for his problem* a "complete and rigorous" solution was out of the question, that the thing to do was, "while maintaining a certain kind of approximation, . . . to carry on . . . a useful analysis."[5]

Walras solved a different, though no less important, problem. He emptied Cournot's problem of its empirical content and produced a "complete and rigorous" solution "in principle," making no pretense that it could be used directly in numerical calculations. His problem is the problem of form, not of content: of displaying an idealized picture of the economic system, not of constructing an engine for analyzing concrete problems.[6] His achievement cannot but impress the reader with its beauty, its grandeur, its architectonic structure; it would verge on the ludicrous to describe it as a demonstration how to calculate the numerical solution to a numerically specified set of equations. The difference is brought out clearly by the further developments along Walras' line that have been — and rightly — regarded as improvements in his system. These have all consisted in making the system still more general and elegant, in eliminating empirically specializing assumptions. The clearest example is, of course, in the theory of production: Walras assumed constant coefficients of production, recognizing that this was an "approximation" and in later editions suggesting the route to generalize the analysis. Pareto generalized Walras' solution to cover variable as well as constant coefficients of production. The recent reintroduction of the assumption of constant coefficients of production in connection with input-output analysis has not been a further development of Walras' pure theory. It has rather been an attempt — so far largely unsuccessful — to use Walrasian constructs in solving Cournot's problem.

Emphasis on pure form has an important role to play in economics in two rather different respects. One, the easier to specify, is the role of mathematics or pure logic in general, namely, to help us to avoid contradictory statements — to avoid mistakes in arithmetic, as it were. This role is immediately recognized and granted, and for that reason tends to be passed over rapidly; yet it deserves to be emphasized how many, how important, and sometimes how difficult to detect, are the fallacies in economics of this kind; fallacies that consist in the assertion that contradictory statements are simultaneously valid, that we can have our cake and eat it too. The ability to think clearly and exactly is a scarce resource for which, unfortunately, there seems no adequate substitute. Walras' discussion of bimetallism (Lessons 31 and 32) and of Ricardo's and Mill's theories of rent and wages (Lessons 39 and 40) are excellent examples, largely peripheral to his own general equilibrium theory, of how useful emphasis on pure form can be. By translating vague statements into symbolic form and using very elementary mathematics indeed, Walras is able to clear away much irrelevant material, show that some widely accepted statements are mutually contradictory, and specify the conditions under which others are valid.

The other respect in which emphasis on pure form has an important role to play is in providing a language, a classificatory scheme to use in organizing materials — labels, as it were, for the compartments of our analytical filing box. This is Walras' great contribution. His general equilibrium system gives a bird's-eye view of the economic system as a whole, which has not only an extraordinary aesthetic appeal as a beautifully articulated abstraction but also a utilitarian appeal as providing relevant, meaningful, and mutually exhaustive categories. This bird's-eye view rests fundamentally on two dichotomies: between services and sources of services or between income and capital; and between the markets for consumer services or goods and for productive services or goods. A third dichotomy might almost be added: between entrepreneurs and consumer units, though this seems somewhat less fundamental. Each consumer unit and entrepreneur is conceived as operating in both markets: in terms of markets for services, a consumer unit sells productive services of the capital sources he owns in the resource market and buys consumer services in the consumption market; an entrepreneur buys productive services in the resource market and sells consumer services in the consumption market either directly or indirectly. The distinction between markets thus leads naturally and directly to the distinction between demand and supply.

This classificatory scheme is developed in considerable detail, with extraordinary skill and ingenuity, great attention being devoted to showing, or attempting to show, that it is internally consistent and exhaustive (*i.e.*, that the system of equations has a solution that tends to be attained and maintained by the operation of market forces). I have described this analysis as involving emphasis on pure form, which I think in a meaningful way it does.

677

Yet I do not mean thereby to imply either that it lacks importance for economics as a substantive science, or that empirical considerations play no role in its construction and use. Quite to the contrary. Walras' picture is not pure mathematics but economics precisely because it was constructed to provide a framework for organizing substantive material of an economic character; the classifications it employs reflect a judgment about the empirically important characteristics of the economic structure; the usefulness of the picture, though not its logical coherence, depends on the extent to which this judgment is confirmed by experience. One cannot read Walras, it seems to me, without recognizing that he was an economist first and a mathematician and logician second; he accomplished what he did not because he was a mathematical genius but despite inferior mathematical equipment — reading the *Elements* gives no reason to doubt the fairness of the examiners who failed him twice in the mathematics examination for entry to the École Polytechnique.[7] In some ways, indeed, "despite" might perhaps be replaced by "because." Walras' necessity to work things out rather cumbrously, from the simplest cases to the more complicated, must have forced him to give much more attention to the economic significance and meaning of his categories than he would have if he had been able to proceed on a still higher level of abstraction. I hasten to add that I do not mean to be urging that bad mathematics is better than good but only that each task requires its own tools. A hand spade may well be better than a modern steam shovel for some kinds of work; pure mathematicians are notoriously bad at simple arithmetic.

Though emphasis on form can and does play a vital role in economic analysis, it can also be mischievous if it is not illuminated by empirical judgment and understanding. An excellent example is Walras' utility analysis of savings. This analysis was first introduced into the fourth edition, which appeared in 1900, about a quarter of a century after the first edition. In this edition, Walras yielded to the temptation, which has claimed so many lesser men, of treating "savings" like a consumer good and simply carrying over mechanically the formal analysis applicable to consumer goods. So he defines a commodity (E) consisting of a perpetual net income stream, a unit of (E) being one unit of *numeraire* per unit of time indefinitely, writes down for each individual a marginal utility function for (E), and regards him as possessing a certain quantity of (E) and maximizing his utility subject to a budget constraint which includes expenditures on (E) along with expenditures on other commodities. He regards this process as yielding a demand function for (E) like other demand functions (pp. 274 and 275).

In symbols, this looks like a simple extension of Walras' general analysis and one is led to ask why it was that he did not discover this obvious yet important extension for a quarter of a century. But the moment one digs beneath the symbols and asks why, as economists, we regard it as important to distinguish savings from current consumption, it becomes clear that Walras' procedure is fallacious and involves precisely the kind of confusion between stocks and flows that Walras elsewhere so carefully avoids and indeed underlines. I can perhaps illustrate this best by Walras' utility function for (E) which, in deriving the demand curve, he writes as

$$\Phi_e(q_e + d_e),$$

where q_e is the initial quantity of (E) possessed, d_e, the quantity purchased or sold during the time unit in question. Now q_e and d_e are of different dimensions and cannot be added; q_e is the number of units of (E) that the individual possesses, *i.e.*, the number of units of *numeraire* per unit of time that the individual can receive indefinitely if he so chooses — for simplicity, let us say the number of dollars per year that is yielded by his existing stock of wealth; d_e is the number of dollars per year that he is going to add to this flow as income on the savings he accumulates during the time period in question (see p. 117), say a year, so that savings during that period are $p_e d_e$, where p_e is the price of a dollar a year indefinitely. In other words, q_e is of the dimension of dollars per year; d_e, of the dimension of dollars per year per year. Let the time period in question be half a year instead of a year; the same numerical value of d_e means that he saves twice as large a fraction of his income. q_e and d_e simply cannot be added: an individual will not be indifferent, as Walras' equation implies that he is, between a situation in which he starts with an income of $10,000 a year and adds $100 a year income to it by saving $2,000 during the year in question, which means that the rate of interest is 5 per cent, and a situation in which he starts with an income of $9,700 a year and adds $400 a year to it by saving $8,000 during the year in question. Savings cannot be assimilated directly to current consumption, precisely because their whole function is to provide a stream of consumer services.

In the earlier editions of the *Elements*, Walras made no attempt to derive the demand for savings from utility analysis. He simply wrote down as an empirical datum an individual savings function, and noted, quite correctly, that in order to derive it from utility considerations it would be necessary "to consider utility under a new aspect, distinguishing present utility from future utility."[8] This was no oversight and the change in the fourth edition no belated discovery of a neglected truth. Surely, the explanation must be that when Walras made the change in the fourth edition, he no longer had his system and its meaning and its role in his bones the way he did when he developed it; he was taken in by considerations of pure form; the substance which the form was to represent was no longer part of him. It would be hard to find a better example of the nonsense to which even a great economist can be led by the divorce of form from substance.

III. CONCLUSION

Walras has done more than perhaps any other economist to give us a framework for organizing our ideas, a way of looking at the economic system and describing it that facilitates the avoidance of mistakes in logic. It is no derogation of this contribution to emphasize that it is not by itself enough for a fruitful and meaningful economic theory; division of labor is appropriate in economic theory too. Economics not only requires a framework for organizing our ideas, it requires also ideas to be organized. We need the right kind of language; we also need something to say. Substantive hypotheses about economic phenomena of the kind that were the goal of Cournot are an essential ingredient of a fruitful and meaningful economic theory. Walras has little to contribute in this direction; for this we must turn to other economists, notably, of course, to Alfred Marshall.

The large and substantial immediate rewards from Walras' concentration on form; the prestige and intellectual appeal of mathematics; the difficulty of making experiments in economics and the consequent laboriousness and seeming unproductiveness of substantive work devoted to filling in our analytical filing boxes — all these have combined to favor the Walrasian emphasis on form, to make it seem not only an essential part of a full-blown economic theory, but that economic theory itself. This conception — or misconception — of economic theory has helped to produce an economics that is far better equipped in respect of form than of substance. In consequence, the major work that needs now to be done is Marshallian rather than Walrasian in character — itself a tribute to Walras' impact.

I am tempted, in concluding this rather discursive commentary, to paraphrase Mill's comment that "A person is not likely to be a good economist who is nothing else." [9] A person is not likely to be a good economist who does not have a firm command of Walrasian economics; equally, he is not likely to be a good economist if he knows nothing else.

NOTES

1. *Elements of Pure Economics*, translated by William Jaffé, published for The American Economic Association and the Royal Economic Society. (Homewood, Ill.: Richard Irwin, 1954. Pp. 374.) All subsequent page references not otherwise identified are to this volume.

2. J. Schumpeter, *History of Economic Analysis* (New York, 1954), p. 827.

3. As Jaffé remarks, the analysis of utility considerations in connection with the theory of capital formation and credit is in parts "obscure to the point of almost complete incomprehensibility." Jaffé gives an extensive reconstruction in an attempt to render the argument intelligible in his translator's note [2] to Lesson 27 (pp. 536–39). I find it difficult to accept this reconstruction in one important respect, namely, Jaffé's interpretation of the argument as applying to a stationary state and his resulting assignment of an essential role to expenditures on the replacement of capital goods. I am inclined to go to the opposite extreme. It seems to me that Walras here, as elsewhere, thought initially

in terms of capital goods that were permanent, required no maintenance or replacement, and gave rise to a permanent flow of services. The question he seems to me to be asking in the section at issue is: given a certain amount of productive power to be used in producing an additional set of permanent capital goods of this kind, what bundle of capital goods will produce the additional stream of consumer goods having the greatest utility. His proof is correct, provided one consistently treats the capital goods as permanent and interprets his differential coefficients or ratios between them as rates of substitution—which seems to me also required in Lesson 26 and to explain what puzzles Jaffé in his translator's note [1] to that lesson (p. 533). The equations labeled [ε] at the bottom of p. 297 are not simultaneously valid; they are alternatives, showing that if (A) is substituted for (T), and all other quantities are unchanged, the quantity of (A) acquired must equal in value the quantity of (T) given up; and so on for every possible pair. That this is intended seems to me even clearer from the wording of earlier editions.

The tendency for Walras to work his argument out initially in terms of permanent capital goods requiring no replacement seems to me to explain also how the difficulty arose which Jaffé deals with in his translator's note [3] to Lesson 27 (pp. 539–41). Having arrived at a result for this case, Walras generalized it without full proof to the case of nonpermanent capital goods, in the process making what Jaffé terms—correctly, I believe—a "slip."

4. Augustin Cournot, *Researches into the Mathematical Principles of the Theory of Wealth* (1838), transl. by Nathaniel T. Bacon (New York, 1897), p. 127.

5. *Ibid.*, pp. 127–28.

6. Walras comments that "when we pass from the realm of pure theory to that of applied theory or to actual practice, . . . the variations in the unknown quantities will be effects of either the first or the second order, that is to say, effects which need or need not be taken into consideration, according as they arise from variations in the special or the general data" (pp. 307–8; see also similar comment on p. 431). In a translator's note, Jaffé cites this sentence as evidence that I "drew too sharp a contrast between Marshall and Walras" in my article "The Marshallian Demand Curve," *Jour. Pol. Econ.* Dec., 1949, LVII, 463–95; reprinted in my *Essays in Positive Economics* (Chicago, 1953), pp. 47–99. He goes on to say, "There one gets the impression that Walras's sole preoccupation was the achievement of 'abstractness, generality and mathematical elegance' (p. 490), while Marshall sought 'an engine for the discovery of concrete truth.' A more valid and important distinction between Walras and Marshall resides in the fact that the former always took great care not to confuse pure theory with applied theory, while the latter gloried in fusing the two"

(p. 542).

In his final sentence, Jaffé speaks like a true Walrasian in methodology. One first constructs a pure theory, somehow on purely formal considerations without introducing any empirical content; one then turns to the "real" world, fills in the empty boxes, assigns numerical values to constants, and neglects "second-order" effects at this stage. As I have argued extensively elsewhere [particularly in "The Methodology of Positive Economics" and "Lange on Price Flexibility and Employment: A Methodological Criticism," both in my *Essays,* pp. 3–43, 277–300, the latter reprinted from this *Review,* Sept., 1946, XXXVI, pp. 613–31], this seems to me a basically false view. Without denying the importance of what Jaffé and Walras call "pure theory" (see my comments below), I deny that it is the whole of "pure theory." More important in the present context, two largely parenthetical comments in the *Elements* to the effect that second-order effects will have to be or can be neglected in application seem a rather thin basis on which to claim that Walras was concerned with the construction of "an engine for the discovery of concrete truth." As I argue in the text, I remain of my original opinion; indeed, I am confirmed therein by the careful rereading of Walras to which I was led by the request to write this article, by Jaffé's critical comment, and by similar comments in reviews of my *Essays.*

7. I am indebted for this tidbit to Richard S. Howey, *The Rise of the Marginal Utility School, 1870–1889,* unpublished Ph.D. dissertation at the University of Chicago, 1955.

8. Jaffé's Collation of Editions, note [h] to Lesson 23, p. 587; my translation from Jaffé's quotation in French.

9. From *On Comte,* p. 82, as quoted by Alfred Marshall, *Principles of Economics,* 8th ed., (London, 1920), p. 771.

28.

CARL G. UHR
University of California, Riverside

Knut Wicksell—

A Centennial Evaluation

Johan Gustav Knut Wicksell was born on December 20, 1851 in Stockholm to a Swedish middle-class family. He died in his 75th year of life on May 3, 1926. During his years of graduate study, 1880–90, and his career as a creative economic theorist, 1890–1915 being his most active period, he was a contemporary of Menger, Böhm-Bawerk, Walras, Marshall, Wagner, and Spiethoff, whose works, apart from those of his colleagues in Sweden, D. Davidson and G. Cassel, influenced his own development and thought in many ways.[1]

Wicksell's "student years" were unusually long.[2] Before he was appointed to the chair of political economy and fiscal law at Lund University in 1900, he was a mature man with a growing family, 49 years of age, and already a writer of renown who, apart from some important articles and tracts, had published three of the five volumes that constitute his major works.[3] Two circumstances contributed to the tardy materialization of his academic career, his relatively late introduction to economics in about 1880 from graduate study of mathematics (which latter he pursued until 1885 when he went abroad for five years to study economics at the universities of England, France, Germany, and Austria), and his early reputation for social and religious unorthodoxy. The latter made his appointment a hotly contested issue and a decided victory for academic freedom.

At Lund his career was very productive. He contributed a stream of

Reprinted from *The American Economic Review*, XLI (December 1951), 829–60, slightly enlarged, by permission of the author and The American Economic Association.

significant articles mainly to the newly launched Swedish economic journal, *Ekonomisk Tidskrift,* and to certain German learned periodicals, and wrote the two volumes of his *Lectures on Political Economy.*[4] In 1916, on reaching mandatory retirement age (65) and pensioned status as a professor emeritus, Wicksell left Lund to return to Stockholm. From that time until his death, he devoted himself to a very busy life of writing in the learned and the daily press on the Swedish inflation problem occasioned by World War I, and to service on a series of government commissions of inquiry into Sweden's monetary and taxation problems.

I. ORIENTATION AND METHOD IN ECONOMICS

Although this sketch of Wicksell's life reveals very little about him that seems unusual other than a tenacious studiousness, the quality of his work as an economist was determined both by his early training in mathematics and by his youthful and life-long attachment to the social reform movement of the 1880's.

His mathematical background accounts for the form and organization of his writing, and often endows the latter with a very formal, abstract character. From mathematics he brought to economics a methodology he was convinced would supersede the sterile empiricism of the German historical school and expose beyond plausibility the doctrinaire extravagances alike of the harmony-economists and their Manchester followers and of their bitter opponents, the Marxist socialists.

This was the deductive method of successive approximation applied with telling effects by Cournot and Walras, whose works he held in high admiration. It permits the economist to abstract from confusing detail and interrelations and isolate the forces at work in simplified, hypothetical cases containing definite elements of the complex reality economic theory seeks to understand. Wicksell was convinced that pursuit of this method was indispensable for theoretical as well as practical progress in economics. It seemed to him that it, and it alone, gave promise of yielding the economist cogent hypotheses which he needs before he can fruitfully approach empiric data for verification or refutation of his theorems, and before he may offer guidance to or interpret the results of public and private economic policy.[5] This was also the reason he avoided statistical work, with the two exceptions of a brief sketch of a theory of index numbers, *Interest and Prices,* Chapter 2 and Appendix (which latter was omitted in the English translation), and a pamphlet, *Läran om befolkningen* (Theory of Population), 1910, in which he developed a method for forecasting the trend and composition of Sweden's population. In both cases he made a contribution, but, on the whole, he was inclined to concentrate on problems of pure theory and to leave to others the task of adapting and testing by practical application.

Few would deny that in his generation Wicksell was uncommonly successful in applying his mathematical method in almost all branches of economic theory. As was to be expected, it served him particularly well in static analysis, as in *Über Wert* and *Lectures-I*. There he was a master craftsman in deepening and extending received theory, in laying bare its limitations, in generalizing it by transforming and reconciling apparently contradictory analyses, such as those of Böhm-Bawerk and of Walras, into unified syntheses. Essential as this was for further progress, it was not here, not in the static equilibrium analysis, that his genius played its important creative rôle.

To the contrary, his greatness rests on the advance he made toward fruitful theoretical solutions of the problems of (1) capital accumulation, (2) the relations between distributive shares in conditions of net investment and technological change, and (3) monetary relations in a "pure credit" system. For all the progress he made in this sphere, which inevitably involved dynamic analyses, his method of successive approximation sometimes got in his way and kept him from making even greater contributions. The too static approximations he employed to deal with dynamic sequences prevented him, at times, from reaching certain insights which were attainable within the same problem-focus, and were discovered by his followers, Lindahl, Myrdal, and Ohlin.

If, however, his mathematical mode of thought determined the form and probably appreciably restricted the scope of his work, it did not detract from the far-reaching implications he was wont to draw from some of his formal demonstrations. Neither did it fetter that agile spirit of freedom and well-nigh prophetic sense of the possibilities of social reform that characterize his outlook and constitute the real meaning of his economic philosophy. Clues to the latter must be sought in the character of the man and in the circumstances and motives that attracted him to economics from other pursuits.

It is said that as a youth Wicksell, who, like most of his contemporaries, was brought up on the moral precepts of the state supported Swedish Lutheran Church, underwent a religious crisis from which he emerged an a-religious philosophical rationalist of the radical type. This tendency was reinforced by his studies and contacts in university life, especially in student activities relating to the social reform movement. In due course he became known not only for his intellectual acumen but also as a gifted speaker. As such he was elected chairman of the Student Corps at Uppsala, 1878–79. This in turn brought him invitations to lecture on diverse subjects to welfare and civic organizations. One of these occasions became a turning point in his life and led to his study of political economy in earnest.

In the spring of 1880 he was addressing a temperance organization on the causes and remedies for alcoholism. Among causes he pointed to the abject poverty and dreariness of home life for the majority of urban workers, a poverty reinforced by the arrival of more and more children. As a remedy he suggested it was up to the medical profession to perfect simple, safe methods of contraception to arrest excessive procreation, and to disseminate the knowledge and application of such methods. Had it not been for the fact that the substance of his lecture was reported in the daily press,

Wicksell might calmly have returned to his mathematical studies. But as it was, what he had to say reached a wider, more articulate public. Since it offended against the mores of the times just as the Darwinian theory of evolution in an earlier day offended against theological dogma, the response was immediate and strong. He was criticized and reviled in the press by professors of medicine, clergymen, essayists, and editors. Overnight he achieved the unenviable reputation of a "moral nihilist" and came to be regarded as the leader of a suspect small intellectual sect known as neo-Malthusians. He defended himself ably and with courage in articles and tracts, all of which added to his notoriety.

In this process he felt the need to make a more methodical study of population questions. So he made the acquaintance of D. Davidson, then a docent in economics at Uppsala. Davidson, who became his life-long friend, introduced him to Malthus by lending him his copy of the *Principle of Population*. From there it was but a short step for him to the study of classical economics in its entirety. This he pursued in conjunction with mathematics until 1885 when, as we have seen, he went abroad to study modern economics. Upon his return to Sweden, Wicksell not only resumed his advocacy of the neo-Malthusian principles he had defended a decade earlier, but also broadened his activity in behalf of the social reform movement.

II.   SOCIAL REFORM PROGRAM OR THEORY OF ECONOMIC DEVELOPMENT

At the close of the 19th century, Wicksell was convinced that the world possessed few additional, unexplored, and unexploited natural resources that would permit continued, rapid growth in numbers without impoverishment. He also thought the industrial revolution and epoch-making inventions of that century represented a unique period in man's economic history, one not likely to be outdistanced by the technological progress to be expected during the 20th and later centuries. For these reasons he thought attainment of stationary population of optimum size[6] throughout the world to be the *sine qua non* for a prospective rise in the mass standard of welfare. Accordingly, he made this condition the basis for most of his speculations concerning the long run or the economic future.

However, granted a discernible tendency for population to become stationary at a size that is optimal in relation to the economy's resources and technology, Wicksell was optimistic about its future economic improvement, a process he was convinced would be hastened and made more harmonious by adoption of certain reforms his economic studies led him to advocate. This was implied in his statement that

. . . the definition of political economy as a practical science is the theory of the manner of satisfying human needs which gives the greatest possible satisfaction to society as a whole, having regard for future generations as well as the present. . . . As soon as we begin seriously to seek for the conditions of the welfare of the whole, consideration for the interest of the proletariat must emerge; and from thence to the proclamation of equal rights for all is only a short step. . . . *The very concept of political economy, or the existence of a science with such a name, implies, strictly speaking, a thoroughly revolutionary programme.*[7]

His "revolutionary programme" contained at least four interrelated parts for a multiple attack on the major problems his analysis had uncovered: problems of (1) monopoly and imperfect competition, (2) inequality of income and wealth, (3) inequality of economic opportunity, and (4) economic instability associated with the trade cycle and with certain abberations of monetary policy and institutions.

A. *The Public versus the Private Sector of the Economy*

His program involved first a substantial expansion of the public sector of the economy, partly at the expense of the private enterprise sector, and chiefly in behalf of perpetuating for the future the freely competitive portion of the latter under more tenable and stable auspices.[8] Expansion of the public sector was in part to take the form of public ownership and operation of "natural" monopolies (public utilities) and also of "artificial" ones, or of "enterprises and industries showing unmistakable tendencies toward formation of cartels."[9]

Monopolistic enterprises should be acquired by local or national governments by properly compensating their private owners. But once acquired, Wicksell insisted they should be publicly operated to give consumers the full benefit of their realizable "economies of scale." This was to be achieved by a combination of taxes and a technique of pricing their output according to marginal unit cost. Their prices were to be reduced by trial and error, and their output and sales expanded according to elasticity of demand, up to an equilibrium point where the sale value of output increment sold after the last price reduction (*i.e.,* output increment times new lower price) exactly equals the increment in total cost of producing the extra output. Since marginal unit cost and price would in most such cases be less than average total unit cost on the corresponding total product, the resulting deficit should be met from taxation.

It is not certain that he would have applied this method universally, for he was aware that complications would arise in all but the simplest cases, but he did not stop to work them out. At any rate, by way of contrast, he thought it irrational for governments deliberately to operate public enterprises for profit as in the case of Prussia's state-owned railways. To his mind the *raison d'être* for public enterprises was to obtain a better allocation and utilization of the nation's resources than private monopoly offers, and not one of using them as engines of indirect taxation.[10]

Secondly, extension of the public sector of the economy was to take the form of a substantial increase in the variety and extent of social services. He considered social services as necessary and justified as a form of secondary or "social" distribution to compensate for income inequalities that arise in the course of primary or "functional" distribution to factor owners according to the marginal revenue productivity of productive factors. For, as he repeatedly said:

On the whole it is a mistake to regard as obvious — as is so often done — that healthy persons capable of work must be able to live from their labor *alone*.[11]

His first concern among social services was for education. He not only wanted the government to make schooling "free" to the public at all levels of academic and vocational instruction, but also to provide subsistence grants for impecunious and worthy students. Further, he stressed the need for a broad program of social security legislation and for national health insurance. He would have devoted the proceeds of most of the progressive income and unearned increments taxes he advocated as support for these activities.[12]

B. Reconstruction of the Fiscal System

The second part of Wicksell's program called for revision of extant tax systems, mostly composed of indirect taxes, and for changes in the political conditions for determining national budgets and the revenue measures needed for their execution. Because of the outrageously regressive incidence of taxes in the 1890's, he urged decreased reliance on excise and tariff duties in the revenue system as a whole and adoption and development of progressive taxes on personal incomes, estates, and corporate profits, as well as a modification of the general property tax to capture an increasing share of "unearned" land value increments. As for high sumptuary excises on liquor and tobacco, he argued for scaling them down to moderate rates and imposing consumer rationing instead, *i.e.*, a "liquor and tobacco control" system, to achieve more equitably the sumptuary ends, and improvement in public health and morals, that they were originally intended to serve.[13]

But tax reform, he realized, must be preceded by political reform to remove all property qualifications for the franchise. Hence he supported the movement for universal suffrage, aware that its achievement would shift political power from the minority of enfranchised property owners to the working class. To make possible an orderly evolution of political relations in this process, he insisted on special safeguards to protect the identity and integrity of political minorities from tyrannization by the majority. For minorities must be preserved to perform their vital task of criticism. The guarantees of a bill of rights were, in his opinion, not sufficient for this. It required more than that, namely, their effective inclusion in the system of representation. Hence he advocated an election system based on proportional representation.[14]

Thus it was both for political and for economic reasons that Wicksell supported the trade union movement and was anxious to extend "free" education to all. Trade unions seemed indispensable for the civic and democratic education of a politically inexperienced working class which suddenly might find itself in possession of national political power and might be maneuvered into perverting a representative, constitutional democracy into mobocracy that has its terminus in dictatorship.

Fully aware that even in a democracy with universal suffrage and proportional representation the potentially all-embracing fiscal power can be captured by narrow, sectional interests at the expense of the general welfare, Wicksell wanted to make doubly sure this would not happen. To that end he urged the following reform in matters involving budgets-and-revenues: (1) Budget proposals must always be accompanied by matching revenue or finance proposals so that expenditures are not approved without regard to the finance requirements they imply. (2) Budget and tax proposals, usually made by the administration and adopted as legislative agenda by simple majority vote in Parliament, must be alterable by amendment by any member or group in Parliament. And only those proposals that are approved by a "qualified majority," *i.e.*, two-thirds of the membership, are to be adopted and embodied in the final budget-and-revenue acts. According to Wicksell, this was necessary both for reasons of equity and on the grounds of the marginal utility calculus.[15]

Following Adam Smith, he believed governments should only undertake functions (*a*) that are not served by private enterprise, and (*b*) that are not served as well by private enterprise. The citizens via their representatives in Parliament must decide what those functions are. Such decisions must rest on a marginal utility calculus comparing the utility of proposed services with the tax burden they imply. In Wicksell's opinion, functions proposed for government action which fail of two-thirds majority approval were not likely to be clearly and unequivocally in the general interest even if supported by ephemeral, bare majorities. Furthermore, functions that are approved must be served to a determinate extent. This involves division of the total budget into separate activities in proportions that, again, must correspond to the current status and expression of the general interest. Finally, in spending for budgeted purposes, government confers general benefits on the public at large and also special benefits on certain segments of that public. Spending for law enforcement may yield only general benefits, but spending for a river improvement yields greater benefits to adjacent property owners than to others. In general, the qualified majority in Parliament must feel that the marginal utility of a proposed government service at least equals the tax burden it imposes to give it approval. If the proposed service yields only general benefits, it should preferably — because of diminishing marginal utility of income — be supported by taxes levied according to the ability principle. If it yields only benefits for some and not for other citizens, it should be supported by taxes levied according to the benefit principle. If it yields both general and special benefits, it should be financed by benefit- and by ability-taxes in the proportions its separate and general benefits bear to the total benefits it confers.[16]

As it happened, Wicksell lived to see some of the foregoing reforms introduced in Sweden. Universal suffrage was achieved during World War I. The growth of the trade union movement and the Social Democratic Party ushered in several of the tax reforms for which he had pleaded and extended social services considerably in the fields of education, social security, public health and health insurance. While his proposal of two-thirds majority approval of budget and revenue acts was not adopted at the national level, where, instead, other innovations of fiscal policy were evolved, it was adopted in principle by a number of provincial and municipal governments. By pointing out this we do not imply that Wicksell and his followers were solely or largely responsible for these reforms. Nonetheless, a certain credit is due him for having foreseen and pleaded for most of them a generation or more before they took place.

C. Monetary Reform

In the third place, Wicksell's reform program called for changes in monetary institutions and policy which, in principle, anticipated by almost fifty years the compromise between monetary nationalism and international exchange stability which has found expression in the International Monetary Fund.

At the institutional level he wanted to strengthen the credit control exercised by discount policy and open-market operations of central banks over private banks. Ultimately he visualized nationalization of the central bank in each country and its replacing private commercial banks by opening affiliates in every town and hamlet. Then he pleaded for abandonment of the gold standard and for effective demonetization of gold. This was to be done by freeing central banks from the obligation to settle payments balances in gold by their entering into international clearings arrangements with each other to redeem each other's notes and drafts at par and sell the same to the public at par. Further to immunize them from the vagaries of gold production and of gold influx and efflux in the course of foreign trade, he thought it necessary that they cease the free minting of gold and abandon the practice of buying and selling gold at fixed mint prices. The world price of gold would henceforth depend chiefly on industrial demand in relation to its supply.[17]

At the policy level, most of his life he thought the aim of central banks in regulating the supply of money, now bank credit money, should be price stabilization, i.e., stabilizing the value of money in terms of the price level of consumption goods. The means to that end were to vary central bank discount rates in the same direction as the consumer price index, thus offsetting a sustained rise in the latter by high discount rates and credit contraction and counteracting its sustained decline by reversing the process. He was convinced that this policy should be pursued both internally and internationally. To the latter end he asked that an international commission of experts work out an international price index to be the guide line for the concerted discount policy of central banks associated in the international clearings union. But, to obviate breakdown of this scheme from the balance of payments disequilibria that various nations develop from time to time as indicated by persistent debit clearings for the nations in question, he urged that, subject to the consent of the central bank majority in the clearings union, they be permitted to adopt discount policies running counter to that of the majority, and, with the cooperation of the latter, to engage in international capital transactions, etc., until the causes of their payments disequilibria had been overcome.

Toward the end of his life, 1925–26, it is true that Wicksell, impressed with his colleague Davidson's penetrating theoretical attack on his price stabilization aim, and further impressed by the monetary upheavals of World War I, modified his emphasis on price stabilization. In the end he had to admit its inconsistency with the conditions of monetary equilibrium which his own analysis had done so much to bring to light. To supplement it, he groped for other, more complex criteria for monetary policy (reminiscent of D. H. Robertson as of 1926), a matter he was unable to resolve to his own satisfaction.[18]

Yet this did not lessen the penetration of his insight into the essential requirements for stable international monetary relations, namely, an institutional arrangement which yields substantially the same exchange stability that was the glory of the gold standard but at the same time provides flexibility where the latter was rigid, i.e., provides an orderly procedure for revaluation of exchange rates when persistent payments disequilibria occur. How much clearer and how much more correct his insight into these relations was than that of most of his contemporaries can best be seen if we recall that Marshall argued for a combination of the symmetallic standard, application of bank rate to restrain activities of speculators, and a tabular standard of value for long-term credit.

D. Countercyclical Credit Policy

The fourth part in Wicksell's program was addressed to the problem of economic instability. It called for government-supported extension of credit in times of depression to maintain a tolerable level of employment by inducing manufacturers to produce to stock when costs are low and to hold resulting inventories off the market until improvement of trade in recovery would make it possible to dispose of them at a gain.

He considered the trade cycle, as distinct from monetary crises (which he attributed chiefly to irrational criteria for monetary management under the gold standard), to be caused by the uneven and unpredictable movement of "real forces," particularly technological innovations and the associated jerky pace of investment in fixed real capital. This process, he thought, could be smoothed substantially by countercyclical production for inventory purposes. But the credit extension needed to finance the latter admittedly represented unusual risks. The banks, committed to his price stabilization policy, could not be expected to carry it out unaided, especially not at the exceptionally low interest rates that must be offered to induce much additional borrowing for inventory production in depression. Hence the government must either supplement bank credit with public credit, or else underwrite the risks and losses the banks may incur in this process.[19]

III. EVALUATION OF WICKSELL'S REFORM PROGRAM

The foregoing account of Wicksell's social reform program should dispel any feeling of contradiction between the abstract treatment that dominates his major works and the concrete aims his analysis indicated to be attainable. Moreover, in broad features it reveals his theory of economic progress. For years he had planned to write a third volume of Lectures (*cf.*, *Lectures-I*, pp. 7–8) to deal with social economy or with the conditions of economic progress, as we might express it today. There he intended to investigate the application of economic theory and precept to the penultimate problem of the science — the maximization of social welfare — under assumptions involving radical change or reform of existing institutions. He never found the energy to complete this task as a systematic exposition. Yet, as we have seen, he left behind enough fragments in his books, his tracts and articles, to give us his vision of the future more rational, more stable political economy.

Thus, in a greater measure than his celebrated contemporaries, Wicksell emerges as a theoretical apostle of the "mixed economy." He labored, more fundamentally than others, in the tradition of J. S. Mill, whose famous dictum seems to have dominated his outlook:

. . . the Laws of Production of wealth partake of the character of physical truths. There is nothing optional or arbitrary in them. It is not so with the Distribution of wealth. That is a matter of human institution solely.[20]

Without sacrificing, indeed while emphasizing, the all-essential rights and freedoms of the individual, Wicksell pointed out clearly some of the paths whereby society may advance in an orderly fashion toward a more nearly optimal allocation of resources, greater income equality, effective equality of opportunity, increasing security and enhanced material welfare. For the system he delineated, for a society with a population of optimum size, a system of public and freely competitive private enterprise, guided by his conception of rational economic policy, gave promise of greater economic stability than prevailed in his own day. It was not a case of his system being designed to eliminate all economic fluctuation, but the behavior of the economy could be expected to be such that average rate of output would be considerably closer to full capacity rate of production than in the past. And its productive capacity could also be expected to continue increasing with the progress of private and social investment and improvements in technology, for the reforms he advocated would not have impaired the inducements for these activities.

It is, of course, easy to criticize his vision of economic progress, especially with the benefit of hindsight. It is clear now that he placed too great reliance on the adjustment powers of the interest rate mechanism, that he made inadequate allowance for risk and uncertainty as impediments to investment, that he was not fully aware of the impact of large-scale deficit finance and huge public debts on contral bank powers of monetary management. This and more can be said against his vision. But then we must remember that his writing largely pre-dates the fateful year 1914. He could not foresee the problems that have come to afflict a society which has exposed itself twice to the holocaust of total war. Who will gainsay that his reliance on interest rate variation and on counter-cyclical production for inventory purposes may not have been more effective than they now seem to most of us in preserving a tolerable degree of economic stability if the pre-1914 society had continued to evolve in peace? And if it had applied but a fraction of the resources and ingenuity it wasted on warfare to the social reforms he advocated?

For all that, Wicksell's greatness as an economist rests much more on his creativeness as a theoretician than on his views concerning economic development. His stature as a theoretician is in turn attributable to the vivid imagination with which he tackled intractable problems, and to the rigorous scientific method he applied in his work. As a result, several of his contributions are of value still, not so much because of the particular conclusions he formulated, for they have mostly been superseded by subsequent work. It is rather because of the highly fruitful points of departure he found from which to approach problems, and because of the flexible framework of analysis he developed, which afforded a wide perspective that enabled others to make further progress.

IV. CONTRIBUTIONS TO ECONOMIC THEORY — STATIC ANALYSIS

A. The Marginal Productivity Theory of Distribution

Considering the state of economic theory as of 1890 it is not surprising that Wicksell sensed the need for a synthesis. With the Austrians, the British neo-classicists, and the Lausanne schools sharing related orientations in value theory but having divergent views on production, capital, and distribution, the time seemed ripe to him to attempt a consistent synthesis between these approaches. In substance this is what Wicksell achieved in *Über Wert* by using the marginal-utility-marginal-productivity theories of Jevons and Menger, adding to these the derived Böhm-Bawerkian analysis of capital, and fusing the product within a Walrasian framework of general equilibrium to reveal the multiple causal interrelations of the theoretical edifice. In this process he became a founder of the marginal productivity theory of functional distribution.

Chronologically Wicksell was the first, in 1893, to demonstrate the "product exhaustion theorem," or the determinacy of functional distribution on the basis of product-exhaustion by imputation of distributive shares to co-operating factors of production in terms of their respective marginal productivity. However, he was content to let the credit for the "theorem" go to Wicksteed who, independently, adduced a more systematic demonstration of it in *Coordination of the Laws of Distribution* the following year.[21]

Wicksell's use of the marginal-utility-productivity theory calls for comment. While he stressed the limitations of marginal utility theory (the impossibility of interpersonal utility comparisons, the difficulties the marginal calculus encounters in commodities in joint demand, in goods produced in joint supply, and with goods that are large and indivisible relative to the individual's budget), he defended it decisively against its critics in an article, "Zur Verteidigung der Grenznutzentheorie," *Zeitschrift der gesammten Staatswissenschaften* (1900), pp. 577 ff. As we have seen, he was also at pains to extend its scope more directly to public finance as the underpinning for his system of "equitable taxation." At the same time he wanted to purify this theory from certain apologetic overtones that had become attached to it.

It is clear that the general equilibrium that arises in perfect competition represents an economic optimum of some sort, especially from the standpoint of production. Given the distribution of income, consumers maximize utility positions relative to ruling prices by spending so as to obtain equimarginal utility per dollar. Producers maximize profit positions (at zero net profits in the long run) by arranging plant to optimal scale, producing the output quantities for which least average costs and marginal costs equal demand price. To do this, they use factors in proportions and quantities such that, given their prices, they obtain equi-marginal value (or revenue) product per dollar of factor outlay.

Walras and later Pareto, not to mention others (J. B. Clark, for instance), concluded that the foregoing equilibrium represented maximization of social welfare.[22] Wicksell objected that since interpersonal utility comparisons can not be made, it is impossible to ascertain which of many possible production-consumption equilibria indicate maximum social welfare. Secondly, the consumer maximization that arises in free competition is relative to (1) the competitively established structure of prices and to (2) the pre-existing distribution of income and wealth. It constitutes no guarantee that a different distribution, for instance, one favoring low income groups and achieved by authoritarian imposition of a set of uniform prices, will not yield a greater quantum of utility. For, as he pointed out:

. . . in normal cases there can always be found a system of uniform prices at which exchange will produce a larger sum of utility than at competitive prices.[23]

Yet, these reservations notwithstanding, Wicksell remained at least a quasi-economic liberal in questions of intervention in "the system of competition" on behalf of increasing social welfare, for

. . . an encroachment on free competition, if it is . . . (to increase social welfare) . . . must be effected *in the right direction*. Unrestricted liberty is infinitely to be preferred to a misguided system of restriction on competition.[24]

However, if this could be said by way of qualification of the marginal-utility-productivity theory on its home grounds, the stationary society of universal free competition, then far greater qualifications were in store for it in the real world where "our assumption of free competition is and can only be incompletely realized."[25]

B. Theory of Price in Imperfect Competition

Wicksell made only slight headway with the theory of imperfect competition because of his inadequate concept of the firm.[26] Nonetheless, using retailing as a form of imperfect competition short of monopoly, he anticipated some of the modern theory of monopolistic competition by showing that free entry in such conditions results in overcrowding — too many, less than optimal-scale retail firms for the good of retailers and their customers alike. He also attributed the existence of fairly fixed, differentiated retail markups to differentiation of firms, since consumers, unable accurately to judge quality of complex merchandise, become dependent on particular retailers as "buyer experts." Hence inelasticity of demand for retail services increases in proportion to the degree of consumer ignorance.[27]

Consideration of imperfect competition led him to delve into isolated exchange where his efforts led to an advance toward the theory of bilateral monopoly. At first (*Über Wert*, pp. 36 ff.), his position was similar to Edgeworth's — exchange ratios and quantities of goods traded at isolated barter are indeterminate within limits of the "contract curve." Decades later, 1925, in his review of Bowley's *Mathematical Groundwork for Economists*, he sensed an error in this theory. He went on to show that if a factor monopolist dominates in bargaining with an end-product monopolist who can not apply monopsony power, then even in bilateral monopoly, factor- and output quantities and prices are determinate. The factor monopolist attains a "real" maximum, and the end-product monopolist only a "relative maximum of normal returns." Thus the charmed circle of indeterminacy of bilateral monopoly was broken, albeit Wicksell was wrong, as Bowley pointed out in his reply, in holding that the converse case of end-product monopoly dominance was indeterminate.[28]

C. Theory of Capital and Interest

Wicksell's most important contribution to static analysis was his revision and reconstruction of Böhm-Bawerk's capital theory. He restated the latter solidly and lucidly on the basis of a stationary state and generalized it by (1) including land in its treatment, (2) introducing into it the assumption of variable production coefficients or factor proportions, and (3) by extending it beyond the confines of a one-commodity economy into a multiple-commodity general equilibrium treatment. As a result, Böhm-Bawerk's cumbersome trinitarian (the "three grounds") interest explanation was transformed into an explicit theory of interest as the marginal productivity of waiting, coordinate with the marginal productivity theories of wages and rent. In this connection, Wicksell also arrived on

694

highly agnostic premises at the conclusion that saving is likely to be interest-inelastic.[29]

Yet, his chief innovation in capital theory was his elaboration of a new, consistent concept of capital structure, actually a method of quantifying real capital both (1) as a determinate time-structure of production capable of variation in two dimensions, "width" and "height," and (2) as a quantification in value terms, a conception he referred to as "the stratification of capital through time" (*Lectures-I*, p. 151). He developed it after first using Böhm-Bawerk's "production period," and later an improved, alternate construct of his own, the "weighted average investment period" (*Lectures-I*, pp. 172 ff.), which, however, was less clear than his structure concept.[30]

The value of Wicksell's formulation was that it made the impact of capital accumulation on the national dividend and on the relations of distributive shares more accessible than they were in earlier versions of "Austrian" capital theory and in "non-Austrian" conceptions of real capital as an aggregate of producers' goods. The essentials of this conception and of the insights it afforded may be sketched as follows.

In a perfectly competitive, stationary society, in equilibrium the quantity of real capital can be viewed genetically as consisting of labor-and-land inputs invested ("saved up") during past periods. The specific capital goods of which it is made up yield, "mature out," the services of their invested inputs in production over more or less long-time-intervals or "maturation terms." Thus the capital structure can be expressed as (1) the number of invested inputs contained in it (or the number of such inputs required for its total replacement) times (2) the time-intervals such inputs must remain invested until they are used up, "mature their services," in production. Given the rates of wages, rent and interest, the value of the quantity of real capital can be obtained by multiplying these inputs by applicable wage and rent rates and by applying to each the rate of interest properly compounded for the maturation term each remains invested. Alternately, one can say that the value of a capital structure equals the sum of the properly discounted values of services its specific capital goods yield over future periods equal to their respective maturation terms.

Stationary conditions imply maintenance of the existing capital structure by replacement investment, which requires that a corresponding portion of society's total labor and land be thus "saved up" or invested in producing replacement goods, all its remaining labor-land being "current" factor services engaged in "direct" production of consumption goods. If interest is 5% and real capital has a corresponding net marginal productivity, then since real capital is "saved up" labor-land, it follows that the marginal productivity of invested factor units must stand in the ratio of 1.05/1.00 to that of "current" factor units. And it is the lower marginal productivity of "current" labor-land that determines the rates of wages and rent.

In equilibrium, at 5% interest rate, the current gross marginal product of real capital, (*i.e.*, its "maturing" services), must for opportunity cost reasons be of a magnitude relative to that of labor-land input required for its replacement, of 1.05 raised by the power of an exponent expressing the maturation term (*e.g.*, in years) during which this current replacement input must remain invested before it, in turn, begins yielding services to production.[31] This was sometimes expressed by saying that capital goods of different maturation terms yield the services of their "oldest saved up" labor-land inputs, and that, in equilibrium, their respective net current yields must stand in a *compound rate relation* to each other, *e.g.*, net yields of .05, .1025, .1576 per unit for goods of one-, two-, and three-year maturity terms, respectively.

One additional property of real capital requires notice, namely, that current replacement input for long-maturity capital is a progressively smaller fraction of the current replacement requirement for the larger number of short-maturity capital goods that, taken in combination, have approximately the same yield. This means that if and when there is an advantage in shifting or converting some short-term into long-term investments, that advantage is reinforced by the fact that *after* the shift is completed, the total requirement of labor-land for replacement work is diminished.[32] Input units thus released from replacement production are then added to the "pool" of "current" factor units producing consumption goods, where they exert downward pressure on wages and rents since they increase the supply of such units, reducing their marginal productivity.

Now society becomes non-stationary in only one respect; its capital structure expands by net investment. This means that more units of labor and land, over and above those usually engaged in replacement work, are withdrawn from consumption goods production to make net new capital goods. This raises wages and rents as supply of "current" services is reduced and their marginal productivity rises, while supply of capital increases and its marginal productivity declines, perhaps by an absolute amount equal to 1% from 5% to 4%.

At first the capital structure tends to increase by *expansion in "width,"* which means that *net investment increases all its capital goods* of different maturation terms *proportionately*. The structure usually contains more units of short- than of long-maturity real capital, and a proportionate increase in all varieties then means a larger absolute increase in the former than in the latter. This *disrupts* the *compound rate relations* that existed between their current yields in the initial equilibrium *in favor of long-maturity capital*. Net yields were .05, .1025, and .1576 per unit before "width" expansion reduced them by an equal absolute amount to .04, .0925, and .1476 per unit for one-, two-, and three-year goods respectively. At these yields three-year and two-year goods are *relatively more profitable* than one-year goods, and this induces expansion progressively in the "height" dimension of the structure.

"Height" expansion means that (1) *further net investment is concentrated* more and more *on long-maturity goods, and* (2) *some preexisting short-term investments are shifted* (by non-replacement and transfer of the corresponding current replacement inputs) *to long-maturity goods*. Accordingly, some labor and land previously engaged in replacement production is released to augment the supply of "current" factor services and exert

696

counterpressure to the wage and rent rise that occurred during "width" expansion. Thus wages and rents recede somewhat and marginal productivity of short-term capital, hence interest, rises somewhat, perhaps from 4.0 to 4.5%. When all penultimate adjustments of numbers of capital goods of different maturity terms in the structure are made and net investment ceases, fully restoring equilibrium, then current net yields of capital goods of different terms will again exhibit the proper compound rate relation to each other, now of .045, .092, and .141 per unit for goods of one-, two-, and three-year terms, respectively.

This was the essence of Wicksell's insight into capital accumulation. Taken in conjunction with his analysis of "cumulative processes" in monetary theory, it gave rise to "capital shortage and vertical maladjustment" theses of business cycles, first propounded by one of his followers, G. Åkerman, in 1924, and later, more elaborately, by Professor F. A. von Hayek.[33] While these theses were stimulated by, and were in a sense a logical outgrowth of Wicksell's work, we must emphasize that he did not share this perspective on business cycles, nor is it likely he would have concurred in the policy recommendations to which they gave rise.

V.   CONTRIBUTIONS TO ECONOMIC THEORY — DYNAMIC ANALYSIS

A. Distributive Shares and the National Dividend in Conditions of Capital Accumulation and Technological Change

Wicksell was the first among modern theorists to subject the question of relative and absolute distributive shares to rigorous analysis. His work was stimulated by reflections on Ricardo's famous chapter "On Machinery" and by Böhm-Bawerk's emphasis on lengthening the production period as a defense mechanism brought into action by rising wages.[34] Wicksell's treatment assumed a perfectly competitive society with a constant labor force and quantity of natural resources. His demonstrations showed the impact on the national dividend and on distributive shares of (1) net investment without technological change, (2) technological change without net capital formation, and (3) technological change and net capital formation proceeding chiefly in the "height" dimension of the structure. His conclusions may be expressed as follows.

Capital expansion in "width" and later, progressively, in "height," always increases the national dividend by the social marginal product of new capital. What happens to the distributive shares of capitalists, on the one hand, and of laborers-and-landowners, on the other, depends on the degree of capital intensity society has achieved, and on the downward (negative) acceleration of the marginal productivity of real capital. If capital intensity is small, both the relative and absolute share of capitalists rises, while the absolute share of labor-land also rises, though more slowly. With slight capital-intensity marginal productivity of capital can not have proceeded far into the stage of diminishing returns, and so the interest rate declines only slightly with net accumulation. But, *ceteris paribus,* accumulation eventually makes society capital intensive. Then the relative and absolute shares of labor-land increase; the relative share of capital declines, its absolute share continuing to increase slowly.

His analysis of technological change in the absence of net accumulation was a refutation of the Ricardian dictum that adoption of labor-saving machinery proceeds regardless of whether the national dividend declines in the process, as long as its adoption is profitable to entrepreneurs. Wicksell showed that technological improvement always increases the national dividend as long as perfect competition prevails. For it increases the average productivity of the factors though not necessarily the marginal productivity of all factors equally. For instance, it may increase that of land more than that of labor and lead to much labor displacement and hardship as land is progressively substituted for labor. But labor displaced by conversion of acreage from grain to pastoral agriculture will offer itself at competitively lower wages and so make grain farming more profitable than it was. This prevents full conversion of acreage into sheep-runs and intensifies cultivation on remaining grain farms. *Ergo,* the national dividend increases and contains more mutton as well as bread with, probably, some wool for export. Yet, he conjectured, most inventions raise the productivity of both labor and land and thus prevent a serious decline in labor's absolute share.

As net accumulation proceeds, labor and land constant, it proceeds progressively in the "height" dimension because long-maturity investments become *relatively* more profitable as wages and rents rise. This retards but can not stop the rise in wages and rent and the decline in capital's relative share. However, if at the same time some technological improvements occur, then, as he said:

> . . . the position is different *where,* as may easily happen, *some technical invention renders long-term capital more profitable (absolutely) than previously.* The consequence must necessarily be — so long as no further capital is saved — a diminution in the "horizontal dimension" and an increase in the "vertical dimension," so that the quantity of capital used in the course of the year will be reduced; an increased quantity of current labor and land will consequently be available for each year's direct production; and, although this need not necessarily cause their marginal productivity and share in the product to be reduced — since the total product has simultaneously been increased by the technical discovery — yet a reduction may clearly result. *The capitalist saver is thus, fundamentally, the friend of labor, though the technical inventor is not infrequently its enemy . . . . That the transformation of circulating into fixed capital, i.e. the change from short-term to long-term investments, may frequently injure labor is beyond doubt.*[35]

Thus technological change, if it enhances the marginal productivity of long-term investments *absolutely,* is likely to reverse the downward trend of the interest rate and the rise in wages and rents that otherwise follow from net accumulation with labor and land constant.

The foregoing shows clearly that Wicksell anticipated by almost three decades several of the conclusions of J. R. Hicks in *Theory of Wages* (1932). Hicks acknowledged his indebtedness to Wicksell's work. To see how close the connection is, one need only recall Hicks's suggestive theory of inventions. It strikes us that Hicks's induced (labor-saving) inventions that would have been profitable without an antecedent change in relative prices (*i.e.*, rise in wages, decline of interest) come to the same thing as Wicksell's "technical invention that renders long-term investment more profitable (absolutely) than previously."[36]

For all the progress Wicksell made with the shares-problem, one aspect of it invites criticism — namely, his constant treatment of it on the assumption of perfect competition, which is useful only for dealing with technologically stationary societies of atomistic enterprise. Once the scene shifts to technologically progressive societies, the problems of large-scale enterprise and imperfect competition inevitably intrude themselves into the analysis. Yet he was well aware of the relation between decline of competition and economies of scale in dealing with the product-exhaustion problem (*Lectures-I*, pp. 126–29, 131, 133). If Wicksell had also pursued his distributive shares discussion on the assumption of imperfect competition, then he might have discovered that oligopolistic market structures are apt to bring forces into existence which threaten the very source of technological progress in the interest of protecting existing investments against obsolescence. It was undoubtedly for lack of a developed theory of the firm that he was unable to effect this integration, in itself not far to seek, between his observations concerning imperfect competition in "value theory" and those of his "theory of distributive shares."

B. *The Wicksell Effect*

In his distributive-share analysis Wicksell stressed a force which is a partial offset to the decline of interest under continuous net accumulation, a phenomenon also observed by the classical economists, especially J. S. Mill, in their speculations concerning the tendency toward a zero interest rate and, presumably, a stationary society. This was the observation that a certain portion of net real saving is absorbed in rising real wages and rent during an interval of capital formation. This seemed a strong guarantee against a zero interest rate, for rising wages and rent could be expected to absorb enough net saving to prevent creation of the quantity of capital that would drive its marginal productivity to zero. Wicksell was rather preoccupied, in three separate demonstrations, with this partial-wage-absorption of saving, so much so that we label it the "Wicksell effect."[37]

He used his demonstrations as an argument against the full applicability to the factor real capital (at both the macro- and the micro-economic level) of "Thünen's law," as he used to call the marginal productivity principle. An increase in real capital, like that of any other factor, augments output by an increment, the social marginal product of capital. If we divide this output-increment by the net real saving that was destined and accounts for the increase in real capital, we obtain the "social marginal productivity rate" of real capital. Now if Thünen's law is to apply, this rate must equal the rate of interest ruling at the end of the period of net capital formation.

Actually it does not, for the social marginal productivity rate of capital is somewhat smaller than the interest rate in proportion to the extent to which rising wages and rent have absorbed some of the net saving. The interest rate, on the other hand, is determined by the marginal productivity of the somewhat smaller quantity of real capital that was created. Now, *per contra*, if society's labor force (or its land) increases, other factors constant, the resulting social marginal product when divided by the labor increment gives us its social marginal productivity rate which, since no similar absorption of labor power has occurred, equals the rate of wages (or rent) at the end of the interval of labor increase. Thus Thünen's law applies fully to labor and land and their remuneration, but it applies to real capital only at the private or micro-economic level.

There were difficulties with Wicksell's argument and proofs, matters we can not enter on here, yet he was substantially right about his "effect" being a phenomenon uniquely associated with changes in the factor real capital. His stress on it was effective in the sense that his proofs were a first attempt which gave rise to a succession of more effective ones to study the process of capital formation in detail.

Essentially, the Wicksell effect points to a host of problems connected with adjustments between the capital structure and (1) changes in income distribution, (2) changes in magnitude and composition of total output (relatively more or less capital goods or consumption goods when total output varies), and (3) changes in income dispositions of individuals (saving versus consumption when income varies) that are called forth by variations in the capital structure itself. These are adjustments which seem to be required to maintain equilibrium or to prevent the "vertical maladjustments" that von Hayek stresses. As such, the Wicksell effect at the real level is a force opposed to that of "forced saving" at the monetary level of analysis in his cumulative processes. If Wicksell had juxtaposed these two forces on a common plane of discourse, he might have arrived at a capital-structure-maladjustment thesis somewhat similar to von Hayek's. For it can be shown, though we must refrain from the attempt here, that von Hayek's "vertical maladjustment," or, in the later versions of his thesis, his "Ricardo effect," represents the swamping of the Wicksell effect that must occur by the increasing momentum of "forced saving" in the upward cumulative process.[38]

C. Monetary Theory

Undoubtedly, Wicksell's greatest contribution lies in the field of monetary theory. During the years 1898–1915 he became the founder of modern monetary analysis. He originated the aggregate demand-supply approach — emphasizing especially the relation of investment to savings — to changes in value of money and associated changes in tempo and scope of economic activity which find expression in fluctuations of price levels, income, and employment. This is not to say that he had an explicit theory of income and employment in the sense of the contemporary "Stockholm" and "Keynesian" schools, for, *inter alia*, he had no clear understanding of the consumption function and its impact on the determination of income. Yet, and herein lies perhaps his greatest merit, he developed the all-essential analytic framework within which these and other "schools" have generated their theories by using substantially the same variables he used, but assigning different values or rôles to them and dismantling some of his restrictive assumptions concerning perfect competition, perfect foresight, and so forth.

Wicksell acknowledged an intellectual debt to the participants of the bullionist controversy at the opening of the 19th century and an even greater debt to those, especially Thomas Tooke, who carried it on at mid-century as the currency-banking school polemic and in the debates surrounding the passage of the Peel Acts. They, together with Marshall and I. Fisher, may be regarded as his forerunners.[39] For it is still true that when Wicksell began his work, monetary theory was confined to varied expressions of the simple quantity theory. Apart from his own contributions, it remained in much the same state in the rest of the world until the 1920's, as is indicated by the success of I. Fisher's work, *The Purchasing Power of Money* (1911), and a second edition as late as 1922.

Monetary discussion was mainly devoted to questions of currency reform, mono- versus bi-metallism, and these versus "tabular" standards of value. Even Marshall with his insight into "real balances" as a prime constituent of the demand for money and his stress on the need for exercise of "bank rate" to restrain speculators and forestall panics, did not transcend the traditional concern over currency standards and the mechanism of payments.[40] In all fairness it can be said that with Marshall and Fisher the problem of value constancy of money was reduced to finding ways and means to make investors reckon in real terms and to bar "speculative" as distinct from "sound" investment. But in their systems there was no direct path from the elasticity and quantity of currency to the forces that act on individual income dispositions and on entrepreneurial production decisions. Keynes, who professed to labor in the Marshallian tradition, belatedly came to recognize this as is shown by his assessment of Marshall's and Wicksell's respective efforts in monetary theory.[41] Since we have already dealt with Wicksell's proposals for reform of monetary institutions, we proceed here to his apparatus of monetary analysis.

1. *Wicksell's Concept of Money and Credit.* In his criticism of the "simple" quantity theory, Wicksell made it clear that monetary analysis must proceed in short-run defiance of Say's law by means of an aggregate demand-supply approach.

Every rise or fall in the price of a particular commodity presupposes a disturbance of the equilibrium between the supply and demand for the commodity. What is true in respect of each commodity separately must doubtless be true of all commodities collectively. A general rise in prices is therefore only conceivable on the supposition that the general demand has for some reason become, or is expected to become, greater than the supply. . . . Any theory of money worthy of the name must be able to show how and why monetary or pecuniary demand for goods exceeds or falls short of the supply of goods in given conditions.[42]

For his purposes, a question of the conditions for value constancy of money and of the causes and consequences of its fluctuation in value, he adopted the following general concept of money:

> . . . money is a quantity in two dimensions, quantity of value, on the one hand, and velocity of circulation, on the other. These two dimensions multiplied together give the "efficiency" of money (a term due to Helfferich) or its power to facilitate the turnover of goods in a given period of time.[43]

This expresses the left side of the Fisher equation of exchange, MV. Although Wicksell studied the forces that account for variation in V, the reciprocal of the extent to which "value storage" occurs in the form of money, his analysis of V was neither complete nor fully integrated with the rest of his system. Briefly, it amounted to an income velocity explanation of the rate of turnover of cash balances.[44] Yet his study of velocity led him to a fruitful insight, that the influence of credit on currency "may under all circumstances be regarded as accelerating the circulation of money," i.e., increasing its "virtual velocity" (Lectures-II, p. 67).

From this he concluded that in a "pure cash" economy V is practically a constant, and the old quantity theory holds without qualification. At the other extreme, a "pure credit" economy (one where checking accounts have almost entirely replaced currency and where the total amount of deposits is fully subject to the policy discretion of the central bank), this V becomes a variable magnitude which may, potentially, approach infinity. Here the "supply of money" is perfectly elastic, and, subject to the central bank discount rate, adapts itself perfectly to the demand for money. Accordingly, he conducted most of his monetary analysis on the assumption of a "pure credit" system for a closed economy. This gave him a great advantage in generalizing his treatment by relegating particular monetary institutions into the background, and, as Ohlin put it, thus "escaping from the tyranny that the concept 'quantity of money' has exercised over monetary theory."[45]

2. *Wicksell's Theory of Monetary Equilibrium and his Norm for Monetary Policy.* Wicksell's apparatus of monetary analysis can be indicated as follows. Aggregate demand consists of money income spent for consumption and money income saved. Aggregate supply has two corresponding categories of goods, output of consumption goods and of capital goods. Changes in the value of money or in the price level must be determined by the interaction of these variables. Savings enter the money market as a supply of investable funds, where, if banks do not indulge in net creation nor in net destruction of deposits, they become available at a loan rate which equates entrepreneurs' investment demand for them to their supply. Investment demand is determined by the "real rate of interest," i.e., by the "expected yield on recently created real capital," the analogue of marginal efficiency of capital. The monetary equilibrium that arises when the loan rate equals the real rate was expressed in this manner:

> The rate of interest at which the *demand for loan capital and the supply of savings exactly agree,* and which more or less corresponds to the expected yield of the newly created real capital, will then be the normal or natural real rate.

It is essentially variable. If the prospects of employment of capital become more promising, demand will increase and will at first exceed supply; interest rate will then rise and stimulate further saving at the same time as the demand from entrepreneurs contracts until a new equilibrium is reached at a slightly higher rate of interest. At the same time equilibrium must *ipso facto* obtain — broadly speaking, and if not disturbed by other causes — in the market for goods and services, so that wages and prices will remain unchanged. The *sum* of money incomes will then usually exceed the value of consumption goods annually produced, but the excess of income — *i.e.*, what is annually invested in production — will not produce any demand for present goods but only for land and labor for future production.[46]

This equilibrium may be disrupted in several ways by his famous "cumulative processes." The real rate and investment demand are highly variable because expected yield of capital is affected by innovation, population growth, opening of new markets, etc. For one of these reasons the real rate rises while the loan rate remains constant. Investment demand rises above the concurrent supply of voluntary savings, but the deficiency is made up by net deposit creation within the pure credit system. Rising investment demand has begun raising prices on capital goods and shifts the distribution of augmented money income in favor of entrepreneurs. The latter, anxious to expand investment on roseate profit prospects, compete for labor and land fully employed elsewhere, and succeed in attracting some of these resources away from consumption goods production at a rise in wages and rents. Thus output of consumption goods declines somewhat while money income and consumption spending of workers and landowners increases. Hence consumption goods' prices rise, and their rise makes profit prospects in capital goods industries even brighter. This induces further expansion there at another rise in wages and rents with further curtailment of consumption output and a subsequent new rise in their prices, etc. This process might go on indefinitely until hyper-inflation ends in a crisis in the course of which the loan rate is raised. It may be raised above the level of the real rate with consequences of cumulative deflation, or it may be raised to equal the latter in which case a new equilibrium arises, most likely at prices that are somewhat higher than in the initial situation.

Wicksell did not insist that cumulative processes necessarily must terminate in crises of hyper-inflation or deflation; nor did he exclude the possibility they may set in motion forces that eventually generate a new equilibrium without crisis. He was content to have demonstrated that the discrepancy between the rates ". . . is enough to explain actual price fluctuations which manifestly cannot be due to variations in the quantity of gold . . . ," (*Lectures-II*, p. 200).

But even in a pure credit system, the banks are not in a position to know the vagaries of the real rate. Yet he insisted their primary duty is to give money value-constancy, *i.e.*, to stabilize the price level. The means to that end is for them to vary the loan-rate in the same direction as the drift of the price level away from its normal index level of 100. The result would not be perfect price stabilization but price fluctuation narrowed to a much smaller range than in the past. Moreover, in conditions short of a pure credit system, he was fully aware the banks can not effectively stabilize the price level by interest rate policy if large, autonomous changes in money quantity occur (for instance, gold in- or efflux for a particular country; for the world as a whole, a sudden rise in gold production or its cessation altogether; or if governments engage in heavy deficit finance and/or fiat issues, or their opposites). But the gold complications were presumably remediable by his international clearings system and the effective demonetization of gold, and, except in times of war, there should be no occasion for serious interference with price stabilization from the side of government finance.

3. *Modification of the Monetary Policy Norm — The Wicksell-Davidson Polemic.* His prescription of price stabilization as the norm for monetary policy rested on a tacit assumption which Davidson was quick to discover. This led to a polemic between the latter and Wicksell in *Ekonomisk Tidskrift,* 1906–1909. While Davidson had the better part of the argument, the issues between them were never properly joined because of the crabbed manner in which both of them argued.[47]

Davidson's point was that price stabilization is only consistent with maintenance of equilibrium if productivity is constant, but if the latter changes, the proper norm is to let prices vary roughly in inverse proportion to the change in productivity. We have initial equilibrium and productivity rises, which means the real rate rises, hence the banks should raise the loan rate accordingly. If this is done, money income remains constant, but increased productivity means larger output which must then be sold at declining prices. Now, if the banks insist on stabilizing prices, then they must reduce the loan rate to prevent the price decline. If so, the loan rate becomes "too low" and lays the basis for an upward cumulative process. For reduction of the loan rate means net deposit creation and an increase in factor payments proportionate to the rise in productivity. This increase in factor incomes is not likely to be divided between saving and consumption in the same proportion as the increase in output is composed of consumption and of capital goods. Most of the extra money income may be spent for consumption at a rise in consumption goods' prices which becomes the basis for an upward process.

It was years later, 1925, after Sweden had tasted severe inflation during World War I, and after Davidson had published the substance of his own monetary analysis in articles in *Ekonomisk Tidskrift,* 1918–23, that Wicksell conceded the strength of his argument. His concession came as an admission that banks can not effectively prevent the inflation that results from "commodity scarcity," *i.e.,* from the equivalent of a decrease in productivity, caused by blockade and other dislocations of warfare.[48] Yet Wicksell did not abandon price stabilization as an imperfect, but to his mind the only practicable criterion for monetary policy. In a peaceful world, he argued, there would be no war-caused "commodity scarcity" nor any other occasion for inflation due to precipitate "decrease in productivity." As for "increase in productivity," he averred such increases are of small scale and are a secular force that does not seriously distort equilibrium relations in the short run. As for Davidson's norm, to let prices vary inversely with changes in productivity, he thought it a counsel of perfection and pointed to the pervasiveness of imperfect competition to block its adoption. Thus he was convinced the practical choice lay between his own norm and no definite norm at all.

4. *Major Characteristics of Wicksell's Monetary Analysis.* Looking back on the foregoing, the salient features of Wicksell's innovation in monetary theory may be summarized as follows:

a. His explanation of cumulative price level fluctuations reversed the alleged relation between changes in money-quantity and the price level as expounded in the quantity theory. It was generally the other way around; the price level rises or falls without corresponding change in money-quantity or in output, but its fluctuation causes a corresponding change in velocity of circulation of money. In the absence of (1) large, autonomous changes in money-quantity (due (i) to the *modus operandi* of the gold standard, or (ii) to major changes in government finance), and in the absence of (2) large, autonomous changes in productivity, price level fluctuations were caused by a divergence between real and loan rates of interest.

b. The driving force behind the movement of prices was a variable investment demand functionally related to the real rate, which latter varies in response to the impact of "real forces," such as innovation, population growth, and so forth.

c. The variability of investment demand implied short-run divergence between aggregate demand and supply. For consumption demand (aggregate income minus saving), does not readily shift out of equilibrium with the supply of consumption goods *except as* total income changes. Hence changes in income were primarily due to a divergence between investment and savings.

d. A moving price level with its attendant changes in circuit velocity of money implies a change in the magnitude and distribution of total money income, and a "forced" change in the allocation of real income between consumption and formation of real capital, a phenomenon which in his day was expressed by the conception of "forced saving" and its opposite.

e. Maintenance of monetary equilibrium and its restoration after disruption was entirely placed on the adjustment powers of central bank discount or interest policy. Optimistically, he considered such policy equally capable of arresting and reversing a deflationary price movement as he, more realistically, thought it capable (in the absence of gold standard, or fiscal interference, or drastic productivity change) of arresting and reversing an inflationary price movement.

f. His analysis proceeded on assumptions of (i) a closed economy with a pure credit system, with (ii) perfect competition on all markets, (iii) high mobility and full utilization of resources, and (iv) near-perfect foresight for all except central bank directors who, because of their deficiency in this regard, must be guided by rational norms of monetary policy.

5. *Transformation of Wicksell's Heritage of Monetary Theory: The Rise of the "Stockholm School."* Shortly after his death, Wicksell's heritage of monetary theory and also that of Davidson, underwent a searching exegesis and expansion by the efforts of younger economists in Sweden, notably Professors Lindahl, Myrdal, and Ohlin, whose labors gave rise to the vigorous, contemporary "Stockholm School." We can not enter into this interesting development here, but it may be useful to point out the primary transformations Wicksell's heritage has undergone in this process.[49]

Lindahl and Myrdal approached the Wicksellian heritage in the conviction that entrepreneurial anticipations are the strategic factor to which most other economic variables respond. Each selected a more refined technique of analysis than Wicksell had used. Lindahl entered on a sequence or intertemporal equilibrium analysis, and Myrdal used a complementary technique of disequilibrium analysis, the *ex ante, ex post* method. The former attempts to find the conditions that influence and determine the direction of entrepreneurial anticipations and then seeks for criteria for policy that will elicit the kind of entrepreneurial behavior that tends to maintain or restore economic stability. The latter asks how, with the *ex post* data on which analysis must proceed, shall we be able to tell whether anticipations have been consistent *ex ante*, and if not, in which direction from *ex ante* equilibrium are we drifting? In both cases a systematic study was made of the Wicksellian apparatus under more realistic assumptions than he had used, assumptions of imperfect competition, imperfect foresight, underutilization of resources, and so forth. Some characteristic conclusions are as follows.

The significant variable, investment *ex ante*, is determined by entrepreneurial anticipations, and it in turn accounts for changes in income, and, via the latter, for the adaptation of savings (by *ex post* gains or losses) to the rate of investment. Since factor prices are not very flexible, income fluctuations account for variations in employment. Thus fluctuating income levels take the place of Wicksell's fluctuating price levels as the important variable. For the price level adapts itself to changes in income, and in adapting itself it effects changes in distribution of income, just as in Wicksell's case it was the quantity of money that adapted itself to the movement in the price level and affected income distribution in that process.

Monetary equilibrium or equality between *ex ante* investment and saving is compatible with price movements provided they are not cumulative and unilateral. It is also compatible with and conditioned upon human and other resource underutilization to a degree corresponding to the extent of market imperfection. Here a price-structure underemployment equilibrium emerges as an alternate to Keynesian underemployment equilibrium based on interest-inelastic investment demand and on a minimum level of interest rate determined by infinite elasticity of liquidity demand for cash balances.

In maintaining and restoring equilibrium, interest rate policy can be of service, for instance, in adapting flexible prices (capital values) to changes in inflexible prices (wage rates), but it can not guarantee full employment.

Its rôle is rather one of removing monetary causes of instability and of adapting the money and credit structure to nonmonetary causes of economic change. The latter must generally be dealt with by nonmonetary measures.

Because of imperfect competition and the coexistence of flexible and inflexible prices, interest changes by themselves are likely to be ineffective in achieving a sufficient approach to economic stability. Therefore, monetary policy requires coordination with other policy, especially with fiscal policy. Moreover, interest rate reduction in depression is unlikely to suffice for initiating recovery. The latter depends more on maintenance of consumption at some level not far below its average level, for instance, by means of public expenditures for social security, unemployment benefits and by private disinvestment. Cushioning of consumption and deferral of replacement investment during the downturn are together likely, after some time, to raise *ex ante* investment demand above the reduced rate of *ex ante* saving and thus provide a basis for recovery.

These and other insights, made available by the intensive and comprehensive work of the Stockholm School, indicate, however sketchily, some broad features of the transformation of the Wicksellian heritage.

VI. CONCLUSION: A COMMENT ON WICKSELLIAN ECONOMIC PHILOSOPHY

Perhaps it is fitting to close this paper with a general remark about the economic philosophy of Wicksell and his followers. That philosophy may be characterized as experimentalist on the positive side and as devoid of orthodoxy on the negative side. Neither he nor his followers have been imbued by strong preconceptions in favor of *laissez faire* systems. They were willing to bid the "unseen hand" farewell and place increasing reliance on deliberate, rationally conceived economic policy as constituting the best prospect for achieving greater stability and internal harmony in the economy. Because their outlook was focussed on, and to some extent enabled them to anticipate, the course of economic change, it avoided doctrinaire allegiance to particular positions and opposition to all others that has vitiated much of the reasoning among various "schools" outside as well as inside the Marxist camp.

It is readily granted that such a frame of mind *per se* is no guarantee against errors and bias in analysis, nor against selection of less-than-best policy alternatives. Yet it preserves and widens the scope for such objectivity as is possible in social science. It conduces to an openmindedness, a willingness to generate and test new approaches, including a certain readiness to take calculated risks where the *a priori* yields no unique answer. Needless to say, such a philosophy, which is the *essence* of the Wicksellian heritage, for all its adaptability does not lack for method and rigorous discipline. Yet, its success seems to rest on its having avoided making a straight-jacket out of discipline and on its having been able to distinguish between its assumptions and reality.

NOTES

1. The writer is especially indebted to Professor Emeritus Emil Sommarin, Wicksell's successor in the chair at Lund University, for biographical information. Our account of Wicksell's career is based in part on private correspondence with Professor Sommarin, in part on his article, "Das Lebenswerk von Knut Wicksell," *Zeitschrift für Nationalökonomie*, Vol. 9 (1930–31), pp. 221–67, and mostly on two chapters in his recent, charming book, *Studenter och Arbetare* (Students and Workers), (Lund, 1947), where he relates Wicksell's rôle in the social reform movements both at Uppsala and at Lund Universities.

2. Wicksell enrolled at Uppsala University in 1869 to study mathematics and physics; earned a B.A. degree in 1872 and later, 1885, a graduate degree, *philosophiae licentiatus*, in mathematics. Such degrees are given to advanced graduate students after comprehensive examinations in which, *inter alia*, preliminary drafts of their doctoral theses are evaluated. Usually such drafts are elaborated into finished form and another set of examinations ensue, resulting in the Ph.D. Wicksell went on instead with economics, in which, after study abroad, 1885–90, and further research in Sweden, he earned another *phil. lic.* at Uppsala, 1894, and his doctorate, 1895, on a thesis in the theory of tax incidence. The latter was incorporated as Part I of his work, *Finanztheoretische Untersuchungen* (Jena, 1896). Finally, 1899, he earned one more degree, *utriusque juris candidatus*, in "fiscal law." This was necessary for him in order to apply for a professorship in economics, for at that time economics was offered as an elective subject by the Faculty of Law. Hence professors of that subject were expected to be well informed and to offer courses on the relation of economics to jurisprudence, especially relating to the fiscal institutions and activities of government. During most of these years Wicksell and his family existed on research grants by Swedish foundations and on what little his writing brought in.

3. *Über Wert, Kapital und Rente* (Jena, 1893), an elegant mathematical treatment of static equilibrium theory, synthesizing the work of the Lausanne and the Austrian schools; *Finanztheoretische Untersuchungen* (Jena, 1896), an elaboration of his doctoral thesis into a lofty and speculative treatment of public finance; *Geldzins und Güterpreise* (Jena, 1898), translated, 1936, as *Interest and Prices*, his epoch-making treatise on monetary theory.

4. *Lectures on Political Economy*, Vol. I, *General Theory* (first Swedish edition, 1901), a revision and elaboration of his earlier analysis in *Über Wert;* and Vol.

II, *Money* (1906), an elaboration of *Interest and Prices*. Both volumes were translated 1934–35; we refer to them as *Lectures-I* and *Lectures-II*. They went through several editions, the latter with some revision, 1915, on points relating to the nature of monetary equilibrium.

5. Wicksell's statements on "method" in economics were always brief; *cf.* the prefaces and introductions to his works, *Über Wert*, pp. i–xxi, and *Lectures-I*, pp. 1–11.

6. He defined "optimum population" as a population of such size that its further increase involves a decrease in "social welfare," *Läran om befolkningen* (Theory of Population), (Stockholm, 1910), p. 42. His neo-Malthusianism recurs also in one of his most important tracts, *Socialiststaten och nutidssamhället* (The Socialist State and Contemporary Society), (Stockholm, 1905), pp. 34 ff., where he pointed out that the very substantial gains a socialist society may achieve by more effective resource utilization and income redistribution are threatened unless protected by a rational population policy.

7. *Lectures-I*, pp. 3–4, italics supplied.

8. *Finanztheoretische Untersuchungen*, p. viii.

9. Wicksell's review of Pareto's *Cours* in *Zeitschrift für Volkswirtschaft, Sozialpolitik und Verwaltung*, Vol. 6 (1897), pp. 161–62 and also his article, "Riksbanken och privatbankerna" (The National Bank of Sweden and Private Banks), *Ekon. Tidskrift* (1919), Part II, pp. 177 ff., and *Finanztheoretische Untersuchungen*, pp. 125–38.

10. *Finanztheoretische Untersuchungen*, pp. 104, 128 ff., 133–35.

11. *Lectures-I*, p. 143; *Finanaztheoretische Untersuchungen*, p. 146.

12. On social security laws, see his articles "Ålderdomskommittens betänkande" (Report of the Old Age Pension Committee), and "Resultatet" (The Result), *Ekon. Tidskrift* (1912), pp. 443–68; (1913), pp. 211–17; further, *Socialistaten och nutidssamhället*, pp. 28 ff., and *Progressiv beskattning* (Progressive Taxation), another tract (Stockholm, 1903), pp. 26 ff.

13. *Våra skatter—Hvilka betala dem och hvilka borde betala?* (Our Taxes Who Pays and Who Ought to Pay Them?), an important tract, issued by Wicksell under the pseudonym of Sven Trygg (Stockholm, 1894).

14. *Den politiska rösträtten och skatterna* (The Political Franchise and Taxation), a tract, 1898; *Finanztheoretische Untersuchungen*, pp. 123 ff.

15. *Finanztheoretische Untersuchungen*, pp. 115, 117, 124, 137, 156 ff.

16. *Finanztheoretische Untersuchun-*

gen, pp. 83–84.

17. *Interest and Prices,* Chap. 12, and *Lectures-II,* Chap. III, Sections 6-G and 6-H, and Chap. IV, Sections 9 and 10.

18. *Cf.* his article, "The Monetary Problem of the Scandinavian Countries" originally written for *Ekon. Tidskrift* (1925), now translated and appended to *Interest and Prices,* pp. 199 ff.

19. *Lectures-I,* "Note on Trade Cycles and Crises," pp. 209–14.

20. J. S. Mill, *Principles of Political Economy,* Ashley edition, pp. 199–200.

21. For a verbal statement of the theorem, see *Über Wert,* pp. xii–xiii; Wicksell's mathematical treatment, *ibid.,* pp. 121–28, and *Lectures-I,* pp. 126 ff. This and Wicksell's rôle in the polemic about the theorem is expertly treated in G. J. Stigler's *Production and Distribution Theories* (1941), Chap. X, and Chap. XII.

22. L. Walras, *Abrégé d'Éléments d'Économie Politique Pure* (Paris, 1938), p. 105, from which a passage is quoted in *Lectures-I,* p. 74, note; V. Pareto, *Manuel d'Économie Politique,* pp. 354 ff., 617–31; K. Wicksell, *Über Wert,* pp. 48–50, *Lectures-I,* pp. 72–83, and his reviews of Pareto's works in *Zeitschrift für Sozialpolitik und Verwaltung,* Vol. VI (1897), pp. 159 ff., and Vol. XXII (1913), pp. 132 ff.

23. *Lectures-I,* p. 80.

24. *Ibid.,* p. 81.

25. *Ibid.,* p. 72.

26. In free competition all his firms were of optimal scale, and in simple monopoly he viewed them as entities for maximizing net revenue by making the proper output adjustment to demand functions of known elasticity. Yet he was aware of the connection between "economies of scale" and decline of competition, an insight he made little use of in particular equilibrium analysis.

27. *Lectures-I,* pp. 86–88.

28. Wicksell's review, *Ekon. Tidskrift,* 1925, was translated as "Mathematische Nationalökonomie" for *Archiv für Sozialwissenschaft,* Vol. 58 (1927), pp. 252–81. Bowley's reply and re-analysis is found in "Note on Bilateral Monopoly," *Econ. Journal,* Vol. XXXVII (1928), pp. 651–65. For a systematic treatment of this entire topic, see W. Fellner, *Competition Among the Few* (New York, 1949), Chaps. IX and X.

29. *Über Wert,* pp. 82–90; *Lectures-I,* pp. 158 ff., 169, 171, 207, 209, 211 ff., and 241.

30. The evolution of Wicksell's capital concept is readily traced in *Über Wert,* pp. 72–80, 93–94; *Finanztheoretische Untersuchungen,* pp. 29 ff.; *Interest and Prices,* pp. 122 ff., and *Lectures-I,* pp. 144–66, 172–84, 204.

31. Goods of one-year maturity term must have a current gross marginal product of 1.05 times, or per unit of, the corresponding replacement inputs; goods of two-year term, a current gross marginal product of $(1.05)^2 = 1.1025$ per unit of current replacement input; goods of three-year term, a gross marginal product of 1.1576 per unit of current replacement input and so forth. Deducting replacement, their respective net current yields or net marginal products are .05, .1025, and .1576 units.

32. Three goods of one-year term each require 1.00 unit labor-land input per annum for current replacement. Their combined current replacement is 3.00 input units and their combined net current yield .15 units. One capital good of three-year term also requires 1.00 input units per annum for current replacement, and its net yield is .1576 units. *After* investment conversion to three-year goods is completed, the labor-land required for replacement is reduced by 2.00 input units per annum per new three-year goods created by the investment shift.

33. G. Åkerman, *Realkapital und Kapitalzins,* Vol. II (Stockholm, 1924), and F. A. von Hayek, *Prices and Production* (1934), *Profits, Interest, and Investment* (1939), and *The Pure Theory of Capital* (1940).

34. *Über Wert,* pp. 101–5; 113–16, and *Lectures-I,* pp. 133–44; 163–66.

35. *Lectures-I,* italics supplied, p. 164.

36. J. R. Hicks, *Theory of Wages,* pp. 121–27.

37. J. S. Mill, *Principles of Political Economy,* Ashley edition, pp. 67–68, 79–90, 713–14. Wicksell's demonstrations occur in *Über Wert,* pp. 112–14; *Lectures-I,* pp. 177–80, and in his review of G. Åkerman's *Realkapital und Kapitalzins,* Vol. I (1923), in *Ekon. Tidskrift* (1923), a review now translated and appended to *Lectures-I,* where wage-absorption-of-saving is discussed verbally, pp. 269 ff., and mathematically, pp. 291 ff.

38. *Cf.* the writer's doctoral thesis, *Knut Wicksell—A Study in Economic Doctrine,* pp. 276 ff., 290–97 (University of California, 1950).

When capital increases by investment of real-savings, other factors constant, its marginal productivity declines, and some of the real-savings are "absorbed" into rising real-wages and rents. The result, *ex post,* is that less real capital has been formed than was intended *ex ante.* This additional real capital raises output by O. If we divide O by the real-saving invested, we obtain the social marginal productivity rate of the saving, a rate which is smaller than the interest rate by reason of "wage and rent absorption" of some of these real savings. Therefore the marginal productivity principle applies to real capital only at the micro- and not at the macro-economic level.

But if labor (or land) increases, other factors constant, no such discrepancy arises between the social-and-private marginal productivity rates of the increasing factor.

The reason is that the services of labor or land cannot be "stored" directly except in the form of real capital, created by investment of real saving. Labor increases by L, and its services apply without leakage in production, yielding an increase in output of O'. When we divide O' by L we obtain the wage-rate, w. The increase in labor, other factors constant, is apt to make this w lower than it was initially, and to increase rent and interest rates. But under perfect competition w equals both the private and the social marginal product of the increasing factor, labor.

39. The relation of Wicksell's to earlier monetary doctrine has received attention by F. A. von Hayek in *Production and Prices*, pp. 1–32, and in Alvin Hansen's *Monetary Theory and Fiscal Policy* (1949), Appendix A and Chaps. 3 and 6, respectively. We should also mention that when D. Davidson pointed out to him, in a note in *Ekonomisk Tidskrift* (1916), that Henry Thornton had expressed a thesis akin to that of *Interest and Prices* in his treatise *Inquiry into the Nature and Effects of the Paper Credit of Great Britain* (1802), pp. 283 ff., Wicksell was delighted and surprised to find that ideas akin to his own were "ancient" enough to antedate Ricardo's writings. This may serve as a reminder to those who regard Wicksell as a "rediscoverer" of Thornton's work, for instance, Professor E. Whittaker in *A History of Economic Ideas*, p. 701. Wicksell's work was evidently done independently and in ignorance of that of Thornton. If anyone is to be credited with rediscovering Thornton, perhaps the honor should go to D. Davidson.

40. A. Marshall, "Remedies for Fluc-tuations in General Prices" (1887), reprinted in *Memorials of Alfred Marshall* (1925), pp. 188–211.

41. J. M. Keynes, *A Treatise on Money*, Vol. I (1930), pp. 186, 192–93, and 198.

42. *Lectures-II*, pp. 159–60.

43. *Ibid.*, p. 19.

44. The quantity of money is the sum of cash balances; the demand for money is a demand for cash balances. The latter has several constituent elements, the most variable of which is a demand for balances to accommodate accumulation of savings which are not simultaneously absorbed in investment; cf. *Interest and Prices*, Chap. 6, and *Lectures-II*, pp. 59 ff.

45. B. Ohlin, in his "Introduction" to *Interest and Prices*, p. xiv.

46. *Lectures-II*, p. 193.

47. This polemic has been sketched by B. Thomas in "The Monetary Doctrines of Professor D. Davidson," *Econ. Journal*, Vol. XLV (March, 1935).

48. For evidence of this concession see *Interest and Prices*, pp. 201, 204–05, 213–15, where one of Wicksell's last articles, "The Monetary Problem of the Scandinavian Countries," originally published in *Ekon. Tidskrift* (1925), has been translated and included as an appendix.

49. The rise of the "Stockholm School," in 1927–35, is related in Ohlin's article, "Some Notes on the Stockholm Theory of Saving and Investment," *Econ. Journal* (1937), reprinted in *Readings in Business Cycle Theory* (1944), pp. 87–130; cf. further the well-known works of E. Lindahl, *Studies in the Theory of Money and Capital*, and G. Myrdal, *Monetary Equilibrium* (1939).

29.

G. F. SHOVE

The Place of

Marshall's "Principles"

in the Development

of Economic Theory

The Editor has asked me, on the occasion of the centenary of its author's birth, to write something about the place of Alfred Marshall's *Principles of Economics* in the development of economic thought.[1] Any attempt to decide what place will finally be assigned to the book in the history of economic ideas would, of course, be foolish. This paper has no such ambitious aim.

Much of what I have to say will be familiar to readers of this *Journal*. But that is inevitable where the ground has already been worked over by some of the leading economists of the present day.[2]

I

"My acquaintance with economics commenced with reading Mill, while I was still earning my living by teaching Mathematics at Cambridge; and translating his doctrines into differential equations as far as they would go; and, as a rule, rejecting those which would not go. . . . That was principally in 1867–8."[3] . . . "While

Reprinted from *The Economic Journal*, LII (December 1942), 294–329, by permission of The Royal Economic Society. At the time of original publication, the author, now deceased, was with Cambridge University.

still giving private lessons in mathematics, he translated as many as possible of Ricardo's reasonings into mathematics; and he endeavoured to make them more general."[4]

Such is Marshall's own account of the beginnings of his work in economics. It gives us the key to a right understanding of the way in which his greatest and most famous book is related to what earlier writers had done, and to what his contemporaries did, in the same field. For the analytical backbone of Marshall's *Principles* is nothing more or less than a completion and generalisation, by means of a mathematical apparatus, of Ricardo's theory of value and distribution as expounded by J. S. Mill.[5] It is not, as many have supposed, a conflation of Ricardian notions with those of the "marginal utility" school. Nor is it an attempt to substitute for Ricardian doctrine a new system of ideas arrived at by a different line of approach. True, the process of completion and generalisation involved a transformation more thoroughgoing than Marshall himself was disposed to admit.[6] Nevertheless, so far as its strictly analytical content is concerned, the *Principles* is in the direct line of descent through Mill from Ricardo, and through Ricardo from Adam Smith. It is of the true Ricardian stock, neither a cross-bred nor a sport.

That Marshall greatly admired Ricardo and was much influenced by him is well known. But the idea that what he did was to effect a "compromise" or "synthesis" between Ricardian doctrines and those of other schools — particularly those associated in this country with the name and work of Jevons and on the Continent with the Austrians — dies hard. In a letter to J. B. Clark dated, 24th March 1908, Marshall wrote:

"One thing alone in American criticism irritates me, though it be not unkindly meant. It is the suggestion that I try to 'compromise between' or 'reconcile' divergent schools of thought."[7]

Apparently such criticism (or interpretation) still persists on the other side of the Atlantic. In a recently published American text-book[8] we read:

"It was left to Marshall to synthesise for general use the ideas of Jevons and others, respecting demand, with those of Ricardo and John Stuart Mill, on cost of production and supply, giving the English-speaking world a broader foundation for value-theory than had been furnished by either of the antecedent schools. . . . While he took over the main conclusions of the Jevonian system . . . Marshall incorporated in his theories the doctrines of Mill on the side of production."

It lingers, too, even in this country. Thus Professor Alexander Gray holds that Marshall

"as a first approach, is perhaps best viewed as representing an endeavour to give Austrian ideas their due place, without becoming swamped in Austrian super-refinements, and then to effect a synthesis of the Austrian ideas with the older Political Economy."[9]

One can easily see how this view arose. It is due to Marshall's unconscionable delay in publishing his results.[10] Indeed, anyone reading through the principal European treatises on economics in the order of their publication[11] and without a knowledge of their inner history could scarcely avoid coming to some such conclusion, unless he paid very particular attention to Marshall's references and acknowledgments.[12] It is mistaken, however, as Lord Keynes' masterly biography clearly brings out. And it obscures what is, to my mind, a central fact in the history of economic thought in this country: that the main line of development from Adam Smith to Marshall is a continuous growth *from a single stem*, with Jevons and (on one side of his work) Malthus standing apart from it. It may therefore be worth while to observe how naturally — one is tempted to say inevitably — the theoretical framework of the *Principles* grows out of an attempt to test, and fill the gaps in, Ricardian doctrines by the use of a mathematical apparatus — in other words, "to translate them into differential equations" and "make them more general." To show this in detail would take too much space. But a few salient examples may be recalled.

(1) Once admit that the (marginal) cost of producing a commodity may vary with the output of it, and the Ricardian theorem that the value of each commodity is equal to its marginal cost no longer solves your problem: for each commodity you have two unknowns — price and output — and only one equation. Now both Ricardo and Mill made this admission as regards "raw produce" or, more generally, commodities "of which so much may be produced at a given cost, but a further quantity not without a greater cost" (Mill's "Third Class").[13] Hence there was an obvious gap in their theory of value. Either another set of equations, relating the selling-price of each commodity and its amount, — the demand equations — must be introduced or you must assume that everything is produced under conditions of constant cost, in which case generality is sacrificed and indeed the whole Ricardo-Mill system, in which diminishing returns in agriculture are pivotal, falls to pieces.

(2) Ricardo habitually treats the proportions in which the different grades of labour, labour and capital, fixed and circulating capital, and capital of different degrees of durability enter into the production of a given commodity — the "technical coefficients" relating to labour and capital — as fixed. In fact they depend, as Marshall saw, not only on the payments required to secure the services of the factors concerned, but also on the scale on which the commodity is to be produced.[14] Indeed, Ricardo himself had argued both in the chapter on "Machinery" which he introduced into the third edition of his *Principles*[15] and in his chapter on "Value"[16] that a fall in the rate of profit necessary to secure command over capital (or, what amounted in his terminology to the same thing, a "rise of wages") would cause resort to more capitalistic methods. But in the main body of his argument this influence is ignored and nowhere are its consequences elaborated either by him or by Mill with any degree of precision. Nor, if my memory serves, does either of them pay any attention to the influence of the scale of production in this respect. Here again there was a gap to be filled. Either the theory of value must be confined to the special case in which the techni-

cal coefficients relating to labour and capital are constants; or another set of equations must be introduced, connecting this time the proportions in which the factors are combined in the production of each commodity with their prices and with the output of the commodity. This leads straight to yet another gap. For how are the prices of the factors determined?

(3) Partly under the influence of Malthus, partly because of the conditions of the time (it was not till the second half of the century that the large rise of real wages in this country clearly emerged as a persistent phenomenon), the Ricardian analysis proceeds in effect on the assumption that the "natural" rate of wages estimated in "corn" or "food and necessaries" or commodities generally (*i.e.*, the rate to which real wages are always tending and at which they will settle in the stationary state — in modern language, "the long-period supply-price of labour") is approximately constant. By Marshall's time it was becoming evident that a rise in the "market" (*i.e.*, current or "short-period") rate of wages need not be entirely absorbed by an increase of population, but may result, to some extent, in a rise in the standard of life, and hence in the level to which commodity-wages will tend in the long run. This carries with it the corollary that a permanent increase in wages may be necessary in order to secure an increased supply of labour. Thus it was becoming obvious that the Ricardian analysis not only lacked generality, but failed to fit the facts. The commodity-wages of the various grades of labour could no longer be equated to so many constants: a set of *differential* equations was needed connecting the wage of each grade with the amount to be supplied.[17] Further, since the amount supplied depends on the amount demanded, the state of the demand must now be given a position co-ordinate with the conditions of supply in the long-period theory of wages. This brings us to the last of the gaps in the Ricardian system to be noticed on the present occasion.

(4) Both Ricardo and Mill held that the market rate of wages (the short-period price of labour), like the market price of goods, is governed by demand and supply, the demand in this case being indentified with the amount of capital, or rather the portion of it which is destined for the maintenance of labour. Mill even went so far as to include labour among the commodities whose value is always determined by demand and supply.[18] And Ricardo had declared that the market rate of wages might remain above the natural rate for an indefinite period.[19] Moreover, he was mainly interested not so much in the "amount" of wages (*i.e.*, wages measured in "corn" or commodities) as in their "value" (*i.e.*, the "quantity of labour" or of "labour and capital" required to produce the real wage at the margin of cultivation),[20] since on his principles it is this which determines the relative shares of labour and capital; and even if the real wage is taken as constant in the long run, the cost of producing it at the margin obviously depends on the position of the margin and hence on the length to which investment is carried. Thus not only in the short period, but in the long period also, wages in the sense which is important in the Ricardian system depend on the conditions governing the supply of capital. But what are these? Neither Ricardo nor Mill explains them at all clearly or definitely. Both hold that

714

there is a minimum rate of profit necessary to secure accumulation and that when the actual rate has fallen to this level, no further accumulation takes place and the stationary state is reached.[21] But they give no indication that it depends on the quantity of capital supplied. In effect they treat it as a *datum*. Yet this makes nonsense of the theorem, common to both, that the rate of profit depends on wages — or, in Mill's phrase, "the cost of labour" — when it is applied to the long period. For if the rate of profit is given from the outset, neither wages nor the cost of producing them has anything to do with it. True, both our authors remark more than once that the supply of capital, the rate at which accumulation proceeds, is stimulated by a rise and checked by a fall in the market rate of profit: Ricardo on the ground that this increases the income of the capitalists and thus augments the source of accumulation — the power to invest;[22] Mill on that ground and also because it enhances the incentive.[23] But vague statements of this kind are not enough to determine the supply of capital. For that purpose we need to put them into the form of a theorem, an equation, establishing a definite relation between the quantity of capital forthcoming and the rate of profit or return.

All these gaps (except perhaps the second) would leap to the eye of anyone trying to "translate" Ricardo's doctrines into differential equations and to "make them more general." Nor were the equations that would fill them far to seek. Readers will have noticed that they are in fact those enumerated[24] in Note XXI of the Mathematical Appendix to the *Principles*[25] and set out in the notes which lead up to that one.

Now Marshall himself has put it on record that his "general theory of distribution (except in so far as it relates to the element of time) is . . . contained" in this Note, "to which the preceding notes, and especially XIV–XX, lead up"[26] and for him the theories of distribution and value were indissolubly interlocked. He adds, "My whole life has been given and will be given to presenting in a realistic form as much as I can of my note XXI."[27] The analysis there set forth is indeed the backbone on which the body of Books V and VI in the final version of the treatise (Books V, VI and VII in the first edition) is built up by the introduction of the highly important and original devices for dealing with the time-element (the gradation of short and long periods, quasi-rent, the prime-and-supplementary cost analysis and the rest) and by a continual testing, illustration and qualification of the pure theory in the light of contemporary and historical fact.

This comes out most clearly in the first edition, where the titles of the books and chapters, as well as the text itself, follow the mathematical framework very closely. In later versions, the connection became somewhat blurred by the author's restless quest after realism and the increasing prominence given to the element of time and to the absence of anything which can properly be called a position of long-period equilibrium where increasing returns prevail.[28] But even in them the mathematical framework can be traced clearly enough by anyone who reads with close attention.

How far Marshall hit on the missing equations for himself and how far they were suggested to him by the work of other writers is, in a sense, a matter for speculation. On the internal evidence alone, it is open to anyone to suppose that some of them at least were suggested by Jevons and the Austrians. But there is no need to suppose anything of the kind. After all, there are a great many passages in which Ricardo and Mill recognise that the price which a commodity can command rises when the quantity offered contracts, and falls when it expands;[29] and from this to the demand equations is a very short step — a step, too, which Cournot had taken long before Menger or Jevons had written a line. Again, in Book IV of his *Principles* (ch. iii) Mill had argued that the price of any factor will fall when an increased quantity of it is applied to a fixed amount of the others, and rise when a fixed quantity of it is combined with an increased amount of the rest. The chapter calls aloud for translation into differential equations, and Marshall praised it highly;[30] what one misses in it is any indication that the price depends on the marginal productivity of the factor — unless, indeed, we can so construe the proposition that when capital and labour increase together their rate of reward will fall because of the operation of the law of diminishing returns at the margin of cultivation. Then, too, as we have already observed,[31] Ricardo had acknowledged more than once that the technical coefficients depend on the price of the factors, and both he and Mill had on occasion contemplated the possibility that the supply price of labour might rise as the amount demanded increased.[32] Taking one thing with another, the keen eye of a mathematician could find plenty of hints in Ricardo and Mill of the direction in which the completion and generalisation of their theories was to be sought.

Further, the external evidence is all against the view that Marshall drew anything of importance from the marginal utility school. He began his work in 1867–8 before Jevons' treatise or Menger's had appeared, and it was on mathematical lines from the first. The outlines of his system are already discernible in his review of Jevons (1872),[33] his article on *Mr. Mill's Theory of Value* (1876),[34] the *Economics of Industry* (1879) — written in collaboration with Mrs. Marshall — and the chapters on *The Pure Theory of Domestic Values* circulated by Sidgwick in 1879; and although these are all of rather later date than the earliest publications of Jevons, Menger and Walras, we have Marshall's own authority for saying that the theory which can be glimpsed in them was not: —

"My main position as to the theory of value and distribution was practically completed in the years 1867 to 1870, when I translated Mill's version of Ricardo's or Smith's doctrines into mathematics."

"My doctrine of quasi-rent, though only gradually developed, took on substance in 1868. . . . That went with my translations of all leading economic doctrines into differential equations; and so far as I can tell there is no broad difference on *that* side between my position before 1870 and now [1900]."[35]

He is quite definite, too, about the sources from which he did derive assistance or suggestions. The "kernel" of his theory of distribution

"is based in the first instance on Adam Smith, Malthus and Ricardo, and in the second on von Thünen as regards substance, and Cournot as regards the form of the thought."[36]

"Under the guidance of Cournot, and in a less degree of von Thünen, I was led to attach great importance to the fact that our observations of nature, in the moral as in the physical world relate not so much to aggregate quantities as to increments of quantities, and that in particular the demand for a thing is a continuous function, of which the "marginal" increment is, in stable equilibrium, balanced against the corresponding increment of its cost."[37]

There is no reason to doubt his word. He was not among the writers who are niggardly in their acknowledgments. He erred, if at all, in the direction of generosity.

We may conclude, then, with Lord Keynes, that "Marshall owed little or nothing to Jevons"[38] and, we may add, nothing of importance to the Austrians. In his theoretical work his debts outside the English classical tradition were to Cournot and von Thünen.

But if the pure theory of the *Principles* sprang, with assistance from Cournot and von Thünen, directly from Ricardo's doctrines, it also, as I have remarked, transformed them. The broad discussion of the effects of progress and taxation on the relative shares of the three great categories of income and on the relative values of wide groups of commodities is replaced by a meticulous examination of the pricing process pursued into every corner of the economic system. The principle of mutual determination everywhere supersedes the idea of a single determinant or a one-way chain of causes. The conditions of demand are everywhere given equal status with those of supply. The determination of "market" values and "natural" values, of value under monopoly and value under competition, of value under constant and under diminishing returns, of rent, wages and profit, is no longer seen as a series of separate problems, sharply distinguished from each other and each with a separate "law" appropriate to itself — all are subsumed under the single unifying idea of the balance at the margin, a balance of small increments of receipts and outgoings, payments and costs, differing in its manifestations and giving different results in different cases, but common to them all, with the principle of substitution acting everywhere as a master-key. All this is entirely foreign to Ricardo's manner of thinking: and to Mill's. If the Ricardian analysis was our starting-point, by the end of the journey we have entered a new world.

Another difference which distinguishes the *Principles* from its forbears, less fundamental but striking all the same, is the prominence given to the equilibrium of the individual firm. This arises partly, no doubt, from the introduction of the principle of substitution, which in industry operates mainly through the individual entrepreneur or the management of the individual concern.[39] But it is also to be accounted for by the now notorious difficulty of reconciling increasing returns with competitive conditions. As Marshall observes:

Cournot "seems not to have noticed that if the field of each of the rivals were unlimited, and the commodity which they produced obeyed the law of Increasing Returns, then the position of equilibrium attained when each produced on the same scale would be unstable. For if one of the rivals got an advantage, and increased his scale of production, he would thereby gain a further advantage, and soon drive all his rivals out of this field. Cournot's argument does not introduce the limitations necessary to prevent this result."[40]

And though in this matter it was Cournot's work rather than Ricardo's that he completed (and developed), the problem is inevitably raised by an attempt to generalise the Ricardian analysis so as to cover the possibility that marginal cost may vary in either direction when output expands. In his solution of it, Marshall uses three expedients (two of them at least entirely novel): external economies, the imperfection of the market and that perpetual shift of advantage from one firm to another under the influence of luck, errors of judgment and the waxing and waning of the managers' efficiency which was given succinct expression in the famous concept of the representative firm. The second and third of these expedients become more prominent or more sharply defined in later versions of the treatise than they had been in the first edition.[41] But all three were present, at least in embryo, from the beginning,[42] and they involved a shift of the centre of interest which opened up a field of speculation and enquiry scarcely touched by previous writers.

So far we have considered Marshall's equations as expressions of purely objective phenomena — that the price of a thing falls when more of it is put on the market, that real wages have to be raised permanently in order to obtain an increase in population, that the amount of investment forthcoming expands or contracts as the return on it rises or falls, that entrepreneurs choose what they consider to be the cheapest method of producing their output, and so on. Neither the mathematical apparatus of the *Principles* nor its main conclusions in the realm of pure theory really require anything more than external data of this kind. But in his search for generality Marshall, as everyone knows, went deeper and saw the behaviour of the marketplace as a reflection of a balancing of divergent motives in the minds of men — "satisfactions" (or the impulse to obtain them) on the one hand and "dissatisfactions" (or aversions from them) on the other, "utilities" and "disutilities." This in his view, was the common element running through all economic behaviour — in our own system of free-enterprise and money-exchange, in the custom-ridden societies of the Middle Ages and the Orient, in barter-economy, in the isolated self-supporting household (if such could be found) and in those other possible worlds at which he allowed himself an occasional glance.[43] It was as an analysis of men's behaviour in a department of life where the strength of their motives is measurable that for him economic theory reached the highest level of generality.

Nor is this surprising in one who grew up when the utilitarian philosophy was still dominant and who came to economics from a study of moral science. The surprising thing is rather that, in spite of the close connection which had always existed in this country between the utilitarians and the economists, it was not till the seventies and eighties of last century that any systematic attempt was made here (avowedly by Jevons[44] and in effect by Edgeworth[45]) to formulate a theory of economics based on the Benthamite

718

pleasure-pain calculus. Marshall, however, was not trying to do that. His system does not rest upon the utilitarian psychology or ethic. From the first he insisted that to say that the strength of the motives at work in the business world is measurable does not imply any assumption as to their character or "quality," still less as to their ethical value.[46] They may be as altruistic as you like; their objective need not be the acquisition of wealth for its own sake; it may equally well be distinction or approval; they need not spring from the desire for pleasure or the avoidance of pain, they may be based on ethical notions about what is "fair" or "right" or "noble."[47] Though in the first edition of the *Principles* the Benthamite terms "pleasure" and "pain" are not infrequently used to denote men's "positive" and "negative" motives,[48] they are jostled even there by more neutral expressions, and as time went on they were almost entirely eliminated. The conception of *measurable* motives — that, and in the end that alone, is what Marshall carried over into economic theory from the utilitarian philosophy.

In so doing he moved still further away from Ricardo. The "supply price" of a commodity now becomes the sum of the prices which have to be paid to "call forth" "the efforts and sacrifices" which are required for making it and constitute its "real cost of production" — a quite un-Ricardian notion.[49] For Ricardo, labour is not a "disutility," but the productive force available to the community, the stuff, so to speak, by means of which commodities are made, and the cost of a thing is the quantity of this force or stuff, together with the quantity of capital, absorbed in its production, not the effort and sacrifice entailed in providing it. And though in his view the minimum rate of profit was the necessary compensation for the "trouble and risk"[50] (to which Mill, following Senior, added the "abstinence"[51]) undertaken by the investor, both he and Mill habitually conceive of the second element in cost also (the capital employed) in objective terms — as the quantity or value of the wages advanced and the length of time for which the advance is made, not as a subjective discommodity or sacrifice.[52] With the emergence of the psychological conception of "real cost" we enter not merely a different world from Ricardo's, but a different universe. As before, however, we have reached it by gradual steps through the endeavour to climb from the Ricardian starting-point into higher and higher levels of generality and unification — the search for "the one in the many, the many in the one." Though one cannot speak with confidence, one may hazard the guess that Marshall began with the objective demand and supply schedules, the phenomena of the market-place, and worked back from them to their psychological basis, not (as was the case with Jevons) the other way about. Certainly he held that of the two steps which "had brought about a great change in the manner of economic thought" in his generation — namely (1) the use of "semi-mathematical language for expressing the relation between small increments of a commodity on the one hand and on the other hand small increments in the aggregate price that will be paid for it"; and (2) "formally describing these small increments of price as measuring corresponding small increments of pleasure" — the former, which had been "taken by Cournot" in 1838, was "by far the more important."[53] And to the end he kept his schedules and curves and equations in a form which was capable of numerical or statistical expression and might afford a basis for those "quantitative studies" which he regarded as "the main task before the rising generation."[54]

II

So much for the mathematical apparatus and the pure theory of the book. But for Marshall pure theory was "a very small part of economics proper and by itself sometimes even — well, not a very good occupation of time."[55] As to mathematics, he thus describes his attitude:

> "I had a growing feeling in the later years of my work at the subject that a good mathematical theorem dealing with economic hypotheses was very unlikely to be good economics: and I went more and more on the rules — (1) Use mathematics as a shorthand language, rather than as an engine of inquiry. (2) Keep to them till you have done. (3) Translate into English. (4) Then illustrate by examples that are important in real life. (5) Burn the mathematics. (6) If you can't succeed in 4, burn 3. This last I did often."[56]

Thus, while the mathematical apparatus translated into English and the non-mathematical extension of it to cover the element of time formed the skeleton of the *Principles*, the bare bones had to be clothed in flesh before they could appear in public or claim to rank as economics proper. To that end, Marshall read widely in history, pored over statistics and reports, travelled and observed; and the *Principles* became a storehouse of information as well as a monument of ingenuity. This mode of treatment is in marked contrast to the method of Ricardo and Mill. It is a throw-back to Adam Smith; and here perhaps the notion that Marshall tried to reconcile divergent schools of thought is not altogether without foundation.

For at the time when he wrote, the whole Ricardian method was under fire from the Historical School. He does not seem to have derived any results of importance directly from this school, and his view of the relation between history and economics differed widely from theirs. But Hegel's *Philosophy of History* was an influence which he shared with them, and there can, I think, be little doubt that sensitiveness to their criticism and anxiety to meet what was sound in it account in some measure for the form which the *Principles* took and for certain features in its general outlook and detailed exposition. Marshall conceded that the Ricardians had confined their attention too narrowly to the facts of their own time and country[57] and that many of their conclusions had not the universality claimed for them by their followers and popularisers;[58] and was constantly on his guard against falling into a similar mistake. He recognised more fully than Mill and much more fully than Ricardo the influence of social customs and institutions on economic behaviour; and tried to weave it into the fabric of his system. He was acutely conscious that the freedom of competition — or, as he would have it, the "freedom of enterprise" — characteristic of the modern economy of the West was a very recent growth and that there were many parts of the world which it had as yet only begun to reach.[59] The historical setting in which he saw the industrial system he was to analyse become somewhat veiled from his readers when the chapters on the growth of free industry, and enterprise with which the first edition opened were relegated to an appendix: but he himself never lost sight of it. His reply to the historians' attack on analytical economics was the same as Jevons': the usefulness of one method does not necessarily imply the uselessness of the other; there is room for both and both are needed.[60] But his solution of the difficulty it raises was different. While Jevons fastened his hopes on a division of labour, a break-up of the science into separate branches or even separate sciences,[61] Marshall's counter-measure was rather by way of a combination of methods — not only history permeated by theory but theory (as in the *Principles*) nourished, modified and illustrated by historical and contemporary fact. If any school of thought outside the Ricardian tradition set its mark on the *Principles* it was the Historical School, rather than the marginal utility school, that did so.

There were other fronts, too, to defend. Closely allied to the historians' assault was the line of attack developed by the "sociologists" — Comte, in particular — who held that "all the aspects of social life are so closely connected that they ought to be studied together" and urged economists "to abandon their distinctive rôle and devote themselves to the general advancement of a unified social science."[62] Then there were the moralists and romantics. Ruskin's fulminations had followed the thunderings of Carlyle, the comparatively good-humoured chaff of the Mudfog sketches (1837–9) had led up to the acid satire of *Hard Times* (1854) and more widely, perhaps, than ever before (though this type of opposition had persisted from the very beginning of the century) "political economists" were now "regarded as cold-blooded beings devoid of the ordinary feelings of humanity"[63] who neglected the imponderables for hard facts and stressed the sordid pursuit of material gain to the exclusion of the tender emotions and higher aspirations of man — as Gradgrinds, in short. Meanwhile, the clear-cut maxims with which Political Economy had been associated in the popular mind had been so riddled with exceptions that they were coming to be accepted, if accepted at all, rather as practical rules of thumb than as scientific laws. Mr. Mill himself had lately (1869) thrown over what had been accounted one of its leading principles without putting anything in its place. A number of other writers (Cairnes, Mcleod and Hearn, for example) had been picking holes of more or less importance in its accepted doctrines. Its practitioners were known to be at variance not only on questions of practical policy, but also about the scope and method of their subject. Altogether, Political Economy had by the seventies lost a good deal of its once proud reputation. In the middle of the decade Bagehot could write:

"It lies rather dead in the public mind. Not only does it not exert the same influence as formerly, but there is not exactly the same confidence in it. Younger men either do not study it, or do not feel that it comes home to them, and that it matches with their most living ideas. . . . They ask, often hardly knowing it, will this "Science," as it claims to be, harmonise with what we know to be sciences, or bear to be tried as we now try sciences? And they are not sure of the answer."[64]

Marshall set himself to rehabilitate it in the general esteem. The *Principles* is an apologia for economics as well as an exposition of it: a kind of counter-Reformation, as one might say, directed against doubts within and denunciation from without the fold.

Hence, I fancy, comes (in part at least) a feature of the book which grates a little on the modern ear: its reiterated insistence of the importance of character in economic affairs and those pious phrases and moralising asides which nowadays seem so out of place in a scientific treatise. Though allowance must be made for Marshall's own temperament (typical of that earnest and self-critical age), it is difficult to resist the impression that his concern to set economics to rights with the moralists shows itself here. But a more scientific influence may also have been at work, derived this time from the sociologists. With the sociologists' doctrines there could, indeed, be no synthesis. For, broadly speaking, they had no doctrines to synthesise. Comte and Herbert Spencer, despite their "unsurpassed knowledge and great genius," could "hardly be said even to have made a commencement with the construction of a unified social science."[65] Marshall's own view was that "the whole range of man's activities in society is too wide and various to be analysed and explained by a single intellectual effort."[66] He refused firmly, as Mill had when he found his feet, to admit that a separate science of economics was impossible. Nor would he accept Mill's suggestion that it must be purely hypothetical, based on the abstraction of certain motives and the assumption that men are governed by them alone, the necessary qualifications being introduced when its abstract principles are applied to concrete problems. It must and could deal with man as he is, seen in the round. Its claim to an autonomous existence was grounded on the fact that it is concerned with a field of activity in which the motive force of the desires, aspirations and emotions springing from man's nature (the whole of it) could be measured: no abstraction from these was necessary.[67] But in his *Logic* Mill had maintained that the general science of society must be founded on what he called "ethology" — a science of human character — and in particular "political ethology" — "the theory of the causes which determine the type of character belonging to a people or an age."[68] May we not find in this line of thought (which was characteristic of the epoch) a partial explanation of much that distinguishes Marshall's *Principles* from earlier and from later work?

At any rate we may be sure that Marshall did not modify his scientific doctrines simply for the sake of appeasement or to curry favour with the critics. "Truth is the only thing worth having: not peace. I never compromised on any doctrine of any kind."[69] He must have been convinced that "the way in which the character of man affects and is affected by the prevalent methods of the production, distribution and consumption of wealth"[70] was of the first importance *scientifically*: otherwise he would not have given it the prominence he did give it. Hegel, the historical school, the sociologists, the moralists and the romantics were all influences making for that conviction. To them must be added yet another element in the intellectual atmosphere of the time: the turn lately taken by the natural sciences.

"At the beginning of last century the mathematico-physical group of sciences were in the ascendant; and these sciences, widely as they differ from one another, have this point in common, that their subject matter is constant and unchanged in all countries and in all ages. . . . As the century wore on, the biological group of sciences were slowly making way, and people were getting clearer ideas as to the nature of organic growth. . . . At last the speculations of biology made a great stride forwards; its discoveries fascinated the attention of the world as those of physics had done in earlier years; and there was a marked change in the tone of the moral and historical sciences. Economics has shared in the general movement; and is getting to pay every year a greater attention to the pliability of human nature."[71]

Perhaps Marshall rather exaggerated the influence of this development on the work of his immediate predecessors, particularly Mill's.[72] His own was profoundly affected by it.

Biological conceptions of growth and decay, elimination and selection, are, as we have seen, brought in to solve even the problem of statical equilibrium. Consciousness that "if the subject-matter of a science passes through different phases of development, the laws of the science must have a development corresponding to the things of which they treat"[73] led to the explicit recognition that economic doctrines must to a great extent be relative to time and place.[74] Further, and more important, Marshall's whole conception of the nature of economic change is coloured by what may be called the biological approach. For him, economic development can never be interpreted in terms of merely mechanical expansion or dynamic movement; it is essentially a process of "organic growth" and the methods of the science must be adapted accordingly. Hence the very restricted sphere (more restricted as time went on) which he assigned to the path-breaking ideas of an "equilibrium price" and an "equilibrium amount." In spite of the care lavished upon them, the long-period supply and demand curves were cast for a minor rôle only. They may serve a useful purpose by provisionally isolating for separate and preliminary analysis some of the forces making for change at a particular moment and indicating the direction of their pressure. They cannot be used to forecast accurately and for any considerable distance into the future the direction in which outputs and values are likely to move, still less the position at which they may be expected to arrive. For any disturbance of the "equilibrium" position is liable to alter the conditions of the problem by modifying tastes, habits and technical knowledge — the swing-back will not follow the same course as the swing-out or return to the point of departure;[75] and, above all, the forces isolated operate in an ever-changing medium which they modify and in turn are modified by. In the struggle for survival, new species of business organisation are constantly emerging and old ones being eliminated according as they are fit or unfit to profit by their environment. With alterations in business organisation man alters too — mentally and morally: the alteration in his character alters the survival-value of the different types of business organisation: and so on endlessly. Marshall's conception of economic change as "organic growth" almost certainly explains why he never developed a mathematical theory of economic dynamics. Quite certainly it reflects the intellectual climate of his age. "The Mecca of the economist lies in economic biology rather than in economic dynamics."[76] The epigram carries its date on its face.

III

Thanks to Jevons and Menger and, in a lesser degree, to Walras, the revival of economic theory had begun before Marshall's work saw the light. But the *Principles* made a big contribution to it, more especially in England. The impact of the book on the public mind has been described by Lord Keynes,[77] and need not be described again. It shows how exactly Marshall had gauged what was wanted at that moment: and how closely his outlook was attuned to the temper of his time. In scientific circles, too, its success was decisive and far-reaching.

In England, it gradually acquired a position if not of such exclusive dominance as Mill's *Principles* had had in the generation after 1850, at least comparable with that. For the part of the field which it covers it became a leading text-book not only in its author's own University but wherever economics was seriously studied. A whole generation of students — more than one, indeed, as academic generations go — was brought up on it. The equilibrium of demand and supply as the all-pervasive element in the pricing process, the balancing of small increments of costs and receipts, "marginal productivity," "elasticity," "substitution," the distinction between long and short periods, "quasi-rent," "prime" and "supplementary" cost, the elegant and serviceable expository device of plane-curves, became the stock-in-trade of the professional economist. Ideas of this sort might very likely have permeated English political economy in any case. They were in the air. But as a matter of plain historical fact their prevalence is due to Marshall. In its country of origin Alfred Marshall's *Principles* stands with Adam Smith's *Wealth of Nations* and Ricardo's *Principles* as one of the three great watersheds in the development of economic ideas: with the usual qualifications, we may divide the history of English political economy into three distinct epochs — the Classical, the Ricardian and the Marshallian or reformed-Ricardian.

That the book powerfully affected theoretical economics in the United States is also evident.[78] Thought in the "Melting-Pot" is naturally somewhat eclectic, and in recent years one major schism at least has developed there. But both directly and through the work of such influential writers as F. W. Taussig and Prof. T. N. Carver (to name only two out of a number), the *Principles* played an important part in forming the ideas of the succeeding generation.[79] To all appearances it must be accounted one of the foundation stones of modern American economics. Let two American witnesses corroborate:—

"Probably it is true that the bulk of the economic writings which have appeared in English since 1890, in their treatment of the problem of value, have been based on the ideas of J. B. Clark and Alfred Marshall, especially the latter. . . . American students, to a large extent, obtained their ideas on the marginal theory of value directly or indirectly from Clark, but . . . even in the United States Marshall's writings had great influence."[80]

"The position of economic theory in the United States is at present [1928] too chaotically diverse to permit any precise generalising. But one might hazard the statement that a large part of it owes more to Marshall than to anyone else. . . . Alfred Marshall . . . still dominates the field of economic theory in a remarkable fashion in England, and to a lesser degree in the United States."[81]

On the Continent of Europe, the effect of the book was much less decisive — partly, no doubt, because of the delay in its publication. By 1890, Central European economics had become largely impermeable to the new Ricardianism. In Austria the pioneering work of the great trio had already established a new and independent tradition, and the ideas and methods which they had introduced had taken too firm a hold to be easily overthrown or radically modified from outside. Böhm-Bawerk and Marshall were, of course, well acquainted with each other's contributions to the thought of the time and some minor inter-actions may perhaps be traced between them, but there was nothing like a fusion or large-scale borrowing on either side.[82] In Germany, the home of the historical school, abstract theory was at a heavy discount and the concessions which Marshall made to the historians' attack on Ricardian method do not seem to have been fully appreciated. At any rate German economic thought continued to develop on non-mathematical and non-analytical lines. Meanwhile, for those continental economists whose bent did lie in the direction of pure theory, Walras had provided a rival system, the more formidable because it displayed its mathematical apparatus to full view in all its undraped attraction instead of relegating it to footnotes and appendices and wrapping it round with realistic qualifications and illustrations and the circumlocutions of ordinary speech. Thus the three streams of economic theory which took their rise in the seventies tended to flow in separate channels — the Austrian school, the Lausanne school and the English or Marshallian — instead of merging into a single flood, though there were, of course, more or less important percolations from one to the other.

This does not mean, however, that the influence of the *Principles* on Continental thought was negligible. On the contrary, it was felt everywhere and in two countries at least which have made distinguished contributions to pure theory — Italy and Sweden — it was very strong. In Italy, as is well known, Marshall's ideas were introduced at an early stage by Pantaleoni — the source in this case being in the first instance the chapters on *The Pure Theory of Domestic Values* circulated by Sidgwick and, in a less degree, *The Economics of Industry*. And though Pareto — a more original thinker than Pantaleoni — built largely on foundations laid by Walras, since his time what may be called the Marshallian tradition, albeit intermingled with other elements, seems on the whole to have got the upper hand of the

725

Walrasian in the work-a-day teaching of the Italian school. In Swedish thought, the Lausanne influence has perhaps been more powerful. But here too the *Principles* left an evident and indelible mark.[83]

Thus outside England and Austria, where the native systems established almost undisputed sway, Marshall's *Principles* and the writings of Walras acted side by side to stimulate and mould the renaissance of theoretical economics in Europe. Without attempting to assess the relative importance of the various influences, it may safely be said that the English work must be given a place in the front rank.

Marshall once defined a "classical" author as one who "by the form or the matter of his words or deeds has stated or indicated architectonic ideas in thought or sentiment, which are in some degree his own, and which, once created, can never die, but are an existing yeast ceaselessly working in the Cosmos."[84] On the first count he easily qualifies for the title. Beyond dispute, the *Principles* contained "architectonic ideas" which were "in some degree his own." How has it stood the test of time?

IV

In some ways it has obviously "dated." Its pious asides and prim moralisings are, as we have already observed, not in the modern taste, and the line of attack against which they were in part a defence has faded out, while ambitious projects for a unified social science (to which, as I have suggested, the stress laid on moral character may have been in some sort a concession) no longer excite the same interest. On that point, Marshall's scepticism is now very generally accepted — except among those who still cling to the doctrines of that other eminent Victorian, Karl Marx. The political attitude, too, which shows through the argument in many places, and occasionally comes to the surface, is not sympathetic to the present generation. Individualism is, for the moment at least, a "creed outworn," and Marshall was individualist to the core. Not that he adhered to the dogmatic maxims of *laissez-faire.* On the contrary, one of the outstanding features of the *Principles* (it had appeared even in the earliest draft) was a logical refutation of *laissez-faire* theory — its practical limitations had, of course, long been recognised. Nor was he among those who defended the distribution of incomes which the existing social system had brought about, either on the ground that it was just or by the plea that it was necessary in order to maintain the supply of capital.[85] He held that "in moderation" what he called the "financial side" of socialism, "predatory" and "rapacious" though it was, might "even be beneficial,"[86] and he was not opposed, in principle at least, to far-reaching measures for diminishing inequalities of wealth, provided that they were carried through by "means which would not sap the springs of free initiative and strength of character."[87] It was the "administrative side" of socialism, the proposal to substitute public management for free enterprise and individual initiative that he viewed with alarm[88] and which led him, in a private letter, to describe the socialistic movement as "by far the

726

greatest present danger to human well-being."[89] This attitude makes very little appeal to most present-day students of economics, young or old. It springs both from the intellectual climate and, what is more significant, from the industrial environment of Marshall's time — more particularly of his earlier years, always of the most crucial period in forming a man's general outlook.

For Marshall's main work was done when competitive capitalism was at the zenith of its achievement. In little more than a century the system of "free enterprise" or "economic freedom" had revolutionised industrial technique, transport and communications and had increased the productive power of the country — indeed its production — out of all knowledge. There were shameful blots on its record, as Marshall was well aware:[90] abuses and a large "residuum" of grinding poverty remained, which he was as anxious as anyone to remove.[91] But since the middle of the century at least it had steadily and substantially (though not without temporary set-backs) raised the real income of the mass of the people in spite of a rapid increase in their numbers. Even after the "good years" had come to an end, and throughout the dragging deflation of the later seventies and eighties, the improvement had gone on (it was not till near the turn of the century, when Marshall was already past middle-age, that a check definitely declared itself). All this had been accomplished through individual initiative, the "restless energy" of business men going their own way and with no great help from Government beyond what was involved in razing obstacles and removing restrictions. Moreover, with his broad historical perspective, Marshall saw it as a brief episode at the end of a long vista of comparative stagnation. With the removal of the barriers of custom and regulation at the end of the eighteenth and the beginning of the nineteenth century, economic development and the wealth of the nation had leapt forward at a pace almost, if not quite, unparalleled.[92] Can we be surprised if for him individual initiative, the "bold" and "free" enterprise of the innovator, was the one thing above all others to be nursed and encouraged in order that progress might continue? or if he was haunted by the fear that in a new form the shackles might be clamped on it once more and technical advance settle down again into the old sluggish *tempo*? Our experience has been different and our outlook has changed with the environment, but one wonders sometimes where the "progressive" intellectuals, so glib now with their sneers at "orthodox" or "apologetic" economics, would have stood if they had been Marshall's contemporaries.

To suppose that Marshall treated the capitalist system as part of the order of nature, or even that he thought of it as having been established once and for all would, of course, be ludicrous. Like Mill, though with less confidence, he looked for the eventual emergence of new forms of organisation and some kind of new social order.[93] His concern was lest they should come in a manner that would throttle enterprise and experiment and before the institutional and technical environment had evolved new motives and new traditions of behaviour that would preserve a driving-force for progress.

"There is strong *prima facie* cause for fearing that the collective ownership of the means of production would deaden the energies of mankind, and arrest economic progress; unless before its introduction the whole people had acquired a power of unselfish devotion to the public good which is now relatively rare."[94]

One of his few ventures into practical politics was the suggestion, designed to reconcile public control with individual initiative, that undertakings which must necessarily have a monopolistic status should be leased for a limited term by public authorities to corporations tendering competitively, the competition turning on the "price or the quality, or both, of the services or goods, rather than on the annual sum paid for the lease."[95] And here and there he caught a glimpse of the way in which current changes in industry might be developing motives and behaviour-patterns by which progress might be preserved under new forms of organisation. In a noteworthy passage, he points to the growth of professional pride, intellectual ambition, the desire for reputation, distinction and group-approval, among the technicians and the new managerial class brought into prominence by large-scale undertakings as forces which might counteract "the tendency to ossification" set up by "the growth of large businesses, and especially those under public control."[96] It is the note of caution, the suspended judgment and the estimate of the speed of social change (comparable with the secular evolution of biological species) which so sharply distinguish his outlook from that of the present generation.

But, after all, what is important and interesting about Marshall is his contribution to science, not his political opinions or his valuation of the capitalist system. Of these there are scarcely any explicit statements in the *Principles*. And though they may have had something to do with the tone of the book and its turns of expression, they did not, I think, have any substantial effect on his scientific conclusions. Except perhaps in one particular — namely, that he was inclined to over-estimate the strength of competition in its struggle against the tendencies making for monopolisation. For he dreaded monopoly almost as much as he dreaded premature socialisation: and largely for the same reason — that it was likely to deaden initiative and keep down constructive ability.[97] Moreover, if monopoly was coming anyhow, the case against socialisation was greatly weakened. There is danger of misjudging him here. The evidence we have now was not at his disposal. Nevertheless, it looks to me as though in this matter the wish was to some extent father to the thought.

Be that as it may, the decay of what may be called "atomic" competition — *i.e.*, competition between a large number of small, closely-knit units — is the main change in industrial structure which distinguishes our time from his and has done more than anything else to render his theoretical analysis inapplicable to the world of to-day. The analysis does not, indeed, proceed on the assumption that competition is perfect. At the outset of his studies Marshall had "believed it was possible to have a coherent though abstract doctrine of economics in which competition was the only dominant force," but he came to "regard that position as untenable from an abstract as well as from a practical point of view,"[98] and, as we have seen, market-imperfection assumed increasing prominence in his treatment of the theory of value as time went on. Nor did he neglect monopoly proper. The pure theory relating to it is worked out, if not completely, at least very fully and with great elegance in Book V, ch. xvi, of the *Principles*. It is the territory between atomic competition and absolute monopoly that the pure theory of the book does not cover at all satisfactorily. And it is precisely this territory which has been so greatly enlarged by the development of the joint-stock company and the advantages (or necessity) of large-scale control. The conflict of interests within the firm; the interpenetration of interests between firms through interlocking directorates, shareholdings, subsidiary concerns and the like; the domination of an industry by a few large units; the inter-mixture of public and private control as seen in the various types of semi-public corporation and of regulating boards and devices; — these are the features of modern industrial structure which find little or no place in the analytical framework of the *Principles* and give it a rather obsolete appearance. References to them are not wanting.[99] Indeed, the tendency for an industry in which internal economies act strongly "to fall almost entirely into the hands of a few large firms"[100] is a recurring theme. But even in that case we are simply told that

"The production of [the] commodity really partakes in a great measure of the nature of a monopoly; and its price is likely to be so much influenced by the incidents of the campaign between rival producers, each struggling for an extension of territory, as scarcely to have a true normal level."[101]

There the matter is left. Partly, no doubt, because it is closely related to the problems raised by combinations and trusts which were expressly reserved for consideration in a later volume;[102] partly perhaps because Marshall held that combinations tended to develop into consolidations approximating to full monopoly.[103] But the last sentence in the passage just quoted suggests that he also accepted the view that value under monopolistic competition is theoretically indeterminate, and concluded accordingly that pure analysis could not accomplish much in that field. At all events, when the promised continuation at last appeared[104] the treatment was almost entirely historical and descriptive and made no attempt to fill the gap in the pure theory. Meanwhile that gap had been widened by a small but highly significant change introduced in the sixth edition of the *Principles*. After the famous "trees of the forest" simile, earlier editions had proceeded "as with the growth of trees, so is it with the growth of businesses . . ."[105] In the sixth, the sentence was re-written so as to read, "so *was* it with the growth of businesses as a general rule before the great recent development of vast joint-stock companies, which often stagnate, but do not readily die. Now that rule is far from universal, but it still holds in many industries and trades."[106] This inconspicuous change of wording really knocks away — so far as a large and growing section of industry is concerned — the main prop on which the reconciliation between atomic competition and increasing returns had rested. For external economies, though they may explain how a diminishing supply-price may arise where internal economies do not exist, do not constitute an effective obstacle to the elimination of the small unit when these do exist: while market-imperfection, through the openings it affords for advertisement, selling-devices, proprietary brands, goodwill and the rest, acts almost as strongly in favour of large-scale businesses as against them.

As yet very little has been done, in England anyhow, towards filling this gap. The development of the scientific analysis has not kept pace with the development of the subject-matter of the science. Recent elaborations of the pure theory of "imperfect competition" have followed closely the lines laid down by Marshall more than forty years ago. The device of setting the cost or supply curve of the individual firm against its own individual demand curve is due to him — as Mr. Sraffa acknowledged in the celebrated article to which its present vogue is due.[107] Moreover, the two leading propositions derived from it and now so familiar in every lecture-room — namely, that in equilibrium (1) the scale of the firm is determined by the equation of the final increment of its receipts with the final increment of its outlay, and (2) the number of firms in an industry by the rule that the total receipts of the firm on the margin of entry must be equal to its total costs — are essentially his.[108] True, the "marginal revenue curve" is a neat and handy tool which has been used with effect both in expounding these propositions and in problems of monopoly, and it has evidently come to stay. But useful as it is, it is no more than a geometrical version of Marshall's algebra. The change which has occurred in this part of the subject is pedagogic. For expository and educational purposes, it has been found convenient to bring the general case in which a firm's output appreciably affects price into the foreground, so as to illuminate the common element running through the particular cases of monopoly, atomic competition in an imperfect market and perfect competition; whereas Marshall preferred to keep all this in the background and to go straight to the special cases which he thought important in a preliminary survey of the forces at work in the industry of his time. This change also has probably come to stay. It means that the *Principles* will lose, is indeed already losing, its pre-eminence as a text-book. But, once again, it is a change in the manner of exposition, not in the substance of the doctrine expounded. It in no wise extends or modifies the theory of the *Principles* so as to cover recent modifications of industrial structure. Markets have not become less perfect in the last fifty years — rather the contrary: the significant developments have been the domination of industry by large units ("oligopoly" — to use the fashionable phrase) and the increasing complexity of the controls. Valuable work has lately been done by various workers (Dr. Zeuthen,[109] Prof. Chamberlin[110] and Mr. Kahn,[111] for instance) on the theory of duopoly and of bi-lateral monopoly and Prof. Pigou's analysis of "exploitation" is an important contribution to the distributional aspect of this type of problem.[112] Nevertheless the general theory of value and distribution as a whole has scarcely advanced at all into that part of the field at which the *Principles* stopped short. It is still concerned almost exclusively with the case of pure monopoly on the one side and on the other with atomic competition, "perfect" or "imperfect."

In England, indeed, there has been some tendency to retreat by confining the theory of imperfect competition to the special (and almost nonexistent) case in which the individual firm produces only one "line" and cannot affect the demand for its output by advertisement and other selling devices:[113] a tendency which illustrates a more general departure from the example set by the *Principles*.

The attempt to fuse realistic study with theoretical analysis has, on the whole, not been followed up. By and large, recent theory, so far as it relates to the problems of value and distribution, is at a higher level of abstraction than Marshall's. The limited rôle which he assigned to mathematics has generally been accepted in his own country, notably by those few economists who have had a mathematical training.[114] (Contrast in this respect the work of Lord Keynes, who came to economics from the Mathematical Tripos, with that of Prof. Pigou, who came to it from history.) But analytical and descriptive work have tended to fall into separate compartments and even into different hands — in accordance with Jevons' forecast rather than with Marshall's practice. Allied to that development is the tendency within the theoretical compartment for mechanical concepts and analogies to regain their primacy. Partly no doubt this has been due to the itch for precise results: not all of us are content to act on the late Prof. Wildon Carr's admirable motto (which might well have been Marshall's), "It is better to be vaguely right than precisely wrong." Partly, perhaps, it may be attributed to the stress laid — unavoidably — in academic teaching on those parts of the subject which the beginner finds most difficult. Would it be fanciful to connect it also with the fact that among the natural sciences physics has once more taken over the lead from biological studies (in the popular imagination at least), and to see in it evidence of some kind of cyclical movement in ideas which affect all scientific enquiries alike? Whatever the explanation, the fact is plain. In those parts of economics with which the *Principles* was concerned, there has been a distinct reversion to Ricardo's method and away from the Marshallian blend of realism and abstraction: a return to the mechanical as against the biological approach. How far this development also will be lasting it is impossible at present to say. There are already some signs of a reaction — in a form which would have been especially welcomed by Marshall — viz., an attempt to check and modify theoretical analysis by the use of statistics. But as yet it has not made much headway.

Meanwhile, the fading out of biological analogies has not been accompanied, as might perhaps have been expected, by any widespread attempt to analyse the process of economic change in terms of dynamics. Some movement in this direction there has been,[115] but up to the present it has not resulted in a wide or far-reaching advance, still less in a re-statement of the theory of value and distribution superseding Marshall's. Yet this is the point at which the apparatus of the *Principles* strikes one as least satisfactory and where its author seems to have been least satisfied with it. Marshall was well aware that the plane curves of demand and supply are not a fully adequate instrument for dealing with an irreversible process in which a change in demand may permanently affect the conditions of supply and vice versa.[116] Hence the very restricted place which he gave to them (and to the corresponding equations) and the stress he laid on the limitations of statical assumptions when the economies of large-scale operations act strongly.[117] Hence also, it may be, the somewhat greater prominence accorded as time went on to the particular equilibrium of individual industries. For, although the device of representing the price that has to be paid for labour and for capital as a function of the aggregate amount required was an improvement on the practice of treating them as constants, the irreversibility of the process to be analysed is even more patent here. The rising long-period supply price of labour definitely depends on the effect of high earnings on habitual standards of life and the rate at which capital is forthcoming is significantly influenced both by the income to which those who supply it have been accustomed and the expectations which experience has implanted in them. It is noteworthy that Marshall, while arguing, after a very cautious survey of the evidence, that labour, capital, and ability-in-command-of-capital had at the time when he wrote definite supply-prices, never actually applied his supply and demand curves to the agents of production. In fact, his apparatus is adapted to display some only of the major influences on which the determination of the system of prices depends. He was constantly feeling his way to a more complete solution. As, for instance, in the following passage:—

"The unsatisfactory character of these results [relating to increasing returns] is partly due to the imperfections of our analytical methods, and may conceivably be much diminished in a later age by the gradual improvement of our scientific machinery. We should have made a great advance if we could represent the normal demand and supply price [of a commodity] as a function both of the amount normally produced and of the time at which that amount became normal."[118]

and in the footnote attached to it, containing suggestions for a three-dimensional diagram. One might have anticipated that an attempt to supply the deficiency would have presented itself to his readers as the outstanding task to be undertaken now that the confusions of the older statical theory had been cleared up and the gaps in it filled.

That so little has been done in this direction may be partly explained by a feature in the economic history of our own time which has tended to divert attention to a matter of much more urgent practical importance — the problem of unused capacity, of workless men and idle or half-idle plant. The extent and persistence of unemployment in the last quarter of a century distinguishes the experience of our generation from Marshall's even more strikingly than the growth of concentrated and complex controls. And here theory has made a big advance, involving what may prove to be a really radical departure from the standpoint adopted in the *Principles*. From that

732

"preliminary volume" monetary factors are excluded by the assumption that the purchasing power of money is constant.[119] This corresponds to and was probably suggested by Ricardo's assumption that the money-stuff, the *numeraire,* is a produced commodity with a constant marginal cost in terms of capital and labour and that the technical coefficients relating to it constitute a kind of norm about which those relating to other commodities are distributed:[120] an assumption which simplified his problem by limiting it to what was in effect a sort of barter-economy and contributed not a little to the traditional separation of the theory of money from the theory of value and distribution. In its Marshallian form (which is in part a reflection of the increased importance of credit-instruments as compared with hard money) its implications are subtler, more far-reaching and in a sense more treacherous because they are less easy to trace. To follow them out in detail or to inquire how far Marshall's assumption succeeded in shutting out monetary influences would take us too far. It must suffice to remark that in determining the scale of the whole system of outputs monetary influences, as we can all see now, play a leading part, and that therefore a theory of general (as distinct from particular) equilibrium must take them into account if it is to explain even approximately the forces at work in the real world to determine the relative values of the commodities which make up the system and the rewards of the agents used in producing them. In explaining the different levels of economic development achieved by different races or in different parts of the world or in widely separated historical epochs and the causes underlying the slow climb from primitive savagery to mechanical civilisation, a somewhat exclusive stress on "prospectiveness" and "self-control," the comparative weight given to present and future benefits, to leisure and acquisition, does no great harm. (The *Principles* is more concerned with explanations of that kind than is commonly supposed.) Moreover, at a time when the capitalist system had not lost its initial *élan* and the underlying psychological and technical conditions were making strongly for further expansion, a theory of value and distribution which provisionally ignored the money mechanism did not involve a very serious distortion of contemporary fact. Even so, it was incomplete and lacked both generality and precision. For it did not cover some of the principal factors on which (on any but a very telescopic view) the rate of progress and hence not only the aggregate volume of investment and output but also the system of relative outputs and prices must always to some extent depend in a monetary economy.

There is some recognition of this in a neglected passage at the end of the *Principles* which points forward to what was to have followed in the later volumes.[121] But it does little more than underline the qualifications of Say's Law, which had been clearly stated in an early essay of Mill's[122] (and rather covered up in his *Principles*) — namely, that the power to buy does not necessarily imply the will to buy and that the periodical recessions of industry are due to people's (more especially business men's) refusal, principally owing to lack of confidence, to lay out the money and credit at their disposal. Unlike Malthus, who had anticipated him by insisting in the teeth of Ricardo's opposition that the interaction of supply and demand is paramount at every point in the pricing process, Marshall did not attempt to apply the supply and demand apparatus to output as a whole. And Malthus' attempt was baulked by his failure to shake himself free from the associations of the Ricardian barter-economy. It was left to Lord Keynes, approaching the problem from the monetary side, to carry this line of thought through to a triumphant conclusion and to revolutionise all our ideas by doing so. The re-integration of the theory of money with the theory of value and distribution which is thus called for has not yet been accomplished. It is too early to say how large a departure from the Marshallian analysis it will involve. That some re-statement will be necessary is already evident.

Thus in two outstanding respects — viz., (1) the comparatively slight treatment of competition and bargaining between large units and of complex industrial controls, and (2) the neglect of aggregate money demand and money cost in the analysis of general equilibrium — the superstructure of the theory contained in the *Principles* shows obvious traces of the conditions prevailing when it was built up.[123] It is a subtle and masterly analysis of the leading forces at work in the determination of relative prices when individualistic capitalism had got well into its stride and had transformed industrial technique but still retained much of its initial expansionist force; and when the new forms of organisation opened up by the principle of limited liability and the monopolistic tendencies inherent in the economy of large-scale operation were making themselves felt but had not yet overrun a great part of the field. Inevitably it is less well adapted to the conditions which have emerged after the passage of more than half a century.[124]

But underlying the superstructure was a broader and more general system of ideas.[125] How far can these still be of service in handling the problems of the present and the coming generation?

Prophecy in such a matter is rash, but at present many of them certainly look like permanent acquisitions. The principle of mutual determination, for instance; the balancing of marginal investments of cost and advantage; the distinction between the short-period and long-period elements in cost; the notion of "elasticity"; are all playing a lively part somewhere or other in the various branches of current economic theory. Witness, for example, Lord Keynes' application of the demand and supply schedules to output as a whole and the part played in his analysis by the balancing of the marginal productivity of capital against the price that has to be paid to compensate for liquidity preference. Witness also the numerous recent discussions of the principles which should govern a collectivist state in determining the amount of investment and the distribution of its resources between alternative uses.[126] And they correspond, surely, to actual phenomena which must persist in one shape or another under any form of organisation and in any social system.

At first sight, it might appear that in a totalitarian *régime* what Marshall seems to have regarded as the most general and universally applicable element in his construction, the psychological conception of real cost, must be ousted by the notion of "opportunity cost." But on second thoughts is that so certain? The last few months have indeed shown clearly enough that the pre-war stresses and strains between the peasants and the industrial or dominant elements in the U.S.S.R. arose partly from the necessity of choosing between "guns and butter." But did they not also represent a conflict between the rival claims of jam to-day and more jam to-morrow — the divergent pulls of the desire to consume now and the advantages offered by long-term investment? and was not the line actually adopted the outcome of some kind of balance between these pulls? Again, two of our most eager admirers of the Soviet régime attribute the inequality of incomes which it has instituted (or preserved) between various grades of labour to the necessity of providing an incentive which would induce workers to undertake prolonged courses of training or to sacrifice their leisure in acquiring technical skill.[127] You may drive out real cost with a pitchfork, but it has an awkward way of coming back.

The main difficulty, in this connection and in others, seems to lie in applying precise scientific methods to the action of large masses, particularly when they are composed of heterogeneous elements whose interests may diverge. It may be that material of this kind is beyond the reach of exact analysis and determinate results. If so, the future of positive economic theory, as distinct from welfare economics, is not bright. The refinements of exact analysis may still be helpful in ascertaining how public authorities and large-scale private associations *ought* to behave — in determining "ideal" outputs, the distribution of resources which would yield "maximum satisfaction" and so on. They will be of little or no use in explaining how they *do* behave — what outputs and what distribution of resources they can in fact be expected to produce. On the other hand, it may be that a solution will be found in the direction to which Marshall's ingenious contrivance of "compromise benefit"[128] and his modest application of it in *Industry and Trade*[129] seem to point. But this is speculation. The economics of group-action, of collective control, massive competition and mass bargaining have yet to be written. What we can say with confidence is that Marshall's *Principles* contributed to the corpus of scientific ideas elements which were not only "architectonic" and "in some sense his own," but are still "an existing yeast working in the Cosmos" and far from dying. On the evidence so far available, its author abundantly deserves the title "classical" even on his own somewhat exacting standard.

NOTES

1. I have had some difficulty in deciding whether in this context "Marshall's *Principles*" should be taken to mean the book as it appeared in 1890 or the more familiar form which it finally assumed. In the event, I have written with two editions before me—the first (1890) and the seventh (1916). Generally speaking, I have used the former when considering Marshall's relation to his predecessors and contemporaries, the latter when considering his work in connection with the problems and ideas of the present day. Page references to the first edition are in square brackets: the rest are to the seventh edition. When the work referred to is not specified it is the *Principles*.

2. Including Lord Keynes in his mem-

oir "Alfred Marshall, 1852–1924" (*Economic Journal*, September 1924: reprinted in *Essays in Biography*; and in *Memorials of Alfred Marshall*, ed. A. C. Pigou—hereafter referred to as *Memorials*); Prof. Pigou ("In Memoriam: Alfred Marshall," in *Memorials*, pp. 81–90); Prof. J. A. Schumpeter ("Alfred Marshall's "Principles": a semicentennial Appraisal": in the *American Economic Review*, June 1941, pp. 236–248).

3. *Memorials*, p. 412.

4. *Ibid.*, p. 20.

5. Marshall had not a high opinion of Mill as an economist. "I incline to regard Petty and Hermann and von Thünen and Jevons as classical, but not Mill" (letter to J. Bonar: *Memorials*, p. 374). "J. S. Mill went so far as to maintain that his occupations at the India Office did not interfere with his pursuit of philosophical inquiries. But it seems probable that this diversion of his freshest powers lowered the quality of his best thought more than he was aware; and though it may have diminished but little his remarkable usefulness in his own generation, it probably affected very much his power of doing that kind of work which influences the course of thought in future generations" (*Principles*, p. [313]). "The genius which enabled Ricardo—it was not so with Mill—to tread his way safely through the most slippery paths of mathematical reasoning . . . had made him one of my heroes" (*Memorials*, pp. 99–100). But it was through Mill that he came to Ricardo.

6. See, *e.g.*, *Principles*, p. [529 n.]. "There is a widely spread belief that [Ricardo's theory of cost of production in relation to value] has needed to be reconstructed by the present generation of economists. The purpose of the present Note is to show cause for not accepting this opinion." There are many passages of similar purport.

7. *Memorials*, p. 418.

8. *A History of Economic Ideas*, by E. Whittaker, Associate Professor of Economics in the University of Illinois. New York and London, 1940. The sentences quoted are on p. 453.

9. *The Development of Economic Doctrine.* (Edition of 1934), p. 364.

10. On this and the reasons for it see Keynes, *op. cit.* (*Memorials*, pp. 26–8 and 33–8).

11. Jevons' *Theory* and Menger's *Grundsätze* both appeared in 1871, nineteen years before the *Principles*. The first part of Walras' *Eléments* was published in 1874, the second in 1877; Böhm-Bawerk's *Kapitalzins-Theorien* in 1884, his *Grundzüge* in 1886, and his *Positive Theorie* in 1889; Wieser's *Ursprung* in 1884, his *Natürliche Werth* in 1889.

12. Even then he might easily be misled. Marshall thus describes his practice as to acknowledgments. "My rule has been

to refer in a footnote to anyone whom I know to have said a thing before I have said it in print, even though I may have said it in lectures for many years before I knew that it had ever occurred to him; I just refer, but say nothing about obligations either way; being quite aware that people will suppose me to imply obligations. Instances are Francis Walker and Fleeming Jenkin" (*Memorials*, p. 416). All the works mentioned in the last note are referred to in the *Principles*.

13. J. S. Mill, *Principles of Political Economy* (Ashley's edition), p. 469.

14. *Principles*, p. [401].

15. *Works* (ed. McCulloch), p. 241.

16. *Ibid.*, p. 26.

17. See below, pp. 731–2, for remarks on the limitations of this method of treating the problem.

18. *Op. cit.*, p. 450.

19. *Works*, p. 51.

20. It is this which he usually has in mind when speaking of a "rise" or "fall" of "wages."

21. Ricardo, *Works*, pp. 67, 68; Mill, *op. cit.*, p. 731.

22. *Works*, pp. 41–2, 201, 253; 53, 143.

23. *Op. cit.*, p. 98. Ricardo's view about the supply of capital fluctuates. Sometimes his argument seems to require the hypothesis that it is constant. Sometimes he inclines to treat it as depending on the rate of profit; sometimes as depending on the excess of aggregate output over what is required to maintain the population at the conventional standard of comfort. On the whole, the last notion perhaps predominates. But he nowhere clearly states that the amount of accumulation is a definite proportion or function of the surplus output. If this hypothesis is introduced, the gap referred to in the text is closed and the Ricardian system becomes, so far as this point is concerned, determinate. In some ways, it is a pity that Marshall did not follow up this strand in Ricardo's thought rather than the idea that the rate of accumulation depends on the incentive.

24. With the addition of a set of equations "each of which equates the supply price for any amount of a commodity to the sum of the prices of corresponding amounts of its factors"—the supply equations corresponding to the Ricardian theorem that value equals cost at the margin in the generalized form which allows for the possibility that marginal cost may vary in either direction as output increases.

25. P. 855. Note XX, p. [745] in the first edition.

26. *Memorials*, pp. 416–7.

27. *Ibid.*, p. 417.

28. The re-arrangement of the book also somewhat obscured the fact that Marshall's theory of value is a theory of

general, not particular, equilibrium. This is obvious enough in the Mathematical Appendix. It also comes out quite clearly in the text of the first edition, where it is not till we reach Book VII, dealing with the pricing of the agents of production, that "Value" appears on a title-page (the full title of this book is "Value: or distribution and exchange," while Book V, dealing with the equilibrium of particular commodities, is called "The Theory of Equilibrium of Demand and Supply"). In the seventh edition, Book V (which embodies the old V and VI) is entitled "General Relations of Demand, Supply and Value." Book VI (corresponding to the old VII) is headed "The Distribution of the National Income," and we are no longer told, as we had been at the beginning of the old Book VII, that only now are we to "deal with the problem of value as a whole" (p. [540]).

29. *E.g.*, Ricardo, *op. cit.*, pp. 66, 94–5. Mill, *op. cit.*, pp. 446–7, 452, 455. Attention may be drawn in particular to Ricardo's striking discussion of taxes on luxuries (*Works*, pp. 144–5) which comes very near to Marshall's position in regard to the effect of elasticity of demand on the yield of a tax.

30. P. 824 and *Memorials*, p. 316.

31. Above, p. 713.

32. See Ricardo, *Works*, p. 284, where, however, the possibility is stated only to be dismissed as a "trifling exception": and Mill, *op. cit.*, p. 719, where it is set aside on the ground that hitherto the day-labourers have treated any increase in their means of living "simply as convertible into food for a greater number of children."

33. Reprinted in *Memorials*, pp. 93–100.

34. *Ibid.*, pp. 119–133.

35. *Memorials*, pp. 416, 417.

36. From an undated note by A. M. printed in *Memorials*, p. 100. The main point of substance for which he was indebted to von Thünen seems to have been the principle of substitution. In the first edition of the *Principles* he calls it "von Thünen's great Law of Substitution" ([p. 704]). Whether the identification of the demand price for a factor of production with its marginal productivity was also suggested by von Thünen is uncertain. But it was evidently not taken from any other source. See *Memorials*, pp. 412–3: "I cannot recollect whether I formulated the doctrine "normal wages" = "terminal" (I got "marginal" from von Thünen's *Grenze*) productivity of labour before I read von Thünen or not. I think I did so partially at least; for . . . [here follows the passage quoted at the head of this paper] . . . . I rejected the wage doctrine in Book II [of Mill's *Principles*], which has a wage-fund flavour: and accepted that in his Book IV, in which he seemed to me

to have been true to the best traditions of Ricardo's method (I say nothing in defence of Ricardo's positive theory of wages), and then to have got very close to what I afterwards found to be von Thünen's position. That was chiefly in 1867–8. I fancy I read Cournot in 1868. I know I did not read von Thünen then: probably in 1869 or 1870. One side of my own theory of wages has been absolutely fixed ever since, to what by title of priority may be called the von Thünen doctrine." One can readily understand why Marshall praised Mill's Bk. IV ch. iii so highly, if it set him on the track which led to his final theory of distribution. I am half inclined to think that it may have been the starting-point of his whole analysis. But the assertion that it is free from the fallacies of the wage-fund doctrine (*Memorials*, 316) surely goes too far. Indeed Mill seems to have arrived at his conclusions that an increase of capital without a change in population raises wages and an increase in population without a change in the amount of capital lowers them by direct inference from that doctrine. At any rate he gives no other reason for accepting them. The doctrine of quasi-rent originated in response to "McLeod's criticisms—now [1902] unjustly forgotten—on the unqualified statement that cost governs value" (*Memorials*, p. 414). But it was Marshall's doctrine, not McLeod's.

37. *Principles*, [p. x].

38. *Memorials*, p. 22.

39. *Principles*, p. 663.

40. *Ibid.*, p. [485–486].

41. For instance, when he first makes his appearance ([pp. 548–9]), the marginal shepherd's net product is equated to the value of the twenty sheep which he adds to his employer's output, without the warning which appeared in later editions that "theoretically a deduction from this has to be made for the fact that, by throwing twenty extra sheep on the market, the farmer will lower the price of sheep generally, and therefore lose a little on his other sheep" (p. 517 n.); and in the first edition the mathematical note which states the principle of substitution in algebraic form (Mathematical Appendix, note XXV in the first edition, note XIV in the seventh) stops short at the end of the first paragraph (which deals with the "Crusoe" case of an individual making things for himself and aiming at his own maximum satisfaction), and accordingly does not include the careful discussion of the comparative magnitude of these two elements in the marginal net product and of their significance when things are being made by a profit-taking entrepreneur for sale on the market (pp. 849–50). But the qualifications were soon introduced (Mr. Guillebaud informs me that they were first inserted in the third edition, dated 1895), and Marshall was too good a

mathematician not to have been aware of them from the outset. One would guess that the note dealing with this point existed substantially in its present form before 1890, the latter part being left out to avoid complicated detail.

42. For the representative firm, see *e.g.*, pp. [375–7], [413–4], [523], and for market-imperfection, pp. [400], [523–4].

43. Pp. [383], [151], [85], [653 n.], [390], [298–9], [513–5], [79 n.], *Memorials*, 169–70.

44. *Theory*.

45. *Mathematical Psychics* (1881).

46. *Principles*, pp. [78–85].

47. Ibid., pp. [82–3], [80], [293–4], 16, [17 n.], 22–7, 92–3. *Memorials*, p. 160–1.

48. *Memorials*, p. 161.

49. Pp. [399–400].

50. *Works*, p. 68.

51. *Op. cit.*, pp. 407, 31–3, 463–6.

52. See Ricardo, *Works*, pp. 51, 22, 24, 25, 18, 123–4, 87; Mill, *op. cit.*, pp. 54, 479–80, 463–6. The nearest approach these authors make to a psychological conception of real cost is in their explanation (on Smithian lines) of the differences between the rates of wages and of profits in different occupations. A psychological interpretation of cost similar to Marshall's is, however, to be found in Senior. See his *Political Economy*, p. 97.

53. P. 101.

54. "The Old Generation of Economists and the New." In *Memorials*, p. 301.

55. *Memorials*, p. 437.

56. *Ibid.*, p. 427.

57. Pp. 762–3, [62–3].

58. Pp. [63ₙ] [66–7].

59. *E.g.*, p. [91].

60. Pp. [76–7]. For Jevons' view, see *Principles of Economics and Other Papers*, pp. 195–6.

61. *Op. cit.*, pp. 197–8, 200–1.

62. Pp. [65], 701.

63. Jevons, *loc. cit.*, p. 190.

64. *Fortnightly Review*, 1876, p. 216. Quoted by Jevons, *loc. cit.*, p. 191, and reprinted in *Collected Works*, Vol. vii, pp. 92–3.

65. P. 770.

66. *Ibid.*

67. Pp. 26–7. *Memorials*, p. 299.

68. *Op. cit.*, pp. 498, 500. Of course, "character" in this context is to be taken as equivalent to the untranslatable term ἦθος, which includes a great deal more than "moral" character in the popular (and narrow) sense. My point is that a belief in the importance of a people's ἦθος in determining its economic behaviour may have helped to reinforce Marshall's insistence on the importance in that connection of the "moral" elements included in the wider term—as well as explaining much else in his handling of economic problems.

69. *Memorials*, p. 408.

70. *Principles*, p. 764 [65].

71. *Ibid.*, p. 764: [64–5].

72. The first edition of Mill's *Principles* was published eleven years before the *Origin of Species*: the third edition (in which the discussion of future changes in the social order took what was to all intents and purposes its final shape) seven years before.

73. *Principles*, pp. [65], 764.

74. *Ibid.*, p. [90].

75. *Ibid.*, pp. [425–7]. In the chapters circulated by Sidgwick the irreversibility of movement along the curves is indicated by barbs on the amount-axis.

76. *Principles*, p. vii.

77. *Memorials*, p. 47.

78. It is difficult for an Englishman to gauge the extent to which the book affected the course of ideas abroad. Tracing "influences" in the thought of a country which one does not know from inside is always risky: one is so apt to get the emphasis wrong and *nuances* elude one. For information about the United States I have relied on the writings of American economists. As regards Germany and Austria, I have been much assisted by a letter from the authoritative pen of Prof. Schumpeter; as regards Italy by a conversation with Mr. P. Sraffa, who knows the economics both of that country and of England from the inside. To both of them, I offer my grateful thanks—and my humble apologies if my attempt to distil what they have told me into a few sentences has resulted in errors.

79. Prof. Carver dissented on some points, but in the main his well-known *Distribution of Wealth* (1904) follows Marshall's method, while the apparatus used to expound the theory of value in Taussig's widely-read *Principles of Economics* is wholly Marshallian.

80. E. Whittaker: *A History of Economic Ideas* (1940), p. 453. Clark, who in years was nearly contemporary with Marshall, seems in the main to have worked independently and though his *Distribution of Wealth* (1899) has some remarkable resemblances to Marshall's work its principal affinities are with the Austrians.

81. P. T. Homan: *Contemporary Economic Thought*, p. 269 and p. x.

82. Marshall's work has, however, not been without influence even in Austria. Prof. Schumpeter writes: "My own generation—starting their University training, say, from 1900 to 1905—did read Marshall in the student stage. I know I did at all events. Later on, especially after the war, he came for a time into his own, though only with a restricted group to which, however, he became a teacher."

83. Among the channels through which it did so, the work of Prof. Cassel may be selected for particular mention. No doubt his explicit references to Marshall are usually critical, but the whole form of

the thought in his *Nature and Necessity of Interest*—the conception of interest as a "price" paid for "waiting" and determined by the demand for and supply of it—is essentially Marshallian and in his *Theory of Social Economy*, a Walrasian analysis is completed and made more general by the introduction of Marshall's principle of substitution—though this is rather oddly described as "supplementary."

84. Letter to J. Bonar, *Memorials*, p. 374.

85. See, for example, *Principles*, pp. 229–30; *Memorials*, p. 463.

86. *Memorials*, p. 462.

87. *Principles*, p. 714.

88. *Ibid.*, pp. 712–13.

89. *Memorials*, p. 462.

90. *Principles*, pp. 11, 177, 749, 750.

91. *Ibid.*, pp. 2, 714–5.

92. For an account of the achievements of nineteenth-century capitalism from a source which is certainly not prejudiced in its favour, see S. and B. Webb, *The Decay of Capitalist Civilisation*, pp. 78–84.

93. See, *e.g.*, p. 752, *Memorials*, p. 367. I doubt whether Marshall thought that the new order would or should be founded on the public ownership of property. As I read them, the indications are to the contrary. In comparing his attitude to the capitalist system (and to socialism) with Mill's, one must remember that Mill's *Principles* belongs to the first half of the century, when the improvement in the position of the mass of the people had not decisively declared itself. So, too, though the first volume of *Das Kapital* was not published till 1867, Marx was then forty-nine years of age and his basic ideas had been formed long before and in a different environment.

94. *Principles*, p. 713.

95. From his presidential address to the Economic Section of the British Association, 1890. *Memorials*, p. 277.

96. *Memorials*, pp. 308–9. From *The Old Generation of Economists and the New* (1896).

97. *Principles*, p. 8.

98. *Memorials*, p. 414.

99. See, for example, pp. 604, 304.

100. P. 397.

101. *Ibid.*; cf. p. 805.

102. Pp. x, v, 660, 722.

103. *Memorials*, pp. 271, 274.

104. *Industry and Trade* (1919).

105. Fifth edition, p. 316.

106. P. 316.

107. *Economic Journal*, Vol. XXXVI, p. 526.

108. The first is clearly stated in the Mathematical Appendix, Note XIV, pp. 848–50. For the second see, in particular, pp. 373, 377, 459–60.

Marshall usually writes of the costs of the "representative" not of the "marginal" firm. But this only makes his theory more general by allowing for the case in which individual firms may rise and fall while the output of the whole industry remains unchanged. When he resorts to a more narrowly statical analysis, the marginal firm, in fact though not in name, duly appears (see his construction of the "particular expenses curve," Appendix H, p. 811 and cp. p. 373).

109. *Problems of Monopoly and Economic Warfare* (1930).

110. *The Theory of Monopolistic Competition* (1933).

111. *Economic Journal*, 1937, pp. 1–20.

112. *Economics of Welfare*, pp. 556–7, 813–4. See also his *Principles and Methods of Industrial Peace* and the corresponding chapter in *Economics of Welfare* (Part III, ch. vi.).

113. This is not true of the United States. Prof. Chamberlin's pioneer *Theory of Monopolistic Competition* treats at length of selling devices and product-differentiation as well as oligopoly.

114. Marshall's hope that economics would attract students trained in the mathematical and physical sciences (*Memorials*, pp. 171–2) has, on the whole, not been fulfilled in his own University. Not only his successor in the chair, but the great majority of the teaching staff at Cambridge since his time have been recruited from the "literary" subjects.

115. *E.g.* in the work of Prof. J. R. Hicks and the Swedish school.

116. See above, p. 723.

117. Pp. 460–1, 805–12.

118. P. 809; cf. p. 463 n.

119. Pp. 62, [9].

120. *Works*, pp. 28–30.

121. Pp. 710–11.

122. *Essays on Unsettled Questions in Political Economy*, pp. 69–72 (2nd ed.).

123. It must be remembered, however, that combinations and money were reserved for later treatment.

124. The relativity of economic doctrine was a well-recognised principle with Marshall. See, for example, *Principles*, p. 37: "Every age and every country has its own problems: and every change in social conditions is likely to require a new development of economic doctrines": also the letter written in 1915 to Mr. C. R. Fay: "A thousand years hence 1920–70 will, I expect, be *the* time for economic historians. It drives me wild to think of it. I believe it will make my poor *Principles*, with a lot of poor comrades, into waste paper" (*Memorials*, pp. 489–90).

125. The task which Marshall set before his own generation of economists was not so much to construct formulae immediately applicable to practical affairs as to build—or rather finish building—an *organon*, an instrument of thought, applicable to a variety of differing problems. See his Inaugural Lecture delivered at

Cambridge in 1885 (*Memorials*, pp. 171; 159–61).

126. *E.g.*, H. D. Dickinson, *Economics of Socialism* (1939); E. F. M. Durbin, *Economic Journal*, 1933, pp. 676–690; M. H. Dobb, *Economic Journal*, 1939, pp. 713–28.

127. S. and B. Webb: *Soviet Communism* (1936), p. 710. Compare pp. 711 and 715 where it appears that wage-rates are adjusted not only to the "difficulty of the work" but to "the sanitary conditions" under which it is done and local variations introduced in order to induce people to move to or stay in the places where they are wanted.

128. *Principles*, pp. 488–493.

129. Pp. 425–6.

30.

NICHOLAS KALDOR

Cambridge University

Alternative Theories

of Distribution

According to the Preface of Ricardo's Principles, the discovery of the laws which regulate distributive shares is the "principal problem in Political Economy". The purpose of this paper is to present a bird's eye view of the various theoretical attempts, since Ricardo, at solving this "principal problem". Though all attempts at classification in such a vast field are necessarily to some extent arbitrary, and subjective to the writer, in terms of broad classification, one should, I think, distinguish between four main strands of thought, some of which contain important sub-groups. The first of these is the Ricardian, or Classical Theory, the second the Marxian, the third the Neo-Classical or Marginalist Theory and the fourth the Keynesian. The inclusion of a separate "Keynesian" theory in this context may cause surprise. An attempt will be made to show however [in a section not reprinted here] that the specifically Keynesian apparatus of thought could be applied to the problem of distribution, rather than to the problem of the general level of production; that there is evidence that in its early stages, Keynes' own thinking tended to develop in this direction — only to be diverted from it with the discovery (made some time between the publication of the *Treatise on Money* and the *General Theory*) that inflationary and deflationary tendencies could best be analysed in terms of the resulting changes in output and employment, rather than in their effects on prices.

The compression of a whole army of distinguished writers, and schools

Excerpt reprinted by permission of the author and of Gerald Duckworth & Co., Ltd., from "Alternative Theories of Distribution," *Review of Economic Studies*, XXIII (2) (1955–56), 83–100; pp. 83–91 excerpted. The original essay will appear in *Essays in Value and Distribution*, being published by Gerald Duckworth & Co., Ltd.

of thought, between Ricardo and Keynes (Marx aside) under the term of Neo-Classical or Marginalist Theory is harder to justify. For apart from the marginalists proper, the group would have to include such "non-marginalists" or quasi-marginalists (from the point of view of distribution theory) as the Walrasians and the neo-Walrasians,[1] as well as the imperfect competitionists, who though marginalist, do not necessarily hold with the principle of Marginal Productivity. But as I shall hope to show, there are important aspects which all these theories have in common,[2] and which justifies bringing them under one broad umbrella.

Ricardo prefaced his statement by a reference to the historical fact that "in different stages of society the proportions of the whole produce of the earth which will be allotted to each of these (three) classes under the names of rent, profit and wages will be essentially *different*."[3] To-day, a writer on the problem of distribution, would almost be inclined to say the opposite — that "in different stages of (capitalist) society the proportions of the national income allotted to wages, profits, etc., are *essentially similar*". The famous "historical constancy" of the share of wages in the national income — and the similarity of these shares in different capitalist economies, such as the U.S. and the U.K. — was of course an unsuspected feature of capitalism in Ricardo's day. But to the extent that recent empirical research tends to contradict Ricardo's assumption about the variability of relative shares, it makes the question of what determines these shares, more, rather than less, intriguing. In fact no hypothesis as regards the forces determining distributive shares could be intellectually satisfying unless it succeeds in accounting for the relative stability of these shares in the advanced capitalist economies over the last 100 years or so, despite the phenomenal changes in the techniques of production, in the accumulation of capital relative to labour and in real income per head.

Ricardo's concern in the problem of distribution was not due, or not only due, to the interest in the question of distributive shares *per se,* but to the belief that the theory of distribution holds the key to an understanding of the whole mechanism of the economic system — of the forces governing the rate of progress, of the ultimate incidence of taxation, of the effects of protection, and so on. It was through "the laws which regulate distributive shares" that he was hoping to build what in present-day parlance we would call "a simple macro-economic model".[4] In this respect, if no other, the Ricardian and the "Keynesian" theories are analogous.[5] With the Neo-Classical or Marginalist theories, on the other hand, the problem of distribution is merely one aspect of the general pricing process; it has no particular theoretical significance apart from the importance of the question *per se.* Nor do these theories yield a "macro-economic model" of the kind that exhibits the reaction-mechanism of the system through the choice of a strictly limited number of dependent and independent variables.

I. THE RICARDIAN THEORY

Ricardo's theory was based on two separate principles which we may term the "marginal principle" and the "surplus principle" respectively. The

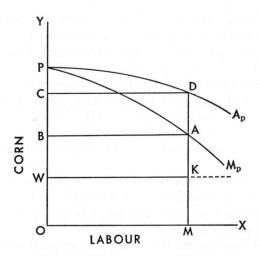

"marginal principle" serves to explain the share of rent, and the "surplus principle" the division of the residue between wages and profits. To explain the Ricardian model, we must first divide the economy into two broad branches, agriculture and industry and then show how, on Ricardo's assumptions, the forces operating in agriculture serve to determine distribution in industry.

The agricultural side of the picture can be exhibited in terms of a simple diagram (Fig. 1), where Oy measures quantities of "corn" (standing for all agricultural produce) and Ox the amount of labour employed in agriculture. At a given state of knowledge and in a given natural environment the curve $p-Ap$ represents the product per unit of labour and the curve $p-Mp$ the marginal product of labour. The existence of these two *separate* curves, is a consequence of a declining tendency in the average product curve — i.e., of the assumption of diminishing returns. Corn-output is thus uniquely determined when the quantity of labour is given:[6] for any given working force, OM, total output is represented by the rectangle $OCDM$. Rent is the difference between the product of labour on "marginal" land and the product on average land, or (allowing for the intensive, as well as the extensive, margin) the difference between average and marginal labour productivity which depends on the elasticity of the $p-Ap$ curve, i.e., the extent to which diminishing returns operate.

The marginal product of labour (or, in classical parlance, the "produce-minus-rent") is not however equal to the wage, but to the sum of wages and profits. The rate of wages is determined quite independently of marginal productivity by the supply price of labour which Ricardo assumed to be constant in terms of corn. In modern parlance, the Ricardian hypothesis implies an infinitely elastic supply curve of labour at the given supply price, OW.[7] The demand for labour is not determined however by the $p-Mp$ curve, but by the accumulation of capital which determines how many labourers can find employment at the wage rate OW. Hence the equilibrium position is not indicated by the point of intersection between the $p-Mp$ curve and the supply curve of labour, but by the aggregate demand for labour in terms of corn — the "wages fund".[8] As capital accumulates, the labour force will grow, so that any addition to the total wage fund, through capital accumulation — the *agricultural* wages fund is indicated by the area $OWKM$ — will tend to be a horizontal addition (pushing the vertical line KM to the right) and not a vertical one (pushing the horizontal line WK upwards).[9]

For any given M, profits are thus a residue, arising from the difference between the marginal product of labor and the rate of wages. The resulting

ratio, $\dfrac{\text{Profits}}{\text{Wages}}$, determines the rate of profit per cent on the capital employed;

it is moreover *equal* to that ratio, on the assumption that the capital is turned over once a year, so that the capital employed is equal to the annual wages-bill. (This latter proposition however is merely a simplification, and not an essential part of the story.)

In a state of equilibrium, the money rate of profit *per cent* earned on capital must be the same in industry and in agriculture, otherwise capital would move from one form of employment to the other. But it is the peculiarity of agriculture that the money rate of profit in that industry cannot diverge from the rate of profit measured in terms of that industry's own product, *i.e.*, the corn-rate of profit. This is because in agriculture both the input (the wage outlay) and the output consist of the same commodity, "corn". In manufacturing industry on the other hand, input and output consist of heterogeneous commodities — the cost per man is fixed in corn, while the product per man, in a given state of technical knowledge, is fixed in terms of manufactured goods. Hence the only way equality in the rate of profit in money terms can be attained as between the two branches is through the prices of industrial goods becoming dearer or cheaper in terms of agricultural products. The money rate of profit in manufacturing industry therefore depends on the corn-rate of profit in agriculture,[10] the latter on the other hand, is entirely a matter of the margin of cultivation, which in turn is a reflection (in a closed economy and in a given state of technical knowledge) of the extent of capital accumulation. Thus "diminishing fertility of the soil," as James Mill put it, "is the great and ultimately only necessary cause of a fall in profit".

To make the whole structure logically consistent it is necessary to suppose, not only that wages are fixed in terms of "corn" but that they are entirely spent on "corn", for otherwise any change in the relation between industrial and agricultural prices will alter real wages (in terms of commodities in general) so that the size of the "surplus", and the rate of profit on capital generally, is no longer derivable from the "corn rate of profit" — the relationship between the product of labour and the cost of labour working on marginal land. Assuming that ("corn") agricultural products are wage-goods and manufactured products are non-wage goods (i.e., ignoring that *some* agricultural products are consumed by capitalists, and *some* non-agricultural products by wage-earners), the whole corn-output (the area $OCDM$ in the diagram) can be taken as the annual wages fund, of which $OWKM$ is employed in agriculture and $WCDK$ in the rest of the economy. Any increase in $OWKM$ (caused, *e.g.*, by protection to agriculture) must necessarily lower the rate of profit (which is the source of all accumulation) and thus slow down the rate of growth.[11] Similarly all taxes, other than those levied on land, must ultimately fall on, and be paid out of, profits, and thus slow down the rate of accumulation. Taxation and agricultural protection thus tend to accelerate the tendency (which is in any case inevitable — unless *continued* technical progress manages to shift the $p–Ap$ and $p–Mp$ curves to the right sufficiently to suspend altogether the operation of the Law of Diminishing Returns) to that ultimate state of gloom, the Stationary State, where accumulation ceases simply because "profits are so low as not to afford (the capitalists more than) an adequate compensation for their trouble and the risk which they must necessarily encounter in employing their capital productively".[12]

II.   THE MARXIAN THEORY

The Marxian theory is essentially an adaptation of Ricardo's "surplus theory". The main analytical differences are: — (1) that Marx paid no attention to (and did not believe in) the Law of Diminishing Returns, and hence made no analytical distinction between rent and profits; (2) that Marx regarded the supply price of labour (the "cost of reproduction" of labour) as being fixed, not in terms of "corn", but of commodities in general. Hence he regarded the share of profits (including rent) in output as determined simply by the surplus of the product per unit of labour over the supply price (or cost) of labour — or the surplus of production to the consumption necessary for production.[13]

There are important differences also as between Marx and Ricardo in two other respects. The first of these concerns the reasons for wages being tied to the subsistence level. In Marx's theory this is ensured through the fact that at any one time the supply of labour — the number of workers seeking wage-employment — tends to exceed the demand for labour. The existence of an unemployed fringe — the "reserve army" of labour — prevents wages from rising above the minimum that must be paid to enable the labourers to perform the work. Marx assumed that as capitalist enterprise progresses at the expense of pre-capitalistic enterprise more labourers are released through the disappearance of the non-capitalist or handi-craft units than are absorbed in the capitalist sector, owing to the difference in productivity per head between the two sectors. As long as the growth of capitalist enterprise is at the cost of a shrinkage of pre-capitalist enterprise the increase in the supply of wage labour will thus tend to run ahead of the increase in the demand for wage labour.

Sooner or later, however, the demand for labour resulting from accumulation by capitalist enterprise will run ahead of the increase in supply; at that stage labour becomes scarce, wages rise, profits are wiped out and capitalism is faced with a "crisis". (The crisis in itself slows down the

745

rate of accumulation and reduces the demand for labour at any given state of accumulation by increasing the "organic composition of capital," so that the "reserve army" will sooner or later be recreated.)

The second important difference relates to the motives behind capital accumulation. For Ricardo this was simply to be explained by the lure of a high rate of profit. Capitalists accumulate voluntarily so long as the rate of profit exceeds the minimum "necessary compensation" for the risks and trouble encountered in the productive employment of capital. For Marx however, accumulation by capitalist enterprise is not a matter of choice but a necessity, due to competition among the capitalists themselves. This in turn was explained by the existence of economies of large scale production (together with the implicit assumption that the amount of capital employed by any particular capitalist is governed by his own accumulation). Given the fact that the larger the scale of operations the more efficient the business, each capitalist is forced to increase the size of his business through the re-investment of his profits if he is not to fall behind in the competitive struggle.

It is only at a later stage, when the increasing concentration of production in the hands of the more successful enterprises removed the competitive necessity for accumulation — the stage of "monopoly capitalism" — that in the Marxian scheme there is room for economic crises, not on account of an excessive increase in the demand for labour following on accumulation but on account of an insufficiency of effective demand — the failure of markets resulting from the inability of the capitalists either to spend or to invest the full amount of profits (which Marx called the problem of "realising surplus value").

Marx has also taken over from Ricardo, and the classical economists generally, the idea of a falling rate of profit with the progressive accumulation of capital. But whereas with the classicists this was firmly grounded on the Law of Diminishing Returns, Marx, having discarded that law, had no firm base for it. His own explanation is based on the assumed increase in the ratio of fixed to circulating capital (in Marxian terminology, "constant" to "variable" capital) with the progress of capitalism; but as several authors have pointed out,[14] the law of the falling rate of profit cannot really be derived from the law of the "increasing organic composition" of capital. Since Marx assumes that the supply price of labour remains unchanged in terms of commodities when the organic composition of capital, and hence output per head, rises, there is no more reason to assume that an increase in "organic composition" will yield a lower rate of profit than a higher rate. For even if output per man were assumed to increase more slowly than ("constant" plus "variable") capital per man, the "surplus value" per man (the excess of output per man over the costs of reproduction of labour) will necessarily increase faster than output per man, and may thus secure a rising rate of profit even if there is diminishing productivity to successive additions to fixed capital per unit of labour.

While some of Marx's predictions — such as the increasing concentration of production in the hands of large enterprises — proved accurate, his most important thesis, the steady worsening of the living conditions of the working classes — "the immiseration of the proletariat"[15] — has been contradicted by experience, in both the "competitive" and "monopoly" stages of capitalism. On the Marxian model the share of wages in output must necessarily fall with every increase in output per head. The theory can only allow for a rise of wages in terms of commodities as a result of the collective organisation of the working classes which forces the capitalists to reduce the degree of exploitation and to surrender to the workers some of the "surplus value".[16] This hypothesis however will only yield a constant share of wages on the extremely far-fetched assumption that the rate of increase in the bargaining strength of labour, due to the growth of collective organisation, precisely keeps pace with the rate of increase in output per head.

III. THE NEO-CLASSICAL THEORIES: MARGINAL PRODUCTIVITY

While Marx's theory thus derives from Ricardo's surplus principle, neo-classical value and distribution theory derives from another part of the Ricardian model: the "marginal principle" introduced for the explanation of rent (which explains why both Marx and Marshall are able to claim Ricardo as their precursor). The difference between Ricardo and the neo-classics is (1) that whereas Ricardo employed the "principle of substitution" (or rather, the principle of "limited substitutability" — which is the basic assumption underlying all "marginal" analysis) only as regards the use of labour relative to land, in neo-classical theory this doctrine was formalized and generalized, and assumed to hold true of any factor, in relation to any other;[17] (2) whereas Ricardo employed the principle for showing that a "fixed" factor will earn a surplus, determined by the gap between the average and marginal product of the variable factor, neo-classical theory concentrated on the reverse aspect — i.e., that any factor variable in supply will obtain a remuneration which, under competitive conditions, must correspond to its marginal product. Thus if the total supply of *all* factors (and not only land) is being taken as given, independently of price, and all are assumed to be limited substitutes to one another, the share-out of the whole produce can be regarded as being determined by the marginal rates of substitution between them. Thus in terms of our diagram, if we assumed that along Ox we measure the quantity of any particular factor of production, x, the quantities of all the others being taken as fixed, $p—Mp$ will exhibit the marginal productivity function of the variable factor. If the actual employment of that factor is taken to be M, AM will represent its demand price per unit, and the rectangle $OBAM$ its share in the total produce. Since this principle could be applied to any factor, it must be true of all (including, as Walras and Wicksell have shown, the factors owned by the entrepreneur himself) hence the rectangle $BCDA$ must be sufficient, and only just sufficient, for remunerating all other factors but x on the basis of their respective marginal productivities. This, as Wicksteed has shown[18] requires the assumption that the production function will be homogeneous of the first degree for all variables taken together — an assumption which he himself regarded as little more than a tautology, if "factors of production" are appropriately defined.[19] From the point of view of the theory, however, the *appropriate* definition of factors involves the elimination of intermediate products and their conversion into "ultimate" or "original" factors, since only on this definition can one assume the properties of divisibility and variability of coefficients. When factors are thus defined, the assumption of constant returns to scale is by no means a tautology; it is a restrictive assumption, which may be regarded, however, as being co-extensive with other restrictive assumptions implied by the theory — i.e., the universal rule of perfect competition, and the absence of external economies and diseconomies.

The basic difficulty with the whole approach does not lie, however, in this so-called "adding-up problem" but in the very meaning of "capital" as a factor of production.[20] Whilst land can be measured in acres-per-year and labour in man-hours, capital (as distinct from "capital goods") cannot be measured in terms of physical units.[21] To evaluate the marginal product of labour it is necessary to isolate two situations containing identical "capital" but two different quantities of labour, or identical amounts of labour and two differing quantities of "capital", in precise numerical relationship.[22]

Marshall, without going into the matter in any detail, had shown in several passages that he was dimly aware of this; and in carefully re-defining marginal productivity so as to mean "marginal *net* productivity" (*net* after deduction of all associated expenses on other "factors") he shied away from the task of putting forward a general theory of distribution altogether.[23]

In fact, in so far as we can speak of a "Marshallian" theory of distribution at all, it is in the sense of a "short period" theory, which regards profits as the "quasi-rents" earned on the use of capital goods of various kinds, the supply of which can be treated as given for the time being, as a heritage of the past. The doctrine of the "quasi-rent" assimilates capital as a factor of production to Ricardian land: the separate *kinds* of capital goods being treated as so many different kinds of "land". Here the problem of the measurement of capital as a factor of production does not arise: since, strictly speaking, no kind of change or reorganization in the stock of intermediate products is permitted in connection with a change in the level or composition of production. It was this aspect of Marshall which, consciously or subconsciously, provided the "model" for most of the post-Marshallian Cambridge theorizing. Prices are equal to, or determined by, marginal prime costs; profits are determined by the difference between marginal and average prime costs; prime costs, for the system as a whole, are labour costs (since raw-material costs, for a closed economy at any rate, disappear if all branches of industry are taken together); ultimately therefore the division of output between profits and wages is a matter depending on the existence of diminishing returns to labour, as more labour is used in conjunction with a *given* capital equipment; and is determined by the elasticity of labour's average productivity curve which fixes the share of quasi-rents.

Marshall himself would have disagreed with the use of the quasi-rent doctrine as a distribution theory, holding that distributive shares in the short period are determined by long-period forces.[24] Clearly even if one were to hold strictly to the assumption that "profit margins" are the outcome of short-period profit-maximisation, this "short-period" approach does not really get us anywhere: for the extent to which diminishing returns operate for labour in conjunction with the capital equipment available to-day is itself a function of the price-relationships which have ruled in the past because these have determined the quantities of each of the kinds of equipment available. The theory does not therefore really amount to more than saying that the prices of to-day are derived from the prices of yesterday — a proposition which is the more true and the more trivial the shorter the "day" is conceived to be, in terms of chronological time.

For the true neo-classical attempt to solve the general problem of distribution we must go to Wicksell who thought that by integrating the Austrian approach to capital with Walrasian equilibrium theory he could provide a general solution, treating capital as a two-dimensional quantity, the product of time and labour. The "time" in this case is the investment period or waiting period separating the application of "original" factors from the emergence of the final product, and the marginal productivity of capital the added product resulting from an extension of "time". This attempt, again, came to grief (as Wicksell himself came near to acknowledging late in life[25]) (i) owing to the impossibility of measuring that period in terms of an "average" of some kind;[26] (ii) owing to the impossibility of combining the investment periods of different "original" factors in a single measure.[27]

In fact the whole approach which regards the share of wages and of profits in output as being determined by the marginal rate of substitution between Capital and Labour — with its corollary, that the constancy of relative shares is evidence of a unity-Elasticity of Substitution between Capital and Labour[28] — is hardly acceptable to present-day economists. Its inadequacy becomes evident as soon as it is realized that the "marginal rate of substitution" between Capital and Labour — as distinct from the marginal rate of substitution between labour and land — can only be determined once the rate of profit and the rate of wages are already known. The same technical alternatives might yield very different "marginal rates of substitution" according as the ratio of profits to wages is one thing or another. The theory asserts in effect, that the rate of interest in the capital market, (and the associated wage rate in the labour market) is determined by the condition that at any lower interest rate (and higher wage rate) capital would be invested in such "labour-saving" forms as would provide insufficient employment to the available labour; whilst at any higher rate, capital would be invested in forms that offered more places of employment than could be filled with the available labour.

Quite apart from all conceptual difficulties, the theory focuses attention on a relatively unimportant feature of a growing economy. For accumulation does not take the form of "deepening" the structure of capital (at a given state of knowledge) but rather in keeping pace with technical progress and the growth in the labour force. It is difficult to swallow a theory which says, in effect that wages and profits are what they are for otherwise there would be too much deepening or too little deepening (the capital/output ratios would be either too large or too small) to be consistent with simultaneous equilibrium in the savings-investment market and in the labour market.

NOTES

1. By the term "neo-Walrasians" I mean the American "linear programming" and "Activity analysis" schools, as well as the general equilibrium model of von Neumann (*Review of Economic Studies*, 1945–46, Vol. XIII (1)) whose technique shows certain affinities with Walras even though their basic assumptions (in particular that of the "circularity" of the production process) are quite different. From the point of view of distribution theory however, the approach only yields a solution (in the shape of an equilibrium interest rate) on the assumption of constant real wages (due to an infinitely elastic supply curve of labour); it shows therefore more affinity with the classical models than with the neo-classical theories.

2. With the possible exception of the "neo-Walrasian" group referred to above.

3. Preface (my italics).

4. "Political Economy" he told Malthus "you think is an enquiry into the nature and causes of wealth—I think it should rather be called an enquiry into the laws which determine the division of the produce of industry amongst the classes who concur in its formation. No law can be laid down respecting quantity, but a tolerably correct one can be laid down respecting proportions. Every day I am more satisfied that the former enquiry is vain and delusive, and the latter only the true objects of the science." (Letter dated 9 Oct., 1820, Works (Sraffa edition) vol. VIII, pp. 278–9.)

5. And so of course is the Marxian: but then the Marxian theory is really only a simplified version of Ricardo, clothed in a different garb.

6. This abstracts from variations in output per head due to the use of more or less fixed capital relative to labour—otherwise the curves could not be uniquely drawn, relative to a given state of technical knowledge. As between fixed capital and labour therefore the model assumes "fixed coefficients"; as between labour and land, variable coefficients.

7. The basis of this assumption is the Malthusian theory of population, according to which numbers will increase (indefinitely) when wages are above, and decrease (indefinitely) when they are below,

the "subsistence level". In Ricardo's hands this doctrine had lost its sharp focus on a biologically determined quantum of subsistence to which the supply price of labour must be tied; he emphasized that habits of restraint engendered in a civilized environment can permanently secure for labour higher standards of living than the bare minimum for survival. Yet he retained the important operative principle that in any given social and cultural environment there is a "*natural* rate of wages" at which alone population could remain stationary and from which wages can only deviate temporarily. The hypothesis of an infinitely elastic supply curve of labour thus did not necessarily imply that this supply price must be equal to the bare minimum of subsistence. Yet this assumption was inconsistent with another (implied) feature of his model discussed below, that wages are not only *fixed* in terms of "corn" but are entirely (or almost entirely) *spent* on corn.

8. Total wages depend on—and are "paid out of"—capital simply because production takes time, and the labourers (unlike the landlords) not being in the position to afford to wait, have their wages "advanced" to them by the capitalists. This is true of fixed as well as circulating capital, but since with the former, the turnover period is relatively long, only a small part of annual wages is paid out of fixed capital; the amount of circulating capital was therefore treated as the proper "wages fund". Despite his analysis of the effect of changes in wages on the amount of fixed capital used relative to labour, i.e., on the proportions of fixed and circulating capital employed in production (Professor Hayek's celebrated "Ricardo effect") for the purpose of his distribution theory this ratio should be taken as given, irrespective of the rate of profit.

9. The feature which the modern mind may find most difficult to swallow is not that capital accumulation should lead to a rise in population but that the reaction should be taken as something so swift as to ignore the intervening stage, where the increase in the wages fund should raise the rate of wages rather than the numbers employed. The adjustment of population to

changes in the demand for labour would normally be treated as a slow long-run effect whereas changes in the demand for labour (caused by capital accumulation) may be swift or sudden. Ricardo however conceived the economy as one which proceeds at a more or less steady rate of growth in time, with the accumulation of capital going on at a (more or less constant) rate; while he conceded that *changes* in the rate of capital accumulation will temporarily raise or lower wages, he assumed that the rate of population growth itself is adapted to a certain rate of capital accumulation which had been going on for some time.

10. The analytical basis for this conclusion, given above, was never, as Sraffa remarks, stated by Ricardo in any of his extant letters and papers though there is evidence from Malthus's remarks that he must have formulated it either in a lost paper on the Profits of Capital or in conversation (cf. *Works*, Vol. I, Introduction, p. xxxi.).

11. The evil of agricultural protection is thus not only that real income is reduced through the transfer of labour to less productive employments, but that owing to the reduction in the rate of profit, industrial prices fall in terms of agricultural prices; income is thus transferred from the classes which use their wealth productively to classes which use it unproductively.

12. Ricardo, *Principles*, p. 122 (Sraffa Edition).

13. Ricardo himself abandoned in the *Principles* the idea that wages *consist* of corn (to the exclusion of manufactures) but whether he also abandoned the idea that the agricultural surplus is critical to the whole distribution process through the fixity of wages in terms of *corn only* is not clear. (Cf. Sraffa, *op. cit.*, pp. xxxii–xxxiii.)

14. Cf. in particular, Joan Robinson, *An Essay in Marxian Economics*, pp. 75–82.

15. It is not clear, in terms of Marx's own theoretical model, why such a progressive immiseration should take place—since the costs of reproduction of labour appear to set an *absolute* limit to the extent to which labour can be exploited. Some parts of *Das Kapital* could however be construed as suggesting that wages can be driven below the (long run) reproduction cost of labour, at the cost of a (long run) shrinkage in the labour force: and with the increasing organic composition of capital, and the rise of monopolies, the demand for labour may show an equally declining tendency.

16. Marx himself would have conceived a reduction in the "degree of exploitation" in terms of a reduction in the length of the working day rather than a rise in real wages per day. In fact both have occurred side by side.

17. As well as of any particular commodity in the sphere of consumption. The utility theory of value is really Ricardian rent-theory applied to consumption demand. In fact, as Walras has shown, limited substitutability in consumption might in itself be sufficient to determine distributive shares, provided that the proportions in which the different factors are used are different in different industries. His solution of the problem of distribution, based on "fixed coefficients" of production (intended only as a first approximation) is subject however to various snags since the solution of his equations may yield negative prices for the factors as well as positive ones and it cannot be determined beforehand whether this will be the case or not. If the solution of the equations yields negative prices the factors in question have to be excluded as "free goods"; and the operation (if necessary) successively repeated until only factors with positive prices are left. Also, it is necessary to suppose that the number of different "factors" is no greater than the number of different "products" otherwise the solution is indeterminate.

18. *The Co-ordination of the Laws of Distribution* (1894).

19. *Ibid.*, p. 53. "We must regard every kind and quality of labour that can be distinguished from other kinds and qualities as a separate factor; and in the same way, every kind of land will be taken as a separate factor. Still more important is it to insist that instead of speaking of so many £ worth of capital we shall speak of so many ploughs, so many tons of manure, and so many horses or footpounds of power. Each of these may be scheduled in its own unit." Under these conditions it is true to say that "doubling all factors will double the product", but since these "factors" are indivisible in varying degrees, it does not mean that the production function is a linear and homogeneous one in relation to incremental variations of output. Also a change in output may be associated with the introduction of *new* factors of production.

20. For a general equilibrium system, capital goods cannot be regarded as factors of production *per se* (in the manner suggested by Wicksteed) otherwise the same things are simultaneously treated as the parameters and the unknowns of the system.

21. Measurement in terms of value (as so many £'s of "capital") already assumes a certain rate of interest, on the basis of which services accruing in differing periods in the future, or costs incurred at differing dates in the past, are brought to a measure of equivalence.

22. The product of the "marginal shepherd" is the difference, in terms of numbers of sheep, between 10 shepherds using 10 crooks and 11 shepherds using 11 slightly inferior crooks, the term "slightly

inferior" being taken to mean that the 11 crooks in the one case represent precisely the same amount of "capital" as the 10 crooks in the other case. (Cf. also, Robertson, "Wage Grumbles," in *Economic Fragments*, 1931.)

23. "The doctrine that the earnings of a worker tend to be equal to the net product of his work, has by itself no real meaning; since in order to estimate the net product, we have to take for granted all the expenses of production of the commodity on which he works, other than his own wages". Similarly, the doctrine that the marginal efficiency of capital will tend to equal the rate of interest "cannot be made into a theory of interest, any more than a theory of wages, without reasoning in a circle". (Cf. *Principles*, 8th edition, Book VI, ch. I, paras 7–8.)

24. Cf., in particular, *Principles*, 8th edition, Book V, ch. V, and 6, and Book VI, ch. VIII, paras. 4.

25. Cf. the concluding passage of his posthumous contribution to the Wieser Festschrift. *Die Wirtschaftstheorie der Gegenwert* (1928) Vol. III, pp. 208–9; also his Analysis of Akerman's Problem, reprinted in *Lectures*, Vol. I, p. 270.

26. Since owing to compound interest, the weights to be used in the calculation of the average will themselves be dependent on the rate of interest.

27. For a more extended treatment cf. my articles on capital theory in *Econometrica*, April 1937 and May 1938; also Joan Robinson, The Production Function in the Theory of Capital, *Review of Economic Studies*, Vol. XXI (1953–54) p. 81, and *Comment* by D. G. Champernowne, *ibid.*, page 112.

28. Cf. Hicks, *The Theory of Wages* (1932) ch. VI, passim.

31.

GARY S. BECKER   WILLIAM J. BAUMOL

Columbia University   Princeton University

The Classical

Monetary Theory:

The Outcome

of the Discussion[1]

I. INTRODUCTORY

Recently a number of economists have shown a revived interest in the monetary theory of the classicists and of the members of the Lausanne School and their successors.[2] It has been maintained that all of these authors held basically common views which have been called "the classical system". Moreover, it has been argued that this system suffers from serious formal shortcomings, in particular that either it is inconsistent or it must leave the absolute price level indeterminate.

We believe a summary of the results of the discussion is now appropriate, and that the conflicting views can be evaluated and to some extent reconciled. Moreover, the arguments can be stated rigorously without recourse to the mathematical apparatus which has been employed. A detailed restatement is therefore included in the belief that the discussion will become available to many who did not follow it before.

For our purposes we may consider the attack on the earlier writers to have been opened by Lange [13], although the discussion, as is indicated below, goes back much further. However, the immediate centre of conten-

Reprinted from *Economica*, n.s. XIX (November 1952), 355–76, considerably modified and enlarged, by permission of the authors and the publisher.

tion is Patinkin's restatement and refinement of the Lange position. We shall therefore describe the Lange-Patinkin version of the classical system and the difficulties which they have shown to be inherent in it. A more satisfactory structure which Patinkin has called "the modified classical system" will then be outlined. Finally, it will be argued through re-examination of some of the classical writings that most of the group probably never held views like those ascribed to them. Indeed, it will appear that "the modified classical system" is a considerably closer approximation to their analysis. No doubt it is true that "the classics", particularly as the term has been used in the discussion, denotes too heterogeneous a group to permit wholesale judgement to be passed on the basis of selections from several members alleged to be representative. Nevertheless, many of the members of that group, among them some of those specifically accused, have passages in their writings which explicitly contradict the charges against them. We do not mean that none of these writers ever expressed himself incorrectly or in a misleading manner on this subject, or that they were all in possession of a full analysis of the logical structure of the problem. It does, however, seem that in most cases where the problem was considered *explicitly*, it was analysed in a manner which is at least formally valid.

II. A MODERN VERSION OF THE CLASSICAL SYSTEM

Consider an exchange economy using (say) paper money as a medium of exchange. An individual who demands (supplies) a commodity gives up (receives) an equal value of the medium of exchange. If we call paper money a good and sum over all individuals, then by definition the total value of *goods*[3] (including money flow) demanded in this economy is identically equal to the total value of goods (including money flow) supplied. In other words, any offer to supply ten dollars worth of goods is made only in expectation of receiving an equivalent value in payment, and this supply therefore also constitutes a demand for ten dollars (either in cash or securities or other commodities). Thus every x dollar supply is automatically also an x dollar demand, and similarly, every demand for y dollars worth of goods must be backed up by an offer to supply in exchange something worth y dollars. Since this is true for *every* supply and *every* demand the total value of all goods (and money) effectively demanded must always be exactly equal to the total value of all goods (and money) effectively supplied — a conclusion which represents little more than an accounting identity. This result, which Lange calls Walras' Law,[4] has nothing whatsoever to do with equilibrium in the various markets, and holds for *all* price configurations.

Suppose that at *any* given set of prices people will supply commodities when and only when they use (and intend to use) the money received to demand other commodities "immediately", i.e., during the period under consideration. Again, by summing over all individuals, we see that at any set of prices the total money demand for *commodities* will be equal to the total money value of the quantity supplied of all *commodities*. It is to be noted that (unlike the case of Walras' Law) demands for and supplies of *money* do not enter into this total which implies that if people sell hats for money they only do so *not* because they want to hold the money, but because they intend to run right down to the corner shoe store to trade that money in for footwear. Thus the result states that commodities in general (and no matter what their prices) will never lack customers, because vendors will *always* want to buy from one another as much (in value terms) as they offer for sale. It is this which Lange and Patinkin have identified with Say's Law. Because it is taken to hold no matter what the price structure and to distinguish it from other versions of the "Law" we shall refer to it as Say's Identity.

Patinkin in discussing his version of the classical system indicates[5] one particular set of circumstances which involves Say's Identity. He states that the classics, particularly the members of the Lausanne School, believed that money has no utility of its own, taking this to imply that in the static classical world there is no reason for any individual to desire any cash balances. Anyone who receives cash will try to exchange all his (useless) money for goods which have utility, so that, if there is a non-zero money supply, prices will rise indefinitely and the money market will be in equilibrium only with infinite prices.[6] Patinkin concludes that a classical economy can operate only if there are no stocks of money, and presents the paradox that this sort of "monetary" economy must in effect be a barter economy with a non-existent money acting only as a unit of account! Moreover, if people have no money stocks and never add, or want to add, to them, Say's Identity clearly holds, as it must in a barter economy, since commodities will be demanded at once in any exchange.

An immediate implication of Say's Identity, or rather an equivalent way of stating it, is that the quantity of money demanded, considered either as a stock or a flow, is independent of the price structure and is always equal to the quantity of money supplied. For at any set of prices, the value of the total quantity of commodities supplied is equal to the total (non-reservation or flow) demand for money. Likewise the value of the total commodity demand is the quantity of money flow supplied. Let us restate this argument in three somewhat oversimplified steps: (i) Say's Identity states that the total demand for commodities x is always the same as the value of commodities supplied (i.e. its supply must also equal x dollars); (ii) but (Walras' Law) x dollars are always supplied to back up a demand for x dollars worth of commodities, and (iii) x dollars are always demanded in return for a supply of x dollars worth of commodities. Therefore, (iv) when supply of commodities equals demand for commodities equals x dollars, it must also be true that supply of money (flow) equals demand for money flow equals x dollars. Clearly the converse must also be true. Thus with Say's Identity the quantity of money flow demanded must always equal the quantity supplied.

But when will the demand for and supply of money flow be equal as Say's Identity requires? This equality would appear to hold if and only if the quantity of money *stock* supplied (the total of the economy's cash balances) is equal to the quantity demanded, because if there is, e.g., an excess supply of cash, people will want to get rid of more money flow than is demanded. Thus, Say's Identity holds if and only if the quantity of money stock demanded is always equal to the quantity supplied.[7]

In our Say's Identity economy, let the money price of all commodities double (the quantity of money remaining unchanged or varying in an arbitrary manner). Since the relative prices of all commodities have remained the same we cannot expect buyers or sellers to make any substitutions among commodities. Only a substitution of money for commodities (an excess supply of commodities) is indicated, commodity prices having risen. But Say's Identity clearly precludes this too. Thus nothing will change with the change in price level.

It follows that the quantity demanded of each commodity will depend only on relative commodity prices. This is what is meant by the Leontief ([15])-Lange-Patinkin contention that the classical supply and demand (excess demand) functions are homogeneous of degree zero *in prices alone*. This rather ponderous nomenclature means only that the quantity of any commodity demanded or supplied is unaffected by a proportional change in prices no matter what is happening to the stock of cash — even if the stock of cash remains constant. It also requires that quantities demanded or supplied and relative prices of commodities, can never, even momentarily, be affected by the quantity of money. In other words, if, *whenever* all prices increase by exactly 12.63 per cent (so that the relative prices of, say, bananas and applejack are unchanged), people do not change any of their demands or supplies, we say that demands and supplies are *homogeneous of degree zero in prices alone*. This is what classical economists have been alleged to have assumed.

The condition that equilibrium exists in all commodity markets can be sufficient at most to determine relative commodity prices. To determine absolute prices we must look at the remaining market — the money market. But the money market is *always* in equilibrium, no matter what the levels of the various prices. Hence, the condition that it be in equilibrium cannot be used to *determine* absolute prices. We conclude that in a Say's Identity economy, relative commodity prices are determinate, commodity quantities demanded and supplied depend only on relative commodity prices, and absolute (money) prices are indeterminate. Money is a "veil" since a good can have importance in the determination of equilibrium in the various markets of an economy only if the market for this good can conceivably be *out* of equilibrium.

In this version of the classical system the analysis of price determination is thus necessarily incomplete as it cannot specify (equilibrium) absolute prices.[8] According to Lange and Patinkin, the classics nevertheless sought to dichotomize the pricing process by determining relative prices in the "real sector" of the economy and absolute prices by introducing an additional relationship — the so-called Cambridge equation or its equivalent in a cash balance or other form of the quantity theory of money. This relates the quantity of money which people wish to hold to the price level by postulat-

756

ing that the quantity of cash the public demands will rise with absolute prices. Thus there would, *ceteris paribus,* be one and only one equilibrium price level corresponding to every level of the supply of cash — that at which people were willing to hold the amount of cash supplied. Clearly this contradicts Say's Identity which, as we have seen, requires that the quantity of cash demanded equal the supply *no matter what the price structure.*[9]

Thus, with the addition of a quantity theory or any other explanation of the absolute price level, this version of the classical system becomes self-contradictory. Without any such addition the system is incomplete in its explanation of the behaviour of the economy.

III. "THE MODIFIED CLASSICAL SYSTEM"

The system just considered may be modified in a simple manner to eliminate the difficulties discussed. Patinkin[10] has called this revised model "the modified classical system". To accomplish this we need merely drop the obviously unrealistic assumption that the quantity of cash demanded is independent of the price structure. We may assume that the quantity of cash demanded will increase with the money value of transactions.

Suppose then that the prices of all commodities double, and that as a result, the quantity of money demanded increases. Since the relative prices of commodities have remained unchanged, there will not be any substitution among commodities. People *will,* however, seek to increase their cash holdings by giving up commodities, i.e., by increasing the quantities of commodities (in money terms) they supply or decreasing the quantities they demand. We can conclude that when there is a significant money market, the demand for commodities cannot depend merely on relative commodity prices, but must also depend on absolute money prices. Thus, any attempt to dichotomize the pricing process by determining relative commodity prices in the commodity markets alone, is impossible (except in a very special sense indicated below) once a significant money market exists. Thus, if any equilibrium is possible, a Cambridge equation, or anything else implying that the quantities of money demanded and supplied are not equal at all price levels, requires that quantities of commodities supplied and demanded must be unaffected by changes in prices alone. This can also be seen as follows: suppose prices, originally in equilibrium, are doubled, the stock of cash remaining constant, and that the quantities of cash stocks and flows demanded now (say) exceed the supply. By Walras' Law the quantity of some commodity supplied must exceed the demand. The demand for or the supply of that commodity must then have changed as a result of the change in price level alone, in violation of homogeneity. Hence, Hickman's system ([8]) which involves both a Cambridge equation and the assumption that the quantities demanded and supplied of all commodities are homogeneous of degree zero in prices alone, must be in error. What he has done, in effect, is assume that the quantity of cash stock demanded can differ from the supply (the Cambridge equation) whereas at the same time (Say's Identity) the quantity of cash flow demanded is identically equal to its supply, so that there are two separate conditions giving equilibrium in the monetary sector of the economy. Brunner has pointed out to us that this last sentence is not quite accurate — Say's Identity is not directly involved in Hickman's argument. However it comes close enough to the source of his difficulty for present purposes.

This argument also indicates that the difficulty in the system attributed by Lange and Patinkin to the classics arises out of the homogeneity assumption, since this precludes inequality in money supply and demand. Say's Identity, since it implies homogeneity, provides a special case of this difficulty. Patinkin seems to have been the first to observe this point.

The situation we are now considering is thus clearly inconsistent with Say's Identity — supply of all commodities does not necessarily equal total demand for all commodities. In particular, these will not be equal if the price structure is such as to cause the quantity of cash demanded to differ from the supply. Nevertheless, the present authors would like to point out that the ambiguous proposition called Say's Law can be interpreted in a way which makes it compatible with an economy in which the absolute price level does matter. This form of Say's Law, which we will call Say's Equality, states in effect that "supply will create its own demand," not despite the behaviour of the price level but because of it. The comparative statics argument is that an excess supply of goods, obtained by disturbing a market equilibrium situation by a cash reduction, will cause the price level to fall to just that point where the excess demand for money is eliminated, since the price level will fall so long as and only so long as there is an excess demand for (insufficient supply of) cash. The foregoing is, in effect, the reasoning behind the cash balance forms of the quantity theory of money and, incidentally, the Pigou effect.

The Cambridge equation implies that for every relative price structure there exists a unique absolute price level at which the money market will be in equilibrium (Say's Equality). This is equivalent to stating that for every set of relative prices there exists a price level which brings about *over-all* equilibrium in the commodity markets, i.e., the total quantity of money offered for commodities is equal to the total value of commodities supplied. Thus it is clear that this version of Say's Law is compatible with determinacy of an absolute price level.

Now assume that we start from a position of equilibrium in all markets. When all commodity prices and every stock of money doubles, the equilibrium is unaffected.[11] No substitutions take place since a proportionate change of commodity prices precludes substitution among commodities, and a substitution between commodities and money is rendered unnecessary, the doubled demand for money being satisfied by the augmented supply. This invariance is to be expected since in the models considered so far a doubling of the stock of money and all prices is strictly equivalent to a change in the unit of account (the "let's call fifty cents a dollar case") and, in effect, involves only a change in the name given the monetary unit.

If we assume that there never exists more than one set of prices compatible with equilibrium (the dangerous uniqueness assumption so often implicitly employed in comparative statics arguments) we arrive at the following comparative statics result: a doubling of the stock of cash *will* double equilibrium prices. Once again money is merely a veil. The phrase is, however, now used in the following comparative statics sense: the quantity of money in circulation affects only the equilibrium price level *and has no effect at all on equilibrium relative commodity prices,* and hence involves no inter-commodity substitution once a new equilibrium is attained. Thus the price system can legitimately be dichotomized into a "real" sector and a monetary sector, but only in a discussion of *equilibrium* relative prices.[12]

IV. THE POSITION OF "THE CLASSICS"[13]

We may sum up the allegations which have been made against the classics in the following three charges:

1. that they believed that cash has no utility of its own in the extreme sense that, in the static model which the classics (meaning in particular the members of the Lausanne School [cf. fn. 2 of this paper]) are alleged to have employed in their monetary analysis, people should, if consistently pursuing their own desires, seek to get rid of all their money as soon as possible;

2. that the classics believed that supplies of and demands for all commodities are homogeneous of degree zero in prices alone and so cannot be affected even momentarily by the quantity of money, and that they sought thus to dichotomize the pricing process, explaining the movement of (equilibrium and non-equilibrium) relative prices in the "real sector" alone, and the price level in the monetary sector by means of a quantity theory (illegitimately) superimposed on the system;[14]

3. finally, that by Say's Law they meant Say's Identity which states that the supply of commodities will create its own demand irrespective of the behaviour of the stock of cash and the price level.

Clearly these charges are not unrelated. Yet it may be worth investigating the attitude of "the classics" on each of these points simply because the authors may conceivably have failed to see the connection and illegitimately have accepted one of these and yet rejected one of the others which follows from it.

In the discussion we trust we have avoided reading too much into the classics in concluding that many of them held views more acceptable than those which have been attributed to them. Certainly we do not mean to imply that they always fully understood the perils they thereby avoided. It may be added that we began our investigation expecting considerably weaker results, and were most surprised to find how clearly many of the classics had expressed themselves on these matters.[15]

V. THE UTILITY OF CASH

Here we may begin with no less an authority than J. B. Say who recapitulates his views on this question by stating, "I have . . . pointed out the various utility of gold and silver as articles of commerce, wherein originates their value; and considered their fitness to act as money, as part of that utility".[16] He had already noted that "paper (money) has a peculiar and inherent value", and, indeed, gone into this point at length.[17]

Ricardo was, of course, less interested in the question of the relation between utility and value. Nevertheless, Marget[18] takes this statement that its employment as money merely adds to the list of uses of bullion to imply that added utility is imparted to metal by its becoming money.

Senior can also be cited to this effect,[19] and Marget[20] points out that Jevons wrote of "the 'utility' of 'that quality of money' which a man 'will desire *not* to exchange' ". Wicksteed[21] speaks of the marginal significance of gold being raised by its use as a medium of exchange, as well as its use as a standard of value. And while Marshall, in speaking of the constancy of the marginal utility of money presumably referred to income rather than cash balances, there is at least one point in the *Principles* in which his money unmistakably means cash,[22] and in which he goes into detail on "the marginal utility of ready money".

Surely Patinkin is not justified in citing Walras as one of those to whom money has no utility. His only reference (indeed his only "damning" reference to Walras) is to the statement "Soit (U) la monnaie que nous considérerons d'abord comme un objet sans utilité propre . . .".[23] This is hardly conclusive, and it may well be meant to indicate no more than the author's intention *at that point* to deal only with monies like paper rather than, for example, gold. In any case, it includes the phrase "d'abord" (to begin with). Indeed it would be most strange for one who has been hailed as a mighty protagonist of the cash balance approach,[24] to find Walras denying utility to cash. But we have better evidence than this. In his *Théorie de la Monnaie* he makes it abundantly clear that he is most pleased that the theory of money provides such a fine and important application of the theory of marginal utility[25] and more than once speaks of the *rareté* of money[26] after having pointed out that this is the term he had appropriated from his father to designate marginal utility.[27]

Pareto is another of the only five "classics" (Walras, Pareto, Wicksell, Cassel and Divisia) whose work is specifically cited by Patinkin as an example of the mishandling of monetary theory. No doubt Pareto's monetary theory is considerably more superficial than that of Walras. Nevertheless even in his case the charges are questionable. As with Walras, Patinkin provides us with only one specific reference to prove that any of his charges apply to Pareto, and again this reference is intended to show that in the Paretan system money has no utility. But the choice of passage is here even more strange. The only reference to money on the page cited is the following: "La monnaie étant une marchandise doit avoir pour quelques individus une ophélimité propre; mais elle peut ne pas en avoir pour d'autres".[28] Surely this is the contradictory of Patinkin's allegation! Indeed, Pareto goes further — in effect reprimanding those others (?) who maintain that money has no utility:

"La monnaie remplit deux rôles principaux: 1° elle facilite l'échange des marchandises; 2° elle garantit cet échange . . . C'est parce qu'on n'a pris parfois en considération que son premier rôle qu'on n'a vu dans la monnaie qu'un simple signe sans valeur intrinsèque".[29]

The list is by no means exhausted, but there seems little point in going on. "The classics" did not generally believe that the holding of cash balances adds nothing to utility beyond that which will eventually be derived by spending the money.

Of course there are those who might appear in some looser statements to have argued otherwise. J. S. Mill did argue that "money, as money, satisfies no want",[30] but he wanted only to point out that money is valuable only because commodities can be bought for it,[31] a homily that should find few dissenters. Divisia more explicitly[32] and Knight by implication[33] have clearly denied a utility to money. In general, however, it seems rather difficult to find classicists taking the extreme form of the position attributed to them by Patinkin.

It may be remarked that the sort of statics which would be required to deprive money of utility in Patinkin's sense would be very special indeed. Transactions demand would be eliminated only if wage payments and all other receipts were staggered in time and amounts so as just to cover the transactions which the recipient desires to make at the moment he desires to make them. This would happen in particular if receipts and payments coincided in a steady stream.[34] Where these requisites do not hold, money derives a "utility" from the goods it can buy, it is true, but because it can buy them at the moment the buyer considers convenient.

VI.   HOMOGENEITY OF DEMANDS AND SUPPLIES IN PRICES ALONE

The "Pigou effect"[35] consists of a rise in the quantities of goods and services demanded with a fall in absolute prices, arising from the resulting increase in purchasing power of all cash holdings. This is a complete denial of the homogeneity postulate, for it permits the demands for goods to be affected by a change in the price level alone, relative prices remaining unchanged. If we are not to call the title of Professor Pigou's article misleading, this effect is part and parcel of the classical stationary state, and there is no more to be said upon the subject.

However, the homogeneity (dichotomization) allegation is really at the heart of the charges under examination, and so is worth some further investigation.[36] First it should be noted that even an unqualified statement that the quantity of money may not affect the quantities of the various commodities demanded and supplied need not mean that the author believes in homogeneity of supplies and demands in prices alone. This may merely be the following (comparative statics) assertion which has been argued above (following Patinkin[37]). If all cash stocks are raised in proportion all prices will rise in proportion, and thus there will be no change in quantities demanded or supplied once a new equilibrium is attained, even in the "modified" classical system. This is not the same as the homogeneity assumption which would never have permitted the quantities of the commodity demanded and supplied to vary even temporarily with the changed stock of cash (no matter how it is injected). What we must then disentangle is which of these, if either, approximates the views of the writers in question.

The literature is quite rich on the effect of an injection of cash, going back to Cantillon and Hume, both of whom make it abundantly clear that they are having no truck with "the homogeneity postulate". Thus Cantillon wrote,

"Through whatever hands the money which is introduced may pass it will naturally increase the consumption; but this consumption will be more or less great according to circumstances. It will be directed more or less to certain kinds of products or merchandise according to the idea of those who acquire the money. Market prices will rise more for certain things than for others however abundant the money may be".[38]

Similarly, Hume wrote,

" . . . we find, that, in every kingdom, into which money begins to flow in greater abundance than formerly, everything takes a new face: labour and industry gain life; the merchant becomes more enterprising, the manufacturer more diligent and skilful, and even the farmer follows his plough with greater alacrity and attention . . .

" . . . though the high price of commodities be a necessary consequence of the encrease of gold and silver, yet it follows not immediately upon that encrease . . . At first, no alteration is perceived; by degrees the price rises, first of one commodity, then of another; till the whole at last reaches a just proportion with the new quantity of specie . . . "[39]

Malthus seems to have accepted Hume's analysis, and indeed to have cited it with approbation, but Ricardo's attitude can at best be described as lukewarm.[40] McCulloch felt that Hume had exaggerated the beneficial effects of an influx of money, but nevertheless contested James Mill's out-and-out denial of the validity of Hume's argument.[41] Note, however, that even if McCulloch (like Walras, as Patinkin himself observes[42]) believed in "just a little non-homogeneity", e.g., believed that prices will rise sufficiently quickly and close to proportionately to render nugatory the impact effects of an influx of cash, he has escaped Patinkin's problems. He has accepted the "modified" classical system, the argument with Hume being only over the time path between the two equilibria which is irrelevant to the present discussion.

J. S. Mill also supported this sort of position,[43] but perhaps the clearest statement is to be found in Marshall's testimony before the Gold and Silver Commission to which the reader is referred.[44]

The case of Wicksell is worth special consideration, especially since he is under particular attack by Patinkin on this point.[45] Wicksell in his writings explicitly employed the device of proceeding from the (over) simple to the complex. Hence it is dangerous to attribute lack of sophistication to him on the basis of isolated passages, since these may be preceded by a warning and adequately qualified later. Thus, as Patinkin points out, at several points[46] Wicksell states that the demand functions for commodities will depend solely on relative prices. But on each occasion the assumption provisionally made is that money serves only as a unit of account and a medium of exchange, and its function as a store of value is explicitly abstracted from.

However, he knew well enough how to deal with homogeneity:

" . . . let us suppose that for some reason or other commodity prices rise while the stock of money remains unchanged, or that the stock of money is diminished while prices remain temporarily unchanged. The cash balances will gradually appear to be *too small* . . . I can rely on a higher level of receipts in the future. But meanwhile I run the risk of being unable to meet my obligations punctually, and at best I may easily be forced by shortage of ready money to forgo some purchase that would otherwise have been profitable. I therefore seek to enlarge my balance . . . through a *reduction* in my *demand* for goods and services, or through an *increase* in the *supply* of my own commodity . . . the universal reduction in demand and increase in supply of commodities will necessarily bring about a continuous fall in all prices. This can only cease when prices have fallen to the level at which the cash balances are regarded as *adequate*."[47]

It is true that Cassel did commit himself to (the macro-economic parts of) the model which Patinkin has called the classical system, and, indeed, the difficulties in which this involved him have been noted before.[48]

In sum there seems to be considerable ground for doubt about the validity of the attack on the classical system. Yet somehow Patinkin's argument is not completely pointless. Somewhere the impression seems to have arisen (and to have gotten into teaching) that this was indeed the nature of the classical system. Indeed, some of the classics themselves have, as we have seen, represented the contrary views as corrections of errors widely held. Keynes' polemics may have contributed considerably. One important source of confusion is, no doubt, the superficial resemblance between the valid comparative statics assertion that equilibrium relative prices may be unaffected by the quantity of cash (if injected into the system in an appropriate manner), and the position ascribed by Patinkin to the classics that relative prices can never be affected by the quantity of cash (however injected), even temporarily.

The nature of the mathematical notation employed may also partly be responsible. The demand and supply functions were usually written as functions of prices alone with no explicit cognizance taken of the quantity of cash or anything else, including money income, all of these having been held in abeyance via *ceteris paribus*. This may indicate merely that an author using this notation had for the moment not thought explicitly about the role of cash, or considered it unimportant at that point. Nevertheless, confusion about demands and supplies being homogeneous of degree zero in prices alone, may have arisen in this manner.

A particularly apt case in point is that of Lange himself who, as Patinkin shows, has gone wrong on just this point in the mathematical appendix to his book.[49] Yet much of the book itself is devoted to an examination of the effects of changes in the stock of cash and the price level on the quantities

of individual commodities demanded and supplied, i.e., to a discussion of
the effects of the absence of homogeneity in prices alone!

VII. SAY'S IDENTITY

This section will necessarily be the most inconclusive in our examination
of the "classical views". This is largely because Say's Law seems to have
been used ambiguously in most cases, the writers for the most part not having considered the relation between the law and the nature of the money
market. Moreover, several different propositions have been referred to as
Say's Law. Say himself, besides formulating the proposition[50] which has
caused so much controversy, confused it with two different, considerably
more innocuous, assertions.

The first is the tautological proposition that there will always be a market for all goods produced where we define a good to be something which
can be sold at a price covering its costs.[51]

The second is the almost Keynesian view that demand will not exist
without production since production creates the income with which goods
can be bought.[52]

However, Say has also advocated the more familiar proposition, and at
one place he makes it clear that he is thinking of the equality rather than
the identity, but in a rather peculiar form.

"Sales cannot be said to be dull because money is scarce, but because other
products are so. There is always money enough to conduct the circulation and
mutual interchange of other values, when those values really exist. Should the
increase of traffic require more money to facilitate it, the want is easily supplied,
and is a strong indication of prosperity . . . In such cases, merchants know well
enough how to find substitutes for the product serving as the medium of exchange
or money [by bills at sight, or after date, bank-notes, running-credits, write-offs,
etc. as at London and Amsterdam] and money itself soon pours in, for this reason,
that all produce naturally gravitates to that place where it is most in demand".[53]

Thus Say is operating with a nearly Wicksellian credit economy in which
price level is indeed indeterminate. But this is so not because the quantity
of money (and credit) has no influence, but rather because the quantity of
circulating medium will vary by just the amount necessary to maintain any
price level!

James Mill, on the other hand, makes a statement typical of many which
were to follow, and which might be used to defend the view that most of
the classics believed in Say's Identity: "When a man produces a greater
quantity of any commodity than he desires for himself, it can only be on one
account; namely, that he desires some other commodity".[54] Unless he here
means money to be considered a commodity or unless, and this is a possibility we cannot rule out, he is assuming implicitly that the price level is
adjusted to the quantity of cash, this would appear to imply acceptance of
the identity. It is, of course, also possible that the problem did not occur to
him.

764

If we compare this with McCulloch (who is sometimes considered the least subtle "classic") it becomes clear that it is not entirely far-fetched to argue that James Mill's statement need not mean that he believed in the identity rather than the equation. Thus McCulloch first argues very much like Mill, only more specifically excluding money:

"It is, however, the acquisition of [other commodities] . . . and not of money, that is the end which every man has in view who carries anything to market".[55]

and argues that therefore the redundance of individual produce must occur because production is misdirected and "is independent of the value of money". However, he at once makes it clear (and repeats this point in detail on the following page) that this is only a long-run equilibrium statement and is so *because the value of money has had time to adjust to the quantity*:

"It must, however, be borne in mind, that in the previous statements we have taken for granted that the value of money . . . has been invariable, or that, at all events, it has not been sensibly affected by sudden changes in its quantity and value. These changes may, as already stated, exert a powerful influence; and have frequently, indeed, occasioned the most extensive derangement in the ordinary channels of commercial intercourse . . . any sudden diminution of the quantity, and consequent rise in the value of money . . . may be such as materially to abridge the power of the society to make their accustomed purchases, and thus to occasion a glut of the market".[56]

Could there be a more forceful rejection of the identity?

J. S. Mill, in the *Principles*, speaks similarly of the "under-supply of money" during a commercial crisis,[57] this again in connection with a discussion of Say's Law, and after having just made the statement (quoted by Keynes in the *General Theory*) that "All sellers are inevitably, and by the meaning of the word, buyers" etc.[58] But the clearest statement on this point is that in J. S. Mill's second essay in his *Unsettled Questions*. We shall offer no quotations from there — it must be read *in extenso*. It is all there and explicitly — Walras' Law, Say's Identity which Mill points out holds only for a barter economy, the "utility of money" which consists in permitting purchases to be made when convenient, the possibility of (temporary) over-supply of commodities when money is in excess demand, and Say's Equality which makes this only a temporary possibility.[59] Indeed, in reading it one is led to wonder why so much of the subsequent literature (this paper included) had to be written at all.

It thus appears that the classics may have been taken too literally by Lange and Patinkin. As was the case in other connections, some of the classics may simply not have considered it worth the effort to point out that they were speaking about long-run equilibrium tendencies. Certainly the cases cited lend support to this view, and we have not found a "classic" who was explicit to the contrary.

The case of Wicksell is also particularly interesting in this connection because of Lange's comments. Lange himself points out that Wicksell (in our terminology) was driven to reject Say's Identity in favour of the Equality. After pointing out how Wicksell was forced to abandon the Identity in order to establish any monetary theory at all, he states,

"He finally appeased his conscience by stating that total demand and total supply must be equal only 'ultimately' but may differ 'in the first place'. With this observation Wicksell, and with him all monetary theorists, gave up Say's law by substituting for the identity an equation which holds only in equilibrium. . . . But this tendency toward equilibrium . . . should not be confused with Say's law."[60]

POSTSCRIPT

We have made several minor changes in this article. Most of these changes are expository, and a few are intended to take account of some of Professor Patinkin's critical comments, in correspondence and in his subsequent writings.[61]

It should be admitted from the outset that this article does Patinkin a serious injustice in that, prior to its publication, he had announced a substantial modification in his position in a long footnote whose significance we had overlooked.[62] He now conceded that the *neo*-classical writers did indeed recognize the role of the value of the stock of cash in determining supplies and demands for commodities in those parts of their writings *where they discussed monetary theory*. But, he maintained, they failed ". . . to carry over recognition of this effect from monetary theory to demand theory."[63] On this issue, we believe that no one has found any conclusive evidence.

To us this is not really surprising because we do not believe that either the classical or neoclassical economists had gone into the problem in any detail. For the issue only arises in conditions of disequilibrium where the cash balance (Pigou) effect provides an adjustment mechanism (see above, pp. 761–64. But the classics were almost exclusively interested in comparative statics (equilibrium questions). It is, therefore, to be expected that classical pronouncements on such matters will be difficult to find.[64]

Our basic position therefore remains unchanged.

1. The classics never really concerned themselves in detail with the issues under discussion and were therefore not in error with respect to them. Moreover, they sometimes did use the real balance effect and they used it correctly. This is not meant to imply that they fully understood the issues and had a fully integrated analysis of the role of cash balances in disequilibrium. But whatever their errors on these matters, they were sins of omission, not sins of commission.

2. The classical and neoclassical analyses of problems of comparative statics are essentially valid, and the Lange-Patinkin discussion is not directly relevant to them.

3. In many well known contemporary writings the dichotomisation fallacy does occur and represents a serious error.

4. Patinkin's work in this area represents a very noteworthy contribution both because of the errors which pervaded recent monetary writings, and, more important, because it fills a major gap in our understanding of the role of money and other assets in the equilibrating mechanism of general equilibrium theory.

NOTES

1. The authors are indebted to Professors Viner and Brunner for their comments and suggestions.

2. See references [1], [8], [12], [13], [14], [31]–[35], and cf. [17], [18] and [36]. But note Patinkin's reservation: "To minimise this [the problem of textual interpretation] . . . I shall confine myself to the mathematical economists of this ['classical'] school". ([31], p. 4).

3. "Commodities" are also considered "goods". Paper money is "a good" only.

4. [13], p. 50.

5. [34], pp. 140–145.

6. This equilibrium possibility is suggested by Brunner ([1], footnote 20, pp. 167–168). Patinkin ([32], footnote 7, p. 135) has argued that infinite prices are not economically meaningful. But surely they can be interpreted to mean that money is not wanted. For when money is worthless, the money price of any useful good must be infinite. Thus, economically, this is identical with the Phipps solution (see [35]) which requires that the price of money be zero. In this case people will throw money away because it will buy nothing. This alone should already raise doubts as to whether any classic ever meant that money has no utility in this sense. But Knight ([11], p. xxii) does believe that money has no utility in a static economy and anticipates Patinkin in pointing out the consequences of this view. Cf. also, e.g., P. N. Rosenstein-Rodan [39], Part II.

7. Note that Say's Identity does not *require* that money have no utility, i.e. that demand (rather than *excess* demand) for money be zero.

8. Cf. Neisser [29].

9. See Lange [13], p. 65, Patinkin [31], pp. 12–16, [32], p. 138. Patinkin's contention goes somewhat further than this, pointing out that with Say's Identity no matter how the stock of cash behaves, the quantity of cash (flow) demanded and supplied must both increase in proportion with prices, i.e. they must both be homogeneous of degree one in absolute prices. This is true since the quantity of money (flow) supplied is the money demand for goods, which is the sum of the demands for the various goods each multiplied by its price. Since the quantity of each good demanded is unaffected by a proportionate change in prices, the sum of these demands each multiplied by its price, i.e. the quantity of money supplied, must change in proportion with the change in prices. The same argument holds for the demand for money, and hence for the excess supply of money. Now the Cambridge equation does not call for the excess supply of cash flows to behave in this manner *irrespective of the level of the stock of cash*. The *form* of the Cambridge relationship is thus in contradiction with the *form* assumed for the money excess supply function. It is this which Patinkin has called "Invalidity I" ([32], p. 138). The next paragraph in this paper summarizes his "Invalidity II" (*Ibid.*, p. 141).

10. [31], pp. 23–26, [32], pp. 143–150 and [33].

11. We require that *every* stock of cash doubles, and not just that the total quantity of cash in the system double, since the effects of an injection of cash will obviously vary with the method employed to introduce it. If given to the miser who sews it into a mattress, the effect will evidently be quite different from that of a gift to someone who spends it at once.

12. There have been some recent attempts to resurrect a system with demand functions that are unaffected by changes in the price level and yet contains a Cambridge-type of equation (see G. C. Archibald and R. E. Lipsey, "Monetary and Value Theory: A Critique of Lange and Patinkin," *The Review of Economic Studies*, Vol. XXVI, October 1958, pp. 1–22; and S. Valavanis, "A Denial of Patinkin's Contradiction," *Kyklos* (1955), pp. 351–368.

For a criticism of the Archibald-Lipsey paper by one of us, see W. J. Baumol, "Monetary and Value Theory: Comment," *The Review of Economic Studies*, to appear in a forthcoming issue. Valavanis' error appears to lie (see p. 356) in treating the Cambridge equation as a technological restraint on the turnover of cash instead of as a behavioral relation. At the very most, purely technological considerations can provide an upper limit to the turnover of cash; they cannot specify an exact value for the price level.

13. We have dropped from the originally published version a section on the role of non-monetary assets because it contained some errors (see D. Patinkin, "Dichotomies of the Pricing Process in Economic Theory," *Economica*, Vol. XXI, May 1954, p. 118) and because it is not important for our purposes. A correct analysis can be found in D. Patinkin, [33], pp. 42–62, and his *Money, Interest and Prices* (Row-Peterson, Evanston, 1956), pp. 137–145.

14. This is what Brunner [1] has called "the complementarity property," meaning thereby that a separate money equation is superimposed on the system to complement the real sector.

15. The authors decidedly do not consider themselves experts in *Dogmengeschichte,* and so are forced to rely heavily on pilfered references coming largely from those extraordinary two volumes ([19]) where, conveniently, Professor Marget subjects closely related allegations to most painstaking examination (see esp. Vol. II, pp. 8–124). No attempt has been made at an exhaustive survey of the literature.

16. [42], p. 228. He is arguing against Garnier, translator of the *Wealth of Nations*. Locke had said this by implication [16], pp. 578–582.

17. *Ibid.*, p. 227, but cf. p. 133, esp. the footnote. It is noteworthy that in later French editions Say decided paper money was of sufficient importance to warrant a separate chapter (see the 6th edition, p. 256, and Chapter XXVI).

18. [19], Vol. II, p. 31, footnote 81, where Turgot and Law are cited to the same effect. For the Ricardo references see [37], pp. 9–10.

19. [43], p. 23 ff. McCulloch argues that coins "exchange for other things, because they are desirable articles, and are possessed of real intrinsic value" [21], (p. 135), but by this he may mean their value as metal, and is willing, though not without hesitation, to exempt drafts, checks and bills from this conclusion. Indeed, elsewhere (p. 217) he has sellers lend or spend their money immediately upon receipt.

20. [19], Vol. II, p. 56, footnote 14.

21. [48], p. 600 (Vol. II).

22. [24], p. 335 and footnote.

23. [44], p. 303.

24. See Marget [17] and esp. [18] for a spirited defence of Walras on these points written some twenty years before the Patinkin articles. After writing this the authors found that Professor Jaffé had, in a paper delivered at a meeting of the Econometric Society, pointed out Patinkin's misinterpretation of Walras on the utility of cash balances. For a summary see [10], pp. 327–8.

25. [45], esp. the introduction, pp. 65–70.

26. *Ibid.*, esp. p. 102. He is presumably speaking of the utility of availability of cash which he distinguished from the utility of money *per se*.

27. *Ibid.*, p. 66.

28. [30], p. 593. It is cited by Patinkin in [34], p. 140, footnote 5.

29. [30], p. 451.

30. [28], p. 6 (Preliminary Remarks). See also Hume [9] ("Of Interest"), p. 321 to the effect that money has "chiefly a fictitious value".

31. Thus compare [27], pp. 69–70

32. [5] Chapter XIX and the Appendix.

33. [11], p. xxii.

34. This can to some extent be arranged artificially by investing money the moment it is received with provision for repayment the (perfectly foreseen) moment it will be needed. But this would only be done to the extent necessary to eliminate demand for cash completely if there were no transactions cost of making and then calling in the investment, and if, in addition, no effort were required in carrying out this transaction. Where these are not abstracted from, it will pay to hold at least small quantities of cash for payments planned for a time shortly after the money has been received, "perfectly" static world or no. It is true that if loans were perfectly safe (the outcomes perfectly foreseen) the distinction between cash and securities might disappear, but not the distinction between the "money-securities" and "real assets", and the latter would still have a positive yield because they are not convenient means of payment and so not perfectly liquid.

35. [36], pp. 349–350. Note the relation to Say's Equality.

36. Various kinds of dichotomization accusations and denials always seem to have flown thick and fast. Locke ([16], p. 582) and Say ([42], p. 226) most emphatically insisted that dichotomization is illegitimate, arguing that, " . . . money . . . is a commodity, whose value is determined by the same general laws, as that of all other commodities". (Say, *op. cit.*, p. 226). Ricardo accuses Malthus and others (not completely specified) of saying that money is a commodity " . . . subject to the same laws of . . . value . . . as other commodities", yet reasoning in an erroneous manner which showed "that they really consider money as something peculiar, varying from causes totally different from those which affect other commodities". [37], pp. 72–3. See also [38], p. 292, and [37], pp. 9–10). Yet this same charge is brought against Ricardo by Cannan ([2], p. 182) and, in effect, Leontief ([15]). Similarly Senior attacked James Mill on this ([43], pp. 8–9), while J. S. Mill explicitly affirmed that the value of money was determined like that of other commodities ([28], Book III, Chapter VII, Section 3, p. 488). To Walras the theory of money provided

" . . . une des premières et des plus déci-
sives applications de mon système d'économie politique pure" (i.e. his marginal utility
theory). (See [45], p. 69); while Ohlin
has lauded Wicksell for "this 'new approach (!)' to monetary theory", for "Until
then, and as a matter of fact for long
afterwards, it was regarded as self-evident
that . . . a change in the general price
level must be due to entirely different circumstances from a change in individual
prices". ([46], Ohlin's introduction, p.
xiii).

37. [31], p. 23, [33], p. 53.

38. [3], p. 179.

39. [9], p. 313.

40. [38], pp. 387–388 and the reference to Malthus given there. For a case
of non-homogeneity in Ricardo, see [38],
p. 179.

41. [21], pp. 556–557. But note that
James Mill did not commit himself to
homogeneity but argued rather that if the
additional money were used to augment
demand, prices would rise at once and rob
this money of its value. See [26], pp.
160–161.

42. [31], p. 12, footnote 5.

43. [28], Book III, Chapter VIII,
Section 2, and the second essay in [27].

44. [23], esp., pp. 38–52. It is noteworthy that at one point Marshall even
included the stock of assets among the
determinants of the demand for cash ([22],
p. 44, as cited by Hansen [7], p. 2). However, Marshall never seems to have done
much with this.

45. [31], p. 12, footnote 5, and [32],
p. 149, footnote 30.

46. [46], p. 23, [47], Vol. I, p. 67,
and Vol. II, p. 22.

47. [46], pp. 39–40 (Wicksell's
italics).

48. See the excellent discussion by
Marget [19], Vol. II, pp. 338–341, also
Wicksell [47], Vol. I, pp. 224–225; Cassel
[4], pp. 150–152.

49. See Lange [12], pp. 99–103. The
Patinkin discussion of this point is in [31],
pp. 18–20. This is not to deny that some
recent mathematical theorists have adopted
monetary analyses involving dichotomization of the real and monetary systems
throughout their works. Indeed Brunner
may well be right when he maintains in a
letter to the authors that such an approach
had recently become well entrenched.

50. Say's Law has been attributed to
James Mill, but this judgement is not universally accepted. Though most of its
components can be found there, the first
edition of the *Traité* which appeared in
1803 had no well organised discussion of
the "Law" (but McCulloch ([20], p. 21),
seems not to have noticed this—note also
the incorrect date given there). Before the
second edition with its extended discussion
of the Law appeared in 1814, James Mill
had published his *Commerce Defended*

([25]) in which the argument is developed
at length.

51. For references see Lange [13],
p. 60, footnote 15, and Neisser [29], p.
385, footnote 4. In particular see Say's
last two letters to Malthus (published
posthumously) and Malthus' reply to the
first of these in [41], pp. 502–515, esp.,
pp. 504–505, 508 and 513.

52. This argument is found in many
places in Say's discussions of the Law. See
[42], pp. 136–137, reproduced in [40],
pp. 340–342, and [41], p. 441.

53. [42], p. 134. The insertion in
brackets is Say's footnote.

54. [26], p. 222.

55. [21], p. 217.

56. *Ibid.*, pp. 218–219. The una-
bridged passage is even more forceful. He
adds, "It is almost unnecessary to lay any
examples of what is, unfortunately, so common before the reader."

57. [28], Book III, Chapter XIV,
Section 4.

58. *Ibid.*, Sections 2 and 3.

59. [27], pp. 46–74, esp., pp. 69 ff.
Mill remarks (p. 74) ". . . these well-
known facts . . . were equally well known
to the authors of the doctrine (Say's Law)
who, therefore, can only have adopted
from inadvertence any form of expression
which could to a candid person appear
inconsistent with it."
Note that on p. 71 a general fall in
commodity prices decreases the demand
for cash not through the transactions demand, but via the expectation that the
price fall will not be permanent.

60. Lange [13], p. 66, Wicksell, [47],
Vol. II, pp. 159–160. See also the passage
quoted above.

61. See "Dichotomies," *op. cit.*, and
Money, op. cit., esp. pp. 373 ff.

62. [32], footnote 30.

63. "Dichotomies," *op. cit.*, p. 117.

64. This interest in comparative statics
also explains why the demand for money
was said to have unit elasticity, for this is
the relevant function in finding the change
in equilibrium resulting from shifts in the
money supply. This is exactly analogous
with the role of commodity demand functions which were developed to analyze
the change in equilibrium resulting from
shifts in commodity supply functions. For
this reason we cannot agree with Patinkin
that the classical monetary demand curve
is different in form from their commodity
demand curves. Patinkin's distinction between *ceteris paribus* (or individual) and
mutatis mutandis (or market) demand
curves seems to us misleading in this respect. For a similar criticism of Patinkin,
see J. M. Buchanan, "*Ceteris Paribus*:
Some Notes on Methodology," *Southern
Economic Journal*, Vol. XXIV, January
1958, pp. 262–264.

BIBLIOGRAPHY

[1] BRUNNER, KARL, "Inconsistency and Indeterminacy in Classical Economics", *Econometrica*, Vol. 19, April, 1951.

[2] CANNAN, EDWIN, *A Review of Economic Theory*, P. S. King, London, 1929.

[3] CANTILLON, RICHARD, *Essai Sur La Nature Du Commerce En Général*, Higgs Translation, Macmillan, London, 1931.

[4] CASSEL, GUSTAV, *The Theory of Social Economy*, translated by Joseph McCabe, Unwin, London, 1923.

[5] DIVISIA, F., *Économique Rationnelle*, Gaston Doin, Paris, 1917.

[6] FISHER, IRVING, *The Purchasing Power of Money*, Revised Edition, Macmillan, New York, 1911.

[7] HANSEN, ALVIN, *Monetary Theory and Fiscal Policy*, McGraw Hill, New York, 1949.

[8] HICKMAN, W. BRADDOCK, "The Determinacy of Absolute Prices in Classical Economic Theory", *Econometrica*, Vol. 18, January, 1950.

[9] HUME, DAVID, *Essays Moral, Political and Literary*, Longmans, Green and Co., London, 1875.

[10] JAFFÉ, WILLIAM, "The *Élements* and its Critics", Abstract of a paper delivered before The Econometric Society, Chicago, December 27, 1950, *Econometrica*, Vol. 19, July, 1951, pp. 327–328.

[11] KNIGHT, F. H., *Risk, Uncertainty and Profit*, London School of Economics and Political Science Series of Reprints of Scarce Tracts in Economic and Political Science, No. 16, London, 1933.

[12] LANGE, OSCAR, *Price Flexibility and Employment*, Cowles Commission Monograph No. 8, The Principia Press, Bloomington, Indiana, 1944.

[13] LANGE, OSCAR, "Say's Law: A Restatement and Criticism" in *Studies in Mathematical Economics and Econometrics; in Memory of Henry Schultz*, edited by Oscar Lange, Francis McIntyre and Theodore O. Yntema, Chicago University Press, Chicago, 1942.

[14] LEONTIEF, WASSILY, "The Consistency of the Classical Theory of Money and Prices", *Econometrica*, Vol. 18, January, 1950.

[15] LEONTIEF, WASSILY, "The Fundamental Assumptions of Mr. Keynes' Monetary Theory of Employment", *Quarterly Journal of Economics*, Vol. LI, November, 1936.

[16] LOCKE, JOHN, *An Essay on the Consequences of the Lowering of Interest and Raising the Value of Money*, Ward, Lock and Co. Edition of *The Works of John Locke*, London, (no date).

[17] MARGET, ARTHUR, "Léon Walras and the 'Cash Balance Approach' to the Problem of the Value of Money", *Journal of Political Economy*, Vol. XXXIX, October, 1931.

[18] MARGET, ARTHUR, "The Monetary Aspects of the Walrasian System", *Journal of Political Economy*, Vol. XLIII, April, 1935.

[19] MARGET, ARTHUR, *The Theory of Prices*, Prentice Hall, New York, Vol. I, 1938, Vol. II, 1942.

[20] McCULLOCH, J. R., *The Literature of Political Economy*, London, 1845.

[21] McCULLOCH, J. R., *Principles of Political Economy*, Fourth Edition, London, 1849.

[22] MARSHALL, ALFRED, *Money, Credit and Commerce*, Macmillan, London, 1923.

[23] MARSHALL, ALFRED, *Official Papers*, Macmillan, London, 1928.

[24] MARSHALL, ALFRED, *Principles of Economics*, 8th Edition, Macmillan, London, 1920.

[25] MILL, JAMES, *Commerce Defended*, Second Edition, London, 1808.

[26] MILL, JAMES, *Elements of Political Economy*, Second Edition, London, 1824.

[27] MILL, JOHN S., *Essays on Some Unsettled Questions of Political Economy*, London, 1844, No. 7 in the Series of Reprints of Scarce Works on Political Economy, London School of Economics and Political Science, London, 1948.

[28] MILL, JOHN S., *Principles of Political Economy*, edited by W. S. Ashley, Longmans, Green, London, 1909.

[29] NEISSER, HANS, "General Overproduction", in *Readings in Business Cycle Theory*, Gottfried Haberler, editor, American Economic Association, Blakiston, Philadelphia, 1944.

[30] PARETO, VILFREDO, *Manuel D'Économie Politique*, 2nd edition, Giard, Paris, 1927.

[31] PATINKIN, DON, "The Indeterminacy of Absolute Prices in Classical Economic Theory", *Econometrica*, Vol. 17, January, 1949.

[32] PATINKIN, DON, "The Invalidity of Classical Monetary Theory", *Econometrica*, Vol. 19, April, 1951.

[33] PATINKIN, DON, "A Reconsideration of the General Equilibrium Theory of Money", *Review of Economic Studies*, Vol. XVIII, 1950–51.

[34] PATINKIN, DON, "Relative Prices, Say's Law, and the Demand for Money", *Econometrica*, Vol. 16, April, 1948.

[35] PHIPPS, CECIL G., "A Note on Patinkin's 'Relative Prices' ", *Econometrica*, Vol. 18, January, 1950.

[36] PIGOU, A. C., "The Classical Stationary State", *Economic Journal*, Vol. LIII, December, 1943.

[37] RICARDO, DAVID, *Letters of David Ricardo to Thomas Robert Malthus*, edited by James Bonar, Oxford, London, 1887.

[38] RICARDO, DAVID, *The Works of*

David Ricardo, McCulloch-Edition, London, 1876.

[39] ROSENSTEIN-RODAN, P. N., "The Coordination of the General Theories of Money and Price", *Economica,* N.S., Vol. III, August, 1936.

[40] SAY, J. B., *Cours Complet D'Économie Politique Pratique,* Third Edition, Paris, 1852.

[41] SAY, J. B., *Oeuvres Diverses,* Paris, 1848.

[42] SAY, J. B., *A Treatise on Political Economy,* Prinsep Translation, Philadelphia, 1853.

[43] SENIOR, NASSAU W., *Three Lectures on the Value of Money,* London, 1840, London School of Economics and Political Science Reprints of Scarce Tracts in Economic and Political Science, No. 4,

London, 1931.

[44] WALRAS, LÉON, *Éléments D'Économie Politique Pure,* Édition Définitive, Pichon et Durand-Auzias, Paris, 1926.

[45] WALRAS, LÉON, *Études D'Économie Politique Appliquée,* Second Edition, Pichon et Durand-Auzias, Paris, 1936.

[46] WICKSELL, KNUT, *Interest and Prices,* Translated by R. F. Kahn, Macmillan, London, 1936.

[47] WICKSELL, KNUT, *Lectures on Political Economy,* Translated by E. Classen, Edited with an introduction by Lionel Robbins, Routledge, London, Vol. I, 1934, Vol. II, 1935.

[48] WICKSTEED, PHILIP H., *The Common Sense of Political Economy,* Edited with an Introduction by Lionel Robbins, Routledge, London, 1933.

Index of Names

Abeille, Louis Paul, 229 (n. 11)

Adams, Henry C., 493

Afanassiev, G., 233 (n. 115)

Aiken, H. D., 487 (n. 2)

Åkerman, Gustaf, 697, 709 (n. 33, 37), 752 (n. 25)

Albertus Magnus, 50–52, 56, 59 (n. 25)

Alexander the Great, 40

Allen, Clark Lee, 33 (n. 70)

Allen, R. G. D., 636, 654 (n. 199, 210)

Allen, William R., 274 (n. 13)

Allix, E., 197 (n. 12), 207 (n. 116), 257 (n. 52)

Alston, L., 521 (n. 61)

Amboise, Georges d', 200 (n. 36)

Ambrose, 12, 47, 59 (n. 9)

Amoroso, Luigi, 582, 593, 593 (n. 4, 6), 594 (n. 10, 21, 36), 595 (n. 39)

Anderson, Benjamin M., Jr., 532

Anderson, James, 401 (n. 178), 447, 598

Angell, James W., 140 (n. 111), 216, 222, 229 (n. 1), 230 (n. 34), 232 (n. 70, 71), 270 (n. 11)

Annenkov, P., 522 (n. 93)

Antonelli, G. B., 652 (n. 148)

Antoninus of Florence, 49, 56–58, 59 (n. 20), 60 (n. 48, 49, 50, 51), 284 (n. 6)

Aquinas, Thomas, 29 (n. 17, 18), 46, 57, 96, 283 (n. 6); and Albertus Magnus, 52; and Aristotle, 13, 37, 41, 54; and Augustine, 13; on economic activity, 41; on economic growth, 38; on international trade, 93; on just price, 13, 54, 55; on justice, 13, 41, 47, 54; on money and exchange, 54–55; on nature and role of the state, 13, 53–54; on society and economic order, 13, 52–53; on usury, 41–42; on value, 49, 278

Archibald, G. C., 767 (n. 12)

Arensberg, C. M., 38 (n. 1)

Argenson, Réné Louis de Voyer de Paulmy, d', 217

Arias, Gino, 285 (n. 17, 18, 20)

Aristophanes, 40

Aristotle, 4, 29 (n. 7, 8, 9), 59 (n. 30), 91 (n. 103), 98 (n. 28), 132 (n. 15), 259 (n. 2), 283 (n. 3, 5), 284 (n. 9), 390 (n. 5), 406 (n. 243); and Cantillon, 108; and scholasticism, 13, 37, 41, 50, 52, 54, 55, 57; on economic activity, 38, 39–40; on economic growth, 38; on

Aristotle—cont.

household management and gain, 12; on inequality, 40; on justice, 39; on money and interest, 40; on order and harmony, 11–12, 40; on property, 12, 40; on societal organization, 11–12, 37–38, 40; on value, 277–78, 282, 288, 293, 294

Arkin, Marcus, 102 (n. 1); author of Selection 6, 141–60

Asgill, John, 136 (n. 63), 208 (n. 138)

Ashley, William J., 32 (n. 51), 135 (n. 50), 197 (n. 13), 207 (n. 122), 255 (n. 20), 256 (n. 47), 273 (n. 12), 428 (n. 22), 450, 647 (n. 26), 709 (n. 20, 37), 736 (n. 13), 770

Augustine, 12–13, 23, 29 (n. 15), 45, 47, 48–49, 50, 55, 57, 59 (n. 10, 17, 24)

Augustus, 6

Auspitz, Rudolf, 634–35, 636, 653 (n. 192)

Ayres, Clarence E., 393 (n. 43)

Babbage, Charles, 619

Bacalan, Isaac de, 207 (n. 117), 222, 223, 229 (n. 12), 232 (n. 79)

Bacon, Francis, 209 (n. 151)

Bacon, Nathaniel T., 593 (n. 2), 594 (n. 18), 681 (n. 4)

Bagehot, Walter, 20, 32 (n. 50), 721–22

Bailey, Samuel, 301, 482 (n. 21)

Baker, W. T., 256 (n. 28)

Balassa, Bela A., 276 (n. 17)

Baldwin, Robert E., 266 (n. 9)

Barbon, Nicholas, 65, 67, 71, 72, 80, 81, 82, 90 (n. 13, 24, 41, 45), 91 (n. 77, 85, 88), 102, 135 (n. 58, 68), 138 (n. 77, 80, 83), 231 (n. 61)

Barker, Ernest, 39 (n. 2), 283 (n. 3)

Barnard, Chester I., 498

Barnett, G. E., 136 (n. 61)

Barone, Enrico, 624, 633, 640, 641, 649 (n. 80), 655 (n. 228)

Barraclough, Geoffrey, 487 (n. 2)

Bassano, Bartolomeo Gamba da, 284 (n. 8)

Bastiat, Frédéric, 21, 32 (n. 56), 668

Baudeau, Nicholas, 163, 171, 172–73, 197 (n. 13, 14), 198 (n. 16, 17, 20, 21, 22), 199 (n. 26, 29, 30, 32), 200 (n. 36, 41), 201 (n. 55, 57), 202 (n. 65, 66, 67),

Subject Index

Advantage, comparative and absolute, 153, 272–74, 375, 451. *See also* International trade

Balance of trade, 43–44, 66–68, 69, 73–74, 93–94, 95, 102, 113, 121, 124, 125–26, 127, 142, 145, 152–53, 189, 217, 218–19, 224–25, 229, 271, 373–76, 423, 689–90. *See also* International trade

Business cycles. *See* Crises and cycles

Cameralism. *See* Mercantilism

Capital, 167, 183, 261, 263–65, 299, 334–35, 415, 421, 422–24, 436, 437, 438–39, 448, 449–50, 464, 472, 473, 474, 478, 494, 507–8, 510, 538, 539, 543–48, 555, 557, 558–71, 598, 603, 666, 668, 669, 695–97, 697–98, 705, 713, 714, 719, 744, 748; accumulation of, 147, 154–55, 178–80, 184, 185, 189, 191, 192, 251, 262, 268, 270, 275, 343, 351, 354, 362, 365, 380, 413, 422, 423, 425, 443, 445–46, 447, 450, 451, 457, 458, 465, 503, 508, 516–17, 544, 560–61, 563, 696–97, 698, 699–700, 714–15, 742, 743, 744, 745, 746. *See also* Interest; Investment; Saving

Cities, formation of, 114–16, 129–30. *See also* Location theory

Comparative advantage (cost). *See* Advantage, comparative and absolute

Competition and competitive markets, 12, 13, 17, 18, 19, 20, 21, 23, 24–26, 53, 70–72, 77–78, 84–85, 155, 182, 261, 263, 275, 292, 327, 444, 451, 457, 473, 525, 526, 578, 579, 580–81, 583, 586–87, 589, 600, 603, 604, 607, 617, 619, 665, 673, 691, 693–94, 695, 698, 699, 705, 717, 720–21, 727, 728, 730, 731, 746, 747, 748

Complementarity, 603, 632, 634–36, 658–59, 665

Consumer surplus, 540, 605, 612, 622, 625, 634, 639

Consumption, 69–70, 113, 161–64, 177, 178, 179, 182–85, 186, 189, 191–92, 193, 195–96, 445, 607–8, 613, 619, 675, 705, 707. *See also* Luxury

Costs, 39, 56, 118, 275, 278, 295, 299, 388, 437, 535, 538–41, 542, 579, 581, 596, 597–98, 599, 600–603, 610, 612, 660, 664–65, 715, 717, 719, 724, 730; marginal, 436, 534–35, 590, 693, 713, 718, 724, 748; opportunity or alternative, 118, 261, 302, 425, 543, 555, 601, 664, 695, 734

Crises and cycles, 86, 455, 456, 459, 460–67, 495, 496, 517, 690, 691, 692, 697, 745–46. *See also* Employment and unemployment; Say's Law

Debt, 124, 142, 149, 155, 183, 185–86, 188, 193, 691

Demand, 261, 262, 274, 275, 290, 292, 293, 297–98, 300, 451, 485, 534, 535, 539, 542, 578–79, 580, 586, 589, 603–4, 607, 608, 614, 616–18, 619, 620, 624, 625, 633, 636–42, 643, 645, 646, 664, 673, 675, 678, 679, 713, 714, 716, 719–20. *See also* Value, supply-and-demand theory of

Distribution, 18, 129–30; Cantillon on, 119–22, 130; classical writers on, 344, 534, 598; Galiani on, 279–80; Keynes on, 741, 742; Malthus on, 356, 364–66; marginalists on, 534, 599, 600–603, 747–50; Marshall on, 716, 748–49; Marx on, 745–47; Menger on, 657, 664–70; mercantilism and, 69–70; J. S. Mill on, 20, 275, 449–50, 691, 714–15; Ricardo on, 265–70, 421–22, 423–24, 431–32, 433–34, 447, 714–15, 741, 742–45, 747; scholasticism on, 38; Smith on, 299, 325; Socratic writers on, 38; von Thünen on, 553–73; Wicksell on, 684, 686–87, 691, 692–94, 694–700, 747, 749. *See also* Interest; Marginal productivity; Profit; Wages

Division of labor, 51, 52–54, 227, 271, 297, 298–99, 317, 325, 385, 408, 417, 444, 446, 449, 451, 558

Duopoly, 577–93, 730. *See also* Imperfect competition; Monopoly

Economic analysis, factors affecting, 2–5, 8, 36–37, 642–46, 720–21, 722–24, 731, 732

PRINTED IN U.S.A.